北京大学中国语言学研究中心

早期北京话珍稀文献集成

主编 刘云

——西人北京话教科书汇编

分卷主编 翟赟 郭利霞 陈颖

官话类编

上

[美] 狄考文 编著

图书在版编目（CIP）数据

官话类编：全二册 / (美) 狄考文编著. —影印本. —北京：北京大学出版社，2017.8
（早期北京话珍本典籍校释与研究）
ISBN 978-7-301-28588-6

Ⅰ. ①官… Ⅱ. ①狄… Ⅲ. ①汉语—口语—对外汉语教学—研究—近代
Ⅳ. ①H195.4

中国版本图书馆CIP数据核字(2017)第195716号

书　　名　官话类编（上下）（影印本）
　　　　　GUANHUA LEIBIAN
著作责任者　［美］狄考文　编著
责任编辑　宋思佳　宋立文
标准书号　ISBN 978-7-301-28588-6
出版发行　北京大学出版社
地　　址　北京市海淀区成府路205号　100871
网　　址　http://www.pup.cn　　新浪微博：@北京大学出版社
电子信箱　zpup@pup.cn
电　　话　邮购部 62752015　发行部 62750672　编辑部 62753027
印 刷 者　北京京华虎彩印刷有限公司
经 销 者　新华书店
　　　　　720毫米×1020毫米　16开本　54.75印张　359千字　1插页
　　　　　2017年8月第1版　2017年8月第1次印刷
定　　价　198.00元（全二册）

总　序

语言是文化的重要组成部分，也是文化的载体。语言中有历史。

多元一体的中华文化，体现在我国丰富的民族文化和地域文化及其语言和方言之中。

北京是辽金元明清五代国都（辽时为陪都），千余年来，逐渐成为中华民族所公认的政治中心。北方多个少数民族文化与汉文化在这里碰撞、融合，产生出以汉文化为主体的、带有民族文化风味的特色文化。

现今的北京话是我国汉语方言和地域文化中极具特色的一支，它与辽金元明四代的北京话是否有直接继承关系还不是十分清楚。但可以肯定的是，它与清代以来旗人语言文化与汉人语言文化的彼此交融有直接关系。再往前追溯，旗人与汉人语言文化的接触与交融在入关前已经十分深刻。本丛书收集整理的这些语料直接反映了清代以来北京话、京味文化的发展变化。

早期北京话有独特的历史传承和文化底蕴，于中华文化、历史有特别的意义。

一者，这一时期的北京历经满汉双语共存、双语互协而新生出的汉语方言——北京话，她最终成为我国民族共同语（普通话）的基础方言。这一过程是中华多元一体文化自然形成的诸过程之一，对于了解形成中华文化多元一体关系的具体进程有重要的价值。

二者，清代以来，北京曾历经数次重要的社会变动：清王朝的逐渐孱弱、八国联军的入侵、帝制覆灭和民国建立及其伴随的满汉关系变化、各路军阀的来来往往、日本侵略者的占领，等等。在这些不同的社会环境下，北京人的构成有无重要变化？北京话和京味文化是否有变化？进一步地，地域方言和文化与自身的传承性或发展性有着什么样的关系？与社会变迁有着什么样的关系？清代以至民国时期早期北京话的语料为研究语言文化自身传承性与社会的关系提供了很好的素材。

了解历史才能更好地把握未来。新中国成立后，北京不仅是全国的政治中心，而且是全国的文化和科研中心，新的北京话和京味文化或正在形成。什么是老北京京味文化的精华？如何传承这些精华？为把握新的地域文化形成的规律，为传承地域文化的精华，必须对过去的地域文化的特色及其形成过程进行细致的研究和理性的分析。而近几十年来，各种新的传媒形式不断涌现，外来西方文化和国内其他地域文化的冲击越来越强烈，北京地区人口流动日趋频繁，老北京人逐渐分散，老北京话已几近消失。清代以来各个重要历史时期早期北京话语料的保护整理和研究迫在眉睫。

"早期北京话珍本典籍校释与研究（暨早期北京话文献数字化工程）"是北京大学中国语言学研究中心研究成果，由"早期北京话珍稀文献集成""早期北京话数据库"和"早期北京话研究书系"三部分组成。"集成"收录从清中叶到民国末年反映早期北京话面貌的珍稀文献并对内容加以整理，"数据库"为研究者分析语料提供便利，"研究书系"是在上述文献和数据库基础上对早期北京话的集中研究，反映了当前相关研究的最新进展。

本丛书可以为语言学、历史学、社会学、民俗学、文化学等多方面的研究提供素材。

愿本丛书的出版为中华优秀文化的传承做出贡献！

王洪君、郭锐、刘云

2016年10月

“早期北京话珍稀文献集成”序

清民两代是北京话走向成熟的关键阶段。从汉语史的角度看，这是一个承前启后的重要时期，而成熟后的北京话又开始为当代汉民族共同语——普通话源源不断地提供着养分。蒋绍愚先生对此有着深刻的认识：“特别是清初到19世纪末这一段的汉语，虽然按分期来说是属于现代汉语而不属于近代汉语，但这一段的语言（语法，尤其是词汇）和‘五四’以后的语言（通常所说的‘现代汉语’就是指‘五四’以后的语言）还有若干不同，研究这一段语言对于研究近代汉语是如何发展到‘五四’以后的语言是很有价值的。”（《近代汉语研究概要》，北京大学出版社，2005年）然而国内的早期北京话研究并不尽如人意，在重视程度和材料发掘力度上都要落后于日本同行。自1876年至1945年间，日本汉语教学的目的语转向当时的北京话，因此留下了大批的北京话教材，这为其早期北京话研究提供了材料支撑。作为日本北京话研究的奠基者，太田辰夫先生非常重视新语料的发掘，很早就利用了《小额》《北京》等京味儿小说材料。这种治学理念得到了很好的传承，之后，日本陆续影印出版了《中国语学资料丛刊》《中国语教本类集成》《清民语料》等资料汇编，给研究带来了便利。

新材料的发掘是学术研究的源头活水。陈寅恪《〈敦煌劫余录〉序》有云：“一时代之学术，必有其新材料与新问题。取用此材料，以研求问题，则为此时代学术之新潮流。”我们的研究要想取得突破，必须打破材料桎梏。在具体思路上，一方面要拓展视野，关注“异族之故书”，深度利用好朝鲜、日本、泰西诸国作者所主导编纂的早期北京话教本；另一方面，更要利用本土优势，在“吾国之旧籍”中深入挖掘，官话正音教本、满汉合璧教本、京味儿小说、曲艺剧本等新类型语料大有文章可做。在明确了思路之后，我们从2004年开始了前期的准备工作，在北京大学中国语言学研究中心的大力支持下，早期北京话的挖掘整理工作于2007年正式启动。本次推出的“早期北京话珍稀文献集成”是阶段性成果之一，总体设计上“取异族之故书与吾国之旧籍互相补正”，共分“日本北京话教科书汇编”“朝鲜日据时期汉语会话书汇编”“西人北京话教科书汇编”“清代满汉合璧文献萃编”“清代官话正音文献”“十全福”“清末民初京味儿小说书系”“清末民初京味儿时评书系”八个系列，胪列如下：

“日本北京话教科书汇编”于日本早期北京话会话书、综合教科书、改编读物和风俗纪闻读物中精选出《燕京妇语》《四声联珠》《华语跬步》《官话指南》《改订官话指南》《亚细亚言语集》《京华事略》《北京纪闻》《北京风土编》《北京风俗问答》《北京事情》《伊苏普喻言》《搜奇新编》《今古奇观》等二十余部作品。这些教材是日本早期北京话教学活动的缩影，也是研究早期北京方言、民俗、史地问题的宝贵资料。本系列的编纂得到了日本学界的大力帮助。冰野善宽、内田庆市、太田斋、鳟泽彰夫诸先生在书影拍摄方面给予了诸多帮助。书中日语例言、日语小引的翻译得到了竹越孝先生的悉心指导，在此深表谢忱。

“朝鲜日据时期汉语会话书汇编”由韩国著名汉学家朴在渊教授和金雅瑛博士校注，收入《改正增补汉语独学》《修正独习汉语指南》《高等官话华语精选》《官话华语教范》《速修汉语自通》《速修汉语大成》《无先生速修中国语自通》《官话标准：短期速修中国语自通》《中语大全》《“内鲜满”最速成中国语自通》等十余部日据时期（1910年至1945年）朝鲜教材。这批教材既是对《老乞大》《朴通事》的传承，又深受日本早期北京话教学活动的影响。在中韩语言史、文化史研究中，日据时期是近现代过渡的重要时期，这些资料具有多方面的研究价值。

“西人北京话教科书汇编”收录了《语言自迩集》《官话类编》等十余部西人主编教材。这些西方作者多受过语言学训练，他们用印欧语的眼光考量汉语，解释汉语语法现象，设计记音符号系统，对早期北京话语音、词汇、语法面貌的描写要比本土文献更为精准。感谢郭锐老师提供了《官话类编》《北京话语音读本》和《汉语口语初级读本》的底本，《寻津录》、《语言自迩集》（第一版、第二版）、《汉英北京官话词汇》、《华语入门》等底本由北京大学图书馆特藏部提供，谨致谢忱。《华英文义津逮》《言语声片》为笔者从海外购回，其中最为珍贵的是老舍先生在伦敦东方学院执教期间，与英国学者共同编写的教材——《言语声片》。教材共分两卷：第一卷为英文卷，用英语讲授汉语，用音标标注课文的读音；第二卷为汉字卷。《言语声片》采用先用英语导入，再学习汉字的教学方法讲授汉语口语，是世界上第一部有声汉语教材。书中汉字均由老舍先生亲笔书写，全书由老舍先生录音，共十六张唱片，京韵十足，殊为珍贵。

上述三类"异族之故书"经江蓝生、张卫东、汪维辉、张美兰、李无未、王顺洪、张西平、鲁健骥、王澧华诸先生介绍，已经进入学界视野，对北京话研究和对外汉语教学史研究产生了很大的推动作用。我们希望将更多的域外经典北京话教本引入进来，考虑到日本卷和朝鲜卷中很多抄本字迹潦草，难以辨认，而刻本、印本中也存在着大量的异体字和俗字，重排点校注释的出版形式更利于研究者利用，这也是前文"深度利用"的含义所在。

对"吾国之旧籍"挖掘整理的成果，则体现在下面五个系列中：

"清代满汉合璧文献萃编"收入《清文启蒙》《清话问答四十条》《清文指要》《续编兼汉清文指要》《庸言知旨》《满汉成语对待》《清文接字》《重刻清文虚字指南编》等十余部经典满汉合璧文献。入关以后，在汉语这一强势语言的影响下，熟习满语的满人越来越少，故雍正以降，出现了一批用当时的北京话注释翻译的满语会话书和语法书。这批教科书的目的本是教授旗人学习满语，却无意中成为了早期北京话的珍贵记录。"清代满汉合璧文献萃编"首次对这批文献进行了大规模整理，不仅对北京话溯源和满汉语言接触研究具有重要意义，也将为满语研究和满语教学创造极大便利。由于底本多为善本古籍，研究者不易见到，在北京大学图书馆古籍部和日本神户外国语大学竹越孝教授的大力协助下，"萃编"将以重排点校加影印的形式出版。

"清代官话正音文献"收入《正音撮要》（高静亭著）和《正音咀华》（莎彝尊著）两种代表著作。雍正六年(1728)，雍正谕令福建、广东两省推行官话，福建为此还专门设立了正音书馆。这一"正音"运动的直接影响就是以《正音撮要》和《正音咀华》为代表的一批官话正音教材的问世。这些书的作者或为旗人，或寓居京城多年，书中保留着大量北京话词汇和口语材料，具有极高的研究价值。沈国威先生和侯兴泉先生对底本搜集助力良多，特此致谢。

《十全福》是北京大学图书馆藏《程砚秋玉霜簃戏曲珍本》之一种，为同治元年陈金雀抄本。陈晓博士发现该传奇虽为昆腔戏，念白却多为京话，较为罕见。

以上三个系列均为古籍，且不乏善本，研究者不容易接触到，因此我们提供了影印全文。

总体来说，由于言文不一，清代的本土北京话语料数量较少。而到了清末民初，风气渐开，情况有了很大变化。彭翼仲、文实权、蔡友梅等一批北京爱国知识分子通过开办白话报来“开启民智”“改良社会”。著名爱国报人彭翼仲在《京话日报》的发刊词中这样写道：“本报为输进文明、改良风俗，以开通社会多数人之智识为宗旨。故通幅概用京话，以浅显之笔，达朴实之理，纪紧要之事，务令雅俗共赏，妇稚咸宜。”在当时北京白话报刊的诸多栏目中，最受市民欢迎的当属京味儿小说连载和《益世余谭》之类的评论栏目，语言极为地道。

“清末民初京味儿小说书系”首次对以蔡友梅、冷佛、徐剑胆、儒丐、勋锐为代表的晚清民国京味儿作家群及作品进行系统挖掘和整理，从千余部京味儿小说中萃取代表作家的代表作品，并加以点校注释。该作家群活跃于清末民初，以报纸为阵地，以小说为工具，开展了一场轰轰烈烈的底层启蒙运动，为新文化运动的兴起打下了一定的群众基础，他们的作品对老舍等京味儿小说大家的创作产生了积极影响。本系列的问世亦将为文学史和思想史研究提供议题。于润琦、方梅、陈清茹、雷晓彤诸先生为本系列提供了部分底本或馆藏线索，首都图书馆历史文献阅览室、天津图书馆、国家图书馆提供了极大便利，谨致谢意！

“清末民初京味儿时评书系”则收入《益世余谭》和《益世余墨》，均系著名京味儿小说家蔡友梅在民初报章上发表的专栏时评，由日本岐阜圣德学园大学刘一之教授、矢野贺子教授校注。

这一时期存世的报载北京话语料口语化程度高，且总量庞大，但发掘和整理却殊为不易，称得上“珍稀”二字。一方面，由于报载小说等栏目的流行，外地作者也加入了京味儿小说创作行列，五花八门的笔名背后还需考证作者是否为京籍，以蔡友梅为例，其真名为蔡松龄，查明的笔名还有损、损公、退化、亦我、梅蒐、老梅、今睿等。另一方面，这些作者的作品多为急就章，文字错讹很多，并且鲜有单行本存世，老报纸残损老化的情况日益严重，整理的难度可想而知。

上述八个系列在某种程度上填补了相关领域的空白。由于各个系列在内容、体例、出版年代和出版形式上都存在较大的差异，我们在整理时借鉴《朝鲜时代汉语教科书丛刊续编》《〈清文指要〉汇校与语言研究》等语言类古籍的整理体例，结合各个系列自身特点和读者需求，灵活制定体例。“清末民初京味儿小说书系”和“清末民初京味儿时评书系”年代较近，读者群体更为广泛，经过多方调研和反复讨论，我们决定在整理时使用简体横排的形式，尽可能同时满足专业研究者和普通读者的需求。“清代满汉合璧文献萃编”“清代官话正音文献”等系列整理时则采用繁体。“早期北京话珍稀文献集成”总计六十余册，总字数近千万字，称得上是工程浩大，由于我们能力有限，体例和校注中难免会有疏漏，加之受客观条件所限，一些拟定的重要书目本次无法收入，还望读者多多谅解。

“早期北京话珍稀文献集成”可以说是中日韩三国学者通力合作的结晶，得到了方方面面的帮助，我们还要感谢陆俭明、马真、蒋绍愚、江蓝生、崔希亮、方梅、张美兰、陈前瑞、赵日新、陈跃红、徐大军、张世方、李明、邓如冰、王强、陈保新诸先生的大力支持，感谢北京大学图书馆的协助以及萧群书记的热心协调。“集成”的编纂队伍以青年学者为主，经验不足，两位丛书总主编倾注了大量心血。王洪君老师不仅在经费和资料上提供保障，还积极扶掖新进，“我们搭台，你们年轻人唱戏”的话语令人倍感温暖和鼓舞。郭锐老师在经费和人员上也予以了大力支持，不仅对体例制定、底本选定等具体工作进行了细致指导，还无私地将自己发现的新材料和新课题与大家分享，令人钦佩。“集成”能够顺利出版还要特别感谢国家出版基金规划管理办公室的支持以及北京大学出版社王明舟社长、张凤珠副总编的精心策划，感谢汉语编辑室杜若明、邓晓霞、张弘泓、宋立文等老师所付出的辛劳。需要感谢的师友还有很多，在此一并致以诚挚的谢意。

“上穷碧落下黄泉，动手动脚找东西”，我们不奢望引领“时代学术之新潮流”，惟愿能给研究者带来一些便利，免去一些奔波之苦，这也是我们向所有关心帮助过“早期北京话珍稀文献集成”的人士致以的最诚挚的谢意。

刘　云

2015年6月23日

于对外经贸大学求索楼

2016年4月19日

改定于润泽公馆

导 读

翟 赟

自马礼逊（Robert Morrison，1782—1834）[①]入华之后，1829年美国公理会海外传道部派裨治文（Elijah Coleman Bridgman，1801—1861）[②]来华，由此拉开了长达一个多世纪的美国对华传教活动的序幕。（张西平，2009：56）晚清时期著名的美国来华传教士狄考文（Calvin Wilson Mateer，1836—1908）就是其中的一员。关于狄考文，很多前贤都做过研究，主要集中于历史、宗教和教育三个方面，尤其关注的是他对近代中国教育的贡献，但对他编写的《官话类编》（*A Course of Mandarin Lessons: Based on Idiom*）这部书不够重视。目前来看，有关《官话类编》的研究成果不多，比较早的有太田辰夫（1964／1995）、邢公畹（1990）、张美兰（2007、2008），近些年来有一些硕士和博士学位论文，如李蕊（2010）、李木谢子（2011）、钱鸿儒（2013）、李银菊（2013）、李婧超（2014）、齐灿（2014）、栗源（2015）。为了让更多人了解《官话类编》，现将该书体例与内容进行简要的梳理和介绍。

一、狄考文及其在华活动

狄考文，美国基督教北长老会传教士。1836年1月9日出生在宾夕法尼亚

① 马礼逊，英国人，西方近代第一位来华传教士，编纂了《通用汉言之法》（*A Grammar of the Chinese Language*）、《华英字典》（*A Dictionary of the Chinese Language*）等，1834年在广州病逝。

② 裨治文，美国第一位来华传教士，晚年主要从事《新旧约全书》的翻译工作，1861年在上海去世。

州（Pennsylvania）坎伯兰县（Cumberland County）一个基督教家庭。1855年进入杰斐逊学院（Jefferson College）学习，1857年毕业。1860年求学于阿立甘（Allegheny）美西神学院。狄考文在1860年12月12日给他母亲的信中写道："我做传教士工作的念头由来已久……自从我进入神学院以后，在某种程度上更坚定了做一名传教士的信心……现在，我差不多已经得出一个结论：对我来说，做一名传教士是我的职责。"（丹尼尔·W. 费舍，2009：24—25）在神学院毕业前两周，即1861年4月5日，狄考文向长老会海外布道会正式递交了赴海外传教的申请书，4月13日得到海外布道会的批准，但传教目的地和启程时间没有确定。之后的一段时间，他在俄亥俄州（Ohio）特拉华镇（Delaware）守旧派长老会教堂（Old School Presbyterian Church）担任牧师。1862年特拉华镇马里恩长老会（the Presbytery of Marion）委任其为专职福音传教士。1863年7月，狄考文携妻子邦就烈[①]（Julia A. Brown，1837—1898）以及郭显德（Hunter Corbett，1835—1920）牧师[②] 夫妇从纽约乘船出发，历时六个月来到中国，开始长达45年的在华传教生涯。1908年9月28日因腹疾在青岛去世，后葬于烟台毓璜顶。（崔华杰，2008；丹尼尔·W. 费舍，2009：12—26）英国浸礼会曾这样评价狄考文："他是一位成功的教育家、一位优秀的行政管理者、一位极具影响力的布道者，同时又是一位卓越的学者。"（丹尼尔·W. 费舍，2009：218）

（一）在华传教活动

入华初期，作为山东布道区"三位伟大的先驱"[③] 之一的狄考文，把宣讲教义、传播福音作为当时最紧迫的任务。狄考文是通过旅行在乡村和城镇间布道。1864年10月开始在农村旅行布道。此后相继在莱州、潍县、青州、

---

① 译名参考丹尼尔·W. 费舍（2009）。

② 郭显德，美国来华传教士，在山东生活、传教56年，1920年1月在烟台去世。

③ 指狄考文、郭显德、倪维思（John Livingston Nevius，1829—1893）。

招远、平度等地传教。城镇布道主要是在街头，利用集市、庙会等人群聚集的场所开展各种布道活动。

由于单纯的旅行布道缺少固定的传教对象，且不能针对个人进行深入持久的宗教引导，狄考文早期的传教活动收效不大，只赢得了为数不多的皈依者。其间狄考文深刻反思自己的传教方式，意识到借助条约权利及西方的坚船利炮扫除传教障碍，只会让当地民众对基督教产生抵触心理，不利于福音传播，也认识到仅仅依靠说教很难实现基督教中国化的目标，需要开办教育，培养传教士。

（二）兴办学校

狄考文在华初期传教受挫，促使其调整传教策略和方法，转向开办教育，以培养不同于中国旧式文人的新式人才，培养高水平的中国籍传教士。

1. 创办登州文会馆

狄考文1863年来到中国，1864年在登州（今山东蓬莱）观音堂创办登州蒙养学堂（Tengchow Boy' s Boarding School，1864—1876），校址和办学规模几经变迁，后来发展为登州文会馆（Tengchow College，1876—1884），1884年美国长老会差会本部批准文会馆升格为大学。① 1904年登州文会馆迁到潍县，与青州英国浸礼会创办的广德书院合并，更名为广文学堂（Kuang-Wen College）。1917年广文学堂与青州的神学学堂、济南的共和医道学堂合并，并迁到济南，这就是齐鲁大学的前身。

文会馆的创办为中国的教育做出了重要贡献。在课程设置方面，除了教学校必备的宗教课程，还有中国儒家经典，同时引进西学课程，其中所开设的自然科学课程“在当时中国的学校中处于领先地位”，所开设的心灵学、是非学和富国策三门社会科学课程“可能是在中国教育系统中最早开设的课程”。（王忠欣，2000：37）登州文会馆促进了中国教育近代化的历程，传

① 也有学者认为是1882年。

播了西方先进的科学文化，培养出了适应中国社会发展需求的新式人才。1898年清政府设立京师大学堂，由当时外务部同文馆总教习丁韪良（William A. P. Martin，1827—1916）[①]聘任八名文会馆毕业生任教习。这足以说明文会馆在当时的影响。

2. 编写教材

1877年，狄考文因在基督教教育方面的突出成就，在传教士大会上被推举为“益智书会”（School and Textbooks Series Committee）委员，负责基督教学校的教科书编译工作。狄考文根据文会馆编写教材的经验和体会，10月在基督教专业期刊《教务杂志》（The Chinese Recorder）上发表文章，探讨新式教科书的编写原则及方法。他认为编写教科书的目的是用来研究和教学的，教科书的编写应该有系统，提供重要事实与原则、问题与解答，教材内容应该涵盖全面，要用通俗的语言进行表述，而且还要努力激发学生的兴趣。（崔华杰，2008：102）

在华期间，狄考文编译的著作很多，如宗教类著作有《谁是耶稣》（1870）、《幼童受洗礼记》（1872）、《创世纪问答》（1875）、《倪维思—狄考文赞美诗集》（1877）等；自然科学类著作有《代数术》（1877）、《形学备旨》（1885）、《代数备旨》（1891）、《笔算数学》（1892）、《术语概要》（1904）、《高等代数》（1908）等；语言学类著作有《官话类编》（1892）、《官话简明教程》（1901）等。

《官话类编》是为了帮助传教士更好地掌握汉语，专为来华传教士编写的汉语教材。据《山东登州文会馆》记载，狄考文刚到登州时，“语言不能传译，乏人，官话课本又无佳音，乃延齐人为傅，苦心学习，随笔记录，必详必慎，以十年之心血，集成一巨著”。“及至全书告竣，陆续复印，一纸

① 丁韪良，来华美国长老会牧师，曾担任过北京同文馆和京师大学堂的负责人，著有《万国公法》《富国策》《格物入门》等书，1916年在北京去世。

内行中外咸惊”，“卒成为一空前绝后之杰作，西人之肆学华语者，莫不奉为至宝”。（李蕊，2010）《官话类编》是20世纪来华传教士学习汉语的必备之书，据说瑞典汉学家高本汉（Klas Bernhard Johannes Karlgren，1889—1978）也是通过自学《官话类编》过了语言关。

（三）主持翻译《圣经》和合本

《圣经》官话和合本（《新旧约全书》官话和合本）之前虽已出版了许多中文译本，但大部分版本是以文言文为基础，且在用词和翻译原则上存在差别，为此重译《圣经》已成为传教士的必然选择。1890年，基督教在华传教士第二次全国大会在上海召开，决议统一圣经汉语译本，成立了文理（文言文）、浅文理和官话三个译本委员会，分别负责三种译本的翻译。狄考文负责官话和合译本的工作，并被任命为官话和合译本委员会主席。1898年开始翻译《新约》，于1907年完成修订并出版。遗憾的是《旧约》只翻译了诗篇部分，狄考文去世了，其余部分的翻译工作在富善（Chauncey Goodrich，1836—1925）主持下到1918年完成，1919年出版，原来译经修订委员会中只有富善一人见证了该书的问世。

《圣经》官话和合本是“中国教会最受欢迎的《圣经》版本”（顾长声，1991：437），影响最大，流行最广，被海内外誉为最规范的白话译本。官话和合本委员会前后共召开了八次会议，每次会议时间都超过两个月，其中一次持续了长达半年之久。在翻译过程中遇到了诸多困难，狄考文倾注了大量心血。正如狄考文70岁生日时在一封题为“致家中挚爱的亲人们”的信中所写的：“我在中国的最后10年所做的重要工作一直以《圣经》官话和合译本为主。这是一项最费力、最艰苦的工作，至今还未结束。”（丹尼尔·W. 费舍，2009：176）

在最初提出的翻译规则中，狄考文主张“字词应当是操官话的平民百姓日常所使用和明白的，书面用语和不大通用的用词应该避免”，“文笔风格应是真正的中文，外国人所撰写或监督的官话往往在用字和习惯上多少有些洋化”。（邢梅，2012：28）富善在悼念狄考文的文章中这样写道：“出于对真理的追求，没有任何人像狄考文博士那样付出如此多的时间和艰辛的工作或者说如此投入。他对译文与原文保持一致、保留原文修辞上的美感所做出的贡献是无与伦比的。”（丹尼尔·W. 费舍，2009：215）

二、《官话类编》概览

主要介绍《官话类编》的版本、编排体例和内容三部分。

（一）版本

狄考文于1867年开始准备编写《官话类编》，直到1892年第一版问世①，花费了25年的时间，在其后的几十年中进行过多次修订与重版印刷。1898年第一次修订，其后有1900年本、1903年本；1905年第二次修订，1906年发行第三版，其后有1909年、1922年重印本。据李蕊（2010）介绍，上海市徐家汇藏书楼藏有 1909 年和 1922 年两个版本。②此次影印使用的版本是《官话类编》1900年本，由上海美华书馆（Shanghai： American Presbyterian Mission Press）出版，781页。

《官话类编》还有两本配套教材，即《官话简明教程》（*A Short Course of Primary Lessons in Mandarin*，1901）和《官话类编》（删节本）（*A Course of Mandarin Lessons (abridged edition): Based on Idiom*，1916）。

① 复旦大学图书馆藏有早期版本，书名页竖排居中标有“官话类编”四字，右边竖排写有“耶稣降世一千八百九十二年”，左边竖排写有“岁次壬辰 美华书馆镌印”，全书200课，188页，只有中文课文，没有前言、目录、作者名讳、英文翻译、注释。

② 据李木谢子（2011）介绍，上海市徐家汇藏书楼还有一本非对外发行的手抄法文本《官话类编》（*Cours de Mandarin*），抄写于1893年。

《官话简明教程》是狄考文在文爱德（Haven Ada）[①] 的协助下于1901年出版的，是一本初级汉语教材。全书共36课，79页，介绍了汉语的发音、笔画、声调、英语拼写与汉语书写的差异、北京音与南京音的对比、给学生的建议等。每课包括字词、会话和注释。每句以英汉对照并配注释的方式排列，分三行，第一行为英文，第二行为中文，第三行为对应汉字的英文单词。

《官话类编》（删节本）是节选《官话类编》前100课另行出版的，299页。其内容与《官话类编》前100课的内容完全相同。据《官话类编》（删节本）前言介绍，由于《官话类编》课文太多，很多学生无法在一年内完成学习，为了满足这部分学生的需求，出版了该删节本。

（二）编排体例

《官话类编》全书200课。就内容编排而言，每页分上下两部分。上面部分左右排列汉语课文和英文翻译部分，汉语课文居左，英文翻译部分居右。汉语课文为右起竖排列文，右下方标句读，每句以“○”间隔，每句右上方有阿拉伯数字标序。翻译部分为横向左起，将随文翻译的英文句子按照汉语课文中的数字编号排列。下面部分依次是语法、词汇、注释。根据课文篇幅及词汇量的多少，语法、词汇、注释三部分的版面有时会有所调整，但是汉语课文及英文翻译部分一直保持在原来的版面位置。

汉语课文的编排，我们可以从邹立文[②] 为此书作的序中看出，序文曰：“此书之成，并非一人之力，曾经分发北京、济南、南京、九江、汉口等处，批过数次，又曾亲往各地，协同诸位名士，详加批阅，终则合此诸批，一一审定，要必以通行者为是，兼有不通行者，则并列之，其列法，北京在

---

① 文爱德，美国公理会传教士，1900年9月25日与狄考文结婚。

② 邹立文，山东平度人，是狄考文夫妇在山东开办的登州男子高等学堂第一届学生，毕业后长期与狄考文合作，参与编译了《形学备旨》《代数备旨》等数学教材。

右，南京在左，如有三行并列，即山东居其中也。是故用此书者，非但可得通行之益，即不通行者，亦可确知南北终有何不同也。”为了照顾各地不同的官话，狄考文调查了北京、济南、南京等地的官话，取其通行者，若三地说法有异，则左中右并列。例如[①]：

①这块（肥皂 / 胰子）不下（脏 / 灰 / 泥）。你这件（事情 / 营生） 不合情理。（第27课）

②我整天（的 / 家）就是（好 / 爱）替古人担忧。（第108课）

③你怎么忽然改了主意呢？（猛过地里 / 冒不通的 / 冷不防的）把我吓了一跳。（第115课）

（三）内容

《官话类编》全书包括初版前言（Preface to First Edition）、第二版前言（Preface to Second Edition）、目录（Contents）、引言（Introduction）、序、凡例、致学习者之建议（Suggestions to the Student）、课文（Lesson）和附录（Supplement）九部分内容。下面扼要介绍初版前言、引言、课文和附录四部分内容。

1. 初版前言

初版前言主要阐述了本书的风格、评价及注意的事项，从梗概（Plan）、文风（Style）、选材（Materials）、随文翻译（Translation）、内容提要（Subjects）、词汇（Vocabularies）、注释（Notes）、方言（Dialects）、拼写系统（System of Spelling）、编排（Arrangement）、索引（Finders）、致谢（Acknowledgment）等方面进行了阐述。

2. 引言

引言部分主要介绍了作者对汉语的研究心得，分别从官话（Mandarin）、

---

① 《官话类编》原文为竖排，本文引用时由于横排无法显示差异表达的范围，故加括号以显示差异表达的界限。

汉字（Characters）、音节（Syllables）、拼音（Spelling）、音节表（Syllabaries）、声调（Tones）、送气音（Aspirates）、韵律（Rhythm）、部首（Radicals）、多音字（Double Readings）、书写（Writing）、学习者建议（Advice to the Student）、解释（Explanations）、总论（General Remarks）等部分加以阐述，并在其后附加了部首列表（Table of Radicals）、笔顺（The Radical Ode）、声调练习（Tone Exercises）、送气音练习（Aspirate Exercises）、北京音列表（Peking Sound Table）、南京音列表（Nanking Sound Table）、九江音列表（Kiukiang Sound Table）、登州音列表（Têngchow Sound Table）、潍县音列表（Weihien Sound Table）、重庆音列表（Chungking Sound Table）。

3. 课文

《官话类编》全书共 200 课，每课句子30个左右，每课包括课文、翻译、语法点、生词、注释五个部分。

（1）课文（Lessons）

课文的选材内容丰富，包括日常饮食起居、官绅商贾、风俗文化、文学艺术、历史宗教等方面。语言材料来源广泛，从中国的“四书五经”到“明清小说”，从天文地理到自然科学，从三皇五帝到民间习俗，可以说包罗万象，涉及中国文化的方方面面。“至若课中散语，非尽自编，更博览《圣谕广训》《好逑传》《西游记》《水浒》《自迩致》等书，择其言语之佳者，按题分列……凡农工商贾、官场日用，无不俱备。”（邹立文序）

关于课文的编写，狄考文曾在一封信中这样写道：“每一课都会举例说明一个在特定范围内选出的习语。……所使用的例句来自各个地区、各个阶层。我还介绍了各种语调的官话，而高层使用的语调主要在第二部分的100篇课文里。不过，该书的主要目的还是帮助人们学习目前正在使用的官话。除俗语外，我尽量回避各种明显的方言，对于任何一个真正官话讲得好的人来说，熟知这些词语虽说不上是必需的但却是十分重要的。……许多俗语使用范围很广，它们给汉语带来了活力和多样性，在很多情况下，它们所表达出的意思是无法用其他方式替代的。在书中，我竭尽全力地想要反映所有地区的特点，而为了做到这一点，很多情况下我都会给出两个或多个表达形式。”（丹尼尔·W.费舍，2009：108）

（2）语法点（Grammar）

这200篇课文，每课围绕一个语法点，反复练习。“依话语之样数，分作二百题目，每题一课，凡话语之种类、式样以及如何变转，如何连接，此二百题俱已赅括。”（邹立文序）

语法点部分主要是对词类和句式的讲解。词类方面，如量词（第1、27、38、42、64、68、100、125、140、147课），代词（第2、3、9、17、21、32、34、36、37、45、48、63、66、84、85、87课），介词（给、替、把、与，第25课；在，第6、26课；把、将，第28课；被、教、叫，第53课），语气词（吗，第8课；喇、咯、啊、哪、咧、哩、呀、哇，第61课；呢，第89课），连词（第78、81、83、94、95、132、133、138、156、157、160、164、165、170、175、176、181、182、193、194课）等。句式方面，如反复问句（第22课），处置句（第28课）、被动句（第53课）、使役句（第71课）。此外还有重叠形式（第68、108、113课），四字格短语（第184、185、186、195、196课），歇后语（第198、199课），谜语（第200课）等。且举第61课为例。

第61课的语法点是重点学习“喇、咯、啊、哪、咧、哩、呀、哇”八个语气词的用法。例如：

①不要说喇，你快去罢。

②我几句话把他顶回去咯。

③请你们都进去坐坐罢。答：我们不坐（哩 / 着喇）。

“喇”用于句末，表示完结，相当于句末表示完结、且读为la的“了”，句中“喇”和“了”的选用因地域与教师的不同而不同；“咯”用于句末，表示确定，与“喇”的区别不大；“哩”不用于北方口语，但在南方有时会作为“喇”的替换词汇出现。①

（3）词汇（Vocabulary）和注释（Notes）

词汇部分列有每课需要掌握的生词 / 生字，先用改造后的威妥玛拼音系统对生词 / 生字作了声、韵、调标音，然后进行英文解释，释义主要关注的是词的基本义。例如：

①保管 *Pao³ kwan³*. Same as 管保.（第68课）

②开眼 *K'ai¹ yien³*. To see the world, *to see the sights*; to learn by experience.（第89课）

③名人 *Ming² jên²*. A noted man, a celebrated character.（第140课）

注释部分主要是对一些特殊的字词，尤其是存在南北地域差异的词和语法表达加以注释。例如：

①用钱感情不如送东西体面。（第58课）

【注释Notes】感情 sometimes forms a phrase, meaning *to stir up or influence others*, but here 感 is the verb and 情 its object. 情 properly means affection, but is here put for the favor, or present, which expresses affection.

---

① 原文为：喇 A final particle indicating completion. It is not essentially different from 了, when 了 is used as a simple final at the end of a clause or sentence and pronounced (as it always is in practice) *la*. There is in fact no certain principle to guide as to which character should be used in any given case，and the usage of different places and teachers differs widely.

咯 A final particle indicating certainty，but in practice not distinguishable from 喇. Teachers vary much in the use of this character.

哩 A final particle found occasionally in books, but not used colloquially in the North. It is sometimes heard in the South instead of 喇.

②跟这里走，（几多 / 多么）顺便。（第85课）

【注释Notes】几多 *How, how many,*—is used in the region of Hankow, and perhaps westward, for 多么. No such combination is known in Central or Northern Mandarin.

此外，还对一些带有文化色彩的词语作了注释，如八仙桌、泰山椅子（第69课），刘玄德（第185课），叔伯（第188课），商纣（第192课），吕洞宾（第196课），诸葛亮、岳飞（第200课）。

4. 附录

附录部分包括词和短语补充列表（List of Supplementary Words and Phrases，626—648页）、对话和演说（Dialogues and Orations，649—741页）、索引（音节索引 Syllable Finder of Characters and Phrases，742—773页；部首索引 Radical Finder of Single Characters，774—781页[①]）三部分。

词和短语补充列表是对课文中重点词语或语法点的补充。对话和演说部分共13篇文章，每篇文章涉及一个话题，其中对话部分包括盘问西事、备造楼房、家务常言、媒人说媒、追讨账目、构讼小品、风水、买卖讲价、生童考试、亲眷相称，演说部分包括太甲悔过、武王誓师、孟子。音节索引是以音节排序为主，笔画排序为辅，并在每个生字 / 词后面标有页码出处；部首索引是将课文中所出现的生字按部首编排，并将多音字分别标注，每个生字后面标有页码出处，方便查找。

三、《官话类编》的特点

综观整部《官话类编》，有以下三方面的特点：

---

① 底本目录页中"Radical Index（部首索引）"标识的起始页码为806，与正文实际页码不符。

（一）《官话类编》是一部实用的官话口语课本

关于《官话类编》的性质，序和凡例中有明确的交代。邹立文在《官话类编·序》中指出："此书之作，原为西人学官话而作也。所谓官话者，非言尽为官场中话，乃言通行之话也。" 狄考文在引言（Introduction）中对官话（Mandarin）进行了界定，指出官话其本质特征上是除了扬子江南岸诸省的北方18 个省份所使用的语言，可分为北方官话、南方官话和西部官话，也可以按照省份划分，如河南官话、山东官话等。北方官话中北京话作为官方语言占统治地位，非常流行，连皇帝都认可。南方官话使用的范围很广，使用人数也多于北方官话。山东官话处于两者之间，近似于普遍。西部官话受北京话的影响很大，但也有自己的特点。

《官话类编·凡例》指出："当知此书，非为人之学文而作，乃为学话而作也。且所编之话语，亦非效法书中句法，特以工雅为贵，乃摹仿口中句法，以自然为贵也。" 这里的"学话"即"学习口语"。狄考文在前言中写道："本书绝大部分内容选自口语，因为该教材的目的就是教授地方口语而不是书面语。当然，在该书中，尤其是后半部分，也收入了相当一部分来自书本的官话和表达形式。"[①]《官话类编·序》："此书之成，并非一人之力，曾经分发北京、济南、南京、九江、汉口等处，批过数次，又曾亲往各地，协同诸位名士，详加批阅，终则合此诸批，一一审定，要必以通行者为是，兼有不通行者，则并列之，其列法，北京在右，南京在左，如有三行并列，即山东居其中也。"

该书200篇日常谈话语体课文，附录中补充的演说语体，课文中左中右

---

① 原文为：The prevalent style is colloquial, because the object of the book is to teach the spoken language as distinguished from the language of books; nevertheless there will be found, especially in the latter half, a considerable mixture of high Mandarin and of expressions taken from books.

并行排列的文字，注释中列举的具有南北地域分布差异的词语以及引言中列出的北京音列表、南京音列表、九江音列表、登州音列表、潍县音列表、重庆音列表，都充分体现了该教材的口语性。

（二）以课文为核心组织教材，将语法、词汇要点融入课文

《官话类编》将语法、词汇融为一体，没有专章讲解语法或词法，而是贯穿在专题课文中。从教材的编排体例看，重心放在课文上，重课文范文部分。每课围绕一个语法点，反复练习，每篇由若干散句组成，按词汇、词法、构词成分、句法等语言问题谋篇设计。（张美兰，2011：254—255）如第22课重点讲授反复问句，由若干散句组成，反复操练该语法点。例如：

①你（想不想家 / 想家不想家）。

②这个刀是（不是你的 / 你的不是）。

③我明天请客，你能来帮忙不能。

④今天算账，（方便不方便 / 便宜不便宜）。

⑤你家大姑娘，出了（门 / 嫁）没有。

⑥客来齐了没有。

⑦赶落太阳，能到不能。

⑧这个信封儿，合式不合式。还有别的（营生 / 事情）没有。

⑨先生在中国（服不服水土 / 服水土不服）。

语法点的编排上，作者很重视语法点的复现率，每次复现的同时，适当地增加语法点的难度。如第1课以最为常用的量词“个”作为切入点，在后面几课中逐渐增加所学量词的难度和数量。从课文的篇幅来看，前七课内容比较简单，都只是单句，句子之间没有任何关系。随着课文篇幅的增加，第8课开始出现了简短的对话，主要是一问一答的形式。

（三）注释和附录内容丰富

《官话类编》的注释和附录内容丰富，尽最大可能为学习者提供学习便利，是一本实用的汉语教材。

第5课的语法点是讲“~子”和“~儿”，注释部分对未婚女子的称呼“闺女、姑娘、小姐、女儿、女子”作了较为详细的注释。例如：

他有两个儿子，一个（闺女 / 姑娘）。

【注释Notes】There is great diversity in Mandarin in the use of terms for girl or young lady. In Shantung the common term is 闺女. The term 姑娘 is also used of the daughters of officers and educated men. In Peking 闺女 is used when speaking of one' s own daughter, while 姑娘 *is used in other cases*. In Southern Mandarin both terms are used with varying frequency, and besides them, as more genteel，小姐（little sister）is used. The terms 女儿 and 女子 are also frequently used, both in the North and in the South, especially for daughter, for which the Chinese has no distinctive word.（山东话普遍称呼为“闺女”。“姑娘”是指官绅及知识分子的女儿。北京话中“闺女”用来指自己的女儿，除此以外的其他场合则用“姑娘”。“小姐”多为南方上流社会用语，“女儿”“女子”南北方通用。）

第39课对不同地区“the sweet potatoes”的称呼作了详细的注释。例如：

外边有个要饭的，可以给他两块冷（山芋 / 地瓜 / 白薯）。

【注释Notes】Sweet potatoes are of comparatively recent introduction into China, and their name is not settled. In Peking they are called both 白薯 and 红薯；in Shantung, they are called 地瓜；in Nanking, 山芋；in Kiukiang, 萝卜薯（read *shao*）；and in Hankow, simply 薯。（北京话称“白薯”“红薯”，

山东话称“地瓜”，南京话称“山芋”，九江话称“萝卜薯”，汉口称“薯”。）

附录部分包括四部分内容，我们以“词和短语补充列表”为例。第40课的语法是讲授趋向补语“出来／去、进来／去”，附录中又补充了与“出来”搭配的动词“爬、剜、温、念、学、翻、找、过、滤、淋、淘”等59个，与“出去”搭配的动词“逃、撵、轰、赶、抬、搬、送、拿、抱”等32个，与“进来”搭配的动词“搬、拿、抬、扛、擒、闯”等16个，与“进去”搭配的动词“放、爬、钉、背、拉、戳”等20个。此外，附录中涉及日常生活的10篇对话,为学习者提供了生活上的便利，具有很强的实用性。

四、《官话类编》的价值

《官话类编》是清末最具影响力的汉语教材之一，在世界汉语教育史中产生过重要影响，具有非常重要的史料价值。

（一）展示了南北官话的语言面貌，为研究南北官话提供了有价值的语料

汉语共同语在晚清时期经历了从南京官话到北京官话的转变，据张卫东（1998a、1998b）研究，这个转变发生在1850年左右（清道光、咸丰年间）。狄考文编写的《官话类编》提供了生动丰富的语汇材料，展示了南北官话的语言面貌，呈现出北京官话和南京官话的异同，为相关研究提供了非常有价值的语料。

明清时期的官话、民国时期的国语和普通话是一脉相承的关系，研究南北官话的差异，有助于揭示普通话的来源问题。郭锐等（2017：3—18）借助《官话类编》所记录的南北官话词汇差异，研究了南北官话词汇与普通话词汇的传承关系。文章指出，晚清时期有南北官话分歧的词汇，有的是北京

官话词汇传继到普通话（A），有的是南京官话词汇传继到普通话（C），有的是来自北京官话和南京官话的词在普通话共存（B）。如表1：

表1 北京官话、南京官话词汇与普通话词汇的传承关系

A		B		C	
北京官话	南京官话	北京官话	南京官话	北京官话	南京官话
白薯	山芋	耗子	老鼠	烙铁	熨斗
白菜	黄芽菜	脑袋	头	日头	太阳
煤油	火油	姑爷	女婿	胰子	肥皂
上头	高头	窟窿	洞	东家	老板
馒头	馍馍	雹子	冰雹	土	灰
多少	几多	分儿	地步	蛇	长虫
抽烟	吃烟	自各儿	自己	见天	天天
喝酒	吃酒	这儿	这里	巧了	好像
给	把	知道	晓得	睄睬	留意

该文根据《官话类编》反映的词汇差异，对有南北官话差异的词汇和普通话词汇进行了统计，有南北官话差异的词汇传承到普通话中的具体数据见表2：

表2 《官话类编》有南北官话差异的词汇与普通话词汇的统计

来源	传至普通话	比例	总比例
北京官话	976	39.2%	52.0%
南京官话	643	25.8%	38.6%
南北共存	318	12.8%	
其他来源	553	22.2%	
	2490	100%	

我们可以看出，除去南北官话共同的词汇，有南北官话差异的词汇中，78%为普通话所继承，只有22%为其他来源，说明普通话的词汇是南北官话的混合体。

（二）为早期北京话研究提供一些实证

刘云（2013）指出："北京话是京味儿文化的载体和重要组成部分，有着深厚的文化底蕴，同时它又与当今的汉民族共同语——普通话有着最紧密的联系，研究意义毋庸赘言。目前的研究现状却不尽如人意，清代和民国时期的北京话研究尤为冷清，无论是研究的广度还是深度都要逊色于日本学者。根结主要在于我们对新材料挖掘的力度不够，仅仅依靠《红楼梦》和《儿女英雄传》，研究很难深入。”《官话类编》是以北京口语为主体的官话教材，记载了当时大量的北京官话口语词，可以更好地为早期北京话的研究提供一些实证，在一定程度上可以弥补材料上的欠缺。例如：

① 西国的狗（天里 / 白天）最老实，到了（夜里 / 下黑 / 黑下）才利害。（第15课）

② 刘仁欣已经赌过咒，管（几早 / 几儿 / 多咱）不和我说话。（第87课）

③ 你这二年在那里念书，家里也省好大的嚼用呢。（第89课）

④ 王先生上回来的信，说在这个月初三要到，今天倒十四咯，还没有来，（光景 / 大约）是有什么讲究啊。（第112课）

⑤ 他光说办土货，没说办洋货呀。答：他（好像 / 巧了）提过，我却（记不得 / 不记得）。（第130课）

（三）为当今国际汉语教育教材的编写提供借鉴

《官话类编》是为适应传教的需要，为来华传教士编写的一部汉语口语教材，在教学对象、教学目的方面都很明确，具有较强的实用性和针对性。

1. 教材的编写方面。来华传教士编写的教材更加重视文化，正如马礼逊所言：“一个人对一个国家的历史、地理、政治制度、宗教制度、当地风俗和看法忽视的部分，就是学习这个国家的语言中的困难……”（卞浩宇，2010）从马礼逊的《通用汉言之法》《华英字典》，到威妥玛的《语言自迩集》，再到狄考文的《官话类编》，这些著作对中国文化作了大量的介绍。

目前在对外汉语的语汇教学中，成语、歇后语、谜语、对联等的教学是难点，仍处于探索之中，而在一百多年前，狄考文已将大量带有文化差异的语汇用英文翻译，并且合理地安排在各章节的教学内容中，这对我们有很大的启示。

2. 配套教材的建设方面。《官话类编》是一本包含初级汉语到高级汉语教学内容的教材，教学内容比较多，学习任务重，为此狄考文编写了配套教材《官话简明教程》和《官话类编》（删节本）。《官话简明教程》就内容而言是《官话类编》的衔接，是本入门教材；《官话类编》（删节本）是节选《官话类编》前100课的内容，该教材的编写反映了狄考文具有汉语分级教学的意识。配套教材的编写，有助于教学内容的衔接，弥补主教材的不足。

《官话类编》作为“来华传教士的首选必备中文教材”（张美兰，2011：252），其在口语性和实用性上的突出特点，以及狄考文编写教材的经验、编写理念和原则、教材建设等方面，能够为今天的国际汉语教育教材的编写提供借鉴。

当然，《官话类编》也存在一些不足。如课文没有注音，句子基本没有考虑语境和语言交际的需求，有的译文翻译欠妥。例如：

> 他指望花几吊钱打官司能转转脸，究竟花了钱还输了官司，真是大姑娘下馆子，人钱两丢。（第198课）
>
> 【翻译 Translation】He hoped that by spending a few thousand cash in a lawsuit，he could put a fair face on the business， but in the end he spent his money and lost his suit. In fact it was the young lady visiting the saloon—girl and money both lost.

作者将“人钱两丢”翻译为“girl and money both lost”欠妥。

五、结　语

《官话类编》是清末最具影响力的汉语教材之一，在世界汉语教育史、中华文化海外传播中产生过重要影响，具有非常重要的史料价值。该书不仅提供了生动丰富的语汇材料，展示了南北官话的语言面貌，呈现出北京官话和南京官话的异同，也为相关研究提供了非常有价值的文献，而且能够为今天的国际汉语教育教材的编写提供借鉴。我们期待更多的学者来关注这部著作，关注明清时期域外汉语教科书。

参考文献

卞浩宇（2010）《晚清来华西方人汉语学习与研究》，苏州大学博士学位论文。

崔华杰（2008）《狄考文研究》，山东师范大学硕士学位论文。

[美] 丹尼尔·W. 费舍（2009）《狄考文传：一位在中国山东生活了四十五年的传教士》，广西师范大学出版社，桂林。

顾长声（1991）《传教士与近代中国》，上海人民出版社，上海。

郭　锐、翟　赟、徐菁菁（2017）汉语普通话从哪里来？——从南北官话差异看普通话词汇、语法来源，《中国言语文化学》第6期。

李婧超（2014）《狄考文〈官话类编〉语音研究》，辽宁师范大学硕士学位论文。

李木谢子（2011）《狄考文的汉语教学——〈官话类编〉研究》，华东师范大学硕士学位论文。

李　蕊（2010）《狄考文〈官话类编〉研究》，上海师范大学硕士学位论文。

李银菊（2013）《近代美国来华传教士狄考文的汉语观——以〈官话类编〉为例》，山东师范大学硕士学位论文。

栗　源（2015）《近代美国来华传教士汉语教材研究——以〈文学官话书〉〈官话类编〉为例》，山东师范大学硕士学位论文。

刘　云（2013）早期北京话的新材料，《中国语文》第2期。

鲁国尧（1985）明代官话及其基础方言问题——读《利玛窦中国札记》，《南京大学学报》第4期。

鲁国尧（2007）研究明末清初官话基础方言的廿三年历程："从字缝里看"到"从字面上看"，《语言科学》第2期。

齐　灿（2014）《19世纪末南北京官话介词、助词比较研究——以〈官话指南〉〈官话类编〉注释为例》，北京外国语大学硕士学位论文。

钱鸿儒（2013）《狄考文〈官话类编〉语汇研究》，浙江财经学院硕士学位论文。

宋代华（2016）《狄考文〈官话简明教程〉研究》，山东师范大学硕士学位论文。

[日]太田辰夫（1964／1995）北京话的文法特点，见《中国语文论集》，汲古书院，东京。

王智玲（2007）《传教士：近代中外文化交流使者——北美长老会传教士狄考文个案研究》，山东师范大学硕士学位论文。

王忠欣（2000）《基督教与中国近现代教育》，湖北教育出版社，武汉。

邢公畹（1990）论汉语的"连锁复句"——对《官话类编》一书连锁复句的分析，《世界汉语教学》第3期。

邢　梅（2012）《〈圣经〉官话和合本句法研究》，复旦大学博士学位论文。

张美兰（2007）美国传教士狄考文对十九世纪末汉语官话研究的贡献，浸会大学林思齐东西学术研究交流研究所研究报告。

张美兰（2008）《官话类编》与十九世纪的汉语官话，《东亚文献研究》（韩国）创刊号。

张美兰（2011）《明清域外官话文献语言研究》，东北师范大学出版社，长春。

张卫东（1998a）试论近代南方官话的形成及其地位，《深圳大学学报》第3期。

张卫东（1998b）北京音何时成为汉语官话标准音，《深圳大学学报》第4期。

张西平（2009）《世界汉语教育史》，商务印书馆，北京。

A COURSE

OF

MANDARIN LESSONS,

BASED ON IDIOM,

BY

REV. C. W. MATEER, D.D., LL.D.

Revised Edition.

SHANGHAI:
AMERICAN PRESBYTERIAN MISSION PRESS.

1900.

TO

STUDENTS OF MANDARIN,

THIS EFFORT

TO REMOVE THE DIFFICULTIES AND OPEN THE WAY TO A MORE THOROUGH ACQUISITION

OF THE

CHINESE SPOKEN LANGUAGE

IS

RESPECTFULLY DEDICATED.

eking, Nanking, Kiukiang, Tengchow and Weihien.

they agree with Peking ircle. In other cases the

TĚNGCHOW sounds are printed in YELLOW. Where they agree with Peking, Nanking or Kiukiang the fact is indicated by a YELLOW circle. In other cases the *characters* are printed in YELLOW.

WEIHIEN sounds are printed in GREEN. Where they agree with Peking, Nanking, Kiukiang or Tĕngchow the fact is indicated by a GREEN circle. In other cases the *characters* are printed in GREEN.

ai	uan	uang	uau	uei	uên	ui	un	ung	ü	üan	üe	üei	üein	üen	üin	ün	üoǐ	ǎh	auh	eih	oh	êh	êoh	ih	iauh	ieih	ioh	iuh	ǐh	oh	uh	uauh	ueh	uêh	üh	üeih	
																						額		一						譯	屋						
	專	壯	抓	追	準		準	中	聚主		決			卷		君	爵	折	紮		折		妯						汁	着	祝			拙	局		Ch
揣	川	牀		吹	春		春	充	取除		缺			犬全		羣	却	撤	察		撤		觸						尺	綽	出				屈		Ch'
																		決																			Chw
																		缺																			Ch'w
								風											法												福						F
壞	換	黃	花	回	混		混	紅	許	喧	穴	靴	喧	喧	訓			赫				赫		吸	瞎	歇	學	畜		合	忽	滑		或		血	H
									須	旋	雪			旋	巡	訓	學							吸			學	畜									Hs
																		或	滑																		Hw
							潤	絨																													J
								絨																													Jr
																																					Jrw
																																					Jw
[illegible]	官	光	瓜	規	棍		棍	工	居	卷	決	噘	卷	卷	君		脚	革				革		及	甲	潔	脚	菊		各	谷	刮		國	局	決	K
快	欵	况	誇	魁	困		困	孔	去	犬	瘸	瘸	犬	犬	羣		却	客	掐			客		乞	恰	怯	郤	曲		渴	哭			闊	屈	缺	K'
																		國	刮																		Kw
																		闊																			K'w
	亂			累	論		論	龍	驢		畧					掄	畧	勒	辣	烈		勒	六	立		烈	掠			落	六				律		L
														戀																							Lw
								夢											抹	滅		麥		密		滅				末	木						M
	煖						嫩	膿	女		虐						虐		納	揑				逆		揑	虐			諾							N
																		額												諤							Ng
																																					Nw
								跭										白	八	憋		白		必		憋				薄	不						P
								朋										迫		撇		迫		匹		撇				潑	僕						P'
	軟			銳	雲				如									熱				熱	肉	日						弱	肉				入		R
	算			碎	孫		孫	送	須				旋		巡			色	颯	洩		色	俗	惜		雪	削	粟		索	俗				恤	雪	S
[illegible]	拴	雙		水	順		順	松	書		說				[illegible]			舌	殺		舌		叔						十	勺	叔				術		Sh
																		說	刷																		Shw
																																					Sr
																																					Srw
																																					Sw
	短			對	敦		敦	冬										得	答	跌		得	督	的		跌				奪	督						T
	團			退	吞		吞	同										特	塔	貼		特	禿	剔		貼				託	禿						T'
	鑽			嘴	尊		尊	宗	聚			嗟			俊			則	雜	節		則	足	疾		節	爵			作	足					絕	Ts
	竄			催	寸		寸	聰	取				全					策	擦	切		策	促	七		切	雀			撮	促						Ts'
									聚						俊		爵																				Tsh
									取	全							雀																				Tsh'
								中																													Tsr
								冲																													Tsr'
																																					Tsrw
																																					Ts'rw
																																					Tsw
																																					Ts'w
																																					Tw
																																					T'w
								翁											襪											惡	屋						W
								用	魚	原	月		原	原	雲	雲	約		押	葉			育							約			月				Y

A Comparative Chart of the Sounds in Five Dialec

PEKING sounds are all printed in BLACK under their proper initials and finals.

NANKING sounds are printed in RED. Where they agree with Peking the fact is indicated by a RED circle. In other cases the *characters* are printed in RED.

KIUKIANG sounds a… or Nanking the fa… *characters* are print…

	a	ai	an	ang	ao	au	e	ei	ein	en	ê	êei	êu	êng	êo	êr	i	ia	iai	ian	iang	iao	iau	ie	iei	iein	ien	in	ing	iõ	iong	iu	iung	ï	ĭ	o	o…
	阿	哎	安	昂	傲	阿					額		恩	哼	偶	兒	衣																			阿	訛
Ch	乍	齋	占	章	兆	乍	這	這	占	眞	這		眞	正	晝		祭	家		占	江	交		姐這			賤	進	井正	角		酒	窘	知	知	斫	摭
Ch'	茶	柴	諂	昌	潮	茶	車	車	諂	臣	車		臣	成	抽		齊	恰	楷	諂	搶	巧		且車			錢	親	清成	卻		秋	窮	池	池		綽
Chw	抓	拽	專	壯		抓		追		準			準																								
Ch'w	欻	揣	川	牀				吹		春			春																								擺
F	法		反	方				非		分		非	分	風	否																					否	佛
H	哈	害	寒	杭	好	哈		赫		很	黑		很	恒	後		希	下	偕	限	向	孝	下	歇	鞋	限	限	欣	形	學	兄	休	兄			火侯	河
H																	希西	下斜	偕	先	向相	孝小	下	些			限	欣心	形性	學		休修	兄				
Hw	花	懷	換	黃		花		回		混			混																								火
J			染	嚷	繞						惹		人	扔																					日		若
J			染	嚷	繞										柔									惹				人									
Jrw			軟																																		
Jw			軟					瑞																													
K	蛤	改	甘	剛	告			給格		根	個		根	更	狗		記	家	界	見	江	交	家	結		見	見	金	經	角	窖	救	窖			哥句	哥
K'	卡	開	看	炕	考	卡		伲刻		肯	刻		肯	坑	口		奇	恰	楷	欠	腔	巧	痂	怯	茄	欠	欠	欽	輕	卻	窮	求	窮			可口	可
Kw	瓜	怪	官	光		瓜		規		棍			棍																								果
K'w	誇	快	欵	况		誇		魁		困			困																								闊
L	拉	來	懶	浪	老	拉		累	連		勒		論	冷	陋		李	倆		連	兩	了		列			連	林	另	畧		留	攏			羅	羅
Lw			亂					累		論																											
M	馬	買	慢	忙	毛	馬		美	面	門	末	美	門	夢	謀		米			面		苗		滅	咩		面	民	名			謬				摩謀	摩
N	那	奶	男	囊	鬧	那		內	念				嫩	能	耨		你			念	娘	鳥		揑			念	您寧	寧	虐		牛	濃			挪	挪
Ng		愛	安	昂	傲			厄		恩			恩		偶																					我	
Nw			煖					餒																													
P	巴	拜	板	邦	包	巴		備別	扁	本	波	倍	本	崩	褒		比			扁		表		別			扁	賓	兵							波	波
P'	怕	派	盼	旁	跑	怕		陪	片	盆	破	陪	盆	朋	掊呸		皮			片		票		撇			片	貧	平							破剖	破
R			染	讓	繞			惹				惹	人	扔	柔																						
S	撒	賽	散	桑	掃	撒		些碎塞	先		色		森	僧	叟		西				相	小			些		先	心	性			修			絲	所搜	索
Sh	傻	曬	山	賞	少	傻	舍	舍	善	身	舍		身	聖	手		西			善				舍			善	心	聖			手		十	時	嗾	
Shw	耍	衰	拴	雙		耍		水					順																								說
Sr	沙	晒	山		捎			色		森				生	搜																				師		
Srw	耍	率	拴	雙				誰																													
Sw	耍	衰	算拴	雙爽				水碎		孫			順																								
T	大	歹	單	當	道	大		得爹	店		得		敦	等	豆		地			店		弔		爹	爹		店		定			丢				多豆	多
T'	他	太	炭	湯	逃	他		退忒	天		忒		吞	疼	頭		替			天		挑		貼			天		聽							妥頭	妥
Ts	雜	在	贊	葬	早	咱		賊則	賤	偺	則		怎	增	走		祭				將	焦			姐		賤	進	井			酒			子	坐走	坐
Ts'	擦	才	殘	倉	草	薩		策且	錢		策		岑	層	湊		齊				槍	俏			且		錢	親	清			秋			次	錯湊	錯
Tsh																	即			尖	將	焦		節				進	井			酒	蹤				
Tsh'																	妻			前	搶	俏		切				親	清			秋	從				
Tsr	扎	齋	跕		找			窄		箴				爭	鄒																						
Tsr'	茶	柴	產		抄			拆		岑				撐	愁																				之		卓
Tsrw	抓	拽		庄				追																											匙		
Ts'rw		揣		窗				吹																													
Tsw	抓	拽	纘專	壯				追罪		尊			準																								
Ts'w		揣	竄川	牀				吹催		寸			春																								
Tw			短					對		敦																											
T'w			團					退		吞																											
W	瓦	外	萬	王		瓦		爲		文		爲	文	翁																						惡	我
Y	牙	挨		羊	要	牙		夜葉	言						有					言				夜			言	音	迎			有				喲	約

PREFACE TO FIRST EDITION.

IT is now twenty-five years since I began to make lessons for beginners in Mandarin. I had at that time little thought of ever printing them, or of the extent to which they would finally grow. At first I made only twenty lessons, but subsequently added a few at a time, until the number reached fifty. The plan originally adopted was substantially that which has now been wrought out to completion. These fifty lessons were copied out and used by beginners for about ten years, when, upon the arrival of a considerable number of new missionaries in Shantung, I revised the lessons already made and added others on the same plan, increasing the number to one hundred and seven. The extent to which these were copied and used, led me about five years ago, to take up the whole work with a view to preparing it for publication. I extended and perfected the plan, added new lessons and thoroughly revised and recast the lessons already made.

Plan. The plan of the course is its distinguishing feature. Each lesson is constructed to illustrate one or more idioms which constitute its "subject;" the word idiom being taken in a somewhat loose and comprehensive sense. The subjects were not evolved by the application to Chinese of Western grammatical principles and ideas, but were gathered directly from the mandarin colloquial by a careful observation of its peculiar forms and methods. They are somewhat heterogeneous, it is true, but not more so than the language they are intended to teach. The plan is believed to afford a number of important advantages, of which the following are the chief:—

1. It facilitates a thoroughly progressive arrangement by which the peculiarities of the language are set forth in a natural order, proceeding from the simpler to the more complex and difficult.

2. The student instead of groping his way through a maze of bewildering idioms, explained in a hap-hazard way in notes and vocabularies, and often falling a victim to hasty and false generalizations, has given to him in each lesson an intelligible idiom, which is fully explained in the subject, and strongly impressed by the abundant illustrations contained in the lesson. These idioms thus become to him so many land marks of progress, and by their acquisition he is made master of the whole structure of the language.

3. The subjects of the lessons, which embrace all the most difficult and important features of the language, being thus singled out and made prominent, are, on this account, much more carefully explained and illustrated than would be the case on a different system.

4. The fact that the lessons are composed of detached and independent sentences, gives opportunity for the introduction of a wider range of subject matter, of style and of idiom than could be secured on any other plan.

5. A large number of the lessons bring to view classes of particles and key words approximately synonymous, yet differing in use and in their shades of meaning. By the study of these lessons the student will acquire a range and variety of expression not easily acquired in any other way. The prime defect of many mandarin speakers is that having got hold of one such word or expression, they are content to ring the changes on it alone, all oblivious to the fact that there are various other cognate forms of similar import yet differing by varying uses and shades of meaning. The result is a monotonous style, wanting both in vigor and perspicuity.

That the plan incidentally involves some disadvantages, is freely admitted. All great gains involve minor losses. The chief disadvantages are the following:—

1. The arrangement according to idioms necessitates the keeping back of certain common and useful forms of expression for an inconveniently long time. This difficulty was frequently felt in arranging the order of the lessons. It drew from my Chinese assistant the remark, that each particular lesson seemed to be clamoring to get in first. The difficulty, however, will not be felt by the learner, and the disadvantage it might otherwise be to him, has been largely obviated by anticipating many such words and phrases, and will be further obviated by following the method of study recommended. (See Introduction: Directions to the student).

2. Lessons which introduce a considerable number of nearly synonymous words are liable to confuse the learner with distinctions for which he is not yet prepared, and which his memory cannot retain. This difficulty, which results from the richness of the language, may be largely obviated by a judicious method of study. While going over the whole lesson carefully, let the student fix in his memory one or two of the more important words for present use, not being too much disturbed that he is not able to retain the others. When subsequently they are heard in conversation or met with in books, they will seem like old acquaintances, and will in this way presently become familiar and their accurate use be acquired.

3. The sentences being disconnected, are harder to understand and more likely to be misunderstood than if they stood in connected discourse. While this is no doubt true, it is largely obviated by accurate translations and by suitable notes and explanations, and is more than compensated by the superior opportunity thus afforded for the ready introduction of every class of idiom and every style of expression.

Style. The prevalent style is colloquial, because the object of the book is to teach the spoken language as distinguished from the language of books; nevertheless there will be found, especially in the latter half, a considerable mixture of high Mandarin and of expressions taken from books. I shall probably be criticised for introducing too much colloquial and too many localisms To this criticism I would reply, that there is much misconception as to the extent to which many of these so called localisms prevail. It does not follow that every expression not commonly seen in Mandarin books, is necessarily local. I have found by investigation that many such expressions are practically general. Moreover, a useful expression that prevails throughout two or three provinces and has an authorized writing, is not to be rejected as local. A man may not himself desire to use all these colloquial forms, yet it is very important to understand them when used by others, as they constantly are by the Chinese. The chief advantage which the Chinaman has in conversation over the average foreigner is his ability to use and to understand these colloquialisms. It must not be supposed, however, that every sort of colloquialism known to the author or his assistants has been introduced. Care has been taken to exclude purely local expressions, especially such as have no authorized writing, as also to exclude, to a considerable extent, that useless colloquial verbiage which characterizes all dialects to a greater or less degree, and which is unnecessary and undesirable in one who would use Chinese to the best advantage.* As far as possible local peculiarities are noted as such and are not repeated.

A more important argument for the use of colloquial is, that general Mandarin, as it is called, is too narrow in its range to answer all the ends of speech, and has constantly to be reinforced from both the colloquial and the *Wên-li.* If the speaker of it attempts to go beyond the narrow range of thought which it covers, he will find himself at a loss for words, and will be compelled to resort to round-about forms and labored explanations, in striking contrast with the straightforward and expressive language of him who commands the abundant resources of the colloquial. He may indeed call in the assistance of the *Wên-li,* if his attainments are adequate, but it will be at the expense of speaking in a pedantic and pretentious style unintelligible to the great majority.

Another point worthy of attention, especially on the part of those who desire to persuade and impress others in public address, is that labored phraseology and paraphrastic expressions are fatal to oratory, which requires not only weighty and impressive thoughts, but also vivid and expressive language which fulfils its office as the arrow flies to the mark.

On the other hand it is not unlikely that I shall be criticised for having introduced too much book language. With reference to this criticism, I would say that very few learn Mandarin who do not at the same time wish to know something of the book style. Moreover, the line of demarcation between Mandarin and *Wên-li* is but vaguely defined. They pass into each other by insensible gradations. It will be found also that the book language of these lessons consists almost entirely of those ready-made and pithy book ex-

* By useless verbiage I mean the ever-recurring and superfluous use of such words as 了, 着, 的, 個, 嗎, 呢, 來, 去, etc

pressions, with which good Mandarin speakers and writers enrich and adorn their style, and which frequent use has made generally intelligible. With these expressions every one who aims to be a good Mandarin speaker, should be familiar.

Materials. The Chinese sentences which constitute the lessons have been gathered from all quarters. After the subjects were made out and arranged, Mandarin literature was searched for suitable illustrations, and what were found were copied under their appropriate lessons. All extant Mandarin literature was considered a legitimate field from which to gather. Much more might have been gathered from Chinese novels but for the difficulty of finding in them any full sentence fairly representing the language of common life. The result of this search was that under most lessons, much more material was gathered than was required, thus giving a choice of the best. Many sentences also were specially constructed by a number of different teachers, particularly in the case of lessons embracing colloquial idioms not often found in books.

The sentences have been chosen not only so as to illustrate the various idioms of the lessons, but pains was also taken to have them embrace as wide a range as possible of words and ideas. In them will be found the language of domestic, social, literary and official life; of art, science, commerce, business, history and religion. It should be remarked however, that there was no intention to *teach* history, science, religion or morals, but simply to exhibit and illustrate the Chinese language. That the lessons do in fact contain much useful information about China and the Chinese people, is an incidental advantage of no mean value.

The manner of their preparation implies that the sentences are truly Chinese in thought, style and idiom. With the exception of some of the short, simple sentences in the first twenty or thirty lessons, the author has scarcely composed a single sentence in the book. Not only so, but in the sentences made to order by teachers, or in emendations made in sentences taken from books, he has left the Chinese teachers to their own spontaneous judgment, *never in any case controlling or overruling them.* Of course the Chinese will not meet the approval of every teacher, for Chinese writers criticise and find fault with each other just as Western writers do.

Translation. The translations are, in the main, literal, being however less and less literal as the lessons advance. But the student must not expect that every word in the English will have its corresponding word in the Chinese The structure of the languages is too radically different to make this a possible thing Strict conformity to the meaning of the original has been more aimed at than elegance of language. Neglect of some of the less important words of the Chinese sentence would oftentimes have greatly enhanced the elegance of the translation. It was felt however that in order to learn the language accurately, the student ought to have a thoroughly faithful and accurate translation as a guide. As far as possible, very colloquial Chinese has been rendered into colloquial English, and more stately Chinese into more elegant English.

Subjects. The statements and illustrations of the subjects have been wrought out with especial care, and contain the most useful and important matter in the book. In them are comprised all the important idioms of the language. They should be carefully noted and studied. The English headings are but brief approximations, and must be taken with some degree of allowance. The subjects were originally worked out in Chinese, and these English headings were an after-thought. In many cases it was found very difficult to give a brief English heading that fairly represented the subject.

Vocabularies. The definitions of words and phrases are brief, but are nevertheless intended to include all the common *Mandarin* uses of the words. The meaning appropriate to the lesson under which the word or phrase occurs, is italicised for the convenience of the learner. This method of giving a full definition, and italicising the one needed, has a number of important advantages which make it a decided improvement over the more common method of simply giving the definition required in the given case. (1) It prevents the student from learning a secondary meaning at the first without knowing it to be such. (2) While learning the one meaning of a character the student has constantly before his mind the fact that it has other meanings, and as he refers again and again to the meaning required, he will unconsciously become more or less familiar with the others. (3) It renders the student independent of a dictionary, thus saving much time and trouble in looking for words. (4) The vocabularies will be found to contain many definitions not given in any dictionary or vocabulary extant.

Notes. The notes are somewhat miscellaneous in their character. The larger number are given to the explanation of unusual idioms and difficult constructions. Phrases too long for convenient definition in the vocabularies, are explained in the notes. Questions concerning the proper characters to be used in particular cases, as also the probable analysis of abnormal phrases, are discussed in the notes. In order to elucidate the meaning of sentences, numerous explanations have been given of historical, political, social, literary, educational, religious and many other matters, so that the student, while learning the language, is also learning many other useful and important things about China and the Chinese. Much time and care have been bestowed on the preparation of the notes, and it is hoped they will prove not the least useful part of the book.

Dialects. In projecting and constructing the lessons the most difficult question that confronted the author was that of dialect. The lessons first made were confined to the Shantung dialects, and to have carried out and finished the course on that plan, would have very greatly lightened the labor involved, but it would have limited the usefulness of the book to a single Province. On the other hand, to have rejected everything, that savored of a difference of dialect, would have compelled a style far too high for colloquial Mandarin, and would thus have defeated the main object in view. The only practicable alternative was to compare and combine a variety of dialects, which onerous task has accordingly been attempted In order to exhibit the practical results, the plan of parallel readings has been introduced. (See Introduction: Explanations.) The lessons have been constructed with reference to the dialects of Peking, Chinanfu, Chefoo, Nanking and Kiukiang,—all that the circumstances of the author enabled him to compass. In order to compare these dialects, the lessons have been twice revised by the aid of Peking teachers, twice by the aid of Nanking teachers, once by the aid of Chinanfu teachers, and once by the aid of a Kiukiang teacher; in addition to which they have been revised, in whole or in part, by one or more of the best foreign speakers of Chinese in these several places. Pekingese has received a larger share of attention than any other dialect, partly because it is the court dialect, but chiefly because there were more published helps by which it may be known.

In carrying out this plan, a vigorous effort has been made to construct a course of lessons free from the predominant influence of any one dialect; although it is perhaps too much to expect that the author and his Chinese assistant should be able to free themselves from all partiality to their own dialect. It should be remembered, however, that those who are acquainted with only one dialect, are not altogether competent judges in the premises, for, missing many of the peculiarities of their own dialect and finding others instead, they naturally attribute the difference to the undue influence of the author's dialect, not knowing that those who speak the dialect of the author will equally miss many of its peculiarities and find others in their stead. It is hoped that the plan pursued will not only make the book useful to all students of Mandarin, but will at the same time afford many valuable hints as to the comparison of dialects.

System of Spelling.

It was with great reluctance that I finally decided to propose a new system of spelling. The preparation of the lessons was well advanced before this step was decided upon, and the elaboration of the system has consumed much time and materially delayed the publication of the work. The most natural thing would seem to have been to use the system already most in vogue: viz., that of Sir Thomas Wade. I found, however, that this system would not spell my own dialect, nor in fact any other dialect than Pekingese, and that unless I left all the other dialects to shift for themselves some other system must be used. It was proposed for a time to give both Wade's and William's spellings, and a specimen page was so printed, but the more the subject was canvassed the more evident it became that such a plan would greatly encumber the book and serve no adequate purpose. Several other plans were canvassed but rejected as unsatisfactory. Inasmuch as in language and idiom the book represents several different Mandarin dialects, it was strongly felt that a system of spelling ought to be provided, adapted to the spelling of these dialects and comprehensive enough to embrace them all without violating its own consistency. As no system now extant fulfilled, or even approximated, these requirements, the author felt constrained to propose a new system. In doing this he has not, however, done what would have been much more simple as well as satisfactory to himself; viz., proposed *de novo* an original system, but has followed strictly in the line of his predecessors, making only such changes as seemed to be demanded by the exigencies of the case. If the system wins its way, it may become an important step towards a general system comprehensive of all Mandarin dialects.

The spelling given in the vocabularies is that heard in Peking. This spelling is chosen, because Pekingese is the court dialect and more popular than any other. In order, however, to afford opportunity for the insertion of a second spelling, a space has, in all cases, been left either after or underneath the Peking spelling. This has considerably increased the space required for the vocabularies, but will, it is believed, be a very valuable feature to all who use another dialect than the Pekingese.

Arrangement.

For the convenience of the student all that concerns each lesson,—Chinese, translation, subject, vocabulary and notes,—are brought together in one place. A convenient and practicable arrangement for accomplishing this end proved to be a matter of no small difficulty, especially as the lessons and their parts were not, and could not be made, of a uniform length. . . . The first twenty lessons are printed in a somewhat larger Chinese type. This was done because, at the first, students find it easier to distinguish the characters when printed in large type.

Indexes.

A full syllabic index has been prepared, including all the words and phrases defined in the vocabularies, subjects and notes. This will enable the learner to find any word or phrase at any time. It is also proposed to prepare and print as soon as practicable, indexes according to the other dialects to which the lessons are specially adapted; viz., Nanking, Kiukiang, Weihien and Têngchow, which will be furnished and bound with the book at a small additional charge. An index of the single characters by radicals, is also added, by means of which characters may be found when the Peking spelling is unknown. Having the single character the phrases under it may also be found.

Acknowledgments.

My first and chiefest acknowledgments are due to my Chinese assistant, Rev. Tso Li Wên (鄒立文), who has given fully four years of constant and diligent labor to the collection and preparation of the Chinese text. He has also investigated with me dialectic differences and has given unstinted and enthusiastic labor to the work in all its details.

Hardly less are acknowledgments due to my wife, who has contributed much in every way to the perfection of the work,—much more than her modesty will allow me to acknowledge.

Special acknowledgments are due to Rev. C. Goodrich, D.D., Rev. J. Wherry, D.D. and Rev. S. E. Meech of Peking, who kindly acted as advisers in the application of the new system of spelling to the Peking dialect. To them every question was referred, and in accordance with their verdict every point was decided.*

I wish also to acknowledge my indebtedness to Rev. C. Goodrich, D.D. of T'ungchow, Rev. J. Wherry, D.D. and Rev. J. L. Whiting of Peking, Rev. P. D. Bergen of Chinanfu, Rev. J. C. Ferguson of Nanking, Rev. F. W. Baller of Ganking and especially to Rev. J. R. Hykes of Kiukiang, for many important criticisms and suggestions, both in general and in particular. Thanks are due to Rev. J. A. Silsby and Mr. A. Kenmure for valuable assistance in correcting and revising the proofs.

Finally, thanks are due to the Board of Missions of the Presbyterian Church and to my own mission in Shantung, for their generous kindness in affording me the time and opportunity to carry forward and complete this undertaking, and see it safely through the Press.

With thankfulness to the kind providence of God which has guided and preserved me and my assistant to the end of this work, do I now send forth the book on its mission; earnestly desiring that it may be of great service to many who are preparing themselves to preach the Gospel to the Chinese. But for the hope that such would be the case, I should not have been willing to turn aside for so long a time from the more congenial work of teaching and preaching.

* See Preface to second edition.

C. W. Mateer.

July 1*st*, 1892.

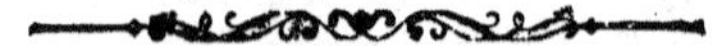

PREFACE TO SECOND EDITION.

BEFORE the author was aware or had begun to make any preparation for a second edition, the announcement came that the first edition was nearly exhausted. The pressure of other engagements has rendered any extended revision impossible. The whole course, however, has been gone over very carefully, and many minor improvements made, and mistakes corrected. This is especially true of the first part of the course, which originally received less careful preparation for the press than did the latter part. The vocabularies in particular have been very carefully revised and corrected.

The system of spelling has not been changed. The author has felt more and more, however, that the application of the system to the Peking dialect did not fairly represent the system in that it was not consistently carried out. After further investigation and correspondence with various parties in the north in whose judgment I had confidence I concluded to go somewhat beyond the views of the Peking friends who gave me their advice for the first edition, and make the application of the system to Pekingese consistent with itself, and in harmony with its application to other dialects. The changes consist in putting *wei* for *ui*, *üen* for *üan*, *yiu* for *yu* and *yien* for *yen*. For discussion see remarks after the Peking sound table, page 43.

The criticism most frequently made on the lessons has been that they are too long and too difficult at the start, and that an introductory series of shorter and easier lessons is needed. In order to meet the requirements of the case a series of thirty primary lessons has been prepared embracing only three hundred characters in all. See Introduction to Primary Lessons.

The plan or order of printing the first twenty lessons has been changed so as to make them uniform with the other portion of the book. Though not wholly satisfactory no improvement on the general plan of arrangement seemed feasible.

Quite a number of additional dialogues and essays have been added in the supplement giving thereby much more exercise in reading Mandarin and introducing the student also to a wide range of special words and phrases.

C. W. MATEER.

Tungchow, April 20, 1898.

CONTENTS.

INTRODUCTION.

LESSONS.

SUPPLEMENT.

LIST OF SUPPLEMENTARY WORDS AND PHRASES.

DIALOGUES AND ORATIONS.

INDEXES.

INTRODUCTION.

MANDARIN.

MANDARIN, or official language as it is called by the Chinese, is in its essential features the language of the people in all the eighteen provinces, except the coast provinces south of the Yang-tsï.* It may be divided into Northern, Southern and Western Mandarin; and is often further distinguished by provinces, as Honan Mandarin, Shantung Mandarin, etc. Northern Mandarin is largely dominated by Pekingese which, being the court dialect, is the most fashionable, and is the accredited language of officials throughout the empire. Southern Mandarin is more widely used and is spoken by a larger number of people than Northern Mandarin. It is not, however, as homogeneous and includes more words and phrases which have no settled writing, being more or less allied to the non-Mandarin dialects of the South. Shantung lies between the two extremes, and its Mandarin may be approximately characterized as Central. The western part of the province is much influenced by Pekingese, with which it has its chief affinities. The eastern portion has hard initial consonants and is in other ways related to Southern Mandarin. The people of this part of the province are the descendants of a large migration from Hupeh and southern Honan.† Being quite off the track of emigration from the North, the dialect has remained comparatively unchanged, not having been affected by the tide which has been flowing from the North for several hundred years. It has fewer words and phrases which cannot be written by significant characters than any other dialect with which I am acquainted, and represents the purest hard sounds now heard in China.

An attempt has been made to adapt the present course of lessons to both Northern and Southern Mandarin. With this end in view they have been repeatedly revised by the aid of teachers from Peking, Chinanfu, Nanking and Kiukiang. No opportunity has been found to make any satisfactory comparison with the Mandarin of Western China. In some cases two or more forms of expression have been found necessary, which have been inserted in parallel lines, the Northern form being on the right and the Southern on the left. These parallel readings generally represent forms of expression, for which there is no equivalent that is everywhere current. For a full explanation of these readings, see Explanations at the end of this Introduction. The student can adopt whichever reading his teacher approves. This method, besides accomplishing the special end in view, has this incidental advantage, that while the student need not learn the forms not current in his

---

* The term 官話, as applied by the Chinese to their own language, seems to imply that originally it sprang up when the people spoke a language different from that of the official class; that is to say, it probably took its rise when a large proportion of the people were not Chinese proper, but aborigines,—subdued and governed by Chinese rulers. It is well known that the Chinese came into China from the North and West This led to their gradually driving the aborigines southward and eastward—a process which has been going on for at least four thousand years. During this process, and especially in its earlier stages, when the aborigines were many and the Chinese few, there was much commingling of races and admixture of language, the conquered learning the language of the conquerors (which they would naturally call "*officer talk*"), yet at the same time modifying it to a large extent, as has ever been the case in similar circumstances. This amalgamation of language prevailed along the head of the wave of conquest, which gradually pushed its way southward and eastward, and as different aboriginal languages were encountered, gave rise to different dialects, resulting finally in what are now the non-Mandarin coast dialects of the South. In the meantime the body of the wave was behind, and being continually reinforced by fresh immigration from the North, it maintained a relatively pure Chinese. This supposition, as to the relation of the southern coast dialects to Mandarin, is strengthened by the fact that these coast dialects depart much more from the written language (which was purely Chinese) than does the Mandarin. All this is quite independent of the numerous changes which during these ages Mandarin has undergone within itself.

† It is related in the Topography of P'êng-lai that at the close of the Yüen dynasty a man named Chang Liang Pi (張良弼), then governor of Hupeh, raised a force of over thirty thousand men, having his head-quarters near 襄陽府. Being left without support, he gathered together the families of his soldiers and gradually retreated to the promontory of Shantung, where he took possession of the country and maintained his independence for a time, but by and by submitted to the new dynasty. Tradition gives the whole number who came with him as about 200,000, and reports that he drove out or killed many of the original inhabitants. The general truth of these statements is attested by tradition pervading the whole people, by the use of pure, hard sounds, and by the different character of the people.

own locality, the fact that they have passed under his eye, will broaden his knowledge of the language and give him an advantage in communicating with persons using a different dialect.

Mandarin is usually distinguished as general or *t'ung-hsing*, local, colloquial and book Mandarin.* *T'ung-hsing* Mandarin consists of all such words and phrases as are everywhere current, and are capable of being written by authorized characters. Local Mandarin consists of all such words and phrases as are local in their use, not commonly found in books, nor capable of being written by authorized characters. Colloquial Mandarin includes all the words and phrases, both *t'ung-hsing* and local, which are in common use in any given locality. Book Mandarin consists of words and phrases taken from the literary style, which are not ordinarily used in speaking but are found in Mandarin books, being used to supplement the deficiencies of the *t'ung-hsing* Mandarin, as well as to add to its dignity and elegance. There are no definite lines of demarcation between these classes of Mandarin. Every man has his own standard.

CHARACTERS.

CHINESE writing is ideographic, and derived, no doubt, from a hieroglyphic original. Its origin, however, is not certainly known, dating back as it does into the obscurity of prehistoric times. The meaning of each character is fixed, but the sound given varies greatly in different places. The great standard dictionary of the Chinese language, prepared under the patronage of the Emperor Kanghi, contains upwards of 41,000 characters, but the greater part of them are either duplicates or obsolete. Dr Williams' dictionary contains over twelve thousand characters, but of these some are duplicates and many are very rarely used. The whole text of the Chinese classics contains 4,754 different characters. There are probably not much over six thousand characters in general use at the present day. Of these many are used only in the literary style. Of characters used in Mandarin there are not over four, or at most five thousand. An average educated Chinese speaker will not use over about two thousand five hundred to three thousand, and the best speakers not over three thousand five hundred to four thousand.

Chinese characters were primarily intended to write the literary style, with is in a sense a language by itself. It is only written, and is incapable of being used as a means of oral communication, except in ready made phrases, for reasons which the student will see as he proceeds. Using these characters to write Mandarin is, to some extent, an adaptation. This adaptation is, however, quite natural and has in turn given new meanings to many characters, while it has also given rise to not a few new characters. The study of Mandarin serves as an invaluable introduction to the study of the literary style or Wên-li 文理.

Many characters have two or more meanings according to the connection in which they are used. These changes of meaning are not more numerous nor more difficult to follow than the same kind of changes in the meaning of words in Western languages. Many characters also have two or more pronunciations or readings. (See Double Readings.)

Chinese characters are concreted symbols, which are never modified for the purpose of inflection or conjugation; hence there is no interdependence of words in respect to case, number, person, mood or tense. The syntax of the language depends entirely upon the order or arrangement of the words. Not only are the characters without any inflection but they are not modified to express related or derivative ideas, as are so many of our primitive nouns and verbs in English. Ideas expressed in English by such terminal syllables as ness, able, ure, ion, ling, er, etc., are expressed in Chinese by the use of two or more independent characters, each preserving its own individuality and joined together by no closer bond than mere juxtaposition.

SYLLABLES.

THE most remarkable thing about Mandarin sounds is the smallness of their number. In the various Mandarin dialects there are on an average only *about* four hundred separate syllables or sounds. The use of tones increases these sounds to about twelve hundred. The words in use are of course many more, say three or four times as many. Hence arises the necessity of repeating the same sound in several

---

* *T'ung-hsing* (通行) means *everywhere current*, and is so much more expressive and convenient than any corresponding English term that I shall take the liberty of using it.

senses. These several senses are distinguished *to the eye* by different characters, as the words *heir* and *air*, or *pair*, *pear* and *pare* in English. If the words were distributed uniformly to the several syllables and their tones, the difficulty arising from so much repetition of the same sound, would be much less than it is, seeing they are in fact very unevenly distributed. Many syllables are wanting in one or more tones, and one or two characters in one tone are often mated by a score or more in another tone. Some syllables have only two or three characters in all, while others have several score. In practice the difficulty is overcome by various devices, the chief of which consists in joining the words in pairs, so that they may mutually designate each other. See Lesson 52.

Mandarin is distinguished by the fact that nearly all its syllables end with a vowel. Its only consonant endings are *n* and *ng*. The Southern non-Mandarin dialects have in addition syllables ending in *k*, *m*, *p* and *t*.

The Chinese language is commonly regarded as monosyllabic, yet many of its syllables have an intermedial vowel and are in fact dissyllables. The Chinese, however, take no account of this fact, and foreigners have followed them in regarding all words as single syllables.

For the purpose of analysis and spelling, the syllables are separated into *initials* and *finals*. The initial consists of the consonant sound or sounds which form the first part of the syllable, and the final, of the vowel or vowel combined with *n* or *ng*, which forms the second part of the syllable. Syllables beginning with a vowel have no initial. The intermedial vowel is regarded as a part of the final. The use of initials and finals offers the best means of analyzing and classifying the sounds of any given dialect, as also of comparing one dialect with another. In native dictionaries the pronunciation of words is indicated by initials and finals. The initial of one character and final of another are taken and joined together to spell the syllable required; thus *ma* and *kên* spell *mên*, *kwei* and *lang* spell *kwang*, etc. This is not an original Chinese idea but was derived from foreigners. Several native dictionaries have also been arranged according to initials and finals as being more convenient for reference than that according to radicals.

SPELLING.

ENGLISH letters cannot be made to represent Chinese sounds perfectly, so that spelling is at best but an approximation. Its use, however, if not a necessity, is at least a very great convenience. A good system of spelling, well adapted to his own dialect, will save the learner much labor and many mistakes. For reasons given in the preface, the author has not used any of the systems of spelling now in vogue, but has constructed a modified system better adapted to the requirements of the case.

The system of spelling used in Dr. Williams' dictionary fails, partly because it is inconsistent with itself, and partly because it adopts a standard, the *Wu Fang Yüen Yin*, which, so far as the spoken language is concerned, is obsolete, not being correct at the present time anywhere in China.

The most popular system, that of Sir Thomas Wade, is inconsistent with itself, quite ignores the relationship of Pekingese to other dialects, and seems to be constructed as if to preclude its application to any dialect except the Pekingese. The most notable characteristic of the system is its want of system.

The system of the China Inland Mission is consistent with itself, and is, in many respects, an excellent one. It is, however, only a system of initials and finals adapted to Southern Mandarin—the power of particular letters being left undefined so that they may be varied according as the key characters vary in different dialects. This plan, while it serves a certain purpose, is but an approximation and is quite inadequate as a general system of spelling.

The system now proposed is based chiefly on the systems of Sir Thomas Wade and the China Inland Mission, and, while supplementing them largely, only departs from them so far as is necessary to secure the end in view. The chief points of superiority claimed for this system are the following, viz. :—

1. It is simple. The powers of the letters are defined almost entirely by referring to their use in English, and as few diacritic marks are used as is possible in the circumstances.

2. It is self-consistent. The spelling of the English language is conspicuously *inconsistent*, but no *system* of spelling, made to order, should deliberately embody in it such a radical defect as this. Consistency is absolutely essential to the intelligent application of the same system of spelling to several dialects, and as a guide to the spelling of all new sounds.

3. It is comprehensive. The system in its present form has a range of initials and finals sufficient to

include at least the dialects of Peking, Weihien, Chefoo, Nanking and Kiukiang, and is capable of easy extension on the same lines.

4. It is discriminating. It brings a number of dialects into accurate comparison, giving to each a complete system of its own, without violating the rights of others. In this way it affords a decided advantage to those who may wish to change their dialect or to learn several dialects.

The following are the principle changes that have been made in the systems of Sir Thos. Wade and the China Inland Mission, with the reasons for making them.

1. Final *o* is made long *o*, and Wade's final *o* is changed to *oă*. Long *o* final is required in Southern and Central Mandarin. The sound indicated by Wade's final *o*, is not really *ō*, but *oă*, as he himself defines it.

2. Final *ï* of the C. I. M. system has been adopted rather than Wade's *ŭ*, because the sound is more nearly allied to *i* than to *u*; moreover, this was the writing originally used for this sound by Edkins, Medhurst and others.

3. *Ss* is changed to *s*, and *tz* is changed to *ts*. *Ss* has simply the power of a single *s* and nothing more, and is therefore superfluous. *Tz* might do for the unaspirated sound, but *z* is by its nature incapable of combining with an aspirate, so that *tz'* is by necessity pronounced *ts'*, which fact is recognized by Sir Thos. Wade when he defines *tz'* as "like *ts'*." Analogy also requires *ts*, because the difference between the two initials now in question is simply and solely in the initial letter *t*, and this fact should be indicated in the spelling.

4. The final *h* of Wade's system is discarded in all cases, because it is required in Southern Mandarin as the distinctive mark of the fifth tone. It has been assigned to this office ever since Chinese sounds began to be spelled with foreign letters.

5. *W* is substituted for *u* in the Northern dialects as it generally represents the sound more accurately, and is more in accordance with the English usage of the letters *u* and *w*. *U* is retained in Nanking, where it marks a pronunciation distinctly different from that heard in the North and West.*

6. The C. I. M. initial *u* and *i* have been replaced by *w* and *y*. It is contrary to the usage of the English letters to use *u* and *i* as initials with the consonantal powers of *w* and *y*.

The following key to the powers of the letters will serve to define the system :—

Vowels.

a, Final or followed by *ng*, as *a* in far, star. In certain syllables of some dialects, when *a* is followed by *n* final, it has the sound of *a* in man as pronounced by Americans. In nearly all dialects *a*, preceded by *w* and followed by *ng*, is broadened to the sound of *a* in fall. The Chinese do not appreciate these variations, but regard the sound as the same. On this account foreign systems of spelling have not felt it necessary to indicate the difference.

ȧ, As *a* in ask, last, as pronounced by Americans.

e, As *e* in met, pen. When standing alone as a final, it is pronounced as if doubled, thus che is pronounced che-e.

ê, As *e* in her, perch. When standing alone as a final, it is also prolonged as if doubled.

i, Final or followed by a vowel, as *i* in machine, ravine. When followed by *n* or *ng*, it is shortened to *i* in chin, pin.

ĭ, Final, as *i* in chin, pin.

ï, The final vowel sound heard in such words as table, noble, etc. when separated from the preceding bl.†

o, As *o* in go, so.

u, As *u* in rule, or *oo* in fool. When followed by *n* or *ng*, it is shortened to the sound of *u* in pull, or *oo* in good. When followed by a vowel, it combines with it and approximates the sound of *w*.

ü, Commonly called French *ü*, is not found in the English language. It is the French rather than the German *ü*, that is, it does not incline so much to long *e* as does the German *ü*.

ae, As *ae* in aerial, save that the accent falls on *a*, and the sounds of the two letters are more nearly joined together. This sound can scarcely be considered Mandarin. It is only heard in the region of Chinkiang and Yangchow, and is probably imported from Soochow. The writing of this sound by the present system would be *eii*, which is a very undesirable combination. *Æ* is adopted because it is

* Before making this change, I addressed a circular to all the missionaries of over five years' residence in Chili, Manchuria and Shantung, asking their opinion as to which letter best represented the sound. Over nine-tenths of the replies were to the effect that *w* was preferable.

† Prof. Bell, the well-known author of "Visible Speech or Universal Alphabetics," says the final *vowel* sound in the words able, noble, etc., corresponds with this sound as he heard it from the lips of several Peking speakers in the Chinese embassy in Washington City.

already in use in Soochow and Shanghai. It is often written *æ*.

ai, As *ai* in aisle or as *i* in mine. In some sections the two vowels are heard separately to a greater or less extent.

ao, As *ou* in loud, proud. Occasionally the vowels are heard slightly separated.

au or *ạ*, As *a* in fall, or as *au* in haul. In Mandarin this sound is only heard in the South, where it takes the place of *a* final in the North. It is heard in Soochow and Shanghai, and is there always spelled *au*.

ei, As *ei* in weight, or as *ey* in grey.

êi, With *ê* and *i* distinct, and with the powers given above. Strike out *n* from money and you have the syllable *mêi*.

êei, With *ê* and *ei* distinct and with the powers given above. Omit *nd* and *ne* from mundane and you have the sound mêei.

êo, With the powers given above, *o* being somewhat more distinct than *ê*; or, the vowel sounds in burrow when all the consonants are withdrawn. The circumflex is sometimes omitted on the ground that the combination sufficiently distinguishes the sound. It is better, however, to write *êo*.

ia, With *i* and *a* distinct, and with the powers given above, the accent being on *a*.

iai, With *i* and *ai* distinct, and with the powers given above, *ai* being accented.

iao, With *i* and *ao* distinct, and with the powers given above, *ao* being accented.

ie, As *ee* in re-enter, re-enroll. When preceded by *y* the *i* is partially occluded and *ie* approximates *e*.

iei, With *i* and *ei* distinct, and with the powers given above, *ei* being accented.

io, As *eo* in re-open.

iu, As *eu* in Peru when the *r* is dropped. In some dialects the accent inclines to the *i* and in some to the *u*. There is, in some dialects, much confusion between *io* and *iu* as finals. They are probably the same final modified by tone and by accidental circumstances.

oǎ, As *oa* in Gilboâ, or in coalesce. The *a* is very short and it is to mark this fact that it is written *ǎ*. Some hear the final sound as short *ŭ* (*u* in hut) and it might perhaps with equal propriety be so written. The sounds of the two letters are not perfectly distinct, but coalesce to some extent, approximating the sound of *ê*. The departure from full *oǎ* is greater or less in different places, and according to different ears. In case of doubt it is better to give the preference to *ê*, leaving *oǎ* as a distinct double sound.

ou, With the vowels distinct, and with the powers given above, or, as *ou* in volute when the *l* is dropped, and the accent thrown on the first syllable. The sound of *u* is comparatively slight, *o* being much the stronger of the two sounds.*

ua, As *ua* in dual with the accent thrown on the *a*.

uai, With *u* and *ai* distinct, and with the powers given above, *ai* being accented.

uei, With *u* and *ei* distinct, and with the powers given above, *ei* being accented.

uê, With *u* and *ê* distinct, and with the powers given above, *ê* being accented.

ui, With the vowels distinct, and with the powers given above—the vowel sounds in gluey.

üa, The *ü* as above, and the *a* flattened to *a* in man, antic. The combination only occurs in final *üan*.

üe, With *ü* and *e* distinct, and with the powers given above. When used as a final the *ü* is accented, and when followed by *n* or *ng*, the *e* is accented.

üei, With *ü* and *ei* distinct, and with the powers given above, *ei* being accented.

Consonants.

The initials *ch*, *k*, *p*, *t* and *ts*, are somewhat softened from their sounds as heard in Great Britain, and much softened from their sounds as heard in America, yet not so much as to quite pass into the corresponding, *j*, *g*, *b*, *d* and *dz*. In some words and in some localities they do, however, become very nearly equivalent to these sounds.

In the initials *ch'*, k', *p'*, *t'* and *ts'*, the aspiration is somewhat stronger than is usual with these letters in America, and very much stronger than is usual in Great Britain. Their force will be obtained approximately by first vocalizing the English letter, and then following at once with the final with an *h* prefixed; thus ch-ha for 茶, or t-ha for 他. An Irishman ought to give these aspirates to perfection.

* Sir Thos. Wade defines the sound of *ou* as, "In reality *êō*, the vowel sounds of burrow when all the consonants are withdrawn." This identifies the sound with that of *êo* in Southern Mandarin, as given above, which is certainly not correct for Pekingese, in which alone the sound is heard. Elsewhere in Northern and Central Mandarin the corresponding sound is either *êo*, or simply *ŏ*. In this case, as in several others, Sir Thos. Wade seems to have been misled in his description of Peking sounds by the Nanking sounds which he had previously learned. It is a question whether after all the final *u* is really anything more than the imperfect *u* necessarily formed by the vocal organs in falling back to their normal position after a full final *ŏ*.

h, Is aspirated a little more strongly than is usual in English. When followed by *i* or *ü* it includes the sound of *y*, making it equivalent to *h* in hue or hew, that is, the Greek *χ*. *h* final is used as the distinctive mark of the fifth or entering tone.

hs, Sir Thos. Wade defines: "A slight aspirate preceding and modifying the sibilant, which, however, is the stronger of the two consonants." A more accurate definition would be, a distinct sibilant preceding and modifying, or obscuring the aspirate. To pronounce it correctly requires that the teeth be somewhat more separated and the tongue brought more to the front than in pronouncing *sh*.* It is *always* followed by *i* or by *ü* in the final. In Pekingese *sh* is never followed by *i* or *ü*.

j, is approximately *s* in fusion, or *z* in brazier. It is only used in Pekingese. The corresponding sound in Southern Mandarin is more guttural and therefore more allied to the untrilled English *r*.

jr, Is a combination of *j* and *r*, which more nearly represents this peculiar initial as heard in Central Mandarin than either *j* or *r* alone.†

k, When followed by *i* or *ü*, includes the sound of *y*, being like *k* in kindness, as formerly pronounced in English, viz., kyindness.

ng, Has the same power as in English, and is used both as a final and as an initial.

r, Not trilled, but as usually spoken in America.

sh, Is in some dialects pronounced just as in English, in others the tongue is somewhat retracted from its normal position in giving *sh* in English.

sr, Place the tongue as if to utter initial *r*, and then, without changing its position, say *s*, followed by the faintest possible *r*.

tsh, As *tsh* in potsherd,—a combination representing the transition sound from *ch* in the North to *ts* in the south, being neither *ch* nor *ts*, but an amalgamation of the two sounds.

tsr, Place the tongue as if to utter initial *r*, and then, without changing its position, say *ts*, followed by the faintest possible *r*.

Both analogy and consistency would require that the syllables 希, hi or hsi, 欣, hin or hsin, 行, hing or hsing, also 幾, ki, 斤 kin, and 經, king, should be spelled hyi or hsyi, kyi, etc., but the general custom in all systems has been to drop the *y*, assuming that it is included in the initials *h* and *k*, as provided above. The student should take special note of this provision, with regard to the power of *h* and *k* before *i* and *ü*.

Remarks.

The above letters and combinations are supposed to provide a consistent spelling for all the sounds found in the dialects of Peking, Chefoo, Weihien, Nanking and Kiukiang. Other Mandarin dialects may contain sounds not provided for, in which case it will be necessary to make new combinations, and perhaps add new diacritic marks. Any additions made should be strictly consistent with the system as already defined.

The sound of many syllables is considerably modified by the tone. Thus in Peking, words ending in *wei* are, in the first and second tones *wi*, and in the third and fourth *wei*. In Têngchow words ending in *ien* are, in the second and third tones *ien*, and in the first and fourth, *ian*. These tonal variations differ greatly in different dialects. It is agreed on all hands that in such cases, it is neither necessary nor desirable to have two spellings. The student will presently learn by experience to make the necessary allowance for such variations. That spelling should be chosen which analogy or history indicates as the fundamental sound. It is a great pity that the usage in this respect is not more uniform and consistent than it is. The fifth tone makes a still more decided change on the fundamental syllable, insomuch that in many cases it is quite dissociated from it; on this account, as well as because this tone is already distinguished by a special terminal letter *(h)*, it is doubtless best to conform the spelling to the sound.

No combinations of English letters can completely represent all the minor distinctions of even one dialect, much less those of a number of dialects. A

* The accuracy of the definition of this sound given by Sir Thos. Wade and followed by Giles is open to question. A careful analysis of the sound will show that the sibilant precedes the aspirate rather than follows it, not however combining with it to form the sound represented by *sh* but retaining its own separate force and followed by the *h* as a distinct sound. The original sound in most cases was *hy* (that is, *h* in hew) and is such still in many places. Within the last two or three hundred years it has been modified by prefixing an *s* without however essentially changing the *hy*; thus, 形 was originally hying (written hing) and has now come to be s-hing. The sound represented by *sh* in English is not a simple joining of *s* and *h* but a new elementary sound, which is also expressed in English by *c* as in emaciate, by *s* as in nauseate and by *t* as in negotiate. The sound now in question differs from it in that *s* and *h* each retains its own special sound following in order. It is doubtless better, however, to *write* the sound *hs* and so avoid confounding it with *sh*. It may be regarded as similar to *wh* in the English words when, what, etc. which are pronounced as if written hwen, hwat, etc.

† Much breath has been spent, both North and South, in discussing whether this initial is *j* or *r*. It is in fact a combination of the two sounds. It begins with *j* and ends with *r*, and *jr* is the best way to represent it, both North and South.

certain margin or suppleness must be given to the spelling of each syllable, especially for the many minor modifications made by change of tone. In every dialect also, there are occasional stray sounds which may be regarded as accidental variations, and need not be provided for in a syllabary of the dialect.

SYLLABARIES.

A SYLLABARY is an alphabetic arrangement of all the syllables in a given dialect, with all the characters ordinarily used in writing that dialect, distributed under these syllables. In some cases the characters are arranged in columns according to their tones, and in others they are simply given in order, the tones being indicated by figures. A good syllabary is a great help in acquiring a correct knowledge of a given dialect. It shows clearly what sounds are in the dialect with the correct spelling of each, which is a very important matter to a beginner, whose ear is not yet trained to distinguish sounds. It also shows the tone of every character, and thus enables the student to verify his own hearing of the sound, and serves also to prompt his memory in the absence of his teacher. It further serves as a valuable *vade mecum* to all who essay to write Chinese, giving so readily the character you want and *know*, but cannot quite recall.

In the nature of the case a syllabary can only include one homogeneous dialect. To attempt more than this is to invite difficulties and defeat the end in view. Every city or district, having a dialect peculiar to itself, should have its own syllabary. It is well worth the while of older residents to prepare a syllabary for the use of beginners, albeit its usefulness is very far from being limited to beginners. The analysis of syllables and tones which its preparation requires, will very likely bring to light some previous mistakes and misapprehensions, and lead to a more consistent and accurate pronunciation of the dialect. For the guidance and help of any who may undertake to make a syllabary, I offer the following suggestions :—

1. Canvass the dialect and gather out as far as possible all the different syllables it contains, choosing a key character for each.

2. Spell these sounds *provisionally* and arrange them in a table by means of the key characters, bringing like initials into the same line, and like finals into the same column.

3. Go carefully over the several initials and finals, and compare all those in the same line or column, and examine closely whether in each case they are really the same. In respect to the finals be especially careful that you are not misled by tonal variations. As far as possible compare characters in the same tone, changing the key characters for this purpose if necessary.

4. Train your teacher to understand what you are doing, especially teach him to understand the idea of comparing sounds by finals, so as to get his assistance in classifying.

5. Having arranged your syllables in alphabetic order with ample spaces, get your teacher to classify by the guidance of the key characters, all the common characters in your dialect,—arranging them by tones under each syllable. If your teacher is able to distinguish clearly the tone from the other elements of the sound, he will do this work without difficulty; if not, you will have to check over his work very carefully.

6. In arranging the characters under the tones, especial care will be required to see that your teacher does not simply follow the Wu Fang Yüen Yin, instead of the real tone of his dialect. A man of moderate scholarship, especially if he be familiar with light literature, will probably do this work better than a literary graduate, because he will more easily free himself from the theoretical tones, and because he will not be so impervious to a new idea.

Until your teacher is really able to throw away the tone-book and trust simply to his *ear*, he will be but a broken reed in the making of a syllabary. The fact that he *says* he understands the distinction between the book tone and the spoken tone, does not prove that he really does do so, or that he is in fact able to depend upon his ear and ignore the book. It is of course understood that purely *wên-li* characters have no established tone in colloquial. For such the teacher will of course refer to the book.

7. This classification of all the common characters of the dialect, will probably elicit the fact that a few rare sounds have been omitted—perhaps that some sounds which are different have been confused, or *vice versâ*. After these corrections are made, make a careful review of the whole work, comparing and testing by means of the initials and finals, to see whether the whole work is at the same time consistent and exhaustive.

8. Only after you have made this thorough analysis and classification of the sounds of your dialect are you ready to settle the final spelling of the several syllables. In doing this, attend to the following points: (1). Use all the English letters *consistently* and according to the powers given them in the table of vowels and consonants. (2). If these sounds are not enough for the emergency, then use new combinations or additional diacritic marks, defining them carefully and making them consistent with the system as it already exists. (3). In spelling words which end in *n*, preceded by an intermedial vowel, note that these endings have a relationship to vowel endings of the same class, thus *tien*, *mien*, *lien*, etc., are related to tie, mie, lie, etc.; yüen, shüen, chüen, etc., are related to yüe, shüe, chüe, etc. Now these syllables, viz., those with intermedial vowels, are the ones which chiefly develope tonal variations by changing *en* to *an*. In such cases, if there be any doubt whether the ending be *en* or *an*, the existence of the corresponding vowel endings in *e* or *a* should determine which is the normal sound and mark the other as a tonal variation. (4). The intermedial *i* in such sounds as lien, liu, etc., should not be dropped when *y* becomes the initial. It is indeed occluded by the cognate sound *y*, but the *final* is still the same as in *lien*, *liu*, etc., and should be so written, retaining the *i*. It will be found that the Chinese consider the final the same, whether it be preceded by *y* or by *l* or by any other initial.

9. Let your syllabary make just as many distinctions of sound as the Chinese make and *no more.* The only exception that I would make to this rule is in the case of the confusion of final *n* and *ng* and initial *n* and *l* in Southern Mandarin. For the sake of facility in consulting dictionaries, and of understanding other dialects in case of removal, it would be well to keep up these distinctions, although they do not exist in your own dialect.

10. A complete syllabary should include double readings. Such double readings as are mere accidental variations unattended by a change of meaning, may be indicated by a star—the character having the same mark under both its readings. Double readings, attended by a change of meaning, should be indicated by numbers at the upper right hand corner of the character, *one* indicating the primary reading and *two* the secondary.

TONES.

TO give a clear and satisfactory exposition of Chinese tones, is a task of no small difficulty. The fact that they differ so greatly in different localities, and are so wholly foreign to the distinctions we are accustomed to make in sounds, coupled with the fact that ears differ as much perhaps as tones, will account, to some extent, for the multifarious and contradictory things which have been written about them. Whether the present attempt to elucidate Mandarin tones, will succeed any better than those which have preceded it, remains to be seen. I shall treat the subject entirely from the practical standpoint.

1. Tones are not musical notes, but are rather intonations or inflections of the voice. There is nothing in Western languages corresponding to them, and they can only be acquired by close attention to, and imitation of, a Chinese teacher. In Southern Mandarin there are five tones, as follows, viz:—1. *Shang p'ing shêng*, or upper level tone; 2. *Hsia p'ing shêng*, or lower level tone; 3. *Shang shêng*, or rising tone; 4. *Ch'u shêng*, or vanishing tone; 5. *Ju shêng*, or entering tone. From Northern Mandarin the fifth tone has disappeared, the characters originally under it being distributed to the other four—chiefly to the second, or lower level tone.* In one or other of these tones all Mandarin words are spoken. Tones are not something added to the sound, but are an original and integral part of it. They do not *modify* the sense in any particular way, nor convey any *special* meaning of any kind. They rather serve to distinguish one word from another, showing that they are two and not one.

* It is a question whether tones were originally an element of the Chinese language proper. It seems not unlikely that they were acquired from the languages spoken by the aborigines who dwelt in the land before the Chinese entered it. This hypothesis is favored by the fact that the aboriginal languages, still extant in China, all have tones, as also the language of the Shan tribes bordering on Burmah. It is also favored by the fact that the non-Mandarin dialects of the South, which are probably the result of admixtures of Chinese with aboriginal dialects, all have *more* tones and lay more *stress* on tones than does the Mandarin. Mandarin shows a disposition to throw off tones, as if they were really foreign to it. Thus within the last four hundred years the fifth or entering tone has entirely disappeared from Northern and Central Mandarin, where it formerly prevailed. The indications are that it will ultimately disappear from Southern Mandarin.

2. It is worthy of special remark that the relationship of tones as such, is not known or recognized by the mass of the Chinese people. They learn the tones as they learn the other characteristics of their sounds—by imitation of their elders; and to their apprehension the different tones of a given syllable are simply different words. Having different sounds and different meanings, and being represented by different characters, their tonal relationship is a thing not thought of. The theoretical knowledge of tones is confined to scholars, and with them it is not a knowledge based on their own spoken language, but is acquired as a theory laid down in their books.

3. Tones have been indicated in various ways by writers on the Chinese language. When indicated on the Chinese character, the most common plan is that adopted by Dr. Williams in imitation of the Chinese method, viz.,—by small semicircles at the four corners of the character. When indicated on the Romanized spelling, the most convenient plan is that adopted by Sir Thos. Wade, viz.,—by the use of numbers at the upper right hand of the spelling. The fifth or entering tone is indicated in the spelling by a final *h*. The following example shows the tones marked in both ways:—

1st tone	or	上平聲	*Shang p'ing shêng*		夫	Fu^{1}.
2nd	„ „	下平聲	*Hsia*	„ „	符	Fu^{2}.
3rd	„ „	上 聲	*Shang shêng*		府	Fu^{3}.
4th	„ „	去 聲	*Ch'u*	„	父	Fu^{4}.
5th	„ „	入 聲	*Ju*	„	福	Fuh.

The tones are usually given by Chinese teachers in the above order, and form a sort of chime, which every learner should acquire, as it will enable him to recognize and locate the tone of any word he may hear.

4. The names of the tones do not truly describe their characters. This is especially true of the two level tones. In a large part of Shantung the 上平 or upper level, is in fact a lower level, and the 下平, or lower level, is an upper level. In Peking the 上平, or upper level, is not properly a level tone at all, nor is the 下平, the former being an upper quick falling tone, and the latter an upper quick rising tone. The term 入, entering, is not a correct description of the fifth tone, which is an abrupt aspirated ending. Dr. Edkins says that the terms 平, 上, 去, 入, "do not in the majority of cases represent the actual effect of the sound on the ear. When first adopted they must have represented the tones of the dialect spoken by the writer who selected them, but when applied according to universal practice, to the sounds given to the same characters in other parts of the empire, they convey no idea of the actual pronunciation." This is perhaps a little strong for Mandarin. In Eastern Shantung, aside from the inversion of the *upper* and *lower* levels, the names are fairly descriptive of the fact.

5. Tones are of two kinds, viz.,—practical and theoretical. The practical tones are those which are actually used by the people in speaking, and differ widely in different localities. The theoretical tones are those which are given in the 五方元音 *Wu Fang Yüen Yin*, or, "Original Tones of the Five Regions." The compiler of this work was from Southern Chili, yet he professes to give the syllables and tones of the Southern Mandarin, which then no doubt extended well to the north. Exactly what he made his standard in fixing the tones, it is not easy to see. At the present time they are not correct anywhere in China, albeit the book is the authorized standard for determining tones throughout the whole empire. Every Chinese scholar is familiar with the tones as given in this book, and when a teacher, who is not specially trained, is asked the tone of a word, he will generally reply according to the book, and not according to the tone that he himself actually uses in speaking. This latter, in fact, he does not generally know, or rather he does not *recognize* it as such. To be of service in teaching a foreigner, a Chinese teacher must be trained to distinguish tones by his ear, rejecting and ignoring the artificial standard of the books. Unless thus trained he will very likely mislead the learner by giving the theoretical instead of the practical tones.*

6. For the purpose of rhyming, tones are divided by the Chinese into two classes, called *p'ing* (平), level, and *tsê* (仄), deflected. The former includes the *shang p'ing shêng* and the *hsia p'ing shêng;* and the latter, the *shang shêng, ch'u shêng* and *ju shêng.* With this distinction every Chinese scholar is familiar. He will readily tell to which class any given word

---

*I once heard a lady in North China complimenting her teacher on the accuracy of his tones, adducing as proof the fact that they invariably agreed with the tones given in Williams' Dictionary. I asked her how about the Ju shêng; she replied that he gave her these as readily as the others. He was in fact giving the theoretical tones, including the Ju shêng, to which he gave a theoretical pronunciation, which he imagined was the Ju shêng. He was thoroughly misleading his pupil as to the real pronunciation of his dialect.

belongs, his standard being not the actual spoken tones, but the *Wu Fang Yüen Yin* and sundry rhyme books based upon it. In writing poetry it is only allowed to rhyme a *p'ing* with a *p'ing* and a *tsê* with a *tsê*. This is in fact the principal, if not the only, purpose that this distinction serves.

7. The tones of words vary in different localities; that is, any given character may be one tone in one place, and another tone in another place. The most frequent change perhaps is from the first tone to the second, and *vice versâ*. The second and fourth tones also often exchange places. These changes of tone are very numerous, and often occur within very short distances, such as would show very little, if any, perceptible change in syllables. The number of these changes is far greater than any one would suppose, who has not made the matter a subject of special inquiry.

8. The manner of rendering the tones differs in different localities; that is, a given tone is not the same sound in one locality that it is in another, *though called by the same name*. It is, so to speak, intoned in a different way. For example, the third tone in Peking, is made by depressing the voice below its natural key and ending with a strong rising inflection. In Eastern Shantung, the same tone is made by beginning in a natural key and ending with a rising inflection. In Chinanfu, the same tone begins high and rises still higher. In fact the four tones, as given in Peking, are all rendered differently in Eastern Shantung; not only so, but in Chinanfu they are rendered still differently from those heard in either place. Each new locality has a new rendering of the tones. These variations know no law, and seem to be practically endless. There is, in many cases, a certain degree of similarity in the rendering of the same tone in different places, yet not such as to make it certainly recognizable, or prevent its being confounded with other tones.

9. The normal tone of a word is often changed by its position in a compound word or phrase, as also by its position in a sentence. Thus the words 東 *tung*^{1} east, and 西 *hsi*^{1} west, are both in the first tone, but when combined in the word 東西, a thing, they are not spoken *tung*^{1} *hsi*^{1}, according to the proper tones, but *tung*^{1} *hsi*^{2}, the tone of *hsi* changing from the first to the second. So also 慈悲, merciful, is not spoken *ts'i*^{2} *pei*^{1}, according to the original tones, but rather *ts'i*^{2} *pei*^{4}, the tone of *pei* changing from the first to the fourth. In like manner 伶巧, ingenious, is not spoken *ling*^{2} *ch'iao*^{3}, according to the normal tones, but *ling*^{2} *ch'iao*^{4}, the tone of *ch'iao*, changing from the third to the fourth. Again, take the expression 你要打我嗎, *Are you going to strike me?* Now 我 is normally in the third tone, but as spoken in this phrase, it changes to the fourth. If its proper tone be retained, the emphasis is thereby thrown on it, and the expression would mean, *Would you* [*dare to*] *strike* ME? Once more, take the sentence 爺有娘有不如己有, *To have a thing in your father and mother's possession is not so good as to have it in your own possession.* Here 娘 is normally *niang*^{2} and 己 is *chi*^{3}, but as spoken in this sentence they both change to the fourth tone. In general it may be said that there are few sentences of any length spoken, in which there are not, for one cause or another, changes in the normal tone of one or more of its words. These changes are complicated and subject to no known general law. The following hints embody as much as the author has learned by experience, and will, it is hoped, be of some service to the student.

(1.) Accented words, both in phrases and in sentences, retain their normal tones.

(2.) Strong emphasis on a word forming part of a clause, is likely to obscure the tone of the succeeding word,—generally changing it to the fourth tone.

(3.) In dual combinations, which include the vast majority of phrases, the first character *generally* takes the accent, and in this case the second character, if not already a fourth tone, generally changes to a fourth tone; that is, to the natural falling inflection

(4.) In case the meaning of the second character of a dual phrase predominates and takes the accent, then it retains its normal tone, and the tone of the first character generally changes, or is at least obscured, especially if it is a level tone.

10. How may an accurate knowledge of tones be acquired, is a question which confronts every student of Chinese. Two distinct methods have been followed, and each has its advocates. One method is to learn the tone of each character as a distinct act of memory in each case, so that the tone is as certainly known as the other elements of the sound. The other method is to regard the tone as an integral part of the sound, which need not be theoretically separated from it, and so proceed to learn both words and sentences by a direct and untrammelled imitation of a teacher, as a Chinese child imitates its parents. Each method has its advantages

and disadvantages. The first method will give greater confidence and accuracy in the use of isolated words, but it imposes a heavy burden on the memory, and its ultimate benefit is neutralized to a considerable extent by the changes required by composition and rhythm, and by the danger that the speaker will adhere too much to the fundamental tone, to the great injury of his speaking. The second method is easier to one who has a good ear, and will make a fluent and natural speaker. There is danger, however, that such a speaker will miss his bearings when he attempts to isolate or emphasize a particular word, especially if it is not a very common one.

On the whole, I would recommend a combination of the two methods. Let the student first practice the tone exercises faithfully with his teacher, until he has caught the chime and can distinguish with certainty the tone of any single word his teacher pronounces. The foundation is now securely laid, and he can go on with confidence to learn words and phrases. In memorizing single words, let the tone always be regarded as an integral part of the sound, so that the word is not regarded as properly heard at all until the tone is heard—for in point of fact *there is no Chinese word without a tone.* In case of uncertainty in catching a tone from a teacher, it is not best to ask him the tone, nor to suffer him to tell you, but have him repeat the word, telling *him* the tone as a check if necessary. In repeating phrases or clauses after the teacher, attention should not be directed chiefly to the tones of the words, but rather to a close and accurate imitation of the sounds, both in general and in particular. If this method is faithfully carried out, the student will come to think less and less about tones, while he will speak the language with greater and greater accuracy. He will in fact acquire the ear of a native, and both hear and speak the language in blissful forgetfulness of tones.

11. Opinions vary as to the relative importance of tones in learning and speaking Chinese. Since they are an integral part of all Chinese speech, their general importance may safely be assumed. Seeing, however, that they vary so much in different localities and yet the people of these several localities understand each other without serious difficulty, it may safely be assumed that their *relative* importance is not so great as is sometimes represented. In order, however, to be understood with readiness and precision, and not offend the ears of the hearers, an accurate rendering of the tones is essential. Even as a basis for acquiring such a style as may be understood in several cognate dialects, the very best thing is the thorough knowledge of the pronunciation of some *one* dialect. The Chinese understand, and can make allowance for, the differing tones of different dialects, but they do not understand Anglicised sounds that have *no tone.* He who neglects tones or other peculiarities of his own dialect, and attempts to acquire what some are pleased to call a "general dialect," will end by not speaking real Chinese at all; *for there is no spoken Chinese without tones, nor any that is free from dialectic peculiarities.*

ASPIRATES.

IN the non-Mandarin dialects of the South there are sounds beginning with *j, g, b, d* and *ds,* also *two* sets of sounds beginning with *ch, k, p, t* and *ts,* which are distinguished as unaspirated and aspirated, the latter being generally written with a reversed elevated comma following the letter. In Mandarin the initials *j, g, b, d* and *ds* are not found, but only the two classes of sounds represented by *ch, k, p, t* and *ts,* distinguished as unaspirated and aspirated. These English letters really represent neither sound correctly. In the one case the aspiration is weaker than Englishmen generally use with these letters, and much weaker than Americans (who aspirate more strongly than Englishmen) generally use. In the other case the aspiration is somewhat stronger than that given to these letters by Americans, and much stronger than that given by Englishmen.

The unaspirated sounds are not really *j, g, b, d* and *ds,* as beginners are apt to imagine, though they approximate these letters, and in a few cases become almost, if not quite, equivalent to them. If the learner has difficulty in properly softening *ch, k, p, t* and *ts,* it would be better to give them flat *j, g, b, d* and *ds,* than to run the risk of confusing them with the aspirates. There is this at least to be said in favor of such a pronunciation, that while the Chinese may not quite approve it, they will not misunderstand it.* It is very important that the

* Seeing that neither *j, g, b, d* and *ds,* nor *ch, k, p, t* and *ts, perfectly* represent the true sounds, it is a question whether in Mandarin it would not be better to write the unaspirated sounds with the former letters and simplify the system of spelling by abolishing that awkward ‘. It is as easy to vary from *j, g, b, d* and *ds,* as it is to vary from *ch, k, p, t* and *ts.*

student of Chinese should get this distinction clearly in mind at first, which he ought readily to do by practising the table of aspirates with a good teacher. Ridiculous and mortifying blunders sometimes result from mistakes in aspirating. I once heard the announcement made from the pulpit that there would be a rooster in the church on a certain evening instead of saying a prayer-meeting, as was intended.

The Chinese do not recognize the relationship existing between aspirated and unaspirated sounds—simply regarding them as independent sounds. They only learn to compare and classify them when taught to do so by foreigners. The aspirates in Mandarin do not vary with different dialects so much as do the tones, but are exceedingly uniform from North to South. When, however, Mandarin is compared with the Southern coast dialects the variations are very great, whole classes of sounds changing from aspirates to unaspirates or *vice versâ*.

RHYTHM.

A Chinese sentence may be constructed with faultless idiom, and each word be pronounced with perfect accuracy, and yet the sentence be almost or quite unintelligible, simply from want of proper rhythmical emphasis. By rhythmical emphasis is meant the relative amount of emphasis given to the several words, their distribution into groups, and the rapidity or slowness with which they are severally spoken. It is highly important to every speaker that he should acquire the art of speaking in correct rhythm, and by consequence, with proper emphasis. Such acquisition will be invaluable in making his speech easily intelligible and in making it sound natural to the Chinese ear. The same thing is true to a greater or less extent of all languages.

In addition to listening carefully to the spoken language heard every day and striving to imitate it, the best way to acquire a proper rhythm is to practice reading closely after a good teacher. Let the teacher read a short clause *in an easy, natural tone*, and the student follow, imitating faithfully both the pronunciation and the rhythmic cadence of the teacher. Then let the teacher read the next clause and the student follow, and so on. The teacher should not read too far at once, lest the student be unable to retain the rhythm in his mind. Special care should also be taken that the teacher does not read in a recitative or affected style. Chinese teachers have a strong proclivity to read in that measured sing-song in which they recite their classics; and oftentimes when told that this is not what is wanted, they become impressed with the difficulty of what is required, and resort at once to a loud pompous style which upsets all proper rhythmical emphasis, and is the farthest possible from the easy natural conversational style that is wanted. If the student has not a trained teacher, he should ask the assistance of a friend who speaks Chinese to explain to his teacher what is wanted, and give him a few lessons on natural reading. Half an hour's practice in reading each day will be a relief from the severer labor of memorizing, and will work wonders in enabling the student to speak Chinese, as the Chinese speak it. It should be remembered, however, that merely reading after a teacher will be useless, if not worse, unless the rhythmical emphasis of the teacher be really and faithfully imitated. This exercise may be profitably varied by reading in concert with the teacher.

RADICALS.

THE Chinese have analysed their numerous written characters so far as to arrange them in two hundred and fourteen classes, each class having a common part called its radical. The Chinese name is 字部, character class, or 字母, character mother. Many of the more complex ones are compounded of those which are simpler. It would be a distinct advantage if the number of the radicals were considerably reduced. The radical was chosen in each case because of its relationship to the meaning of the character, to which it generally gives more or less of a clue. The other part of the character has been named the phonetic by foreign sinologues, because in most cases it determines, or at least suggests, the sound. The Chinese have no special name for it. Nearly all modern characters are made up distinctly of a radical and a phonetic, the one indicating the meaning and the other the sound. The same is true of many ancient characters, but not by any means of all.

The meaning, form and order of these two hundred and fourteen radicals, should be memorized. It will be a hard task, but it will repay the student well. Over one hundred and sixty of them are themselves characters in common use, and will require to be learned in any case. Moreover, all characters are built up from them, and the student will find that after learning them, Chinese characters will lose to a great extent their strange unmeaning look, and will become more familiar and intelligible. These radicals and their combinations will become so many hooks on which the memory can fasten, and so retain the characters in its keeping. The best time to learn the radicals is at the very outset, before attempting to learn other characters. The mind is then fresh and unoccupied, and will retain what it gets with a much firmer grasp than it will that which is crammed into it after it is already sated with five hundred or a thousand characters.

These radicals are, in a sense, the Chinese alphabet—the only one, at least, that they possess. Most native dictionaries are arranged in the order of these radicals, particularly the great standard imperial dictionary of Kanghi. Most foreign dictionaries of Chinese are syllabic, but in all cases of uncertainty as to the standard spelling of a character, recourse has still to be had to a radical index. In looking up characters by radicals, it will save much time and vexation to know either the order of these radicals or the number of each one. Many, perhaps most, students of Chinese have undertaken to learn the numbers. This is no light task in the first place, and it is a rare thing that the numbers are retained permanently in the memory, save in the case of comparatively few radicals which are in constant demand. The Chinese do not learn the radicals by number, but, having them arranged in groups according to the number of their strokes, they learn the order in which they stand. This is no doubt the better and more effective way,—being in fact the way we use our own alphabet in consulting a dictionary. In order to assist the memory and lighten the task of learning these radicals in their order, the Rev. J. A. Silsby of Shanghai has, at the request of the author, woven the 214 radicals into a mnemonic radical ode, which is appended at the end of the table of radicals.

How to recognize the radical of a character is a question of some importance to a beginner. Unfortunately no invariable rule can be given, but the following directions will be of some service :—

1. Consider whether the character itself is or is not a radical.

2. The great majority of characters consist more or less evidently of two parts, either right and left, or upper and lower, or inner and outer (a top and a side joined counts an outer). In case one of these parts is a radical and the other not, then that which is a radical, is the radical of the character; as, 站, 完, 固, etc.

3. If both parts be radicals, then :—

(*a*) The left hand part is the radical, except in the case of 刀, 力, 攴, 斤, 殳, 彡, 欠, 戈, 斗, 邑, 見, which generally stand on the right.

(*b*) The lower part is the radical, except in the case of 艹, ⺮, 亠, 穴, 日, 西, 雨, 爪, 父, 山, ⺌, which generally stand at the top.

(*c*) The outer part is the radical. This class is comparatively small.

4. It may be observed in general :—

(*a*) That the most prominent radical in a character is likely to be its governing radical.

(*b*) Some radicals almost always govern the character in which they appear; as, 艹, ⺮, 見, 疒.

There are of course some exceptions to these rules, yet they are quite as true as such rules generally are. For characters to which no rule applies, reference may be had to the list of difficult characters usually given in both native and foreign dictionaries.

DOUBLE READINGS.

MANY Chinese characters have two readings, and a few have three readings. The most of these changes of reading are attended by a change of meaning Those which are not attended by a change of meaning, are mere accidental variations, the remnants probably of dialectic admixtures. In some dialects there are many more of them than in others. I have tried in all cases to give the reading, which is most prevalent, favoring the colloquial rather than the book reading.*

Of readings which vary the meaning with the sound, the variation, in by far the greater number of cases, is tonal; in a comparatively few cases one character is read in two syllables. No general principle characterizes these changes, though a large number of those depending on tone, consist in the change from verb to

* On an average, about one character in five has a double reading, and of these double readings, about three-fourths are attended by a change of meaning, the other fourth being accidental variations.

noun, or from noun to verb or adjective, similar to such words as con′-flict and conflict′ or gal′-lant and gallant′ in English. It still remains true, however, in Chinese as in English, that by far the larger number of such changes of meaning are *not* attended by any change of pronunciation. I have not noted all the double readings given in Dr. Goodrich's Pocket Dictionary, because many of them are peculiar to Peking. I have noted all which seemed to prevail in as many as two dialects. In other cases, viz.,—those in which the distinction seemed local, or was inconsistent in different dialects, I have adhered to that reading which was judged to be the primary reading of the character. For the variations made in such cases by different dialects the student will have to depend on his teacher. It is very likely also that some of the distinctions which have been made, will be found to be incorrect in some dialects. In some cases also the subsequent use of a word will be found inconsistent with the general distinction of meaning as first made. This inconsistency generally arises from the effect of composition.*

The whole subject of double readings is surrounded with difficulties. If only one dialect be considered, it is *comparatively* easy to fix the readings, though even then there is more or less both of uncertainty and inconsistency. When, however, three or four or more dialects are considered together, there is no small amount of confusion and contradiction. If each dialect of Mandarin had such a carefully prepared vocabulary as Dr. Goodrich has given to the Pekingese, then an intelligent and valuable comparison might be made. As it is at present, only a general approximation is possible.

I have made no attempt whatever to conform the spelling of double words, or of phrases, to the tonal changes introduced by composition. For these the student will have to depend on his teacher and on his ear.

WRITING.

WRITING Chinese will be found a useful exercise for every student. It will be a grateful relief from the tedium of direct memorizing, while it will serve to give a more accurate knowledge of the characters and help to fix them in the mind. The Chinese consider that a character is not *really* learned until it can be, not only recognized, but also written. The best way to learn to write, is to get a teacher to write a copy of simple characters in large hand, place this underneath the *thin* Chinese paper and trace the characters as Chinese schoolboys do. Use a Chinese pen and write in regular Chinese order and style, taking lessons from your teacher's example. You will soon see that your teacher writes the left hand side before the right, and the top before the bottom, and that he makes the horizontal strokes before the perpendicular stroke which crosses them, etc. Having acquired the art of tracing characters in a fair hand and in proper order of strokes, proceed to copy out a part or all of the lesson for the day. All the while you are copying, you will be having an exercise in recalling and fixing the characters in your mind.

The difficulty in writing is not in learning to handle the pen properly and write neatly, but in knowing what character should be used in each case, and in recalling readily and accurately its form and composition. How much time it will pay the student to spend in writing Chinese, will depend on his special gifts, together with the requirements of the work in which he expects to engage. Every student can learn to write a fair Chinese hand, and will find it quite an advantage to be able to do so, but to be a *ready writer*—recalling all needed characters readily and using them accurately, requires natural aptitude, together with constant and long-continued practice.

ADVICE TO THE STUDENT.

READ over the Introduction carefully. You will not understand it all, but it will serve to give you a useful general idea of the work you are undertaking. Reading it over once or even twice is not sufficient. It should be carefully studied and re-read from time to time until it is fully understood. Give special attention to the system of spelling and to the powers of the letters as there defined. You cannot spell words properly or consistently until you are familiar with the powers to be given to the letters.

---

* This is one of the perplexing things that beset the path of one who undertakes to make a vocabulary. A Chinese scholar gives a clear and evident general distinction between the two readings of a character, and all seems plain. The trouble comes when it is discovered that the distinction will not carry out consistently, but is contradicted by usage. For instance see 難 and 勝.

I wish to emphasize this point strongly. I have known students who, after one or even two months' study of Chinese, did not know the powers of the letters they were attempting to use. A student who imagines that he can spell Chinese words without any special system, will soon find himself involved in confusion and inconsistency, and will presently be unable to tell what sound he meant to express by his own writing.

2. Learn the radicals thoroughly according to the directions given with the Table of Radicals.

3. Practice the tone exercises until you have mastered the "chime" and can distinguish readily the tone of any character your teacher pronounces. At the same time also practice the aspirate exercises until you have mastered the difference between an aspirated and an unaspirated sound.

4. Having fitted yourself thus far, begin with the lessons proper and learn them carefully until the Chinese can be given readily by looking at the English. Review frequently, and so continue until about sixty lessons have been well mastered, which will require six or eight months of steady work.

5. Having laid this foundation, strike out with more boldness. Take a new lesson each day and get it as well as you can, and so go on without halting or turning back, till you have gone over one hundred and ninety-six lessons. I give this advice for several reasons :—

(*a*). It will relieve the tedium, perhaps discouragement, of bald, hard, committing to memory, and will bring something fresh each day.

(*b*). The same characters and phrases will be turning up again and again, so that by the time you are through, you will be gratified to find that though imperfectly learned at their first appearance, many of them have nevertheless "stuck."

(*c*). This plan will give you a comprehensive view of all the important idioms in the language and avoid the danger of missing some entirely by stopping short of the end.

6. Having reached the end, return to the sixtieth lesson and review *thoroughly*, which you can now do with ease and with a fuller comprehension of the various idioms brought to view.

7. As soon as you can put two words together, begin to talk, not only with your teacher during hours of study, but at other times, with all the Chinese about you. Be sure that the more you talk, making the best use you can of the phrases you have learned, and picking up others, the faster you will learn Chinese. Talking will take the place of exercises in translating English into Chinese, and your key will be the fact of your being understood.

8. Cultivate assiduously the art of hearing how the Chinese around you speak. Have an interrogation point permanently attached to your ears. When your mind is alert to hear how the Chinese speak their language, and to compare what you hear with what you yourself say, then and then only will you have acquired the art of learning Chinese. He who unconsciously continues to say a thing *one way*, when he is constantly hearing the Chinese say it *another way* will never learn Chinese well. I would urge on every one the *extreme importance* of keeping his ears wide open so as to hear, to imitate, and to appropriate.

9. Do not assume that the English spelling really represents the true pronunciation of your dialect. *He who does this will certainly speak with a marked foreign brogue.* The true pronunciation of each syllable should be learned from your Chinese teacher. The spelling, being approximately correct, will serve to *recall* the sounds, but should never be allowed to *determine* them. He who depends on the spelling for the pronunciation of the words will certainly not pronounce accurately.

10. Speak distinctly and not too fast. Foreigners are often better understood than the Chinese themselves, chiefly because they enunciate more distinctly and speak more slowly.

11. Try to avoid long and involved sentences. Break up your thoughts into short sentences. This is the chief secret of perspicuity in Chinese.

12. Be content to turn your thoughts around and split them up, and do them over into Chinese style. They may seem to you to have lost much in the process, but they will be far more forcible to the Chinese than in the foreign form in which you would prefer to have them. He who would use the Chinese language effectively, must learn to think as well as to talk in Chinese.

13. Do not fail to learn to read, as well as to speak, Mandarin. The two things naturally go hand in hand and mutually help each other. The additional labor involved in learning to read whilst learning to speak, is not great. Even ladies whose time is limited, will not find the task nearly so great as is often imagined. It is needless to say that ability to read will be a great power in the hands of its possessor. It is worthy of remark that one who does not learn to read, scarcely ever learns to speak *well*.

14. Learn as much colloquial as you can and do not be afraid to use it. It is a mistake to suppose that colloquial is necessarily inelegant, or unacceptable to the ears of the people. There are times when a stately literary style is becoming, as in conversation with officials or with educated men, but for the varied wants of everyday life, it is far from being the most useful or effective. In preaching, a certain amount of dignity is no doubt important, but this is not in the least inconsistent with a free use of colloquial. The freshness, directness and pithiness which the colloquial adds to "general Mandarin," are almost, if not quite, essential to really effective public address. In preaching especially, an elegant classical style with its high-sounding book phraseology, is worth but little as compared with an attractive colloquial style, which will catch the ears and win the hearts of the people.

15. Unless for special reasons, always learn the dialect of the place in which you reside. You will learn it more easily, as every one you meet will be your teacher, and you will avoid the confusion and discouragement of trying to learn one dialect while you are hearing another. The very best foundation on which to build a knowledge of several dialects, or of "general Mandarin," is an accurate knowledge of some one dialect.

16. Remember that the chief thing in learning a language is memory. The Western mind is given to reasoning and philosophizing, but the exercise of this faculty is largely thrown away in learning a new language, especially such an unscientific language as the Chinese. Don't begin, therefore, by attempting to investigate the logical principles that underlie the structure of the language, but take it on faith, and make it your chief business to *cram* the words and phrases of the lessons as fast as possible. This is the shortest and surest road to success.

17. Do not stop learning Chinese at the end of one or two years. Cultivate the habit of *listening* to the language of the Chinese whom you hear speaking. Seize every *new* expression and appropriate it, investigating it with your teacher if necessary. If you allow yourself to fall into the habit of passing new words and expressions by, simply gathering the speaker's meaning in a general way from the words you already know, you will presently cease to hear any new words at all, and your knowledge of Chinese will remain practically stationary.

EXPLANATIONS.

ALL *single* characters are defined in the vocabularies, but *phrases* which first occur and are defined in the subject, are not afterwards repeated in the vocabulary.

2. As a rule all the leading Mandarin meanings of characters and phrases are given, but meanings confined to the *Wên-li*, are not generally given. The more primitive meaning is usually given first, and the others in order.

3. Many Chinese characters are used with almost equal facility as nouns and as verbs, as adjectives and as adverbs. In such cases the vocabulary has not detailed the meaning in the several parts of speech, but gives only that one which is most normal to the character, leaving the others to be inferred from the connection in each case.

4. *That meaning of a word or phrase which occurs in the given lesson, is printed in italics.* Sometimes on account of the structure of the sentence, the translation contains none of the meanings in exact form. In such cases none are italicized. When a character is used in a phrase which greatly modifies its proper meaning, so as to make it doubtful on which of its meanings the phrase is founded, then none is italicized. When two or three meanings given to a character are practical equivalents, none is italicized.

5. When a character has two readings attended by a difference of meaning, the second reading is noted at the end of the definition. The word *also* indicates that the other reading has not yet appeared, and the word *see*, that the other reading has already appeared and been defined.

6. When a character has two readings not attended by any change of meaning, they are both noted in the vocabulary when it is first defined, but when it subsequently occurs in phrases, only one reading, the most common or suitable one, is given.

7. The spellings in the vocabularies are in accordance with the Peking sounds, but a space is left after or underneath each spelling for the writing in of a second spelling to suit the student's particular dialect. The student should not write in these spellings hap-hazard, but *first master the system of spelling as applied to his own dialect* and then write them in carefully, going to a syllabary in cases of doubt (if he is so fortunate as to have a syllabary of his dialect). If he has an index for his dialect, this will afford a guide in all cases. It will be found that a large proportion of Pekingese spellings apply equally to

other dialects. The best and most labor-saving plan is to underscore the Peking spellings which prove to be correct, and erase the others, writing in the correct spelling. If this is done with the learning of each lesson, it will save much time and confusion on review.

8. In the subjects and vocabularies (N.) stands for Northern Mandarin; that is, that which is spoken in Peking and vicinity; (C.) stands for Central Mandarin which, in this case, is limited to that spoken in Eastern Shantung; (S.) stands for Southern Mandarin, which means, in this case, that spoken on the lower Yangtze, especially that of Nanking. These indications are only approximate, and being in some cases given on the authority of one teacher, are not always to be depended on. When a phrase is local, but the limits of its use are unknown to the author, it is marked (L.); that is, local. Words and phrases the use of which is confined to classical or book style, are marked (W.); that is, *Wên-li*. All words and phrases which are unmarked, are supposed to be *t'ung-hsing*, or at least approximately so. A wider examination will no doubt show that some of these are also more or less local.

9. In the duplicate readings in the Chinese text, the one on the right hand is the Northern form, and the one on the left, the Southern. In some cases three readings are given, which are arranged in order with the Northern one on the right. In some cases a duplicate reading consists of a Northern and Central, or a Central and Southern—the other section not being represented, for want of information. In all such cases the more northerly reading is to the right. In a few cases both forms are *t'ung-hsing*, but are not equally applicable in the given connection. In such cases attention is called to the matter in the notes. These parallel readings are *supposed* to be synonymous. That they differ slightly in many cases, is unavoidable. The translation conforms to the right hand reading. When the difference is considerable, a second translation, conforming to the other reading, is given in parenthesis.

11. Duplicate readings, especially in the case of common phrases, are not generally repeated in full. One reading is used alone and then the other, preference being given to that which is supposed to have the wider range of use.

GENERAL REMARKS.

GRAMMATICAL science has never been applied to the Chinese language. There are of course principles of construction embedded in it, but they have never been developed and systematized. Educated Chinese have no guide in writing or speaking their language save their own ear and the particular precedents established by usage. As a consequence *the language, as at present spoken, has in it many anomalous forms and usages which are really at variance with the underlying principles of the language.*

2. In China, literary taste and skill have thus far expended themselves almost entirely on the *Wên-li*. Elegance in speaking is neither taught nor cultivated. Teachers correct and criticize with great pains the *Wên-li* essays of their pupils, but allow them to speak any way they choose. In talking, every man is a law unto himself, and individual peculiarities abound to a phenomenal extent.

3. The introduction of Christianity and of Western thought into China is giving a marked stimulus to Mandarin literature; and mission schools cultivate care and correctness in speaking as well as in writing. These things are a beginning, and will certainly increase and develope in the future, and they will tend gradually to elevate and purify the Mandarin. The tendency of the times also is towards a lower and more diffusive style of *Wên-li*, approximating, in some measure, the model of the spoken language. There is little doubt that ultimately Mandarin, enriched, corrected and dignified, will come to be the written, as well as the spoken, language of China.

4. Chinese has generally been regarded as a very difficult language to learn. The difficulty chiefly concerns the writing. The spoken language is of course more difficult to an English speaker than a cognate European language, but not more difficult than other Asiatic languages.

5. To pick up a limited knowledge of colloquial, which will answer for household or business purposes, is quite easy; but to acquire a fluent, idiomatic and comprehensive knowledge of the language, answering to all the departments of life, requires diligent and persevering study.

6. Four things are important in order to speak good Chinese:—

(*a*). To put the words and clauses in their proper idiomatic order.

(*b*). To give to the words and phrases their proper rhythmical emphasis.

(*c*). To give to the words their correct syllabic pronunciation.

(*d*). To give the aspirates and tones correctly.

These things I regard as important in the order in which they have just been enumerated.

TABLE OF RADICALS.

IN the following table the radicals are arranged in classes according to the number of strokes in each, and in the order in which they usually stand in dictionaries. They are numbered in order from one upwards—albeit the Chinese never number them. Each radical is spelled according to the Peking sound, and space is left for writing in a second spelling. The meanings given are brief and suggestive, rather than exhaustive. A considerable number of the radicals are contracted or modified in composition. The modified form is given in each case at the side of the full form. Some forty six or seven of the radicals are obsolete as independent characters, being now only used as radicals in composition. They are indicated in the table by an asterisk (*).

The best way to learn the radicals is *first* to learn the shape and meaning, associating these things together; then proceed to learn the sound and the order. If the student uses another dialect than Pekingese, he should get a competent person to write in the spelling according to his own dialect. The radical ode which follows the table will, no doubt, furnish the easiest method of learning the order. If however any one is inclined to learn the order direct, he will find that the easiest way is to sing the radicals over and over until he is familiar with the names and order. Then have them written out on a sheet of paper and sing them over, guided by the characters alone. Finally sing them over entirely from memory. They will need frequent rehearsing in order to keep from forgetting them.

1 Stroke.

No.	Sound	Name	Radical	Meaning
1	*I*^{1}	(一橫)	一	One, unity.
2	*Kun*^{3}	(一竪)	丨*	to pass through, an upright.
3	*Chu*^{3}	(一點)	丶*	a point, a dot.
4	*P'ie*^{3}	(一撇)	丿*	a stroke to the left.
5	*I*^{1,4}		乙	a curve, one.
6	*Chüe*^{2}		亅*	a barb, a crook.

2 Strokes.

No.	Sound	Name	Radical	Meaning
7	*Êr*^{4}	(兩橫)	二	two.
8	*T'ou*^{2}		亠*	a cover, a hat.
9	*Jên*^{2}	(單立人)	人 亻	a man.
10	*Jên*^{2}		儿*	a man, the legs of a man.
11	*Ju*^{3,4}		入	to enter, into.
12	*Pa*^{1,2}		八	eight.
13	*Chiung*^{3}	(三道框)	冂*	a limit.
14	*Mi*^{4}	(禿寶蓋)	冖*	to cover, a cover.
15	*Ping*^{1}	(兩點水)	冫*	ice, icicle.
16	*Chi*^{1,3}		几	a bench.
17	*K'an*^{3}		凵*	a receptacle, a box.
18	*Tao*^{1}	(立刀)	刀 刂	a knife, a sword.
19	*Li*^{4}		力	strength.
20	*Pao*^{1}		勹*	to wrap.
21	*Pi*^{3}		匕	a spoon, a ladle.
22	*Fang*^{1}	(三道框)	匚*	a chest, a case.
23	*Hsi*^{3}	(三道框)	匸	to conceal.
24	*Shï*^{2}		十	ten.
25	*Pu*^{3}		卜	to divine.
26	*Chie*^{2}	(硬耳刀)	卩* 㔾	a seal, a joint.
27	*Han*^{4}	(禿偏上)	厂*	a ledge, a cliff.
28	*Si*^{1}		厶*	selfish, perverse.
29	*Yiu*^{4}		又	and, again.

3 Strokes.

No.	Sound	Name	Radical	Meaning
30	*K'ou*^{3}		口	a mouth.
31	*Wei*^{2}	(四道框)	囗*	an enclosure.
32	*T'u*^{3}	(土堆)	土	earth.
33	*Shï*^{4}		士	a scholar, a sage.
34	*Chï*^{3}		夂*	a step, to follow.
35	*Ts'wei*^{1}		夊*	walking slowly.
36	*Hsi*^{1,2}		夕	evening.
37	*Ta*^{4}		大	great.
38	*Nü*^{3}		女	woman, daughter.
39	*Tsï*^{3}		子	son, child.
40	*Mien*^{2}	(寶蓋)	宀*	a roof.
41	*Ts'un*^{4}		寸	an inch.
42	*Hsiao*^{3}		小	small, little.
43	*Wang*^{1}		尢* 尣 尪	weak, lame.
44	*Shï*^{1}		尸	a corpse.
45	*Ch'ê*^{4}	(半草)	屮*	a sprout.

46 *Shan*^{1} 山 a hill, a mountain.
47 *Ch'wan*^{1} (三 臥 人)巛 川 mountain streams.
48 *Kung*^{1} 工 labor, a workman.
49 *Chï*^{3} 己 self.
50 *Chin*^{1} (大 巾 旁)巾 a napkin.
51 *Kan*^{1} 干 to oppose, a shield.
52 *Yao*^{1} 幺* small, tender.
53 *Yien*^{3} (偏 上)广* a roof, a shelter.
54 *Yin*^{3} 廴* moving on.
55 *Kung*^{3} 廾* joined hands.
56 *I*^{4} 弋 a dart.
57 *Kung*^{1} 弓 a bow, archery.
58 *Ch'i*^{4} (橫 山)彐 彑 a pig's head, pointed.
59 *Shan*^{1} (三 撇)彡 hair, plumagé.
60 *Ch'i*^{4} (雙 立 人)彳* a step.

4 Strokes.

61 *Hsin*^{1} 心 ⺗ the heart.
„ (竪 心) 忄
62 *Kê*^{1} 戈 a spear.
63 *Hu*^{4} 戶 a door.
64 *Shou*^{3} 手 the hand.
„ (提 手) 扌
65 *Chï*^{1} 支 a branch, a prop.
66 *P'u*^{1} (反 文)攴 攵* to rap, to tap.
67 *Wên*^{2} 文 literature, ornament.
68 *Tou*^{3} 斗 a peck, a bushel.
69 *Chin*^{1} 斤 an axe, a catty.
70 *Fang*^{1} 方 square.
71 *Wu*^{2} 无 旡 without, not.
72 *Jï*^{4} 日 the sun, a day.
73 *Yüe*^{1,4} 曰 to speak.
74 *Yüe*^{4} 月 the moon, a month.
75 *Mu*^{4} 木 wood, a tree.
76 *Ch'ien*^{4} 欠 to owe, to be deficient
77 *Chï*^{3} 止 to stop.
78 *Tai*^{3} 歹 歺 bad, vicious.
79 *Shu*^{1} 殳 a pole; to kill.
80 *Wu*^{2,4} 毋 to deny; do not!
81 *Pi*^{3} 比 to compare.
82 *Mao*^{2} 毛 hair, wool.
83 *Shï*^{4} 氏 family name.
84 *Ch'i*^{4} 气 breath, vapour.

85 *Shwei*^{3} 水 氺 water.
„ (三 點 水) 氵
86 *Hwoă*^{3} 火 fire.
„ (四 點 火) 灬
87 *Chao*^{3} 爪 爫 claws.
88 *Fu*^{4} 父 father.
89 *Yao*^{2} 爻 crosswise.
90 *Ch'iang*^{2} 爿* a bed, a frame.
91 *P'ien*^{4} 片 a slice, a splint.
92 *Ya*^{2} 牙 a tooth.
93 *Niu*^{2} (提 牛 旁)牛 a cow, an ox.
94 *Ch'üen*^{3} 犬 a dog.
„ (反犬 or 犬猶) 犭

5 Strokes.

95 *Hsüen*^{2} 玄 sombre, black.
96 *Yü*^{4} 玉 a gem, a precious [stone.
„ (斜 玉) 王
97 *Kwa*^{1} 瓜 a melon, a gourd.
98 *Wa*^{3} 瓦 a tile.
99 *Kan*^{1} 甘 sweet.
100 *Shêng*^{1} 生 to live, to produce.
101 *Yung*^{4} 用 to use.
102 *T'ien*^{2} 田 a field.
103 *P'i*^{3} 疋 a roll of cloth.
104 *Ni*^{1,4} (病 字 旁)疒* disease.
105 *Poă*^{1,4} 癶* back to back.
106 *Pai*^{2} 白 white.
107 *P'i*^{2} 皮 skin, bark.
108 *Min*^{3} (皿 堆)皿 a dish, a platter.
109 *Mu*^{4} 目 罒 an eye.
110 *Mao*^{2} 矛 a halberd, a lance.
111 *Shï*^{3} 矢 an arrow, a dart.
112 *Shï*^{2} 石 a stone.
113 *Shï*^{4} 示* ⺬ 礻 [a revelation a divine omen.
114 *Jou*^{3} 禸* a footprint.
115 *Hê*^{2} (禾 木)禾 grain of any kind.
116 *Hsüe*^{2,4} (穴 字 頭)穴 a cave, a den.
117 *Li*^{4} 立 to set up, to erect.

6 Strokes.

118 *Chu*^{2} (竹 字 頭)竹 the bamboo.
119 *Mi*^{3} 米 rice.
120 *Sï*^{1} (絞 絲)糸* 糹 raw silk.
121 *Fou*^{3} 缶 crockery.

122 *Wang*^{3} 网*罒⺳ a net.
123 *Yang*^{2} 羊 a sheep.
124 *Yü*^{3} 羽 wings, feathers.
125 *Lao*^{3} 老 old.
126 *Êr*^{2} 而 still, yet.
127 *Lei*^{3} 耒 a plow.
128 *Êr*^{3} 耳 the ear.
129 *Yü*^{4} 聿 a pen, a pencil.
130 *Jou*^{4} 肉月 flesh, meat.
131 *Ch'ên*^{2} 臣 a statesman.
132 *Tsï*^{4} 自 self.
133 *Chï*^{4} 至 to, to arrive.
134 *Chiu*^{4} 臼 a mortar.
135 *Shê*^{2} 舌 the tongue.
136 *Ch'wan*^{3} 舛 to oppose, error.
137 *Chou*^{1} 舟 a boat, a ship.
138 *Kên*^{4} 艮 perverse, limited.
139 *Sê*^{4} 色 color.
140 *Ts'ao*^{3} 艸*艹 grass, herbs.
141 *Hu*^{1} 虍*a tiger.
142 *Ch'ung*^{2} 虫 an insect.
143 *Hsüe*^{3,4} 血 blood.
144 *Hsing*^{2} 行 to go, to travel.
145 *I*^{1} 衣衤 clothes.
146 *Hsi*^{1} 襾西 to cover, west.

7 Strokes.

147 *Chien*^{4} 見 to see, to perceive.
148 *Chüe*^{3} 角 a horn, a corner.
149 *Yien*^{2} 言 words, to speak.
150 *Ku*^{1,3} 谷 a valley.
151 *Tou*^{4} 豆 beans, pulse.
152 *Shï*^{3} 豕 a pig, swine.
153 *Chai*^{4} 豸 a reptile.
154 *Pei*^{4} 貝 a shell, precious.
155 *Ch'ï*^{3,4} 赤 flesh color, naked.
156 *Tsou*^{3} 走 to go, to walk.
157 *Tsu*^{2} 足 the feet, enough.
158 *Shên*^{1} 身 the body.
159 *Ch'ê*^{1} 車 a cart, a coach.
160 *Hsin*^{1} 辛 bitter.
161 *Ch'ên*^{2} 辰 time.
162 *Choa*^{4} 辵*辶 to go, to run.
163 *I*^{4} 邑 a region, a city.
„ (右耳刀) 阝
164 *Yiu*^{3} 酉 ripe, must, wine.
165 *Pien*^{4} 釆 to pluck, to sort out.
166 *Li*^{3} 里 a Chinese mile.

8 Strokes.

167 *Chin*^{1} 金 metal, gold.
168 *Ch'ang*^{3} 長镸 long.
169 *Mên*^{2} 門 a door, gate.
170 *Fou*^{4} 阜 a mound, plenty.
„ (左耳刀) 阝
171 *Tai*^{4} 隶* to reach to, to attain.
172 *Chwei*^{1} 隹 birds.
173 *Yü*^{3} 雨⻗ rain.
174 *Ch'ing*^{1} 青 blue sky.
175 *Fei*^{1} 非 no, wrong.

9 Strokes.

176 *Mien*^{4} 面 the face.
177 *Kê*^{2} 革 raw-hide.
178 *Wei*^{2} 韋 leather.
179 *Chiu*^{3} 韭 leeks.
180 *Yin*^{1} 音 sound.
181 *Yie*^{4} 頁 a leaf, the head.
182 *Fêng*^{1} 風 wind.
183 *Fei*^{1} 飛 to fly.
184 *Shï*^{2} 食 to eat.
185 *Shou*^{3} 首 the head, first.
186 *Hsiang*^{1} 香 incense.

10 Strokes

187 *Ma*^{3} 馬 a horse.
188 *Ku*^{3} 骨 a bone.
189 *Kao*^{1} 高 high.
190 *Piao*^{1} 髟* hair.
191 *Tou*^{4} 鬥 to quarrel, to fight.
192 *Ch'ang*^{4} 鬯* herbs, essences.
193 *Li*^{4} 鬲 a tripod, an urn.
194 *Kwei*^{3} 鬼 a demon, a ghost.

11 Strokes.

195 *Yü*^{2} 魚 a fish.
196 *Niao*^{3} 鳥 a bird.
197 *Lu*^{3} 鹵 crude salt.
198 *Lu*^{4} 鹿 a deer.

199 *Moä*[4]	麥	wheat.
200 *Ma*[2]	麻	hemp.

12 Strokes.

201 *Hwang*[2]	黃	yellow.
202 *Shu*[3]	黍	millet.
203 *Hê*[4]	黑	black.
204 *Chï*[4]	黹	embroidery.

13 Strokes.

205 *Min*[3]	黽	frogs.
206 *Ting*[3]	鼎	a tripod.
207 *Ku*[3]	鼓	a drum.
208 *Shu*[3]	鼠	a rat, a mouse.

14 Strokes.

209 *Pi*[2]	鼻	the nose.
210 *Ch'i*[2]	齊	regular, even.

15 Strokes.

211 *Ch'ï*[3]	齒	front teeth.

16 Strokes.

212 *Lung*[3]	龍	a dragon.
213 *Kwei*[1]	龜	a tortoise, a turtle.

17 Strokes.

214 *Yoä*[4]	龠	a flute, a pipe.

THE RADICAL ODE.

BY REV. J. A. SILSBY.

THE following ode will relieve the student of much labor in learning the meaning and order of the radicals. It will serve as a continuous ladder, with suggestive and ever-varying rounds, which the student can mount with vastly greater ease than he can climb the bare pole of arithmetical numbers. Not only is the first acquirement made easier, but the memory will retain the ode more firmly and recall it more readily than it will the bare numbers.

HOW TO BEGIN.

One Stroke.

Beginning with [1]*unity*, just as you ought, — [1] 一
You next make an [2]*upright*, and then make a [3]*dot;* — [2] 丨 [3] 丶
Make a [4]*stroke to the left*, then a [5]*curve* and a [6]*crook*, — [4] 丿 [5] 乙 [6] 亅
And you've summed up the use of one stroke in a book.

A RIDDLE.

Two Strokes.

[7]*Two* [8]*hats* on one [9]*man!* See, that [10]*tramp* walking fast, — [7] 二 [8] 亠 [9] 人 [10] 儿
[11]*Enters* slyly at [12]*eight*, ere the [13]*limit* is passed. — [11] 入 [12] 八 [13] 冂
A [14]*cov'ring* of [15]*ice* hides a [16]*bench* and a [17]*box*, — [14] 冖 [15] 冫 [16] 几 [17] 凵
A [18]*sword* of great [19]*strength* is [20]*wrapped up* in old socks, — [18] 刀 [19] 力 [20] 勹
A [21]*spoon* in a [22]*case* is [23]*concealed* with [24]*ten* knives; — [21] 匕 [22] 匚 [23] 匸 [24] 十
[25]*Divine* what this means, and then ask the old wives,— — [25] 卜
Why that [26]*seal* on the [27]*cliff*, made by some [28]*selfish* hoax, — [26] 卩 [27] 厂 [28] 厶
Should let a [29]*conjunction* end up the two strokes. — [29] 又

CONSOLATION FOR AN UNFORTUNATE WIDOW.

Three Strokes.

Three smacks on the [30] *mouth!* an [31] *enclosure* how sweet!	30 口	31 囗		
Which [32] *earth's* greatest [33] *sage* [34] *follows* [35] *slowly* to greet.	32 土	33 士	34 夂	35 夊
This [36] *evening* [37] *great* [38] *lady,* your [39] *son* had a fall	36 夕	37 大	38 女	39 子
From a [40] *roof* that was forty-one [41] *inches* too [42] *small.*	40 宀	41 寸	42 小	
He is [43] *lame,* not a [44] *corpse,* and some [45] *sprouts* from the [46] *hill,*	43 尢	44 尸	45 屮	46 山
Washed in [47] *streams* by the [48] *workmen,* will keep him quite still.	47 巛	48 工		
Wrap [49] *self* in a [50] *napkin;* make [51] *shields* for the [52] *tender;*	49 己	50 巾	51 干	52 幺
Give [53] *shelter* to orphans; [54] *move* on, their defender!	53 广	54 廴		
Joined [55] *hands* follow Cupid's [56] *dart,* shot from his [57] *bow:*	55 廾	56 弋	57 弓	
Eat [58] *pig's head;* don [59] *plumage;* his [60] *footsteps* you know.	58 彐	59 彡	60 彳	

SUNDRY REFLECTIONS.

Four Strokes.

If your [61] *heart* be once pierced by a [62] *spear* as you stand,	61 心	62 戈		
Then the [63] *door* of eternity's surely at [64] *hand.*	63 戶	64 手		
When you've mastered this [65] *branch* of the language, be sure	65 支			
You've but [66] *tapped* at the portal of [67] *literature.*	66 攴	67 文		
Though we measure with [68] *bushels* and [69] *catties* and [70] *squares,*	68 斗	69 斤	70 方	
Yet [71] *without* the [72] *sun's* light we could not sell our wares.	71 无	72 日		
Why [73] *speak* of the [74] *moon* with such rapture my dove?	73 曰	74 月		
To the shade of the [75] *wood* do we [76] *owe* our first love.	75 木	76 欠		
[77] *Stop,* [78] *vicious* man, [79] *kill* not! [80] *Deny* not my prayer;	77 止	78 歹	79 殳	80 毋
Can life be [81] *compared* with those locks of red [82] *hair?*	81 比	82 毛		
One's [83] *family name* is as dear as his [84] *breath;*	83 氏	84 气		
Through [85] *water* and [86] *fire* he'll defend it till death.	85 水	86 火		
The [87] *claws* of a kitten, my [88] *father* once said,	87 爪	88 父		
Should never scratch [89] *crosswise,* nor climb on a [90] *bed;*	89 爻	90 爿		
And a [91] *splint* twixt the [92] *teeth,* puts an end to all jokes,	91 片	92 牙		
While an [93] *ox* and a [94] *dog* will end up the four strokes.	93 牛	94 犬		

SAD DEATH OF TWO JEWELERS.

Five Strokes.

Two [95] *sombre* [96] *gem* merchants once ate a [97] *cucumber:*	95 玄 96 玉 97 瓜
They slept on some [98] *tiles*, and how [99] *sweet* was their slumber!	98 瓦 99 甘
But [100] *to live* was no [101] *use;* in a [102] *field* at their ease,	100 生 101 用 102 田
In [103] *dry goods* rolled up, they were killed by [104] *disease.*	103 疋 104 疒
[105] *Back to back* they were laid, dressed in [106] *white;*—'twas their wish,	105 癶 106 白
With the [107] *skin* of the cucumber placed in a [108] *dish!*	107 皮 108 皿
Then an [109] *eye*, [110] *lance* and [111] *dart* were engraved on a [112] *stone,*	109 目 110 矛 111 矢 112 石
As an [113] *emblem divine* of the [114] *foot-prints* now flown;	113 示 114 禸
This stone, midst the [115] *grain* in a [116] *cavernous den,*	115 禾 116 穴
Was [117] *erected* to finish five strokes of the pen.	117 立

AN ECCENTRIC OLD STATESMAN.

Six Strokes.

"Our [118] *bamboo* and [119] *rice*, [120] *silk* and [121] *crocks*, I am told,	118 竹 119 米 120 糸 121 缶
Our [122] *nets*, [123] *sheep* and [124] *quills* must be taxed as of [125] *old.*	122 网 123 羊 124 羽 125 老
And [126] *yet* we [127] *plow* on for this fool with long [128] *ears!*"	126 而 127 耒 128 耳
"Stick a [129] *pen* in his [130] *flesh*," cried a boatman with jeers.	129 聿 130 肉
The [131] *statesman* [132] *himself* now [133] *arrived* with a [134] *mortar,*	131 臣 132 自 133 至 134 臼
The [135] *tongue* that [136] *opposed* him he'd smash and make shorter!	135 舌 136 舛
The [137] *boat's* [138] *perverse* skipper, with red [139] *colored* face,	137 舟 138 艮 139 色
He tied up with [140] *grass*, and dismissed in disgrace.	140 艸
But when [141] *tigers* and [142] *insects* drew [143] *blood*, he thought best	141 虍 142 虫 143 血
To [144] *travel* for [145] *clothing* and skip to the [146] *west.*	144 行 145 衣 146 西

BEWARE OF THE SERPENT.

Seven Strokes.

Seven strokes we now [147] *see*, and a [148] *horn*,—fateful [149] *word!*	147 見 148 角 149 言
In the [150] *valley* [151] *beans* grow, and of [152] *pigs* a whole herd;	150 谷 151 豆 152 豕
Great [153] *reptiles* their [154] *precious* young offspring are feeding;	153 豸 154 貝
With legs bare and [155] *naked* a lad [156] *walks* unheeding;	155 赤 156 走
His [157] *foot* gets a sting and his [158] *body* soon dies;	157 足 158 身
A [159] *coach* brings his mother: how [160] *bitter* her cries!	159 車 160 辛
'Tis high [161] *time* to [162] *run* from a [163] *region* so vile,	161 辰 162 辵 163 邑

Where [164]*wine* [165]*plucks* its victims for many a [166]*mile*. — 164 酉 165 釆 166 里

FLEETING RICHES.

Eight Strokes.

Eight strokes! and now [167]*gold*, after [168]*long* labor gained, — 167 金 168 長
Doth open the [169]*doorway* of [170]*plenty* [171]*attained.* — 169 門 170 阜 171 隶
But riches like [172]*birds*, when the [173]*rain* hides the [174]*blue*, — 172 隹 173 雨 174 青
If I am not [175]*wrong*, will fly quickly from you. — 175 非

FOOLISH ANGER.

Nine Strokes.

Nine strokes on the [176]*face* with a [177]*raw-hide* or [178]*leather*, — 176 面 177 革 178 韋
Or e'en with a [179]*leek*, will raise [180]*sounds* in all weather. — 17· 韭 180 音
For [181]*leaves* in the [182]*wind*, when they [183]*fly* far away, — 181 頁 182 風 183 飛
Don't [184]*eat* off your [185]*head*, nor burn [186]*incense* all day. — 184 食 185 首 186 香

GOOD ADVICE.

Ten Strokes.

Ten strokes on a [187]*horse*, with a [188]*bone* raised on [189]*high*, — 187 馬 188 骨 189 高
Will wear off his [190]*hair*, and soon cause him to shy. — 190 髟
Don't [191]*fight* about [192]*essences* cooked in an [193]*urn*, — 191 鬥 192 鬯 193 鬲
Or you'll find yourself doomed with the [194]*demons* to burn. — 194 鬼

FISHING AND HUNTING.

Eleven Strokes.

Eleven fresh [195]*fish* and a [196]*bird* caught with [197]*salt.* — 195 魚 196 鳥 197 鹵
A [198]*deer* which eats [199]*wheat*, tied with [200]*hemp*, calls a halt. — 198 鹿 199 麥 200 麻

GOING TO MARKET.

Twelve Strokes.

Twelve [201]*yellow* [202]*millet* stalks next you will see, — 201 黃 202 黍
A [203]*black* silk [204]*emdroidery* purchased by me. — 203 黑 204 黹

EXPLOIT OF SOME FROGS.

Thirteen Strokes.

Thirteen little [205]*frogs* on a [206]*tripod* once sat, — 205 黽 206 鼎
But jumped on a [207]*drum*, when they saw a big [208]*rat.* — 207 鼓 208 鼠

RESULT OF A FIGHT.

Fourteen and Fifteen Strokes.

Fourteen were the [209]*noses* all [210]*even* in height, — 209 鼻 210 齊
Fifteen were the [211]*teeth*, which were lost in a fight. — 211 齒

THE DRAGONS END IT.

Sixteen and Seventeen Strokes.

Sixteen [212]*dragons* sat on a [213]*tortoise* last June, — 212 龍 213 龜
Playing seventeen [214]*flutes;* and that winds up my tune. — 214 龠

TONE EXERCISES.

THE following tone exercises are not intended as a means of learning the tone of particular words, but as a means of acquiring the special *intonation* peculiar to each tone, and of learning the chime formed by these tones when given in regular order. Two tables are given, one for Northern and one for Southern Mandarin. All the syllables are not represented in the table, because in some cases it was impossible to find characters agreeing in the different dialects. Many syllables are originally deficient in one or more tones. A few of these are given, but the majority are not. The number of syllables given are abundant for the purpose for which the table is intended. Some syllables seem to be repeated, which shows that in another dialect the given syllable divides into two. The student should go over these exercises carefully with his teacher a number of times, or until he can give and distinguish each tone with certainty, and can chime them together to the satisfaction of his teacher. This will soon be accomplished if he has an average ear, and will give strict attention to the business in hand. No phrases are given in illustration of the tones of the several syllables, because this is not considered to be the most profitable method of study. The tones of particular words are best learned in connection with the characters taken separately, as they occur in the course of the lessons, and the modifications made by composition and collocation are best learned from words and phrases as they stand together in sentences. Every lesson is, in this sense, a tone exercise.

NORTHERN TABLE.

嗷	渣	乂		彰	昌	招	遮	眞	琛	征	稱	雞	唧	欺	棲	加	槍	交	蹺	嗟	尖	千	牽	知
熬	閙	茶	纏		嘗	着	哲		臣		成	吉	即	旗	臍		墻		喬	捷		錢	鉗	姪
襖			謟	鞝	廠	沼	者	枕	紖	整	逞	己	擠	起		甲	搶	絞	巧	姐	剪	淺	遣	
傲	乍	杈	韂	丈	唱	兆	浙	震	趁	政	秤	記	祭	氣	砌	價	嗆	叫	竅	借	箭	倩	欠	智

癡	侵	驚	輕	楸	究	抽	居	區	捐	圈	噘	諸	樗	初	穿	裝	窗	忠	充			翻	方	非
持	秦		擎			綢	局	渠		拳	决		除	雛	船		牀		蟲	兒	罰	煩	房	肥
尺	寢	景	頃	酒	久	醜	舉	曲	捲	犬	蹶	煑	杵	楚	喘	奘	闖	腫	寵	爾	法	反	紡	匪
叱	唚	敬	慶	就	救	臭	句	去	眷	勸	[illegible]	住	處	畜	串	壯	創	仲	銃	二	鏺	飯	放	廢

紛	夫	咳	憨	蒿	哏	劐	齁	忽	歡	荒	灰	昏	烘	西	希	鰕	箱	香	消	枵	些	先	掀	星
墳	扶	孩	含	毫	痕	活	喉	胡	環	皇	回	魂	紅	席	翕	匣	詳	降			邪		弦	
粉	府	海	罕	好	很	火	吼	虎	緩	謊	悔	渾	哄	璽	喜		想	响	小	曉	寫	癬	險	擤
忿	父	亥	汗	浩	恨	禍	後	戶	患	滉	惠	掍	横	細	戲	下	象	向	笑	孝	瀉	線	限	姓

興	須	暄	醫			該	剛	康	高	摳	姑	枯	官	光	誆	規	虧	空	鍋	[illegible]		撈		撩
刑	徐	懸	移	人	儒			扛							狂		揆		國	藍	狼	勞	梨	聊
			以	忍	汝	改	堈	沆	稿	口	古	苦	管	廣		詭		孔	果	懶	朗	老	理	了
幸	序	楦	意	刃	褥	盖	杠	炕	告	叩	固	褲	慣	逛	框	貴	愧	控	過	爛	浪	澇	利	料

　遛　嚕　媽　顢貓　濛眯　摸囔　　　妞　疤般潘包抛
零留羅爐龍麻埋瞞毛煤蒙迷綿魔囊鐃尼年牛挪拔　盤雹袍
領柳捋櫓朧馬買滿卯美猛米免抹攮惱你撚鈕諾把板　飽跑
另六洛路弄罵賣慢貌昧夢密面默齉鬧膩念拗糯罷半盼抱礮

烹　批標飄邊偏拼兵波坡噗三桑蘇雖商燒賒身升失詩書梳
朋鼻皮　嫖　便貧　駁婆葡　　俗隨　韶舌神繩十時熟孰
捧筆劈表漂匾諞品秉播笸普傘嗓　髓賞少捨審省　使暑菽
碰敝庇鰾票遍片牝病簸破舖散喪塑碎尚邵赦慎賸式試恕數

衰縧嗒獃丹貪當湯滔燈低梯挑搷天廳多拖偷督端吞通猜簪
　　達　　談　糖逃　敵題條　田亭奪駝投毒　屯同才偺
摔死打歹膽坦黨躺討等底體朓點餂梃朶庹　賭短　統彩攢
率四大代旦炭蕩燙套鐙地替糶店　聽剁橐透鍍斷褪痛菜贊

餐遭操謅忖宗齜彎汪威溫窩烏丫央腰　煙音英迂寃暈憂癰
殘　槽　村　瓷頑王惟文　無牙羊遙爺顏銀迎魚原雲油容
慚早草走存總跐晚枉委穩我武雅養咬野眼引影禹遠允有永
儳造糙奏寸粽次萬旺位問臥物軋樣要夜硯印硬欲願運右用

SOUTHERN TABLE.

哀安鏖乂章昌昭抄真稱抽之癡忠充諸樞專川　番方非紛風
挨昂熬茶　腸　潮　呈紬　馳　蟲　除　椽而煩房肥墳馮
矮唵襖　掌敞找炒診逞丑台恥腫寵煮杵囀喘耳反訪匪粉捧
愛暗傲岔丈唱兆　鎮秤臭至滯衆銃住處篆串二飯放肺忿鳳
　　　察　　　　　　　姪赤　　　黜

敷　憨蒿齁亨希蝦香驍掀興呵轟呼花荒歡輝昏喧衣該甘堪
扶孩寒毫侯痕　遐降爻嫌形河洪湖划皇環回魂懸移
釜海罕好吼很喜　响曉顯　火哄虎　幌緩毀渾　倚改敢砍
富害旱浩後恨係下向孝限幸賀鬨戶化晃宦惠混楦義蓋幹勘
福　　　　　隙瞎　　　　盒　忽滑　　　　　益

虧揆傀愧
規鬼貴
筐狂況
官管貫
誇胯跨
瓜寡卦刮
區渠去屈
居舉句局
枯苦庫哭
姑古故骨
空孔控
科可課渴
歌果箇各
輕擎慶
金錦近
謙虔遣欠
交皎叫
加賈架夾
欺奇起氣乞
機蟣記極
坑肯掯
摳口叩
勾狗彀
高稿告
康慷炕

迷米謎蜜
蒙猛孟
梅美昧
棉免面
毛卯貌
巒滿慢
埋買賣
嗎麻馬罵抹
驢旅慮律
雷壘類
爐魯路祿
龍攏弄
留柳溜
靈領令
涼兩亮
犂理吏立
樓簍陋
拈年碾念
連臉煉
鐃腦鬧
囊攮齉
拿那那納
圈權犬勸
娟捲眷
昆綑困

擻叟嗽
先涎鮮線
些邪寫謝洩
桑嗓喪
薩灑靸
仁荏認
瓤壤讓
鋪菩普鋪僕
婆頗破潑
波簸薄
貧品聘
兵丙並
飄嫖縹票
批皮痞屁劈
朋捧碰
奔本笨
鞭扁變
拋袍跑砲
包保抱
潘盤泮
邦榜棒
班板扮
疤靶霸拔
摸魔麼磨末
明敏命

兜斗豆
天田舔掭
顛典店
滔逃討套
湯堂躺燙
貪檀坦炭
鐺擋蕩
胎臺泰
獃歹代
打大達
宣旋選鏇
雖隨髓碎
蘇數訴俗
松竦宋
心醒姓
箱想象
西洗細席
衰摔帥
詩時始市拾
身神審甚
收手受
賒蛇捨赦
燒韶少紹
傷裳賞尚
沙傻殺

楸酒就
青晴請親
晶井靜
槍牆搶嗆
漿獎匠
雌詞此次
資子字
妻臍砌戚
躋擠祭疾
撐層蹭
千前淺倩
姐借截
操曹草糙
糟早躁
餐殘慘燦
猜才彩菜
通同桶痛
東董洞
拖駝妥脫
多朵剁奪
廳亭挺聽
丁頂定
佻條挑跳
梯題體替剔
低底地笛

淵元遠願
迂魚雨寓
雍榮甬用
憂由有右
英迎影映
音銀引印
烟言眼厭
耶爺野夜頁
腰搖舀耀
央羊癢樣
枒牙啞訝鴨
溫紋刎問
威惟委味
汪亡枉旺
彎頑晚萬
烏無五務屋
推頹腿退
端短斷
圖土兎禿
都覩杜篤
村存忖寸
趨徐取趣
粗芻楚醋族
租阻助足
宗總粽

ASPIRATE EXERCISES.

In order to facilitate the acquisition of the distinction between aspirates and non-aspirates the following tables of exercises have been arranged. It was found impossible to make one table answer for both Northern and Southern Mandarin; hence one is given for each. Each table gives all the syllables to which the distinction applies. In all dialects a few syllables capable of making the distinction are deficient either in the aspirate or the unaspirate. These of course are not given. Some syllables seem to be repeated, which is caused by the splitting of the syllable by a different dialect. In all cases, except those which are specially marked, the tone of the two characters is the same, thus eliminating this complication, whilst the distinction of aspiration is being acquired.

The student should go over this table repeatedly with his teacher, carefully imitating his pronunciation. In general the greater danger lies in not aspirating strongly enough the aspirated sound. It should be specially noted by the student, that mere stress or force of voice is not necessarily aspiration. It is the position of the tongue, not the amount of breath, that makes the difference. Let the student get a clear apprehension of what aspiration means and the whole difficulty vanishes.

NORTHERN TABLE.

2	3	1	1	1	4	1	2	1	1	1	3	2	4	2	1	1	1	1	1	
閘	展	張	招	遮	振	爭	疾	機	家	江	矯	潔	見	直	金	精	京	揪	究	迴[3]
茶	諂	昌	超	車	趁	撐	齊	欺	掐	腔	巧	茄	欠	遲	欽	清	輕	秋	丘	窮[2]

1	4	4	2		4	1	1	1	3	1	1	3	1	4	4	1	3	1	3	3
州	眷	句	決	[1]君	駐	專	莊	追	準	忠	該	赶	綱	告	個	歌	訳	更	狗	古
抽	勸	去	瘸	[2]羣	處	穿	窗	吹	蠢	充	開	砍	康	靠	刻	科	肯	坑	口	苦

1	4	1	1	4	3	1	4	4	4	4	4	4	4	1	4	3	3	1	1	4
瓜	怪	官	光	貫	滾	工	過	罷	敗	扮	謗	報	貝	奔	迸	筆	表	憋	編	殯
誇	快	寬	誆	愧	綑	空	闊	怕	派	判	胖	砲	配	噴	碰	撇	漂	撇	偏	聘

	1	3	3	1	4	1	3	4		3	4	1	1	1	1	4	2	3	1	1
兵[1]	波	補	打	呆	蛋	當	島	得	登[1]	底	掉	爹	顛	丁	多	豆	毒	短	堆	敦
平[2]	坡	普	塔	胎	炭	湯	討	忒	滕[2]	體	跳	帖	天	聽	拖	透	徒	疃	推	吞

1	3	3	4	1	3	4	4	4	4	1	1	4	4	1	4
東	紮	宰	讚	臧	早	仄	贈	坐	奏	租	躦	最	尊	宗	自
通	擦	採	謲	倉	草	測	蹭	錯	湊	粗	攛	脆	村	聰	次

SOUTHERN TABLE.

1	3	1	1	1	1	4	1	1	1	1	1	3	1	1	1	3	3	4	1	4
齋	展	張	招	渣	遮	振	貞	周	知	卓	忠	主	專	庄	追	準	改	幹	剛	告
差	諂	昌	超	叉	車	趁	稱	抽	痴	綽	冲	處	穿	窗	吹	蠢	愷	看	康	靠

5	3	1	5	1	3	5	5	4	1	4	5	1	3	1	3	1	4	1	4	5
革	狗	根	及	江	狡	甲	結	見	斤	竟	脚	鳩	果	公	古	瓜	怪	官	逛	國
客	口	坑	乞	腔	巧	恰	怯	欠	欽	慶	却	邱	可	空	苦	誇	快	寬	況	闊

4	4	1	4	4	4	4	3	4	5	4	4	5	1	5	3	4		5	4	4
貴	棍	君	拜	扮	半	謗	保	罷	別	辯	倍	白	奔	必	表	殯	兵[1]	薄	布	代
愧	困	羣	派	盼	判	胖	跑	怕	撇	片	配	迫	烹	匹	摽	聘	平[2]	潑	鋪	太

1	3	3	5	5	1	4	5		5	4	1	1	1	3	1	1	3	5	1	3
丹	擋	島	答	跌	顛	豆	得	登[1]	的	吊	丁	多	冬	宰	簪	髒	早	節	尖	奏
貪	倘	討	蹋	貼	天	透	特	疼[2]	剔	跳	聽	拖	通	采	餐	倉	草	切	千	湊

5	1	5	1	1	1	3	1	3	4	5	1	1	4	1	4	1	5	3	1	1
則	爭	疾	將	焦	津	井	楸	子	坐	爵	宗	租	聚	鑽	罪	尊	毒	短	堆	敦
策	撐	七	槍	鍬	親	請	秋	此	錯	雀	聰	粗	趣	攛	脆	村	禿	疃	推	呑

PEKING SOUND TABLE.

The following List of Syllables represents the application of the new system of spelling to Peking dialect.

The points of departure from the system of Sir Thos. Wade are briefly as follows :–

1. Final *o* is changed to *oă*.
2. *U* when followed by a vowel is changed to *w*.
3. Final *ŭ* and final *ih* are both changed to *ĭ*.
4. *Ss* is changed to *s* and *tz* to *ts*, so that ssŭ becomes *sĭ* and *tzŭ* becomes *tsĭ*.
5. *Yeh* and *yen* and *yu* are changed to *yie* and *yien* and *yiu*.
6. Final *h* is discarded in all cases.
7 Üan is changed to üen.

☞ See remarks at the end of the table.

阿 A, Nga	兆 Chao	楷 Ch'iai	角 Chioă	除 Ch'u	君 Chün
哎 Ai, Ngai	潮 Ch'ao	江 Chiang	卻 Ch'ioă	追 Chwei	羣 Ch'ün
安 An, Ngan	這 Chei	槍 Ch'iang	酒 Chiu	吹 Ch'wei	爵 Chüoă
昂 Ang	這 Chê	交 Chiao	秋 Ch'iu	準 Chun	却 Ch'üoă
傲 Ao	車 Ch'ê	巧 Ch'iao	窘 Chiung	春 Ch'un	抓 Chwa
乍 Cha	眞 Chên	姐 Chie	窮 Ch'iung	中 Chung	欻 Ch'wa
茶 Ch'a	臣 Ch'ên	且 Ch'ie	知 Chĭ	充 Ch'ung	拽 Chwai
齋 Chai	正 Chêng	賤 Chien	池 Ch'ĭ	聚 Chü	揣 Ch'wai
柴 Ch'ai	成 Ch'êng	錢 Ch'ien	拙 Choă	取 Ch'ü	專 Chwan
占 Chan	祭 Chi	進 Chin	綽 Ch'oă	卷 Chüen	川 Ch'wan
諂 Ch'an	齊 Ch'i	親 Ch'in	晝 Chou	犬 Ch'üen	壯 Chwang
章 Chang	家 Chia	井 Ching	抽 Ch'ou	决 Chüe	牀 Ch'wang
昌 Ch'ang	恰 Ch'ia	淸 Ch'ing	主 Chu	缺 Ch'üe	擉 Ch'woă

額	Ê	訓	Hsün	刻	K‘ei	兩	Liang	那	Na	跑	P‘ao
恩	Ên	學	Hsüoă	根	Kên	了	Liao	奶	Nai	倍	Pei
哼	Êng	乎	Hu	肯	K‘ên	列	Lie	男	Nan	陪	P‘ei
兒	Êr	回	Hwei	更	Kêng	連	Lien	囊	Nang	本	Pên
法	Fa	混	Hun	坑	K‘êng	林	Lin	鬧	Nao	盆	P‘ên
反	Fan	紅	Hung	哥	Kê	另	Ling	內	Nei	崩	Pêng
方	Fang	花	Hwa	可	K‘ê	畧	Lioă	嫩	Nên	朋	P‘êng
非	Fei	懷	Hwai	狗	Kou	留	Liu	能	Nêng	比	Pi
分	Fên	換	Hwan	口	K‘ou	羅	Loă	你	Ni	皮	P‘i
風	Fêng	黃	Hwang	古	Ku	陋	Lou	娘	Niang	表	Piao
佛	Foă	火	Hwoă	苦	K‘u	路	Lu	鳥	Niao	票	P‘iao
否	Fou	衣	I	棍	Kun	論	Lun	揑	Nie	別	Pie
夫	Fu	染	Jan	困	K‘un	龍	Lung	念	Nien	撇	P‘ie
哈	Ha	讓	Jang	工	Kung	驢	Lü	您	Nin	扁	Pien
害	Hai	繞	Jao	孔	K‘ung	戀	Lüen	寧	Ning	片	P‘ien
寒	Han	惹	Jê	瓜	Kwa	畧	Lüe	虐	Nioă	賓	Pin
杭	Hang	人	Jên	誇	K‘wa	掄	Lün	牛	Niu	貧	P‘in
好	Hao	扔	Jêng	怪	Kwai	畧	Lüoă	挪	Noă	兵	Ping
赫	Hê Hei	日	Jï	快	K‘wai	亂	Lwan	耨	Nou	平	P‘ing
很	Hên	若	Joă	官	Kwan	馬	Ma	奴	Nu	波	Poă
恆	Hêng	柔	Jou	欵	K‘wan	買	Mai	嫩	Nun	破	P‘oă
河	Hê	如	Ju	光	Kwang	慢	Man	濃	Nung	剖	P‘ou
後	Hou	瑞	Jwei	況	K‘wang	忙	Mang	女	Nü	布	Pu
希	Hsi	潤	Jun	規	Kwei	毛	Mao	虐	Nüe	普	P‘u
下	Hsia	絨	Jung	魁	K‘wei	美	Mei	虐	Nüoă	撒	Sa
向	Hsiang	輭	Jwan	果	Kwoă	門	Mên	煖	Nwan	賽	Sai
孝	Hsiao	蛤	Ka	闊	K‘woă	夢	Mêng	訛	Oă	散	San
些	Hsie	卡	K‘a	拉	La	米	Mi	偶	Ou	桑	Sang
限	Hsien	改	Kai	來	Lai	苗	Miao	巴	Pa	掃	Sao
欣	Hsin	開	K‘ai	懶	Lan	滅	Mie	怕	P‘a	色	Sê
形	Hsing	甘	Kan	浪	Lang	面	Mien	拜	Pai	森	Sên
學	Hsioă	看	K‘an	老	Lao	民	Min	派	P‘ai	僧	Sêng
休	Hsiu	剛	Kang	累	Lei	名	Ming	板	Pan	傻	Sha
兄	Hsiung	炕	K‘ang	勒	Lê	謬	Miu	盼	P‘an	曬	Shai
須	Hsü	告	Kao	冷	Lêng	摩	Moă	邦	Pang	山	Shan
旋	Hsüen	考	K‘ao	李	Li	謀	Mou	旁	P‘ang	賞	Shang
雪	Hsüe	給	Kei	倆	Lia	慕	Mu	包	Pao	少	Shao

舍 Shê	算 Swan	爹 Tie	草 Ts'ao	宗 Tsung	翁 Wêng
身 Shên	大 Ta	貼 T'ie	賊 Tsei	從 Ts'ung	我 Woă
聖 Shêng	他 T'a	店 Tien	則 Tsê	鑽 Tswan	武 Wu
時 Shï	歹 Tai	天 T'ien	策 Ts'ê	竄 Ts'wan	牙 Ya
手 Shou	太 T'ai	定 Ting	怎 Tsên	妒 Tu	挨 Yai
書 Shu	單 Tan	聽 T'ing	參 Ts'ên	土 T'u	羊 Yang
水 Shwei	炭 T'an	丟 Tiu	增 Tsêng	對 Twei	要 Yao
順 Shun	當 Tang	多 Toă	層 Ts'êng	退 T'wei	言 Yien
耍 Shwa	湯 T'ang	妥 T'oă	子 Tsï	敦 Tun	夜 Yie
衰 Shwai	道 Tao	豆 Tou	次 Ts'ï	吞 T'un	音 Yin
拴 Shwan	逃 T'ao	頭 T'ou	坐 Tsoă	冬 Tung	迎 Ying
雙 Shwang	得 Tei	雜 Tsa	錯 Ts'oă	同 T'ung	約 Yoă
說 Shwoă	得 Tê	擦 Ts'a	走 Tsou	短 Twan	有 Yiu
絲 Sï	忒 T'ê	在 Tsai	湊 Ts'ou	團 T'wan	用 Yung
索 Soă	等 Têng	才 Ts'ai	祖 Tsu	瓦 Wa	魚 Yü
搜 Sou	疼 T'êng	贊 Tsan	粗 Ts'u	外 Wai	原 Yüen
素 Su	地 Ti	殘 Ts'an	嘴 Tswei	萬 Wan	月 Yüe
碎 Swei	替 T'i	葬 Tsang	催 Ts'wei	王 Wang	雲 Yün
孫 Sun	弔 Tiao	倉 Ts'ang	尊 Tsun	爲 Wei	
送 Sung	挑 T'iao	早 Tsao	寸 Ts'un	文 Wên	

REMARKS.

1. In the first edition in substituting *w* for *u* an exception was made in case the *u* was followed by i (that is in *ui*). In this edition the adoption of *w* for *u* is made uniform. It is conceded that neither letter is equally applicable in all cases, but in any given dialect it is better to adhere to the one or the other throughout.

2. Of the final *i* in *ui* Sir Thos. Wade says "it is ei in some tones," that is to say the difference as between *i* and *ei* is tonal. Now the fact that in other cognate dialects *ei* prevails very largely and in some entirely, points to the conclusion that *ei* is the normal sound and *i* the tonal variation. Moreover a discriminating analysis will I think show that the final sound in (hui) 灰[1] 回[2] 悔[3] 惠[4] is not really different from that in (kuei) 虧[1] 魁[2] 傀[3] 愧[4] or that in (lei) 勒[1] 雷[2] 纍[3] 類[4]. So far as any difference exists it is merely a matter of less or more tonal variation between i and ei. Chinese teachers also *when they comprehend the idea of classifying sounds* will not fail to classify these finals together. If Sir Thos. Wade had given attention to these facts he might have avoided making a distinction between Pekingese and other dialects which does not really exist.

3. The fact that final *eh* (not preceded by an intermedial vowel) occurs in only one syllable, viz., *yeh,* of itself raises the suspicion that it is misclassified. The analogy of *mieh, lieh, tieh,* etc., indicates that it should be spelled *yieh* (or, dropping the *h, yie.*) The *i* is indeed to a considerable extent occluded by its union with the cognate initial *y*, yet analogy indicates its presence, and in some tones it is quite discernible. In most of the dialects of central and southern Mandarin the *i* is often quite unmistakeable. The Chinese in Peking as elsewhere regard 烈, 滅· 貼, etc., as having the same final as 也.

The syllable *yen* is the only one with simple *en* as its final which likewise raises a suspicion that it also is misclassified. It belongs in fact with lien, mien, tien, hsien, pien, etc., and should be spelled *yien.* The *i* is of course occluded by its union with *y* yet analogy shows that it is there and in some tones its presence is clearly perceived.

On the same principles *yu* should be spelled *yiu.* The general concensus of opinion in central and southern dialects has always been that this final is analogous with liu, miu, tiu, hsiu etc., not with lu, mu, tu, su, etc. In this opinion I coincide and have accordingly made the change. The *i* is of course largely occluded in practice, but should not be dropped out of the writing.

4. Of the finals in *ien* and *üan* Sir Thos. Wade says that in some tones *ien* changes to *ian* and that in some tones *üan* changes to *üen*, and further that the two have the same peculiarity with regard to the final sound. It seems very strange under these circumstances that he did not spell them both *en* or both *an.* The fact that we have a number of final *ie* and a number of final *üe* but no final *ia* or *üa,* creates a very strong presumption that *en* is the normal sound and *an* the tonal variation. The distribution of the two endings amongst the different tones varies much in different dialects and not unfrequently in the same dialect, but the fact still remains that the one is the normal and the other the variant, whilst both analogy and usage indicate that the ending which is normal in the one case is also in the other and that in both cases this is *en.* Chinese scholars when they understand the point will not admit that the two endings are different either theoretically or practically.

5. Sir Thos. Wade's final *ih* and his final *ŭ* have been combined in one (viz., ĭ) for the reason that the distinction between them is more imaginary than real, being merely the effect of differing initials. A slight distinction is perhaps made in Peking city, but certainly not such a distinction as is indicated by Sir Thos. Wade's description of the power of i in ih, viz.,—"as *i* in chin, chick, thing." Practically no distinction is heard in Chili out of Peking. The conclusion that the two finals are really the same was reached by my Peking advisers after very careful investigation and comparison. In southern Mandarin the two endings are regarded as identical.

6. In his Pocket Dictionary, Dr. Goodrich has changed Sir Thos. Wade's *ko, k'o* and *ho,* to *kê, k'ê,* and *hê,* "as more accurately representing the Peking sounds." I have in this second edition followed him in making this change, albeit I have since felt that it is probably introducing a distinction where there is no real difference. The question is whether the remaining sounds of the class, viz., 摩 波 破 and 彿 should not follow the same rule.

7. Final *ün,* represents a sound which is practically the same in Peking that it is in other Mandarin dialects. The general concensus of opinion in central and southern Mandarin is that it is better written *üin.* Sir Thos. Wade says of it: "It is inflected as if an *i,* very faint and rapidly pronounced intervened between *ü* and *n.*" In some of the dialects of Central China the *i* is by no means "faint." Whether the difference between Pekingese and other dialects is in this case sufficient to justify a different spelling, I question. I have, however, allowed it to stand unchanged.

NANKING SOUND TABLE.

The following list of syllables represents the application of the new system of spelling to the Nanking Dialect. *U* is retained, because it represents the sound more accurately than *w.* Syllables containing it are pronounced so as to bring out the vowel force of *u*—often making the syllable sound like a dissyllable. The addition of—*h* to a syllable indicates the existence of a fifth tone, spelled by the addition of *h* to the regular spelling. All fifth tones which modify the spelling of the fundamental syllable, together with all whose fundamental syllable is unknown, are inserted in alphabetic order.

See remarks at the end of the table.

阿 A	安 An	傲 Ao	齋 Chai	占 Chan	章 Chang
哎 Ai	昂 Ang	阿 Au	柴 Ch'ai	諂 Ch'an	昌 Ch'ang

兆 Chao
潮 Ch'ao
乍 Chau—h
茶 Ch'au—h
這 Che—h
車 Ch'e—h
眞 Chên
臣 Ch'ên
正 Chêng
成 Ch'êng
晝 Chêo
抽 Ch'êo
知 Chï—h
池 Ch'ï—h
着 Choh
綽 Ch'oh
中 Chong
充 Ch'ong
主 Chu—h
除 Ch'u—h
揣 Ch'uai
專 Chuan
川 Ch'uan
壯 Chuang
牀 Ch'uang
抓 Chuau
追 Chuei
吹 Ch'uei
拙 Chuêh
準 Chuên
春 Ch'uên
額 Êh
恩 Ên, Êng
偶 Êo
兒 Êr
反 Fan
方 Fang
法 Fauh
非 Fêei
分 Fên
風 Fêng
否 Fêo
夫 Fu—h
害 Hai
寒 Han
杭 Hang
好 Hao
哈 Hau
赫 Hêh
很 Hên
恒 Hêng
後 Hêo
希 Hi—h
偕 Hiai
向 Hiang
孝 Hiao
下 Hiau—h
歇 Hieih
限 Hiein
欣 Hin
形 Hing
學 Hioh
兄 Hiong
休 Hiu—h
火 Ho—h
紅 Hong
乎 Hu—h
懷 Huai
換 Huan
黃 Huang
花 Huau—h
回 Huei
或 Huêh
混 Huên
許 Hü
靴 Hüei—h
喧 Hüein
訓 Hüin, Hüing
衣 I—h
改 Kai
開 K'ai
甘 Kan
看 K'au
剛 Kang
炕 K'ang
告 Kao
考 K'ao
革 Kêh
客 K'êh
根 Kên
肯 K'ên
更 Kêng
坑 K'êng
狗 Kêo
口 K'êo
記 Ki—h
奇 K'i—h
界 Kiai
楷 K'iai
江 Kiang
腔 K'iang
交 Kiao
巧 K'iao
家 Kiau—h
痂 K'iau—h
絜 Kieih
怯 K'ieih
見 Kiein, Kieing
欠 K'iein, K'ieing
金 Kin
欽 K'in
經 King
輕 K'ing
脚 Kioh
郤 K'ioh
窘 Kiong
窮 K'iong
救 Kiu
求 K'iu
哥 Ko—h
可 K'o—h
工 Kong
孔 K'ong
古 Ku—h
苦 K'u—h
怪 Kuai
快 K'uai
官 Kuan
欵 K'uan
光 Kuang
况 K'uang
瓜 Kuau—h
誇 K'uau
規 Kuei
魁 K'uei
國 Kuêh
闊 K'uêh
棍 Kuên
困 K'uên
居 Kü—h
去 K'ü—h
噘 Küei—h
瘸 K'üei—h
卷 Küein
犬 K'üein
君 Küin
羣 K'üin
來 Lai
懶 Lan
浪 Lang
老 Lao
拉 Lau—h
列 Leih
連 Lein
勒 Lêh
冷 Lêng
陋 Lêo
李 Li—h
兩 Liang
了 Liao
林 Lin
另 Ling
留 Liu
羅 Lo—h
龍 Long
路 Lu—h
亂 Luan
累 Luei
論 Luên
驢 Lü—h
買 Mai
慢 Man
忙 Mang
毛 Mao
馬 Mau—h
滅 Meih
面 Mein Meing
美 Mêei
麥 Mêh
門 Mên
夢 Mêng
謀 Mêo
米 Mi—h
苗 Miao
民 Min
名 Ming
謬 Miu
摩 Mo—h
母 Mu—h
奶 Nai
男 Nan
囊 Nang
鬧 Nao
那 Nau—h
揑 Neih
念 Nein
能 Nêng
你 Ni—h
娘 Niang
鳥 Niao
寧 Ning
牛 Niu
挪 No—h
濃 Nong
奴 Nu
煖 Nuan
女 Nü
阿 O—h
翁 Ong
拜 Pai
派 P'ai
板 Pan
盼 P'an
邦 Pang
旁 P'ang
包 Pao
跑 P'ao
巴 Pau—h
怕 P'au
別 Pei—h
撇 P'eih
扁 Pein Peing
片 P'ein P'eing
倍 Pêei
陪 P'êei
白 Pêh
迫 P'êh
本 Pên
盆 P'ên
崩 Pêng
朋 P'êng
褒 Pêo
掊 P'êo
比 Pi—h

皮 P‘i—h	些 Sei—h	素 Su—h	挑 T‘iao	將 Tsiang	短 Tuan
表 Piao	先 Sein	算 Suan	定 Ting	槍 Ts‘iang	團 T‘uan
票 P‘iao	色 Sêh	碎 Suei	聽 T‘ing	焦 Tsiao	對 Tuei
賓 Pin	森 Sên	孫 Suên	丢 Tiu	俏 Ts‘iao	退 T‘uei
貧 P‘in	僧 Sêng	須 Sü—h	多 To—h	進 Tsin	敦 Tuên
兵 Ping	叟 Sêo	雪 Süeih	妥 T‘o—h	親 Ts‘in	吞 T‘uên
平 P‘ing	曬 Shai	旋 Süein	冬 Tong	井 Tsing	武 U—h
波 Po—h	山 Shan	巡 Süin	同 T‘ong	清 Ts‘ing	外 Wai
破 P‘o—h	賞 Shang	歹 Tai	在 Tsai	酒 Tsiu	萬 Wan
布 Pu—h	少 Shao	太 T‘ai	才 Ts‘ai	秋 Ts‘iu	王 Wang
普 P‘u—h	傻 Shau—h	單 Tan	贊 Tsan	子 Tsï	瓦 Wau—h
染 Ran	舍 She—h	炭 T‘an	殘 Ts‘an	次 Ts‘ï	爲 Wêei
讓 Rang	身 Shên	當 Tang	葬 Tsang	坐 Tso—h	文 Wên
繞 Rao	聖 Shêng	湯 T‘ang	倉 Ts‘ang	錯 Ts‘o—h	挨 Yai
惹 Rêei	時 Shï—h	道 Tao	早 Tsao	宗 Tsong	羊 Yang
熱 Rêh	句 Shoh	逃 T‘ao	草 Ts‘ao	從 Ts‘ong	要 Yao
忍 Rên	書 Shu—h	大 Tau—h	咱 Tsau—h	祖 Tsu—h	牙 Yau—h
扔 Rêng	衰 Shuai	他 T‘au—h	擦 Ts‘au—h	粗 Ts‘u—h	夜 Yei—h
柔 Rêo	拴 Shuan	爹 Tei—h	姐 Tsei—h	鑽 Tsuan	言 Yein Yeing
日 Rïh	雙 Shuang	貼 T‘eih	且 Ts‘ei—h	竄 Ts‘uan	音 Yin
弱 Roh	水 Shuei	店 Tein Teing	賤 Tsein Tseing	嘴 Tsuei	迎 Ying
絨 Rong	順 Shuên	天 T‘ein T‘eing	錢 Ts‘ein Ts‘eing	催 Ts‘uei	有 Yiu
如 Ru—h	西 Si—h	得 Têh	則 Tsêh	尊 Tsuên	約 Yoh
軟 Ruan	相 Siang	特 T êh	策 Ts‘êh	寸 Ts‘uên	用 Yong
銳 Ruei	小 Siao	等 Têng	怎 Tsên	聚 Tsü	魚 Yü
潤 Ruên	心 Sin	疼 T‘êng	增 Tsêng	取 Tsü	月 Yüeh
賽 Sai	性 Sing	豆 Têo	層 Ts‘êng	嗟 Ts‘üei—h	原 Yüein
散 San	修 Siu	頭 T‘êo	走 Tsêo	全 Ts‘üein	雲 Yüin
桑 Sang	絲 Sï	地 Ti—h	湊 Ts‘êo	俊 Tsüin	
掃 Sao	所 So—h	替 T‘i—h	祭 Tsi—h	妒 Tu—h	
撒 Sau—h	送 Song	弔 Tiao	齊 Ts‘i—h	土 T‘u—h	

REMARKS.

1. In Nanking, initial *n* and *l* are not distinguished. Some of the people say *l* and some say *n*, and all are unconscious of the difference. Both syllables are given in the table according to the usage of general Mandarin. If students of Nankingese will take pains to acquire this distinction and keep it up, it will do their Nankingese no harm, and will be a very great advantage in case of removal to another dialect, or in conversing with persons from the North or West.

2. Final *n* and *ng*, especially when following *i*, are confused in the same manner as initial *n* and *l*. Both syllables are given in the table according to the usage of general Mandarin, and

for the same reason as in the case of initial *l* and *n*.

3. There is a difference of opinion in Nanking as to whether 這, 車 and 舍 should be spelled with *e* or *ê*. The older spelling is *ê*, the newer, *e*. Personally I hear the sound rather *e* than *ê*. All the other syllables with this final, are confined to the fifth tone and become *êh*, save 月 which inclines strongly to *eh*.

4. Final *ên* is not so clearly *ê* as in Pekingese, but rather a sound between *en* and *ên*. The balance of opinion is in favor of writing it *ên*.

KIUKIANG SOUND TABLE.

哎	Ai	準	Chwên	乎	Hu—h	結	Kieih	來	Lai	民	Min
阿	An	春	Ch'wên	紅	Hung	茄	K'iei—h	懶	Lan	名	Ming
章	Chang	專	Chwoan	壞	Hwai	見	Kien	浪	Lang	摩	Mo—h
昌	Ch'ang	川	Ch'woan	黃	Hwang	欠	K'ien	老	Lao	滿	Moan
兆	Chao	耳	Êr	花	Hwau—h	金	Kin	拉	Lau—h	墓	Mu—h
潮	Ch'ao	反	Fan	或	Hwâh	欽	K'in	勒	Lâh	夢	Mung
乍	Chau—h	方	Fang	回	Hwei	經	King	累	Lei	您	N'
茶	Ch'au—h	法	Fauh	混	Hwên	輕	K'ing	論	Lên	奶	Nai
折	Châh	非	Fei	換	Hwoan	脚	Kioh	陋	Lêo—h	男	Nan
轍	Ch'âh	分	Fên	衣	I—h	卻	K'ioh	李	Li—h	囊	Nang
這	Chei	否	Fêo	改	Kai	救	Kiu—h	兩	Liang	鬧	Nao
車	Ch'ei	夫	Fu—h	開	K'ai	求	K'iu—h	了	Liao	那	Nau—h
占	Chein	風	Fung	甘	Kan	窮	K'iung	烈	Lieih	內	Nei
諂	Ch'ein	害	Hai	看	K'an	哥	Ko—h	連	Lien	嫩	Nên
真	Chên	寒	Han	剛	Kang	可	K'o—h	林	Lin	耨	Nêo
臣	Ch'ên	杭	Hang	炕	K'ang	古	Ku—h	另	Ling	愛	Ngai
晝	Chêo—h	好	Hao	告	Kao	苦	K'u—h	掠	Lioh	安	Ngan
抽	Ch'êo—h	哈	Hau	考	K'ao	工	Kung	留	Liu	昂	Ngang
知	Chï—h	赫	Hâh	卡	K'au—h	孔	K'ung	羅	Lo—h	傲	Ngao
池	Ch'ï—h	很	Hên	革	Kâh	怪	Kwai	亂	Loan	額	Ngâh
着	Choh	後	Hêo	客	K'âh	快	K'wai	龍	Lung	恩	Ngên
綽	Ch'oh	火	Ho—h	根	Kên	欵	K'wan	買	Mai	偶	Ngêo
中	Chung	希	Hsi—h	肯	K'ên	光	Kwang	慢	Man	我	Ngo—h
充	Ch'ung	皆	Hsiai	狗	Kêo	況	K'wang	忙	Mang	你	Ni—h
主	Chü—h	向	Hsiang	口	K'êo	瓜	Kwau—h	毛	Mao	娘	Niang
除	Ch'ü—h	孝	Hsiao	記	Ki—h	誇	K'wau	馬	Mau—h	鳥	Niao
揣	Ch'wai	下	Hsiau—h	奇	K'i—h	國	Kwâh	美	Mei	揑	Nieih
壯	Chwang	血	Hsieih	界	Kiai	闊	K'wâh	麥	Mêh	念	Nien
床	Ch'wang	限	Hsien	江	Kiang	規	Kwei	門	Mên	寧	Nin or Ning
抓	Chwau	欣	Hsin	腔	K'iang	魁	K'wei	謀	Mêo	虐	Nioh
拙	Chwâh	形	Hsing	交	Kiao	棍	Kwên	米	Mi—h	牛	Niu
鈌	Ch'wâh	學	Hsioh	巧	K'iao	困	K'wên	苗	Miao	挪	No—h
追	Chwei	休	Hsiu—h	家	Kiau—h	官	Kwoan	咩	Miei—h	煖	Noan
吹	Ch'wei	兄	Hsiung	痂	K'iau—h	寬	K'woan	面	Mien	膿	Nung

女 Nü	波 Po—h	舍 Shei	湯 T‘ang	葬 Tsang	子 Tsï
啊 O	破 P‘o—h	善 Shein	道 Tao	倉 Ts‘ang	次 Ts‘ï
拜 Pai	半 Poan	身 Shên	逃 T‘ao	早 Tsao	坐 Tso—h
派 P‘ai	盤 P‘oan	手 Shêo—h	大 Tau—h	草 Ts‘ao	錯 Ts‘o
板 Pan	布 Pu—h	時 Shï—h	他 T‘au—h	咱 Tsau—h	鑽 Tsoan
盼 P‘an	普 P‘u—h	嗾 Sho—h	得 Tâh	薩 Ts‘au—h	竄 Ts‘oan
邦 Pang	踫 Pung	書 Shü—h	特 T‘âh	則 Tsâh	宗 Tsung
旁 P‘ang	朋 P‘ung	衰 Shwai	兌 Tei	策 Ts‘âh	從 Ts‘ung
包 Pao	讓 Rang	雙 Shwang	退 T‘ei	罪 Tsei	冬 Tung
跑 P‘ao	繞 Rao	耍 Shwau—h	敦 Tên	崔 Ts‘ei	同 T‘ung
巴 Pau—h	熱 Râh	說 Shwâh	吞 T‘ên	怎 Tsên	外 Wai
怕 P‘au—h	惹 Rei	瑞 Shwei	豆 Têo—h	寸 Ts‘ên	萬 Wan
白 Pâh	人 Rên	順 Shwên	頭 T‘êo—h	走 Tsêo—h	王 Wang
迫 P‘âh	柔 Rêo—h	拴 Shwoan	地 Ti—h	湊 Ts‘êo—h	瓦 Wau—h
倍 Pei	雲 Ruên	西 Si—h	替 T‘i—h	祭 Tsi—h	爲 Wei
陪 P‘ei	日 Rïh	相 Siang	吊 Tiao	齊 Ts‘i—h	文 Wên
本 Pên	弱 Roh	小 Siao	挑 T‘iao	將 Tsiang	惡 Wo—h
盆 P‘ên	染 Roan	些 Siei—h	爹 Tiei—h	槍 Ts‘iang	丸 Woan
褒 Pêo	如 Rü—h	先 Sien	鐵 T‘ieih	焦 Tsiao	武 Wu—h
呸 P‘êo	賽 Sai	心 Sin	店 Tien	俏 Ts‘iao	翁 Wung
比 Pi-h	散 San	性 Sing	天 T‘ien	姐 Tsiei—h	挨 Yai
皮 P‘i—h	桑 Sang	削 Sioh	定 Ting	且 Ts‘iei—h	羊 Yang
表 Piao	掃 Sao	修 Siu—h	聽 T‘ing	賤 Tsien	要 Yao
票 P‘iao	撒 Sau—h	絲 Sï	丟 Tiu	錢 Ts‘ien	牙 Yau—h
別 Pieih	色 Sâh	所 So—h	多 To—h	進 Tsin	液 Yei—h
撇 P‘ieih	碎 Sei	算 Soan	妥 T‘o—h	親 Ts‘in	有 Yêo—h
扁 Pien	森 Sên	送 Sung	短 Toan	井 Tsing	言 Yien
片 P‘ien	叟 Sêo—h	歹 Tai	團 T‘oan	清 T‘s‘ing	音 Yin
賓 Pin	賞 Shang	太 T‘ai	在 Tsai	爵 Tsioh	迎 Ying
貧 P‘in	少 Shao	單 Tan	才 Ts‘ai	雀 Ts‘ioh	喲 Yo—h
兵 Ping	傻 Shau—h	炭 T‘an	贊 Tsan	酒 Tsiu	用 Yung
平 P‘ing	舌 Shâh	當 Tang	殘 Ts‘an	秋 Ts‘iu	

REMARKS.

1. Initial *l* and *n* are occasionally confused, but for the most part they are distinguished in the same way as in general Mandarin.

2. With respect to final *n* and *ng*, syllables in *an* and *ang* are generally distinguished; final *ĕn* is used exclusively, final *ĕng* disappearing entirely; final *in* and *ing* are confused to some extent, especially in the native city, but the dialect, as a whole, makes the same distinction that is made in general Mandarin.

3. *K* before *i* approximates *ch*, especially in the aspirates, but still is decidedly not *ch* as heard in Pekingese. The syllable *k‘iung*, in particular, becomes practically *ch*, and might, with propriety, be so written.

4. Final *â*, or *âh*, is confined to the 5th tone

and is peculiar to the Kinkiang dialect. Rev. J. R. Hykes, D.D., who has arranged the syllabary as here given, regards it as the 5th tone of syllables in ai. It is so regarded by native scholars in Kinkiang. Judging from analogy it looks as if it were rather the Kinkiang modification of *êh*, as heard in other Southern Mandarin dialects. It is a singular fact that nearly all 5th tones in *êh* are without a fundamental syllable.

5. In the syllables 占 and 善 the vowel is a full clear *ei*, and quite different from 見, *chien*, and others of the same class.

6. The termination *ên* is not as distinctly *ên* as in Pekingese, but tends more or less towards *en*. This is especially the case with the syllable 人, which is in fact *ren*.

In the syllable 雲 *ruên* the *u* is quite short and cannot be represented by *w*. In fact the difference between 人 and 雲 is expressed by *ren* and *rên*.

TÊNGCHOW SOUND TABLE.

阿	A	哼	Êng	休	Hiu	根	Kên	古	Ku	浪	Lang
哎	Ai	兒	Êr	兄	Hiung	肯	K'ên	苦	K'u	老	Lao
安	An	法	Fa	後	Ho	更	Kêng	工	Kung	累	Lei
昂	Ang	反	Fan	乎	Hu	坑	K'êng	孔	K'ung	勒	Lê
傲	Ao	方	Fang	紅	Hung	記	Ki	居	Kü	論	Lên
章	Chang	非	Fei	許	Hü	奇	K'i	去	K'ü	冷	Lêng
昌	Ch'ang	分	Fên	穴	Hüe	家	Kia	决	Küe	李	Li
兆	Chao	風	Fêng	喧	Hüen	恰	K'ia	瘸	K'üe	倆	Lia
潮	Ch'ao	否	Fo	訓	Hüin	界	Kiai	卷	Küen	兩	Liang
祭	Chi	夫	Fu	花	Hwa	江	Kiang	犬	K'üen	了	Liao
齊	Ch'i	哈	Ha	懷	Hwai	腔	K'iang	君	Küin	列	Lie
姐	Chie	害	Hai	換	Hwan	交	Kiao	羣	K'üin	連	Lien
且	Ch'ie	寒	Han	黃	Hwang	巧	K'iao	瓜	Kwa	林	Lin
賤	Chien	杭	Hang	回	Hwei	結	Kie	誇	K'wa	另	Ling
錢	Ch'ien	好	Hao	混	Hwên	怯	K'ie	怪	Kwai	畧	Lioă
進	Chin	黑	Hê	火	Hwoă	見	Kien	快	K'wai	留	Liu
親	Ch'in	很	Hên	衣	I	欠	K'ien	官	Kwan	隴	Liung
井	Ching	恆	Hêng	蛤	Ka	金	Kin	欵	K'wan	陋	Lo
清	Ch'ing	希	Hi	磕	K'a	欽	K'in	光	Kwang	羅	Loă
酒	Chiu	下	Hia	改	Kai	經	King	况	K'wang	路	Lu
秋	Ch'iu	偕	Hiai	開	K'ai	輕	K'ing	規	Kwei	龍	Lung
爵	Choă	向	Hiang	甘	Kan	角	Kioă	魁	K'wei	驢	Lü
綽	Ch'oă	孝	Hiao	看	K'an	郤	K'ioă	棍	Kwên	馬	Ma
踪	Chung	歇	Hie	剛	Kang	救	Kiu	困	K'wên	買	Mai
主	Chü	鞋	Hiei	炕	K'ang	求	K'iu	果	Kwoă	慢	Man
除	Ch'ü	限	Hien	告	Kao	窘	Kiung	闊	K'woă	忙	Mang
全	Ch'üen	欣	Hin	考	K'ao	窮	K'iung	拉	La	毛	Mao
額	Ê	形	Hing	個	Kê	勾	Ko	來	Lai	美	Mei
恩	Ên	學	Hioă	刻	K'ê	口	K'o	懶	Lan	末	Mê

門 Mên
夢 Mêng
米 Mi
苗 Miao
滅 Mie
面 Mien
民 Min
名 Ming
謀 Mo
墓 Mu
那 Na
奶 Nai
男 Nan
囊 Nang
鬧 Nao
內 Nei
您 Nên
能 Nêng
你 Ni
娘 Niang
鳥 Niao
揑 Nie
念 Nien
寧 Ning
牛 Niu
濃 Niung
耨 No
挪 Noă
奴 Nu
膿 Nung
女 Nü
偶 O
巴 Pa
怕 P'a

拜 Pai
派 P'ai
板 Pan
盼 P'an
邦 Pang
旁 P'ang
包 Pao
跑 P'ao
倍 Pei
陪 P'ei
波 Pê
破 P'ê
本 Pên
盆 P'ên
崩 Pêng
朋 P'êng
比 Pi
皮 P'i
表 Piao
票 P'iao
別 Pie
撇 P'ie
扁 Pien
片 P'ien
賓 Pin
貧 P'in
兵 Ping
平 P'ing
剖 P'o
布 Pu
普 P'u
撒 Sa
賽 Sai
散 San

掃 Sang
桑 Sao
碎 Sei
色 Sê
森 Sên
僧 Sêng
儍 Sha
賞 Shang
少 Shao
西 Shi
舍 Shie
善 Shien
心 Shin
聖 Shing
手 Shiu
勺 Shoă
松 Shung
書 Shü
說 Shüe
尋 Shüin
絲 Sï
摟 So
索 Soă
素 Su
送 Sung
耍 Swa
衰 Swai
拴 Swan
雙 Swang
水 Swei
順 Swên
大 Ta
他 T'a
歹 Tai

太 T'ai
單 Tan
炭 T'an
當 Tang
湯 T'ang
道 Tao
逃 T'ao
兌 Tei
退 T'ei
得 Tê
忒 T'ê
敦 Tên
吞 T'ên
等 Têng
疼 T'êng
地 Ti
替 T'i
弔 Tiao
挑 T'iao
爹 Tie
貼 T'ie
店 Tien
天 T'ien
定 Ting
聽 T'ing
丟 Tiu
豆 To
頭 T'o
多 Toă
妥 T'oă
雜 Tsa
擦 Ts'a
在 Tsai
才 Ts'ai

贊 Tsan
殘 Ts'an
葬 Tsang
倉 Ts'ang
早 Tsao
草 Ts'ao
罪 Tsei
崔 Ts'ei
則 Tsê
策 Ts'ê
怎 Tsên
岑 Ts'ên
增 Tsêng
層 Ts'êng
子 Tsï
次 Ts'ï
走 Tso
湊 Ts'o
坐 Tsoă
錯 Ts'oă
祖 Tsu
粗 Ts'u
宗 Tsung
聰 Ts'ung
抓 Tswa
No character. Ts'wa
拽 Tswai
揣 Ts'wai
專 Tswan
川 Ts'wan
壯 Tswang
牀 Ts'wang
追 Tswei
吹 Ts'wei

準 Tswên
春 Ts'wên
妒 Tu
土 T'u
冬 Tung
同 T'ung
瓦 Wa
外 Wai
萬 Wan
王 Wang
爲 Wei
文 Wên
我 Woă
武 Wu
翁 Wung
牙 Ya
挨 Yai
羊 Yang
要 Yao
矮 Yei
夜 Yie
言 Yien
音 Yin
迎 Ying
有 Yiu
約 Yoă
用 Yung
魚 Yü
月 Yüe
原 Yüen
雲 Yüin

REMARKS.

1. The dialect of Têngchow is remarkable for the small number of its syllables and for the clearness with which they are distinguished. The sounds also depart less from normal English sounds than those of most Mandarin dialects—the only elementary sound in it not heard in English being ü.

2. The hard sounds are all pure hard—

showing no tendency whatever towards *ch*; nor does *h*, when followed by *i* or *ü*, show any tendency to change to *hs*. Both *ch* and *sh* are pronounced quite as they are in English.

3. It is important for the learner to take especial note of the fact that *k* and *h*, followed by *i* or *ü*, are pronounced as if a *y* intervened between the consonant and the vowel.

4. The double readings, due to accidental variation, are very few. This is, no doubt, due to the comparative isolation of the promontory, and the absence of admixture of other dialects. Pekingese has more than ten times as many such variations.

5. The termination *iu* shows a strong tendency to pass into *éo* or *io*. In some tones of certain syllables the final *o* is quite distinct. The predominant sound, however, is *iu*.

6. The termination *ien* changes in the 1st and 4th tones to *ian*, and the termination *üen* changes in the 1st and 4th tones to *üan*. It is evident, however, from analogy that *en* is the normal sound, and *an* the tonal variation.

7. In the 1st and 4th tones *ing*, after *ch* and *k*, tends to pass into *iêng*—a tonal variation which need not be recognised in a table of sounds.

8. The syllables ch‘üen and shüin are stray-sounds from some outside dialect, and are confined,—the former to 全 and the latter to 巡 and one or two other characters.

WEIHIEN SOUND TABLE.

阿	A	反	Fan	兄	Hiung	乎	Hwu	坑	K‘eng	去	K‘ü
章	Chang	方	Fang	西	Hsi	衣	I	狗	Kêo	卷	Küan
昌	Ch‘ang	非	Fei	斜	Hsia	染	Jran	口	K‘êo	犬	K‘üan
兆	Chao	分	Fen	先	Hsian	嚷	Jrang	記	Ki	君	Küin
潮	Ch‘ao	風	Fêng	相	Hsiang	繞	Jrao	奇	K‘i	羣	K‘üin
眞	Chen	否	Fêo	小	Hsiao	柔	Jrêo	家	Kia	脚	Küoa
臣	Ch‘en	佛	Foă	些	Hsie	惹	Jrie	恰	K‘ia	却	K‘üoă
晝	Chêo	夫	Fu	心	Hsin	人	Jrin	界	Kiai	瓜	Kwa
抽	Ch‘êo	哈	Ha	性	Hsing	如	Jru	見	Kian	誇	K‘wa
占	Chian	害	Hai	修	Hsiu	絨	Jrung	欠	K‘ian	怪	Kwai
諂	Ch‘ian	寒	Han	誦	Hsiung	輭	Jrwan	江	Kiang	快	K‘wai
這	Chie	杭	Hang	須	Hsü	若	Jrwoă	腔	K‘iang	官	Kwan
車	Ch‘ie	好	Hao	旅	Hsüan	蛤	Ka	交	Kiao	欵	K‘wan
正	Ching	赫	Hei	雪	Hsüe	磕	K‘a	巧	K‘iao	光	Kwang
成	Ch‘ing	很	Hen	巡	Hsüin	改	Kai	結	Kie	况	K‘wang
知	Chĭ	恆	Hêng	紅	Hung	開	K‘ai	怯	K‘ie	規	Kwei
池	Ch‘ĭ	候	Hêo	許	Hü	甘	Kan	金	Kin	魁	K‘wei
拙	Choa	希	Hi	喧	Hüan	看	K‘an	欽	K‘in	棍	Kwen
綽	Ch‘oa	下	Hia	穴	Hüe	剛	Kang	經	King	困	K‘wen
主	Chü	偕	Hiai	訓	Hüin	炕	K‘ang	輕	K‘ing	果	Kwoă
除	Ch‘ü	限	Hian	花	Hwa	告	Kao	救	Kiu	闊	K‘woă
專	Chwan	向	Hiang	懷	Hwai	考	K‘ao	求	K‘iu	古	Kwu
川	Ch‘wan	孝	Hiao	換	Hwan	格	Kei	窘	Kiung	苦	K‘wu
準	Chwen	蝎	Hie	黃	Hwang	刻	K‘ei	窮	K‘iung	拉	La
春	Ch‘wen	欣	Hin	回	Hwei	根	Ken	工	Kung	來	Lai
兒	Êr	形	Hing	混	Hwen	肯	K‘en	孔	K‘ung	懶	Lan
法	Fa	休	Hiu	火	Hwoă	更	Kêng	居	Kü	浪	Lang

- 老 Lao
- 冷 Lêng
- 陋 Lêo
- 李 Li
- 倆 Lia
- 連 Lian
- 兩 Liang
- 了 Liao
- 列 Lie
- 林 Lin
- 另 Ling
- 界 Lioă
- 留 Liu
- 蘢 Liung
- 羅 Loă
- 路 Lu
- 龍 Lung
- 驢 Lü
- 界 Lüe
- 亂 Lwan
- 累 Lwei
- 倫 Lwen
- 馬 Ma
- 買 Mai
- 慢 Man
- 芒 Mang
- 毛 Mao
- 美 Mei
- 門 Men
- 夢 Mêng
- 謀 Mêo
- 米 Mi
- 面 Mian
- 苗 Miao
- 滅 Mie
- 民 Min
- 名 Ming
- 摩 Moă
- 墓 Mu
- 那 Na
- 奶 Nai
- 男 Nan
- 囊 Nang
- 鬧 Nao
- 內 Nei
- 能 Nêng
- 耨 Nêo
- 艾 Ngai
- 安 Ngan
- 昂 Ngang
- 傲 Ngao
- 厄 Ngei
- 恩 Ngen
- 偶 Ngêo
- 你 Ni
- 念 Nian
- 娘 Niang
- 鳥 Niao
- 揑 Nie
- 甯 Ning
- 牛 Niu
- 濃 Niung
- 挪 Noă
- 奴 Nu
- 膿 Nung
- 女 Nü
- 煖 Nwan
- 餒 Nwei
- 巴 Pa
- 怕 P'a
- 拜 Pai
- 派 P'ai
- 板 Pan
- 盼 P'an
- 邦 Pang
- 旁 P'ang
- 包 Pao
- 跑 P'ao
- 倍 Pei
- 陪 P'ei
- 本 Pen
- 盆 P'en
- 崩 Pêng
- 朋 P'êng
- 剖 P'êo
- 比 Pi
- 皮 P'i
- 扁 Pian
- 片 P'ian
- 表 Piao
- 票 P'iao
- 別 Pie
- 撇 P'ie
- 賓 Pin
- 貧 P'in
- 兵 Ping
- 平 P'ing
- 波 Poă
- 破 P'oă
- 布 Pu
- 普 P'u
- 撒 Sa
- 賽 Sai
- 散 San
- 桑 Sang
- 掃 Sao
- 塞 Sei
- 叟 Sêo
- 僧 Sêng
- 賞 Shang
- 少 Shao
- 身 Shen
- 善 Shian
- 舍 Shie
- 聖 Shing
- 手 Shiu
- 十 Shï
- 勺 Shoă
- 書 Shü
- 順 Shüin
- 絲 Sï
- 索 Soă
- 沙 Sra
- 晒 Srai
- 山 Sran
- 梢 Srao
- 色 Srei
- 森 Sren
- 生 Srêng
- 搜 Srêo
- 師 Srï
- 疏 Sru
- 耍 Srwa
- 率 Srwei
- 拴 Srwan
- 雙 Srwang
- 誰 Srwei
- 朔 Srwoă
- 素 Su
- 送 Sung
- 算 Swan
- 碎 Swei
- 孫 Swen
- 大 Ta
- 他 T'a
- 歹 Tai
- 太 T'ai
- 單 Tan
- 炭 T'an
- 當 Tang
- 湯 T'ang
- 道 Tao
- 逃 T'ao
- 得 Tei
- 忒 T'ei
- 等 Têng
- 疼 T'êng
- 豆 Têo
- 頭 T'êo
- 地 Ti
- 替 T'i
- 店 Tian
- 天 T'ian
- 弔 Tiao
- 桃 T'iao
- 爹 Tie
- 貼 T'ie
- 定 Ting
- 聽 T'ing
- 丟 Tiu
- 多 Toă
- 妥 T'oă
- 雜 Tsa
- 擦 Ts'a
- 在 Tsai
- 才 Ts'ai
- 贊 Tsan
- 殘 Ts'an
- 葬 Tsang
- 倉 Ts'ang
- 早 Tsao
- 草 Ts'ao
- 賊 Tsei
- 偺 Tsen
- 增 Tsêng
- 層 Ts'êng
- 走 Tsêo
- 湊 Ts'êo
- 即 Tshi
- 妻 Ts'hi
- 尖 Tshian
- 前 Tsh'ian
- 將 Tshiang
- 鎗 Tsh'iang
- 焦 Tshiao
- 俏 Tsh'iao
- 節 Tshie
- 切 Tsh'ie
- 進 Tshin
- 親 Tsh'in
- 井 Tshing
- 清 Tsh'ing
- 酒 Tshiu
- 秋 Tsh'iu
- 踪 Tshiung
- 從 Tsh'iung
- 聚 Tshü
- 取 Tsh'ü
- 全 Tsh'üan
- 俊 Tshüin
- 爵 Tsüoă
- 雀 Ts'üoă
- 子 Tsï
- 次 Ts'ï
- 扎 Tsra
- 茶 Ts'ra
- 齋 Tsrai
- 柴 Ts'rai
- 站 Tsran
- 產 Ts'ran
- 找 Tsrao
- 抄 Ts'rao
- 窄 Tsrei
- 拆 Ts'rei
- 箴 Tsren
- 岑 Ts'ren
- 爭 Tsrêng
- 撐 Ts'rêng
- 鄒 Tsrêo
- 愁 Ts'rêo
- 之 Tsrï
- 匙 Ts'rï
- 卓 Tsroă
- 錯 Ts'roă

助 Tsru	追 Tsrwei	尊 Tswen	敦 Twen	武 Wu	用 Yung
楚 Ts‘ru	吹 Ts‘rwei	寸 Ts‘wen	吞 T‘wen	牙 Ya	魚 Yü
中 Tsrung	祖 Tsu	妒 Tu	凡 Wa	挨 Yai	原 Yüan
冲 Ts‘rung	粗 Ts‘u	土 T‘u	外 Wai	羊 Yang	雲 Yüin
抓 Tsrwa	宗 Tsung	冬 Tung	萬 Wan	要 Yao	約 Yüoă
No character. Ts‘rwa	聰 Ts‘ung	同 T‘ung	王 Wang	夜 Yie	
拽 Tsrwai	鑽 Tswan	短 Twan	爲 Wei	言 Yian	
揣 Ts‘rwai	竄 Ts‘wan	團 T‘wan	文 Wen	音 Yin	
庄 Tsrwang	罪 Tswei	對 Twei	翁 Wêng	迎 Ying	
窗 Ts‘rwang	催 Ts‘wei	退 T‘wei	我 Woă	有 Yiu	

REMARKS.

1. Syllables which in most other Mandarin dialects begin with initial *s* and *ts*, are in Wei-hien divided into two sets, one set having simply *s* and *ts* as in other dialects, and the other set having *s* and *ts* modified by *r*.

2. The characters under the Pekingese initial *hs* divide into two classes, one taking *hy* and the other *hs*, the former embracing characters read *hy* in Southern Mandarin, and the latter those read *si*.

3. *Tsh* represents a sound which is neither *ch* nor *ts*, but a combination of the two. It is always followed by *i* or *ü*, whilst *ts* alone is never followed by *i* or *ü*.

4. All final *n's* are nasal, so that the *n* is scarcely audible.

5. In final *en* the sound of the vowel is obscured by the strong nasal, so that it is difficult to tell whether it should be written *en* or *ên*. There is a difference of opinion as to which is the better writing.

6. The syllables *chen*, *ch‘en* and *shen* show a strong tendency towards *chin*, *ch‘in* and *shin*, and the syllables *ching*, *ch‘ing* and *shing* show a similar tendency towards *chêng*, *ch‘êng* and *shêng*. In both cases the sounds are really admixtures of the clear *i* of the district to the east, with the *e* or *ê* of the region to the west.

7. In the syllables *chü*, *ch‘ü* and *shü* the *ü* is not pure, but lies between *ü* and *u*.

CHUNGKING SOUND TABLE.

The following list of syllables represents the application of the system of spelling to the dialect of Chungking. It was prepared by a committee appointed by the missionary community in Chungking. The following remarks concerning it were also prepared by this committee:—

1. The syllables spelled *ai*, *an*, *ang*, *ao*, *ê*, *ên*, *ou (eo)* and *oă (o)* in Peking are preceded by *ng* in Chungking.

2. Where the initial *ch* is followed by the vowels *a, ei, ê, ou (eo)* ï, *oă (o) u* (except 足 and 族), the letter *w* and the final *ung* (in Chungking), this *ch* is changed to *ts*. Both spellings are given in the table, so as to be in accord with general mandarin usage, and both are equally understood. *Ch* is sometimes heard with these syllables by men from other parts of the province.

3. The sounds 足 *choo*, 族 *ch‘oo*, 贖 *shoo* and 育 *yoo* have been spelled with *oo* instead of *u* as better representing the sounds, and more readily learned by the beginner.

4. The final *g* of Pekingese is not sounded in syllables with the vowels *ê* and *i*, as 正 *Chên*, 成 *Ch‘ên*, 兵 *Pin*, 平 *P‘in*, etc.

5. The *j* of Pekingese is a decided *rough r* in Chungking, but is given differently by different Chinese.

6. *L* and *N* are almost always interchangeable, being sometimes used interchangeably on the same character.

7. A number of characters represented by *i* in Pekingese are *Ni* or *Li* in Chungking.

8. The sounds 盾 *Tun* and 吞 *T‘un* are included under *Tên* and *T‘ên* as being practically the same sounds.

9. *Hu* of Pekingese becomes *Fu* in Chungking.

10. In the talk of the people of Chungking such sounds as 惹 and 熱 would seem to be truly represented by *rei* and *rê*. This is also the case with the sounds 舍 *sei* and 舌 *sê*. The difference is largely due to the tones of the two characters, and as *ê* is regarded as the true sound these

characters have been included under *rê* and *sê* respectively.

11. With the exception of *shoo*, all syllables commencing with *sh* in Pekingese, are sounded without the *h*, though it is retained in some other districts of Sï-chuan.

12. *O* seems to fairly give the sounds of both 阿 and 窩, therefore *wo* is omitted in the table. While these two characters seem to demand something more than *o*, the *w* is not equivalent to that in 完 or 文 or 五.

阿	A or au	今	Chin	追	Chwei, Tswei	序	Hsü	古	Ku	流	Liu
哎	Ai	欽	Ch'in	吹	Ch'wei, Ts'wei	削	Hsüe	苦	K'u	落	Lo
扎	Cha, Tsa	覺	Chio	準	{Chwun Tswun}	玄	Hsüen	工	Kung	陸	Lu
茶	Ch'a, Ts'a	卻	Ch'io	春	{Ch'wun Ts'wun}	巡	Hsüin	孔	K'ung	倫	Lun
債	Chai, Tsai	九	Chiu	二	Er	戶	Hu and Fu	瓜	Kwa	弄	Lung
柴	Ch'ai, Ts'ai	求	Ch'iu	乏	Fa	宏	Hung	誇	K'wa	旅	Lü
占	Chan, Tsan	龔	Chiung	凡	Fan	化	Hwa	怪	Kwai	亂	Lwan
諂	Ch'an, Ts'an	窮	Ch'iung	方	Fang	懷	Hwai	快	K'wai	累	Lwei
章	Chang, Tsang	之	Chï, Tsï	非	Fei	宦	Hwan	官	Kwan	馬	Ma
昌	Ch'ang, Ts'ang	尺	Ch'ï, Ts'ï	浮	Feo	皇	Hwang	寬	Kw'an	買	Mai
兆	Chao, Tsao	捉	Cho, Tso	分	Fên	回	Hwei	光	Kwang	滿	Man
潮	Ch'ao, Ts'ao	戳	Ch'o, Ts'o	夫	Fu	惑	Hwê	況	Kw'ang	忙	Mang
者	Chei, Tsei	足	Choo	奉	Fung	魂	Hwun	桂	Kwei	毛	Mao
車	Ch'ei, Ts'ei	族	Ch'oo	哈	Ha	一	I	盔	Kw'ei	美	Mei
拆	Chê, Tsê	主	Chu, Chu	孩	Hai	嘎	Ka	國	Kwê	貿	Meo
徹	Ch'ê, Ts'ê	出	Ch'u, Ts'u	汗	Han	卡	K'a	濶	K'wê	墨	Mê
眞	Chên, Tsên	中	Chung, Tsung	行	Hang	改	Kai	棍	Kwun	門	Men
臣	Ch'en, Ts'en	充	Ch'ung Ts'ung	好	Hao	開	K'ai	困	Kw'un	米	Mi
舟	Cheo, Tseo	句	Chü	后	Heo	干	Kan	拉	La	妙	Miao
仇	Ch'eo, Ts'eo	去	Ch'ü	黑	Hê	看	K'an	來	Lai	滅	Mie
吉	Chi	决	Chüe	很	Hên	岡	Kang	藍	Lan	免	Mien
七	Ch'i	瘸	Ch'üe	合	Ho	炕	K'ang	郎	Lang	民	Min
甲	Chia	捐	Chüen	西	Hsi	告	Kao	老	Lao	謬	Miu
恰	Ch'ia	犬	Ch'üen	下	Hsia	考	K'ao	樓	Leo	末	Mo
戒	Chiai	君	Chüin	懈	Hsiai	勾	Keo	勒	Lê	木	Mu
江	Chiang	羣	Ch'üin	相	Hsiang	口	K'eo	冷	Lên	某	Mung
强	Ch'iang	爪	Chwa, Tswa	小	Hsiao	革	Kê	力	Li	那	Na
交	Chiao	拽	Chwai, Tswai	邪	Hsie	克	K'ê	倆	Liang	乃	Nai
巧	Ch'iao	揣	Ch'wai, Ts'wai	仙	Hsien	根	Ken	了	Liao	南	Nan
姐	Chie	專	Chwan, Tswan	心	Hsin	肯	K'en	列	Lie	囊	Nang
切	Ch'ie	川	{Ch'wan Ts'wan}	學	Hsio	哥	Ko	連	Lien	腦	Nao
件	Chien	壯	{Chwang Tswang}	休	Hsiu	可	K'o	林	Lin	嫩	Nên
千	Ch'ien	床	{Ch'wang Ts'wang}	凶	Hsiung	給	Ki or Kê, Chi	畧	Lia	哀	Ngai

安	Ngan	包	Pao	人	Rên	太	T'ai	偺	Tsan	同	T'ung
昂	Ngang	抛	P'ao	日	Rï	丹	Tan	參	Ts'an	段	Twan
拗	Ngao	貝	Pei	若	Ro	坦	T'an	臧	Tsang	團	Tw'an
額	Ngê	丕	P'ei	入	Ru	當	Tang	倉	Ts'ang	兌	Twei
恩	Ngên	褒	Peo	絨	Rung	唐	T'ang	早	Tsao	推	Tw'ei
偶	Ngeo	北	Pê	軟	Rwan	刀	Tao	草	Ts'ao	翁	Ung
我	Ngo	柏	P'ê	銳	Rwei	叨	T'ao	走	Tseo	瓦	Wa
尼	Ni	本	Pên	閏	Rwan	斗	Teo	湊	Ts'eo	外	Wai
娘	Niang	盆	P'ên	撒	Sa	偷	T'eo	賊	Tsê	完	Wan
鳥	Niao	比	Pi	顋	Sai	得	Tê	册	Ts'ê	王	Wang
揑	Nie	疋	P'i	三	San	忒	T'ê	怎	Tsên	未	Wei
年	Nien	表	Piao	桑	Sang	灯	Tên	曾	Ts'ên	文	Wen
虐	Nio	票	P'iao	掃	Sao	疼	T'ên	子	Tsï	五	Wu
寧	Nin	別	Pie	手	Seo	地	Ti	此	Ts'ï	丫	Ya
牛	Niu	撇	P'ie	舌	Sê	梯	T'i	左	Tso	挨	Yai
挪	No	便	Pien	僧	Sên	刁	Tiao	錯	Ts'o	央	Yang
奴	Nu	片	P'ien	贖	Shoo	佻	T'iao	租	Tsu	吆	Yao
農	Nung	彬	Pin	十	Sï	迭	Tie	粗	Ts'u	掖	Yi
女	Nü	品	P'in	勺	So	貼	T'ie	最	Tsui	也	Yie
暖	Nwan	波	Po	書	Su	典	Tien	脆	Ts'ui	言	Yien
內	Nwei	坡	P'o	宋	Sung	天	T'ien	尊	Tsun	引	Yin
阿	O	不	Pu	刷	Swa	丁	Ting	寸	Ts'un	又	Yiu
八	Pa	鋪	P'u	衰	Swai	廷	T'ing	宗	Tsung	岳	Yo
怕	P'a	[足夆]	Pung	拴	Swan	丟	Tiu	從	Ts'ung	育	Yoo
拜	Pai	朋	P'ung	雙	Swang	多	To	鑽	Tswan	用	Yung
派	P'ai	然	Ran	水	Swei	拖	T'o	攛	Ts'wan	玉	Yü
半	Pan	嚷	Rang	順	Swun	咱	Tsa	掇	Tswê	元	Yüen
盼	P'an	饒	Rao	大	Ta	擦	Ts'a	杜	Tu	月	Yüê
邦	Pang	柔	Reo	他	T'a	在	Tsai	土	T'u	勻	Yün
胖	P'ang	熱	Rê	代	Tai	才	Ts'ai	東	Tung		

COMPARATIVE CHART.

The foregoing five tables are combined in a comparative chart in colors and inserted as a frontispiece. This chart shows in detail the relation of the several dialects to each other. So far as possible the same key characters have been retained throughout. The preparation of the chart has entailed much labor, and its printing considerable expense.

官話類編序

此書之作、原爲西人學官話而作也、所謂官話者、非言盡爲官場中話、乃言通行之話也、狄公有志於此書、由來久矣、自二十年前、即有所積蓄、近來五六年間、與僕專作此事、嘔心吐膽、不知凡幾、論此書之作法、係依話語之樣數、分作二百題目、每題一課、凡話語之種類式樣以及如何變轉如何接連、此二百題、俱已賅括、至若課中散語、非盡自編、更博覽聖諭廣訓、好逑傳、西遊記、水滸、自邇致等書、擇其言語之佳者、按題分列、且語中所論、則甚周徧、凡農工商賈官場日用、無不俱備、總爲發明 各題之用法而加之於諸事也、故學者如能學熟此二百課、其話語已足用矣、如能精通此二百題、而說話之妙訣、則已得矣、且此書之成、並非一人之力、曾經分發北京濟南南京九江漢口等處、批過數次、又曾親往各地、協同諸位名士、詳加批閱、終則合此諸批、一一審定、要必以通行者爲是、兼有不通行者、則並列之、其列法北京在右南京在左、如有三行並列、即山東居其中也、是故用此書者、非但可得通行之益、即不通行者、亦可確知南北終有何不同也、即所繙之英文以及所講所註者、亦經南北有名之西士批閱、務求與漢語適合、字義恰對、並爲南北酌定字音、使各方知其共有幾音、而各音係何聲氣、復按字音字部、將書中所用之字與話、各作一指要錄、令學者便於觀查、故此編既成、於有志學官話者、豈特爲小補哉、時在光緒十八年、歲次壬辰、夏季中澣、

鄒立文序

例言

夫人之教話、原非中國之常事、故所請之先生、未必盡得要訣、今余不揣鄙陋、畧舉數端、以誌於下、

一 當知此書、非爲人之學文而作、乃爲學話而作也、且所編之話語、亦非效法書中句法、特以工雅爲貴、乃摹倣口中句法、以自然爲貴也、爲先生者、宜詳辨之。

一 此書所記之四聲、非憑五方元音而定、乃憑北京之語音而定、蓋中國之四聲、處處不同、論及說話、各當以本地之聲氣爲準、不可拘於五方元音、亦不可拘於此書、祇當推敲本地之語音、憑己之耳韻、聽其爲何聲、卽言其爲何聲也。

一 中國書中、雖有五聲之說、然而北方祇有四聲、蓋入聲獨南方有之、而北方諸省、已將此聲混於餘四聲內、故在北方教話之先生、可將入聲之說、置之不論、祇留心分辨四聲可也。

一 若學者請先生誦讀、自己隨而學之、則先生誦讀之時、務要出於自然、使其輕重快慢、各得其當、聲音不可太高、亦不可故作腔調、一如誦經讀文者然。

一 如學者吐字不淸、未得字之眞音、先生則當立卽示明、使其說得恰對、蓋於初時學錯、以後雖欲改之、亦深難矣、卽於平素說話之間、亦當爲之留意、一有不對之處、卽當言明、不可聽其錯誤、而絕不理也。

一 書中並列之句、皆係不通行者、先生可擇其行者教之、如俱不行、而另有他話與之意同、亦可隨意示明。

一 西人學習官話、原非易事、未免常有忘記與錯亂之時、爲先生者、應當耐性、屢說覼述、教示不倦、方爲善於教導者也。

一 書中旣無話不說、所用之字、未免有希見罕用者、雖覺生索、却經名士批過、大都憑衆人之識見而定、故有以爲非者、亦未可憑一人之識見而改也、其中亦有無心之錯字、書後業已指明、先生從而改之可也。

A COURSE

OF

MANDARIN LESSONS.

Suggestions to the Student.

1.—Begin by reading over the introduction carefully, especially the "Explanations" and "Advice to Students." You will find there many things you ought to know when commencing the study of Chinese.

2.—Take especial pains to acquire at the very outset a good working knowledge of the system of spelling as applied to your own dialect. *Do not begin to spell at random.*

3.—Listen very carefully to your teacher, so that you may hear the sounds correctly. When you can *hear* a sound correctly you will generally be able to speak it correctly.

4.—Do not neglect the tones *at first*, but try to get them from the very start. If your teacher cannot distinguish the tones as such get some one to *teach* him. Practice on the tone table will be time profitably spent.

5.—It will pay every student of Chinese to learn the radicals, and the *best time* to learn them is at the very outset.

6.—Do not be afraid to use what you have learned. Get it off on all occasions, no matter who hears or who laughs.

第一課

一[1]個人。○兩[2]個男人。○三[3]個女人。○四[4]個先生。○五[5]個師母娘。○六[6]個學生。○七[7]個字。○八[8]個門。○九[9]個月。○十[10]個學堂房。○十[11]一個錢。○十[12]二個月是一年。○三[13]十天是一個月。

Translation.

1 One person. 2 Two men.
3 Three women. 4 Four teachers.
5 Five ladies. 6 Six pupils.
7 Seven characters. 8 Eight doors.
9 Nine months.
10 Ten school rooms (or schools).
11 Eleven cash.
12 Twelve months are one year.
13 Thirty days are a month.

LESSON I.

The General Classifier.

There is in Chinese a large class of words joined with substantives as classifiers, there being some sort of affinity, real or imaginary, on which the classification is based. In general, each noun has a fixed classifier, though a few nouns have two or more. We have in the case of a few nouns in English a somewhat similar usage: thus we say, a flock of sheep, a pane of glass, a loaf of bread, a piece of work, two stalks of corn, etc. When these classifiers happen to correspond to similar forms in English, they may be translated; in all other cases they are untranslatable. Pidgin English has summed up the whole class in the one word "piece." Thus, "one piece man," is the English equivalent of 一個人, *i*¹ *kê*⁴ *jên*².

Classifiers are only used when a definite number is spoken of, and hence have been by some called *numeratives.** Beyond this merely negative rule, no definite directions can be given for the use of these classifiers. The only adequate rule is usage.

Most concrete nouns take a classifier; but some do not, especially such as express time, space, or quantity; such as, day, year, inch, mile, ounce, catty, etc. These classifiers will be illustrated at length in a number of future lessons.

The present lesson is limited to 個, which may be called the general classifier. It is applied to such nouns as have no special classifier, and *may*, upon occasion, be applied to almost any noun, as a substitute for the special classifier. The idea of 個 is that of mere individuality, and hence it is by far the most extensively used of its class. It is the only classifier that can be applied to an abstract noun. It is often written 箇, and its abbreviated form is 个.

些 may be regarded as the plural of 個. As such it is joined with 這 *chê*⁴ and 那 *na*⁴, as in the next lesson. When used alone it is always used indefinitely, as in (22), (23) and (24). It is often preceded by *one*, the two words together meaning *some*.

* I prefer the term *classifier*, because these words are only adjunct to the matter of enumeration, which is still effected by the proper numerals. Their primary office is to classify.

Vocabulary.

個 *Kê*⁴. One, a single one; a unit; the general classifier:— See Sub.

些 *Hsie*¹. A little, a few; somewhat; an adjective of comparison often answering to the English termination *er*. Forms the plural of 個:—See Sub.

一 *I*¹. *One;* the first; the same; at once; a, an; a few; the whole.

二 *Êr*⁴. *Two;* the second; the cardinal number two.

兩 *Liang*³. *Two;* a couple, a few; a pair, double; an ounce, a tael of silver.

三 *San*¹. *Three;* thrice. Also read *sa*¹.

四 *Sï*⁴. *Four;* all around.

五 *Wu*³. *Five;* a perfect number.

六 *Liu*⁴. *Six.* Often read *lu*⁴ by literary men.

七 *Ch'i*¹. *Seven.*

八 *Pa*¹. *Eight.*

九 *Chiu*³. *Nine.*

十 *Shï*². *Ten;* complete.

人 *Jên*². *A man;* mankind; human; a person —Les. 52.

七[14]天是一個禮拜。○一[15]千
個錢是一吊。○一[16]百五十
個人。○十[17]九個小錢。○二[18]
百四十個女人。○一[19]百零
六個錢。○一[20]年零八個月。
○十[21]一個月、零七天。○先[22]
生有好些個錢。○門[23]口有
些個好些堂有好些
一些女人。○學[24]房有一大
些學生。○門[25]口有五六個

14 Seven days are a week.
15 One thousand cash are a string.
16 One hundred and fifty men.
17 Nineteen small cash.
18 Two hundred and forty women.
19 One hundred and six cash.
20 A year and eight months.
21 Eleven months and seven days.
22 The teacher has a good many cash (or, much money).
23 There are some women at the door.
24 There are good many scholars in the school room.
25 There are five or six persons at the door.

男 *Nan*². A male (of the human species); *masculine;* a son.

男人. *A man;* a husband.

女 *Nü*³. *A woman;* a girl; a wife; a lady; female (of the human species).

女人. *Nü*³ *jên*². *A woman;* a wife.

先 *Hsien*¹. *Before;* former; previous; early; in front.

生 *Shêng*¹. To bear, to produce; to beget; *to be born;* to excite; to live, to exist; unripe, raw; unacquainted.

先生 *A teacher.* A style of address applicable to all educated men, and generally applied to any genteel stranger. It is the nearest equivalent of Mr. that the Chinese language affords.

師 *Shï.* A leader; a model; *a teacher,* a master; a metropolis.

娘 *Niang*². A girl, a young lady; *a mother;* a wife.

師娘 Wife of an educated man; *Mrs.*

母 *Mu*³. *A mother;* female.

師母 Wife of an educated man:—Note 5.

學 *Hsüe*² or *hsiao*². *To learn;* to imitate; learning, science, doctrines; a school or place of learning.

學生 *Hsüe*² *shêng*¹. *A pupil, a scholar;* a disciple, a follower.

字 *Tsï*⁴. *A written character;* a word; a writing; a name; a title.

門 *Mên*². *A gate, a door;* an opening; a profession; an occupation; a class.

月 *Yüe*⁴. The moon; *a month.*

房 *Fang*². *A room;* a house: an office or bureau; a wife.

堂 *T'ang*². *A mansion, a hall;* an official room; a court; a church, hospital or large shop; the persons assembled in a hall.

學堂 *Hsüe*² *t'ang*². A school room, a school.

學房 *Hsüe*² *fang*². Same as last:—Note 10.

錢 *Ch'ien*². *Copper cash;* money; wealth; the tenth part of a tael, a mace.

是 *Shï*⁴. *The verb to be;* is, am, are; it is so, yes; absolute right; this.

年 *Nien*². A year, annual.

天 *T'ien*¹. Heaven; the sky, the air; *a day;* a season; Providence; God.

禮 *Li*³. *Worship;* a ceremony, a rite; propriety; offerings; ceremonial gifts.

拜 *Pai*⁴. To reverence, to kneel to; *to worship;* to visit, to pay one's respects to.

禮拜 Worship; *a week;* the Sabbath day.

千 *Ch'ien*¹. *A thousand;* an indefinite number; many.

吊 *Tiao*⁴. To hang; to suspend or lift,—as by a cord; *a string of cash,* equal in most places to a thousand, but in some places to five hundred, or even less,—as in Manchuria.

百 *Pai*³. *A hundred;* the whole of a class; numerous; all.

小 *Hsiao*³. *Small;* petty, mean; junior, inferior; a concubine.

零 *Ling*². *A fraction;* a remainder; a cipher showing that one place is vacant.

人。○[26]一千六百零八個男人。○[27]一年有三百六十五天。○[28]三千零零五個錢。○[29]李太太、有十八九個學生。○[30]李老爺、是個好人。○[31]房老爺、有三吊五百錢。

26 One thousand six hundred and eight men.

27 There are three hundred and sixty-five days in a year.

28 Three thousand and five cash.

29 Madam Li has eighteen or nineteen pupils.

30 Li Lao Yie is a good man.

31 Fang Lao Yie has three thousand five hundred cash.

有 *Yiu*^{3}. *To have, to possess;* to be, to exist; in replies,—yes.

好 *Hao*^{3}. *Good;* right, proper; fit; fine, graceful; very. Also read *hao*^{4}.

好些 *Hao*^{3} *hsie*^{1}. A good many, a considerable number :—Note 22.

口 *K'ou*^{3}. The mouth; *an entrance or opening;* a hole; a port for trade; speech; pronunciation. A classifier :—Les. 68.

門口 *Mên*^{2} *k'ou*^{3}. A gateway; the recess outside of a gate.

些個 *Hsie*^{1} *kê*^{1}. / **一些** *I*^{1} *hsie*^{1}. } Some; a few :—Note 22-3.

大 *Ta*^{4}. *Great, big;* noble; chief, elder; very; entirely. Also read *tai*^{4}.

一大些 *I*^{1} *ta*^{4} *hsie*^{1}. A great many, a large number.

李 *Li*^{3}. A plum; *a common surname.*

太 *T'ai*^{4}. Too; very, extreme :—Les. 24. *A term of respect,* mostly applied to women.

太太 Wife of an officer or of a titled gentleman, Madam. Applied by way of compliment to very old women of any rank.

老 *Lao*^{3}. Old, aged, venerable; *a term of respect, Sire;* out of date; stale; in Pekingese, a long or protracted time. An intensive :—Les. 142.

爺 *Yie*^{2}. A father; *a grandfather.* A title used in addressing divinities, officers and titled gentlemen.

老爺 Sir, Your Honor,—applied to all inferior officers, and to men of wealth who have honorary degrees; a maternal grandfather.

Notes.

2 Chinese has two words for *two;* viz, 二 and 兩. The former is the regular cardinal number, is generally used when speaking of abstract numbers and takes no classifier; while the latter is used of persons and things. The appropriate place of each can only be learned from usage.

3 女人. *A female man,* as 男人 is *a masculine man.* 人 is generic for the race, though commonly used as masculine.

5 The wife of an educated man is called 師娘 in the North, and in the South 師母. In Nanking 師娘 is also used, but is considered a little less respectful than 師母, being applied to the wives of tradesmen and shop-keepers.

10 Both 學房 and 學堂 are intelligible anywhere, but the former prevails in the North and the latter in the South.

11 The Chinese has no such contracted forms as eleven, twelve, twenty, thirty, etc., but the numbers are given in full.

12 Verbs in Chinese have no modification for number; hence 是 is used alike for singular and plural.

13 The student will notice that the classifier is used with 月, but not with 年 or 天. There is no accounting for such freaks of usage.

16 The "and" is supplied. In Chinese, numerals are strung together without any connecting word.

17 "Small cash" are counterfeit cash made smaller or thinner than the legal coin, and are slipped in between the others and counted as good cash. When receiving money in small sums the receiver throws out these small cash, and demands that they be replaced with good ones. Brokers make a business of buying these small cash at a discount and paying them out a few in each hundred for good ones. These 小錢 are also called 私錢 *Sï*^{1} *chien*^{2}, *illicit cash.*

19 The omission of a digit in the midst of a number is indicated in Chinese by the word 零. When two or more places are omitted, two *ling's* are generally used (always in mathematical language):—(28). *Ling* is also used when a lower denomination follows a higher,—as (21).

22 The use of 個 after 些 is an anomalous form current in Peking, but largely confined to Peking and its vicinity.

23 Lit.—*The door mouth has some women;* i.e., *there are some (or several) women at the door.* The verb 有, *to have,* is frequently used in this way for the verb *to be.* 一些 is rarely heard in Peking, being replaced by 些個. In Southern Mandarin the 一 is often omitted and 些 used alone.

25 The "or" is understood. Whenever two digits follow each other in this way, "or" is understood between them.

29 The 十 here belongs to both 八 and 九; or in literal English *ten, and eight or nine.*

第二課

這[1]個人、沒有學問。○那[2]個人、
沒有錢。○這[3]個音、不好聽。○
這[4]些小錢、不好好用使。○這[5]個筆、
不大好。○這[6]些字難學。○那[7]
個落地地方不好。○這[8]個人、不會
說官話。○那[9]個人有病、不能
吃飯。○這[10]些東西、實在不好好
用使。○不[11]要開那個門。○那[12]些
人、沒有飯吃。○那[13]個學生、會

TRANSLATION.

1 This man has no learning.
2 That man has no money.
3 This syllable is not pleasant to hear.
4 These small cash are not good to use (will not pass).
5 This pen is not very good.
6 These characters are hard to learn.
7 That place is not good.
8 This man cannot speak Mandarin.
9 That man is ill, and unable to eat.
10 These things are really not usable.
11 Do not open that door.
12 Those men have nothing to eat.

LESSON II.

DEMONSTRATIVE PRONOUNS.

這 This, 那 That } These words, when not followed by a special classifier, are generally followed by 個 or 些. Sometimes the 個 and 些 are omitted, the sense remaining approximately the same. When followed by 些 the meaning is plural; viz, *these* and *those*. The 些 sometimes takes an 一 before it, which modifies the sense a little, making it equivalent to *this or that lot of*, etc. Thus, 這些東西 means *these things*, but 這一些東西 means rather, *this lot of things*.

VOCABULARY.

這 *Chê*^{4}, *chei*^{4}. This; here; now; this place or thing. The second pronunciation is colloquial, and probably a contraction of 這一.

那 *Na*^{4}, *nei*^{4}. That; there; that place, or thing, or time. The second pronunciation is colloquial, and probably a contraction of 那一. Also *na*^{3}.

沒 *Moǎ*^{4}, *mei*^{2}. To die; to disappear; not yet; *no, not.* In Mandarin 沒 is always followed by 有, expressed or understood, and, except when 有 is used as a principal verb, always puts the idea in the perfect tense.

問 *Wên*^{4}. *To ask;* to hold responsible; to examine a case; to convict.

學問 *Hsüe*^{2} *wên*^{4}. *Learning;* scholarship; knowledge; information.

音 *Yin*^{1}. A sound of any kind; a musical note, a tone; *the sound of a word.*

不 *Pu*^{4}. *Not, no;* with adjectives it answers to the prefixes, *un, dis,* etc. The tone varies with the collocation.

聽 *T'ing*^{1}. *To hear;* to listen, to understand. Also *t'ing*^{4}.

使 *Shï*^{3}. To order; to send; *to use;* to cause, to effect; if; supposing that:—Les. 132. An instrumental verb:—Les. 54.

用 *Yung*^{4}. *To use,* to employ; to cause; to need; useful; so as to. An instrumental verb:—Les. 54.

筆 *Pi*^{3}. *A pen,* a pencil, a style; a stroke in a character; an item in an account.

難 *Nan*^{2}. *Hard, difficult;* irksome; to be hard on, to harrass, to persecute. Also *nan*^{4}.

地 *Ti*^{4}. The earth; a place, a spot; the ground, the floor.

方 *Fang*^{1}. A square; a place; a rule; a prescription; to compare; then, thereupon; a classifier:—Les. 147.

寫好些字。○這[14]個人、不說實話。○那[15]個人、不會寫字。○這[16]個字、實在不好寫。○那[17]個人、不要這些小錢。○這[18]些話、實在難學。○請[19]先生寫這個字。○那[20]個學生、不聽說。○太[21]太不能吃這個飯。○這[22]個地方、有好些個〔一大些〕人。○那[23]個小學生、不大老實。○那[24]個地方、沒有好人。○那[25]個地方、沒有

13 That scholar can write a good many characters.
14 This man does not speak the truth.
15 That man cannot write.
16 Truly this character is not easy to write.
17 That man will not take these small cash.
18 These words are truly hard to learn.
19 Will you (teacher) please write this character?
20 That scholar does not mind what he is told.
21 The lady cannot eat this food.
22 There are a good many people in this place.
23 That small pupil is not very steady.
24 There are no good men in that place.
25 There is not a good man in that place.

地方 *A place;* an occasion; a situation to work or to live; a tax collector.

落 *Loă*⁴. *To descend, to fall;* to let down; to enter on an account; to begin,—to write. Also *lao*⁴ and *la*⁴.

落地 Same as 地方, but used only in the South.

會 *Hwei*⁴. To collect; to know how; *can,*—used of acquired ability; a fraternity; a joint-stock company; a church; a short time.

能 *Nêng*². Power; ability; to be able; *can,*—used of natural ability; competent; talented.

說 *Shwoă*¹. *To speak, to say;* to narrate; to reprove; words, sayings. Also *shwei*⁴.

官 *Kwan*¹. An officer of any class; official; the government.

話 *Hwa*⁴. Words, talk; *spoken* as opposed to *written* language; to speak.

官話 Official language; the court dialect, Mandarin.

病 *Ping*⁴. *Illness, disease;* a defect; a fault; a vice.

喫 吃 *Ch'ï*¹. *To eat;* to drink; to suffer, to bear. The second is a short form of writing in common use.

飯 *Fan*⁴. A meal; *food;* rice or millet (cooked).

東 *Tung*¹. *East;* sunrise; the place of honor; master or owner.

西 *Hsi*¹. *West;* western; foreign.

東西 *A thing;* a worthless fellow.

實 *Shï*². *Real, solid;* true, honest; the results; the kernel; the multiplicand or dividend.

在 *Tsai*⁴. *To be in or at;* at, in, within; present; depending upon; to be alive.

實在 Really; truly; verily; in fact; well!

要 *Yao*⁴. *To want;* to need; to require from; to dun; necessary, important; to intend; to be about to; sign of future:—Les. 13.

開 *K'ai*¹. *To open;* to explain; to begin; to start; to write out; boiling hot. An auxiliary verb:—Les. 74.

寫 *Hsie*³. *To write;* to compose; to disburden; to dissipate.

實話 *Shï*² *hwa*⁴. The truth; the facts.

聽 *T'ing*⁴. To hearken to; *to obey;* to let; to follow; to hear a cause, to await; according to, as. See *t'ing*¹.

聽說 *T'ing*⁴ *shwoă*¹. To obey; to be obedient.

請 *Ch'ing*³. To request; to invite; *please;* to engage or hire,—as a teacher, etc.

老實 *Lao*³ *shï*². Honest; trustworthy; steady; gentle (of an animal).

窮 *Ch'iung*². Exhausted; *poor;* to exhaust, to search out; the end.

個好人。○那[26]個地方、沒有一個好人。○這[27]個地方、沒有窮人。○這[28]個學生要六個錢。○這[29]個老先生實在窮。

26 There is not a single good man in that place.

27 There are no poor people in this place.

28 This pupil wants six cash.

29 This old teacher is exceedingly poor.

NOTES.

3 The verb *to be* is here understood. Its omission is very common.

4 使 is very common in Northern Mandarin, but not in the South, where 用 is always used.

5 不大好. *Not great good ;* i.e., *not very good.*

7 地方 is everywhere current, 落地 is only used in the South.

9 飯 is added to 吃 in order to specialize the syllable *ch'i*, as that *ch'i* which has 飯 for its object, thus distinguishing it from other words of the same sound. The object combines with the verb and need not appear in the translation. This is a very common idiom. In the fifteenth sentence we have another example in 寫字. See Lesson 51.

12 沒有飯吃. Lit., *No have rice to eat ;* i.e., have nothing to eat.

19 Lit., *I invite the teacher to write this character.* "Teacher" is here used instead of "you," for the sake of politeness.

20 聽說. Lit., *hear saying ;* i.e., *obey orders.* Both words are here used out of their primary senses. 聽, *to hear,* is used in the sense of *listen to, to obey ;* and 說, *to speak,* is used in the sense of commands or instructions. The former changes its tone, but the latter does not.

24 The plural is here implied, as it often is. The 25th sentence shows how the singular is expressed, and the 26th shows how the addition of an 一 emphasizes the singular.

LESSON III.

PERSONAL PRONOUNS.

我 I, or me.

你 You, or thou, or thee.

他 He, she, him, her, it ;—used freely of men and beasts, but sparingly of things. As in Chinese nouns have no distinction of gender or case, one pronoun answers for all.

們 The sign of the plural ; usually added only to the personal pronouns, but sometimes to other words denoting persons. It is never added to words, denoting things. The second and third personal pronouns are often used in the plural without 們. In polite language 們 is often added to 我 and 你 when only one is meant. This is especially the case in Pekingese.

The above are the regular personal pronouns. There are besides these a number of colloquial pronouns which will be introduced by and by :—Les. 84.

VOCABULARY.

我 *Woă*³. . . . . . . I, me, mine, we, us ; the *ego.*

你 *Ni*³. You, thou, your. When formally addressing superiors 你 is generally replaced by the title of the person addressed.

他 *T'a*¹. He, she, him, her, it ; that one ; the other.

們 *Mên*¹. . . . . . . Sign of the plural :—See Sub.

早 *Tsao*³. . . . . . . *Early ;* soon ; beforehand.

朝 *Chao*¹. The dawn, the morning, early. Also *ch'ao*².

早飯 *Tsao*³ *fan*⁴. . . . . . . Breakfast :—Note 2.

朝飯 *Chao*¹ *fan*⁴ . . . . Breakfast.

來 *Lai*². *To come ;* to effect ; the future. An auxiliary verb :—Les. 10 and 113.

明 *Ming*². Bright ; evident ; brilliant ; *intelligent ;* to make plain ; the dawn.

白 *Poă*², *pai*². White ; *plain,* easy to comprehend ; obvious ; without rank ; without price, freely ; in vain. The second reading is confined to Pekingese.

明白 Evident ; plain ; *to understand ;* satisfactory,—as a bargain ; intelligent, shrewd.

第三課

他[1]没没有吃早朝飯。○我[2]有三百錢。○他[3]們不能來。○我[4]没有錢。○他[5]不會寫這個字。○我[6]不明白這個字。○先[7]生要你說實話。○他[8]不能不告訴你。○你[9]們可以等一等。○我[10]們没有地方寫字。○他[11]不會開這個門。○那[12]個時候、我不能去。○這[13]個禮拜、我不能來。○你[14]去告訴他、等一等。○我[15]們還没吃午晌中飯。○這[16]個事、你不能不管。○這[17]個事情、你不可好告訴他。

Translation.

1 He has not eaten breakfast.
2 I have three hundred cash.
3 They can not come.
4 I have no money.
5 He can not write this character.
6 I do not understand this character.
7 The teacher wants you to speak the truth.
8 He can not but tell you.
9 You may wait a little.
10 We have no place to write.
11 He can not open this door.
12 At that time I can not go.
13 This week I can not come.
14 You go and tell him to wait a little.
15 We have not yet eaten dinner.
16 You can not but attend to this affair.
17 You must not tell him of this business.

告 *Kao*^{4}. To announce to a superior; *to tell of;* to accuse or impeach; to proclaim.

訴 *Su*^{4}. *To tell, to inform;* to state in reply or defense.

告訴 *To inform, to tell.* In this combination *su*^{4} is frequently corrupted into *sung*^{4}.

可 *K'ê*^{3}. *To be willing, to permit;* to be able; may, can, might; fitting; accurate. Before a verb it forms a verbal adjective:—Les. 180. Also *k'ê.*

以 *I*^{3}. To use; *to take;* to regard as, by; so as to; an instrumental verb:—Les. 145.

可以 *Can, may;* will do, will answer the purpose; as a reply,—yes:—Les. 70.

等 *Têng*^{3}. An order or class; equal, like; *to wait;* to want immediately; such like, etc.; a sign of the plural:—Les. 188.

等一等 Lit., wait one wait; i.e., wait a little, presently; hold!

時 *Shï*^{2}. *Time;* a season; an hour; an occasion, an opportunity.

候 *Hou*^{4}. To wait; to expect; *a time.*

時候 Time, duration; *a certain time.*

去 *Ch'ü*^{4}. To go (somewhere); to go away, to leave; to separate, to reject; past, gone. An auxiliary verb:—Les. 10.

還 *Hwan*^{2}. To return; to revert; to repay; *still,* even, furthermore, yet, also, and. As a conjunction it is often read *Han*^{2} or *Hai*^{2} or *Ha*^{2}. It sometimes merely serves to intensify, and is incapable of translation.

晌 *Shang*^{3}. Noontide, noon.

午 *Wu*^{3}. Midday, noon; the hour which begins at eleven and ends at one o'clock.

中 *Chung*^{1}. *The middle,* the center; in the middle of, within; medium; to accomplish, to be sufficient. Also *chung*^{4}.

晌飯 *Shang*^{3} *fan*^{4}. The noontide meal, dinner:—Note 15.

午飯
中飯 } The noontide meal, dinner:—Note 15.

正 *Chêng*^{4}. Correct, just, legal; upright, not awry; principal; orthodox; exactly; *at the time just;* plus (+). Also *chêng*^{1}.

事 *Shï*^{4}. *An affair;* business; that which is done, an act; to serve; to manage.

這18個飯、我實在不能吃。○這19個時候、他們正吃飯。○這20個東西、我不能給你。○這21個事情、我實在不知道(曉得)。○他22不明白這個道理。○請23先生給我三吊(一吊五百大錢)。○這24個事情、我們不能不告訴先生。○這25個時候、他們還沒有吃夜飯(沒吃晚飯)。○你26可以告訴他、禮拜四來。○明27天是禮拜六、我們不學話。

18 I really can not eat this food.
19 They are just now eating.
20 I can not give you this article.
21 This business I positively do not know.
22 He does not understand this doctrine.
23 Please, teacher, give me three thousand cash, (or, one thousand five hundred big cash.)
24 We can not but tell the teacher of this affair.
25 At this time they have not yet eaten supper.
26 You may tell him to come on Thursday.
27 To-morrow is Saturday, we shall not study.

情 *Ch'ing*². The seven passions taken together; . . . . viz., 喜 joy, 怒 anger, 哀 sorrow, 懼 fear, 愛 love, 惡 hatred and 欲 concupiscence; the desires; the emotions, the passions; *the facts or circumstances of an affair;* a case.

事情 An affair; business; a matter.

管 *Kwan*³. A tube; a flute; to rule, to control; . . . . *to care for, to manage;* a classifier:—Les. 42.

給 *Chi*³, *kei*³. To give; to supply; sign of the . . . . dative:—Les. 25. The reading *kei*³ is confined to Pekingese; in Central Mandarin it is often, perhaps generally, read *k'i*³.

知 *Chi*¹. *To know*, to be aware of; sensible of; . . . . . . to inform; knowledge, wisdom.

道 *Tao*⁴. *A road or path;* a doctrine or prin- . . . . ciple approved by the mind; the right way, duty; to speak, to talk; Taoism.

知道 To know, to be aware of; to care.

理 *Li*³. To govern, to regulate; to erect; *rea-* . . . . *son,* abstract right; a principle; to think of; to regard.

道理 Reason; *doctrine;* what is right.

曉 *Hsiao*³. Clear, luminous; the morning, the . . . . dawn; *to understand, to know.*

得 *Tê*². *To get, to obtain;* to succeed; to be- . . . . come, to accomplish. An auxiliary verb:—Les. 43. Also *tei*³.

曉得 To know, to comprehend.

晚 *Wan*³. *Evening,* twilight; late, tardy; the . . . . latter or last.

夜 *Yie*⁴. . . . . . . *Night;* darkness.

晚飯 *Wan*³ *fan*⁴. . . . . } Supper.
夜飯 *Yie*⁴ *fan*⁴. . . . . }

NOTES.

2 In speaking, the 有 is very often omitted after 沒, especially in the North. When writing, however, teachers will generally insist on using it; especially is this so in the South. As often in Chinese, the practice belies the theory. When 有 is omitted, the 沒 is generally read *mei*, which is presumably a contraction for 沒有; albeit in the North *mei* is frequently heard with 有 following. 朝飯 for "breakfast" appears to be used only in Shantung.

8 We have here two negatives making a strong affirmative, which is a common Chinese idiom.

9 The "you" is emphatic; that is, the person addressed is contrasted with some one who is *not* required to wait: unless so used the 你們 would generally be omitted.

14 等一等 is in the infinitive by the construction of the sentence, which is the only sign the infinitive has in Chinese.

15 In Peking, 午飯 is used, and in the South, 中飯, while 晌飯 is used in Shantung. In Chinanfu, however, 晌午飯 is generally used.

16 The object is here placed before the verb, which is quite a common idiom in Chinese. It gives prominence to the object and force to the expression.

17 不可 means *must not,* and has more or less the force of a command. It is entirely *t'ung hsing* (通行); i.e., everywhere current. 不好 means, *ought not,* or

第四課

我[1]的錢不彀。○老[2]爺的話不錯。○你[3]不要管我的事。○他[4]的學問不大。○他[5]不懂得我的話。○你[6]不該說他母親的不是。○這[7]個東西是我的。○我[8]不能隨他的便。○他[9]不明白我的意思。○師[10]母娘的衣裳、實在好看。○李[11]先生的意思、正對。

Translation.

1 My money is not sufficient.
2 Your Honor's words are correct.
3 Do not meddle in my affairs.
4 His scholarship is not good.
5 He does not understand my language.
6 You ought not to speak of his mother's faults.
7 This article is mine.
8 I can not accommodate myself to his convenience.
9 He does not comprehend my idea.
10 Your clothes are very beautiful, Madam.
11 Mr. Li's idea is exactly right; [or, your idea, Mr. Li, is exactly right.]

should not, and implies an impropriety. It is extensively used in this sense both in Central and Southern Mandarin, but is not often heard in Pekingese.

21 **知道** is rarely heard in Nanking or the South; **曉得** almost entirely superseding it. **曉得** is also used in the North, but somewhat sparingly.

23 In a large part of North China it is the custom to call ten cash twenty, fifty a hundred, and so on, in all cases (except in numbers under ten) giving a number which is double the actual number of the cash; and sums of cash when so designated are called **小錢**, *small cash*. When, on the contrary, it is desired not to reckon double, but to call a cash a cash, they say **大錢**, *large cash*. Numbers under ten are not doubled, but the word **大** is added by way of distinction. The **小錢** are also called **京錢**, *capital cash*, because this method of reckoning originated in Peking. In places near the border line between these methods of reckoning, the terms "large" and "small" are applied to all sums of cash. Elsewhere it is understood,—in the North that any given sum of cash is double, and in the South that it is the real number. Thus we see that **小錢** may mean either counterfeit cash, or cash reckoned double, according to circumstances.

25 **晚飯** is used both in Pekingese and in Southern Mandarin, but **夜飯** is generally used in Shantung.

26 The days of the week are numbered as so many days after the Sabbath. The Sabbath itself is called **禮拜日**, or more commonly simply **禮拜**. This terminology was introduced by the Roman Catholics.

27 **學話** *learn words*, i.e., have a lesson.

LESSON IV.

The Possessive Particle.

的 is the common sign of the possessive case. It serves for both our forms of the possessive; viz., the *'s* and the *of*. It is often omitted and the possessive implied by the mere juxtaposition of the words. This is especially the case when two possessives follow each other.

的 has other important uses which will appear by and by:—Les. 18, 23 and 39.

Vocabulary.

的 *Ti*[1]. *Sign of the possessive*:—see Sub.; also . . . . . . Lessons 18, 23 and 39. Also *ti*[4].

彀 *Kou*[4]. To draw a bow to its full; *enough*, ... adequate.

錯 *Ts'oă*[4]. To confuse; to mistake or err; *wrong*, ... *to be wrong*; excepting.

懂 *Tung*[3]. Disturbed; *to understand, to perceive*. Read *twin*[3] in some places.

懂得 *Tung*[3] *tê*[2]. To understand, to comprehend. . . . .

該 *Kai*[1]. To owe money; *ought, should*; what . . . . is proper or right; the aforesaid.

親 *Ch'in*[1]. To love, to be attached to; to show . . . . affection for; *a relative*, kin; one's own. Also *ch'ing*[4].

母親 *Mu*[3] *ch'in*[1]. . . . Mother.

12 你先生的意思、不大合式。○ 13 他的意思、容易明白。○ 14 這不是他男人的事。○ 15 他没有(没)明白你的話。○ 16 這個東西、不合我的式。○ 17 我不知道這個地方的規矩。○ 18 先生的話、我聽不明白。○ 19 李先生的學堂(學房)没有規矩。○ 20 這個人的官話、實在好

12 Your teacher's idea is not quite suitable.

13 His idea is easily understood.

14 This is not her husband's business.

15 He did not understand your language.

16 This thing does not suit me.

17 I do not understand the customs of this place.

18 I do not understand what you say, [or, the teacher says.]

19 Mr. Li's school-room has no discipline.

20 This man's Mandarin is exceedingly pleasant to hear.

不是 *Pu*² *shï*⁴. A fault; a sin; a wrong. Note .... in this phrase 不 is read *pu*².

隨 *Swei*². To follow, *to comply with;* to permit; .... as, according to; whenever.

便 *Pien*⁴. To accord with; *convenient*, opportune; at hand, ready; then, so, just:—Les. 190. Also *p'ien*².

意 *I*⁴. Thought, intention, *idea;* meaning, motive; opinion.

思 *Sï*¹. ...... *To think*, to consider; to desire.

意思 Intention; sentiments, opinion; *meaning.*

衣 *I*¹. *Clothes*, garments; a case or covering of ...... any kind.

裳 *Shang*¹. ..... Skirts, petticoats; *clothes.*

衣裳 Dress, clothes (personal, not bed-clothes).

看 *K'an*⁴. *To see, to look at;* to examine; to .... regard as, to estimate; mock,—as a mock persimmon. Also *k'an*¹.

好看 *Hao*³ *k'an*⁴. Good to see, beautiful, admirable. 好 is joined to many other words in the same way as, 好聽, good to hear, 好吃 good to eat, etc.

對 *Twei*⁴. Parallel scrolls; *to correspond, to suit;* .... to compare, to respond; consistent with; opposite; a pair. A classifier:—Les. 140.

合 *Hè*². To shut the mouth; to unite, to combine; suitable; *according to;* harmonious; together; the whole; product (math.). A classifier:—Les. 140.

式 *Shï*⁴. ...... A form, *a pattern;* an example.

合式 According to pattern; *suitable; appropriate.*

容 *Yung*², *jung*². To contain; *to tolerate* or .... bear with; to pass over, to forgive; air, manner; face, countenance.

易 *I*⁴. *Easy;* without care; remiss; the mutations of nature, change; to exchange.

容易 Easy, facile.

規 *Kwei*¹. A pair of compasses; a regulation, ... a law; a *custom.*

矩 *Chü*⁴. A carpenter's square; a law; *a custom;* a pattern.

規矩 Custom; *usage;* propriety; order, method.

樣 *Yang*⁴. A model, a pattern; manner, style; .... way, fashion; *sort.*

氣 *Ch'i*⁴. Vapor, steam; gas; *air, breath;* the .... vital principle; the ether; *spirit, temper;* any feeling that produces excitement, as anger, hatred, etc.; air, aspect.

生氣 *Shêng*¹ *ch'i*⁴. To get angry, to be excited .... by passion.

力 *Li*⁴. *Strength* of body or mind; energy; ...... properties or powers of anything.

力氣 *Physical strength*, prowess; force.

比 *Pi*³. *To compare;* to assort; to equal; an ...... illustration:—Les. 58.

國 *Kwoă*². A state, *a country*, a kingdom, a .... nation; governmental.

中國 *Chung*¹ *kwoă*². The Middle Kingdom, ... China.

外 *Wai*⁴. ...... Outside; *foreign;* extraneous.

外國 Each and all foreign countries.

課 *K'ê*⁴. ...... *A lesson*, a task; a series.

多 *Toă*¹. *Many*, numerous; much; mostly; .... very, excessive:—Les. 48.

聽。○我[21]們的老爺、沒有這樣的規矩。○請[22]老爺不要生氣、這是我的錯。○他[23]女人的力氣、比他的大。○中[24]國的字、比外國的難寫。○這[25]一課的生字、不大多。

21 Our master has no such custom.

22 Please, sir, do not get angry ; this is my mistake.

23 His wife's strength is greater than his.

24 Chinese characters are more difficult to write than foreign ones.

25 There are not very many new characters in this lesson.

NOTES.

2 *Your honor*, is but a make-shift translation. The 老爺 is used for the sake of etiquette, to avoid the use of the pronoun. This polite form is used in addressing officials, superiors, strangers, etc. It is, however, far from being universal custom in every day life, especially in the familiar intercourse of family and friends. As the English language does not afford any adequate means of rendering such indirect address, I shall hereafter translate simply by the pronoun "you" as the equivalent of the title, whatever it may be.

3 不要 *not want*, is a common and mild form of forbidding. The 你 is best omitted in the translation.

14 The 個 is here omitted, as it often is, especially when not followed by its noun.

16 我的 is here interjected between the parts of the compound term 合式.

20 A more elegant translation would be, *This man speaks Mandarin beautifully.*

21 The attachés of an official all speak of him as 我們的 so-and-so, meaning thereby "the official with whom we are connected."

23 Lit.—*His wife's strength compared with his is great.* This is the ordinary method of formal comparison. There are a variety of other forms of comparison, for which see Les. 58, 99. The term 女人 is here used for wife, as it often is when there is no occasion or desire to show any special respect.

LESSON V.

THE ENCLITICS 子 AND 兒.

子 A child, a son.

兒 An infant, a son.

Both of these characters are added to words to individualize them, and mark them as nouns. Some words take one and some take the other, while many take either at pleasure. A few nouns never take either of them. The two answer substantially the same purpose. 子 is a little more dignified than 兒. 兒 has in most cases more or less of a diminutive force. 子 is more used in Southern Mandarin, and 兒 in Northern Mandarin, especially in Pekingese.

Both 子 and 兒 are more used in spoken than in written Mandarin. Their excessive use, especially that of the latter, marks an uneducated man, or a careless speaker. 兒 is usually spoken so as to coalesce with the word to which it is joined ; thus 錢兒, is not pronounced *Ch'ien-er*, but *Ch'ier*. Many of the Chinese are scarcely conscious of the fact that they are adding this 兒 to their words. In Nanking, especially, most teachers will aver that it is not used, and will protest against writing it, while in fact it is much used, though not so much as in Peking.

兒 is also used in forming adverbs of time and place :—Les. 9 and 16.

VOCABULARY

子 *Tsï*³. *A child*, a son; a boy, a lad; an heir; ....a seed or kernel; a sage :—see Sub.

兒 *Êr*².... An infant; a son; a boy:—see Sub.

桌 *Choâ*¹.... A table, a stand.

乾 *Kan*¹. Dry ; exhausted ; *clean.* Also read ....*ch'ien*².

淨 *Ching*⁴. Pure, undefiled; *clean;* only, simply; ....net :—See Les. 49.

乾淨 Clean, unspotted ; trifling, dainty.

法 *Fa*³. A law, a statute; *an art, a method;* ......the rules or methods of any science; legal punishment :—Les. 103.

第五課

這[1]個桌子不乾淨。○他[2]的
法子不合式。○你[3]不可學
他的樣子。○他[4]有兩個兒
子、一個姑娘(閨女)。○那[5]些花兒、
實在好看。○這[6]些椅子不
好坐。○我[7]不要這個小房
子。○他[8]的家裏(老婆)不會過日
子。○他[9]不能不過窮日子。
○三[10]兩銀子、該換五吊多

TRANSLATION.

1 This table is not clean.
2 His plan is not suitable.
3 You must not follow his example.
4 He has two sons and one daughter.
5 Those flowers are certainly beautiful.
6 These chairs are not fit to sit on (or, not comfortable).
7 I do not want this small house.
8 His wife can not economize.
9 He can not but be a poor man.
10 Three ounces of silver ought to sell for over five thousand cash.

姑 *Ku*^{1}. *A polite name for women*, especially . . . . . . young and unmarried women; lenient, yielding.

閨 *Kwei*^{1}. Women's apartments; *unmarried* . . . . *girls;* feminine.

姑娘 *Ku*^{1} *niang*^{2}. A girl, an unmarried lady; . . . . Miss; a daughter:—Note 4.

閨女 *Kwei*^{1} *nü*^{3}. A virgin, a girl, a young . . . . lady; a daughter.

花 *Hwa*^{1}. *A flower*, a blossom; variegated; to spend . . . . . . money; pleasure; vice; raw cotton.

椅 *I*^{3}. . . . . . . A chair, a seat.

坐 *T'soă*^{4}. To sit, to squat; to sit in judgment, ...to remain; to set, to place.

婆 *P'oă*^{2} . . . . . . *An old woman;* a mother.

老婆 *Lao*^{3} *p'oă*^{2}. *A wife;* an old woman; a . . . . .woman servant:—Note 8.

老太 *Lao*^{3} *t'ai*^{4}. An old woman; an old lady, ...(Nankingese.)

家 *Chia*^{1}. A household, *a family;* home; do- . . . . .mestic; a sect; a profession. An enclitic:—Les. 72.

裏 or **裡**. *Li*^{3}. A lining; inside, inner, in; with- . . . . . . .in. Both forms are used.

家裡 Home; family; *wife;* wife and children.

過 *Kwoă*^{4}. To pass by or over; to exceed, to . . . . .surpass; *to spend time;* to transgress; a transgression; beyond, further; excessive; than, rather; an auxiliary verb:—Les. 41.

日 *Jï*^{4}. The sun; *a day;* days, times; the day . . . . . .for a thing.

過日子 To make a living; *to live;* to be thrifty, to economize.

銀 *Yin*^{2}. . . . . . . Silver; money; cash.

換 *Hwan*^{4}. To remove; *to exchange*, to change; . . . . .to barter.

頭 *T'ou*^{2}. *The head;* front; top; chief; first; . . . . .best; the beginning or entrance; the end. A classifier:—Les. 38. Also Les. 47, 143.

老頭 *Lao*^{3} *t'ou*^{2}. An old man; the old man of . . . . .the house.

歲 *Swei*^{4}. . . . . . *A year of one's age;* years, age.

孩 *Hai*^{2}. . . . . . . A child; a youth; a boy.

生日 *Shêng*^{1} *jï*^{4}. . . . . .Birthday.

出 *Ch'u*^{1}. *To go out;* to issue, to put forth; to . . . . .surpass; to eject; to sacrifice; to beget; to be born. An auxiliary verb:—Les. 40.

出門 or **出門子** *Ch'u*^{1} *mên*^{2} *tsï*^{3}. To go from . . . . home, to travel; *to get married* (said of the woman):—Note 16.

閣 *Kê*^{2}. An upper room; a balcony; *female* . . . . . . *apartments;* a council chamber.

出閣 To marry, to wed, (said of the woman.)

尖 *Chien*^{1}. Tapering, pointed; wedge-like; *a* . . . . *point*, the apex.

刀 *Tao*^{1}. A sword; *a knife;* a quire of paper rang- . . . . . . ing from fifty to two hundred sheets.

快 *K'wai*^{4}. Glad, cheerful; prompt, quick, ... rapid; *sharp*, keen.

辮 *Pien*^{4}. . . . . . . To plait, to braid; *the queue.*

錢。○[11]他該我兩吊多錢兒。○[12]那個老頭子兒、没有兒子。○[13]這個老婆子、老太有七十多歲。○[14]他的孩子没有力氣。○[15]李老爺的兒子、明天過生日。○[16]衣先生的女兒、還没出門子、閣。○[17]這個筆没有尖兒。○[18]我的小刀兒、不大快。○[19]外國人没有辮子。○[20]不要開書房的門兒、門。○

11 He owes me more than two thousand cash.
12 That old man has no son.
13 This old woman is over seventy years of age.
14 His child has no strength.
15 To-morrow is Mr. Li's son's birthday.
16 Mr. I's daughter is not yet married.
17 This pen has no point.
18 My pocket knife is not very sharp.
19 Foreigners have no queues.
20 Do not open the school-room door.

書 *Shu*¹. *A book;* a letter; documents; to write; ....the canon of History.

書房 *Shu*¹ *fang*². A school room; a study; a ....library.

杏 *Hsing*⁴.......... An apricot.

三 *Sa*¹. Three, a contraction of 三個. See *san*¹. ......

賣 *Mai*⁴... *To sell;* to betray; to make game of.

僱 *Ku*⁴...... To hire; to engage the services of.

媽 *Ma*¹. An old woman; a mother; *a waiting* ....*woman.*

老媽 *Lao*³ *ma*¹. *A servant woman;* a nurse; ....among the Manchus,—mother.

看 *K'an*¹. To watch, to guard, to look after .... to tend:—See *k'an*⁴.

娃 *Wa*². A baby, an infant. Usually doubled, ... 娃娃:—Note 23.

叫 *Chiao*⁴. *To call;* to cry out; to name; to ....sing,—as an insect; to tell to do; to cause, to let; sign of passive:—Les. 53.

名 *Ming*². A name; *the given name;* a person; .... fame, reputation; a title.

小名 *Hsiao*³ *ming*². A small or pet name:— ....Note 24.

學名 *Hsüe*² *ming*²..........A school name.

Notes.

4 There is great diversity in Mandarin in the use of terms for girl or young lady. In Shantung the common term is 閨女. The term 姑娘 is also used of the daughters of officers and educated men. In Peking 閨女 is used when speaking of one's own daughter, while 姑娘 is used in other cases. In Southern Mandarin both terms are used with varying frequency, and besides them, as more genteel, 小姐 (little sister) is used. The terms 女兒 and 女子 are also frequently used, both in the North and in the South, especially for daughter, for which the Chinese has no distinctive word.

8 The term 老婆 is often used (generally in Shantung) by the common people for wife, but is more or less disrespectful. When thus used the accent is thrown on the 老, also 子 or 兒 is frequently added. 家裏 means properly *home,* but is often used for that which is most important in a home; viz., a wife. The expression 過日子 is very suggestive, in view of the hand to mouth way in which the most of the Chinese live.

12 After 老頭 the 子 and 兒 are used indifferently. When 兒 is used, the two words are often pronounced as if the *êr* were in the middle of the *t'ou*²; namely, *lao t'rou*². In this case, as in other similar cases of corrupt pronunciation, it is not necessary to imitate the corruption.

13 老婆子 here means an old woman, the emphasis being on the 婆. With an odd perversity, they put the emphasis on the 老 when the woman is young, and not when she is old. 有 not 是 is generally used in speaking of ages.

15 The first birthday of a child is specially observed. Afterwards little notice is taken of birthdays, except in the case of old people and officials.

16 出閣 is the more correct term, though 出門子 is much used in some places. In Kiukiang 出門子 is only applied to the marriage of a widow while in Chinanfu it is used of harlots. If 子 be omitted, or if it be replaced by 兒, the phrase means *to go on a journey.*

21 這些杏子、賣三個(三二)錢一個。○

22 一天不過能學二十五六個生字(字兒)。○

23 李師娘(母)要僱一個老婆(老媽兒)、看孩子(娃娃)。○

24 他的小名兒叫年子、他的學名兒我不曉得(知道)。

21 These apricots sell for three [large] cash apiece.

22 One can learn only twenty-five or six new characters in a day.

23 Mrs. Li wishes to hire an old woman (or, a nurse) to take care of her baby.

24 His little name is called Nien-tsï; his school name I do not know.

18 小刀兒 means a pocket knife, while 刀 or 刀子 means a large knife, or a sword.

21 三個錢一個. *Three cash [for] one.* The Chinese inserts no word answering to our word "for."

23 The prevalent term for *nurse* is 老媽, though 老婆兒 or 老婆子 is used in some places in this sense. In Nanking 媽媽 is also used in the same sense. In the South 娃娃 is commonly applied to little children, in the North only to babies, or (more commonly) to earthen dolls.

24 Boys at birth receive a 小名, or more elegantly, a 乳名 *ju³ ming², milk name.* When they start to school, a new name is given them by the teacher, which becomes their proper name through life. If they never go to school, a new name is usually given them by their parents before their manhood, which is called a 大名. The parents, especially the mother, often call them by their "little name" as long as they live. Besides these two names, young men usually take a 號 *hao⁴* or *title,* and many of them also receive a 外號 *wai⁴ hao⁴, nickname.* It is considered the proper thing to address a grown man by his *hao⁴*, especially in writing.

LESSON VI.

THE COMMON PREPOSITION OF PLACE.

在 At, in:—it precedes the noun and is generally followed by a postposition after the noun; as if we should say in English, *to the wall-wards,* instead of, towards the wall. The most frequent postpositions are 裏, 外, 上 and 下. 在 is sometimes omitted or understood, as in 18 and 24.

VOCABULARY.

上 *Shang⁴*. Above, upon; high, ancient; before; superior; excellent, exalted; Heaven; imperial; on, near. Also *shang³*.

下 *Hsia⁴*. *Below, underneath*; low, vulgar; poor in quality; next; a time; once; to descend; to fall,—as rain.

父 *Fu⁴*. *A father;* an ancestor; a senior.

父親 *Fu⁴ ch'in¹*. Father.

城 *Ch'êng²*. A citadel; *a walled city;* the wall of a city.

住 *Chu⁴*. To stop, to cease; *to dwell, to live in*; to endure. An auxiliary verb:—Les. 75.

躺 *T'ang³*. *To lie down;* to sprawl.

牀 *Ch'wang²*. *A bed;* a lounge; a sled.

樓 *Lou²*. A loft; a tower; *an upper floor or story;* a house of two or more stories.

底 *Ti³*. The bottom; *below, underneath;* low, menial; to the end; the original draft.

底下 *Ti³ hsia⁴*. Beneath, underneath:—See Les. 120, Sub.

鋪 *P'u¹*. *To spread out;* to arrange, or lay out in order; bedding.

看書 *K'an⁴ shu¹*. To read, to study.

打 *Ta³*. *To strike,* to beat; to fight; to bastinade; to do, to make; to cause; by, in, through:—See Les. 124.

敲 *Ch'iao¹*. To pound, to tap, *to rap on;* to beat,—as a drum.

打門 *Ta³ mên²*. To knock at the door:—Note 10.

敲門 *Ch'iao¹ mên²*. To knock at the door.

叫門 *Chiao⁴ mên²*. To halloo; *to knock at the door:*—Note 10.

炕 *K'ang⁴*. To dry, to bake; *a brick bed or divan heated by a fire underneath.*

紡 *Fang³*. To spin, to twist into thread.

第六課

我[1]的父親不在家。○我[2]的母親還在。○他[3]們在城裏住。○我[4]住在東門外。○他[5]兩個人躺在牀上。○在[6]樓底下没有人。○李[7]師娘在樓上鋪牀。○李[8]先生在家裏看書。○在[9]上有天、在下有地。○不[10]用叫打敲門、他不在家。○他[11]母親生有病病躺在炕上。○大[12]姑娘、在家裏紡棉線花。○小[13]女兒、在院子裏看孩子。○你[14]的帽子、不好放在地下。○我[15]的衣裳在樓上。○在[16]桌子

TRANSLATION.

1 My father is not at home.
2 My mother is still living.
3 They live in the city.
4 I live outside the east gate.
5 They two are lying on the bed.
6 There is no one down-stairs.
7 Mrs. Li is up-stairs making the beds.
8 Mr. Li is at home (or, in the house) reading.
9 Above is heaven, below is the earth.
10 You need not knock at the door; he is not at home.
11 His mother is lying on the *k'ang* sick.
12 The eldest daughter is in the house spinning.
13 The younger daughter is in the yard watching the baby.
14 You should not put your hat on the floor.
15 My clothes are up-stairs.
16 There are a good many books on the table.

線 *Hsien*⁴. *Thread*, either cotton, woollen, silk, or flaxen; a fine cord; a clue, a trace; a ray,—as of light; a streak or vein.

棉 *Mien*². . . . . . . The cotton plant.

棉花 *Mien² hwa¹*. Cotton, raw cotton, cotton wool.

小女兒 *Hsiao³ nü³ êr²*. A little girl; *a younger daughter*.

院 *Yüen*⁴. A walled enclosure; *a yard;* a public institution,—as a hospital, an asylum, a college, etc.

帽 *Mao*⁴. A cap, hat, or head covering of any kind.

放 *Fang*⁴. To let go, to liberate; to indulge; *to lay down*, to put, to open out; to send forth; to stretch, to extend.

地下 *Ti⁴ hsia⁴*. Below, on the ground, on the floor.

鋪 *P'u*⁴. A shop, a workshop; *a store;* a stage of ten *li* on official roads.

店 *Tien*⁴. *A large shop;* a storing and forwarding office; an inn:—Note 17.

街 *Chie*¹. . . . . . . A thoroughfare, a street.

買 *Mai*³. . . . . . . To buy, to purchase.

買賣 *Mai³ mai⁴*. . . . Business, trade:—Les. 50.

少 *Shao*³. *Little*, not much; few; a little while; seldom; slightly; to owe; wanting. Also *shao*⁴.

擱 *Kê*¹. *To lay on, or down;* to put or place carefully; to hinder; to run aground.

碎 *Swei*⁴. To break to pieces; a piece; *fragments, bits.*

零碎 *Ling² swei⁴*. Fragments, broken pieces; *odds and ends*, remnants.

窗 *Ch'wang*¹. . . . . . . *A window;* a window sash.

臺 *T'ai*². A turret; a fort; *a stand;* a platform, a pulpit; a title of respect to officers and others.

窗臺. A window-sill.

要飯 *Yao⁴ fan⁴*. To ask for food from door to door, to beg:—Note 23.

做 *Tsou*⁴, *tsoa*⁴. To do, to act, to perform. Often interchanged with 作.

上有好些〔老些〕書。○他[17]父親的鋪子〔店〕、在大街上。○東[18]街上的買賣不少。○在[19]學堂裏、有二十多個學生。○在[20]城裏有一百多學房〔學堂〕。○這[21]些書可以擱在桌子上。○這[22]些零碎東西、你可以擱在窗臺上。○有[23]一個老頭子、在門外要飯。○院[24]子裏的花、實在好看。○他[25]們兩個在書房裏看書。○李[26]老爺的兒子、在西門外做買賣。

17 His father's shop is on the great street.
18 There is no little business on the east street.
19 There are over twenty pupils in the school-room.
20 There are over one hundred schools in the city.
21 You may put these books on the table.
22 These odds and ends you may put on the window-sill.
23 There is an old man outside the gate begging.
24 The flowers in the yard are truly beautiful.
25 They two are in the school-room studying.
26 Mr. Li's son is doing business outside the west gate.

NOTES.

2 在 is here used as a verb meaning *to be alive.* This is the common way of saying that any one is still alive, and 不在 of saying that he is dead.

5 I have translated this sentence as referring to present time; but for any thing that appears in the words themselves, it might with equal propriety be rendered, *they were lying on the bed.* The correct sense must be gathered from the connection. The want of tense endings in Chinese leaves a great deal of the language in this uncertain state.

6 在樓底下 Lit., *at the loft underneath.* The 底 might be omitted, and in some sections generally is omitted. 人 at the close of this sentence is equivalent to *one.* It is constantly used in this indefinite sense for, *any one, any body,* etc. :—Les. 52.

9 在上 *At the above.* The absence of a noun leaves 上 as the noun. The same is true of 下 in the next clause. This form of expression is often used to call heaven and earth (embracing the Chinese idea of God) to witness to the sincerity of the speaker.

10 Both 打 and 敲 are used of knocking at the door. In some places one is more used, and in other places the other. 敲 is the more proper and elegant of the two words. 叫門, *to call the gate,* is also largely used in the same sense. The book term is 叩門 *k'ou⁴ mên²*.

12 Might also be translated *my eldest daughter,* etc.: which is correct, would depend on who is the speaker. In some places 棉 is omitted, and 紡花 used alone.

14 Note the difference between 底下 (6) and 地下.

17 In the South 店 is used for *shop* instead of 鋪子, and an inn is called 客棧 *k'ê⁴ chan⁴* or 客寓 *k'ê⁴ yü⁴*.

23 要飯 is commonly used for begging, though 討飯 *t'ao³ fan⁴* is more accurate.

LESSON VII.

SIGN OF THE PAST TENSE.

了 is added to verbs to denote that the action is complete, and hence past. In speaking it is generally shortened into *la*³. It is also used as an auxiliary verb :—Les. 88.

已經 denotes past time, but always with a reference to the present, or to some given past or future time; thus answering to both the perfect and pluperfect tenses. It is stronger, however, than *have* and *had,* and for this reason *already* is frequently added in translating. 已經 immediately precedes the verb, except as separated by the negative particle. When it precedes a verb 了 always follows, though 了 is often used without a preceding 已經.

The future perfect form is too complicated for this lesson.

第七課

張[1]先生的錢舖錢店、已經倒了黃了。○我[2]在街上、買了三斤棉花。○我[3]已經吃了飯。○大[4]老爺已經走了。○他[5]的事情、已經說明白了。○我[6]已經等了三天。○丁[7]先生的母親、已經死了。○他[8]在城裏、住了好些日子。○沒[9]有法子、事情已經壞了。○他[10]們的買賣做賠賒了。○張[11]老爺的錢、已經花淨了。○他[12]做了一年買賣、賺了尋了一百五十兩銀子。○做[13]完了活、你可以來告

Translation

1 Mr. Chang's bank is already bankrupt.
2 I bought three catties of cotton (or, cotton wool) on the street.
3 I have already eaten.
4 The Prefect has already gone.
5 His business is already satisfactorily settled.
6 I have already waited three days.
7 Mr. Ting's mother is already dead.
8 He lived in the city a long time.
9 There is no help for it, the business is already ruined.
10 They have done a losing business.
11 Mr. Chang's money is already all spent.
12 He did business one year and cleared one hundred and fifty taels.
13 When you have finished your work, come and tell me.

Vocabulary.

了 *Liao*³. *Fixed, concluded;* to bring to an end; to complete; intelligent:—See Sub., also Les. 88.

已 *I*³. Now, already, just:—See Sub. At the end of a clause,—no more, enough.

經 *Ching*¹. To pass through or by; *already, then:*—See Sub. To manage; laws, canons; classical books. Also *ching*⁴.

張 *Chang*¹. To extend; to increase; to proclaim; to boast, *a surname.* A classifier, Les. 42.

錢舖 *Ch'ien*² *p'u*⁴. A bank, a broker-shop.

錢店 *Ch'ien*² *tien*⁴. A bank, a broker-shop; Southern.

黃 *Hwang*². Yellow; the imperial color; blasted; *to fail in business.*

倒 *Tao*³. To fall over or down; *to fail in business,* to empty:—Les. 91. Also *tao*⁴.

斤 *Chin*¹. An axe; *a catty,*—equal to one and one-third English pounds.

走 *Tsou*³. To go; to walk; to run; to travel; to go away, to depart.

大老爺 *Ta*⁴ *lao*³ *yie*². A title of respect higher than 老爺:—Note 4.

丁 *Ting*¹. A full-grown man; an individual; a *surname.*

死 *Si*³. *To die;* dangerous, mortal; urgent, intense; firm, fixed; a closed passage; an auxiliary verb:—Les. 183.

壞 *Hwai*⁴. To spoil, to injure; to perish; *spoiled,* rotten; dilapidated.

賠 *P'ei*². To make up a deficiency, *to lose*; to confess a fault and make amends.

賒 *Shê*². To lose money in trade.

賺 *Chwan*⁴. To sell at a profit; to gain; to earn; to cheat.

尋 *Hsin*², *hsün*². To seek, to investigate; commonly, usually; *to gain,* to make money.

完 *Wan*². To finish; *finished,* completed; entirely:—Les. 101.

活 *Hwoă*². Living, lively; cheerful; to be alive; open; moveable; *work,* livelihood.

忘 *Wang*²˒⁴. *To forget;* to neglect.

訴我。○我[14]已經吃彀了。○這[15]個字我忘記了。○他[16]在鄉裏、住了一年。○這[17]一課、我們已經學熟了。○先[18]生已經放了學。○已[19]經過了時候、先生還沒來。○這[20]些話、我們已經學了兩天。○我[21]五點半鐘到了家。○他[22]已經寫了三點鐘的工夫、還沒寫完。○等[23]他來了、可以請他到客堂(客房)坐一會兒。○你[24]當小心那個火、不要燒了房子。○他[25]的孩子、已經不上學了。

14 I have already eaten enough.
15 I have forgotten this character.
16 He lived in the country a year.
17 This lesson we have already well learned.
18 The teacher has already dismissed school.
19 It is already past the time, and the teacher has not yet come.
20 We have already been learning these sentences for two days.
21 I reached home at five and a half o'clock.
22 He has already been writing three hours, and has not yet finished.
23 When he comes you may invite him into the parlor to sit a while.
24 You should be careful of that fire and not burn the house.
25 His boy has already quit school.

記 *Chi*⁴. *To remember;* to record, to note down; a history; a mark, a sign.

忘記 To forget.

鄉 *Hsiang*¹. A village; *the country;* a region; rude, rustic.

熟 *Shu*², *shou*². Ripe, mature; cooked, well cooked; *acquainted with;* intimate.

點 *Tien*³. A black spot, a speck; a dot, a comma; *an hour* by a foreign clock; a little, a particle; speckled; to punctuate; to erase; to nod; to light,—as a lamp; to kindle.

半 *Pan*⁴. To divide in two; a half.

鐘 *Chung*¹. A bell; a clock,—so called because it strikes.

到 *Tao*⁴. To arrive at, *to reach;* to go or come to:—Les. 76.

工 *Kung*¹. *Work;* skill; a workman; a job, a piece of work; a day's work.

夫 *Fu*¹. *To assist;* a husband; a man; a distinguished man; an exalted lady.

工夫 *Time spent in doing anything;* leisure; time; work; skill acquired by practice.

客 *K'ê*⁴ *A guest, a visitor;* a stranger; a passenger; a merchant; a dealer; a customer.

客堂 *K'ê*⁴ *t'ang*². A reception room, a guest room, *a parlor.*

客房 *K'ê*⁴ *fang*². A guest room, a parlor.

一會 *I*¹ *hwei*⁴. A short space of time, *a while;* presently, after a little.

當 *Tang*¹. What is suitable or just; *ought;* adequate to bear responsibility; to act as, to be; to meet; to occur; when, at the time of; as, then:—Les. 90. Also *tang*⁴.

心 *Hsin*¹. *The heart;* the mind; the will; affections, desires; the middle.

小心 *Hsiao*³ *hsin*¹. To be careful, cautious, prudent.

火 *Hwo*³. *Fire,* flame; excitement; anger; fever; inflammation.

燒 *Shao*¹. *To burn;* to kindle; to roast, to grill; hot, feverish.

上 *Shang*³. To go up, to ascend; to exalt; to hand up; the third tone. See *shang*⁴.

第八課

林¹先生來了嗎。○你²不認識（認得）我嗎。○火³爐裏還有火嗎。○你⁴的父母好嗎。○飯⁵還不熟嗎。○你⁶看我怕你嗎。○這⁷些銀子彀了嗎。○撒⁸謊（扯謊）還不算罪嗎。○你⁹不是張先生的兄弟嗎。○先¹⁰生吃了飯嗎、答已經吃了。○

Translation.

1 Has Mr. Lin come?
2 Do you not know (recognize) me?
3 Is there still fire in the stove?
4 Are your father and mother well?
5 Is the rice not yet cooked?
6 Do you think I am afraid of you?
7 Is this silver sufficient?
8 And is not lying to be considered a sin?
9 Are you not Mr. Chang's younger brother?
10 Have you eaten? Ans. I have already eaten.

Notes.

1 There is some uncertainty whether 黃 for "bankrupt" should not rather be written 荒 *hwang*¹ and read *hwang*². 倒 is the more widely used of the two forms.

4 The prefix 大 is not considered as properly belonging to a Hsien magistrate, though generally given to him. It is given of right to a Prefect and to sundry military officers. 大人 is given to a Tao T'ai and a Governor.

5 說明白了 means to discuss and agree upon a bargain, or a business arrangement of any kind:—See Les. 109.

7 Might with equal propriety be rendered, *has already died.*

9 The natural object of the verb here stands as its nominative, and by virtue of its position makes the verb passive. This is a very common idiom,—more common, in fact, than the regular passive with 被:—Les. 53. There are several other examples in this lesson.

11 花淨 Lit. *spent clean*; i.e., *all spent.*

13 完 is frequently added to verbs as an auxiliary to mark the completion of the action:—Les. 101.

15 This sentence might follow the English order, and read 我忘記了這個字, but is more thoroughly Chinese as it is.

19 The translation supplies "it is" and "and," illustrating how Chinese often does without such little words as these, so frequent and so useful in English.

20 話 commonly means *words*, but in this connection should be translated *sentences.*

LESSON VIII.

The Direct Interrogative Particle.

嗎 The sign of a direct question; i. e., a question that may be answered by yes or no. The Chinese do not indicate a direct question, as we do, by a rising inflection, but by the addition of this special word at the end of the interrogative clause. The character 麼, *moǎ*, is often written instead of 嗎, and some teachers will insist on always writing 麼, but incorrectly.*

麼 is joined to other particles (see Les. 17 and 36) to ask an *indirect* question, of which it is the proper sign. In speaking, both sounds (*ma* and *moǎ*) are heard, *ma* being the more frequent.

* Note.—嗎 formerly meant to revile, but is now entirely superseded by 罵, leaving 嗎 as the proper and distinctive sign of a direct question. Pedantic teachers object to it because it is a modern and colloquial character.

Vocabulary.

嗎 *Ma*¹. Direct interrogative particle:—See Sub.

林 *Lin*². A forest, a grove; *a surname.*

認 *Jên*⁴. *To know well;* to recognize; to acknowledge, to confess.

識 *Shï*⁴. To know; *to recognize;* to be versed in; knowledge.

認識 To know; to be acquainted with.

認得 To know, to recognize.

爐 *Lu*². Any vessel for holding fire; *a stove;* a furnace. A classifier:—Les. 140.

火爐 *Hwoǎ*³ *lu*². A stove.

怕 *P'a*⁴. *To fear*, to dread; lest, perhaps.

你[11]不會講這個字嗎。○已[12]經給了你、你還來要嗎。○你[13]還敢說不該我這個錢嗎。○從[14]北京來了信、你不知道(曉得)嗎。○已[15]經賠了不是、你還要告嗎。○你[16]的錢不彀、不好跟東家(對老板)借一點嗎。○你[17]念了四年的書、還不認識

11 Can you not explain this character?
12 Having given you, do you still come and ask [for more]?
13 Do you even dare to say that you do not owe me this money?
14 Do you not know that a letter has come from Peking?
15 I having apologized, do you still intend to bring suit?
16 If your money is insufficient, why not borrow a little of your employer?
17 Have you gone four years to school and yet do not know this character?

撒 *Sa*¹......To let loose; to let go. Also *sa*³.

扯 *Ch'ê*³. *To pull apart;* to tear; to drag or ....haul.

謊 *Hwang*³......Falsehood, *lies;* exaggeration.

撒謊 To tell lies, to lie.

扯謊 " " " " "

算 *Swan*⁴. To count, to reckon; to estimate, *to* ....*regard;* a calculation, a scheme.

罪 *Tswei*⁴. A crime, *a sin*, a fault; a violation ....of law or order; punishment; retribution; suffering.

兄 *Hsiung*¹. *An elder brother;* a senior, used ....after names as a term of respect.

弟 *Ti*⁴. *A younger brother;* a junior; a cousin. ......

兄弟 *A younger brother* or cousin:—Note 9.

答 *Ta*¹. *An answer;* to answer; to respond ......to; to recompense.

講 *Chiang*³. To converse; *to explain;* to dis- ....course, to preach; to discuss; to make a bargain.

敢 *Kan*³. *To dare, to venture;* presuming, bold. ....With 不, in polite phrase,—I can not, I would not presume.

從 *Ts'ung*². To follow; to comply with; *from;* ....by; through; whence.

北 *Pei*³...... The north, northern.

京 *Ching*¹. Great, exalted; *the capital*, the ....metropolis.

北京 The northern capital, Peking.

信 *Hsin*⁴. Sincerity; truthfulness, faith; to be- ...... lieve, to trust; *a letter;* a message, news; to accord with, to follow.

跟 *Kên*¹. The heel; to follow; to follow up an ...... inquiry; *to apply to.* In Pekingese, —with, together with, and.

板 *Pan*³. A board or plank; an engraved block; ...... a bastinado; fixed, obstinate.

老板 *Lao*³ *pan*³. The head of a shop or busi- .... ness. A Southern word.

東家 *Tung*¹ *chia*¹. The master of a household; ....*employer;* the responsible or moneyed partner of a firm:—Note 16.

借 *Chie*⁴. To lend; *to borrow;* to avail of, by; ...... supposing, for example.

念 *Nien*⁴. To reflect, to consider; *to chant, to* ...... *read aloud;* to memorize; thoughts.

打算 *Ta*³ *swan*⁴. To consider; to plan; *to ex-* .... *pect*, to intend.

飽 *Pao*³...... *Satiated*, full; satisfied.

眼 *Yien*³. The eye; a hole, an opening; a fault; ...... the centre. A classifier :—Les. 140.

見 *Chien*⁴. To perceive by the senses; *to see;* ...... to observe; to visit; to endure; an opinion; a mental view:—Les. 102 and 122.

親眼 *Ch'in*¹ *yien*³......With one's own eyes.

看見 *K'an*⁴ *chien*⁴...... To see; to perceive.

不好過 *Pu*⁴ *hao*³ *kwoă*⁴. Hard to make a living; .... *unwell*, ailing; sick.

疼 *T'êng*². To pain, *to ache;* to love intensely; ....to have a fondness for; to feel for.

識這個字嗎。○他[18]還没有走嗎、答 他打算明天走。○客[19]已經吃飽了嗎。○張[20]老爺不在家、你不曉得嗎。○他[21]没親眼看見、還敢這樣說嗎。○先[22]生不大好好過嗎。答 是、我的頭疼。

18 Has he not yet gone? Ans. He proposes to go to-morrow.
19 Have the guests already finished eating (eaten to the full)?
20 Do you not know that Mr. Chang is not at home?
21 If he had not seen with his own eyes, would he venture to speak thus?
22 Are you not well? Ans. No, my head aches.

NOTES.

6 看 here means, *to think.* Seeing, being the chief means of acquiring knowledge and forming judgment, is put figuratively for the act of judging.

7 The plural form is used in Chinese because the silver consists of irregular pieces which are to be weighed.

8 Lying is not practically regarded by the Chinese as an offence against morals, though it is so in theory. The term 罪 comes very far short of expressing the Christian idea of sin. 還 is only approximately translated by *and.* It expresses surprise, and adds emphasis to the question.

9 兄弟 means *younger brother,* though 兄 alone means *elder brother,* and 弟 alone means *younger brother.* There is no accounting for this anomalous combination. When the order is inverted; viz., 弟兄, the phrase means *brothers,* including both older and younger.

13 還, if read without special emphasis, is intensive, and may be rendered *even.* If, however, it be emphasized, it assumes its proper meaning, and must be rendered, *still.* "Do you *still* dare to say," etc.

16 The conditional idea is here implied, as is often done in Chinese. It is indicated, partly in the order of the sentence, and partly by the emphasis given in speaking. (21) is similar. In ancient times the eastern side of the house, or court, was occupied by the proprietor, or host, the west being given to guests; hence the meaning of 東家. For this use of 家 see Les. 72.

20 The first clause is spoken affirmatively, and the second interrogatively. *Mr. Chang is not at home; don't you know?*

22 不大好 *not very well.* 大 after a negative is often thus used as an intensive, equal to *very.* 不好過 Lit., *not passing over well;* i.e., *not in good health.* It is Southern Mandarin, and somewhat stronger than 不大好. Notice how the English idiom requires the answer to be "no," while the Chinese makes it "yes."

LESSON IX.

HERE AND THERE.

這裡 Here, in this place.
這兒 " " " "
The first is the proper and regular form, and should always be used in public discourse, or when dignity is important. The second is the short colloquial form. It is much more used in Northern than in Central and Southern Mandarin. It is not heard at all in Nanking.

那裡 There, in that place.
那兒 " " " "
These two forms correspond to those above, and the same remarks apply.

此地 In this place, here. Used chiefly in Southern Mandarin, where it largely supersedes 這裡.

VOCABULARY.

此 *Ts'i*[3]. .... This, here; now:—Les. 63.

成 *Ch'êng*[2]. To finish; to become; to fulfil one's part; to terminate; complete; *the results;* the quality of a thing:—Les. 101.

年成 *Nien*[2] *ch'êng*[2]. The harvest, the crops.

說話 *Shwoa*[1] *hwa*[4]. To talk, to speak, to converse.

閒 *Hsien*[2]. Repose, leisure; at ease, unoccupied; *idle,* indolent; vacant.

閒話 *Hsien*[2] *hwa*[4]. *Chit chat;* gossip; conversation.

冷 *Lêng*[3]. *Cold,* chilly; indifferent; offended; lonesome; unusual.

熱 *Jê*[4]. Hot; to heat; feverish; ardent, *interested;* zealous.

第九課

請[1]先生在這裏坐。○這[2]裏沒有你的事情。○你[3]那兒裏的年成好嗎。○[4]這兒此地是個規矩地方。○那[5]裏沒有火爐。○他[6]不在這裏住。○你[7]們不要在這裏說話。○在[8]那兒不好說閒話。○這[9]裏熱、那裏冷。○這[10]裏熱鬧鬧熱、那裏凊靜。○你[11]這些傢伙傢使、可以放在這裏。○[12]這裏此地的木匠、沒有好手藝。○這[13]裏是住家、不是講書堂。○過[14]晌午、先生可以在這裏寫字。○這[15]裏的買賣

TRANSLATION.

1 Will you please sit here?
2 There's nothing here that concerns you.
3 Is it a good year with you?
4 This is an orderly place.
5 There is no stove there.
6 He does not live here.
7 You must not talk here.
8 It's not proper to gossip there.
9 It is hot here and cold there.
10 It is bustling here and quiet there.
11 These tools of yours you may put here.
12 The carpenters of this place are not skillful.
13 This is a dwelling house; not a chapel (or, a preaching hall).
14 You may write here this afternoon.
15 The business here is large; there, it is small.

鬧 *Nao*⁴. *Bustle*, tumult; to scold, to rail, to make a disturbance.

熱鬧 Bustling, busy; interesting.

鬧熱 The same. Southern.

凊 *Ch'ing*¹. *Pure, clear;* incorruptible; clear,—as a tone; settled,—as an account.

靜 *Ching*⁴. *Still, quiet;* mild, peaceable; silent; pure; impassable.

凊靜 Quiet, undisturbed.

傢 *Chia*¹. Tools, furniture.

伙 *Hwoă*³. Goods, furniture.

傢伙 Household furniture; *utensils;* tools; a bold, reckless fellow.

傢使 *Chia*¹ *shï*³. *Utensils;* tools. Local in Shantung.

木 *Mu*⁴. Wood; wooden.

匠 *Chiang*⁴. *A mechanic*, an artisan.

木匠 A carpenter; a joiner.

手 *Shou*³. The arm; *the hand;* a hand, a person; skill; actions, doings.

藝 *I*⁴. *Skill in doing;* expert; a craft, an art; an accomplishment.

手藝 Manual skill, handicraft, workmanship.

住家 *Chu*⁴ *chia*¹. *A dwelling house;* to be at home.

講書堂 *Chiang*³ *shu*¹ *t'ang*². A preaching place, a chapel, a church.

過晌 *Kwoă*⁴ *shang*³. The afternoon.

過午 *Kwoă*⁴ *wu*³. The afternoon.

情理 *Ch'ing*² *li*³. Reason; right; common sense:—Note 17.

纔 *Ts'ai*². Near in time; just, just now; *and then;* thereupon:—Les. 65.

害 *Hai*⁴. To injure, to hurt; to damage; *fearful* of; very, extremely.

害怕 *Hai*⁴ *p'a*⁴. *To fear;* to be frightened.

藏 *Ts'ang*². *To hide*, to conceal; to store up; stores. Also *tsang*⁴.

躲 *Toă*³. *To conceal oneself*, to hide; to slip away, to escape.

好說 *Hao*³ *shwoă*¹. *Easy to speak;* proper, grammatical. In answer to a compliment,—You flatter me.

强 *Ch'iang*². Violent, headstrong; firm; relying on force; sturdy; an excess, a remainder; *better than*, superior to:—Les. 58. Also *ch'iang*³, *chiang*⁴, and *chiang*¹.

大、那裏的買賣小。○木16匠的傢伙、不在這裏。○17這兒(此地)的人、實在不說(講)情理。○他18在這裏、坐了半天纔走了。○他19害了怕、這裏兒藏、那裏兒躲。○這20裏的話、比那裏的話好說。○你21們那裏的規矩、比我們這裏好強。○木22匠師傅(司務)在那裏嗎、答我没看見。○他23是在這裏、是在那裏、我一點兒不曉得。○我24已經找徧了、實在不知道他放在那裏。

16 The carpenter's tools are not here.

17 The people here are very unreasonable.

18 He sat here half a day before he left.

19 He was afraid and hid himself here and there.

20 The language here is easier to speak than the language there.

21 Your customs there are better than ours here.

22 Is the carpenter there? Ans. I have not seen him.

23 Whether he is here or whether he is there I have not the least idea.

24 I have already searched everywhere; I have really no idea where he put it.

傅 *Fu*^{4}. To superintend; a tutor, a teacher; a skilled workman; to lay on,—as colors.

司 *Sï*^{1}. To control, to preside over.

務 *Wu*^{4}. To bend the mind to, to strive; *business*, duty; must, by all means.

師傅 *Shï*^{1} *fu*^{4}. A teacher, an instructor; one who has pupils or apprentices; a *master workman*, a head-man.

司務 *Sï*^{1} *wu*^{4}. Same as preceding, but used only in the South.

一點兒 *I*^{1} *tien*^{3} *ĕr*^{2}. Read *i*^{2} *tier*^{3}. A very little; in the least.

找 *Chao*^{3}. To supply what is deficient; *to look for*, to seek, to search for; to accuse, to hold responsible.

徧 *Pien*^{4}. *Everywhere;* the whole; entire; to pervade.

NOTES.

1 This sentence would be equally good if written 請先生坐在這裏.

3 Lit., *Is you there's year good?* The Chinese takes the liberty of putting "there" in the possessive case.

4 規矩 is properly a noun, but is here used as an adjective. It is a very common thing for Chinese words and phrases to be used as several parts of speech. Such transitions must not surprise the learner.

11 A 的 is implied after 你. This idomatic form gives almost exactly the same force as the form of the translation. 傢伙 is used both in the North and South:—See 傢什. 傢使 is chiefly used in Shantung.

12 好 drops out of the translation. It might be preserved by turning the sentence about thus: *The skill of the carpenters of this place is not good.*

13 住家, *a live-home;* i.e., *a private residence.* This sentence would be appropriately used to visitors or strangers who were intruding into private rooms or buildings where it was not convenient to have them go, a chapel being understood to be a public place where any one may go.

14 過午 is Southern and 過晌 Northern, though either would probably be understood in most places. 過晌午 is also heard in some places, but the Nanking teacher rejects all these and insists on 中飯後.

17 In this connection 講 is more widely used than 說. 情理, the affections and the reason—the humane sentiments combined with the principles of abstract right, forming the ideal "ought."

18 "Half a day" is here, as often, used as an exaggeration, meaning a considerable time, or at least more time than befitted the circumstances. The turn of the sentence here requires 纔, *then*, to be translated *before.*

19 了 is elegantly inserted between the parts of 害怕 instead of coming after it. "Hid himself here and there;" lit., *hid here and skulked there.*

21 There ought of right to be a 的 after 這裏 and before 强, and it would often be so said. The fact that it *can* be omitted and the incongruity not be noted by a Chinese teacher, shows that no proper analysis is applied to their spoken language.

22 師傅 means properly a master or teacher in any art or profession. It is used throughout the North. Teachers along the *Yangtse* reject it, however, and substitute 司務, which would be wholly inadmissible in the North.

第十課

請[1]先生起來。○賊[2]偷了我的衣裳去了。○張[3]先生的牲口、跑去了。○可[4]以喊叫兩個人來擡轎轎子。○這[5]些傢傢伙使可以撤去。○他[6]已經搬去了。○他[7]的衣裳箱子、已經搬來了。○桌[8]子上有土灰、可以撢去。○大[9]狗搶奪了了小狗的食去。○這[10]三個箱子、還沒有發去嗎。○他[11]沒有力氣、不能起來。○有[12]一個人、從西院子過來。○我[13]的兄弟、帶了一百兩銀子去。○他[14]的錢已

TRANSLATION.

1 Will you please get up? (or, Will the gentleman please rise?)
2 A thief stole away my clothes.
3 Mr. Chang's animal ran away, (or, has run away.)
4 You may call two men to carry the chair.
5 You may take away these dishes.
6 He has already moved away.
7 His box of clothing has already been brought.
8 There is dust on the table, brush it off.
9 The big dog snatched away the little dog's food.
10 Have these three boxes not yet been forwarded?
11 He has no strength, he can not get up.
12 A man came over from the west court-yard.
13 My younger brother took with him a hundred taels of silver.
14 He has already drawn his money.

LESSON X.

THE AUXILIARY VERBS 來 AND 去.

There is in Chinese a large class of auxiliary verbs which are joined to other verbs to qualify or limit their meaning. Of these the simplest are 來 to come, and 去 to go. They are auxiliary verbs of direction, and may be joined to any verb containing the idea of motion.

VOCABULARY.

起 *Ch'i*³. To rise, *to stand up;* to begin; to raise up; to open out the meaning; the origin:—Les. 29 and 126.

賊 *Tsei*², *tsê*². *A thief*, a robber, a bandit; an insurgent, a rebel.

偷 *T'ou*¹. *To steal*, to pilfer; underhand, secret.

牲 *Shêng*¹. Sacrificial animals,—the horse, ox, lamb, cock, dog and hog.

牲口 *Shêng*¹ *k'ou*³. Domestic animals, especially work animals,—the horse, cow, mule and donkey.

跑 *P'ao*³. To run, to gallop; *to run off*, to flee; to walk; to travel.

喊 *Han*³, *hsien*³. *To call*, to call to; to vociferate, to halloo.

擡 or **抬** *T'ai*². *To carry between two persons;* to lift; to elevate; to praise.

轎 *Chiao*⁴. A sedan chair, a palanquin.

撤 *Ch'ê*⁴. *To remove from;* to recall; to set aside.

搬 *Pan*¹. To remove; *to transport;* to move; to bandy, to discuss.

箱 *Hsiang*¹. A box; *a trunk;* a casket.

灰 *Hwei*¹. Ashes; soot; *dust;* lime; ash-colored; disheartened.

土 *T'u*³. Earth, soil, clods; *dust;* territory, lands; native; local.

撢 *Tan*³. *To brush off with a duster*, to dust; a feather duster.

狗 *Kou*³. *A dog;* petty, contemptible; vile.

經支去了。○請[15]王先生、明天帶捎我的綿衣裳來。○說[16]來說去、還是那些話。○他[17]們四個人、擡轎去接王大人。○生[81]子已經跑去告訴他母親了。○這[19]些東西、你還沒送去嗎。○這[20]是兩個錯字、可以點去。○你[21]借了我的筆去、明天要送來。○丁[22]先生的兒子、從關東寄捎了了信來。○他[23]借了我的大襖去、當了五百錢。○王[24]老三的兒子、在這裏跑來跑去、實在討厭。

15 Will Mr. Wang please bring along my wadded clothes to-morrow?

16 He talked and talked, but it was still the same thing over and over.

17 They four went as chair-bearers to meet General Wang.

18 Shêng-tsï has (or, had) already run off to tell his mother.

19 Have you not yet taken these things [to their destination]?

20 These are two erroneous characters; you may strike them out.

21 The pen which you borrowed of me you must return to-morrow.

22 Mr. Ting's son has sent a letter from Manchuria.

23 He borrowed my overcoat and pawned it for five hundred cash.

24 Wang the Third's boy is here running back and forth most provokingly.

奪 *Toa*². To take by force, *to snatch;* to carry off; to criticise.

搶 *Ch'iang*³. To rob by violence; *to snatch;* to dispute and struggle for.

食 *Shï*². To eat; *food;* a meal; bait; to take back one's word, to retract.

發 *Fa*¹. To send forth; *to dispatch;* to prosper; to grow rich; to ferment; to show forth; to issue, to pay out money:—Les. 73.

帶 *Tai*⁴. A sash, a girdle, a garter; a bandage; a tape; a zone; connected with; *to take along with,* to conduct:—Les. 110.

支 *Chï*¹. A branch, to pay out; *to draw money;* to diverge; to withstand.

捎 *Shao*¹. To select; to take along with; *to send by another:*—Note. 15.

綿 *Mien*². *Soft, cottony;* wadded; floss; drawn out as a thread; enduring; connected.

綿衣裳 *Mien*² *i*¹ *shang*¹. Wadded garments.

王 *Wang*². A king, a ruler; royal; *a surname.* Also *wang*⁴.

接 *Chie*¹. *To receive;* to succeed to, to take; to unite; to join on; to graft.

送 *Sung*⁴. To accompany, to see a guest to the door; to send; *to go on purpose to take;* to make a present; to give as a free gift.

關 *Kwan*¹. To shut,—as a gate; to bar; a custom house or *barrier;* a suburb; to belong to, to concern; consequences, results.

關東 *Kwan*¹ *tung*¹. East of the **山海關**, or end of the great wall on the Gulf of Pechili, Manchuria.

寄 *Chi*⁴. To lodge, to transfer; to entrust to, *to send a letter or message.*

襖 *Ao*³. An outer garment, a robe, a coat.

當 *Tang*⁴. *To pawn,* to pledge; to consider or regard as; instead of, for, as; suitable, proper:—Les. 90. See *tang*¹.

討 *T'ao*³. To manage; to search; to ask for, to beg; to bring upon; *to provoke.*

厭 *Yien*⁴. Satiated; distasteful, hateful; to dislike, to loathe.

討厭 Hateful, *disagreeable,* provoking.

第十一課

拿[1]一杯水來。○拿[2]一點柴伙來生火。○你[3]去拿個燈來。○拿[4]手巾擦去（揩去）眼淚。○他[5]盡淨拿實話哄人。○紙[6]没有了、可以拿錢去○買。○拿[7]自來火（取燈）（洋火）來點燈。○拿[8]熱水還洗不乾淨嗎。○可[9]以拿我的片子去請他。○没[10]有座座

TRANSLATION.

1 Bring a cup (or, glass) of water.
2 Bring a little wood and kindle the fire.
3 You go and bring a lamp.
4 Take your handkerchief and brush away the tears.
5 He just deceives people by means of the truth.
6 The paper is all used up: you may take [some] cash and go and buy [more].
7 Bring a match and light the lamp.
8 Can you not wash clean, even with warm water?
9 You may take my card and go and invite him.

NOTES.

4 The translation fails to convey fully the direction, or command, implied in the Chinese. The use of 叫 implies that there are professional chair-bearers within "call." Where there are none such, the term 找 *chao*³, *to seek*, would most likely be used.

9 食 food, is used in Mandarin only in certain phrases.

10 In the South 隻 *chi*¹ is generally used as the classifier of "boxes."

15 捎 means, *to bring, take or send along with*, the implication being that the purpose of going is aside from the matter in question. It is not used in Southern Mandarin, where 帶 takes its place, although 帶 only serves to replace it in part.

16 說來說去 is a highly idiomatic expression, meaning to repeat over and over again, or to talk around a thing without coming to the point. There is nothing in the sentence to indicate whether the time is past or present; whether it should be translated in the third person or in the second. It defies all attempts at a literal translation.

17 When an official in travelling approaches a city over which he has jurisdiction, etiquette requires that officials of a lower rank go outside of the city to a greater or less distance to "receive" him. A military officer entitled to be addressed as 大人 would generally be of rank corresponding to that of Brigadier General.

19 Note how the object is here placed first.

21 This sentence *implies* a relative clause, without formally expressing it. See Les. 46.

22 Here 帶 will not replace 捎, and 寄 is somewhat bookish.

23 It is a common practice in China to borrow clothing, or other articles, for the purpose of "making a raise" by pawning them.

24 The sons of a family are numbered according to their ages, and are frequently designated by these numbers added to the family name, either with or without an intervening 老. The eldest, however, is not called 王一 or 王老一, but 王大 or 王老大. The use of 老 does not indicate that the person in question is old, but simply that in age he is the third. A child in arms may be so called. Not only are the sons of one man thus numbered, but the sons of brothers, living together, are all counted as own brothers and numbered in the order of their ages.

LESSON XI.

THE INSTRUMENTAL VERB 拏.

拏 or 拿 *to take, to bring*, is much used as an instrumental verb. It nearly always takes after it either 來 or 去. It is sometimes rendered as a verb, but is often best rendered by an instrumental preposition. The frequent use of instrumental verbs, of which there are a number, is a characteristic feature of Chinese construction. See Les. 28, 54 and 145.

VOCABULARY.

拿 *Na*². To lay hold of, to seize; to arrest; *to take; to bring*:—See Sub.

拏 *Na*². Same as 拿. The two forms are used indiscriminately.

杯 *Pei*¹. A cup; a goblet; *a tumbler.*

水 *Shwei*³. *Water;* a fluid; a stream; clear limpid; pliant.

柴 *Ch'ai*². Brush; *firewood;* fuel.

柴伙 *Ch'ai*² *hwoă*³. Firewood; fuel.

生火 *Shêng*¹ *hwoă*³. To light or kindle a fire.

位兒、可以去拿椅子來。○
[11]你拿我的東西去送人、
還有這個理嗎。○[12]那牆
上有灰、可以拿笤箒來
掃去。○[13]拿鉛筆寫字、還
能擦去。○[14]拿手打他、還
不行嗎。○[15]到八點鐘、你
可以拿燈籠去接我。○
[16]他拿我的話、不當話。○

10 There are no seats: go and bring some chairs.
11 Is it reasonable for you to take my things to make presents to other people?
12 There is dust on that wall, bring a broom and sweep it off.
13 If you write with a lead pencil, you can rub it out.
14 Will it not answer to strike him with your hand?
15 At eight o'clock you may bring a lantern to meet me.
16 He paid no attention to what I said.

燈 *Têng*¹. . . . . *A lamp;* a lantern.

巾 *Chin*¹. *A napkin;* a neckcloth; a cap or . . . . turban.

手巾 *Shou*³ *chin*¹. *A handkerchief;* a towel; a . . . . napkin.

擦 *Ts'a*¹. To scatter; to brush; *to wipe;* to . . . . rub; to scour.

揩 *Ch'ie*¹. *To brush away,* to wipe lightly with . . . . the hand. In Shantung read *ts'ai*¹.

淚 *Lei*⁴. . . . . . . *Tears;* to weep.

眼淚 *Yien*³ *lei*⁴. . . . . . . Tears.

盡 *Ching*⁴. . . . Entirely, wholly; just. Also *chin*⁴.

哄 *Hung*³. The hum of a crowd; to cozen, *to* . . . . *deceive;* to coax, to soothe.

紙 *Chï*³. . . . . . . *Paper,* stationery; a document.

取 *Ch'ü*³. To lay hold of; *to take,* to bring, to . . . . exact; to select.

洋 *Yang*². . . . . The ocean; *foreign;* vast, wide.

自 *Tsï*⁴. From, commencing at; *self,* myself; . . . . . . personally:—Les. 21.

取燈 *Ch'ü*³ *têng*¹. . . . . . . Matches:—Note 7.

洋火 *Yang*² *hwoă*³. . . . . . . Matches.

自來火 *Tsï*² *lai*² *hwoă*³. . . . . . . Matches.

洗 *Hsi*³. . . . . . . *To wash;* to purify; to rinse.

片 *P'ien*⁴. A leaf, a flake; a strip; *a card;* a . . . . section. A classifier:—Les. 125.

座 *Tsoă*⁴. *A seat,* a place to sit; a divan. A . . . . classifier:—Les. 100.

位 *Wei*⁴. A seat, a throne; position, dignity; . . . . proper. A classifier:—Les. 27.

座位 A seat, *a place to sit;* an honorable seat; dignity.

牆 *Ch'iang*². . . . . . A wall of stone, brick or mud.

笤 *T'iao*². . . . . A coarse broom.

箒 or 帚 *Chou*³. . . . . . A broom.

笤箒 A corn broom.

掃 *Sao*³. *To sweep,* to brush; to clean up; to clear off, to rid. Also *sao*⁴.

鉛 *Ch'ien*¹. . . . . . . *Lead;* leaden.

鉛筆 *Ch'ien*¹ *pi*³. . . . . A lead pencil.

行 *Hsing*². To go, to walk; to act, to do; to . . . . prevail; to be customary; to serve as, *to answer.* Also *hsing*⁴, and *hang*².

籠 *Lung*². *A cage;* an open basket; to cover; . . . . to entrap.

燈籠 *Têng*¹ *lung*². . . . . . . A lantern.

鞭 *Pien*¹. *A whip;* a lash, a cut or stroke of . . . . a whip; to flog.

小人 *Hsiao*³ *jên*². *The mean man,* a depraved . . . . and contemptible fellow,—a classical term; a boy, a child.

作 *Tsoă*⁴. *To act, to do;* to become; to behave; . . . . to make; to stimulate; work. Also *tsoă*¹ and *tsu*³.

下作人 *Hsia*⁴ *tsoă*⁴ *jên*². A worthless fellow; . . . . a blackguard.

貨 *Hwoă*⁴. . . . . . . *Goods;* merchandize; stock.

常 *Ch'ang*². Constant, ordinary; ever, always; . . . . *habitually;* a rule, a principle.

這[17]個牲口不走、可以拿鞭子打他。○你[18]上書房去拿我的帽子來。○我[19]看你淨盡拿不是當理說。○你[20]不好拿下作人當拿小人來比我。○李[21]老三拿四千八百兩銀子來買貨。○他[22]常拿中國的貨、當外國貨賣。○林[23]師傅、你不要拿我的傢伙傢使、做你的活。

17 This animal will not go; you should whip him up.

18 Go to the school-room and bring my hat.

19 In my opinion you are just putting wrong for right.

20 You must not take me to be a mean fellow.

21 Li the Third brought four thousand eight hundred taels of silver to buy goods.

22 He constantly sells native goods for foreign goods.

23 Mr. Lin, you must not take my tools to do your work.

NOTES.

1 In this first sentence 拿 is a principal verb. So also in the third.

4 We might with equal propriety translate, "Take *a* handkerchief and wipe away *your* tears." The Chinese could readily express the "your" by inserting 你的, but they would rarely do so except for the sake of special emphasis. 擦, *to wipe, to scour*, is not often used of tears, the more common word being 揩, *to brush, or wipe away*, and which in Shantung is read *ts'ai*[1] and in Nanking *k'ai*[1].

5 "Just" is only an approximate rendering of 淨 or 盡, which is much used, as here, with the general sense of *entirely, wholly*, etc. The 盡 suits the meaning best, and is preferred at Nanking, where also its ordinary reading is correct. The idea in the sentence is, that the speaker creates an impression in advance, which is contrary to the facts, and then states the facts in such a way that they are disbelieved.

6 The 人 at the close is used indefinitely :—Les. 52.

7 取燈 is the literary name for matches, 自來火 is the commercial name, and 洋火 the name most commonly used by the people. Besides these names, matches are in some places called 觸燈, ts'u[3] têng[1], *strike lamps*.

9 A card in the hand of a messenger is the proof that he is authorized to speak for the party whose card he bears.

10 The form of the sentence implies that more than one chair was wanted; hence, "some" is supplied in the translation.

11 人 is here used in contrast with 我, and hence means *other people*, or *another man*. 還 is used intensively.

13 The subjunctive idea is implied rather than expressed. The sentence might perhaps with equal propriety be rendered, *Writing done with a lead pencil may be rubbed out.*

15 拿燈籠去接我. *We* should certainly say "come" rather than go. The Chinese in such cases always speak from the standpoint of the person addressed.

16 Lit., *He took my words not as words*; i.e., *disregarded what I said*. For this and similar uses of 當, see Les. 90.

20 Lit., *You ought not to take a mean man to measure me*; i.e., you should not liken me to a mean man. 好 and 當 do not convey quite the same meaning; the former refers to propriety, the latter to duty.

LESSON XII.

THE COMMON CONNECTIVES.

和 With, together with, and. The Chinese language has no equivalent for "and." This word 和 is made to do duty for it, and foreigners are generally inclined to use it too much. The Chinese very often allow mere juxtaposition to suggest or imply the idea we convey by "and."

也 In *Wên-li* (文理 the literary style) a final particle marking the completion of the idea. In Mandarin it means, *also, likewise*. Before 是 it serves to strengthen the idea, but is not generally translatable :—See 17. Before 不 it implies a doubt, or alternative, which is sometimes, though not always, equal to *whether*. When used twice in succession the first is untranslated and the second rendered *and also*.

又 Again; moreover; still. Followed by 不 it is disjunctive.

再 Again, a second time; henceforth.

This lesson only introduces the common uses of these words, without attempting to illustrate them fully. There are also a number of other words of the same class :—See Les. 110.

第二十課

我[1]和他不合式。○不[2]可和人打仗打架。○我[3]已經再三和他說了。○你[4]說這話、也有情理。○我[5]和他沒有來往。○他[6]不還錢、又不見面。○我[7]和你兩個一路去不好嗎。○我[8]的父親在家裏、和客說話。○他[9]嘴裏是一樣、心裏又是一樣。○善[10]人和惡人、天生是仇敵。○丁[11]百萬又和他兄弟打架。○拿[12]爐灰擦、也不能擦乾淨。

Translation.

1 He and I are not on good terms.
2 You must not fight with people.
3 I have already spoken to him repeatedly.
4 There is some reason in what you say.
5 I have no intercourse with him.
6 He will not pay me, nor even see me.
7 Wouldn't it be well for us to go together?
8 My father is at home talking with the guests.
9 In his mouth is one thing, in his heart another.
10 The good and evil are by nature enemies.
11 Ting Pê Wan has had another quarrel with his younger brother.
12 It cannot be scoured clean, even with ashes.

和 *Hê*², *hwoă*². Harmony, agreement; to be at peace; to mix; to unite; *with*, etc.:—see Sub.

也 *Yie*³. Also, and, likewise:—see Sub.

又 *Yiu*⁴. Also, and; furthermore; and then; again:—see Sub:—Les. 170.

再 *Tsai*⁴. Repeated, a second time; then; again; still, henceforth; in any case; certainly.

仗 *Chang*⁴. Weapons; to fight, to come to blows; a *fight;* to rely on, to trust.

架 *Chia*⁴. A frame, a stand, a rack; staging; to support; *to ward off.* A classifier:—Les. 125.

打仗 *Ta*³ *chang*⁴. To fight a battle; to fight; to come to blows:—Note 2.

打架 *Ta*³ *chia*⁴. To fight, to fisticuff.

再三 *Tsai*⁴ *san*¹. Again and again, repeatedly.

往 *Wang*³. *To go;* to go away, to go towards; past, gone; formerly.

來往 *Lai*² *wang*³. To and fro; intercourse, communication, dealings.

面 *Mien*⁴. The countenance, *the face;* the surface; the side; the front; honor; reputation:—Les. 26 and 125.

路 *Lu*⁴. *A road,* a path; a way of duty or action; a sort, a class.

一路 *I*¹ *lu*⁴. The whole way; a sort, or kind; the same kind:—Les. 106.

嘴 *Tswei*³. A bird's bill; *the lips;* the snout; a mouth; a spout; an aperture.

善 *Shan*⁴. *Good,* virtuous; goodness, merit; meet, docile; skilful, expert.

惡 *Ê*⁴. *Bad,* vicious; *evil;* ugly, vile; wickedness. Also *wu*⁴ and *ê*³.

天生 *T'ien*¹ *shêng*¹. By birth, by nature; *naturally,* originally.

仇 *Ch'ou*². *An enemy,* a competitor; hatred, enmity, revenge.

敵 *Ti*². An opponent, a competitor; *an enemy;* an equal; to withstand; to fight.

仇敵 *An enemy,* a foe; an antagonist.

萬 *Wan*⁴. A myriad; ten thousand; many; every one; all:—Les. 104.

爐灰 *Lu*² *hwei*¹. Ashes.

回 *Hwei*². To revert; to return; to repeat, to review; to repent; *a time,* a turn; a chapter in a novel; Mohammedan:—Les. 41 and 64.

緊 *Chin*³. To bind fast; *urgent, pressing;* instant; confined, tight.

13 我已經告訴你三回、你又忘記（忘）了嗎。
14 這個禮拜、你不去也不要緊。
15 他不是個好人、你再不可和他交往。
16 和他說話、該大一點聲兒（聲氣）。
17 你和他說到天亮、也是無益。
18 你的女人不講情理、你也不講情理嗎。
19 他的房子和地、也不過能值一千吊錢。
20 我已經告訴你不用再來、你又來了嗎。
21 他已經定

13 I have already told you three times: have you forgotten again?

14 It is no matter, even if you do not go this week.

15 He is not a good man: you must have no more dealings with him.

16 When you speak to him you should raise your voice a little.

17 Talk to him till daylight and it will be of no avail.

18 Are you going to talk unreasonably as well as your wife?

19 His house and land are not *worth* over one thousand strings of cash.

20 Have you come again, after I told you you need not come any more?

21 He has already made up his mind: it is useless to exhort him.

要緊 *Yao^4 chin^3*. . . . . . . Urgent; *important.*

交 *Chiao^1*. To join; to deliver up; to communicate with; to copulate; trade; *intercourse, friendship.*

交往 *Chiao^1 wang^3*. The intercourse of friendship; dealings.

聲 *Shêng^1*. A sound; *a voice;* accent, tone; reputation; to make known.

聲氣 *Shêng^1 ch'i^4*. . . . . Sound, *voice.*

亮 *Liang^4*. . . . . . *Clear,* bright; lustrous; open.

無 *Wu^2*. None; not having; *without,* wanting:—Les. 121.

益 *I^{2,4}*. To increase; more; to benefit; *beneficial;* advantageous; full:—Les. 123.

無益 Useless, unprofitable.

值 *Chï^2*. To meet, *to be worth;* to sell for; value, price; worth while.

定 *Ting^4*. To fix, to settle, *to decide;* really, certainly; at rest, fixed:—Les. 116.

主 *Chu^3*. A ruler, lord, *master;* a host; to rule; to show what is to be.

主意 *Chu^3 i^4*. Will, *determination;* to decide, to make up the mind.

勸 *Ch'üen^4*. *To exhort;* to admonish; to encourage; to advise.

同 *T'ung^2*. Together; all; united; *the same,* alike; identical; to unite, to harmonize; and, with, etc.:—Les. 110.

爹 *Tie^1*. Papa, daddy.

睛 *Ching^1*. . . . . . The pupil of the eye; the iris.

眼睛 *Yien^3 ching^1*. . . . . . The eye; the eyes.

耳 *Er^3*. . . . . . *The ear;* a handle, an ear.

朵 *Toă^3*. A cluster; *a lobe;* a head of flowers; a pendant. A classifier:—Les. 125.

耳朵 The ear lobe; the ear.

聾 *Lung^2*. . . . . . . Deaf; hard of hearing.

同窗 *T'ung^2 ch'wang^1*. . . . . . . A school-mate.

戚 *Ch'i^4*. To pity; mournful; related to, akin, *relatives,* kindred.

親戚 *Ch'in^1 ch'i^4*. Relatives not of the same surname.

NOTES.

2 **打架** is the more general and proper term for "to fight." **打仗** is, however, largely used in Shantung and elsewhere in this sense.

4 **也** is represented by *some* in the translation. It gives the idea of a concession on the part of the speaker that "you" *also* have some show of reason on *your* side; as if we should say, *Well, yes, what you say is reasonable.*

7 The addition of **兩個** is a common idiom. It conveys the idea that you and I are to be companions. The **一路**, which is the Southern form, does not give quite the same sense. With it the translation should be, *Wouldn't it be well for me to go along with you?*

10 **天生** *Heaven born;* i.e. *by nature.* The sentiment of the sentence is too strong for Chinese ethics.

了主意、勸他也是無益。○我[22]的兒子、和他的女兒同歲(同年)。○他[23]的老父(爹)親、眼睛也花了、耳朵也聾了。○告[24]訴他、和告訴我是一樣。○他[25]是我的同窗、又是我的親戚。○王[26]太太又來了、林師娘可以和他講一會道理。

22 My son and his daughter were born the same year.

23 His old father's eyes are dim and his ears deaf.

24 To tell her is the same as to tell me.

25 He is my schoolmate and also my relative.

26 Old Mrs. Wang has come again. You (Mrs. Lin) may preach to her a while.

---

13 In the South 記 is always used with 忘; in the North it is often, perhaps generally, omitted.

16 大 is here translated as a verb. We might, however, supply a verb and translate, *When you speak to him you should speak with a little louder (greater) voice.*

18 The first clause does not affirm what is said, but assumes it as a fact.

19 也 is lost in the translation. It was introduced into the sentence by something that preceded, and with which the assertion concerning the worth of the property is brought into comparison. Its force may be approximated by emphasizing the word worth. 能 would be omitted by many. Its presence implies a hypothesis :—" in case they were sold."

22 When speaking of age, 歲 is commonly used. In this sentence Nanking Mandarin prefers 年, which is only so used, however, when joined with 同. Notice that in this sentence the verb to be is omitted.

24 It is here assumed that the person referred to is a woman; hence 他 is rendered " her."

LESSON XIII.

COMMON FUTURE FORMS.

就 To approach; just now, forthwith.

必 Certainly; must, determined on.

要 To want, to need.

These three words are all used to express the future. The first expresses what will immediately or speedily follow;—often equal to, *just now*, *at once*, *forthwith*, etc.

The second expresses what will necessarily or certainly follow;—often equal to, *surely*, *must*.

The third expresses what will probably follow, or what the person intends should follow; generally rendered simply *will* or *shall*.

要 is often joined with 就 or 必, in which case it largely loses its own special signification.

These words do not always require "will" or "shall" in the translation. They are often equivalent to, *about to*, *going to*, etc. The future is often implied without any special word, by the mention of a future time; as, 我明天去, *I to-morrow go; i.e.*, I shall go to-morrow.

VOCABULARY.

就 *Chiu*^{4}. To approach; to accompany; to complete, to finish; to accommodate; then,—in time or in argument; *just now, at once:*—See Sub., also Les. 44.

必 *Pi*^{4}. A strong affirmative; *certainly will:*—See Sub. Must; necessarily; positively :—Les. 104 and 116.

教 *Chiao*^{1}. To instruct, *to teach ;* to command. Also *chiao*^{4}.

館 *Kwan*^{3}. An inn; a club house; an assembly hall; an exchange; a saloon, a restaurant; a school-room ; *a school.*

天父 *T'ien*^{1} *Fu*^{4}. Heavenly Father :—a Christian term.

保 *Pao*^{3}. *To protect;* to defend; to be surety for, to warrant; to keep safe; to insure.

護 *Hu*^{4}. *To protect;* to aid; to escort.

保護 *To protect*, to guard; to screen from.

本 *Pên*^{3}. The origin, root; source; cause; radical; the beginning; native; *capital*, principal; proper, own; this; the present; a volume; a document. A classifier :—Les. 42.

第十三課

等[1]一等我就去。○他[2]要到這裏來教學（教館）。○不[3]用害怕、天父必保護你。○李[4]先生一會兒就來。○他[5]的買賣、必要賠錢（貼本）。○不[6]多時候、木匠就要收工（散工）。○過[7]三四個禮拜、我要回家。○我[8]家去住七八天、就回來。○這[9]個事、我要先和你說明白。○你[10]可以先走、我隨後就到。○這[11]本三字經、不多日子就念會了。○等[12]兩三天、我必要去見他。○客[13]來了、我就必來告訴你。○還[14]沒寫完嗎、答 眼看（眼見）就寫完了。○用[15]電線

TRANSLATION.

1 Wait a little and I will go.
2 He intends to come here to teach school.
3 You need not fear: the Heavenly Father will certainly protect you.
4 Mr. Li will come presently.
5 His business will certainly be a losing one.
6 In a short time the carpenters will quit work.
7 After three or four weeks I shall return home.
8 I will go home and stay seven or eight days and then return.
9 I want to have a clear understanding with you about this matter beforehand.
10 You may go ahead: I will be there presently.
11 I can master this Trimetrical Classic in a few days.
12 Wait two or three days and I will certainly go and see him.
13 When the guests come I will certainly come and tell you.
14 Have you not yet finished writing? Ans. I shall finish in a moment.

三字經 *San*¹ *Tsï*⁴ *Ching*¹. The Trimetrical Classic, — a primer containing an epitome of Chinese philosophy and history.

散 *San*⁴. *To scatter;* to dissipate; to disperse, to separate. Also *san*³.

收 *Shou*¹. To receive; *to quit work;* to collect, to gather; to harvest; to wind up.

後 *Hou*⁴. *After, subsequent;* behind in place; then, next; in future; an heir.

隨後 *Swei*² *hou*⁴. Forthwith, presently, at once.

念會 *Nien*⁴ *hwei*⁴. To memorize, to master:—Note 11.

眼看 *Yien*³ *k'an*⁴. About to; *on the point of,* on the verge of; evidently.

眼見 *Yien*³ *chien*⁴. The same.

電 *Tien*⁴. Lightning; electricity.

電線 *Tien*⁴ *hsien*⁴. A telegraph wire or line; the telegraph.

立 *Li*⁴. To stand up; to set up; to institute, to establish; to appoint; to draw up a contract; *just now,* soon.

立時 *Li*⁴ *shï*². Instantly, at once, forthwith:—Les. 162.

傳 *Ch'wan*². To transmit; to hand down; to promulgate, *to propagate;* to summon, to subpœna. Also *chwan*⁴.

好事 *Hao*³ *shï*⁴. Virtuous deeds; deeds of benevolence or charity; alms.

存 *Ts'un*². To preserve; *to maintain;* to retain; to lay by, to keep; to file; to put on deposit; a balance to credit.

躭 or **耽** *Tan*¹. To obstruct; to prevent; *to hinder.*

誤 *Wu*⁴. To mistake, to be in error; *to hinder;* an unintentional wrong, a fault.

躭誤 To hinder, to prevent; *to spend in vain;* to miss an opportunity.

捎打信、立時就到了。○我[16]就要在這裏傳道理。○要[17]作好事、必要先存好心。○不[18]先說明白了、這個法子就不行。○這[19]個法子要怕不行。○這[20]個法子必不行。○不[21]要躭誤工夫、起來就走、○已[22]經換了轉了東北風、我看必要下雨。○我[23]劃出出上拼上一夜不睡、趕天亮也必送去。○不[24]用再去請他、等一會兒他就來。○我[25]看他的買賣、快要關門歇了。○王[26]心淸在安息日上、必要到講書堂。

15 A letter sent by telegraph is there at once.
16 It is my purpose to propagate religion here.
17 If you would act right you must first have a right heart.
18 If you do not first have a clear understanding this plan will not work.
19 This plan will probably not succeed.
20 This plan will certainly not succeed.
21 Do not waste time: go as soon as you get up.
22 The wind has changed to the north-east: I think it will certainly rain.
23 Even if I give up the whole night to it I will not fail to deliver it to you by day-light.
24 You need not go again to invite him: wait a little and he will come.
25 In my opinion his business will soon close up.
26 Wang Hsin Ch'ing will certainly be at church on the Sabbath.

轉 *Chwan*³. To turn over or about; to reverse; to turn over to; on the contrary, on the other hand; to comprehend; *to veer—as the wind:*—Les. 112. Also *chwan*⁴.

風 *Fêng*¹. *The wind;* air; manner, style; fashion, example; fame, reputation.

雨 *Yü*³. Rain; a shower.

劃 *Hwoă*¹. To split open; to rend; to give up, to risk, *to sacrifice:*—Note 23.

拼 *P'in*¹. To reject; to brush away; to risk, to stake; *to sacrifice.*

睡 *Shwei*⁴. *To sleep;* to nod or doze.

趕 or **赶** *Kan*³. To pursue; to hurry; to drive; *by,* by the time:—Les. 144.

歇 *Hsie*¹. To rest; to stop, to leave off; to take a vacation; *to quit business.*

關門 *Kwan*¹ *mên*². To shut the door; *to quit* or *wind up business.*

安 *An*¹. Quiet; *rest;* peace; at ease; to tranquilize; to place; to put to rights.

息 *Hsi*². A respiration; to breathe; to sigh; *to rest;* to put a stop to; interest.

安息日 *An*¹ *hsi*² *ji*⁴. The Sabbath day.

Notes.

2 This sentence might mean, *He wants to come here to teach.* Which meaning the speaker intended would be indicated by the emphasis and the connection. 教館 is rarely heard in the North, and 教學 as rarely in the South.

6 收工 is more widely used than 散工. The 收 is used from the standpoint of gathering tools, etc., and putting them in order for leaving.

11 Nothing in the sentence indicates whether "I" or "you" or "he" should be used in translating. 念 means *to chant, or drone,* and 念會 means to rhyme over till you "know it," as school boys say; that is, to memorize.

13 客來了 *The guests having come;* i.e., *when the guests come.*

14 眼看 *eye seeing;* i.e., *in sight, just at hand;* nearly always followed by 就. The two forms are quite equivalent.

16 The translation does not quite give the full force of the 就: the idea is that just now and here I purpose to propagate religion.

17 Might with equal propriety be rendered, *Whoever would act right must first have a right heart.*

19 要, as here used, is more or less local: it should be read with a slight emphasis, and expresses a strong presumption; whereas 怕 properly expresses apprehension.

第十四課

若[1]是你去、我也要去。○ 若[2]是先
生知道、他必要打你。○ 若[3]没有
人挑唆、事情早成了。○ 你[4]若等
用、我就給你。○ 若[5]是他不先提、
你也不要提。○ 你[6]的兄弟若不
出頭、別人還能出頭嗎。○ 若[7]是
他不還你、我就還你。○ 罪[8]人若
不悔改、死後必下地獄。○ 若[9]没
有事情躭悮、六天我就回來了。

TRANSLATION.

1 If you go I also will go.
2 If the teacher knew it he would certainly whip you.
3 If no one had meddled, the affair would have been concluded long ago.
4 If you are waiting to use it, I will just give it to you.
5 If he does not first mention it, you need not mention it.
6 If your younger brother does not take the lead (or, come to the front), can any one else do so?
7 If he does not repay you, I will repay you.
8 If sinners do not repent, after death they will go to hell.
9 If there is nothing to prevent, I shall return in six days.

---

22 換 is more common in the North, 轉 in the South though both forms would probably be understood either North or South.

23 The expression 剹上, or 出上, or 拼上, has a peculiar force very near to our word *sacrifice;—I will sacrifice the whole night*, etc. The three forms are not precisely equal in force, nor are they everywhere alike current. 剹 is most used in the North, 拼 in the South. In Kiukiang 𢶍不得 also is used in the same sense, but how analyzed it is not easy to see.

LESSON XIV.

THE COMMON SIGN OF THE SUBJECTIVE.

若 If, should, supposing.

若是 If, should, supposing.

As a conjunction, 若 means the same without 是 that it does with it. Whether 是 is added or not depends chiefly on euphony.

There are a number of other words of similar meaning and use, which will be introduced by and by:—See Les. 132.

This lesson illustrates in a measure how the Chinese language expresses moods and tenses without any endings or even special forms.

VOCABULARY.

若 *Joă*[4]. Like; as; same as; *if, perhaps, supposing*:—See Sub.

挑 *T'iao*[3]. To provoke, *to irritate;* to tease; to mix, to stir up; to rip open; to carry,—as a lantern. Also *t'iao*[1].

唆 *Soă*[1]. *To incite;* to set at variance.

挑唆 To sow discord; *to incite to contention.*

提 *T'i*[2]. To raise up; to bring to notice; *to mention;* to summon; to remit. Also *ti*[1].

出頭 *Ch'u*[1] *t'ou*[2]. To take the lead, to put oneself forward, to take the responsibility.

別 *Pie*[2]. To separate; to distinguish; to depart; different from, *another.* Also *pie*[4].

罪人 *Tswei*[4] *jên*[2]. A sinner:—a Christian term

悔 *Hwei*[3]. *To repent;* to regret.

改 *Kai*[3]. *To change,* to alter; to reform, to amend.

悔改 To repent and reform; *to repent.*

獄 *Yü*[4]. A prison, a jail.

若[10]是明天再不學、我必要罰你。○幸[11]虧你來帮助、你若是不來、我們就沒有法子。○若[12]王老三真說了這些話、他實在沒有良心。○我[13]們在路上若不坐那一會兒、這個時候早到了。○若[14]是他不罵我、我還能打他嗎。○他[15]若真窮到這個地步(分兒)、還能這樣胖嗎。○若[16]是天分好、二年也能學會了。○他[17]又應許二十還錢、若是到了日子、

10 If by to-morrow you still have not learned it, I shall certainly punish you.

11 It's fortunate you came to our help: if you had not come we should have been in a dilemma.

12 If Wang the Third really said these things, he certainly has no conscience.

13 If we had not sat down that time on the road, we should have been there before this time.

14 If he had not reviled me, would I have struck (or, thrashed) him?

15 If he were really as poor as this, would he still be so fat?

16 If his talents are good, he can learn it even in two years.

17 He has again promised to pay by the twentieth: if at that time he still does not pay, I shall strip off his clothes.

地獄 *Ti⁴ yü⁴*. Hell:—a Buddhist term adopted by Christianity.

悞 *Wu⁴*. To deceive; false; *to hinder*. Constantly interchanged with 誤.

罰 *Fa²*. A punishment; to fine; *to punish*.

幸 *Hsing⁴*. *Fortunate*, lucky; blessed.

虧 *K'wei¹*. To wane, to be wanting; a deficiency; a defect; to injure; *owing to;* in consequence of; happily.

幸虧 Fortunately; *luckily;* a happy chance.

帮 *Pang¹*. *To help;* to assist; to add on a piece; a company, a set:—Les. 140.

助 *Chu⁴*. To assist, to help.

帮助 To assist, to help, to aid.

眞 *Chên¹*. True; sincere; genuine; *in reality;* truly, in fact.

良 *Liang²*. *Good*, gentle, mild; excellent of its kind; natural, instinctive.

良心 *Liang² hsin¹*. Conscience, the moral nature; a desire to do right.

罵 *Ma⁴*. To rail at, to scold; *to call names;* to revile.

分 *Fên⁴*. A part, a share; *rank*, lot; the duties of a station. Also *fên¹*.

步 *Pu⁴*. To walk; *a step*, a station; a pace of five Chinese feet, a way, a course. A classifier:—Les. 125.

地步 *Ti⁴ pu⁴*. Rank; *position;* footing; circumstances.

胖 *P'ang⁴*. *Fat;* hearty.

天分 *T'ien¹ fên⁴*. Natural endowments, talents gifts.

應 *Ying¹*. That which is right, ought; suitable, proper; *to assent*. Also *ying⁴*.

許 *Hsü³*. To grant, to allow; to acquiesce; to permit; *to promise;* to betroth; many, very:—Les. 130.

應許 To *promise;* to consent.

剝 *Poa¹*, *pa¹*. To skin; to peel off; to uncover; *to tear off;* to fleece.

肯 *K'ên³*. To be willing; to assent, *to allow*.

待 *Tai⁴*. To wait; to expect; *to treat*, to behave towards.

管保 *Kwan³ pao³*. To guarantee, *to warrant;* you may be sure.

府 *Fu³*. A library; a store-house; an encyclopedia; a palace; *a mansion*.

府上 *Fu³ shang⁴*. A gentleman's house; your residence.

望 *Wang⁴*. To hope for, to expect; *to look towards;* to gaze at; hopes.

拜望 *Pai⁴ wang⁴*. To pay one's respects to, to call on.

再不還、我要剝他的衣裳。○若[18]是有人這樣待你、管保你也是不肯。○若[19]是知道府上在這裏兒、就早過來拜望了。

18 If any one should treat you in this way, I'll guarantee you also would protest.

19 If I had known your residence was here, I should have come over before this to call upon you.

NOTES.

1 Or, *If you go I also want to go.*

2 This sentence might be rendered, *If the teacher had known it he would certainly have whipped you*, or, *If the teacher finds it out he will certainly whip you.* These distinctions which the English expresses so admirably, the Chinese does not express, although it might be made to express, or at least indicate them; thus the first, by inserting 早 *tsao,*[3] *early,*—若是先生早知道, etc.; and the second by inserting 後來 *hou*[4] *lai,*[2] *afterwards,*—若是先生後來知道, etc.

6 The Chinese might with equal propriety be arranged, 若你的兄弟不出頭, etc., and this is the *grammatical* order. The Chinese, however, do not hesitate, in order to throw emphasis on the subject, to leave the first words without any logical construction. The grammatical incongruity is something they neither understand nor appreciate.

9 The use of 了 at the close implies that the return would be within, or by the end of, the six days; without it the meaning *might* be that the party would *start* back in six days.

13 Lit., *at this time early have arrived;* i.e., *before this time.* Notice how the Chinese language attains to the idea of "should have been."

15 分兒 will not pass in the South, though 地步 is equally good in the North.

17 "*Strip off his clothes;*" i.e., to hold for security.

LESSON XV.

INTENSIVES.

最 Excessively, exceedingly, very. More used in the South than in the North.

頂 The top; the best or highest in character or quality,—thus making the superlative. Less used in Southern than in Northern Mandarin.

挺 To stretch, used as a kind of super-superlative in place of 頂. It is a question whether *t'ing* is not simply 頂, aspirated in order to strengthen it.

很 Excessive; joined to adjectives, it form an intensive, often equivalent to a superlative. It is often preceded by 得 or 的, in which case the two words follow the adjective they qualify. The literal meaning is, *to the point of excess*, but in use the meaning is not essentially different from that of 很 alone.

至 Very; most; wholly. As an intensive it is used chiefly with adjectives of time or quantity.

誠得 Very, exceedingly. This term is much used in Central Mandarin, but not at all in the South, and but little in the North. There are sundry other intensives:—See Les. 137.

VOCABULARY.

頂 *Ting*[3]. The top, the summit; the crown; to carry on the head; to put one thing for another; to serve as; *very, in the highest degree:*—see Sub. A classifier:—Les. 125.

最 *Tswei*[4]. To carry to the extreme; *very, exceedingly:*—see Sub.

很 *Hên*[3]. Stern, harsh, etc., often used for 狠; very, excessively:—see Sub.

誠 *Ch'êng*[2]. Sincere; real; perfect in virtue; *really, verily, certainly.*

誠得 *Ch'êng*[2] *tê*[3]. Very, exceedingly:—see Sub.

挺 *T'ing*[3]. To straighten; to stiffen; resolute, decided; *very, exceedingly.*

至 *Chi*[4]. To arrive at, to reach: the end, the summit; to, at, even to; respecting; *the greatest degree of, most, very:*—see Sub., also Les. 144.

利 *Li*[4]. *Sharp, acute;* advantageous; fortunate; gain, profit; interest; to benefit.

利害 *Li*[4] *hai*[4]. Severe, stern; violent; *fierce;* powerful.

第十五課

他[1]的狗頂利害。○這[2]個人最論理(講理)、公道的很。○我[3]的大師傅、誠得會(很會弄)做飯。○王[4]老二的身量挺頂高。○你[5]的小刀子兒快得很。○我[6]看你至多有三十歲。○寫[7]這本書、至少也要得三個月的工夫。○張[8]五的心眼兒最詭詐。○他[9]至早是禮拜四來、至遲晚是禮拜六、○這[10]個小姑娘眞淘氣、我頂不喜歡他。○你[11]這個瘡、該常用水洗、至少一天一回。○這[12]些藥挺頂利害、至多一點鐘吃一回。○還[13]

Translation.

1 His dog is exceedingly fierce.
2 This man is very reasonable;—exceedingly just.
3 My cook can prepare first-class food.
4 Wang the Second's stature is exceedingly tall.
5 Your pocket-knife is extremely sharp.
6 I take you to be, at most, thirty years old.
7 To write this book will take, at the very least, three months' time.
8 Chang the Fifth's heart is very deceitful.
9 At the earliest he will come on Thursday; at the latest on Saturday.
10 This little girl is very provoking (or, mischievous): I dislike her exceedingly.
11 This boil of yours you should frequently wash with water;—at least once a day.
12 This medicine is very powerful: at most, take it but once an hour.

論 *Lun*⁴. To discourse upon; to discuss; to reason, to think over; to estimate; an essay; *according to;* as to, with reference to.

公 *Kung*¹. Public, common; general; just, *equitable;* the male of animals; husband; a "duke;" Sir, Mr.

公道 *Kung*¹ *tao*⁴. *Just,* righteous; fair, impartial; cheap.

大師傅 *Ta*⁴ *shï*¹ *fu*⁴. A head cook, a steward.

弄 *Lung*⁴, *nung*⁴, *nou*⁴. To do; to handle; to manage; to toy or trifle with; *to prepare or cook food.*

身 *Shên*¹. *The body;* the main part of a thing; oneself; a lifetime:—Les. 147.

量 *Liang*⁴. *A measure,* a limit; capacity to eat or drink; size; calibre. Also *liang.*²

身量 Stature, size.

高 *Kao*¹. High; *tall;* loud; eminent; excellent; old; high-priced; good.

心眼 *Hsin*¹ *yien*³. *Disposition,* character; plans, tricks.

詭 *Kwei*³. *To deceive,* to cheat; malicious; perverse.

詐 *Cha*⁴. To deceive, to impose upon; *artful,* cunning, false.

詭詐 *Crafty;* deceitful; treacherous.

遲 *Ch'ï*². Slow, dilatory; *late;* to delay.

淘 *T'ao*². To scour; to wash in a sieve; to stir about; to clean out, *to excite.*

淘氣 *T'ao*² *ch'i*⁴. *Provoking;* troublesome; mischievous; fidgety:—Note 10.

喜 *Hsi*³. Joy, delight; *to be pleased with;* to give joy to; to rejoice.

歡 *Hwan*¹. Joy (in expression); glad, merry; *to rejoice;* to gladden.

喜歡 To be pleased with, *to like;* to rejoice.

瘡 *Ch'wang*¹. A sore, *a boil,* an ulcer. In some places, the itch.

一回 *I*¹ *hwei*². Once, one time:—Les. 64.

藥 or 葯 *Yao*⁴. *Medicine,* physic, drugs, chemicals; gunpowder.

大道 *Ta*⁴ *tao*⁴. *The main road,* a highway; fundamental truth.

是走大路道好、小路道難誠找得得難很找。○我[14]打算十五六到家、至遲晚不過十七日。○這[15]本書頂高貴貴重、你要小心用他。○送[16]他這些禮物、也很可以。○他[17]們弟兄三個、最多有四十畝地。○這[18]個洗臉盆、至少也值四百錢。○西[19]國的狗、白天天裏最老實、到了夜下黑裏黑下纔利害。○眞[20]神是天地的主宰、最尊貴、最聰明、最能幹。○這[21]個布頂好頂好、我也要去買他的.

13 It is better, after all, to go the main road; the small road is exceedingly hard to find.

14 I propose to reach home on the fifteenth or sixteenth, or, at the latest, by the seventeenth.

15 This book is very precious, you must be careful how you use it.

16 To make him these presents will answer very well.

17 The three brothers have, at most, but forty mow of land.

18 This wash-basin is worth, at the very least, four hundred cash.

19 Western dogs are very docile in the day-time: it is only when night comes that they are fierce.

20 The true God is Lord of heaven and earth, very great, very wise and very powerful.

21 This cloth is first-rate; I also will go and buy of him.

小道 *Hsiao^{3} tao^{4}*. . . . . . . A by-road, a path.

貴 *Kwei^{4}*. Honorable; dignified; a term of . . . . respectful address; dear, high priced; *precious;* to honor, to value.

重 *Chung^{4}*. Heavy; weighty; severe; heinous; . . . . grave; *to honor;* to regard as important. Also *ts'ung^{2}*.

貴重 To value highly; *precious;* honorable; dignified.

高貴 *Kao^{1} kwei^{4}*. Highly valued, *precious;* . . . . *rare:*—Note 15.

物 *Wu^{4}*. A thing; matter; *an article;* goods; . . . . . . a creature, a being, the *non ego.*

禮物 *Li^{3} wu^{4}*. . . . . *Presents;* offerings.

弟兄 *Ti^{4} hsiung^{1}*. . . . . . . Brothers, brethren.

畝 *Mu^{3}*. A Chinese acre,—about one-sixth of . . . . . . an English acre.

臉 *Lien^{3}*. The cheek; *the face;* the countenance; . . . . reputation; honor.

盆 *P'ên^{2}*. . . . . . . A tub; a basin.

白天 *Pai^{2} t'ien^{1}*. . . . . . . Day-time, daylight.

黑 *Hei^{1}*. . . . . . . Black; *dark;* cloudy; obscure.

黑下 *Hei^{1} hsia^{4}*. . . . . At night, at dark.

下黑 *Hsia^{4} hei^{1}*. . . . . At night, at dark.

神 *Shên^{2}*. The gods; *god*—in the heathen sense, ... a supernatural (good) being; the human spirit; superhuman, divine. Used by many for God.

眞神 *Chên^{1} Shên^{2}*. . . . . The true God.

宰 *Tsai^{3}*. To rule; a steward; a minister of state; . . . . *a ruler;* to slaughter and dress.

主宰 *Chu^{3} tsai^{3}*. . . . . . . A ruler, the chief ruler.

尊 *Tsun^{1}*. High, honorable; *eminent;* to honor; . . . . to dignify. A classifier:—Les. 140.

尊貴 *Tsun^{1} kwei^{4}*. Honorable, lofty; great, ... *exalted.*

聰 *Ts'ung^{1}*. Discriminating; *quick of apprehension* or perception.

聰明 *Ts'ung^{1} ming^{2}*. Discriminating; clever, ... *intelligent;* wise.

幹 *Kan^{4}*. *Skill, capability;* to attend to; to . . . . . . follow a calling; affairs, business.

能幹 *Nêng^{2} kan^{4}*. Ability; *power;* might.

布 *Pu^{4}*. *Cloth* of any kind; to spread out; to . . . . . . diffuse; to publish.

第十六課

今[1]天日很暖和、天氣也
清亮。○高[2]大大媽娘的病、
今天好些。○今[3]天兒是
初三、明天兒是初四。○
你[4]明天日去去上逛市集、可以
買五斤魚來。○他[5]們
如今還在那裏嗎。○
現[6]在正好收割莊稼。
○明[7]天兒個是安息日。

Translation.

1 It is very mild to-day, and the air is bracing.
2 Mrs. Kao's disease is somewhat better to-day.
3 To-day is the third, to-morrow will be the fourth.
4 When you go to market to-morrow you may buy five catties of fish.
5 Are they, at present, still there?
6 It is just now time to reap the harvest.
7 To-morrow will be the Sabbath.

2 The second clause is in apposition with the first, and supplementary to it. The clauses should be separated by a short pause.

3 In some places, especially in the South, 弄飯 completely supplants 做飯.

7 得 as here used is read *tei*³ in Peking, but retains its normal sound in Shantung. It is never used in this way in the South, 要 being used instead.

9 晚, in the sense of late, is rarely used in the South, being nearly always replaced by 遲.

10 淘氣 Lit., *stir up anger;* i.e., *provoking, vexatious,* in which sense it is used in most places. In some places, however, notably in Peking, it is used in the sense of *mischievous, fidgety,* which leaves out of view all reference to the person affected. The "anger" excited is evidently that of the party affected by the "mischief."

11 的 is to be understood after 你, and in similar cases is often expressed. The construction is thoroughly Chinese; viz., *your this boil,* for, *this boil of yours.*

13 The 還 at the beginning of this sentence implies that a mistake had been made in going by the small road, or at least a question is raised as to which road to take.

15 高貴 as used in Shantung means *precious, rare,* in the sense of being hard to get or hard to replace. In Peking it is only so used of persons. It is replaced in the South by 貴重, which adds to its ordinary meaning that of rarity or preciousness.

16 很可以 Lit., *very can do;* i.e., *will do very well.*

19 下黑 or 黑下. Both forms are used in the North, the one in some places, the other in other places. In the South 夜裡 is chiefly used, 黑下 being heard in some places.

21 頂好 is repeated for emphasis, which is a very common idiom. The 他 at the close refers to the person of whom the cloth was bought.

LESSON XVI.

Common Time Particles.

今日 or 今天 To-day.
明日 or 明天 To-morrow.
昨日 or 昨天 Yesterday.

The two forms are used indifferently in most places. In Nanking the forms with 日 are rarely used.

今兒 or 今兒個 To-day.
明兒 or 明兒個 To-morrow.
昨兒 or 昨兒個 Yesterday.

These are colloquial forms in constant use. The addition of 個 is peculiar to Pekingese.

前日 or 前天 Day before yesterday.
後日 or 後天 Day after to-morrow.
前兒 or 前兒個 Day before yesterday.
後兒 or 後兒個 Day after to-morrow.

The addition of 個 is peculiar to Pekingese.

現在 } Now, at present. The two forms are
如今 } substantially equivalent, which one is used being chiefly a matter of euphony. If there be any difference, it is that the first is more definitely immediate than the second.

後來 Afterwards, in future, then.
以後 Afterwards, subsequently.

There are many other ways of marking time. See Les. 117 to 120.

8 我的肚子昨日（天）疼了一天。○

9 明兒（天）晚上（下晚）、我要請客。○

10 前兒個（日、天）我去見（會）他、他不在家。○

11 現在饅頭（饝饝）已經蒸得（好）了。○

12 在二月裏我見了他、以後再沒見他。○

13 後來的事情、你還能先知道（曉得）嗎。○

14 現在已經到了時候、我要去考書。○

15 若是今兒個（天）僱妥了牲口、明兒個（天）我就起身。○

16 王大人有信說、

8 Yesterday my belly ached the whole day.

9 To-morrow evening I want to invite company.

10 Day before yesterday I went to see him and he was not at home.

11 By this time the bread is sufficiently steamed.

12 I saw him in the second month, and I have not seen him again since.

13 And can you foreknow that which is future?

14 The time has now fully arrived; I must go and hear my class.

15 If I succeed in hiring animals to-day, I shall start to-morrow.

16 General Wang has sent word saying that he will come to see me day after to-morrow.

VOCABULARY.

今 *Chin*^{1}. . . . . . . Now, presently.

前 *Ch'ien*^{2}. To advance; *before in time or place;* . . . . in the presence of; the former; previously; the south side.

如 *Ju*^{2}. *As, like;* as if; according to; if, per- . . . . . . haps; to equal:—Les. 99.

昨 *Tsoă*^{2}. . . . . *Yesterday;* recently.

現 *Hsien*^{4}. To manifest; *now,* at present; current; . . . . plain, apparent; for the occasion.

暖 *Nwan*^{3}. . . . . Warm; bland, mild.

暖和 *Nwan*^{3} *hê*^{2}. . . . . *Warm;* to warm.

天氣 *T'ien*^{2} *ch'i*^{4}. *The air,* the atmosphere; . . . . the weather.

清亮 *Ch'ing*^{1} *liang*^{4}. Refreshing, bracing, cool; . . . . pure.

大娘 *Ta*^{4} *niang*^{2}. A father's elder brother's . . . . wife; applied at large as a term of respect to any elderly woman, *Mrs.*

大媽 *Ta*^{4} *ma*^{1}. Same as 大娘. Southern.

集 *Chi*^{2}. To flock together; to gather; to col- . . . . . lect; to compile; *a market or fair.*

赶集 *Kan*^{3} *chi*^{2}. To go to market:—Note 4. . . . .

市 *Shi*^{4}. . . . *A market;* to trade; a crowd; vulgar.

魚 *Yü*^{2}. . . . . . . A fish.

初 *Ch'u*^{1}. To begin; *the first,* the beginning:— . . . . Note 3.

割 *Kê*^{1}. To cut; to divide; *to reap;* to deduct, ... to take off.

收割 *Shou*^{1} *kê*^{1}. . . . . To reap, to harvest.

莊 *Chwang*^{1}. *Growing grain;* sedate, serious; . . . . well-behaved.

稼 *Chia*^{4}. Farming, husbandry; *standing grain;* . . . . a sheaf.

莊稼 *Standing grain;* the crops; farming.

肚 *Tu*^{4}. *The belly,* the abdomen; the temper or . . . . mind. Also *tu*^{3}.

晚上 *Wan*^{3} *shang*^{4}. . . . . The evening.

下晚 *Hsia*^{4} *wan*^{3}. . . . . . . The evening.

饅 *Man*^{2}. . . . . Steamed bread or cakes; bread.

饅頭 *Man*^{2} *t'ou*^{2}. Bread,—always steamed by . . . . the Chinese, but in foreign families the term is used of baked bread.

饝 *Moă*^{2}. Steamed cakes or rolls. In use always . . . . . . doubled.

蒸 *Chêng*^{1}. Steam, vapor; *to cook by steaming;* . . . . to distil; to decoct.

考 *K'ao*^{3} A deceased father, ancestors; *to exa- . . . . mine* a candidate or a pupil; to question.

考書 *K'ao*^{3} *shu*^{1}. To hear a recitation. A . . . . foreign term:—Note 14.

妥 *T'oă*^{3}. Secure, safe, firm; *satisfactory,* all . . . . right; ready:—Les. 109.

他後天日來見我。○保[17]住子很結實、後來必是個好漢子。○你[18]在這裏住一宿夜、明日再走不好嗎。○看[19]他現在這樣用心、以後必有出息。○野[20]地裏的草、今日還在、明日就丟在爐裏。○我[21]從前沒見他、今天兒纔見了。○這[22]個事情、今日兒個不能定規、可以等到明日兒個再說。○如[23]今電報已經行在中國、以後火輪車也必要行。

17 Pao Chu-tsï is very hardy: in due time he will certainly be a robust man.

18 Will it not do for you to stay here to-night and go on again to-morrow?

19 Seeing he is so diligent now, he will no doubt turn out well hereafter.

20 The grass of the field to-day is, and to-morrow is cast into the oven.

21 I never saw him before: I have only just seen him to-day.

22 This business cannot be settled to-day: wait till to-morrow and we will talk about it again.

23 The telegraph has already become an accomplished fact in China, and railroads will succeed by and by.

起身 *Ch'i*³ *shên*¹. To start to go anywhere, to . . . . set off.

結 *Chie*¹. A knot; to knot, to tie; to bind by a . . . . contract; to set, to stiffen; *strong, vigorous;* to bear,—as fruit. Also *chie*².

結實 *Chie*¹ *shï*². To bear fruit; strong, tough, ... vigorous, *robust.*

漢 *Han*⁴. A noted Chinese dynasty; Chinese; . . . . *a large strong man;* a man.

好漢子 *Hao*³ *han*⁴ *tsï*³. A strong man, a fine . . . . portly fellow.

宿 *Su*⁴, *hsü*¹. A stage where one rests for the . . . . night; a night's rest; *to pass the night,* to lodge; a constellation.

出息 *Ch'u*¹ *hsi*². . . . . *Outcome,* profit.

野 *Yie*³. A waste; *a common;* a desert; the . . . . country; savage, wild; rustic, rude.

草 *Ts'ao*³. Herbs, *grass;* weeds; straw; hastily, ... carelessly; the running hand; a rough draft, female.

丟 *Tiu*¹. To cast away; to throw aside; *to throw* . . . . . . *or pitch;* to lose.

定規 *Ting*⁴ *kwei*¹. To decide, to settle, to fix. . . . .

報 *Pao*⁴. To recompense; to revenge; to inform, ... to report; *a gazette,* a newspaper.

電報 *Tien*⁴ *pao*⁴. The telegraph; a telegram. . . . .

輪 *Lun*². *A wheel,* a disk; a revolution; to . . . . rotate, to take turns.

車 *Ch'ê*¹. A wheeled carriage; a cart, a barrow. . . . . . . Read *chü*¹ in *Wên-li.*

火輪車 *Hwoa*³ *lun*² *ch'ê*². A railroad car; the . . . . cars.

NOTES.

2 In many places 一 would be inserted before 些.

3 初 is applied to the first ten days of the month to distinguish them from the second and third ten; hence 初三 is the *third,* as distinguished from the 13th and 23rd. As we have no such distinction in English, the 初 disappears in the translation.

4 In North China, markets are held in all the principal towns and villages every five days. They are always arranged so that the markets in a given neighborhood come in rotation. Tradesmen and small dealers *follow* these markets, usually attending one each day. Hence 赶集 comes to mean *to go to market.* Such markets are not prevalent in the South, where the business is mostly done by shopkeepers.

6 Peking teachers object to 好 as here used, and would change to 現在正是收割莊稼的時候. This, however, gives a slightly different sense; viz., *it is just now (in the midst of) harvest time.*

8 一天 one day; that is, the whole day.

11 The use of 得 in this connection is Pekingese.

13 還 is here intensive.

第十七課

他[1]爲甚麼打你呢。○他[2]是你的什麼人。○你[3]的大姐姐(大姐)爲甚麼不來做針線呢。○你[4]們這裏娶媳婦(奶奶)、行甚麼禮呢。○你[5]今天不快活(開味)、是爲甚麼呢。○弄[6]壞了我的傢伙(傢什)、爲甚麼不來告訴我呢。○你[7]們爭鬧(別字眼)、是爲甚麼事呢。○現[8]在銀子甚麼行市呢。○你[9]今天、從什麼地方動身呢。○這[10]個事情、爲甚麼到如今纔說呢。○你[11]有病、爲甚麼不早調治呢。○我[12]說

TRANSLATION.

1 Why did he strike you?
2 What [relative] is he of yours?
3 Why does your oldest sister not come to sew?
4 Here when you marry a wife, what ceremony do you have?
5 Why is it that you are not happy to-day?
6 Having spoiled my tools, why did you not come and tell me?
7 What is it you are wrangling about?
8 What is the price of silver at present?
9 From what place did you start to-day?
10 Why have you delayed till now to speak of this business?
11 If you were sick, why did you not seek treatment before this?

14 In this sentence 要 expresses both intention and necessity. 考書 is a term used in foreign schools: in native schools they have no occasion to use such a term; they use only 背書 *pei⁴ shu¹*,—*repeat the books*, and 講書 *chiang³ shu¹*,—*explain the books*.

15 僱妥 *to hire satisfactorily;* that is, in this case, *to succeed in hiring*.

16 The Chinese seems to say that 王大人 received a letter; nevertheless, the meaning here is that a letter has come from 王大人. In a different connection 王大人有信 might mean that *Wang Ta Jên* had received a letter.

22 再說 *Again speak*,—a common phrase for postponing any business, and including a promise to attend to it at some future time.

LESSON XVII.

COMPOUND RELATIVE AND INTERROGATIVE PARTICLES.

甚麼 or **什麼** What, anything, something. The second is the colloquial form. In use, the final *n* of 甚 is always elided, and 什 is in most places pronounced in the same way as 甚. The 麼 is sometimes spoken *ma* (嗎), but is never so written.

When 爲 precedes 什麼 the combination means, *because of what;* i.e., *why*. When followed by 人 the combination means *who*.

什麼 is also used indefinitely, meaning *any*, *at all;* or with a negative, *none*, *not at all*.

Colloquially, 什麼 is in many places contracted into *sha²*. In other places 麼 is used alone for 什麼. Neither of these corruptions is heard in Eastern Shantung, but they prevail in the middle and western parts of the province, as well as in many other places, both North and South.

呢 the sign of an indirect question. Theoretically every indirect question should end with 呢. Practically it is very often omitted, and there seems to be no rule governing its use. It is more used in some places than in others. It has but a limited use in Western Mandarin. See also Les. 89.

話、你爲甚麼不留心聽呢。○你[13]甚麼時候要走、可以來告訴我一聲。○你[14]身上有甚麼病嗎。○你[15]身上有甚麼病呢。○我[16]今年八十三歲、甚麼也不能管了。○這[17]個東西、不好做甚麼。○尊[18]敬長上、不是甚麼難事。○你[19]好不好（甚麼好）等一等、我先

12 Why do you not pay attention when I speak?

13 Whenever you wish to go, come and give me word.

14 Have you any disease?

15 What disease have you?

16 This year I am eighty-three, and can not attend to any thing at all.

17 This article is not good for any thing.

18 To show respect to your elders is not any thing difficult.

19 Could you wait a little and allow me first to go and attend to a little something?

VOCABULARY.

甚 *Shên*². What:—see Sub., also Les. 188. Also read *shên*⁴.

什 *Shï*². A file of ten soldiers; used as a contracted form of 甚.

麼 *Moă*², *ma*². An interrogative particle joined with various words in asking indirect questions:—see Sub.

呢 *Ni*¹. An interrogative particle ending any question not answered by yes or no:—see Sub., also Les. 89.

爲 *Wei*⁴. For, *on account of;* because, wherefore:—Les. 77. Also *wei*².

姐 *Chie*³. An elder sister.

大姐 *Ta*⁴ *chie*³. Eldest sister.

大姐姐 *Ta*⁴ *chie*³ *chie*³. Eldest sister.

針 *Chên*¹. *A needle;* a pin; a stitch; to prick; to stab with a needle.

針線 *Chên*¹ *hsien*⁴. Needle-work, sewing.

娶 *Ch'ü*³. To take a wife, to marry.

媳 *Hsi*². A son's wife.

婦 *Fu*⁴. *A wife;* a married woman; a female.

媳婦 A daughter-in-law; a wife.

奶 *Nai*³. The breasts, the udder; to suckle; to suck; milk; a nurse.

奶奶 A paternal grandmother; also applied to any elderly lady; a wife (Nankingese).

快活 *K'wai*⁴ *hwoă*². Cheerful, in good spirits, *happy.*

味 *Wei*⁴. *Taste,* flavor; a delicacy.

開味 *K'ai*¹ *wei*⁴. To enjoy oneself; *cheerful;* to like; to have an appetite.

傢什 *Chia*¹ *shï*². Utensils, *tools,* fixtures:—Note 6.

爭 *Chêng*¹. *To wrangle,* to contest; to strive for precedence.

爭鬧 *Chêng*¹ *nao*⁴. *To wrangle,* to quarrel, to fight.

別字眼 *Pie*² *tsï*⁴ *yien*³. *To altercate,* to dispute, to quarrel.

行 *Hang*². A row; a series or order; a guild, a trade; *a mercantile establishment,* a store. See *hsing*², from which it is often distinguished by inserting a dot, thus—行; or by a small circle, thus,—行. A classifier:—Les. 42.

行市 *Hang*² *shï*⁴. The market price, the current rate.

動 *Tung*⁴. *To move;* to excite; to shake; to begin; to take action:—Les. 91.

動身 *Tung*⁴ *shên*¹. To move; to start.

調 *T'iao*². To harmonize; to mix; *to regulate;* to stir up, to incite. Also *tiao*⁴.

治 *Chï*⁴. To govern, to rule; *to heal, to cure;* to oversee; to condemn.

調治 To treat a disease; to cure.

留 *Liu*². To detain,—as a guest; to keep back; to leave; *to hold on to;* to delay.

留心 *Liu*² *hsin*¹. To be careful, to give good heed; to bear in mind.

一聲 *I*¹ *shêng*¹. One sound; *a call;* a cry, a shout, etc.

去做一點甚麼。○[20]你是甚麼人、敢這等大模大樣。○[21]他的本事、和他父親不差甚麼。○[22]北屋的炕不好燒、常冒煙、不知是甚麼毛病。○[23]那個人眞不知道甚麼、我爲他費了多少事、臨走管任甚麼也沒說。

20 Who are you, that you dare to put on such airs?

21 His ability is about equal to that of his father.

22 The k'ang in the north room does not draw well; it is constantly smoking. I do not know what defect it has.

23 That man really does not know anything. I have taken any amount of pains on his account, yet when he was about to start he said nothing at all.

敬 *Ching*⁴. To honor, *to show respect to;* reverent; to worship.

尊敬 *Tsun*¹ *ching*⁴. To show respect to; to honor.

長 *Chang*³. Senior; *an elder;* a superior; to grow; to swell. Also *ch'ang*².

長上 *Chang*³ *shang*⁴. Elders; superiors.

模 *Moă*², *mu*². A mold; *a pattern*, a model.

大模大樣 *Ta*⁴ *mu*² *ta*⁴ *yang*⁴. An ostentatious manner; braggadocio.

本事 *Pên*³ *shï*⁴. *Ability*, capacity,—including both natural and acquired qualities; resources.

差 *Ch'a*¹. To mistake; *to differ;* a fault, a difference; a discrepancy:—Les. 57. Also *ch'ai*² and *ts'ï*².

屋 *Wu*¹. *A house;* a room, an apartment.

好燒 *Hao*³ *shao*¹. To burn well,—of fuel; *to draw*,—as a k'ang, or a stove.

冒 *Mao*⁴. To rush forward heedlessly; *to rush or stream out;* to feign; heedless.

烟 or 煙 *Yien*¹. *Smoke;* tobacco or opium,—as smoked.

毛 *Mao*². *Hair*, fur, feathers; mould; tare of goods.

毛病 *Mao*² *ping*⁴. A fault; a peccadillo; *a defect;* an idiosyncrasy; a disease.

費 *Fei*⁴. *To spend*, to use; to lavish; outlay; waste; trouble.

多少 *Toă*¹ *shao*³. How much? a great deal, *ever so much.*

臨 *Lin*². To look down on; to approach; to descend; at the point of, *about to;* whilst.

任 *Jên*⁴. A trust, a duty; to bear, to sustain; *to allow*, to give rein to:—Les. 83.

任甚麼 *Jên*⁴ *shên*² *moă*². No matter what; anything at all.

管甚麼 *Kwan*³ *shên*² *moă*². The same, but not *t'ung hsing.*

NOTES.

3 做針線, *to do needle thread;* i.e., *to sew, to do needlework.*

4 娶媳婦 means literally, *to marry a daughter-in-law.* When a girl is first married, and for some years, at least, her duty as a daughter-in-law completely overshadows her duty as a wife; hence she is not usually called a wife, but a daughter-in-law. The proper word for wife is 妻 *ch'i*⁴ which, however, is rarely used in the North, though frequently heard in the South.

6 傢什 is equivalent to 傢伙, but is not so widely used. Though written 傢什, it is generally pronounced as if written 傢使.

7 別字眼, *to distinguish character eyes;* i.e., *to dispute about words, to jangle.* 眼 is often put for the important or central part.

8 We might insert 是 in this sentence, thus,—現在銀子是什麼行市呢,—and the English learner has a strong feeling that it should be there. Chinese, however, while it will tolerate it, prefers to omit it. The same remarks apply to the 17th sentence, and to many others.

10 The order of this sentence might be changed as follows;—爲什麼到如今纔說這個事情呢,—and thus agree with the English order; but the Chinese prefers to set forth the object first.

12 The "when" is implied in the order of the words.

14 This use of 甚麼 is thoroughly colloquial, but seems to be quite general. It is to be spoken without any emphasis.

15 甚麼 is here used normally, and is to be emphasized.

16 The force of 也 is untranslatable. The 甚麼 is to be strongly emphasized.

第十八課

我[1]要買好的、不要壞的。○他[2]要白的、不要黑的。○粗[3]的、細的、不好合在一塊兒。○可[4]以先用那些零碎的。○客[5]嫌酒凉(冷)再要熱的。○那[6]個胖的、是他女兒。○這[7]些桃兒(桃子)不大好、生的多、熟的少。○他[8]一家人、沒有一個不伶俐的。○你[9]是甚麼人、答小的叫同喜。○教[10]友也不能一樣、有眞的、有假的。○沒[11]有再好的嗎、答沒有、這還不算好的嗎。○有[12]軟和的、可以給我一個。○世[13]上的人、

TRANSLATION.

1 I want to buy good ones; I don't want spoiled ones.
2 He wants the white, not the black.
3 It is not proper to mix the coarse and the fine together.
4 First use those odds and ends.
5 The guest complains that the wine is cold, and asks that the next be hot.
6 That fat one is his daughter.
7 These peaches are not very good: there are more green ones than ripe ones. (Lit., the green are many, the ripe are few.)
8 There is not one of the whole family that is not clever.
9 Who are you? Ans. Your servant is called T'ung-Hsi.
10 Nor are church members all alike;—some are true and some are false.
11 Have you no better ones? Ans. No: are not these to be considered good ones?
12 If you have any *soft* ones you may give me one.
13 Of men the intelligent are few, the stupid many.

19 In the first clause **甚麼** is used to modify the abruptness of the request; as if we should say, *would it be at all convenient for you,* etc. This use of **甚麼** is more or less local. Some teachers would prefer the sentence written **你等一等好不好**, etc., which is neither better nor worse, save that it throws a little more stress on the *waiting*. The first means, *can you wait a little?* the second, *can you not wait a little?*

20 **模樣** is separated, and **大** repeated for rhetorical effect.

21 The proper structure of this sentence would demand **的** after father, but the Chinese omit it without feeling the incongruity.

23 Note how the pronoun is omitted where the English requires it.

LESSON XVIII

的 JOINED TO ADJECTIVES.

When **的** is joined to an adjective it turns it into a noun of quality, approximating in sense to "the" joined to an adjective of quality in English; as **好的**, *the good*, **壞的**, *the spoiled*, etc. The translation, however, will vary very much with the circumstances of the case.

VOCABULARY.

粗 *Ts'u*¹. Rough; large; *coarse;* vulgar; gross, ... vile.

細 *Hsi*⁴. Fine; *small;* delicate; trifling; subtle; .... careful.

塊 *K'wai*⁴. ...... A lump; a piece:—Les. 27.

一塊兒 *I*¹ *k'wai*⁴ *êr*². *All together,* all at once; .... together with, in company with:—Les. 105.

嫌 *Hsien*² *To dislike;* to find fault with, to .... have an aversion to; fastidious.

酒 *Chiu*³. All spirituous liquors,—fermented, ... malted and distilled.

凉 *Liang*². ...... Cool, *cold;* distant, cool.

桃 *T'ao*². ...... A peach.

伶 *Ling*². ...... Active; *clever.*

聰明的少、糊塗的多。○在[14]家裏穿舊的、出門穿新的。○那[15]一家有兩個媳婦、一個標緻[俊]的、一個醜的。○我[16]看這是個公的、那是個母的。○長[17]的不合式、若是沒有短的、可以不買。○他[18]一家人、老的老、小的小、一個中用的也沒有。○家[19]裏有現成的東西、現做也不費事。○院[20]子裏的樹、有高的、有矮的、有大的、有小的、有活的、有死的。

14 At home wear the old [clothes]: when you go abroad wear the new.

15 There are two daughters-in-law in that family; one pretty and one homely.

16 I think this one is a male and that one a female.

17 The long are unsuitable. If there are no short ones you need not buy.

18 The old are too old and the young are too young: there is not one capable person in the whole family.

19 There is ready material in the house: to make it when needed will be no trouble.

20 Of the trees in the yard some are high and some low, some large and some small, some alive and some dead

俐 *Li*⁴. . . . . . *Clever*, talented; neat.
伶俐 *Talented*, smart; shrewd, quick-witted.
小的 *Hsiao*³ *ti*¹. Your humble servant:—Note . . . . .9.
友 *Yiu*³. . . . A companion, *an associate;* a friend.
教 *Chiao*⁴. To cause to do:—Les. 71; a sect; *a* . . . . *church;* doctrine, tenets. See *chiao*⁴.
教友 One who belongs to the same society or church; *church members;* membership.
假 *Chia*³. *False;* feigned; to avail of, to borrow; . . . . if, supposing:—Les. 123. Also *chia*⁴.
軟 *Jwan*³. *Soft*, weak, tender; yielding; limber, ... pliable.
軟和 *Jwan*³ *hŏ*². *Soft*, pliable; tender-hearted. . . . .
世 *Shï*⁴. An age, a generation; *the world;* . . . . . . mankind; times; hereditary.
塗 *Tu*¹. . . . . . . Dull, stupid. Also t'u².
糊 *Hu*². . . . . . To paste; sticky; *foolish*, stupid.
糊塗 Foolish, silly; *stupid;* demented.
穿 *Ch'wan*¹. To perforate; to string, to run on . . . . or through,—as cash on a string; to put on,—as clothing, *to wear*.
舊 *Chiu*⁴. *Old;* worn out, spoiled; ancient, ... venerable:—Les. 97.

新 *Hsin*¹. . . . . . . To renew; *new;* fresh; recent.
俊 *Chün*⁴. . . . . . Superior; handsome, *pretty*.
標 *Piao*¹. A signal, a flag; a sign-board; a . . . . ticket; a warrant; to make a signal; to display; to inscribe; fine, *beautiful*.
緻 *Chï*⁴. . . . . . . Fine in texture; soft, *elegant*.
標緻 Pretty, handsome, lovely.
醜 *Ch'ou*³. Ugly, deformed, *homely;* disagree- . . . . able; shameful.
長 *Ch'ang*². *Long*,—in time or distance; con- . . . . stant; to excel. See *chang*³.
短 *Twan*³. *Short* in time or distance; brief; a . . . . short-coming; few; wanting.
中 *Chung*⁴. To hit the centre; to happen accord- . . . . ing to; to fall into,—as a trap; fit, *suitable*. See *chung*¹.
中用 *Chung*⁴ *yung*⁴. *Capable*, efficient; with a . . . . negative,—worthless.
現成 *Hsien*⁴ *ch'êng*². Ready; ready-made; . . . . *ready to hand*.
費事 *Fei*⁴ *shï*⁴. To spend effort; to take pains; . . . . laborious, *troublesome*.
樹 *Shu*⁴. . . . . . *A tree;* plants in general.
矮 *Ai*³. . . . . . *Low*, squat; short, small; to lower.

第十九課

地[1]是圓圓的。○你[2]快快的去請他來。○我[3]慢慢的（一會兒）就去。○他[4]是暗暗的說你的不是。○這[5]個人常常和他兄弟打架。○張[6]先生不會辦事、常常上當。○明[7]天我要早早（早些）的起身。○你[8]說這個話、明明不合情理。○往[9]往有人看錯了這個事。

Translation.

1 The earth is round.
2 Do you go quickly and ask him to come.
3 I shall go presently.
4 He is covertly finding fault with you.
5 This man is constantly fighting with his younger brother.
6 Mr. Chang does not know how to do business. He is constantly being cheated.
7 To-morrow I want to start early.
8 What you say is plainly contrary to reason.
9 Men frequently make a mistake in this matter.

Notes.

5 In the South 凉 is very little used, 冷 quite taking its place. If 冷 were used in this connection in the North, it would imply that the wine was not only not hot (as it should be according to Chinese ideas), but cold—excessively cold.

7 In Peking 桃 never takes 子, and in Nanking it never takes 兒. In Chinanfu either may be used. In some places neither is used.

9 The question is supposed to be asked by a magistrate of one appearing before him. In such cases the party addressed generally speaks of himself as 小的, *the little one*, unless he is a literary man, when he calls himself 童生 *t'ung² shêng¹*, or if he has a degree, simply 生.

10 也 indicates that the sentence is in addition to some previous statement, and, combined with the negative, has the force of "nor." The 能 does not appear in the translation. Its use intimates a difference in Christians *as a matter of course*.

12 *If*, is here clearly implied.

16 This sentence has reference to fowls, or to birds.

18 It would seem as if 太 (Lesson 24) ought to be joined with the second 老 and 小, and it might be so said; the correlation of the clauses, however, allows of its omission, which adds to the sprightliness of the style.

19 Note the opposite meanings which the two 現 here have.

20 Or, *there are high ones and low ones, etc.*

LESSON XIX.

Adjectives Reduplicated for Emphasis.

Adjectives are often repeated for the sake of emphasis. This idiom is important and ever recurring. Most adjectives and some adverbs may be so repeated. Adjectives when repeated generally become adverbs.

For the reduplication of verbs, see Les. 33.

Vocabulary.

圓 *Yüen²*. *Round*, circular; spherical; to make round; to interpret a dream.

慢 *Man⁴*. Remiss; *slow;* sluggish, dilatory; supercilious.

慢慢的 Slowly; gradually; *presently;* by and by.

暗 *An⁴*. Dark; obscure; gloomy; secret; *covert*, stealthy; to one's self, mentally.

辦 *Pan⁴*. To administer; *to manage;* to transact, to do; to provide.

上當 *Shang⁴ tang⁴*. *To get cheated*, to be victimized, to fall into a trap:—Note 6.

往往 *Wang³ wang³*. *Frequently*, every little while:—Les. 108. Sub.

輕 *Ch'ing¹*. Light; to think lightly of; to slight; frivolous; *gently;* young.

笨 *Pên⁴*. Stupid; dull of apprehension; awkward, clumsy; unwieldy.

蠢 *Ch'un³*. Simple, foolish, *stupid*, doltish.

再[10]要你輕輕的關這個門。○這[11]個孩子頂蠢笨、上學也是白白兒的。○不[12]用着急、慢慢的就明白了。○稱[13]了高高的一百二十斤。○没[14]有大進項、也不過僅僅的彀花費。○你[15]打聽明白了、可以悄悄兒的來告訴我。○人[16]過了四十歲、身子漸漸

10 Hereafter I want you to shut this door gently.

11 This child is extremely stupid: it is useless for him to go to school.

12 Don't get impatient: by and by you will understand.

13 It weighed one hundred and twenty catties, good weight.

14 He has no great income,—no more than barely enough to cover expenses.

15 When you have found out clearly, come quietly and tell me.

16 When a man has passed forty, his strength gradually declines.

着 *Chao*[2], *choă*[2]. To become; to attain to; to cause, to send, to order; to place; yes, truly, exactly so; a move in chess. Les. 20. Sub.

急 *Chi*[2]. *Impatient*, anxious; hurried; uneasy; in extremity.

着急 Anxious, excited; eager; *impatient*.

稱 *Ch'êng*[1]. To style, to call; to praise, to compliment; *to weigh*. Also *ch'êng*[4] and *ch'ên*[4].

進 *Chin*[4]. To advance, to make progress; *to enter*, to go in, up, or on.

項 *Hsiang*[4]. The neck; a sort, an item, a class; a term (in algebra); *money*, funds.

進項 Income, receipts.

僅 *Chin*[3]. . . . . . . *Barely;* scarcely; only.

花費 *Hwa*[1] *fei*[4]. . . . . . . Expense, outlay.

打聽 *Ta*[3] *t'ing*[4]. To make inquiry, to find out by inquiring.

悄 *Ch'iao*[3]. . . . . . Secret; *quiet;* private; anxious.

悄悄的 Secretly; clandestinely; *quietly;* be quiet, keep still.

漸 *Chien*[4]. . . . . . *Gradually*, step by step; slowly.

衰 *Shwai*[1]. To wear away, to decay, *to decline;* to fade. Also *ts'wei*[1].

敗 *Pai*[4]. To destroy; to ruin; to suffer defeat; *enfeebled;* damaged.

衰敗 To decay; *to fail, to grow infirm;* to suffer defeat.

頽 *T'wei*[1]. . . . . . . *Broken down*, ruined.

衰頽 To go to ruin; *to grow infirm.*

苦 *K'u*[3]. Bitter; unpleasant; painful; *urgent;* afflictions, sufferings.

苦苦的 *Earnestly*, urgently; severely.

哀 *Ai*[1]. To grieve for; to pity; to lament; *to beseech;* urgent, importunate; alas!

哀告 *Ai*[1] *kao*[4]. To beseech, *to entreat;* to importune.

强 *Ch'iang*[3]. To compel, *to force;* to constrain; to strengthen. See *ch'iang*[2]; also read *chiang*[4], and *chiang*[1].

强嘴 *Ch'iang*[3] *tswei*[3]. To deny in the face of evidence, to asseverate.

俇 *Chiang*[4]. . . . . . . Unsubmissive, obstreperous.

嘴俇 *Tswei*[3] *chiang*[4]. Unreasonable talk; contradictory.

離 *Li*[2]. To leave, *to separate from;* to be absent; to scatter; from, away from:—Les. 57.

遠 *Yüen*[3]. . . . . . **Distant**; *to keep away from.*

逃 *T'ao*[2]. . . . . . . *To abscond*, to flee; to escape.

逃學 *T'ao*[2] *hsüe*[2]. . . . . To play truant.

應該 *Ying*[1] *kai*[1]. . . . . . . Ought to, duty bound.

蹧 or **遭** *Tsao*[1]. *To meet;* to endure; to experience; a time:—Les. 64.

蹋 *T'a*[4]. . . . . . . To stamp; to tread on.

蹧蹋 To destroy wantonly; *to abuse;* to spoil.

紛 *Fên*[1]. . . . . . *Confused;* many things at once.

紛紛不一 *Fên*[1] *fên*[1] *pu*[4] *i*[1]. Confused, contradictory.

悶 *Mên*[4]. Sad; *melancholy*, heavy-hearted; lonely; a feeling of oppression.

樂 *Loă*[4]. Joy, pleasure, fun; to rejoice, *to be happy;* to be pleased with. Also *yoă*[4].

悶悶不樂 *Mên*[4] *mên*[4] *pu*[4] *loă*[4]. *Melancholy*, discouraged.

就衰敗了(衰頹了)。○我[17]的意思、還是苦的去哀告他。○明[18]明是你的錯、你還這樣强嘴(嘴⿰亻夅)。○我[19]勸你以後要離他遠遠的。○他[20]這樣的逃學、應該重重的打他。○你[21]的孩子也多多的、你還能說他不蹧蹋人的東西嗎。○街[22]上的話、紛紛不一。○你[23]常這樣悶悶不樂、最容易生病。

17 My idea is to go again and earnestly entreat him.

18 Clearly it is your fault; and yet you asseverate in this way.

19 I recommend you hereafter to keep far away from him.

20 You ought to whip him severely for having played truant in this way.

21 Your children also are quite numerous: would you venture to assert that they never abuse anybody's things?

22 The reports on the street are contradictory.

23 When a man is all the time so melancholy as this, it is very easy to become sick.

Notes.

1 Peking teachers object to doubling 圓, but Southern teachers approve.

3 Both forms are in general use. If 一會兒 be used, the translation should be *presently*, instead of *by and by*.

6 上當 Some would write 檔, but the general custom of Chinese books is to write simply 當. The derivation of the meaning is not certain. Perhaps it is from the idea of a pawn or surety, implying that the party found himself suddenly placed in the power of another; or perhaps from the idea of an opening or empty space, implying that the party took for reality that which proved to be "thin air."

7 早些, properly, *a little earlier*.

13 The general custom in China, in weighing all kinds of coarse commodities, is to weigh with the end of the scale beam considerably above the level, and there is generally some contest on the part of the purchaser to get it higher. Steelyards are nearly always made to weigh light in anticipation of this custom.

16 If the sentence were rendered, *His strength will gradually decline*, it would show more clearly the force of the 就, but it would not give the whole idea of the sentence so well.

20 We might with equal propriety render, *If he plays truant in this way, you ought to whip him severely.*

21 人 is used indefinitely for *anybody*.

22 Such expressions as 紛紛不一, and 悶悶不樂 in the next sentence, are taken from the book language. Mandarin is constantly spiced by such ready-made phrases, appropriated from the book language. By use they become familiar to the unlearned as well as the learned.

LESSON XX.

The Auxiliary Verbs 着 and 之.

着 is the most important and widely used of all the auxiliary verbs. It expresses the carrying of the action of the principal verb into effect. It often gives the force of the present participle. It may be joined to almost any active verb; but is much more frequently joined to some than to others.

In Peking, when 着 immediately follows the verb, it is read *choă*^{2}; but when 不 or 得 intervenes, it is always read *chao*^{2}. This distinction of reading is confined to Pekingese.

之 is a *Wên li* particle having various uses, one of which corresponds in a measure to the use of 着 as an auxiliary in Mandarin. It is used in Shantung and elsewhere as a substitute for 着, which, in Eastern Shantung, it largely replaces. It can not, however, be used with a negative, as 着 can. It is probably an old form which has been superseded by 着 in most places. It is sometimes heard both in Nanking and in Kiukiang.

第二十課

某[1]人仗着他有力氣。○那[2]個人想之着打你。○你[3]該等着先生的空兒。○說[4]着容易、做着難。○黑[5]夜你該鎖着那個後門。○他[6]專靠着他父親的錢、過日子。○這[7]些話要緊、你該留心聽之着。○你[8]不要指着這個、說那個。○婦[9]人該順着他的丈夫。○你[10]不認得路、可以找個人來引領着你。○他[11]們兩個在門口坐着說話。○王[12]先生覺覺得着我待他不公道。○他[13]不肯照

TRANSLATION.

1 The man referred to presumes on the fact that he is strong.
2 That man has a mind to beat you.
3 You ought to wait the teacher's leisure.
4 To talk is easy; to perform is difficult (or, talking is easy; performing is difficult).
5 You ought to lock that back door at night.
6 He depends entirely upon his father's money for a living.
7 These words are important; you should pay attention to them.
8 Do not address this one when you are speaking of that one.
9 A woman ought to obey her husband.
10 If you are not acquainted with the road, you should get a man to guide you.
11 They two are sitting at the door talking.
12 Mr. Wang feels that I treated him unjustly.

VOCABULARY.

之 *Chï*[1]. To go, to proceed; belonging to; sign of possessive in *Wên li*:—see Sub. He; she; it; this; that; also used as an expletive.

某 *Mu*[3], *mou*[3]. A certain person, so-and-so,—used when it is not convenient to use the name.

想 *Hsiang*[3]. To think on; to reflect; to remember; *to plan;* to expect; to wish.

空 *K'ung*[4]. An empty place, a crevice; vacant, unoccupied; time, *leisure;* a deficiency, a defalcation. Also *k'ung*[1].

黑夜 *Hei*[1] *yie*[4]. Night; *at night.*

鎖 *Soă*[3]. A lock; *to lock.*

專 *Chwan*[1]. Singly, *solely;* bent on; special.

靠 *K'ao*[4]. To lean upon, *to rely on;* to trust to; to be near; adjoining.

指 *Chï*[3]. A finger or toe; *to point at;* to refer to; to direct; to rely upon.

婦人 *Fu*[4] *jên*[2]. A married woman, a wife.

順 *Shun*[4]. To comply, to yield to; *to obey;* dutiful; convenient.

丈 *Chang*[4]. A rod of ten Chinese feet; *a senior;* one worthy of respect.

丈夫 *Chang*[4] *fu*[1]. *A husband;* a man (*vir*), a knight; a brave man.

領 *Ling*[3]. A collar, a necktie; to receive from, to take:—Les. 79; to direct; *to lead,* to act as guide. A classifier:—Les. 125.

引 *Yin*[3]. To draw out; *to lead, to guide;* to induce; to introduce; to thread,—as a needle; to quote; an introduction or preface.

覺 *Chüe*[2], *chioă*[2]. To perceive; to be sensible of, *to feel;* to awaken, to arouse. Also *chiao*[4].

覺得 *Chüe*[2] *tê*[2]. To feel, to be sensible of.

照 *Chao*[4]. To enlighten, to shine; to front towards; to care for; to accord with; *according to,* as; a pass, a permit.

主人 *Chu*[3] *jên*[2]. Master, employer.

碰 *P'êng*[4]. To run against; to bump; *to meet;* to happen on.

作 *Tsu*[3]. To let out, to tell:—See *tsoă*[4] and *tsoă*[1].

作聲 *Tsu*[3] *shêng*[1]. To tell, to divulge, to let out a secret:—Note 14.

着他主人的意思行。○若[14]在路上碰着他、不要作聲。○暫[15]且留着、也不礙事。○穿[16]着雨衣、下雨也不關妨事。○你[17]不按着規矩不行。○守[18]着甚麼、學甚麼。○我[19]的小刀子、已經找着了。○[20]好好生慎看孩子、不要磕着跌着他。○他[21]的孩子、跟着李先生念書。○他[22]不想着還錢、你跟他要、也是白費工夫。○正[23]對着門、有對我生財四個字、貼在牆上。

13 He is not willing to act according to his master's wishes.
14 If you meet him on the road, don't mention it.
15 It's no matter if you do keep it for the present.
16 When you have on rain clothes, it is no matter if it does rain.
17 It will not do for you not to follow the rule.
18 Men imitate those with whom they associate.
19 My pocket knife has already been found (or, is already found).
20 Take good care of the baby, and do not let him fall down.
21 His son goes to school to Mr. Li.
22 He does not intend to pay: it is a waste of time for you to dun him.
23 Exactly opposite the door there are pasted on the wall the four characters, "May he who is opposite me make money."

暫 *Chan*⁴. A short time, briefly; for the time . . . . being, temporarily.

且 *Ch'ie*³. Moreover, also, yet; further, be- . . . . sides:—Les. 138.

暫且 Temporarily, for the time being.

礙 *Ai*⁴. *To hinder*, to impede; to embarrass; to . . . . . . obstruct.

妨 *Fang*¹. *To hinder*, to oppose; an impedi- . . . . ment.

礙事 *Ai*⁴ *shï*⁴. Matter; *consequence;* hindrance; . . . . generally used with a negative.

關事 *Kwan*¹ *shï*⁴. . . . . . . Same as 礙事.

妨事 *Fang*¹ *shï*⁴. . . . . . . Same:—Note 16.

按 *An*¹. To act according to; as, according to. . . . . . . Also *an*⁴.

守 *Shou*³. To keep; to guard; to obey; to at- . . . . tend to; to protect; *to associate with.*

好生 *Hao*³ *shêng*¹. Carefully, attentively. 生 is . . . . the form found in books, but the phrase is universally spoken *hao*³ *shing*⁴.

慎 *Shên*⁴. To act carefully; *cautious;* attentive; . . . . considerate.

好慎 *Hao*³ *shên*⁴. . . . . . . Same as 好生.

磕 *K'ê*¹. . . . . . . *To strike against;* to knock.

跌 *Tie*¹. To slip and fall, to tumble; to stumble; . . . . *to fall:*—Les. 92.

念書 *Nien*⁴ *shu*¹. *To go to school;* to study; to . . . . repeat over and over.

財 *Ts'ai*². . . . . . *Riches*, wealth; property, goods.

貼 *T'ie*⁴·¹. To attach to; *to paste to*, to post; to . . . . make up a loss; adjacent.

NOTES.

3 The idea is, Do not pretend to be speaking to this one when you really mean that one;—do not whip one man over another man's shoulders.

11 Or, *They two were sitting at the door talking.* See Note, Les. 6. (5.)

14 In many places 作聲 is read *tsu*⁴ *shêng*¹. It is also often written 做聲, and pronounced *tsoă*⁴ *shêng*¹. It should be noted that 作 and 做 are both read *tsoă*⁴ in Peking; but in most places the latter is read *tsou*⁴. The two characters are by no means interchangeable.

15 Or, if referring to a person, *It is no matter if you do detain him for the present.*

16 妨事 is Southern Mandarin, though occasionally heard in the North. 關事 is frequently written 管事, and 礙事 is more widely understood than either of these forms.

18 Or, *Men take to that with which they are constantly brought in contact.*

20 磕 is here used causatively, not meaning to strike, but to cause, or allow, the child to fall down and strike itself on the ground. Chinese verbs are often so used.

23 When it is desired to isolate a clause, or expression, and use it as a substantive, it is followed by a statement of the number of characters it contains. These characters are pasted up by the shopkeeper himself; but they read as if expressing the good wishes of the party on whose wall they are pasted.

第二十一課

我[1]自己的錢不彀。○打[2]發你自己去、我不放心。○先[3]正自己、後正人。○他[4]自己打自己的嘴巴子。○應[5]當愛人如己。○他[6]是我知己的朋友。○自[7]己不知道自己的毛病。○我[8]自己不好意思和他說。○這[9]不是合夥的買賣、是我自己一各個兒的。○自[10]盡和殺人、是一樣的罪。○不[11]能給你、我自家要留着使喚用。○這[12]個事情、

TRANSLATION.

1 My own money is not sufficient.
2 I do not feel easy to send you alone.
3 Correct yourself before you correct others.
4 He slaps his own mouth (i.e., he talks inconsistently).
5 You should love others as yourself.
6 He is my confidential friend.
7 One does not know one's own faults.
8 I do not like to speak to him myself.
9 This is not a partnership business; it is my own.
10 To commit suicide is as great a sin as to commit murder.
11 I cannot give it to you; I want to keep it for my own use.
12 You ought to decide this thing yourself.

LESSON XXI.

THE REFLEXIVE PRONOUN.

自 Self; my own, his own, etc.

己 Self; private; selfish.

自己 Self. This term is joined with the several personal pronouns to make *myself, thyself,* etc. It is also used alone in these same senses, the antecedent being understood. It may sometimes also be translated, *oneself.* It is frequently written, and more frequently spoken, 自家. Both 自 and 己 are used alone, but always in ready-made book phrases. When thus used, the 自 precedes the verb with which it is joined, while 己 follows it.

自各兒 or 自己各兒 His own, her own, etc. The second form is strongly colloquial. The Nanking equivalent is 自己一個:—Les. 66.

VOCABULARY.

己 *Chi*³. . . . . . Self, oneself; private; special.

各 *Kê*⁴. . . . . . . Each, every, all:—Les. 66.

打發 *Ta*³ *fa*¹. To send, to dispatch; to satisfy, ... to please.

放心 *Fang*⁴ *hsin*¹. To set the mind at rest, to . . . . be free from anxiety.

巴 *Pa*⁴. To adhere; a crust; a clamp; *the jaw;* . . . . . . a tail. Also *pa*¹.

嘴巴 *Tswei*³ *pa*⁴. The lower jaw; *the mouth.* . . . .

應當 *Ying*¹ *tang*¹. Ought, should, duty bound, ... under obligation.

知己 *Chi*¹ *chi*³. . . . . . . Intimate, confidential.

愛 *Ai*⁴. *To love,* to take delight in; to wish; to . . . . . . be sparing of, to grudge.

朋 *P'êng*². . . . . . A friend, a companion.

朋友 *P'êng*² *yiu*³. . . . . . A friend, an associate.

夥 *Hwoa*³. A band, a company; a comrade, *a* . . . . *partner;* numerous.

合夥 *Hê*² *hwoa*³. *A partnership;* to enter into . . . . a partnership.

盡 *Chin*⁴. To exhaust; *finished,* ended; empty; . . . . all, entirely; to the uttermost:—Les. 101 and 158. See *ching*⁴.

自盡 *Tsï*⁴ *chin*⁴. To end one's own life, to . . . . commit suicide.

殺 *Sha*¹. . . . . . To kill; *to murder:*—Les. 183.

殺人 *Sha*¹ *jên*². . . . . To commit murder.

喚 *Hwan*⁴. . . . . To call, to hail, to bid, to name.

使喚 *Shï*³ *hwan*⁴. To employ, to use, to utilize . . . . (C. and N.).

掛 *Kwa*¹. To be connected with, involved in; *to* . . . . *brush against,* to jostle. Also *kwa*⁴

該是你自己拿主意。○[13]不關他的事、是我自家的錯。○[14]沒有人拐掛着他、是他自己跌倒了。○[15]天地不能自己造自己。○[16]這是他哥哥的眼鏡、不是他自家的。○[17]人靠着自己的功勞、不能得救。○[18]不用人送他、他自己能去。○[19]你若不親自去、我怕這個事情、不能辦妥當。○[20]他如今有二十來畝地、若是安分守己、也可以過

13 He is not responsible; it was my own mistake.

14 Nobody touched him; he fell down of himself.

15 Heaven and earth could not create themselves.

16 These are his elder brother's spectacles, not his own.

17 A man cannot be saved by trusting in his own merit.

18 He does not need any one to go with him: he can go himself.

19 If you do not go yourself, I fear this business can not be satisfactorily arranged.

20 He now has upwards of twenty mow of land: if he is frugal and temperate he can make a living.

拐 *Kwai*³. To swindle, to decoy; to kidnap; to round a corner; a right angle. Read *kwai*¹,—*to brush against*, to jostle (L).

造 *Tsao*⁴. To make, to build; *to create;* to act; to commence.

哥 *Ke*¹. *An elder brother;* used as a suffix to show respect.

哥哥 An elder brother:—Note 16.

鏡 *Ching*⁴. A metallic mirror; a looking-glass; *a lens.*

眼鏡 *Yien*³ *ching*⁴. Spectacles.

功 *Kung*¹. *Merit;* achievements; virtue.

勞 *Lao*². To toil, *to labor;* to trouble; wearied, distressed, burdened.

功勞 Meritorious deeds, merit.

救 *Chiu*⁴. To rescue, *to save;* to liberate.

親自 *Ch'in*¹ *tsï*⁴. *Oneself;* in person, *in propria persona.*

妥當 *T'oă*³ *tang*⁴. Satisfactory, in proper order or condition.

安分 *An*¹ *fên*⁴. To do one's duty; to fill one's proper station; *to be frugal.*

守己 *Shou*³ *chi*³. To restrain oneself, *to be temperate.*

吃虧 *Ch'ï*¹ *k'wei*¹. *To suffer loss;* to get the worst of the bargain.

埋 *Man*². To conceal; to lay up; to accuse. Also *mai*⁴.

怨 *Yüen*⁴. To hate, to feel bitter; *to murmur at;* malice; a wrong.

埋怨 To hold a grudge against; *to find fault with,* to murmur at.

欺 *Ch'i*¹. To cheat; *to deceive;* to insult; to befool; to ridicule.

欺哄 *Ch'i*¹ *hung*³. *To deceive,* to impose upon.

底細 *Ti*³ *hsï*⁴. The facts, the real state of the case.

底裏 *Ti*³ *li*³. The same as 底細 (W).

約 *Yüe*¹, *yoă*¹. To bind by contract, to agree with; to restrain; *to estimate;* a treaty; a deed; condensed; about, nearly:—Les. 96.

摸 *Moă*¹, *mu*¹. To feel after, to seek; *to guess;* to follow a pattern.

約摸 To estimate, to guess, *to speak at random.*

表 *Piao*³. The exterior; to manifest, *to make known;* a signal; any instrument with a scale,—as a thermometer or a watch; a permit; kindred of a different name.

表明 *Piao*³ *ming*². To make known, to show; *to tell, to publish.*

表白 *Piao*³ *pai*². To show, to *publish.*

跟從 *Kên*¹ *ts'ung*². To follow.

克 *K'ê*⁴. To be able; *to subdue;* to repress.

克己 *K'ê*⁴ *chi*³. To govern oneself, *to deny oneself.*

背 *Pei*¹. To carry on the back. Also *pei*⁴.

十字架 *Shï*² *tsï*⁴ *chia*⁴. The cross—from its resemblance to the character 十.

日子。

21 這是你自己找着吃虧、還來埋怨我嗎。

22 你該小心、不要自己欺哄自己。

23 自己不知道底細、不好約摸着說。

24 不用自己表表明白、好不好、人早曉得了。

25 有人要跟從我、就當克己、背着十字架跟從我。

21 You brought this loss on yourself; and yet you come complaining against me.

22 You should be careful and not deceive yourself.

23 You should not speak at random, when you do not know the bottom facts in the case.

24 You need not publish it yourself: whether good or bad, people already know.

25 If any man will follow me, let him deny himself, and take up his cross, and follow me.

---

2 放心 Lit., *to let down, or lay down, the heart*; similar to our phrase "to set the heart at rest."

3 人 is here used for *others*, in opposition to *self*. So also in (5).

8 不好意思 is a very common phrase, which will not bear a literal analysis. It expresses a slight feeling of shame or embarrassment.

12 Lit., *This thing is yours to decide.*

14 是 might be omitted, but as used it adds emphasis to the clause following it.

16 哥 is not repeated as adjectives are, for emphasis, but probably for the purpose of distinguishing the word from others, or as an indication of endearment. Names of relatives show a special tendency to double in this way: thus we have,—姐姐 *chie*³ *chie*³, elder sister; 妹妹 *mei*⁴ *mei*⁴, younger sister; also 媽媽 *ma*¹ *ma*¹, mother; 爹爹 *tie*¹ *tie*¹, father; 爺爺 *yie*² *yie*², grandfather; 奶奶 *nai*³ *nai*³, grandmother, etc. 父 and 母, however, are never repeated.

20 二十來. It is hard to see how this phrase comes to mean *upwards of twenty*. The 來 is nearly always pronounced *la*, and 個 is often added. In Peking it means *about twenty*—less or more; elsewhere it always means upwards of twenty, though not usually over twenty-five.

21 吃虧 is an infinitive clause, the object of the verb 找.

23 底裏 is not used in the North, save in one or two ready-made phrases. It is used in the South, but is a little bookish.

24 Note how the subjunctive idea is implied in 好不好.

LESSON XXII.

AFFIRMATIVE-NEGATIVE QUESTION.

Besides the form with 嗎, a direct question is very often asked by putting the idea first in the affirmative, and then in the negative, implying or offering an alternative in the answer; somewhat as we do in English when we add "or not" to a direct question.

This form of question is much used, and is somewhat less categorical than with 嗎.

VOCABULARY.

想家 *Hsiang*³ *chia*¹. . . . . To be homesick.

忙 *Mang*². . . . . . . Busy, occupied; *hurried*.

帮忙 *Pang*¹ *mang*². *To help do extra work;* to assist:—Note 5.

賬 *Chang*⁴. . . . . *An account;* a debt; a charge.

宜 *I*². . . . . . . Right; fit, proper; *suitable*.

便宜 *Pien*⁴ *i*². . . . . . . *Convenient;* serviceable.

方便 *Fang*¹ *pien*⁴. . . . . Convenient.

嫁 *Chia*⁴. . . . . . To marry a husband.

出嫁 *Ch'u*¹ *chia*⁴. To get married (of the woman).

齊 *Ch'i*². Even, uniform; on a level; complete; to equalize; at once; *all*.

陽 *Yang*². The superior of the dual powers of nature; *the sun;* day; heaven; male; virility; the front; this world or life.

太陽 *T'ai*⁴ *yang*². . . . . The sun.

封 *Fêng*¹. To appoint, to constitute officially; to seal; *an envelope*, a sealed packet. A classifier:—Les. 125.

信封 *Hsin*⁴ *fêng*¹. . . . . A letter envelope.

營 *Ying*². To plan, *to attend to;* to get a living; an intrenched camp; military.

第二十二課

紙[1]還有沒有。○你[2]早一點兒去好不好。○你[3]想家不想家。想不想家 ○這[4]個刀是你的不是。不是你的 ○我[5]明天請客、你能來幫忙不能。○今[6]天算賬、便宜不便宜、方便不方便 ○你[7]家大姑娘出了嫁沒有。出了門 ○客[8]來齊了沒有。○趕[9]落太陽能到不能。○這[10]個信封兒合式不合式。○還[11]有別的事情沒有。營生 ○先[12]生在中國、服水土不服。服不服水土 ○李[13]師母的喉嚨、今天好了沒有。○先[14]生的胳

TRANSLATION.

1 Is there any more paper?
2 Would it not be better for you to go a little earlier?
3 Are you homesick?
4 Is this knife yours?
5 I am going to invite company to-morrow: can you come and help me?
6 Is it convenient to settle accounts to-day?
7 Is the eldest daughter of your family married yet?
8 Have the guests all arrived?
9 Can we arrive by sunset?
10 Is this envelope suitable or not?
11 Have you still any other business?
12 Does the climate in China agree with you?
13 Is Mrs. Li's throat well to-day?
14 Does your upper arm still pain you?

營生 *Ying² shêng¹*. To make a living; an affair, *a piece of business;* work.

服 *Fu²*. Clothing; *to yield to;* to submit; to subdue; to agree to; to swallow.

水土 *Shwei³ t'u³*. Climate.

服水土 Acclimated, to stand the climate.

喉 *Hou²*. The throat, the gullet.

嚨 *Lung²*. The throat, the œsophagus.

喉嚨 The throat.

胳 *Kê¹*. The fore-arm.

膊 *Poă⁴*. The humerus, the upper arm.

胳膊 The upper arm; the arm. Also written 胳膀.

脚 *Chiao³*, *chioă³*. *The foot;* the base; conveyance; freightage.

凍 *Tung⁴*. To freeze; frost-bitten; cold.

賤 *Chien⁴*. Mean, ignoble; *cheap;* to depreciate, to regard lightly.

便 *P'ien²*. Advantage; *cheap*. See *pien⁴*.

便宜 *P'ien² i²*. Advantage; *cheap*.

米 *Mi³*. Rice or millet after being hulled.

大米 *Ta⁴ mi³*. Rice,—as distinguished from millet (小米).

乾飯 *Kan¹ fan⁴*. Rice or millet boiled dry.

到底 *Tao⁴ ti³*. In the end; *after all;* finally; positively.

火盆 *Hwoă³ p'ên²*. A brazier; *an earthen bowl for holding live coals.*

滅 *Mie⁴*. To destroy; to exterminate; to put out or *to go out,*—as fire.

熄 *Wu³*. To smother,—as fire, *to put out* or to go out. Also *wu⁴*.

保人 *Pao³ jên²*. *Bail,* security, an endorser, a backer.

商 *Shang¹*. *To consult,* to deliberate; to trade; a merchant.

議 *I⁴*. *To deliberate;* to discuss; to criticize.

商議 To consult with, to consider; to speak in behalf of.

廚 *Ch'u²*. A kitchen, a cook-house.

鍋 *Kwoă¹*. An iron kettle, a skillet.

破 *P'oă⁴*. To break, to tear, *to split;* to destroy; to solve; to storm:—Les. 102.

補 *Pu³*. *To repair;* to patch; to make up; to aid, to strengthen. Also *p'u¹*.

小爐匠 *Hsiao³ lu² chiang⁴*. A tinker, a traveling smith.

整 *Chêng³*. To adjust; *to repair,* to mend; to reform; the whole of, entire.

整治 *Chêng³ chi⁴*. To repair, to put in order.

拾 *Shi²*. To gather up; to bring together; to clear away; to arrange; ten.

收拾 *Shou¹ shi²*. To put in order; *to repair;* to gather up and take away.

膊、還疼不疼。○那[15]個飯壞了沒壞。○這[16]個禮拜的衣裳、洗完了沒有。○今[17]天實在冷、你的脚冷不冷(凍不凍)、○這[18]兩天銀子行市、長了沒有。○四[19]百錢買這本書、你看便宜不便宜(賤不賤)。○大[20]米乾飯、先生吃不吃。○他[21]說要來、到底來了沒有。○這[22]個意思、先生明白不明白。○我[23]給你三吊錢、彀不彀。○我[24]要再說、請先生聽着、看對不對。○火[25]盆裡的火、熄(滅)了沒有。○你[26]不放心、我找個保人行不行。○我[27]要和他商議一點事情、不知道他有工夫沒有。○厨[28]房的鍋破了、我去找個補鍋的(小爐匠)來、收拾(整治)他好不好。

15 Has that food spoiled?
16 Have you finished washing this week's clothes?
17 It is very cold to-day: are your feet frozen (or cold)?
18 Has the price of silver advanced these few days?
19 Four hundred cash for this book; do you not think it cheap?
20 Do you eat dry rice?
21 He said he would come; but, after all, has he come?
22 Is this idea clear to you?
23 If I give you three thousand cash, will it be enough?
24 I will say it again. Please listen and see whether it is correct or not.
25 Has the fire in the fire-pan gone out?
26 If you are uneasy, would it do for me to get some one as security?
27 I want to consult him about a small matter: I wonder if he has time.
28 The kettle in the kitchen is cracked (or, broken): shall I not get a tinker to come and mend it?

NOTES.

2 好不好 has a different meaning here from what it had in the last lesson, and is read with a different emphasis.

3 你想家不想家 is the proper and more prevalent form; that is, the rule in all cases is, to complete the affirmative form *before* the negative is begun. The second form is much used in Shantung, and also to some extent in other places; though most teachers, if asked, would say that the first is the right one; because they have been accustomed to see it so in books. To adhere in all cases to the book form sounds labored and awkward.

4 To give the meaning in the translation, a slight emphasis should be thrown on 你. By a different emphasis the sentence might be made to mean, *This knife is yours, is it not?* To give this meaning the emphasis should be thrown, in the first form on the first 是, and in the second form on the second 是.

5 帮忙, *to assist the hurry;* i.e., to help with any extra work. Properly applied to assistance rendered freely; but often used of temporary work that is paid for.

7 Instead of repeating the principal verb in the negative form, 有 is made to stand for it. This is a common form.

13 For anything that appears in this sentence, it may have been addressed to Mrs. Li; in which case the meaning would simply be, *Is your throat well to-day?*

17 凍 properly means *frozen*, but is used in many places as an exaggeration for *very cold,—freezing cold.*

20 大米乾飯 is a Northern expression. In the South 飯 alone expresses it all, for the reason that they have no 小米, *millet;* and 飯, when used alone, is understood to mean *dry rice.*

27 不知道 *do not know*, is the common way of expressing "I wonder." The 道 is often omitted.

28 The Southern form in 補鍋的, *a mender of kettles:*—Les. 39. In the North a 小爐匠 is a traveling tinker who carries a forge and a small kit of blacksmith tools, and mends crockery, as well as iron, brass and tin ware.

LESSON XXIII.

的 JOINED TO VERBS.

When 的 follows a verb it gives it the force of a participial noun, or makes it equivalent to a relative clause. Thus, the first sentence might be rendered literally, *His going is very quick;* and the second, *The money which he earned was not much.* While this is the analysis of this idiom-

第二十三課

他[1]走的很快。○他[2]掙的錢不多。○伏[3]天下的雨很大。○這[4]個月花的錢不少。○這[5]個刀磨的不快。○我[6]的父親、病得的不輕。○客[7]堂、掃的不乾淨。○你[8]看我這個畫兒、畫的好不好。○這[9]個字繙的不大對。○你[10]慢慢的說、我就聽得的清楚。○他[11]用的這個比方恰對。○我[12]怕你說得的荒唐。○他[13]學的多、又溫習的熟。○你[14]學的

Translation.

1 He goes very fast.
2 He did not make much money.
3 The summer rains were very great.
4 There has been not a little money spent this month.
5 This knife is not ground sharp.
6 My father is very sick.
7 The parlor is not swept clean.
8 Look at this painting of mine, [and see] whether it is well painted.
9 This word is not translated quite right.
10 If you speak slowly, I shall hear distinctly.
11 He used this comparison very appositely.
12 I fear you are speaking rashly: (or, I fear you spoke rashly.)
13 He learned much, and also learned [it well.

atic usage, a good English rendering will take a variety of forms, according to the connection.

得 may often be substituted for 的 without appreciable change of meaning. Such substitution is more frequent in the South than in the North. It is possible that 得 was the original form.

Vocabulary.

掙 *Chêng*^{4}. *To make money by labor*, to earn; to break or tear away.

伏 *Fu*^{2}. To fall prostrate, to humble oneself; to suffer, to conceal; *the hot season.*

伏天 *Fu*^{2} *t'ien*^{1}. The hot season, July 19 to August 18.

磨 *Moǎ*^{2}. To rub, *to grind;* to sharpen; to argue; trials; a time:—Les. 64. Also *moǎ*^{4}.

畫 *Hwa*^{4}. A picture, *a painting;* a mark, a line; a stroke in a character. Also *hwa*^{2}.

畫 *Hwa*^{2}. To draw a line; *to paint or draw;* to line off. See *hwa*^{4}.

繙 *Fan*^{1}. To open out; *to translate,* to interpret.

楚 *Ch'u*^{3}. Sharp, painful; orderly; plain, *distinct,* clear.

清楚 *Ch'ing*^{1} *ch'u*^{3}. Clear, *distinct;* in order; settled,—as an account.

比方 *Pi*^{3} *fang*^{1}. *A comparison;* an illustration; for instance.

恰 *Ch'ia*^{4}. Luckily, opportunely; *exactly;* just; at the exact moment.

荒 *Hwang*^{1}. Barren, waste; *reckless,* careless; empty; famine.

唐 *T'ang*^{2}. To boast; dissolute.

荒唐 Unsteady; unreliable; wild; *rash.*

溫 *Wên*^{1}. Warm, tepid; mild, genial, kind; to practice, *to become familiar with.*

習 *Hsi*^{2}. *To practice;* skilled; custom, habit.

溫習 To repeat again and again, to practice.

肉 *Jou*^{4}. Flesh; *meat;* fat, fleshy; corporeal; substantial. Also *ju*^{4}.

煮 *Chu*^{3}. To boil in water, to cook.

爛 *Lan*^{4}. Bright, brilliant; *cooked tender;* soft, mellow; tattered; rotten.

湊 *Ts'ou*^{4}. To gather together, to collect; *to happen or hit upon.*

巧 *Ch'iao*^{3}. Skilful, ingenious; wily, shrewd; *opportune.*

湊巧 *Opportune,* in the nick of time; lucky.

櫃 *Kwei*^{4}. A chest; a locker; a bureau; a safe; a cupboard; *a sideboard.*

正當 *Chêng*^{4} *tang*^{4}. Square; level; *straight, not awry.*

蓋 *Kai*^{4}. A cover, a roof; to cover, to roof; *to build a house.*

體 *T'i*^{3}. The body, the limbs; a solid; the substance; to feel for; *becoming;* to embody; to realize; to pervade.

官話、殼用的不殼用的呢。○這[15]個肉煮得的
不爛。○你[16]來的實在湊巧。○這[17]個櫃櫃子、安
的不正當正。○王[18]大老爺的房子、蓋得的實在
體講面究。○我[19]在路上、躭誤的工夫不少。○路[20]
太太生得的和氣、唱的詩也頂好。○你[21]新將娶
的兒媳婦、如意不如意。○纔[22]買的那個新
爐子、做的眞巧。○我[23]有甚麼得罪先生的
地方、請寬恕我。○我[24]賺的、沒有他的三分
之一。○我[25]年輕的時候、家裏有錢、吃的是
好的、穿的也是好的。

14 Is the Mandarin you have learned sufficient for ordinary use?
15 This meat is not boiled tender.
16 Your coming is truly opportune.
17 This sideboard is not set straight.
18 Wang Ta Lao Yie's house is very elegantly built.
19 I spent a deal of time on the road.
20 Lady Lu is naturally amiable, and also sings hymns exceedingly well.
21 Does the wife you have just taken for your son please you?
22 That stove you have just bought is certainly ingeniously made.
23 If I have in any wise offended you, I beg you to pardon me.
24 What I cleared was (or, is) not one-third of what he cleared.
25 When I was young our family was rich; I ate good food and wore good clothes.

體面 *T'i^{3} mien^{4}*. Genteel; honorable; *elegant;* fine-looking.

究 *Chiu^{1}*. To examine into, to search out; after all, finally, in the end:—Les. 127.

講究. *Chiang^{3} chiu^{1}*. To explain; to discuss. In the South,—that which elicits commendation, fine, *elegant.*

和氣 *Hé^{2} ch'i^{4}*. Peaceable, *amiable.*

唱 *Ch'ang^{4}*. *To sing;* to call out,—as a roll.

詩 *Shï^{1}*. A poem, an ode, a hymn.

將 *Chiang^{1}*. To take, to hold; an auxiliary verb:—Les. 28; *to take a wife* (L.); to accommodate; to avail of; soon, presently; sign of future:—Les. 55. Also *chiang^{4}*.

如意 *Ju^{2} i^{4}*. Satisfactory, *pleasing,* agreeable, gratifying.

得罪 *Tê^{2} tswei^{4}*. *To offend,* to sin against; I beg your pardon.

寬 *K'wan^{1}*. Broad; spacious; *forgiving,* indulgent; to extend.

恕 *Shu^{4}*. *To pardon;* to excuse; indulgent; benignant.

寬恕 *To forgive;* to be lenient, to be generous.

年輕 *Nien^{2} ch'ing^{1}*. Young, youthful.

NOTES.

2 Or, *He is not making much money.*

11 Might also be rendered. *The comparison which he used was very apposite.* The 這個 is here thrown in between the parts of the clause in a highly idiomatic way that should be noted by the learner:—(see also 22.)

14 Or, *Have you learned sufficient Mandarin for ordinary use?*

17 正當 appears to be used only in Central Mandarin.

19 躭誤工夫 sometimes means *to be detained,* but more frequently it means *to spend time,* or *to waste time.*

21 The proper and everywhere current form is 娶. 將 is local in Shantung.

24 沒有他的 is elliptical for 沒有他賺的.

LESSON XXIV.

INTENSIVES OF EXCESS.

太 Too, excessive, very. The composition of this character indicates a sort of afterthought, in the form of a supplement to the character 大; by a dot "great" is made to be "too great."

第二十四課

1今天太熱。○2你說的太快。○3你的衣裳忒骯髒癩歹。○4我的鐘太慢。○5如今天太短。○6我今日太乏了。○7那些水太涼。○8那個人的心忒毒了。○9學的太多、學不熟。○10以後講的、太煩絮了。○11早晨上沏泡的茶太釅厚。○12那個小姑娘、生的過於精明細。○13明天出殯、太急促了。○14先生寫字、費工夫太大。○15他做的過快、不大仔細。○16我

Translation.

1 It is too hot to-day.
2 You speak too fast.
3 Your clothes are too dirty.
4 My clock is too slow.
5 The days now are too short.
6 I am too tired to-day.
7 That water is too cold.
8 That man's heart is too malignant.
9 If you learn too much you will not learn it well.
10 Afterwards there was too much repetition in his discourse.
11 The tea made this morning was too strong.
12 That little girl is by nature too precocious.
13 To have the funeral to-morrow will be too hurried.
14 You take too much time in writing.

忒 Too, excessive; an exaggeration of 太:—mostly used of things that are in some way displeasing.

過於 Too, excessive. 過 is sometimes used alone in the same sense.

過逾 Both words mean to pass over, or to go beyond, and together mean, *too much, beyond measure*. The accent is on the second character, while in 過於 it is on the first.

過分 Beyond duty or propriety, outrageous.

Vocabulary.

忒 *T'ê*^{4}. ...... An excess; too, very:—see Sub.
於 *Yü*^{2}. ...... In, at, on; with, by; as, so; than.
逾 *Yü*^{4}. To pass over; to go beyond; to exceed; ...... to omit; still, more.
癩 *Lai*^{1}. ...... Foul, filthy (L.). Also *lai*^{4}.
歹 *Tai*^{3}. ...... *Bad*, vicious; perverse.
癩歹 Unkempt; soiled, dirty (L.).
骯 *Ang*^{1}. ...... Dirty.
髒 *Tsang*^{1}. ...... Filthy; to *dirty*, to defile,
骯髒 Filthy, *dirty*, foul, nasty.
乏 *Fa*^{2}. To be in want of; deficient; exhausted, ... weary, *tired;* half-witted, stupid.
毒 *Tu*^{2}. ...... Poisonous; *malignant;* cruel.
煩 *Fan*^{2}. Troubled; annoyed; perplexed, *con-* ...... *fused;* grieved; urgent.
絮 *Hsü*^{4}. To repeat, *to reiterate;* prolix; to ...... wad,—as a quilt; gossamer, fleecy.
煩絮 *Repetitious*, tautological.
晨 *Ch'ên*^{2}. ...... Morning, dawn.
早晨 *Tsao*^{3} *ch'ên*^{2}. ...... The morning.
早上 *Tsao*^{3} *shang*^{4}. ...... The morning.
沏 *Ch'i*^{1}. ...... To steep or *make* tea (Pekingese).
泡 *P'ao*^{4}. To steep, to soak; *to draw,—as tea.* ...... Also *p'ao*^{1}.
茶 *Ch'a*^{2}. ...... Tea,—the plant or the infusion.
釅 *Yien*^{4}. ...... Strong,—as tea or coffee.
厚 *Hou*^{4}. Thick; generous, liberal; large, sub- ...... stantial; intimate; *strong,*—as tea.
精 *Ching*^{1}. Unmixed; fine, subtle; expert, prac- ...... ticed; *smart*, ready; the essence; semen; an apparition.
精明 *Ching*^{1} *ming*^{2}. *Smart*, clever, quick-wit- ...... ted, sharp; shrewd.
精細 *Ching*^{1} *hsi*^{4}. *Smart*, clever, sharp; alert. ......
殯 *Pin*^{4}. ...... To carry to burial; a funeral.
出殯 *Ch'u*^{1} *pin*^{4}. To observe funeral rites; *to* ...... *have a funeral.*
促 *Ts'u*^{4}. ...... To urge; *urgent*, pressing; close.
急促 *Chi*^{2} *ts'u*^{4}. ...... *Hurried*, hasty.

的嘴太直、說話常得罪人。○若[17]是太貴、可以少買一點。○這[18]個學生、過逾的拙笨。○教[19]學館不可過鬆、也不可過嚴。○丁[20]家木的學問很好、可惜忒也張狂了。○人[21]不可不打算、也不可過於打算。○他[22]有不是、是不錯的、你也說的太過了。○送[23]他這點禮物、過於輕了。○世[24]上的利害人、沒有像你這樣過分的。○和[25]熟人交往、不必過於拘謹。○我[26]看你譏誚他、太過逾了。○他[27]蹧蹋我太過分了、我不能讓他。

15 He works too fast, and is not very careful.
16 My manner of speaking is too straightforward: I am constantly offending people in my talk.
17 If it is very dear, buy a little less.
18 This pupil is excessively stupid.
19 In teaching it is not best to be too lax, nor yet too strict.
20 Ting Chia Mu's scholarship is very good: it is a pity he is so arrogant.
21 A man should make plans; yet he should not plan too much.
22 He was to blame it is true, and you also spoke too severely.
23 To give him this trifling present, is too meagre.
24 Of all the violent men in the world, you are the most outrageous.
25 It is not best to be too punctilious in our intercourse with intimate friends.
26 In my opinion, you ridicule him too excessively.
27 He insults me too outrageously; I shall not submit to it [him].

仔 *Tsï*³. . . . . . . To carry; *careful.*

仔細 *Tsï*³ *hsi*⁴. . . . . Careful, particular.

直 *Chï*². Straight; upright; outspoken; *straightforward;* purposely.

拙 *Choä*¹. . . . . . . *Stupid;* unskillful, clumsy.

鬆 *Sung*¹. To relax; *slack,* loose; easy-going; flabby, spongy.

嚴 *Yien*². Severe, stern, *strict;* extreme; majestic, dignified; close,—as a door.

惜 *Hsi*¹. To compassionate; *to regret;* to be sparing.

可惜 *K'ê*³ *hsi*¹. To be regretted; *what a pity!* Alas!

狂 *K'wang*². Mad, raving; insane; rash, excitable; *proud,* insolent; violent.

張狂 *Chang*¹ *k'wang*². Boastful; *arrogant;* pretentious.

像 *Hsiang*⁴. *Like,* similar, as; a likeness; an image, an idol.

拘 *Chü*¹. To grasp and hold; to restrain; to embrace; *to adhere to.*

謹 *Chin*³. . . . . . . Diligent, *careful;* respectful.

拘謹 Cautious, conservative; *punctilious.*

譏 *Chi*¹. . . . . . *To ridicule;* to mock; to satirize.

誚 *Ch'iao*⁴. . . . . . *To blame,* to scold, to upbraid.

譏誚 *To ridicule,* to jeer at.

讓 *Jang*⁴. *To yield,* to allow; to esteem others; to waive; retiring; courteous.

NOTES.

3 癩歹 is very forcible, but more or less local. In the South 髒 is used alone.

7 那些水 might, with equal propriety, be 那個水. The plural form usually indicates a limited quantity, while the singular is quite indefinite.

8 Lit., *This man's heart is too poisonous;* said of one who has no regard for the rights and feelings of others.

11 沏 is Pekingese. 泡 is Central and Southern Mandarin. 厚 is Nankingese.

16 Lit., *My lips are too direct.* We attribute speech to the tongue, the Chinese, to the lips.

18 拙 is Nankingese. In the North 拙 is not applied to the mind.

21 過於打算 refers to one who is always changing his plans, or is too sanguine in his planning.

26 We have in 太過逾, a duplicate intensive, which, however, is more elegant in Chinese than the redundant expression "too excessively" is in English.

第二十五課

他1臨走、留這五百錢給把夥計。○可2以
給替我拿一壺開水來。○請3你要緊的
給我辦討個家口小。○你4自己不會寫、我
替你寫。○你5能給我找個地方處不能。
○我6的大襖、不能借給把他。○沒7有錢
不要緊、我賒給與你。○耶8穌替萬人贖
罪。○請9先生給我寫個仿格影本子。○我10
給他提拔鞋、也是不配的。○你11給替我衲
鞋底、我給替你緝褂子。○客12到明天要
走、你給與他平上三兩銀子。○王13先生

TRANSLATION.

1 When he was starting, he left these five hundred cash for the servants.
2 Bring a pitcher of hot water for me.
3 Please do not fail to bespeak a wife for me.
4 If you can not write it yourself, I will write it for you.
5 Can you find a situation for me?
6 I can not lend him my overcoat.
7 If you have no money, no matter; I will trust you.
8 Jesus made atonement for the sins of all men.
9 Will you please write a copy for me?
10 I am not worthy to pull up his shoes.
11 If you quilt my shoe soles, I will hem your coat.
12 The guest will leave to-morrow; do you weigh for him three taels of silver.

LESSON XXV.

THE DATIVE.

給 To give; hence,—to, for; when it follows the verb it means *to*, and when it precedes it, *for*. It is nearly always read *kei*3 in Pekingese. Though properly unaspirated, it is generally aspirated in Central and Southern Mandarin. In Nanking, when used as the sign of the dative it is read *kĕ*3.

替 To substitute; hence,—instead of, for. It always precedes the verb.

把 To take (see Les. 28), is much used along the Yangtse for **給**, when **給** means *to*, but never when it means *for*. This use of **把** is not properly Mandarin, but is allied to the Southern coast dialects.

與 To, the *Wên-li* equivalent for **給** as a sign of the dative. Colloquially it is not so used in the North, but is used to some extent in the South, especially in the region of Hankow.

In the South, **替**, **把** and **與** largely supersede **給**, which is, however, the regular and recognized Mandarin form.

VOCABULARY.

替 *T'i*4. To take the place of; to do for or instead of; in behalf of; for.

把 *Pa*1. To take; to take hold of, to seize; to regard as:—an instrumental verb, Les. 28. *To*:—see Sub. Also *pa*3 and *pa*4.

與 *Yü*3. To give; to transfer; as, rather; with, and; *to*:—see Sub., also Les. 110.

計 *Chi*4. To plan, to consider; to compute; a stratagem; *a comrade.*

夥計 *Hwo*3 *chi*4. A comrade, a companion; *the employés in a shop.*

壺 *Hu*2. A pot, a jug, a pitcher:—Les. 174.

開水 *K'ai*1 *shwei*3. Boiling water.

家口 *Chia*1 *k'ou*3. Family; *wife.*

家小 *Chia*1 *hsiao*3. A wife.

處 *Ch'u*4. *A place;* a state; a circumstance:—Les. 98. A classifier:—Les. 125. Also *ch'u*3.

地處 *Ti*4 *ch'u*4. A place, a locality; *a situation;* a berth (L.).

賒 *Shê*1. To buy or sell on credit; *to trust;* to borrow.

耶 *Yie*2. Father; a Wên-li final particle implying doubt.

替我代了一個月的館。○不14用你自己來拿、一會兒我就給你送去。○你15這些洋錢、換賣給我好不好、答好、我正打算託你給我換賣。○這16是王大老爺的信、到了北京、可以交與給他。○我17自己不能定規、請你替我拿個主意。○堯18的天下、讓給舜。○我19有一個最熱鬧的故事、你坐下我說給你聽。○你20打算兩不找、我不能換把給你。○那21些釘子、你給我拿來擱在窗臺上。○我22們日用的飲食、今日賜給我們。○保23子他媽娘、在南街給王二爺當媽老媽媽、

13 Mr. Wang taught school a month in my stead.

14 You need not come for it yourself: I will take it to you presently.

15 Would you sell (i.e., in exchange for cash) me these dollars of yours? *Ans.* All right; I was just about to ask you to sell them for me.

16 This is Wang Ta Lao Yie's letter; when you reach Peking you can give it to him.

17 I can not come to a decision myself: will you please make the decision for me?

18 Yao yielded the empire to Shun.

19 I know a very interesting story: sit down and I will tell it to you.

20 If you expect to trade even, I can not trade with you.

21 Bring those nails and put them on the window-sill for me.

22 Give us this day our daily bread.

23 Pao-tsï's mother is nurse on the South street for Wang Êr Yie.

穌 *Su*¹. . . . . . . To revive, to come to life again.

耶穌 Jesus.

贖 *Shu*². . . . . . A pledge; *to redeem*, to ransom.

影 *Ying*³. . . . . . . A shadow; *a picture*, an image.

仿 *Fang*³. To imitate; a model; *a copy to write by*.

格 *Kê*². To examine thoroughly; to influence, to affect; to reach; a line, *a rule;* a limit.

仿格 A copy to write by:—Note 9.

影本 *Ying*³ *pên*³. . . . . The same.

拔 *Pa*². *To pull up;* to extirpate; to draw,—as a sword; to pinch and pull the skin as a counter-irritant, to cup; to excel.

鞋 *Hsie*². . . . . . . Shoes, gaiters.

配 *P'ei*⁴. An equal; a wife; to pair, to match; to accompany; *to be worthy of.*

衲 *Na*⁴. . . . To line, to pad; *to quilt;* a cassock.

幧 *Ch'iao*¹. . . . . To hem.

褂 *Kwa*⁴. . . . . An upper garment, a coat.

平 *P'ing*². Even, level; equitable; ordinary; peaceful; to level; *to weigh in scales.*

代 *Tai*⁴. To substitute; *for*, in place of; a generation; a dynasty.

託 *T'oa*¹. To charge with; to entrust to; *to ask one to do for;* to rely upon.

堯 *Yao*². A celebrated sovereign of China, said to have reigned 103 years, beginning B. C. 2357.

舜 *Shun*⁴. An ancient emperor, whose reign began B. C. 2255.

天下 *T'ien*¹ *hsia*⁴. All under heaven, the world; China; *the sovereignty.*

故 *Ku*⁴. The cause or reason of a thing; therefore; on purpose; of course; *old;* original; former; an affair.

故事 *Ku*⁴ *shï*⁴. A legend, *a story*, an adventure, a singular or amusing affair.

兩不找 *Liang*³ *pu*⁴ *chao*³. To trade even, no boot.

釘 *Ting*¹. . . . A nail, a spike, a peg. Also *ting*⁴.

飲 *Yin*³. . . . . . To drink; *drink.* Also *yin*⁴.

飲食 *Yin*³ *shï*². . . . . . Food and drink.

賜 *Sï*⁴, *t'sï*⁴. *To give*, to bestow; a benefit, a gift from a superior.

南 *Nan*². . . . . . . South.

媽媽 *Ma*¹ *ma*¹. Mamma;—in some places, grandmother, in other places *a nurse:*—Les. 5, Note 23.

第二十六課

[1]我看見他們在土地廟後說話。○[2]正在眼前、你還不看見嗎。○[3]我在裏面、他在外面。○[4]在地裏頭有火。○[5]外頭實在冷。○[6]我的家眷住在裏邊。○[7]這裏頭的房子、是你的嗎。○[8]萬老四的狗、常在外邊咬雞。○[9]你的兩個孩子、我纔看見在樓後頭。○[10]我打算在院子西

Translation.

1 I saw them behind the T'u-ti temple talking.
2 Right before your eyes, and you don't see it?
3 I was inside, and he outside.
4 There is fire inside the earth.
5 It is very cold outside.
6 My family live within.
7 Is the house in here yours?
8 Wan the Fourth's dog is constantly out biting [people's] chickens.
9 I just now saw your two children behind the house.
10 I propose to build a side room on the west side of the yard.

Notes.

1 On leaving a Chinese inn, it is customary to give a small "tip" to the servants; not, however, so much as five hundred cash, unless one has been at the inn a number of days.

3 Marriages in China are arranged by go-betweens. This is a request to some one not to neglect the business entrusted to him. 辦, in the North, and 討, in the South, are used only with reference to a second wife. In some places 家口 means either wife, or wife and children; in other places it is confined to the latter meaning.

9 A 仿格, or 影本, is a page of "copy" written by the teacher in a large, fair hand. This copy the pupil places underneath his thin paper and traces the characters.

12 Chinese ideas of hospitality require that, in sending away a guest from a distance, you should make him a present of something for his journey.

18 It is related of the ancient emperor *Yao*, that he yielded the empire to his friend *Shun*, instead of leaving it to his son; which the Chinese regard as an unparalleled example of patriotism. The use of 天下 for China is a specimen of Chinese egotism.

22 This is from the translation of the Lord's prayer. The clause 日用的飲食 means literally, *the drink and food, used day by day*. It is high Mandarin, not readily understood save by constant use.

23 保子他娘 is a somewhat inelegant colloquial form, equivalent to 保子的娘.

LESSON XXVI.

Beside the postpositions of place, 裏, 外, 上, 下, given in Lesson 6, there are also such as 前, 後, 左, 右, etc., all which take after and combine with themselves the words 頭, *head*, 面, *face*, and 边, *border*. We say, inside, outside, etc.; but the Chinese go further and say, in-head, out-head, in-face, out-face, etc. The meaning in the several cases is substantially the same. Which form is most suitable in any case can only be learned by practice. The usage varies considerably in different places.

Vocabulary.

邊 or 边 *Pien*^{1}. . . . . . Edge; border; boundary.

廟 *Miao*^{4}. . . . . . A temple—great or small.

土地 *T'u*^{3} *ti*^{4}. . . . . . A local divinity:—Note 1.

眷 *Chüen*^{4}. To love; to care for; kindred; . . . . . . *family*.

家眷 *Chia*^{1} *chüen*^{4}. *Family*, household; wife.

咬 *Yao*^{3}. *To bite*, to chew; to involve in a . . . . . . crime; to bark.

雞 *Chi*^{1}. . . . . . A chicken; a cock.

廂 *Hsiang*^{1}. . . A side building; a suburb:—Les. [188.

廂房 *Hsiang*^{1} *fang*^{2}. A small house at the side . . . . . . of the court between other houses.

背 *Pei*^{4}. The back; the rear; to turn the back . . . . . . on; to repudiate, to falsify; *in the shade;* to repeat. See *pei*^{1}.

撇 *P'ie*^{1}. To skim off; to throw aside; to leave . . . . . . behind, *to forget;* a stroke down and to the left in writing:—See Radical 4.

拴 *Shwan*^{1}. To bind up; to fasten or tie to; *to* . . . . . . *hitch*.

馬 *Ma*^{3}. . . . . . *A horse;* warlike; cavalry.

邊、蓋個廂房。○在[11]房子東面背風、實在暖和。○我[12]的衣裳、撇在裏邊。○在[13]大門前拴的馬、是你少爺的不是。○王[14]老三、在東巷衚衕儘裏邊的那個門裏住。○上[15]面是正面、下面是反面。○大[16]孩子在炕裏邊哭、小孩子在炕外邊笑。○有[17]人想告你、要你裏邊的衣服、連外邊的也由他拿去、○抽[18]屜裏邊、你也找了嗎。○他[19]們在裏頭說、我在外面聽見了。○請[20]先生上邊坐。○該[21]讓先生在前頭走、你們在後頭跟着。○你[22]的鞋、可

11 At the east side of the house it is sheltered from the wind, and is quite warm.
12 I forgot my clothes inside.
13 The horse hitched in front of the large gate is your young master's, is it not?
14 Wang the Third lives in the innermost door in the east alley.
15 The upper side is the right side; the lower side is the wrong side.
16 The big child was on the inner side of the k'ang crying, and the little one on the outer side laughing.
17 If a man thinks to accuse you, wanting your inside coat, let him take the outside one also.
18 Did you also search in the drawer?
19 They were talking inside, and I heard them outside.
20 Please take the upper seat.
21 You should allow the teacher to go before, and you follow after.
22 You may take off your shoes without, at the side of the door.

少 *Shao*⁴. Young, juvenile; *a youth;* secondary; ....to be second:—See *shao*³.

少爺 *Shao*⁴ *yie*². ...... The son of an official.

衚 *Hu*². ...... A side street.

衕 *T'ung*⁴. ...... A side street.

衚衕 A side street, an alley (Pekingese).

巷 *Hsiang*⁴, *hang*⁴. .... An alley.

儘 *Chin*³. To finish; completely; all; *the utmost:*—Les. 137.

反 *Fan*³. To return; to turn over; *to reverse;* to rebel; but, on the contrary:—Les. 112.

哭 *K'u*¹. .... *To cry*, to weep, to bemoan.

笑 *Hsiao*⁴. .....*To laugh;* to smile; to ridicule.

衣服 *I*¹ *fu*². ...... Clothing, dress.

連 *Lien*². To connect; to join; following; even, still; and, *together with:*—Les. 110.

由 *Yiu*². The origin or antecedents; from, through; the cause or instrument; *to let*, to permit:—Les. 83.

抽 *Ch'ou*¹. To take or *draw out;* to select, to allot; to smoke,—as a pipe.

屜 *T'i*⁴. ...... A pad, a saddle-cloth; a buffer.

抽屜 A drawer.

聽見 *T'ing*¹ *chien*.⁴ To hear; to perceive by hearing; to listen:—Les. 51.

脫 *T'oa*¹. *To take off*, to undress; to escape, to evade; to avoid.

旁 *P'ang*². ...... *The side;* sideways; near.

旁邊 *P'ang*² *pien*¹. At or by the side; the side.

颳 *Kwa*¹. .....*To blow;* to drive with the wind.

左 *Tsoă*³. *The left;* second in position, a deputy; depraved, heretical.

右 *Yiu*⁴. ...... *The right;* to honor; to aid.

上頭 *Shang*⁴ *t'ou*². Upon; above; overhead; the term by which inferiors designate their superiors, and the apartments in which they live, "topside."

上邊 *Shang*⁴ *pien*¹. .... The same.

開飯 *K'ai*¹ *fan*⁴. To set forth or serve a meal.

罩 *Chao*⁴. To cover over; to shade; a hollow cover; an air-pump receiver.

燈罩 *Têng*¹ *chao*⁴. A lamp shade, a lamp chimney.

骨 *Ku*³. *A bone;* the skeleton or hard part of anything.

骨頭 *Ku*³ *t'ou*². ...... A bone:—Les. 47.

髮 *Fa*³. .... Hair, the **hair** on the head.

頭髮 *T'ou*² *fa*³. .... Human hair.

以脫在外頭門旁邊。○在[23]外邊颳大風、實在難走。○不[24]是在書架子裏頭、是在書架子高上頭面。○男[25]的該在左邊、女的該在右邊。○這[26]南邊的天氣太熱。○上[27]頭邊還沒有開飯嗎、答已經開了。○這[28]個燈罩裏面不乾淨。○人[29]的頭裏頭有骨頭、外頭有頭髮。

23 A strong wind is blowing outside and it is very hard walking.
24 If it is not inside the book-case, it is on the top.
25 The man ought to be on the left, and the woman on the right.
26 The climate here in the South is too hot.
27 Has the meal not yet been served to the family (or, guests)? *Ans.* It has.
28 This lamp chimney is not clean inside.
29 On the inside of one's head are bones, and on the outside, hair.

NOTES.

1 土地. The lowest god in China with magisterial functions. There is a *T'u³ ti⁴* temple, or shrine, in or near every village, and also one in every Hsien city. The gods in these many temples are all different individuals, though they all have the same birthday, on which they are worshipped; viz., the second day of the second month. It is to this temple that the soul first repairs after death.

7 這裡頭的房子. Lit., *this inside's house;* i.e., *the house which is here within.*

17 The sentence is taken without change from the Mandarin N. T. It would be smoother colloquial if 着 were added to 想.

20 The English speaker is strongly inclined to put 在 before the 上, and the Chinese will allow it, but prefers to omit it.

24 This sentence might be taken indicatively; viz., *It is not in the inside of the book-case; it is on the top.* Which meaning it would convey, would depend wholly on the manner of saying it. The use of 高頭 in the sense of *on top*, or *above*, is exclusively Southern.

25 男的 and 女的 might, with equal propriety, be translated in the plural.

29 This sentence well serves to illustrate some of the uses of the word 頭.

LESSON XXVII.

FOUR COMMON CLASSIFIERS.

This lesson illustrates four of the most common classifiers:—See subject to Lesson 1. Other Classifiers will be illustrated in a number of future lessons:—See Les. 38, 42, 68, 100, 125, 140 and 147.

把 A handful,—classifier of things which have a handle, or can be held in the hand.

塊 A piece,—classifier of things in pieces, lumps or fragments.

件 To divide,—a classifier of wide application, used in general of particular articles regarded as separate wholes.

位 A seat of dignity,—classifier of persons, especially of such as are regarded as worthy of respect.

For full list of words falling under each of these classifiers, see Supplement.

VOCABULARY.

把 *Pa³*. A handful, a bundle:—See Sub. See . . . . . . *pa¹* also *pa⁴*.

件 *Chien⁴*. To divide; an article, an item, a . . . . piece:—See Sub.

錐 *Chwei¹*. . . . . . . *An awl;* to pierce.

剪 *Chien³*. To clip, to snip, to shear; shears, ... scissors, tongs.

鐵 *T'ie³*. . . . . . . Iron; firm, resolute.

皮 *P'i²*. Skin; leather; fur; bark; a covering; . . . . tare of goods.

菜 *Ts'ai⁴*. . . . . . . Edible vegetables.

園 *Yüen²*. A yard; a garden; a park; a large . . . . shop or saloon.

胰 *I²*. . . . . . . The caul; soap.

肥 *Fei²*. . . . . . . Fat, plump; rich; fertile.

皂 *Tsao⁴*. . . . . . . Black; lictors, runners.

肥皂 A kind of coarse native soap.

泥 *Ni²*. . . . Mud, mire; mortar; clods, earth; *dirt*

切 *Ch'ie¹*. . . . . . To cut, to slice. Also *ch'ie⁴*.

第二十七課

這[1]把錐子沒有尖兒。○那[2]把剪子不好使用。○這[3]塊鐵太長。○這[4]件皮襖實在體面。○這[5]塊地正好作菜園。○那[6]件東西不能很貴。○這[7]塊胰子肥皂不下泥灰髒。○你[8]這件營生事情不合情理。○請[9]你切一塊西瓜給我。○外[10]頭來了三位老爺。○二[11]位太太已經走了。○這[12]瓶裏的水、可以倒在那把壺裏。○我[13]這把斧子、已經壞了。○你[14]買的那塊洋布、太枵薄了。○這[15]把椅子底下有灰土、

TRANSLATION.

1 The awl has no point.
2 That pair of scissors is not usable.
3 This piece of iron is too long.
4 This fur coat is very genteel.
5 This piece of land would just suit for a vegetable garden.
6 That article can not be very expensive.
7 This piece of soap does not take out the dirt.
8 This business of yours is not according to reason.
9 Please cut me a piece of watermelon.
10 Three officers have arrived without.
11 The two ladies have already gone.
12 The water in this bottle you may pour into that pitcher.
13 This ax of mine is already spoiled.
14 That piece of foreign [cotton] cloth which you bought is too thin.

瓜 *Kwa*^{1}. . . . . . Melons, cucumbers, gourds, etc.
西瓜 *Hsi*^{1} *kwa*^{1}. . . . . . . A watermelon.
瓶 *P'ing*^{2}. . . . . . . A pitcher, a jug, a bottle.
倒 *Tao*^{4}. To invert; to pour out; to empty, to vacate; on the contrary; but, still, then:—Les. 112. See *tao*^{3}.
斧 *Fu*^{3}. . . . . . . An ax, a hatchet, a cleaver.
洋布 *Yang*^{2} *pu*^{4}. Foreign cotton cloth, long cloth.
枵 *Hsiao*^{1}. . . . . Hollow; thin.
薄 *Poă*^{2}, *pao*^{2}. Thin, subtile; a thin leaf; poor, mean; to extend, to reach. Also *poă*^{4}.
枵薄 Thin; thinness; thickness.
晌午 *Shang*^{3} *wu*^{3}. . . . . Midday, noon.
中時 *Chung*^{1} *shï*^{2}. . . . . The same.
中上 *Chung*^{1} *shang*^{4}. . . . . The same.
數 *Shu*^{3}. To enumerate, to count; to censure. Also *shu*^{4} and *soă*^{4}.
臭 *Ch'ou*^{4}, *hsiu*^{4}. An offensive smell, stench; putrid, tainted; disreputable.
終 *Chung*^{1}. The end, finis; all, the whole; the utmost; dead; to die:—Les. 127.
終身 *Chung*^{1} *shên*^{1}. . . . . Life-time, life.
談 *T'an*^{2}. To talk about, to discuss; to chat; conversation; chit-chat.
閒談 *Hsien*^{2} *t'an*^{2}. To talk familiarly, to chat; to gossip.
鍘 *Cha*^{2}. . . . . . . A hinged shear or cutter.
鍘刀 *Cha*^{2} *tao*^{1}. . . . . A straw cutter.
竈 *Tsao*^{4}. . . . . . . A furnace, a kitchen range.
竈臺 *Tsao*^{4} *t'ai*^{2}. . . . . A kitchen range.
鍋臺 *Kwoă*^{1} *t'ai*^{2}. . . . . The same.
菜刀 *Ts'ai*^{4} *tao*^{1}. A cleaver, a meat chopper.
鏟 *Ch'an*^{3}. A shovel, a scoop, a scraper; to level off, to scrape.
勺 *Shao*^{2}, *shwoă*^{2}. To ladle out; a ladle; a spoon; a spoonful.
炊 *Ch'wei*^{1}. . . . . To cook; a small broom.
刷 *Shwa*^{1}. . . . . . A brush; to brush; to scrub.
炊箒 *Ch'wei*^{1} *chou*^{3}. A small broom or whisk used to wash dishes.
刷箒 *Shwa*^{1} *chou*^{3}. . . . . The same.
鍤 *Ch'a*^{1}. . . . . . A fork; a large pin.
匙 *Ch'ï*^{2}. A spoon; a key,—in which sense it is in Peking read *shï*^{2}.
羹 *Kêng*^{1}. . . . . . Soup, porridge.
調羹 *T'iao*^{2} *kêng*^{1}. A spoon,—usually made of wood or porcelain.

可以拿一把笤箒來掃去。○[16]晌午（中時、中上）買的銀子是八件、你數了沒有。○[17]那塊肉已經臭了。○[18]這是你終身的一件大事、有話不妨說。○[19]我們是一塊土的人、不可爲一件小事打架。○[20]我纔見二位先生、在屋裏閒談。○[21]我要買一把鍘刀、不知有現成的沒有。○[22]竈鍋臺上、有一把菜刀、一把鏟子、一把勺子、一把刷炊箒。○[23]我有六把刀子、六把鍤子、還有十二把匙子（調羮）、不知彀不彀。

15 There is dust under this chair; bring a broom and sweep it away.
16 Of the silver bought at noon there were eight pieces · did you count them?
17 That piece of meat is already tainted.
18 This is the great affair of your life; if you have any thing to say, do not hesitate to speak.
19 We are natives of the same place, and must not fight about a small matter.
20 I just now saw the two gentlemen in the room chatting.
21 I want to buy a straw knife: I wonder if they are to be had ready-made.
22 On the cooking range are a meat chopper, a scraper, a dipper, and a whisk.
23 I have six knives and six forks, and also twelve spoons: I wonder if they are enough.

Notes.

7 下 is here used as a verb, meaning to remove, or take out, the dirt. Foreign soap is called 胰子 in the North, and in the South, 肥皂, or 胰子肥皂.

15 椅子底下 means beneath the chair, not the under side, or part, of the chair, which would be, 椅子下邊.

16 晌午 is the form used in the North, while 中時 and 中上 are used in the South.

18 Said by an officer to a girl brought before him in a matter concerning her marriage engagement.

23 Foreign spoons are called 匙子 in some places; in other places they are called 羮匙, *soup spoons*, or 調羮 *stirrers*; and in others, 勺子, *dippers*. The Chinese use spoons much less than we do, and they are generally made either of China-ware or of wood.

LESSON XXVIII.

The Instrumental Verbs 把 and 將.

把 is used instrumentally of anything that can be taken or held in the hand, and often, by accommodation, of other things. Whether used as a classifier or as an instrumental verb is known by the connection.

將 as an instrumental verb is very similar in meaning to 把, but is a little more bookish, and is often used of affairs, and of mental operations.

These words may sometimes be rendered by *take*, but are generally best untranslated.

Vocabulary.

袷 *Chia*³. . . . . Lined, double.

另 *Ling*⁴. Separate; additional; another; *besides*, furthermore.

托 *T'oă*¹. To support with the hand, to bear up; the length of the extended arms, a fathom.

襟 *Chin*¹. . . . . . The lapel of a coat; *a collar.*

托襟 The round collar on a woman's dress.

托領 *T'oă*¹ *ling*³. . . . . The same. (N.).

護領 *Hu*⁴ *ling*³. . . . . The same. (S.).

掌 *Chang*³. *The palm of the hand;* a hoof, a paw; to grasp; to rule, to control.

巴掌 *Pa*⁴ *chang*³. *The palm of the hand;* a slap, a box.

帳 *Chang*⁴. . . . . . A curtain, a screen; a plan.

第二十八課

孩[1]子把火弄滅熄了。○把[2]我的袷襖、放
在皮箱裏。○把[3]這些傢伙拿去、擱在
櫃裏。○我[4]要把這件掛子、另換個新
托領托襟護領。○可[5]以把火爐放在外頭。○他[6]
生氣把我打了兩巴掌。○你[7]去把帳
子掛上。○我[8]將這件事告訴你、你不
要聲張張揚。○張[9]先生家去了、你去把他
請來。○把[10]這些混髒水拿去、倒在街上。
○可[11]以把鑰匙、放在抽屜裏頭。○你[12]
纔放鎗、把孩子嚇哭了。○他[13]不肯把

TRANSLATION.

1 The child has poked out the fire.
2 Take my double coat and put it in the leather trunk.
3 Take away these dishes and put them in the cupboard.
4 I intend to put a new collar on this gown.
5 You can set the stove outside.
6 He got angry and struck me two blows with the palm of his hand.
7 Go and hang up the curtains.
8 I will tell you this affair, but you must not spread it abroad.
9 Mr. Chang has gone home. Do you go and ask him to come.
10 Take away this dirty water and pour it out on the street.
11 You can (or, may) put the key in the drawer.
12 Your shooting off that gun just now frightened the baby till it cried.

掛 *Kwa*^{4}. *To hang up*, to suspend; to dwell upon, ... to be anxious about. See *kwa*^{1}.

揚 *Yang*^{2}. To spread; *to publish;* to scatter, ... to winnow; to raise or lift up.

聲張 *Shêng*^{1} *chang*^{1}. To noise abroad, to publish.

張揚 *Chang*^{1} *yang*^{2}....... The same.

混 *Hun*^{2}.... Turbid, muddy; *dirty*. Also *hun*^{4}.

鑰 *Yao*^{4}, *yoă*^{4}, *yüe*^{4}....... A bolt, a key.

鑰匙 *Yao*^{4} *shi*^{2}.......... A key.

鎗 *Ch'iang*^{1}.......... *A gun*, a pistol; a spear.

嚇 *Hê*^{4}, *hsia*^{4}. To threaten, to intimidate; to .... scare, *to frighten.*

武 *Wu*^{3}..... Military, martial; majestic, fierce.

武藝 *Wu*^{3} *i*^{4}. Military tactics; *skill,*—of any .... kind.

拳 *Ch'üen*^{2}..... *The fist;* to grasp in the hand.

踢 *T'i*^{1}...... *To tread on;* to kick.

蹬 *Têng*^{4}........ To step, *to tread;* to kick.

踢蹬 To spoil, to ruin; to squander.

腹 *Fu*^{3,4}. The belly, the abdomen; the seat of .... the mind; *intimate*, dear.

心腹 *Hsin*^{1} *fu*^{3}. In the heart; intimate, *confidential;* the bosom; the mind.

驢 *Lü*^{2}....... An ass, donkey.

趙 *Chao*^{4}....... A long time; *a surname.*

驕 *Chiao*^{1}..... *Proud*, haughty; to be proud of.

傲 *Ao*^{4}....... *Proud*, uncivil; to treat rudely.

驕傲 *Proud;* overbearing; to disdain.

叭 *Pa*^{4}....... The cry of a cockatoo.

叭哥 *Pa*^{4} *kê*^{1}........... The cockatoo.

賭 *Tu*^{3}....... To wager, to bet; *to gamble.*

業 *Yie*^{4}. *Estate*, patrimony; calling, profession, ... trade. In books,—a sign of the past.

家業 *Chia*^{1} *yie*^{4}.....Family inheritance, *estate.*

牢 *Lao*^{2}......... A corral; a jail; *firm*, strong.

搖 *Yao*^{2}. *To move to and fro;* to shake; to .... ring,—as a bell; tossed, disturbed.

搖椅 *Yao*^{2} *i*^{3}.......... A rocking-chair.

舅 *Chiu*^{4}....... A maternal uncle.

舅舅 A maternal uncle. See Les. 21, Note 16.

一下 *I*^{1} *hsia*^{4}......One time, *one stroke*, once.

東洋車 *Tung*^{1} *yang*^{2} *ch'ê*^{1}......A jinricksha.

馬褂 *Ma*^{3} *kwa*^{4}..........A short outside coat.

鈕 *Niu*^{3}....... A knob; *a button;* a pivot.

襻 *P'an*^{4}....... *A loop;* a belt, a band.

鈕襻 A button loop.

釦 *K'ou*^{4}....... *A button;* a clasp; to button.

釦門 *K'ou*^{4} *mên*^{2}. A button loop, a button hole. ....

自己的武藝教給人。〇一[14]拳一脚、將人打死。〇我[15]的母親死去、把我撇了。〇李[16]子把我的那把剪子弄壞踢蹬了。〇不[17]要將心腹話告訴人。〇你[18]上東街、把王老三的小驢兒借來。〇趙[19]二爺太驕傲、把人看不在眼裏。〇你[20]把那個哵哥籠子、給我拿來。〇丁[21]少爺常常賭錢、把那家業踢蹬蹧踢淨了。〇你[22]該將這個意思、牢記在心。〇把[23]那把大搖椅子、放在桌子旁邊。〇你[24]快去將這件事、告訴你的舅舅。〇在[25]街上、有個東洋車碰我一下、把馬褂子上的鈕襻兒、釦門兒、掙壞了兩個。

13 He is not willing to teach his skill to others.
14 Between fist and foot he killed the man.
15 My mother died and left me.
16 Li-tsï ruined that pair of shears of mine.
17 Do not tell to others what is told you in confidence.
18 Do you go over to the East Street and borrow Wang the Third's donkey.
19 Mr. Chao the Second is too proud: he can not see other people.
20 Bring here that cockatoo's cage for me.
21 Mr. Ting's son is all the time gambling, and has wasted all his estate.
22 You ought to keep this thought always in mind.
23 Put that large rocking-chair beside the table.
24 Go quickly and tell your (maternal) uncle of this affair.
25 A jinricksha ran against me on the street, and tore out two of the button-holes (loops) on my coat.

Notes.

4 Lit., *I intend to take this piece of gown, and besides [the original one] exchange a new collar.*

6 The Chinese is similar in structure to the vulgar English,—"He got angry and took and struck me."

8 Or, *If I tell you this affair, you must not spread it abroad.*

10 混水 is not used in the South. It means *muddy* rather than *dirty* water.

14 一拳一脚 is spirited and very expressive. It does not necessarily mean, *one* stroke and *one* kick, but a few strokes and kicks.

16 李子 is a girl's name. It is common to name girls after fruits and flowers.

17 心腹話, *words from the heart and belly;* i.e., *confidential secrets.* The Chinese regard not only the heart, but also the belly, as the seat of knowledge.

18 When 小 precedes 驢, an 兒 is always used after it, thus showing the diminutive force of 兒.

19 把人看不在眼裡 Lit., *takes men and sees them not in his eyes;* i.e., *disregards them.*

LESSON XXIX.

The Auxiliary Verb 起.

起 is joined as an auxiliary to verbs indicating motion upwards and, by accommodation, to many others. It sometimes has an inceptive force, and sometimes denotes progressive action, but is more frequently used simply to express the completion of the action. It is generally followed by 來. In Peking 起來 is often replaced by 得. For full list of verbs commonly followed by 起, see Supplement.

Vocabulary.

廳 *T'ing*¹. . . . . *A hall,* a parlor; a court room.

廳房 *T'ing*¹ *fang*². The central and main building in a compound; a reception room or hall.

羊 *Yang*². . . . . A sheep, a goat.

腿 *T'wei*³. . . . . The leg, the thigh.

弔 *Tiao*⁴. To condole, to pity; to suspend, *to hang up,*—as by a cord.

第二十九課

趙[1]老爺的廳房、還沒有蓋起來。○請[2]你明天早一點起來、我有一件事託你。○把[3]羊腿吊起來。○房(屋)[4]子裏太熱、可以把窗戶支撐起來。○這[5]個藥、該用水和起來喝。○請[6]你把這些賬、給我算起來。○傳[7]來把起(得了)來了沒有。

先生的書架子、做起來了(得了)沒有。○把[8]這些散錢、給我穿起來。○孩[9]子醒了、可以抱起他來。○把[10]這個畫兒掛起來。○我[11]的筆掉在地下、請你給我撿(拾)起來。○這[12]些方甎、該按規矩稞起來。○大[13]褂子還

TRANSLATION.

1 Mr. Chao has not yet finished building his main hall.
2 Will you please get up a little earlier to-morrow; I have some business to entrust to you.
3 Hang up that leg of mutton.
4 It is too warm in the room: you may raise the window.
5 This medicine is to be taken mixed with water.
6 Please reckon up this account for me.
7 Is Mr. Fu's book-case finished?
8 String up these loose cash for me.
9 The baby has wakened; you may take him up.
10 Hang up this picture.
11 My pen has fallen on the floor: please pick it up for me.
12 These square bricks ought to be piled up in order.
13 The large coat is not yet hemmed.
14 The officer gave the order, and they were put in confinement.

戶 *Hu*⁴. *A door of one leaf; an opening;* an individual; a household.

窗戶 *Ch'wang*¹ *hu*⁴. A window.

撐 *Ch'êng*¹. *To prop;* to fasten open; to pole,—as a boat.

喝 *Hê*¹. *To drink,* to sip; a gurgling sound. Also *hê*⁴.

散 *San*³. To fall apart or into disorder; *scattered;* a medicinal powder; odds and ends. See *san*⁴.

醒 *Hsing*³. *To awake;* to arouse; to startle.

抱 *Pao*⁴. To infold; *to hold in the arms;* to compress; to cherish; to harbor.

掉 *Tiao*⁴. To shake; *to fall into or down,* to slip or fall off:—Les. 92.

撿 *Chien*³. *To gather up;* to collate, to sort.

甎 *Chwan*¹. A brick.

方甎 *Fang*¹ *chwan*¹. A square brick or tile for paving.

稞 *Toa*⁴. A stack of grain; *to pile up.*

吩 *Fên*¹. To order, to direct.

咐 *Fu*⁴. To enjoin.

吩咐 To command, *to order;* to charge.

押 *Ya*¹. To stamp, to sign; to arrest; *to guard;* to suppress; to pawn,—in an unlicensed pawn shop; to mortgage. Also *ya*².

折 *Chê*², *shê*². To break in two; to annul; to break off; to decide, *to discriminate;* to fold; to abate, to discount; to barter.

証 *Chêng*⁴. To testify, to prove; *to remonstrate with.*

折証 To dispute, to wrangle.

競 *Ching*⁴. To strive; to wrangle, to quarrel.

爭競 *Chêng*¹ *ching*⁴. To dispute, to contend, to wrangle.

字紙 *Tsi*⁴ *chï*³. Paper with characters on it, either written or printed.

拉 *La*¹. To pull, to drag, to tug; *to take by the hand;* to buy on credit; to bring up.

扶 *Fu*². *To help,* to assist, to support; to defend; to lean upon.

站 *Chan*⁴. *To stand up;* to stand still, to stop; a stage of a journey.

捲 *Chüen*³. *To roll up;* to curl; to seize.

疊 *Tie*². *To fold;* to reiterate; to reduplicate.

包 *Pao*¹. *To wrap up;* to contain; to undertake, to contract; to warrant; to plate; a bundle.

袱 *Fu*². A cloth for wrapping bundles.

包袱 A wrapper; a bundle.

沒稭得了(起來了)。○官[14]吩咐一聲、把他們押起來了。○這[15]些零錢、合起來是七十五個。○你[16]說起這個、我就想起一件事來。○他[17]們兩個爭競(折証)一會兒、就罵起來了。○我[18]走了不多時候、就下起雨來了。○把[19]那些字紙、都拾起來。○耶[20]穌拉着孩子的手、扶他起來、孩子就站起來了。○這[21]些衣裳、該捲的捲起來、該疊的疊起來、後來用包袱包起來。

15 These remnants of cash amount in all to seventy-five.

16 Your speaking of this reminds me of a certain affair.

17 They two, having disputed a while, began to swear at each other.

18 I had gone but a little while when it began to rain.

19 Gather up all that paper with characters on it.

20 Jesus took the child by the hand and assisted her to rise, and she stood up.

21 Roll up such of these clothes as should be rolled up, and fold such as should be folded, and then tie them up in a bundle (large handkerchief).

Notes.

1 蓋起來. If the emphasis be thrown on 蓋, the meaning is simply, *built;* if on 起來, the meaning is, *finished building.* When 起 is used alone, it necessarily takes the emphasis and the meaning is, *finished building.*

4 支 is used in the North, 撐 in the South. The former means to *hoist,* the latter more properly means to *prop.*

8 穿. Some would write 串, as the more proper character, though its tone is not correct. If used, it should be read *ch'wan*^{1}.

10 Foreign pictures in frames are generally classified by 個, rather than by 張:—Les. 42.

14 一聲, *One sound;* that is, he gave one short peremptory order.

16 就 here means *at once,* as it often does:—Les. 44.

18 起來 *seems* inappropriate here. It is used inceptively.

19 It is considered a sin and a shame to defile paper with characters on it, and a meritorious thing to gather it up carefully and burn it, thus preventing its being trodden under foot, or defiled by others. Written characters, being handed down from the sages of antiquity, are regarded as sacred and hence to defile them is a species of sacrilege.

21 The form of expression in this sentence is very common in Chinese.

LESSON XXX.

上 and 下 as Auxiliary Verbs.

上 is added as an auxiliary to verbs expressing motion upwards, and 下 to verbs expressing motion downwards. They are not confined, however, to verbs of motion but are used freely with many others. Besides the idea of motion, they sometimes express the success or practicability, of the action.

To both of them 來 and 去 are frequently added.

Vocabulary.

套 *T'ao*^{4}. *To encase;* to include; a wrapper, *a case;* a snare, a trap; tedious, conventional. A classifier:—Les. 42.

筆帽 *Pi*^{3} *mao*^{4}. A brass cap to protect the point of a Chinese pen.

筆套 *Pi*^{3} *t'ao*^{4}. . . . . .The same.

剁 *Toa*^{4}. . . . . . . To chop, to mince; *to cut off.*

節 *Chie*^{2}. . . . . . . A limit of time, a festival; *a verse,* a section; temperance, moderation; to regulate. A classifier:—Les. 147. Also *chie*^{3}.

抄 *Ch'ao*^{1}. To hunt up; *to write out,* to transcribe; to confiscate.

盤 *P'an*^{2}. A platter, *a plate;* a market; an affair; to coil, to wind; to examine, to question.

牛 *Niu*^{2}. . . . . . A cow, an ox; kine.

構 *Kou*^{4}. To drag, to pull; to implicate; *to reach up to.*

第三十課

把[1]你的鞋提上。○這[2]兩個字沒寫、請先生寫上。○不[3]要乾了筆、該把筆套帽兒套上。○孩[4]子要上炕、你可以把他拉上來。○拿[5]刀把骨頭剁下來。○把[6]這一節書抄下來。○可[7]以把這個盤子拿下去。○把[8]那塊牛肉給我搆下來。○樓[9]上沒有座位、你把這兩把椅子搬上去。○我[10]是大人派下來的。○水[11]缸裏有一把勺匙子、你去撈上來。○半[12]天的工夫、纔求下來了。○在[13]下邊桌子上有筆硯、請你給我送上來。○這[14]是天上掉下

TRANSLATION.

1 Pull up your shoes.
2 These two characters have not been written. Please write them.
3 You should put the cap on the pen, and not allow it to get dry.
4 The child wants to get on the k'ang; pull him up.
5 Take a chopper and chop off the bone.
6 Write out this verse.
7 You may take away this plate.
8 Take down that piece of beef for me.
9 There are no seats upstairs; take up these two chairs.
10 I am come down by appointment of His Excellency.
11 There is a spoon (dipper) in the water kang. Do you go and rake it out.
12 It was half a day before my entreaties prevailed.
13 There are writing materials on the table below. Please bring them up for me.

派 *P'ai*^{4}. A branch, a tribe; *to appoint*, to depute; to send; to distribute to each.

缸 *Kang*^{1}. A large jar for water, etc.

撈 *Lao*^{1,2}. *To hook or haul out of the water*, to dredge, to grapple for.

求 *Ch'iu*^{2}. To ask, *to beg*; to pray; to search for, to aim at.

下邊 *Hsia*^{4} *pien*^{1}. Below; down-stairs; the apartments of inferiors:—see Note 24, Les. 33.

硯 *Yien*^{4}. An inkstone.

筆硯 *Pi*^{3} *yien*^{4}. Pen and ink, writing materials,—pen, ink, paper, etc.

富 *Fu*^{4}. *Rich*, affluent; abundant.

富貴 *Fu*^{4} *kwei*^{4}. Riches and honor; wealth, *opulence*.

壓 *Ya*^{4}. *To bring into subjection*; to conquer, to repress; to intimidate. Also *ya*^{1}.

玩 *Wan*^{2}. *To play or toy with*; to ramble; to dawdle; to practice.

耍 *Shwa*^{3}. *To play with*, to trifle; to make game of; to fence; to work at a trade.

玩耍 *To play*, to amuse one's self; to dally with.

玩玩 To play, to amuse one's self:—Les. 33.

腦 *Nao*^{3}. *The brain*; gum camphor.

袋 *Tai*^{4}. *A bag*; a pocket; a purse.

腦袋 *The head*; the wits; the mind.

輩 *Pei*^{4}. *A generation*; a class, a sort.

老輩 *Lao*^{3} *pei*^{4}. Grandfather; ancestors.

祖 *Tsu*^{3}. Grandfather; ancestors, forefathers.

祖上 *Tsu*^{3} *shang*^{4}. Ancestors.

降 *Chiang*^{4}. *To descend*; to send down; to fall; to reduce in rank. Also *hsiang*^{2}.

天使 *T'ien*^{1} *shï*^{3}. A heavenly messenger, an angel.

玻 *Po*^{1}. A transparent glaze.

璃 *Li*^{2}. A vitreous substance like glass.

玻璃 Glass.

鴉 *Ya*^{1}. A raven, a crow.

鵲 *Ch'iao*^{3}, *ch'io*^{4}. The magpie, jackdaw and jay.

鴉鵲 The magpie.

喜鵲 *Hsi*^{3} *ch'iao*^{3}. The magpie.

落 *Lao*^{4}. *To alight*,—as a bird; to fall,—as a price. See *lo*^{4}, also *la*^{4}.

來的富貴。○正[15]上學的時候、不好出去玩玩玩耍。○你[16]要壓下我來、我要壓下你去。○我[17]兄弟從馬上棹下來、把頭腦袋磕破了。○杏[18]子兒下來的早、桃子兒下來的遲晚。○這[19]個房子、是他老輩子祖上留下來的。○我[20]看見一位天使、從天上降下來。○這[21]個窗戶棹了一塊玻璃、你可以把他安上去。○外[22]頭有一個鴉喜鵲、纔從樹上落下來。

14 This opulence has fallen down from heaven.
15 During school hours it is not right to go out of school to play.
16 You want to put me down, and I want to put you down.
17 My younger brother fell off a horse and cut his head open.
18 Apricots get ripe early, peaches, late.
19 This house was handed down to him from his ancestors.
20 I saw an angel coming down from heaven.
21 There is a pane of glass out of this window. You may put it in.
22 There is a magpie outside which has just flown down from the tree.

NOTES.

1 The Chinese are much given to wearing their shoes turned down at the heels; hence the occasion of this language.

3 乾 is properly an adjective, but is here used as a verb; yet it does not mean *to dry the pen*, as would seem most natural, but *to allow it to get dry*.

6 這節書, *this verse of book*. The word 書 is added in order to limit the word 節.

14 This is a strong way of saying that the good fortune referred to was both great and unexpected.

17 腦袋, for the head, is Pekingese. Its metaphorical use is more general.

20 天使, for angel, is a Christian term.

22 喜鵲, is the more general term; though 鴉鵲 is also widely used.

LESSON XXXI.

NEGATION AND AFFIRMATION WITH AUXILIARIES.

When a negative is inserted after the principal verb and before the auxiliary, the meaning is not that the action does not take place, but rather that it can not take place; i.e., the negative applies to the auxiliary, not to the principal verb. When it is desired to affirm strongly in opposition to a previous negation, the clause is repeated with 得 substituted for the negative:—Les. 43.

These forms give a peculiar and admirable force, which we can not fully express in English.

VOCABULARY.

得 *Tei*³. Must, ought. See *tê*². This distinction of pronunciation is not *t'ung hsing*.

必得 *Pi*⁴ *tei*³. . . . Must, necessarily:—Les. 104.

謄 *T'êng*². *To copy*, to transcribe; to transfer; to vacate, to empty.

筲 *Shao*¹. . . . . . An osier or wooden bucket.

桶 *T'ung*³. . . . . . A tub, a cask; *a bucket*, a pail.

提 *Ti*¹. . . . . . To lift up, to carry. See *t'i*².

溜 *Liu*¹. To flow; to issue forth; to float, to wander; smooth. Also *liu*⁴.

提溜 To carry with the hand,—as a bucket, etc.

擰 *Ning*³,². To haul about, to twist; to pinch. *To carry in the hand.* (s.)

硬 *Ying*⁴. . . . *Hard;* stiff; obstinate; unfeeling.

挖 *Wa*¹. . . . . *To excavate*, to dig out; to gauge.

辰 *Ch'ên*². A Chinese hour; the hour from 7 to 8 o'clock A.M.

時辰 *Shï*² *ch'ên*². A Chinese hour,—equal to two English hours.

時辰表 *Shï*² *ch'ên*² *piao*³. . . . . A watch.

第三十一課

這[1]個表我買不起。○你[2]給我買的鞋太小、我
穿不上。○我[3]們今天必得走、你留也是留不
下。○一[4]天的工夫、謄不起來。○他[5]的嘴拙、怕
說不上來。○這[6]一桶筲水、我提溜不了提溜不上擡不起來。○地[7]凍
的頂硬、挖不下去。○你[8]跟着他走、我看你跟
不上。○現[9]喫現做、必做不下來。○我[10]的小刀
掉在水裏、撈不上來。○時[11]辰表是外國來的、
中國人做不上來。○瘦[12]子人的褲子、胖子人穿不
上下去。○這[13]些雞蛋白清打不起沫潑子兒來。○四[14]五
歲的孩子、自己還不會下來下不來嗎。○我[15]不應他、

TRANSLATION.

1 I can not afford to buy this watch.
2 The shoes you bought for me are too small; I can not get them on.
3 We must go to-day. You can not detain us if you would.
4 I can not copy it in the space of one day.
5 His tongue is thick; I fear he will not be able to say it.
6 I can not carry this bucket of water.
7 The ground is frozen too hard; I fear you can not excavate it.
8 If you go with him, it is my opinion you will not be able to keep up.
9 If you depend on preparing this food after it is ordered, you will certainly not be able to do it in time.
10 My pocket knife has fallen into the water, and I can not get it out.
11 Watches come from abroad. The Chinese can not make them.
12 A fat man can not put on a lean man's trousers.
13 The whites of these eggs will not beat into a froth.
14 Is a boy four or five years old not able to get down himself?

瘦 *Shou*^{4}, *sou*^{4}. . . . . . . *Lean*, thin, poor.
褲 *K'u*^{4}. . . . . . . Trousers, pantaloons.
蛋 *Tan*^{4}. . . . . . . *An egg;* a testicle.
潑 *P'oă*^{1}. To scatter, to splash; to drip; *froth;* . . . . . to waste; to dissipate; resolute, gamey.
沫 *Moă*^{4}. . . . . . . *Froth*, foam; bubbles.
英 *Ying*^{1}. . . . . . . Flourishing; excellent; brave.
英國 *Ying*^{1} *kwoă*^{2}. . . . . Great Britain.
密 *Mi*^{4}. Thick, dense, close; *fine*, small; hidden; . . . . . . intimate; secret.
細密 *Hsi*^{4} *mi*^{4}. . . . . Fine; delicate; close.
坑 *K'êng*^{1}. *A pit, a hollow;* a quarry; a mine; . . . . to entrap; to wrong.
頭晌 *T'ou*^{2} *shang*^{3}. . . . . The forenoon.
上半天 *Shang*^{4} *pan*^{4} *t'ien*^{1}. . . . . . . The same.
填 *T'ien*^{2}. *To fill up;* to make up a deficiency, ...to repay; to add on.
丸 *Wan*^{2}. . . . . . . *A pill;* a small ball; a bullet.
丸藥 *Wan*^{2} *yao*^{4}. . . . . .Pills.
咽 *Yien*^{4}. . . . . *To swallow*, to gulp. Also *yien*^{1}.

喘 *Ch'wan*^{3}. *To breathe;* to breathe hard, to . . . . pant.
歎 *T'an*^{4}. . . . .To sigh, to moan. *To breathe.* (s.)
鹽 *Yien*^{2}. . . . . . . Salt, saline.
錁 *K'ê*^{4}. *A small ingot of silver or gold;* paper . . . . money.
鹽錁 A small shoe of silver of about ten taels.
銀錁 *Yin*^{2} *k'ê*^{4}. . . . . .The same.
色 *Sê*^{4}, *shê*^{4}, *shai*^{3}. Color, hue; manner; expres- . . . . .sion of face; kind; *quality;* lust, venery.
成色 *Ch'êng*^{2} *sê*^{4}. . . . . Quality, touch.
足 *Tsu*^{2}, *chü*^{2}. The foot; enough, *sufficient;* to . . . . satisfy; entirely, in full.
一身 *I*^{1} *shên*^{1}. . . . . .The whole body.
腰 *Yao*^{1}. The loins; *the small of the back;* the . . . . . . kidneys; the waist; the middle.
伸 *Shên*^{1}. To stretch, to expand; *to straighten;* . . . . .to explain; to redress.
膀 *Pang*^{3}. . . . . . The upper arm, the humerus.

實在覺得下不去。○英[16]國話難學、怕你學不上來。○我[17]的眼已經花了、細密針線做不上來。○這[18]個坑、一上半天頭晌還填不起來嗎。○這[19]丸藥你若咽不下去、可以用水送下去。○我[20]有個心疼的病、到疼起來、一點氣也歎喘不上來。○有[21]現成的樣子、還做不上來嗎。○這[22]個銀鹽錁、成色不足、換不上行市。○張[23]老三的奶奶老婆一身病、腿站不起來、腰直伸不起來、頭擡不起來、胳膊髈子也揚不起來。

15 I felt that I could not but promise him.

16 English is hard to learn. I fear you will not be able to learn it.

17 My eyes have already failed, so that I can not do fine sewing.

18 Can you not fill up this pit in a whole forenoon?

19 If you can not swallow these pills, use some water to wash them down.

20 I am subject to pain in my stomach; and when the pain comes on, I can not get my breath at all.

21 Can you not make it, even when you have a ready-made pattern?

22 The quality of this ingot is below par. It will not exchange for market price.

23 Chang the Third's wife is diseased all over. She can not stand on her legs, nor straighten her back, nor hold up her head, nor lift up her arms.

Notes.

9 現吃現做 means, to prepare food after it is ordered, or after the guest arrives and is ready to eat. 現 is constantly so used of anything done on or for the occasion, excluding previous preparation.

11 In this sentence 做不上來 indicates want of skill, and in the 9th, 做不下來 indicates want of time; but this distinction between 上 and 下 is merely accidental.

12 Some teachers insist on using 上, and others on using 下. In the former case, the conception is of pulling the trousers on to the legs, and in the latter, of putting the legs into the trousers.

13 沫 is the better and more widely used word for *froth*. The two terms for *the white of an egg* are both widely used.

14 下不來 is rejected by Southern teachers.

15 下不去 is similar in form (but not in elegance) to the slang phrase, "it won't go down."

20 心疼的病 seems to say that the pain is in the *heart*, but *heart* is here put for the stomach.

22 鹽錁 is so called because it is used in the payment of the salt tax. Sometimes written 元錁 from its similarity to the larger 元寶 of fifty taels.

LESSON XXXII

Definite Locatives.

這 and 那 are joined with the words 頭, 面, 邊 and 處 to express *this* and *that* end, face, side or place. These forms are much more used in Chinese than are the corresponding forms in English. They may often be translated simply by *here* and *there*.

這頭 This end. } Applied to things having
那頭 That end. } length; also to parties opposed to each other.

這面 This face. } Applied to thin articles with
那面 That face. } faces; also to opposing parties.

這邊 This side or edge. } Applied to the bor-
那邊 That side or edge. } ders, or margins, of things, and to places.

這處 This place, or neighborhood. } Slightly
那處 That place, or neighborhood. } bookish.

Vocabulary.

窄 *Tsê*³, *chai*³. *Narrow;* straightened; narrow-minded, mean.

朝 *Ch'ao*². The imperial court; the sovereign; a dynasty; towards, *facing*. See *chao*¹.

窊 *Wa*¹. A low place; hollow, *concave*. Often written 凹.

河 *Hê*². *A river;* a canal; a creek.

兵 *Ping*¹. *A soldier*, troops, martial; a pawn.

第三十二課

這1邊寬、那邊窄。○這2邊兒厚、那邊兒
楞薄、○這3頭大、那頭小。○這4頭粗、那頭
細。○這5面兒朝上、那面兒朝下。○這6
面平、那面窊。○河7這邊有賊、那邊有
兵。○我8那邊實在亂雜、鬧人不斷。○
這9面兒還光滑一點些。○這10邊兒亮、那
邊兒黑。○那11地處方的人不好交。○這12
面向陽、那面背陰。○這13邊兒理正、那
邊兒理偏。○桌14子這邊有抽屜、那邊
沒有。○人15說和事、不好護着這頭、說

TRANSLATION.

1 This side is wide, and that side is narrow.
2 This side is thick, and that side thin.
3 This end is large, and that end small.
4 This end is coarse, and that end fine.
5 This is to be the upper side, and that the lower side.
6 This side is level; that side is concave.
7 On this side of the river there were robbers; on that side, soldiers.
8 There is a deal of confusion over where I am: there are idlers around all the time.
9 This side is somewhat smoother.
10 Here it is light, and there, dark.
11 The people there are not fit to associate with.
12 This side faces the sun; that side is shaded.
13 On this side the argument is fair; on that side it is forced.
14 The table has a drawer on this side; on that side it has none.

亂 *Lan*⁴, *lwan*⁴. Disorder; *confusion;* anarchy, ... rebellion; tangled.

雜 *Cha*², *tsa*². Mixed; *confused;* heterogeneous, ... miscellaneous.

亂雜 *Confused;* disorderly; promiscuous. Note 8.

斷 *Twan*⁴. To break or snap in two; to put a . . . . stop to; *to discontinue;* to decide; certainly, positively:—Les. 116.

光 *Kwang*¹. Light, brilliance; honor, glory; naked; . . . . *smooth;* only, solely:—Les. 49.

滑 *Hwa*². *Smooth;* slippery; polished; knavish, ... cunning; to slip and fall.

光滑 *Smooth;* polished; shining.

向 *Hsiang*⁴. Towards, *facing;* an intention; . . . . hitherto, heretofore; the points of the compass:—Les. 119.

陰 *Yin*¹. A shadow, *shady;* dark; cloudy; hades; . . . . . . the inferior of the dual powers of nature; female; secret, private; supernatural.

偏 *P'ien*¹. Deflected; excessive; *partial,* prejudic- . . . . . . ed; bent on, determined:—Les. 112.

婿 *Hsü*⁴. . . . . A son-in-law.

女婿 *Nü*³ *hsü*⁴. . . . . A son-in-law.

姑爺 *Ku*¹ *yie*². Son-in-law,—a title given to a . . . . man by the servants and younger members of his wife's family.

說和 *Shuo*¹ *hê*². To make up a quarrel; *to* . . . . *act as mediator.*

怪 *Kwai*⁴. Strange, monstrous; supernatural; a . . . . ghoul; to take offense at, to be surprised; *very,* unusually:—Note 18, also Les. 142.

冰 *Ping*¹. . . . . *Ice;* clear; crystallized.

鐵匠 *T'ie*³ *chiang*⁴. . . . . A blacksmith.

濟 *Chi*³,⁴. To aid, to relieve; to effect, to further; . . . . to stop; clever, *excellent.*

不濟 *Pu*⁴ *chi*⁴. . . . . Inferior, poor, scrubby.

分 *Fên*¹. To divide, to separate; to apportion; . . . . to share; to distinguish; a tenth; a candareen or tenth of a mace. See *fên*⁴.

分明 *Fên*¹ *ming*². . . . . Clearly, manifestly.

翻 *Fan*¹. *To turn over;* to change; to reverse; . . . . a bout; a set; fickle.

騰 *T'êng*². . . . To ascend; to transfer; to vacate.

翻騰 To turn over, to rummage, to overhaul. In this phrase **騰** is, in most places, read *têng*².

陣 *Chên*⁴. To set in array, a rank; an army; a . . . . battle; *a burst, a time.*—Les. 100.

隔 *Kê*², *chie*². A division; to separate, to put or . . . . keep asunder; *to prevent.*

釘 *Ting*⁴. . . . . . . To nail; *to fasten.* See *ting*¹.

擱板 *Kê*¹ *pan*³. . . . . A shelf; a mantel.

透 *T'ou*⁴. *To pass through;* to comprehend; . . . . through; thoroughly:—Les. 102.

那頭。○是[16]姑爺(女婿)這頭兒告了呢、是姑娘(女兒)那頭兒告了呢。○這[17]是正面、那是反面。○炕[18]這頭怪熱、那頭冰涼。○這[19]地方(處)的鐵匠頂不中用(不濟)、一個好手藝的沒有。○你[20]分明是向着那一邊兒、又上這邊兒來做甚麼呢。○我[21]的鏡子、這面好照人、那面好看畫兒。○這[22]裏的莊稼、比我們那邊的晚些。○你[23]翻騰我的抽屜做甚麼、這裏頭沒有你的東西。○昨[24]天下了一陣大雨、把我隔在河那邊。○你[25]看你釘的這個擱板、這頭高着有二分。○這[26]邊有個小眼、往外透(撒)氣。

15 When acting as mediator, it is not right to shield one side, and blame the other.
16 Was it the son-in-law's side that brought the suit, or was it the daughter's? [wrong.
17 This is the right side, and that, the
18 This end of the k'ang is very hot, and that end is cold as ice.
19 The blacksmiths of this place are very poor: there is not a good one among them.
20 You are manifestly partial to that side; what are you coming over here for?
21 This mirror of mine reflects your person on this side, and shows you a picture on that side. [with us.
22 The crops are later here than over
23 What are you rummaging my drawer for? There is nothing of yours in here.
24 Yesterday there came a great rain, which cut me off on that side of the river.
25 Look at this shelf which you have put up. This end is about two-tenths of an inch higher (than that end).
26 There is a small hole on this side, which lets out the air.

NOTES.

8 亂雜 is often inverted (viz., 雜亂) without appreciable change of meaning.

9 The two forms are quite equivalent; which is used being a mere matter of taste.

12 Lit., *This side faces the light; that side backs the shade.*

18 怪. Properly, *monstrous, frightful*, but often used as a species of intensive, meaning *excessively, very, rather*. It is only applied to things that are disagreeable or unexpected, and its use may perhaps be explained by considering it an exaggeration; just as the words "horrid" and "frightful" are often used in colloquial English. When so used its tone in most places changes to *kwai*¹.

19 不濟 is a very expressive phrase, which is widely used, though not, perhaps, entirely *t'ung hsing*. It is found in the Sacred Edict.

21 The Chinese are fond of having pictures set in the backs of their mirrors.

25 二分. The parts, or tenths, are understood to be parts of an inch, without specifying the fact.

26 往外撒氣 Lit., *go out leak air*. A relative must be supplied by which to connect the clauses.

LESSON XXXIII.

REDUPLICATION OF VERBS.

Verbs are repeated, partly for emphasis, and partly to specialize the action expressed. In many cases 一 is inserted between the words, by which the second verb is turned into a verbal noun;—thus 看一看, *to look a look*, or, as we say, "to take a look." It is very likely that the original and full form is that with 一, and that the 一 has been omitted in some cases for the sake of brevity. The meaning is substantially the same, whether 一 is inserted or not.

VOCABULARY.

停 *T'ing*². *To stop*, to cease; to delay; suitable, fit, satisfactory.

景 *Ching*³. Bright, luminous; *aspect, view*; a sight, a curiosity; style, form.

光景 *Kwang*¹ *ching*³. *State of affairs;* circumstances; scenery; sights.

曬 or 晒 *Shai*⁴. To dry in the sun; *to sun;* to beam upon.

第三十三課

客[1]堂的鐘停了、你去開上開上他。○我[2]們來看看事情的光景。○[3]可以拿去曬一曬。○少[4]坐坐再走不好嗎。○謝[5]謝李先生、這樣費心。○快[6]去望望你父親來了沒有。○不[7]必明說、可以畧畧的題一題。○你[8]去聽聽、他們在那裏說甚麼。○這[9]頭寬一點、可以用斧子砍一砍。○他[10]來坐了一坐、就急急的走了。○你[11]家去看看、要緊早早的回來。○刷[12]刷鍋、把那些脂油煉一煉。○

TRANSLATION.

1 The clock in the parlor has stopped. Do you go and wind it.
2 We have come to take a look at the state of the affair.
3 Take it away and sun it.
4 Why not sit down a little before you go?
5 Thank you, Mr. Li, for taking all this trouble.
6 Go quickly and look if your father has come (or, is coming).
7 You need not tell it out plainly: you can allude to it in a general way.
8 Do you go and listen to what they are saying over there.
9 This end is a little wide. Take an ax and hew off some.
10 He came and sat for a while, and then went off in a hurry.
11 When you go home for a visit, be sure and come back early.
12 Wash the kettle, and then try out that fat.

謝 *Hsie*⁴. . . . *To thank;* to resign, to quit; to fade.

費心 *Fei*⁴ *hsin*¹. *To take trouble,* to be accommodating; thank you.

畧 *Lüe*⁴, *liao*⁴, *liao*³. To plan; to seize, to capture; to abridge; a resumé; *in general,* rather, slightly, approximately:—Les. 177.

題 *T'i*². A theme, a proposition, a subject; a heading; *to mention;* to discuss.

砍 *K'an*³. To chop, *to cut off;* to cut with a sword or edged weapon; to fell.

脂 *Chï*¹. . . . . . . *Fat,* lard, grease; suet.

油 *Yiu*². . . . . Oil; *fat;* slippery; shining; to oil.

脂油 Lard, *fat.*

煉 *Lien*⁴. . . . . . . To refine, to smelt; *to try out,* or to separate.

秤 *Ch'êng*⁴. . . . . . . A steelyard, a balance.

數 *Shu*⁴. *A number;* a list, an account; several; destiny, fate. See *shu*³, also *soă*⁴.

彀數 *Kou*⁴ *shu*⁴. . . . . . Enough for the purpose.

聞 *Wên*². To hear, to learn from report; *to smell;* news, fame.

嘗 *Ch'ang*². *To taste,* to test, to prove; usually, formerly, ever:—Les. 192.

鹹 *Hsien*². . . . Saltish; *salted;* bitter.

修 *Hsiu*¹. To adorn; *to clean up;* to repair; to adjust; to cultivate; to chasten.

甲 *Chia*³. . . . . The chief, number one; to excel; armor; a scale, *a finger-nail;* C in music.

指甲 *Chï*³ *chia*³. . . . . Finger or toe nails.

消 *Hsiao*¹. To melt; *to pass away;* to cancel; to allay; to digest; to exhaust; required, necessary.

灑 or 洒 *Sa*³, *sha*³, *shai*³. *To sprinkle;* to scatter; to spill, to slop over.

加 *Chia*¹. *To add,* to superadd; to increase; to confer upon; to inflict.

烙 *Loă*⁴, *lao*⁴. To burn in or brand; to bake; *to iron clothes* or press a seam.

烙鐵 *Loă*⁴ *t'ie*³. A branding iron; a soldering iron; *a flat iron.*

燙 *T'ang*⁴. *To iron* or smooth out; to scald, to burn or blister.

逛 *Kwang*⁴. To ramble; to visit; *to walk for pleasure.*

戀 *Lien*⁴, *lüen*⁴. *To long for,* to dote on, to hanker for; loving.

捨 *Shê*³. To let go, *to give up;* to abandon; to renounce; to give alms.

戀戀不捨 Unable to give up, captivated.

揚揚得意 *Yang*² *yang*² *tê*² *i*⁴. Self-satisfied, elated.

梳 *Shu*¹. . . . . .A coarse-toothed comb; to comb.

抹 *Ma*¹. To wipe, to wipe off or out; to rub off; *to dust.* Also *moă*³.

拿13秤來稱一稱、看看彀數不彀。○你14不信聞聞、是臭了不是。○做15的時候、你沒嘗嘗鹹不鹹嗎。○今16天我要去見見他、問問他爲甚麼怪着我。○把17你的小刀借給我使用一使用、修修我的指甲。○現18在他正生大氣、可以等他消消氣再說。○先19用水灑一灑、再加烙鐵烙燙一烙燙。○這20樣好天、你該出去逛逛、散散心。○他21到如今、還是戀戀不捨的。○看22他那個樣子、眞是揚揚得意。○早23晨起來、洗洗臉、梳梳頭、掃掃地、擦抹擦抹桌子、這是一套兒的事情。○你24在下邊等一等、我上去給你問問。

13 Bring the steelyards and weigh it, and see if it is full weight.

14 If you don't believe it is spoiled, smell it.

15 When you made it, did you not taste whether it was salt or not?

16 I intend to go to see him to-day and ask him why he is offended at me.

17 Lend me (the use of) your knife to trim my finger-nails.

18 He is very angry just now; wait till his passion cools and we will see about it.

19 First sprinkle with water, and then iron with a flat iron.

20 In such pleasant weather as this, you ought to go out for exercise and recreation.

21 Even to this time she can not give him up.

22 Judging from his appearance he is quite elated.

23 When you get up in the morning, the first things in order are, to wash your face, and comb your hair, and sweep the floor, and dust the table.

24 Wait in the rear, till I go in and inquire.

NOTES.

1 上 is the more general word for winding a clock or watch. In Nanking 開 is used.

4 In the translation, 再 is rendered *before*. A more literal translation would preserve its normal meaning; thus,—*Would it not be well to sit down a little and then go?*

7 Some teachers insist on 提, instead of 題, in this sentence. The usage varies. There is authority for using both characters in the sense of *to mention*.

16 怪 is translated in the passive, though the construction is not properly passive. 怪 means *to take offence*, and hence, *to be offended*.

17 In Peking the tone of 指 changes in 指甲, to *chi*^{1}.

18 We speak of anger cooling; the Chinese, of its melting.

19 烙鐵 is properly either a branding iron, or a small goose for pressing seams; but the term is often used of foreign flat-irons. The second character changes its sound in many places to *t'i*^{4}, in Peking to *t'ie*^{4}. 加烙鐵, *add an iron*; i.e. *proceed, in addition, to iron them.*

21 戀戀不捨. A book phrase, in which the first character is repeated and the opposite idea added with a negative. Phrases made on this model are common.

22 揚揚得意. A book phrase, meaning *to toss the head with a self-satisfied air.*

23 抹 is not read *ma* by the dictionaries; but the syllable *ma* is everywhere used, both North and South, in the sense of *to wipe off*, the idea of cleansing or removing being prominent; and 抹 seems to be the best character to which to attach this meaning. The tone differs in different places. Read *mo*^{3}, it means *to rub on*, the idea of adding something being prominent.

24 In a yamen, or wherever there are servants or employés, to go into the presence of the officer, or head of the house, is to 上去; and his office, or residence, is referred to as 上邊: hence, also, the houses, or apartments, allotted to inferiors, are spoken of as 下邊. *In the rear*, seems to be our best approximation. It should be noted, however, that with the Chinese the apartments of subordinates are frequently, perhaps generally, in the front.

LESSON XXXIV.

THE INTERROGATIVE PERSONAL PRONOUN.

誰, who, is applied only to persons. It is properly interrogative, but is also used to mean *some one, somebody*, and with a negative, *nobody* or *anybody*. It is not much used along the Yangtse, 那個 being used instead. It is understood, however, and but a short distance northwards begins to be heard. Its use is one of the characteristics of a pure Mandarin.

第三十四課

1 那個(誰)在門外。○
2 你來找那個(誰)。○
3 這是那個(誰)告訴你的。○
4 外頭有那個(誰)叫門。○
5 那個(誰)在客堂拊琴。○
6 那個有痲子的是甚麼(誰、)人。答 是姓張的。○
7 那個(誰)有粉不搽在臉上呢。○
8 這些玩藝兒、是那個(誰)的。○
9 那個(誰)在家裏看門。○
10 那個(誰)在廚房裏、答 沒有那個(誰)。○
11 這是誰的仿圈(鎮紙)、答 我不曉得是誰的。○
12 喫誰的向誰。○
13 你看今天能下雨不能、答 那個誰知道。

TRANSLATION.

1 Who is outside the door?
2 Whom have you come to look for?
3 Who was it that told you this?
4 Who is outside calling at the door?
5 Who is in the parlor playing the organ?
6 Who is that pock-pitted man? *Ans.* It is the man Chang.
7 Who has paint and does not rub it on her face?
8 Whose playthings are these?
9 Who is at home keeping house?
10 Who is in the kitchen? *Ans.* No one.
11 Whose is this paper-weight? *Ans.* I do not know whose it is.
12 Every man stands up for his own employer.
13 Do you think it will rain to-day? *Ans.* That, who can tell?

VOCABULARY.

誰 *Shwei*^{2}. . . . . . Who? whose? whom? See Sub.

那 *Na*^{3}. . . . Which? who? See *na*^{4}, also Les. 45.

拊 *Fu*^{3}. To pat; to lay the hand on; *to play* a . . . . . . stringed or keyed instrument.

琴 *Ch'in*^{2}. A lute or harpsichord; applied to . . . . the *piano, organ*, etc.

痲 *Ma*^{2}. . . . . . . Numb, paralysed; *pock-marks*.

姓 *Hsing*^{4}. . . . . . . A surname; a clan.

粉 *Fên*^{3}. *Powder* of any kind, meal; chalk, pow- . . . . dered soapstone; to whitewash.

搽 *Ch'a*^{2}. . . . *To rub on*, to smear, to spread over.

看門 *K'an*^{1} *mên*^{2}. . . . To keep the gate; *to watch*.

玩藝 *Wan*^{2} *i*^{4}. . . . . Toys, *playthings*.

圈 *Ch'üen*^{1}. *A circle;* a small circle; to encircle; . . . . to draw small circles as marks of punctuation or of emphasis. Also *chüen*^{4}.

仿圈 *Fang*^{3} *ch'üen*^{1}. An oblong brass ring used . . . . as a paper weight.

鎮 *Chên*^{4}. *To press down;* to keep in subjec- . . . . tion; to guard; a large mart.

鎮紙 *Chên*^{4} *chi*^{3}. . . . . Same as 仿圈. (s.)

姜 *Chiang*^{1}. . . . . A surname.

玉 *Yü*^{4}. . . . . A gem, a pearl; precious; perfect.

山 *Shan*^{1}. . . . A mountain, a hill; wild, untamed.

羞 *Hsiu*^{1}. . . . *To be ashamed;* to blush; confused.

恥 *Ch'ï*^{3}. . . . . . Disgraced; *ashamed;* to blush.

羞恥 *Shame*, mortification; modesty.

嚷 *Jang*^{1}. To chatter, *to clamor about;* to let out . . . . a secret. Also *jang*^{3}.

吵 *Ch'ao*^{3,1}. . . . . *To clamor*, to wrangle.

饑 *Chi*^{1}. . . . . . Dearth; famine; hunger; straits.

饑荒 *Chi*^{1} *hwang*^{1}. Famine, scarcity; want of . . . . money, indebtedness; a difficulty, *a scrape*, straits.

外人 *Wai*^{4} *jên*^{2}. . . . . . . An outsider, a stranger.

牌 *P'ai*^{2}. A shield; a signboard; a tablet; a . . . . permit; *a notice;* cards, dominoes.

村 *Ts'un*^{1}. . . . . . A hamlet, a village; to sneer at, ... to gibe.

鄉村 *Hsiang*^{1} *ts'un*^{1}. . . . . A country village.

體貼 *T'i*^{3} *t'ie*^{4}. To put one's self in the place . . . . of another, to feel for, to sympathize; *to appreciate*.

滋 *Tsï*^{1}. Humid; *juicy;* sap; numerous; to fer- . . . . . tilize; to moisten; to grow; to stir up.

滋味 *Tsï*^{1} *wei*^{4}. . . . . . . Taste, *feeling*, sensation.

切 *Ch'ie*^{4}. *Urgent*, earnest; important; all, the . . . . whole :—Les. 105. See *ch'ie*^{1}.

囑 *Chu*^{3}. . . . To order; to enjoin upon, *to charge*.

囑咐 *Chu*^{3} *fu*^{4}. . . . . *To charge*, to enjoin.

隨便 *Swei*^{2} *pien*^{4}. At pleasure, *as you like*, at . . . . your convenience.

○姜[14]玉山一點羞恥也沒有、他管(任)誰也不怕。○你[15]聽聽街上直吵嚷吵嚷、誰和誰鬧饑荒呢(嗎)。○那[16]個人的臭名兒、誰不知道呢。○這[17]裏沒有外人、不是你是誰。○誰[18]肯說自己(誰)的瓜兒苦。○誰[19]的門口能掛個無事牌呢。○同[20]在一個鄉村、那個認不得那個(誰不認得誰)。○誰[21]也不能體貼我心裏的滋味。○這[22]不是我的不是、答不是你的不是是誰的。○你[23]當嚴嚴切切的囑咐他、隨便那個(任誰)不要告訴。○這[24]時候他們正在氣頭上、誰也不肯讓誰。

14 Chiang Yü Shan has no shame at all. He fears nobody.
15 Listen to that incessant clamor on the street. Who is making a row with whom?
16 Who does not know that man's bad reputation?
17 There was no other (outside) person here. If it was not you, who was it?
18 Who is willing to admit that his own melons are bitter?
19 Who can hang up a "no trouble notice" at his door?
20 All living in the same village; who does not know every body?
21 No one can appreciate the feelings of my heart.
22 This is not my fault. *Ans.* If it is not your fault, whose is it?
23 You should strictly charge him not to tell anybody.
24 Just now they are in the height of their anger, and no one will yield to any other.

NOTES.

3 這 here refers to the thing told, not to the person telling it. The 的 at the end may be omitted. Its use or omission does not alter the sense, but changes the grammatical structure. Without it the translation should be, *Who told you this?*

7 粉 here means the white lead with which Chinese women paint their faces. The idea of the proverb is that one who has merit naturally wishes to display it.

12 A neat way of expressing the idea, that it is to every one's interest to stand up for the man through whom he gets his livelihood.

14 管 is colloquial, and prevails in Central Mandarin. 任 is more elegant, but is slightly bookish in the South, where 隨便 is chiefly used (23).

15 The translation given supposes the sentence to end with 呢. If 嗎 be used, the translation of the last clause should be, *Is it some one having a row with some one?* The emphasis thrown on the 誰 and on the 饑荒 should be quite different for the different interrogative endings.

18 誰 is here equivalent to 自己. Its use in this connection is less general than that of 自己.

19 This sentence grows out of the custom of hanging tablets over the door with complimentary or sentimental inscriptions. Few families are so happy that they can hang up an inscription setting forth that they are free from care.

22 This sentence affords a good exercise in emphasis.

24 氣頭上 Lit., *On the top of their anger.*

LESSON XXXV.

INDEFINITE PRONOUNS.

都 All. Its sense is comprehensive. When referring to two things previously spoken of, it is to be rendered *both;* when used, as it frequently is, with a single person or thing, it has the force of *even;* and when preceded by 各 it means severally. It is frequently joined with the other indefinite pronouns as an expletive. It follows the noun.

凡 Every body. Its sense is distributive.

衆 All. Its sense is collective. It is ordinarily applied only to persons. It precedes the noun.

大衆 All, the whole crowd.

大家 All, the whole family or party.

攏總 All, all together, the whole lot, *in toto.*

通統 All, every single one.

通身 All together, *en masse.*

For other words of this class, see Les. 158.

第三十五課

[1]他一家老少都病了。○[2]念書寫字、都得要專心。○[3]人老了、腰腿都不中用。○[4]凡事不可不知趣。○[5]你家裏都有甚麼人呢。○[6]衆位都來了嗎。○[7]除了這個、都可以拿去。○[8]這裏攏總有三千多兵。○[9]他那些話、通身都是假的。○[10]你的兩個孩子、都有天分。○[11]大家的見識不同。○[12]他不論待誰、都是刻薄。○[13]我家裏一個大錢都沒有。○[14]你在這裏都認得誰、答 誰都不認得。○[15]山東省、攏總有一百零八縣。○[16]他是甚麼時候走的、大

TRANSLATION.

1 His whole family, old and young, are sick.
2 In both reading and writing, one should give undivided attention.
3 When a man gets old, both his back and his legs are unserviceable.
4 In every thing, a man should have a just appreciation of the time and the circumstances.
5 Who all are there in your family?
6 Have all [the gentlemen] come?
7 You may take away all except this.
8 There are here, in all, over three thousand soldiers.
9 That talk of his is all false.
10 Your two children are both gifted.
11 Our opinions do not all agree.
12 He treats every body meanly.
13 I have not a single cash in the house.
14 Whom all do you know in this place? *Ans.* I do not know any body at all.
15 The Province of Shantung has, in all, one hundred and eight hsiens.
16 At what time he left, none of us know.

都 *Tu*^{1}, *tou*^{1}. A metropolitan city; all, every one; in general:—See Sub.

凡 or 凢 *Fan*^{2}. All, everybody; common, vulgar; the world; mortal; earthly.

衆 *Chung*^{4}. A concourse; the majority; all; the whole; many:—See Sub.

攏 *Lung*^{3}. To seize; to collect together; to operate on; to draw near, to comb.

總 *Tsung*^{3}. To unite in one, to comprehend; all, the whole; generic; generally, still, in any case; must be; a president:—Les. 104.

通 *T'ung*^{1}. To go through; to perceive; to make known; to communicate; to pervade; current; everywhere, general; the whole of.

統 *T'ung*^{3}. To gather into one; the whole, general, entire; to control; a clue.

專心 *Chwan*^{1} *hsin*^{1}. Undivided attention; a single purpose; intent on.

趣 *Ch'ü*^{4}. To run quickly; to show alacrity; to regard pleasurably; *taste, flavor;* graceful, elegant.

知趣 *Chï*^{1} *ch'ü*^{4}. To know the flavor, to have a sense of the fitness of things.

除 *Ch'u*^{2}. To exclude, to deduct; to divide (math.); besides, *except:*—Les. 135.

見識 *Chien*^{4} *shï*^{2}. *Opinion,* sentiments; experience; discernment.

刻 *K'ê*^{4}. Insulting; *oppressive;* one-eighth of a Chinese hour, or fifteen minutes; a little while. Also *k'ê*^{1}.

刻薄 *K'ê*^{4} *poă*^{2}. To insult, to oppress, *to treat meanly.*

山東 *Shan*^{1} *tung*^{1}. Province of Shantung.

省 *Shêng*^{3}. *A province;* to diminish; to use sparingly, to save; to avoid; frugal. Also *hsing*^{3}.

縣 *Hsien*^{4}. A county,—the district ruled by one magistrate.

京城 *Ching*^{1} *ch'êng*^{2}. The capital.

井 *Ching*^{3}. *A well;* a pit; an excavation; a plot of ground.

果 *Kwoă*^{3}. *The fruit of trees;* really, truly; results, effects; reliable:—Les. 136.

指頭 *Chï*^{3} *t'ou*^{2}. *A finger,* a toe.

般 *Pan*^{1}. Sort, *class;* manner.

家都不曉得。○我[17]的眼鏡、都是隨身帶着。○京[18]城裏沒有河水、喫的都是井水。○這[19]是大衆的事、我自己不敢作主。○凡[20]不結好果子的樹、就砍下來、丢在火裏。○要[21]得衆人的心、那實在難。○孩[22]子們不能都一樣、十個指頭還能一般齊／還有長短嗎。○不[23]可凡事都隨從衆人。○風[24]颳翻了船、把船上的人通統／通身都淹死了。○這[25]些東西都亂七八蹧／七亂八蹧的、可以把他收拾好了。○這[26]個學生萬惡滔天、連先生他都敢罵。○你[27]們兩家鬧饑荒、／鬧出葛籐來告狀、都是他挑唆的。○看[28]牌、壓寶、擲骰子、他攏總／通統都會。○他[29]辦這件事、是甚麼時候兒、甚麼地方兒、甚麼緣故、甚麼法子、我都知道。

17 I always carry my spectacles with me.
18 There is no river water in the capital. All the water used is well water.
19 The business concerns [us] all. I can not venture to decide it myself.
20 Every tree that bringeth not forth good fruit is hewn down, and cast into the fire.
21 It is a very difficult thing to please every body.
22 Children can not be all alike. Can the ten fingers be all of the same length ?
23 You must not follow the crowd in every thing.
24 The wind capsized the boat, and every body on board was drowned.
25 These things are all in confusion. Arrange them in proper order.
26 This scholar is outrageous. He even dares to swear at his teacher.
27 You two families getting into a quarrel and going to law, is all of his getting up.
28 Card playing, thimble-rigging and dice throwing;—he is skilled in all of them.
29 I know all about when, and where, and why, and how, he did this thing.

一般 *I¹ pan¹*. . . . . .Alike, the same. Les. 106.
隨從 *Swei² ts'ung²*. . . *To follow*, to accord with.
船 *Ch'wan²*. . . . . A ship, a boat, a junk.
淹 *Yien¹*. To soak, to steep; to overflow; *to* . . . . *drown;* to tarry long.
淹死 *Yien¹ si³*. . . . . To drown :—Les. 183.
亂七八蹧 *Lan⁴ ch'i¹ pa¹ tsao¹*. Topsy-turvy, ... helter-skelter, all in confusion :—Note 25.
滔 *T'ao¹*. . . . . . . To overpass, to reach beyond.
萬惡滔天 *Wan⁴ oă⁴ t'ao² t'ien¹*. Wicked be- . . . . yond bounds, outrageous, incorrigible.
葛 *Kĕ²*. A long creeping vine; connections. As . . . . . .a surname read *kĕ³*.
籐 *T'êng²*. . . . . . . A trailing plant; the rattan.
葛籐 Intercourse; a difficulty, an embarrassment; *a scrape;* a hanger-on.
狀 *Chwang⁴*. Form, appearance; to accuse; *an* . . . . *accusation*, an indictment.
告狀 *Kao⁴ chwang⁴*. To accuse, to indict; *to go* . . . . *to law.*
壓 *Ya¹*. . . *To press down*, to weight. See *ya⁴*.
寶 *Pao³*. Precious; a gem; a coin; *a treasure ;* . . . . a complimentary term :—Les. 171.
壓寶 To play at thimble-rig :—Note 28.
看牌 *K'an⁴ p'ai²*. . . . . To play cards.
擲 *Chï¹*. *To throw down* or at; to fling away, to . . . . reject; to shovel,—as earth.
骰 *Shai³*. . . . . Dice.
緣 *Yien², yüen²*. A facing, a binding; correspond- . . . . ing with something previously existing, a subtle affinity; *because, therefore.*
緣故 *Yien² ku⁴*. . . . . . . The cause, the reason.

第三十六課

你1這麽大的人、還害怕
嗎。○你2不可這樣欺負
你的兄弟。○任3怎麽說、
他也不聽。○那4麽一些些個
補襯、你都用了嗎。○我5
的孩子、從來沒有這樣麽
哭。○他6那恁麽麽蹧蹋你、你
不要再忍耐他。○你7識
那恁麽麽些字、還不會記賬
嗎。○那8麽樣着我不算。○

TRANSLATION.

1 Such a great fellow as you, and still afraid?
2 You ought not to impose upon your brother in this way.
3 No matter what you say, he will not listen.
4 What! have you used up all that lot of patches?
5 My baby has never cried so before.
6 Having abused you in that way, you should not suffer him any longer.
7 Knowing so many characters as that, can you still not keep accounts?
8 In that case, I will decline.

NOTES.

2 In Northern Mandarin necessity is generally expressed by 得, rather than by 要. In the South 要 is used.

13 都 in this sentence is used somewhat like our phrase, "at all,"—*I have not a cent at all in the house.* Its use in this way is common, but not elegant. The sentence in the lesson is taken from a Pekingese book, yet a first-class Pekingese teacher, in reviewing this lesson, threw out the 都 and wrote 也.

17 都 here means, *at all times;* i.e., *always.* 隨身, *following* [my] *body;* i.e., *with me.*

18 吃的水, *the water eaten;* i.e., all the water used for domestic purposes.

21 得衆人的心, *to get the hearts of all;* i.e., *to be acceptable,* or *pleasing, to all.*

22 有長短, *have some long and some short.*

25 亂七八蹧. The original and proper order of this phrase undoubtedly is, 七亂八蹧, *seven disorders, eight accidents;*—a most expressive term for *confusion.*

26 萬惡滔天 is a book phrase; lit., *ten thousand vices overtopping the heavens;*—applied hyperbolically to a bad boy. 都 here includes all others, with the teacher as climax.

28 壓寶 is a method of gambling much practised in some parts of China. It is somewhat similar to the game, or trick, called thimble-rig.

LESSON XXXVI.

MODEL PARTICLES.

這麽 / 這樣 } Such, in this way, so, thus.

那麽 / 那樣 } Such, in that way, so.

The more common and colloquial form is that with 麽. When so used as to involve a comparison, the comparison is completed by *as this,* in the case of 這麽; and by *as that,* in the case of 那麽.

恁麽 / 恁樣 } Such, in that way, so.

The book pronunciation of 恁 is *jên*³, but as here used it is read *nin*³ or *nên*³ (the final *n* is elided in use). It is a question whether 那 should not always be written, and read as 恁. The use of 恁, however, is not without authority.

怎麽 / 怎樣 } How, in what manner.

The normal use of 怎 is interrogative (see next lesson), but it loses its interrogative force in some cases;—as when used in two correlative clauses (11, 15); or when preceded by such words as 任, 管, 不論, etc., (3, 13); or when immediately following a negative, (14.) In some parts of Shantung, and perhaps elsewhere, 怎麽 is often incorrectly used instead of 這麽.

VOCABULARY.

怎 *Tsên*³. An interrogative particle generally . . . . . . .followed by 麽; why? what?—See Sub.

恁 *Nin*³. . . . . . . Thus, so, such:—See Sub.

負 *Fu*⁴. To carry on the back; to bear, to suffer; . . . . . . to turn the back on; to abuse; *to slight;* to be defeated; minus (math.).

欺負 *Ch'i*¹ *fu*⁴. . . . . *To insult;* to oppress.

9 這點工夫、不能做那麼些活。○
10 我沒想到（料想）他能這麼痛快（爽快）。○
11 官怎麼問、他怎麼答。○
12 我這麼問他、恁麼（那麼）問他、到底沒問明白。○
13 這是頂要緊的事、不論怎麼（管那麼的）樣、必要商議妥當。○
14 你的年紀還不怎麼老、心就不聽使（用）了嗎。○
15 我一點不管、你們看怎麼樣、就怎麼樣。○
16 依你這麼說、他們兩家的媒、我就不用作了。○
17 那個學生眞懶惰、不論怎麼着（隨便怎麼樣）他也不念書。○
18 這麼滑的

9 I can not do all that work in this little time.
10 I did not anticipate he could be so prompt.
11 He answered according to whatever the officer asked.
12 I questioned him in this way and in that way; and, after all, I did not find out.
13 This is a very important matter: we must, by all means, come to some satisfactory understanding.
14 You are not yet very old; is your mind failing?
15 I do not care in the least. Do just as you think best.
16 According to what you say, there is no use in my acting as go-between for these two families.
17 That scholar is essentially lazy. No matter what you do, he will not study.
18 With such a slippery road as this,

補 *P'u*¹. To spread, to arrange—used for 鋪 in ..... the phrase 補襯. See *pu*³, also *p'u*³.

襯 *Ch'ên*⁴.......... Inner garments; padding.

補襯 Rags; pieces of old cloth used for making pasteboard.

從來 *Ts'ung*² *lai*²...... Heretofore:—Les. 119.

忍 *Jên*³. Fortitude; patience; to bear, *to suffer* ...... *patiently;* to repress; hard-hearted.

耐 *Nai*⁴.... *To bear with;* to suffer; to forbear.

忍耐 *To be patient,* to forbear; long-suffering.

料 *Liao*⁴. To estimate, *to judge of;* to arrange .... in order; materials; grain, pulse; strass, colored glass; ability, skill.

料想 *Liao*⁴ *hsiang*³. *To anticipate,* to expect, to .... deem.

想到 *Hsiang*³ *tao*⁴. To think of; to expect, ... *to anticipate:*—Les. 91.

痛 *T'ung*⁴. Pain, ache; acute feeling; to com- .... miserate; distressed.

痛快 *T'ung*⁴ *k'wai*⁴. Cheerful, buoyant; *prompt,* .... ready; hearty.

爽 *Shwang*³. Cheerful; light-hearted; healthy, ... vigorous; sudden; ready, *quick.*

爽快 *Shwang*³ *k'wai*⁴. Cheerful, healthy, vigor- .... ous; quick, *prompt.*

紀 *Chi*⁴. To arrange and record; annals; *a year,* ...... a period.

年紀 *Nien*² *chi*⁴.............. *Age;* years; time.

聽 *T'ing*⁴. To hearken to, *to obey;* to wait; ac- .... cording to, as. See *t'ing*¹.

依 *I*¹. To rely on, to trust to; to conform to; ..... to accede to; *according to,* as.

媒 *Mei*²........ *A go-between,* a match-maker.

懶 *Lan*³...... Lazy; remiss; disinclined to.

惰 *Toă*⁴...... Indolent, remiss.

懶惰 Lazy; disinclined to exertion; averse.

趔 *Lie*⁴........ To slip, to stumble.

趄 *Ch'ie*⁴...... Weak; *to hobble.*

趔趄 The unsteady motions produced by slipping or stumbling.

獃 *Tai*¹. Foolish, silly; to stare vacantly; *to* ...... *loiter,* to tarry; a simpleton.

挑 *T'iao*¹. *To carry on a pole on the shoulder;* to .... select, to choose. See *t'iao*³.

擔 *Tan*⁴. The burden carried on a pole, *a load;* .... a picul. Also *tan*¹.

肩 *Chien*¹....... *The shoulder;* to sustain; firm.

肩膀 *Chien*¹ *pang*³............. The shoulder.

肩頭 *Chien*¹ *t'ou*². The top of the shoulder. .... See Les. 47.

跭 *Pêng*⁴, *fêng*⁴.......... *To jump;* to rebound.

非 *Fei*¹. No, *not;* wrong; bad; shameless, vi- .... cious:—Les. 121 and 135.

路道、不能不打趔趄。○你[19]這麽停獃着着、是個甚麽意思呢。○你[20]挑這麽重的擔子、不怕壓壞了肩膀兒肩頭嗎。○這[21]個孩子氣的亂跭、這麽哄也不好、那麽哄也不好、非打不行。○恁[22]樣的大胖孩子、死了實在可惜。

one can not but walk unsteadily.
19 What do you mean by loitering (or, stopping) in this way?
20 Are you not afraid of injuring your shoulder by carrying such a heavy load?
21 This youngster is hopping mad (jumping up and down with anger). No kind of coaxing does any good. Nothing will serve but to whip him.
22 What a pity that such a fine, fat child should die.

NOTES.

3 怎麽 is here rendered *what*, though the force of the thought is *how*. We might render, *No matter how you put it.*

4 More literally, *As many rags as that, and you have used them all up!* The 一 might be omitted, but its use adds emphasis.

8 More literally, *In that case, you may count me out.*

9 這點 is a contraction for 這麽點, or 這麽一點. The 麽 is not unfrequently dropped out in this way.

13 不論怎麽樣. Here 麽 and 樣 are both used, and this is a not infrequent form. 管那麽的 is a phrase much used in some parts. It answers to the English, *by all means.* 那 is here read *Na*[3]. For the use of 的 see Les. 80.

16 Or, *Acccording to the way you represent it.*

19 The two forms are not quite equivalent. 停 means, *to stop or refuse to proceed;* whereas 獃 means, *to be absent-minded, or to loiter listlessly.*

21 氣的亂跭 "*hopping mad.*" Some would write 迸, but I find no authority for using this character in this sense; while the meaning of 跭 is quite suitable, and it is also read *pêng*[4], as well as *fêng*[4]. The double way of putting the coaxing is a characteristic Chinese idiom; while the use of the word 哄 intimates that Chinese *coaxing* is chiefly *deceiving.*

LESSON XXXVII.

INTERROGATIVES OF MANNER AND PLACE.

怎麽 How? why?
那麽 How? why?
Notice, that when 那 is used interrogatively it takes the third tone.

那裏 } Where? The two forms are quite
那兒 } equivalent in meaning, but the second is colloquial and somewhat undignified. It is rarely heard in the South.

VOCABULARY.

避 *Pi*[4]. To flee from; *to avoid;* to hide; to shirk; ..... to stand aside.
諱 *Hwei*[4]. .... To *shun;* to avoid; to taboo.
避諱 To avoid sacred names; *to avoid a delicate or forbidden subject;* to keep clear of.
鈴 *Ling*[2]. .... A small bell; a hand bell.
襪 *Wa*[4]. ...... Stockings, socks.
抓 *Chwa*[1]. To scratch; to tear with claws; to .... seize; to catch; to grab.
鐲 *Choa*[2]. .... A bracelet, a wristlet.
推 *T'wei*[1]. *To push away;* to secede; to shirk; to ...... decline; to resign; to extend; to infer.
磨 *Moa*[4]. .... A millstone; *a mill.* See *moa*[2].
推磨 To grind flour at a mill.
收成 *Shou*[1] *ch'êng*[2]. The proceeds of the year, ... the harvest.
心口疼 *Hsin*[1] *k'ou*[3] *t'êng*[2]. Pain in the stomach, dyspepsia.
孫 *Sun*[1]. .... A grandson; *a surname.*
迂 *Yü*[1]. .... Vague; addled, *stupid.*
滯 *Chi*[4]. To obstruct, to stop; an impediment; ...... *dull witted.*
迂滯 *Stupid,* obtuse, doltish; obstinate.
執 *Chi*[2]. To seize; to lay hold of; to keep; to ...... manage; to maintain; *obstinate,* set.
拘執 *Chü*[1] *chi*[2]. .... Obstinate, *immovable.*
進學 *Chin*[4] *hsüe*[2]. To get the first degree, to .... graduate.

第三十七課

[1]你怎麼沒去作禮拜。○[2]怎麼一點避諱不知道呢。○[3]搖了鈴、你怎麼沒聽見呢。○[4]你的襪子在那裏找着了呢。○[5]我託你那件事、怎麼樣呢。○[6]來了客、你怎麼不來告訴我呢。○[7]你在那裏兒抓的呢。○[8]我的鐲子你曉得在那裏嗎呢。○[9]怎麼還沒弄做好了飯呢、答我去推磨就躭誤了。○[10]說是要你快來、怎麼來的這麼遲晚呢。○[11]他從那裏來、要往那裏去呢。○[12]今年收成怎麼樣、答不怎麼樣、中平中平兒的。○[13]你如今怎麼這麼瘦呢、答我有個心口疼的病、喫不下飯去。○[14]孫三是個聰明人、怎麼在這件事上、這麼拘迂執滯呢。○[15]做活怎麼不按着

TRANSLATION.

1 Why did you not go to church?
2 Why is it that you have not sense enough to avoid an unpleasant subject?
3 The bell has rung. How is it that you did not hear?
4 Where did you find your stockings?
5 What about the business I entrusted to you?
6 When the stranger came, how is it that you did not come and tell me?
7 Where did you catch it (or, arrest him)?
8 Do you know where my bracelets are?
9 How is it that you have not yet gotten the meal ready? *Ans.* I was hindered by going to grind at the mill.
10 You were told to come quickly: how is it that you have come so late?
11 Where did he come from, and where is he intending to go?
12 How is the harvest this year? *Ans.* Nothing extra: only ordinary.
13 How is it that you are so lean these days? *Ans.* I have dyspepsia, and have no appetite.
14 Sun the Third is an intelligent man: how is it that in this business he is so stupid (immovable)?

為 *Wei*^{2}. To do, to effect; *to act;* to play the part of; to regard as. See *wei*^{4}.

行為 *Hsing*^{2} *wei*^{2}. Conduct, deportment, character.

品 *P'in*^{3}. A kind, rank, order; a rule or guide; *actions;* a part in music. Also *p'in*^{2}.

行 *Hsing*^{4}. Doings, conduct, character. See *hsing*^{2} and *hang*^{2}.

品行 Deportment, character, conduct.

橫 *Hêng*^{2}, *hung*^{2}. *Crosswise,* transverse; to lie across. Also *hêng*^{4}.

豎 or 竪 *Shu*^{4}. To erect; to stand upright; upright; *perpendicular;* chaste.

言 *Yien*^{2}. A word; a remark; a phrase; speech, talk; sayings; *to say.*

語 *Yü*^{3}. To talk with; *to tell;* words; phrases, sentences; language.

言語 Words, conversation; *to speak,* to tell.

仲 *Chung*^{4}. In the middle; *a surname.*

添 *T'ien*^{1}. *To add;* to increase; to throw in.

豫 or 預 *Yü*^{4}. At ease; satisfied; to prearrange, *to prepare;* beforehand; already.

備 *Pei*^{4}. To prepare; *to provide for;* ready: complete; entirely; all; wholly.

豫備 To prepare, *to provide;* to anticipate.

坐月 *Tso*^{4} *yüe*^{4}. To lie in, to be confined:—Note 22.

庇 *Pi*^{4}, *p'i*^{4}. To shelter, to cover; *to protect.* Properly *pi*^{4}, but usually spoken *p'i*^{4}.

護庇 *Hu*^{4} *p'i*^{4}. To shield; to protect.

禍 *Hwo*^{4}. Evil, misery; calamity, *disaster,* woe; the judgments of Heaven.

跳 *T'iao*^{4}. To leap, *to jump;* to hop, to dance; to palpitate.

時候呢。○他[16]的學問不怎麼樣、那兒能進學呢。○我[17]有意僱他看門、他的行爲怎麼樣呢。○聽[18]說那位馬先生的本事很好、不知他的品行怎麼樣。○這[19]些話你怎麼不早說呢。○橫[20]說豎說你都不肯、你打算怎麼樣呢。○你[21]這麼直哭、不論怎麼問、你也不言語、到底是怎麼着/的呢。○仲[22]先生、我今天不能來上學/進館、問怎麼/那麼不能來、答我的女人添了一個小孩子、我得/要給他豫備坐月子的東西。○這[23]是怎麼話說/怎麼說呢、大家都這麼護庇你、你怎麼必得往禍坑裏跳呢。

15 How is it that you do not do your work at the proper time?
16 His scholarship is only so, so. How could he get a degree?
17 I have a mind to hire him as a gate-keeper. What is his general character?
18 I hear that Mr. Ma's abilities are very good, but I do not know what is his general deportment.
19 Why is it that you did not speak of these things sooner?
20 No matter what is said, you dissent. What do you propose to do?
21 You do nothing but cry. No matter what one asks you, you make no reply. What is the matter with you, anyhow?
22 Mr. Chung, I can not come to school to-day. *Q.* Why? *Ans.* My wife has presented me with a baby, and I must prepare for her the things necessary for her confinement.
23 What do you mean! When we are all protecting you in this way, why is it that you persist in courting disaster?

NOTES.

1 We might with equal propriety translate, *Why have you not gone to church?* The Chinese fails to mark the distinction between the imperfect and perfect tenses. 怎麼 is here equivalent to *why*, although its proper meaning is *how*. The same thing is true of "how" in the English phrase, "How is it that, etc.?" The sentence might be rendered, *How is it that you have not gone to church?*

8 If this sentence be made to end with 呢, the emphasis falls on "where"; if with 嗎, it falls on "know."

10 It is quite uncertain by whom the person was told to come quickly, but it is implied that it was either by the speaker, or by some one sent or instructed by him.

12 The force of 不怎麼樣 is, that there was nothing noteworthy about the crops, either good or bad; that is, they were average crops.

18 Note that 行爲 may be applied to any one; but 品行 is properly applied only to persons of some social standing.

20 橫說豎說, *speak crosswise, or speak perpendicular*; i.e., *speak as you will.*

21 怎麼的 is the common Southern form. It is sometimes heard in Peking, especially when the cause, or reason, is required; while 怎麼着 is used when manner is spoken of. See Les. 80, Sub.

22 坐月子. *A woman's confinement; also the month following it.* During this month the mother is supposed to sit on her k'ang, eat certain kinds of food, and be served by her husband and sisters-in-law. Such language sounds strange in the mouth of one who is a pupil in school; but it must be remembered that *boys* get married in China, and that such subjects as this are spoken of by them with the utmost freedom.

23 Lit., *what sort of a speech is this?*—expressing both surprise and reproof. 怎麼必得往禍坑裏跳呢. *Why must you go and jump into the pit of woe?* i.e., *why do you persist in bringing disaster on yourself?*

LESSON XXXVIII.

FOUR COMMON CLASSIFIERS.

條 A branch,—classifier of things distinguished for length, rather than for breadth or thickness.

隻 Single,—classifier of single things as distinguished from pairs, also of some animals.

頭 Head,—classifier of various animals.

匹 A pair,—classifier of horses, and of kindred animals; though the usage in different places is far from uniform.

For full list of nouns falling under each of these classifiers see Supplement.

第三十八課

[1] 王老二眞是一條好漢子。○

[2] 我看這條街總有三里多長。○

[3] 寶子的兩隻鞋都穿歪了。○

[4] 他騎着一頭/匹大騲驢。○

[5] 那條狗不知跑了那裏去了。○

[6] 我的兩隻眼睛、疼的/得要命。○

[7] 若走那條路、少說也能/要遠五里。○

[8] 一條繩子不彀、可以用兩條。○

[9] 這隻/條牛你要賣嗎。○

[10] 一個人有一百隻羊、失迷/迷失了一隻。○

[11] 明天不能走、我兩隻脚都磨起泡來了。○

[12] 李小姐帶着兩隻金鐲子/鐲頭。○

[13] 這條/隻腿筋骨疼、那條/隻腿生

Translation.

1 Wang the Second is truly a portly fellow.

2 I think this street must be over three *li* long.

3 Both of Pao-tsï's shoes are worn crooked.

4 He was riding a large she-ass.

5 I wonder where that dog has run to.

6 Both my eyes pain me beyond endurance.

7 If we go by that road it will be further by at least five *li*.

8 One rope is not sufficient; use two.

9 Do you want to sell this cow?

10 A certain man had a hundred sheep, and he lost one (or, one got lost).

11 I can not go to-morrow. I have rubbed blisters on both my feet.

12 Miss Li wears two gold bracelets.

13 I have rheumatism in this leg, and on that one there is a boil.

Vocabulary.

條 *T'iao*^{2}. A branch; a switch; an item; a section, a law. A classifier:—See Sub.

隻 *Chï*^{1}. One of a sort or of a pair; single. A classifier:—see Sub.

匹 *P'i*^{1}. A pair; a mate. A classifier:—see Sub. Also *p'i*^{3}.

里 *Li*^{3}. A place; a village; an alley with gates; a measure of three hundred and sixty paces, approximately equal to one-third of a mile.

歪 *Wai*^{1}. Deflected; askew, awry; *crooked*, aslant; depraved, wicked.

騎 *Ch'i*^{2}. *To ride;* to sit astride.

騲 *Ts'ao*^{3}. The female of equine animals.

命 *Ming*^{4}. To command; to charge; an ordinance, a decree, commands, orders; fate, destiny, lot; *life;* living creatures.

要命 *Yao*^{4} *ming*^{4}. To take the life; deadly, fatal; *unendurable*, terrible.

繩 *Shêng*^{2}. A cord, a string, *a rope;* a line.

失 *Shï*^{1}. *To lose;* to neglect; to err, to miss; to slip; to fail.

迷 *Mi*^{2}. To delude; to fascinate; *confused;* stupefied; blinded; infatuated.

失迷 To lose one's way; lost, confused.

迷失 The same.

泡 *P'ao*^{1}. A bubble, *a blister:*—See *p'ao*^{4}.

小姐 *Hsiao*^{3} *chie*^{3}. Younger sister; *Miss,*—used in the South, also in Chinese novels.

金 *Chin*^{1}. Metal; metallic money; gold; precious; noble, honorable.

鐲頭 *Choă*^{2} *t'ou*^{2}. A bracelet:—Les. 47.

筋 *Chin*^{1}. *The sinews;* the nerves; strong.

筋骨疼 *Chin*^{1} *ku*^{3} *t'êng*^{2}. Rheumatism.

島 *Tao*^{3}. A hill in the sea, *an island.*

打魚 *Ta*^{3} *yü*^{2}. To fish:—See Les. 124.

瓦 *Wa*^{3}. Tiles; earthenware; pottery.

瓦匠 *Wa*^{3} *chiang*^{4}. A mason, a bricklayer.

偏口魚 *P'ien*^{1} *k'ou*^{3} *yü*^{2}. The sole.

蟲 *Ch'ung*^{2}. Worms, *snakes*, snails, insects.

長蟲 *Ch'ang*^{2} *ch'ung*^{2}. A snake.

蛇 *Shê*^{2}. *A serpent;* treacherous, subtle.

鴨 *Ya*^{1}. A duck.

鵝 *Oă*^{2}, *ê*^{2}. The domestic goose.

攤 *T'an*^{1}. To open out; to share, to fall to; to divide amongst; a stall, *a stand.*

菜攤 *Ts'ai*^{4} *t'an*^{1}. A stand for selling meat and vegetables.

瘡。○你14可以補一補這隻破襪子。○在15長山島前、有兩隻船打魚。○姜16瓦匠從房子上掉下來、跌壞了一隻胳膊(膀子)。○你17看是這匹馬的力氣大、是那匹馬的力氣大呢。○大18師傅上街買了三條偏口魚。○孩19子的兩手、都凍的冰凉(冰冷)。○你20快去看看、南牆跟底下有一條大長蟲(蛇)。○河21裏有十隻鴨子、六隻鵝。○我22買了七隻小雞兒、兩隻公的、五隻母的。○菜23牀子(攤子)出着五隻山雞(野雞)、十隻野貓(兎子)、兩隻鹿。○張24二爺家裏過的很寬綽(寬餘)、養着一頭(隻)牛、一匹(頭)驢、兩匹(頭)騾子。○你25把院子裏那個小哈吧狗(匹小吧狗)給我抓來。

14 You may darn (mend) this torn stocking.

15 There are two boats fishing to the south of the Ch'ang Shan Island.

16 Chiang, the mason, fell off the house and broke one of his arms.

17 Do you think that this horse has the greater strength, or has that one?

18 The cook went on the street and bought three soles.

19 Both of the child's hands are as cold as ice.

20 Go quickly and see! There is a big snake at the foot of the south wall.

21 There are ten ducks and six geese in the river.

22 I bought seven little chickens,—two cocks and five hens.

23 On a huckster's stand were spread out five pheasants, ten rabbits (or, hares) and two deer.

24 The family of Mr. Chang the Second are in very good circumstances. They keep a cow, and a donkey, and two mules.

25 Catch that small Peking dog in the yard for me.

菜牀 *Ts'ai⁴ ch'wang²*. . . . . The same.

山雞 *Shan¹ chi¹*. . . . . A pheasant.

野雞 *Yie³ chi¹*. . . . . The same.

貓 *Mao¹,²*. . . . . A cat.

野貓 *Yie³ mao¹*. The wild cat. In Peking,—*a hare.*

兎 *Tu⁴*. . . . . A rabbit; a hare.

鹿 *Lu⁴*. . . . . A deer; a stag.

綽 *Ch'oă⁴, ch'ao¹*. Gentle, kindly; generous; spacious; vague; many.

寬綽 *K'wan¹ ch'oă⁴*. Wide, ample; liberal; *in easy circumstances.*

餘 *Yü²*. Overplus; remainder; remnant; the rest; besides:—Les. 172.

寬餘 *K'wan¹ yü²*. *In easy circumstances;* ample; abundant.

養 *Yang³*. To nourish; to bring up, to rear; *to support;* to provide for; to develop.

騾 *Lo²*. . . . . A mule.

哈 *Ha³*. To sip; to laugh. Used as a phonetic and frequently read *ha³* and *k'a¹,⁴*.

吧 *Pa¹*. . . . . Large-mouthed.

哈吧狗 *Ha³ pa¹ kou³*. The pug-nosed Peking dog.

吧狗 *Pa¹ kou³*. . . . . The same.

NOTES.

1 條, applied to a man, implies that the individual is very tall, and inasmuch as 條 is not ordinarily applied to men, it suggests a tinge of ridicule.

9 Cows are generally classified either by 隻, or 頭 (24), though 條 is used in Hankow.

13 A leg is classified by 條, because it is long; and by 隻, because it is one of a pair. The latter is the more dignified.

15 When applied to hills, houses, streets, etc., 前 means *south.* Following the noun, it means *south of;*—as, 山前, *south of the hill*; when preceding the noun it means, *the south, southern;*—as, 前街, *the southern street.* In the same way, 後 means *north.*

19 冰凉 *ice cold.* See Les. 141.

25 Lit., *You take that little Peking dog in the yard, and catch him for me.*

第三十九課

檯[1]轎的來了沒有。○送[2]信的走了沒有。○趕[3]脚的要酒錢。○我[4]僱人、是要個能管賬的。○這[5]個刀子把兒、是個鹿角的。○我[6]們做要手藝的、不能穿好衣裳。○做[7]執事的、應當恒心執事。○外[8]邊有個要飯的、可以給他兩塊冷白薯(地瓜、山芋)。○管[9]事的不在家、我們不能作主。○[10]糴糧買草(買米買柴)、都是當家的事情。○種[11]莊稼的、出力不少、掙錢不多。○[2]先生蓋房子、是要蓋土坯(砌土墼)的、是要蓋甎(砌甎)的呢。○[13]做(弄)飯的叫廚子、

Translation.

1 Have the chair-bearers come?
2 Has the letter-carrier (postman) gone?
3 The muleteer wants a cumshaw.
4 I desire that the man I hire should be able to keep accounts.
5 The handle of this knife is deer horn.
6 We mechanics can not wear good clothes.
7 He that ministers, should do it with perseverance.
8 There is a beggar without. You may give him a couple of cold sweet potatoes.
9 The manager is not at home. We can not take the responsibility.
10 To lay in grain and buy fuel, is the business of the head of the family.
11 The farmer works hard, and gets but little money.
12 Do you intend to build your house of sun-dried brick, or of burned brick?
13 The man who cooks is called a ch'u-

LESSON XXXIX.

的 Denoting the Agent. 的 Denoting the Material

的, when added to a verb and its object, indicates the agent, corresponding to the English termination *er*, in such words as letter-carrier, fortune-teller, book-keeper, etc. In English the number of terms so formed is limited, but in Chinese 的 serves this purpose with entire regularity, wherever you wish to apply it.

的, when added to nouns of material, turns them into descriptive adjectives, corresponding to the English termination *en*, in such words as, golden, leaden, earthen, wheaten, etc. In English the number of adjectives formed in this way is limited, but in Chinese the usage is entirely uniform with respect to all such nouns.

Vocabulary.

趕脚 *Kan³ chiao³*. To follow and drive a beast of burden; to be a muleteer.

酒錢 *Chiu³ ch'ien²*. A bonus to an employé, a cumshaw:—Note 3.

管賬 *Kwan³ chang⁴*. . . . To act as book-keeper.

角 *Chiao², chiao³, chüe²*. *A horn;* a corner; an angle; a cape; a quarter; one-tenth of a dollar. A classifier:—Les. 125.

執事 *Chi² shï⁴*. A superintendent; *a deacon:*—Note 7. [See *pa¹*, and *pa³*.

把 *Pa⁴*. . . . . . A handle, something to hold by.

恒 *Hêng²*. . . . Constant; perpetual; *persevering.*

恒心 *Hêng² hsin¹*. . . . . Persevering.

薯 *Shu³*. . . . . . . A yam; *the sweet potato.*

芋 *Yü⁴*. . . . . The taro.

白薯 *Pai² shu³*. The sweet potato. (Peking):—Note 8.

地瓜 *Ti⁴ kwa¹*. . . . . The same. (Shantung).

山芋 *Shan¹ yü⁴*. . . . . . . The same. (Southern).

管事 *Kwan³ shï⁴*. . . . . . . To superintend.

糴 *Ti²*. . . . . To purchase grain for use.

糧 or **粮** *Liang²*. Rations; *grain;* provisions; taxes (in grain.)

當家 *Tang¹ chia¹*. To act as head of the family; the master of the house, a husband:—Note 10.

種 *Chung⁴*. To sow, to plant; *to cultivate;* to propagate. Also *chung³*.

伺候飯的叫擺桌子擺檯的。○你[14]是個做甚麼的人、答我是個修理鐘表的。○我[15]是個念書的、不懂得用兵的事。○我[16]們的茶壺、都是鍍包銀的、財主也有鍍包金的。○他[17]們弟兄五個、有四個做生意的。○街[18]旁有個算命的、擺着攤兒。○你[19]這個菸袋嘴子、我乍見當是個玉石的、細看還是個琉璃燒料的。○外[20]頭是甚麼人吵鬧呢、答是跟班的和趕車的吵鬧。○天[21]堂是頂榮華的地方、城牆是十二樣寶石的、城門是珍珠的、城裏的房屋和街道、都是精金的。

tsï, and the man who waits on table is called a pai-t'ai-ti.

14 What is your occupation? *Ans.* I am a watch-maker.

15 I am a literary man, and do not understand military affairs.

16 Our tea-pots are all silver-plated. Some of the rich have theirs plated with gold.

17 Of the five brothers, four are business men.

18 A fortune-teller has put up his stand at the side of the street.

19 At first sight, I took this pipe mouth-piece of yours to be stone; but on looking more closely, I see it is glass.

20 Who is making that disturbance outside? *Ans.* It is the servants wrangling with the carters.

21 Heaven is a most glorious place: the walls of the city are of twelve kinds of precious stones; the gates are of pearl; the houses and the streets are all of pure gold.

出力 *Ch'u¹ li⁴*. . . . . To exert one's self.
砌 *Ch'i⁴*. . . . . . A stone step; ornamental tiles; to . . . . lay brick or stone, to build up.
坯 *P'ei¹, p'i¹*. . . . . . . Unburnt tiles or brick.
墼 *Chi³*. . . . . . . Sun-dried brick, mud brick.
土坯 *T'u³ p'ei¹*. . . . . Unburnt brick.
土墼 *T'u³ chi³*. . . . . . . Sun-dried mud brick.
厨子 *Ch'u² tsï³*. . . . . A cook.
伺 *Ts'ï⁴, sï⁴*. . . . . To wait upon, to serve.
伺候 *Ts'ï⁴ hou⁴*. . . . . . . To wait upon, to serve.
擺 *Pai³*. *To spread out*, to move; to scull; to sway . . . . . . to and fro; to strut; a pendulum.
檯 or 枱 *T'ai²*. . . . *A table*, a stage:—Note 13.
修理 *Hsiu¹ li³*. . . . . To regulate; *to repair*.
鍍 *Tu⁴*. . . . . . . To gild, to plate:—Note 16.
財主 *Ts'ai² chu³*. . . . . A rich man.
生意 *Shêng¹ i⁴*. . . . . Business, occupation.
算命 *Swan⁴ ming⁴*. . . . . To tell fortunes.
乍 *Cha⁴*. At first; *at first sight;* unexpectedly, ... suddenly; for the moment.
菸 or 烟 *Yien¹*. . . . . . . Tobacco; tobacco leaves.
菸袋 *Yien¹ tai⁴*. . . . . . . A tobacco pipe.
石 *Shï²*. . . . . . . *A stone;* a rock; hard; a picul.
玉石 *Yü⁴ shï²*. . . . . A gem, a pearl.
琉 *Liu²*. . . . . A fine kind of glass.
琉璃 *Liu² li²*. . . . . Clouded glass; glaze.
燒料 *Shao¹ liao⁴*. . . . . Clouded glass.
吵鬧 *Ch'ao³ nao⁴*. To scold and wrangle; to . . . . make a disturbance.
班 *Pan¹*. To distribute; *a rank*, an order; a . . . . set; a troop:—Les. 140.
跟班 *Kên¹ pan¹*. Attendants, servants of an . . . . officer.
天堂 *T'ien¹ t'ang²*. The heavenly hall, *heaven*, ... the abode of the blessed—a term introduced into China by Buddhism.
榮 *Yung², jung²*. . . . . *Glory*, splendor; honor.
華 *Hwa²*. Flowery, elegant; *glorious*, beautiful; . . . . ornate; China.
榮華 *Glory*, splendor, effulgence, grandeur.
珍 *Chên¹*. . . *Precious;* rare; excellent; valuable.
珠 *Chu¹*. . . . . . . *A pearl;* a bead; fine, excellent.
珍珠 A pearl.
房屋 *Fang² wu¹*. . . . . Houses, buildings
街道 *Chie¹ tao⁴*. . . . . A street.

第四十課

我[1]說的話、你能聽出來嗎。○
你[2]進去把他叫出來。○請[3]先
生給我點出句子來。○門[4]窄
擡不進去。○把[5]鍋給我騰倒取出
來。○我[6]的雞跑出去、不曉得
是誰抓去了。○沒[7]有掩藏的
事、不露出來的。○先[8]刷出傢傢
伙什來、再上街也不遲。○靛[9]缸
裏拉不出白布來。○他[10]是好
人隊裏挑出來的。○這[11]個瓶瓶

Translation.

1 Can you understand what I say?
2 You go in and call him out.
3 Will you please punctuate it for me?
4 The door is too narrow; it can not be carried in.
5 Empty the kettle for me.
6 My chicken has run out. I wonder who has nabbed it.
7 There is nothing hidden that shall not be revealed.
8 There will be time enough to wash up the dishes before you go on the street.
9 You can not get white cloth out of an indigo dye pot.
10 He is rejected from the company of virtuous men.

Notes.

3 Muleteers, boatmen, and all, in fact, who are hired to do transient jobs, expect, in addition to the price agreed upon, a small present, which is called 酒錢. The idea probably is that the employer in such cases ought to "treat," but this being inconvenient, he gives a few cash for the party to treat himself.

4 個 is here to be construed with 人, understood, at the end of the sentence.

7 The term here rendered "minister," means rather, *a manager,—one who has charge of some special business.* The same term is elsewhere used in the N. T. for *deacon.*

8 Sweet potatoes are of comparatively recent introduction into China, and their name is not settled. In Peking they are called both 白薯 and 紅薯; in Shantung, they are called 地瓜; in Nanking, 山芋; in Kiukiang, 蕃蒻薯 (read *shao*); and in Hankow, simply 薯.

10 當家的事情. A full construction would require 當家的的事情; but one 的 is elided, and the other made to do duty for both. The 當家的 is ordinarily the father, or head, of the family; but in case of his death or disability, another member is appointed to control the business of the family. This is generally the elder brother, but not always. The term is also frequently used by women as the ordinary designation of their husbands. 糴 is used only of buying grain.

13 擺檯的 is used to designate the servant who spreads the table and waits upon it. The term is only used in connection with foreigners.

16 Both 鍍 and 包 are used for electroplating, the terminology being as yet unsettled. To gild by fire in the old way is 鍍.

LESSON XL.

The Auxiliary Verbs 出 and 進.

出來 Come out. } 出去 Go out. } As an auxiliary, 出 is nearly always followed by 來 or 去, and corresponds in a measure to the use of the word "out" after verbs; but it is used much more freely than "out" is in English.

進來 Come in. } 進去 Go in. } As an auxiliary, 進 is also nearly always followed by 來 or 去, and corresponds in a measure to the use of the word "in" after verbs in English. It is not nearly as much used as 出.

Vocabulary.

句 *Chü*[4]. *A stop*, a period; a sentence, a phrase; a line in verse. A classifier:—Les. 42.

掩 *Yien*[3]. To screen; to cover, *to conceal;* to hide from observation.

掩藏 *Yien*[3] *ts'ang*[2]. *To hide;* secret.

露 *Lou*[4]. To disclose, to expose; *to reveal;* to protrude. Also *lu*[4].

靛 *Tien*[4]. Indigo; indigo color.

塞梓頂緊、拔不出來。○洗[12]出衣裳來、該把齷齪髒水倒出去。○要[13]把好的揀出來、把壞的扔丟出去。○這[14]一點賬最容易算、怎麼算不出來呢。○我[15]察不出他有甚麼罪來。○扒[16]出心來給他吃了、也賺討不出好來。○他[17]姊妹兩個、我認不出那個是那個來。○天[18]要下雨、可以把轎子打進去。○李[19]掌櫃老板的來了、答可以請他進來。○十[20]個人掙出來的銀子錢、也不彀你一個人花費的。○吳[21]大人的門軍太利

11 The stopper of this bottle is very tight. I can not pull it out.

12 When you have washed the clothes you should pour out the dirty water.

13 Select the good ones, and throw the bad ones away.

14 This little account is very simple; how is it that you can not reckon it up?

15 I can not find that he has any fault.

16 If I should tear out my heart and give him to eat, I could not please him.

17 Of these two sisters, I can not distinguish which is which.

18 It is going to rain. You had better take in the sedan chair.

19 Mr. Li has come. *Ans.* Invite him to come in.

20 The earnings of ten men would not be enough for you to spend.

21 Gen. Wu's gate-keeper is too strict. You will certainly not get your

---

隊 *Twei*^{4}. A rank, a file; a group, a company; . . . . *a crowd*. A classifier of companies.

塞 *Sê*^{1}. . . . A stopper, a plug, a cork. Also *sê*^{4}.

梓 *Tsu*^{3}. . . . . . . A plug, a cork. (c. and s.)

齷 *Wu*^{1}. . . . . . . Small; sordid; crowded.

齪 *Ts'u*^{4}. . . . . . . To grate the teeth.

齷齪 Worried, vexed; fretful. (N.) Rubbish, filth; *dirty*, foul. (s.)

揀 *Chien*^{3}. . . . . *To select*, to choose, to pick out.

扔 *Jêng*^{1,3}. To discard, to abandon; to reject, ... *to throw away*.

察 *Ch'a*^{2}. To examine, *to inquire into judicially;* . . . . to scrutinize; to discover.

扒 *Pa*^{1}. To divide; to pull apart; *to tear* or *cut* . . . . *out*. Also *p'a*^{2}.

姊 *Tsï*^{3}. . . . . . . An elder sister.

妹 *Mei*^{4}. . . . . A younger sister.

姊妹 Sisters, a sister :—Note 17.

掌櫃 *Chang*^{3} *kwei*^{4}. Superintendent, manager, ... head-man, boss.

吳 *Wu*^{2}. . . . . To talk; a surname.

軍 *Chün*^{1}. . . . . . . An army; *a soldier;* military.

門軍 *Mên*^{2} *chün*^{1}. A guard at a gate, a military officer's gatekeeper.

稟 *Ping*^{3}. To report to a superior; to receive . . . . from heaven; *a petition*.

帖 *T'ie*^{1,3,4}. A writing scroll, *a writing;* a billet; . . . . a card; a placard :—Les. 147.

稟帖 *A petition;* a report.

受 *Shou*^{4}. To receive; to contain; to endure; . . . . to bear; *to suffer* :—Les. 79.

魔 *Moă*^{2}. . . . . A devil, a demon.

鬼 *Kwei*^{3}. The soul of a dead man before it is . . . . . . formally enshrined or deified; a ghost; a goblin; a demon, *a devil;* any monstrous thing.

魔鬼 Devils, the devil.

惑 *Hwoă*^{4}, *hê*^{4}. *To delude*, to blind the mind; . . . . to unsettle another's mind, to excite doubt or suspicion.

迷惑 *Mi*^{2} *hwoă*^{4}. To delude; to beguile; to ensnare, to befool; a delusion.

圈套 *Ch'üen*^{1} *t'ao*^{4}. . . . . A snare, *toils*.

刑 *Hsing*^{2}. To imitate; a pattern; punishment; . . . . torture; castigation; penal; law.

刑罰 *Hsing*^{2} *fa*^{2}. . . . . . . Punishment; torture.

實情 *Shï*^{2} *ch'ing*^{2}. . . . . . . The facts, the truth.

歡喜 *Hwan*^{1} *hsi*^{3}. To rejoice, to be glad; satisfied; *pleased*.

叔 *Shu*^{2}. . . . . A father's younger brother.

大叔 *Ta*^{4} *shu*^{2}. . . . . . . The senior 叔.

害、你的稟帖、必傳不進去、答我有法子能傳進去。○22已經受了魔鬼的迷惑、難逃出他的圈套來。○23不加刑罰給他、問不出實情來。○24人歡喜不歡喜、都可以從眼睛裏看出來。○25大叔若是到底不管、實在是把我弄得出不來進不去的。

petition sent in. *Ans.* I have a plan by which it can be sent in.

22 When you have been ensnared by the devil, it is hard to escape his toils.

23 Without torturing him you will not get the truth out of him.

24 Whether a man is pleased or not, can always be seen from his eyes.

25 If you, uncle, positively will not do anything, you will put me in a very embarrassing position.

NOTES.

2 進 is here used as a principal verb. The subject of the lesson is illustrated by 出.

3 點出句子來. Lit., *point out the clauses;* i.e., *punctuate it.*

4 擡不進去. Note how the verb is left without either subject or object, both of which must be supplied from the context.

5 倒 does not here mean to lift the kettle and *pour out* the contents, but simply to *empty it.* In like manner, 取 does not mean to *take out* the kettle, but simply its contents.

7 不露出來的. The 的 here makes the clause relative, the antecedent being the clause, 掩藏的事. See Les. 23.

9 A proverb applied to one from a vicious or disreputable family.

10 A witty saying, meaning that the person referred to, so far from being a *good man,* is *refuse,* whom good men have eliminated from their company.

15 甚麽 is without emphasis. If emphasized the meaning would be, I can not find out what fault he has.

17 姊妹 means properly, *sisters,* but is often used in the singular, either of an elder or younger sister. It is also sometimes used to mean both brothers and sisters; i.e., all the children of a family.

19 In the North, 掌櫃 is generally used of *the head-man* of any business. In the South, 老板 is used in place of it, and is also heard at sea ports in the North. 掌櫃 may be, and often is, an employé, in the office of *head-man;* but 老板 is *the proprietor.* Women frequently call their husbands 掌櫃, that is the head-man of the house.

20 It really requires both 銀子 and 錢 to cover the idea of "money."

25 This sentence does not properly illustrate the subject of the lesson; but it has both 進去 and 出來 used in a very idiomatic way, 把我弄的出不來進不去的, *So circumstance me that I can neither go out nor come in;* i.e., *neither retreat nor advance.* The order is often changed to 進不來出不去的.

LESSON XLI.

THE AUXILIARY VERBS 過 AND 回.

過, as an auxiliary verb, expresses the idea of *over,* either in respect of time, or of place. It generally takes 來 or 去 after it. When followed by 來, it indicates motion *over* and *towards:* when followed by 去, it indicates motion *over* and *away from.* In many cases the original idea of *motion* is lost in that of *change.*

回, as an auxiliary, expresses the idea of *turning back.* It also generally takes 來 or 去 after it. When followed by 來, it indicates motion *back* and *towards;* when followed by 去, it indicates motion *back* and *away from.* The range of its use is more limited than that of 過.

For full list of verbs followed by each of these auxiliaries see Supplement.

VOCABULARY.

竅 *Ch'iao⁴.* An orifice, an aperture; a cavity; . . . . .the mind; the avenues by which the mind acquires knowledge; the *key* or *clue.*

心竅 *Hsin¹ ch'iao⁴.* Power to comprehend, the . . . . .understanding.

姪 *Chi².* . . . . . . A nephew, the son of a brother.

賴 *Lai⁴.* To depend upon, to rely on; to assume; . . . . . . *to pretend,* to trump up; to accuse falsely; to deny, to ignore.

賴學 *Lai⁴ hsüe².* . . . . .To play truant (s).

第四十一課

請[1]先生把這個錯字改過來。○乍[2]學中國話、實在難(開心竅)轉過竅來。○你[3]的姪兒(賴)逃學跑了、你該把他找回來。○這[4]是我經手借的、我還給他送回去。○這[5]一頭不合式、該倒過來。○你[6]去找個(誰)人和你兩個、把這個箱子挪過去。○在[7]那裏修理好了、還請你給我帶回來。○這[8]面沒有那個字、可以翻過來看看。○你[9](好)該拿梅先生的秤砣(要)玩嗎、快快的給他送回去。○這[10]隻雞鬭不過那隻雞。○這[11]樣的嘴、

TRANSLATION.

1 Please correct this erroneous character.

2 When you first begin to learn Chinese it is very hard to get the clue.

3 Your nephew has run away from school. You ought to find him and bring him back.

4 This was borrowed through my instrumentality, and I will also return it to him.

5 This end does not fit. It should be reversed.

6 Go and find a man (some one) to help you move over this box.

7 When it is repaired, will you please bring it back again for me?

8 There is no such character on this page. Turn over and look.

9 Is it right (proper) for you to take Mr. Mei's steelyard weight to play with? Return it to him at once.

10 This rooster is not a match for that one in a fight.

經手 *Ching*^{1} *shou*^{3}. To have experience of; . . . . *agency*, instrumentality.

挪 *Noă*^{2}. . . . . . . *To move;* to shift; to transfer.

梅 *Mei*^{2}. . . . . . A plum, a prune; *a surname.*

砣 *T'oă*^{2}. A weight at the end of a string; *a steelyard weight;* a sounding lead.

鬭 *Tou*^{4}. *To fight;* to contend for victory; to incite to contention; to play at.

吃飯堂 *Ch'ï*^{1} *fan*^{4} *t'ang*^{2}. . . . . . . Dining-room.

飯廳 *Fan*^{4} *t'ing*^{1}. . . . . Dining-hall.

傘 *San*^{3}. . . . . . . An umbrella, a parasol.

覺 *Chiao*^{4}. Sleep, the unconsciousness of sleep. . . . . See *chioă*^{2}.

睡覺 *Shwei*^{4} *chiao*^{4}. To sleep; to lie down to sleep.

首 *Shou*^{3}. *The head;* a chief; the beginning; . . . . foremost. A classifier:—Les. 147.

飾 *Shï*^{1}. To adorn, to ornament, to set off; to gloss over; to deceive; *an ornament.*

首飾 Head ornaments; jewelry.

匣 *Hsia*^{2}. A chest, a coffer, a casket, a small covered box.

定親 *Ting*^{4} *ch'in*^{1}. To settle a marriage engagement.

青 *Ch'ing*^{1}. Green (of grass); *blue* (of the sky or ocean); black (of cloth); glossy.

紅 *Hung*^{2}. . . . . . . *Red;* fiery; ruddy.

煤 *Mei*^{2}. . . . . *Coal,*—especially hard coal; soot.

煤油 *Mei*^{2} *yiu*^{2}. . . . . . . Coal oil, kerosene.

火油 *Hwoă*^{3} *yiu*^{2}. . . . . . . Kerosene.

海 *Hai*^{3}. . . . . . . The sea; marine; capacious.

上海 *Shang*^{4} *hai*^{3}. Shanghai; to go to the seashore.

朱 *Chu*^{1}. . . . . . Vermilion red; *a surname.*

嫖 *P'iao*^{2}. Trifling, licentious; to follow lewd women; *to lead the life of a rake.*

回頭 *Hwei*^{2} *t'ou*^{2}. . . . To turn about; *to reform.*

匪 *Fei*^{3}. Illegal, seditious; robbers, brigands; dissolute, *vicious;* no, not so.

類 *Lei*^{4}. . . . . Species, sort, *kind;* to class with.

匪類 Vagabonds, profligates; vice, *dissipation.*

昏 *Hun*^{1}. Dusk, dark, obscure; confused, muddled; *to faint,* to become insensible.

甦 *Su*^{1}. . . . . . *To revive;* to come to life again.

甦醒 *Su*^{1} *hsing*^{3}. *To revive;* to regain one's senses; to rise from the dead.

衞 *Wei*^{4}. To escort for protection or honor; to guard; a military station; an outpost; *a local name for Tientsin.*

我說不過他。（說他不過。）○孫[12]師娘在喫飯堂（飯廳）裏、你去請過他來（請他過來）。○你[13]去的時候、可以把他的傘帶過去。○那[14]裏沒有地方睡覺、你搬過來不好嗎。○先[15]生用過飯了嗎、答 偏過了。○他[16]們奪了去的、我們今天還要奪回來。○南[17]莊上拿着首飾匣子來定親、又碰（頂）回去了。○他[18]說過來說過去、到底沒說出個青紅皂白來。○這[19]把笤箒、是你從廂房拿過來的、可以再送過去。○這[20]十個煤油（火油）箱子、是在上海發錯了、我還要發回去。○朱[21]老大如今回過頭來、凡喫喝嫖賭匪類的事、一點也沒有他。○那[22]一夜他病的頂重、昏過去了、好一會子纔甦醒過來了。○十[23]個京油子、說不過一個衞嘴子。

11 With such a tongue as his, I am no match for him.
12 Mrs. Sun is in the dining-room: go and invite her over.
13 When you go over you can take along his umbrella.
14 There is no place there to sleep. Would it not do for you to move over here?
15 Have you eaten? *Ans.* I have.
16 What they took from us, we must get back again to-day.
17 The folks of the south village brought a box of jewelry to settle the betrothal, but were sent back [with a refusal].
18 He talked the business over and over, and, after all, expressed no definite opinion.
19 This broom is one you brought over from the side house. You had better take it back again.
20 These ten boxes of kerosene oil were sent from Shanghai by mistake. I must send them back again.
21 Chu Senior has now reformed, and avoids every form of dissipation and profligacy.
22 That night he was very seriously ill. He fainted, and it was a long time before he revived again.
23 Ten oily-mouthed Pekingese can not get ahead of one tonguy Tientsinese.

NOTES.

2 It is a traditional idea that the mind receives knowledge through apertures in the heart, and the more of these apertures a man has, the quicker is his power of apprehension. 比干 (now canonized as the god of wealth) was reported to have seven such apertures in his heart, and the tyrant 紂王 had his heart cut out to see if it was so. 開竅 is to have these openings freed of obstruction, thus admitting the light which gives knowledge. 轉過竅來 is to have these openings turned in the right direction, that so the light may find due entrance.

10 The 難 at the close of this sentence might be omitted without detriment.

11 The more usual form is 說不過他. 說他不過 is an elegant transposition, which is also used in colloquial in some places.

12 Chinese houses have no distinctive "dining-room." The terms 吃飯堂 and 飯廳, are only used in connection with foreign houses. 請過他來 is not precisely the same as 請他過來. In the first, the stress naturally falls on the word 請; in the second, it falls on 過. The first means *to bring her over* [by inviting]; the second means simply *to invite her to come over*,—her coming, or not, being no concern of the party inviting.

15 用, as here used for *eating*, is in some places quite colloquial, and in others it has something of the stateliness of the word "partake." 偏過了, *I have the advantage of you in that I have already eaten*;—used when one happens on others while eating, or about to eat.

17 A present of jewelry to the bride elect, is always necessary to the settlement of a marriage contract. In this case the friends of the intended groom went with the presents in due form, supposing, or assuming, that the proposal was satisfactory; and were sent back again crestfallen, as is indicated by the use of the word 頂 or 碰.

18 沒說出個青紅皂白來 *did not express a blue, red, black or white*; i.e., *said nothing to the point; expressed no definite opinion or decision.*

21 凡吃喝嫖賭, etc., *has nothing to do with such vices as gluttony, drunkenness, licentiousness and gambling.* These terms are linked together as a comprehensive summary of dissipation, and are all included in the term 匪類.

23 This is a pithy fling at the people of Tientsin. 油子 and 嘴子, as here used, are slang.

第四十二課

請[1]再給我訂一本仿。個仿本個字本 ○ 給[2]學生買東西、該另記一本賬。○ 我[3]那部康熙字典、是六套。○ 請[4]先生給我講講這句書。○ 你[5]和他兩個把那張牀擡上來。○ 好[6]體面講究一本書、可惜已經破了。○ 今[7]天你出去、給我買十管筆、兩錠塊墨、五十張毛邊紙。○ 我[8]有一個朋友、送了兩張地圖給我。○ 人[9]至少該有兩套衣服、好換着糨漿洗。○ 他[10]說那一句話、我半天沒會過意來。○ 一[11]本千字文、正有二百五十句。○ 這[12]

TRANSLATION.

1 Please make another copy-book for me.
2 When you buy things for the scholars, you should keep the account in a separate book.
3 That Kanghi's dictionary of mine is in six *t'ao*.
4 Will you please explain this sentence [for me?
5 Do you and he go and carry up that bedstead.
6 A very good-looking book: what a pity it is torn!
7 When you are out to-day, buy for me ten pens, two sticks of ink, and fifty sheets of *mao-pien* paper.
8 I have a friend who made me a present of two maps.
9 A person should have at least two suits of clothes in order to change for washing.
10 When he made that remark, it did not occur to me for half a day what he meant.
11 The One Thousand Character Classic

LESSON XLII.

CLASSIFIERS.

本 The root,—classifier of volumes of a book.

行 A row,—classifier of things in rows.

部 The sum,—classifier of books considered as wholes; i.e., as works or treatises, irrespective of the number of volumes.

張 To extend,—classifier of things presenting a large or plain surface.

管 A reed,—classifier of long tubular things.

套 A wrapper,—classifier of book covers and of things in suits, or sets.

句 A sentence,—classifier of clauses and sentences.

錠 An ingot,—classifier of pieces of silver and sticks of ink.

For full list of nouns which take these several classifiers see Supplement.

VOCABULARY.

部 *Pu*⁴. The sum; a class or division; a section; . . . . . . a radical; a tribunal; a Board. See Sub.

錠 *Ting*⁴. A platter; an ingot; a stick of medi- . . . . cine or ink. See Sub.

訂 *Ting*¹. . . . . . To bind into a book. Also *ting*⁴.

仿本 *Fang*³ *pên*³. . . . . A copy-book.

字本 *Tsï*⁴ *pên*³. . . . . The same.

康 *K'ang*¹. . . . . . . Peace; vigorous; excellent.

熙 *Hsi*¹. . . . . Bright, glorious; harmonious.

康熙 The emperor Kanghi:—Note 3.

典 *Tien*³. A canon; a statute or code; a law, an . . . . ordinance; *a precedent*, a reference; records; to mortgage, to lease; to manage.

字典 *Tsï*⁴ *tien*³. . . . . A dictionary.

墨 *Mei*⁴, *mo*⁴. . . . . *Ink;* dark, black; writings.

毛邊 *Mao*² *pien*¹. A kind of heavy brown writ- . . . . ing paper.

圖 *T'u*². A diagram, a chart, *a map;* to plan, ... to plot; to wish for, to aspire after.

地圖 *Ti*⁴ *t'u*². . . . . A geographical map.

部格物入門、是木板印的。○馬13老爺有一
張山水畫兒、值二十兩銀子。○這14部化學、
該找人打一個套。○請15先生給我打勒一個
仿格子、要八個字一行。○我16那部舊天文、
不知誰借去了。○用17不着多工夫、也不過
說三五句話。○請18你把那部書、給我套起
來。○李19天保那個小學生、眞好天分、一天
能念九十行生書。○這20張桌子不穩當、可
以找甚麽墊起來。○買21一部形學、要得七角
五分洋錢。○我22要你給我做兩張書案、一

has just two hundred and fifty lines in it.

12 This book of natural philosophy is printed from wooden blocks.

13 Mr. Ma has one landscape painting which is worth twenty taels.

14 You should find some one to make a *t'ao* for this chemistry.

15 Please, teacher, rule for me a *kê-tsï* with eight characters in each column.

16 I wonder who borrowed that old astronomy of mine.

17 It will not require long; I only wish to speak a few words.

18 Please put that book in the *t'ao* for me.

19 That little scholar Li T'ien Pao is certainly gifted. He can commit to memory ninety lines in one day.

20 This table is not steady. Find something to prop it up.

21 It requires seventy-five cents to purchase a geometry.

22 I want you to make for me two book-

糨 *Chiang*¹. . . . . *To starch.* Also *chiang*⁴.

漿 *Chiang*¹. Congee; starch; broth; syrup; pus; . . . . *to starch.*

糨洗 *Chiang*¹ *hsï*³. . . . . . . To wash and iron.

文 *Wên*². Lines, veins; striæ; variegated; elegant; . . . . . . civil; *literary;* scholarly; ornamental; a form,—as of prayer. A classifier:—Les. 125.

千字文 *Ch'ien*¹ *tsï*⁴ *wên*². The One Thousand . . . . Character Classic.

格物 *Kê*² *wu*⁴. To scrutinize the nature of . . . . things; natural science, physics.

入 *Ju*⁴. *To enter;* to penetrate; to pay in or re- . . . . ceive; to progress; income.

印 *Yin*⁴. A seal, a stamp; to seal, *to print,* to . . . . take an impression of.

化 *Hwa*⁴. To alter; to transform; to influence; . . . . to melt, to transmute, *to decompose.*

化學 *Hwa*⁴ *hsüe*². . . . . . . Chemistry.

勒 *Lê*¹, *lei*¹. To rein in; to restrain; to tie up; . . . . to exact unjustly; to strangle.

天文 *T'ien*¹ *wên*². . . . . . . Astrology; *astronomy.*

穩 *Wên*³. Firm, constant; secure, *stable;* to put . . . . or set down; repose.

穩當 *Wên*³ *tang*⁴. . . . . . . *Steady,* safe, secure.

墊 *Tien*⁴. To advance money; to make good; *to* . . . . *wedge up,* to shore up; a cushion.

形 *Hsing*². *Form,* figure, shape; body; manner, ... style; material; to give form to.

形學 *Hsing*² *hsüe*². The science of form, geo- . . . . metry.

案 *An*⁴. *A table,* an official desk; a case in law; . . . . . . the records of a case; an affair.

書案 *Shu*¹ *an*⁴. . . . . A study table.

凳 *Têng*⁴. . . . . . . *A bench;* a stool; a form.

蘇 *Su*¹. . . . . . . A species of thyme.

州 *Chou*¹. A district larger than a *hsien;* a con- . . . . tinent; a region.

蘇州 Suchow. Capital of Kiangsu Province.

相 *Hsiang*⁴. To look at; to prognosticate; *a minis-* . . . . *ter of state;* similar. Also *hsiang*¹.

相公 *Hsiang*⁴ *kung*¹. A minister of state (an- . . . . cient); the son of a gentleman; in Peking,—an actor.

鑼 *Loa*². . . . . . . A gong.

鼓 *Ku*³. *A drum;* to arouse; to encourage; to . . . . . . bulge, to swell; to warp.

鑼鼓 Gong, drum, cymbals, etc.,—used as an accompaniment in singing or acting.

瓷 *Ts'ï*². . . . . . Glazed crockery, China-ware.

張圓桌、六條凳子、一張籐牀。○我[23]前一回到蘇州、給王三相公買了一套鑼鼓、用了十三吊四百錢、又買了三套瓷盆、兩吊二百五十個錢一套。

tables, one round table, six benches and one cane bedstead.

23 The last time I went to Suchow I bought for Mr. Wang the Third a set of brass musical instruments, costing thirteen thousand four hundred cash, and two nests of stone-ware basins, costing two thousand two hundred and fifty cash for each nest.

NOTES.

1 The use of the classifier causes the dropping of the second character of 仿本, which is the more general term. Those who decline to drop the final 本, use the general classifier above.

3 Kanghi's dictionary is so called because made in the reign, and by the order, of the Emperor Kanghi, the second and most illustrious emperor of the present dynasty. A 套 is a number of volumes enclosed in one case. Large works are usually put up in 套 of six or eight volumes each.

5 The words 兩個 are inserted to indicate that the two are to form the pair which are necessary in order to 抬 a thing. They might, however, be omitted without special damage to the sentence.

6 The first clause is a rhetorical inversion for 一本好體面書, by which stress is thrown on the 好體面.

7 The sentence might also be rendered,—*Go out to-day and buy me ten pens, etc.* Which meaning was intended would depend wholly on the pauses made and inflection used.

9 In Peking, 漿 is generally written for *to starch;* but doubtless the proper term is 糨. When read in the 4th tone it means *starch,* and in the 1st tone, *to starch.* Where hard sounds are used, the sound of 漿, being soft, is incorrect. The term 糨洗 is a singular inversion of the natural order.

10 會 here means *to apprehend,* which is one of its more unusual meanings.

11 The book called 千字文 consists of one thousand common characters, arranged in two hundred and fifty measures of four each, no character being repeated.

12 入門, *entering the door,* is a common term in the titles of books which are introductory or elementary. 木板 *a wooden block, or board, engraved with characters for printing.* 木 is added to distinguish this style of printing from that with moveable types, which are called 活板. An electrotype plate is a 銅板, a stereotype is a 鉛板.

14 化學 and 形學 (21) are names given by foreigners.

17 三五句話, *three or five clauses of words.* 三兩句, *three or two clauses,* is also sometimes used in the same way.

19 生書. A book, or portion of a book, which has not been previously seen, or learned.

21 When dollars were first used in China, there were no fractional coins, and the dollars were chopped into sectors and used instead; and from this came the term 角, which now means a dime or 10 cent piece.

22 Instead of putting their books in book-cases, the Chinese usually pile them on long tables at the side of the room.

LESSON XLIII.

THE AUXILIARY VERB 得.

得, as an auxiliary verb, expresses completion under the aspect of practicability, feasibility or propriety. With a negative it strongly reverses these ideas. It is not infrequently inserted between the principal verb and another auxiliary, in which case it adds to the force of the affirmation:—Compare Les. 31. In speaking, it is often heard *tai,* which is simply a corrupt pronunciation. 的 is sometimes substituted for it, with very little, if any, change of meaning.

VOCABULARY.

邪 *Hsie*^{2}. Deflected from the right; depraved, corrupt, evil; heretical; corrupting; magical, demoniacal; *haunted.*

免 *Mien*^{3}. *To avoid;* to escape from; to evade; to let off, to excuse, to forgive.

憂 *Yiu*^{1}. Grief, *sorrow;* anxiety; low-spirited, melancholy; mourning.

解 *Chie*^{3}. To open; to untie; to extricate; *to dissipate;* to dispel; to explain; to release. Also *chie*^{4} and *hsie*^{4}.

渴 *K'ê*^{2}. *To thirst;* to long for, to put after.

近 *Chin*^{4}. *Near;* recent; soon; to approach; similar.

謠 *Yao*^{2}. A tale, a *rumor;* a false report.

第四十三課

那[1]個房子邪、住不得。○看[2]不得他外面老實。○忍[3]得一時氣、免得百年憂。○這[4]點小事、不值得耽誤老爺的工夫。○兩[5]脚站得牢、不怕大風搖。○你[6]不知道、那也怨不得。○遠[7]水救解不得近渴。○那[8]都是謠言、信不得的。○這[9]句話也說得過去。○你[10]家裏這樣潮濕、怪不得你生長瘡疥。○逃[11]了王法、逃不得鬼神。○你[12]惹他、怪不得他生氣。○了[13]不得了、馬棚上起來火了。○他[14]是一個小媳婦、凡事由不得

TRANSLATION.

1 That house is haunted and is not habitable.

2 Do not be deceived by his outward docility.

3 Restraining momentary anger may save a hundred years of sorrow.

4 It is not worth while trespassing on your time with this trifling affair.

5 He who stands firmly on his feet, need not fear the force of a strong wind.

6 If you did not know, you are not then to be blamed for it.

7 Water at a distance will not quench (save from) thirst near at hand.

8 Those are all flying rumors unworthy of belief.

9 This mode of speech will answer the purpose.

10 With such a damp house as this, it is no wonder you have the itch.

11 You may evade the law, but you can not escape the gods.

12 You provoked him. No wonder he got angry.

13 What *shall* we do? the stable has caught fire.

謠言 *Yao^2 yien^2*. False reports, *exciting rumors*, alarming stories.

潮 *Ch‘ao^2*. The tide; *damp*, moist.

濕 *Shï^1*. Wet, soaked; *damp*, humid.

潮濕 Damp, humid.

怪不得 *Kwai^4 pu^4 tê^2*. No wonder, well I never, sure enough.

疥 *Chie^4*. A small sore; *the itch*.

王法 *Wang^2 fa^3*. Statute law; the law of the land; punishment, order.

鬼神 *Kwei^3 shên^2*. Demons and gods; *the gods;* supernatural beings in general.

惹 *Jê^3*. *To provoke*, to stir up, to excite; to induce, to bring upon.

棚 *P‘êng^2*. A shed, *a stable;* a tent.

疑 *I^2*. To doubt; *to surmise;* to hesitate.

嫌疑 *Hsien^2 i^2*. Suspicion.

教化 *Chiao^4 hwa^4*. Education, civilization.

上天 *Shang^4 T‘ien^1*. *Heaven* (personified), the powers above, Deity, God.

瞞 *Man^2*. *To deceive;* to hoodwink; to conceal the truth.

銅 *T‘ung^2*. Copper; *brass*.

倫 *Lun^2*. Regular, invariable; *natural relationships;* right conduct; species, class.

人倫 *Jên^2 lun^2*. The five relations; viz.,—husband and wife, father and son, brother and brother, prince and officer, friend and friend.

雜亂 *Tsa^2 lan^4*. Same as **亂雜**:—Les. 32.

本分 *Pên^3 fên^4*. *Duty*, obligation; the things becoming any station.

醉 *Tswei^4*. Intoxicated, *drunk;* stupefied.

顧 *Ku^4*. To attend to, *to regard;* to reflect on; to assist, to patronize.

制 *Chï^4*. To govern; to limit; to hinder; *to cause to do*, to control; to test.

鄰 *Lin^2*. Near, contiguous; *a neighbor;* a neighborhood.

舍 *Shê^4*. To lodge; a shed, a cottage, *a dwelling;* my. Also *shê^3*.

鄰舍 A neighbor; neighbors.

坊 *Fang^1*. An alley; *a hamlet;* a neighborhood; an honorary portal; a factory.

街坊 *Chie^1 fang^1*. Next door neighbors.

孝 *Hsiao^4*. *Duty to parents and seniors;* mourning apparel; time of mourning.

他。○事[15]急了、避不得嫌疑。○教[16]化最是少不得的。○欺[17]得別人、欺不得上天。○我[18]有一把舊銅壺、用使不得了。○瞞[19]得過人、瞞不過神。○眞[20]的假不得、假的眞不得。○人[21]倫二字、是雜亂不得的。○那[22]個人用不得、他不守本分、常喝醉酒。○我[23]對你說一句話、使得使不得。○凡[24]人在初生的時候、一刻也離不得父母。○我[25]這二年、窮的實在過不得了。○人[26]護顧自己、也得於理上下得去。○我[27]寫的字太不好、實在見不得人。○你[28]

14 She is the youngest daughter-in-law, and nothing is under her control.

15 The business is urgent. One can not stop to guard against suspicion.

16 Education is most essential.

17 You may defraud others: you can not defraud Heaven.

18 I have an old brass tea-pot, but it is not usable.

19 You may deceive man (or, men): you can not deceive God (or, the gods).

20 The genuine can not be made counterfeit, nor the counterfeit, genuine.

21 The human relations must not be confused.

22 That man is not fit to be used. He will not behave himself. He is continually getting drunk.

23 Will you allow me to speak a few words with you?

24 Every one, when he is first born, is dependent every moment on his father and mother.

25 I have been so poor these two years, that I really have no way of living.

26 In looking out for himself, a man

孝順 *Hsiao⁴ shun⁴*.... Dutiful to parents, *filial*.

盼 *P'an⁴*. *To look towards;* to long for, to expect.

盼望 *P'an⁴ wang⁴*. *To look for*, to hope for, to long for.

耀 *Yao⁴*......To illumine; effulgence, *splendor*.

榮耀 *Yung² yao⁴*......Splendor, *glory;* honor.

攆 *Nien³*........ To follow after, to pursue.

拽 *Chwai⁴*. To throw away, to cast aside, to throw. Also *yie⁴*.

NOTES.

2 More literally, *It will not do to trust to his appearance of docility.*

3 A proverb somewhat *Wên-li* in style.

5 A proverbial couplet in rhyme.

6 那 may here be regarded as standing for the matter referred to, and be rendered *it;* i.e., *what you have done;* or, it may be regarded as combining with 也 to form a conjunctive adverb, meaning, *then, in that case.* The translation given combines these views. It might *seem* most natural to make it stand for the first clause, and so render, *Your not knowing, is a thing you are not to be blamed for.* This, however, is not the correct sense.

9 Note how 說 here takes three auxiliary verbs after it, each of which adds to and modifies the force of the principal verb. If the 過 were dropped out, the translation should be, *This language is admissible.*

10 疥 is the general and proper term for *itch;* but in the South it is rarely used, 瘡, which properly means a boil, or sore, of any kind, being substituted for it.

11 A common saying in the mouths of those who would exhort people to virtue. The term 鬼神 is a comprehensive classification of all spiritual beings. As a class, the 鬼 are inferior, subject to authority, uncanonized, and evil. As a class, the 神 are superior, exercise authority, are canonized, and good. A canonized 鬼 becomes a 神. The attendants and messengers of the 神 are 鬼. Used impersonally, as a philosophical term in Chinese cosmogony and metaphysics, it refers to the (supposed) inferior and superior powers of nature, viewed from the spiritual side. 陰 and 陽 characterize these same powers from the physical side.

13 了不得 is a common exclamation, used when anything disastrous or alarming suddenly occurs. It properly expresses the idea that matters are beyond all remedy, but is often used as a mere exaggeration. The addition of a 了 at the end serves still further to strengthen the expression :— See Les. 88, Vocab.

14 This might also simply mean a *young* daughter-in-law, referring to her being recently married and young.

16 The 最 is transposed for rhetorical reasons. The regular colloquial form would be, 是最少不得的 The sentence is from the Sacred Edict.

17 The use of 別人, in the first clause, shows that 上天 is regarded as personal. This use of the word 人 is the only means that Chinese colloquial has of expressing personality.

制不了我那裏去。制不得我怎麼樣○若[29]是快一點走、兩天也能回得來。○我[30]和你作了十來年的鄰舍街坊、現在你走了、我實在捨不得。○你[31]看不孝順的人、那裏養得出好兒子來。○我[32]如今盼望天上的榮耀、心裏歡喜的了不得。○那[33]賊見我趕得很急、拽扔下東西就跑了。

must still keep within the bounds of reason.

27 My writing is too poor: it really is not fit to be seen.
28 You can do nothing at all to me.
29 If you go with some speed, you can get back in two days.
30 We have been neighbors for over ten years, and now that you are going away I am very loth to give you up.
31 Look at the undutiful man. How can he bring up a good son?
32 I am now looking for glory on high, and my heart is filled with joy inexpressible.
33 The thief, seeing that I was pursuing him hotly, dropped the goods and fled.

19 If the speaker were a polytheist, he would of course be understood as using 神 in the plural; but if a monotheist, he would be understood as using it in the singular. The want of a plural form leaves all such distinctions to be inferred from the circumstances or connection. Fewer mistakes are made in consequence than one would be ready to suppose.

22 酒 is here somewhat redundant. It is added to give additional force and perspicuity.

26 In some places the accent in 護自己, is thrown on the 己, contrary to the usual custom with the term 自己. The first 得 expresses necessity, being put for 必得. When 上 and 下 are used together, they generally mean above and below. Here, however, 上 attaches to 理, and 下 is used as a principal verb.

27 見不得人 *not* [*fit*] *to be seen by men.* The logical subject; viz., 人, is made the object, thus turning the verb into the passive form. 人 is used indefinitely:—Les. 52.

28 制不了 This phrase seems to be quite *t'ung hsing*, but there is a difference of opinion as to the proper writing. Some would write 治. The form 那裏去, or, as it is often spoken, 那兒去, is Pekingese. Teachers say that its peculiar meaning in this connection comes from the custom of banishing offenders beyond the borders.

33 The sound and meaning here given to 拽 are not recognized by the dictionaries. The word is very widely used, being found in Northern, Central and Southern Mandarin, and this character is established as the most suitable writing.

LESSON XLIV.

就.

就 has already been illustrated (Les. 13) as a sign of the immediate future, and has also been several times used, meaning *at once*. It has, however, a variety of other uses, of which the following is an approximate classification:—

1. It is used as a principal verb, meaning *to approach, to take advantage of, to be ready, to accommodate one's self to*. (5) (13).
2. It is added as an auxiliary to a few verbs, giving the idea of, *ready, satisfactory*. (15) (26).
3. Before an active verb, and referring to past time, it means, *just, then, at once, etc.* (3)(6).
4. Joined with 是 it forms the much used phrase 就是, which has a variety of uses not easy to classify:—

(1) At the opening of a sentence it means, *even, even if*. (1) (14).

(2) In a subordinate clause it draws a conclusion, or states a consequence; and may be rendered, *but, but somehow, so, etc.* (4) (11).

(3) At the end of a sentence it marks a decision, coupled with a concession; sometimes having the force of such phrases as, *might as well, so I will, etc.*, but is often untranslatable. (18) (29).

(4) As a reply, it means, *that's so, all right, so be it*. (28). See Les. 70.

就 is one of the most important and ever recurring characters in colloquial Mandarin, and its skillful management marks an accomplished speaker.

第四十四課

你[1]就是生氣、也是無益。○我[2]實在惡心、就是嘔不上來吐不出來。○你[3]怎麼說的、就當怎麼做。○他[4]不論做甚麼都風快很快、就是太冒失。○收[5]拾出飯來、可以就着熱鍋温熰一點水。○他[6]見事情不對、就拿起腿來走了。○這[7]句話就是繙不出來。○不[8]管他肯不肯、就是這麼着。的○人[9]在得時的時候、說怎麼樣就怎麼樣。○就[10]是不願意、也要將就一點。○他[11]心裏明白、就是說不出來。○鄭[12]先生温柔和平、凡事都肯將就就俯人。○就[13]着你的掃箒、把我的門口也掃一掃。○他[14]就是藐視我、我也不怕。○已[15]經定規就了、到這初

TRANSLATION.

1 Even if you do get angry, it will do no good.
2 I am exceedingly nauseated, but somehow I can not vomit.
3 You ought to do just as you said you would.
4 Whatever he does, he does very rapidly; the trouble is, he is too precipitate.
5 When you take out the rice, you can take advantage of the hot kettle to warm a little water.
6 When he saw the business was going wrong, he left without ceremony.
7 Somehow I can't translate this sentence.
8 No matter whether he is willing or not, this is the way it must be.
9 When a man is in favor [with the powers that be], whatever he says is law.
10 Even if you are not willing [to this arrangement], you should make some allowance.
11 He understands it, but somehow he can not express himself.
12 Mr. Chêng is mild and peaceable, and in every thing willing to make allowance for people.
13 I will take advantage of your broom to sweep before my door also.

惡 *Ê*^{3}....... Nausea. See *ê*^{4}, also *wu*^{4}.
惡心 *Ê*^{3} *hsin*^{1}......... Nauseated.
嘔 *Ou*^{1}...... *To vomit*, to spit out. Also *ou*^{3}.
吐 *T'u*^{4}....... To vomit. Also *t'u*^{3}.
風快 *Fêng*^{1} *k'wai*^{4}. Quick as the wind, very quick, ... *very rapid*. Les. 149.
冒失 *Mao*^{4} *shï*^{1}. Rash, imprudent, *precipitate;* .... fool-hardy.
熰 *Wu*^{4}....... To warm, to steam. See *wu*^{3}.
得時 *Tê*^{2} *shï*^{2}...... *In favor*, in luck.
願 *Yüen*^{4}. To wish, to desire; *to be willing;* a .... vow, a votive offering:—Les. 59.
願意 *Yüen*^{4} *i*^{4}............ Willing, agreed.
將就 *Chiang*^{1} *chiu*^{4}. To put up with, to tolerate, ... *to make allowance for.*
鄭 *Chêng*^{4}........... Serious; *a surname.*
柔 *Jou*^{2}. Flexible, pliant; soft; *mild*, gentle; ...... complaisant; a flat in music.
温柔 *Wên*^{1} *jou*^{2}.......... *Mild*, gentle, meek.
和平 *Hê*^{2} *p'ing*^{2}......... *Peaceable*, amiable.
俯 *Fu*^{3}.... To stoop; to bow down; *to condescend.*
就俯 *Chiu*^{4} *fu*^{3}. *To accommodate to;* to make .... shift; to make the best of.
掃 *Sao*^{4}...... A coarse broom. See *sao*^{3}.
掃箒 *Sao*^{4} *chou*^{3}. *A broom of coarse grass, or* .... *bamboo;* the sao^4 chou^3 plant.
藐 *Miao*^{3}. To slight, to look down upon, *to express contempt in the looks;* small.
視 *Shï*^{4}...... To inspect, *to look at;* to regard.
藐視 *To show contempt*, to disdain; to act superciliously; to treat scornfully.
庚 *Kêng*^{1}..... To alter; to bestow; *age*, years.
柬 *Chien*^{3}...... To select; to abridge; *a card.*
庚帖 *Kêng*^{1} *t'ie*^{3}. A card containing the horoscope of a betrothed person.

六日、要(換庚帖/下媒柬)○ [16]這件東西就是找不着、我看他到底從那裏出來。○ [17]他們就是要了我的命、我也要去見見他。○ [18]不用你來洗、我就手替你洗出來就是了。○ [19]我和他說的(妥妥/就就)兒的、怎麼他又反復了呢。○ [20]他正誇海口、你想他就是伶俐、半年還能念一部四書嗎。○ [21]我就就着他的話、把他說的閉口無言。○ [22]酒席已經預備就了、去請他、他就是不來。○ [23]粗(糙/拉)針線他還能做、就是(紉針紉不上/穿針穿不上)、○ [24]天祥的哈喇、我看八百錢一尺、是大價、不知爲什麼他(就/還)是不賣。○ [25]飯(得/就好)了沒有、答、(得/就好)了。○ [26]價錢我和他講就了、二百六十個錢一斤。○ [27]我不是喫你的

14 I do not care if he does treat me with contempt.
15 It is already settled, that on the sixth of this month the betrothal papers are to be exchanged.
16 I can not find this thing anywhere. We'll see where it finally will turn up.
17 Even if they take my life, I mean to go and see him.
18 You need not come to wash them. While I am at it, I can wash them for you just as well as not.
19 I settled it definitely with him. How is it that he has changed his mind?
20 He was simply talking large. Even if he is bright, do you think he could commit the whole of the Four Books in half a year?
21 I just took up his own words, and shut his mouth so completely that he had not a word to say.
22 The feast is quite ready; but when I went to invite him, for some reason he would not come.
23 She can still do coarse sewing. The trouble is she can not thread her needle.
24 As I look at it, eight hundred cash per foot is a high price for T'ien Shang's broadcloth; yet for some reason he will not sell.
25 Is the rice (food) ready? *Ans.* It is ready.

媒柬 *Mei2 chien3* ... A betrothal card.

就手 *Chiu4 shou3*. Along with, at the same time, *while one's hand is in.*

復 *Fu4*. Again, a second time; to return; to reply; to restore.

反復 *Fan3 fu4*. Back and forth; *to change the mind*, to go back on one's self.

誇 *K'wa1* ... To boast, to brag; *to exaggerate.*

誇海口 *K'wa1 hai3 k'ou3*. To brag, to boast extravagantly.

四書 *Sï4 shu1*. The Four Books; viz., 大學, The Great Learning; 中庸, The Doctrine of the Mean; 論語, The Analects; 孟子, The Works of Mencius.

閉 *Pi4*. *To close a door;* to shut, to exclude; to lay up; to stop up, to obstruct.

閉口無言 *Pi4 k'ou3 wu2 yien2*. To shut the mouth and be silent; nothing to say.

席 *Hsi2* ... A mat; a table; *an entertainment.*

酒席 *Chiu3 hsi2* ... *A feast*, a banquet.

糙 *Ts'ao4* ... Rude, *unworkmanlike;* inferior.

粗糙 *Ts'u1 ts'ao4* ... *Coarse;* rude.

粗拉 *Ts'u1 la1* ... The same. (L.)

紉 *Jên4* ... To thread a needle.

祥 *Hsiang2*. *Good luck;* happiness; a favorable omen from the gods.

喇 *La1*. To talk fast; a final particle:—Les. 61. Also *la3*.

哈喇 *K'a1 la1* ... Broadcloth:—Note 24.

尺 *Ch'ï3* ... The Chinese foot of ten 寸, *ts'un4*.

價 *Chia4* ... Price; value.

價錢 *Chia4 ch'ien2* ... Price.

心思 *Hsin1 sï1*. Thought, *idea*, opinion; intention; to consider, to reflect.

愁 *Ch'ou2* ... Mournful, sad, apprehensive.

兒孫 *Êr2 sun1* ... Children and grandchildren.

飯長大的、你打不得、答你罵我我就打得。○若28是不對我們的心思、他也不能强留、若是不對他的心思、我們還能强住嗎、答就是。○我29也不願意常說他、他若是到底不改、我不用他就是了。○我30看你現在喫不愁、穿不愁、兒孫又都知道過日子、也就是了。

26 The price I have settled with him at two hundred and sixty cash per catty.

27 I was not raised on your rice: you have no right to whip me. *Ans.* If you insult me, I have a right to whip you.

28 If it does not suit our wishes, he will not constrain us to stay; and if it does not suit his wishes, shall we insist on staying? *Ans.* Of course not.

29 Nor am I willing to keep constantly scolding him. If, after all, he does not change, I will just discharge him.

30 You have no anxiety about food or clothing, and your children and grandchildren are all doing well; it seems to me you ought to be satisfied.

NOTES.

2 惡心 properly means a *wicked heart*, but is put figuratively for nausea.

6 拿起腿來走了, *took up his legs and left*;—a colloquial phrase, meaning that he left suddenly and without notice. It is sometimes shortened into 拿腿走了.

9 得時 is here applied to one who is in the confidence and favor of a superior, so that his advice prevails and he can get whatever he wishes.

12 將就 and 就俯 are not precisely equivalent. 將就 is *to tolerate or make allowance for the peculiarities of others*; while 就俯 *is to adapt or accommodate one's self to the peculiarities of others*. In many places 就俯 becomes 俯就.

13 This sentence is an indirect apology for taking the broom. The use of 也 implies that the owner of the broom had just finished sweeping before his own door.

15 這初六日. The use of 這 points to the 6th of the *current* month. The 庚帖 is a folded card of red paper, on which is written the proposal, or its acceptance, as the case may be. The age of the party is given by means of the eight characters, marking the year, month, day, and hour of his (or her) birth; hence the name, *age card*. See Les. 117, Note 31. The exchanging of these cards by the hands of the go-betweens (媒人), constitutes the marriage engagement. The 媒柬 is a similar paper, and is used for the same purpose, but does not generally contain the eight 庚字 or *age characters*. 柬帖 is another name for the same.

16 就 here expresses the speaker's impatience with a peculiar elegance and force, which the translation fails to convey.

19 就就, as here used, is not entirely *t'ung hsing*; it means *to the point of perfect readiness*, and differs slightly in meaning from 妥妥. The order of the last clause would more regularly be, 他怎麼又反復了. The 怎麼 is put first in order to give it additional emphasis.

20 誇海口, *brags with a mouth like the sea.*

21 就 is here repeated, but not as in the 19th sentence. The emphasis there required, is very different from that required here. The first 就 is an adverb, the second a verb.

22 The fact that 酒席 is the common, and in fact the only, colloquial term for a feast, is very significant. The second part of the sentence is only intelligible in view of the Chinese custom of sending round, when the feast is all ready, to invite the guests a second time.

24 哈喇 is probably the result of an attempt to say "cloth." The pronunciation of 哈 is very various. In Nanking, cloth is called *ha la*.

25 Of the three forms given, 得 is Pekingese, the other two are Central and Southern. 飯 may refer to rice specifically, or it may include the whole meal.

30 喫不愁穿不愁 is an inversion of the more natural order, 不愁喫不愁穿, made for the purpose of giving emphasis to the words 喫 and 穿. 知道過日子 *know to make a living*; i.e., they are not lazy or dissipated, but diligent and thrifty.

LESSON XLV.

那 WITH THE CLASSIFIERS.

那, which? is joined with all the classifiers. An 一 is often inserted between the 那 and the classifier, and *properly* belongs there in all cases. When emphasis is desired it is always inserted.

Thus used, 那 is not always strictly interrogative, but passes into the declarative form in the same way, and very much in the same circumstances, as "which" does in English.

第四十五課

1 那個人生來就是惡人呢。
○ 2 誰知道那一塊硯臺是他的。
○ 3 這四條個小狗、你看中那一條個呢。
○ 4 你說要找個姓秦的、到底是那個姓秦的。
○ 5 那一個套兒合式、就用那個。
○ 6 這兩件大褂衫子子、你看那一件的針線好呢。
○ 7 你來請先生坐赴席席、是請那一位呢。
○ 8 你認認這些筆、那一管是你的。
○ 9 這三把椅子、我實在認不出那一把是他的來。
○ 10 你們學格物、現在學那一本

TRANSLATION.

1 Who is by birth a bad man?
2 Who knows which inkstand is his?
3 Which of these four pups do you fancy?
4 You say you want to find a man by the name of Ch'in; but which of the Ch'ins?
5 Just use whichever *t'ao* is suitable.
6 Of the sewing of these two large gowns, which is better?
7 Which gentleman is it that you have come to invite to the feast?
8 Examine these pens and see which is yours.
9 I really do not know which one of these three chairs is his.
10 Which volume of the natural philosophy are you now studying?

VOCABULARY.

硯臺 *Yien⁴ t'ai²*. . . . . An ink stone.

看中 *K'an⁴ chung⁴*. To be pleased with; *to prefer*.

秦 *Ch'in²*. An ancient kingdom; name of a dynasty; *a surname*.

衫 *Shan¹*. An unlined garment,—coat, shirt or jacket.

赴 *Fu⁴*. *To go to*, to repair to; to attend; to hasten.

赴席 *Fu⁴ hsi²*. . . . . To attend a feast.

坐席 *Tsoa⁴ hsi²*. To sit at a feast, to go to a feast.

辯 *Pien⁴*. To dispute; *to argue;* to criticize; to discriminate.

辯論 *Pien⁴ lun⁴*. . . . . . . To discuss, *to debate*.

希 *Hsi¹*. Rare, seldom; sparse; to expect; *to delight in;* almost, nearly:—Les. 57.

罕 *Han³*. . . . . . *Rare*, scarce; seldom, infrequent.

希罕 Rare, uncommon; *to prize*, to delight in.

圈 *Chüen⁴*. An enclosure; a prison; *a fold;* a snare. See *ch'üen¹*.

正 *Chêng¹*. . . . . . The first (month). See *chêng⁴*.

芽 *Ya²*. . . . . A germ, *a sprout;* the beginning.

白菜 *Pai² ts'ai⁴*. . . . . Cabbage.

黄芽菜 *Hwang² ya² ts'ai⁴*. . . . . Cabbage.

奬 *Chiang³*. To exhort, to encourage; *to commend;* to praise, to laud.

誇奬 *K'wa¹ chiang³*. To praise, to eulogize; to boast, *to brag*.

葡 *P'u²*. . . . . The vine (grape).

萄 *T'ao²*. . . . . Used for its sound in 葡萄.

葡萄 The grape, grapes.

棗 *Tsao³*. The buckthorn or jujube, commonly called "*date*" in China.

彙 *Hwei⁴, lei³*. . . . . . *A class*, a series; to sort.

字彙 *Tsï⁴ hwei⁴*. A vocabulary, an abridged dictionary.

獅 *Shï¹*. . . . . The lion.

虎 *Hu³*. . . . . . *The tiger;* brave, fierce, cruel.

老虎 *Lao³ hu³*. . . . . A tiger.

熊 *Hsiung²*. . . . . *The bear*. (L.)

種 *Chung³*. . . . A seed; a sort, *a kind*. See *chung⁴*.

獸 *Shou⁴*. . . . . . *A wild animal*, a beast; brutal.

野獸 *Yie³ shou⁴*. . . . . . . A wild beast.

兇 *Hsiung¹*. . . . . Inhuman; cruel; *fierce*.

猛 *Mêng³*. *Fierce;* resolute; cruel; severe; suddenly, unexpectedly:—Les. 115.

兇猛 *Fierce*, savage, ferocious, raging.

呢。○這[11]些銀子、你嫌那一錠成色不足。○先[12]生聽這兩個人辯論、是那一個有理。○我[13]聽他的話、無論那一句都有滋味。○你[14]看那匹馬好、你就騎那匹。○這[15]三張畫兒、你喜歡〔希罕〕那一張呢。○可[16]以到羊圈裏去看看、那一隻肥就宰那一隻。○今[17]日是正月那一天、答十三。○這[18]一擔黃芽菜〔白菜〕兩頭兒都好、你要那一頭兒呢。○你[19]常誇獎的那個學生、是那一個、答就是那個頂小的。○這[20]裏有葡萄、也有棗子〔棗兒〕、你願意喫那一樣呢。○書[21]舖裏有兩部字彙、一部新的、一部舊的、先生要買那一部呢。○獅[22]子、老虎、熊、這三種野獸、無論那一種都是最兇猛的。

11 Which of these pieces of silver is it with the quality of which you are dissatisfied?

12 Of the two whom you have heard debate, which do you think is in the right?

13 To my ears, every word he said was interesting.

14 Just ride whichever horse you like best.

15 Which of these three pictures do you prize the most (prefer)?

16 Go and look among the flock of sheep and dress whichever one is fat.

17 What day of the first month is this? *Ans.* The thirteenth.

18 Both ends of this load of cabbage are good. Which end do you want?

19 Which is the scholar you are always bragging about? *Ans.* That smallest one.

20 Here are both grapes and dates. Which would you prefer to eat?

21 There are two dictionaries in the book-store; one new one, and one second-hand. Which do you wish to buy?

22 The lion, the tiger and the bear; all these three kinds of wild beasts are very fierce.

NOTES.

1 If the 呢 were omitted, this sentence would more naturally be taken to mean, "*That man was by birth a wicked man.* The two meanings might of course be distinguished by careful emphasis, even without the 呢. Every interrogative sentence in this lesson *might* end with a 呢; and if the language were regular and consistent with itself, would do so. As it is, some do, and some do not. The sentences are just as the Chinese teachers have made them.

2 Perspicuity would seem to require 呢 at the end of this sentence. Its meaning, as written, is entirely uncertain. It might be translated just as truly, *Who would have thought it? That inkstand was his!* As spoken, the meaning would be indicated by the emphasis.

4 The first 個 is here used somewhat as we use "one," meaning a man named so-and-so. The use of 到底 implies that there had been some misunderstanding about the person.

6 The Chinese here makes the comparison by simply asking which is good:—See Les. 58.

9 Note how far the auxiliary 來 is separated from 出, and from the principal verb, 認.

11 Lit., *These* [*pieces of*] *silver, you dislike which piece* [*because*] *its touch is not full.*

13 Lit., [As] *I heard his words, no matter which, all were interesting.*

20 棗子 is Southern; 棗兒 is universally used in the North.

LESSON XLVI.

THE COMPOUND RELATIVE.

所 A place,—a compound relative pronoun meaning *what, that, who, that which, the things which.* The clause it introduces usually comes between the subject and the predicate, and in all such cases ends with 的. In other cases the 的 is sometimes omitted, or replaced by 着.

第四十六課

[1]我所念(讀)的書、都忘記了。○[2]他所說的都是實話。○[3]你所提的事、我已經知道了。○[4]老年人所經練的多、所見聞的也廣。○[5]少所見、多所怪。○[6]你所喫的鹽、比他喫的米還多。○[7]我所奇怪的、是他撒(扯)謊撒(扯)得這樣圓全。○[8]我所學的有限、所記得的也不清楚。○[9]他就是把所有的東西都變賣了、也不彀還所欠的債。○[10]這是他所該辦的事、來羅唆我做甚麼。○[11]你所安(鋪)排的章程怕(要)不行。○[12]這就是所說的那位小令郎嗎。○[13]我所預備的、他一點也沒問。○[14]一年所打的糧食、不彀

TRANSLATION.

1 I have forgotten all the books I learned.
2 Every thing that he says is true.
3 What you have mentioned I already knew.
4 The experience of old men is large, and their observation, wide.
5 He who has little experience has many surprises.
6 You have eaten more salt than he has rice.
7 What surprises me is that he tells his lies with such proficiency.
8 What I learned was but little, and what I remember is not distinct.
9 Even if he should sell off all he has, it is not enough to pay off the debts he owes.
10 This is something that he should attend to. Why do you come bothering me about it?
11 The plan you proposed will not work, I fear.
12 Is this your little son that you spoke of?
13 He did not examine me on any thing that I had prepared.

VOCABULARY.

所 *Soă*³. A place, a locality; the cause by which:—see Sub. A classifier:—Les. 125.

讀 *Tu*². To read aloud; to read carefully; *to study*. Also *tou*⁴.

練 *Lien*⁴. To experiment on; *to practice;* to train, to drill; to select.

經練 *Ching*¹ *lien*⁴. Experience.

見聞 *Chien*⁴ *wên*². Observation.

廣 *Kwang*³. Broad, *wide;* spacious; extensive; large; liberal; Cantonese.

奇 *Ch'i*². Extraordinary, *surprising*, wonderful; strange; unnatural. Also *chi*¹.

奇怪 *Ch'i*² *kwai*⁴. Remarkable, wonderful, *surprising*.

全 *Ch'üen*². *Complete;* entire; unbroken, perfect; all, the whole:—Les. 158.

圓全 *Yüen*² *ch'üen*². Complete.

限 *Hsien*⁴. A limit: a restriction; a few, *a little;* to limit, to set bounds to; to assign.

變 *Pien*⁴. To transform, *to change;* a turn in affairs; a revolution; metamorphosis.

變賣 *Pien*⁴ *mai*⁴. To sell off, to turn into money.

欠 *Ch'ien*⁴. To be deficient; *to owe;* wanting.

債 *Chai*⁴. A debt, an obligation.

囉 *Loă*². Prattle; *troublesome.*

囉唆 *Loă*² *soă*¹. Troublesome, embarrassing; *to bother*, to trouble, to worry.

排 *P'ai*². To place in order, *to arrange;* to adjust; to stretch; a row, a line.

安排 *An*¹ *p'ai*². To arrange, to dispose; *to propose, to plan*, to intend.

鋪排 *P'u*¹ *p'ai*². To arrange, to distribute; *to plan.*

章 *Chang*¹. A statement; statutes, *rules;* an essay; a chapter, a section; variegated.

程 *Ch'êng*². A rule, a pattern; *a regulation;* a task; a road, a stage; to estimate.

章程 *A plan;* a set of rules; procedure; policy.

半年喫的。○就[15]是你自己所花的錢、也該記賬。○他[16]所應許的、都落了空。○我[17]們所說的、是我們知道的、我們所見証的、是我們看見的。○你[18]們在那邊所說的私體己話、我在這邊都聽見了。○他[19]年中所出的錢多、所入的錢少、還能不拉饑荒、虧空嗎。○我[20]所算的數、和你所算的、正差十三個錢。○那[21]一夜進去一些個強盜、把他所積攢的、都搶了去了。○人[22]所說的話、所作的事、連心裏所存的意思、沒有神所不知道的。○天[23]主是無所不在、無所不知、無所不能的神。

14 The grain gathered in one year is not sufficient for a half year's food.
15 Even what you spend yourself, you ought to keep an account of.
16 What he promised all came to nothing.
17 We speak that which we know, and testify to that which we have seen.
18 I heard here all the private conversation you had over there.
19 The expenditures of the year exceeded the receipts. How could he help running into debt?
20 The amount, as I have reckoned it, differs from your count by just thirteen cash.
21 That night some thieves broke in and robbed him of all he had saved.
22 There is nothing that a man says, nothing that he does, not even any of the thoughts of his heart, that God (or, the gods) does not know.
23 The Lord of Heaven is the omnipresent, omniscient and omnipotent God.

令 *Ling*[4]. A law, an order; to command, to bid; .... to cause, to cause to do:—Les. 71; *good, worthy;* your:—a term of honor:—Les. 171.
郎 *Lang*[2]. A young gentleman; a son; *a term .... of respect;* masculine; strong.
令郎 Your son, a son.
糧食 *Liang*[2] *shï*[2]. .... Grain (garnered).
空 *K'ung*[1]. Empty, void; a hole, an opening; the .... firmament; *emptiness.* See *k'ung*[4].
落空 *Loa*[4] *k'ung*[1]. .... To come to nothing.
見証 *Chien*[4] *chêng*[4]. ...... *To testify;* testimony.
體己 *T'i*[3] *ch'i*[2]. *Private,* personal; secret, con- .... fidential:—Note 18.
私 *Sï*[1]. *Private;* selfish; partial; secret; under- ...... hand; illicit.
防 *Fang*[2]. A dyke, a levee; a defense, a .... protection; to ward off; *to guard against.*
私防 Illicit savings; *private,* secret.
虧空 *K'wei*[1] *k'ung*[4]. .... Debt, deficiency.
拉饑荒 *La*[1] *Chi*[1] *hwang*[1]. To run into debt.
拉虧空 *La*[1] *k'wei*[1] *k'ung*[4]. .... The same.
盜 *Tao*[4]. ..... *A robber,* a highwayman; to rob.
強盜 *Ch'iang*[2] *tao*[4]. ...... A robber, a bandit.
積 *Chï*[1,2]. .... To accumulate; *to store up.*
攢 *Tsan*[3], *ts'wan*[2]. ...... To collect, to pile up.
積攢 To amass; *to accumulate;* to hoard.
天主 *T'ien*[1] *Chu*[3]. ..... The Lord of Heaven.

NOTES.

2 Or, *Everything that he said was true.*

6 A forcible way of expressing, that one is a great deal older and more experienced than another.

11 要 See Les. 13, Note 19.

18 體己 is widely used, but is not *t'ung hsing.* Note that 己 is here read *Ch'i*[2]. In Peking the phrase is heard *t'i*[3] *hsi*[1], but the writing of *hsi*[1] is not apparent.

21 搶了去了 We have here one 了 added to the principal verb, and another to the auxiliary. This is often done for emphasis, but is not elegant. Both the 了 should be spoken *la*[3].

22 This sentence was made by a Christian teacher.

23 In these neat phrases 所 may be taken, either in its original sense as a noun meaning *place,* or as a relative pronoun meaning *that which,* and the sense will remain the same; thus showing how the 所 passes from the one meaning to the other.

第四十七課

我[1]的指頭疼。○你[2]不該拿拳頭打他。○今日陰天、 今天天陰看不見日頭。○給[4]了他一大塊饅頭、他還嫌少。○鞋[5]小必得加楦頭排一排。○有[6]一隻大火輪船、纔攏了碼頭。○路[7]上這些小石頭、實在討厭。○還[8]沒買犁鏵、 鑱頭 犁頭怎麽耕地呢。○老[9]太太有兩個丫頭伺候他。○我[10]家裏煮了一鍋芋頭、你愛喫不愛喫呢。○可[11]以找四塊甎

Translation.

1 My finger hurts.
2 You ought not to have struck him with your fist.
3 It is cloudy to-day. The sun is not visible.
4 I gave him a large piece of bread, and yet he is dissatisfied.
5 These shoes are small. It will be necessary to stretch them with a last.
6 A large steamer has just come alongside the wharf.
7 These small stones on the road are very annoying.
8 I have not yet bought a plow-share. How can I plow?
9 The old lady has two maid-servants to wait on her.
10 I have in the house a kettle of taros cooked. Are you fond of them?

LESSON XLVII.

The Specific Suffix 頭.

頭 The head,—is added to many nouns to specialize them. No rule can be given as to what words will take 頭 after them. In general it may be observed, that words involving the idea of a lump, or of a point, take 頭 after them. Whenever the addition of 頭 makes any special modification of the meaning the combination is defined; in other cases it is not.

For full list of words taking 頭 after them, see Supplement.

Vocabulary.

楦 *Hsüen*⁴. . . . *A last;* to stuff, to fill in a cavity.
碼 *Ma*³. Weights; a yard (meas.); an emporium, a mart, *a jetty;* abbreviated numerals.
碼頭 *Ma*³ *t'ou*². . . . . A jetty, *a wharf;* a mart.
火輪船 *Hwoă*³ *lun*² *ch'wan*². A steamship, a steamboat.
犂 *Li*². . . . . . *A plow;* dark; piebald.
鏵 *Hwa*². . . . . A spade; *a plow point* or share.
鑱 *Ch'an*¹. . . . To carve, to chip; *a coulter point.*
鑱頭 *Ch'an*¹ *t'ou*². . . . A plow point, a coulter.
犂頭 *Li*² *t'ou*². . . . . The same.
耕 *Ching*¹, *kêng*¹. . . . . . . To till; to plow.
丫 *Ya*¹. . . . . .A fork; *a slave girl;* a daughter.
舌 *Shê*². . . . . *The tongue;* the clapper of a bell.
脣 or **唇** *Ch'un*². . . . . The lips.
嘴脣 *Tswei*³ *ch'un*². . . . . The lips.
腫 *Chung*³. . . . . *To swell,* swollen; boastful.
波 *Poă*¹. . . . . . . A wave, a ripple; ruffled; vast.
稜 *Lêng*². . . . . . . A corner, an edge; an angle.
羅 *Loă*². A net; a sieve; gauze; to spread out, to arrange; to bolt,—as flour.
波稜蓋 *Poă*¹ *lêng*² *kai*⁴. The knee; the knee-pan.
波羅蓋 *Poă*¹ *loă*² *kai*⁴. . . . . The same.
間 *Chien*¹. A space, an interval; between; *in the midst of;* in, during; to set apart. A classifier:—Les. 68. Also *chien*⁴.
中間 *Chung*¹ *chien*¹. . . . . Between; in the midst.
節 *Chie*³. . . . *A joint,* a knot, a length:—See *chie*².
枕 *Chên*³. *A pillow;* a rest for the back; a socket. Also *chên*⁴.
枕 *Chên*⁴. *To pillow on,* to lean on; contiguous. See *chên*³.
駒 *Chü*¹. . . . . . A colt,—under two years.
轆 *Lung*². . . . . .A halter.

頭、把這個火爐墊起來。○他[12]的舌頭有病、連嘴脣子都腫了。○[13]波稜蓋(波羅蓋)兒、是腿中間兒的骨頭節兒。○這[14]個枕頭太高。○人[15]子沒有枕頭的地方。○那[16]個騾駒子、把籠頭掙壞了。○這[17]個堵頭(懷頭)小一點、要一個大些的。○他[18]的對頭利害、誰敢多嘴管這閒事。○這[19]事的盡頭就是死。○王[20]日新在濟南府車行裏當把兒頭(把頭)、一年掙五十多吊。○他[21]家裏有個碓臼、就是沒有杵頭子(碓頭)。○他[22]借了二十吊錢、給人三畝地作押頭。○我[23]要鏇四條桌子腿、用甚麼木頭好呢、答楸木就好。○這[24]麼一匹小高麗馬、怎麼必得帶轡頭呢、答你那裏知道、不帶轡頭、就是沒有法子騎他。

11 Get four pieces of brick and put them under the feet of this stove to raise it up.
12 His tongue is diseased, so that even his lips are swollen.
13 The knee is the joint in the middle of the leg.
14 This pillow is too high.
15 The son of man hath not where to lay his head.
16 That mule colt has broken his halter.
17 This end piece is a little small. I want one somewhat larger.
18 His opponent is violent. Who would venture to meddle in this business which does not concern him?
19 The end of these things is death.
20 Wang I Hsin is acting as head-man in the stage company in Chinanfu at a salary of over fifty thousand cash a year.
21 He has a mortar in the house, but is short a pestle.
22 He borrowed twenty thousand cash and mortgaged three acres of land as security.
23 I want to turn four table legs: what wood is the best to use? *Ans.* Walnut is the best.
24 What necessity is there for having a bridle for such a little Korean pony? *Ans.* But you see, without a bridle it is impossible to ride him.

堵 *Tu*³. To obstruct; *to close up*, to stop; to fill in. A classifier:—Les. 140.

堵頭 *Tu*³ *t'ou*². A shutter, a plug; the end of a coffin, end of a drawer, etc.

懷 *Hwai*². To cherish; to think of; to put or carry in the bosom; to harbor, to remember against; the bosom, the heart.

懷頭 *Hwai*² *t'ou*². The ends of a coffin; a stop-gap; *an end piece.*

對頭 *Twei*⁴ *t'ou*². An opponent.

多嘴 *Toă*¹ *tswei*³. To intermeddle with the tongue, to criticize the affairs of others.

閒事 *Hsien*² *shï*⁴. *Anything extraneous to duty;* an unimportant affair, a private affair.

車行 *Ch'ê*¹ *hang*². A cart company:—Note 20.

把頭 *Pa*³ *t'ou*². A head-man.

碓 *Twei*⁴. A mortar; a pestle. A foot-pestle. (s.)

臼 *Chiu*⁴. A mortar.

碓臼 A mortar,—of wood, stone or metal.

杵 *Ch'u*³. A pestle, a beater.

碓頭 *Twei*⁴ *t'ou*². A pestle (s).

押頭 *Ya*¹ *t'ou*². Property or goods given in pledge.

鏇 *Hsüen*⁴. To turn in a lathe.

楸 *Ch'iu*¹. The catalpa:—Les. 147, Note 15.

麗 *Li*⁴. Elegant, graceful; beautiful, bright.

高麗 *Kao*¹ *li*⁴. Korea.

轡 *P'ei*⁴. A bridle; the reins of a bridle.

第四十八課

1 你手裏有幾個栗子。
○ 2 那隻花牛(犂牛)賣了多少(幾多)錢。
○ 3 他們來了幾個人、答來了十數人。
○ 4 老兄還有多少盤纏。
○ 5 先生有幾位令郎。
○ 6 多少改一改就行了。
○ 7 已經有若干日子、我沒見他的信。
○ 8 你是多少(幾多)錢買的、我還給你多少(幾多)錢。
○ 9 老爺家裏、一年得(要)多少耗費、答要(得)六七百吊錢。
○ 10 多少差池(差)一點、也不要緊。
○ 11 先生是行幾、答我是排行第九。

Translation.

1 How many chestnuts have you in your hand?
2 How much did that black piebald cow sell for?
3 How many of their men have come? *Ans.* Over ten have come.
4 How much travelling money have you still?
5 How many sons have you?
6 By altering it slightly it will answer.
7 I have had no letter from him for a long time.
8 I will give you as much as you paid for it.
9 How much do you require for home expenses per year? *Ans.* I need six or seven hundred strings of cash.
10 If it misses by a little, no matter.
11 Which of the brothers are you? *Ans.* I am the ninth.

Notes.

2 There is no indication of time in this sentence. It might also be rendered, *You ought not to strike him with your fist.*

5 鞋小 These two words here illustrate how, under certain circumstances, the Chinese language can be exceedingly brief.

8 This sentence might with equal propriety be rendered, *How can I plow when I have not yet bought a plow point?* Which construction was intended would be indicated by the manner of speaking. Of the three terms for *plow point*, the first is Pekingese, the second Central, and the third Southern. The article referred to is a triangular point of cast iron, which serves in place of both coulter and share. A Chinese plow is one of the rudest of their many rude implements.

11 In the North a 甎頭 is a brickbat, or piece of a brick, but in the South it is a whole brick.

13 Of the two terms for knee, the first is Northern and the second Southern. In neither term are the first two characters properly significant. There are also other colloquial terms for knee. The book term is 膝 *hsi*[1].

15 This sentence is introduced to illustrate, by contrast, the use of 枕 as a verb, with 頭 as its object.

20 A 車行 is an association of carters, which controls the whole business of carting in a city. They generally exact a fee from all carts entering the city which are not connected with them. 把頭 is variously used in different places, but always means a head-man of some kind. In the South 包頭 is used instead.

21 杵 is the proper word for a pestle, but is not used in the South. 碓 is rather the stone head on the wooden handle of the pestle than the whole pestle.

23 楸 is used with different prefixes for several kinds of trees. 核桃楸 is walnut.

LESSON XLVIII.

Numeral Adjectives.

幾個 How many? some, a few. Any special classifier may be substituted for 個. As an interrogative, 幾 is generally applied to comparatively small numbers.

多少 How many? how much? a little, slightly (6); much, a great deal (18).

幾多 How many? Used in the South instead of 多少, but never heard in the North.

若干 How many? how much? a good many, a great many. Rarely used interrogatively in Mandarin.

數 Some, several, a few.

第 A series,—prefixed to a number makes it an ordinal.

○你[12]打算卸多少煤、答我打算卸五噸。○會[13]中能事的、不過有數人。○你[14]臨走要緊拿着幾個錢、好買幾個火燒、燒餅。○你[15]的孩子今年幾歲、答五歲。○明[16]天不能起身我還有若干事情、沒辦妥當。○你[17]這個要飯的、實在不知多少足。○我[18]爲他那件事、不知操了多少心。

12 How much coal do you propose to take? *Ans.* I propose to take five tons.
13 There are only a few men of ability in the society (church).
14 When you start, be sure to take a few cash to buy some biscuits.
15 How old is your child this year? *Ans.* Five years.
16 I can not start to-morrow, I have a lot of business not yet arranged.
17 You are a beggar that does not know when he has enough.
18 I can not tell how much anxiety of mind I have had on account of that affair of his.

VOCABULARY.

幾 *Chi*^{3}. How many? how much? a little, several:—see Sub. Also *chi*^{1}.

干 *Kan*^{1}. A shield; to offend; to provoke; arms; concerning; consequence; a stem, the ten stems or horary characters,—甲, 乙, 丙, 丁, 戊, 己, 庚, 辛, 壬, 癸; *a few, some.*

第 *Ti*^{4}. A series, *an order;* a degree; a section; but, yet, merely:—see Sub.

栗 *Li*^{4}. . . . . . . *The chestnut;* firm, durable.

老兄 *Lao*^{3} *hsiung*^{1}. . . . . . Sir,—a term of respect.

纏 *Ch'an*^{2}. To bind up; to bandage; to involve; to implicate; to bother.

盤纏 *P'an*^{2} *ch'an*^{2}. . . . . Road money.

耗 *Hao*^{4}. *To spend;* to consume, to use up; to make void; a rat, a mouse.

耗費 *Hao*^{4} *fei*^{4}. . . . . . . To expend; expenses.

池 *Ch'ï*^{2}. A pond, a tank; a moat. *Regular, even.* (L.)

差池 *Ch'a*^{1} *ch'ï*^{2}. . . . . . Different from. (C. and S.)

卸 *Hsie*^{4}. To lay aside; to put off, to undo; to vacate; *to unload;* to take delivery of.

噸 *Tun*^{4}. A ton,—a new character made to express the foreign word "ton."

餅 *Ping*^{3}. . . . . . . A cake; a biscuit.

燒餅 *Shao*^{1} *ping*^{3}. . . . . A baked cake.

火燒 *Hwoă*^{3} *shao*^{1}. . . . . A baked cake.

知足 *Chï*^{1} *tsu*^{2}. . . . . . To be satisfied, contented.

操 *Ts'ao*^{1}. To hold; to manage; to drill; to exercise, *to put forth;* to restrain. Also *ts'ao*^{4}.

操心 *Ts'ao*^{1} *hsin*^{1}. To take trouble, to charge the mind with, *to be anxious.*

兌 *Twei*^{4}. . . . . *To exchange,* to barter.

舖底 *P'u*^{4} *ti*^{3}. . . . . Shop fixtures, outfit.

生財 *Shêng*^{1} *ts'ai*^{2}. The same. (S.) To make money, to grow rich.

醫 *I*^{1}. . . . . . . To heal; to cure; *medical.*

醫道 *I*^{1} *tao*^{4}. *Medicine;* the practice of medicine, medical science.

糶 *T'iao*^{4}. . . . . To sell (only used of grain).

春 *Ch'un*^{1}. . . . . *Spring,* vernal; joyous.

乾 *Ch'ien*^{2}. Heaven; superior; a father; stable, firm. See *kan*^{1}.

隆 *Lung*^{2}. High, eminent, surpassing; exalted; abundant, rich.

乾隆 K'ienlung,—the fourth emperor of the present Tartar dynasty.

皇 *Hwang*^{2}. Great, imperial, august; a sovereign, *an emperor.*

皇上 *Hwang*^{2} *shang*^{4}. The emperor; His Imperial Majesty.

劉 *Liu*^{2}. . . . . . . To kill; *a surname.*

墉 *Yung*^{1}. . . . . . . A redoubt; an adobe wall.

劉墉 A high official under the emperor K'ienlung, a native of Southern Shantung.

街市 *Chie*^{1} *shï*^{4}. . . . . A market street.

目 *Mu*^{4}. The eye; a principal man, a leader; *an index;* the mind; to designate; to eye.

題目 *T'i*^{2} *mu*^{4}. . . . . . . A text, a theme, a subject.

翰 *Han*^{4}. . . . . . . A pencil, a quill; writings.

約翰 *Yoă*^{1} *han*^{4}. . . . . John.

脚力 *Chioă*^{3} *li*^{4}. . . . . Freight, carriage.

○我[19]還有若干的貨沒賣、又不知得等多少日子、纔能把舖底兌出去（生財盤給人）。○請[20]掌櫃的看看、我還欠着多少（幾多）銀子、答沒有多少（幾多）、也不過十兩八兩的。○他[21]在醫道上、用了數十年的工夫。○秦[22]三不知有多少糧食、直糶了一春、家裏還有若干。○乾[23]隆皇上、問劉墉說、你看這街市上、有多少人呢、劉墉說、也不過是名利兩個人。○題[24]目在約翰第一書、第二章、第三節。○買[25]價若干、脚力若干、請賜一回音。

19 I have still a great many goods unsold, and I can not tell how long it may be before I can dispose of my shop fixtures.

20 Please, cashier, look and see how much I still owe. *Ans.* It is not much,—not over eight or ten taels.

21 He has spent several tens of years at medicine.

22 I wonder how much grain Ch'in the Third has. He has been selling all the spring, and he still has a great deal left.

23 The Emperor K'ienlung asked Liu Yung, saying, "How many people do you think there are on this market street?" Liu Yung answered, "Only the two men, Fame and Gain."

24 The text is in first John, second chapter and third verse.

25 Please write me a reply stating the price and the freight.

NOTES.

1 Note that 栗, *a chestnut*, takes 子 after it, as also 李, *a plum*, but 梨, *a pear*, does not take 子 after it.

2 犂牛 is not used in the South, and 花牛 is not its exact equivalent. 犂牛 is a black cow with white spots, and 花牛 is a spotted cow of any color.

4 The meaning of 盤纏 is probably derived from the custom of carrying money in a belt encircling the waist. In colloquial the combination 盤纏錢 is often heard.

11 行 here refers to the order of succession in ages. It is sometimes confined to own brothers, and sometimes includes cousins of the same family name.

12 卸 We say, "How much will you have?" or, "How much will you take?" but the Chinese attribute to the buyer the act of the seller, and say, *How much will you unload?* In like manner they say of meat or cloth, *How much will you cut?* and of silver, *How much will you weigh?*

13 事 is here used as a verb meaning to *transact or manage business.*

14 火燒 are unleavened cakes, baked on both sides in a small oven. They are round, about an inch thick and from four to six inches in diameter. They are sometimes made with sugar or dates in the inside. In the South 燒餅 is applied to the same kind of a cake, but in the North it is only applied to such as have sugar in them, or sesame seed on the outside. The usage varies very much in different places.

15 In inquiring ages 幾 is only used of children, or of young persons in their teens.

17 Not to know 多少, is not to know the quantity befitting the circumstances. If 知足 is here equivalent in meaning to 不知多少 (of which I am not sure), then it is used somewhat out of its usual sense. The use of 你這個 gives a tinge of impatience.

19 兌 Here means to sell or dispose of as a whole, instead of selling off in detail.

20 We say "eight or ten;" the Chinese say *ten or eight.* The 兩 has to be inserted twice, otherwise the *ten or eight* would be eighteen. 的, at the end, is really superfluous. It gives to the Chinese something like the force of the English expression, "a matter of eight or ten taels."

21 It is worthy of note that 數 is thus used only with the round numbers ten, hundred, thousand, and myriad. When it precedes the number, as here, it means *several* tens, *several* hundreds, etc.; but when it follows, as in (3), it means *over or upwards* of ten, but usually *about* a hundred or a thousand.

23 不過 *not over, only*:—See next Les., Sub.

25 The style of this sentence is not colloquial, but such as would be used in a letter. 請賜一回音, *Please give one return word;* i.e., *Please write me a reply.*

第四十九課

光[1]你自己來了嗎。○我[2]們兩個(倆)只僱一個牲口。○他[3]光會挑眼。○光[4]你說不足憑。○只[5]有一篇沒謄起來。○他[6]淨撒謊(扯謊)一句實話沒有。○人[7]過日子、只在勤儉二字。○他[8]光說好話、不作好事。○我[9]腰裏只帶着(的)二百錢。○那[10]個學生背書光(寡)是重、若是不管他、怕要成個結吧(結吧)子。○你[11]父親和你哥哥都願意、怎麼單顯着你不肯呢。○第[12]三日頂頭風很大、一天不過走了五十里路。○不[13]可但聽一面

TRANSLATION.

1 Are you the only one that has come?
2 We two will only hire one donkey between us.
3 He does nothing but find fault.
4 Your word alone is not sufficient proof.
5 There is only one leaf not yet copied.
6 He is always lying, there is no truth in him.
7 Making a living depends wholly on two things; viz., diligence and economy.
8 He always talks well, but never does well.
9 I have brought only two hundred cash in my pocket.
10 That scholar is given to repeating when he recites his lesson. If he is not controlled, I fear he will become a stutterer.
11 Why do you put forward your dissent, when your father and older brother are both willing?
12 The third day there was a very strong head wind, and we only went fifty *li* during the whole day.

LESSON XLIX.

RESTRICTIVE PARTICLES.

只 Only, merely, nothing but, wholly. Also used as a conjunction:—Les. 95.

光 Only, alone, nothing but, given to, even. 光 is colloquial, but entirely *t'ung-hsing*.

寡 Only, etc.,—the same as 光. Used chiefly in Central and Southern Mandarin.

淨 Simply, only, nothing but.

單 Only, simply, nothing but.

單單 Simply, solely, specially.

但 Only, simply, merely. As here used, 但 is not appreciably different from 單, save that its use seems to be limited to certain connections. It is also used as a conjunction:—Les. 95.

不過 Not exceeding, nothing more than, only.

VOCABULARY.

只 *Chi*³,¹. Only, merely, nothing but; but, yet, however.

寡 *Kwa*³. Few, seldom; rare; alone; a widow; but, only:—see Sub.

單 *Tan*¹. Single, alone; odd,—as a number; a bill, a receipt; only, but, simply.

但 *Tan*⁴. Only; simply; but, yet; whenever.

倆 *Lia*³. Two,—an abbreviation for 兩個.

挑眼 *T'iao*¹ *yien*³. To pick flaws.

憑 *P'ing*². To lean on, to trust to; *proof*, evidence; according to:—Les. 83.

篇 *P'ien*¹. *A leaf*,—of a book; a section; books. A classifier:—Les. 147.

松 *Sung*¹. The pine; enduring.

勤 *Ch'in*². *Diligent;* attentive; laborious.

儉 *Chien*³. Temperate, frugal, *economical*.

背書 *Pei*⁴ *shu*¹. To turn the back to the teacher and recite a lesson, to repeat.

重 *Ch'ung*². To double; *to repeat*, to do over; again. See *Chung*⁴.

結吧 *Chie*¹ *pa*¹. To stutter, to stammer.

顯 *Hsien*³. Manifest, conspicuous; to exhibit, *to make manifest;* to render illustrious.

頂頭 *Ting*³ *t'ou*². Opposing, contrary.

之詞。○不[14]用提人情枉費、就是光喫也不彀。○先[15]生單單喫這一樣、不喫別的嗎。○那[16]個不可託、你怎麼單單託他呢。○他[17]天天淨在烟館裏、正經事一點不幹。○他[18]不過對你說玩話、你不要信他。○你[19]單顧眼前、不顧背後。○我[20]只知道一件事、就是知道自己不知道甚麼。○這[21]幾天他們不講究別的、淨講究怎樣得功名。○欒[22]老四說話太利害、光吹鬍子葫蘆瞪眼的。○凡[23]事不求有功、只求無過。○我[24]手下沒有現錢、只有兩吊錢的票子。○劉[25]先生取人、是但看人的外貌。○

13 It will not do to listen only to one side.
14 It is not enough for food alone, to say nothing of the claims of society and other incidental expenses.
15 Do you only eat this one kind, and eat nothing else?
16 Rather entrust it to anybody than to him.
17 He spends every day in the opium den and pays no attention whatever to legitimate business.
18 He is only talking in fun to you, you must not believe him.
19 You regard only the present moment, caring nothing for the future.
20 I know only one thing,—that is, I know that I myself do not know anything.
21 These few days they talk of nothing else save of how to get a degree.
22 Lwan the Fourth talks too violently. He is all the time vociferating with glaring eyes.
23 Seek for merit in nothing; it is enough if you do not offend.
24 I have no ready money at hand; I have nothing but a two thousand cash bank-note.

詞 *Ts'ï*². An expression, a phrase; words, language; a poem; a writing.

人情 *Jên*² *ch'ing*². Natural feeling, mercy; good-will; *the presents and acknowledgements which express good-will.*

枉 *Wang*³. To do or suffer wrong; a wrong, a grievance; *needless*, to no purpose.

枉費 *Wang*³ *fei*⁴. To spend to no purpose; money spent for unnecessary things; *incidental expenses.*

正經 *Chêng*⁴ *ching*¹. *Legitimate*, proper, right; really, verily.

玩話 *Wan*² *hwa*⁴. . . . . Jesting, *in fun.*

眼前 *Yien*³ *ch'ien*². Before the eyes, in the presence of; *the present*, now:—See Les. 118, Sub.

背後 *Pei*⁴ *hou*⁴. Behind the back, in private; hereafter, *the future.*

功名 *Kung*¹ *ming*². . . . . . An honorary degree.

欒 *Lwan*². . . . . A common surname.

吹 *Ch'wei*¹. . . . . . *To blow*, to breathe; to praise.

鬍 *Hu*². . . . . The moustache, the beard.

葫 *Hu*². . . . . . . A gourd, a calabash.

蘆 *Lu*². . . . . A reed, a hollow-stemmed plant.

葫蘆 A gourd, a calabash.

瞪 *Têng*⁴. To raise the eyebrows and stare; to *glare on.*

現錢 *Hsien*⁴ *ch'ien*². . . . . . . *Ready cash;* coin.

票 *P'iao*⁴. . . . . A warrant; a ticket; *a bank-note.*

貌 *Mao*⁴. Outward mien; style, form, *appearance;* the face, the visage.

財命 *Ts'ai*² *ming*⁴. . . . . Luck in business.

增 *Tsêng*¹. . . . . . *To add*, to increase, to augment.

增光 *Tsêng*¹ *kwang*¹. To increase one's reputation, to shed lustre on.

疑惑 *I*² *hwoa*⁴. *To suspect*, to doubt; in suspense.

勞心 *Lao*² *hsin*¹. *To weary the mind*, mental toil; study.

勞力 *Lao*² *li*⁴. *To weary the body;* physical toil; to labor.

掙[26]錢不掙錢、那但看他的財命怎樣。○若[27]是進了學、不但你一家增光、就是一村也都增光。○不[28]只我一個人在家裏、怎麼單疑惑是我偷的呢。○我[29]的事情、是光勞心、不勞力、他的事情、是光勞力、不勞心。

25 In choosing men, Mr. Liu is wholly guided by their appearance.

26 Whether he makes money or not, depends entirely on what luck he has.

27 If you get a degree, you will not only add lustre to your own family, but you will shed lustre on the whole village.

28 I was not the only person at home. Why do you specially suspect me of stealing it?

29 My business wears only on my mind, not on my body: his wears only on his body, not on his mind.

NOTES.

2 倆. This contraction is not used in the South.

3 The use of 會 here is a little peculiar. It conveys the idea that the person is addicted to finding fault, or that this is his "forte."

6 Or, *what he says is all lies, there is not a word of truth in it.*

8 好事 commonly means *benevolent* or *charitable acts*, the accent being on 好; but here it means *to do right*, the accent being on 事.

9 的 and 着 are here practically equivalent, the grammatical structure being, however, somewhat different. The Chinese frequently wear in front, connected with their girdle, a broad quilted or leather pouch, which answers the double purpose of a pocket and a purse. Its proper name is 跨兜子 K'wa[4] tou[1] tsi[3]. It is often referred to, as here, by the term, 腰裏, *on the waist*. A string of cash is often carried by simply hanging it across the ordinary belt.

12 五十里路 *fifty li of road*. The 路 is added for euphony.

13 一面之詞 is a book phrase adopted into the colloquial; hence the use of 之.

16 Lit., *Who can not be trusted? Why do you specially entrust it to him?* That is, is there no one else to whom you could entrust it, that you go out of your way to entrust it to him? This is the Chinese interrogative way of expressing the idea given in the translation.

22 吹鬍子 *to blow the moustache,*—to talk so excitedly that the saliva is blown out on the moustache. 吹葫蘆 *to blow a gourd,*—to talk in a loud vociferous way.

23 This is a popular ethical principle, attributed to some of the Taoist philosophers. It would hardly commend itself to a Western mind.

25 取人 *to take a man;* i.e., to choose, to select, to form an opinion of.

LESSON L.

QUALITY BY OPPOSITES.

When two adjectives of opposite meanings are joined together they form an abstract noun of quality; thus, much-little means quantity, far-near means distance, etc. The same principle is also applied to verbs, as come-go for intercourse, buy-sell for business, etc. The lesson illustrates nearly all the common nouns thus formed. Not all opposites joined together are used in this way. They are often joined for enumeration 22, or for contrast 23,—of which the lesson contains a number of examples.

VOCABULARY.

是非 *Shi[4] fei[1]*. Right-wrong; *moral;* strife; .... trouble; criticism.

好歹 *Hao[3] tai[3]*. Good-evil; character; sense, ... propriety; *somehow*, any way.

糊弄 *Hu[2] lung[4]*. To sham, *to stave off;* to make .... believe; to befool, to cozen.

小米 *Hsiao[3] mi[3]*.......... Millet, canary seed.

粥 *Chu[1], chou[1]*. Soft boiled rice or millet, con- .... gee, *gruel.*

熬 *Ao[2,1]*. *To cook by boiling;* to simmer, to de- .... coct; to endure, to persist.

稀 *Hsi[1]*. Loose, open; thin, scattered; *thin,* .... fluid; very, fully.

稠 *Ch'ou[2]*.......... *Thick*, dense; viscid, stiff.

稀稠 Thin-thick, thickness, *consistency*, viscidity.

津 *Chin[1], ching[1]*.......... A ford; saliva; sap.

天津 *T'ien[1] chin[1]*.......... Tientsin.

第五十課

人[1]都有個是非之心。○好[2]歹糊弄起來就得是
了。○這[3]個小米粥、煮熬的稀稠的不稀不厚正好。○天[4]
津的買賣、沒有上海的大。○你[5]若不信、我敢
和你賭個輸贏。○小[6]驢那能駝得了駝上這個馱
子、你沒掂掂他的輕重嗎。○我[7]在門外聽了
一回、一點動靜沒有。○買[8]我們的東西、都是
包管來回包用回換。○水[9]路和旱路的遠近、能差正訛一半。
○你[10]怎麼說話一點輕重沒有。○你[11]這麼大、
還不知尊卑上下嗎。○這[12]個斧子把兒、粗細
正合式。○他[13]做什麼、一點緊慢沒有。○你[14]先

TRANSLATION.

1 All men have a moral faculty.
2 Stave the matter off somehow or other, and it will be all right.
3 This millet gruel is cooked to exactly the right consistency.
4 The business of Tientsin is not so great as that of Shanghai.
5 If you don't believe, I am ready to lay a wager with you.
6 How can a donkey carry such a load as this? Have you not tried the weight?
7 I listened a while outside the gate; there was not the least sound [stir].
8 All who buy our goods have the privilege of returning them.
9 The distance by water and by land differs by as much as (just) one half.
10 How is it that you speak without the least judgment?
11 As big as you are, and yet you do not understand the respect due to your seniors!
12 The handle of this ax is exactly the right thickness.
13 He never gets in a hurry in what he [does.

輸 *Shu*[1]. . . . To overturn; *to lose*, to be defeated.

贏 *Ying*[2]. An overplus; profit, gain; to conquer, ... *to win;* to excel.

輸贏 Lose-win; a venture; a chance, *a wager*.

駝 *T'oá*[2]. . . . . A camel; *to carry*,—as a beast.

馱 *Toá*[4]. . . . . The load carried by an animal.

掂 *Tien*[1]. To heft in the hand, *to lift and estimate* . . . . . . *the weight;* to bob up and down.

輕重 *Ch'ing*[1] *chung*[4]. Light-heavy; *weight;* . . . . *judgment;* discretion.

動靜 *Tung*[4] *ching*[4]. Motion-rest, motion; stir; . . . . noise; *sound.*

包管 *Pao*[1] *kwan*[3]. To warrant, to assure, to . . . . *guarantee.*

來回 *Lai*[2] *hwei*[2]. Go-return; the round trip; . . . . *return of goods.*

包用 *Pao*[1] *yung*[4]. To guarantee a thing to be . . . . suitable.

回換 *Hwei*[2] *hwan*[4]. To return, to send back; to . . . . revert; *to exchange.*

旱 *Han*[4]. . . . . . . Drought; dry; *land travel.*

遠近 *Yüen*[3] *chin*[4]. . . . . . . Far-near; *distance.*

訛 *Oá*[2], *ê*[2]. To deceive, to defraud; false, erroneous. *To differ.* (s.)

卑 *Pei*[1]. . . . . . Base; plebeian; *inferior;* humble.

尊卑 *Tsun*[1] *pei*[1]. High-low, rank, position; *the* . . . . *respect due to age.*

粗細 *T's'u*[1] *hsi*[4]. Coarse-fine; size, *thickness;* . . . . fineness; coarseness.

緊慢 *Chin*[3] *man*[4]. Activity-indolence; *hurry,* . . . . excitability; for the time being.

探 *T'an*[4]. To feel and search; to explore; to . . . . sound; *to try;* to spy out, to inquire.

深 *Shên*[1]. *Deep;* profound, abstruse; old, long; . . . . intense; very, extremely.

淺 *Ch'ien*[3]. *Shallow;* superficial; light,—as a . . . . color; easy, simple.

深淺 Deep-shallow; *depth.*

大小 *Ta*[4] *hsiao*[3]. Big-little; *size;* capacity; calibre, station, *place.*

軟硬 *Jwan*[3] *ying*[4]. Soft-hard; hardness; *stiffness*, rigidity.

下去探探水的深淺。○你[15]穿穿這件馬褂子、看看大小怎麼樣。○這[16]管筆軟硬怎麼樣呢。○貨[17]有高低、不要光聽賣多少錢。○這[18]兩句詩、意思很好、就是平仄不對。○標[19]緻醜醜俊陋不很要緊、只要他會過日子。○長[20]短和枵厚厚薄都彀了、就是寬窄不彀。○中[21]國的冷熱、南北不同。○看[22]他身量的高矮、沒有二十歲、也有十八九了。○損[23]益兩樣、若不留心分別、那就不知好歹了。○我[24]看他有一件大毛病、就是作事不知進退。○人[25]若居心驕傲、不知自己的大小、必常惹出是非來。

14 Do you go down first and try the depth of the water.
15 Put on this short coat and see how about its size.
16 How is this pen for stiffness?
17 Goods differ in quality. Do not merely regard the price asked.
18 The sentiment of this couplet is very good, but the tones are not correct.
19 Looks are of no great importance, only so that she is thrifty.
20 The length and thickness are both sufficient, but the width is not sufficient.
21 The temperature of China is not the same in the North and in the South.
22 Judging by the height of his stature, if he is not twenty, he must be eighteen or nineteen.
23 When a man takes no pains to distinguish between loss and gain, he may be said to be without common sense.
24 In my opinion he has one serious fault; viz., he has no idea of prudence in what he does.
25 If a man is proud in mind and without a just estimate of himself, he is sure to be constantly getting into trouble.

低 *Ti*¹. To lower; to droop; to sink; *low;* below; humble; common.

高低 *Kao*¹ *ti*¹. High-low; height; rank; *quality;* station.

仄 *Tsê*⁴. . . . Aslant, oblique, inclined, *deflected.*

平仄 *P'ing*² *tsê*⁴. . . . . Level-deflected; *tone.*

醜俊 *Ch'ou*³ *chün*⁴. Ugly-pretty; beauty, comeliness; *looks.*

陋 *Lou*⁴. . . . . .Low, mean; *ill-favored;* sordid.

醜陋 Ugly, *homely*, unsightly, repulsive.

長短 *Ch'ang*² *twan*³. . . . . . Long-short; *length.*

厚薄 *Hou*⁴ *po*²*.* . . . . Thick-thin; *thickness.*

枵厚 *Hsiao*¹ *hou*⁴. . . . . . . Thin-thick; *thickness.*

寬窄 *K'wan*¹ *chai*³. Wide-narrow; *width*, amplitude, breadth.

冷熱 *Lêng*³ *jê*⁴. . . . . Cold-hot; *temperature.*

高矮 *Kao*¹ *ai*³. . . . . High-low; *height*, size.

損 *Sun*³. To diminish; to abridge; to wound; to spoil; to injure; *loss;* damage.

分別 *Fên*¹ *pie*². . . . . . To separate, to distinguish.

退 *T'wei*⁴. To draw back, *to retreat;* to back out, to refuse; to excuse; to yield.

進退 *Chin*⁴ *t'wei*⁴. Advance-retreat; *prudence;* judgment.

居 *Chü*¹. To live in, to reside; *to remain in a condition;* dwelling.

居心 *Chü*¹ *hsin*¹. To have or maintain a certain state of mind.

NOTES.

1 之 takes the place of 的, because 是非之心 is a book construction.

2 It is a question whether 好歹, as here used, illustrates the subject of the lesson. The sentence, however, illustrates an important principle of Chinese polity.

3 Though the two forms are somewhat different, the idea expressed is the same. The first, or right hand form, might be rendered more literally, *The consistence to which this millet is cooked is just right;* and the second, *This millet gruel is so cooked that it is neither too thin nor too thick, but just right.* This method of using two negatives with words of opposite qualities, is a common way of expressing that a thing is medium, or just right.

第五十一課

應[1]當愛惜光陰。○你[2]沒有念書、怎麼會寫字呢。○他[3]哭的眼淚、把衣裳都濕了。○困[4]苦、艱難、最能磨煉人的心性。○我[5]願意憐憫誰、就憐憫誰。○眼[6]看兩週生日的孩子、還不會說話。○他[7]的主意、一點也不堅固。○找[8]鎚子來打砸一一打砸、就結實了。○女[9]兒已經過了門、就是後悔、也不能更改。○這[10]

Translation.

1 You ought to improve your time.
2 If you have never been to school, how can you write?
3 The tears he wept wet all his clothes.
4 Poverty and hardship are very effective in disciplining a man's character.
5 Whom I wish to have mercy on, I will have mercy on.
6 A child almost two years old, and yet not able to talk!
7 His resolution is not at all stable.
8 Get a hammer and pound it and it will be firm.
9 When a girl is once married, there is no undoing it, even if she does repent.
10 Verily, it is fatiguing to travel in this hot season.

4 天津. The proper and general pronunciation of 津 is *chin*[1], but in this name the general custom in Chili is to pronounce it *ching*[1].

6 The original reading of 駄 was t'oă, and its meaning, *to carry a burden*; but it is now rarely used in this sense, being superceded by 駝. It is generally read and used as given in the vocabulary,

8 包管來回 is a set form for expressing the idea that goods are sold with the privilege of returning them, if not satisfactory. The expression 包用回換 is Southern, and means to guarantee the exchange of an article unsuitable in size.

9 能 and 正 give a different sense. 能 implies a sort of estimate or opinion of the speaker, approximately expressed by the phrase *as much as*; while 正 fixes it at *just* this amount.

11 Not to know, in this case, implies censure. The 上下 repeats the idea of 尊卑, and is added both for emphasis and for rhythm.

13 一點緊慢沒有, *He has not the least fast or slow;* that is, he neither can nor will hurry.

18 Tones are divided into two classes, called 平 and 仄. The former includes the 上平聲 and 下平聲, that is the two *level* tones; and the latter, the 上聲, 去聲 and 入聲, that is the three deflected tones. The rules of Chinese versification require that level tones should be rhymed together, and deflected tones together.

19 會過日子 is a very expressive phrase. It includes the ability, diligence and thrift which make the most of every thing.

LESSON LI.

Definitive Combinations.

Chinese being a monosyllabic language, and the number of syllables limited, the consequent repetition of the same syllable renders it absolutely necessary that some means should be adopted to distinguish the different meanings of the same syllable. This is done to the eye in writing, by the different composition of the characters, analogous to different spellings in English, as *here* and *hear*. In speech it is done by combining with the given syllable another defining syllable or word, this combination forming, practically, a dissyllabic word.

There are three principal classes of these combinations.

First.—A word of similar meaning is added, so that each serves to distinguish the other. This device is used, with verbs,—as in 看見; with nouns,—as in 規矩; and with adjectives,—as in 明白.

Second.—The object is added to the verb where it would not otherwise be needed, and where other languages would regard it as redundant,—as in 說話, 吃飯, etc.

Third.—A defining word is prefixed,—as in 頭髮. English has a somewhat similar use in a few words,—as in *eyebrow, wheel-barrow.*

Illustrations of all these classes have occurred in previous lessons, as it was impossible to avoid such constantly recurring forms. This lesson has been deferred to this place that the student might be better able to understand and appreciate its principles. The constant use of these combinations in Mandarin forms one of the prime distinctions between it and Wen-li.

伏天走路、實在辛苦。○書11內雜亂無章、一點次序沒有。○街12上有個賣蜂蜜的、要八十個錢一斤。○你13不能喫喝酒、還不能喫飯嗎。○他14黑夜夜裏不能睡覺、這是個大事。○不15用寫信、我述說給他聽就是了。○李16老八常常給人說壞話、我很厭惡他。○你17這個東西、實在少教訓、你怎麼這樣輕薄先生呢。○你18知道他常生氣、要緊要躲避他一點兒。○外19頭天陰陰天、有月亮也看

11 The book is all in confusion; there is not the least order in it.
12 There is a man on the street selling honey. He asks eighty cash per catty.
13 If you can not drink wine, can you not eat?
14 His not being able to sleep at night is a serious matter.
15 It is not necessary to write a letter. I will tell it over to him which will answer every purpose.
16 Li the Eighth is continually slandering people. I thoroughly detest him.
17 You scape-grace! You are certainly ill-bred. How is it that you are so disrespectful to your teacher?
18 Knowing that he is given to getting angry you should by all means keep out of his way.
19 It is cloudy out of doors; you can not see, even with the moon.

Vocabulary.

愛惜 *Ai*⁴ *hsi*¹. To love fondly; to spare; to begrudge; *to improve* time.

光陰 *Kwang*¹ *yin*¹. Time.

困 *K'un*⁴. Exhausted, wearied; distressed; *needy;* to go to sleep; to besiege; to enslave.

困苦 *K'un*⁴ *k'u*³. *Poverty;* trouble.

艱 *Chien*¹. Difficult; distressing; *hardship.*

難 *Nan*⁴. *Difficulty;* embarrassment, adversity, suffering. See *nan*².

艱難 Difficulty, straits, trials, *hardship.*

磨煉 *Moă*² *lien*⁴. *To discipline;* to train; to refine; to learn by experience.

性 *Hsing*⁴. Nature, *disposition*, spirit; property, quality; faculty.

心性 *Hsin*¹ *hsing*⁴. Natural temper; *character*, disposition.

憐 *Lien*². *To pity*, to commiserate.

憫 *Min*³. To mourn for; *to pity.*

憐憫 To pity; *to have mercy on;* to commiserate.

週 *Chou*¹. To revolve, to turn round; *a year.*

週歲 *Chou*¹ *swei*⁴. A full year.

堅 *Chien*¹. *Stable*, firm, strong; durable, lasting; resolute, constant.

固 *Ku*⁴. Secure; constant; pertinacious; *fixed;* assuredly.

堅固 *Firm, stable*, immovable, fixed.

鎚 *Ch'wei*². *A hammer;* a mallet; a club.

砸 *Tsa*². *To pound;* to knock; to crush; to shiver to pieces.

過門 *Kwoă*⁴ *mên*². To get married (of the woman).

後悔 *Hou*⁴ *hwei*³. To be sorry for, to repent; to change the mind.

更 *Kêng*¹. To change, to alter; to repair, *to amend.* Also *kêng*⁴, and *ching*¹.

更改 *Kêng*¹ *kai*³. To alter, to change; to amend; *to undo.*

辛 *Hsin*¹. Bitter, *toilsome;* grievous.

辛苦 *Hsin*¹ *k'u*³. Toil, weariness, *fatigue*,—especially that of a journey.

內 *Nei*⁴. Inner, *internal*, interior; *in;* inclusive; among; a wife.

次 *Ts'ï*⁴. Second, inferior; *order;* a time.

序 *Hsü*⁴. *Order*, precedence, a preface.

次序 *Regular order*, order of precedence.

蜂 *Fêng*¹. *A bee;* a hornet, a wasp, etc.

蜜 *Mi*⁴. *Honey;* nectar; honeyed.

蜂蜜 Honey.

述 *Shu*⁴. To narrate; *to tell in order.*

述說 *Shu*⁴ *shwoă*¹. To tell over in order, to rehearse.

惡 *Wu*⁴. To hate, *to dislike;* averse to. See *oă*⁴, and *ê*³.

厭惡 *Yien*⁴ *wu*⁴. *To detest*, to abominate.

訓 *Hsün*⁴. To instruct; *instruction*, precepts.

不見。○看20這人的外貌、眞是温柔和平、那能做出這樣的狠毒(惡毒)事來呢。○不21過三年沒見面、他的頭髮和眉毛(眼眉)都白了。○人22的言語行爲、就是人心(內心)的形像。○他23們倆、一個剛強、一個軟弱(柔弱)、不能一塊兒辦事。○若24有歡喜的事、不知不覺就快樂、若有悽慘的事、不知不覺就悲傷。

20 Judging from this man's appearance he is eminently kind and peaceable. How could he do so cruel a thing as this?

21 It is not over three years that I have not seen him, and his hair and eyebrows are all white.

22 A man's words and deeds are the counterpart of his mind.

23 They two,—the one firm and the other yielding, can not do business together.

24 When one has cause for rejoicing he unconsciously becomes joyful, and when he has cause for sorrow he unconsciously becomes sad.

教訓 *Chiao*[1] *hsün*[4]. To teach, *to instruct* (with authority), to discipline.

輕薄 *Ch'ing*[1] *poă*[2]. *To treat disrespectfully*, to condemn, to slight.

躱避 *Toă*[3] *pi*[4]. To avoid, *to keep out of the way of*, to shun; to flee from.

月亮 *Yüe*[4] *liang*[4]. The moon.

狠 *Hên*[3]. *Cruel*, harsh; intractable.

狠毒 *Hên*[3] *tu*[2]. *Cruel*, relentless; savage.

惡毒 *Oă*[4] *tu*[2]. *Cruel*, savage, brutal

眉 *Mei*[2]. The eyebrows.

眼眉 *Yien*[3] *mei*[2]. The eyebrows. (L).

眉毛 *Mei*[2] *mao*[2]. The eyebrows.

形像 *Hsing*[2] *hsiang*[4]. Likeness; image; *counterpart*, figure.

剛 *Kang*[1]. Hard, *unyielding*; intrepid; sharp (music); recently, just now; Les. 65.

剛强 *Kang*[1] *ch'iang*[2]. *Firm*, resolute; headstrong; violent.

弱 *Joă*[4], *jao*[4]. Weak, feeble; pliable, *yielding*; decayed.

軟弱 *Jwan*[3] *joă*[4]. Weak, yielding; infirm; delicate; debilitated.

柔弱 *Jou*[2] *joă*[4]. *Pliable*; tender; delicate.

快樂 *K'wai*[4] *loă*[4]. Glad, *joyful*, happy.

悽 *Ch'i*[1]. Grieved, *sad*; vexed.

慘 *Ts'an*[3]. Hard-hearted, cruel; *wounded in mind*; miserable.

悽慘 *Sorrowful*, sad; grieved; melancholy.

悲 *Pei*[1]. To feel for; *grieved*, sorrowful.

傷 *Shang*[1]. To injure, to wound; to distress, *to grieve*, mortified.

悲傷 Distressed in mind, sorrowful, *sad*.

Notes.

2 Or, *You have never been to school; how can you write?*

11 雜亂無章 is a book phrase meaning *without order or method; in confusion.* Adding a word of opposite meaning with a negative, is a common rhetorical device of Chinese style.

12 蜂蜜 is honey, but 蜜蜂 is a honey bee.

13 When one has declined wine, this language is used by way of insisting on his eating the more.

15 "*Which will answer every purpose,*" is an approximate paraphrase of 就是了.

16 給人說壞話 *To disseminate evil reports about a man, or to speak evil of a man privately, so as to do him an injury.*

17 少教訓 expresses the idea that the boy has not been properly taught by his parents or teachers, and also that he has not profited by his teaching; hence it means *ill-bred, unmannerly.* 訓 is sometimes omitted and 少教 used alone. 少調教 is also used in some places. The tone of 教 is in violation of the distinction of tones usually made. See *chiao*[1] and *chiao*[4]. My Peking teacher says in explanation that simply *to teach* is *chiao*[1] but that *to teach with authority* is *chiao*[4].

19 Judging by analogy from 日頭, we would expect to find 月頭 instead of 月亮,—which however is never used; again, judging by analogy from such words as 眼淚, we would expect 月亮 to mean moonlight, while in fact it simply means the moon. It illustrates the principle of the lesson, but not any of the three classes specified.

22 內 is doubtless added to 心 in order more clearly to distinguish it from 身, the body, which in many places has the same sound as 心.

第五十二課

他[1]騙人是好手。○這[2]正是支吾糊倒人的話。○他[3]不能虧負人。○不[4]可損人利己。○你[5]這不是特意的要氣人嗎。○我[6]不會做糊弄人的事。○這[7]個大胖孩子、眞希罕人。得人喜○打[8]人打個死、救人救個活。○他[9]弟兄們、常欺負人。○在[10]家不敬人、出門沒人敬。○那[11]是欺負人、沒有影子兒的事情、他淨哄人。○學[12]着難爲人、有甚麼好處呢。○他[13]這麼欺人詾人、不能讓他。○不[14]要多帶東西、路上光光是累人。○[15]老王王老婆婆子子、善會挑唆人打架。○好[16]事不怕人、

TRANSLATION.

1 He is an adept at swindling.
2 This language is purely evasive.
3 He can not wrong any one.
4 You should not injure others to benefit yourself.
5 Are you not thus purposely stirring up anger?
6 I am incapable of doing anything to befool people.
7 This great fat baby is truly captivating.
8 When you strike, strike hard; and when you help, help effectively.
9 These brothers are constantly insulting people.
10 If you are not respectful at home, you will not be respected abroad.
11 He is simply deceiving you, there is not a shadow of such a thing.
12 What good is there in learning to worry people?
13 We can not allow him to impose upon us in this way.
14 Do not take along many things, they are only an incumbrance on the road.
15 The old woman Wang is very clever at stirring up a fight.

LESSON LII.

人 AS A PERSONAL SUFFIX.

The word 人 is added to verbs to generalize them. It may sometimes be rendered *people*, or *a man*, but is generally untranslated; or rather, its force is comprehended in words which express the idea of the verb and it combined. When a contrast is expressed or implied, it is equivalent to *others*. When joined to verbs expressing emotions, they become causative; as 氣人, in (5,) and 希罕人, in (7.) Sometimes both uses are found in the same word,—as 恨人, in (27,) and in (28.) This use of 人 is very extensive. It may in fact, if occasion require, be added to almost any transitive verb.

VOCABULARY.

騙 P'ien4. To take advantage; to cheat; *to swindle;* to defraud; to straddle.

好手 Hao3 shou3. Skilled in any art; an expert, *an adept.*

吾 Wu2. . . . . I, my (w.); to excuse; *to delay.*

支吾 Chi1 wu2. *To evade;* to make excuses; to prevaricate.

糊倒 Hu2 tao3. *To make all sorts of excuses;* to tergiversate.

虧負 K'wei1 fu4. To be deficient; *to wrong,* to defraud.

利己 Li4 chi3. To benefit oneself, to act selfishly.

特 T'ê4. A mate; single; special; *purposely;* specific:—Les. 159.

特意 T'ê4 i4. . . . . *On purpose;* specially.

難爲 Nan2 wei2. To harrass; *to worry,* to annoy; to maltreat; difficult.

好處 Hao3 ch'u4. *Good,* benefit, advantage:—Les. 98.

詾 Hsiung1. To scold, to abuse, *to browbeat;* trouble, calamity.

累 Lei4. To involve, to implicate; *to trouble; to encumber;* to embarrass. Also *lei3*.

纏磨 Ch'an2 mo2. . . . . . . *To pester,* to tease.

怕人沒好事。○你[17]這個纏磨人的毛病、眞討人嫌。○[18]攤碰着那樣無用的老婆、你說愁人不愁人呢。○你[19]輕看人、人還能重看你嗎。○他[20]那個耍笑人的脾氣、到老也不能改。○看[21]他凍的那個樣兒、眞可憐人。○沒[22]有體貼人的心、那能作出照應人的事來呢。○這[23]種藥不可多喫、多喫能彀毒傷人。○恭[24]敬人、是交朋友頂要緊的道理。○[25]我懶怠去見他、他光是吹擇呼人人。○他[26]牢籠人的法子、百發百中。○哄[27]人和恨人、是最容易犯的兩樣毛病。○從[28]來沒看

16 Virtue does not fear the light; that which fears the light is not virtuous.
17 This habit you have of pestering people is exceedingly offensive.
18 But doesn't it worry a man to have such a worthless wife as that fall to his lot?
19 When you look down upon others, will others esteem you?
20 That disposition he has to make fun of people, he will not amend as long as he lives.
21 It is really pitiable to see him suffering so from the cold.
22 How can one show kindness to others when he has no feeling of sympathy for them?
23 This kind of medicine should not be taken in large doses; if taken in large doses it is injurious (poisonous).
24 The most important principle in our intercourse with friends is to be courteous.
25 I am loth to go to see him; he is given to storming at people.
26 His methods of entrapping people are invariably successful.

輕看 *Ch'ing¹ k'an⁴.* To look down upon, to despise, to esteem lightly.

重看 *Chung⁴ k'an⁴.* To have regard to, *to esteem.*

耍笑 *Shwa³ hsiao⁴.* To ridicule, *to make fun of;* to hoax.

脾 *P'i².* The spleen; digestion; *disposition.*

脾氣 *P'i² ch'i⁴.* *Disposition,* temperament, idiosyncrasy, peculiarity.

可憐 *K'ê³ lien².* To pity, to have mercy on.

應 *Ying⁴.* A response; an echo; to fulfil, *to respond;* to promise: See *ying¹.*

照應 *Chao⁴ ying⁴.* To protect; to care for; *to show kindness;* to entertain.

能彀 *Nêng² kou⁴.* *Can;* able to.

恭 *Kung¹.* To treat with veneration; to revere; *to show respect;* decorous, reverent.

恭敬 *Kung¹ ching⁴.* *To show respect,* to reverence, to honor.

怠 *Tai⁴.* Rude, idle; *lazy;* remiss.

懶怠 *Lan³ tai⁴.* Disinclined, loth.

呼 *Hu¹.* An expiration; to call out to; *to speak to;* to invoke; to cry aloud.

吹呼 *Ch'wei¹ hu¹.* To talk loud, *to storm at,* to blow up.

擇 *Ch'êng¹.* To rebuff; to insult; *to scold.*

牢籠 *Lao² lung².* *To entrap;* to dupe; to impose upon; to victimize.

恨 *Hên⁴.* *To hate,* to dislike; to be indignant; spite; vexed, sorry.

犯 *Fan⁴.* To offend; *to transgress,* to violate; to be exposed; to assault; an accused criminal; worth while:—Les 91.

躁 *Tsao⁴.* Hasty, flurried; nervous, irascible; damp, muggy.

急躁 *Chi² tsao⁴.* *Worried;* irritable; out of patience.

歇息 *Hsie¹ hsi².* *To rest;* to stop.

催 *Ts'wei¹.* *To urge,* to press; to importune.

量 *Liang².* To measure; to estimate, to consider; the quantity or size of; *to think over.* See *liang⁴.*

體量 *T'i³ liang².* *To feel for,* to sympathize with.

巫 *Wu¹.* *A sorceress,* a witch, a medium.

見這樣累人的孩子、一時也不下手懷、眞是恨人。○問[29]了半天、也沒問出一句話來、實在急躁人。○來[30]家還沒歇息過來、你就又催他走、怎麼這麼不體量人呢。○他[31]女人是個巫婆、最能愚弄惑弄人。○古[32]語說、善門難開、善門難閉、你看賙濟人是個容易事嗎。○人[33]若有了作賊的名聲、不但自己本家丟人、就是親友、也都跟着丟人。○我[34]們從外國乍來的時候、一句話也不會說、實在悶人急人、

27 To deceive and to hate are two faults very easily committed.

28 I have never seen such a troublesome child; it will not leave one's arms for a moment. Truly it is vexatious.

29 I am out of all patience; after questioning him for half a day I have found out nothing.

30 He has just got home and is not yet rested, and you forthwith urge him to go again? Why are you so inconsiderate?

31 His wife is a sorceress and well versed in the art of deceiving.

32 The old saying is: The door of charity is difficult to open, and equally difficult to shut. Do you think relieving the poor is an easy thing?

33 When a man has the reputation of being a thief, not only is his own family disgraced, but his relations and friends are involved in the disgrace.

34 When we first arrive from the foreign country we can not speak a single word, which is very embarrassing.

巫婆 *Wu¹ p'oă²*. . . . . *A sorceress*, a witch.
愚 *Yü¹˒²*. Simple, stupid, rustic; used in letters . . . . for the pronoun I; *to cheat*, to befool.
愚弄 *Yü² lung⁴*. . . . . *To deceive*, to befool.
惑弄 *Hwoă⁴ lung⁴*. . . . . . . To beguile, to befool.
古 *Ku³*. . . . . . Ancient, *old;* of old; antiquity.
古語 *Ku³ yü³*. . . . . . *An old saying;* a tradition.
賙 *Chou¹*. . . . . . To give alms.
賙濟 *Chou¹ chi⁴*. To give alms, to relieve the . . . . poor.
名聲 *Ming² shêng¹*. . . . . . *Reputation;* fame.
本家 *Pên³ chia¹*. Original home; native place; . . . . *own family.*
丟人 *Tiu¹ jên²*. To disgrace oneself, to be put . . . . to shame.

NOTES.

4 損人利己 is a neat and expressive book phrase, often heard in colloquial. The 損人 carries with it a telic force, so that the proper connection is not *and*, but *in order that*. When 人 is correlated with 己, it always means *others*.

5 這 here refers to whatever the person in question had been doing or saying. 氣, which is usually a noun, is here used as a verb and, as expressing an emotion, is used causatively.

6 The inability here is such as depends on moral causes.

8 Approximately equal to *what is worth doing at all is worth doing well*. Note the force of 個.

9 他, being in apposition with 弟兄們, is plural. The 們 may be said to be added to both words at once.

15 In 老王婆子, the 老 is placed first to emphasize it. When 善 is used in the sense of *skilful*, it is nearly always followed by 會.

18 老婆 is here used somewhat depreciatingly for *wife*. Marriage is regarded as a lottery, as is intimated in the use of the word 攤. The Chinese has a touch of grim humor which the translation does not bring out.

23 能穀 is quite *t'ung-hsing*, but is much more used in Northern than in Central and Southern Mandarin.

26 百發百中 *In a hundred arrows, a hundred hit the centre*,—a ready-made Wen-li phrase, expressing with equal elegance and force the idea of *invariably*.

28 下 is used as a verb. 下手 does not form a phrase as it usually does. 恨 is used causatively and conveys very strongly the idea of *vexation*.

31 A 巫婆 is a sorceress who, by burning incense, making motions and repeating prayers and incantations, induces her patron divinity to visit her and give the assistance or information which she desires.

32 The difficulty in beginning charity is that the clamors of the beneficiaries will not allow one to stop. These clamors, if not responded to, easily pass into violence.

33 In this sentence, which is from the Sacred Edict, 親友 is Wen-li rather than Mandarin. For Mandarin it should be expanded into 親戚, 朋友.

第五十三課

我[1]被你害苦了。○
我[2]的腿教叫狗咬了。○
太[3]陽被叫雲彩遮了。○
好[4]人常被壞人蹧踢。○
他[5]叫我說的閉口無言。○
劉[6]先生被叫我得罪了。○
兩[7]個孩子、都被你慣壞了。○
聽[8]說姜瓦匠的腿、教石頭砸斷折了。○
凡[9]動刀的、必被刀所殺。○
他[10]叫我辱罵的不輕。○
不[11]要說大話、免得被人嗤笑。○
好[12]好一部書、可惜叫蟲子蛀咬了。○
李[13]大有輸了官司、功名也被革了。○
他[14]的銀子、被強盜搶去、心裏很憂愁。○
我[15]

Translation.

1 I have been grievously injured by you.
2 My leg has been bitten by a dog.
3 The sun is hidden by clouds.
4 Good men are constantly being vilified by the wicked.
5 I reproved him so that he had not a word to say.
6 Liu Hsien Shêng was offended by me; (or, I offended Liu Hsien Shêng.)
7 Both children have been spoiled by you.
8 I hear that Chiang the mason's leg has been broken by a stone.
9 Every one that takes the sword shall be killed by the sword.
10 He was roundly berated by me.
11 Do not talk boastfully, and you will avoid being ridiculed.
12 What a pity that such a fine book should be worm-eaten.
13 Li Ta Yu lost his suit and his degree was also taken away.
14 He was very much grieved because his silver was carried off by robbers.

LESSON LIII.

Passive Forms.

被, to suffer,—is used to form the passive, and is the regular and proper passive form of the language. In the North its use is largely confined to the more stately language of books and of literary men. In the South it is much more extensively used, being the ordinary form used on all occasions.

教, to teach, or **叫**, to call,—is also used to form the passive, and, in the North, is the generally used colloquial form. It is only occasionally used in the South. Peking teachers generally use **叫**, while Shantung teachers prefer **教**. In purely Chinese Mandarin books the two characters seem to be used indiscriminately.

教 is the older, and **叫** the more modern form.

Vocabulary.

被 *Pei*4. A bed quilt or comforter; to suffer; by, from; sign of passive:—see Sub.

雲 *Yün*2. *Clouds*, fog; shaded; numerous.

彩 *Ts'ai*3. *Variegated*, colored; beautiful, gay.

雲彩 A cloud.

遮 *Chê*1. To screen; to shade; *to hide*, to intercept; to protect.

慣 *Kwan*4. Habitual, accustomed to; addicted to; inured to; *to indulge.*

辱 *Ju*4,2. To insult; to dishonor; *to rail at;* to outrage, to debauch.

辱罵 *Ju*4 *ma*4. To rail at, *to berate.*

嗤 *Ch'ï*1. To laugh; to laugh at.

嗤笑 *Ch'ï*1 *hsiao*4. To laugh at; *to ridicule;* to sneer at.

蛀 *Chu*4. Insects that eat books or furs; *to eat as these insects do.* (L.)

官司 *Kwan*1 *sï*1. *A lawsuit*, a case in court.

革 *Kê*2. Skin, hide; armor; to change; to degrade from office; *to strike off.*

憂愁 *Yiu*1 *ch'ou*2. *Grieved*, sorry, sad.

的袍子、被火燒了一個大窟窿。○醋[16]瓶不知叫誰打碎了。○王[17]老四眞有本事、你們都被他哄了。○可[18]惜你聽他的話、教他躭誤了。○人[19]善被人欺、馬善被人騎。○若[20]不被人挑唆、他不能這樣生氣。○王[21]長通那個酒徒、已經被衙役捉拿去了。○他[22]等叫我打了一拳、我等叫他踢了一脚。○若[23]以後教人問起來、我們有甚麼話回答呢。○在[24]這裏有一本聖書、多日沒見、必是叫誰拿去了。○告[25]人的、叫作原告、所告的人、叫作被告。○皂[26]班的王頭、私下訛詐了二十吊錢、現在被人揭告了。○不[27]知誰家的狗、進

15 A large hole (or, cave) was burned in my gown by the fire.

16 I wonder by whom the vinegar bottle was broken.

17 Truly Wang the Fourth is sharp; you were all deceived by him.

18 It is a pity you listened to his advice, and thus were hindered by him.

19 When a man is good he is imposed upon, and when a horse is good he is ridden.

20 If he had not been stirred up by some one, he would not have gotten so angry as this.

21 That drunkard Wang Chang T'ung has already been arrested by the constables.

22 I struck him a blow, and he gave me [a kick.

23 If hereafter we are questioned by any one, what have we to say?

24 There was a Bible here, but I have not seen it for a long time; it must be that some one has taken it away.

25 The man who brings suit is called the plaintiff, and the man against whom suit is brought is called the defendant.

26 Wang, one of the head lictors, illicitly extorted twenty thousand cash, and is now being prosecuted for it.

27 A dog whose owner I do not know,

袍 *P'ao*². . . . . . . A long dress coat.

窟 *K'u*¹. . . . . . . A cellar, *a hole* in the ground.

窿 *Lung*². . . . . . . A cavity, an orifice.

窟窿 An orifice, a hole.

洞 *Tung*⁴. A cave, a dell; a gorge; a cavity, *a* . . . . *hole;* to see through.

醋 *Ts'u*⁴. . . . . . . Vinegar, pickle.

徒 *T'u*². A follower, a disciple; a retainer; *a* . . . . . . *low fellow;* empty; futile, in vain.

酒徒 *Chiu*³ *t'u*². . . . . A drunken fellow.

衙 *Ya*². . . . . *A court-house,* a tribunal; an office.

役 *I*⁴. To minister to, to serve; *underlings,* . . . . policemen.

衙役 Official attendants; underlings in a yamên, *constables.*

捉 *Choa*¹. . . . . . . To seize; *to arrest;* to catch;

回答 *Hwei*² *ta*². . . . . . . *To answer,* to respond.

聖 *Shêng*⁴. Intuitively wise and good, *holy, sa-* . . . . *cred;* sage, wise.

聖書 *Shêng*⁴ *shu*¹. The Holy Scriptures, the . . . . Bible.

原 *Yüen*². A plateau; *origin,* beginning; natural; . . . . originally, really:—Les. 126.

原告 *Yüen*² *kao*⁴. . . . . The plaintiff.

被告 *Pei*⁴ *kao*⁴. . . . . The defendant.

皂班 *Tsao*⁴ *pan*¹. . . . . Policemen; *lictors*

私下 *Si*¹ *hsia*⁴. . . . . Private, *illicit,* clandestine.

訛詐 *Oa*² *cha*³. To accuse falsely; to extort, to . . . . squeeze.

揭 *Chie*¹. To lift up,—as a cover, to raise up; to . . . . bring to mind; to state to superiors.

揭告 *Chie*¹ *kao*⁴. To reveal and accuse, to . . . . charge, *to prosecute.*

偷嘴 *T'ou*¹ *tswei*³. . . . . . To steal food.

棍 *Kun*⁴. . . . . . *A stick;* a club; a knave.

索 *Soa*³. . . A cord, a *rope.* Also *soa*² and *soa*⁴.

來偷嘴、教我打了一棍子、趕出去了。○ 28劉國富眞教人哄怕了、明明對他說的是實話、他還疑惑是謊話。○ 29頭一回被蛇咬了、第二回見了黑索、也是害怕的。

came in to steal something to eat, when I struck him a blow with a stick and drove him out.

28 Liu Kwoă Fu has been deceived until he is over suspicious. Even when you tell him the plain truth he suspects it is a lie.

29 He who is once bitten by a serpent, is startled the next time at the sight of a black rope.

Notes.

7 慣壞 To spoil by indulging in the practice of vicious habits.

12 蛀 is more or less *wên*, 咬 being largely used in the same sense.

15 洞 as here used is exclusively Southern. It is used in the North of a rat hole, or of any hole or cavity in a solid, which is used to contain or secrete something, but not of a hole which perforates.

19 A common saying made humorous by a play on the words 欺 and 騎, which have the same sound, differing only in tone.

22 The active form gives the sense accurately and briefly. The sentence may be translated passively thus: *He was struck a blow by me, and I was struck a kick by him.*

26 皂班 is one of the divisions or classes of underlings in a *yamên* whose business it is to act as lictors or executioners. The classes are usually divided into sections, each having a head. These headmen are distinguished by their surnames. Hence 王頭 is that one of the headmen of the lictors whose name is Wang.

27 偷嘴 *to steal a mouth;* i.e., *to steal something to put in the mouth.*

28 哄怕了 applied to one who from being repeatedly deceived, becomes excessively suspicious.

LESSON LIV.

The Instrumental Verbs 使 and 用.

使 and 用 are both in common use as instrumental verbs. They may sometimes be translated as verbs, but are generally best rendered by an instrumental preposition. In most cases the sense is quite the same whether 使 or 用 be used, though there is often a choice in regard to rhythm; also in certain phrases or connections one is used and not the other. In Southern Mandarin 用 is used almost exclusively, 使 being rarely heard.

Vocabulary.

杴 *Hsien*¹. . . . A pole; *a wooden shovel*, a shovel.

雪 *Hsüe*³. . . . . . *Snow;* snowy; to whiten.

撮 *Ts'oă*¹,⁴. To take with the fingers; to gather . . . . up, *to scrape up;* to manipulate; to make a resumé; a pinch; a handful.

碗 *Wan*³. . . . . . A deep dish, a bowl.

舀 *Yao*³. . . . . . To bale out; *to dip up or out.*

裁 *Ts'ai*². *To cut out garments;* to cut, to trim; . . . . to diminish; to regulate, to plan.

縫 *Fêng*.² . . . . . . *To sew*, to stitch. Also *fêng*⁴.

裁縫 A tailor.

鐵裁縫 *T'ie*³ *ts'ai*² *fêng*². A sewing machine.

文章 *Wên*² *chang*¹. . . . . A literary essay.

調 *Tiao*⁴. A tune; rhythm, *style;* to transfer, to . . . . move:—See *t'iao*².

鉸 *Chiao*³. . . . . . A pivot, to shear, *to cut off.*

摩 *Moă*¹. *To stroke with the hand;* to handle; to . . . . feel for. Also *moă*².

挲 *Soă*¹, *sa*¹. . . . . . To rub in the hand.

摩挲 *To stroke affectionately;* to toy with.

搓 *Ts'oă*¹. *To rub between the hands*, to twist; to . . . . scrub by rubbing.

摩搓 *Moă*¹ *ts'oă*¹. *To stroke with the hand*, to . . . . fondle, to toy with. (s.)

鉋 *Pao*⁴. . . . . . *A plane; to plane*, to level off.

推鉋 *T'wei*¹ *pao*⁴. . . . . . A carpenter's plane.

第五十四課

可[1]以用使木杴、把這些雪鄉撮出去。○用[2]個碗舀一點水來。○西[3]國做針線、用鐵裁縫的多。○請[4]你把這些藥、用紙包起來。○洗[5]臉有愛用使熱水的、有愛用使冷涼水水的。○我[6]們這裏、沒有石頭砌牆、都是用土打牆。○我[7]做文章、就是用慣了這個調兒。○他[8]是用電線打的信、不能樣樣細說。○你[9]若再、用左手使剪子、我就給你剪鉸下個指頭來。○寫[10]信給先生、必該用張講體究面紙。○王[11]老爺歡喜這孩子、就用手摩摩搓挲他的頭。○捨[12]不得使好筆、怎能寫好字呢。○這[13]塊板不平、用鉋推子鉋給我鉋推鉋推。○這[14]本書就是用鉛字活板印的、你看清楚不清楚呢。○若[15]是胰子刷不

TRANSLATION.

1 Take the wooden shovel and clear away this snow.
2 Take a bowl and dip up some water.
3 In western countries most people do their sewing on sewing machines.
4 Please take some paper and wrap up these medicines.
5 For washing the face some like to use hot water, and some like to use cold.
6 We have no stones here for building walls; all our walls are made of pounded earth.
7 In writing essays, I have become habituated to this style.
8 He sent word by telegraph, and could not go into particulars.
9 If you use the scissors with your left hand again, I will cut off one of your fingers.
10 When you write to your teacher, you should use a sheet of nice paper.
11 Wang Lao-yie was pleased with the child and stroked its head with his hand.
12 When you are too stingy to use a good pen, how can you do good writing?
13 This board is not level (even); take a plane and plane it for me.
14 This book was printed with movable lead type. See how distinct it is.
15 If it will not brush clean with soap, then try a little acid on it.

活板 *Hwoă*^{2} *pan*^{3}. A form or page of movable type, movable type.

强水 *Ch'iang*^{2} *shwei*^{3}. Mineral acids.

試 *Shï*^{4}. *To try;* to experiment; to test; to tempt; to examine; trained.

本地 *Pên*^{3} *ti*^{4}. *Native;* this place.

紅花 *Hung*^{2} *hwa*^{1}. The safflower.

染 *Jan*^{3}. *To dye;* to taint; to infect; to catch a disease; to soil; to imbue; to vitiate.

品紅 *P'in*^{3} *hung*^{2}. Auiline red.

風爐 *Fêng*^{1} *lu*^{2}. A small earthen furnace.

糞 *Fên*^{4}. Ordure, dung; *manure;* vile, refuse.

膠 *Chiao*^{1}. *Glue;* gum; *to glue;* sticky; obstinate; stupid.

粘 *Chan*^{1}, *nien*^{2}. To paste, to stick, *to glue.*

天文鏡 *T'ien*^{1} *wên*^{2} *ching*^{4}. A telescope.

星 *Hsing*^{1}. A star, *a planet;* a spark; a dot.

土星 *T'u*^{3} *hsing*^{1}. The planet Saturn.

環 *Hwan*^{2}. *A ring;* a bracelet; to encircle.

戒 *Chie*^{4}. To warn, *to caution;* to guard; to refrain from; precepts.

戒尺 *Chie*^{4} *ch'ï*^{3}. *A ferule;* a ruler.

戒方 *Chie*^{4} *fang*^{1}. *A ferule;* a ruler. (s.)

體統 *T'i*^{3} *t'ung*^{3}. *Dignity,* propriety; becoming, decorous.

知府 *Chï*^{1} *fu*^{3}. The magistrate who presides over a 府, *a prefect.*

捐 *Chüen*^{1}. To subscribe money, to contribute; *to buy a title or an office.*

科 *K'ê*^{1}. A class; a rank; a gradation; a rule; to classify; *an examination.* Les. 68.

科甲 *K'ê*^{1} *chia*^{3}. Literary graduates above the rank of 舉人; viz., 進士 and 翰林.

淨、可以再用一點强水試一試。○[16]本地的好紅布、都是用紅花染的、不會用品紅染。○[17]手中一個大錢沒有、還想着買這個買那個、你使甚麼買呢。○[18]一個人做飯喫、是用火爐子風爐子便宜。○[19]種莊稼不使糞、怎能長出好莊稼來呢。○[20]不用使釘子釘、用膠粘上膠上就行了。○[21]用天文鏡看土星、見外邊有一個大光環套着、實在好看。○[22]先生打學生、該用戒尺戒方、若是拳打脚踢、就失了先生的體統了。○[23]如今的人、有錢就有功名、你看仲經堂、硬用銀子捐了一個知府、那些窮科甲、還能好做甚麼呢。

16 All native cloth of good red color is dyed with red flowers. We do not know how to use aniline red.

17 You haven't a cash on hand, and yet you want to buy this and buy that. What will you buy it with?

18 Cooking for one person is most conveniently done with a furnace.

19 When you farm without using manure, how can you grow a good crop?

20 You need not nail it; gluing it will answer the purpose.

21 When you look at Saturn with a telescope, you see around it a large ring of light which is very beautiful.

22 When a teacher whips a pupil he should do it with a ferule. If he strikes with his fist and kicks with his foot, he loses his dignity.

23 With people nowadays, to have money is to have a degree. Look at Chung Ching Tang, how he bought, out and out, the office of prefect. What can these impecunious graduates do?

NOTES.

1 For *shovel* some would write 掀, but the balance of authority is in favor of the character in the text. There is great diversity in regard to the word meaning *to shovel*. As used in eastern Shantung, 擲 expresses the idea perfectly, but its use is local. 撮 is widely used, but it means *to scrape up* (usually into a dust pan or 簸箕), rather than to shovel. Chinanfu teachers reject both words and write 除, while Kiukiang and Hankow teachers write 鏟.

4 Lit., *Please take these medicines and wrap them up with paper.*

8 In scientific books the telegraph is generally called 電報. When it was introduced into China the people dubbed it 電線.

9 Chinese parents constantly threaten their children in just such a reckless way as this. The children soon learn to know what such threats amount to.

10 Note how this sentence, as also the 12th, 19th, 21st and 22nd, all have hypothetical clauses introduced in the translation by "when," without in any case having a hypothetical particle.

14 The translation does not fully bring out the force of 就. Its use implies that the subject had been referred to before, and the speaker takes this opportunity of showing a specimen of the printing: as when we say, "there, this book, etc."

18 The "furnace" here referred to is the small earthen furnace used by the Chinese, having holes in the bottom, and a raised rim for supporting a tea-kettle or a stew-pan. These furnaces burn either charcoal or grass and sticks and are fanned or blown with a small bellows; hence the name, *wind furnace*, which is used in the South.

20 The translation only *implies* the instrument, which is fully *expressed* in the Chinese.

22 戒尺 means *a ferule*, both in the North and in the South, but in the South it is only applied to the ferules used by officers, while 戒方 is applied to the ferule used by a teacher.

23 硬 here means, *sole, sheer;* that is, the party bought his office by the sheer use of money, overriding all the proprieties of the case. The theory of Chinese examinations is that they are for the purpose of bringing to light the talented men, and a high degree is theoretically a passport to office. As is generally the case in China, theory and practice differ. Money will get almost any office without a literary degree, and the degree without the use of money rarely, if ever, procures an office. The government openly sells its titles and offices, and the money paid for them is facetiously spoken of as *contributed*. 甲, being the first of the ten stems, or cyclical characters, is used to denote first in rank, meaning that they excel the others with whom they are examined, and hence are rewarded with a degree.

第五十五課

如[1]今正在將成未成的時候。○他[2]的
病將來不能好。○你[3]們待〔要〕要回去嗎。
○耶穌道理、將來必要傳遍天下。○
託[5]他我不放心、將來必得〔得〕我自己去。
○你[6]磨拳頭擄髈子〔伸手擄胳膊〕的做甚麼呢、你
還得〔待、要〕打我嗎。○看[7]風雨表這樣下落〔降〕、
天將要下雨。○請[8]你寬容我、我將來
必要還清。○你[9]想他從小就自是、將
來還能有大出息嗎。○他[10]到中國、現
在將近三十年了。○聽[11]他的口氣、將

TRANSLATION.

1 It is just now on the point of being settled.
2 He probably can not get well of his disease.
3 Are you about to return?
4 The Christian religion will certainly be preached in all the world.
5 I am not satisfied to entrust it to him. I will probably have to go myself.
6 What are you showing your fists and rolling up your sleeves for? Are you going to strike me?
7 Judging from the way the barometer is falling, it is just going to rain.
8 Please have patience with me and I will pay thee all.
9 Seeing he has been so self-willed from his youth, do you think there is any great outcome in him?
10 It is now nearly thirty years since he came to China.
11 Judging from his talk, he is intending

LESSON LV.

將, 待 AND 得 INDICATING FUTURITY.

In addition to its use as an instrumental verb, (Les. 28,) 將 is also used to express the near future, combining with it more or less of the idea of probability. It generally takes 來 after it, which does not sensibly modify its meaning(2,)(9.) The combination, however, often takes after it either 必 (17,) or 要 (11,) or 必要 (4,) by which the meaning is modified in each case.

When 將 is used alone with an intransitive or neuter verb, it expresses simple proximity (10,) (16,)(23,)

待 is used in some places to express futurity, including the idea of purpose or oughtness. In other places 得 is used in the same way. In a general way it may be said that 待 is used in Central and 得 in Southern Mandarin. 待 is used occasionally in the North, but is always followed by 要.

The use of both 待 and 得 is quite colloquial, albeit they frequently give a shade of meaning which no other word will quite replace. It is a question whether 待 is not in this case simply a mispronunciation of 得.

VOCABULARY.

未 *Wei*[4]. *Not yet*, never; the hour from 1 to 3 o'clock P. M.—Les. 152.

遍 *Pien*[4]. Everywhere; *all*, the whole; entire; to go around, to pervade:—Les. 64 and 86.

擄 *Lu*[1]. *To strip;* to wipe off; to rub down.

風雨表 *Fêng*[1] *yü*[3] *piao*[3]. A barometer.

下落 *Hsia*[4] *lao*[4]. To fall, to descend.

下降 *Hsia*[4] *chiang*[4]. To descend.

寬容 *K'wan*[1] *jung*[2]. To be lenient, *to be merciful*, to be indulgent.

自是 *Tsï*[4] *shï*[4]. Self-opinioned: self-*willed;* arrogant, overbearing.

口氣 *K'ou*[3] *ch'i*[4]. Manner of speaking, *talk*, phraseology.

追 *Chwei*[1]. To pursue; *to trace or follow up;* to press for a debt; to overtake; to reflect on.

追究 *Chwei*[1] *chiu*[1]. To follow up; *to investigate;* to ferret out.

養活 *Yang*[3] *hwoa*[2]. To nourish; *to support.*

啞 *Ya*[3]. Dumb, silent.

來是要做買賣、不打算多念書。○ 12 沒有影兒(子)的事情、還(要待)追究甚麼呢。○ 13 你不能掙錢、只能花錢、將來誰養活你呢。○ 14 一個沒過門的親戚、將待(還能)怎麼樣呢、只好喫他這個啞吧虧。○ 15 我有苦難、他不幫助我、將來他有苦難、我也不幫助他。○ 16 初九日、天將亮的時候、差人把他拏去了。○ 17 現在中國打水、是用扁擔(擔杖)繩子、轆轤、水車、將來必有換水龍的。○ 18 隨他的便、他要待走我也不留他、他要待住下我也不攆他。○ 19 這件事左右兩

to go into business, and does not propose to carry his education very far.

12 What is there to investigate? There isn't a shadow of such a thing.

13 You can not earn money; you only know how to spend it. By and by who is going to support you?

14 What can I do with one who is a prospective relative? I will just have to bear the loss in silence.

15 When I am in trouble he will not help me: by and by when he is in trouble I shall not help him.

16 Just before daylight on the ninth, he was arrested by the officers of the law.

17 In China, at present, water is raised with a carrying pole, a rope, a windlass, or a water-wheel; by and by some will certainly change to pumps.

18 Let him follow his own convenience. If he wishes to go I will not keep him, and if he wishes to stay I will not send him off.

啞吧 *Ya³ pa¹*. . . . . . . Dumb, *silent*.

苦難 *K'u³ nan⁴*. . . . Distress, *trouble*, calamity.

差 *Ch'ai¹*. To send (a person); to commission; one . . . . sent; *an official messenger;* a waiter. See *ch'a¹*, also *ts'ï²*.

差人 *Ch'ai¹ jên²*. *An official messenger;* a constable.

打水 *Ta³ shwei³*. *To draw water* and carry it to . . . . the place where it is wanted.

扁 *Pien³*. . . . *Flat*, thin; to flatten; a signboard.

扁擔 *Pien³ tan⁴*. . . . . . . A flat carrying stick.

杖 *Chang⁴*. . . . . . . A staff, a cane; a club; *a pole*.

擔杖 *Tan⁴ chang⁴*. A carrying stick with a chain . . . . and hook at the ends.

轆 *Lu⁴*. . . . A grooved wheel; a pulley; a *roller*.

轤 *Lu²*. . . . . . . A windlass; a pulley.

轆轤 A windlass.

水車 *Shwei³ ch'ê¹*. A chain or elevator pump:— . . . . Note 17.

龍 *Lung²*. . . . *A dragon*, a sea serpent; imperial.

水龍 *Shwei³ lung²*. . . . *A pump;* a fire engine.

攆 *Nien³*. To expel summarily, to put or turn . . . . out, to drive out.

默 *Moă⁴*. . . . . Dark; secret, *quiet;* in the mind.

悄默聲 *Ch'iao³ moă⁴ shêng¹*. *To keep quiet;* on . . . . the sly; *silence!*

好 *Hao⁴*. To love, *to be fond of;* to be addicted . . . . to. See *hao³*.

帶累 *Tai⁴ lei⁴*. *To encumber*, to obstruct; to . . . . clog, to impede.

陷 *Hsien⁴*. To fall into, to sink; *to involve;* to . . . . entrap, to enveigle.

帶陷 *Tai⁴ hsien⁴*. . . . . . . To encumber, impede.

舉 *Chü³*. To raise with the hands, to lift up; *to* . . . . . . *recommend;* to begin; to move; a proposition, an affair; all, the whole.

薦 *Chien⁴*. . . . . To introduce, *to recommend*.

舉薦 To recommend, to mention with favor.

丟臉 *Tiu¹ lien³*. To lose face, to be put to . . . . shame.

推脫 *T'wei¹ t'oă¹*. *To make excuse;* to evade; . . . . to draw back, to shirk.

然 *Jan²*. Certainly, yes, *so;* but, then, however:— . . . . added to many words to give emphasis or express certainty:—see Les. 94, 97, 115, 116.

不然 *Pu⁴ jan²*. Not certainly, no; *otherwise;* . . . . if not.

一時 *I¹ shï²*. At one time, at once, on the spur . . . . of the moment.

接待 *Chie¹ tai⁴*. . . . . . . To receive; *to entertain*.

難、不知將來怎麼辦纔好。○我[20]待要
要回他幾句話、又怕得罪他、待要要
悄默聲兒不作聲的、眞就是咽不下去。○
你[21]這樣好喫懶做的、將來要帶帶陷累
你丈夫窮一輩子。○我[22]待要要舉薦
他、又怕他給我丟臉、待要要不舉薦
他、實在沒法推脫。○你[23]們將到的
時候、可以坐下喫兩袋菸、先差人
給他個信、不然、去這麼些人、怕他
一時沒法接待。

19 This business is beset with difficulties. I do not know how it will be best to manage it.

20 If I should make any reply to him, I fear I should offend him; yet I really can not swallow it in silence.

21 So gluttonous and lazy as this, you will most likely keep your husband poor all his life.

22 I am afraid to recommend him, lest he puts me to shame; yet if I do not, I have no way of excusing myself.

23 When you get nearly there you can sit down and smoke a couple of pipes of tobacco, while you send some one forward to give him word; otherwise, I fear he may find it difficult to entertain so many on the spur of the moment.

NOTES.

7 下落 or 下降 is an inversion of the usual order, the auxiliary being made the principal verb. The difference is, that the usual order is commonly transitive, while the inverted order is always intransitive.

14 一個沒過門的親戚, *a relative who has not yet crossed the door;* i.e., the young lady through whom the affinity is to take place is not yet married. 他這個啞吧虧, *this dumb loss of his;* i.e., this loss which he has inflicted on me, and which I must bear in silence. By a characteristic metonymy the dumbness and loss, which really pertain to the speaker, are construed with the other party.

15 The 也 might be represented in the translation by an *also*, but the sense is better expressed and the sentence smoother without it.

17 When wells are shallow, the bucket is let down on the hook of the *tan chang* into the well, and drawn up by hand. When the well is too deep to reach the water in this way, a rope is tied to the bucket and the water drawn up hand over hand. In watering gardens and in case of deep wells, a windlass is used. In raising water from a river or canal for irrigation, a species of inclined chain pump is used. It is usually driven by a large horizontal wheel with cogs, turned by an ox or donkey.

21 The phrase 好吃懶做, *hankering after good eating and lazy at work*, is most commonly applied to girls and young women. It expresses the worst fault a virtuous woman can have.

23 Note the different use of 差人 from that in 16. The two words there form a phrase; here they do not.

LESSON LVI.

THE DISJUNCTIVE CONJUNCTION.

或 is the regular word meaning *or*, but is not nearly so much used as we use *or* in English. In many, perhaps in the majority of, cases the disjunctive idea is implied in the structure of the clauses, as (11); numerous such cases have already occurred in previous lessons. 是 is often joined with 或 for the sake of rhythm.

Whether—or, is formally expressed by 或 repeated, but is also frequently expressed by correlate clauses, without any special word (9), (15.)

Either—or, is sometimes expressed by one 或 (14); sometimes by two (6), (8).

或者, *or else*, is a Wen-li phrase, but not unfrequently used in Mandarin. It also means *perhaps, possibly*.

When a double question is asked, giving an alternative, the second clause is often introduced by 還, which, in such cases, means *or*, (4), (13), (16). It generally gives a slight preponderance to the second alternative.

第五十六課

或[1]去、或不去、等明天再說。○用[2]一點鹼、或是肥皂、就洗乾淨了。○可[3]以去問問他、或是或非就明白了。○是[4]都要現錢呢、還是要幾張票子呢。○這[5]個藥一天喫四回、或是五回都可以。○或[6]銀子或當頭、求你借點給我。○你[7]快說、或東或西、到底是怎麼樣。○或[8]多或少、該給他幾個酒錢纔對。○我[9]現在沒有主意、不曉得是這麼的着好、是那麼的着好。○客[10]是要喝湯呢、還是要喝茶呢、(答)或湯或茶都可以。○你[11]學官話的書、是寫的呢、是印的呢。○身[12]

Translation.

1 Wait till to-morrow before deciding whether to go or not.
2 Use a little soda or a little soap, and it will wash clean.
3 You can go and ask him, and you will know whether it is so or not.
4 Do you want it all in copper cash, or do you want a few notes?
5 This medicine may be taken either four or five times a day.
6 Lend me a little I pray you, either of money or of something to pawn.
7 Whether this or that, say quickly how it is.
8 Whether much or little, you ought by rights to give him a cumshaw.
9 I am undecided at present whether it is best this way or that way.
10 Does the gentleman wish to drink rice water or tea? *Ans.* Either will do.
11 Is the book from which you are learning Mandarin written or printed?
12 When you are physically so weak as this, you ought to eat more good food, or take some tonic medicine.

Vocabulary.

或 *Hwoa*⁴. Doubtful; moreover, perhaps, if, may; or, either:—see Sub.

者 *Chê*³. This, that which; what;—a *Wen-li* particle with many uses. It takes the place of 這, and of 的 as used in Les. 23 and 39. It is occasionally used in Mandarin.

鹼 *Chien*³. Barilla or impure soda,—it is about half caustic and half carbonate.

當頭 *Tang*⁴ *t'ou*². Something pawned, or given in pledge.

湯 *T'ang*¹. Broth, soup, gravy; *rice water;* a warm spring.

身體 *Shên*¹ *t'i*³. The body, the physical frame.

補藥 *Pu*³ *yao*⁴. Tonic medicine, tonics.

礦 *Kung*³. Ore; *a mine;* the matrix of a gem.

虛 *Hsü*¹. Vacant, empty; untrue; *simulated;* unsubstantial; exhausted; humble; space; unconditioned; abstract.

勢 *Shï*⁴. Authority; influence; dignity; strength; *form;* condition.

虛張聲勢 *Hsü*¹ *chang*¹ *shêng*¹ *shï*⁴. To make a demonstration or feint, to make a flourish of trumpets.

帝 *Ti*⁴. A ruler, a potentate, an emperor; *a god;* the Supreme Ruler; Heaven.

關帝 *Kwan*¹ *ti*⁴. The god of war.

戲 *Hsi*⁴. To play, to jest, to make fun; *a theatrical play,* a comedy.

蓬 *P'êng*². Overgrown, tangled. (w.)

萊 *Lai*². A thistle; untilled land. (w.)

蓬萊 A district or county in Eastern Shantung.

遊 *Yiu*². To saunter, to ramble; to travel for amusement, to make a circuit.

遊逛 *Yiu*² *kwang*⁴. *To saunter about,* to take a walk, to visit for pleasure.

逛景 *Kwang*⁴ *ching*³. To view the country, *to enjoy the scenery,* to travel for pleasure.

素 *Su*⁴. Plain; simple; pure; contented; heretofore, formerly; *usually.*

平素 *P'ing*² *su*⁴. Commonly, *ordinarily.*

體這樣軟弱、應該多喫一點好飯、或是喫一點補藥。○聽[13]說你們那裏要開銀礦、這是真的嗎、還是假的呢。○你[14]光空口說空話白話不行、必得留下個當頭押頭或是找出個保人來。○信[15]上只說他病了、也沒告訴是病的輕、還是病的重。○在[16]王大人看、他們是真要打仗嗎、還是虛張聲勢呢。○你[17]是要上關帝廟去聽戲呢、還是要上蓬萊閣去遊逛逛景呢。○他[18]平素不是失信的人、今日沒來、必是病了、或者是遇見要緊的事、不能脫身。○不[19]知他念書是希圖圖需成名呢、還是要預備做生

13 I hear that you people are going to open a silver mine. Is it true? or is it false?

14 Mere empty talk will not do. You must either leave a pledge or find security.

15 The letter simply said he was sick, not telling whether his sickness was severe or not.

16 In Your Excellency's opinion are they really going to fight? or are they simply making a feint?

17 Do you want to go to the temple of the god of war to hear a theatrical play? or do you want to go to P'êng Lai Kwoă to saunter about (enjoy the view)?

18 He is ordinarily not a man who breaks his word. His not coming to-day must be owing to sickness, or else some important business has turned up so that he can not leave.

19 I do not know whether he is studying in order to get a degree, or whether he is preparing himself to go into business.

失信 *Shï¹ hsin⁴*. To break one's word, to violate a promise.

遇 *Yü⁴*. To meet; to occur, to happen.

遇見 *Yü⁴ chien⁴*. To meet; *to happen on.*

脫身 *T'oă¹ shên¹*. To escape; to find leisure; *to leave.*

需 *Hsü¹*. Required, needful; usual; necessary.

圖需 *T'u² hsü¹*. To desire; to want; *to aim;* to seek after.

希圖 *Hsi¹ t'u²*. To desire; to seek for; *to scheme.*

成名 *Ch'êng² ming²*. To get a degree.

付 *Fu⁴*. To give to, *to hand over*, to pay.

交付 *Chiao¹ fu⁴*. To transfer; to deliver to; to hand over to; *to commit to.*

音信 *Yin¹ hsin⁴*. News, word,—specially that which comes by word of mouth.

壽 *Shou⁴*. *Age*, years; birthday; aged.

壽數 *Shou⁴ shu⁴*. Age in years; *life.*

天命 *T'ien¹ ming⁴*. Fate, *the decree of Heaven;* the endowment of heaven.

稱呼 *Ch'êng¹ hu¹*. To designate, to call; *to address.*

上帝 *Shang⁴ ti⁴*. The Ruler Above, *the Supreme Ruler*. Used by many for God.

NOTES.

1 The translation implies that the person to go was the person addressed. The Chinese, however, leaves this quite undecided. It might also mean, *whether I go or not, wait till to-morrow to consider.*

4 Bank-notes are largely used in China, but their circulation is entirely local. Usually they are only current in the city in which they are issued.

7 或東或西 *whether east or whether west;* i.e., *either this or that.*

10 The water in which rice has been boiled is much used as a drink,—especially just after meals. It is usually called 飯湯.

14 The 空 is twice used for emphasis. The Southern form replaces the second 空 with 白, but in other connections 說白話 means *to fib, to tell "white" lies.*

17 關帝, *the Chinese god of war*, also called 武帝

意。○我[20]知道你的行爲、你也不冷、也不熱、我願你或冷也或熱。○哈[21]拿定了主意、把丈夫交付天主、盼望天不亮的時候、他可以回家、或者得着他的音信。○人[22]的壽數長短、都是天命所定。○眞[23]神可以怎麽稱呼呢、答或稱呼天父、或稱呼天主、或稱呼上帝、都可以。

20 I know your works, that you are neither cold nor hot, I would you were either cold or hot.

21 Hannah made up her mind to commit her husband to God, hoping that by daylight he would come home, or else that she would get word from him.

22 Whether a man's life be long or short, is fixed by the decree of Heaven.

23 How is the true God to be addressed? *Ans.* Either Heavenly Father, or Lord of Heaven, or Supreme Ruler, may be used.

His name as a man was 關羽. He lived in the second century, in 解州, in the province of Shansi, and is reputed to have been originally a seller of bean-curd. He subsequently joined Liu Pei, and in course of time became a celebrated general. He was finally taken prisoner and put to death by beheading. He was canonized by Hwei Tsung, of the Sung Dynasty, in the 12th century A.D., and in the Ming Dynasty was raised to the rank of 帝. The present dynasty has put especial honors upon him, conferring on him the pompous title 協天大帝 *The Great Sovereign (or God), Peer of Heaven,* and causing many temples to be built to him. He has a temple in nearly every village. Theatricals are generally held in connection with temples. Each temple has some set day in the year, on which special worship is offered and theatrical performances are given. These theatrical displays are in fact a part of the worship, being supposed to be pleasing to the gods.

蓬萊閣 A noted temple at Têngchow, built on a high rock overlooking the sea. 逛景 does not form a phrase in the same way as 遊逛, which consists of two verbs of similar meaning. 逛景 is a verb with its object, and means, *to look at the view, to survey the scenery.*

22 或 might be twice inserted; thus, 人的壽數或長或短, which would make the meaning more explicit. In order to make the meaning clear as the sentence stands, it is necessary to speak the words 長短 slowly and emphatically, each with its proper tone, and with a distinct pause between them.

LESSON LVII.

Approximation.

Mandarin has a large variety of words to express the general idea of approximation, each having its own peculiar use and shade of meaning. In regard to a number of these phrases the usage differs in different places, and some of them are decidedly colloquial.

差不多 Almost, about.

差不許多 Almost, very nigh, very little difference. (N. and C.)

差不幾多 Almost, very little difference. (S.)

差不離 Nearly, somewhere about, near the mark, fair, passable.

差不離形 About, not far from the mark.

差不來往 or 不差來往 Approximately.

希乎 or 希乎希 Nearly, all but.

差一點 Nearly, within a little.

差不着一點 } Almost, all but, within a hair's breadth.
差沒一點 }

不錯 Correct, all right, no mistake:—Les. 70.

不離 Not far off, fairly good, all right.

不離經 The same.

不大離 Not very far off, not so bad, fair, near the mark.

不大離經 The same. (S.)

不大離形 The same. (N. and C.)

不大差什麽 No great difference, about the same.

幾乎 or 幾幾乎 Nearly, almost, well nigh, very near.

第五十七課

這[1]件子太破了、那一件還不大離經(不大離)。○你[2]是多日沒見他的字、這以後寫的眞正不錯。○我[3]看你二位的年紀、差也差不多。○我[4]的烟袋、昨日差一點叫人拔了去。○別[5]的莊稼都不離經(不離)、就是蕎麥瞎(蹧)了。○如[6]今英文、差不多通行天下。○前[7]天榮喜從樓梯上掉下來、幾幾乎跌斷(絕)了氣。○就[8]是不能背的一點不差、也要得不大離形兒。○這[9]一路紙、比那一路紙怎麼樣呢、答不差往來(差不來往、差不許多)。○他[10]們兩個的手藝、不大差甚麼、都是好手。○[11]回來回來、你再添一添、差不離形(差不離)我就賣給你。○我[12]們纔到了河中間、

TRANSLATION.

1 This [garment] is too ragged; that one is fairly good.

2 You have not seen his writing for a long time; of late he has been writing very well indeed.

3 I judge the ages of you two gentlemen differ very little, if they differ at all.

4 Yesterday a man very nearly snatched away my pipe.

5 All the other crops are fairly good, but the buckwheat is a failure.

6 The English language is now current almost all over the world.

7 The day before yesterday Yung Hsi fell down stairs and was stunned almost to death.

8 Even if you can not repeat it exactly, yet you ought to come very near it.

9 How does this class of paper compare with that? *Ans.* They are approximately the same.

10 There is no considerable difference in their skill; they are both good workmen.

11 Come back, come back! Add a little more, and if you come anywhere near the price, I'll sell to you.

12 Just when we had reached the middle of the river, a great rise of water

VOCABULARY.

幾 *Chi*¹. A few; *nearly*, almost; minute; subtle; chance; to be near, to approximate. See *chi*³.

乎 *Hu*¹˒². A final interrogative particle expressing doubt, or surprise, but often used as a mere expletive.

眞正 *Chên*¹ *chêng*⁴. Really, truly, *indeed.*

蕎 *Ch'iao*². Buckwheat.

麥 *Mai*⁴, *moă*⁴. Wheat.

蕎麥 Buckwheat.

瞎 *Hsia*¹. Blind; ignorant; reckless. *To fail*, to come to nought, to miscarry. (N., C.)

英文 *Ying*¹ *wên*². The English language.

通行 *T'ung*¹ *hsing*². Everywhere current.

梯 *T'i*¹. A ladder; *stairs;* a step-ladder, steps.

樓梯 *Lou*² *t'i*¹. A stairway, a ladder to an upper story or loft.

絕 *Chüe*². To cut off; to interrupt; to sever; *to exterminate;* very, extremely:—Les. 116.

沖 *Ch'ung*¹. To strike or dash against; *to carry away* (by water); to steep.

傳言 *Ch'wan*² *yien*². A report, a rumor.

寸 *Ts'un*⁴. An inch (Chinese); a very little.

家當 *Chia*¹ *tang*⁴. Patrimony, property, *wealth*, fortune.

家私 *Chia*¹ *sï*¹. The same.

撞 *Chwang*⁴, *ch'wang*⁴. To pound; to beat upon; *to strike or run against;* to cheat.

撞倒 *Ch'wang*⁴ *tao*³. To strike and overturn, to push over:—Les. 91.

崖 *Ai*², *yai*². A precipice; *a bank;* a shore.

坡 *P'oă*¹. A declivity; a slope; a hill; a terrace, *a bank.*

趕緊 *Kan*³ *chin*³. *Diligent*, assiduous; to hurry, to push.

上緊 *Shang*⁴ *chin*³. The same.

估 *Ku*¹. *To estimate*, to reckon, to consider, to set a price, to appraise. Also *ku*⁴.

就下來了大水、差沒一點(希乎希)被水沖去。○那[13]不是一年半年的人、就是沒有五十歲、也差不幾多(差不多)。○我[14]聽見一個傳言說、他在路上翻了車、幾希乎叫車壓死。○不[15]用再寬二寸、我看再寬一寸、就不大離經形了。○論[16]他弟兄兩個的家家私當、也差不多、就是老大的家口多一點。○兩[17]個孩子、都叫牲口撞倒了、差差不着一點(一點)掉在坡崖子底下。○若[18]上趕緊緊的做、我估量着、做不起來、也不差甚麼。○昨[19]天晚上、我和他說了一會兒、說來說去、差一點鬧撑(弄扭、弄結)了。○你[20]看劉希孔、和王作清、在場中的文章怎麼樣呢、答不離、都

came and we were all but carried away.

13 That man is not in his teens; if not fifty, he is not very far from it.

14 I heard a report that on the way his cart upset, and he came very near being crushed to death.

15 It need not be two inches broader. If it is one inch broader it will, I think, be about right.

16 As to wealth, the two brothers are about the same, but the elder has somewhat the larger family.

17 Both children were knocked down by the animal, and came within a very little of falling down the bank.

18 If we work diligently, I calculate we can finish, or at least come very near it.

19 I talked with him a while yesterday evening, and our talk came very near ending in a quarrel.

20 What do you think of the essays Liu Hsi K'ung and Wang Tsoă Ch'ing wrote for the examinations? *Ans.* Very fair. Both have a prospect of getting their degree.

估量 *Ku*^{1} *liang*^{4}. To consider, *to calculate*, to guess, to appraise.

扭 *Niu*^{3}. *To twist*, to wrench; to wring; to sprain; to wriggle.

鬧撑 *Nao*^{4} *ning*^{2}. To get into a quarrel.

弄扭 *Lung*^{4} *niu*^{3}. The same. (c.)

弄結 *Lung*^{4} *chie*^{1}. The same. (s.)

孔 *K'ung*^{3}. Excellent; the peacock.

塲 or **場** *Ch'ang*^{3}. An open plot of ground; *an arena* for drill, examinations, theatricals, etc. Also *ch'ang*^{2}.

指望 *Chï*^{3} *wang*^{4}. Hope, *prospect*.

自從 *Tsï*^{4} *ts'ung*^{2}. From the time.

元 *Yüen*^{2}. First, original, primary; *large, great;* a dollar.

元寶 *Yüen*^{2} *pao*^{3}. A shoe or ingot of silver containing about fifty taels.

象 *Hsiang*^{4}. The elephant; *form*, image; an emblem, a resemblance.

氣象 *Ch'i*^{4} *hsiang*^{4}. *Aspect*, mien, air.

舉動 *Chü*^{3} *tung*^{4}. Actions; *bearing*, behavior; a move.

親事 *Ch'in*^{1} *shï*^{4}. *A marriage alliance*, matrimonial affairs.

炸 *Cha*^{4}. To burst, *to fly to pieces;* bits. Broken coal (N.) Also *cha*^{2}.

裂 *Lie*^{4}. To crack open; *to split;* to tear.

炸裂 To split in pieces, to burst, *to fall through.*

癨 *Hwoă*^{4}. The rapid disease, the cholera.

癨亂病 *Hwoa*^{4} *lwan*^{4} *ping*^{4}. Cholera.

瘋 *Fêng*^{1}. Leprosy; palsy; *rabid;* insane, demented; any nervous disease.

合算 *Hoă*^{2} *swan*^{4}. To reckon up, to take the aggregate; *on the whole;* profitable, paying.

圍 *Wei*^{2}. To surround; to invest; *to besiege;* a wall round a village, a fortification.

一連 *I*^{1} *lien*^{2}. One after the other, *consecutive*, together with; even also:— Les. 105.

有進學的指望。○世[21]上眞有些會說話的人、差不多離的話、叫他一說、就說活了。○自[22]從他兒子捎帶了兩個元寶來、就大改氣象、在舉動言語之間、覺着正經不錯。○這[23]門親事、若不是我去的早、差不多又炸裂散了。○他[24]纔得了家信說、他父親前日害癨亂病幾乎死了。○正[25]走到十字路口、從南來了一條大瘋狗、差一點把我咬着。○請[26]問老兄、這兩條路走那條好呢、答南路近一點、北路好走一點、合算起來、差不幾許多多。○長[27]毛來的時候、我那莊上的圍子、被他一連困了五天、幾幾乎就困破了。

21 Truly there are some men in the world who know how to talk. They will take up almost anything, and say it so as to make it seem real.

22 Ever since his son sent him the two ingots of silver, his aspect has greatly changed; both in his bearing and in his talk he feels himself decidedly worthy of regard.

23 If I had not gone early, this marriage proposal would, most likely, have fallen through again.

24 He has just received a letter from home, saying, that the day before yesterday his father was seized with cholera and came very near dying.

25 Just when I had reached the street crossing, there came from the southward a large, rabid dog, and he came very near biting me.

26 Will you please tell me, my friend, which of these roads I had better go? *Ans.* The south road is a little nearer, the north road is a little better; but, on the whole, there is very little difference.

27 When the rebels came, they besieged the wall of our village for five consecutive days, and came very near breaking it.

Notes.

1 The classifier 件 is here put for the noun, and hence takes the 子. Such an abbreviation is only allowable in colloquial.

3 差也差不多 *Differing, still do not differ much,*—a common idiomatic form.

7 跌斷了氣 *To fall so as to break or stop the breath;* i.e., *the life.* For a temporary suspension of breathing, a different word is commonly used. 斷 and 絕 are auxiliaries, used with only a few verbs. Pekingese prefers 摔斷了.

9 The second 紙 might be omitted without detriment to the sentence.

11 This is the language of one who has just refused an offer, and the customer has started to go.

13 一年半年, an exaggerated form of expressing that one is not young.

15 再 does not here mean *again,* but *in addition.*

17 It is worthy of note that 差一點 means practically the same as 差沒一點 or 差不着一點, notwithstanding the fact that the one *seems* to say the opposite of the others.

21 差不多的話 *Words which are almost;* i.e., almost any story or incident which has even the least semblance of truth or reality. 說活了, lit., *to speak alive;* i.e., they can talk so well that in their mouths the most improbable things put on the aspect of reality.

22 舉動言語之間 is a Wên-li phrase which use has made intelligible, although it would be somewhat pedantic, if used in addressing an uneducated man. 正經不錯, lit., *proper and no mistake;* i.e., *both self-satisfied and self-important.*

23 門 is the classifier of 親事, and its use as a classifier is almost limited to this one thing. 炸裂 is usually pronounced as if written 炸離.

24 家信 may be either a letter from home, as in this case, or a letter addressed to those at home. 害 is to be taken passively.

25 十字路口, *the place where two streets cross,*—the term being derived from the character 十. In some places 路 is omitted, and in others 街 is substituted for it.

26 請問老兄 is a polite manner of addressing a stranger, when asking for information of any kind.

27 長毛 is abbreviated from 長毛賊, *long-haired robbers.* This is the name generally given by the Chinese to the adherents of the great Taiping rebellion of 1850 to 1865. They were so called because they did not shave their heads, as the Chinese are all required to do by the present Tartar dynasty. In some parts of China—notably in Shantung, the larger villages generally have adobe walls around them, as a protection against armed robbers. In some cases walls (generally of stone) are built for greater protection on the tops of hills by several villages in common, and to these the people flee with their valuables in case of danger. 我那莊, *that village of ours.*

第五十八課

他[1]明白、你更明白。○我[2]比不上他的能幹。○爹[3]有娘有、不如自己有。○綿[4]襖不及皮襖暖和。○這[5]塊洋錢、比那塊強。○你[6]看那個強、答我看這個強。○人[7]是比萬物更尊貴的。○火[8]棍兒短、強似手撥攦。○點[9]蠟燭不及點燈上合算。○作[10]首領的、更不可犯規。○用[11]錢感情、不如送東西體面。○城[12]裏的風氣、大不及城外的好。○我[13]看他的學問、趕不上你的。○打[14]他、不如拿個理去和他講。○這[15]個房子、比那個房子好多了。○可[16]以多做一點飯、賸下強其似不彀。○要[17]叫這個人回頭、比登天還難。○他[18]的病、眼

Translation.

1 He understands, but you understand better.
2 I can not compare with him in ability.
3 For your father or mother to own a thing is not so good as for you to own it yourself.
4 A wadded coat is not so warm as a fur coat.
5 This dollar is better than that one.
6 Which do you think is the better? *Ans.* I think this one is the better.
7 Man is more exalted than all things else.
8 A short poker is better than to stir the fire with one's hand.
9 It is not as economical to burn candles as it is to burn a lamp.
10 Still more should not one who is a leader violate the rules.
11 To return a favor with money is not so genteel as to send a present.
12 The air in the city is not nearly so good as it is outside.
13 I do not think his scholarship comes up to yours.
14 To beat him is not so good as to try the effect of reason.
15 This house is much better than that one.
16 You may cook a little more rice. It is better to have some left, than not to have enough.

LESSON LVIII.

The Comparative Degree.

Formal comparison is made with 比, of the use of which there have been frequent instances in previous lessons. There are, however, a variety of other words and ways, by which comparison is effected.

更 To change,—as a comparative, is equal to *more*, or to the termination *er*. It precedes the adjective which it qualifies. It is often used in connection with 比, (1), (19).

强 Violent,—as a comparative, *better*, *superior*. (5). It follows the noun it qualifies, and is generally used in connection with 比 (5), or joined with 如 or 似 or 其, as below.

更强 Still better, much better; better. (19.)

似 Like,—is often used to form a direct comparison. It follows the adjective with which it is joined. (24.)

其 That,—is used colloquially in the same way as 似, but is not *t'ung hsing*. (24)

如 As,—may also be used alone in the same way, but usually takes 强 before it, or is joined with a negative, as below.

强其 (16), **强似** (8)(35), **强如** (28) } Better than, superior to. The first form is local, the other two are general.

不及 Not as good as, inferior to,—a much used form.

不如 Not equal to, not up to. (4) (9)

多 or **得多** following an adjective is equal to *much*,—much better, much higher, etc. (15) (29)

赶不上, **跟不上** } Not equal to, not up to. (13) (21)

Comparison may also be effected without any special word. (20)

看着一天比一天好了。○[19]爲甚麽但揀那個、這個不比那個更好强嗎。○[20]好歹是在各人看着、我看這個沒有那個好。○[21]我使這旱乾筆、跟不上那水筆好使。○[22]像這樣沒有良心的人、眞正不如禽獸了。○[23]我那些弟兄們、連外人都不如。○[24]他分這四層意思、一層深其似一層。○[25]好的都擺在上面、往下一個不如一個。○[26]你的事、比我的事還更要緊嗎。○[27]俗語說、十賒不如一現、又說、十鳥在樹、不如一鳥在手。○[28]見人有錯、在背地裏告訴他、强如在衆人跟前說出來。○[29]前院天子井那

17 To lead this man to reform is harder than to ascend to heaven.
18 His disease is evidently improving every day.
19 Why do you specially select that one? Is not this one better than that one?
20 Whether good or bad depends on how each individual looks at it. As I see it, this is not as good as that.
21 For my use this dry pen is not equal to that wet one.
22 In very deed, a man so devoid of conscience as this is not as good as a beast.
23 Those brothers of mine are not even equal to strangers. [form a climax.
24 These four divisions which he makes
25 The good ones are all put on top; as you descend they get poorer and poorer. [mine?
26 Is your business more important than
27 There is a proverb which says, Ten credits are not so good as one cash [sale]; and another which says, Ten birds in the tree are not so good as one in the hand.
28 When you see a fault in a man, it is better to tell him in private, than to speak of it in public.

VOCABULARY.

更 *Kêng*⁴. More, still; again:—see Sub. See .... *kêng*¹, also *ching*¹.

及 *Chi*². To reach to; to connect:—see Sub.; effective, practicable, availing:—Les. 92; and, with, also; about, concerning; at, to.

似 *Si*⁴. Like, similar to, resembling:—see Sub.; ...... as, as if:—Les. 99.

其 *Ch'i*². A *Wên-li* pronoun having many uses:— ...... he, she, it; that, the one; whoever; there; if, then, etc.; used in Mandarin in many phrases taken from books:—Les. 146.

綿襖 *Mien*² *ao*³........ A wadded coat.

洋錢 *Yang*² *ch'ien*².... Foreign money; a dollar.

萬物 *Wan*⁴ *wu*⁴.......... All things.

撥 *Pŏ*¹. To spread; to separate; to distribute; .... to transfer, *to turn over to.*

搣 *La*¹.......... To turn over; *to pull about.*

撥搣 To turn over, *to stir about,* to scatter.

蠟 *La*⁴...... *Wax;* waxy, glazed; a candle.

燭 *Chu*²...... *A candle,* a torch, a light.

蠟燭 A candle.

上算 *Shang*⁴ *swan*⁴........ Profitable, paying.

首領 *Shou*³ *ling*³.......... A leader, a chief.

感 *Kan*³. To move the feelings; to affect, to act ...... on physically or mentally; to rouse, to excite; to be grateful; *to return a favor.*

風氣 *Fêng*¹ *ch'i*⁴..... *The air;* custom, fashion.

賸 *Shêng*⁴..... *Overplus,* remainder; leavings.

登 *Têng*¹..... *To ascend,* to begin; to record.

禽 *Ch'in*²... Birds, flying and feathered creatures.

禽獸 *Ch'in*² *shou*⁴. Birds and beasts, a comprehensive term for the whole animal creation.

層 *Ts'êng*². A layer, a story; a step; a degree; .... *a division.* A classifier:—Les. 100.

俗 *Su*²..... *Common,* vulgar; lay; the world.

俗語 *Su*² *yü*³....... A common saying.

鳥 *Niao*³.......... A bird, the feathered tribe.

背地 *Pei*⁴ *ti*⁴...... *In private;* secretly.

跟前 *Kên*¹ *ch'ien*². At the feet; in the presence .... of, *before.*

有後天井(院子)大、前天井(院子)小得多了。○30這件事很纏手、不及你親自去看看。○31兒子孝、不如媳婦孝、女兒孝、不如女婿孝。○32用手做的傢伙、總不及用機器做的光滑(滑錫)。○33得意的黧貓歡似虎、失時的鳳凰不如雞。○34你看財帛比你的心血更重、你一個大錢、比割你身上一塊肉更疼。○35我看現在的時勢、莫妙於(莫強似)凡事不管、自己多麼清靜、又少得罪多少人呢。

29 The front court as large as the back court! The front court is much smaller.

30 This business is very much involved. It would be better for you to go in person and see about it.

31 A dutiful daughter-in-law is better than a dutiful son. A dutiful son-in-law is better than a dutiful daughter.

32 After all, tools made by hand are not so nicely finished as those made by machinery.

33 A brindled cat in high spirits disports itself like a tiger: a phœnix in unpropitious circumstances is not equal to a chicken.

34 You regard money as of more value than your heart's blood. To take away a cash hurts you more than to cut out a piece of your flesh.

35 It seems to me that in the present state of affairs, the best way is to decline all responsibilities. What an amount of trouble it saves, and how many people it saves offending.

天井 *T'ien[1] ching[3].* A court between two houses, a court-yard.

纏手 *Ch'an[2] shou[3].* Intricate, *involved*, embarrassing.

機 *Chi[1].* Change; origin; moving power; natural cause; contrivance; *a machine;* a loom; a stratagem; opportune.

器 *Ch'i[4].* A vessel; *a tool*, an implement.

機器 *A machine*, an instrument; apparatus.

錫 *T'ang[4].* To smooth, to polish.

滑錫 *Hwa[2] t'ang[4].* Smooth; slippery; polished; *finished.*

得意 *Tê[2] i[4].* *In good spirits;* satisfied.

黧 *Li[2].* A blackish yellow color, dun.

失時 *Shï[1] shï[2].* Out of luck or favor; *in unfavorable circumstances.*

鳳凰 *Fêng[4] hwang[2].* A fabulous bird of felicitous omen, the phœnix.

帛 *Poă,[4,2].* White silk; *wealth.*

財帛 *Ts'ai[2] poă[2].* Money, wealth.

血 *Hsüe,[4] hsie[3].* *Blood;* related by blood.

時勢 *Shï[2] shï[4].* The times; *state of affairs.*

莫 *Moă[4].* Do not, no need of:—Les. 82; perhaps; *not so;* nothing; nothing like.

妙 *Miao[4].* *Excellent*, wonderful, admirable; subtle, mysterious; supernatural.

Notes.

1 The "but" in the translation is implied by the connection. The sentence might also be taken hypothetically, and be rendered, *If he understands, you still more.*

9 蠟燭, *wax candles*, is the most general and most perspicuous term for candles. Chinese candles are usually made of a mixture of tallow and lard, by dipping, and are finally dipped once or twice in wax, thus giving them a thin skin of wax, which protects the soft inside and forms a cup to retain the molten grease. In some places, as in Peking, candles are called simply 蠟, *wax;* in other places they are called 蠟燈, *wax lamps.*

11 感情 sometimes forms a phrase, meaning *to stir up or influence others*, but here 感 is the verb and 情 its object. 情 properly means affection, but is here put for the favor, or present, which expresses affection.

14 個 is used to specialize the particular reason, or principle, involved in the case.

17 登天 *ascend to heaven,*—an expression to denote something that is impossible. 登 is used in Mandarin only in set phrases.

18 一天比一天好了, *one day compared with one day good; i.e., improving day by day.* Note that the Chinese says the *disease* is improving.

第五十九課

誰[1]願意爲他白効勞呢。○若[2]不爲喫穿二字、誰還肯幹營生(活)呢。○你[3]是願受打、是願受罰、答小的情願受罰。○罰[4]你請一桌客、你甘心情願不甘心不情願呢。○進[5]教是在自己甘心願意、沒有强逼人進教的。○可[6]以用幾個小紙撚兒訂起來、我不愛那些大紙撚兒。○說[7]和事的給他斷了三百吊錢、他又情願讓他二十吊。○一[8]年二百兩銀子的東脩、你還不肯住(就)下、你想要掙多少呢。○不[9]用理他、他願意愛意也是這麼樣、不願意愛意也是這麼樣。○我[10]不管他心焦

TRANSLATION.

1 Who is willing to work for him for nothing?

2 If it were not for the sake of food and clothing, who would be willing to work?

3 Would you prefer to be beaten, or to be fined? *Ans.* I would prefer to be fined.

4 If fined to the extent of feasting one table, would you be willing or not?

5 Joining the church must be of your own free will. No one joins the church by compulsion.

6 Use some small paper cords and bind it [the book] up. I do not like those coarse paper cords.

7 The arbitrators awarded him three hundred tiao, and even of this he, of his own accord, abated twenty tiao.

8 Getting a salary of two hundred taels a year, and yet you will not remain! How much do you expect to earn?

9 Pay no attention to him: so it must be, whether he likes it or not.

10 I do not care whether he is worried or not. I can not suffer him to treat me so rudely as this.

---

21 The 旱筆, or 乾筆, is a pen of which only a very small portion is wet with the ink, and it is allowed to dry when not in use. In the case of the 水筆, the whole head of the pen is wet, and is kept from drying when not in use by being covered with the brass tube or "cap" provided for the purpose. The "dry pen" is used chiefly in the South.

24 The translation gives the sense. A more literal translation would be,—*each division is more profound than the preceding one.*

29 天井 means properly a narrow court between two houses, in allusion probably to the patch of sky seen from the bottom of a well. It has, however, come to be used in many places instead of 院子, *yard.* In other parts of the country it is scarcely used at all.

33 Paraphrase thus:—"When in the mood, a brindled cat will put on the air and mien of a tiger; while the *fêng hwang*, though naturally a magnificent bird, is, when in unfavorable circumstances, no better than a chicken." The meaning is, that everything depends on circumstances.

LESSON LIX.

ASSENT AND DISSENT.

願 and 愛, and their combinations, are chiefly used to express willingness or assent; but various other words are used with a negative to express unwillingness or dissent.

願意 Willing, to acquiesce, to agree. (1) (5)

情願 Of one's own free will, voluntarily. (7)

愛意 Willing; inclined, disposed. (9)

甘願 Freely, of one's own accord. (15)

甘心 Satisfied, willing, assisting. (4)

甘心樂意 Freely, cordially. (13)

不肯 Unwilling, dissatisfied. (8) (11)

不服 To dissent, to demur, to protest. (12)

不讓 To disallow, to restrain, to resent. (14)

不依 To disallow, to withstand; to demand satisfaction. (18)

不答應 To refuse, to resent, to demur. (18)

不受 or 不受頭 To refuse to submit. (10)

不心焦(焦心)、他這樣衝撞(唐突)我、我就不能答應(受頭)。○11這就是他打了我的孩子、若是我打了他的孩子、他再不肯干休。○12你但逞他的威風、滅我的志氣、我心裏就是不服。○13人孝順父母、應當甘心樂意、不可出於勉强。○14你出去撞騙人、不用掛我的幌子(招牌)、若是再指着我的名子去撞騙、我一定不讓。○15那是我甘願送給他、是他硬强拿去了。○16我也不愛踢毽兒、也不愛打毬

11 In this case, it is he that struck my child. If I had struck his child, he would never have been willing to drop it.

12 You are all the time boasting of his power, in order to weaken my resolution, but I am determined not to yield.

13 A man should honor his parents of his own free will, and not as the result of constraint.

14 When you set out to swindle people, I don't want you to hang out my sign. If you ever again attempt to swindle people in my name, I will certainly make it hot for you.

15 I give it to him of my own accord! He took it away by main force.

16 I do not like to play shuttlecock, nor to play ball; the thing I like is to play chess.

VOCABULARY.

甘 *Kan*¹. Sweet; pleasant, agreeable; luscious; delightsome; *willing, voluntary.*

効 *Hsiao*⁴. *To toil*, to labor earnestly, to exert oneself; exertions.

効勞 *Hsiao*⁴ *lao*². To toil, *to work for.*

逼 *Pi*¹. To press upon; *to urge or force arbitrarily;* to ill-use.

强逼 *Ch'iang*³ *pi*¹. To compel, to force.

進教 *Chin*⁴ *chiao*⁴. To join the Church, to become a Christian.

撚 *Nien*³. To fumble over; to toy with; *to roll and twist with the fingers.*

紙撚 *Chï*³ *nien*³. *A twisted paper string or cord;* a lamp-lighter.

束 *Su*⁴, *shu*⁴. To bind, to restrain, to coerce.

脩 *Hsiu*¹. Dried meat; to prepare.

束脩 A teacher's salary.

焦 *Chiao*¹. Scorched; anxious, *worried.*

心焦 *Hsin*¹ *chiao*¹. *Worried*, vexed.

衝 *Ch'ung*¹. *To rush against;* to excite; to collide with.

衝撞 *Ch'ung*¹ *chwang*⁴. To butt against; to interfere with; to offend; *to treat rudely.*

突 *T'u*⁴, *tu*⁴. Abruptly; to rush; *insolent*, audacious:—Les. 115.

唐突 *T'ang*² *t'u*⁴. *To treat rudely.*

答應 *Ta*¹ *ying*⁴. To reply; to respond; *to assent,* to agree to.

受頭 *Shou*⁴ *t'ou*². *To submit to.* (L.)

休 *Hsiu*¹. To rest; *to cease;* to desist; to divorce; prosperous; stop, do not:—Les. 82.

干休 *Kan*¹ *hsiu*¹. To quit, *to drop*, to relinquish; to submit.

逞 *Ch'êng*³. To presume on, to rely on; *to boast;* presumptuous, reckless.

威 *Wei*¹. Majesty; grave, *imposing*, lordly.

威風 *Wei*¹ *fêng*¹. Majesty; *prowess.*

志 *Chï*⁴. The will; inclination; purpose, *determination*, aim; topographies; annals.

志氣 *Chï*⁴ *ch'i*⁴. Determination, *resolution;* will; courage.

樂意 *Lo*⁴ *i*⁴. *Heartily; willing*, cordial.

出於 *Ch'u*¹ *yü*². To proceed from.

勉 *Mien*³. To force oneself, *to constrain;* to urge; to animate.

勉强 *Mien*³ *ch'iang*³. *To constrain;* to compel; to insist on.

撞騙 *Chwang*⁴ *p'ien*⁴. To cheat, to humbug, *to swindle.*

幌 *Hwang*³. A curtain, *a sign*, an advertisement.

招 *Chao*¹. To beckon; to invite; to excite; to confess, to admit; *a sign-board.*

就是愛下棋。○保[17]子爹、孩子直鬧（不肯）、快來抱他去、我好做（弄）飯。○北[18]莊李有年的女兒、是這東莊趙四的媳婦、前日叫他婆婆暴（惡）打了一頓、氣的吊死了、他的街坊鄰居、通統不服、都願意李有年來不依他、把趙四折蹬（盤弄）的水盡鷄飛、這纔甘心、以後經人調處（調說）了、趙四只拿出三十吊錢、李有年就肯了、若是這件事挪在我身上、就是給我三百吊、我也是不答應的。

17 Pao-tsï's papa, the baby is very cross; come and carry him out while I get the dinner.

18 The daughter of Li YuNien, of the village to the north, is daughter-in-law to Chao the Fourth, of the village to the east. Day before yesterday her mother-in-law gave her a violent beating, and she got so angry that she hanged herself. The neighbors were all up in arms, and were anxious that Li YuNien should take the matter up, and not be satisfied till he had squeezed out of Chao the Fourth every cash he had. Afterwards, through the intervention of middle-men, Li YuNien agreed to let off Chao the Fourth on payment of only thirty thousand cash. If it had been my affair, I would not have assented if he had paid me three hundred thousand cash.

招牌 *Chao¹ p'ai²*. . . . . A signboard, a sign.

一定 *I¹ ting⁴*. *Certainly*, positively, inevitably:—Les. 116.

硬强 *Ying⁴ ch'iang³*. *By force*, compulsory, peremptory.

毽 *Chien⁴*. . . . . . A shuttlecock.

踢毽 *T'i¹ chien⁴*. To play shuttlecock,—using the foot as a battledoor.

毬 *Ch'iu²*. . . . . . *A (play) ball;* a balloon.

打毬 *Ta³ ch'iu²*. . . . . To play ball.

棋 *Ch'i²*. . . . *Chess;* checkers, fox and geese, etc.

下棋 *Hsiâ⁴ ch'i²*. . . . . To play chess, etc.

暴 *Pao⁴*. A scorching heat: stormy; cruel, *violent*, oppressive.

暴打 *Pao⁴ ta³*. . . . . .To beat violently.

惡打 *Oâ⁴ ta³*. . . . . To beat cruelly.

頓 *Tun⁴*. To bow the head, to stamp; a resting place; to rest; a meal; a turn, *a time;* a stop, a period; staccato:—Les. 64.

鄰居 *Lin² chü¹*. . . . . . . A neighbor, neighbors.

折蹬 *Chê² têng⁴*. To harass; to persecute; *to use up,* to destroy.

盤弄 *P'an² nung⁴*. To coil up; to entangle; to embarrass; to use up.

飛 *Fei¹*. . . . . . . *To fly,* to go swiftly; sudden.

處 *Ch'u³*. To dwell; to occupy the place of; *to attend to;* to do what is proper. See *ch'u⁴*.

調處 *T'iao² ch'u³*. To rearrange; *to adjust or compromise a quarrel.*

調說 *T'iao² shwoâ¹*. To arrange terms of compromise, to make peace.

NOTES.

3 罰 usually means simply punishment, but here, being contrasted with 打, it is used to signify *a fine.* It is not an uncommon thing for officials to give light offenders the choice of a beating or a fine.

4 This is the language of one who is acting as mediator. It is a common thing for the offender to make amends by giving a feast to the parties interested.

6 紙撚 here refers to the little paper strings which all Chinese teachers know how to make, and which they use to bind small books for temporary use.

8 束脩 is only applied to the salary of a teacher. It is derived from the ancient custom of making presents of meat, etc., instead of paying a salary in money.

10 心焦不焦 is the Central and Southern form. In this case 心焦 does not form a phrase, as it does in the other form.

14 不讓 here means, as it often does, *to resent forcibly, to call to account and demand satisfaction.*

15 The force of 那裡 is very hard to transfer to writing in English. It can only be expressed by the tone of surprise and indignation given to the English words.

16 Chinese boys play ball very little. Their chief game with a ball consists simply in striking the ball with the hand time after time, so as to keep it rebounding from the ground.

17 Chinese women generally speak of, or to, their husbands through the names of their children. 不肯 is a forcible way of expressing that the child is unmanageable.

18 水盡鷄飛 *Water exhausted and goose flown,*—a figure to express the utter exhaustion of resources; *bankrupt.*

第六十課

悄¹悄(靜靜)兒的罷。答請。○你²管你的罷。○請³兩便罷、答請。○想⁴是有人得罪他了罷。○你⁵這麼做、我不能讓你、答你不讓罷。○改⁶日再見罷。○有⁷話快快的說罷。○他⁸實在不借、就罷。○你⁹放心罷、不能哄你。○罷¹⁰了、事到如今、說也無益。○你¹¹這樣黑乾枯瘦(黃皮刮瘦)的、必是有點症候罷。○陰¹²涼兒裏坐着涼快(涼涼)罷。○隨¹³你罷、你看着好就好。○這¹⁴裏是住家的、你快走罷。○壺¹⁵裏的水彀不彀、答彀了罷。○打¹⁶死他、不過償他的命罷了。○閒¹⁷着再

Translation.

1 Keep quiet.
2 Do you mind your own business.
3 Well, good day. *Ans.* Good day.
4 I think some one must have offended him.
5 If you act in this way I will have to demur. *Ans.* Demur as much as you like.
6 We will see each other again.
7 If you have anything to say, say it quickly.
8 If he positively will not lend, so be it.
9 Do not be alarmed, I shall not deceive you.
10 Let it go. After the matter has come to this pass, it would be useless to speak of it.
11 You have such a sallow and shrivelled look. It must be that you have some ailment.
12 Sit down in the shade and cool off.
13 As you like: if you are content, it is all right.
14 This is a private house. Please go out at once.

LESSON LX.

The Final Particle 罷.

罷 is a final particle of great expressiveness, and with a wide variety of uses. It does not always stand at the close of a sentence, but it generally, if not always, marks the end of an idea. The following is an approximate classification of its uses:—

1 It emphasizes an injunction (9), or an invitation (12), or command. (1) (14)

2 It softens a command. (34) (38)

3 It asks a question which is coupled with a doubt. (20) (38)

4 It modifies an assertion by suggesting a doubt, (15) (38), or a query. (4) (28)

5 It marks a conclusion more or less definite. (13) (19)

6 When specially emphasized it marks a peremptory decision (8), or expresses defiance. (5)

7 Followed by 了, it emphasizes a decision. (10) (16)

8 When repeated (sometimes trebled), it becomes an exclamation expressing impatience (32), or a concession. (36)

9 Repeated with 了, it expresses impatience (26), or surprise. (40)

10 When followed by 呀, it becomes a term of importunate, or peremptory entreaty. (29)

Though the use of 罷 is well recognized in general Mandarin, yet its use in Western Mandarin is limited. In the larger number of the sentences in the lesson a Chung-k'ing teacher changed the 罷 to 嗎, the propriety of which it is impossible to reconcile with general Mandarin.

Vocabulary.

罷 *Pa*⁴. To cease, to stop; to discontinue; to .... finish. A particle used to emphasize a command, etc.:—see Sub.

改日 *Kai*³ *ji*⁴. .... Another day, *again.*

枯 *K'u*¹. ... Decayed, rotten; withered, *dried up.*

枯瘦 *K'u*¹ *shou*⁴. ... ... Lean, *shrivelled,* thin.

刮 *Kwa*¹. To pare, *to scrape;* to rub; to even .... off; to scrape by or against.

來說話罷。○不[18]用送、都請回罷。○若[19]是你們都
願意、就是這麼樣着罷。○今[20]兒夜裏、我住在這裏
可以罷。○你[21]實在不肯、有甚麼法子你去使使去罷。
○你[22]的病好了沒有、答現在算好了罷。○先[23]試
試看罷、若是不行再說。○過[24]的得去就罷了、不可
逞強。○現[25]成的便飯、將就喫點兒罷。○罷[26]了罷
了、你真算好的。○不[27]用着急、再少等一會兒罷。
○誰[28]說話這麼大的喉嗓嚨子、必是那個討厭的、又
來了罷。○罷[29]呀老爺、限我十天的期限罷、答好、就
是罷。○快[30]拉倒罷、管閒事還有甚麼上便算宜嗎。○

15 Is the water in the kettle sufficient? *Ans.* I think so.
16 If I kill him, I have only to give my life for his.
17 When you have time come again and chat a while.
18 You need not escort me. Please return.
19 If you are all willing, so let it be.
20 Can I stay here over night?
21 If you are still dissatisfied; then go and do your uttermost.
22 Are you quite recovered from your illness? *Ans.* Yes, practically.
23 First try it, and if it will not work we'll consider further.
24 If you can at all put up with it, it will be better to drop the matter and not push it to extremes.
25 Common fare, ready to hand. Waive a point and eat a little.
26 Well done! Good for you!
27 Do not get impatient; wait just a little longer.
28 Who is it that is speaking with such a stentorian voice? It must be that that hateful fellow has come again.
29 Come now, Your Excellency, allow me ten days time. *Ans.* All right. So be it.

黑乾枯瘦 *Hei¹kan¹ k'u¹ shou⁴*. Sallow and . . . . shrivelled.

黃皮刮瘦 *Hwang² p'i² kwa¹ shou⁴*. Yellow and . . . . thin.

症 *Chêng⁴*. . . . . . . A chronic disease, a malady.

症候 *Chêng⁴ hou⁴*. Disease, *ailment;* complaint; . . . . malady.

陰凉 *Yin¹ liang²*. . . . . Shade, shady.

凉快 *Liang² k'wai⁴*. *To cool off;* cool; refresh- . . . . ing; chilly.

償 *Ch'ang²*. To pay back, to indemnify; to atone; . . . . *to replace.*

請回 *Ch'ing³ hwei²*. Please return; good day, ... good-bye.

逞强 *Ch'êng³ ch'iang²*. To rely on one's strength . . . . or prowess; *to push to extremes;* to stake on one supreme effort.

便飯 *Pien⁴ fan⁴*. . . . . Ordinary food.

嗓 *Sang³*. . . . *The throat;* larynx; the windpipe.

呀 *Ya¹*. . . . A final emphatic particle :—Les. 61.

期 *Ch'i¹,²*. A set or fixed time; *time,* period, ... season; to expect, to hope for.

拉倒 *La¹ tao³*. To desist, to give up, to drop; to . . . . cease, to be all over with; stop it, enough! begone!

颺 *Yang²*. Driven by the wind; whirled; *to win- . . . . now;* to publish; to waft.

場 *Ch'ang²*. *A threshing floor;* a time :—Les. 64. . . . . A classifier :—Les100. See *ch'ang³*.

颺場 To winnow the grain on the threshing floor by tossing it up in the face of the wind, which thus blows the chaff away from the grain.

簸 *Po³*. . . . . . . To clean grain with a 簸箕.

簸 *Po⁴*. . . . . . . *A winnowing fan;* a dust pan.

箕 *Ch'i¹, chi¹*. . . . . . *A wicker scoop,* a dust pan.

簸箕 *A wicker scoop for cleaning grain;* a dust pan.

罷休 *Pa⁴ hsiu¹*. To cease, to give up; to drop, ... *to pay no attention to.*

饒 *Jao²*. Abundant; surplus; indulgent; to favor, ... to excuse, *to overlook;* to pardon.

瑟 *Sê⁴*. . . . . . . A lute.

約瑟 *Yüe¹ Sê⁴*. . . . . . Joseph.

趁 *Ch'ên⁴*. To avail of, to embrace, to improve . . . . an opportunity.

一面 *I¹ mien⁴*. One face, one side; *once.*

該31給你多少錢、纔算公道、答不要緊、先生看着罷。○罷32罷、就在這裏住下罷。○我33待要不等他罷、又怕他來、待要等他罷、又怕他不來。○沒34有風怎麼颺場呢、答實在沒有風、就用簸箕簸罷。○知35道就說知道、不知道就說不知道罷、撒謊扯謊作甚麼呢。○他36罵你、你就罷罷休了嗎、答罷罷、他是喝醉了、看他父親的面上、饒了他罷。○孩37子在外頭哭、你去叫他來家家來罷。○燒38的水開了沒有、答開了罷、回開了、就拿來罷。○聽39說街上的魚很便宜、我去買幾斤罷、答好、若是眞便宜、買個十來斤罷。○罷40了罷了、我兒子約瑟還在、趁着我還沒死、要去見他一面。

30 Drop it at once. Is there anything to be gained by meddling in other people's business?

31 How much do you consider that I ought in justice to give you? *Ans.* It is not important: whatever you please.

32 So be it then. Let us stop here.

33 If I do not wait for him, I fear he may come. On the other hand, I fear if I wait for him, he may not come after all.

34 How can one winnow without wind? *Ans.* If there really is no wind, then use a winnowing fan to clean it.

35 If you know, then say so; and if you do not know, say so. Why do you lie about it?

36 When he reviles you, do you pay no attention? *Ans.* Oh, he's drunk. For his father's sake I will overlook it.

37 The child is out of doors crying. Do you go and call him into the house.

38 Is the water you are heating boiling? *Ans.* I think so. *Reply.* If it is, then bring it in.

39 I hear that in the market, fish are very cheap. Shall I go and buy a few catties? *Ans.* All right; if they are really cheap, you may buy ten or more catties.

40 Well, well; my son Joseph is still alive. I will go and see his face before I die.

NOTES.

3 This is a polite form of leave taking, but is not much used in common life. The meaning is, let each follow his own convenience.

4 Or, *It must be that some one has offended him.*

6 Another form of leave taking, more or less indicative of friendship. The first two characters are often omitted, and 再見罷 used alone. The Chinese affords no words answering to our admirable words, "good-bye," and "farewell."

11 症候 is used in some places in the sense of *a plague or contagious disease*, but its general use is as given above.

12 This is the greeting of one sitting in the shade, to a passer-by.

14 住家 *Live home*, i.e., *a private residence.*

16 Such foolish and reckless language as this is not infrequently heard from the Chinese.

17 The common language of a woman to a caller who is about to leave.

18 This is the language of a guest, politely declining the honor of being escorted to the gate (or further) by the host. The 都 is not distinctly given in the translation. Its use implies that several persons were addressed.

21 使去 In this case 去 is not an auxiliary verb, but both 使 and 去 are principal verbs, so that 使去 and 去使 are quite equivalent. In Shantung 使 would generally be used alone, without 去.

23 In conversation the 若是 would often be omitted.

24 得 is the more common and more correct form.

25 This is the language of a housewife, or a host, to a casual guest happening in at meal-time.

26 This style of speech might also be used ironically, in which case it should be translated, *Yes, yes, no doubt you're a prodigy.*

29 We have illustrated in this sentence how 就是 is used in a reply. See Les. 44, Sub.

33 罷 here expresses most forcibly the indecision and hesitation of the speaker.

36 The double 罷 in the reply has a peculiar force, which no one English word will express. It marks the apologetic purpose of the speaker to let the matter pass.

38 燒的水 is put for 你所燒的水, *the water which you are heating.*

40 罷了罷了 renders Jacob's expression of mingled satisfaction and surprise with admirable force.

第六十一課

我[1]要得走喇。○你[2]管你的就是得咯。○好[3]啊、就是那麽的着罷。○我[4]們在天上的父啊。○快[5]念罷。先生要背書咧喇。○纔[6]回來嗎、家裏都好啊。○不[7]要說喇、你快去罷。○天[8]不早喇、你得趕快的走啊、○他[9]不過仗着嘴會說罷咧。○誰[10]敲門哪、答我啊、快開開罷。○我[11]幾句話把他頂回去咯。○日[12]頭晌午偏西錯了、可以起身走喇。○已[13]經給你這麽些、中得喇、你去罷。○若[14]再來、我叫看街的攆轟你、你聽明白喇。○家[15]裏

TRANSLATION.

1 I must go (or, I am going).
2 It will be enough for you to attend to your own business.
3 All right. So let it be.
4 Our Father which art in heaven.
5 Get your lesson quickly. The teacher is just now going to hear it.
6 Have you just now returned? Are they all well at home?
7 Stop talking and go at once.
8 It is getting late; you should be off immediately.
9 He simply depends on his fluency of speech.
10 Who is knocking? *Ans.* I am. Make haste and open the door.
11 With a few words I silenced him.
12 It is past noon. We had better be going.
13 Having given you this much, you ought to be satisfied. Be off with you.
14 If you come again, I'll have the policeman drive you off. Do you understand?

LESSON LXI.

EUPHONIC ENDINGS.

Mandarin abounds in final particles, used to round off the close of the sentence, or to emphasize certain ideas and emotions. It is very difficult to define or distinguish these particles accurately in English. Their proper use can only be acquired by imitation, and by close attention to the manner in which the Chinese use them. The usage also varies not a little in different places. Few, if any, foreign speakers use them as much as the Chinese do.

喇 A final particle indicating completion. It is not essentially different from 了, when 了 is used as a simple final at the end of a clause or sentence and pronounced (as it always is in practice) *la*. There is in fact no certain principle to guide as to which character should be used in any given case, and the usage of different places and teachers differs widely.

咯 A final particle indicating certainty, but in practice not distinguishable from 喇. Teachers vary much in the use of this character.

啊 A final sound having a variety of uses:—
1 It concludes a formal address or an invocation. (4) (29)
2 It concludes an inquiry. (6) (17)
3 It emphasizes an injunction or a declaration. (8) (30)

哪 A final particle very nearly if not quite equivalent in meaning and use to 啊. Careful observation of the use of this particle points to the conclusion that it is simply a variation in sound from 啊, occasioned by the preceding word ending in the letter *n*. Notice how in (29) and (30) the two words change places, for no apparent reason save the ending of the preceding word.

咧 A euphonic ending which in the North is used only after 罷. (9) (19) In the South it is sometimes used instead of 喇. (5)

哩 A final particle found occasionally in books, but not used colloquially in the North. It is sometimes heard in the South instead of 喇. (16) (26)

呀 A final particle giving a strong emphasis, either to an inquiry (21), or to an assertion. (25)

哇 A final particle sometimes used instead of 啊, to emphasize an assertion or an injunction.

鎖着門哪、我媽帶着鑰匙走喇。○請[16]你們都進去坐坐罷、答我們不坐着哩喇。○你[17]要和我一塊兒走啊、還是要先走哪。○你[18]看這些衣裳、都長了白毛翳毛霉翳咯、快拿出去晾晾罷。○他[19]也是個人罷咧、還能不按着道理行嗎。○像[20]你這樣的人、可算是伸竪得大拇指頭的喇。○請[21]說爽快爽撇話罷、你是願意呀、是不願意呀。○他[22]這麼俊俏、麻俐、能幹、料理家務、眞是好喇。○你[23]沒喫早飯罷、答沒呢、沒家那裏有哇、○

15 The house is locked up and my mother has gone away with the key.
16 Will you please walk in and be seated? Thanks; we will not sit down.
17 Do you wish to go with us, or do you prefer to go ahead?
18 See, these clothes are all moldy. Take them out at once and air them.
19 He also is a man. Will he then act contrary to reason?
20 A man like you may be considered as having a will of his own.
21 Please speak to the point. Are you willing or not willing?
22 She is so graceful, so quick and so capable, and manages the household admirably.
23 Have you not had your breakfast? *Ans.* No. Where have I anything to eat?
24 A youth becomes a man at sixteen, and he is now seventeen; can he then be considered small?

VOCABULARY.

咯 *Loă*4. A final particle taking the place of 喇:—see Sub.
啊 *A*1, *Ê*1. A common final particle:—see Sub.
咧 *Lie*1,3. The chatter of birds; a final particle:—see Sub.
哪 *Na*1,4. A final particle:—see Sub.
哩 *Li*1,4. A final particle found in books, and used in South China.
哇 *Wa*1. To retch, to vomit; a final particle:—see Sub.
趕快 *Kan*3 *k'wai*4. Quickly, make haste.
轟 *Hung*1. Any rumbling noise—as thunder; to blast, to explode; to hustle or *drive off;* to eject; to blow up.
翳 *I*1. To screen, to intercept; to overshadow; a screen; *a flake, a pellicle, a coat.*
霉 *Mei*2. Humid, damp; *moldy;* mildew.
霉翳 Mold.
翳毛 *I*1 *mao*2. Mold.
白毛 *Pai*2 *mao*2. Mold.
晾 *Liang*4. To dry in the open air, to air.
拇 *Mu*3. *The thumb,* the great toe.
大拇指頭 *Ta*4 *mu*3 *chï*3 *t'ou*2. The thumb, the great toe.
爽撇 *Shwang*3 *p'ie*1. Quick, prompt. (s.)
俏 *Ch'iao*4. Similar; handsome, *pretty;* sprightly, nimble.
俊俏 *Chün*4 *ch'iao*4. Handsome, pretty, elegant, *graceful.*
麻 *Ma*2. Hemp; *quick,* sprightly, lively.
麻俐 *Ma*2 *li*4. Ready; *quick;* clever.
料理 *Liao*4 *li*3. *To manage,* to regulate.
務 *Wu*4. To labor strenuously, to attend to; concerns; duty, *affairs;* must; necessary.
家務 *Chia*1 *wu*4. *Household affairs,* family duties; family.
沒家 *Moă*4 *chia*1. A corrupt form of 沒有:—Note 23.
手爐 *Shou*3 *lu*2. A brazier for warming the hands.
老成 *Lao*3 *ch'êng*2. Experienced, prudent, *discreet, staid.*
穩重 *Wên*3 *chung*4. Sedate, gentle, *steady.*
姻 *Yin*1. A bride, a betrothed girl; *affinity;* relationship.
姻緣 *Yin*1 *yüen*2. The fate or affinity which brings lovers together; *a match.*
天理 *T'ien*1 *li*3. The law of heaven, the principles of right, moral truth.

十[24]六歲成丁、他現在已經十七喇、這還算小嗎。○[25]王大哥在家裏嗎、(答)沒在家呀、(問)沒在家上那裏去喇、(答)趕集去喇。○[26]那個人講究的很哩、喫要喫好的、穿要穿好的。○[27]聽說你四百錢買了一個手爐、是新的啊、是舊的呢、(答)是個半新不舊的。○[28]那撒母耳少年老成、也聰明、也穩重。你若把女兒給他、眞是好姻緣喇。○[29]李四啊、爲人都有個天理良心哪、你這樣蹧蹋好人、是有罪的呀。○[30]張三哪張三哪、我們姓張的臉、都叫你自己丟了啊。

25 Is brother Wang at home? *Ans.* No, he is not at home. *Ques.* If he is not at home where has he gone? *Ans.* He has gone to market.

26 That man is very stylish; he insists on having high living and fine clothes.

27 I hear you have bought a hand stove for four hundred cash. Is it a new one or an old one? *Ans.* It is second hand, but as good as new.

28 That young man Samuel is discreet, clever and steady; if you give him your daughter it will certainly be an excellent match.

29 Li Sï! all men have a heaven-implanted conscience for the guidance of life. In thus wronging a good man you are committing a sin.

30 Chang San! Chang San! Alas, you have brought disgrace on our whole Chang family.

NOTES.

2 and **13**. The use of 得, as in these sentences, is decidedly Pekingese, though understood elsewhere, and occasionally used. 中 is used in many places in the same way, but is not *t'ung-hsing*.

5 背書 usually means *to recite*, but here it is used causatively, meaning to cause to recite; i.e., *to hear the recitation*.

9 In speaking the words 說罷咧, the two latter must be joined closely to the first and to each other, like a word of three syllables accented on the first.

11 頂回去. It is implied that the other party came with a plausible story, when a few words served to "shut him up."

14 轟你. *Shoot you out;* i.e., *drive you out or off.* A Northern word.

20 伸得大拇指頭 *To put up an erect thumb.* The Chinese hold up the thumb as a sign of resolution or of defiance; hence the meaning of this phrase.

21 In many places two 呢 would take the place of the final particles here used.

23 沒家 is a corrupt form of 沒有 used as a reply, the 家 being in most places pronounced *ka* or *kê*. It is much used in Central Mandarin. 沒呢 is used in many places in the North, but is not *t'ung-hsing*. See Les. 89.

24 成丁 *To become a man.* A youth is supposed to attain to manhood at sixteen,—to be capable of taking a wife, bearing arms, etc.

26 講究 is here used, as in the South, in the sense of 體面.

27 A 手爐 is a small brazier with a perforated cover for holding live coals. It is used for warming the hands in cold weather

LESSON LXII.

相 THE AUXILIARY OF RECIPROCITY.

相 To inspect,—is placed before the verb to which it is auxiliary. It may be joined with any transitive verb, and in most cases gives the idea of *mutual or reciprocal.* In some cases it is reflexive, and in others it simply strengthens the idea of the verb and makes up the euphony of the sentence. The idea of reciprocity is often strengthened by the addition of 互. As an auxiliary 相 is used both colloquially and in books.

第六十二課

我[1]來有一點事相求。○他[2]們倆人、互相安慰。○這[3]兩個人的面貌相似。○大[4]家坐着談談、很相得。○該[5]定規在那個地方相會。○我[6]的秉性、和你的正相反。○不[7]許他們相罵相打。○請[8]老爺過去、有事相商。○一[9]身的血脈、都是相通的。○那[10]兩個地方相隔不遠。○這[11]兩個人的話、一點也不相合。○我[12]做好人、你就怒目相看嗎。○在[13]半路上相遇、不能說許多話。○夫[14]妻二人、應該互相幫助。○你[15]不願意就罷、我也不能相強。○他[16]姊妹兩個的高矮、相差不過一寸。○老[17]兄所說的、和我的意見相同。○

TRANSLATION.

1 I have come to make a request of you.
2 They two mutually comfort each other.
3 These two persons' faces resemble each other.
4 They all sat down and talked together very agreeably.
5 We should decide where we will meet.
6 My natural disposition is exactly the opposite of yours.
7 Do not allow them to rail at and fight with each other.
8 Will your honor please go over? There is something to be consulted about.
9 The circulation of the blood is connected throughout the whole body.
10 Those two places are not far apart.
11 The language of those two men does not at all agree.
12 Do you look upon me angrily because I am good.
13 Meeting on the road as we did, we could not speak at length.
14 Husband and wife should mutually help each other.
15 If you are not willing, that is the end of it: I will not force you.
16 The two sisters do not differ in height by more than an inch.
17 What you say agrees with my opinion.

VOCABULARY.

相 *Hsiang*¹. To inspect; mutually, reciprocally; by turns:—see Sub. See *hsiang*⁴.

互 *Hu*⁴.... *Reciprocal, mutual;* responsive; with.

慰 *Wei*⁴... To soothe, *to comfort*, to tranquilize.

安慰 *An*¹ *wei*⁴...... To appease, *to comfort.*

面貌 *Mien*⁴ *mao*⁴. *The face*, countenance, physiognomy, looks.

相似 *Hsiang*¹ *sï*⁴...... Similar, *to resemble.*

相得 *Hsiang*¹ *tê*². Pleased; *agreeable;* suited, gratified.

秉 *Ping*³. To grasp, to maintain; imparted by Heaven; *natural.*

秉性 *Ping*³ *hsing*⁴. Nature; *natural disposition*, temperament.

脈 *Moä*⁴.... *The pulse;* streaks or veins; descent.

血脈 *Hsüe*⁴ *moä*⁴. The blood, *the circulation of the blood;* race; life blood.

怒 *Nu*⁴......... *Anger*, passion, rage; incensed.

怒目相看 *Nu*⁴ *mu*⁴ *hsiang*¹ *k'an*⁴. To look at angrily. (w.)

意見 *I*⁴ *chien*⁴......... *Opinion*, idea, notion.

妻 *Ch'i*¹....... A wife, a consort. Also *ch'i*⁴

反悔 *Fan*³ *hwei*³. To break a contract or promise; *to repudiate.*

天然 *T'ien*¹ *jan*²......... Natural, *instinctive.*

性情 *Hsing*⁴ *ch'ing*². Disposition, temper; *nature;* properties.

相好 *Hsiang*¹ *hao*³. *Friendly*, on good terms, intimate.

端 *Twan*¹. The origin, the end, the extremity; elementary principles; *correct*, upright; grave, modest. A classifier:—Les. 140.

常[18]在一塊兒辦事、不可相欺。○那[19]是兩相情願的事、還能反悔嗎。○他[20]們大家都是相親相愛的。○父[21]母和兒女相親、這是天然的性情。○我[22]已經給他賠過不是、如今照常相好。○你[23]和有益的朋友相交、將來品行就端方了。○弟[24]兄們有了東西、應該相讓、不該相爭。○你[25]的忠言、和他的私慾、兩不相投。○前[26]言不達後語、就是說、前後的話不相符合。○凡[27]是相敬相信的朋友、來往都是相迎相送。○今[28]有張王二人、同時起身、走一條路、張姓一天走八十里、王姓一天走七十五里、間過了五天、二人相隔若干里。

18 Constantly doing business together, we should not deceive one another.

19 That is something we mutually agreed to, and can it be repudiated?

20 They all love one another.

21 That parents and children should be attached to each other is an instinct of nature.

22 I have already made an apology, and now we are as friendly as ever.

23 If you associate with helpful friends your deportment will become correct.

24 When brothers get anything [in common] they should mutually prefer one another and not quarrel.

25 Your faithful words and his selfish desires do not harmonize.

26 Former words are inconsistent with subsequent language; that is to say, the first and last assertions do not agree.

27 All honored and faithful friends when visiting always meet each other on arrival and escort each other on departure.

28 Two men, Chang and Wang, started together to travel the same road. Chang traveled eighty *li* per day, and Wang seventy-five *li* per day; after five days how many *li* were they apart?

端方 *Twan¹ fang.¹* . . . *Correct,* upright, proper.

忠 *Chung¹*. Loyal, *faithful;* sincere; unselfish; . . . . honest, upright.

慾 *Yü⁴*. . . . . . . Inordinate desire; lust; *covetous.*

私慾 *Sï¹ yü⁴*. . . . . . . Lust, desire; *selfishness.*

投 *T'ou²*. To throw down or into; to deliver to; . . . . to cast off; to have recourse to; to intrust; *to harmonize* with; to bid for.

達 *Ta²*. To pass through; to penetrate; *to correspond;* to inform; to transfer to; to advance; all, everywhere.

符 *Fu²*. A check, a voucher; to correspond with, ... *to agree;* to verify; a charm.

符合 *Fu² hê²*. . . . . . . To correspond, *to agree.*

迎 *Ying²*. *To meet and receive as a guest;* to . . . . meet, to occur; a meeting.

NOTES.

1 The use of 相 here implies that the request is one that concerns both the speaker and the person spoken to.

6 秉性 is slightly *Wên.*

12 怒目相看 is an expression in the book form, not used in colloquial.

15 能 here indicates moral ability, hence it is rendered *will.*

19 兩相情願 The introduction of 兩 intimates that there were two parties, both of whom were willing. The euphony of the sentence joins 相 with 兩 rather than with 情願, with which it is logically connected.

20 The compound verb 親愛 is here separated, and 相 used with each part. This is a common and very forcible idiom.

23 The sentiment of this sentence is based on a saying of Confucius in the Analects, 益者三友,友直,友諒,友多聞, *"There are three friendships which are advantageous;—friendship with the upright; friendship with the sincere; and friendship with the man of much information."*

26 前言不達後語 is *Wên* in style. Note how 言 and 語 are correlated.

27 If you know that a guest is coming, it is polite to go out and meet him, and when he leaves, politeness requires you to accompany him to the door, or to the gate, or, in special cases, a short distance on his way.

第六十三課

我[1]和他不分彼此。○這[2]麼一辦、彼此都好。○朋[3]友應當彼此相愛。○你[4]們彼此都要將就一點兒。○我[5]們兩家、彼此沒有穿換/拉扯。○當[6]把善事彼此談論。○兩[7]莊的人彼此照應。○我[8]們倆、彼此很對勁兒/合脾氣。○聽[9]他們的口供、正是彼此刁賴/相賴。○大[10]家彼此相帮相助。○沙[11]景潤和黃桂香、彼此賠禮、已經和好喇。○衆[12]人彼此對看、沒有話說。○他[13]們彼此推讓、誰也不肯上坐。○我[14]先把你的話、如此如彼都告訴他了。○他[15]們兩個、心裏彼此懷恨。○夫[16]妻中有不是的事、也要彼此包容忍耐。○常[17]在一塊兒、彼

Translation

1 There is no distinction of *meum* and *tuum* between us (i.e., all mine is his and his is mine).
2 By this arrangement both are satisfied.
3 Friends ought mutually to love each other.
4 You must forbear a little with each other.
5 Our two firms have no dealings with each other.
6 We should converse together on some profitable theme.
7 The people of the two villages assist each other.
8 We two are very well mated in disposition.
9 Judging from their testimony, they are just recklessly accusing each other.
10 They mutually help one another.
11 Sha Ching Jun and Hwang Kwei Hsiang mutually made apologies and were reconciled.
12 They all looked at each other but had nothing to say.
13 Each one declined in favor of the other, no one being willing to take the upper seat.
14 I first gave him a detailed account of what you said.
15 In their hearts they two hate each other.
16 When differences occur between

LESSON LXIII.

彼此, The Pronominal of Reciprocity.

When the words 彼 and 此 are used separately they mean, *that* and *this*, *there* and *here*, *then* and *now*, etc.; but joined together, as in this lesson, they mean *mutually*, *reciprocally*. They are much used in connection with 相, of the last lesson, one form strengthening the other. When followed by 都, they may be rendered *both*. There is no accounting for the order of these words. The natural order would certainly seem to have been 此彼. When they are separated, as in (14), the natural order asserts itself.

Vocabulary.

彼 *Pi*³. . . . . That, those; there; the other.

穿換 *Ch'wan*¹ *hwan*⁴. *Dealings*, intercourse, communication.

拉扯 *La*¹ *ch'ê*³. . . . . . . The same.

談論 *T'an*² *lun*⁴. *To converse*, to discuss, to argue, to debate.

勁 *Chin*⁴. Muscular, strong, robust; stiff; *disposition*, character.

對勁 *Twei*⁴*chin*⁴. To suit, to be fitting; *agreeable*, appropriate.

供 *Kung*¹. To confess; to testify; to declare; to make a deposition. Also *kung*⁴.

口供 *K'ou*³ *kung*¹. . . . . . . *Testimony*, witness.

刁 *Tiao*¹. Perverse, seditious; unscrupulous, *reckless;* wicked, artful.

刁賴 *Tiao*¹ *lai*⁴. *To accuse recklessly*, to recriminate, to implicate others.

此那能一點過錯錯過沒有呢。○ 18 他們彼此的事、根本來歷我都曉得。○ 19 這個說是這麼樣、那個說是那麼樣、彼此都有話說。○ 20 海角天涯、是彼此相隔很遠的意思。○ 21 那時候、必有許多人厭棄我的道理、彼此互相陷害、互相怨恨。○ 22 一家子、大是大、小是小、上是上、下是下、彼此相安。○ 23 無論甚麼事情、若是太有理、人就不相信喇、你看我和李九那件事、明明他是無故的欺負我、到我去遞呈子的時候、官說必是我先得罪了他、兩家彼此有仇、他纔打我、後來那個呈子、到底不准。

husband and wife they should mutually bear and forbear.

17 Being constantly together, how can they avoid giving some little offence to each other?

18 I know perfectly the origin and history of their mutual affairs.

19 One says it was this way, and the other says it was that way; each has his own story.

20 "The corner of the ocean and the limit of heaven," expresses the idea that things are very widely separated.

21 At that time many shall reject my doctrine, and shall betray one another and hate one another.

22 When in a family great and small, superiors and inferiors, keep their places there is mutual harmony.

23 No matter what it is, if it be too plausible, men will not believe it. Look at that affair between me and Li the Ninth. Manifestly he abused me without cause; yet when I went to enter suit against him, the magistrate said I must have previously offended him so that there was enmity between us, on account of which he beat me; and so finally he refused to entertain the suit.

沙 *Sha*¹. . . . Sand, gravel; reefs; gritty; friable.

潤 *Jun*⁴. To moisten, to bedew; to instill into; . . . . . . to enrich, to benefit; increase, profits.

桂 *Kwei*⁴. . . . . . . Cinnamon; cassia.

香 *Hsiang*¹. Fragrant; reputable; perfume; in- . . . . cense. Much used in names.

賠禮 *P'ei*³ *li*³. . . . To make amends, *to apologize.*

推讓 *T'wei*¹ *jang*⁴. To yield the precedence, to . . . . give way to, *to decline.*

懷恨 *Hwai*² *hên*⁴. *To hate*, to cherish enmity, ... to hold spite.

包容 *Pao*¹ *jung*². To be generous, to make allowance for, *to forbear.*

過錯 *Kwoă*⁴ *ts'oă*⁴. A fault, a transgression, *an* . . . . *offence.*

錯過 *Ts'oă*⁴ *kwoă*⁴. . . . . . . The same.

根 *Kên*¹. Root; origin, source; cause; the base; . . . . . . fundamental. A classifier:—Les. 68.

根本 *Kên*¹ *pên*³. *Origin*, source; foundation; . . . . proof, evidence.

歷 *Li*⁴. To pass over or through or away; to expe- . . . . . rience; arranged in order; *successive.*

來歷 *Lai*² *li*⁴. . . . Antecedents; *history;* annals.

涯 *Ai*², *yai*². . . . . Bank, shore, water line; *limit.*

棄 *Ch'i*⁴. To throw away, *to reject;* to discard; . . . . to abandon.

厭棄 *Yien*⁴ *ch'i*⁴. *To reject with disdain*, to cast . . . . off, to throw away.

陷害 *Hsien*⁴ *hai*⁴. To victimize; to implicate; . . . . *to betray.*

怨恨 *Yüen*⁴ *hên*⁴. . . . . *To hate*, to detest.

遞 *Ti*⁴. . . . To transmit; *to hand in;* to change.

呈 *Ch'êng*². To state to a superior, to present; . . . . a plea, a suit, *an accusation.*

准 *Chun*³. To permit, to authorize, *to allow;* to . . . . approve, to grant,—as a petition.

第六十四課

我[1]已經商議他兩回。○淨[2]白跑了一趟。○他[3]欺負我不只一次喇。○這[4]一下子砸了鍋喇。○他[5]被我羞辱了一頓。○這[6]一遭、我叫他氣的眼珠子都藍了。○我[7]勸過他一回、他不肯聽。○頭[8]一次講書、還算可以。○一[9]番一番的太煩數了。○前[10]五年我來一回。○兩[11]點鐘怎麼只響了一下呢。○

Translation.

1 I have already consulted with him twice.
2 I had the whole trip for nothing.
3 He has imposed upon me not only this once.
4 I have lost my living this time.
5 I gave him a *meal* of disgrace.
6 He made me so angry this time that my eyeballs turned blue.
7 I exhorted him once, but he would not listen.
8 As a first effort at preaching it is very fair.
9 Time after time, it is too troublesome.
10 I came once five years ago.
11 It is two o'clock, how is it that it struck only one?

Notes.

1 To hold all you have at the service of your friend is the ideal friendship.

2 The 一 may be omitted, but the sentence is much more forcible with it.

5 家 is here used as "house" is used in English, to designate a business firm. 穿換 is used of the intercourse of business firms. Social intercourse is expressed by 來往. In some places 來往 is used in both senses.

8 The two forms here given are not precisely synonymous. 對勁兒 includes suitability in other respects besides disposition, to which 脾氣 is limited.

13 上坐 *To take the higher or more honorable seat.*

14 如此如彼 *As this as that;* i.e., *one by one in order.*

16 The use of 也 implies that the sentence is in addition to something which preceded it. It is from the Sacred Edict.

20 海角天涯 is a book phrase, occasionally heard in colloquial.

22 子 is not infrequently added to 家. 大是大小是小、上是上下是下 *Great is great and small is small, upper is upper and lower is lower;* i.e., *each knows and keeps his proper place.* This peculiar form of repetition represents a common idiom.

LESSON LXIV.

Adverbial Numerals.

一回 One return,—one time, once.

一次 One order,—one time, once.

一遭 One meet,—once. Much used in Northern and Central Mandarin, but rarely heard in the South.

一番 One repeat,—one turn or time, once.

一趟 One course,—one time, one. Often written 一蹚. Authorities differ as to which is the proper character.

一下 One down,—a time, a stroke; at once.

一下子 At one time, at once.

一頓 One meal,—a spell, a time, once.

一合 One union,—a round, an onset, a tilt. Used chiefly in books, and applied to horsemen.

一發 One send off,—a time, once.

一程子 One road,—a spell, a while, a stage; the distance from one stopping place to another.

一陣 One burst,—a spell, a time.

一遍 One whole,—a round, a time, once.

一向 One direction,—a while, for some time; formerly.

一氣 One breath,—a spell, a heat, once.

一磨 One rub,—a time, once.

一場 One arena,—a time, a bout, a round.

These several terms are to some extent interchangeable, yet each has its own shade of meaning, and its appropriate place can only be learned by experience.

Other numerals than *one* may be joined with any of these words.

我[12]從小只看見過一遭海市。○這[13]一遭我算認得你喇。○一[14]頓水餃子(扁食)、把肚子鐣壞了。○我[15]看了一遍、不大難學。○長[16]毛賊第二番來、比頭一番還利害。○是[17]在這裏住下呀、還是再走一程呢。○二[18]位將軍、大戰了三十二合、沒分勝敗。○一[19]回相見一回老、能得幾時爲弟兄。○人[20]能點個翰林、也算不枉念了一回書。○他[21]做了一氣(一程)子買賣、把本錢都賠淨了。○我[22]種了一回牛痘、後來又出(生)了一回天花(天喜)。○張[23]大哥、這一向不知流落那裏去了。○一[24]年這麼一遭、能不給大爺(大爺爺)磕幾個頭嗎。○你[25]的心口還疼嗎、答早晨疼了一陣、現在又好了。○一[26]遭生、

12 From my youth I have only once seen the mirage.
13 I rather think I know you this time.
14 That mess of meat dumplings has overloaded my stomach.
15 I looked over it once, it is not very hard to learn.
16 The second time the long-haired robbers came they were worse than the first time.
17 Shall we stop here, or shall we go on another stage?
18 The two generals fought thirty-two tremendous tilts, and the victory was still undecided.
19 Each time we meet we are older: how little time there is for the enjoyment of fraternal affection!
20 If a man can attain the degree of Han-lin, he may consider that his life of study has not been in vain.
21 He went into business for a time, and lost all his capital.
22 I was vaccinated, and afterwards had the small-pox the natural way.
23 I wonder where brother Chang has drifted to by this time.
24 Should we not once in a year knock heads to your honor?
25 Does your stomach still pain you? *Ans.* It pained me a spell this morning, but is now well again.

VOCABULARY.

逷 *T'ang*^{4}. To pass by; to fall; the track in which horses run; *a time, a heat, a course, a row.*

番 *Fan*^{1}. To repeat; to change; *a time, a turn;* rude, uncivilized; foreign.

羞辱 *Hsiu*^{1} *ju*^{4}. To put to shame, to insult, *to disgrace;* to outrage.

藍 *Lan*^{2}. . . . . . . *Blue;* indigo.

講書 *Chiang*^{3} *shu*^{1}. To expound the classics; to discourse on a text; *to preach.*

數 *Soă*^{4}. Worried, flurried, *distracted:*—see *shu*^{4}, and *shu*^{3}.

煩數 *Fan*^{2} *soă*^{4}. . . . . . . Involved; *troublesome.*

響 *Hsiang*^{3}. To resound; *to ring;* noise, clamor, echo.

海市 *Hai*^{3} *shï*^{4}. . . . . The mirage.

扁食 *Pien*^{3} *shï*^{2}. . . . . Meat dumplings.

餃 *Chiao*^{3}. . . . . Meat dumplings.

鐣 *Ch'êng*^{1}. To gormandize; the sense of oppression caused by eating too much, *to overload the stomach.*

將軍 *Chiang*^{1} *chün*^{1}. A commandant, *a general,* a chieftain.

戰 *Chan*^{4}. . . . . . . *To fight,* to join battle; war.

勝 *Shêng*^{4}. To get the victory; to excel; to rise superior to, to sustain; adequate.

翰林 *Han*^{4} *lin*^{2}. A graduate of the third degree, *a Han-lin.*

本錢 *Pên*^{3} *ch'ien*^{2}. . . . . . . First cost; *capital.*

痘 *Tou*^{4}. . . . . . . The small-pox.

牛痘 *Niu*^{2} *tou*^{4}. . . . . . . The cow-pox; *vaccine.*

兩遭熟、三遭就是老主顧。○這[27]一程走的太快、把我弄累乏倦了。○你[28]這一程子往那裏去來、怎麼沒有見你呢。○我[29]看他這一次來、比前一次還胖一點。○這[30]樣做一會歇一會、不如一氣做完了。○姓[31]張的那個老婆子一磨一磨的常來騷擾我。○我[32]只打了他一下、他就儘量罵了我一頓、我也沒法兒還口。沒能反腔沒有的回嘴○你[33]不用掛心、我先和他鬧一場再說。○[34]那一場麥子、已經打了兩遍、還沒打淨。○彗[35]星出現、有幾年一次的、有幾十年一次的、有幾百年一次的。○這[36]孩子眞沒有個記性、昨兒個他媽窯他撒賴、打了他一大頓、今兒個他又忘記了。

26 The first time a stranger, the second time acquainted, and the third time an old customer.

27 I (or, we) have gone this stage too fast, I find myself quite wearied.

28 Where have you been for some time? How is it that I have not seen you?

29 In my opinion he is somewhat fatter than he was the first time.

30 This way of working a while and resting a while is not as good as to finish at one heat.

31 That old woman Chang comes constantly, time after time, and worries me.

32 I struck him only one blow, whereupon he exhausted his whole vocabulary of abuse upon me, and I was unable to get the better of him.

33 You need not be concerned; after I have had a bout with him we'll talk about it.

34 I have threshed that wheat on the floor twice, and it is not yet clean.

35 Comets appear, some once in several years, some once in several tens of years, and some once in several hundreds of years.

36 Truly this child has no memory. Yesterday his mother gave him a sound beating for his contrariness, and to-day he has forgotten it.

天花 *T‘ien1 hwa1*. . . . . The small-pox.

天喜 *T‘ien1 hsi3*. . . . . The small-pox.

流 *Liu2*. To flow; to circulate, to diffuse; *to wander*, to become reckless; vagrant, shifting; a class, a set.

流落 *Liu2 loa4*. To wander, to rove, to roam, *to drift;* a prodigal.

心口 *Hsin1 k‘ou3*. . . . . The pit of the stomach.

主顧 *Chu3 ku4*. . . . . . . *A customer;* a patron.

倦 *Chüen4*. . . . . . . Tired, fatigued, *wearied.*

騷 *Sao1*. To disquiet; to fidget; perturbed, grieved; the male of animals.

擾 *Jao3*. To incommode, *to embarrass;* to confuse, to annoy.

騷擾 *To harass*, to annoy; to embarrass.

儘量 *Chin3 liang4*. To carry to the uttermost, *to exhaust;* to do one's best.

腔 *Ch‘iang1*. A tune; the brogue or dialect of a place; conceited, vain.

反腔 *Fan3 ch‘iang1*. To turn the tune, *to get the better of.*

還口 *Hwan2 k‘ou3*. To answer back, to retort, to rejoin.

回嘴 *Hwei2 tswei3*. . . . . The same.

掛心 *Kwa4 hsin1*. To be anxious, *to be concerned about.*

彗 *Hwei4*. . . . . . . A besom; *a comet.*

彗星 *Hwei4 hsing1*. *A comet;* a star of ill omen.

出現 *Ch‘u1 hsien4*. *To appear;* to come forth, to manifest.

記性 *Chi4 hsing4*. . . . . Memory.

撒賴 *Sa1 lai4*. To pretend to be injured; to impose upon, to levy blackmail; to importune; *to act contrarily.*

第六十五課

我[1]出門纔回來、家裏還沒安排/安置好。○你[2]纔知道他有個倔彊脾氣嗎、這幾年還强的多喇。○剛/纔[3]說曹操、曹操就到。○我[4]方纔聽見一個信兒說、學院/學臺初三日從青州起馬/上馬。○我[5]纔來的時候、他剛/彊會說話、如今已經成了大漢子喇。○李[6]奇文哥在這裏嗎、答眞不湊巧、他等了你一點多鐘、剛纔/彊纔走喇。○他[7]這麼大的年紀、

TRANSLATION.

1 I was away and have just returned, and have not yet put the house in order.

2 Have you just now found out that he is stubborn? He is much improved these last few years.

3 As soon as you speak of Ts'ao Ts'ao, he is at hand.

4 I have just now heard a report that the examiner will leave Ch'ing-chou [for this place] on the third.

5 When I first came he was just able to talk; now he has come to be a full grown man.

6 Is Mr. Li Ch'i Wên here? *Ans.* How very unlucky! He waited for you over an hour, and has just now gone.

NOTES.

2 淨 is here translated *all.*

4 Lit., *I have smashed the kettle this time.* In China everything is cooked in a kettle, and to smash this kettle means nothing to eat. Used when one loses a position or opportunity on which his living depends.

6 The Chinese assert that when a man is filled with suppressed anger his eyes turn *blue.*

12 海市 *A sea market;* i.e., streets and people pictured in the clouds over the sea.

13 Said to one by whom you have been cheated, and meaning that you will be on your guard against him in the future.

14 For meat dumplings, 扁食 is the more proper and widely used term. 水 is added to 餃 because the dumplings are boiled in water. They are also called 煑餃子, and in Shantung *ku[1] tsi[3]*. 肚子 usually means the bowels rather than the stomach, but is here used indefinitely for both. It requires both *overloaded* and *disordered* to convey the meaning expressed by 餺壞了.

19 A saying which originated in the words of a celebrated official, reproving two brothers for going to law about the division of their father's estate.

20 The prime idea of seeking an education in China is to get a degree, and by this means become an official, and so get rich.

22 In many places the more familiar term for vaccination is 種花.

24 大爺 here means, not an uncle (as it usually does), but simply a man of wealth or high standing who has servants and other employés. In speaking, the accent is thrown on 爺. In the South 大爺爺 is used in the same way. "Your Honor," is only an approximate rendering. The occasion of the *k'oă t'ou* is probably the New Year, and is insisted on in expectation of a present.

26 The language of a shop-keeper to a new customer.

34 一場 does not here illustrate the lesson, being used in its primary and literal sense.

35 Comets are colloquially called 掃箒星, *broom stars.*

LESSON LXV.

THE IMMEDIATE PAST LIMITED BY THE PRESENT.

纔 Just now, immediately preceding. In previous lessons 纔 has already been used in the sense of *before; in order that.*

剛 Just this moment. Not often used alone.

剛纔 or **纔剛** Just, just now, just this moment. The two forms are interchangeable. The former, perhaps, indicates the more immediate present. The former is preferred in the South, the latter in the North.

方 A little ago, just now; recently. 方 is not quite as colloquial as 纔. It is also used like 纔 to mean *before; in order that.*

方纔 Just now, just a moment ago.

剛剛 Just this very moment. For still further emphasis the 剛剛 is sometimes preceded by 纔, and sometimes followed by it. 方 and 纔 are not doubled as 剛 is.

彊 is used in the South in the same way and with the same sense as 剛 in the North. In Central Mandarin both forms are used, 剛 predominating;—See Les. 177.

他女人怎麼纔二十多歲呢、答這是續弦後婚。○我8昨天眞是好時運、一天也沒叫雨淋給雨沰着、纔剛彊到家、就下大了。○纔9出鍋屜的饅頭、喫兩個再走罷。○借10光老先生、有一個背包袱的、從這裏過去了沒有、答剛剛纔過去喇。○從11多少日子、你就吵嚷吵嚷着說媳婦、現在說妥中了沒有、答那裏說妥中了呢、剛纔有點邊兒、又叫仇人打了破頭楔喇。打破了搗翻了○就12這麼樣、他是不肯給出力的、必得在他手裏行點賄賂賄纔行。○你13就是不怕拉饑荒、空方纔還的不大離喇、你又拉了這麼些。○若14有知己的

7 When he is so old as this, how is it that his wife is just in her twenties? *Ans.* This is a second marriage.

8 I was very fortunate indeed yesterday. It did not rain on me the whole day; but I had barely gotten home when it began to rain heavily.

9 Rolls just from the kettle;—eat a couple before you go.

10 May I trouble you, old gentleman? Did a man carrying a bundle on his back pass by here? *Ans.* He has just this moment passed by.

11 You have been stirring round this long time to get a wife. Is it now satisfactorily settled? *Ans.* It is far from settled. Just when it was in a fair way to be arranged, it was broken up by an enemy.

12 Simply leaving matters thus, he will not make any exertion. It will first be necessary to put a bribe in his hand.

13 You are not the least afraid to run into debt. Having just now fairly paid up, you go again and contract all this debt.

Vocabulary.

置 *Chï*^{4}. To dismiss, to put aside; to establish; to place, *to arrange;* to buy, to lay in.

安置 *An*^{1} *chï*^{4}. . . . . . To arrange, *to put in order.*

倔 *Chüe*^{2,4}. . . . Obstinate, perverse, opinionated.

彊 *Chiang*^{4}. *Stubborn,* impracticable, obstinate. The same as 强. Also *chiang*^{1}.

倔彊 *Stubborn,* impracticable, mulish, headstrong.

彊 or 强 *Chiang*^{1}. Barely; nearly, almost; scarcely, just, just now:—See *chiang.*^{4} Peking teachers often write 將 for the meanings here given to 强, but 將, being everywhere *soft,* is not allowable where hard sounds are used.

曹 *Ts'ao*^{2}. Officials; judge of appeals; a company, a class; sign of the plural in *Wên-li.*

曹操 *Ts'ao*^{2} *Ts'ao*^{1}. A famous brigand and general:—See Note 3.

學院 *Hsüe*^{2} *yüen*^{4}. . . . . . . A literary chancellor.

學臺 *Hsüe*^{2} *t'ai*^{2}. . . . . The same.

青州 *Ch'ing*^{1} *chou*^{1}. A departmental city in central Shantung.

婚 *Hun*^{1}. . . . A bridegroom; to marry; *marriage.*

後婚 *Hou*^{4} *hun*^{1}. . . . . A second marriage.

續 *Hsü*^{4}. To second; to join on; to keep up; tied together, continuous.

弦 *Hsien*^{2}. . . . . . . A lute or fiddle string.

續弦 To marry a second wife.

運 *Yün*^{4}. To revolve; to move in a circuit; to transport; a turn, a chance; luck, *lot.*

時運 *Shï*^{2} *yün*^{4}. . . . . *Fortune,* luck.

淋 *Lin*^{2}. To drop; *to wet,—as by rain;* to sprinkle. Also *lin*^{4}.

沰 *Toä*^{4}. . . . To drop, to drip; to wet, *to rain on.*

借光 *Chie*^{4} *kwang*^{1}. May I trouble you, please Sir.

楔 *Hsie*^{1}. . . . . . . A wedge.

破頭楔 *P'oä*^{4} *t'ou*^{2} *hsie*^{1}. A wedge driven into a crack or split.

搗 *Tao*^{3}. To beat with a mallet, to pound in a mortar; to reel, *to wind.*

搗翻 *Tao*^{3} *fan*^{1}. To tangle, to jumble, *to thwart,* to knock to pieces.

賄 *Hwei*^{4}. . . . . . . Riches; *a bribe,* hush money.

賂 *Lu*^{4}. . . . . To bribe, to corrupt.

人、方可託他帶去、若沒有就罷。○我[15]病了剛纔起來、身上一點力氣沒有、好歹扎掙着纔走了去了。○我[16]們今天走的早一點、起身的時候、日頭剛剛出來。○聽[17]說那塊壞骨頭、跌斷了腿、把我歡喜的沒法、這纔眞是現報喇。○纔[18]來的那位馬老爺、是個甚麼前程呢、答是個世襲的守備。○人[19]當血氣方剛的時候、應當自戒、不可和人爭鬪。○他[20]纔要伸手拿、我就喝了一聲、一下把他嚇獃了、嘴裏亂哦哦、也說不出句話來。

14 If you have a confidential friend, you may entrust it to him to bring; if not, no matter.

15 I have been ill and have just gotten up. I have no strength at all. It was only by special exertion that I was able to come.

16 We started a little earlier to-day. When we left the sun had but just appeared.

17 I am delighted beyond measure to hear that that worthless villain has fallen and broken his leg. Without doubt this is a manifest retribution.

18 What rank has that Mr. Ma who has just now come? *Ans.* He is a hereditary major.

19 When a man first attains the strength of his manhood, he ought to restrain himself, and not fight with people.

20 When he was on the point of putting forth his hand to take it, I gave one shout, which frightened him out of his wits. He muttered something with his lips, but was unable to say anything.

賄賂 *A bribe*, a present intended as a bribe.

拉空 *La*^{1} *k'ung*^{4}. . . . . . To run in debt.

拉饑荒 *La*^{1} *chi*^{1} *hwang*^{1}. To contract debts with no means of paying.

扎 *Cha*^{2}. To brace up, to put forth effort, to strain. Also *cha*^{1}.

扎掙 *Cha*^{1} *chêng*^{4}. To brace oneself for a vigorous effort, to put forth all one's strength; to try one's best.

現報 *Hsien*^{4} *pao*^{4}. Immediate and manifest retribution.

前程 *Ch'ien*^{2} *ch'êng*^{2}. Honorary degree, rank, previous standing.

襲 *Hsi*^{3}. Double, repeated; to attack by stealth; to plagiarize; *hereditary.*

世襲 *Shï*^{4} *hsi*^{3}. . . . . . Hereditary rank.

守備 *Shou*^{3} *pei*^{4}. . . . . A military title, a major.

血氣 *Hsüe*^{4} *ch'i*^{4}. *Physical vigor*, constitution; the animal feelings, the flesh.

自戒 *Tsï*^{4} *chie*^{4}. *To restrain oneself;* temperance; watchfulness.

爭鬪 *Chêng*^{1} *tou*^{4}. . . . . *To fight*, to brawl.

哦 *O*^{1}. . . . . To chant, to hum; *to mutter.*

NOTES.

3 曹操 was a noted usurper of the Han dynasty. For military strategy and unprincipled artifice and usurpation, he is the most noted character in Chinese history. The sentence is a saying analogous to, "Speak of the devil and he will appear."

4 起馬 or 上馬. *To start;*—a term only applied to officials, and no doubt fixed in the language when it was the custom of mandarins to travel on horseback. They now ride in chairs with four or eight bearers. Although not so said, it is fairly implied, that the examiner was starting *towards* the place of the speaker.

9 屜 is here used of the platter on which the rolls are laid in the kettle while steaming. The sentence is the call of a huckster by the wayside.

10 A question or inquiry preceded by some polite expression, such as is here used, will nearly always elicit a respectful reply. An abrupt question often fails to do so.

11 從多少日子 *From many days;* i.e., *for a long time.* 打破頭楔 *To make a crack or split by driving in a wedge,*—used metaphorically of one who interferes and breaks up or defeats any business or scheme. A Peking expression.

第六十六課

中[1]國每五年閏兩個月。○各[2]人的孩子各人親。○你[3]逢來就該敲門。○每[4]樣要一點兒。○衙[5]門每逢三八放告。○各[6]式各樣的都有。○你[7]每月能掙多少錢。○我[8]們是各管各事。○各[9]人當盡各人的本分。○從[10]前他每逢進京、必來看看、現在已經五六年沒有來喇。○他[11]每日在廳前、伺候呼喚。○師[12]傅領進門、修行在

Translation.

1 In every five years China intercalates two months.
2 Every man loves his own child.
3 Every time you come you should knock at the door.
4 I will take a little of each kind.
5 In the yamên there is opportunity every third and eighth day to enter suit. [hand.
6 Every kind and style are kept on
7 How much money can you earn each month? [affairs.
8 Each one of us attends to his own
9 Every man ought to do his own duty.
10 Formerly whenever he came to the capital he always came to see us; but five or six years have now passed that he has not come.
11 He was every day at the door of

13 你就是不怕拉饑荒 The force of 就 is hard to express in English. Paraphrase thus:—*The thing you are not afraid to do is to run in debt.*

16 走的早一點 might also mean, *We started a little too early.*

17 那塊壞骨頭 *That piece of rotten bone,*—a coarse phrase used to signify that a person is thoroughly worthless and detestable. 歡喜的沒法 *To be delighted beyond all power of expressing or containing the emotion.* Men are not wanting in China who feel no shame in proclaiming their spite as is here done.

19 剛 does not here form a phrase with 方, but is used independently as a verb, meaning *to become strong or mature.*

20 一下 here means *all at once, suddenly.* 亂 is frequently prefixed to verbs to express wild or irregular action.

LESSON LXVI.

Distributive Pronouns.

各 Each, every. } 各 is *each* inclusive of all,
每 Each, every. } while 每 is *each* severally.

When 各 is repeated, the second 各 is rendered *own.* (8) (9)

各自 Each his own, each for himself. (16)

自各 I myself, you yourself, he himself. (17)

In colloquial 自各 is often expanded into 自各兒 or 自己各兒.

逢 To meet,—though not properly a distributive, becomes one when applied to time, or to the repetition of an act, and means, *every time, as often as.*

每逢 Every time, as often as.

In Central and Southern Mandarin 逢 is freely used alone, but in Peking it is rarely used save in combination with 每.

Vocabulary.

每 *Mei*³. *Each, every; each one;* constantly; always.

逢 *Fêng*². To meet unexpectedly; to happen, to occur; *every time, as often as, whenever.* Also *p'ang*².

閏 *Jun*⁴. *To intercalate;* intercalary.

衙門 *Ya*² *mên*². *A yamên,* a government office, an official establishment.

放告 *Fang*² *kao*⁴. To receive indictments.

呼喚 *Hu*¹ *hwan*⁴. *To call,*—as a servant.

修行 *Hsiu*¹ *hsing*⁴. To reform, *to practise virtue.*

恤 *Hsü*¹˒⁴. To feel for, *to commiserate;* pity, sympathy.

憐恤 *Lien*² *hsü*⁴. To pity, *to compassionate.*

歸 *Kwei*¹. To return; *to revert;* to restore; to betake oneself to; to belong to; to go home; to divide by one figure.

各人。○王13老爺很憐恤人、有逢求必應。○把14這幾綹線、各歸各色。○每15逢冬天、我就咳嗽。○將16軍不下馬、各自奔前程。○這17個事情、得你自各兒(自己)去。○軍18營中、每逢三六九操演。○中19外各國、人情自然相同。○我20要賞你們每人一塊洋錢。○我21們這裏是逢四九趕集、你們貴莊呢、答我那敝莊兒上、是逢五排十。○兩22個人從那兒分手、各走各路。○每23逢禮拜六、我要算賬。○坡24上有王家的花園、內

the audience room waiting on [his master's] call.

12 The teacher explains first principles; to practise them rests with the person himself.

13 Mr. Wang is very compassionate; he responds to every plea.

14 Take these few skeins of thread, and assort them according to their colors.

15 I have a cough every winter.

16 The generals did not dismount, but each pursued his own road.

17 This business requires that you should go yourself.

18 In the encampment they drill every third, sixth and ninth day.

19 In all countries, Chinese and foreign, human nature is necessarily the same.

20 I wish to make you each a present [of a dollar

21 We here, hold markets on every 4th and 9th. How is it in your honorable village? *Ans.* In my unworthy village the markets are set for every 5th and 10th.

22 From that time the two separated, and each one went his own road.

綹 *Liu*^{3}. . . . . . . A skein of silk.

冬 *Tung*^{1}. . . . . . . *Winter;* the end; to store up.

咳 *K'ê*^{2}. . . . . . . *To cough,* to hack. Also *hai*^{1}.

嗽 *Sou*^{4}. . . . . . . *To cough;* to expectorate.

咳嗽 *To cough,* to hack and cough.

奔 *Pên*^{1,4}. To run, to go; *to hasten;* to follow; . . . . to be busy with; to fly, to hurry.

軍營 *Chün*^{1} *ying*^{2}. . . . . An encampment.

演 *Yien*^{3}. Ample, extended, *to practise,* to exercise; to perform; to drill.

操演 *Ts'ao*^{1} *yien*^{3}. . . . . . . *To drill,* to parade.

自然 *Tsï*^{4} *jan*^{2}. That which exists or acts of . . . . itself; natural, *necessary,* spontaneous; certainly, of course.

賞 *Shang*^{3}. *To give a reward,* to confer on; a . . . . prize, a reward.

敝 *Pi*^{4}. Bad; *unworthy;* a demeaning term for . . . . . . *my, mine;* to stop, to close:—Les. 171.

分手 *Fên*^{1} *shou*^{3}. To go apart, *to separate;* to . . . . take leave of.

異 *I*^{4}. Different, diverse; unusual, *rare;* heterodox; to regard as strange, to marvel at.

酒病 *Chiu*^{3} *ping*^{4}. *Given to wine,* intemperate.

喝醉 *Hê*^{1} *tswei*^{4}. *To get drunk,* to become in- . . . . toxicated.

佛 *Fê*^{2}, *Fu*^{2}. . . . . Buddha.

忌 *Chi*^{4}. To shun, *to avoid,* to keep aloof from; . . . . . . to dread; to dislike, to be jealous.

忌口 *Chi*^{4} *k'ou*^{3}. To refrain from eating meats, ... to fast.

戒口 *Chie*^{4} *k'ou*^{3}. . . . . . . The same.

揭短 *Chie*^{1} *twan*^{3}. *To find fault with;* to re- . . . . proach for a fault; to publish the shortcomings of others; to slander.

防備 *Fang*^{2} *pei*^{4}. To prepare for; *to be on guard* . . . . *against;* to be beforehand with.

巡 *Hsün*^{2}. *To go round and inspect;* to patrol; . . . . to cruise.

撫 *Fu*^{3}. To rub, *to quiet;* to soothe; to cherish; . . . . . to manage; to play,—as on a lute.

巡撫 The governor of a province.

閱 *Yüe*^{4}. To examine, *to inspect;* look over; to . . . . read over carefully.

閱邊 *Yüe*^{4} *pien*^{1}. To make a tour of inspection. . . . . Note 30.

公館 *Kung*^{1} *kwan*^{3}. An official stopping place, ... *a reception room;* a pub-

有各種異草奇花。○ 他[25]有個酒病、逢喝酒就喝醉了。○ 佛[26]道兩家、每逢初一十五、就必忌口。○ 各[27]人說各人的理來、不可彼此揭短。○ 不[28]常有病的人、每逢得病就不輕。○ 我[29]們各自防備、不被他偷也就是了。○ 巡[30]撫下來閱邊、各府州縣、都得預備公館、大小官員、也要行點敬意。○ 三[31]嫂子不要爲喫穿作難、你若眞有守節的心、我每年帮你五十兩銀子過日子就是了。

23 I wish to settle accounts regularly every Saturday.

24 On the declivity is the flower garden of the Wang family in which is every kind of rare plant and curious flower.

25 He has a weakness for wine, so that every time he drinks it he is certain to get drunk.

26 The two sects, Buddhists and Taoists, require to abstain [from meat] every first and fifteenth of the month.

27 Let each man state his own case, and not each find fault with the other.

28 When one who is generally healthy gets sick, his sickness is always severe.

29 It behoves us each to be on his guard that he does not steal from us.

30 When the governor goes round on a tour of inspection, it is necessary for every prefect and magistrate to prepare reception rooms for him, and officers of all grades are expected to make presents.

31 My third sister-in-law, do not be troubled about food and clothing. If you really desire to remain a widow, I will help you each year, to the extent of fifty taels.

lic hall; the head-quarters of a company or society.

員 *Yüen*^{2}. . . . . . . Any officer civil or military.

官員 *Kwan*^{1} *yüen*^{2}. *Officers of all ranks;* . . . . grandees.

敬意 *Ching*^{4} *i*^{4}. An expression of respect, *a* . . . . *present,* a largess.

嫂 *Sao*^{3}. *An elder brother's wife;* a woman, a . . . . lady, a matron.

作難 *Tsoă*^{4} *nan*^{2}. *To be in trouble,* to be embar- . . . . rassed, to be in straits.

守節 *Shou*^{3} *chie*^{2}. To remain a widow, to be true . . . . to a deceased husband.

Notes.

1 The month, in China, is determined by the changes of the moon, thus giving only about three hundred and fifty-four days to twelve months. In order to make up the loss, a month is intercalated as often as necessary,—about two in five years. The month intercalated varies, being settled by the Astronomical Board in Peking.

5 **每逢三八**; that is, the 3rd, 8th, 13th, 18th, 23rd and 28th of every month. This is the established custom in all yamêns. An indictment *may* be presented at other times by paying a special fee.

8 **人** is to be understood after each **各**. If fully expressed it would be **各人管各人的事**.

12 The original reference is to the cultivation of virtue, but the sentence is often used, by accommodation, of ordinary learning, and even of manual skill.

16 This sentence, from a standard novel, is often quoted and applied to the affairs of ordinary life, **前程** being taken in its metaphorical sense.

21 In North China, markets are held in the cities and in all large villages once in five days, and those in the same vicinity are arranged so as not to come on the same days. Note the different form of expression when the market occurs on the fifth and tenth. This form is probably used to avoid the juxtaposition of five and ten, which would make fifty. When the month has only twenty-nine days, the market that would have come on the 30th comes on the first of the following month.

24 **異草奇花** is a book expression but, as used in this connection, would be understood by most people.

26 **家** here means a school or sect. When spoken of as a religious observance, **忌口** means to abstain from meats, but when used in connection with the administration of medicine, it means to abstain from anything that may be incompatible with the medicine. Abstinence from meats on the 1st and 15th is mostly confined to the priests, and is not always observed by them.

29 Lit.,—*that we are not stolen by him.* The meaning is, however, *that our goods are not stolen by him.* **也就是了** *The best we can do, etc.*

30 The **府, 州, 縣**, are three grades of cities in a descending series. Each governor is expected to make a tour of

第六十七課

他[1]處處不肯給人方便。○人[2]人都這麼說、我也不知是眞是假。○你[3]天天打這裏過、都是往那裏去呢。○這[4]種軟簾紙、囫圇的少、差不多張張都有毛病。○羅[5]先生說話、實在淸楚、句句字字、沒有聽不眞切的。○月[6]月掙八吊錢、年年還得拉空賬嗎。○他[7]是回遭回遭圖小利、圖慣了。○你[8]說的句句都是實話、最可嘆的、就是人都能說不能行。○醜[9]事家家有、不漏是好手、誰敢保那些沒有丟醜的、都比他好强呢。○此[10]地、是我們南

TRANSLATION.

1 He will not oblige in anything.

2 Everybody says so, but I do not know whether it is true or false.

3 You pass by here every day; where are you always going?

4 There is scarcely any of this *jwan lien* paper whole, almost every sheet has some defect.

5 Mr. Loă speaks very clearly, there is not a sentence nor a word that is not distinctly heard.

6 You earn eight thousand cash every month, and yet you run into debt year by year!

7 He is always looking out for small gains until it has become a habit.

8 What you say is every word true, but the unfortunate thing is that while all can preach, they can not practise.

9 Every family has some disgraceful secret; they who do not let it out are clever. Who would venture to assert that they whose shame is not known are any better than he is?

inspection to all the principal places in his jurisdiction at least once, during his incumbency of three years. Officials resident on his route have to provide entertainment for him and his retinue, and all officers are expected to make him a present. If any should omit it, or give too little, he would soon find that there was some reason justifying his removal.

31 The highest attainment of female virtue is for a young widow to remain a widow for life, and this idea is extended to, and finds its highest exemplification in, the case of a girl whose betrothed dies before marriage. In point of fact, however, in the middle and lower classes, the majority of young widows do marry again, and it is but a rare thing that a girl whose betrothed dies before marriage, remains unmarried for life.

LESSON LXVII.

DISTRIBUTION BY REPETITION.

The idea of *each* or *every* is often expressed by repeating the word of which it is affirmed; as 人人 every man, 天天 every day, etc. This idiom is analogous to the English, man by man, day by day, etc. We have thus seen that repeating *an adjective* emphasizes it, Les. 19; repeating *a verb* specializes the idea and intensifies it, Les. 33; and repeating *a noun* makes it distributive.

VOCABULARY.

簾 *Lien*[2]. . . . . . A curtain, a screen, *a scroll.*

軟簾 *Jwan*[3] *lien*[2]. . . . . A kind of writing paper.

囫 *Hu*[2]. . . . . . Round, whole.

圇 *Lun*[2]. . . . . . Finished.

囫圇 *Whole,* entire, complete.

壯 *Chwang*[4]. Stout, *robust,* hardy, healthy; . . . . manly; flourishing; to incite.

整壯 *Chêng*[3] *chwang*[4]. Regular, orderly; entire, ... *whole.* (s.) [Les. 109.

眞切 *Chên*[1] *ch'ie*[4]. . . . . . Plain, *distinct,* clear.

拉賬 *La*[1] *chang*[4]. To run up an account, *to go* . . . . *into debt.*

嘆 *T'an*[4]. . . . . To sigh, to groan; *sad;* to praise.

漏 *Lou*[4]. To leak, to drip; to disclose, *to let out;* . . . . . to forget, to omit; to smuggle.

京的平常(凡常)話、人人都這樣講。○神[11]的十條誡、條條我都犯了、我的罪愆、高過我的頭頂。○凡[12]在回教的人、個個都齊鬍子。○劉[13]景清很會畫畫、他所畫的像、就和照的像差不多。○若[14]天下個個都是好兒子、好兄弟、天下自然常常太平。○地[15]圖是將地的形勢、一一畫清。○我[16]本處人、都傳說他的事、家家戶戶沒有不知道的。○興[17]極必衰、衰極必興、天下萬國、處處都是一理。○俗[18]語說、件件(樣樣)通、件件(樣樣)鬆、就是說人要精於那一樣、必得專於那一樣。○書[19]中的大旨、我還記得、要章章節節都背出來、節節都講

10 *T'sï ti* is a common phrase with us in Nanking; every one uses it.

11 I have broken all the ten commandments of God. My sins have gone over the top of my head.

12 Every Mohammedan cuts his beard square.

13 Liu Ching Ch'ing is very good at painting pictures. The portraits he paints are almost equal to photographs.

14 If all in the world were good sons and good brothers, the world would, of course, be always peaceful.

15 A map is a distinct drawing of the several features of the earth.

16 His affairs are reported among all our people; there is not a family or household that does not know them.

17 When anything has flourished to the utmost, it must decline; and when it has declined to the utmost, it must begin to flourish. Throughout the world, the same principle everywhere prevails.

18 The saying runs, "He that is jack of all trades is master of none": that is to say, he who would excel in anything must give his whole attention to it.

19 The general scope of the book I still

敢保 *Kan³ pao³*. To guarantee, to assure, to warrant, to wager.

丟醜 *Tiu¹ ch'ou³*. To expose oneself to contempt, to disgrace oneself.

平常 *P'ing² ch'ang²*. Ordinary, *common*, usual, customary.

凡常 *Fan² ch'ang²*. The same. (s.)

回教 *Hwei² chiao⁴*. The Mohammedan religion:—Note 11.

誡 *Chie⁴*. *A command*, a precept; a warning.

愆 *Ch'ien¹*. A fault, *an error;* a failure.

罪愆 *Tswei⁴ ch'ien¹*. A transgression, *a sin*, a short-coming.

頭頂 *T'ou² ting³*. The top of the head.

太平 *T'ai⁴ p'ing²*. *Peaceful*, quiet.

形勢 *Hsing² shï⁴*. Aspect; outline, contour; shape; *configuration*.

傳說 *Ch'wan² shwoă¹*. *To report*, to pass from mouth to mouth; a rumor; a tradition

興 *Hsing¹*. To rise, *to flourish;* prevailing, fashionable; to hoax. Also *hsing⁴*.

極 *Chi²*. *The utmost point*, the extremity; extremely; to reach the end, to exhaust.

旨 *Chï³*. Intention, purpose; *scope*, sense; imperial will, a decree, an order.

筆直 *Pi³ chï²*. Straight, *straight as a line*, direct:—Les. 149.

一直 *I¹ chï²*. *Straight*, direct; forthwith, immediately:—Les. 162.

疃 *T'wan³*. A village, a hamlet. Used only in Central and Western Mandarin.

岔 *Ch'a⁴*. A fork in the road; a branch, a divergence; to mistake, to go wrong.

批 *P'i¹*. *To criticize*, to revise; to give judgment on a communication from an inferior.

號 *Hao⁴*. *A mark*, a sign; a style or appellation; a signal, a call, a summons; to mark; to label. A classifier:—Les. 147. Also *hao²*.

記號 *Chi⁴ hao⁴*. *A mark*, a sign; a token, a motto.

出來、我實在不能。○
20 從這裏上辛店、打那裏走呢、答出了村疃、步步往西北走、一點岔道沒有、一筆直直的就去喇。○
21 我見中國書上、有點點的、有圈圈的、是什麼意思呢、答那是批書的記號、最好的就圈圈、次一等的就點點。

remember, but to repeat every chapter and expound every verse, is really more than I can do.

20 Which way do you go from this to Shin Tien? *Ans.* When you get out of the town, go on directly northwest; there is no fork in the road, just go on straight as a line (pen).

21 I notice dots and circles on Chinese books; what is the meaning of them? *Ans.* They are the marks of the critic. Where the style is very good he makes circles, where it is not quite so good he makes dots.

NOTES.

3 都 here refers to the number of times, and hence, means *always*.

4 種 is dropped out in the translation. If you should translate, as would seem natural, *this kind of jwan lien paper, etc.*, you would miss the meaning, which is not that this particular kind of *jwan lien* paper is faulty, but that *jwan lien* paper in general, is faulty.

9 他 here refers to some one who had been mentioned before. 强 is commonly used for "better" in Central and Northern Mandarin, but is not often so used in the South.

10 此地 is generally used by the non-mandarin dialects south of the Yang-tse for 這裡. It is sometimes used in the North, but its constant use marks any dialect as, by so much, an impure Mandarin. The use of 講 for 説 is also characteristically Southern.

12 The classifier is repeated instead of the noun. Almost any classifier *may* be thus repeated instead of the noun, though, in many cases, the general classifier, 個, is substituted for the specific classifier. Mohammedans are commonly designated as 回回教, but they, generally, speak of themselves as 在教, which accounts for the phraseology here used. They are also called 回子, but this term is not considered respectful.

13 畫畫 is a repeated word, but does not illustrate the lesson. It is introduced here to put the learner on his guard. The first 畫 is a verb, and the second, a noun. The Chinese language, especially the *Wên-li*, is very partial to this form of expression. See also 21.

15 一一 *One by one*, that is, each one in order,—the common form of expressing this idea.

17 This sentence sets forth a stock idea of Chinese philosophy.

18 This proverb is the exact equivalent of our "Jack of all trades and master of none," and is more briefly and elegantly expressed.

20 打那裡 *By which way?* As here used, 打 is quite *t'ung hsing*, but a number of other forms are in use in various places. I have heard 把 and 跟 and 起, also *ma* and *man* and *ka*. 從 also, is properly used in this sense, though not often so used colloquially.

LESSON LXVIII.

CLASSIFIERS.

棵 Classifier of trees.

科 A class or order,—classifier of herbs, grains and shrubs. There is much confusion in the use of these two classifiers. I have given the distinction which seems most natural, and which is commonly observed.

乘 A span or team,—classifier of sedan chairs and vehicles other than those on wheels.

雙 Double,—classifier of things in pairs.

口 Mouth,—classifier of members of a family, kettles, hogs, etc.

副 An assistant,—classifier of buttons and of things in sets, also of doses of medicine. In writing, 付 is not infrequently used instead of 副.

劑 A dose,—classifier of doses of medicine (S).

間 A partition,—classifier of rooms or compartments. Note 28.

根 Root,—classifier of strings, sticks, and, generally, of things long and narrow.

堆 A pile,—classifier of things in heaps.

疋 Classifier of pieces of cloth.

輛 A chariot,—classifier of wheeled vehicles,

第六十八課

我[1]有十雙絨襪子。○李[2]潤發家裏、有八口人。○還[3]少兩雙筷子。○管[4]保一副（保管一劑）藥就好了。○我[5]典了三間房子。○可[6]以抽一根綫給我。○後[7]園裏、有十二棵櫇菓樹、八棵梨樹。○這[8]科金銀花、實在香。○他[9]兩口子要分家。○把[10]那根頭髮揑（捻）下來。○石[11]頭、是二千八百斤爲一堆。○一[12]根草、有一根草的露水養。○八[13]個大錢、買了一副鈕（釦）子。○今[14]天我要用這口鍋煮衣裳。○他[15]一科莊稼沒有、就是仗着手藝過日子。○再[16]過三天、我要回家、可以給我僱一

TRANSLATION.

1 I have ten pairs of woollen stockings.
2 Li Jun Fa has a family of eight.
3 We are still short two pairs of chopsticks.
4 I will guarantee that one dose of medicine will cure him.
5 I leased a house of three rooms.
6 Draw out a thread and give me.
7 There are twelve apple trees and eight pear trees in the back yard.
8 This honeysuckle is exceedingly fragrant.
9 The two heads of the family are going to separate.
10 Pluck out that hair.
11 Two thousand eight hundred catties of stone make one cord.
12 Every blade of grass has its own dew to nourish it.
13 I bought a set of buttons for eight cash.
14 I intend to use this kettle to-day to boil the clothes.
15 He hasn't a stalk of grain, but depends entirely on his trade for a living.

VOCABULARY.

雙 *Shwang*^{1}. A pair, a couple; both; double; even:—see Sub. Also *shwang*^{4}.

副 *Fu*^{4}. An assistant, a deputy, a vice, an alternate; a duplicate:—see Sub.

棵 *K'ê*^{1}. Used only as a classifier:—see Sub.

堆 *Twei*^{1}. A pile, a heap, a mound; to heap up, to store:—see Sub.

乘 *Ch'êng*^{4}. A span, a team:—see Sub. Also *ch'êng*^{2}.

疋 *P'i*^{3}. Used only as a classifier:—see Sub.

輛 *Liang*^{4}. A chariot:—see Sub.

絨 *Jung*^{2}. Floss; velvet; woollen cloth; *worsted;* nap, down; punk.

筷 *K'wai*^{4}. Chopsticks.

劑 *Chi*^{4}. To trim, to cut even; to portion out; *a dose*, a prescription:—see Sub.

保管 *Pao*^{3} *kwan*^{3}. Same as 管保.

綫 *Hsien*^{4}. The same as 線.

櫇 *P'in*^{2}, *p'ing*^{2}. A water plant.

菓 *Kwoa*^{3}. Fruit, berries, nuts, etc.

櫇菓 A species of apple—quite large, but spongy and insipid.

梨 *Li*^{2}. Pears—of which there are many kinds in China.

揑 *Nie*^{1}. To take with the fingers, to pluck; to knead; to fabricate, to trump up.

捻 *Nie*^{1}, *nien*^{3}. To pinch, *to nip,* to hold with tongs or nippers; to twist.

金銀花 *Chin*^{1} *yin*^{2} *hwa*^{1}. The honeysuckle.

分家 *Fên*^{1} *chia*^{1}. To divide the inheritance; *to live separately.*

兩口子 *Liang*^{3} *k'ou*^{3} *tsï*^{3}. Husband and wife.

露 *Lu*^{4}. *Dew*, mist; to bless:—See *lou*^{3}.

露水 *Lu*^{4} *shwei*^{3}. Dew.

苫 *Shan*^{2}, *chan*^{1}. To thatch; a coarse grass used for thatch; a mat.

苫子 A rude mule litter covered with matting.

駝轎 *T'oa*^{2} *chiao*^{4}. A mule litter.

紗 *Sha*^{1}. *Silk gauze;* crape.

顏 *Yien*^{2}. Countenance, visage; *color,* hue.

顏色 *Yien*^{2} *sê*^{4}. *Color,* hue.

光潤 *Kwang*^{1} *jun*^{4}. Smooth, polished; shining, *brilliant.*

乘駝(苫)轎(子)。○
17 你看那一疋紅紗、顏色兒鮮光明潤不鮮光明潤。○
18 我南山上的穀、叫你的牛喫了二三十科。○
19 我看見他圈裏、養着兩口大肥豬。○
20 在家裏穿着這雙舊鞋罷、那雙新的、留着出門。○
21 山東娶親、有用兩乘(頂)轎的、有用四乘(頂)轎的。○
22 你今天出去、可以給我買三疋白布、一疋灰色紬子。○
23 前院子有五科花兒、兩科月月月(季)紅、兩科玫瑰、一科牡丹。○
24 十來口人喫飯、只這一口鍋弄(做)、實在不方便。○
25 買了兩科黃(白)芽菜、用錢六十文、八根(科)蔥、用錢十二文。○
26 王

16 In three days I am going home. You may hire a mule litter for me.
17 Look at that piece of red silk gauze; is not the color brilliant?
18 Twenty or thirty stalks of my millet on the south hill were eaten up by your cow.
19 I saw that he kept two big, fat hogs in the sty.
20 Wear this pair of old shoes at home, and keep that pair of new ones to go out with.
21 At weddings in Shantung, some use two sedan chairs and some, four.
22 When you go out to-day, you may buy for me three pieces of white cotton cloth, and one piece of ash colored silk.
23 There are five flowering bushes in the front yard,—two monthly roses, two red roses and one shrub peony.
24 With upwards of ten persons to eat and only this one kettle to cook in, the cooking is very inconvenient.
25 I bought two heads of cabbage for sixty cash and eight onions for twelve cash.

鮮 *Hsien*¹. Fresh, new; *bright*, clean. Also *hsien*³.

鮮明 *Hsien*¹ *ming*². New, *bright*, brilliant, resplendent.

穀 *Ku*³. Grain; cereals; *millet*.

豬 or 猪 *Chu*¹. A hog, a pig.

娶親 *Ch'ü*³ *ch'in*¹. To take a wife.

紬 *Ch'ou*². *Coarse silk*, pongee; a clue, a thread; to investigate, to follow up.

季 *Chi*⁴. A season of the year, *a period;* a younger brother.

月季 *Yüe*⁴ *chi*⁴. The monthly rose.

月月紅 *Yüe*⁴ *yüe*⁴ *hung*². Same. (s.)

玫 *Mei*². A bright red pearl, a garnet.

瑰 *Kwei*⁴. A red pearl; rare, admirable.

玫瑰花 The red rose.

牡 *Mu*³. The male of quadrupeds, of a few birds, and of some plants; a bolt, a piston.

丹 *Tan*¹. *Carnation color;* cinnabar; a medicinal concoction, a pill; sincere, loyal.

牡丹花 The shrub peony.

蔥 *Ts'ung*¹. Onions.

大車 *Ta*⁴ *ch'ê*¹. A freight cart.

轎車 *Chiao*⁴ *ch'ê*¹. A passenger cart.

小車 *Hsiao*³ *ch'ê*¹. A wheelbarrow.

黃泥 *Hwang*² *ni*². *Clay*, earth.

聘 *P'in*⁴. To ask; *to betroth;* to espouse.

聘禮 *P'in*⁴ *li*³. Betrothal presents.

定禮 *Ting*⁴ *li*³. Betrothal presents.

戒指 *Chie*⁴ *chi*³. A finger-ring.

墜 *Chwei*⁴. To sink, to descend; to fall, to crumble; a pendant, *an ear-ring*.

鉗 *Ch'ien*². Pincers, nippers, tongs; *a clasp:*—see Note 29.

耳挖 *Êr*³ *wa*¹. An ear-pick or scoop.

簪 *Tsan*¹. A pin or skewer to fasten the hair, a hair-pin.

陪 *P'ei*². To assist; to accompany; *to match;* to act as second or mate.

被擱 *Pei*⁴ *kê*¹. A low cabinet on which the bedding is laid during the day. It stands across the head of the *k'ang* or bed.

燈臺 *Têng*¹ *t'ai*². *A lamp stand;* a lamp-post; a light-house.

鋪蓋 *P'u*¹ *kai*⁴. Bedding.

太太拿着一些頭繩子、給大學生每人一根黑的、小學生每人一根紅的。○27西邊車店裏、今日兒晚上、來了八輛大車、五輛轎車、十三輛小車。○28在他大門外、有九堆石頭、一堆黃泥、一堆細沙、聽說要蓋兩間廂房。○29他都送的什麼聘定禮呢、答有兩疋藍粗洋布、一疋紅洋機布、一副鐲鐲頭子、四兩個副戒指、兩副鉗墜子、一根耳挖子、三根簪子。○30那頭陪送的甚麼呢、答一口大櫃、一口小櫃、兩個皮箱、兩把椅子、一個被擱子、一個大鏡子、再是銅盆、燈臺、鋪蓋、枕頭、樣樣都有。

26 Mrs. Wang took some hairstrings and gave the large pupils each a black one and the small pupils each a red one.

27 There arrived this evening at the cart inn to the west, eight freight carts, five passenger carts and thirteen wheelbarrows.

28 Outside his front gate are nine piles of stone, a heap of clay and one of fine sand. I hear he is going to build two side rooms.

29 What all did they bring for betrothal presents? *Ans.* Two pieces of strong blue foreign cloth, one piece of fine red foreign cloth, one pair of bracelets, two pairs of finger-rings, two pairs of ear-rings, one ear-pick and three hair-pins.

30 What outfit was given with the bride? *Ans.* One large clothes press, one sideboard, two leather trunks, two chairs, one cabinet and one large mirror, besides wash-basin, lamp stand, bedding and pillows, all complete.

NOTES.

1 Woollen stockings are of foreign manufacture. The Chinese do not *knit* their stockings, but make them of cotton cloth.

5 *Lease* is not quite an accurate translation of 典, which is an indefinite lease in consideration of a round sum paid down at the first, but the property is subject to redemption by the owner at any time, or after the lapse of some specified time, usually three years. If not redeemed within forty years, it is not redeemable except in the case of land with graves on it. 典 is not properly (as sometimes translated) to *mortgage*, which is expressed by 押, although in drawing a mortgage the term 典 is used, for the reason that 押 is illegal. There is in this case, however, no possession given as in the case of a real 典. Thus a *mortgage* in China is a lease given, but held in abeyance by the lessee, with power to take possession in case of failure to pay as promised.

9 口 may here be regarded either as a classifier of 家 understood, or as a noun standing for *member of a family*. 分家 properly means to divide the inheritance between brothers, but is sometimes used, as here, of the separation of husband and wife.

12 The idea is that in the economy of nature, man included, the wants of everything are provided for.

14 Or, *I want to use this kettle, etc.* Which meaning was intended would be indicated in speaking by the stress put on 用. Boiling clothes, in washing them, is a foreign custom.

16 The 苫子 is used only in North China, and there only in hilly country where carts cannot be used.

21 In the case of two chairs, one is for the bride, the other for the groom. In the case of four, the two extra chairs are, one for the 將迎客, the other for the 送迎客. The former, who rides in the front chair, is an elderly woman of the groom's friends, the latter, who rides in the rear chair, is an elderly woman of the bride's family. For 頂 as a classifier see Les. 125. It was not intended to introduce it here, but the Pekingese called for it.

26 The Chinese say *head strings* for hair strings.

27 Wheelbarrows are extensively used in North and West China for the transportation of goods.

28 A pile, or cord, of building stone is in some places understood to mean a definite quantity of from 2,400 to 2,800 catties, in other places it is like a pile of earth or sand, quite indefinite. 兩間廂房 *a side building of two rooms.* 間 does not necessarily nor properly mean *a room*, but, rather, the space enclosed between two girders in the roof which are supported by posts in the wall, and with which the partitions usually coincide. The size of houses is indicated by the number of these *chien*.

29 洋機布 is, in some places, a particular quality of foreign cotton cloth, fine and strong, in other places it simply means foreign cotton cloth of any quality. Ear-rings are called 鉗子 in Peking, because they clasp into the ear.

第六十九課

前[1]幾天、我教蔣炳文好罵。○你[2]不看眼目神行事、好沒眼色。○他[3]客廳屋裏、有兩張八仙桌子、四把泰山椅子、一張條几、都擺設的好齊整的。○這[4]架薔薇、開的實在多、可惜好快要謝喇。○逢[5]樂羣有個好體面女兒、就是脚大一點兒。○王[6]三爺說話、好大口氣。○你[7]說你是好人、我看你是個好混帳人。○你[8]去罷、好快要上學喇。○好[9]大膽子一個大膽的李鵬九、我的事情、他就敢做主嗎。○[10]他三天沒念會一號書、今日教先生好一頓打。前天上的書、今天還沒有背過來、給先生一頓好打。○這[11]幾個錢、他還捨

TRANSLATION.

1 I was soundly berated by Chiang Ping Wên a few days ago.

2 Why did you not suit your actions to the circumstances? You have not the least discernment.

3 He has in his drawing-room two square tables, four arm-chairs and one long sideboard, all very neatly arranged.

4 This climbing rosebush has on it a great many roses. I am sorry they are about to drop off.

5 P'ang Loă Ch'ün has a very fine looking daughter, except that her feet are a little large.

6 Wang San Yie speaks in a very pompous style.

7 You say you are a good man. As I see it, you are a good rascal.

8 Be off; it is time to go to school.

9 That Li P'êng Chiu is mighty bold that he should venture to control my affairs.

10 In three days he has not learned one lesson, and to-day the teacher gave him a good flogging.

LESSON LXIX.

MISCELLANEOUS USES OF 好.

In addition to its ordinary normal use, 好 has a great variety of peculiar uses most of which are brought together in this lesson. They cannot be analysed or classified. 好 is a little like the English word *well*, "*only more so.*" Like other words, however, it has its proper place and should not be made to do service on all occasions.

VOCABULARY.

蔣 *Chiang*³...... An aquatic plant; *a surname.*

炳 *Ping*³...... Bright, luminous.

眼目 *Yien*³ *mu*⁴. The eyes; *the expression of the eyes.*

眼神 *Yien*³ *shên*². The expression of the eyes as indicative of the thoughts or the feelings.

眼色 *Yien*³ *sê*⁴. Discrimination, *discernment,* judgment, sense; a wink, a hint.

客廳 *K'ê*⁴ *t'ing*¹. Reception hall, parlor, *drawing-room.*

客屋 *K'ê*⁴ *wu*¹..... Parlor, *drawing-room.*

仙 *Hsien*¹. A human soul with divine powers, a genius, a fairy.

八仙桌 *Pa*¹ *hsien*¹ *choă*¹. A square dining table seating eight persons:—Note 3.

泰 *T'ai*⁴........ Exalted; honorable; liberal.

泰山 *T'ai*⁴ *shan*¹. The most noted sacred mountain in China, situated sixty miles south of Chinanfu, in Shantung.

泰山椅 *T'ai*⁴ *shan*¹ *i*³. A high backed arm-chair:—Note 3.

几 *Chi*¹.... A bench; a low table; *a side table.*

條几 *T'iao*² *chi*¹. A long narrow table, *a sideboard.*

設 *Shê*⁴. To institute; *to arrange,* to set out in order; to suppose; if:—Les. 132.

……不得花、眞好小器(氣)。○
12現在疼的輕一點、就是早起(上)疼了一陣好的。○
13我給你抬着送去罷、答好說、不敢勞駕。○
14我看你好不知趣、人家都哭、你怎麼在那裏笑呢。○
15不多時候、飯就好喇、等吃一點再走罷。○
16好(不)容易交一個朋友、你就(好)輕易得罪他嗎。○
17你去借條口袋來、我明天好去趕集。○
18不(這)說(就)催促你喇、答好說、躭誤你用喇。○
19別的都好說、就是這些孩子、沒有地方交代(託)。○
20先和他好說、他若實在不肯、再應許賠他、

11 He even grudges to spend these few cash. Really, he is niggardly.

12 The pain is a little lighter now, but this morning it was awfully severe for a while.

13 Let me take it for you. *Ans.* Thanks, I could not think of troubling you.

14 It seems to me you are wholly wanting in a sense of the fitness of things. Why do you stand there and laugh when others are weeping?

15 Dinner will be ready before long. Wait and eat a little before you go.

16 Is it so easy to make a friend that you should lightly offend him ?

17 You go and borrow a bag, so that I can attend market to-morrow.

18 I beg pardon for pushing you. *Ans.* Not at all. I am sorry to have inconvenienced you.

19 The other matters can be readily arranged, but there is no one to whom I can entrust these children.

20 First try to persuade him, and if he

擺設 *Pai*³ *shê*⁴. To spread out in order, *to arrange*, to display.

齊整 *Ch'i*² *chêng*³. Uniform, even, *neat*, orderly, regular.

薔 *Ch'iang*². A red rose.

薇 *Wei*². A kind of fern, greens.

薔薇 A climbing rose, the cinnamon rose.

逄 *P'ang*². A surname. See *fêng*².

羣 *Ch'ün*². A flock, a herd; a company, *a multitude;* the whole.

混 *Hun*⁴. Mixed, disorderly; *to do or act in a heedless or reckless manner*, to shift, to eke out, to slur over. See *hun*².

混帳 *Hun*⁴ *chang*⁴. Unreasonable; vicious, recreant; worthless.

膽 or 胆 *Tan*³. The gall; courage, *boldness.*

鵬 *P'êng*². A fabulous bird.

小器 *Hsiao*³ *ch'i*⁴. Mean spirited, narrow minded, stingy, *niggardly.*

小氣 *Hsiao*³ *ch'i*⁴. Same.

早起 *Tsao*³ *ch'i*³. The morning.

駕 *Chia*⁴. A chariot; to drive or sit in a chariot; to mount, to ascend; *to avail of.*

勞駕 *Lao*² *chia*⁴. To trouble one,—a polite phrase of apology.

輕易 *Ch'ing*¹ *i*⁴. For small cause, *lightly;* rarely, seldom:—Les. 161.

口袋 *K'ou*³ *tai*⁴. A bag, a wallet.

催促 *Ts'wei*¹ *ts'u*⁴. To drive, to urge; to dun, *to push;* to insist on.

交代 *Chiao*¹ *tai*⁴. To deliver to, to hand over; *to entrust to.*

交託 *Chiao*¹ *t'oa*¹. To put in the hands of, *to entrust to;* to consign to.

漓 *Li*². Water dropping, the pattering of rain.

漓溜羅嗦 *Li*² *liu*¹ *loa*² *soa*¹. Prolonged and confused, complicated.

羅裏羅嗦 *Loa*² *li*³ *loa*² *soa*¹. Same.

蔡 *Ts'ai*⁴. A small feudal state; *a surname.*

惠 *Hwei*⁴. Kindness, grace, *liberality;* charity, favor; to be kind to, to bestow.

卿 *Ch'ing*¹. A noble, a lord.

淵 *Yuen*¹. A whirlpool; an abyss; *vast.*

博 *Poa*²,⁴. Ample, spacious; intelligent, *learned;* to barter; to gamble.

淵博 Profound in learning.

提拔 *T'i*² *pa*². To raise up, to assist, *to help.*

情趣 *Ch'ing*² *ch'ü*⁴. Taste, savor, relish, satisfaction.

也還不遲。○請[21]放心罷、那個人很好說話、敢保不能不答應。○那[22]個人就是好說話、說起來、漓溜囉唆囉裏囉唆、沒有說完的時候。○把[23]信寫好了、可以念給我聽聽、再封起來。○這[24]場官司、他也不過花了十幾吊錢、答好錢哪、花了四十多吊咧。○蔡[25]惠卿先生、好淵博體面的學問、寫的字也不錯。○我[26]花錢費事的提拔他、還落了許多的不是、一尋思想起來、好沒滋味情趣。○這[27]一課很不好做、也不知好學不好學。

positively refuses, it will be time enough to agree to pay damages.

21 Please do not worry. That man is very reasonable. I guarantee you he will be willing.

22 That man is an inveterate talker; when he once begins, he strings it out without end.

23 When you have finished writing the letter, read it to me before you seal it up.

24 He did not spend more than ten or fifteen thousand cash in this lawsuit. *Ans.* He didn't, eh? He spent over forty thousand.

25 Mr. Ts'ai Hwei Ch'ing is a man of very fine scholarship; his handwriting, also, is quite good.

26 I spent money and effort to help him along and yet a great deal of fault is found with me. I feel vexed whenever I think of it.

27 This lesson was very hard to make. I don't know whether it will be easy to learn, or not.

NOTES.

2 Although no interrogative form is expressed, the interrogation is implied in the first clause. In Chinese, reproof is generally in the interrogative form. The sentence might, of course, be taken in the direct indicative form, but, in that case, would hardly justify the emphatic expression that follows.

3 八仙桌 *Eight fairy table,* a high sounding name for a square table that will seat eight persons. 泰山椅子 *Tai Shan chairs,* high backed chairs with arms at the sides. *Tai Shan* is used as a fancy name in allusion to the high back of the chair.

7 There is here a play on the word 好,—*a good rascal; i.e.,* one that is fully up to the standard of ordinary rascality, *a grand rascal.*

9 The name is made emphatic by being put in this peculiar way.

10 一號 *one mark; i.e., one lesson.* Chinese teachers usually mark lessons by pasting a small strip of red paper at the point to which the lesson extends. This paper is called a 號, and is put for the lesson which is marked by it. A different phraseology prevails in the South where 上 is used for setting a lesson, but there is no way of expressing the noun "lesson." Hence the Southern teacher insisted on recasting the whole sentence as given,—avoiding, as will be noticed, the use of the noun "lesson." 好一頓打 and 一頓好打 express the same idea. Teachers differ in their choice of the two forms.

13 The term 抬, here used, implies that there was a third party who carried the other end of the pole. 好說 is the common response to a compliment, or to expressions of thanks or of self-depreciation. 不敢勞駕 *not venture to trouble your carriage,*—the word carriage being put by metonomy for the person. People worthy of honor are supposed to ride in carriages.

16 The meaning, strange to say, is substantially the same whether the negative be used or not.

17 The word 一 is elided colloquially before 條.

18 不說催促你喇 This is the language of one who, having vigorously urged payment, now receives the money. The force of 不說 is,—I will omit the usual apologetic forms for having inconvenienced you by my urgency. The sentence may also be used of a borrowed article.

22 好說話 Notice the different meaning of this phrase in this, and in the preceding sentence; also the different tone of 好.

23 可以 is omitted in the translation. It is often used in Chinese when its equivalent is not needed in English. It serves to soften what might otherwise seem too much like a command.

24 好錢哪 A very idiomatic expression not readily analysed. It is, perhaps, put for 好多錢. The translation gives the exact force.

25 The Southern teachers reject 體面 and substitute 淵博, which, in the North, is decidedly *Wén.* If it be used, the translation should be *profound* instead of *respectable.*

第七十課

請[1]先生給我寫個信皮兒、好不好、答好啊。○把[2]這個帽子、好生愼收着、不要叫烟燻喇、答是喇。○今[3]兒張家出殯、請問太太願意出去瞧瞧熱鬧嗎、答可以。○古[4]人都說是太陽轉、到底不是太陽轉嗎、答不是。○我[5]娶親那一天、把你的靴子、借給我穿穿、好不好、答好、現成。○請[6]老爺看看、這個樣子中不中、答中、行不行、答行、這個樣子就不錯。○等[7]他來的時候、你可以把我的話告訴

TRANSLATION.

1 Would you be so kind, sir, as to address an envelope for me? *Ans.* Certainly.

2 Put this hat carefully away, and do not allow it to become tainted with smoke. *Ans.* All right.

3 The Chang family have their funeral to-day. We would enquire if you, madam, wish to go and see the display. *Ans.* I believe I will.

4 The ancients all said that the sun revolved [round the earth]. After all, does the sun not revolve? *Ans.* No.

5 Would you be willing to lend me your boots to wear on my wedding day? *Ans.* Certainly. They are at your service.

6 Will the gentleman please examine whether this manner [of doing it] will answer? *Ans.* Yes, it will answer very well.

LESSON LXX.

YES AND NO.

是 Yes. The Chinese use the substantive verb 是 as their most common affirmative. It corresponds more nearly than any other word in the language to our word *yes*, though in many places it will not replace *yes*.

是的 Yes. This form is generally used in the South, and sometimes, in the North.

是是 Yes, yes. An emphatic assent. It is generally used by inferiors assenting to the commands of superiors—Aye, aye, sir. It is also used to indicate impatience—yes, I know.

就是 So be it, all right. See Les. 44.

喳 or **嗻𠴨** Yes, sir, or madam,—a Manchu word. It is rarely heard away from Peking, save in yamêns, where everybody apes it.

好 or **好啊** A cordial assent,—very well, all right.

行 or **行啊** It will do, it will work. Often marks a concession more or less reluctant.

中 or **中啊** It will do, so be it; that will do, that's enough. 啊 is generally added to 好, 行 and 中, and sometimes to 是, but is spoken lightly.

可以 A qualified assent, that is, *consent*, you may, all right. This term has given rise to the pidgin English phrase, "can do."

對 That's so, you're right. An emphatic assent.

是喇 The 喇 is added sometimes for euphony, and sometimes for emphasis. It is added in like manner to 好, 行, 中, and especially to 對.

不 No. It applies to the present and the future. When past time is referred to, 沒 or 沒有 is used instead. A light 啊 is often added to 不.

不是 No. Generally less emphatic than 不 without 是.

不行 Won't work, cannot allow it, "no go."

不中 Won't do, cannot allow it. Used in Shantung but is not *t'ung hsing*.

不錯 No mistake, that's so, of course.

一點不錯 Not the least mistake, precisely, to be sure.

那是不錯 That's certain, that's so, of course.

也好啊 } **也可以** } The use of 也 marks some change of thought or idea, in consequence of which the assent is given.

Affirmation and negation are often expressed by simply repeating the principal verb of the interrogative sentence, with or without 不, as the case may be, as in 你懂得官話嗎 答懂得, *Do you understand Mandarin? Ans. I do.* This principle is in fact illustrated in (1), (5), (6).

他、答是。是的。○你[8]要慢慢的套他、若是逼問的急了、他還不曉得你是什麼心思、你想他敢告訴你嗎。答不錯。○還[9]是二分利嗎、我聽說是分半利、答不。○你[10]只管拿給他看看、若是如意、他就留下、不如意、還是我的東西、答就是。○若[11]事中沒有他的牽連、怎麼每逢提起來、他就吃覺驚呢、答一點不錯。○婆[12]婆不苦待媳婦、也就彀了、還能叫媳婦倒管着嗎、答那是不錯的。○你[13]若不和他立下合同、以後他必反覆、答對喇、我早聽說、他有那樣的毛病。○在[14]這裏要玩幾天再走罷、答不啊咯、明天是我堂兄的三週年、今天必得家去。○他[15]不給錢、我們不好上他

7 When he comes, you may tell him what I said. *Ans.* Yes, I will.

8 You will have to pump him gradually. If you interrogate him too eagerly, he will not know what your purpose is, and do you think he will tell you? *Ans.* Of course not.

9 Is the interest two per cent [per month]? I heard it was one and a half per cent. *Ans.* No.

10 Don't hesitate to bring it for him to see. If it pleases him, let him keep it; and if it does not please him, he need not take it. *Ans.* All right.

11 If he were not concerned in the affair, why should he be alarmed every time it is mentioned? *Ans.* That's so.

12 It is sufficient if the mother-in-law does not abuse her daughter-in-law; can she be expected to let her daughter-in-law rule over her? *Ans.* Of course not.

13 If you do not have a written agreement with him, he will certainly go back on you. *Ans.* That's so. I have heard that he has that weakness.

14 Stay here and recreate a few days before you go. *Ans.* No, I must go home to-day. To-morrow is the third anniversary of my cousin's death.

VOCABULARY.

信皮 *Hsin⁴ p'i²*. The outside of a letter; the paper in which a note is enfolded and which serves as an envelope.

熏 *Hsün¹*. Vapor, fumes; to fumigate, *to smoke;* to perfume; to suffocate.

烑 *Ch'iao³*. *To smoke,* to soil.

請問 *Ch'ing³ wên⁴*. *To enquire;* a polite form of question,—please tell me.

瞧 *Ch'iao²*. *To look at,* to glance at, to take a peep at.

轉 *Chwan⁴*. A revolution; to turn round, *to revolve,* to circulate; to go round a corner. See *chwan³*.

靴 *Hsüe¹*. A boot.

逼問 *Pi¹ wên⁴*. *To interrogate,* to cross question; to demand an answer.

只管 *Chï³ kwan³*. Only, simply; *without hesitation,* freely, just:—Les. 83.

牽 *Ch'ien¹*. To drag along; to pull,—as a boat, to lead, to induce; *to implicate.*

牽連 *Ch'ien¹ lien²*. *To be concerned* or implicated in, connected with.

瓜葛 *Kwa¹ kê²*. *Concerned,* entangled in, involved, implicated.

苦待 *K'u³ tai⁴*. To treat with severity, to maltreat, to abuse.

驚 *Ching¹*. Frightened, terrified, *alarmed.*

吃驚 *Ch'ï¹ ching¹*. Startled, *alarmed.*

覺驚 *Chioa² ching¹*. To feel alarmed; *to manifest alarm:*—Note 11.

合同 *Hê² t'ung²*. *Agreement,* contract, indenture, covenant.

堂兄 *T'ang² hsiung¹*. A first cousin of the same family name.

週年 *Chou¹ nien²*. A full year, the whole year, *anniversary.*

館子去請客、和他頂(抵)賬嗎、答一點不錯、這就是個好法子。〇我[16]再限你們三天的期(限)、若再拿不了人來、我要重重的責治你們、答喳喳(是是)、大老爺的恩典。〇上[17]房已經叫別人包(佔)去喇、先生看看這個房子(屋)、行不行、答行啊。〇我[18]們不賺(尋)他的就罷了、還能賠着賣給他嗎、答那是不錯的。〇李[19]文運要借兩吊錢的盤費、託我來商議、先生願意借給他不願意、答可以、你去請他來罷。〇我[20]看六十里路、僱兩個牲口、至多用六百錢、答不行、這正是個忙時候、六百錢沒有去的。〇聽[21]說他的功課很忙、從早到晚、一點閒空沒有、是嗎、答對(是)喇(的)、他沒有閒空是不錯的。〇你[22]拿不了、就把這個蒲

15 If he will not pay, suppose we get up a company and go to his restaurant and have a feast on account. *Ans.* To be sure: that is a good idea.

16 I will give you three days more. If you then fail to produce the man, I'll punish you severely. *Ans.* Aye, aye, your honor is very gracious.

17 The best room is already occupied. Please, sir, look at this room and see if it will answer. *Ans.* It is all right.

18 It is enough if we do not make anything off him; we can not sell to him at a loss. *Ans.* Of course we can't.

19 Li Wên Yün wants to borrow two thousand cash for travelling expenses, and asks me to speak with you and ask whether, or not, you are willing to lend it to him. *Ans.* Well, yes. Go and call him in.

20 It seems to me that six hundred cash, at the most, should hire two animals for sixty li. *Ans.* It can't be done. This is a very busy time. No one is willing to go for six hundred cash.

21 I hear that his studies keep him very busy, so that he has no leisure from morning till night. Am I correct? *Ans.* You are indeed. That he has no leisure is emphatically true.

館 *Kwan*^{3}. . . . . . . Same as 舘.

請客 *Ch'ing*^{3} *k'ê*^{4}. To invite company, to make . . . . a party, *to have a feast.*

抵 *Ti*^{3}. To oppose, to ward off; to sustain, to . . . . . . bear; *to substitute for,* to atone.

頂賬 *Ting*^{3} *chang*^{4}. *Against a debt,* in lieu of . . . . the money, in settlement.

抵賬 *Ti*^{3} *chang*^{4}. *In settlement of an account,* to . . . . compound a debt by property given instead of money.

責 *Tsê*^{2}. To reprove, to reprimand; *to punish,* to . . . . . . fine; a charge, duty, responsibility.

責治 *Tsê*^{2} *chï*^{4}. . . . . *To punish,* to chastise.

喳 *Cha*^{1}. . . . . . . Yes, sir. See Sub. Also *ch'a*^{1}.

恩 *Ên*^{1}. . . . . . . Favor, *grace,* mercy; kindness.

恩典 *Ên*^{1} *tien*^{3}. Favor, bounty, *grace,* mercy. . . . .

上房 *Shang*^{4} *fang*^{2}. The rooms which in an inn . . . . face the entrance.

佔 *Chan*^{4}. To usurp, to trespass upon, to arrogate; . . . . . . to take possession of, *to occupy.*

盤費 *P'an*^{2} *fei*^{4}. . . . . Travelling expenses.

功課 *Kung*^{1} *k'ê*^{4}. . . . . *Studies,* lesson, task.

閒空 *Hsien*^{2} *k'ung*^{4}. . . . . . . Spare time, *leisure.*

蒲 *P'u*^{2}. . . . . . . The cat-tail rush, calamus.

團 *T'wan*^{2}. A lump, a mass; *round,* globular; . . . . to collect, to group; to surround; united, agreeing together.

蒲團 A rush mat, a [round] mat of any kind; specially the mat on which priests sit when they *recite prayers.*

蒲墊 *P'u*^{2} *tien*^{4}. A rush mat, a mat of any . . . . kind.

智 *Chï*^{4}. *Wisdom,* knowledge, prudence, discre- . . . . tion.

團墊子留下、以後我給你帶捎去不好嗎、
答也好可以。〇23一吊五百錢你賣不賣、
答不行中、啊那些錢買不了。〇24我欠你的
十吊錢、這個月先還你六吊、那四吊
到八月再還、好不好、答也行好啊。〇25從
來說、秤不離砣、客不離貨、你可好以離
了貨、去幹別的事嗎、這一回、幸虧叫
人騙得不多、若是再有第二回、你必
得自己墊上、答是是、不經一失事、不長
一智、那能再有第二回呢。

22 If you can not take all, had you not better leave this mat and I will send (take) it to you by and by? *Ans.* Well, all right.

23 Will you take fifteen hundred cash? No, that money will not buy it.

24 Of the ten thousand cash I owe you, I will pay six thousand this month, and then, may I wait till the eighth month to pay the other four thousand? *Ans.* Yes, that will do.

25 It has always been said, "The steelyards can not be separated from the weight, nor the merchant from his goods." Is it proper for you to leave the goods, to look after other things? This time, fortunately, not much was taken, but if you do so a second time, you will have to make it good yourself. *Ans.* All right. "Without experience (mistakes) no wisdom is gained." I will not do so a second time.

NOTES.

11 覺驚 This phrase is widely used, but it is hard to see how it can apply to external appearance, as it does here. Some would write 脚驚 and others (where soft sounds prevail) 着驚.

14 On the first three anniversaries of any one's death paper money is burnt at the grave and also at home in front of the tablet. The first and third anniversaries are regarded as the most important.

16 This is the language of an officer to his underlings urging them to catch some transgressor.

17 The 上房 is the most desirable room in an inn. The term must be carefully distinguished from

22 As used in the North, 帶 would here necessarily mean that the party was going himself and would *take the mat along*, whereas 捎 means to send by another.

25 客 Here, the merchant or agent who has goods in charge and who travels with them. In Peking 事 and 失 are read nearly or quite alike, and which should here be used is more or less doubtful, as either will give a good sense. In eastern Shantung 事 is *Sï*^{4} and 失 is *Shï*^{2}, and the latter is unequivocally the correct word.

LESSON LXXI.

THE CAUSATIVES 教, 使, 令 AND 給.

教 or **叫**, in addition to its primary meaning, and its use to form the passive (Les. 53), is also much used as a causative. This causative sense is often modified so as to include the idea of instruction or direction to do or act. In the North the idea of causing often passes over to that of permitting or allowing as (2), (3).

使, in addition to its use as an instrumental verb (Les. 54), is often used causatively. Its causative force is a little stronger than that of 教 and it is a little more bookish.

令 To command, is used in certain connections only, for 教. It is always followed by 人, or by a pronoun, and is only used in connection with the expression of some emotion.

給 (read kê) is largely used in Southern Mandarin in a causative sense, taking the place to some extent of both 教 and 使. It is never so used in Central or Northern Mandarin.

第七十一課

誰[1]教你這麼樣做。○先[2]生不叫許上街。○我[3]不
能教你吃虧。○不[4]要叫父母擔憂。○叫[5]他
明天一早上工。○你[6]實在教我丟臉。○叫[7]
厨房早些把飯預備下。○翠[8]瑛說話。叫人
聽不出來。○教[9]我看、不如由他罷。○他[10]調弄
弄聳人、叫人不能防備。○依[11]你的意思、叫
我怎麼辦呢。○你[12]不管他、這就是教他學
壞了。○纔[13]說的事、你不可叫人曉得、答是
的。○他[14]叫你怎麼樣、你就怎麼樣嗎。○來[15]
了這麼些人、教我沒法子安排。○王[16]世官、

TRANSLATION.

1 Who directed you to act so?
2 The teacher does not allow you to go on the street.
3 I cannot allow you to suffer loss.
4 Do not grieve your father and mother.
5 Have him go to work early to-morrow morning.
6 You have caused me deep mortification.
7 Let the cook prepare the meal a little earlier.
8 Ts'wei Ying talks in such a way that one cannot understand her.
9 In my opinion, it would be better to let him have his way.
10 His arts of deception are such that one cannot guard against them.
11 According to your idea, what would you have me do?
12 Your not controlling him is the very cause of his ruin.
13 You must not allow any one to know what we have just been saying. *Ans.* No, I will not.
14 Do you do just whatever he wants you to do?

VOCABULARY.

擔 *Tan*¹. To carry with a pole; *to bear*, to sustain; to undertake; to be responsible for. See *tan*⁴.

擔憂 *Tan*¹ *yiu*¹. To be heavy-hearted, *to grieve*, to mourn.

一早 *I*¹ *tsao*³. Early in the morning.

上工 *Shang*⁴ *kung*¹. To begin work, to go to work.

翠 *Ts'wei*⁴. The feathers of the kingfisher.

瑛 *Ying*¹. The lustre of pearls.

聳 *Sung*³. To excite, to stir up, to egg on.

調弄 *Tiao*⁴ *nung*⁴. To cozen, to bamboozle, to befool, *to deceive*.

弄聳 *Lung*⁴ *sung*³. To cozen, *to dupe*, to practise upon.

可恨 *K'ê*³ *hên*⁴. Hateful, *detestable*, abominable:—Les. 180.

舒 *Shu*¹. To unroll, to open out; tranquil, at ease; lax, easy; *comfortable*.

坦 *T'an*³. A level place; *tranquil*, quiet.

舒坦 *Comfortable*, pleasant, at ease.

受用 *Shou*⁴ *yung*⁴. *Comfortable*, at ease.

屈 *Ch'ü*¹. To bend, to stoop; to contract; to subject; *to wrong*, to oppress.

受屈 *Shou*⁴ *ch'ü*¹. To suffer wrong; to be subjected to injustice.

莫非鴉 *Moa*⁴ *fei*¹ *ya*¹. Morphia.

難受 *Nan*² *shou*⁴. Distressed, pained, grieved; *uncomfortable*, miserable.

安穩 *An*¹ *wên*³. *Quiet*, peaceful, tranquil; steady, stable.

殺威 *Sha*¹ *wei*¹. *Severe*, austere, harsh, imperious, commanding.

殺氣 *Sha*¹ *ch'i*⁴. A severe expression, a harsh appearance; *murderous*.

回信 *Hwei*² *hsin*⁴. A letter in reply, an answer, a response.

掛念 *Kwa*⁴ *nien*⁴. To be anxious, to be solicitous.

觸 *Ch'u*⁴, *ch'oa*⁴. To butt, to gore; to push; to run against; to offend; to oppose; to excite, *to quicken*.

觸動 *Ch'oa*⁴ *tung*⁴. To stir up, to excite, *to quicken;* to provoke.

一點正經事不做、眞令人可恨。○你17要仔細告訴他、給使他放心。○叫18父母受舒用坦幾日、方盡兒子的本分。○你19們教我這樣被受屈、實在下不去。○給20他一點莫非鴉吃、給使他睡覺就好了。○他21教我難受、我也不能教他安穩。○他22臉上有殺氣威、看見就令人害怕。○到23如今沒見回信、叫我不能不掛念他。○這24是上天觸動你的靈機、教你這樣聰明。○我25的父母、也叫請間師師母娘

15 So many have come that I have no way of providing for them.
16 Wang Shï Kwan has no legitimate business at all. He is truly a detestable fellow.
17 You must tell her carefully so as to relieve her mind.
18 Only by making your father and mother comfortable for a season will you be discharging your duties as a son.
19 I certainly cannot allow myself to be wronged by you in this fashion.
20 Give him a little morphia to make him sleep, and he will be all right.
21 He made me feel badly, and I'll take care that he doesn't get much comfort.
22 He had a severe (murderous) expression on his face so that whoever looked at him felt afraid.
23 Up to this time I have had no answer [to my letter] so that I cannot help feeling anxious about him.

靈 *Ling*². The spiritual part, spirit; ethereal, *intelligent;* efficacious; powerful.

靈機 *Ling*² *chi*¹. The "intelligent machine," the mind, the springs of thought; *the faculties.*

惦 *Tien*⁴. To think of, to remember.

惦記 *Tien*⁴ *chi*⁴. To think of, to call to mind, to bear in remembrance.

扛 *K'ang*². *To carry on the shoulder;* to withstand, to sustain, to bear.

杠 *Kang*⁴. A pole, a cross-bar, a lever.

詳 *Hsiang*². To examine; to discourse upon; minutely, *in detail.*

詳細 *Hsiang*² *hsi*⁴. Carefully, minutely, *in detail;* trusty, reliable.

臊 *Sao*⁴. Bashful, ashamed. Also *sao*¹.

害臊 *Hai*⁴ *sao*⁴. *Ashamed,* mortified.

害羞 *Hai*⁴ *hsiu*¹. Put to the blush, *ashamed,* mortified.

蘭 *Lan*². Orchideous plants; scented, elegant; joyous, delightful; adopted.

褥 *Ju*⁴. *A mattress,* a cushion, a rug.

安歇 *An*¹ *hsie*¹. *To rest,* to go to rest, to sleep peacefully.

均 *Chün*¹. In equal parts, just, *even;* all, altogether; to adjust.

匀 *Yün*². Equal, *even;* a little; to divide off, to allot.

均匀 Alike, equal, uniform, *even;* seasonable.

拈 *Nien*². To take in the fingers, to pick up, *to draw,*—as a lot.

鬮 *Chiu*¹. A lot, a cut, a ticket.

拈鬮 To cast lots, to draw cuts.

碰命兒 *P'êng*⁴ *ming*⁴ *êr*². To run the risk, to take one's chance.

命兒攤 *Ming*⁴ *êr*² *t'an*¹. Same.

運氣 *Yün*⁴ *ch'i*⁴. *Chance,* luck, fortune, lot, fate.

遺 *I*². *To will,* to bequeath; to leave behind, to forget, to neglect; surplus.

遺命 *I*² *ming*⁴. Dying commands, *a will,* a testament.

長孫 *Chang*³ *sun*¹. The eldest grandson in the male line.

效 *Hsiao*⁴. To imitate, to copy; to verify; *effect,* efficacy; result.

功效 *Kung*¹ *hsiao*⁴. Efficacy, *effect,* result; merit.

變化 *Pien*⁴ *hwa*⁴. To change, to transform.

吉 *Chi*². Fortunate, *auspicious;* prosperous.

吉利 *Chi*² *li*⁴ *Auspicious,* lucky, propitious, hopeful.

喪 *Sang*⁴. To lose; to be bereft of; forgotten, lost; to die; to ruin; *unlucky,* baneful. Also *sang*¹.

喪門 *Sang*¹ *mên*². *Unlucky,* ill-omened:—Note 35.

安好、答謝謝、叫他們惦想記着。○我[26]叫你去找一根扁擔、怎麼扛了一根杠子來呢。○請[27]先生詳細一點講、叫他慢慢就說明白了。○我[28]打你、不是要叫你疼、是要叫你害羞躁。○背[29]着人拿東西、不教給人知道、這就是偷。○這[30]件事實在難、叫我一點主意沒有。○二[31]人說完了話、戶蘭給他鋪上褥子、叫他安歇。○若[32]實在分不均勻、可以抓鬮叫/拈鬮憑他們各人碰命兒/命兒攤的運氣。○我[33]父親臨死、留的遺命、叫除出三十畝地、給長孫。○耶[34]穌教的大功效、就是能變化人心、使得人改惡為善。○吉[35]利話、他一句不說、淨說一些喪門話、叫人不願意聽。

24 It is Heaven that has quickened your faculties so that you have this wisdom.

25 My father and mother, also, send their kind regards. *Ans.* Thank you. They are very thoughtful.

26 I sent you to get a *pien-tan*, how is it that you come carrying a *kang-tsï?*

27 Please explain it in detail, and let him hear it step by step, and he will understand.

28 I whip you, not to make you suffer pain, but that you may be ashamed.

29 Stealing is the taking of people's things behind their backs and without their knowledge.

30 This is a very embarrassing affair. I haven't the least idea what to do.

31 When the two were done talking, Hu Lan spread mattresses for them and bade them [lie down to] rest.

32 If you positively cannot divide it evenly, you may draw cuts and let each one take his chance.

33 Just before his death, my father made a will directing that thirty mow of land be set apart for his eldest grandson.

34 The chief effect of Christianity is that it is able to change the heart, causing men to turn from evil and become virtuous.

35 He did not speak one auspicious word, but just a lot of ill-omened talk which we were loth to hear.

NOTES.

2 The Southern form 許, is entirely *t'ung hsing* and in very common use. It is a little stronger than the other form, differing from it much as *permit* does from *allow*. See Les. 130.

3 This sentence might also mean, *I will not cause you to suffer loss.* The meaning intended will depend on the connection.

5 一早, *one early*, is emphatic. It means *very early*, or as early as the circumstances will permit.

7 Kitchen is put by metonomy for cook. This is a common idiom; thus heaven 天 for *God*, audience hall 朝廷 for *Emperor*, learning court 學院 for *examiner*, etc.

18 受用 may also be used in the North.

19 Lit., *Your causing me to suffer wrong in this way, will certainly not go down.*

22 殺威 is more or less local. 殺氣 is more general, and its meaning is much stronger.

26 A 扁擔 is a pole for one person to carry over the shoulder with burdens suspended from the ends; the 杠子 is a pole for two persons to carry a burden suspended between them.

32 拈鬮 is the book form, while in the North 抓鬮 is the form commonly used. They differ in meaning, much as "cast lots" differs from "draw cuts." The latter part of the sentence expresses a very common idea, yet I found it impossible to get two teachers from different places to agree as to how to say it. 碰命兒 is the Peking form, 命兒攤 is the Shantung form, while the Nanking teacher rejected both and recast the whole clause.

33 遺命 is a book expression. There is no legal provision in China for either making or executing a will. The case referred to here was probably nothing more than verbal directions.

35 According to the meaning here used 喪 should be read *Sang*^{4}, it is, however, generally read *Sang*^{1}.

第七十二課

你[1]成整天家作甚麽。○人[2]家都冷眼兒看你。○他[3]們二人是乾親家。○走[4]的時節時家、不要忘了鎖門。○你[5]要殷勤事奉兩個老人家。○他[6]二姨姨母是個財主家。○你[7]的大姑娘、有婆家沒有。○該[8]人家的錢、舌頭就短喇。○他[9]兩個小的時節時家、是同窗。○這[10]個人、叫大家夥兒都容不下。○說[11]了半天、你還是個內行行家嗎。○我[12]常想着做買賣、就是找不着個

TRANSLATION.

1 What are you all the time doing?
2 Everybody looks coldly upon you.
3 They two are sworn relatives.
4 When you go, do not forget to lock the door.
5 You ought to minister diligently to the old folks.
6 Her second maternal aunt is wealthy.
7 Is your oldest daughter betrothed?
8 When you are in debt to a man, your tongue is short.
9 They two were schoolmates when they were young.
10 None [of us] can put up with this fellow.
11 After all this talk you turn out to be an expert, eh!
12 I have been waiting this long time to go into business, but cannot find a monied partner.

LESSON LXXII.

THE ENCLITIC 家.

The character 家 is added to certain words for the purpose of merging the individual in the family or class, thus generalizing them. It is added to man, woman, and to all terms denoting family relationships, to various offices, to time, etc. It may be compared to "kind" used as a suffix in such words as mankind, womankind, etc.; but is by no means equivalent to it.

VOCABULARY.

成天家 *Ch'êng² t'ien¹ chia¹*. Continually, all the time:—Les. 108.

整天家 *Chêng³ t'ien¹ chia¹*. Same:—Note 1.

親 *Ch'ing⁴*. A relative by marriage:—Note 3. See *ch'in¹*.

親家 *Ch'ing⁴ chia¹*. A relative by marriage.

乾親家 *Kan¹ ch'ing⁴ chia¹*. A relative by adoption:—Note 3.

人家 *Jên² chia¹*. Others in contrast with oneself, other people; *everybody;* the person referred to.

冷眼 *Lêng³ yien³*. To look on with displeasure, *to look coldly at*, askance.

時節 *Shï² chie²*. A time, the time which, a period of time.

時家 *Shï² chia¹*. Same:—Note 4.

殷 *Yin¹*. Abundant, full; particular; *diligent*.

殷勤 *Yin¹ ch'in²*. *Diligent*, attentive.

奉 *Fêng⁴*. To receive respectfully; to deliver to; to reverence; *to serve;* obediently.

事奉 *Shï⁴ fêng⁴*. To wait upon, to serve, *to minister to*.

姨 *I²*. A mother's sister, a maternal aunt.

姨母 *I² mu³*. Same.

婆家 *P'oă² chia¹*. Mother-in-law, mother-in-law's family.

大家夥 *Ta⁴ chia¹ hwoă³*. The whole company, all concerned. (L.)

行家 *Hang² chia¹*. One skilled in any art, an expert.

內行 *Nei⁴ hang²*. Versed in the secrets of a business or art, expert.

搶嘴 *Ch'iang³ tswei³*. Forward to talk, impertinent, *unmannerly*.

搶頭 *Ch'iang³ t'ou²*. Same.

搶先 *Ch'iang³ hsien¹*. Same (s.)

東家。○如[13]今官家的事情、也是半公半私的了。○怎[14]麼一個孩子家、說話這麼搶嘴。頭先○人[15]家都厭惡他、他自己一點兒不覺。○一[16]個男子漢、半天家說不出句話來、實在躁人。○婦[17]道家不可承喫承穿、也得幫助他丈夫過日子。○替[18]人家說話、都要實在、不可胡說亂巴道的。○我[19]素來不該人家的、不欠人家的。○不[20]可嫌人家好歹、佔人家便宜。○新[21]姑女爺婿到正月初三日、都上丈人家去拜年。○人[22]

13 At the present time official business has also come to be half legitimate and half illicit.

14 How is it that a mere child puts in his talk in such an unmannerly way?

15 Everybody detests him, but he does not, in the least, realize it.

16 I tell you it tries one's patience, when a full-grown man can't get a sentence out in a whole half day.

17 It will not do for women to think only of food and dress, they should also help their husbands to get along in life.

18 When you speak for others, you should speak the truth, and not talk recklessly.

19 It is not my custom to be in debt, nor to be in arrears to any man.

20 You should not find fault with people, nor sponge upon them.

21 On the third of the first month every new son-in-law goes to visit his wife's relatives to pay his respects.

男子漢 *Nan3 tsï3 han4*. A man as distinguished from a woman, a man with decided masculine qualities.

婦道家 *Fu4 tao4 chia1*. Women, wives.

承 *Ch'êng2*. *To receive;* to undertake; to assist; to contest, to compete; to support, to uphold; to open up; to succeed, second to.

胡 *Hu2*. What! How? The Mongols; used for 糊,—*confused*, muddled.

胡說巴道 *Hu2 shwoă1 pa1 tao4*. To talk wildly or *recklessly*.

胡說亂道 *Hu2 shwoă1 lan4 tao4*. Same.

素來 *Su4 lai2*. Heretofore; commonly, *customarily*.

新女婿 *Hsin1 nü3 hsü4*. A bridegroom.

新姑爺 *Hsin1 ku1 yie2*. A bridegroom.

丈人 *Chang4 jên2*. Father-in-law.

拜年 *Pai4 nien2*. To pay one's respects at the New Year.

子弟 *Tsï3 ti4*. Sons and younger brothers; young people of the family:—Note 22.

冤 *Yüen1*. Oppression; injustice, *wrong*.

冤家 *Yüen1 chia1*. One from whom wrong has been received, *an enemy*.

搬家 *Pan1 chia1*. *A household-moving*, to flit, to migrate.

檢 *Chien3*. To sort, to collate; *to examine;* to revise; to compose; to pick up.

管家 *Kwan3 chia1*. A head-man, a steward.

檢點 *Chien3 tien3*. To look over carefully, to count over; *to oversee*.

綠 *Lü4, lu4*. Green, the color of leaves.

說白道綠 *Shwoă1 pai2 tao4 lü4*. To discuss people's characters, to gossip, *to defame*.

說白道黑 *Shwoă1 pai2 tao4 hei1*. Same:—Note 25.

結親 *Chie2 ch'in1*. To make a marriage alliance.

娘家 *Niang2 chia1*. A married woman's mother's family.

乳 *Ju3*. *Milk;* the breasts; to suck; to suckle.

乳名 *Ju3 ming2*. A pet name:—Note 27.

叫作 *Chiao4 tsoă4*. Named, called.

蓮 *Lien2*. The lotus,—consecrated to Buddha.

勾 *Kou1*. To mark off and reject; to entice, to inveigle; to hook on, to connect by a hook; the short side of a right-angled triangle.

一筆勾消 *I1 pi3 kou1 hsiao1*. To erase by a stroke of the pen, to strike out; *to ignore*.

薙 *T'i4*. To shave the head.

家興、是子弟、人家敗、也是子弟。○他[23]們倆是寃仇家、不可請讓在一張桌子上。○大[24]戶人家搬家、必派幾個老管家檢點。○他[25]正在那裏、張家長、李家短、說白道黑綠的。○我[26]和他結親作親家、把女兒配許給他兒子、很對心思。○我[27]娘家姓李、我的小乳名、叫作李翠蓮。○從[28]前我待他的好處、他算一筆勾消、如今和我成了寃家

22 The prosperity of a family depends on the rising generation, and, also, the decadence of a family proceeds from them.

23 They two are enemies, and must not be invited to sit at the same table.

24 When wealthy families move, they always appoint several old stewards to oversee.

25 He is over there criticising this one and that one, defaming people's characters.

26 For me to contract a marriage alliance with him, giving my daughter to his son, suits my wishes exactly.

27 My mother's name was Li, and my little name was Li Ts'wei Lien.

28 He wholly ignores all my former kindness, and has now become my enemy.

尙 *Shang*⁴. To esteem, to honor; to control; . . . . still, furthermore, yet.

和尙 *Hê² shang⁴*. A Buddhist priest. Read *hê²* . . . . *ch'ang⁴* in some places.

出家 *Ch'u¹ chia¹*. To take a vow of celibacy, ... to enter the priesthood.

僧 *Sêng¹*. . . . . . . A Buddhist priest; a lama.

僧家 *Sêng¹ chia¹*. Priests, the Buddhist priest- . . . . hood.

俗家 *Su² chia¹*. . . . . The laity, *the world*.

誼 *I²*. That which is right, proper or fit, *friend-* . . . . . *ship*, acquaintance.

情誼 *Ch'ing² i²*. . . . . . . *Favor*, kindness.

奬賞 *Chiang³ shang³*. . . . . *Reward;* prize.

國家 *Kwoă² chia¹*. . . . . . . State, *country*.

政 *Chêng⁴*. . . . . To rule; *government*, laws.

儒 *Ju²* . . . . Scholars, literati, the learned.

儒家 *Ju² chia¹*. The learned class, *Confucianists*, ... the literati.

欲 *Yü⁴*. To wish for, to long for; aspiration, ... hopes; lust, *appetite*, passion.

NOTES.

1 成天家 or 整天家 Both forms of this much used phrase are regarded as correct. In some places the aspirated form is chiefly used, and in some places the unaspirated. In some places, both North and South, 成天 is frequently used without the 家, and, in the North especially, 的 is often substituted for 家. See Les. 108, Sub.

3 親 is read Ch'ing⁴ only when followed by 家. 乾親家 *Dry relatives;* i.e., relatives not really such, but made such by adoption. The Chinese practise a species of adoption in the case of brothers and sisters, also parents and children. It is simply a mutual choice, accompanied by the giving of presents, and implying a promise or vow of mutual faithfulness. The vow is sometimes formally expressed, and ratified by a feast. When a member of one family enters into such a relationship with a member of another family, the two families become 乾親家.

4 時家 though not often used in the South, is readily understood. In the North it is more used in some places than in others. It may be applied to any verb or noun indicating time. Where not used, 時節 takes its place, but requires a 的 before it, which the 時家 does not. The construction of 了 is, *Do not forget to have locked the door.*

5 老人家 is a respectful way of referring to any one's parents. It is also used as a term of respect when addressing any elderly person (30).

6 This sentence might with equal propriety, and without perceptible change of meaning, be given 他二姨家是財主.

7 Lit., *Has your eldest daughter a mother-in-law?*

10 這個人 is used emphatically, and expresses a shade of contempt. 大家夥兒 *all the persons concerned*, is much used in some places, but is not *t'ung hsing.*

11 行家 One thoroughly versed in any business, art, or profession, *an expert.* The conversation had disclosed what the speaker had not previously suspected, viz., that the party addressed was an expert.

17 承吃承穿 *Receive food and receive dress*, that is receiving all and doing nothing, only thinking of food and dress.

22 子弟 *Sons and younger brothers*, including also *their* sons—a general term including all of the family younger than oneself, but primarily supposed to be used by the eldest brother, who is regarded as the head of the family.

23 讓 means properly *to yield or give place to*, hence as used by the host with reference to guests, it means *to seat or place at table.*

24 大戶人家 *A family with a large doorway*, that is a large and wealthy family.

25 張家長李家短 etc., 說 must be supplied. 張 and 李 being very common names are used at large for

了。○薙[29]頭當和尚、就叫出家、自稱爲僧家、稱人爲俗家。○爲[30]我的事情、叫你老人家受驚、這個情誼、叫我怎麼報呢。○獎[31]賞是國家的善政、也是皇上的恩典。○儒[32]家的功夫、是養氣、道家的功夫、是煉氣、養氣煉氣、都是清心寡欲的意思。

29 To shave the head and become a Buddhist priest is called, "leaving the family." They call themselves the priesthood, and call others the world.

30 That you, good sir, should be worried on account of my affairs, is a favor I am wholly unable to requite.

31 Rewards conferred promote the good government of the country, and are, at the same time, an expression of imperial favour.

32 The effort of Confucianism is to nourish the vital principle; the effort of Taoism is to refine the vital principle; both aim at purifying the heart and diminishing the appetites.

any one, as we say Jones and Brown. It is not easy to see why 黑 should not always be used, yet 綠 is used in many places. 道 is used in the sense of 說.

27 小名 is the colloquial, 乳名 is the book form.

29 Buddhist priests shave the entire head, and in this respect differ from Taoist priests, some of whom (those who marry) wear the hair as other Chinese do, others (those who do not marry) allow *all* the hair to grow, and wear it in a knot on the top of the head. Buddhist priests are not allowed to marry, hence the phrase 出家.

32 氣 refers here to the divine essence which is held to constitute the soul, and of which the physical breath is the emblem and vehicle. This divine essence, or vital principle, the Confucianist regards as good, and seeks to *nourish* and preserve it as the path to virtue and longevity. The Taoist regards it as evil, especially as being corrupted by association with the body, and seeks to *purify* and refine it, as the passport to immortality. 清心寡欲 is a ready-made book phrase. 清 and 寡 are to be taken as verbs.

LESSON LXXIII.

發 Expressing Development.

發 To send forth,—is joined with many words to express the idea of becoming, developing, etc. It is especially joined to such words as express qualities perceived by the senses. It may often be rendered by *become*, or *grow*, or *get*. In many cases English affords no exact equivalent.

發黃 To be or become yellow.

發家 To enrich one's family:—Note 2.

發財 To make money, to get or grow rich.

發亮 To appear lustrous, to shine.

發紅 To be or become red, to grow red.

發壞 To become addicted to vicious practices, to develop a vicious character; to spoil, to ferment.

發亂 To become confused, to be in a state of confusion.

發狂 To become or grow reckless, or violent.

發瘋 To suffer an attack of convulsions, to be subject to fits.

發怯 To be or become timorous, to give way to fear.

發怒 To become or grow angry, to get in a passion.

發軟弱 To become or grow weak, to betray weakness.

發誓 To take an oath, to swear.

發笨 To become stiff, to grow clumsy.

發花 To become or grow dim or indistinct (of the eyes).

發慌 To become excited or confused, to grow nervous.

發悶 To feel gloomy; to have a sense of distress or uneasiness.

發利害 To grow severe; to become unruly; to storm, to make an ado.

發威 To become violent, to rage; to assume an air of authority and anger.

發硬 To become hard; to grow stiff.

發僵 To be or become obstinate; to grow stiff, to be clumsy.

第七十三課

你[1]的舌頭發黃。○外[2]財不發家。○這[3]樣買賣、不能發財。○好[4]墨寫的字發亮。○說[5]起來、他臉上發紅。○發[6]壞的地方、沒有我。○他[7]的事多、心裏發亂。○年[8]輕的人、最容易發狂。○人[9]不得外財不發。○我[10]的外甥、抽(發)瘋死了。○該[11]大起膽來、不要害怕(發怯)。○有[12]人發怒、就和

TRANSLATION.

1 Your tongue is yellow.
2 Illegitimate gains do not advance a man's estate.
3 It is impossible to get rich at this kind of business.
4 Writing done with good ink, shows a lustre.
5 When you speak of it, his face grows [red.
6 I am free from vicious practices.
7 His mind is confused with the multitude of his affairs.
8 It is very easy for the young to become reckless.
9 Without illegitimate gain, no one gets rich.
10 My nephew died of epilepsy.
11 You should brace up your courage, and not yield to fear.

發虛 To feel languid or exhausted.

發現 To become manifest; to be aroused or awakened (of conscience).

發飽 To have a feeling of distention or fulness, flatulence.

作飽 The same:—Note 24.

發酸 or 作酸 To be or become sour; to have a sour taste.

發心口疼 To have or suffer an attack of dyspepsia or indigestion.

發涼 To become cold, to feel cold.

發冷 To seem or feel cold:—Note 26.

發暈 or 作暈 To be or become or feel dizzy.

發乾 or 作乾 To be or become or feel dry.

發慈悲 To be compassionate, to show pity, to be moved with a feeling of compassion.

發驕傲 To be or become or grow proud.

發瘧子 or 發瘧疾 To have or suffer from ague.

發熱 To be or feel hot or feverish.

發痲 To become or feel numb.

發糊塗 To become foolish or silly; to be stupefied; to become bewildered.

發齁 To wheeze, to be asthmatic.

發脹 To be distended, to feel a sense of fulness.

發板 To be or feel stiff; to be or grow intractable.

For further list of words joined with 發, see Supplement.

VOCABULARY.

外財 *Wai⁴ ts'ai²*. *Illegitimate gain;* money acquired by a stroke of good fortune.

甥 *Shêng¹*. . . . . Relatives of a different surname.

外甥 *Wai⁴ shêng¹*. The children of one's own sisters and wife's sisters.

抽瘋 *Ch'ou¹ fêng¹*. *To fall in an epileptic fit,* attacked by convulsions.

怯 *Ch'ie⁴*. . . . . . *Timorous;* nervous.

酵 *Chiao⁴*. . . . . Yeast, leaven.

發酵 *Fa¹ chiao⁴*. To raise, to ferment; baking powder, *bicarbonate of soda.*

蘇打 *Su¹ ta³*. . . . . . . Bicarbonate of soda.

誓 *Shï⁴*. . . . . *To take an oath;* a vow, an oath.

慌 *Hwang¹*. Hurried, *nervous,* frightened; to move unsteadily, to wabble.

消停 *Hsiao¹ t'ing²*. To do leisurely, *to do at one's ease* or convenience.

發作 *Fa¹ tsoâ⁴*. *To get in a passion,* to storm; to inflame and swell, to become acute :—Note 20.

猛獸一樣。○這[13]一回的饅頭、沒發好。○可[14]以再加上一點發酵(蘇打)。○你[15]若不發軟弱、就沒有這些事情。○先[16]生不要信他、他發誓是假的。○人[17]老了。手脚發笨、眼睛也發花。○到[18]了塲裏、不要發慌、只管消停着做罷。○我[19]這兩天、心裏發悶。○[20]不發威(不發利害、不發作起來)、他是不能怕的。○冬[21]天人手發僵硬、難以寫字。○你[22]這樣發虛、該吃一點補藥纔好。○我[23]那時良心發現、覺得罪重。○你[24]肚子作飽不作飽(發飽不)、答天天夜裏作(發)飽。○嘴[25]裏作酸不作酸(發酸不)、答嘴裏常作(發)酸。○昨[26]天新娘子(新媳婦)發(害)心口疼、手脚

12 Some men when they get angry, are like wild beasts.
13 The bread, this time, did not rise well.
14 You may add a little more soda.
15 If you had betrayed no weakness, there would have been none of these things.
16 Do not believe him, sir, the oath he takes is false.
17 When a man is old, his hands and feet become stiff, and his eyes, dim.
18 When you reach the examination hall, do not get nervous, but write [your essay] at your ease.
19 I am feeling gloomy these few days.
20 If you do not storm, he will not be afraid.
21 In the winter one's hands grow stiff, so that writing becomes difficult.
22 In this exhausted condition, it would be well for you to take a little tonic.
23 At that time my conscience was aroused, and I felt the weight of my sins.
24 Does your belly feel distended? *Ans.* It feels so every night.
25 Do you have a sour taste in your month? *Ans.* I constantly have a sour taste in my month.
26 Yesterday the bride had a pain in her stomach, so that both her hands and feet became cold.

冬天 *Tung*[1] *t'ien*[1]. Winter, the winter season.

僵 *Chiang*[1]. Prostrate; *stiffened.*

難以 *Nan*[2] *i*[3]. Hard, difficult.

酸 *Swan*[1]. *Sour,* acid; irritating, grieved; numbness or weakness of the muscles.

暈 *Yün*[4]. A halo; foggy; obscure; *dizzy.*

慈 *Ts'i*[2]. Maternal affection; kindness, *tenderness;* mercy.

慈悲 *Ts'i*[2] *pei*[1]. *Compassion,* forbearance, mercy.

救主 *Chiu*[4] *chu*[3]. A saviour, the Saviour (a Christian term).

前進 *Ch'ien*[2] *chin*[4]. To advance; *advancement,* promotion.

瘧 *Yao*[4], *yoă*[4], *yüe*[4], *nüe*[4]. Intermittent fever, ague.

疾 *Chi*[2]. Sickness, disorder, ailment.

瘧疾 Intermittent or remittent fever, ague.

汗 *Han*[4]. Sweat, perspiration.

出汗 *Ch'u*[1] *han*[4]. To perspire, to sweat.

賭氣 *Tu*[3] *ch'i*[4]. *To resolve or vow in anger to do a thing,* to do in spite of all hindrances, to do with the might.

永 *Yung*[3]. Perpetual, *everlasting;* final.

永遠 *Yung*[3] *yüen*[3]. Endless, *everlasting,* eternal.

齁 *Hou*[1]. *To breathe hard,* asthma; a special intensive:—Les. 148.

齁病 *Hou*[1] *ping*[4]. Asthma:—Note 35.

傷風 *Shang*[1] *fêng*[1]. To take cold.

脹 *Chang*[4]. To swell up, to enlarge; dropsical; tenseness, *fullness.*

罐 *Kwan*[4]. *A jar,* a crock, a mug, a cruse.

火罐 *Hwoă*[3] *kwan*[4]. A small cup used for cupping, also to hold medicines.

都發了冷涼。○[27]睡躺了這些日子、起來不能不作發暈。○我[28]嘴裏作發乾、請給我一點水喝。○天[29]父大發慈悲、給人一位救主、○人[30]發驕傲、最容易躭誤自己的前進。○人[31]發瘧疾子、是有時發冷、有時發熱。○我[32]的兩條腿、都不出汗、常覺着發痲。○他[33]病的不輕、好幾天淨發糊塗、說話也不清楚。○我[34]大哥賭氣、上了關東、他說不發大財、永遠也不回來。○你[35]這麼喘、是有個發齁的病嗎、答 沒有齁病、是傷了風。○我[36]沒有甚麼大病、就是腦子發脹、身上發板、用火罐子給我拔一拔、就好了。

27 Having been confined to your bed all these days, you cannot but feel dizzy when you first get up.

28 My mouth feels dry, please give me a little water to drink.

29 Our Heavenly Father in His great compassion gave unto men a Saviour.

30 When a man becomes proud, he is very apt to hinder his own advancement.

31 When one has ague, he sometimes feels cold, and sometimes hot.

32 Both my legs are destitute of perspiration, and constantly feel numb.

33 His illness is not slight; for several days he has been constantly in a stupor, his speech, also, is indistinct.

34 My eldest brother went off to Manchuria in a fit of anger, saying that unless he made a fortune, he would never return.

35 Is your shortness of breath on account of asthma? *Ans.* No, I have no asthma; I have caught a cold.

36 I have no illness of any consequence, but I have a fullness in my head, and my body feels stiff. If you will cup me, I shall be all right.

NOTES.

1 In this sentence, the translation fails to convey the force of 發. It might be paraphrased, *your tongue has developed a yellow color.*

2 發家 *To advance the interests of the family:* riches are held by families rather than by individuals. This use of 發 is not quite analogous to its use in this lesson.

6 Lit., *Becoming bad place has not me*, that is I am free from all participation in any kind of vice. The more usual and natural order would be, 我沒有發壞的地方. The inversion is for the purpose of throwing emphasis on the clause, 沒有我.

9 財 is to be understood after 發. The explanation of the seeming inconsistency between this and the second sentence seems to be that this is the sentiment of the average man who believes that dishonesty is the best policy, while the first is the sentiment of the virtuous man who believes in a righteous providence; or the inconsistency may be explained, by taking this sentence to mean, *without a stroke of extra good fortune, no one gets rich.*

10 抽瘋 is more widely used than 發瘋.

11 大 is here made to do service as a verb.

13 發 is here used of the raising of bread, and does not illustrate the principle of the lesson. The same is true of 發酵 in the next sentence.

18 Although not distinctly so stated, the "arena" here referred to is evidently the examination hall, and the thing to be done is the writing of a literary essay.

20 發作. In this phrase 發 takes the accent, which shows that it is used as a leading verb, and not as in other places in this lesson.

21 In this connection, 僵 is much more widely used than 硬.

24 作飽 *To become full.* This use of 作 for 發 is very common in Southern Mandarin, but is never heard in the North. 發飽不 is put for 發飽不發飽. The word or words that would follow a negative are not infrequently dropped in this way, and emphasis is thrown on the negative. This is especially the case in Central and Northern Mandarin.

26 In general, Southern Mandarin shows a strong predilection for 冷. The distinction which most teachers in the North would give to the two words in this connection, is that 發涼 means *feels cold to others*, and 發冷 means *feels cold to the person himself.*

27 In the South 睡 is used as a euphemism for prolonged sickness, and 躺 in the North.

31 It is a singular fact that in Pekingese the syllable to which this character 瘧 belongs has a great variety of readings. In eastern Shantung this character and others of its class have but one reading, viz., yoă.

35 齁病 is asthma in Shantung, as also in the South. In Peking asthma is 咳嗽喘.

第七十四課

把[1]這張紙裁開。○那[2]條路走不開車。○雲[3]彩都
散開了。○可[4]以用剪子剪𨭉開。○拿[5]刀來、把西瓜
切開。○這[6]孩子老離不開他媽。○叫[7]木匠來、把
這個箱子開打開。○要[8]歸正道、應當丢開世俗。○
這[9]把鑰匙開不開。○拿[10]熅烙斗鐵把這些摺兒熅烙開。
○叫[11]那個娃小娃子、給我滾開。○把[12]這個盒蓋揭開。
○這[13]麽大的風、還颳不開天。○剩[14]的那塊洋錢、
可以給他們兩下劈分開。○他[15]兩個人打架、我拉
不開。○鋪[16]上檯桌布單子、把傢伙擺開。○我[17]嘴角上
生瘡、張不開嘴。○我[18]的信、不知叫誰拆開看了。

Translation.

1 Cut this sheet of paper in two.
2 That road is not wide enough for a cart.
3 The clouds have all scattered.
4 You can cut it apart with scissors.
5 Bring a knife and cut the watermelon.
6 This child never leaves its mother.
7 Call the carpenter to open this box.
8 If you would return to the right path, you should give up the world.
9 This key will not open it.
10 Bring a smoothing iron and iron out these wrinkles.
11 I want that boy to make himself scarce.
12 Open the lid of this box.
13 So strong a wind, and yet not clear up the sky!
14 The dollar that is left, you may divide between the two.
15 The two are fighting, and I cannot part them.
16 Spread the table cloth, and set out the dishes.
17 I have a sore on the corner of my mouth, so that I cannot open my lips.
18 I wonder who opened my letter and read it.

LESSON LXXIV

The Auxiliary 開.

開 to open, is added as an auxiliary to such verbs as will take the qualifying idea of opening or spreading out. It frequently carries with it an inceptive force. For list of words taking this auxiliary see Supplement.

Vocabulary.

𨭉 *Chiao*3. To cut with shears, to shear. Same as 鉸.

世俗 *Shï*4 *su*2. Common or worldly customs.

熅 *Yün*4. To smooth out by heat, *to iron.*

斗 *Tou*3. A measure of ten 升,—varying in different places from about a gallon to over a bushel; a vessel; the great dipper.

熅斗 A hollow smoothing iron heated by a charcoal fire inside.

摺 *Chê*2. To double up; a fold, a crease, *a wrinkle;* a folded paper or book; a mat bin, a long strip of matting; a memorial, a dispatch.

滾 *Kun*3. To bubble; to boil; *to roll over and over*, to tumble.

盒 *Hê*2. A small box with a cover, a casket.

剩 *Shêng*4. What is left, another form of 賸.

劈 *P'i*1. To cut open, to split; *to divide.*

桌單 *Choā*1 *tan*1. A tablecloth.

檯布 *T'ai*2 *pu*4. Same. (s.)

拆 *Ch'ai*1, *ts'e*4. *To break open;* to take to pieces, to take apart; to rip; to pull down, to destroy.

三[19]間房子、怕住不開。○把[20]這塊板、從這裏鋸截開。○不[21]必找剪子、用手就撕開了。○神[22]所配合的、人不可以分開。○誰[23]敞開了那個門、答是風颳開了。○你[24]給人家說的事情、說開了沒有。○他[25]們的賬目不清、算不開了。○這[26]個寃仇、就是神仙也解不開。○四[27]音聲你會分不會、答四音聲都可以分得開。○這[28]幾條板凳、坐不開這麼些人。○我[29]今兒很睏、睜不開眼喇。○凡[30]能推脫的、他總想法子推脫了。○先[31]生急等茶喫喝、就是燒水不老開不水開。○我[32]看你酒上很親、一時也離不開。○我[33]請人寫了一副對聯、你

19 I fear three rooms will be insufficient to accommodate us.

20 Take this board and saw it in two at this place.

21 It is not necessary to get scissors, you can tear it with your hand.

22 Whom God hath joined together, let not man put asunder.

23 Who left that door open? *Ans.* The wind blew it open.

24 Did you get the business arranged which you undertook to settle for them?

25 Their accounts are not clear. They are unable to get a settlement.

26 Even the divine genii could not break up this feud.

27 Are you able to distinguish the four tones? *Ans.* I can distinguish all the four tones.

28 These few benches will not seat so many people.

29 I am very sleepy to-day, I cannot keep my eyes open.

30 Everything that can possibly be evaded, he is sure to find a way to evade.

31 The teacher is impatient for his tea, but, somehow, I cannot get the water to boil.

截 *Chie*². To cut off, *to saw off;* to obstruct, to intercept, to keep in check.

鋸 *Chü*⁴. A saw; *to saw;* to mend with clamps or staples.

撕 *Si*¹. . . . . *To tear,* to rip, to rend.

配合 *P'ei*⁴ *hê*². To match, *to mate;* suitable, fit.

敞 *Ch'ang*³. A high level space; spacious; to display; *to open.*

說開 *Shwoá*¹ *k'ai*¹. To begin to speak; to open out on, to enlarge on; *to arrange any business by exhortation or argument.*

賬目 *Chang*⁴ *mu*⁴. . . . . Accounts.

寃仇 *Yüen*¹ *ch'ou*². Enmity, animosity; *a feud;* a deadly enemy.

神仙 *Shên*² *hsien*¹. Divine genii, immortals :—Note 26.

板凳 *Pan*³ *têng*⁴. . . . . A bench, a stool.

睏 *K'un*⁴. . . . . . To sleep, to nod; *sleepy.*

睜 *Chêng*¹. . . . . To open the eyes; to stare.

聯 *Lien*². *Connected,* associated; to combine, to join in order.

對聯 *Twei*⁴ *lien*³. Parallel mottoes or distiches written on scrolls.

進京 *Chin*⁴ *ching*¹. To go to or visit the capital.

閃 *Shan*³. To flash; to evade, to dodge; *to make room for.*

世面 *Shï*⁴ *mien*⁴. New or strange things, *the sights,* the world.

綾 *Ling*². . . . . . Thin silk damask, lining satin.

綾羅 *Ling*² *loá*². . . . . Silk gauze.

綢 *Ch'ou*². To bind, to wrap round; *thin fine silk,* levantine.

緞 *Twan*⁴. . . . . Satin.

綢緞 Silk and satin, silks generally.

粳 *Ching*¹, *kêng*¹. Long white rice, unglutinous rice.

粳米 *Ching*¹ *mi*³. . . . . Same.

麪 *Mien*⁴. *Flour* of wheat or other grain; dough; vermicelli.

白麪 *Pai*² *mien*⁴. . . . . Wheaten flour

打開看看好不好呢。○怎34麼把那部
書、放擱在書架子高上頭呢、答書架子裏
頭擱不開。○有35話為甚麼放在心裏、
直去和他講明說開就是了。○這36麼
大條路、你怎麼單揀這裏走呢、快閃
開些罷。○將37來我有空、可以走開的
時候、我要進京一遭、見見世面。○富38
貴人家、穿的是綾羅綢緞、吃的是粳
米白麪、那些穿粗布舊衣的人、在大
街上遇見、自然躲開。

32 I see you are very fond of wine. You cannot do without it at all.

33 I got a man to write a pair of scrolls for me. Open and look at them: what do you think of them?

34 Why did you put that book on top of the bookcase? *Ans.* It will not go into the bookcase.

35 If you have anything to say, why do you keep it to yourself? Better go directly to him, and tell him plainly.

36 Why is it that with such a wide road as this, you yet insist on going here? Give place at once.

37 When I have time, and can get away, I am going to make a visit to the capital and see the sights.

38 The rich dress in silks and satins, and feast on white rice and wheaten flour. When those who wear coarse and dingy clothes meet one of them in the street, they naturally give way to him.

NOTES.

2 車 is the real subject of the verb, yet it comes after it. The sentence shows how completely Chinese sometimes inverts the English order.

6 老 as here used, is peculiar to Pekingese.

7 開開 The first 開 is the principal verb, the second, an auxiliary, or the two may be taken as a duplicated verb:—Les. 33.

10 Most Chinese teachers will insist that to iron ought to be 熨 yü, and not 熅. The fact is, however, that the word is not spoken yü but yün, and on this account, no doubt, 熅 has superceded 熨, and rightly so.

11 滾 as here used is highly contemptuous. Why it should be so, is not readily explained. The translation is not a whit more forcible, nor more wanting in dignity, than the Chinese.

26 神仙 According to Taoist mythology there are five classes of 仙, viz., 鬼仙, 人仙, 地仙, 神仙 and 天仙.

27 Nanking says 音 for "tone," but the more general term is 聲. The modesty of the speaker accounts for the use of 可以.

28 板凳 is properly *pan*[3] *têng*[4], but in Peking is frequently spoken *pan*[3] *t'êng*[4] and in other places *pan*[3] *ts'êng*[4].

31 等 often means, as here, *to need, to want immediately.*

35 講明說開 is a rhetorical reduplication. Chinese abounds in such forms.

LESSON LXXV.

THE AUXILIARY 住.

住 To live, to endure,—is added as an auxiliary to such words as will take the qualifying idea of enduring, or sustaining continuously. For list of words taking this auxiliary, see Supplement.

VOCABULARY.

揪 *Chiu*[1]. . . . To seize, *to hold;* to pinch and pull.
擋 *Tang*[3]. To impede, to obstruct, *to stop;* to . . . . .withstand, to screen, to ward off.
捶 *Ch'wei*[2]. . . . . . To beat, *to pound,* to cudgel.
糨 *Chiang*[4]. . . . . . Starch, paste. See *chiang*[1].
糨糊 *Chiang*[4] *hu*[2]. . . . . Same.
力量 *Li*[4] *liang*[2]. . . . . . . *Strength,* vigor, ability.
搽 *Ch'a*[2]. . . . . . *To rub on;* to paint, to smear.
持 *Ch'ï*[1]. To seize hold of, to grasp; to hold on, ...*to maintain;* to manage; to resist.
支持 *Chï*[1] *ch'ï*[2]. *To withstand,* to bear up . . . . .against; to direct.

第七十五課

我[1]一個人揪不住他。○賊[2]叫官兵擋住了。○人[3]心是靠不住
的。○拿[4]捶板布石、把他壓住了。○底[5]下加塊板子、就托住了。○
這[6]點事情、難不住他。○必[7]得厚稠糨糨糊子、纔能貼住。○你[8]的嘴太
散快、什麼事都藏不住。○這[9]匹馬口硬、我勒不住。○你[10]能堵住
誰的嘴呢。○怕[11]自己的力量、支持不住。○逢[12]搽上藥、就扛忍不
住疼。○殷[13]勤人、一時也閒不住。○我[14]的本事、敵不住他。○那[15]
把傘太小、遮不住身子。○定[16]不住年景收不收。○放[17]心罷、我
都記住喇。○喫[18]了止疼藥、也止不住疼。○這[19]塊木頭太細、怎
能架得住呢。○這[20]是險要的地方、我一個人把守不住。○那[21]
個人嘴散淺、一句話也留盛不住。○你[22]作父親、還管不住孩子嗎。

TRANSLATION.

1 I cannot hold him alone.
2 The rebels were stopped by the imperial soldiers.
3 The human heart is unreliable.
4 Put the mangle on it to press it down.
5 It can be supported by putting a board underneath.
6 This little affair is not sufficient to trouble him.
7 It will require thick paste in order to hold it.
8 You are too communicative, you cannot keep anything to yourself.
9 This horse is hard in the mouth, I cannot hold him.
10 Whose mouth can you shut up?
11 I fear my own strength will not bear the strain.
12 Every time the medicine is applied the pain is intolerable.
13 A diligent man cannot endure to be idle a moment.
14 My abilities are no match for his.
15 That umbrella is too small; it will not shelter one.
16 It is uncertain whether the year will be a plentiful one or not.
17 Never fear: I can remember it all.
18 I took a dose of pain-killer, but it did not stop the pain.
19 This piece of wood is too slender; it is quite insufficient to bear the strain.
20 This is a dangerous and important place; I am not able to guard it alone.
21 That man is too communicative, he cannot keep a single thing.

年景 *Nien² ching³*. The harvest, the season, *the year*.

止 *Chï³*. *To cease*, to desist; to remain, to wait; but, only; conduct.

險 *Hsien³*. . . . A precipice; *dangerous*, hazardous.

險要 *Hsien³ yao⁴*. Perilous; *a dangerous but important juncture or position.*

把守 *Pa³ shou³*. . . . . *To guard*, to defend.

盛 *Ch'êng²*. To fill into a vessel; *to hold*, to contain. Also *shêng⁴*.

圈籠 *Ch'üen¹ lung²*. To surround, *to entrap*, to ensnare.

才 *Ts'ai²*. . . . Talent, *endowment*, ability, genius.

口才 *K'ou³ ts'ai²*. The gift of speech, *eloquence*.

成家 *Ch'êng² chia¹*. To take a wife; to set up for oneself.

立業 *Li⁴ yie⁴*. To attain a competency, to make one's fortune.

摘 *Chai¹, tsê.⁴* To pick, as fruit, *to pull;* to deprive of; to choose; to select.

牙 *Ya²*. . . . . . . *A tooth*, a tusk; a bud; an agent.

捱 *Ai²*, *yai²*. To suffer, to bear, to endure, *to stand.* Also *ai¹*.

董 *Tung³*. . . . . . . To store up, *a surname.*

涵 *Han²*. To steep, to submerge; capacious; large-hearted, lenient.

昌 *Ch'ang¹*. . . . . . . Brilliant, elegant, prosperous.

兇手 *Hsiung¹ shou³*. . . . . A murderer.

○他[23]想之用圈籠圈子套我、那能圈籠套得住呢。○我[24]看你大大的對不住我。○這[25]麼大的風、燈籠那能點得住呢。○說[26]話能戀得住人、纔算眞有口才。○人[27]若能守得住、再沒有不成家立業的。○摘[28]個牙能有多麼疼呢、我不信我挨不住。○殺[29]董涵昌的那個兇手、已經拏住了。○國[30]若自相分爭、國必站立不住。○他[31]的脾氣不好、一個朋友也交不住。○[32]白日天裏還不怎麼樣、就是黑夜夜裏受不住。○這[33]永遠受不完的苦、我怎能忍得住呢。○我[34]的妹夫、受得了一個雞爪瘋、大小東西、都拿不住。○若[35]眞有喜樂的事、誰也禁不住笑、眞有悲傷的事、誰也禁不住哭。○俗[36]語說、一不扭拗衆、我一個人、怎能扭拗得過住了衆人呢。

22 You are the father, and yet cannot govern your own child!
23 He proposes to entrap me, but he will not succeed in doing it.
24 I consider that you have treated me very badly.
25 With such a strong wind how can you expect to keep a lantern lighted?
26 A man is accounted really eloquent when he can so speak as to captivate people.
27 If a man can preserve what he inherits, he will not fail to advance his fortunes.
28 What great pain can there be in having a tooth pulled? I do not believe that I cannot stand it.
29 The murderer who killed Tung Han Ch'ang, has been arrested.
30 A kingdom divided against itself cannot stand.
31 His disposition is so bad that he cannot retain a single friend.
32 In the daytime it is not so bad, night is the time that I cannot endure it.
33 This suffering which never ends, how can I endure it?
34 My brother-in-law has the chicken-foot palsy. He can hold nothing either large or small.
35 When there is anything really joyful, no one can help laughing; when there is anything really sorrowful, no one can help crying.
36 The proverb says, "One cannot hinder all." How can I, a single person, obstruct [the business of] all?

分爭 *Fên*[1] *chêng*[1]. To dispute, to quarrel, *to contest.*
站立 *Chan*[4] *li*[4]. . . . . . . *To stand;* to endure.
白日 *Pai*[2] *ji*[4]. . . . . Daytime, daylight.
天裡 *T'ien*[1] *li*[3]. . . . . Same. (s.)
夜裡 *Yie*[4] *li*[3] . . . . .A night, in the night.
妹夫 *Mei*[4] *fu*[1]. . . . . .A younger sister's husband.
爪 *Chwa*[3], *chao*[3]. *Claws,* talons; to scratch; to hold in the claws.
雞爪瘋 *Chi*[1] *chwa*[3] *fêng*[1]. A species of palsy or paralysis in which the fingers become contracted and stiff.
喜樂 *Hsi*[3] *loa*[4]. Rejoicing; *joyful,* lighthearted, cheery.
禁 *Chin*[4]. To prohibit, to forbid, *to restrain;* to impose upon. Also *chin*[1].
拗 *Niu*[4], *ao*[4]. To break off, to twist; obstinate, perverse; to impede, *to obstruct.*

Notes.

2 Rebels in China are practically bands of robbers, hence 賊 often means rebels. The rebels in the T'ai P'ing rebellion were generally called 長毛賊, *long-haired rebels.*

4 捶板石 or 捶布石 A smooth squared stone, on which starched clothes are pounded with wooden clubs to smooth and stiffen them. 板 is used with reference to the shape of the stone, and 布 with reference to the purpose for which it is used. Neither term is known in the South, for the reason that there clothes are not treated in this way.

5 Or, *Put a board underneath and it will support it.*

第七十六課

我[1]們一天忙到黑晚。○苦[2]終自有甜來到。○沒[3]料到今天下雨。○一[4]天怕他赶不到。○做[5]到老、學到老、還有三分學不到。○可[6]以僱脚子、把貨發到通州去。○灰[7]塵四起、直樸到臉上來。○挨[8]到這個時候、我纔想起來了。○叫[9]他們搬到別的地方去住。○老[10]兄甚麼時候來的、答剛纔來到。○你[11]說到這個、我不能帮助你們。○藏[12]珍寶的地方、那些賊沒搜到。○鄆[13]道一、自從和王元典那個壞蛋、交往上了、不知不覺的、就走到下流去了。○不[14]是說你病了嗎、怎麼跑到這裏來呢。

TRANSLATION.

1 We were busy from morning till night.
2 After the bitter naturally comes the sweet.
3 It did not occur to us that it might rain to-day.
4 I fear he cannot push through in a day.
5 One learns as long as he lives, and still leaves much unlearned.
6 You may hire conveyances and forward the goods to Tungchow.
7 The dust rose on all sides and puffed in their faces.
8 After all this time, I have only now thought of it.
9 Let them move to some other place to live.
10 When did you come? *Ans.* I have but just arrived.
11 In the matter you refer to, I cannot help you.
12 The robbers did not ransack the place where his jewels were.
13 From the time that Yün Tao I began to associate with that worthless fellow, Wang Yüen Hsing, he has insensibly fallen into vicious habits.

7 糨 takes 子 after it in some places, and in some it does not. The Southern term is 糨糊.

12 扛 is the more colloquial form, and very widely used.

14 A literal translation would require "him" at the end instead of "his." The sentence, in order to give a logical structure, ought to end with a 的. The Chinese are not generally sensible of such incongruities.

18 止疼藥 *Stop pain medicine,*—the name given to Perry Davis' Pain Killer, which has been extensively sold in China.

20 險要 In this phrase the two words are different in meaning and both significant, hence a full translation requires two words.

24 Or, more literally, *I should think you would have no face at all to see me.*

27 守得住 as here used, means to preserve intact the inheritance received from one's fathers. The form in the Sacred Edict is 守的住, which is a form rarely, if ever, heard amongst the people. 成家立業 The composition of this phrase shows how closely family and fortune are united in the Chinese mind.

29 兇手 *Murderous hand—a murderer.* 手 is often joined with verbs or adjectives to characterize an individual by his conduct, or by his trade, thus 吹手 *a musician,* 鎗手 *a spearman,* 起手 *a pickpocket,* etc.

30 自 is used for 自己. The 己 is excluded by the close union formed with 相, although 相 is logically connected with the following 分爭.

32 天裡 is in some places always said 白天裡.

34 得 is more widely used than 受, despite the fact that 受 is evidently more appropriate.

LESSON LXXVI.

THE AUXILIARY 到.

到 To arrive at, is added as an auxiliary to such words as will take the qualifying idea of continuance, or of extension to some point of time or place. For list of words taking this auxiliary see Supplement.

○你[15]敬我一尺、我敬你一丈、你敬我一丈、我擡舉你到天上。○已[16]經送到這裏、請回去罷。○我[17]寄捎了兩封信給李先生、一封也沒寄捎到。○大[18]家約會九點鐘齊、怎麼就誤到如今呢。○我[19]沒想到還有這些難爲。○天[20]下的事情、只有說不到的、沒有做不到的。○你[21]天天這麼遊手好閒的、懶到幾時是個頭兒／纔收頭呢。○我[22]若信他、倚靠他、他的功勞、就歸到我的身上。○你[23]去迎客、迎到那裏呢、答 迎到二十里堡。○我[24]十八歲那一年、從春天一直病到秋天。

14 You were reported sick, were you not? How is it that you are running around here?

15 You honor me a foot, and I'll honor you a rod; you honor me a rod, and I'll exalt you to heaven.

16 Having accompanied me so far, please return.

17 I sent two letters to Mr. Li, but neither of them reached him.

18 We all agreed to be on hand by nine o'clock; how is it that you are so late as this?

19 It had not occurred to me that there would be these difficulties.

20 In human affairs, many things occur which no one ever anticipated.

21 You are idly lounging around in this way every day. When will your indolence come to an end?

22 If I believe on him, and trust him, his merit will accrue to my account.

23 When you went out to meet your guest, how far did you go? *Ans.* I went to the twenty *li* station.

24 The year I was eighteen I was sick

甜 *T'ien*². . . . . *Sweet*, savory; agreeable.

通州 *T'ung*¹ *chou*¹. Tungchow, a *fu* city forty . . . . *li* south-east of Peking.

塵 *Ch'ên*². *Dust*, particles; traces; the age, the . . . . world; vice and pleasure.

灰塵 *Hwei*¹ *ch'ên*². . . . . Dust, dirt.

樸 *P'u*¹. To lean against; to strike against; to flap, ... to clap; to rush suddenly, *to puff*.

四起 *Sï*⁴ *ch'i*³. . . . . To rise on all sides.

挨 *Ai*¹, *yai*¹. Side by side, in order; to push, to . . . . crowd; to lean on, to trust to; *to put off;* to postpone. See *ai*².

珍寶 *Chên*¹ *pao*³. . . . . . Pearls, *jewels*, treasures.

搜 *Sou*¹. To search, to make thorough and dili- . . . . gent search, *to ransack;* swift, quick.

鄆 *Yün*⁴. An ancient city in the kingdom of Lu; . . . . *a surname.*

壞蛋 *Hwai*⁴ *tan*⁴. A bad egg, *a worthless fellow*, ... a good-for-nothing, a scamp.

不知不覺 *Pu*⁴ *chï*¹ *pu*⁴ *chüe*². *Insensibly*, un- . . . . consciously.

下流 *Hsia*⁴ *liu*⁴. . . . . *Vicious*, vulgar, mean.

約會 *Yoä*¹ *hwei*⁴. *To agree to meet;* to call a . . . . meeting.

遊手 *Yiu*² *shou*³. *To idle away time*, to loiter, ... to dawdle.

好閒 *Hao*⁴ *hsien*². Lazy, indolent; *to lounge*, ... to loaf.

收頭 *Shou*¹ *t'ou*². To end, *to come to an end*, ... to finish up.

倚 *I*³. To rely on, to trust to, to depend upon; . . . . a fulcrum.

倚靠 *I*³ *k'ao*⁴. *To trust to*, to rely on; to lean . . . . upon, to rest.

堡 *P'u*⁴, *pu*³'⁴. . . . . . . *A guard station*, a hamlet.

春天 *Ch'un*¹ *t'ien*¹. . . . . Spring.

秋 *Ch'iu*¹. . . . . Autumn; a season, sad.

秋天 *Ch'iu*¹ *t'ien*¹. . . . . Autumn.

花子 *Hwa*¹ *tsï*³. . . . . *A beggar*, a mendicant.

討飯 *T'ao*³ *fan*⁴. *To beg for bread*, to be a . . . . beggar.

讀書 *Tu*² *shu*¹. . . . . . *To study*, to go to school.

辦理 *Pan*⁴ *li*³. . . . *To do*, to transact, to manage.

蝎 *Hsie*¹. . . . . A scorpion.

螫 *Chê*¹. *To sting;* a sting; poisonous. Also . . . . . . *shï*⁴.

○他[25]對你提到我的事情沒有、答一點也沒提。○昨[26]天有個花子、跑到門口討飯、沒給他什麼、他就罵起來了。○讀[27]書有三到、就是眼到、心到、口到。○俗[28]語說、到了河邊再脫鞋、意思、就是等事情臨到眼前、再打算怎樣辦理。○昨[29]天晚上、我叫蝎子螫了一下毒鉤子、直疼到今天早上纔好了。○過[30]了大街、我們來到城隍廟、那裏有說書的、變戲法的、耍猴子的、唱小曲的、賣畫眉的、鬪鵪鶉的、甚麼玩意兒都有。

continuously from spring to autumn.

25 Did he speak to you of my affairs? *Ans.* He did not mention them.

26 Yesterday a beggar came to the door wanting something to eat, and when nothing was given him, he began to revile.

27 There are three requisites to study—the eyes, the mind and the tongue.

28 The saying runs, When you have reached the river it is time enough to take off your shoes, which means, wait till the thing is actually at hand before you plan what you will do.

29 Yesterday evening a scorpion stung me, and it pained me continuously until this morning before it ceased.

30 Crossing the great street we came to the Ch'êng Hwang temple, where were story telling, sleight of hand performing, monkey shows, song singing, thrush venders, quail fighting and every kind of amusement.

鉤 *Kou*¹. A hook; a claw, *a barb*, a clasp; to ....hook; to detain; to tempt, to entice; to sew in a lining.

隍 *Hwang*². The moat or ditch around a city .... wall.

城隍 *Ch'êng*² *hwang*². The tutelar god of a .... city:—Note 30.

說書 *Shwoa*¹ *shu*¹. To recite stories—usually ....the imaginary exploits of noted characters, heroes, robbers, rebels, etc.

戲法 *Hsi*⁴ *fa*³. *Sleight of hand*, tricks, leger- .... demain, jugglery.

猴 *Hou*². .... *A monkey;* tricky, unreliable.

曲 *Ch'ü*³. ... *Songs*, ditties, ballads. Also *ch'ü*¹.

畫眉 *Hwa*⁴ *mei*². .... The grey thrush.

鵪 *An*¹. .... The quail.

鶉 *Ch'un*². .... The quail.

鵪鶉 The quail.

玩意 *Wan*² *i*⁴. Toys, play-things; *amusements*, ...in fun, in play.

NOTES.

1 晚 is more widely used in this connection than 黑.

2 A proverb, expressing the idea that when misery has reached its limit, happiness follows in natural order. 自 is a contraction for 自然. As usual with proverbs, the style is terse and bookish.

4 趕不到 Said of one accomplishing a journey.

5 Lit., *Work till old age—learn till old age, and yet there will be three parts* [in ten] *unlearned.*

6 脚 includes both packmules and carts, but usually refers to the former. 脚子, in the South, means coolies who carry burdens. In some places 脚子 also means a small boat—a ship's boat.

7 Bunyan's original is, "The dust began so abundantly to fly about that they had almost been choked."

11 This sentence might also mean: *Having spoken in this way, I will not help you.* All depends on the circumstances and on the emphasis given by the speaker.

13 壞蛋 *A spoiled egg,*—a figure for a worthless renegade, more expressive than elegant, and much stronger than the corresponding expression in English.

15 Not used in direct address to the other party, but only put so for the purpose of illustration or exhortation.

16 Said out of politeness by a guest to the person escorting him.

18 齊 *even, uniform; i.e., all present.*

21 遊手好閒 *Swinging the hands and delighting in idleness,*—an expressive book phrase in common use.

27 有三到 *Three things at it,*—that is the eye, the mind and the mouth, must all be brought into service and kept to it. The sentence does not properly illustrate the principle of the lesson.

28 The idea is, don't anticipate trouble before it comes. "Sufficient unto the day is the evil thereof."

第七十七課

你[1]為甚麼來的這樣遲晚呢。○不[2]要因為一點小事生氣。○因[3]朋友的臉面、不好意思不去。○為[4]着一半句話、也不犯記在心裏。○我[5]們為的是這口氣、不是為這幾兩銀子。○他[6]那個租錢、為甚麼付不上來呢。○我[7]名叫羣、因為我們多的緣故。○人[8]為財死、鳥為食亡。○為[9]個蒼蠅、破個扁食。○人[10]的心術難以知道、因為藏在裏頭。○他[11]不上你的門兒、必是因為你得罪了他。○賊[12]還能憑空的咬他嗎、逢咬他、必有所因。○他[13]們兩家不和、是因之着賭錢的根。○你[14]為甚麼單來找我的不是呢。○他[15]們因為話不投機、打的頭破血流出。○這[16]個孩子的眼睛、是因着出生疹子、被風掭吹壞了。

Translation.

1 Why are you so late as this in coming?
2 Do not get angry on account of a small matter.
3 On account of my friend's feelings, I am ashamed not to go.
4 A matter of a few words; it is not worth keeping in mind.
5 What we want is to get revenge, not to get these few taels.
6 Why is it that he cannot pay that rent of his?
7 My name is legion; for we are many.
8 Men die for money, and birds lose their lives for food.
9 To smash a dumpling on account of a fly.
10 The devices of the heart are hard to know, for they are hidden within.
11 That he does not enter your door, must be because you have offended him.
12 Would the thief accuse him without any cause? If he accuses him, there must be some occasion.
13 The strife between the two families took its rise in gambling.
14 Why are you always finding fault with me?
15 Because of a misunderstanding, they fought till their heads were cut and bleeding.
16 This child's eyes were destroyed by exposure to the wind when he had measles.

30 城隍 Lit., *city moat*, but popularly used as the title of the tutelar god of the city. Each walled city in China has such a god and a temple in his honor. These temples are generally the finest temples in the city and kept in the best repair, and are the most resorted to by worshippers. There is no one individual god known as Ch'êng Hwang at large, but each city has its own—a deified man acting as patron god of the city. They are supposed to be appointed and rotated from time to time. Each city god has the same rank in the unseen world that the chief officer of the city over which he presides has in this world. In some cases the courts of this temple are the constant scene of a sort of Vanity Fair, in others, only on the occasion of the regular festivals in honor of the god.

LESSON LXXVII.

Causal Particles.

因 To proceed, to rely on, for, because, since.

為 To do, to become, for, because, since, on account of.

因為 For, because, since, inasmuch as.

因着 or 因之 Same as 因 alone.

為着 Same as 為 alone.

為了 Same as 為 alone,—only used in Southern Mandarin.

為什麼 Because of what; *i.e.*, why, wherefore.

為的是 For the purpose of, why.

○住地方
[17]謀衣食、不可因爲一時不順心、就說拉倒。○
他[18]做買賣不發財、就是因爲用度太大了。○因[19]
爲我沒招呼讓他喫飯、他就說我眼中無人。○不[20]
必因着孩子家爭吵吵嘴、兩家就失了和氣、○我[21]因
爲是你們的叔叔、不得不再三囑咐再四叮嚀你們。○你[22]
怎麼認得張二爺呢、答我在烟臺開漿糨洗鋪、因
之洗衣裳、纔認得他。○兄[2]弟應當恭敬哥哥、因
爲他的年紀長、名分大。○我[24]因今日的快樂、將
這一年的憂愁、全忘了。○他[25]給你錢、你爲甚麼
不要、你天天東跑西遶、爲的是什麼呢。○爲[26]什

17 When you are working for another you should not be ready to throw up your place because, on a single occasion, things do not go right.

18 He does not get rich at his business simply because his expenses are too great.

19 Because I did not invite him to eat, he says I am too proud to notice [common] people.

20 It is not necessary to destroy the harmony of the two families because the children have had a quarrel.

21 Because I am your uncle I cannot help charging you again and again.

22 How do you come to be acquainted with Chang Êr Yie? *Ans.* I kept a washing shop at Chefoo and, by washing for him, came to know him.

23 The younger brother should show respect to the elder, because he is older in years and superior in rank.

24 Because of this day's joy, I have forgotten all the sorrows of the whole year.

25 Why did you not take the money when he offered it to you? For what are you striving every day?

VOCABULARY.

因 *Yin*[1]. To proceed, to rely on; a cause, a reason; because of, for, on account of; by means of, in consequence of; then, so.

租 *Tsu*[1]. . . . . . . *Rent*, rental; to rent, to lease.

租錢 *Tsu*[1] *ch'ien*[2]. . . . . *Rent*.

亡 *Wang*[2]. . . . . . . *To die*, to perish; lost.

蒼 *Ts'ang*[1]. The green of plants, azure of the sky; hoary, old.

蠅 *Ying*[2]. . . . . A fly, the house-fly.

蒼蠅 The house-fly, flies in general.

術 *Shu*[4]. An art, a craft, a trick, *a device*, a mystery.

心術 *Hsin*[1] *shu*[4]. *Device*, design; disposition, character.

上門 *Shang*[4] *mên*[2]. *To visit* [socially], to call on.

憑空 *P'ing*[2] *k'ung*[1]. *Without cause* or evidence, for nothing.

賭錢 *Tu*[3] *ch'ien*[2]. *To gamble*, to play for money, to bet.

投機 *T'ou*[2] *chi*[1]. *To understand*, to get the clue, to see the point.

疹 *Chên*[3]. Pustules or pimples, rash; *measles*, scarlet fever, etc.

撩 *Liao*[2]. To take hold of; to manage; to play with; to incite, to seduce, *to inflame;* to fell a seam, to overseam. Also *liao*[4].

謀 *Mou*[2]. A stratagem, an artifice; to deliberate, to scheme, *to plan*, to plot.

衣食 *I*[1] *shi*[2]. . . . Food and clothes, a livelihood.

順心 *Shun*[4] *hsin*[1]. *To one's mind*, agreeable, acquiescent.

度 *Tu*[4]. A measure; a degree, a limit, a rule; capacity; to arrange; *to spend or pass time;* to ford. Also *toa*.[4]

用度 *Yung*[4] *tu*[4]. . . . . *Expenses*, living.

招呼 *Chao*[1] *hu*[1]. . . . To call, *to invite*, to beckon.

爭吵 *Chêng*[1] *ch'ao*[3]. *To quarrel*, to wrangle, to bicker.

吵嘴 *Ch'ao*[3] *tswei*[3]. *To quarrel*, to scold, to wrangle.

麼不託人帶來呢、答因爲信中有要緊的事情、等不得了。○ 27 他沒告假、怎麼走了呢、答因爲老爺欠安、他不便告假。○ 28 應當愛惜光陰、因爲光陰不能爲你留得住。○ 29 端午節喫糯米糭子、是因爲屈原、被小人讒謗、自己跳在汨羅江淹死了、後來託夢給人、叫包一些糭子、丢扔在江中、這纔興起端午節、喫糭子的風俗來。

26 Why did you not send it by some one? *Ans.* Because there are important matters in the letter which could not wait.

27 How came he to go without asking leave of absence? *Ans.* Because you were not feeling well, he thought it would be inconvenient to ask you.

28 You ought to improve the time, because time will not wait for you.

29 The reason balls of glutinous rice are eaten on the dragon-boat festival, is that Ch'ü Yüen, when falsely accused by bad men, threw himself into the Miloă river and was drowned; afterwards he directed some one, in a dream, to make some rice balls and throw them into the river. From this arose the custom of eating rice balls on the dragon-boat festival.

再四 *Tsai⁴ sï⁴*. . . . . . Again and again. (s.)
叮 *Ting¹*. . . . . . . To enjoin; to bite, to sting.
嚀 *Ning²*. . . . . To direct.
叮嚀 To charge, to enjoin. (w.)
名分 *Ming² fên⁴*. *Rank*, station, office; the duties . . . . pertaining to any station.
逩 *Pên⁴*. . . . . . . To run, *to hasten*, to rush.
欠安 *Ch'ien⁴ an¹*. . . . . Indisposed, *unwell*.
假 *Chia⁴*. *Leave of absence*, furlough. See *chia³*. . . . . . .
告假 *Kao⁴ chia⁴*. . . . . .To ask leave of absence.
端午 *Twan¹ wu³*. The dragon-boat festival on the . . . . fifth day of the fifth month.
江 *Chiang¹*. . . . . . . A deep rapid river.
江米 *Chiang¹ mi³*. . . . . .Glutinous rice.
糯 *Noă⁴*. . . . . Glutinous rice.
糯米 *Noă⁴ mi³*. . . . . Same.
糭 *Tsung⁴*. Glutinous rice dumplings with fruit . . . . or meat inside, and wrapped in leaves for cooking.
讒 *Ts'an²*. . . . . . . To traduce, to slander.
謗 *Pang⁴*. . . . . . . To vilify, to slander.
讒謗 *To accuse falsely*, to slander, to traduce.
汨 *Mi⁴*. . . . . . . Name of a river. Also *ku³*.
夢 *Meng⁴*. . . . . To dream; a dream.
風俗 *Fêng¹ su²*. . . . . .*Custom*, vogue, tradition.

NOTES.

4 一半句話 *Half of a sentence*, that is, a few words or sentences. 犯 is here used in the sense of *worth while*. This use is general, but somewhat anomalous. Some teachers would write with 煩, as being more suitable to the meaning, though not the right tone.

5 Note how different is the meaning of 口氣, from the *phrase* 口氣 in Les. 55. The two characters here stand separately, each with its own meaning.

8 食 here refers to the bait set to catch the bird.

9 A widely known proverb, meaning to incur serious loss for a small cause.

12 咬 *to bite*, is used figuratively of the accusation of a prisoner against an accomplice. Such accusations are often procured by torture, and are not infrequently false. 所因 *that which because; i.e., some cause or occasion.*

15 話不投機 Lit., *words failed to transmit the rationale or idea.* 頭破血出 *Head broken and blood flowing*, a ready made phrase.

16 疹子 is used generically for any rash attended by fever, and includes scarlet fever, measles and chicken-pox.

17 謀衣食 is the less used, and more pedantic expression. 說拉倒 "*To throw up a situation*," "*to give warning.*" In this connection 拉倒 is quite *t'ung hsing.*

19 沒讓他吃飯 does not mean, *did not allow him to eat*; but, *began to eat before him without offering a share to him by way of apology.* When you begin to eat in another's presence, or when any one approaches where you are eating, politeness requires that you invite him to share with you. This invitation is a mere civility, it being understood that it will be declined. 眼中無人 is a book phrase.

第七十八課

前[1]幾天放了兵餉、所以銀子賤了。○我[2]是從南路來的、所以沒遇見他。○你[3]已經哄了我好幾回、因此我再不聽你。○昨[4]夜因爲睡的太遲晚、所以今天沒有精神、光想之着打盹駭盹。○這[5]件事所以難成、是因爲有人挑唆。○上[6]半天我的頭疼、所以不能考書。○我[7]們知道他是誤殺、故此敢來給他作見証。○以[8]後因爲推脫不開、所以纔應承了。○我[9]覺得有你在那裏、所以我就沒管。○如[10]今的人、多是嘴甜心苦、所以不可輕易

TRANSLATION.

1 A few days ago the soldiers received their pay and hence silver is cheap.
2 I came by the south road and therefore did not meet him.
3 You have already deceived me several times; therefore I shall not listen to you again.
4 I retired very late last night; hence I have no animation to-day, but am all the time nodding.
5 The reason this affair is hard to consummate, is because there is some one meddling with it.
6 In the forenoon my head ached and therefore I could not recite.
7 We know that he killed him accidentally; therefore we are bold to testify for him.
8 Afterwards, because he could find no excuse, he gave the promise.
9 I knew that you were there and therefore I paid no attention.
10. At the present time, the majority of men are deceitful, therefore it is not well to be too credulous.

21 再四 is not commonly used, but is the form in the Fortunate Union, from which the sentence is taken. 叮嚀 also is not often used colloquially, the common expression being 囑附.

25 東跑西逩 *Run east and rush west, to hasten hither and thither with work or business*, a common and expressive phrase.

29 端午 is colloquial, but *t'ung hsing.* The book term is 端陽. 屈原 a statesman of the kingdom of Ts'u, B. C. 314. He was falsely accused by a jealous rival and disgraced, and in his grief committed suicide by jumping into the 汨羅 Miloă river. As the name of a river the proper reading of 汨 is *mi*, but the other reading *ku*[3] is often confused with it.

LESSON LXXVIII.

ILLATIVE PARTICLES.

所以 The reason or cause; therefore, hence.

因此 } For this cause, on this account,
爲此 } therefore.

故此 On this account, consequently, therefore.

因這個緣故 or 爲這個緣故 For this reason.

因而 And so, and hence, and on this account. A book term, the use of which in conversation is somewhat pedantic.

VOCABULARY.

而 *Ér*². And, and yet, also; still, moreover; as if, contrariwise. Much used in *Wên-li* but rarely in Mandarin, save in certain combinations.

餉 *Hsiang*³. Rations, pay of soldiers; taxes, duties, revenue.

兵餉 *Ping*¹ *hsiang*³. *Soldiers' pay or wages;* money for this purpose.

精神 *Ching*¹ *shên*². That (supposed) divine essence which gives life and vigor to the soul, life, *animation,* spirits, vivacity.

盹 *Tun*³. Dull, heavy, sleepy; *a nod.*

打盹 *Ta*³ *tun*³. *To nod,* to doze; to be sleepy, to be drowsy.

相信。○我11因爲他不知好歹、所以再不管他的閒
事。○他12喫那些不當喫的東西、故此生病。○我13有
一點要緊的用項、所以必得支錢。○從14前他們倆
就和一個人一樣、以後買賣倒了、賬目有些不清、
爲此兩家纔弄鬧扭擰了。○趙15硯田因爲五十歲得子、
所以道喜的人很多。○我16時常思想你、眼淚淌流乾、
因此瞎了雙眼。○他17告李先生這些事情、一點憑
據沒有、所以必是誣告。○你18平常不交往人、所以
你有苦難、人都不願帮助。○迦19猶道、我因爲閱歷
過這事、故此會猜破這謎兒。○因20爲皇上年輕、不能

11 Since he does not know when he is well treated, I shall therefore have nothing more to do with his affairs.
12 He eats improper food, therefore he is ill.
13 I have a little pressing need, and therefore am compelled to draw my money.
14 Formerly they two were of one mind in everything; afterwards their business failed and their accounts became involved, and, on this account, the two families got into a quarrel.
15 Because Chao Yien T'ien has had a son born to him at fifty, therefore a great many are presenting congratulations.
16 I have wept my eyes dry thinking constantly of you: on this account both eyes have become blind.
17 There is not the least proof of the things he charges against Mr. Li; he is undoubtedly accusing him falsely.
18 Ordinarily you are not neighbourly, therefore, when you are in trouble, people are not inclined to help you.
19 Chia Yiu replied, "Because I have passed through this experience, therefore I can solve this riddle."

憁 *Ch'ung*⁴. . . . . . To come abruptly; *to nod.* (s)
憁盹 *Ch'ung*⁴ *tun*³. . . . . . . To nod. (s).
誤殺 *Wu*⁴ *sha*¹. . . . . . . To kill by accident.
應承 *Ying*¹ *ch'êng*². To agree, to assent, *to promise.*
用項 *Yung*⁴ *hsiang*⁴. Use, utility, function; *need*, requirement.
田 *T'ien*². . . . . . . A field; fields, lands.
道喜 *Tao*⁴ *hsi*³. . . . . To congratulate.
時常 *Shï*² *ch'ang*². Constantly, continually, customarily.
思想 *Sï*¹ *hsiang*³. *To think of*, to reflect, to consider.
淌 *T'ang*⁴. To run—as water, to flow, to course, to drip.
據 *Chü*⁴. To occupy, to lean on; testimony, *evidence;* according to, from; to reject.
憑據 *P'ing*² *chü*⁴. . . . . *Proof*, evidence.
誣 *Wu*¹. . . . . . *To accuse falsely*, to calumniate.
誣告 *Wu*¹ *kao*⁴. *To accuse falsely*, to trump up charges.

迦 *Chia*¹. . . . . Used only in names.
猶 *Yiu*². Resembling, like; as if, same as; still, even; thus, so.
閱歷 *Yüe*⁴ *li*⁴. *To pass through*, to experience; to look over, to examine.
猜 *Ts'ai*¹. To suspect; to guess, to conjecture, *to solve.*
謎 *Mi*²,⁴. . . . . . . *A riddle*, an enigma, a puzzle.
破謎 *P'o*⁴ *mi*². To propose a riddle, to solve a riddle:—Note 19.
后 *Hou*⁴. A ruler; the sovereign; *empress* or queen, a feudal prince.
太后 *T'ai*⁴ *hou*⁴. . . . . . . The Emperor's mother.
垂 *Ch'wei*². To hang down, *to suspend;* to let fall; to reach to; to condescend.
評 *P'ing*². To discuss; to criticize, to review; *to judge of.*
評論 *P'ing*² *lun*⁴. To discuss, *to give an opinion*, to criticize.
禿 *T'u*¹. . . . . . *Bald*, bare; blunt; unscrupulous.
暴病 *Pao*⁴ *ping*⁴. . . . . . . A violent disease.

治國、所以太后、纔垂簾聽政。○古21人評論說、這和尙眞是利害、因此蘇東坡道、不禿不毒、不毒不禿。○我22們正走到半路、有人趕着來送信說、他母親得了個急促暴病、因這個緣故、他又回去了。○他23是個男人、怎麼叫他劉老婆呢、答他的聲音很尖、又常和女人一塊兒說話、爲這個緣故、人就給他一個綽外號、叫劉老婆。○這24家去報喪、報的太遲晚、那家來弔喪、弔的更遲晚、因而兩家漸漸疎淡、現在已經不上門兒咯。

20 On account of his youth the Emperor cannot assume the reins of government, hence it is that Empress-mother hears causes from behind the curtain.

21 The opinion of the ancients is that these Buddhist priests are very outrageous; therefore Su Tung P'oă says, "He who is not bare-pated is not venomous; he who is not venomous is not bare-pated."

22 When we were just half-way, a man overtook us with a message, saying his mother had taken a violent disease, so on this account he returned again.

23 Why is he called Old Woman Liu when he is a man? *Ans.* His voice is very sharp and he is constantly with the women talking to them, on which account people have nicknamed him Old Woman Liu.

24 This family gave notice of the funeral too late, and that family were still later in offering their condolences, and on this account the two families became gradually estranged, so that they have now ceased to enter each other's doors.

促病 *Ts'u⁴ ping⁴*. A sudden and violent disease.

急病 *Chi² ping⁴*. . . . . Same.

聲音 *Shêng¹ yin¹*. . . . . .Sound, *voice*, cry.

外號 *Wai⁴ hao⁴*. . . . . A nickname.

綽號 *Ch'ao¹ hao⁴*. . . . A nickname, fancy name.

喪 *Sang¹*. To mourn for parents; *a funeral;* time of mourning. See *sang⁴*.

報喪 *Pao⁴ sang¹*. To report a death and give notice of burial:—Note 24.

弔喪 *Tiao⁴ sang¹*. To present condolences at or before a funeral.

疎 *Su¹*. Open, coarse; distant, sundered, *estranged;* careless, remiss.

淡 *Tan⁴*. Insipid, flat; weak, watery; *distant—as an offended friend;* light—as a color.

疎淡 *Estranged*, cool, separated.

NOTES.

1 Chinese soldiers are usually paid at considerable intervals, and when they are paid each one wants to sell his silver for copper cash, to be used in paying debts. This sudden demand for cash, especially in small places, makes silver cheap.

4 Notice that 睡的太晚 does not mean *slept too late in the morning*, but, *went to bed too late in the evening.* Sleeping late in the morning is expressed by saying 起來的晚.

6 I have translated as if this were the language of a pupil. It would however be equally appropriate in the mouth of a teacher. 考書 means properly *to examine a class*, but is also used to mean *being examined or reciting.*

8 The force of 纔, as here used, is difficult to bring into an English translation. See also 14.

9 In many places the 有 would be omitted.

10 嘴甜心苦 *The mouth sweet and the heart bitter; i.e., using fair words to conceal an evil purpose, deceit, guile, imposture.*

14 他們倆就和一個人一樣 Lit., *They two were all the same as if one person; i.e., they agreed in everything.*

15 It is implied that the man had no son previously.

19 破謎 is occasionally used (as here) to mean, *to guess a riddle;* but generally it means, *to propound or make a riddle.* See Les. 200.

第七十九課

他[1]因爲偷嘴、不知挨了多少罵。○人[2]都是願愛享福、還有願愛受罪的嗎。○先[3]下手的爲强。後下手的遭殃。○若[4]是蒙恩不報、就叫忘恩負義了。○這[5]個孩子實在乖、一點也不淘氣、養着這等省心的孩子、大人少喫多少累呢。○你[6]弄出錯漏子兒來、我喫不住。○出[7]外離鄉的人、到患害病的時候、就更想家。○俗[8]語説、周瑜打黃蓋、一

Translation.

1 There is no telling how much scolding she has had to bear for eating things on the sly.

2 All men wish to enjoy happiness. Are there any who wish to suffer?

3 He who strikes the first blow gets the advantage; he who strikes second gets the worst of it.

4 When a man receives a favor and does not return it, he is said to be ungrateful.

5 This child is peculiarly good; it is not the least troublesome. When such a good baby as this falls to one's lot, how much toil it saves.

6 If you stir up a difficulty, I shall not be able to endure it.

7 When one away from home gets ill,

---

20 垂簾聽政 *Suspend a curtain and hear government affairs.* The Empress is not supposed in etiquette to meet her ministers face to face, but to hear their reports and give her orders, sitting behind a curtain. The expression is decidedly *Wên-li* in style.

21 蘇東坡 A celebrated statesman and literary genius of the Sung dynasty. This saying of his is an alliterative play on the words 禿 and 毒, and refers to the custom of Buddhist priests of shaving their heads. The sarcasm of the saying is that no treachery or dishonesty is worthy of the name as compared with that of a priest, and that no man who is not treacherous and dishonest will be a priest.

24 Upon the death of any one, a messenger is sent to inform the relatives and kindred of the fact, and to announce the date of the funeral. This is called 報喪. In the case of rich or official families a written or printed paper is sent. Upon the day of the funeral, kindred and friends present their condolences, worship before the coffin, make a small contribution of cash and partake of the feast provided. This is called 弔喪.

LESSON LXXIX.

Receptive Verbs.

受 To receive, to bear,—very widely used and limited by no special circumstances.

挨 To bear,—pain, evil or abuse, generally inflicted by another.

遭 To meet with,—misfortune, pain or loss

吃 To eat; i.e., suffer,—loss or trouble.

害 To be injured by,—disease, pain or shame.

患 To be afflicted with,—disease.

蒙 To receive,—favor, grace or kindness.

享 To receive, i.e., enjoy,—happiness, peace or prosperity.

領 To receive from,—a benefactor or superior.

Vocabulary.

享 *Hsiang*³. To accept as the gods do sacrifices; . . . . to enjoy; to receive gratefully.

福 *Fu*². Blessings conferred by the gods, *happiness*, felicity; prosperity.

蒙 *Mêng*². Dull, ignorant; to cover over, to conceal; to receive thankfully, to be obliged:—see Sub. Also *mêng*³.

患 *Hwan*⁴. Evil, misfortune, calamity, affliction; . . . . to suffer, to be afflicted:—see Sub.

受罪 *Shou*⁴ *tswei*⁴. To bear suffering, *to suffer*:— . . . . Note 2.

下手 *Hsia*⁴ *shou*³. To make a beginning; to take hold; to set to, *to take the initiative*; a second place, a sub-foreman.

殃 *Yang*¹ . . . Misfortune, judgment, *retribution.*

忘恩 *Wang*⁴ *ên*¹. To forget a favor, *to be ungrateful.*

個願打、一個願挨。○憐[9]恤人的人、是有福的、
因為他們必要蒙憐恤。○我[10]和他不是別旁外人、
不必計較誰吃虧、誰得便宜。○張[11]家那個養探童
養養媳婦、太受氣喇、天天挨打挨罵的、一點好
時候沒有。○昨[12]天大人看操看好了、今天兵
丁都去領賞去喇。○這[13]十年之內、我領了三
回賑、頭一回是領飯、第二回是領糧、第三回
是領錢。○用[14]胰子洗衣裳、人又省力、衣裳也
少喫受虧傷。○好[15]時候、他逍遙自在的要好懶、到這
時候受遭罪、誰可憐他呢。○這[16]樣破費你、我很

he is all the more homesick.

8 The saying is, "When Chiu Yü beats Hwang Kai, there is one willing to lay on and one willing to stand it."

9 Blessed are the merciful; for they shall surely receive mercy.

10 He does not stand in the same relation to me as others. It is not necessary to discuss who loses or who gains.

11 That *t'ung-yang* daughter-in-law of the Chang family is *too* much abused. She is beaten and scolded every day and has no comfort of her life.

12 The general was pleased with the parade yesterday, and to-day the soldiers have all gone to receive rewards.

13 Within these ten years I have received famine relief three times. The first time I received cooked rice; the second time, grain; and the third time, money.

14 By using soap to wash clothes, the person washing saves labor, and the clothes receive less injury.

15 When he was well-to-do, he took his ease and indulged his indolence; now that he has come to grief, who will pity him?

16 I am greatly indebted to you for

義 *I*^{4}. Equity, righteousness, uprightness; *free,* charitable, superior, excellent; adopted.

負義 *Fu*^{4} *i*^{4}. *To abuse kindness;* to render evil for good.

乖 *Kwai*^{1}. Perverse, contrary, bad-tempered, sulky; crafty, tricky; odd, *peculiar.*

省心 *Shêng*^{3} *hsin*^{1}. Trouble-saving, *good,* obedient.

漏子 *Lou*^{4} *tsï*^{3}. A mistake, *a difficulty.* (s.)

出外 *Ch'u*^{1} *wai*^{4}. *To leave home;* to go abroad, to travel.

離鄉 *Li*^{2} *hsiang*^{1}. *Away from home,* in a strange place; a stranger.

害病 *Hai*^{4} *ping*^{4}. Sick, *ill;* taken sick.

患病 *Hwan*^{4} *ping*^{4}. Same.

周 *Chou*^{1}. To make a circuit; to extend everywhere; plenty; honest; entirely; close, fine; a surname.

瑜 *Yü*^{2}. Lustrous; excellent.

較 *Chiao*^{4}. *To compare;* rather; in general.

計較 *Chi*^{4} *chiao*^{4}. To compare notes, *to discuss,* to argue, to bargain.

童 *T'ung*^{2}. A boy, a lad; a young student; *a virgin;* undefiled; youthful.

童養 *T'ung*^{2} *yang*^{3}. To support a betrothed girl before her marriage.

探養 *T'an*^{4} *yang*^{3}. Same:—Note 11.

受氣 *Shou*^{4} *ch'i*^{4}. Ill-treated, *abused.*

看操 *K'an*^{4} *ts'ao*^{1}. To review troops, to superintend the drilling of soldiers, *to witness a parade.*

兵丁 *Ping*^{1} *ting*^{1}. Soldiers.

賑 *Chên*^{4}. To relieve those in want; charity, bounty, *relief.*

逍 *Hsiao*^{1}. To ramble, to saunter at ease.

遙 *Yao*^{2}. Distant, remote.

逍遙 To saunter carelessly, *at one's ease.*

自在 *Tsï*^{4} *tsai*^{4}. Natural, *easy;* self-possessed, composed; comfortable.

領情、就是不喫不喝、也和喫了喝了一樣。○古17語說、打了不罰、罰了不打、我還能又挨打、又受罰嗎。○李18榮春一個好人、就是沒得好報、從小遭了許多顛險(磨折)。○他19訛你這幾吊錢、也富不了他、你出這幾吊錢、也窮不了你、不過暫且受點急急促。○官20司不是好打的、你看金狗家、誰不說是胎裏帶來的家當(紅的日子)、後來遭了一塲官司、弄的家產盡絕。

having taken so much trouble on my account. Though I do not eat or drink, it is the same as if I did.

17 There is an old saying, "When a man is beaten he is not fined; when fined, he is not beaten." Must I take a beating and be fined besides?

18 Li Jung Ch'un is a good man, but his virtue has not had a due reward. From his youth he has met with a great many misfortunes.

19 These few thousand cash out of which he has defrauded you, will not make him rich, nor will your paying them make you poor; it will simply put you to some temporary embarrassment.

20 Lawsuits are not profitable. Look at Chin Kou: who would not say that he had by birth a rich inheritance? Presently he got involved in a lawsuit and used up his patrimony completely.

好懶 *Hao*^{4} *lan*^{3}. To delight in idleness, *to indulge indolent habits.*

耍懶 *Shwa*^{3} *lan*^{3}. *To spend time in idleness,* to dilly-dally, to loiter.

破費 *P'oă*^{4} *fei*^{4}. To waste, *to spend lavishly*; to put to expense; to thank.

領情 *Ling*^{3} *ch'ing*^{2}. To receive a favor, *to be obliged,* under obligation to.

顛 *Tien*^{1}. To upset, *to overturn;* to ruin.

顛險 *Tien*^{1} *hsien*^{3}. Calamities, *misfortunes,* difficulties.

磨折 *Moă*^{2} *chê*^{2}. Trial, trouble, difficulty, *misfortune:*—Note 18.

胎 *T'ai*^{1}. The pregnant womb, *congenital;* a receptacle.

胎裡紅 *T'ai*^{1} *li*^{3} *hung*^{2}. Born in affluence, a splendid inheritance.

產 *Ch'an*^{3}. To produce, to bear; birth, parturition; productions; *estate;* occupation.

家產 *Chia*^{1} *ch'an*^{3}. Family inheritance, estate, property, *patrimony.*

盡絕 *Chin*^{4} *chüe*^{2}. Ended, used up; entirely, *completely.*

占 *Chan*^{1}. *To divine or foretell by a lot,* divination. Read *chan*^{4} when used for 佔.

卦 *Kwa*^{4}. A divining mark or diagram, a sign.

占卦 To cast lots, to divine, *to foretell.*

破財 *P'oă*^{4} *ts'ai*^{2}. *To lose money* or property, to meet with financial disaster.

口舌 *K'ou*^{3} *shê*^{2}. Evil reports, scandal, detraction, calumny.

平等 *P'ing*^{2} *têng*^{3}. Equal in rank.

喊叫 *Han*^{3} *chiao*^{4}. To cry aloud, to shout, *to call out.*

救火 *Chiu*^{4} *hwoă*^{3}. Fire! fire! to put out a fire.

閂 *Shwan*^{1}. *The bolt or bar across a door;* to bolt a door.

NOTES.

1 偷嘴 is applied to children or young daughters-in-law who take things to eat on the sly, also to dogs or cats which steal food.

2 愛 is much used in the North in the sense of *wishing or being willing,* but is not so used in the South, where 願 takes its place. 願 is also used in the North, but in such connections generally takes 意 after it. 受罪, *to receive sin; i.e.,* to receive the consequences of sin, viz., *suffering.* 罪 is much used in this sense, showing how strongly the connection between sin and suffering is impressed on the human mind.

3 遭殃 *To meet with retribution,* that is, in this case, *to get the worst of it.* The term is somewhat belittled by its use in this connection. It is chosen for the rhyme, and also to

○我[21]叫那算命占卦的先生、給我批了一個八字、說、我這步時運不好、不是破財、就是遭口舌是非。○蒙[22]恩和蒙情、有個要緊的分別、若是得了在上的好處、就該說是蒙恩、得了平等人的好處、就該說是蒙情。○王[23]五正在夢中、聽見外頭喊叫救火、吃了一驚、慌的連門閂也摸不着了。

21 I got that fortune-teller to tell my fortune by the eight characters. He said my fortune was not propitious, that I would either lose my money or suffer from evil reports.

22 There is an important difference between receiving grace and receiving a favor. If you get good from a superior, it should be spoken of as receiving grace; if you get good from an equal, it should be spoken of as receiving a favor.

23 Wang Wu Chêng, when in the midst of a dream, heard some one outside calling out, "fire! fire!" and was so frightened that in his alarm he could not even find the bolt of the door.

intimate that he who is behindhand gets the legitimate desert of his failure to be first.

5 大人 is here used for parents. A 省心的孩子 is one who does not cry nor fret nor get into mischief; for which we have no special word in English, other than to say that he is a "good" child.

7 患 is the more elegant book form, 害 the more colloquial.

8 周瑜, a noted general in the time of the three kingdoms, an adherent of the house of Wu. The story is that 周瑜, in order to deceive 曹操 with whom he was at war, beat 黃蓋, one of his own generals unmercifully, he consenting to be so beaten. 黃蓋 then went over to 曹操, and pretended that he had deserted 周瑜 on account of this shameful and unmerited beating, and wanted an opportunity to get revenge. 曹操 was deceived by him, and in consequence of his treachery suffered defeat. The proverb is used of those who resort to similar tricks, or who willingly endure pain for some coveted end.

10 The three forms have substantially the same meaning, save that 外人 suggests the idea of a relative, which the others do not necessarily do.

11 Parents who are poor, or who are tired of keeping their betrothed daughters, sometimes send them to the home of their future mother-in-law, months or even years, before they are to be married; albeit such a course is considered very ungenteel. Betrothals are also sometimes made, having this arrangement definitely in view, especially in the case of the death of the girl's mother. The lot of such girls is proverbially hard. The most general term for such a girl is, 童養媳婦, *a daughter-in-law supported as a child or virgin.* The term used in Shantung is 探養媳婦, *a daughter-in-law supported beforehand.* The term in Nanking is simply 養媳婦, *a supported daughter-in-law.*

17 It is not regarded as legitimate for a Chinese official both to fine a man and to beat him.

18 李榮春 and 一個好人 are in grammatical apposition. 顛險 is a book term not often heard in colloquial. 磨折 is colloquial, but as used in the North is always reversed, viz., 折磨.

21 The eight characters referred to are those which mark the year, month, day and hour of birth—two for each, according to the Chinese cyclical method of indicating dates. See Les. 117, Note 31. Prognostications are made on the basis of these characters. 步 is here the classifier of 時運. 口舌 and 是非 are rhetorically correlated, and mutually limit each other.

LESSON LXXX.

THUS.

這麼的 } **這麼着** } Thus, then, in *this* case. The final 的 is the ancient and original form, still much used in Central and Southern Mandarin. In Eastern Shantung it is used exclusively, the form with 着 not being heard at all. 着 is the more modern form, used in Pekingese and the North, and also introduced to a considerable extent in the South. The same is true of 的 and 着 following 那麼 and 怎麼.

那麼的 or **那麼着** Thus, then, in *that* case.

這麼 Is not infrequently used as a contraction for 這麼的 or 這麼着.

恁麼的 A colloquial form of 那麼的. This form is not often found in books, but is widely used in colloquial.

這樣 or **這麼樣** Thus, in *this* case.

恁樣 or **恁麼樣** Thus, in *that* case.

這麼一來 In these circumstances, therefore.

第八十課

麻[1]刀/紙筋、又沒有了、答這麼着/的、還得/還要去買。○他[2]親兄弟不管、恁/那麼的我也不管。○我[3]看給他五百錢、虧他一點、答這麼該給他多少呢。○若[4]他父親不死、必還叫他念幾年書、這麼一來、就不用想喇。○我[5]來登門/上門認錯、你還不肯、這麼着/的、你待/你要怎麼樣罷。○屈[6]了原告也不好、屈了被告也不好.如是換上青衣小帽、暗暗去私訪。○我[7]已經和他約定/就了、一塊兒去下大場、今天聽說他丁了憂、這麼/這樣一來、我只得自己一個/自各兒去。○不[8]撒謊對不住朋友、撒謊對不住良心、如是他早早就躲開了。○若[9]是一遍學不會、

Translation.

1 The cut rope (paper stiffening) is all used up again. *Ans.* In that case, you will have to go and buy more.

2 If his own brother declines to interfere, in that case neither will I interfere.

3 I think that to give him five hundred cash would be a little short. *Ans.* How much then should I give him?

4 If his father had not died, he would certainly have had him study several years yet; but now it is of no use to think of it.

5 I have come to you and confessed my fault, and yet you are dissatisfied; what then are you going to do about it?

6 To wrong the plaintiff would not do, and to wrong the defendant was equally unjust: so he disguised himself in common clothes and a small hat and went out to make inquiry.

7 I had already agreed to go with him to the provincial examination, but to-day I hear he is in mourning, so that now I shall have to go by myself.

8 Unless he told a lie he would offend his friend, and if he told a lie he would violate his conscience, so he got out of the way beforehand.

如是 Thus, then, so, in that case. This is the most elegant form of saying *thus*, and is the form most frequently used in books.

於是 And so, thereupon, then, well then. In use, 如是 and 於是 are much confused, especially in dialects in which they are read alike.

如此 Thus, so, so that, in that case,—nearly equivalent to 如是.*

Vocabulary.

麻刀 *Ma² tao¹*. Old rope for strengthening mortar:—Note 1.

紙筋 *Chï³ chin¹*. Paper pulp used for the same purpose.

登門 *Têng¹ mên²*. To go to or enter a man's house. (w.)

認錯 *Jên⁴ ts'oă⁴*. To own a fault, to admit, *to confess*.

訪 *Fang³*. To search out, *to inquire into*.

私訪 *Sï¹ fang³*. *To inquire secretly*, to detect, to spy.

青衣 *Ch'ing¹ i¹*. Dark clothing, the blue clothes worn by the common people.

大場 *Ta⁴ ch'ang²*. The examinations at the provincial city, or at the capital.

丁憂 *Ting¹ yiu¹*. To mourn for a parent:—Note 7.

* As will be seen, the various phrases constituting this lesson are very similar in meaning, and no doubt the learner will be perplexed to know exactly when and how to use each one. This cannot be acquired from definitions, nor by the mere force of memory, but will come gradually by practice and observation. The lesson will call attention to the various phrases, and serve as a guide and prompter in their use. The same remarks apply to a large number of other lessons.

就兩遍、兩遍學不會、就三遍、這麽樣、還有到底學不會的嗎。○現10在黃大人、陞了兩廣總督、老太爺感恩不盡、於是拿出五萬銀子、放飯施捨。○他11們個個人都是如此。○昨12天晚上、他還猶疑不定的、不知是去好、是不去好、答這麽着（恁麽的）、你再去問問他、他若不去、我們好快走啊。○待13姊妹們、你願打就打、願罵就罵嗎、這麽樣、你把我放在那裏呢。○他14有急難、我出上工夫衞護（顧）他、如今我家有事、他連面也不照、這麽一來、我就和他絕了交、那樣的朋友、有也是五八（五八、）四沒有也是四（四十。）八五○諸15葛亮在葫蘆峪、埋下地雷火礮、預

9 If you cannot learn it by one repetition, then repeat it twice; and if you cannot learn it by repeating twice, then repeat it three times. Is there anything you cannot in this way finally learn?

10 His Excellency, Mr. Hwang, has been advanced to the Governor-Generalship of the two Kwang, and his father, as an expression of his gratification, has set apart fifty thousand [taels of] silver to distribute food and charity among the poor.

11 They are every one so.

12 Yesterday evening he was still hesitating, not knowing whether it was better to go or not. *Ans.* In this case, do you go again and ask him, so that if he is not going, we may go at once.

13 In your intercourse with your sisters, can you beat and revile them as you please? Have you no regard for my feelings?

14 When he was in straits, I spent time in defending him; now, when my family are in difficulty, he does not so much as show his face. I will, therefore, cut his acquaintance. That style of friend, to have him is five times eight, and not to have him is four times ten.

陞 *Shêng*¹. . . . . To ascend; *to rise in office.*

督 *Tu*¹. . . . *To govern;* to oversee; to admonish.

總督 *Tsung*³ *tu*¹. . . . . A governor-general.

老太爺 *Lao*³ *t'ai*⁴ *yie*². The father of an officer or of one who has a high literary degree.

感恩 *Kan*³ *ên*¹. . . . . . . To be thankful, *grateful.*

放飯 *Fang*⁴ *fan*⁴. To distribute food to the poor.

施 *Shï*¹. To expand; to distribute, to diffuse; to give, *to bestow.*

施捨 *Shï*¹ *shê*². . . . . To bestow charity.

猶疑 *Yiu*² *i*². . . . . . . To be in doubt, *to hesitate.*

急難 *Chi*² *nan*⁴. *A strait,* an emergency, a pressing difficulty.

衞顧 *Wei*⁴ *ku*⁴. . . . . . . To protect, *to defend.*

衞護 *Wei*⁴ *hu*⁴. . . . . Same.

絕交 *Chüe*² *chiao*¹. To have no more to do with, *to cut the acquaintance of.*

諸 *Chu*¹. All, every; in *Wên-li* a final particle of doubt or interrogation; at, in; a surname.

峪 *Yü*⁴. . . . . A ravine, a gully.

埋 *Mai*². To bury, to cover over; *to conceal;* to hoard. See *man*².

雷 *Lei*². . . . . *Thunder;* to beat a drum.

地雷 *Ti*⁴ *lei*². . . . . *A mine,* a blast.

礮 or 砲 *P'ao*⁴. . . . . . . *A great gun,* a cannon.

懿 *I*⁴. . . . . Virtuous, accomplished. (w.)

將 *Chiang*⁴. A leader, a general; the king in chess. See *chiang*¹.

恰巧 *Ch'ia*⁴ *ch'iao*³. Opportune, timely, *in the nick of time,* lucky.

淹沒 *Yien*¹ *moä*⁴. To drown out, to wet; *to overflow,* to overwhelm.

騰挪 *T'êng*² *noä*². To transfer; to arrange for, *to find time;* to postpone.

河道 *Hê*² *tao*⁴. The banks or bed of a river.

備轟死司馬懿、和他的兵將、以後司馬懿走到那裏、恰巧下了大雨、把地雷火礮都淹濕沒了、於是諸葛亮、嘆了一聲說、罷了罷了、眞是謀事在人、成事在天。○我[16]看叫天福去、不如叫寶恩去、因爲寶恩、還能騰挪一點工夫、他又認得道兒、答這麼樣你看着罷、怎麼好、就怎麼的着。○那[17]河道窄的地方、水流的很快、必沖起許多泥來、河道寬的地方、流的必慢、水中的泥、必漸漸沉下、河心就漸漸地高了、如此大水一來、必從這河心高的地方、漫出堤來。○鄭[18]天存已經混到頭兒創底鋪下了架子喇、今天我在街上、見他脚上

15 Chu Kê Liang, in the valley of gourds, concealed subterraneous mines and fire guns intending to blow up Sï Ma I with his soldiers and generals; but subsequently, when Sï Ma I came to the place, just in the nick of time it rained a great rain and overflowed his mines and guns; upon which Chu Kê Liang said with a sigh, "Well, well; after all, it is true that man proposes but Heaven disposes."

16 It would be better, I think, to have Pao Ên go rather than T'ien Fu because Pao Ên can find the time; he also knows the road. *Ans.* Well, just as you like; do whatever seems best.

17 Where the bed of the river is narrow and the water runs very swiftly, it will necessarily take up much mud. Where the bed of the river is wide, the water will, of course, run slowly and the mud will gradually fall down, thus slowly filling up the channel of the river. Hence, when a flood comes, at the places where the bed of the river is thus filled up, the water will overflow the banks.

18 Chêng T'ien Ts'un has come to the end of his tether. I saw him to-day on the street shivering with the

河心 *Hê² hsin¹*. The bottom or channel of a river.

沉 *Ch'ên²*. To sink, *to fall to the bottom;* to be lost, to perish; heavy, weighty.

漫 *Man⁴*. *To overflow*, to well up; wide spreading, diffused, vague.

堤 *Ti¹*. A dyke, a bund, a levee, *a bank.*

創 *Ch'wang⁴,³*. To create, to transform; to found; *to essay*, to follow a business.

底鋪 *Ti³ p'u¹*. Resources all exhausted, down to first principles.

遢 *T'a⁴*. Careless, slovenly.

遢拉 *T'a⁴ la¹*. To shuffle with the feet.

趿 *Sa¹,⁴*. To tread shoes down at the heel; to wear them so.

披 *P'ei¹*. *To throw over the shoulders,* to put on; disheveled. Also *p'i¹*.

袖 *Hsiu⁴*. *The sleeve*; to put into the sleeve.

洒 *Hsi¹*. To shudder with cold:—Note 18.

央 *Yang¹*. To beg earnestly, *to entreat.*

央及 *Yang¹ chi²*. To beg hard, to importune, to crave, *to entreat.*

大烟 *Ta⁴ yien¹*. Opium (as smoked).

膏 *Kao¹*. Grease; ointment, *paste;* plasters; rich food.

廣膏 *Kwang³ kao¹*. Foreign opium:—Note 18.

臘 *La⁴*. A sacrifice three days after the winter solstice; *the 12th month.*

祭 *Chi⁴*. To sacrifice to the gods; an offering.

辭 *Ts'ï²*. Words, speech, phraseology; to refuse, to decline; to depart, *to take leave of.*

小婆子 *Hsiao³ p'oa² tsï³*. A secondary or inferior wife, a concubine.

小奶奶 *Hsiao³ nai³ nai³*. Same. (s.)

邋拉着跋的破鞋頭、腿上穿的燈籠褲子、身上披的一件沒有袖子的小掛兒、凍的恓恓恓恓的、直央及我、我腰裏帶的五六十個錢、叫我都給了他喇、答 有錢怎麽單給他呢、你忘了他做買賣的時候、吃的是粳米白麪、穿的是綾羅綢緞、吃大烟必得吃廣膏、臘月二十三日祭辭竈、買三隻鴨子、四隻雞、他小婆子奶奶還嫌不好吃、這樣、他現在受罪、還算多了嗎。

cold, shuffling his feet along in a pair of worn-out shoes, having on his legs a pair of tattered pants, and on his shoulders a shortcoat without sleeves. He entreated me without ceasing, and I gave him all I had in my pocket—some fifty or sixty cash. *Ans.* If you have money to give, why give it to him? Have you forgotten when he was in business, how he ate the best rice and finest flour and wore silk and satin and would smoke only foreign opium? Also, how on the twenty-third of the twelfth month, in sacrificing to the kitchen god, he bought three ducks and four chickens, and yet his concubine found fault with them as unfit to eat? In view of all these things, are his present sufferings more than he deserves?

NOTES.

1 麻刀 is old ropes chopped into bits, rubbed up so as to disentangle the fibre, and used in mortar as we use hair. In some places, especially in the South, old paper is soaked into pulp and used for the same purpose.

4 Peking teachers would change to 他父親若是, etc., but teachers in Central and Southern Mandarin regard the form in the text as equally good, if not better.

5 登門認錯 is a ready-made book phrase, often used by educated people.

6 In difficult cases, Chinese magistrates not infrequently disguise themselves and go out at night, or for several days together, to see what they can find out.

7 丁憂 *To sustain grief; i.e.*, to mourn for the death of a parent. Three years is the allotted time for mourning for a parent, during which time officers are excused from duty, and candidates do not attend the examinations.

9 The final 的 might with perhaps equal propriety be referred to the person, and the clause be rendered: *Is there any one who cannot in this way finally learn it?*

10 兩廣 that is, 廣東 *Kwantung*, and 廣西 *Kwangsi*. In the phrase 感恩不盡 the object of the verb is so closely united to it, that it refuses to be displaced by the auxiliary. In 五萬銀子 the 兩 is omitted, as in such cases it often is.

13 The language of a man or of his mother to his wife, remonstrating against her treatment of her sisters-in-law.

14 The last clause of this sentence is the Chinese version of "Six of one and half-a-dozen of the other." The Northern form goes by multiplication, the Southern by addition. Other numbers are sometimes used in the same way.

15 諸葛亮 otherwise called 孔明, one of the greatest generals known in Chinese history. He was the faithful adherent of 劉備 *Liu Pei*, and finally secured him in possession of the throne, A.D. 220. 劉備 said of him, 孔明眞神人也, *K'ung Ming is truly a divine man!* It is not certainly known what was the character of the explosives he used, certainly not such as are used in modern warfare. 司馬懿 Commander of the armies of the kingdom of Wei. The historian of the three kingdoms says of him, that he 用兵如神, *handled an army like a god.*

16 怎麽好就怎麽着 *As is best so be it.* A common phrase for "Do as you think best." 那 is often substituted for 怎, the sense being practically the same.

18 混到頭兒 *Run through to the end*—"come to the end of his tether;" 創底鋪喇 *come to the bottom spread*—"down to the bed rock;" 下了架子 *the scaffolding fallen down*—"played out." The three phrases, Northern, Central and Southern, mean substantially the same thing. 混 *confused*, here a verb, *to act in a senseless and heedless manner.* 鞋頭 Shoes with the heels turned down and worn as heel-less slippers. 燈籠褲子 Trousers that are so thin, and have so many holes in them, that the light and air go through them as they do through a paper lantern. 恓恓恓恓的 The word is repeated to imitate the shuddering sound expressive of cold. The phrase is to be spoken in two couplets. 廣膏 *Canton paste or cake*, so called because foreign opium was first introduced at Canton, and because it comes in the form of thick paste or cake. 辭竈 *to take leave of the kitchen god.* This is done in every family on the twenty-third of the twelfth month, by presenting to him offerings and prayers. 祭竈 is the form used in some places.

第八十一課

今[1]天有風、却不涼快。○你[2]不曉得、我卻曉得。○那[3]個人可是利害、却最講論理。○車[4]子是他的、他却不在車子上。○他[5]們明知賈有連是賊、卻不肯報官。○遇[6]了荒年、你們怎樣過呢。○像[7]這樣的好人、世上却不多有。○看[8]他臉上很願意、可沒明說出來。○自[9]己好清靜、却常會到別人家裏去攪擾。○他[10]不過身量小、歲數却不小了。○鍾[11]教友很好唱詩、唱的却不好。○我[12]該你的、現在可不能還你。○你[13]想這個錢、不是他吞了、却是誰。○我[14]到你家裏去吃飯、你可不要過厚費。○

Translation.

1 There is a breeze to-day, but it is not cool.
2 You do not know, but I know.
3 That man is severe, it is true; but very amenable to reason.
4 The cart is his, but he is not in it.
5 They, knowing clearly that Chia Yiu Lien is a thief, are yet unwilling to inform the magistrate.
6 If you meet with a year of famine, then how will you live?
7 There are, however, not many as good men as this in the world.
8 Judging from the expression of his face he is very willing, but he has not yet plainly said so.
9 Delighting in quiet himself, he is yet constantly (capable of) going to other peoples' houses to raise a disturbance.
10 He is not young, it is only that he is small of stature.
11 Our fellow-Christian Chung loves very much to sing, but he sings poorly.
12 I owe you, but I cannot pay you at present.
13 If he did not embezzle this money, who do you suppose did?
14 I will accept your hospitality, but do

LESSON LXXXI.

The Exceptive Conjunction.

卻 or **却** To reject,—properly a verb, but chiefly used as a conjunction to introduce an exceptive or adversative clause; but, but then, however, yet, and yet.

可 Can,—is used in the same way and with substantially the same meaning as **卻**. Thus used it changes its tone to k'ê², and appears to be simply a colloquial substitute for **卻**. Southern Mandarin generally adheres to **卻**. Both words are often used when they amount to little more than a mere expletive or catchword.

却有一件 or **一樣**, But there is one thing.

却有一宗 or **一椿**. The same.

Vocabulary.

卻 or **却** *Ch'üe⁴, ch'iao⁴*. To decline, to reject; but then, however. The original form was 卻, but 却 is now extensively used.

可 *K'ê²*. But, then, but then, however:—see Sub. See *k'ê³*.

賈 *Chia³*. A surname. Also *ku³*.

荒年 *Hwang¹ nien²*. A year of famine.

攪 *Chiao³*. To stir up; to disorder; to annoy; to excite.

攪擾 *Chiao³ jao³*. To embroil, *to raise a disturbance*, to make a rumpus.

歲數 *Swei⁴ shu⁴*. Age (of a person).

鍾 *Chung¹*. A small cup; *a surname*.

吞 *T'un¹*. To swallow whole, to gulp; to seize, to appropriate, *to embezzle*.

厚費 *Hou⁴ fei⁴*. To be bountiful, to spend lavishly, *to go to extra expense*.

繡[15]球花好看、卻不很香。○我[16]有一個法子、卻不知行不行。○沒[17]本事、卻生事、生出事來、無本事。○聽[18]說東鄉也下了雨、卻不及這邊兒下的大。○你[19]有家下家口奶奶沒有、答已經定了親、却還沒娶。○他[20]心裏想着朦混弄人、卻朦混弄不住。○他[21]的漢丈也不很大、生的卻很崑魁壯偉。○明[22]明是他殺的、沒有証見、可不能問罪。○這[23]可奇怪喇、人已經臭爛歸土、怎麼還能復活呢、答奇怪是是奇怪、這却是將來必有的事。○衆[24]位到我家裏來、我也不能不准衆位的情面、却可有一件、他若再來尋事、我却是

not go to any extra expense

15 The hydrangea is a beautiful flower, but not very fragrant.

16 I have a plan, but I do not know whether it will succeed or not.

17 Without capacity, you yet have a capacity for getting into difficulties; and when you have gotten into a difficulty, you are without any capacity to get out.

18 I hear that it also rained east of the city, but not so much as it did here.

19 Have you a wife? *Ans.* I am engaged, but not yet married.

20 He is planning to hoodwink [us], but he will not succeed.

21 His stature is not great, it is true, but he is very stalwart.

22 It is clear that he killed him, yet without testimony he cannot be convicted.

23 But this is strange! After a man has decayed and returned to dust, how can he live again? *Ans.* Strange it certainly is, but it is something that will surely come to pass.

24 Since you gentlemen have come to my house, I cannot but accede to

過費 *Kwoă*⁴ *fei*⁴. . . . . Same. (s.)
繡 *Hsiu*⁴. . . . To embroider; variegated, figured.
球 *Ch'iu*². . . . . A sphere, a ball, a globe.
繡球 The hydrangea.
生事 *Shêng*¹ *shï*⁴. To make trouble, *to get into difficulty.*
家下 *Chia*¹ *hsia*⁴. . . . . A wife.
朦 *Mêng*². . . Dim, indistinct; to cajole, to humbug.
朦混 *Mêng*² *hun*⁴. To mislead, *to hoodwink*, to humbug; obscure.
朦弄 *Mêng*² *lung*⁴. . . . To cajole, *to hoodwink.*
漢丈 *Han*⁴ *chang*⁴. . . . . *Stature*, size.
魁 *K'wei*². . . . . Chief, highest; *best of its class.*
偉 *Wei*³. . . . . . Fine-looking; *strong*, powerful.
魁偉 Robust, *stalwart*, athletic.
崑 *K'un*¹. . . A peak. Extraordinary, elegant. (s.)
崑壯 *K'un*¹ *chwang*⁴. Robust, *stalwart*, athletic. (s.)
証見 *Chêng*⁴ *chien*⁴. . . . . . . Evidence, *testimony.*
問罪 *Wên*⁴ *tswei*⁴. *To convict*, to condemn, to regard as guilty.
臭爛 *Ch'ou*⁴ *lan*⁴. . . . . Rotten, *decayed.*

復活 *Fu*⁴ *hwoă*². *To come to life again*, to rise from the dead.
情面 *Ch'ing*² *mien*⁴. Face, feelings; influence:—Note 24.
尋事 *Hsin*² *shï*⁴. To raise a disturbance, *to make trouble*, to annoy.
宗 *Tsung*¹. Ancestors; family; a clan; kind, class, sort; *a matter;* to honor.
樁 *Chwang*¹. A post, a stake; a pile; classifier of affairs.—Les. 125.
摔 *Shwai*³. *To throw*, to swing about, to fling, to toss, to jerk. Also *shwai*¹.
睰 *Kwoă*¹. . . . . . To see dimly; *to give attention.*
睬 *Ts'ai*³. . . . . To pay attention, to notice.
睰睬 To notice, to heed, to pay attention.
在意 *Tsai*⁴ *i*⁴. *To notice*, to pay attention, to regard, to heed.
貌相 *Mao*⁴ *hsiang*⁴. Features, physiognomy, visage, *looks.*
德 *Tê*². Virtue, goodness; energy, virtue; power, quality; to flourish.
德行 *Tê*² *hsing*⁴. Virtue, morals, well-doing, *worth.*

找你們。○你25實在願意去、我也不擋你、卻有一宗椿、若是到了那裏想家、可不要埋怨我。○26剛纔是誰摔扔拋進一塊石頭去、答纔有兩個孩子、往東跑了、我却沒聒睬不在意他們摔扔拋石頭。○27看不得他的貌相不如人、德行却是人所不及的。

your wishes; but one thing you must remember, if he comes again to make trouble, I will hold you responsible.

25 If you really want to go, I will not hinder you; but there is one thing, if after you get there you are homesick, you must not reflect on me.

26 Who was it that just now threw in a stone? *Ans.* Two boys just now ran towards the east, but I did not notice that they threw any stones.

27 Do not be deceived by the inferiority of his looks; in sterling worth he has few equals.

NOTES.

3 可 here makes a concession to something previously said by another. We might translate, *Yes, he is severe, it is true, etc.*

4 Putting 他 before the 却 gives it emphasis.

9 會 as here used, is very expressive, and is very widely used. The Peking teacher objects to it and substitutes 常, which, however, does not give the force of 會.

12 Notice how 現在 precedes the conjunction, although it belongs to the conjunctive clause.

17 This sentence is a play on the word 事, and is a smart or pithy saying.

19 A wife is known by a variety of epithets. The proper term, which distinguishes her as *wife*, is 妻 or 妻子, but it is not used to any extent in colloquial. When the idea of sex is prominent she is called simply 女人. When spoken of in a careless or depreciating way she is called 老婆. When classed with, or in relation to a husband, she is called 婦 or 婦人. When the family idea is prominent she is called 家裡, or 家下, or 家眷, or 內人, or 賤內. When dignified by the rank of her husband, she is called 師娘, or 太太, or 夫人. The term 奶奶, which refers to motherhood, is used for *wife* only in the South.

20 人 is here used as an enclitic, but this does not at all interfere with its application to the person speaking. The structure of the sentence does not make it certain whether the reference was to the speaker or to some one else.

21 也 is here rendered, *it is true*. Its exact force could only be known from the preceding sentence, or from the idea which gave rise to it.

22 問罪 is put for 定罪—the process for the result. This use probably grows out of the custom of charging the crime on the supposed criminal, demanding of him a confession, and enforcing it by torture.

23 怪是怪 *Strange it is*, or, *true it's strange*, a common idiomatic form.

24 衆位 *All you gentlemen*. The classifier is put for its noun. 情面 *The face of the feelings*, that is, the face as the exponent or representative of the feelings or sentiments of the mind.

26 Mandarin has no *t'ung hsing* word meaning *to throw*. The three terms given in the text are all more or less local.

LESSON LXXXII.

FORBIDDING.

别 Don't, you must not,—much used colloquially in Central and Northern Mandarin, and also not infrequently in books. It is used in some places in the South, but not in others; thus it is used in Nanking, but not in Kiukiang. In Eastern Shantung it is read *pai*⁴. It is in reality a contraction of 不要.

休 to reject; do not by any means,—a book term only used colloquially in certain phrases and connections. In some places, however, it is much used colloquially; thus in Northern Shantung it quite takes the place of 别, being spoken *ho*.

莫 Do not, you should not, there is no need that,—mostly confined to certain phrases and connections. In some parts of the South, however, as in Kiukiang, it is in constant use and quite takes the place of 别.

不要 Do not want, do not,—much used everywhere, especially in the South, where it takes the place of 别 in the North.

不用 Need not, do not. A milder form than any of the preceding.

不可 Must not, should not, ought not.

不許 Must not, thou shalt not,—gives an authoritative prohibition.

不准 Do not allow; to forbid.

不消 Need not, not worth while.

漫 To overflow, do not, you need not—always joined with a word meaning *to say*.

第八十二課

你[1]莫別揪着我。○會[2]首們不准開賭。○背[3]地裏不要議論人。○求[4]你好歹莫別露出來。○快[5]喫飯罷、莫別生氣喇。○醜[6]婦是我妻、休想美貌的。○你[7]莫別笑話基督徒、他是好人。○不[8]要這樣客氣。○莫[9]說別人、就是我也知道。○這[10]本電氣鍍金、別住手兒、三天就抄起來了。○聞[11]名休見面、見面大有限。○依[12]我說、你不消花那項錢。○你[13]們都出去玩兒罷、別在這裏嚷吵嚷。○只[14]可商議、不可强派。○要[15]小心提擰溜着、別洸洸蕩出來。○我[16]怎麼講的、你就當怎麼回、不許隨口糊謅。○只[17]管自己門前雪、休管別人瓦上霜。○再[18]不要叫他來喇、我看

TRANSLATION.

1 Don't you take hold of me.
2 The headmen do not allow any gambling.
3 Do not disparage men behind their backs.
4 I beg of you, in any case, do not let it leak out.
5 Be quick and eat, and don't fret.
6 If one has a homely wife, he should not keep thinking of pretty women.
7 Do not laugh at Christian; he is a good man.
8 Don't be so formal.
9 Not to speak of others, even I know it.
10 Do not stop, and in three days this book on electroplating will be copied.
11 It is better not to meet the man of whose reputation you have heard, for if you meet him face to face, you will find him decidedly commonplace.
12 As I see it, you had better not spend that money.
13 Out with you all to your play, and don't stay here making a noise.
14 You can only consult together, you cannot peremptorily appoint.
15 Carry it carefully and don't splash it over.
16 You ought to give it just as I explained it. I cannot allow any random guess that comes uppermost.

VOCABULARY.

別 *Pie*^{4}. Do not, you must not;—see Sub. See . . . . . . *pie*^{2}.

會首 *Hwei*^{4} *shou*^{3}. The chairman of a committee . . . . or society; headmen, leaders.

開賭 *K'ai*^{1} *tu*^{3}. *To gamble*, to open a gambling . . . . room.

議論 *I*^{4} *lun*^{4}. To discuss, to canvass; to criticize, ... *to disparage*.

美 *Mei*^{3}. . . . . . . Delicious; *beautiful;* excellent.

美貌 *Mei*^{3} *mao*^{4}. . . . Beautiful, *pretty*, handsome.

笑話 *Hsiao*^{4} *hwa*^{4}. *To laugh at*, to ridicule, to . . . . make fun of; in fun.

基 *Chi*^{1}. . . . Foundation; possessions, patrimony.

基督徒 *Chi*^{1} *tu*^{1} *t'u*^{2}. The name given to . . . . Bunyan's Christian.

客氣 *K'ê*^{4} *ch'i*^{4}. *Formal*, conventional, distant; modest, simpering, bashful.

電氣 *Tien*^{4} *ch'i*^{4}. . . . . Electricity.

鍍金 *Tu*^{4} *chin*^{1}. . . . . . To gild; *to electroplate*.

住手 *Chu*^{4} *shou*^{3}. . . . . *To stop*, to cease, to desist.

聞名 *Wên*^{2} *ming*^{2}. . . . To hear of by reputation.

見面 *Chien*^{4} *mien*^{4}. *To see face to face*, to have . . . . an interview with.

洸 *Kwang*^{1}. . . . To oscillate, to wabble; unsteady.

蕩 *Tang*^{4}. Vast; vagrant, dissipated; to squan- . . . . der; to shake, to agitate.

洸蕩 To wabble; to slop over, to splash out.

隨口 *Swei*^{2} *k'ou*^{3}. . . . . To talk at random.

謅 *Tsou*^{1}. . . . . Jest, raillery; to exaggerate, to lie.

那個人不大準(詳)成(細)。○漫[19]說是二百八、就是三百也是你的錢。○我[20]託你抄(找)持幾個玻璃瓶子、你別忘記了。○各[21]照本位、不許亂坐。○再[22]往火爐裏添煤、別拉(撒)落(在)地下。○別[23]看他常常有病、一點也不少做活。○要[24]甚麼吃、可以在外邊要、莫(休)進來。○衙[25]門口、朝南(八字)開、有理無錢休進來。○我[26]囑咐你不要脫衣裳、你却不聽、這不是凍着喇。○要[27]擤鼻(子)涕、或是吐痰、可以到外邊去、不准弄在地板上。○來[28]來來、別住筷子、好歹總得吃飽啊。○這[29]樣不識抬舉的東西、你不用理他、看看他有甚麼本事。○罷[30]罷罷、他也別嫌你、你也別嫌他、

17 Simply sweep the snow from before your own door; don't meddle with the frost on your neighbor's roof.

18 Don't let that man come again. I think he is not to be trusted.

19 You need not mention two hundred and eighty. If you said three hundred, you still might keep your money.

20 Do not forget those few glass bottles I asked you to get for me.

21 Let each one take his own seat; to sit at random is not allowed.

22 When you put coal in the stove again, do not spill it on the floor.

23 Don't let the fact that she is constantly ailing influence you. She does not [on this account] do any the less work.

24 If you want something to eat, ask for it outside, but don't come in.

25 The door of the yamên faces the south (opens like the character eight): having right but not money, do not enter.

26 I charged you not to strip off your clothes but you did not mind, and now you have caught cold.

27 If you want to blow your nose or to spit, you should go out and not soil the floor.

28 Come on, come on, don't lay down

糊謅 *Hu² tsou¹*. *To talk at random;* to tell barefaced lies.

霜 *Shwang¹*. *Frost*, efflorescence.

準 *Chun³*. To adjust; to measure; a rule, a gauge; accurate; *certain*, sure.

準成 *Chun³ ch'êng²*. Accurate; certain, sure; reliable, *trusty*.

抄持 *Ch'ao¹ ch'i²*. *To get up*, to make a raise of, to rake up. (L.)

落 *La⁴*. To forget, to leave behind, *to drop;* to be late. See *lao⁴* and *loa⁴*.

拉落 *La¹ la⁴*. To scatter, *to spill*, to draggle.

擤 *Hsing²*. To blow or wipe the nose with the hand.

鼻 *Pi²*. The nose.

涕 *T'i⁴*. Tears; to weep; *mucus from the nose*.

鼻涕 Mucus from the nose, snivel.

地板 *Ti⁴ pan³*. A board floor, *the floor*.

痰 *T'an²*. Phlegm, mucus from the lungs.

抬舉 *T'ai² chü³*. To exalt, to honor; to compliment; *to treat well*.

隨機應變 *Swei² chi¹ ying⁴ pien⁴*. To adapt oneself to circumstances:—Note 31.

倒針 *Tao⁴ chên¹*. To backstitch.

跑針 *P'ao³ chên¹*. To run (a seam).

縣太爺 *Hsien⁴ t'ai⁴ yie²*. His honor the magistrate:—Note 32.

光棍 *Kwang¹ kun⁴*. "A bare pole," a bachelor; a rowdy, a rough; *a daredevil*, a sharper; exemplary, unassailable; spruce, comely.

佾 *Ch'iao⁴*. Silly, half-witted.

冒犯 *Mao⁴ fan⁴*. To offend, to anger, to affront, *to provoke*.

奸 *Chien¹*. Crafty, traitorous, wicked.

奸邪 *Chien¹ hsie²*. Malicious, *wicked*.

兇惡 *Hsiung¹ ê⁴*. Vicious, villainous; *evil*, sinful; wicked.

着忙 *Choa² mang²*. *Hastily*, in a hurry; flurried.

我看你們兩個、都彀人受的。○南[31]北的風氣不同、作官的也當隨機應變、不可板上釘釘。○漫[32]道他是個衙役、就是個縣太爺、他能把我怎麼樣呢。○媽[33]媽告訴要倒針縫、不要跑針縫。○你[34]不要小看了他、他是此地出名的大光棍、大小事情、有他出來、沒有過不去的。○他[35]父親殺了一輩子牛、養了這麼個現世報的偢乏孩子、不會說話、冒犯了先生、請先生休怪他。○休[36]入奸邪人的道、莫走兇惡人的路。○二[37]姑娘、見遮思克在門後藏着、就說、快叫看門的來瞧瞧、遮思克赶緊出來、忙着說、別別別別的家別別別的家、我愛這個地方、求你別叫看門的知道。

your chopsticks. You must make the best of it and eat your fill.

29 A fellow like this who does not know when he is well treated! You need not pay any attention to him and we will see what he can do.

30 Enough, enough; he need not find fault with you, nor you with him. As I see it, either of you is as much as a man can stand.

31 The customs are different in the North and the South, and an official should adapt himself to the circumstances and not insist on having his own way.

32 What if he is a constable! Even if he were a magistrate, what could he do to me?

33 Mother said to backstitch it, not to run it.

34 Don't you look upon him with contempt. He is the most noted daredevil of this place. Any affair, great or small, in which he comes to the front, is sure to go through.

35 His father was a beef-butcher all his life, and has his reward in the bringing up of this silly son, who does not know what he ought to say and has provoked you. Please, sir, do not take offence at him.

36 Enter not into the path of the wicked, and go not in the way of evil men.

37 When the two young ladies saw Jessica hidden behind the door, they said, "Let us call the door-keeper to come and see." Jessica came out hastily and said excitedly, "Don't, don't. I love this place. Please don't let the door-keeper know."

NOTES.

2 The reference is to the directors or managers of a market or festival.

6 A saying commonly attributed to the Emperor Yao.

9 The 就 and 也 join together to give the force of *even*.

10 電氣鍍金 *Gilding by electricity*,—the title of the book.

11 Or, *When you hear of a man's reputation, don't spoil the impression by meeting him. If you meet him, you will find the reality very little.*

12 項 is here used as a classifier of 錢. *The sort of money, or that sum of money.*

16 In Chinese schools the teacher explains the classics in common language, and then calls on the pupil at the next recitation to reproduce the substance of his explanation; this repetition or reproduction is expressed by 回.

17 A proverb, the meaning of which is, don't trouble yourself to correct other people's faults, but rather give attention to your own.

18 不大準成, 不大詳細 Both these phrases are here used somewhat out of their usual sense. They are applied to any one whose conduct or character is suspicious. The former is the more widely used.

19 In even tens, over a hundred, the 十 is often omitted. The 錢 is also left to be inferred from the connection

20 抄持 is more or less local, but very expressive.

21 The language of a teacher to his pupils, or of an officer to the candidates in the examination hall.

25 All yamêns in China face the south, they also all have two flaring walls in front approximating the form of the character 八. This rhyme or proverb is intended to express the idea that so surely as yamêns face the south, or have flaring walls in front, so surely is money more potent than right.

26 這不是凍着喇 This indirect interrogative form of affirmation frequently cannot be preserved in

第八十三課

他[1]任甚麼都不管。○你[2]想去、只管去。○憑[3]你去辦、兩個法子都好。○我[4]任憑他說、也沒有作聲。○這[5]個話、不管在那裏、也說得過去。○憑[6]他來多少回、總不許他進來。○別[7]管怎麼樣、你可得給我錢。○任[8]憑怎麼樣、我總比你長幾歲。○無[9]論是誰勸他、他就是不聽。○不[10]拘大事小事、都要謙

TRANSLATION.

1 He pays no attention to anything at all.
2 If you want to go, just go.
3 Go and arrange it as you like. Both plans are good.
4 I let him talk and said nothing.
5 This statement will pass anywhere.
6 No matter how often he comes, by no means let him come in.
7 No difference what you say, you must give me the money.
8 No matter how you put it, I am still several years older than you.
9 No matter who exhorts him, he will not listen.
10 In everything, whether great or small, be conciliatory and not self-opinionated.

a correct translation. Such forms are much more frequently used in Chinese than in English.

27 弄 here expresses the idea in a form which no English translation will reproduce.

28 Said by a host to his guests at the beginning of a fresh course. The 來來來 is a cordial invitation to each one to take up his chopsticks and begin to eat. 好歹 is used apologetically.

29 不識抬舉 Not to appreciate an honor or compliment, but, on the contrary, to take it as a want of courage or spirit, and so presume upon it.

31 隨機應變 *Follow the turn of affairs and respond to the change* [by a corresponding change of plan]; that is, *to adapt oneself to circumstances, to be equal to the occasion.* 板上釘釘 *To drive a nail in a board,* that is, a nail driven in a board is fixed once for all, and is unchangeable. There is perhaps also a pun or play on the word 板, which often means, *stiff, obstinate.* The phrase is just the opposite of 隨機應變.

32 縣太爺 A respectful designation of the Hsien magistrate. Formerly magistrates were addressed as 太爺, but this title is now generally superseded by that of 大老爺.

35 養了 etc., Lit., *Has raised this present-life-recompense half-witted son.* Buddhism has disseminated everywhere in China the Brahmanical notion that butchering cattle for beef is a great sin. The recompense in this case was a half-witted son.

37 別家 is the Peking form. In some places 別的 is said as if written 別得, which was probably the orginal form. Nanking rejects both forms and uses a triple 別, which is also widely used, but not to the exclusion of the other forms.

LESSON LXXXIII.

CONCESSIVES.

任 To allow, to permit; any,—as 任什麽 anything, 任誰 anyone, etc.

憑 According to; as [you] like; it rests with.

任憑 To allow; to suffer; to let; no matter.

任管 Same as 任憑,—but local.

管 or **不管** No matter; be as it will; as [you] please; any. The addition of 不, strange to say, makes very little difference in the meaning.

無管 Same as 不管.

只管 Just, simply, freely, without hesitation.

隨管 No matter; as [you] please.

論 As to, with reference to.

不論 or **無論** No matter; irrespective of; whether.

不拘 No difference; no matter; irrespective of; in any case.

無拘 Same, but local.

別管 It matters not; no difference; by no means.

隨 As [you] like, as [you] please. When thus used it is, in Central Mandarin, frequently read *ts'ui*.

隨便 As [you] like, at [your] convenience. Much used in the South.

由 To allow, to let, to give way to.

讓、不可自是。○任[11]憑(管)你怎樣求他、他的心連動也不動。○我[12]還要拜望他去、見不見憑他。○[13]無(不)拘甚麼事、只要熟練(悉)、就容易了。○他[14]沒說到我們跟前、管他怎麼說罷。○不[15]論大小生意、要價還價、都要臉色和平。○李[16]大爺實在顢頇(柔綿)、別管怎麼催他、他也不上火。○論[17]標緻(俊)也不很標緻(俊)、就是頭上脚下(管那裏)(隨那裏)都長的周正。○我[18]早知道今日受苦、不拘怎麼樣也要留幾個錢、今日用。○武[19]大郎忍氣吞聲、由他咒罵、心裏只依着兄弟的言語。○我[20]只管盡到了自己的心、以後聽天由命也就是了。○若[21]見他罵人、

11 Entreat him as you will, his sympathies are not even touched.

12 I still am going to call on him. He may see me or not as he likes.

13 No matter what it is, only get accustomed to it and it becomes easy.

14 Since he has not said it in our presence, let him talk as he pleases.

15 In business, whether great or small, both in asking and in offering a price, a pleasant expression of countenance should always be preserved.

16 Uncle Li is emphatically apathetic (easy-going). No matter how you hurry him he never gets excited.

17 As to looks, she is not very pretty, but she is well-proportioned in every respect.

18 I knew beforehand that we should be in want at this time, hence I was determined, in any case, to keep a few cash for the present emergency.

19 Wu the Elder restrained his anger and kept silent and let her abuse him, keeping in mind his brother's words.

20 I simply act according to the best of my ability, and leave the rest to Heaven and fate.

21 If you see him reviling any one or

VOCABULARY.

謙 *Ch'ien*¹. Respectful, unassuming, modest; *yielding;* humble.

謙讓 *Ch'ien*¹ *jang*⁴. Yielding, complaisant, obliging, *conciliatory.*

悉 *Hsi*²·¹. Fully, minutely, thoroughly.

熟練 *Shu*² *lien*⁴. Experienced, practiced, conversant, *accustomed to.*

熟悉 *Shu*² *hsi*². Practiced, *accustomed to,* familiar with, pat.

要價 *Yao*⁴ *chia*⁴. *To ask a price,* the price asked.

還價 *Hwan*² *chia*⁴. To make an offer, (in response to a price asked.)

臉色 *Lien*³ *sê*⁴. *Expression,* color

顢 *Man*¹. A large full face.

頇 *Han*¹. A large face.

顢頇 Sluggish, dilatory; *apathetic;* shameless, brazen-faced.

柔綿 *Jou*² *mien*². Compliant, *easy-going,* submissive, passive.

上火 *Shang*⁴ *hwo*³ *To get excited;* to become angry.

周正 *Chou*¹ *chêng*⁴. Complete, symmetrical, *well-proportioned,* shapely.

忍氣 *Jên*³ *ch'i*⁴. *To restrain anger,* to control one's temper.

吞聲 *T'un*¹ *shêng*¹. To hold the tongue, *to keep quiet,* to be silent.

咒 *Chou*⁴. To curse, to imprecate, to swear; a charm, a litany.

咒罵 *Chou*⁴ *ma*⁴. To curse, to revile, to execrate, *to abuse.*

漆 *Ch'i*¹. *Varnish,* lacquer; to varnish; black.

烏 *Wu*¹. The crow; black, dark, *dull.*

膽量 *Tan*³ *liang*⁴. *Courage,* bravery.

賦 *Fu*⁴. To levy a tax; to spread out; *a kind of verse;* a ballad, an idyl.

典故 *Tien*³ *ku*⁴. A precedent, an authority, *a quotation,* an allusion.

俗氣 *Su*² *ch'i*⁴. *Commonplace,* hackneyed.

和孩子打架、無論他是不是、就先打他。○這[22]個漆實在不好、不論漆幾遍、總是發烏、一點也不亮。○人[23]的膽量大小、是天生的、一點也不由人。○我[24]們念書的人、無論是作文章、是作詩賦、必得有典故、纔不俗氣。○媽[25]啊、我的褂子、買上個綠花洋布托領（托襟、護領）好不好。答 隨你罷。○不[26]論做甚麼、外行總是不行。○人[27]若有驕傲、吝嗇、這兩樣毛病、再別管有多少好處、也帶掉（贅累壞、白贅上）了。○楊[28]崑山真是寬宏大量、無論人怎樣毀謗他、都能安然受着、總不見他發作。○不[29]用等、我們各人隨

fighting with other children, no matter whether he is in the right or in the wrong, first whip him.

22 This varnish is exceedingly poor; no matter how many coats you put on, it is still dull and without the least luster.

23 The amount of a man's courage is the bestowment of nature; it is not in the least under his own control.

24 We scholars, whether writing an essay or composing poetry, must make quotations in order not to be common-place.

25 Mother, may I buy a green print collar for my gown? *Ans.* Just as you like.

26 No matter in what line it is, an inexperienced hand will not succeed.

27 Let a man have these two faults, pride and stinginess, and no matter how many excellences he has they go for nothing (are all vitiated).

28 Yang K'un Shan is truly a generous and magnanimous man. No matter how people vilify him, he is able to bear it all with equanimity, never showing any vexation.

外行 *Wai⁴ hang²*. One outside of a profession, ... untrained, *inexperienced*.

吝 *Lin⁴*. . . . . *Stingy*, sordid, parsimonious.

嗇 *Sê⁴*. . . . . . Harvest; avaricious, *stingy;* frugal.

吝嗇 *Stingy*, mean, niggardly.

贅 *Chwei⁴*. To hamper, to encumber, *to throw in;* . . . . an appendage, an encumbrance.

贅累 *Chwei⁴ lei⁴*. To encumber, to embarrass, to . . . . obstruct, to clog, *to vitiate*.

白贅 *Pai² chwei⁴*. Thrown in, superfluous, ... useless, *for nothing*. (c.)

帶掉 *Tai⁴ tiao⁴*. To neutralize, to render null; . . . . to spoil, *to vitiate*. (s.)

宏 *Hung²*. . . . . Vast, ample, wide.

寬宏 *K'wan¹ hung²*. Liberal-minded, *generous*, ... large-hearted.

大量 *Ta⁴ liang⁴*. *Magnanimous*, open-handed, ... of large capacity, gifted.

毀 *Hwei³*. To break down, to destroy, to abolish, ... to ruin; to slander, *to vilify*.

毀謗 *Hwei³ pang⁴*. To defame, to calumniate, to . . . . slander, *to vilify*.

安然 *An¹ jan²*. Peacefully, tranquilly, *with* . . . . *equanimity*.

涵養 *Han² yang³*. *Self-control*, magnanimity, ... patience, long-suffering.

矜 *Ching¹*. To pity; to regret; boastful, vaunt- . . . . ing; *passionate*, impatient.

闊 *K'woă⁴*. . . . . . . Broad, *ample;* liberal, lavish.

開通 *K'ai¹ t'ung¹*. Clear-headed, clever, *judi-* . . . . *cious*.

開脫 *K'ai¹ t'oă¹*. . . . . The same. (s.)

開闊 *K'ai¹ k'woă⁴*. . . . . The same. (s.)

無怪 *Wu² kwai⁴*. . . . . No wonder.

盡力 *Chin⁴ li⁴*. With the might, to the utmost, ... *one's best*.

歇手 *Hsie¹ shou³*. . . . *To stop*, to desist, to quit.

河路 *Hê² lu⁴*. . . . . . . River travel.

平安 *P'ing² an¹*. . . . . . . Peaceful, *safe*, secure.

壯班 *Chwang⁴ pan¹*. Official guard:—Note . . . . 35.

擺治 *Pai³ chï⁴*. To operate on, to put through, ... to ply; to maltreat, *to torture*.

佈 *Pu⁴*. To spread out, extend; to arrange; . . . . . . to publish.

擺佈 *Pai³ pu⁴*. To spread out, to arrange; to . . . . maltreat, *to torture*.

便罷。○請[30]你要緊的想着、(別管怎麼着 管怎麼的 隨便怎麼樣)不要忘記了。○人[31]若用到了涵養的工夫、不拘碰着甚麼事、也不能改他那不矜不躁的樣子。○王[32]六不論說話辦事、眞是開(通脫闊)無怪他父親常誇獎他。○不[33]拘誰託他一件事、他不應就罷了、他若是點了頭、必要替你盡力的辦、不成不肯歇手。○船[34]主說、現在河路很不平安、不如按着站數走妥當、答隨他們罷、怎麼妥當就怎麼走。○壯[35]班問孫通子要班規錢、(隨管 隨便)怎麼樣難爲他、擺佈治他、他就是不出油兒。

29 You need not wait; we will each go at his own convenience.

30 Please bear it carefully in mind, and do not by any means forget it.

31 When a man is thoroughly schooled in self-control, no matter what happens, it cannot disturb his calm and dispassionate manner.

32 Without question, Wang the Sixth is judicious both in speaking and acting. No wonder his father is constantly boasting of him.

33 No difference who applies to him for assistance, if he does not promise, that is the end of it; but if he assents, he will do his best and will not cease till he has accomplished it.

34 The captain says that just now river travel is very unsafe; to go by the regular stages will be the more satisfactory. *Ans.* Just as they like: proceed in whatever way is thought best.

35 The *chwang pan* demanded the usual fees of Sun T'ung Tsï, but in spite of all their maltreatment and torture, he refused to disgorge.

NOTES.

1 不管 as here used is not intended to illustrate the subject of the lesson; this is done by 任.

5 This sentence might perhaps be taken as referring to language simply, and be translated, *This language or phraseology will pass current anywhere.* In this case, however, 這個話 should rather be 這句話, and 說得過去 should be simply 說得, or 說得去.

12 As here used, 拜望他去, is not quite equivalent to 去拜望他. The order is changed in order to throw stress on the 去.

18 今日 *To-day,*—put indefinitely for *the present,* which, however, is not a colloquial but a book usage.

19 大郎 properly, *eldest son,* but here used simply as a name. This 武大郎 lived in the Sung Dynasty, and was noted for his imbecility and deformity of person. He had no given name—was not considered worth one, being simply called *the elder Wu.* He had a virago of a wife, who, with the aid of one of her paramours, finally murdered him. He had, however, a brother of distinguished ability called 武松 who afterwards avenged his death. He is one of the characters in the "History of Robbers," from which this sentence is taken. He is frequently introduced in theatrical plays, hence his name is familiar to the people. The person here spoken of as reviling him was his wife.

20 聽天由命 *Yield to heaven and submit to fate*—a book phrase which combines the ideas of *providence and fate.*

21 無論他是不是 is an abbreviation for 無論是他的是, 是他的不是, *no matter whether it is his right or his wrong.* This is an approved maxim of Chinese parental policy.

24 Elegance of style in Chinese depends largely on the constant use of classical figures, allusions, and quotations.

25 綠花洋布 Note the three qualifying adjectives in succession.

27 帶掉 is the Nanking form. 掉 is an auxiliary verb much used in the South:—Les. 92.

29 The use of 等 in the first clause, shows that the convenience referred to was that of going or starting away, hence *go* is supplied in the translation.

31 涵養的工夫 Time and effort spent in schooling the temper and acquiring the art of self-control. 到了, that is, to the point of a thorough acquirement. 不矜不躁 *Not passionate, not fretful,*—a book phrase.

32 誇獎他 does not here mean to praise him, as it might seem to do, but to boast of him to others.

35 壯班 a class or section of the 衙役 in a magistrate's office, who are his special guard, and are entrusted with the business of arresting and confining prisoners in civil cases. When a man is arrested, he is required by custom to pay a fine to the 班, or class, arresting him, which is more or less, according to the ability of the prisoner. If he refuses to pay, or to pay as much as is required, all sorts of cruel devices are resorted to in order to extract it from him. He is at the mercy of these rapacious underlings. 不出油 *Will not give out the oil,*—a significant figure taken from the extracting of oil from beans by pressure.

第八十四課

[1]咱我們歇歇罷。○衆[2]位、我偺們走罷。○明[3]天是我俺們大哥的生日、○您[4]的公事都完了嗎。○您[5]您納的少爺、不是在戶部有差使嗎。○你[6]你納這麼坐了、叫我怎麼坐呢。○他[7]他納這些年有病、誰照應家裏呢。○咱[8]我們那點兒不如他。○俺[9]先生是個出名的秀才。○咱[10]們所見的、全不錯。○人[11]欺負咱們、咱們也要有些包涵。○酒[12]多喇、咱們停一會兒再喝罷。○偺[13]們倆相隔忒遠、不能常在一塊兒。○咱[14]們家裏

TRANSLATION.

1 Let us take a rest.
2 Well, gentlemen, shall we go?
3 To-morrow will be our elder brother's birthday.
4 Is your business all finished?
5 Is not your son employed in the Board of Revenue?
6 If you sit thus, where will you have me sit?
7 During these years of illness who took charge of his family?
8 Are we not in every respect as good as he?
9 Our teacher is a well-known graduate.
10 All that we saw was unexceptionable.
11 When others insult us, we should have some self-restraint.
12 We have drunk too much. Let us wait a little before drinking again.
13 We two are too widely separated to be frequently together.
14 Have you all forgotten our old home custom?

LESSON LXXXIV.

COLLOQUIAL PRONOUNS.

In addition to the regular Mandarin pronouns, there are, especially in Central and Northern Mandarin, a number of colloquial pronouns in common use.

偺 We, we folks, our, us. The speaker classes himself with those present, or with others of like station, occupation or opinion. The character is not authorized by the dictionaries, but is in general use. 喒 is sometimes incorrectly written for it.

咱 Same meaning as 偺. It was probably adopted to write the shortened form of pronouncing 偺 *tsan*, viz., *tsa*.

In Peking 偺 and 咱 always have the plural termination, 們, joined with them. In Central Mandarin it is generally omitted. Its use seems to add nothing, as the words are essentially plural. Neither 偺 nor 咱 is used to any extent in Southern Mandarin.

偺家 We, us,—an old colloquial form used in the Ming Dynasty, and found in books, but now obsolete.

俺 We, us,—used especially when the speaker wishes to particularize himself. It is used in Central Mandarin and in certain localities both North and South. It is not infrequently found in Mandarin books. 偺 frequently includes those addressed, while 俺 always excludes them.

您 You, you folks. In Peking this word is used as a term of respect,—*You, sir*, or, *you, madam*. It is also often read as if written 您納, the *na* being spoken very lightly. In Shantung it always includes a plural idea, and expresses no special respect. It never takes 們 after it. In some places it is read *nĕn*², in others *nin*², and in others *na*³, and in Southern Mandarin a nasal *n*. It is much more used in some places than in others.

你納 or **您納** You, sir, you [my senior]. This form is exclusively Pekingese, and is explained as a contraction for 你老人家.

納 is sometimes added to 他 in the same way.

佢 *K'ei* is used along the *Yang-tsï* as a colloquial substitute for 他, but it belongs to the Southern coast dialects, not to Mandarin.

的老舊規矩、你們都忘了嗎。○咱[15]們五六年沒有見面、你的鬍子都白了。我[16]看你很面熟、咱們是在天津說過話不是。○只[17]您弟兄兩個(哥兒倆)來了嗎、答我們(俺)父親也來了。○咱[18]們這兒的小河很窄、有浮橋就可以過去。○咱[19]們兩個這盤子(件)買賣、對付不了(接就不上、圓就不來)。○俺[20]家裏擀的麪條子、進去吃兩碗罷。○這[21]種小人乍富的脾氣、很可以不理他。○人[22]家的錢在咱手裏、不能由得咱用。○我[23]想咱們用人、總是樸實有眼力見兒(眼色)的纔好。○偺[24]們今天兒商量半天纔定規、以後永不改了。○他[25]媽一點奶也沒有、你能給俺僱個奶媽子不能。○

15 We have not seen each other for five or six years; your beard is quite gray.
16 Your face is very familiar: we had a talk together in Tientsin, had we not?
17 Did only you two brothers come? *Ans.* Our father also came.
18 This little stream of ours is very narrow: you can cross it on a moveable bridge.
19 We cannot come to an agreement about this piece of business of ours.
20 We have made vermicelli at our house; come in and have a bowl or two.
21 We can very well afford to disregard the pride of newly gotten wealth in this class of petty natures.
22 Another's money in our hands is not at our disposal.
23 In my opinion, the best man for our use, after all, is a plain man of sound judgment.
24 We deliberated a long time to-day before we decided: hereafter we will never reverse it.
25 His mother hasn't a drop of milk: can you hire a wet nurse for us?

VOCABULARY.

偺 *Tsan*². . . . . . . We, we folks :—see Sub.
咱 *Tsa*². . . . . An elided form of 偺 :—see Sub.
俺 *An*²˒³. . . . . . . I, we, us :—see Sub.
您 *Nin*². . . . . . . You, you folks :—see Sub.
納 *Na*⁴. To receive; to pay over to; to be affected . . . . . . by; a pronominal enclitic :—see Sub.
公事 *Kung*¹ *shï*⁴. Public affairs, *business;* a . . . . wedding or funeral.
戶部 *Hu*⁴ *pu*⁴. . . . . . . The Board of Revenue.
差使 *Ch'ai*¹ *shï*³. Engagement, commission, ... *employment.*
出名 *Ch'u*¹ *ming*². *Well-known,* celebrated, ... distinguished.
秀 *Hsiu*⁴. . . . . . Flourishing, cultivated, elegant.
秀才 *Hsiu*⁴ *ts'ai*². A graduate of the first . . . . degree, bachelor of arts.
包涵 *Pao*¹ *han*². . . . . . Patience, *self-restraint.*
面熟 *Mien*⁴ *shu*². *The face familiar,* known by . . . . sight.
浮 *Fou*². To float; light, volatile; *unsubstantial,* . . . . . . fleeting. Also *fu*².
橋 *Ch'iao*². . . . . . . A bridge; a cross-piece.
浮橋 A bridge of boats, *a moveable bridge.*
對付 *Twei*⁴ *fu*⁴. To match, to adjust, to adapt; . . . . *to agree;* to bargain, to buy.
接就 *Chie*¹ *chiu*⁴. To adapt, to accommodate; . . . . to come to terms, to agree.
圓就 *Yüen*² *chiu*⁴. . . . . . . The same.
擀 *Kan*³. . . . . To roll out,—as dough is rolled.
麪條 *Mien*⁴ *t'iao*². . . . . . . Vermicelli, noodles.
乍富 *Cha*⁴ *fu*⁴. . . . . . . Sudden wealth.
樸 *P'u*³˒². . . . . . . Sincere, *plain,* substantial.
樸實 *P'u*³ *shï*². *Plain, unadorned;* honest, ... simple-minded.
眼力見兒 *Yien*³ *li*⁴ *chien*⁴ *êr*². Discretion, ... *judgment,* cleverness, shrewdness, discernment. (N.)

天[26]氣不穩妥、要颳大風、趁着還沒颳、咱們快快些走罷。○我[27]估量是這兒的人、喜歡咱們來、故此奏這樂器。○就[28]是你的口頭語、也不可這樣大放無拘、你不論在誰眼前、都好自稱偺老子嗎。○揭[29]陽鎮上、沒有一個曉事的好漢、抬舉咱家。○俺[30]家裏做針線、可就有的是人喇、前日他姑嫂五個、給我做大綿襖、我在正間裏、刷了兩個鍋的工夫、他們把綿花就鋪絮上了、翻過來的時候、這個縫大襟、那個打邊子、這個煞胳肢窩、揢襖裉、那個上領條兒、緣袖口的緣袖口、釘鈕釦子門的釘鈕釦子門、不到半天、就做起來了。

26 The weather is unsettled: we are going to have a high wind: let us go quickly before it begins to blow.

27 I presume it is that the people here are pleased with our coming, and therefore make this music.

28 Even if it is a favorite expression of yours, it will not do for you to use it recklessly. Is it proper for you, no matter whom you are addressing, to be always styling yourself "your old father"?

29 There is not in Chie Yang Chên a single efficient man to uphold us.

30 There is no lack of folks to sew in our family. Day-before-yesterday they, five sisters-in-law, made me a wadded gown. While I was in the kitchen washing out the two kettles, they put in the wadding; and as soon as it was turned, this one stitched up the overlap, that one laid the chalk lines, another closed the seams under the arms, and another put on the collar-binding; one bound the cuffs and another sewed on the button-loops, and in less than half a day it was finished.

商量 *Shang¹ liang²*. To consult, to compare notes, *to deliberate*.

奶媽 *Nai³ ma¹*. A wet nurse.

奏 *Tsou⁴*. To memorialize the throne, to bring forward; to play or make music.

樂 *Yoă⁴*, *yüe⁴*. Music, *musical*. See *loă⁴*.

樂器 *Yoă⁴ ch'i⁴*. Musical instruments.

口頭語 *K'ou³ t'ou² yu³*. *A pet phrase*, a peculiarity of speech.

曉事 *Hsiao³ shï⁴*. Able, clear-headed, efficient. (w.)

正間 *Chêng⁴ chien¹*. The middle room facing the front:—Note 30.

大襟 *Ta⁴ chin¹*. The lapel of a garment.

煞 *Sha⁴*. Baleful, malign, to the point of death, very; *to close up*, to shut up; to end.

肢 *Chï⁴*. The upper arm. Used only in the phrase 胳肢窩.

窩 *Woă¹*. A nest, a lair; a den; *a hole, a depression*, a nook; a shrine.

胳肢窩 *Kê¹ chï⁴ woă¹*. The armpit.

領條 *Ling³ t'iao²*. The binding around the collar.

揢 *Kê⁴*. To sew or stitch together the parts of a garment, to close up; to twist together the strands of a thread or rope.

裉 *K'ên⁴*. The gusset under the arm.

袖口 *Hsiu⁴ k'ou³*. *The wristband;* a cuff.

釘 *Ting¹*. To sew on as a button or loop; to patch; to mend shoes.

NOTES.

1 Oı, *Shall we take a rest?* All would depend on the manner of speaking.

2 This sentence might also be spoken so as to mean, *Gentlemen, let us go.*

6 Addressed by a host to his guests who had already taken, or were about to take the lowest seats.

12 The Chinese *seems* to say that the wine is abundant, but the sense is that much wine has been drunk.

13 The use of 倆 implies intimacy. It would not be used by the speaker in the sixteenth sentence.

14 都 might also be rendered *quite*, or, *altogether*,—*Have you quite forgotten* etc. Southern teachers object to 舊 and say 老. The two words are here approximate equivalents. 舊 is what has been practiced before and so is not *new;* 老

第八十五課

這[1]簍柚子、有幾多多麼重。○跟[2]這裏走、幾多多麼順便。○府[3]上到這裏幾多多麼遠、答三十里路地。○你[4]看人家那個孩子、多麼聽說。○這[5]個井有多深呢、答六丈多深。○你[6]的二千金、現在多大歲數。○天[7]壇有多高呢。○火[8]輪車一天、能走多麼遠呢、答一天能走二千里路。○給[9]你這些、你還嫌少、你想要多少呢。○他[10]只會闖禍、一點

TRANSLATION.

1 How heavy is this basket of pomeloes?
2 How much more convenient it was to have come this way!
3 How far is it from your residence to this place? *Ans.* Thirty *li.*
4 See how obedient that child of his is.
5 How deep is this well? *Ans.* It is over sixty feet deep.
6 How old is your second daughter?
7 How high is the altar of heaven?
8 How far can a railway train travel in a day? *Ans.* It can travel two thousand *li.*
9 Even when I give you all these, you yet find fault with them for being too few! How many do you propose to ask for?
10 He is always getting into trouble.

is what has been practiced for a long time and so is not *recent.*

17 哥兒倆 The 兒 stands for the correlative word, that is, 弟. So also in the similar phrases 爺兒倆, *father and son*, or *daughter*, and 娘兒倆, *mother and son*, or *daughter*. 哥兒倆 is the address of one of the same age or station; 弟兄兩個 is the language of an elder or a superior.

18 浮橋 is properly a floating bridge of boats, but is often applied to any temporary or moveable bridge. Such bridges are often made of rough planks laid endwise on wooden benches, and are taken away during the prevalence of high water.

19 盤 is the classifier of business. Its use probably comes from the use of the 算盤, or abacus. Peking teachers reject both the Central and Southern forms. They also disallow the use of 上來 with 對付, which, however, would be quite appropriate in most localities.

22 A Chinaman's untrustworthiness is nowhere more conspicuous than in the liberty he takes with other people's money entrusted to him to keep, or to carry.

26 快些 Properly, *a little quicker*, but used here simply as an intensive implying no comparison. 些 is often so used in the South, rarely in the North.

28 偺老子 is a Peking expression and somewhat slangy. "*Your daddy*" would perhaps give about the flavor of it.

29 揭陽鎮 A large market village in Honan, mentioned in the History of Robbers, from which the sentence is taken.

30 有的是 *Plenty of*, "*lots of*," a very idiomatic form of expressing this idea. 姑嫂 The daughter-in-law calls her husband's sisters 大姑子 and 小姑子, and they call their elder sisters-in-law, 嫂子. The terms by which each designates the other are joined together as the common designation of all. 正間 is the middle room, which, in the homes of the common people, has a cooking range on either side, and is, in fact, the kitchen. 翻過來, etc. The seams are first sewed up, and the cotton wadding spread on, and the garment is then turned inside out. 打邊子 is to measure and strike the chalk lines by which the quilting is to be done.

LESSON LXXXV.

多 AS AN INTERROGATIVE.

多 is applied interrogatively to many adjectives, as *how* is in English, as 多大 *how great*, 多長 *how long*, etc. 麼 is often inserted after the 多, and joined with it. This was probably the original form, the use of 多 alone being a contraction.

As in English so in Chinese, this interrogation often passes into an exclamation.

VOCABULARY.

簍 *Lou*³. . . . *A basket*, hamper, a market basket.
柚 *Yiu*⁴. . . . . The pomelo or shaddock.
順便 *Shun*⁴ *pien*⁴. *Convenient*, direct; smooth, ... compliant.
千金 *Ch'ien*¹ *chin*¹. A thousand taels of gold, ... priceless, inestimable; a complimentary term for another man's daughter.
壇 *T'an*². . . . . *An altar*, an arena.

不知道天多高、地多厚。○看[11]人家這匹馬、跑的多麼快。○他[12]已經多遠來了、還可以叫他空手回去嗎。○早[13]知道劉芳齡要去、託他帶着、多麼省事呢。○你[14]估量這棵梧桐樹、有多高、能鋸幾節呢。○從[15]曲阜縣、到沂州府、有多遠呢。○[16]這麼(好乾淨這一點)一點點兒的東西、能有多麼重呢。○他[17]頭一個女人、多麼排場、這個差的多了。○你[18]的眼睛不好使(用)嗎、你看這頭多粗、那頭多細。○他[19]光告訴叫做一張床、沒告訴多長多寬。○你[20]如今正是得時的時候、吃的有多麼好、穿的有多麼好。○人[21]家韓青山的內人(老婆、夫人)、多麼會說、眞是女中的魁首。○

He hasn't the least common sense.

11 See how fast this horse of his can run.

12 Having come a long distance it will not do to send him home empty-handed.

13 If we had known that Liu Fang Ling was going, how much it would have saved to get him to take it!

14 How high do you estimate this *wu t'ung* tree to be? and how many lengths will it make (saw)?

15 How far is it from Ch'üfu Hsien to Ichou Fu?

16 A trifling little bit of a thing like this, what weight can it have?

17 How lady-like his first wife was. This one is vastly inferior.

18 Is your eyesight not good? See how large this end is and how small that one is.

19 He simply told me to make a bed, but did not say how long or how wide.

20 You are just now enjoying the smiles of fortune. How excellent are your food and your clothing.

21 That wife of Han Ch'ing Shan's, how she can talk! Verily, she takes the palm among women.

22 Are you not afraid you will be drowned, going into the water in this way when you do not know how

---

天壇 *T'ien*¹ *t'an*². The altar of heaven at Peking:—Note 7.

闖 *Ch'wang*³. To rush out, or in, or against; to dash forward; suddenly.

闖禍 *Ch'wang*³ *hwoă*.⁴ To bring on calamity, *to get into trouble.*

空手 *K'ung*¹ *shou*³. *Empty-handed,* destitute of, unsupplied.

芳 *Fang*¹. Fragrant, excellent. (w.)

齡 *Ling*². A person's age, years. (w.)

省事 *Shêng*³ *shi*⁴. *To economize labor,* to save trouble.

梧 *Wu*². *Stereulia Platanifolia.*

桐 *T'ung*². Allied to the above.

梧桐 The national tree of China; it has large leaves and a graceful top. The wood is valued for coffins because it resists decay, and for musical instruments because it is dense and resonant.

曲 *Ch'ü*¹·⁴. Crooked, bent; tortuous, false; to wrong, to oppress. See *ch'ü*³.

阜 *Fou*⁴. A mound of earth, abundant. (w.)

曲阜 A city in southern Shantung noted as the site of Confucius' grave.

沂 *I*². A river in south-eastern Shantung.

沂州 *I*² *chou*¹. A prefectural city on the 沂 river.

排場 *P'ai*² *ch'ang*³. Neat, orderly; well-behaved. *lady-like.*

床 *Ch'wang*². The same as 牀.

韓 *Han*². An ancient state; *a surname.*

內人 *Nei*⁴ *jên*². Wife:—Note 21.

夫人 *Fu*¹ *jên*². Wife, lady:—Note 21.

魁首 *K'wei*² *shou*³. A leader, *a first-class man,* an honor man, facile princeps.

浮 *Fu*². To swim. See *fou*².

浮水 *Fu*² *shwei*³. To swim.

莊稼漢 *Chwang*¹ *chia*⁴ *han*⁴. *A farmer,* a rustic.

不22知水有多麼深、你就下去、不怕淹死嗎、答不怕、我會浮水。○你23們念書的人、風也吹不着、雨也淋(灑)不着、日頭(太陽)也曬不着、比我們這些莊稼漢、多麼自在呢。○你24看領兵的元帥、得勝回營的時候、一到營門、幾萬兵一齊跪接、傳下令來、一齊答應、那個威武多大。○我25這腿上的疙瘩醫治不好、還是天天長、不知要長多麼大、寔在彀我受的。

deep it is? *Ans.* Never fear. I know how to swim.

23 You literary men, the wind cannot blow on you, nor the rain wet you, nor the sun scorch you. How much more comfortable you are than we farmers.

24 See the general in command when he returns to his encampment after a victory. When he reaches the gate, the whole army kneel together to receive him, and when the command is given, all respond together. How imposing is the spectacle!

25 This boil on my leg is not improving under treatment. It continues to enlarge every day. It is hard to say how large it is going to be. It is as much as I can stand.

帥 *Shwai*4. A leader, *a commander-in-chief;* ....the king in chess.

元帥 *Yüen*2 *shwai*4....... A general.

得勝 *Tê*2 *shĭng*4. *To get the victory*, to conquer, ...to triumph.

一齊 *I*1 *ch'i*2....... All together:—Les. 105.

跪 *Kwei*4....... To kneel, to bow down to.

跪接 *Kwei*4 *chie*1......To receive on the knees.

威武 *Wei*1 *wu*3.... *Imposing*, stately, majestic.

疙 *Kê*1.......... A pimple, a boil.

瘩 *Ta*1.......... A sore, a boil.

疙瘩 A raised sore or boil; a lump or swelling; a wheal; a knot on a string.

醫治 *I*1 *chï*4....... To heal, to cure; to treat.

NOTES.

1 幾多 *How, how many,*—is used in the region of Hankow, and perhaps westward, for 多麼. No such combination is known in Central or Northern Mandarin.

2 Or, *How much more convenient it is to go this way.*

3 路 is joined to 里 as an expletive. In the North 地 is often used in the same way. The usage is similar to the phrase "*a distance of thirty li.*"

4 人家 is here used pronominally for the person or persons referred to.

7 天壇 is a large square stone altar, which stands in the grounds of the temple of heaven at Peking. It is directly south and in front of the round temple commonly called the "Temple of Heaven." It is about thirty feet high, level and paved on the top, and has cut stone steps on each of the four sides.

10 不知天多高地多厚 *Does not know how high is the heaven nor how deep is the earth*, that is, he is utterly lacking in judgment, has no sense of the fitness of things.

12 The interrogative is used for emphasis, and is best rendered into English in the indicative.

13 The structure of this sentence is such as to imply an *if*.

14 A 節 is understood to be the length for a coffin, that being the purpose for which logs are supposed to be primarily intended.

16 乾淨 is here used as opposed to *bulky* or *cumbersome*. It is so used in Central and Southern Mandarin but not in the North. The sentence is the language of one who is skeptical about the great weight of a small box or parcel.

21 人家 is prefixed to this sentence for the purpose of suggesting a contrast with the speaker's own wife or family—a shade of thought which no English translation will convey. 內人 is preferred in this connection by Peking teachers. They aver that it expresses nothing either of respect or of disrespect, but its common use by the husband when speaking of his wife, shows that it is depreciatory. It is not used in Shantung, though known as a book term. 老婆 is quite *t'ung hsing*, but more freely used in some places than in others. Its use evinces want of respect, rather than expresses any special disrespect. 夫人 is properly applied only to the wife of a person of rank, but has come into use, in some places, of any genteel woman. It is rarely used in Shantung.

23 In Nanking 日頭 is hardly ever used, 太陽 being almost always used instead.

第八十六課

怎[1]麼弄的滿屋裏這麼些煙。○洗[2]澡是渾身都洗。○他[3]是個飄流人、滿處打野食（饑荒）吃。○耶[4]穌是普天下的救主。○你[5]想他賣了家廟的樹、合族的人、還能讓他嗎。○天[6]已經陰滿了、是要下普（大）雨的樣子。○有[7]理走遍天下、無理寸步難行。○今[8]天不知受了一點甚麼風氣、滿身起了些疙瘩。○這[9]個孩子、一點不討人喜歡、哭起來滿地直滾。○你[10]看你弄的滿臉是灰、就和一個小鬼兒一樣。○只[11]要碰着個好父母官、這就是闔縣的造化。○王[12]家莊、為這個人命案子（案）、合疃（村）都嚇跑了。○誰[13]把蒲團子（墊子）藏在

Translation.

1 How have you come to fill the whole room with all this smoke?
2 To bathe is to wash the whole body.
3 He is a tramp wandering from place to place picking up a living?
4 Jesus is the Saviour of the whole world.
5 Seeing he has sold the trees in the family temple, do you suppose the clan will allow it to pass?
6 The sky is already clouded all over, it looks as if we were about to have a general rain.
7 With right on your side, you can go anywhere; without right, it is hard to move an inch.
8 I wonder what malarial affection I have caught to-day; my whole body is covered with wheals.
9 This boy is not at all prepossessing; when he takes a fit of crying he just lies down and rolls on the ground.
10 Just look! You have gotten your whole face covered with dirt. You look just like a little imp.
11 Only let a good parental magistrate fall to your lot, and it is a boon to the whole district.
12 On account of this murder case, the whole village of Wangchia Chwang has been frightened into flight.

LESSON LXXXVI

Totality.

This lesson is distinguished from Les. 35, as the word *whole* is distinguished from the word *all*.

滿 The whole, complete, entire; when used of place,—everywhere.

合 The whole, all of a number of persons.

闔 All, the whole. The same practically as 合. In some connections one character is preferred, and in some the other.

渾 The entire body or family,—rarely, if ever, used with any other words than 身 and 家.

普 Everywhere, universal, all.

遍 The whole, entire; everywhere.

Vocabulary.

滿 *Man*³. Full; stuffed; entire; complete; Manchu:—see Sub.

渾 *Hun*². Turbid, polluted, dirty; the whole, the entire mass:—see Sub. Also *hun*⁴.

普 *P'u*³. Great; all, everywhere, universal.

闔 *Hê*². A two-leaved door, a family; all, the whole:—see Sub.

澡 *Tsao*³. To bathe or wash the body.

洗澡 *Hsi*³ *tsao*³. To bathe the whole body.

飄 *P'iao*¹. Swayed or rocked by the wind; graceful, airy.

飄流 *P'iao*¹ *liu*². To wander, to roam.

野食 *Yie*³ *shï*². Prey, *picking*:—Note 3.

家廟 *Chia*¹ *miao*⁴. Family or ancestral temple:—Note 5.

族 *Tsu*². *A clan;* a family; kindred; class.

寸步 *Ts'un*⁴ *pu*⁴. A step an inch long,—the least distance, *an inch*.

這裏、叫我滿那裏(處)去找。○14爲姑娘送嫁、比
不得兒娶媳婦、給他四百錢就滿行。○15掃
地的時候、該先灑上一點水、免得滿屋起
浮土(暴土、彈灰)。○16這時遍地都凶荒、約瑟就開了倉、
糶糧給伊及人。○17李老八、看不得他外面
老實、心裏更猴(滿肚子是猴、滿心裏是鬼)。○18爲這一點小事、還值
得你們渾家子(合家)不依嗎。○19基督徒見了、渾
身發料。○20每逢三六九、上朝的日子、滿朝
文武、都得到齊。○21有一個花子(乞丐)名叫拉撒
路、遍身生瘡、被人放在財主門前。○22昨天

13 Who hid the straw mat here? I have been hunting it everywhere.

14 A present made on the marriage of a daughter is very different from one made on the marriage of a son. If you give four hundred cash, it will be quite sufficient.

15 When sweeping the floor, you should first sprinkle some water on it, and thus avoid filling the room with dust.

16 At this time there was famine in the whole land, and Joseph opened the store houses and sold grain to the people of Egypt.

17 It will not do to be misled by Li the Eighth's guileless exterior; his heart is brimful of duplicity.

18 Is it worth while for the whole of you to take offence on account of this little affair?

19 When Christian saw them, he trembled all over.

20 At every audience on the third, sixth and ninth, the whole court, civil and military, are required to present themselves.

21 There was a beggar named Lazarus, whose whole body was full of sores,

造化 *Tsao⁴ hwa⁴*. To create, to make; the Creator; *a boon*, a blessing, luck.

人命 *Jên² ming⁴*. A human life, a case of life and death.

彈 *T'an²*. To fillip, to thrum; to snap, to throw, to shoot; to press down. Also *tan⁴*.

彈灰 *T'an² hwei¹*. . . . . Dust. (s.)

浮土 *Fou² t'u³*. . . . . Dust.

暴土 *Pao⁴ t'u³*. Dust. Read *pu⁴ t'u³* in many places.

凶 *Hsiung¹* Unfortunate, unlucky; adverse; *calamitous*, malignant.

凶荒 *Hsiung¹ hwang¹*. . . . . . . Famine, want.

伊 *I¹*. A *Wên-li* third personal pronoun, but used in the southern coast dialects.

伊及 *I¹ chi²*. . . . . Egypt.

料 *Tou³*. To shake; to shiver; *to tremble;* to arouse, to excite.

上朝 *Shang⁴ ch'ao²*. To have an audience, to go to meet the Emperor.

乞 *Ch'i⁴·³*. . . . . . . To beg, to ask alms.

丐 *Kai⁴*. . . . . . To ask alms; a mendicant.

乞丐 A beggar:—Note 21.

燋 *Chao², chê²*. . . . . . To take fire; *to burn.*

驚動 *Ching¹ tung⁴*. To wake up, *to stir up;* to alarm, to arouse.

族長 *Tsu² chang³*. The eldest man of a family or clan, *an elder.*

地畝 *Ti⁴ mu³*. . . . . . *Land,* area of land.

絲 *Sï¹*. . . . . Raw silk; floss; *a cord,* a line; wire.

蹝 *Lung⁴*. . . . . To walk unsteadily.

踵 *Chung³*. . . . . The heel, to follow at the heels.

蹝踵 Heels over head.

踜 *Lêng²*. . . . . . . A slip, a pitch of the body.

蹭 *Ts'êng⁴*. To miss one's footing, to stagger, *to tumble.* Also *ts'eng.⁴*

踜蹭 A headlong fall, a somersault.

栽 *Tsai¹*. . . . . To set out, to plant.

獃子 *Tai¹ tsï³*. . . . . *A simpleton,* a silly fool.

爬 *P'a²*. *To crawl,* to creep, to climb, to scale; to scrape, to scratch; an iron rake.

黑夜夜裏那一把火、直燒燔了一個多時辰、把閤城的人、都驚動起來了。○我23開的滿工錢給他、臨走又送了他兩塊洋錢、這還對不起他嗎、答滿對得起他。○我24們不如商議族長、叫合莊按着地畝、拔出二十吊錢來、買一套鑼鼓。○滿25地都是絲繩、動動脚跌一個躘踜踵蹭左邊去、一個面磕地、右邊去、一個倒栽葱、把個獃子跌得身麻脚軟、頭暈眼花、爬也爬不起來。

who was laid at the rich man's gate.

22 That fire, night before last, burned for over two hours, stirring up all the people in the city.

23 I gave him his full wages, and when he was about to go, I gave him a present of two dollars. Is there anything illiberal in that? *Ans.* That was treating him very liberally.

24 Let us consult the elders and have the whole village contribute according to their land, a sum of twenty thousand cash to buy a set of musical instruments.

25 The ground was covered with snares so that with every step he stumbled and fell. If he went to the right, he fell flat on his face; if to the left, he turned a somersault, until with his tumbling, the simpleton's body was numb and his feet weak, his head dizzy and his eyes dim, insomuch that he was not able to crawl to his feet again.

Notes.

3 饑荒 is here used in the sense of hunger, which is the only sense it has in the South. In the North 打饑荒 means "to raise the wind," in order to meet some sudden demand for money. 打野食 is usually spoken of beasts and birds, but is here used facetiously of one who lives by what he manages to get by hook or by crook from day to day.

5 家廟, also called 祠堂 *Ts'ï⁴ t'ang²* and 影房 *Ying fang*. It is common for large families to have a special family temple in which the ancestral tablets are kept and where the whole family or clan go to worship their ancestors. There are no idols in such temples.

7 A very common saying. The average Chinaman makes large professions of acting according to *reason*.

8 滿身起了些疙瘩 *My whole body has raised* [in] *wheals.* 風氣 The Chinese do not understand modern ideas of malaria, but they have a strong belief that certain poisons are conveyed by the air.

9 直 is much used, as here, to express the continuance or incessant repetition of an action.

11 Magistrates are often called (and like to be called) 父母官, *parental officers*, implying that they have towards the people the feelings of parents, and govern them like parents do their children, which is generally as far as possible from the fact.

12 A large part of a village are often arrested on account of a murder, and few who are arrested get off without some loss.

14 送嫁 To make a present on the occasion of the marriage of a daughter. It usually consists of money, or of money accompanied by some article of female adornment.

15 Mandarin colloquial seems to have no really *t'ung hsing* word for "dust."

17 The belly, as well as the heart, is frequently spoken of as the seat of intellectual and moral qualities. 猴 is used figuratively for *craft* and *cunning*. 鬼 is used in the same way, but includes less of the idea of cunning and more of that of viciousness.

21 乞丐 for *beggar*, is *Wên-li*, being rarely if ever heard in colloquial. The common and *t'ung hsing* term is 花子.

22 那一把火 *That handful of fire.* The use of 把 as a classifier, probably implies a reference to the start of the fire.

24 Such assessments are frequently made for the repair of temples, for theatrical plays, etc., and public opinion compels everyone to pay.

25 This sentence is from the 西遊記, which records the fabulous adventures of a Buddhist priest, called Hsüen Chwang, but commonly known as 唐僧 *T'ang Sêng*, who went to the West in the seventh century in search of sacred books. The person referred to as a 獃子 is 猪八戒 *Chü¹ pa¹ chai⁴*, who was *T'ang Sêng's* disciple or attendant. He is here presented as in circumstances somewhat similar to those of Christian when passing through the Valley of the Shadow of Death. 躘踵 is an obsolete form, which is now written 踜蹭, in conformity with its modern pronunciation. 倒栽葱 *An onion planted head down*, that is, *the heels in the air, a somersault.* In Chinese the root or bulb of an onion is called its "head," and when set out it is of course planted "head" down. In the phrase 把個獃子 the 個 is equal to 那個 *that or the.*

第八十七課

[1]你多會子兒叫我、我就能多會子兒來。○[2]親家蓋房子、幾時動工呢、答擇的三月初五的日子。○[3]你淨賴人、我多咱應過你。○[4]幾時得了機會、請你勸勸他。○[5]這樣耽擱工夫、到多咱纔能做起來呢。○[6]劉仁欣已經賭過咒、管多咱幾兒幾早不和我說話。○[7]離家這麽遠、到幾時能得團圓呢。○[8]你要進京嗎、多咱會子兒早晚兒走、你告訴我、我好給你餞行。○[9]這是多會子兒幾咱的事呢、答我記不清是多會子兒幾咱、只知是在六月間。○[10]若問他要罷、又怕傷了和氣薄了仁義、若不問他要罷、他管

TRANSLATION.

1 I can come whenever you send for me.

2 Kinsman, when do you begin work on your house? *Ans.* The fifth day of the third month has been selected.

3 You are making an entirely false demand. When did I promise you?

4 Whenever you get an opportunity, please exhort him.

5 Wasting time in this way, when will you be able to finish?

6 Liu Jên Hsin has already taken an oath that he will never speak to me.

7 Separated from home so far as this, when shall I enjoy the family circle?

8 You are going to the capital are you? When you go, let me know that I may give you a send-off.

9 When did this happen? *Ans.* I do not remember distinctly when: I only know it was in the sixth month.

10 If I ask him for it, I fear I may offend him; if I do not ask him for it, he will never try to pay me.

LESSON LXXXVII.

WHEN.

幾時 How much time; *i.e.*, when, whenever.

幾兒 Same. Northern, and strongly colloquial.

多咱 When,—a widely used term, but not entirely *t'ung hsing*. It is never heard in Eastern Shantung. Along the Yangtze it takes a 子 after it.

幾咱 A Southern form of 多咱, which in some places quite supersedes it.

麽咱 Another Southern form of 多咱.

多會 When, whenever. In the North it nearly always takes after it an enclitic 兒, which in the South is replaced by 子. It is quite *t'ung hsing*, but more used in some places than in others.

多早晚兒 How much sooner or later; *i.e.*, when,—a Peking expression.

多早 A contracted form of 多早晚兒, used in the South.

幾早 Same as 多早.

VOCABULARY.

咱 *Tsan*^{1}. . . . . A time, a period of time.

動工 *Tung*^{4} *kung*^{1}. To begin work, to break . . . . ground.

擇 *Chai*^{2}. . . . . . *To select*, to choose; to pick out.

機會 *Chi*^{1} *hwei*^{4}. *Opportunity*, occasion, opening; . . . . nick of time.

欣 *Hsin*^{4}. . . . . Delight; merry, elated.

耽擱 *Tan*^{1} *kê*^{1}. To loiter, *to waste time*, to . . . . miss an opportunity.

賭咒 *Tu*^{3} *chou*^{4}. To bet or promise with an . . . . oath, to take an oath.

團圓 *T'wan*^{2} *yüen*^{2}. A complete circle; harmo- . . . . niously united; *the whole family*, altogether.

餞 *Chieu*^{4}. . . . . A present of food on parting.

多喒幾時也不想着還。○李[11]先生幾時來的、答我昨天來的、問幾時回去、答住個三五天就走。○七[12]王爺、多喒麼喒從北京起的身、答十一從北京起的身、問多喒麼喒到的旅順口、答十五到的旅順。○省[13]城裏候補的官、總有八九百、若不捐些花樣、熬到幾時能補鈌呢。○我[14]爲他費了多少心機、得罪了多少仇人、以後他還勾通別人去告我、所以我多喒幾早想起來、多喒幾早寒心。○我[15]的兩個媳婦、脾氣正相反、大的差不多管多喒會不在家、小的差不多管多喒會不出門。○他[16]信上寫的、幾時領的憑、幾時出的京、我算計着、現在該到了任了。○先[17]

11 When did you come, Mr. Li? *Ans.* I came yesterday. *Ques.* When do you return? *Ans.* I will go in four or five days.

12 When did the Seventh Prince start from Peking? *Ans.* He left Peking on the eleventh. *Ques.* When did he reach Port Arthur? *Ans.* He arrived at Port Arthur on the fifteenth.

13 In the provincial capital there are fully eight or nine hundred expectant officials. If one did not purchase his advancement, how long do you suppose he would have to wait for a position?

14 How much trouble I took on his account, and how many enemies I made! yet he afterwards leagued with others to bring suit against me, so that whenever I think of it I feel disheartened.

15 The dispositions of my two daughters-in-law are exactly opposite: the elder is almost never at home; the younger almost never goes from home.

16 His letter states when he received his commission and when he left the capital: I estimate that by this time he ought to be at his post.

17 Sir, when will you return from your

餞行 *Chien*⁴ *hsing*². To give a feast or a present of food to one starting on a journey.

仁 *Jên*². Benevolence, charity; humanity, *kindness;* a kernel, a pit.

仁義 *Jên*² *i*⁴. Good-nature, amiability, brotherly love, *friendship.*

旅 *Lü*³. A guest, a sojourner; a multitude.

旅順 *Lü*³ *shun*⁴. Port Arthur on the Gulf of Pechili.

省城 *Shêng*³ *ch'êng*². The capital city of a Province.

候補 *Hou*⁴ *pu*³. An expectant official, one waiting for an appointment.

花樣 *Hwa*¹ *yang*⁴. Money spent to secure, or to hasten an appointment.

鈌 *Ch'üe*¹. A defect, a deficiency, *a vacancy;* a situation, an office.

補鈌 *Pu*³ *ch'üe*¹. To fill a vacancy, to supply a place, *to get a position.*

心機 *Hsin*¹ *chi*¹. Thought, consideration, study; anxiety, *trouble.*

勾通 *Kou*¹ *t'ung*¹. To plot against, *to league with,* in collusion with.

寒 *Han*². Cold, shivering, *chill;* poor, plain.

寒心 *Han*² *hsin*¹. Cast down, depressed, *disheartened.*

領憑 *Ling*³ *p'ing*². To receive credentials or a commission.

算計 *Swan*⁴ *chi*⁴. To reckon, *to estimate;* to count up.

則 *Tsê*². A rule, a law; a pattern; *a standard;* wherefore, and so; there, in that case.

回想 *Hwei*² *hsiang*³. *To recollect;* to look back, to recall; to reflect.

巴 *Pa*¹. To expect, to long for; oh that, would that. See *pa*⁴.

巴結 *Pa*¹ *chie*¹. *To look forward to,* to strive for, to long and labor for; to curry favor with, to act the flunkey, to fawn upon.

生這一次出門、幾時回來、答不定幾時、多則三個月、少則兩個半月。○18回想我在學房念書的時候、心裏常常盼巴望結到趕多喒進了學就好了、以後進了學、又盼巴望結到趕多喒中了舉就好了、以後中了舉、又盼巴望結到趕多喒點了翰林就好了、如今點了翰林、還盼巴望結到趕多喒放了學差就好了、就是以後放了學差、還不曉得能足意不能。○19甲戌、你的爆熚要能放到幾時呢、你這幾天把我震的、實在彀受的。

present tour? *Ans.* It is uncertain when: at the most, in three months; at the least, in two months and a half.

18 I recollect that when I was in school studying, I was always thinking that when I should get my first degree, I should be satisfied: afterward when I obtained it, I thought when I should reach the degree of *chüjên* I should be satisfied, but afterwards when I became a *chüjên*, I then thought that when I should be elected a *hanlin* I should be satisfied; and now that I am elected a *hanlin*, I still want to be appointed literary chancellor. In case I should hereafter be appointed literary chancellor, I do not know whether I should be satisfied.

19 Chia Hsü, when will your fire-crackers all be fired off? You have been stunning my ears these few days beyond endurance.

中舉 *Chung⁴ chü³*. To attain the degree of *chüjên.*
學差 *Hsüe² ch'ai¹*. The office of Literary Chancellor:—Note 18.
足意 *Tsu² i⁴*. *Satisfied*, content.
戌 *Hsü¹*. The eleventh hour, 7 to 9 P.M.
爆 *Pao⁴, p'ao⁴*. To snap, to pop, *to burst;* to crackle, to sputter.
熚 *Chang¹*. An explosion of flame, a flash.
爆熚 A fire-cracker. Also read *p'ao⁴ chang¹*.
震 *Chên⁴*. To shake, to quiver, to tremble; to shock, *to stun*, to startle; to threaten.

NOTES.

2 擇日子 is the technical term for selecting a lucky day. Such a selection is made for almost every important undertaking, such as commencing work on a new building, opening a new business, getting married, etc. The selection is made by a professional prognosticator.

3 你淨賴人 Peking teachers would write 竟 instead of 淨. The idea, however, of *purely, simply, entirely*, which is the idea intended, is more naturally derived from the primary meaning of 淨, than from that of 竟; moreover, it should be noted that the word is *t'ung hsing*, and the sound of 淨 is everywhere correct, while the sound of 竟 is only correct where soft sounds prevail. Where hard sounds prevail, 竟 is not recognized as having the meaning in question, and if so used will be misunderstood; thus 你竟賴人, would be taken to mean, *You are after all making a false demand.*

6 管 joined with any of the time particles in the lesson, and followed by a negative, means, *no matter when;* i.e., *never.*

10 傷了和氣 *Wound the peace*, 薄了仁義 *Make thin the goodwill or friendship*, that is, *to give offence*. 了 is used as an auxiliary; see next lesson.

11 個 serves to combine the three or five days into one space or period. The two 的 in this sentence, and the four in the next, have practically the force of so many 了.

13 Officials out of office, and literary graduates who are approved as suitable for appointment, are called 候補, *vacancy waiters*. They all reside in the provincial capital, each striving by the use of money and wire-pulling to advance his own interests. Without the liberal use of money no appointment can be secured. Money spent in bribing is facetiously said to be "contributed" (捐), the theory being that it is *contributed* to the necessities of the government.

14 得罪仇人 Lit., *to offend an enemy;* i.e., to offend anyone so as to make an enemy of him. 寒心 *Cold hearted*, but means much more than to feel *cool* towards the person offending. It expresses that peculiar feeling of pain or depression experienced when a friend proves false or faithless.

15 *Elder* and *younger* here refer not to actual age, but to the wives of older and younger sons.

16 到了任 *Reached his duty*, that is, the post of duty to which he was appointed.

17 多則……少則 *At most …… at least*, a book form often used colloquially. See Les. 170.

18 The sole ambition before a student in China is to get a degree, and then get an office, and so get money and power. Every school-boy has this set before him as the pinnacle of his ambition. The proper term for literary chancellor is 學台. The term 學差 refers to the *office* rather than to the *person*. It is the most lucrative office in a province.

第八十八課

炭[1]已經完了喇。○敢[2]保(包你)錯不了。○你[3]贏不了我。○這[4]件事了不了。○這[5]也算不了個大事。○我[6]看賸不了許多。○喫[7]飯是天天少不了的。○事[8]大事小、見面就了。○他[9]要反悔、也反悔不了。○今[10]天做不了、也不礙事。○老[11]兄的厚情、總說不了。○若[12]是學不會、永遠不肯丟(了)手。○人[13]都說是屈他、我看是屈不了他。○躭[14]誤不了我使喚就得了(不誤我用就中了)。○好[15]人受蹧蹋、是免不了的。○我[16]聽着也不是不入味(熱盆)、就是心裏太笨(魯笨)、記不了這麼些事情。○你[17]所用不了的、可以送給我。○那[18]塊地、三

TRANSLATION.

1 This charcoal is already used up.
2 I guarantee there will be no mistake.
3 You cannot get the better of me.
4 This affair cannot be settled.
5 This cannot be considered any great affair.
6 I judge there will not be very much left.
7 Eating is an every-day necessity.
8 Whether an affair be great or small, meet face to face and it is soon settled.
9 He cannot retract it if he would.
10 It is of no consequence even if you cannot finish it to-day.
11 Your bountiful kindness, elder brother, is beyond expression.
12 I'll never give it up until I learn it.
13 Everybody says he is wronged; but as I see it, he suffered no wrong.
14 It is sufficient if it does not interfere with my using it.
15 That good men should suffer abuse is unavoidable.
16 It is not that I am not an interested hearer, but my mind is too dull, I cannot remember so many things.
17 What you do not need you may bring to me.

LESSON LXXXVIII.

了 AS AN AUXILIARY VERB.

Besides its use as a tense ending (Les. 7), 了 is also used as a regular auxiliary verb, being joined to such verbs as will take the qualifying idea of completion or of possibility. Its force comes out most clearly when joined with a negative. These two uses, though different, pass into each other, and are oftentimes not easily distinguished. When 了 is an auxiliary it cannot be read or spoken *la* as it always *can* (and generally *is*) when it is a tense ending. In Southern Mandarin 掉 is often used as an auxiliary instead of 了. Some of the uses of 了 as a principal verb are also introduced into the lesson.

VOCABULARY.

炭 *T'an*[4]. . . . *Charcoal;* embers; bituminous coal.

許多 *Hsü*[3] *toa*[1]. A great many, a large number, ... a great deal, *very much.*

了手 *Liao*[3] *shou*[3]. To quit, *to give up*, to leave . . . . off, to abandon.

丟手 *Tiu*[1] *shou*[3]. . . . . To quit, *to give up.*

入味 *Ju*[4] *wei*[4]. *Interested,* attentive, enlisted, ... appreciative.

熱盆 *Jê*[4] *p'ên*[2]. *Interested,* attentive; enthu- . . . . siastic, ardent, earnest.

魯 *Lu*[3]. . . . . Stupid, dull.

魯笨 *Lu*[3] *pên*[3]. . . . . Stupid, *dull.*

結 *Chie*[2]. To conclude, to finish, *to settle up;* . . . . . the end. See *chie*[1].

了結 *Liao*[3] *chie*[2]. To finish, to put an end to, ... *to settle*, to close up.

十兩銀子買不了。○他[19]的大烟、說斷可斷不掉了。○已[20]經了結的事、怎麼又提起來呢。○我[21]在暹羅所看見的事、一輩子也忘記不掉了。○這[22]些話、若是外人聽了去、可就了不得了。○我[23]常想着來看看、就是不來得不來了。○可[24]惜了兒的、眼看着他這個人、是要成個要飯的了。○這[25]些硝強水酸怕一個瓶瓶子裝不了。○做[26]一條汗巾、用不了這塊綢子。○我[27]聽他講了半天、心裏還是不大了瞭亮。○這[28]種行貨、值不了那那麼些些個錢。○二[29]人搖着三板、嗷欸喲喲哎乃呀呀的搖了半天、也沒能到得了。○

18 Thirty taels of silver will not buy that piece of ground.
19 He says he is going to break off opium, but he cannot break it off.
20 Why call up again business which is already settled?
21 I cannot in all my life forget the things I saw in Siam.
22 It will be a sorry business if outsiders get to hear these things.
23 I have long been wanting to come to see you, but somehow I could not get away.
24 It is a thousand pities that this man is on the verge of becoming a beggar.
25 I fear one bottle will not hold this nitric acid.
26 It will not require all of this piece of silk to make a sash.
27 I heard him explaining for half a day, and yet my mind was not very clear.
28 This style of inferior goods is not worth that much money.
29 The two men rowed their sampan puffing and blowing for half a day, but were unable to reach the place.

暹 *Hsien*^{1}. . . . . To advance. (w.)
暹羅 *Hsien*^{1} *loă*^{2}. . . . . Siam.
了不得 *Liao*^{3} *pu*^{4} *tê*^{2}. Irreparable, no help for it; *a bad business;* an exclamation of apprehension or sorrow, my stars! alas! what shall I do!—Les. 43, Note 13.
硝 *Hsiao*^{1}. . . . . Saltpetre, nitre.
硝强酸 *Hsiao*^{1} *ch'iang*^{2} *swan*^{1}. Nitric acid, aqua fortis.
裝 *Chwang*^{1}. To dress; to put into; to pack, to load; *to hold;* to pretend.
汗巾 *Han*^{4} *chin*^{1}. An ornamental handkerchief, a sash:—Note 26.
瞭 *Liao*^{3}. . . . . A clear eye, far-sighted.
了亮 *Liao*^{3} *liang*^{4}. Intelligible, plain, *clear,* perspicuous.
瞭亮 *Liao*^{3} *liang*^{4}. . . . . The same.
行貨 *Hsing*^{2} *hwoă*^{4}. *Inferior* or second-rate goods.
欸 *Ao*^{3}. The call used by workmen working together:—Note 29.
乃 *Ai*^{3}. . . . . The same. Also *nai*^{3}.

嗷 *Ao*^{1}. A note or sound of wailing or distress; *a responsive call.*
喲 *Yüe*^{1}. . . . An exclamation of surprise or pain.
哎 *Ai*^{4}. An exclamation of surprise, or distress, or regret.
攬 *Lan*^{3}. . . . To grasp, to monopolize; to secure.
包攬 *Pao*^{1} *lan*^{3}. To take upon oneself, to assume, *to take the responsibility.*
簡 *Chien*^{3}. To condense, to abridge; brief, terse; to treat rudely; to choose.
簡直 *Chien*^{3} *chï*^{2}. *Direct,* straightforward, in short, point-blank.
直絕 *Chï*^{2} *chüe*^{2}. Direct, point-blank, *just;* entirely.
推辭 *T'wei*^{1} *ts'ï*^{2}. To excuse oneself; to refuse, *to evade.*
卷 *Chüen*^{4}. A roll, a scroll, *a book;* section of a book:—Les. 147. Also *chüen*^{3}.
夏 *Hsia*^{4}. . . . . . Summer; *a surname.*
草草了事 *Ts'ao*^{3} *ts'ao*^{3} *liao*^{3} *shï*^{4}. To do heedlessly, careless, *makeshift,* slovenly.

看30見人家有辦了不了的事、他就包攬着
給人家辦了。○你31簡直直絕的不用推辭、就是
推辭、也推辭不了。○敢32保那些臢飯已
經壞了、答如今天氣還不大熱、壞不了不得壞
罷。○我33看他的文章、進不了不得進學、也不過
是草草了事、沒遞白頭有交白卷子就是了。○
聽34說夏文德的官司、已經了了、不知是
眞是假、答那能了了呢、若找不出個頂
案的來、永遠也了不不得了。○壞35了醋喇麻了夥
計、老爺回家來了、這可了也了不得了。

30 When he sees any one in a difficulty, he takes the responsibility of managing the business for him.

31 Do not try to evade it at all, for you cannot evade it if you would.

32 I'll warrant that rice that was left over is spoiled. *Ans.* The weather is not yet very warm, it can hardly be spoiled.

33 I don't believe his essay will get him a degree; it was nothing more than a makeshift, gotten up to avoid handing in a blank.

34 I hear that Hsia Wên Tê's lawsuit is concluded. I wonder if it is true? *Ans.* How could it be concluded? Unless some one is found on whom to fix the charge, it can never be concluded.

35 The vinegar is spoiled, my good fellow! his worship has come home. We are in for it, sure enough.

NOTES.

4 了 is here both principal verb and auxiliary.

8 A common saying, the meaning of which is, that for the settlement of a difficulty there is nothing like meeting face to face. The 了 at the end is not an auxiliary but a principal verb.

9 The use of 也 requires the first clause to be taken subjunctively. If 也 were changed to 却 the sentence would mean, *he wants to retract but cannot.*

14 使喚 is much used in Shantung. It is also used in Peking, but less frequently, and in a somewhat more restricted sense.

21 In Southern Mandarin 掉 sometimes takes the place of 了. See Les. 92.

22 The 去 after 聽了 seems like an encumbrance. It is used to suggest the idea of the secret getting "out."

24 可惜了兒的 is a common colloquial phrase, in which the addition of 了兒的 adds greatly to the expressiveness of 可惜. It serves as a sort of superlative.

26 汗巾 *A sweat napkin,* not however practically used for this purpose, but carried by women purely as an ornament. It is long like a sash, made of silk, and often elegantly embroidered. It is either carried in the hand, or across the arm.

27 For 了亮 some would write 燎亮 or 瞭亮.

29 嗷喲哎呀 is an approximate writing of the responsive *heigh ho* made by the Chinese when rowing or carrying. 欸喲乃呀 is a book form for the same thing. The dictionary gives ai^1 as the correct reading of 欸, but says that in this particular phrase it is to be read ao^3. In common use it is constantly confounded with 欵 or, as more correctly written, 款. The Nanking teacher would write 哎喲嚇喝, as best representing the sounds in the South.

30 辦不了 *Unable to do,* not, *unable to finish,* as the phrase might mean in a different connection.

33 草草了事 *Coarsely finish the thing,—to dash off in a careless or indifferent manner.* A book expression in common use. The 草草 is used perhaps with a reference to the hasty writing of the 草字 or *grass character.* 遞白頭卷子 *To hand in a blank paper,* instead of an essay. This is sometimes done by careless and indifferent scholars, when they can get no clue at all to the treatment of the theme. 頭 is omitted in the South.

34 When any one is charged with a crime and the proof of his guilt is insufficient, he is very likely to lie in prison until some one else is found, upon whom the crime can be fixed.

35 壞了醋了 *Spoiled the vinegar.* A phrase borrowed from the process of making vinegar, in which care is required that the process of fermentation does not go too far, and so destroy the vinegar. 了也了不得了 is a highly idiomatic form. The first 了 is reduplicated in order to strengthen the force of the expression 了不得, thus making the expression equivalent to 了不得, 了不得.

第八十九課

[1]太太叫你快些過去呢。○[2]快到十二點鐘了罷、答還早呢。○[3]你們的賬都收齊喇、答差遠着的呢。○[4]他家裏還養着騾子呢、還用打算賙濟他嗎。○[5]孩子那去喇、答在牀上睡覺呢。○[6]我很願意到西國去開開眼、可就是去不了呢。○[7]我那個兄弟、和寶叔同年歲、若站在一處、只怕那個還高些呢。○[8]知道有這個字、可老想不起來呢。○[9]我怎麽不留他、留他留不住呢。○[10]如今聽起大奶奶這個病來、定不住還是喜呢、嫂子且別叫人混治、若治錯了、可了不得。○[11]他若有個好歹、你再要娶這一個媳婦兒、這麽個模様兒、這麽個性情兒、只怕打着燈籠、也沒處去找呢。○[12]有喜事呢、大

TRANSLATION.

1 The lady sends for you to go over quickly.

2 It must be nearly twelve o'clock? *Ans.* Not by a long while.

3 All your outstanding accounts are collected, I suppose? *Ans.* Not by a great deal.

4 Hem! They keep a mule. Why think of giving alms to them?

5 Where has the child gone? *Ans.* Why, it's on the bed asleep!

6 I would like very much to visit the West and see the sights, but I just cannot go.

7 That brother of mine is the same age as Uncle Pao, but if they should stand together, I suspect that he is somewhat taller.

8 I know there is such a character, but somehow I cannot recall it.

9 What's the reason I did not invite him! He would not stay when I did invite him.

10 Judging from what I hear of the lady's sickness, it is not unlikely that it is an occasion of congratulation. You must not allow it to be treated at random. If it should be wrongly treated, it would be a sad affair.

11 If anything should happen to her, and you should want to marry another such wife, of such a form and such a disposition, I suspect you could not find her even with a lantern in your hand.

LESSON LXXXIX.

MISCELLANEOUS USES OF 呢.

呢 has already been defined in Les. 17 as the sign of an indirect question, which is its primary and most important use. It has, however, a variety of other uses which are difficult to classify, and which differ somewhat in different places.

1 It concludes expressions of surprise, indignation, or reproof (1 to 5).

2 It concludes expressions of uncertainty, or perplexity (6 to 12).

3 It concludes expressions marking a suddenly occurring thought, with an implied query as to why the thought did not occur sooner (13 to 17).

4 It gives preponderance to one side of a statement involving an alternative, or a comparison (18 to 21).

5 It concludes an emphatic reply, which contains a query expressed or implied (22 to 25).

6 Standing alone with a noun, it propounds a question, taking the place of the full interrogative form (26, 27).

In all these cases a careful scrutiny will probably show some sort of a query expressed or implied. 呢 is much more used in some places than in others. Where its use is most prevalent, it is often heard when it seems to serve no other purpose than simply to round out the sentence.

家都慶賀、有喪事呢、大家都帮助。○可13不是呢嗎、到底是我看錯了。○前14日先生吃了兩個餑餑、還沒給錢呢、答可是呢、你不提起來、我就忘記了。○可15是呢、我還忘了問、大嫂子和孩子們都好嗎。○我16送了外甥女過去、到底便宜些、答正是呢、你去比誰都妥當。○在17這山上歇伏、比在城裏凉快多喇、就是天天下山買東西、很不便當、答可不是呢。○爲18什麼忙亂痛哭呢、這女孩兒不是死、是睡覺呢。○你19這二年在那裏念書、家裏也省好大的嚼

12 If there is a wedding, all should offer congratulations. If there is a funeral, all should come to help.

13 Sure enough! After all, I was mistaken.

14 You have not yet paid for the two rolls you ate yesterday. *Ans.* That's so. If you had not mentioned it, I should have quite forgotten it.

15 Sure enough! I quite forgot to ask. Are your wife and children all well?

16 After all, it will be more convenient if I go and take my niece. *Ans.* That's so. It will be better for you to go than for any one else.

17 During the dog-days it will be much cooler to rest here on the hill than in the city, but it will be very inconvenient going down every day to buy supplies. *Ans.* That's a fact.

18 Why make ye this ado and weep? The damsel is not dead, but sleepeth.

19 You having been there these two years at school, your family must have saved considerable expenditure.

VOCABULARY

西國 *Hsi*¹ *kwoă*². *Western nations*, a general term for foreign countries.

開眼 *K'ai*¹ *yien*³. To see the world, *to see the sights;* to learn by experience.

只怕 *Chï*³ *p'a*⁴. It's to be feared, *I suspect;* but, peradventure:—Les. 131.

模樣 *Mu*² *yang*⁴. *Form*, fashion, appearance, style, pattern.

喜事 *Hsi*³ *shï*⁴. An occasion of rejoicing, a wedding.

慶 *Ch'ing*⁴. To wish joy, *to congratulate*, to bless; happy, lucky.

賀 *Hê*⁴. To congratulate with a present.

慶賀 *To offer congratulations*, to felicitate.

喪事 *Sang*¹ *shï*⁴. A funeral, a burial.

餑 *Poă*¹. A steamed cake or roll; a baked sweet cake:—Note 14.

可是 *K'ê*³ *shï*⁴. *Sure enough*, really, to be sure.

可不是 *K'ê*³ *pu*⁴ *shï*⁴. That's so, *sure enough*, you're right:—Les. 173.

看錯 *K'an*⁴ *ts'oă*⁴. To mistake, *to be mistaken*, to be deceived.

大嫂 *Ta*⁴ *sao*³. The eldest brother's wife,—largely used as a term of respect by friends and acquaintances, Mrs.

外甥女 *Wai*⁴ *shêng*¹ *nü*³. A niece of a different surname.

歇伏 *Hsie*¹ *fu*². To take a summer vacation.

便當 *Pien*⁴ *tang*⁴. *Convenient*, opportune.

忙亂 *Mang*² *lwan*⁴. Hurry, confusion, bustle, *ado*.

痛哭 *T'ung*⁴ *k'u*¹. To wail, *to weep*.

嚼 *Chüe*², *chiao*²˒⁴. To chew, to bite; *to eat;* to ruminate; food; bit of a bridle.

嚼用 *Chiao*² *yung*⁴. Living; *expenditure*.

駱 *Loă*⁴. A camel.

駱駝 *Loă*⁴ *t'oă*². A camel, a dromedary.

壁 *Pi*⁴. A partition wall; a screen; a division.

隔壁 *Kê*² *pi*⁴. Next door neighbor; *adjoining;* in the next room.

酒館 *Chiu*³ *kwan*³. A wine shop, a saloon.

癤 *Chie*¹. A pimple, *a boil*.

香几 *Hsiang*¹ *chi*¹. *An incense stand* or table, a long narrow table.

用呢。○ 20 我又告訴你們、駱駝穿過針的眼、比財主進神的國、還容易呢。○ 21 你如今要鬧出了這個學房、若再要找這樣一個地方、我告訴你說罷、比登天還難呢。○ 22 那裏隔壁、就是一個酒館、答那纔正合我的式呢。○ 23 你沒去請他來喝酒嗎、答請他他不來呢。○ 24 叫他們都上這裏來、答還沒吃完飯呢。○ 25 怎麼不坐下呢、答大腿上長了一個癤子、坐不下呢。○ 26 洋取火燈呢、答洋取火燈在香几子上。○ 27 他大舅、已經應許管他衣裳、和

20 Again I say unto you, it is easier for a camel to go through the eye of a needle than for a rich man to enter into the kingdom of God.

21 You are on the point of losing your place in the school by your misconduct. But I tell you if you try to find another place like this, it will be harder than ascending to heaven.

22 There is a wine-shop adjoining. *Ans.* That suits me exactly [do you know].

23 Did you not ask him to come and take some wine? *Ans.* I invited him, but he would not come.

24 Tell them all to come here. *Ans.* But they have not yet finished eating.

25 Why do you not sit down? *Ans.* How can I when I have a boil on my thigh?

26 The matches? *Ans.* The matches are on the incense stand.

27 His maternal uncle has already promised to find his clothes, his pens, ink, paper and books, and his two younger paternal uncles have prom-

大舅 *Ta⁴ chiu⁴*. . . . . The eldest maternal uncle.

資 *Tsï¹*. Property, goods; necessaries, *a fee;* a . . . . . . quota; to avail of.

學資 *Hsüe² tsï¹*. . . . . . Teachers' fees, *tuition.*

官鹽 *Kwan¹ yien²*. Government salt:—Note . . . . 28.

去年 *Ch'ü⁴ nien²*. . . . . Last year.

鹽店 *Yien² tien⁴*. . . . . A salt dépôt.

巡役 *Hsün² i⁴*. Constables, police, *revenue . . . . officers.*

贓 *Tsang¹*. . . . . . . *Stolen or illicit goods,* plunder.

坑害 *K'êng¹ hai⁴*. To entrap, to ill-use, *to . . . . harass,* to wrong.

作 *Tsoă¹*. To bring to pass, to incur; a work- . . . . man; workmanship:—See *tsoă⁴*, and *tsu³*.

作死 *Tsoă¹ sï³*. To destroy oneself, *to bring on . . . . death.*

NOTES.

1 The underlying query is, why have you not *already* gone over?

2 還早呢 implies that the party addressed is badly mistaken.

3 A query is suggested in the first clause, by the inflection given in speaking. In the reply 着 would in many places be omitted.

4 The two 還 seem repetitions as written, but would be no objection to the sentence as spoken.

5 The question is understood to be put in a tone of doubtful anxiety. 那去 is a contraction for 那裡去. The use of 呢 at the close gives to the reply the force of a surprised query, as to why the question should have been asked.

7 同年 is not used in the North of persons' ages, but 同歲. It there means *the same year,* but not *the same age.*

10 大奶奶 is the title by which the lady in question was known in the family, not that she bore this relationship to the speaker. 喜 is put for 喜病, the 病 having been introduced above. 喜病 is the common term for the sickness of pregnancy. 且 as here used is an affectation of book style.

11 好歹 is not unfrequently used to express the disastrous termination of an uncertain event. In case of sickness, as here, it is a euphemism for death. 這一個媳婦兒 is put for 這麼一個媳婦兒, or 這麼個媳婦兒, which latter form is that in which it would almost certainly be spoken, save that in some places 兒 would be omitted, or replaced with 子. 媳婦兒 is in some places applied specifically to women of ill fame.

筆墨書紙、他兩個叔叔、應許管先生飯、快叫孩子去念兩天罷、問學資呢、答學資都算我的。○說[28]起吃官鹽來、我要問你一件事、聽說你們貴處去年把鹽店燒了、還殺了二十多個巡役、是眞的嗎、答可不是呢嗎、你想他們爲不一點點兒的事情、就給人家栽鹽贓、坑害人家、若光栽男人的贓、也還罷了、最可恨的、是常栽女人的贓、這不是他們自己作死嗎。

ised to board the teacher: now just decide to send him to school awhile. *Ques.* But how about tuition? *Ans.* I will be responsible for that.

28 Speaking of using government salt, I want to ask you a certain thing. I hear that last year at your place you burned the salt dépôt and killed over twenty revenue officers. Is this true? *Ans.* Of course it is. Just consider that for the least thing they would fabricate a false charge of smuggling, and harass people. If they only made such false charges against men, it might be borne; but the outrageous part of it is that they were continually making such false charges against women. They brought about their own destruction.

13 Whether 嗎 or 呢 be used, the meaning is not perceptibly different, and both forms are practically *t'ung hsing*. Peking teachers prefer 嗎, but do not exclude 呢; in Shantung and the South the reverse is generally true. There is very little difference of meaning between 可是 and 可不是; the former is the direct affirmative, the latter the interrogative affirmative.

14 餑 is always doubled in use, and has different meanings in different localities. The query suggested by 呢 serves to soften the abruptness of the affirmation.

16 Properly, 外甥 applies only to males, but in practice is often made to include females as well. In other cases 女 or 女兒 or 閨女 is added by way of distinction.

21 說罷 is thrown in for emphasis. In 登天的 the 的 is superfluous and would better be omitted.

26 取燈呢 is equivalent to 取燈在那裡呢.

27 Teachers in country villages usually "board round." 兩天 is often used for a short but indefinite time.

28 貴處 is a polite form of referring to any one's native place:—Les. 171. 不點兒 is a contraction for 不大一點兒, which full form is also often used. 栽鹽贓 *Plant salt plunder,* to hide or scatter salt on the premises of another person, and then accuse him of surreptitiously dealing in salt. Salt is a government monopoly in China and the occasion of enormous oppression and abuse. 自己作死, *To bring about one's own death,* by conduct which can have no other result.

LESSON XC.

VARIOUS USES OF 當.

當 has two tones. In the 1st tone it means *ought,* in the 4th tone it means *to pawn.* In addition to these senses, which we have had in previous lessons, it has a variety of uses not readily apprehended and classified by the learner, to whom it seems to change its face nearly every time it turns up.

In the 1st tone it means, to serve in any capacity (1), (5), (25), (34); in the presence of, at (6), (7), (9), (10), (20), (27); at the time of, or at that time (11), (13), (14), (15), (19), (23), (28); to bear (12), (16), (17), (18), (21).

In the 4th tone it means, to pawn, (35); to suppose or consider, (2); to regard as (3), (30), (31), (32); the same, native (4), (22), (24), (26), (29); to hinder (8), (33).

This distribution of meanings between the two tones is only approximate, as the usage differs somewhat in different places.

第九十課

[1]一人身不能充當二役。○他[2]當認是你不去呢。○你[3]拿我們當客待嗎。○當[4]天去、不能回來。○當[5]今的皇上是光緒。○他[6]的女人、叫他當官賣了。○咱[7]們有話、應該說在當面。○年[8]輕的人、總免當不了嬉戲。○當[9]場不讓父、舉手不留情。○你[10]怎麽當安息日做活呢。○那[11]個當口兒、我身上就有了病喇。○勞[12]動先生們來看我、實在不敢當。○正[13]當吃飯的時候、不好上人家家裏去。○當[14]那日天那雪、直下到一更天。○若[15]當時不圖省事、現在那有這些囉唆呢。○當[16]家不得不儉、待客不得不

TRANSLATION.

1 One person cannot serve in two capacities.
2 He supposed you were not going.
3 Are you going to treat us as guests?
4 We cannot go and return the same day.
5 The present emperor is Kwang Hsü.
6 He sold his wife by permission of the magistrate.
7 If we have anything to say, we should say it face to face.
8 Young people will have their fun.
9 In open competition a man does not give place even to his father. When a man raises his hand to strike, he discards sentiment.
10 How is it that you are working on the Sabbath day?
11 Even at that time I was suffering from [illness.
12 I really am not worthy that you gentlemen should have taken the trouble to come to see me.
13 It is not a proper thing to go into any one's house just at meal-time.
14 On that day the snow fell continuously until the first watch.
15 If at the time we had not been so anxious to save labor, we should not have had all this inconvenience.

VOCABULARY.

充 *Ch'ung*¹. To fill full, to satiate; *to act in the capacity of;* extreme.

當天 *Tang*⁴ *t'ien*¹. The same day [of which something else is predicated].

當今 *Tang*¹ *chin*¹. The reigning [emperor]; *the present,* existing.

緒 *Hsü*⁴. A thread, a clue, a beginning; a rule, a guide; to succeed to.

光緒 *Kwang*¹ *Hsü*⁴. The reigning Emperor Kwang Hsü.

當官 *Tang*¹ *kwan*¹. In the presence of the magistrate, *by official authorization or permission.*

當面 *Tang*¹ *mien*⁴. Before the face, *face to face,* in the presence of.

嬉 *Hsi*¹. ...... To ramble; to play, *to laugh.*

嬉戲 *Hsi*¹ *hsi*⁴. To laugh, to giggle; *to have fun,* to play.

當兒 *Tang*¹ *êr*². *A space or point of time;* an opening, a gap.

當口 *Tang*¹ *k'ou*³. .... The same.

勞動 *Lao*² *tung*⁴. *To put to trouble,* to inconvenience, to disturb.

敢當 *Kan*³ *tang*¹. .... To dare, to assume.

不敢當 *Pu*⁴ *kan*³ *tang*¹. Unwilling to bear [responsibility]; *unworthy of* [a compliment].

當日 *Tang*¹ *ji*⁴. On that day, the said day or time; once upon a time.

當日 *Tang*⁴ *ji*⁴. .... The same day.

更 *Ching*¹. A watch of the night. See *kêng*¹ and *kêng*⁴.

當時 *Tang*¹ *shï*². ... At that time, the said time.

當時 *Tang*⁴ *shï*². *At the time,* at the same time, immediately.

豐 *Fêng*¹. Abundant; copious; fertile; prolific; *bountiful.*

罪名 *Tswei*⁴ *ming*². Reputed guilt, *misdeeds,* misbehavior.

豐。○你[17]自己的罪名、還當不起、怎麼還要管別人的閒事呢。○你[18]們彼此的重擔、要互相擔當。○當[19]伏天、走這麼遠的路、實在彀受的。○昨[20]日你當眾人面前、所起的誓、今日就忘記了嗎。○將[21]來各人的報應、各人當、誰也替不得(了)誰。○你[22]娶親、是要吃當日酒啊、是吃連朝(二日)酒呢。○若[23]早知道他的手不穩(老)、當初誰肯舉薦他呢。○當[24]時和他說明、免得以後瑣碎(麻繁)(滴打)。○王[25]小那個不識數的貨、叫(給)李大拿着當鎗放了(拿着他去作惡人了)(巧指使了)。○[26]為當年的買賣賬、又沒到臘月、還值得動打嗎。○[27]北邊牆上(在北牆)、當中的那個小像、是甚麼人呢。答 那是我的父親。○當[28]漢平帝元始元年、耶穌在猶太國降生。○前[29]二年、我從驢上掉下來、把胳髈

16 As the head of the house you should be economical, but as a host you must be bountiful.

17 You cannot bear the burden of even your own misdeeds: why then do you want to meddle in other people's affairs?

18 Bear ye one another's burdens.

19 To travel so far as this in midsummer, is just all I can stand.

20 Have you forgotten to-day the oath you took yesterday in the presence of all?

21 Every man will have to bear his own recompense. No one can take the place of another.

22 At your wedding do you propose to have the feast on the same day or the next day?

23 If it had been known before that he would steal, who would have recommended him in the first place?

24 Arrange it with him distinctly at the time and avoid subsequent entanglement (after-clap.)

25 That numskull of a Wang the Less was used as a cat's paw by Li the Elder.

26 On account of this year's debt, and not yet having come to the last month, is it the proper thing to come to blows?

27 Whose is that middle likeness on the north wall? *Ans.* That is my father's.

擔當 *Tan1 tang1*. . . . . *To bear*, to endure.

報應 *Pao4 ying4*. . . . . *Recompense*, retribution.

連朝 *Lien2 chao1*. . . . . On successive days. (s.)

當初 *Tang1 ch'u1* At first, *in the first place*, ... originally.

瑣 *Soa3*. Fragments; minute; petty; troublesome, annoying.

瑣碎 *Soa3 swei4*. In fragments; troublesome, embarrassing, *entangling*.

繁 *Fan2*. . . . . .Numerous; troublesome.

麻繁 *Ma2 fan2*. *Entangled*, complicated, embarrassed; troublesome.

滴 *Ti1*. . . . A drop; to drop, *to dribble;* to ooze.

滴打 *Ti1 ta3*. To drop, to dribble; to prolong, *to string out*, after-clap.

指使 *Chi3 shi3*. To point out, to direct, to order; . . . . to manage, *to make use of*.

當年 *Tang4 nien2*. . . . . .This year.

動打 *Tung4 ta3*. To begin to strike or beat, *to come to blows*.

當中 *Tang1 chung1*. . . . . . . .In the middle.

始 *Shï3*. The beginning, the first, the start, ... then, before.

元年 *Yüen2 nien2*. . . . . . . First year [of a reign].

猶太 *Yiu2 t'ai4*. . . . . .Judea, Jewish.

降生 *Chiang4 shêng1*. To descend and be born, ... to be born into the world from a previous state of existence.

傻 *Sha3*. . . . . .*Half-witted*, lackbrained, doltish.

憨 *Han1*. . . . . .Obtuse, *dull-witted*, soft.

傻蛋 *Sha3 tan4*. A fool, an idiot, a mooncalf, *a simpleton*.

憨蛋 *Han1 tan4*. A blockhead, a ninny, a numskull, *a simpleton*.

膊子跌觸了、當時也沒覺得很疼、以後却受了好罪。○他30怕惹仇人、我們就不怕惹仇人嗎、他當是我們都是傻憨蛋喇。○我31看王連科那個人、永遠也不能回頭、無論怎樣勸戒他、他只當作耳旁邊風。○人32在病重的時候、心裏都是很急躁的、所以他說甚麼不中聽的話、你權當沒聽見、不可生他的氣。○這33回可上了你的當咯。○他34姐夫、和他妹夫、都在衙門裏當差、一個當更夫、在監牢獄裏打更、一個當火夫、在厨房裏拉二脚子當下手。○我35明天也該進城去當當、就是沒有工夫、問我替你捎帶着去當罷、答那怎麼好呢、對不要緊、我當不了上當鋪去贖當。

28 Jesus was born in Judea, in the first year of Yüen Shï, of Han P'ing Ti.

29 Two years ago I fell off a donkey and sprained my arm. At the time I did not feel much pain, but afterwards I suffered a great deal.

30 If he is afraid of making enemies, are not we also afraid of making enemies? He thinks we are a set of simpletons.

31 I don't believe that man Wang Lien K'ê will ever reform. No matter how you exhort him, he pays no attention at all.

32 When anyone is very sick his mind is always irritable. If, therefore, he says anything unbecoming, you must not get angry at him, but pass it by as if you had not heard.

33 I have certainly been deceived by you this time.

34 His two brothers-in-law both have positions in the yamên; one is watchman in the jail, the other is second fireman in the kitchen.

35 I ought to go to the city to-morrow to pawn a pawn, but I have no time. *Ans.* Let me take it along and pawn it for you. *Ques.* How could I trouble you? *Ans.* Never mind. I must go to the pawnshop any way to redeem a pawn.

勸戒 *Ch'üen⁴ chie⁴*. *To exhort*, to caution, to admonish.

耳旁風 *Er³ p'ang² fêng¹*. Hearsay, rumor, *idle tales*.

耳邊風 *Er³ pien¹ fêng¹*. The same.

中聽 *Chung⁴ t'ing¹*. *Becoming*, seemly, pleasant.

權 *Ch'üen²*. Weight; authority, influence; exigency; to balance, to weigh.

權當 *Ch'üen² tang⁴*. *To consider as if*, to make believe, to feign.

姐夫 *Chie³ fu¹*. Elder sister's husband.

當差 *Tang¹ ch'ai¹*. To fill an inferior office; to act under the authority of another; *to fill the position of a servitor.*

更夫 *Ching¹* (or *kêng¹*) *fu¹*. A watchman.

監 *Chien¹*. To oversee, to superintend; *a prison.* Also *chien⁴*.

監牢獄 *Chien¹ lao² yü⁴*. A prison.

打更 *Ta³ ching¹*. To act as watchman.

火夫 *Hwoa³ fu¹*. A fireman; *an under-cook.*

當鋪 *Tang⁴ p'u⁴*. A pawnbroker's shop.

贖當 *Shu² tang⁴*. To redeem a pawn.

NOTES.

2 當 is the more general form.

6 Men frequently sell their wives in China, though it is not regarded as a proper or lawful thing to do. Sometimes when a wife has been guilty of some grave misconduct, she is sold to another man with the approval of the magistrate. In this sentence 太太, or 師娘, or 夫人, could not be substituted for 女人, though 老婆 might.

9 A proverbial saying in book style. 當場 refers probably to the examination hall, the meaning being that when competing for a degree each man does his best, regardless of who may be worsted,—even a father not being exempt.

14 In the South 當日 is used only in the sense of *once upon a time*, but in the North, it takes the additional meaning of, *that day, the said day* or time.

第九十一課

我1想着之快些走、就是走不動。○若2是錐子
扎擱不動、可以用鑽鑽子鑽。○那3個人胖的搰遛
錐擸不動。○牲4口走弄乏倦了、趕也趕不動。○這5
是自然的理、誰能駁倒了呢。○那6盤副小磨、
一個人也推動了。○你7們抬不動、犯我可以
下去走幾步。○這8麽大的一匹騾子、二百
斤還馱不上動嗎。○我9讓他抱着後腰、他也
摔不倒我。○你10這個小人兒、還能挑動這
麽重的擔子嗎。○好11鈍鋸、鋸子連一塊木板、
也鋸不動。○你12看東西不多、一個人却拿

Translation.

1 I am anxious to go fast, but the fact is I am not able.
2 If an awl will not penetrate it, you may use an auger and bore it.
3 That man is so fat that he cannot waddle along.
4 The animal is tired out. Urging does not move him.
5 This is a necessary truth: who can overthrow it?
6 That small mill one man is able to turn.
7 If you are not able to carry me, I might get down and walk a few steps.
8 Such a large mule as this, and yet cannot carry two hundred catties?
9 I will give him a back hold, and yet he cannot throw me down.
10 Is such a little man as you able to carry such a heavy load as this?
11 What a dull saw! it will not even cut a piece of board.
12 You think there are not many things, and yet one man cannot carry them all.

22 The principal wedding feast is sometimes held on the day of the wedding, sometimes on the day following, and sometimes the feast continues two days. 二日 means a feast on the second day, but 連朝 means a feast for two successive days. 兩日 is also used with the same sense as 連朝. If both days be included, the translation should be,—*Do you propose to have a one day's feast or a two days' feast?*

23 手不老實 *Hand not trusty*, or 手不穩 *hand not steady*, that is, "light-fingered."

25 那個不識數的貨 *That commodity that cannot count ten.* The application of 貨 to a *person* is of course depreciatory in the highest degree. 巧指使 *To use ingeniously*, to make a cat's paw of; 拿着當鎗放了 *to shoot one off as a gun*, to make a tool of. The Southern form sounds flat, though vouched for by two Nanking teachers.

26 Custom does not allow a creditor to use forcible measures in collecting a debt until in the last month. There is *practically* no legal method of collecting a debt in China. It has to be done by the sheer force of irrepressible dunning, reaching in extreme cases to the use of violence.

28 平帝 was the emperor's title, 元始 the name or designation of his reign, which in former times was changed from time to time according to the emperor's fancy, so that one reign was by this means divided into several parts or terms. In modern times this custom has fortunately fallen into disuse.

29 觸 seems to be the proper character for *sprain*, though it does not give quite the proper sound in all places. The use of 跌 seems to give a somewhat different sense, meaning rather *to bruise* than *to sprain*.

34 打更 *To strike the watch*, which is done by Chinese watchmen by beating on a kind of wooden drum. 拉二脚子 *Takes the second foot*; 二 indicates the second place, and 脚 is used with reference to his being required to run to do this or that at the bidding of his superiors.

35 當當 *To pawn a pawn.* The first 當 is a verb, the second a noun.

LESSON XCI.

The Auxiliary Verbs 動, 倒 and 犯

動 To move,—is added as an auxiliary to such words as will take the qualifying idea of motion.

倒 To invert,—is added as an auxiliary to such words as will take the qualifying idea of inversion.

犯 To oppose, to endure,—is added as an auxiliary to such words as will take the qualifying idea of endurance. The use of 犯 is local in Eastern Shantung, but it gives a phase of meaning which no other word will express.

不犯了。○我13的牙不好濟、硬東西、一點也咬不動。○想14要求他做點甚麼、沒有求動的時候。○眞15有主意的人、別人引誘不動。○人16在年輕的時候、就是失腳、也跌不倒。○他17不肯來、我拉也拉不動他。○不18知誰丟扔一塊石頭、在正當道兒大路口上、一下把我絆倒了。○請19你幫助我、磨挪磨挪這個書架子、我自己磨挪不動。○若20是這個禮拜、你作好孩子、我要買個搬不倒兒給你。○反21賊來的時候、那些跑不動的人、有許多被他們殺了。○我22看見你把他推倒了、你怎麼說、是他自己跌倒了

13 My teeth are poor, I cannot masticate anything hard.

14 If you wish to ask him to do anything for you, you will never prevail.

15 A man who really has a mind of his own cannot be enticed by others.

16 When a man is young, even though he makes a mis-step, he will not fall.

17 He is not willing to come, and I am not able to drag him.

18 I wonder who threw a stone in the middle of the road? It tripped me and threw me down.

19 Please help me to move this book-case. I am not able to move it myself.

20 If you are a good child this week, I will buy you a doll.

21 When the rebels came, a great many who were not able to run were killed by them.

22 I saw you push him down. Why do you say that he stumbled and fell down of himself?

VOCABULARY.

扎 *Cha*¹. *To pierce*, to stab; to make paper images; ...... to paint a wall. See *Cha*³.

攮 *Nang*³. To ward off, to stab, to pierce, *to* .... *penetrate.*

鑽 *Tswan*⁴. A skewer, an awl, a drill, a gimlet, ... *an auger*. Also *tswan*¹.

鑽 *Tswan*¹. To pierce, to drill, *to bore*. See *tswan*⁴.

搰 *Ku*⁴. To mix, to stir, *to twist*. Read *hu*¹ in ...... Chinese dictionary.

擁 *Yung*³,¹. To hug; to crowd, to throng; *to* .... *push or press forward.*

搰擁 To squirm, to wriggle; *to waddle;* to evade.

遛 *Liu*¹,². To linger; to lead about; to walk .... leisurely; to glide, *to shuffle.*

駁 *Poă*². To dispute, *to controvert;* to repel, to ...... send back; to transfer, to tranship.

鈍 *Tun*⁴. .... Blunt, *dull;* stupid, obtuse.

誘 *Yiu*⁴. To encourage; to draw on, *to entice*, to ...... allure; to tempt.

引誘 *Yin*³ *yiu*⁴. *To lead on to evil, to entice*, to .... tempt, to allure.

失脚 *Shï*¹ *chiao*³. *To make a mis-step*, to slip, ... to stumble.

大路口 *Ta*⁴ *lu*⁴ *k'ou*³. The middle of the .... road.

絆 *Pan*⁴. *To trip up*, to throw down; to stumble; to hinder; to fetter; a loop.

搬不倒 *Pan*¹ *pu*⁴ *tao*³. A self-righting doll .... or puppet:—Note 20.

反賊 *Fan*³ *tsei*². .... *Rebels*, robbers.

塋 *Ying*². .... A tomb, a cemetery.

墳 *Fên*². .... A grave, a tomb.

塋地 *Ying*² *ti*⁴. ... A burial ground.

墳地 *Fên*² *ti*⁴. .... Same.

打坑 *Ta*³ *k'êng*¹. To dig a hole in the ground, ... *to dig a grave.*

壙 *K'wang*⁴. A vault, *a grave;* a desert, a .... solitude.

開壙 *K'ai*¹ *k'wang*⁴. .... To dig a grave.

刨 *P'ao*². .... To grub, *to dig.*

盧 *Lu*². .... A pan, a vessel; a surname.

生鐵 *Shêng*¹ *t'ie*³. .... Cast iron.

呢。○咱[23]們那塊墳塋地、淨是石頭、每逢開打壙坑、人都嫌刨不動。○盧[24]二爺吃大烟、吃的光賸了一個骨頭架子、差不多風颳倒了。○舊[25]生鐵鑄的器具發硬、鏇也鏇不動、鑽也鑽不動、若是新生鐵鑄的、却很好好中拾撩掇治。○那[26]把茶壺、把給他三百錢、還不曉得買得倒來、買不倒來咧。○從[27]來說、好心感動天和地、你有這樣的好心、天老老天爺爺不能不保佑你。

23 That burying ground of ours is nothing but stones. Every time a grave is to be dug, they take exception to it as being impossible to dig.
24 Lu Êr Yie has smoked opium till there is nothing left of him but a skeleton. The wind would almost blow him over.
25 Articles cast of old iron are hard; they can neither be turned nor drilled; but if cast of new iron, they are very easy to work.
26 I do not know whether three hundred cash will be sufficient to purchase that tea-pot or not.
27 It has ever been said that "a benevolent heart moves heaven and earth." Seeing you have acted with such a benevolent purpose as this, God will certainly protect you.

鑄 *Chu*⁴. . . . . To cast.
具 *Chü*⁴. Prepared, arranged; all; to present . . . . . to; *an implement*, a utensil.
器具 *Ch'i*⁴ *chü*⁴. Implements, tools, *articles*, ... vessels.
撩治 *Liao*² *chï*⁴. *To operate on;* to put through; . . . . to manage; to put in order.
掇 *Toă*⁴. . . To arrange, to gather up. Also *ts'oă*³.
拾掇 *Shï*² *toă*⁴. To gather up, to put in order, ... to repair, *to dress up*.
感動 *Kan*³ *tung*⁴. To excite, *to move;* to . . . . quicken, to inspire.
老天爺 *Lao*³ *T'ien*¹ *Yie*². . . God:—Note 27.
天老爺 *T'ien*¹ *Lao*³ *Yie*². . . . . Same.
佑 *Yiu*⁴. . . . . . . To aid, to help; *to protect*.
保佑 *Pao*³ *yiu*⁴. . . . . . . *To protect*, to defend.

NOTES.

1 快些 is here taken simply as an intensive in accordance with its use in Southern Mandarin. See Les. 84. Note 26.

2 None of the terms here used for *piercing with an awl* is correct in Eastern Shantung, where the term is *nań* (no settled character).

3 搰擁 means properly *to wriggle*, and 遛, *to glide*, but neither is *t'ung hsing* in this connection. Kiukiang would say *hwai*⁴ (no character) and Hankow, 歪 *wai*¹ *to sidle*.

6 副 is Southern but not exclusively so. It is used in the North when the millstones are regarded as *a pair*. 盤 refers rather to the mill as a whole.

8 Two hundred catties is considered a moderate load for a pack-mule. 馱不上 is rejected in many places, yet it expresses a shade of meaning not given by 馱不動. The latter means properly, unable to move with the burden, while the former means unable to bear the fatigue of continuously carrying the burden.

9 抱着後腰 *To clasp around the waist.*

11 鋸 is the most general term for *to saw*, but in Western Shantung it is never used, 割 being used instead. A board is supposed to be easy to saw, hence the force of 連. 好鈍 *Good dull*; i.e., *very dull*, *"good and dull."*

12 犯 refers to the *person*, meaning that he is not able to carry so many; 了 refers to the *things*, meaning that they are too many for one person to carry, and that some will have to be left.

18 Neither of the forms given is usual in Shantung where 正道眼兒 would be used. 一下 here means *all at once*, both time and manner being included.

20 搬不倒 A doll or puppet without feet, but having a round base and loaded in such a way that when pushed over it will right itself.

23 墳地 and 塋地 differ much as our graveyard and cemetery; the former is the place of graves, the latter is the burying place. 打坑 is the more widely used term, though it applies to other things than digging a grave, whereas 開壙 is specific for digging a grave.

25 Almost all castings made by the Chinese are made of old iron, and are consequently very hard.

27 天 and 地 are here used in a semi-personal sense. 老天爺 *The old Heavenly Grandfather* or 天老爺 *the Heavenly old* (or great) *Grandfather*. The former prevails in the North, the latter in the Centre and South. In many cases 爺 becomes 爺爺. The 老 is sometimes omitted and 天爺 used. This term in its various forms probably expresses the nearest approximation the Chinese people have to the idea of the true God. Whenever a man is driven by stress of circumstances to call to Heaven for help he calls upon 老天爺. Nevertheless it is undoubtedly true that particular gods are sometimes called 老天爺, especially is this true of 玉皇上帝. This use of "grandfather" accords with the ground idea of Chinese theogony, that all gods were once men.

第九十二課

明[1]天怕來不及、○趕[2]着寫、還趕得及。○他[3]沒跑迭、掉贏叫我捉住了。○這[4]麽些客吃飯、一個人伺候不及。○趁[5]他不及料的時候、我要給他個冷不防。○擦[6]上點肥胰子、就洗掉喇。○水[7]流不迭、淌不掉流不贏就漫出河堤來。○眼[8]看就到了金花的百歲、帽子上的鈴鐺、怕預備不及。○求[9]天父看救主的功勞、赦掉我的罪孽。○[10]話沒說完、說話不迭話沒有說及他就一步闖進來了。○到[11]這步田地、後悔也後悔不及了。○該[12]早下手、現做還能做得及嗎。○孩[13]子沒躲迭、及就被馬撞倒了。○你[14]們有能辦的、去辦罷、我知道

TRANSLATION.

1 I fear I cannot finish it to-morrow.
2 If you hurry, you can finish writing in time.
3 He did not run fast enough, and I caught him.
4 One man cannot serve so many guests.
5 I want to give him a surprise before he is aware of what I am doing.
6 Rub on a little soap, and it will wash out.
7 The water having no place to escape, broke over the banks of the river.
8 Chin Hwa's hundredth day is just at hand. I fear we will not be able to get ready the bells for his hat.
9 I pray the heavenly Father, for the sake of the Saviour's merits, to forgive my sins.
10 Before we could finish speaking, he rushed in with a bound.
11 Having reached this pass, retreat is out of the question.
12 You ought to begin early; you cannot do it up on the spur of the moment.
13 The child not escaping in time, was knocked down by the horse.
14 Any of you who has the ability may

LESSON XCII.

THE AUXILIARY VERBS 及, 迭 AND 掉.

及 To reach, to extend to,—added as an auxiliary to denote the bare or possible completion of an action, or with a negative the impossibility of completion. When used affirmatively it generally takes 得 as a sub-auxiliary.

迭 To alternate, to exchange,—added as an auxiliary to denote that an action was not or could not be accomplished within the limits of the time. It is most frequently used with a negative. It is rarely used in the South, being replaced by 掉 or 贏. In Peking 當 is frequently added to it (17).

掉 To fall, to lose, to fail,—added as an auxiliary to such words as will take the qualifying idea of falling, losing, or failing. It is much more frequently used in the South than in the North.

贏 To excel,—is used in the region of Hankow as an auxiliary in the place of 迭. It is not used in general Mandarin.

VOCABULARY.

迭 *Tie*². To alternate, to exchange; to get time, ... to compass; instead of:—See Sub.

迭當 *Tie² tang⁴*. .... To get time.

冷不防 *Lêng³ pu⁴ fang²*. Unexpected, sudden; .... *unawares:*—Les. 115.

百歲 *Pai³ swei⁴*. The hundredth day of a child's .... age:—Note 8.

鐺 *Tang¹*. A pedlar's gong; the clang of a gong, ... the tinkle of a bell.

鈴鐺 *Ling² tang¹*. ...... A small bell.

赦 *Shê⁴*. ..... To pardon, *to forgive*, to reprieve.

我辦不及了。○剛15纔一甩手、把我的頂針黹甩掉了、滿家裏找、也沒找着。○那16盒子帶不了來、是一時收拾不及。○衣17裳還沒有穿及迭當、就被捕役拿住了。○別18說是他、就是神仙、也忙不及迭。○這19件事、可以等我回來再說罷、現在迭不的辦不及辦喇。○你20想他病了半點鐘、就死了、請大夫醫生郎中怎能請得及呢。○人21不該從火輪車路上走、因爲火輪車來的太快、要躲也躲不及迭。○這22些毛病、他已經習慣成自然、要叫他一下子都除掉了、這是强他所不能的。○三23天以內、我不敢應你這麼些錢、就是應了、也湊不及。○沒24到危險地方、還可以

go and manage it: I know that I cannot manage it.

15 Just now in giving my hand a fling I flung away my thimble. I have searched the whole room for it and have not found it.

16 The reason he could not bring the box was because it could not be gotten ready at once.

17 Before he could get on his clothes, he was arrested by the constables.

18 Say nothing of him; even the genii could not have gotten through with it.

19 Let this business lie over still I come back; I have not time to attend to it now.

20 Just think of it. He died after an illness of only half an hour. How could we call a physician in time?

21 One should not walk on the railroad track, for the cars come so rapidly that one cannot get out of the way in time.

22 These vices have been practiced until they have become a second nature. To require him to give them all up at once, will be forcing him to do what he is not able to do.

23 I cannot venture to promise you that much money within three days, and

---

孽 *Nie*^{4}. The consequence of sin, retribution; .... misfortune.

罪孽 *Tswei*^{4} *nie*^{4}. .... *Sin*, the evil of sin.

田地 *T'ien*^{2} *ti*^{4}. Land, ground; state, condition; .... place, point, *pass*.

甩 *Shwai*^{3}.... To throw away; *to fling*, to throw.

頂針 *Ting*^{3} *chĭn*^{1}. .... A thimble.

黹 *Chï*^{3}. .... To embroider.

頂黹 *Ting*^{3} *chï*^{3}. .... A thimble. (s.)

捕 *Pu*^{3}. .... To capture, to seize, *to arrest*.

捕役 *Pu*^{3} *i*^{4}. ...... *A constable*, a policeman.

醫生 *I*^{1} *shêng*^{1}. ...... A physician, a doctor.

大 *Tai*^{4}. .... Great:—Note 20. See *ta*^{4}.

大夫 *Tai*^{4} *fu*^{1}. An honorary official title con- .... ferred on various ranks of high officers; *a physician*:—Note 20.

郎中 *Lang*^{2} *chung*^{1}. The senior secretary of any .... one of the six Boards:— a physician;—Note 20.

習慣 *Hsi*^{2} *kwan*^{4}. To acquire a habit, to ha- .... bituate:—Note 22.

以內 *I*^{3} *nei*^{4}. .... Inside of, *within*.

危 *Wei*^{2,1}. ...... *Dangerous*, hazardous, perilous.

危險 *Wei*^{2} *hsien*^{3}. ...... *Dangerous*, perilous.

橫豎 *Hêng*^{2} *shu*^{4}. In every direction, *on all* .... *sides*, in every way; probably, most likely:—Les. 130.

招架 *Chao*^{1} *chia*^{4}. To fence, *to guard*, to ward .... off.

廢 *Fei*^{4}. To set aside, to annul; *to destroy*; ...... useless, void; corrupt, degenerate.

律 *Lü*^{4}. ...... A law, a statute.

律法 *Lü*^{4} *fa*^{3}. ...... *A law*, a statute.

先知 *Hsien*^{1} *chï*^{1}. .... A prophet.

成全 *Ch'êng*^{2} *ch'üen*^{2}. To complete, *to fulfil*, ... to consummate.

躲避、到了那個分兒上、就躲避不及了。○我25看見有十來個人、打一個姓李的、那姓李的、橫豎招架、也招架不及迭住。○不26要想我來、是要廢掉律法、和先知的道理、我來不是要廢掉、正是要成全。

even if I should promise, I could not raise it.

24 Before you reach the point of danger, it is possible to escape. When the danger is at hand, there is no time for escape.

25 I saw upwards of ten men attacking a man named Li. The man Li guarded himself on all sides, but was unable to ward them off.

26 Think not that I am come to destroy the law and the prophets. I am not come to destroy but to fulfil.

NOTES.

1 Or, *I fear I cannot finish it in time for to-morrow.*

5 不及料 is equivalent to 料不及. A plainer and less bookish expression would be 料不到. The sentence is taken from a Chinese novel.

8 The Chinese celebrate the one-hundredth day of a child's age. Why it is called 百歲 is not certain. Some teachers would prefer to write it 百晬. The most likely explanation is, that the term expresses a wish that each day may represent a year, and that thus the child may live to be a hundred years old. It is customary on this occasion for the maternal grandmother to present the child with a fancy hat and shoes, sometimes with a whole suit. The hat is often ornamented with silver jewelry and little bells.

9 看 here means *to regard.* It is thus used where we would say "for the sake of." 赦掉 is perfectly proper and fitting in this connection but not as common as 赦免 or 饒赦.

12 Or, *You ought to have begun early; beginning now will it be possible to complete it?*

16 The literal would be,—*The not being able to bring that box was in that it could not be gotten ready in time.* 因爲 might be inserted after 是 without detriment to the sentence.

18 忙不迭 *Unable to do it even by hurrying.*

20 大 is only read *tai*, in the phrases 大夫, 大王, 大黃 and sometimes 大學. This was probably the original pronunciation in all cases. It is the only pronunciation given by K'anghi. 大夫 is used in the North for physician, but not in the South. It is heard in Western, but not in Eastern Shantung. How it came to supplant the more regular and proper term 醫生, is not certainly known. It was probably at first applied to the court physicians, who had official rank, and thence passed into general use. 郎中 is the common term in the South, and is also found in books. It probably came into use in the same way as 大夫.

22 習慣成自然 *A habit acquired becomes natural.* 習慣 is rarely used save in connection with the whole expression.

24 那分上 *That point;* i.e., *the point of danger.*

25 住 is no doubt *t'ung hsing* in this connection, but 迭 is also quite proper and is widely used, and expresses a somewhat different idea. If 住 be used the translation should be, *was unable to withstand them.*

LESSON XCIII.

INITIAL INTERJECTIONS.

Chinese colloquial abounds in exclamatory words expressive of various emotions, many of which it is difficult to render into English. The proper characters to use are in a number of cases more or less uncertain, and the meanings attached to them vary much in different localities. The tones of these characters are especially variable and uncertain.

阿 Oh! Ah! Whew!—expresses a suddenly occurring thought, coupled sometimes with pleasure, sometimes with displeasure.

哦 The same,—Southern teachers prefer this character.

哎呀 Heigh ho! Hurrah!—expresses either astonishment or exultation.

哎喲 Oh! Alas! Ah me!—expresses consternation, or sorrow, or suffering.

嘻 Pshaw! Fudge! Humph!—expresses impatience, or disgust, or indignation.

哏 Bosh! Plague on it! Confound it!—expresses strong disgust and indignation.

嚇 Bosh! Bah!—expresses disgust, or indignation, or contempt. It is used chiefly in the South.

呸 or 啐 Tush! Humph!—expresses the strongest kind of impatience and contempt. Its use is an insult. No word in English is adequate to translate it.

呀呀呸 An emphatic form of 呸. It is explained as a sort of catching of the breath in

第九十三課

1阿哦、我想起來喇。○ 2哎呀、好大一條長蟲蛇、○ 3把你的大紅襖、脫給我穿着罷、答喡、我俺不。○ 4嘚嚇、這不是糊鬧嗎、那有同姓結親的呢。○ 5呸呸、你叫我的小名、你叫得起嗎。○ 6哎喲、我的媽呀、媽媽、娘啊、可要了我的命喇。○ 7阿哦、還是這麼着的嗎、這回我可明白喇。○ 8喡、好歹混幾天就得是喇、管那些做甚麼呢。○ 9啊、他說至晚遲到今天來、怎麼又沒來呢。○ 10家去見了你嬸子嬸嬸、替我問他好啊、唵、答啊、是喇。○ 11嗐、我們年紀相彷的人、就剩下他跟和我了、別人都不在喇。○ 12阿哦、他已經走了嗎、我還有回信叫他捎帶呢。○ 13哎喲、不好喇、房子上起了火喇。○ 14媽啊、你的

Translation.

1 Oh! I have just thought of it.
2 Heigh ho! what a monstrous snake.
3 Won't you spare me your large red coat to wear? *Ans.* Och! I won't.
4 Bosh! That's all nonsense. People of the same family name don't intermarry.
5 Humph! What right have you to be calling me by my little name?
6 Oh, my mother! It will kill me.
7 Ah! It's this way, is it? This time I understand it.
8 Pshaw! Make-shift somehow for a few days, and it will all be right. Why trouble yourself about such things?
9 What's up? He said that at the latest he would come to-day. How is it that after all he has not come?
10 When you go home and see your aunt, remember me to her; do you hear? *Ans.* Aye; I will.
11 Ah me! Of us who were of about the same age, only he and I are left; all the rest are gone.
12 Ah! Has he already gone? I wanted to send a reply by him.
13 My oh! It's dreadful! The house is on fire.
14 Oh, Mother! I have broken your large mirror! *Ans.* Oh my! What a

order to give forcible ntterance to the 呸. It is found in Mandarin books, and is much used in theatrical plays. I have heard children use it in their quarrels.

啊 A—h!—expresses hesitation, or doubt, or surprise.

唵 Eh? A word (or grunt) much used in colloquial when emphasizing an idea, especially in charging anyone. It follows each clause or point made by the speaker, as much as to say, Do you hear? Do you understand?

嗐 Ah me! Alas! confound it!—expresses sadness, or wonder, or dissatisfaction. Its use varies in different places.

嗐 Oh my! Bless my heart! What a pity!—expresses surprise coupled with sorrow or pity.

哼 Humph! Hem!—expresses slight contempt or discontent.

唉 Aye, all right, that's so,—expresses full approval or assent.

嘘 or 嗤 Tut, tush, fie,—expresses displeasure or reproof.

噫 Well; well, well; really; sure enough,—expresses gratification, or amusement, or ridicule. In *Wên-li* it means, Ah me, alas.

吡 Shoo,—mostly applied to driving away fowls, but sometimes used to children, or in contempt to young people or even to adults.

Vocabulary.

阿 *A*¹, *ê*¹. . . . An exclamation of surprise. Also *a*³.
阿 *A*³, *ê*³. . . . An exclamation of doubt. See *a*¹.
喡 *Wei*⁴. . . . . . . Pshaw, fudge, och;—see Sub.
嘚 *T'ei*². . . . . . . Bosh, plague on it:—see Sub.
呸 *P'ei*¹,⁴. . . . . . . .To sputter; tush:—see Sub.
呸 *P'ei*⁴. . . . . Same. (s.)

大鏡子、叫我打喇、答噯、可惜、你怎麼給我打了呢。○15哼、像那樣的邋遢手、邁態手、憨包、還想着進學啊、我看他淨癡心妄想。○16你快叫我聲爺爺、我買塊糖給你喫、叫爺爺、答唉、好孩子。○17借光老大爺、間老爺爺、這是上周村的大道不是、答啊、你說甚麼、我的耳朶聾啊。○18哎嚉、我若是再到賭錢場、我就是個四條腿的驢。○19啈嚏、人家要快快的學書、你這麼跟着直打攪、是個甚麼道理呢。○20你能捨得三吊多錢、穿個哈喇馬褂子嗎、答嗐、三吊來錢、我就捨不得了嗎。○21叱、去罷、別在這裏鬧喇。○22我問你一件事情、是馬慶雲、拐了人家一個媳婦來嗎、答嚇嚉、那裏的事、這纔是活蹧蹋人喇。○23若是找不着、我

pity! How did you come to break it?

15 Humph! Such a blockhead as he, and yet thinks of getting a degree! In my opinion he is indulging a vain expectation.

16 Now you call me grandpa once and I'll buy you a piece of candy to eat. (Calls) Grandpa. *Ans.* Good! You are a nice boy.

17 May I trouble you, my aged friend? is this the great road to Chou-ts'un? *Ans.* A—h? What did you say? I am hard of hearing.

18 Pshaw! If I go again into a gambling house, you may set me down for an ass.

19 Tush! When other people want to get their lessons quickly, what reason is there in your continually interrupting them in this way?

20 Can you afford to spend over three thousand cash for a broadcloth coat? *Ans.* Humph! Do you suppose I can't afford a matter of three thousand cash?

21 Shoo! Begone with you, and don't make a disturbance here.

22 I want to ask you something. Is it so that Ma Ch'ing Yün has kidnapped another man's wife? *Ans.* Tut, tut! Nonsense! What an unconscionable slander!

23 If I can't find it, I'll demand it of you. *Ans.* Humph! Why will you

啊 $A^{3,1}$, $\hat{e}^{3,1}$. Exclamation of surprise or doubt. Not practically distinguished from 阿.

唵 $\hat{E}^2$. Eh?:—see Sub. Also an^1.

嗐 Hai^4. Ah me, alas:—see Sub.

噯 Ai^1. An exclamation of surprise and regret:—see Sub.

哼 $H\hat{e}ng^1$. To groan, to grunt; humph, hem:—see Sub.

唉 Ai^2. A reply—that's right, so so, yes:—see Sub. Also ai^1.

嚉 Tei^2. Humph, bah:—see Sub.

嚏 $T'ai^2$. Tut, tush:—see Sub.

啈 $T'\hat{e}^2$. Same. (s.)

噫 I^1. A sound expressive of surprise or admiration, or of pain and sorrow:—see Sub.

叱 $Ch'i^4$. To hoot at, to scold; to shoo—as chickens:—see Sub.

糊鬧 Hu^2 nao^4. *To make believe*, to sham; to make much ado about nothing; to act the fool.

嬸 $Sh\hat{e}n^3$. A father's younger brother's wife.

不在 Pu^4 $tsai^4$. Dead, deceased (used only of adults).

邋 La^4. To exceed; filthy.

邋遢 La^4 $t'a^4$. Filthy, slovenly, slatternly, dowdy; *good-for-nothing*, miserable.

邁 Mai^4. To advance, to exceed; old, senile.

態 $T'ai^4$. Figure, configuration; air, gait; circumstances.

邁態 Inefficient, impotent, *good-for-nothing.* (L.)

憨包 Han^1 pao^1. *A blockhead*, a ninny, a goose. (s.)

是跟你要、答呀呀呸、你爲甚麼跟我要呢、我是給你看東西的嗎。○24這個大騾子、是您的嗎、答嚷、我俺若是有這麼個大騾子、就成了財主喇。○25嗐嗯、今天出去看燈、眞喪晦氣、不知叫那個忘八蛋把我的辮子、鉸剪了半截子去。○26噫、你看他那兩隻小脚、怎能在繩子上、走來走去呢、答嗐、這也不是一日的工夫。○27健壯的壯字、該在甚麼部裏呢、答該在士字部裏、對阿哦、我當是在爿字部、或是土字部裏、怪不得察不着喇。○28嚏、你那裏知道、他不是眞來要甚麼吃啊、是來瞅道瞧門路兒、預備來偷你的呀。○29我勸你別尋死啊、你看你的老婆孩子、不是都喫你、穿你嗎、你若死了、他們都倚靠誰

demand it of me? Is it my business to watch your things?

24 Is this big mule yours? *Ans.* No, I am sorry to say it's not. If I had a big mule like that, I'd be a rich man.

25 Plague on it! I was unlucky, sure enough! In going out to see the illuminations to-night some vile rascal cut off the half of my queue.

26 Well, really! Just look at those two little feet! How in the world can they walk back and forth on that rope? *Ans.* That's so! You may be sure that was not learned in one day.

27 Under what radical should *chwang* of *chien chwang* be? *Ans.* It should be under the radical *shï*. Well! I thought it was under *ch'iang* or under *t'u*. No wonder I could not find it.

28 Tush! Don't you know that his coming in to beg is simply in order to spy out a way by which he can steal from you?

29 I beg of you don't think of suicide. Look at your wife and children! Are they not dependent on you for food and clothing? If you die, whom will they have to depend upon?

癡 *Ch'ï*¹. . . . . Stupid, silly; crazy, idiotic.

癡心 *Ch'ï*¹ *hsin*¹. *Infatuated*, beside oneself, foolish.

妄 *Wang*⁴. Disorderly, incoherent; reckless; *foolish*, absurd; false.

妄想 *Wang*⁴ *hsiang*³. To long for what is unattainable, *vain hopes*.

糖 *T'ang*². . . . . Sugar, candy.

借問 *Chie*⁴ *wên*⁴. Please tell me, *may I inquire*.

賭錢場 *Tu*³ *ch'ien*² *ch'ang*³. A gambling house, a betting ring.

打攪 *Ta*³ *chiao*³. To discompose, *to interrupt*, to bother, to pester.

喪氣 *Sang*⁴ *ch'i*⁴. *Unlucky*, ill-starred; depressed in spirits.

晦 *Hwei*⁴. . . . . Obscure; *unlucky*, unpropitious.

晦氣 *Hwei*⁴ *ch'i*⁴. . . . . . *Ill-luck*, misfortune.

忘八蛋 *Wang*² *pa*¹ *tan*⁴. A rascal, a reckless villain:—Note 25.

半截 *Pan*⁴ *chie*². . . . . A large piece, the half.

健 *Chien*⁴. Strong, *robust;* persevering, indefatigable; constant.

健壯 *Chien*⁴ *chwang*⁴. Robust, strong, able-bodied.

士 *Shï*⁴. . . . A scholar, a gentleman; an officer.

爿 *Ch'iang*². . . . . A couch; the 90th radical.

門路 *Mên*² *lu*⁴. Opening, *way of access;* a method, a means.

尋死 *Hsin*² *si*³. To commit suicide, to make away with oneself.

保舉 *Pao*³ *chü*³. *To recommend*, to give a good report of.

呢、答嚏嗐、現在顧不了（不管）那些喇。○30你從前保舉了他、他現在怎麼還疑惑你讒謗他呢、答哼誰知道呢。○31老頭子病到那個樣兒、要點水喝、都沒有人舀給他、想什麼喫、也沒有人給他弄做、今天我去看他、他對我直哭、答喨那纔是苦命喇。○32你要麻俐的走啊、唵、在街上不要和人打架、唵、到你姐姐家、就一直上你姐姐房屋裏去啊、唵、別先到他婆婆房屋裏去、唵、和你姐姐說、咱媽媽說喇、（我媽說喇）你不用想家、再等不多日子、就來接搬你、好愼生想着、別忘記喇、唵。

Ans. Hem! What do I care for that now?

30 You heretofore recommended him; how does it come that he now suspects you of speaking evil of him? *Ans.* Humph! Who knows?

31 The old man so sick as that! and yet when he wants a drink, there is no one to get it for him; when he wants something to eat, there is no one to cook it for him. When I went to see him to-day he cried and cried. *Ans.* Ah me! His is indeed a bitter lot.

32 Now you go briskly, eh? don't fight with anybody on the street, eh? and when you get to your sister's, go straight into her room, eh? don't go first into her mother-in-law's room, eh? say to your sister that mamma says she must not get homesick, that after a few days we will go for her. Be sure and remember and don't forget, eh?

NOTES.

2 In Northern and Central Mandarin snakes are commonly called 長虫. 蛇 is a book term and generally means a venomous snake or serpent. It is used colloquially in the South and also in many parts of the North.

3 俺不 "*I won't*" is a very pat phrase, especially with children.

4 It is contrary to custom for persons of the same name to marry, although it is sometimes done.

5 The use of the "little name" implies familiar acquaintance, and, generally, superior age or station.

6 When a Chinaman gets into great straits he invariably calls his mother. The three forms of calling mother represent in the general, Northern, Central, and Southern custom, although there are many local variations.

9 啊 is here 1st tone and denotes surprise joined with a little anxiety. The translation given is only an approximation to the meaning.

10 問他好啊 Here 啊 is merely a euphonic ending. The 啊 below is a responsive recognition that the speaker is heard, after which the reply follows.

11 跟 as here used is local in Peking and the North.

15 The three terms here used are not quite synonymous. 邋遢 means properly, *dirty, slovenly*, but is used in Pekingese in the sense of, *inferior, good-for-nothing;* 邋態 is used in Shantung, but not in the North. It is also heard in the region of Hankow. Though local, it is a very expressive term; 憨包 is a Southern term and in this connection is the strongest of the three.

16 快 as here used has very little force. I have rendered it *now.*

17 周村 is a large unwalled town in Central Shantung, having an extensive trade and much wealth. The first 是 should be emphasized, indicating that the speaker presumed that the road referred to *was* the road to Chou Ts'un.

18 四條腿 is added for emphasis, and to make more striking the contrast between the man and the *beast.*

19 人家 is used from the standpoint of the party addressed, and means *other people*, including the speaker. 學書 is descriptive of "getting a lesson" in the Western sense. The term is not used in native schools.

22 活 is used to convey the idea that the slander is wholly without foundation. It is "made out of whole cloth."

24 No single English word will express the sigh of regret here expressed by 喨.

25 嗐, as here used, is given with a short, strong emphasis, very different from that of (11.) 看燈 refers to going out to see the lanterns on the eve of the 15th of the first month. The Chinese says *to-day*, but it has to be rendered *to-night.* 忘八蛋 *One who has forgotten, or is destitute of, the eight virtues*, and thus properly beyond the pale of humanity. 蛋 is used as a term of reviling in allusion to its being the undeveloped and unrecognizable possibility of a being. Though decidedly inelegant, this term is refined in comparison with the language often heard. There are few Chinese who, in the circumstances here referred to, would not use a stronger term than this one, which is in fact a mild substitute for the stronger one used by the writer of the sentence. A gentleman should never use even this term.

26 This sentence refers to the female acrobats sometimes seen in China.

29 It would seem more natural to say 吃你的, 穿你的, but the idea is much more vivid without the 的.

32 This is a fair specimen of a Chinese woman charging a son or a nephew. It is not in the least overdone.

第九十四課

他[1]雖年輕、却是秀才。○你[2]雖然這麼說、那能這麼做呢。○他[3]雖然有不是、我也有點兒過錯。○王[4]老四、脾氣雖不好、心田却不錯。○他[5]雖然不能出門、還可以管家裏的事。○孩[6]子雖然種過花兒牛痘、也難保再就不出。○他[7]雖是個伶俐人、却辦些糊塗事。○他[8]的房子、雖然窄小、家裏擺設的、却像個富家。○吃[9]大烟的人、雖然父母上了停牀停了牀、他還要過癮喇。○雖[10]然天長、有的是工夫、却不如早早做出來。○丁[11]老三乾空是個財主、待人却很刻薄。○大[12]清國的皇帝、雖是旗人、漢人作官的却不少。○雖[13]然是

TRANSLATION.

1 Although he is young, he is nevertheless a graduate.
2 Although you speak thus, yet of course you will not do so.
3 Although he is in the fault, I also am somewhat to blame.
4 Although Wang the Fourth's temper is bad, his heart is all right.
5 Although he cannot go abroad, he can manage things at home.
6 Although the child has been vaccinated, yet you cannot be sure that he will not take [the disease] again.
7 Although he is a clever man, he has done some silly things.
8 Although his house is contracted, yet inside, the rooms are furnished like those of a wealthy family.
9 The opium smoker must satisfy his craving even when his father and mother are on their deathbeds.
10 Although the day is long and there is plenty of time, yet it will be better to do it early.
11 It is all to no purpose that Ting the Third is a rich man, he still treats people very meanly.
12 Although the emperor of China is a Manchu, yet not a few of the officials are Chinese.

LESSON XCIV.

CORRESPONDING CONJUNCTIONS.

雖 or 雖然 Although. The use of 然 does not change the meaning, being added merely for euphony. 雖 requires an answering clause, which is generally introduced by one of the three words 却, or 也, or 還. Thus:—

雖.....却 Although...yet, nevertheless.
雖.....也 Although...yet also, yet even.
雖.....還 Although...yet still.

Somtimes the answering word is omitted and the relation implied in the structure of the sentence (18). In *Wên-li* 然 is not joined with 雖, but is used to introduce the answering clause. This usage is occasionally introduced in book Mandarin (25).

乾 Exhausted, is sometimes used instead of 雖, but with a somewhat different meaning viz., to no purpose, in spite of, even if. In the South 乾 is not thus used, but 空 empty, is used in the same way, and with the same meaning.

VOCABULARY.

雖 *Swei*¹. Although, if, even of, supposing:—see Sub.

心田 *Hsin*¹ *t'ien*². The heart viewed as the source of the affections and purposes, natural bent.

窄小 *Chai*³ *hsiao*³. Narrow, *contracted.*

停牀 *T'ing*² *ch'wang*². A deathbed:—Note 9.

癮 *Yin*³. A rash; *the craving of an appetite,*—especially that for opium or drink.

過癮 *Kwoa*⁴ *yin*³. To pass over or stop the craving by satisfying it.

聰明過人、却也要得心地乾淨、方能叫人敬服。○他[14]們的買賣、雖然貼賠了、也不過是貼賠了工夫、却沒貼賠錢。○我[15]的老父親、雖然有信、不叫我掛念他、我却不能不掛念他。○這[16]鐵中玉、雖只一人、他動起手來、幾十人也打不他過不他過。○你[17]們各人、雖有明白的道理、却還要聽你母親的教訓。○他[18]雖然沒有欺負我、我看見他欺負那些老實人、我心裏實在氣不忿。○看[19]你的飯量、也不大離、怎麼乾吃不長上肉臕呢。○雖[20]然交朋友、有勸善規過的道理、也當看他

13 Although you are superior to others in intelligence, yet you must have a virtuous mind in order to command the respect of others.

14 Although their business was a losing one, it was only time that was lost, they did not lose money.

15 Although my old father writes for me not to be anxious about him, yet I cannot but be anxious.

16 Although this T'ie Chung Yü is only one man, yet if he once sets to, thirty or forty men cannot master him.

17 Although all of you know some things, yet you should still heed your mother's instruction.

18 Although he has not imposed upon me, yet when I see him imposing on well-meaning people, I really cannot restrain my anger.

19 Your appetite seems to be very fair. How is it that in spite of your eating you do not get fat?

20 Although exhortation and reproof belong to the duties of friendship, yet it is necessary to consider the character of the individual in question.

21 Although the mother scolds her little son with her mouth, yet she em-

皇帝 *Hwang*² *ti*⁴. . . . . An emperor.

旗 *Ch'i*². . . . . A flag, *a banner,* a standard.

旗人 *Ch'i*² *jên*². Bannermen, Tartars :—Note 12.

漢人 *Han*⁴ *jên*². Chinese,—especially as distinguished from the Tartars.

心地 *Hsin*¹ *ti*⁴. . . . . Same as 心田 above.

敬服 *Ching*⁴ *fu*². *To respect,* to honor, to esteem.

忿 *Fên*⁴. . . . Anger ; resentment ; *indignation.*

氣不忿 *Ch'i*⁴ *pu*⁴ *fên*⁴. Indignant, unable to restrain one's anger :—Note 18.

飯量 *Fan*⁴ *liang*². Capacity for eating, *appetite.*

臕 *Piao*¹. . . . . . . *Fat,* obesity, corpulence.

勸善 *Ch'üen*⁴ *shan*⁴. *To exhort to virtue,* to preach morality.

規過 *Kwei*¹ *kwoa*⁴. *To reprove,* to admonish for a fault. (w.)

憎 *Tsêng*¹'⁴. . . . . . To dislike, to hate, to detest.

憎嫌 *Tseng*⁴ *hsien*². To dislike, to find fault with, *to scold.*

摟 *Lou*³. *To embrace;* to carry off, to elope with. Also *lou*¹.

摟抱 *Lou*³ *pao*⁴. *To embrace,* to fold in the arms, to hug.

親熱 *Ch'in*¹ *jê*⁴. To caress, *to kiss;* dear, loving, affectionate.

出相 *Ch'u*¹ *hsiang*¹. Worthy of note or imitation, *remarkable,* special.

妖 *Yao*¹. Strange, ominous, monstrous; *unusual;* a phantom, a ghost, a fiend.

妖巧 *Yao*¹ *ch'iao*³. . . . . . . Odd, *witty,* singular.

千古 *Ch'ien*¹ *ku*³. *Antiquity,* of old, from ancient times.

雄 *Hsiung*². The male of birds and insects ; brave, martial, *heroic.*

英雄 *Ying*¹ *hsiung*². *A hero,* a knight ; of noble and courageous mind.

的爲人。○母21親和小兒、口裏雖然憎嫌、還是用手摟抱、用嘴親熱他。○張22二那個人、模樣雖不出相、最能說個妖巧話、說着這個、譏誚着那個。○他23雖是一個小女子、却有千古大英雄的度量。○這24時候、亞伯身體雖然倦乏了、還不能睡着、因爲他想到明天要辦的事、不由得心裏發跳。○我25兒雖如此說、然冤家可解不可結。○曹26州府、那是久反之地、出賊最多、所以在道路上、不多遠就有一個卡防、預備護送客旅、凡是城池、鎭店、也都有官兵彈壓、雖然如此、總擋不住他們搶奪。

braces him with her arms and kisses him with her lips.

22 Although there is nothing remarkable in the personal appearance of that man, Chang the Second, yet he has a great faculty for saying witty things, speaking of one while he ridicules another.

23 Although she is a little girl, she has the ability of the great heroes of antiquity.

24 Although at this time Abel was very weary in body, he still could not sleep, for he was thinking of what was to be done on the morrow, and in spite of himself his heart kept palpitating.

25 Notwithstanding what you say, my son, still it is better to remove enmity than to incur it.

26 That Ts'aochou-fu has long been a rebellious place which produces many robbers, therefore there are guards stationed on the road at short distances for the purpose of escorting travellers, and every city and market-town also has a guard of soldiers to protect it; and yet, notwithstanding all this, they cannot be restrained from robbing.

度量 *Tu*⁴ *liang*². Capacity, *ability*; calibre; penetration, judgment.

亞 *Ya*³'⁴. Deformed, secondary, inferior,—much used in names as a phonetic.

伯 *Po*². The third rank of nobility, an earl; a title of respect. Also *pai*³.

久 *Chiu*³. Enduring, *a long time*, of old.

道路 *Tao*⁴ *lu*⁴. *A road*, a way; a method, a resort.

卡 *Ch'ia*³. A guard-house, a small police or customs station. Also *ch'ia*².

卡防 *Ch'ia*³ *fang*². A guard-house, a watch station.

護送 *Hu*⁴ *sung*⁴. *To escort*, to accompany with a guard, to give safe conduct.

客旅 *K'ê*⁴ *lü*³. A traveller, a stranger.

城池 *Ch'êng*² *ch'i*². A walled city.

鎭店 *Chên*⁴ *tien*⁴. A market-town.

彈壓 *T'an*² *ya*⁴. To keep in order, to restrain; *to protect*, to guard.

搶奪 *Ch'iang*³ *to*². *To rob*, to plunder; to carry off violently.

Notes.

6 To vaccinate is variously designated. Besides the two terms used in the text, both 種痘子 and 種洋痘 are used. The 再 might be omitted with advantage; as used it regards the effect of vaccination as if it were a species of small-pox.

9 停牀 is a special bed prepared for one who is dying. The Chinese have a strong prejudice against allowing any one to die on a *k'ang* or on a bed; they say that the soul will have to carry the *k'ang* or bed on its back and cannot get out of the house until a necromancer is employed to assist it. He takes a rooster and by means of sundry incantations conducts the soul out of the house. Hence as soon as it appears that anyone is about to die, they move him off the bed or *k'ang* to some temporary bed on the ground or on benches in the middle of the room. The most common way is to take a door off its hinges (a thing very easily done with Chinese doors) and lay it across a couple of benches and stretch the dying person on it. 過癮 means practically to take a smoke, by which means the uneasy craving is relieved, and so "*passes by*."

12 旗人 The Manchus are divided by the reigning dynasty into eight banners or clans, under which they are officered and marshalled. As commonly used by the Chinese the term includes all the Tartars.

15 有信 here means *has sent a letter*, or *a letter has arrived from*. In other connections it generally means to *receive a letter*.

第九十五課

我[1]固然錯了、但你說我的話太利害。○明[2]明是他起的事、但是他却不出頭。○我[3]哥哥是笑在臉面上、然而心裏愁苦得很。○莊[4]稼雖仗着雨水均勻、但是也得人去修鋤葺理、○凡[5]說話行事、雖要認眞、只是不可認眞太過。○我[6]很不願意借錢給人、但他再三央求、我也沒有法子。○但[7]是東西已經壞了、你就是不割捨捨不得、還能怎麽樣呢。○平[8]常誰不知道和平好呢、但到被人衝撞的時候、就由不得自己了。○若[9]但看那個人的外面、實在老實、然而心裏却詭詐得很。○兒[10]女固然應當孝順、然而爲父母的、

TRANSLATION.

1 I was wrong, it is true; but your reproof is too severe.

2 Clearly it was he who originated the affair, yet nevertheless he refuses to bear the responsibility.

3 My elder brother has a smile on his face, nevertheless, in his heart he is very much distressed.

4 Although the crops depend on seasonable rains, yet they require men to cultivate them.

5 Although we should always be sincere in word and deed, yet it is not well to be too simple-minded.

6 I am very loth to lend money, yet he has begged me again and again until I have no alternative.

7 But the article is already ruined, so that even though you do begrudge it, what can you do?

8 In ordinary circumstances, who does not know that it is best to be pacific? but when you are offended by some one, you lose your self-control.

9 If you regard only that man's exterior, he is certainly trusty; nevertheless, in his heart he is exceedingly treacherous.

10 Children should of course obey their

16 幾十人 *Several tens of men.* 打他不過 an obsolete form of 打不過他. It is still heard in some places along the Yang-tse.

18 那些 does not mean any particular individuals, but well-meaning people in general. 氣不忿 is to be understood as if written 氣的不得不忿, for which it seems to be a contraction.

20 勸善規過 is a ready-made book expression. 他 stands for 朋友, and the use of 的 makes 爲人 a noun meaning *character*. A more colloquial form of speech would be 當看他爲人怎麽樣.

21 用嘴親熱他 does not refer to kissing in the proper sense, of which the Chinese are generally ignorant, but to rubbing the face with the nose and lips, which Chinese mothers are in the habit of doing.

23 This is said of 冰心小姐, *Miss Icy-heart*, the heroine of the "Fortunate Union."

25 In speaking, an 啊 should be inserted after 兒. This sentence is also from the "Fortunate Union."

LESSON XCV.

DISJUNCTIVES.

但 or **但是** But, but yet, still. The 是 is added or not as the rhythm of the sentence requires.

只是 But, but then, but only.

但是一件
但有一件
只是一件 } But there is one thing, but it must be borne in mind.

却但是一件 But then it must be remembered, but the fact is, nevertheless.

然 But, yet. Not often used alone in Mandarin save as the correlative of 雖 as noted in the preceding lesson.

然而 But, yet, nevertheless, yet on the other hand. Essentially *Wên-li*, but frequently used in Mandarin books—very rarely in colloquial,

也不要惹兒女的氣。○官[11]司雖然定了案、但是有勢力的人、還能再翻過來。○人[12]的天分、雖然次些、但是若肯勤學、也能趕得上人。○凡[13]和人初交、不能一點疑惑沒有、然而日久、就放心了。○文[14]章雖然難學、但若仔細摹倣、也能學個不大離（出色）。○張[15]兄說得有理、但是你的經紀、總不如他。○你[16]不聽勸、我也不能逼着你聽、但只是一件、以後你喫虧的時候、却不要來找我。○你[17]說的這些話、雖都是大道理、然君子少、小人多、明白的少、不明白的多。○我[18]怎麼不責備他呢、但他那一張嘴、就像一把快刀、我還說不得一句、他早說

parents, yet, on the other hand, parents should not provoke their children to anger.

11 Although a lawsuit has been decided, yet one who has influence may still get it reversed.

12 Although a man's talents may be somewhat inferior, yet if he will study with diligence, he can still attain to mediocrity.

13 When a man first makes an acquaintance, he cannot avoid having some misgivings; but as time progresses he becomes confident.

14 Although it is hard to learn to write a *wên-chang*, yet if any one will carefully follow the pattern, he may become fairly proficient.

15 What you say, Brother Chang, is true, still your skill is by no means equal to his.

16 If you will not give heed, I cannot compel you, but there is one thing [you must bear in mind], hereafter when you suffer the consequences, you must not come to me for help.

17 Although what you say is very true, still good men are few and mean men many; the intelligent are few and the foolish many.

18 What is the reason I did not reprove her? But that mouth of hers is like a sharp sword. Before I could speak a single sentence, she had already rattled off ever so

VOCABULARY.

固然 *Ku⁴ jan²*. Certainly, unquestionably, *of course, it is true.*

愁苦 *Ch'ou² k'u³*. *Distressed*, troubled, sorrowful, miserable.

鋤 *Ch'u²*. A hoe; *to hoe*, to cultivate.

修鋤 *Hsiu¹ ch'u²*. *To cultivate with a hoe*, to dig about.

葺 *Ch'i¹*. To repair, to put in order, *to dress.*

葺理 *Ch'i¹ li³*. To repair, to dress, *to cultivate.* (s.)

認眞 *Jên⁴ chên¹*. *Sincere*, frank; honest, true, faithful.

央求 *Yang¹ ch'iu²*. *To beg*, to importune, to beseech.

割捨 *Kê¹ shê³*. *To give up*, nothing loth:—Note 7.

兒女 *Êr² nü³*. Children.

勢力 *Shï⁴ li⁴*. Power, *influence.*

日久 *Jï⁴ chiu³*. In the course of time, by-and-by, *as time progresses.*

摹 *Mu²*. To follow a pattern, to imitate.

倣 *Fang³*. To imitate, *to copy;* a copy, a model; like, resembling.

摹倣 To imitate, to follow a pattern or model.

出色 *Ch'u¹ sê⁴*. Superior, first-rate, above the average, *proficient.*

經紀 *Ching¹ chi⁴*. Experience, *detective skill;* a broker, a specialist.

出無數的大道理來、教我無處開口。○燕[19]窩魚翅、雖是最高貴的海味、但是沒有雞湯和肉、調和起來、也是不怎麼受喫。○領[20]洋賑的、不分大口小口、每人領錢一百四、領義賑的、每大口領六百、每小口領三百、因此有人說、洋賑不如義賑、但是一件、洋賑是從頭年起、每七天一領、直放到麥秋後爲止、義賑是從三月起、只放一次就完了、比較起來、還是領洋賑好。○用[21]西國人在海關收稅、俸祿更多、好像不如用本國人、却但是一件、西國人比本國人、更有本事、也更忠心、所以皇上情願多出俸祿、也要用西國人。

much plausible talk, giving me no chance to open my mouth.

19 Birds' nests and fish fins, although they are the rare delicacies of the sea, yet if not mixed with chicken broth and meat, they are not specially palatable.

20 Those who received foreign relief, received one hundred and forty cash for each person, whether child or adult. Those who received the imperial bounty, received for each adult six hundred cash, and for each child three hundred, hence some say the foreign relief was inferior to the imperial bounty. But it must be remembered that the foreign relief began before the New Year, one distribution in seven days, and continued without interruption until after the wheat harvest. The imperial bounty began in the third month and stopped after only one distribution, so that, comparing the two, the foreign relief was after all the better.

21 To use foreigners at the ports to collect duties, requires higher salaries, and it seems as if it would be better to use natives, but the fact is that foreigners have more ability and are more honest, hence it is that the Emperor prefers to give higher salaries and use foreigners.

君 *Chün*¹. A prince, a sovereign; *honorable, superior,* a term of respect.

君子 *Chün*¹ *tsï*³. The ideal or superior man:—Note 17.

燕 *Yien*⁴. A swallow, a martin.

燕窩 *Yien*⁴ *wo*¹. A swallow's nest, *edible bird's nest.*

翅 *Ch'ï*⁴. A wing, *a fin.*

魚翅 *Yü*² *ch'ï*⁴. Sharks' fins.

海味 *Hai*³ *wei*⁴. A delicacy of the sea.

調和 *T'iao*³ *hê*². *To mix,* to blend; to mediate, to make peace.

受吃 *Shou*⁴ *ch'ï*¹. Good to eat, *palatable.*

頭年 *T'ou*² *nien*². Before the New Year.

麥秋 *Mai*⁴ *ch'iu*¹. Wheat harvest.

比較 *Pi*³ *chiao*³. To compare.

海關 *Hai*³ *kwan*¹. A custom house.

稅 *Shui*⁴. *Duties on goods,* tariff.

俸 *Fêng*⁴. *Salary,* emoluments; wages.

祿 *Lu*⁴. *Official salary,* emoluments, pay; prosperity.

俸祿 The emoluments of office, *salary.*

忠心 *Chung*¹ *hsin*¹. Faithful, devoted; *honest,* reliable.

NOTES.

2 却 is in fact superfluous, yet the colloquial very often adds it in this way after 但是, as *nevertheless* is added in the translation. 出頭 *To come to the front;* i.e., *to bear the responsibility.*

3 The use of 臉 prevails in the South, that of 面 in the North.

4 雨水 means properly *rain water,* and is generally so used, but in the present case it means simply rain. 均勻

第九十六課

醫[1]生多半是年紀大的好。○請[2]放心罷、大諒（諒來）沒有事情。○書[3]中雖然有些小毛病、大畧還算清楚。○他[4]到如今不來、大半是不來了。○若[5]衆人都說某人好、大槪就是一個好人。○我[6]家的事情、大半是我哥哥管。○大諒（諒想）[7]你不惹他、他也不能打你。○流[8]水賬已經算了兩遍、大槪錯不了（不得錯）。○大[9]約放債的人、都是有勢力的。○病[10]到這個分兒上、大料（大約）是不能好了。○世[11]上的邪事、大槪都能戀得住人。

Translation.

1 For the most part, elderly physicians are the best.
2 Please set your heart at rest. There will probably be no trouble.
3 Although there are some small defects in the book, yet for the most part it is clear.
4 Not having come by this time, it is most likely he will not come.
5 If everybody says that a certain man is good, most likely he is a good man.
6 Our family affairs are, for the most part, controlled by my elder brother.
7 Probably if you had not irritated him, he would not have struck you.
8 The day book has already been counted over twice, it is probably correct.
9 Those who lend money generally have some official influence.
10 His illness having reached this stage, it is not likely he can recover.
11 The vices of the world are, in general,

may be used of the uniform distributions of rain either over a certain territory or over a certain time. In the latter case, as here, it means *seasonable.*

7 但 at the beginning of this sentence refers back to something preceding. 割捨 is nearly always used with a negative, meaning, *to be loth to part with, to grudge.* It is widely used, but not *t'ung hsing.* In Peking it is generally heard 割捨不得.

9 The 但 in the first clause is an adverb meaning *only,* and as such does not illustrate the theme of the lesson. As 然而 is used in Mandarin, 却 usually and naturally follows it. It *may* be omitted, however, as in (3.)

10 The sentiment of this sentence is Christian. No heathen would ever give expression to such a sentiment.

12 但是若 This combination or juxtaposition of conjunctions is considered somewhat inelegant, especially by Peking teachers. It represents, however, a collocation of human thought common to all languages, and is very frequently heard in colloquial. It may sometimes be avoided, without the loss of the idea, by a careful manipulation of the clauses. In order to avoid it here, the Peking teacher would drop the 但是. This, of course, is allowable, but it loses part of the idea and very much weakens the opposition of the clauses. The 人 at the beginning of the sentence is specific, the one at the end, general.

17 君子 *A royal man,* that is a virtuous and honorable man—one who embodies the highest excellencies of human character, which, theoretically, are supposed to inhere in a Prince. The term is much used in the classics and is translated by Dr. Legge as "*the superior man.*"

18 The interrogation of the first clause is equivalent to a strong affirmation. The Chinese does not indicate whether a man or a woman is referred to. Woman's reputed gifts would indicate that it was a woman, though the phrase 無數的大道理 sounds like the language of a man who has some knowledge of books.

19 不怎麽受吃 *Not to any extent bear eating,* 怎麽 has practically the force of *specially* or *particularly.* In many places 什麽 would be substituted for 怎麽.

20 The cash here referred to is 京錢, that is, double count.

LESSON XCVI.

Approximation.

大半 or **多半** The great half,—for the most part, mostly, generally, most likely.

大槪 Great summing up,—on the whole, generally, probably.

約 Approximately, about.

大約 Great agreement,—for the most part, generally, most likely.

大畧 Great approximation,—about, for the most part, most likely.

大料 Great anticipation,—in all probability, most likely. (N.)

○ 大[12]約年老的人、血氣自然衰弱。○ 天[13]陰的不厚(沉)、又起了風、諒來(想必)沒有大雨。○ 凡[14]說話帶諂媚(呵奉)的、大約沒有正經人。○ 聶[15]大人上(往)上海、大概不能久住。○ 世[16]上人、好姿質的總少、大半都是中等的。○ 牲[17]口在夏天、大概沒有帶鈴鐺的、因爲怕招瞎眼蝨(蠅子)、○ 如[18]今的人、大半有一分權柄、就加上三分驕傲。○ 李[19]老師、這幾天也不說、也不笑、想必是有甚麼心事。○ 昨[20]夜約在四更天的時候、有一個賊來撬(撥)門、被我趕跑了。○ 王[21]二上關東、六年沒有信、諒

such as have power to fascinate.

12 In general, when men grow old, their vigor naturally declines.

13 The clouds are not heavy (thick), a wind has also sprung up, there will probably not be much rain.

14 Generally when any man's talk savors of flattery, he is not a reputable person.

15 When General Nie goes to Shanghai, he will not probably remain long.

16 Of mankind, the talented are few; the great majority are mediocre.

17 In the summer, animals do not commonly wear bells, lest they draw the flies.

18 It is mostly the case, at the present time, that when a man gets any degree of authority, his pride increases in a three-fold ratio.

19 Prof. Li neither speaks nor smiles these few days. I fancy there is something weighing on his mind.

20 Last night, about the time of the fourth watch, a thief came and tried the door, but I drove him away.

21 Wang the Second went to Manchuria, and for six years there has been no word of him. Probably he is dead.

大諒 Great supposition,—Most likely, belike, probably. (N.)

諒來 Probably, most likely. Quite *t'ung-hsing*, but more used in Central than in Northern or Southern Mandarin.

諒想 Probably, I presume, I suppose. (s.)

諒必 Most likely, I presume, I expect.

想必 I suppose, I presume, I fancy. *T'ung-hsing*, but more used in the South than in the North.

This lesson is closely allied to Lesson 130.

VOCABULARY.

諒 *Liang*⁴. To believe; to suppose, to guess; .... probably, likely:—see Sub.

概 *Kai*⁴. To level, to adjust; a summing up; all, ... the whole.

流水賬 *Liu*² *shwei*³ *chang*⁴. A day book, a blotter:—Note 8.

放債 *Fang*⁴ *chai*⁴. .... To lend money.

衰弱 *Shwai*¹ *joǒ*⁴. Weak, *feeble*, debilitated, ... decrepit.

諂 *Ch'an*³. *To flatter*, to fawn upon; adulation, ... sycophancy.

媚 *Mei*⁴.... Smirking, smiling; *to flatter*, to pet.

諂媚 *To flatter*, to cajole, to act the sycophant.

呵 *Hê*¹, *ha*¹. To expel the breath; to pant, to .... yawn; to flatter; a final particle.

呵奉 *Hê*¹ *fêng*⁴. To flatter, to act the sycophant, ... to curry favor with. (s.)

聶 *Nie*⁴....... To whisper; a surname.

姿 *Tsï*¹...... Fascinating; *talents*, endowments.

質 *Chï*⁴,³,². *Substance*, matter, to establish by .... evidence, to confront; honest, sincere, real; disposition.

來是已經死了。○[22]烟筒釜臺烟衝不見冒烟、想必是還沒生火。○諒[23]必有些過節兒、我們猜算不到。○這[24]是前五年的事、雖然不能說得一點不差、大畧却是如此。○我[25]在這裏存着五吊八百錢、對不對、答大畧是那個數目、看看賬就知道了。○他[26]每逢支錢、必上摺子、摺子上沒有、想必是沒支。○外[27]頭來了一個人、身量不高、大約四十多歲、要見先生、答阿、想必是李先生、可以請他進來。○這[28]塊蔓菁、大約再等七八天、就好拔了。○天[29]生的賊骨頭、若不動大刑、大料諒他是不肯招的。

22 There seems to be no smoke issuing from the chimney. I presume the fire is not yet kindled.

23 Most likely some things have occurred which we did not anticipate.

24 This affair happened five years ago, and although I cannot say exactly, yet it was about this way.

25 I have here deposited to my credit five thousand eight hundred cash; is that correct? *Ans.* Yes, it is probably about that amount. By looking at your account I will know.

26 Every time he gets money it is put on his pass book. If it is not on the pass book, I presume he has not received it.

27 A man has arrived without who wishes to see you. He is not very tall and is about forty years old. *Ans.* Oh, I presume it is Mr. Li. You may invite him in.

28 After about seven or eight days more, this patch of turnips will be ready for gathering.

29 Thieving is bred in that fellow's bones, and it is not likely that he will be willing to confess without the application of the severest torture.

姿質 Endowments, parts, *talents*, cleverness.

中等 *Chung^1 têng^3*. . . . . . Mediocre, average.

夏天 *Hsia^4 t'ien^1*. . . . . Summer.

蝱 *Mêng^2*. . . . . *A horse-fly;* a gad-fly.

瞎眼蝱 *Hsia^1 yien^3 mêng^2*. A horse-fly:—Note 17.

柄 *Ping^{3,4}*. . . . . . A handle, a crank; *authority.*

權柄 *Ch'üen^2 ping^3*. *Authority,* power, control, prerogative.

老師 *Lao^3 shï^1*. An instructor, *a professor;* superintendent of education:—Note 19.

心事 *Hsin^1 shï^4*. *Something weighing on the mind,* trouble, embarrassment.

撬 *Ch'iao^4*. . . . . . . To raise with a lever, *to pry.*

筒 *T'ung^{2,3}*. . . . A tube, a pipe.

烟筒 *Yien^1 t'ung^2*. A smoke pipe, a stove pipe, a flue:—Note 22.

釜 *Fu^3*. . . . . A caldron, a boiler, a kettle.

釜臺 *Fu^3 t'ai^2*. A chimney, a flue:—Note 22.

烟衝 *Yien^1 ch'ung^1*. An outlet for the smoke, a flue:—Note 22.

過節 *Kwoä^4 chie^2*. To keep a feast day; to exceed the bounds of propriety; *an occurrence,* a complication, a hitch.

猜算 *Ts'ai^1 swan^4*. To conjecture, to guess; *to anticipate,* to look for.

數目 *Shu^4 mu^4*. . . . . Number.

蔓 *Man^2*. . . . . A turnip. Also *wan^4*.

菁 *Ching^1*. . . . . Luxuriant; a turnip.

蔓菁. *A turnip,* a beet.

NOTES.

4 Note that the first 不來 is past, and the second one future.

5 It is uncertain whether this sentence was intended to enunciate a principle, or to apply to a particular individual. In the latter case it should be rendered, *If everybody says that Mr. So and So is a good man, he most likely is a good man.*

8 流水賬 A running account written in the order in which the business is done. A cash book is a 銀錢流水賬.

9 It is a sort of a necessity in China that he who would lend money should have some 勢力, otherwise he would

第九十七課

他[1]雖不來、你仍然該去。○實[2]指望到今年就寬裕綽了、誰知今年仍是受窮。○他[3]就是長到一百歲、在你手裏、仍舊是個孩子。○仍[4]然是你該得去、因為別人不認得門兒。○世[5]俗說、人死了為鬼、不知人死了、仍舊是人。○我[6]給他改正了一回、仍舊還是不好。○有[7]道的人、雖然受苦難堪、然而仍有他的快樂。○這[8]些椅子、你們從那裏搬來的、還要照舊送回去。○我[9]們得救、雖不倚靠律法、却仍舊要得按律法行事。○說[10]來說去、該怎麼辦的、仍舊還是要

TRANSLATION.

1 Although he does not come, you should still go.
2 I had certainly hoped to have plenty this year, and behold I am still suffering from poverty.
3 Even if he grows to be a hundred years old, in his relation to you he will still be a child.
4 After all you will have to go, for no one else knows the door.
5 The world says that when a man dies, he becomes a demon; but the fact is when a man dies, he is still a man.
6 I corrected it for him once, and still it is not right.
7 A man who has received the truth, although he may suffer grievous trials, yet nevertheless has his joys.
8 Take these chairs back to the place from whence you brought them.
9 Although we are not saved by trusting in the law, yet it is still necessary to live according to the law.
10 After all your talk, you will still have to do it as it ought to be done.

presently find himself without any money to lend. 勢力 here means power to coerce payment, to have such influence with those in authority as will enable one to use a certain degree of violence with impunity.

15 In some places 上 is used for going to a place, without regard to up or down. In other places 往 is used.

17 瞎眼蝱 A species of horse-fly, popularly regarded as blind, because of the peculiar appearance of its eyes. It is supposed to be guided by the sound of the bells in finding the animals.

19 老師, also called 教官, theoretically an official teacher appointed in each *Hsien* city to teach the graduates of his district. The office is a sinecure so far as teaching is concerned. He simply exercises the functions of a superintendent, and is entitled to certain fees. He has charge of the Confucian temple and offers sacrifices at the required seasons. The 老師 in a *Fu* city is the general superintendent of those in the *Hsien* cities. There are also military 老師.

22 There is no *t'ung hsing* term for "chimney," for the reason, probably, that in a large part of China there are no chimneys. In Eastern Shantung chimneys are general, and the distinctive name is 釜臺. A 烟筒 is a stove pipe, though the term may perhaps in some places be applied to a chimney. 烟衝, as used in the South, is simply a horizontal hole in the wall for the exit of the smoke. Stove pipe is so called by foreigners.

26 Pass books are extensively used by Chinese shop-keepers and bankers.

28 這塊蔓菁 *This piece of turnips*, that is, this piece of land which is sown in turnips.

29 Probably spoken by an underling, and intimating that the party spoken of was an old thief accustomed to being flogged and fortified against it.

LESSON XCVII.

STILL.

還 As before, still, yet. This word belongs properly in this lesson, but from necessity it has already been so frequently used that it is useless to illustrate it further.

仍 As before, still, nevertheless.

仍舊 As of old, as before, all the same, still.

仍然 As ever, still. Practically the same as 仍舊, but a little more elegant.

照舊 As before, as heretofore, still.

依舊 As before, as heretofore. A little bookish.

仍舊還是 After all, still. A much used, but somewhat redundant expression.

怎麼辦。○這[11]一夜、仍舊馬不停蹄、走到天明。○我[12]見有許多賭錢的人、已經[起誓發願|賭咒發誓]的、再不賭了、以後仍然還是去賭。○睜[13]開兩個眵[瞎窟窿|眼]、就得掃地、[擦|抹]桌子、[刷|洗]鍋、[做|弄]飯、明天起來、照舊還是那一套。○這[14]一[遭|回]、和王瑞亭清了賬、要緊叫他立個[清楚字據|清白帖子|清白單子]、若不然的時候、以後仍舊還是不清。○[15]若打了自己的孩子、他雖然暫時冷淡、不多時候、仍又親熱。○一[16]個人的見識、總有看不到的地方、所以只請一位先生批過、仍舊怕不[妥當|熨貼]。○騾[17]子能

11 He continued to ride on the whole night, his horse's feet not stopping till the dawn.

12 I have known a great many gamblers vowing, with an oath, never to gamble again, and yet they afterwards went back to their gambling as before.

13 The moment I get my bleared eyes open, it is—sweep up—wipe off the table—wash the kettle and get breakfast,—and to-morrow when I get up, it will be the same round over again.

14 After this settlement with Wang Jwei T'ing, be sure and have him write you a receipt in full. If you do not, it will afterwards turn out that you still have no settlement.

15 When you punish your own child, although he may be estranged for the time being, he will presently be as affectionate as ever.

16 One man's judgment is, in any case, imperfect, therefore to ask only one teacher's criticism is, after all, unsatisfactory.

VOCABULARY.

仍 *Jêng*^{2}. .... As, as before, still, again.

裕 *Yü*^{4}. *Plentiful*, superabundant; liberal; .... overmuch.

寬裕 *K'wan*^{1} *yü*^{4}. Abundant, in easy circumstances, *plenty;* generous, liberal.

改正 *Kai*^{3} *chêng*^{4}. *To correct*, to adjust, to .... alter.

堪 *K'an*^{1}. *To sustain*, to bear; able, adequate; .... worthy of, fit.

蹄 *T'i*^{2}. .... A hoof, *a foot;* a horse-shoe.

起誓 *Ch'i*^{3} *shï*^{4}. .... To swear, to take an oath.

願 *Yüen*^{4}. .... Sincere, faithful; a promise, *a vow.*

發願 *Fa*^{1} *yüen*^{4}. ...... To make a vow, to vow.

眵 *Ch'ï*^{1}. Blurred (eyes), purulent eyelids, ... *bleared.*

瑞 *Jwei*^{4}. A signet; a keep-sake; felicitous, ... auspicious.

亭 *T'ing*^{2}. .... A pavilion, an arbor; straight, even.

字據 *Tsï*^{4} *chü*^{4}. A paper given in proof, a .... certificate, *a receipt.*

淸白 *Ch'ing*^{1} *poà*^{2}. Plain, clear; intelligible; *in* .... *full*, quit claim, final.

暫時 *Chan*^{4} *shï*^{2}. Temporarily, *for the time* .... *being*, for the present.

冷淡 *Lêng*^{3} *tan*^{4}. Cool, *estranged*, alienated; .... indifferent.

熨 *Yü*^{4}. To smooth out, *to adjust*, to settle. .... Also *yün*^{4}.

熨貼 *Yü*^{4} *t'ie*^{4}. All right, *satisfactory*, in order, ... O. K.

折算 *Chê*^{2} *swan*^{4}. To average; to sum up, *to* .... *aggregate.*

大烟鬼 *Ta*^{4} *yien*^{1} *kwei*^{3}. .... An opium sot.

酷 *K'u*^{1}. Hard-hearted, cruel; extreme, radical; .... bitter, *relentless.*

挖酷 *Wa*^{1} *k'u*^{1}. To berate, to taunt, *to reprove*, ... to reproach, to upbraid.

保標 *Pao*^{3} *piao*^{1}. *To convoy*, to guarantee safe .... delivery, to insure.

况 *K'wang*^{4}. Moreover, furthermore, still more; .... a time; an event.

景况 *Ching*^{3} *k'wang*^{4}. *Condition of things*, state .... of affairs, circumstances.

祖母 *Tsu*^{3} *mu*^{3}. ...... Paternal grandmother.

有二十年的好站時頭候、驢只有十來年的好站時頭候、所以折算起來、仍舊還是養騾子上算。○18我家裏那個大烟鬼、不知叫我挖酷了多少回、罵了多少頓、仍舊擋不住他喫抽烟、你說愁人不愁人呢。○19我不用人保標、若是命裏該有事、就是有保標的、也仍舊免不了。○20去年我回家看看、家裏的景況、還都依舊未改、就是我的祖母不在了。

17 A mule may have twenty years of effective service, but a donkey has only ten or more years, so that in the aggregate, it is after all more profitable to keep mules.

18 That opium sot of ours—I don't know how often I have reproved him, or how many times I have berated him, and yet it does not prevent his smoking all the same as before. Isn't it vexatious?

19 I don't want anybody as escort. If I am fated to have trouble, even if I have an escort, it cannot after all be prevented.

20 Last year I went home for a visit; the condition of everything at home was just the same as before, save that my grandmother had died.

NOTES.

3 The Chinese hold that parental authority and filial obedience continue without change through life. The same is also true of the authority of elder brothers and uncles.

4 門 at the end of a clause nearly always takes 兒 after it. Though not always written, it is, at least in the North, nearly always spoken.

5 The souls of dead men are commonly spoken of as 鬼, albeit a man never speaks of the souls of his dead parents or ancestors as 鬼 but as 神, they being regarded as deified. Christianity, however, cannot afford to allow that a dead man is a 鬼, much less that he is or may become a 神.

9 The Southern teachers here as often insist on 要 for 得. The meaning, however, is somewhat different. 要 states a charge or requirement of the speaker; 得 expresses the requirement or necessity of the case.

10 說來說去 here means, *to talk in a roundabout way for the purpose of making a point.* It sometimes means simply to *keep up a conversation.*

11 馬不停蹄 *Horse's feet not stopping*—an expression found in novels.

12 The 的 after 瞀 might be omitted without changing the sense, though the construction would be somewhat modified.

13 眵 *Sticky, bleared,*—is here used of the unpleasant, sticky sensation in the eyes often experienced when getting up early, or before one is satisfied with sleep. It gets especial force from the fact that in China poor eyes are the rule rather than the exception. The Peking equivalent is more expressive than elegant. The Nanking teacher rejects both forms, and says 把眼睛一揉, *giving my eyes a rub,* which sounds very tame. Tidy housekeepers in China no doubt wash the kettle after cooking a meal, but the general use of the phrase 刷鍋做飯 shows that the reverse order is the common practice.

14 若不然的時候 Lit., *If-not-so's time* i.e., *in case you do not.*

18 大烟鬼 *Great smoke devil;* i.e., *besotted opium smoker.* 鬼 is used as a term of reproach and contempt. The underlying idea is that the man has lost the proper characteristics of manhood, and become a demon in depravity. There are other terms of the same class, as 看錢鬼, *a miser,* 賭錢鬼, *a gambler.*

19 保標 *To convoy or escort money, treasure, or other valuables.* It is done either by soldiers, constables, or professional fighting men.

20 依舊未改, a ready-made expression, somewhat bookish.

LESSON XCVIII.

THE AUXILIARY 處.

處 is added to many adjectives and participles for the purpose of turning them into abstract nouns of quality or condition, thus 難處, the state or quality of being difficult, 好處 the state or condition or quality of being good, etc. This use of 處 is somewhat similar to that of the English termination *ness* in such words as goodness, usefulness, bitterness, etc. The words with which 處 is most commonly joined are those given in the lesson; if, however, occasion requires, it may be joined to almost any adjective or participle.

第九十八課

各[1]人有各人的難處。○他[2]經過好些險處。○你[3]看那裏是什麽去處。○大[4]處不算、小處算。○你[5]的好處、我一輩子忘不了。○人[6]往高處走、水往低處流。○你[7]又找我的錯、有甚麽益處。○孫[8]先生的長處、是善於講書。○沒[9]有用處、就是便宜我也不要。○鄭[10]天保出門、到處和店家磨牙。○出[11]處不如聚處多。○那[12]個地方地處落地的風俗、過於浮華。○你[13]們這樣癡傻說癡傻笑、有什麽樂處呢。○人[14]說我的短處、心裏就不自在。○你[15]們有好處大家享、有苦處大家受。○我[16]們的心、實是污穢到了極處。○先[17]生若得工夫、請到我們寓下處去坐坐罷。

TRANSLATION.

1 Every man has his own difficulties.
2 He has passed through many perils.
3 Go and see what kind of place that is.
4 He is particular about the small [expenses], not the great [ones].
5 I will not forget your kindness as long as I live.
6 Men seek high places [as] water seeks [the] low.
7 What profit is there in again joining issue with me?
8 Mr. Sun's strong point is in his excellent expositions.
9 It is of no use, so that, even if it is cheap, I do not want it.
10 When Chêng T'ien Pao travels, he quarrels with the inn-keepers wherever he goes.
11 There are more in the market than there are in the factory.
12 The fashions of the place are excessively gay.
13 What is there so funny that you are talking and laughing in such a silly fashion?
14 When anyone speaks of our shortcomings, we feel uncomfortable.
15 When you have blessings share them in common, and when you have adversities bear them in common.
16 Truly our hearts are utterly unclean.
17 If you get time, please come to our lodgings and visit us.

難處 Difficulty, strait, troublesomeness.

險處 Danger, peril, risk, precariousness.

去處 A place to go to; a place; on occasion.

大處 That which is great or important; greatness, magnitude.

小處 That which is small or unimportant; smallness, littleness, inferiority.

好處 Benefit, advantage; kindness; blessing; virtue, merit.

高處 That which is high; pre-eminence; highness, altitude.

低處 That which is low; inferiority; lowness.

益處 Benefit, profit, profitableness.

長處 Superiority, pre-eminence; forte.

用處 Use, usefulness.

到處 Every place, everywhere. A contraction of 所到之處, and not quite in line with the lesson.

出處 The place in which a thing is produced and from which it proceeds; origin, factory.

聚處 The place where things are collected; a market, a rendezvous, a focus.

地處 A place, a situation. (L.)

樂處 An occasion of rejoicing; gladness, enjoyment.

短處 Short-coming, deficiency, fault; shortness.

苦處 Suffering, adversity; bitterness.

極處 The extreme, the uttermost.

寓處 Dwelling-place, residence, lodgings.

下處 The same.

明處 That which is public, in public.

暗處 That which is private, in private, in secret; darkness.

損處 Injury, harm, detriment, injuriousness.

○他[18]在明處是一樣、在暗處又是一樣。○這[19]是一種太平藥、吃了一點害損處也沒有。○人[20]有短處、大概沒有不遮掩的。○老[21]兄進京的時候、要緊給我找個地處方。○你[22]在這裏十來多年、沒有甚麼得罪人的處去所處、○凡[23]廟會的日子、男女混雜、也沒有人整理、有許多不便宜處。○他[24]若不在衙門裏、可以上他寓處去找他。○我[25]有甚麼奇處兒、比我好的多着的呢。○他[26]今天在這裏、明天在那裏、沒有一定的住處。○那[27]個人、雖然沒有甚麼大好處、可也沒有甚麼大壞處。○有[28]話應該說在當面、光背地裏啣嘟咕囔、有甚麼益處。○小[29]

18 He is one thing in public, and quite another in private.

19 This is a mild medicine; taking it will not do the least harm.

20 There is hardly a man having a fault who does not try to conceal it.

21 When you go to the capital, be sure and find a situation for me.

22 You have been here upwards of ten years without giving occasion of offense to any one.

23 On the occasion of fairs at the temples, men and women are mixed together without any one to control them, which gives rise to a great deal of inconvenience.

24 If he is not in the yamên, you can go to his lodgings and look for him.

25 What is there remarkable in me? There are plenty of better men than I am.

26 He is here to-day and there to-morrow. He has no certain abiding-place.

27 Although that man has no great virtues, neither has he any great vices.

28 If you have anything to say, you should say it to his face. What use is there in always grumbling behind his back?

害處 Injury, harm.

奇處 That which is remarkable or wonderful, strangeness.

住處 Place of abode, residence.

壞處 Bad habits, vices, viciousness.

趣處 Enjoyment, satisfaction, happiness.

錯處 Mistake, fault.

乖處 Perverseness; craftiness; shrewdness; peculiarity.

巧處 Ingenuity, skilfulness, cleverness.

便宜處 Convenience, fitness, opportuneness.

可惡處 That which is hateful; detestableness, hatefulness.

VOCABULARY.

磨牙 *Moŏ*² *ya*². To dispute, to jangle, to wrangle, *to quarrel.*

聚 *Chü*⁴. To assemble, to gather together, *to collect*, to converge.

浮華 *Fou*² *hwa*². Luxurious, dissolute, *gay.*

傻說 *Sha*³ *shwoŏ*¹. To talk foolishly; nonsense, *silly talk.*

癡說 *Ch'ï*¹ *shwoŏ*⁴. The same.

傻笑 *Sha*³ *hsiao*⁴. To laugh as a simpleton, *to giggle.*

癡笑 *Ch'ï*¹ *hsiao*⁴. The same.

汚 *Wu*¹. Filthy, *unclean;* polluted, vile.

穢 *Hwei*⁴. *Filthy*, dirty; obscene, vile; to defile.

汚穢 *Unclean*, defiled, polluted.

寓 *Yü*⁴. *To dwell*, to lodge; a residence; a lodging place; allegory.

遮掩 *Chê*¹ *yien*³. To hide, *to conceal*, to cover up, to screen.

處所 *Ch'u*⁴ *soŏ*³. A place, *occasion.* (s.)

混雜 *Hun*⁴ *tsa*². *Mixed up*, confused.

的不肯說人的短處、答不要你偏說短處、他有好處、你不能彀說嗎。○那30些喫喝嫖賭的人、當時雖然覺得有些樂趣處、却不曉得還有苦處在後頭哩。○這31是由得自己的事情、還有甚麼難處呢。○張32耀文是本分人、小錯處他固然不能沒有、若說他有大壞處我却不信。○哄33騙人、這也是常有的事、他那個可惡處、就是單哄騙他至契的朋友。○像34張天德、那纔是眞乖巧呢、任憑人家用甚麼法子、他不上人家的當、這是他的乖處、他想出個法子來、人家却必上他的當、這是他的巧處。

29 I would rather not tell tales on other people. *Ans.* I don't want you specially to tell tales on him; if he has any virtues, can you not speak of them?

30 Although men who are given to profligacy think they have some enjoyment at the time, yet they do not consider that the bitterness will come by and by.

31 This is a matter that rests with yourself. What difficulty is there?

32 Chang Yao Wên is a well-behaved man. Minor faults, of course, he has, but the report that he has great vices I do not believe.

33 Deception is a matter of constant occurrence, but the hateful thing about him is that he makes a point of deceiving his especial friends.

34 Give me a man like Chang T'ien Tê for real shrewdness and skill. No matter what artifice you try, he is not to be caught—this is his shrewdness: but when he sets a trap for you, you are certain to be caught—this is his skilfulness.

整理 *Chêng*³ *li*³. To put in order, to set right; *to control;* to straighten up.

嘟 *Tu*¹. To mutter, to grumble.

囔 *Nang*². To speak indistinctly.

嘟囔 To grumble and mutter in an undertone.

唧 *Chi*¹·². To hum as an insect, *to babble, to mutter.*

咕 *Ku*³. To mumble, to stammer.

唧咕 *To grumble and mutter*, to murmur.

哄騙 *Hung*³ *p'ien*⁴. *To deceive*, to cheat, to impose upon, to hoax, to cozen.

可惡 *K'ê*³ *wu*⁴. *Hateful*, detestable; odious, abominable.

契 *Ch'i*⁴. A covenant, a bond; *devoted to*, sacred to. Also *hsie*⁴.

至契 *Chï*⁴ *ch'i*⁴. Very intimate, devotedly attached, bosom friends.

乖巧 *Kwai*¹ *ch'iao*³. *Shrewdness*, address, cunning, subtlety.

Notes.

3 去處 is fairly *t'ung-hsing*, but its use is much more prevalent in some places than in others.

4 This common saying is very nearly equivalent to our "Penny wise and pound foolish."

7 Bunyan's original is, "You lie at the catch again; this is not for edification."

8 善於 *good at*, is a *Wên-li* form, extensively used in colloquial.

11 The meaning is that the place to see large quantities of any article, and to buy it cheaply, is in the market, where it is collected for sale, not in the place from which it comes, or the factory in which it is made.

12 地處 is, for the most part, local in the region of Chinanfu.

14 我 is here used *generally*, which is expressed in English by using the plural.

22 十來多. In the South 多 is not added to 十來, as it frequently is in the North. The common Southern form is 十多.

23 Chinese women are very much secluded, save at religious fairs and at theatricals, where custom gives them great liberties.

29 For the use of 偏, see Les. 112.

第九十九課

二[1]人的面貌相似。○你[2]這話實在不明白、好像小孩子的話似的一樣。○好[3]生氣的人、比如一個爆燵、見火就響。○你[4]別一定不信、他說的也似乎有理。○美[5]國的天氣、和中國的類似彷彿。○人[6]若喪了良心、好比瞎子、最難走着正路。○鄭[7]牧師走道、常低着頭、彷彿心裏想甚麼似的一樣。○人[8]做慣了惡事、就好比從山上往下跑、要停住、也是不能的。○你[9]嫌我不會辦事、比方這事在你身上、諒來你也是要

TRANSLATION.

1 The faces of the two are similar.

2 This language of yours is very unintelligible, it is just like the talk of a child.

3 A man who gets angry easily is like a fire-cracker; whenever the fire touches it, it explodes.

4 Don't be too strong in your disbelief; what he says seems reasonable.

5 The climate of the United States is similar to that of China.

6 When a man's conscience is dead he is like a blind man, it is very hard to keep the right road.

7 Pastor Cheng always keeps his head down when he walks, as if he were considering something in his mind.

8 A man who has fallen into the habit of doing evil, is like a man running down hill; he cannot stop if he would.

9 You find fault with me for incapacity, but suppose this business were

LESSON XCIX.

COMPARISON.

比 To compare,—like, compared with.

比方 Compare-place,—for example, suppose.

如 Like, as.

比如 Compare-like,—for example, suppose, like.

好比 Good to compare,—for instance, as if, like, much like.

如同 Like-same,—just as, as if, similar to.

似 Like, similar to.

相似 Alike, similar.

似乎 To be like, to seem as.

似的 A colloquial enclitic added at the end of a clause to fill out the force of the previous comparison. It is very much used in some places, and but little in others. It has no equivalent in good English. "Like" is sometimes used in colloquial English in a similar way, as, "He seems tired like."

類似 Class-like,—similar to, nearly like. It is a local term much used in Shantung. It is sometimes varied to **類乎似**, or **類似乎**.

像 A likeness,—like, similar.

像似 Similar-like,—just like, very like, as if.

好像 Good-similar,—just like, very like, as if, for instance.

都像 All-like,—for example, for instance.

彷彿 Similar to, as if, like.

即如 Such as, for example. (w.)

譬如 By way of illustration, similar to, may be compared to.

VOCABULARY.

彷 *Fang*³. . . . . To be like :—See Sub.

彿 *Fu*². . . . . .Like, similar,—only used in **彷彿**.

譬 *P'i*⁴. . . *To compare;* a comparison, a parable.

美國 *Mei*³ *Kwoä*². America; the United States . . . . .of America.

牧 *Mu*⁴. . . . . . . *To shepherd;* to superintend.

這樣辦。○人[10]的性情、喜好爲惡、如同吸鐵石吸鐵一似般的。○這[11]宗族、譬如一棵樹、長起來千枝萬葉、都是一個根上生出來的。○懶[12]惰人走路、如同脚上帶着脚鐐一般。○世[13]路難行錢作馬。○用[14]德律風達信、正如對面說話一樣、○如今[15]天的冷熱、和昨天的彷彿。類似乎昨天。○比[16]方我不用人帶領路、你細細的告訴我、都是打那裏走、行不行。○我[17]想人沒受聖靈的感化、好像蠟燭沒點火似的、自己黑暗、也不能照人光明。○人[18]心似鐵、官法如爐。○能[19]用相似的理、將所要說的理顯明出來、這就爲比喻。○樹[20]有葉子、就譬如人有肺、都是爲端

yours, it is likely that you would manage it in the very same way.

10 Man's nature delights in doing evil, just as a loadstone attracts iron.

11 One's ancestry may be compared to a tree which, when grown, has a multitude of branches and leaves all of which spring from the one root.

12 A lazy man walks as if he had hobbles on his feet.

13 Life is a hard road to travel (like a road), and money is the horse.

14 Sending a message by telephone is just like speaking face to face.

15 The temperature to-day is similar to that of yesterday.

16 Suppose I should not employ any one to guide me, but you should tell me carefully all about how to go; would that answer?

17 In my opinion, a man who has not received the influence of the Holy Spirit is like a candle which is not lighted. It is dark itself, and cannot give light to others.

18 The heart of man is like iron, the law is like the furnace.

19 A comparison consists in the use of a similar idea to set forth the idea which you wish to explain.

20 The leaves of trees may be compared

牧師 *Mu⁴ shï¹*. . . . . A Christian pastor.

走道 *Tsou³ tao⁴*. . . . . *To walk*, to travel.

喜好 *Hsi³ hao⁴*. *To delight in*, to be enamored . . . . of, to love.

吸 *Hsi¹*. To draw in the breath, to inspire; to . . . . suck; *to attract*, to draw.

吸鐵石 *Hsi¹ t'ie³ shï²*. . . . . A loadstone.

宗族 *Tsung¹ tsu²*. Ancestors, *ancestry*, ancestral clan:—Note 11.

枝 *Chï¹*. . . . . . . A branch, a twig:—Les. 100.

葉 *Yie⁴*. . . . *A leaf*, blade; a thin plate of metal.

鐐 *Liao⁴*. . . . . . . A fetter, a shackle.

脚鐐 *Chiao³ liao⁴*. . . . Fetters, shackles, gyves.

對面 *Twei⁴ mien⁴*. . . . . Face to face.

聖靈 *Shêng⁴ Ling²*. . . . . The Holy Spirit.

感化 *Kan³ hwa⁴*. *To influence*, to inspire; to . . . . transform; to convert.

黑暗 *Hei¹ an⁴*. . . . . Darkness.

光明 *Kwang¹ ming²*. . . . *Light;* bright, shining.

顯明 *Hsien³ ming²*. To manifest, *to set forth*, ... to make clear.

喻 *Yü⁴*. . . . To instruct, *to explain*, to admonish.

比喻 *Pi³ yü⁴*. An illustration, *a comparison*, a . . . . parable.

肺 *Fei⁴*. . . . . The lungs.

螺 *Lŏ²*. . . . Spiral univalves; spiral, screw-like.

螄 *Sï¹*. . . . . A gasteropodous mollusk.

螺螄. A whelk, a periwinkle.

龜 *Kwei¹*. . . . . A tortoise, a terrapin.

烏龜 *Wu¹ kwei¹*. *A black tortoise;* a whore- . . . . monger, a satyr.

比作 *Pi³ tsŏ⁴*. . . . . . . To compare to or with.

銀錢 *Yin² ch'ien²*. . . . . *Money*, specie, wealth.

糞土 *Fên⁴ t'u³*. . . . . . *Dung*, filth.

臉面 *Lien³ mien⁴*. *Reputation*, honor, self-re- . . . . spect, face, influence.

義氣 *I⁴ ch'i⁴*. . . . Uprightness, integrity, *honor*.

氣用的。○我21不叫這些小人兒、在這裏吵鬧、他們就說、羊群（螺螄）裏跳（揀）出駱駝（烏龜）來喇、這不是把我比作一個駱駝（烏龜）嗎。○銀22錢如糞土、臉面（義氣）值千金。○有23一個姓張的啞吧孩子、跟李先生學着說話、起初是一竅不通、這幾天似乎懂點門路喇。○我24今天看見一個說相聲的、說得眞好、他學女人說話、聽着恰像女人的聲音、學孩子說話、聽着恰像孩子的聲音。○打25抱不平、是甚麼意思呢、答比如摩西、看見伊及的督工人、暴打一個以色列人、他心裏就懷不平之氣、下手打那督工人、這就叫打抱不平。○看26劉安的相貌、如同徠獃

to the lungs of men ; both are used for breathing.

21 I would not let these youngsters make a noise here, whereupon they said, "A camel has jumped out of the flock of sheep," ("A black turtle found among periwinkles"). Is not this comparing me to a camel (turtle)?

22 Money is as dung ; reputation (honor) is worth thousands of gold.

23 A dumb boy named Chang is Mr. Li's pupil in learning to articulate. His mind was utterly blank at first, but these few days he seems to be getting a little idea of learning.

24 I saw a polyphonist to-day who performed first-rate. When he imitated a woman speaking, it sounded exactly like a woman's voice ; when he imitated a child talking, it sounded exactly like a child's voice.

25 What is the meaning of [the phrase] vindicating the oppressed? *Ans.* For example: when Moses saw the Egyptian task-master cruelly beating an Israelite, his mind was affected with a sense of the injustice, and he at once interfered and beat the task-master. This is what is called vindicating the oppressed.

起初 *Ch‘i^3 ch‘u^1*. *At first*, in the beginning, primarily :—Les. 126.

說相聲 *Shwoă^1 hsiang^4 shêng^1*. To mimic sounds and voices :—Note 24.

相貌 *Hsiang^4 mao^4*. Countenance, physiognomy, *face*.

列 *Lie^4*. To arrange in order ; to marshal ; a rank, a series ; regularly ; severally.

徠 *Lai^2*. To induce, to encourage. (w.)

徠獃臭 *Lai^2 tai^1 ch‘ou^4*. A clown, *a booby ;* a dirty beast, a dowdy.

能耐 *Nêng^2 nai^4*. Ability, potency, efficiency, *capacity*.

能爲 *Nêng^2 wei^2*. Ability, capacity, force.

才幹 *Ts‘ai^2 kan^4*. *Ability*, talent, capacity.

名號 *Ming^2 hao^4*. A name, *a title*, an appellation.

開頭 *K‘ai^1 t‘ou^2*. To begin, to *lead off*, to date from :—Les. 126.

萬世 *Wan^4 shï^4*. Ten thousand generations, the ages, forever.

失落 *Shï^1 loă^4*. To lose, to let slip.

NOTES.

5 The second 的 in this sentence would be left out by many speakers without at all feeling the incongruity of the construction.

9 在你身上 *On your body ;* i.e., *concerned you.*

11 The initial 這 simply marks the subject of discourse. When a Chinese teacher is asked to define 宗族 he always does so by explaining the two words separately, which makes the term as a whole not a little confusing. It means ancestors, or ancestry, or ancestral clan, according to circumstances. It is a book, rather than a colloquial, term. 千枝萬葉 is an expression in the studied form of books.

13 世路 does not here form a phrase, as elsewhere, but means simply, *the course or way of life.* This is the Peking form of the saying and does not illustrate the lesson. Compare, "Money makes the mare go."

臭一般、一點不像有能爲耐的樣子、但是和他細談起來、就曉得他眞是個有才幹、有志氣的人。○萬27事只有天作主、算來半點不由人、這話一點不錯、卽都如像秦始皇、他取那名號、就是打算從自己開頭、往下直傳到萬世、那知道打算的很遠、却失落的很快、剛到二世、就被滅了。

26 Liu An has the face of a booby; he does not look as if he had the least capacity, but if you get into conversation with him, you will find that he is a man of ability and decision.

27 The saying is quite true, that "all events are controlled by the will of heaven; the plans of men are entirely futile." For example, Ch'in Sï Hwang took this title with the idea that from him, as the first, the succession would continue throughout the ages; but although his plans were very far-reaching they were very soon overturned, for in the second generation the dynasty was broken up.

18 The structure of this sentence is *Wên*: it becomes Mandarin only by being quoted and used as a common saying. 官法 does not mean simply the law, but all the means and methods by which officers control the people.

21 小人兒 The use of 兒 gives a diminutive touch similar to our word "youngster." Neither of the comparisons here used seems specially apt.

23 一竅不通 *Not a single orifice open*, that is, utterly stupid or blank.

24 說相聲的 A small showman who stands behind a curtain and exhibits his powers of mimicry for the entertainment of the listeners.

25 打抱不平 To interfere for the righting or the revenging of the wrongs of others.

26 徠獃臭 is a widely used phrase, but has different meanings in different places.

27 秦始皇 Lit., *Ch'in the First Emperor.* He destroyed the feudatory system of ancient times and consolidated all the petty states into one empire. He declared himself Emperor, taking the term "First Emperor" as his title. He was a man of ability, but made himself infamous by his celebrated edict ordering all books to be burned, and the chief scholars of the land to be buried alive (焚書坑儒). His son was a man of inferior ability and lost the empire bequeathed to him.

LESSON C.

CLASSIFIERS.

陣 A rank,—classifier of things that come with a sudden start, as wind, rain, smoke.

座 A seat,—classifier of hills, walled towns, temples, pagodas, etc.

場 An arena,—classifier of rain, wind, and of affairs which involve contention or emulation, as lawsuits, quarrels, examinations, etc.

枝 A twig,—classifier of slender things, as pens, pencils, arrows, etc.

鋪 To spread out,—classifier of things spread out, as beds, matting, etc.

桿 A staff,—classifier of guns, spears, steelyards, etc.

盞 A shallow cup,—classifier of lamps and wine cups.

顆 A kernel,—classifier of small round things, as beads, pearls, etc.

穗 An ear of grain,—classifier of heads or ears of grain.

粒 A grain,—classifier of things in grains, as sand, grain, etc.

牀 A bed,—classifier of bedclothes.

層 A layer,—classifier of stories, strata, tiers, specifications, etc.

掛 To hang up,—classifier of things hung up, as watches, saddles, necklaces, etc., also, in the South, of bunches of grapes.

嘟嚕 A bunch,—classifier of fruit in bunches, as grapes, bananas, etc.

第一百課

這[1]陣風颺的實在涼。○前[2]面那座山、生長的實在古怪。
幾[3]乎惹出一場大事來。○恩[4]姐戴着三枝石榴花
兒。○這[5]鋪張牀太短、伸不開腿。○他[6]們那場官司、經人
說和了。○那[7]是一桿行秤、每斤足十六兩。○光[8]點一
盞燈不彀、可以再點兩枝蠟蠟燭。○這[9]場雨、下的正是
時候。○我[10]纔買了一根枝菸袋、你看值多少錢。○上[11]古
迦南地的葡萄、一嘟嚕掛彀兩個人抬的。○景[12]州城西
門裏、有一座十三層的高塔。○今[13]年十分年成、叫這
塲風颺去了一半。○一[14]座青石橋、兩邊都是朱紅欄
杆。○我[15]家裏有兩鋪炕、兩鋪張牀、冬天睡炕、夏天睡牀、

TRANSLATION.

1 This wind blows decidedly cool.
2 That mountain in front of us has a very strange conformation.
3 I came near stirring up a serious affair.
4 Sister Grace is wearing three sprigs of pomegranate flowers.
5 This bed is too short; one cannot stretch out his legs.
6 By the interposition of a third party that lawsuit of theirs has been compromised.
7 That is a standard steelyard; every catty is full sixteen ounces.
8 To light one lamp only is not sufficient, you may light two candles in addition.
9 This rain came just at the right time.
10 I have just bought a pipe. How much do you think it is worth?
11 In ancient times one bunch of the grapes of Canaan was enough for two men to carry.
12 Inside the west gate of the city of Chingchou, there is a high pagoda of thirteen stories.
13 This year gave promise of full crops, but the half was destroyed by this storm of wind.
14 A black stone bridge with a vermilion red balustrade on either side.
15 We have in our house two *k'angs* and

VOCABULARY.

桿 *Kan*³. A staff, a handle, a lever, a club, a pole:—see Sub.

盞 *Chan*³. A shallow cup for oil or wine:—see Sub.

顆 *K'ê*¹. A kernel, a crystal:—see Sub.

粒 *Li*⁴. A grain, a particle:—see Sub.

穗 *Swei*⁴. An ear, a head, a spikelet:—see Sub.

嚕 *Lu*³. Protuberant; a bunch.

嘟嚕 *Tu*¹ *lu*³. To hang down, to pout, to be down in the mouth; a bunch, a cluster:—see Sub.

前面 *Ch'ien*² *mien*⁴. *In front of*, in the foreground, before.

古怪 *Ku*³ *kwai*⁴. Antique; *strange*, old, singular, exceptional, grotesque.

戴 *Tai*⁴. *To wear on the head or face;* to bear; to honor.

榴 *Liu*². The pomegranate.

石榴 *Shï*² *liu*². The pomegranate.

上古 *Shang*⁴ *ku*³. Ancient times, anciently.

塔 *T'a*³. *A pagoda*, a tower, a pillar.

十分 *Shï*² *fên*¹. Complete, *full*, perfect; the whole, entire:—Les. 137.

朱紅 *Chu*¹ *hung*². *Vermilion red*, bright red.

欄 *Lan*². A railing, *a balustrade;* a pen, a cage, a paled enclosure.

杆 *Kan*¹. A club, a staff; a pole, *a post*.

欄杆 *A balustrade*, a railing, a paling.

淒 *Ch'i*¹. Bleak; shivering; sad, *mournful*.

淒涼 *Ch'i*¹ *liang*². Sad, *melancholy*, lonely.

菊 *Chü*². The aster, the marigold, the daisy, the chrysanthemum.

長壽菊 *Ch'ang*¹ *shou*⁴ *chü*². The marigold.

○凡16是一座城、裏邊就有一座城隍廟。○昨17兒晚上、一陣風一陣雨的、那個聲兒、眞是淒涼。○南18園裏有一科萬長壽菊、開了七枝花兒、實在好看。○有19些散勇、偷了三百多桿洋鎗、現在被官兒捉住了。○這20五顆珠子、是我父親在蘇州買的、二百銀子一顆。○北21京城內有座樓、叫作翠雲樓、樓上樓下、大小有百十個閣子。○一22穗穀穀子、大約有三千顆粒、一穗高秫粱秫、大約有一千顆粒、一穗麥子、大約有一百顆粒、一穗稻子、大約有八十顆粒。○西23屋那張鋪牀上、有一牀毯子、一牀氈氈子、一牀皮褥子、兩牀綿褥子、兩牀被單子、三牀被被子。○西24國客店、大概都是四五層的

two beds. In the winter we sleep on the *k'angs*, and in the summer, on the beds.

16 Every walled city has in it a temple to Ch'êng Hwang.

17 Yesterday evening the sound of the successive gusts of wind and rain was decidedly melancholy.

18 In the south garden is a marigold on which seven flowers have opened. It is very beautiful.

19 There were some discharged soldiers who stole over three hundred foreign guns. They have just been arrested by the officers.

20 These five pearls were bought by my father in Soochow for two hundred taels each.

21 In the city of Peking there is a tower called the Emerald Cloud Tower, in which there are, above and below, great and small, upwards of a hundred balconies.

22 A head of millet has, on an average, about three thousand grains; a head of sorghum has about one thousand grains; a head of wheat has about one hundred grains, and a head of rice about eighty grains.

23 On the bed in the west room there is a carpet rug, a felt rug, a fur rug, two cotton mattresses, two sheets and three quilts.

萬壽菊 *Wan4 shou4 chü2*. . . . . The same.

勇 *Yung3*. Brave, courageous, valorous; fierce; . . . . *a soldier*, a brave.

粱 *Liang2*. . . . . Millet.

高粱 *Kao1 liang2*. Barbadoes millet, a species of . . . . sorghum. *Sorghum vulgare*.

秫 *Shu4*. . . . . . The same. Generally doubled.

稻 *Tao4*. . . . . *Growing rice*, paddy; rice.

毯 *T'an3*. . . . . . A rug, carpet, drugget.

氈 *Chan1*. . . . . Felt of all kinds.

客店 *K'ê4 tien4*. *An inn*, a hotel, a lodging- . . . . house.

被單 *Pei4 tan1*. . . . . A bed sheet.

齊全 *Ch'i2 ch'üen2*. *Complete*, perfect, finished; . . . . in full, all.

痢 *Li4*. . . . . Dysentery, flux.

痢疾 *Li4 chi2*. . . . . . Dysentery.

傷寒 *Shang1 han2*. . . . . Typhus or typhoid fever.

餓 *Ê4, ngê4*. . . . . Hungry, starving.

餓死 *Ê4 si3*. . . . . . To starve to death.

道光 *Tao4 Kwang1*. The sixth Emperor of the . . . . present dynasty, who reigned from 1821 to 1851.

凍死 *Tung4 si3*. . . . . To freeze to death.

NOTES.

2 The Chinese speak of hills as if they had grown, sometimes using 生, and sometimes 長, a result, no doubt, of their evolution ideas.

7 A 行秤 is a steelyard representing the standard weight current among the business men of a given place, and professing to give full sixteen ounces to the catty. In point of fact, however, the majority of such steelyards weigh light, when tested by the legal standard.

9 正是時候 Most learners will be inclined to say 在 for 是, and in fact 在 might be used without impropriety, but 是 is the more common and truly idiomatic form.

大樓、每人一間房、裏頭預備的手巾、臉盆、鏡子、鋪盖、樣樣齊全、所以住店、就和在家一樣。○饡[25]不死的痢疾、餓不死的傷寒、我姐姐那一年得傷寒病、一連八天、一顆粒米也沒下去、到底還沒餓死呢。○道[26]光十五年正月二十六日、下了一場大雪、有五尺多深、因為那一天是個好日子、所以娶親的、有許多凍死的、也有娶錯了的。

24 In western countries the inns are mostly four or five stories high; each guest has a room which is furnished with towel, wash-basin, mirror and bedding, all complete, hence staying in an inn is the same as if at home.

25 There is no danger of eating too much in dysentery, nor too little in typhoid fever. The year my sister had the fever, she did not eat a grain of rice for eight days, and yet she did not starve.

26 In the fifteenth year of Tao Kwang, on the twenty-sixth of the first month, there was a great fall of snow of over five feet deep. Because that day happened to be a lucky day, many who were getting married were frozen to death, and some even brought home the wrong wife.

---

10 菸袋 Not *tobacco bag or pouch*, as would seem most natural, but *tobacco pipe*. The 袋 refers to the *bowl* of the pipe.

11 In some places 穗 is used as the classifier of grapes.

12 景州 A city in Chili, about seven hundred li south of Peking. If 十三層的高塔 were transposed to 十三層高的塔, it would mean, *a pagoda thirteen stories high.*

13 The "*gave promise*" is not formally expressed, but is implied in the structure of the sentence.

17 Note here the peculiar force of 的, marking, as it does, the alternate succession of wind and rain. The phrase 那個聲兒 may be connected, either with the clause above or with the clause following, making a slight difference in meaning, which is difficult to present in an English translation.

19 散勇 *Scattered soldiers.* Soldiers are often discharged far from home, and with little or no money. They then become vagrants, ready for every species of crime.

20 二百銀子 The 兩 is left out for brevity—a common practice in colloquial.

22 高粱 Is *t'ung-hsing*, but refers mostly to the grain as growing or on the threshing floor. After it is garnered or ground into flour, it is, in most places, called 秫 or rather 秫秫. This distinction, though common, is not universal.

25 饡不死 etc, *A dysentery cannot be stuffed to death nor a typhoid fever starved to death;* that is, dysentery is a disease in which the patient need not fear eating too much, and fever is one in which he need not fear eating too little. The construction is peculiar and not easy for a beginner to analyse.

26 The fact that the day was a lucky one carries with it the necessary implication that there were many weddings on that day, which accounts for the seeming absurdity of saying that because it was a lucky day many who were getting married were frozen to death. In the excitement and dangers incident to rescuing various parties from the snow and resuscitating those who were half frozen, some of the brides were carried to the wrong place.

LESSON CI.

THE AUXILIARY VERBS 盡, 定, 完 AND 成.

盡 To exhaust,—added as an auxiliary to such words as will take the qualifying idea of exhaustion or completion.

定 To fix,—added as an auxiliary to such words as will take the qualifying idea of certainty or stability.

完 To finish,—added as an auxiliary to such words as will take the qualifying idea of finishing or completing.

成 To effect, to complete,—added as an auxiliary to such words as will take the qualifying idea of completion or maturity.

第一百一課

這[1]是會上議定的章程、不能更改。○學[2]臺到泰安、現在考完了沒有。○凡[3]事當留餘步、說盡了、却不可做盡了。○已[4]經講定了價、不好再少給錢。○世[5]間的大事、必得趁着個好機會、纔能辦成。○等[6]他說完了、你再說、不要這樣插嘴、截(隔)人的話。○我[7]纔從王天保那裏來、他一(言)定是不肯、所以你總(要)得想法子開消。○這[8]麼一點事情、三天還做不完、眞齷(躁)齪人。○怪[9]不得我們老了、你看這些後生、幾年都長成大漢子了。○若[10]沒有甚麼要緊的事情、可以等他背完了書、我再請他出來。○依[11]我看、你不表明更好、一表明、是假也弄成眞了。○若[12]叫甯老爺知

TRANSLATION.

1 This is the settled policy of the society and cannot be changed.

2 Has the chancellor completed the examinations since his arrival at T'ai An?

3 Some allowance must be made in everything. One may speak radically, but must not act radically.

4 Having settled the price it will not do afterwards to pay less.

5 In matters of importance in this world, one must seize the favorable opportunity if he would succeed.

6 Wait till he has finished speaking before you begin. You must not interpose your talk and interrupt people in this way.

7 I have just come from Wang T'ien Pao's. He absolutely refuses, therefore you will have to find some method of liquidation.

8 Such a little matter as this not finished in three days! Really you are too provoking.

9 No wonder we are growing old. Look at these young folks how, in a few years, they have come to be full grown men.

10 If you have no important business, suppose you wait till he has finished hearing his recitations and I will then ask him to come out.

11 As I see it, it would be better for you not to examine into it. As soon as you make an ado about it, what

VOCABULARY.

泰安 *T'ai⁴ an¹*. A Fu city situated at the foot of the sacred mountain, 泰山.

餘步 *Yü² pu⁴*. Something held in reserve, an *allowance*, a loophole.

插 *Ch'a¹*. To insert, to thrust into; to interfere or meddle; *to interrupt*.

插嘴 *Ch'a¹ tswei³*. To interrupt in speaking.

言定 *Yien² ting⁴*. Positively, unequivocally, *absolutely*.

開消 *K'ai¹ hsiao¹*. To pay off, to settle up, to discharge, *to liquidate*.

甯 *Ning⁴*. A surname.

後生 *Hou⁴ shêng¹*. Children; *young folks*.

往常 *Wang³ ch'ang²*. *Hitherto*; usual, ordinary.

詩經 *Shï¹ ching¹*. The book of poetry,—originally collated by Confucius.

二五眼 *Êr⁴ wu³ yien³*. Mean, scrubby, shabby, beggarly.

二五不當 *Êr⁴ wu³ pu⁴ tang⁴*. Same.

兆 *Chao⁴*. An omen, a sign; a trillion.

菓木 *Kwoa³ mu⁴*. Fruits generally.

蹭 *Ts'êng⁴*. *To rub past*, to miss by a little. See *tsêng⁴*.

蹭工 *Ts'êng⁴ kung¹*. To kill time, to dawdle, to dilly-dally, *to idle time*.

下緊 *Hsia⁴ chin³*. To hurry up; diligent.

决 *Chüe²*. *To decide*, to settle; positively.

道、他們却不了得不了成。○學[13]堂房往常的規矩、都是念完了四書、再念詩經、如今也有先念詩經、後念四書的。○劉[14]玉子的親事、你給他辦成了沒有、答嗯、他那個二五不眼當的樣子、誰肯和他結親呢。○王[15]兆舉那個病、死也不死得不死了活、也不活得不活成。○雖[16]說人的良心、已經喪盡、却仍有發現的時候。○這[17]園裏的菓木、趕明天怕摘不完、你還直蹭工、不下上緊的摘。○辦[18]事總得決斷、不可猶豫不定。○黃[19]泉路上無老少、誰能保定自己、必要活到明天呢。○現[20]在酒也喝完了、飯也喫完了、從來說、客去主人安、我們不如告辭散了罷。○要[21]戒忌大烟、必得拿定了主意、至死一口不喫、但是姚謹德、

is false will be regarded as true.

12 If Ning Lao Yie finds it out, they will be in a strait.

13 Hitherto the general custom in schools has been to finish committing the Four Books before taking up the Odes; but there are some now-a-days who first commit the Odes and afterwards the Four Books.

14 Did you get that marriage engagement of Liu Yü-tsï's settled? *Ans.* Humph! who would be willing to make a marriage alliance with such a scarecrow as he is?

15 That disease of Wang Chao Chü's is such as to keep him lingering along more dead than alive.

16 Although we may say a man has lost all conscience, yet the time will come when his conscience will revive.

17 I fear you will not get the fruit in this orchard all gathered by to-morrow, and yet you are persistently idling away time and not pushing the work.

18 In business you should decide promptly, and not hesitate in uncertainty.

19 The grave makes no distinction of old or young. Who can guarantee that he himself will certainly live until to-morrow?

20 We have now finished drinking the wine and eating the food. It is an old saying, "When the guests are gone the host is at rest." We would

决斷 *Chüe*³ *twan*⁴. *To decide;* positive, decided, determined, certain.

猶豫 *Yiu*² *yü*⁴. Undecided, wavering, *hesitating,* uncertain.

泉 *Ch'üen*². . . . A spring, a fountain.

黃泉路 *Hwang*² *ch'üen*² *lu*⁴. *The grave;* Hades:—Note 19.

告辭 *Kao*⁴ *ts'ï*². To take leave, to ask to be excused.

姚 *Yao*². . . . Handsome, *a surname.*

皮肉 *P'i*² *jou*⁴. . . . The body, the physical man.

家財 *Chia*¹ *ts'ai*². . . . Property, *patrimony.*

順從 *Shun*⁴ *ts'ung*². To obey, *to follow the wishes of another,* to gratify.

子孫 *Tsï*³ *sun*¹. . . . Descendants, posterity.

豪 *Hao*². Eminent, superior; martial, brave; a leader, *a champion.*

傑 *Chie*². . . . One eminent for virtue and prowess.

豪傑 *A hero,* a knight, a champion.

機謀 *Chi*¹ *mou*². *Strategy;* manœuvre; trick, wile, device.

磡 *K'an*³. . . . A ledge, a dike, *a sill.*

象牙 *Hsiang*⁴ *ya*². . . . An elephant's tusk, ivory.

扇 *Shan*⁴. . . . *A fan;* leaf of a door, window, etc.

股 *Ku*³. The thigh, the rump; a share in business; a chapter, a head; a proportion, a quota; *a strand, a rib.*

鑡 *Ch'a*¹. To break off, to snap in two. [Not aspirated in Shantung.] Also *ch'a*².

齊各鑡 *Ch'i*² *kê*⁴ *ch'a*¹. Snapped off, square off, square in two.

腕 *Wan*⁴. . . . A flexible or universal joint.

脚腕 *Chiao*³ *wan*⁴. . . . The ankle-joint.

踒 *Wo*¹. . . To double up; to wrench, *to sprain.*

是一個愛惜皮肉（惜皮愛肉）的人、所以我看定他戒（忌）不了。〇爲[22]父母的喪事、費盡家財、那赶上父母在堂、叫父母喫點子、穿點子、順從他、不惹他生氣呢。〇俗[23]語說、十分精明使九分、留着一分給子孫、十分精明使盡了、養的兒孫不如人、所以從古有許多英雄豪傑、用盡他的機謀、誰也制不得了他、但他養的兒孫、多有二五不知一十的。〇我[24]從家裏往外一走、叫門檻絆了一跌、把我的象牙扇股子、齊各鎚的跌成兩截兒、把脚腕子蹽得也腫了。

better tender our acknowledgments and take our departure.

21 In order to break off opium, one must resolve not to touch it if he dies [for want of it]. But Yao Chin Tê is a very self-indulgent man. I am confident he cannot break it off.

22 To spend all your patrimony on your father's and mother's funerals is by no means as good as to give them something to eat and something to wear while they are still alive, and to follow their wishes and not provoke them to anger.

23 The saying is, "Use only nine parts of your shrewdness, reserve one part for the benefit of your children." If you use your shrewdness to the utmost, your children will be inferior. Hence it is that from ancient times there have been many champions and heroes whom, if they put forth all their strategy, no one could match, who yet have brought up children most of whom did not know that twice five make ten.

24 As I was going out at the door I stumbled and fell over the door sill, breaking the ivory frame of my fan square in two, and wrenching my ankle so that it is quite swollen.

Notes.

1 Note the difference between 議定 and 一定. The first means *settled, decided upon*, the second *fixed, certain*. They are only distinguished by a tone, and are easily confused in speaking.

3 留餘步 *To make some abatement from the strict rule of equity or prerogative as a measure of conciliation or of precaution.*

7 開消 is sometimes used of satisfying an obligation or demand other than monetary. The proper translation in this place depends on what it was that Wang T'ien Pao absolutely demurred to.

11 表明 *To make manifest*, here means to take up some charge or slander, deny it and demand investigation for the purpose of clearing oneself.

15 In its literal construction the Chinese says that the *disease* is "more dead than alive." The meaning, however, is that the *person* is in this condition on account of the disease. Such a grammatical incongruity is not appreciated by the average Chinese speaker or writer.

14 二五眼 is a widely used colloquial phrase, the writing and analysis of which are uncertain. Some prefer to write 二無眼, that is *both eyes gone, good for nothing at all.* The other form may mean, *Won't pawn for ten* [*twice five*] *cash.*

16 Or, *there are still times when it revives.*

18 猶豫不定 *A state of uncertainty*,—a book phrase, but in common use.

19 黃泉路 *The yellow spring road*, a poetical description of the grave.

20 Social enjoyment has but little to do with a Chinese feast. It is simply a feast of eating and drinking. When this is over the sooner the guests go the better.

21 愛惜皮肉 *To be tender of oneself, to be afraid of any hardship or physical pain, self-indulgent.* 惜皮愛肉 is a rhetorical transposition of the same phrase.

22 那 is interrogative and a contraction for 那裡; 在堂 *in the hall*, that is, *alive.*

23 精明 here means *shrewdness*, especially such as involves craft in overreaching others. It is often replaced in this connection by 精細. The proverb expresses a superstition that a man of great shrewdness, who uses his abilities to the utmost to overreach others, and to protect himself from suffering the least wrong, will have stupid children.

24 絆了一跌. In Peking 跌 is read *tsai*[1] in this connection.

第一百二課

這[1]部書我從來沒看見。○若[2]遇見人家說體(貼)己話、就該閃開。○王[3]天雲的腿、教(給)狗咬破了。○有[4]雨布蓋着、大約不能淋(濕)透了。○我[5]在天津的時候、瞧見李中堂、上道臺衙門去赴席。○這[6]幾天實在冷、我們的水缸水甕、在家裏都凍破了。○從[7]多日找他、也找不着、今天恰巧叫(給)我碰見了。○神[8]的事、誰能參透了呢。○張[9]大文的文章、原作就好、叫先生這一改、倒改壞了。○我[10]聞見這屋裏有點邪(惡)味(氣)、你們不聞見嗎。○先[11]使兩家把話說透了、還有不能了的事嗎。○這[12]不是爲打架門毆、你就是停幾天、也停不壞。○雨[13]衣還沒有穿迭(及)當、

TRANSLATION.

1 I have never seen this book before.
2 If you happen upon persons speaking together privately, you should keep away from them.
3 Wang T'ien Yün's leg was torn by a dog.
4 Being covered with a waterproof cloth, it will not likely be wet through.
5 When I was in Tientsin, I got a sight of Li Chung-t'ang as he was going to the Taotai's office to a feast.
6 It has been very cold these few days; our water jar was burst even in the house.
7 After having searched for him for a long time without success, I luckily met him to-day.
8 Who can comprehend the ways of God?
9 Chang Ta Wên's essay was originally very good, but it has been ruined by the teacher's corrections.
10 I smell a little bad odor in this room; do you not smell it?
11 Let the two families first fully understand each other, and there is nothing that can not be settled.
12 This is not a case of assault and battery, there will be no harm done if you do wait a few days.
13 Before I could get on my rain coat I was wet through all over.

LESSON CII.

THE AUXILIARY VERBS 見透, AND 破.

見 To perceive,—added as an auxiliary to such words as will take the qualifying idea of perception.

透 To pass through,—added as an auxiliary to such words as will take the qualifying idea of penetrating.

破 To split, to detect,—added as an auxiliary to such words as will take the qualifying idea of splitting, or of detecting.

VOCABULARY.

貼己 *T'ie¹ chi³.* Partial to self; personal, *private,* intimate.

中堂 *Chung¹ t'ang².* A minister of state:—Note 5.

道臺 *Tao⁴ t'ai².* The intendent of circuit, commonly called Taotai, an officer next in rank above a Chifu, and having functions partly civil and partly military.

甕 *Wêng⁴.* A water pot or amphora.

參 *Ts'an¹.* *To examine,* to compare; to mix, to mingle; to prepare; to visit a superior; to impeach. Also *ts'ên¹* and *shên¹.*

原作 *Yüen² tsoă⁴.* The original copy or model, *the original.*

邪味 *Hsie² wei⁴.* A mouldy mephitic smell, *a bad odor,* a stench.

渾身都濕透了。○我[14]沒防備、叫他一把、把我的衣裳撕破了。○還[15]有七八里路、一上這個山嶺、就望見喇。○王[16]金堂那個人、成事不足、敗事有餘、好事他也能辦壞了。○我[17]請他、就是要他講醫書給我聽、他若是識不透那些字、怎麼能講得透呢。○從[18]來沒遇見像你這樣不懂理的、你是一個男子漢、怎麼和人家的女人打罵呢、你忘了男不和女鬥的話嗎。○再[19]給我做襪子、要肥一點兒、這雙太瘦、還沒等着穿破、就先撐破了。○那[20]座廟已經狼狽(破爛)了多年、這遢我去看見、又修的煥然一新(湛新)的。○話[21]不說不知、木不鑽不透、把話說開了、就和木頭鑽透

14 I was not on my guard when, with one clutch, he tore my clothes.

15 We have still seven or eight li; when we have ascended this hill we can see it.

16 That man Wang Chin T'ang has more capacity for failing than he has for succeeding; he can make a mess of the most feasible business.

17 The very purpose for which I engaged him was to explain [certain] medical books to me. If he does not know all the characters, how can he explain the books?

18 I have never met such a senseless fellow as you. How is it that you, a man, fight and wrangle with another man's wife? Have you forgotten the saying, "A man must not fight with a woman?"

19 When you make me another pair of stockings, I want them a little wider; these are too tight; they burst before they were worn out.

20 That temple had been in ruins many years, but when I visited it this time, it was repaired and glittering in a brand new dress.

21 "Words unspoken remain unknown; wood not bored is still unpenetrated." Speaking things out plainly is like boring through the wood.

22 When one has seen through the ways

惡氣 *Ê*⁴ *ch'i*⁴. *An offensive smell;* a poisonous gas.

毆 *Ou*¹. *To fisticuff,* to maul; to wrangle.

鬥毆 *Tou*⁴ *ou*¹. To fight, to brawl; *assault and battery.*

嶺 *Ling*³. A ridge, a mountain range.

山嶺 *Shan*¹ *ling*³. A range of hills or mountains; *the crest of a hill.*

破爛 *P'o*⁴ *lan*⁴. Torn, tattered; dilapidated, *in ruins.*

狼 *Lang*². A wolf; cruel, fierce.

狽 *Pei*⁴. An animal similar to a wolf, a jerboa.

狼狽 Destroyed, broken down, used up, *in ruins:*—Note 20.

煥 *Hwan*⁴. Brilliant, resplendent. (w.)

湛 *Chan*⁴. Deep; to steep, to imbibe; very, *exceeding:*—Les. 142.

煥然湛新 *Hwan*⁴ *jan*² *chan*⁴ *hsin*¹. Resplendently new, shining in a new dress:—Note 20.

煥然一新 *Hwan*⁴ *jan*² *i*¹ *hsin*¹. The same.

點火 *Tien*³ *hwo*³. To strike a match, to strike a fire with flint and steel.

斜 *Hsie*², *hsia*². *Oblique,* inclined, awry; diagonal; distorted.

夢見 *Mêng*⁴ *chien*⁴. To see in a dream, to dream of.

失火 *Shï*¹ *hwo*³. To take fire, to have a conflagration:—Note 25.

謀合 *Mou*² *hê*². To scheme, *to plan,* to plot together.

局 *Chü*². Contracted, confined; *an affair,* an enterprise; a company, a club; a manufactory; a depôt; head-quarters.

了一樣。○看[22]破世事懶睜眼。○趕[23]脚的去點火吃菸的工夫、牲口就在前頭驚了、馱子也翻了、把我的兩個皮箱、都跌摔壞咯。○這[24]孩子的眼、從小帶點斜、以後好了、今年上學念書的時候、叫先生一巴掌又打壞了。○我[25]昨天黑夜、做了一個夢、夢見又失火、又吃包子、必主今天要生氣、答說破大吉、說破了就好喇。○昨[26]天大家謀商合量的事情、已經有七八成、誰料想有個局外人、一句話弄壞了。○管[27]倉的監督、和看倉的差役花戶、通同作弊、將倉裏的米、偷出了許多、現在叫大人查破了。

of the world, he is loath to open his eyes.

23 While the muleteer went to light his pipe, the mule going on took fright, and, overturning his load, broke both of my leather trunks.

24 From childhood this boy's eyes had a slight squint, but by and by they became right. While he was going to school this year, the teacher gave him a box on the ear which made them as bad as ever.

25 I had a dream last night in which I dreamed that the house caught fire, and that I was eating dumplings, which certainly means that I will get in a passion to-day. *Ans.* "Whatever is solved becomes good fortune;" having solved it, it will be all right.

26 The business we were all planning yesterday was in a fair way to succeed, when an outsider unexpectedly came along and by a single word spoiled it all.

27 The overseer of the storehouses and the subordinates in charge all conspired together and stole a large quantity of the rice in the storehouse. Their superior officer has just now found it out.

局外 *Chü wai*⁴...... An outsider, a looker-on.

倉 *Ts'ang*¹. *A granary, a storehouse;* hurried, ... flurried. [See *chien*¹.

監 *Chien*⁴......To examine, to inspect; to revise.

監督 *Chien*⁴ *tu*¹. *An overseer,* a superintendent, ... an inspector; a bishop.

花戶 *Hwa*¹ *hu*⁴. The people; tax-payers. *Subor- ... ... dinate keepers of the imperial store-house.* (N.)

差役 *Ch'ai*¹ *i*⁴. Attendants, retainers, *subor- ... ... dinates.*

通同 *T'ung*¹ *t'ung*². All, the whole:—same as ... ... 通統.

弊 *Pi*⁴...... *Corrupt,* vicious; deteriorated.

作弊 *Tsoă*² *pi*⁴. To cheat, to embezzle, to ... ... swindle, *to steal public funds.*

查 *Ch'a*²........ To examine, to inquire into.

NOTES.

2 The reason why 見 is added to words meaning to meet, is that meeting brings the object to the perception of the senses.

3 咬破 is to bite so as to produce a bleeding wound.

4 The Chinese use oiled cotton cloth to protect them from the rain. 淋 limits the meaning to *rain,* while 濕 leaves it indefinite as to how the water comes, whether by raining, splashing or soaking. 淋, however, is not used in the South.

5 李中堂, usually called by his proper name, 李鴻章. The term 中堂 is an official title, corresponding approximately to *minister* or *cabinet officer,* usually translated Grand Secretary. There are four—two principal (正) and two vice (副), two being Chinese and two Manchus.

7 從多日 *From many a day;* i. e., *for a long time.*

8 A heathen reading this sentence would doubtless take 神 in the plural. As Chinese has no plural form, the distinction of singular and plural has to be gathered from the context, or from general usage. Ambiguities of this kind are frequent in Chinese.

16 成事不足敗事有餘. *In capacity to accomplish he is deficient, of capacity to ruin he has an excess.* 好事 *A good thing;* i. e., any business or affair, that is free from embarrassing circumstances.

20 In Peking 狼狽 is only applied to persons, but in general Mandarin it is also applied to houses, and generally to anything in a state of disorder or ruin. 煥然潛新 is somewhat bookish. 然 is used as a 虛字, or *empty character,* as characters used for the sake of euphony are called.

第一百三課

他[1]鋪排這麼些活、我們怎麼個做法呢。○各[2]人有各人的筆法。○現[3]在天朝的海防、大概都用德國兵法。○算[4]法有四個大法子爲根本、就是加法、減法、乘法、除法。○你[5]又受了他的搪(拖)拖喇、像你這樣的要法、永遠也要不出錢來。○變[6](玩耍)戲法的、都是用的手法、不是用的什麼邪法。○他[7]講的一點次序也沒有、叫人怎麼個聽法、怎麼個記法呢。○先[8]生打學生、雖說應當、也但看是怎麼個打法。○

Translation.

1 How can we get through with so much work as all this which he has laid out for us?

2 Every man has his own handwriting.

3 At the present time the soldiers on the coast defence in the Celestial Empire, for the most part use the German drill.

4 Arithmetic has four chief rules which are fundamental, viz., addition, subtraction, multiplication and division.

5 You have been again imposed upon by him, have you? With this way of collecting, you will never get anything.

6 Jugglers always depend upon sleight of hand, not upon anything supernatural.

7 There is not the least order in his exposition, how can one either understand or remember it?

8 Although it is admitted that a teacher should whip his pupils, yet all depends on how he whips.

---

21 The idea of the sentence is that mutual misunderstandings disappear when the parties speak plainly face to face.

22 A proverb, signifying that to know the world is to be disgusted with it.

24 一巴掌 *One slap.* 打 is omitted in anticipation of its use just below.

25 失火 *To lose fire,* that is, to forget or neglect the fire, and so allow it to grow into a conflagration. 主 is used as a verb to express the idea of *meaning* or *signifying.* Its use corresponds to our phrase, "*which is a sign.*" The Chinese suppose that if a dream portending ill fortune is understood in advance of its accomplishment, it then becomes an omen of good fortune.

LESSON CIII.

The Modal Affix.

法 is much used as an affix to verbs, to denote the manner of the action. It is sometimes also joined to nouns, which it practically turns into verbs,—thus 兵法 means *drill,* but must be analysed, as *the method of drilling soldiers, or of soldiering.* In all cases 法 is without accent, and in speaking tends to take an enclitic 子 or 兒. When it takes the accent it is not an affix. In all cases in which 法 makes any special modification of the meaning of the verb, a definition is given in the vocabulary. For list of words taking 法, see Supplement.

Vocabulary.

做法 *Tsoŭ⁴ fa³.* Method of doing or working, style.

筆法 *Pi³ fa³.* Style of writing, chirography.

天朝 *T'ien¹ ch'ao².* The Celestial Empire, China:—Note 3.

海防 *Hai³ fang².* Coast guard or defence.

德國 *Tê² kwoŭ².* The German Empire.

兵法 *Ping¹ fa³.* Method of drilling, drill.

算法 *Swan⁴ fa³.* Mathematics, *arithmetic:*—Note 4.

加法 *Chia¹ fa³.* Method of adding, addition in mathematics.

減 *Chien³.* To diminish; *to subtract.*

減法 *Chien³ fa³.* Subtraction.

乘 *Ch'êng².* To ride, to mount; to take advantage of; *to multiply.* See *ch'êng⁴.*

過[9]日子要儉省是不錯的、但若是太儉省了、也不是個正經過法。○這[10]麽一些個零碎東西、又沒有個簍子、叫我怎麽個拿法呢。○一[11]樣的事情、各人有各人的辦法、不能拘定一個死法子。○這[12]樣礙口的話、叫我怎樣說法呢。○您[13]的孩子打人罵人、你一點兒也不管、慣孩子還有這樣的慣法嗎。○王[14]顏歐柳的字、寫法雖不一樣、却都有骨力。○先[15]生怎樣的教法、學生就怎樣的學法、所以古語說、師傅不明徒弟拙、眞是不錯。○中[16]國一個字、常見有五六個念法、又有七八

9 It is true that one should be economical in his way of living, but to be too saving is not a proper manner of living.

10 All these odds and ends of things and no basket! How am I to carry them?

11 Though the business be the same, each man has his own way of managing it. You cannot establish one invariable rule.

12 How can I use such unbecoming language as this?

13 Your children beat and insult others, and yet you pay no attention to them! What reason is there in indulging children to such an extent as this?

14 Although Wang, Yien, Ou and Liu's styles of writing are not the same, yet they are all vigorous.

15 As the master teaches so the pupil learns; hence the old saying, "An inferior master makes a stupid pupil," is quite correct.

16 In Chinese it constantly occurs that one character has five or six pronunciations and seven or eight meanings, so that the Chinese literary style is very difficult to learn.

乘法 *Ch'êng² fa³.* . . . . Multiplication.

除法 *Ch'u² fa³.* . . . . Division.

搪 *T'ang².* . . . To extend; to ward off; to evade.

拖 *T'oă¹.* To drag along; to hang down; to lead; to implicate; *to protract.*

搪拖 To evade, to postpone, *to impose upon by false promises.*

要法 *Yao⁴ fa³.* Manner of collecting money, manner of dunning.

手法 *Shou³ fa³.* . . . . . . Skill or sleight of hand.

邪法 *Hsie² fa³.* . . . Sorcery, *magic*, witchcraft.

儉省 *Chien³ shêng³.* To save, *to be economical*, to be frugal.

過法 *Kwoă⁴ fa³.* . . . . . Style or mode of living.

礙口 *Ai⁴ k'ou³.* *Unbecoming* (language), not fit to be spoken.

歐 *Ou¹.* . . . . A surname.

柳 *Liu³.* . . . . . Willow; striped; *a surname.*

寫法 *Hsie³ fa³.* *Style of writing*, handwriting, penmanship.

骨力 *Ku³ li⁴.* . . . . . . Strength, *vigor*, firmness.

徒弟 *T'u² ti⁴.* A disciple, *a pupil*, an apprentice.

念法 *Nien⁴ fa³.* Mode of reading, *pronunciation.*

講法 *Chiang³ fa³.* Mode of explaining, or preaching; *meaning*, definition.

文理 *Wên² li³.* . . . . . The literary or book style.

家法 *Chia¹ fa³.* *The rules of a family*, family government.

國法 *Kwoă² fa³.* *The laws of a country*, statutes, government.

民 *Min².* The people—as distinguished from the officials.

子民 *Tsï³ min².* The people, the subjects of a government, *citizens.*

徐 *Hsü².* . . . . . . Grave; slow; *a surname.*

索 *Soă⁴,¹.* To search; *to demand*, to exact. See *soă³* and *soă².*

勒索 *Lê¹ soă¹.* To constrain, *to extort*, to "squeeze."

尋常 *Hsun² ch'ang².* . . . . Ordinary, usual.

委 *Wei³.* *To sustain*; to delegate, to depute; a wrong, a grievance; to reject.

個講法、所以中國文理、是最難學的。○俗[17]語說、家有家法、國有國法、又說、人隨王法草隨風。你既是大清國的子民、還能不守大清國的王法嗎。○徐[18]安仁那個勒索法、眞是非同尋常。○問[19]官司、必得委曲婉轉的、問出底理原情來、方見官的斷才、若不論曲直、上堂就打、這樣的問法、誰還不會呢。○西[20]國的樂法、是用兜類米乏叟拉替七個音編成的、中國是用凡工尺上一四合七個音編成的。

17 It is a common saying, "The familr has its rules, and the country its laws"; also, "Men yield to the laws as the grass to the wind." Seeing you are a Chinese subject can you do otherwise than obey Chinese laws?

18 Such extortion as that of Hsü An Jên's is certainly exceptional.

19 In trying a case in court, if the officer would show his skill as a judge, he must ask questions in an indirect and specious way so as to bring out the bottom facts of the case. If, without regard to the merits of the case, he begins to beat as soon as the parties appear—who could not try a case in this way?

20 The western system of musical notation involves the use of the seven syllables; do, re, mi, fa, sol, la, t'i. The Chinese system involves the use of the seven syllables, fan, kung, ch'i, shang, i, sï, hê.

委曲 *Wei³ ch'ü¹*. . . . . *Indirect*, circuitous.

婉 *Wan³*. . . . . Yielding, obliging, *winsome*.

婉轉 *Wan³ chwan³*. Plausible, *specious*, roundabout.

原情 *Yüen² ch'ing²*. Original idea, original facts or circumstances.

斷才 *Twan⁴ ts'ai²*. Judicial faculty, capacity for judging and deciding.

問法 *Wên⁴ fa³*. Mode of asking; *style of hearing a case at law.*

樂法 *Yüe⁴ fa³*. Musical notation, system of music.

兜 *Tou¹*. A bib, a pouch, a sling; to carry in a fold of the dress, or in an apron.

叟 *Sou³*. . . . . . An old man, venerable sir. (w.)

編 *Pien¹*. To braid, to plait; *to arrange;* to compose (a book or tune).

Notes.

1 The use of 個, as here, is a little peculiar. It gives an emphasis somewhat similar to the use of the word "sort" in English,—as if we should translate, *He has laid out all this work for us, in what sort of a way can we get it done?* It is so used several times in this lesson. When used in this way it is nearly always followed by 法, expressed or understood.

3 天朝 *Heavenly Dynasty.* This is the high sounding title by which the Chinese delight to call their own country, and which has given rise to the term "Celestial Empire."

4 算法 is often used vaguely for mathematics in general, but is here, as often, restricted to arithmetic. Strictly speaking 乘 is to multiply by several digits, whilst 因 signifies to multiply by one digit. Also 除 properly means "long division," whilst 歸 signifies "short division." 乘 and 除 are constantly used, however, to signify the processes of multiplication and division at large.

5 Kiukiang rejects both 搪拖 and 拖 and says 搪抵.

6 In 戲法 and 邪法, the 法 is emphasized, and does not properly fall within the lesson. 手法 illustrates the lesson.

9 正經過法 *Regular or proper mode of living.* When economy is pushed to such an extreme as to interfere with health and decency, it is not a 正經過法. The use of 也 implies a contrast with the opposite extreme of extravagance.

11 死法, with the accent on 死, means *manner of dying, or of suffering death*, but with the accent on 法, it means, *one invariable and unalterable rule.*

13 慣 means properly *to acquire a habit*, but here, *to indulge in, or allow the acquisition of a bad habit.*

14 王顏歐柳 are the names of four renowned penmen, living in different ages. Fac-similes of their

第一百四課

請[1]他明天務必早來。○這[2]件事你總要得原諒我。○那[3]把芭蕉扇子、你必定得給我找出來。○說[4]話務總總要須得在論論理。○學[5]生必得常有先生管着。○你[6]總要得把錢張羅下。○你[7]們做丈夫的、須要疼愛婦人。○交[8]友待客、總要恭敬。○他[9]待我這個仇、我必要報。○你[10]是我的學生、總要須得守我的學規。○事[11]情若待要了、必須你親自去見他。○這[12]是誰的主意、我總要追究出來。○若[13]要拿他、須要看看動靜。○[14]若待要叫我消解恨、必得把他殺了。○最[15]好的法子、必須行得實在方好。○瘟[16]疹之後、必要

TRANSLATION.

1 Ask him to be sure to come early to-morrow.

2 You must certainly excuse me in this matter.

3 You must not fail to find that palm-leaf fan for me.

4 You must talk reasonably.

5 It is necessary that scholars should constantly have a teacher to control them.

6 You must, by some means, collect the money.

7 You who are husbands should love your wives.

8 In intercourse with friends, and in receiving guests, one must not fail to be respectful.

9 I shall certainly repay this enmity with which he has treated me.

10 You are my pupils, and you must keep my rules.

11 In order to bring the affair to an end, you will have to go and see him yourself.

12 I am determined to find out who originated this idea.

13 If you want to arrest him, you must look well to the circumstances.

14 Nothing but his death will appease my hatred.

15 The best plan needs to be executed in earnest in order to make it a success.

penmanship are used in schools as copies. The Chinese lay great stress on good penmanship.

16 常見 *might* stand at the opening of the sentence, instead of in its present position. The statement is a little exaggerated. It applies to *Wên-li* far more than to Mandarin.

17 法, in this sentence, means *rule* or *law* and scarcely comes under the lesson. 大清 is the dynastic title of the present Tartar dynasty.

18 非同尋常 *Not as usual;* i. e., *exceptional.* A ready-made phrase in the literary style.

19 底理原情 *Primary reason* and *original motive.*

LESSON CIV.

WORDS AND PHRASES DENOTING NECESSITY.

務必 }
務要 } Should, must, certainly must, be sure and, by all means. Often used to express a wish or a charge.

必得 }
必要 } Must, positively must, without fail, necessary. Southern Mandarin avoids 得 and prefers 要.

須 Ought, requisite, must. Rarely used alone in Mandarin, and then usually in proverbs, or in expressions taken from books.

必須 Must, have to, necessary.

須要 Should, ought, must. A bookish term.

總 In any case, no matter how,—a word of many uses. To denote necessity it is joined with 要, 得 and 須.

總要 Must, must in any case, bound to.

總得 Must, should, by all means, whether or not.

總須 Must, certainly must.

切 (with a negative) By no means, not for anything.

萬 (with a negative) Must not, not for the world, be sure not.

千萬 Same as 萬, but stronger.

退脫皮。○所[17]有犯法的、總得究辦。○凡[18]讀書的、務要立志。○望[19]兄長留心、切不可輕看仇敵。○這[20]兩個箱子、必要得綁結實了纔好馱。○孝[21]順父母的道理、人人須要盡心竭力。○萬[22]不可因爲自己聰明、笑話人家糊塗。○雖[23]然回家的心、都是急的、但你身上還沒復元、千萬不可以走。○東[24]西你收了沒有、務必寫一回信給我。○若[25]要叫人尊重、總須得不慢待人。○孩[26]子們、必得哄着他一點兒、不可常嚇呼他。○你[27]要往那個地方去、務必上衙門請一張路票。○凡[28]人作事、總要得自己有主意、不可光隨喜從人。○要[29]爲人上人、須受苦中

16 After epidemic scarlet fever, the patient's skin is sure to peel off.

17 It is important to bring all law-breakers to justice.

18 Every student should fix his determination.

19 I trust you will be cautious; by no means allow yourself to despise your enemy.

20 These two boxes must be securely bound in order to satisfactory carriage.

21 In filial piety every one should exert himself to the utmost.

22 You must never, because you yourself are clever, ridicule others for being stupid.

23 Although the desire to return home is always strong, still you must not think of starting before you have regained your strength.

24 You must not fail to write and tell me whether you have received the things or not.

25 If you would gain the esteem of men, you must not treat them contemptuously.

26 It is necessary to coax children a little; you should not be always threatening them.

27 If you wish to go to that place, be sure you go to the yamên and procure a passport.

Vocabulary.

須 *Hsü*^{1}. To wait; necessary, requisite; ought, should; partially, somewhat.

原諒 *Yüen*^{2} *liang*^{4}. *To excuse*, to overlook, to make allowance for.

芭 *Pa*^{1}. A fragrant plant.

蕉 *Chiao*^{1}. The plantain or banana.

芭蕉 The banana palm.

張羅 *Chang*^{1} *lo*^{2}. To publish, to noise abroad, to tell; *to collect* (money), to scrape together, "to raise the wind." To manage. (N.)

疼愛 *T'êng*^{2} *ai*^{4}. *To love ardently*, a warm affection for.

婦人 *Fu*^{4} *jên*^{2}. *A wife*, a married woman.

學規 *Hsüe*^{2} *kwei*^{1}. *The rules of a school*, discipline; fees paid on taking the first degree.

解恨 *Chie*^{3} *hên*^{4}. To appease resentment or enmity; to be appeased.

消恨 *Hsiao*^{1} *hên*^{4}. The same.

瘟 *Wên*^{1}. An epidemic, a pestilence.

瘟疹 *Wên*^{1} *chên*^{3}. Epidemic scarlet fever or measles.

究辦 *Chiu*^{1} *pan*^{4}. To prosecute, *to bring to justice*, to try and punish.

兄長 *Hsiung*^{1} *chang*^{3}. Elder brother,—a polite term of address.

綁 *Pang*^{3}. To tie, *to bind*, to bandage.

盡心 *Chin*^{4} *hsin*^{1}. Earnest, with the whole heart, to do one's best.

竭 *Chie*^{2}. *To exhaust, to exert to the utmost*; used up, finished.

竭力 *Chie*^{2} *li*^{4}. *To exert the strength to the utmost*, to do one's best.

復元 *Fu*^{4} *yüen*^{2}. To return to the original state, to restore, *to regain*.

苦。○喫[30]了人的桑、總得給人家做個繭。○各[31]樣兒的東西上、必得愛惜儉省、纔是過日子的道理呀。○若[32]人犯不齊、十天半月必須伺候、憑你有天塌的大事、也不得回去。○切[33]不可去賭錢喫酒、不可和人打架、不可暗地積攢銀錢、疼自己的老婆孩子、不顧爹娘。○若[34]看見路上有小紙包、彷彿銀子似的、千萬不要去撿拾、或見別人撿拾了、也千萬不要眼熱、因爲這都是騙人的法子、你當牢記在心。○無[35]論是頭役、是總頭役、都不可靠、萬別信他爲

28 In whatever he does, a man should make up his own mind and not always follow the lead of others.

29 He who would rise superior to others must endure the severest toil.

30 When you have eaten a man's mulberry leaves, you must not fail to make a cocoon for him.

31 To be frugal and economical in all things--this is the secret of prosperity.

32 If the accused are not all present, you will have to remain in waiting ten days or a fortnight. No matter how momentous your business you could not return.

33 You must not gamble nor drink; you must not quarrel with people; you must not be too fond of your wife and children, laying by money for them to the neglect of your father and mother.

34 If you see a small parcel on the road resembling a packet of silver, by no means pick it up; nor allow yourself to covet it if you see another person pick it up; for these are all tricks for cheating people. Be sure you bear this well in mind.

尊重 *Tsun*¹ *chung*⁴. To honor, *to respect*, to hold in esteem.

慢待 *Man*⁴ *tai*⁴. To treat discourteously *or with contempt*, to dishonor.

頌 *Sung*⁴. . . . . . *To praise*, to eulogize, to extol.

哄頌 *Hung*³ *sung*⁴. To coax, to divert, to conciliate. (L.)

嚇呼 *Hê*⁴ *hu*¹. *To threaten;* to frighten:—Note 26.

路票 *Lu*⁴ *p'iao*⁴. . . . . A pass, *a passport*.

隨喜 *Swei*² *hsi*³. *To follow*, to assent to, to chime in with. (L.)

桑 *Sang*¹. . . . The mulberry tree, *mulberry leaves*.

繭 *Chien*³. . . . . . . The cocoon of the silkworm.

人犯 *Jên*² *fan*⁴. Accused persons, prisoners awaiting trial:—Note 32.

塌 *T'a*¹. . . . To give way and fall, to fall down.

暗地 *An*⁴ *ti*⁴. . . . . . . *In secret*, clandestine.

眼熱 *Yien*³ *jê*⁴. *To covet*, to desire, to crave, to lust after.

頭役 *T'ou*² *i*⁴. The head men in each *pan* (班) of underlings.

公門 *Kung*¹ *mên*². . . . A public office, a yamên.

䠷 *T'iao*³. . . . . A tall man, a giant.

NOTES.

8 交友待客 is a ready-made phrase. If it were made for the occasion its brevity would render it obscure.

11 了 is not here a past particle, but is used in its proper sense as a principal verb.

12 The natural order is inverted in order to emphasize the first member. Otherwise it would have been said 我總要追, etc.

19 仇敵 is here not a private enemy, but an enemy in war.

23 都 is here practically equal to *always*. It is really an indefinite pronoun standing for 回家的心.

26 The vicious practice of the Chinese of coaxing or quieting children by making false promises or threats, is plainly embodied in the word 哄. The term 哄頌 is local in Shantung. 嚇呼 is read both *hê*⁴ *hu*¹ and *hsia*⁴ *hu*¹; with the former reading it means *to threaten*, with the latter, *to startle, to frighten.*

27 The use of 請 implies that the passport is a favor granted in response to a polite request.

29 Or, "*There is no excellence without great labor*",—a proverbial saying constructed, as are nearly all such sayings, on the *Wên-li* model. A more colloquial form is 不受苦中苦難成人上人.

貼己的朋友、你若看他爲公門中的人、能替你拿主意、幫助你寫呈子、又能給你挖門打門路子、就離喫虧不遠喇。○常[36]聽說劉玉堂的事、這劉玉堂是個甚麼樣的人呢、答 是個細高挑兒、兩撇鬍子、有四十多歲、說話作事、都很光棍、總不留空子、叫人挑出不是來。

35 No matter whether it be a principal underling or the head of the underlings, none are trustworthy; be sure you do not trust them as confidential friends. If you think that because they are in the office they can advise you and help you to present your case, and can find a way to influence the officer in your favor, you are in a fair way to be fleeced.

36 I am continually hearing of Liu Yü T'ang's affairs; what kind of a man is this Liu Yü T'ang? *Ans.* He is a tall, slender man with a long mustache, and over forty years of age. He is very plausible in all that he says and does, giving no opportunity for any one to find any fault.

32 This language is addressed by an underling to one involved in a law suit, and who is compelled to wait in the yamên the officer's convenience. 人犯 is not applied to *condemned* criminals, who are called 犯人 or 囚犯. 天塌的大事 *An affair as important as the falling of the heavens,*—a high sounding hyperbole.

33 Confucian ethics considers it a great fault to neglect parents in order to provide for wife and children. A man must love his parents *more* than he does his wife and children. The sentence is from the Sacred Edict.

34 A common trick of Chinese foot-pads is for one to go before the unwary traveller and drop a packet, which always contains bogus money, while the other follows after and overtakes the traveller, and makes the picking up of the packet the occasion of getting into his confidence, or in some way robbing him.

35 挖門子 Either to take a bribe, promising to influence the officer on behalf of the party, or to act as go-between in negotiating a bribe with the magistrate or his advisers.

LESSON CV.

Aggregation by the use of 一.

一 One,—is prefixed to a variety of words to express the general idea of aggregation, or of being together.

一共 One all,—all together, in all, the sum total, collectively.

一概 One summing up,—all, the whole, nothing but.

一同 One together,—with, together with, all together, in one lot or company.

一塊 One piece,—together, together with, at one time, in one place. In speaking 一塊 nearly always takes 兒 after it.

一堆 One pile,—together, at the same time, at once. 一堆 is a widely used colloquial term, but not *t'ung-hsing*. Save when used in its primary sense it always takes after it an enclitic 兒.

一切 One whole,—every one, all included, the whole.

一連 One connection,—together, including; in succession, continuously.

一齊 One even,—all, all together, all at once, en masse, in a body.

一處 One place,—together. A book term not often used in colloquial.

一併 One equality,—altogether, entirely, in toto, the whole lot.

一色 One color,—all, the whole. Used only in reference to colors.

一乾 One heaven,—all, entirely, every one. (C.)

一總 One sum,—all, in toto.

It should be noted that these various phrases nearly always come just before the principal verb.

第一百五課

我[1]一共欠你多少錢。○他[2]所說的、一概不可憑信。○請[3]你和我們一同住下。○中[4]國一共有三萬萬人。○我[5]們兩個是一塊(堆)兒進的學。○洪[6]水的時候、一連下了四十天雨。○你[7]們一齊使勁(用勁)兒就掀動喇。○這[8]一切的話、旁人我都沒告訴。○大[9]家夥兒一齊動手、不多的時候就完了。○大[10]小衙門、當刑名師爺的、一概(乾)是紹興人。○他[11]是一塊兒來的、你怎麼把他挑出來呢。○一[12]連放了兩個火砲、一個打在水裏、一個直打到鴨嘴灘。○大[13]老爺今天比限、各屬的地方(鄉約、鄉保)一齊來了、我看見跪了滿滿的一大堂。○世[14]上一切所有的

TRANSLATION.

1 How much do I owe you in all?
2 You must not believe anything that he said.
3 I invite you to stop with us.
4 China has in all three hundred millions of inhabitants.
5 We two took our degree at the same time.
6 At the time of the flood it rained continuously for forty days.
7 If you make a simultaneous effort, you can raise it.
8 I have not reported any of this conversation to anyone else.
9 If we all together put our hands to the work, it will be finished very soon.
10 In both superior and inferior yamêns, the criminal lawyers are all natives of Shaohsing.
11 He came at the same time, how is it that you single him out?
12 They fired two shots in succession, one fell in the water and one sped on to Duckbill sandspit.
13 To-day his worship urges payment [of taxes], and the various collectors have all come. I saw a whole court-room-full kneeling before him.
14 All the people in the world are the descendants of Adam and Eve.

VOCABULARY.

共 *Kung*⁴. All, in all, altogether; to sum up; with, altogether; the same; to live with; to include.

併 *Ping*⁴. Even, equal; to equalize; together, unitedly. Not distinguished from 並.

憑信 *P'ing*² *hsin*⁴. *To believe implicitly*, to confide in, to trust.

洪 *Hung*². An inundation, *a flood;* vast.

洪水 *Hung*² *shwei*³. A deluge, *the flood.*

使勁 *Shï*³ *chin*⁴. To exert strength, to try hard, *to make vigorous effort.*

用勁 *Yung*⁴ *chin*⁴. The same.

掀 *Hsien*¹. To lift, *to raise up*, to set up; to open; to whirl.

旁人 *P'ang*² *jên*². Others, other people.

動手 *Tung*⁴ *shou*³. *To take hold,* to bear a hand; to begin.

刑名 *Hsing*² *ming*². A legal adviser in the lower courts, a prosecuting attorney:—Note 10.

師爺 *Shï*¹ *yie*². An officer's assistants, with whom he associates on terms of equality.

比限 *Pi*³ *hsien*⁴. To urge payment of taxes:—Note 13.

紹 *Shao*⁴. To connect, to join. (w.)

紹興 *Shao*⁴ *hsing*³. Shaohsing,—a Fu city in Chekiang.

灘 *T'an*¹. Rapids; *a sandbank*, the beach.

屬 *Shu*²'³. Connected with, tributary to; pertaining to, depending on; kinship; sort, *grade;* actual, existing.

人、都是亞當夏娃的後代。○家[15]裏待客的事情、一概在我、你只照應外邊就好得喇。○他[16]一連三天都沒有飯吃、肚中饑餓的了不得。○你[17]和他在一塊兒、住了許多日子、還不知道他的脾氣嗎。○我[18]的兒、你常和我在一塊處兒、我一切所有的、都是你的。○請[19]借兩個元寶給我、一等我回來的時候、本利一併奉還。○姑[20]娘做新娘子(媳婦)那一天、從頭到脚、一色是紅的。○若[21]將吃飯穿衣人情零用、一概都算在內、每年總得二百吊錢。○王[22]濟仁叫路截(斷道)(擋路)的一杠子砸倒了、把他的衣裳鋪蓋、一總扛了去咯、光剩了一個半死不活的人。○這[23]一切的事情、都是從他

15 In the house, the whole responsibility of attending to the guests rests with me. If you will simply look after the outside matters, it will be sufficient.

16 For three days together he had nothing whatever to eat, so that he felt excessively hungry.

17 You lived with him a long time, and don't you yet know his peculiarities?

18 My son, thou art always with me, and all that I have is thine.

19 Please lend me a hundred taels, and when I return, I will repay you in full both principal and interest.

20 On the day that a girl becomes a bride, she is dressed in red from head to foot.

21 If food and clothing, the claims of society and incidental expenses, are all included, it will require fully two hundred strings of cash a year.

22 A robber with one stroke of a club knocked Wang Chi Jên down, and carried off all his clothes and bedding, leaving him half dead.

23 This whole difficulty was stirred up by his wife.

24 After the resurrection the bodies and souls of the righteous together go to the enjoyment of eternal happiness.

鄉約 *Hsiang¹ yoă¹*. Police officer, justice of the peace; a tax collector, a publican :—Note 13.

地方 *Ti⁴ fang¹*........ The same.

鄉保 *Hsiang¹ pao³*........ The same.

後代 *Hou⁴ tai⁴*...... Posterity, *descendants.*

饑餓 *Chi¹ ê⁴*......... Hungry.

奉還 *Fêng⁴ hwan²*. To return with thanks, to repay, *to pay in full.*

新娘子 *Hsin¹ niang² tsï³*. A bride, a newly married woman. (s.)

路截 *Lu⁴ chie²*...... A highway robber.

斷道 *Twan⁴ tao⁴*..... To rob on the highway.

擋路 *Tang⁴ lu⁴*........ The same.

釁 *Hsin⁴*. A flaw; *an occasion of offence or quarrel;* a feud; an omen.

魂 *Hun²*. *The soul,* the spiritual part, the manes; the mind, the wits.

靈魂 *Ling² hun²*. The soul, the spirit, the life :—Note 24.

抄家 *Ch'ao¹ chia¹*. To confiscate a man's property and estate.

滅門 *Mie⁴ mên²*. To put a man together with all his family to death, to exterminate.

房產 *Fang² ch'an³*...... Property in houses.

入官 *Ju⁴ kwan¹*. To accrue to the government, *to revert to the state.*

販 *Fan⁴*.... To buy and sell, *to deal in,* to traffic.

斷宰 *Twan⁴ tsai³*. To forbid the slaughter of animals :—Note 26.

倒運 *Tao³ yün⁴*....... *Unlucky,* ill-starred.

水師 *Shwei³ shï¹*. *Naval,* a title given to various officers connected with the navy or coast defence.

女人起釁。○復[24]活以後、義人的身體和靈魂、一同去享永福。○王[25]大老爺犯了抄家滅門的罪、所有的房產田地、一併入了官了。○姜[26]太公販猪羊貴、販羊猪貴、猪羊一齊販斷宰、眞是倒運。○水[27]師營的兵、實在整齊、看上邊一概是灰色小襖、看下邊一色是靴子、說要往前、都一齊往前、說要退後、都一齊退後、就是他們的脚、也是一齊起一齊落、彷彿一個人的脚聲兒。○場[28]上的麥子曬乾喇、你去把他收拾在一堆兒、預備往家裏扛。○主[29]考因爲考期臨近、要避徇情的嫌疑、所以傳出話來說、這幾天凡有投帖請見的、一概不許通報。

25 Wang Ta Lao Yie was guilty of crimes punishable by confiscation of his property and extermination of his family, hence all his houses and lands reverted in toto to the state.

26 When Chiang T'ai Kung dealt in hogs, sheep rose in price; when he dealt in sheep, hogs rose in price; when he bought both at once, butchering was forbidden. He was certainly unlucky.

27 The appearance of the soldiers in the marine encampment is exceedingly uniform. Above you see only their grey coats, and below, only their boots. At the order to advance they all move forward together, and at the order to retire, they all move backward together. Even their feet all rise together and all go down together as though it were the sound of but one man's foot.

28 The wheat on the threshing floor is quite dry. You go and gather it into a pile ready to be carried home.

29 Because the time for examinations is near at hand, the examiner, in order to avoid the suspicion of favoritism, has sent out word forbidding to report to him any who, during these few days, send in their cards or solicit an audience.

整齊 *Chêng³ ch'i².* .... Regular, even, *uniform;* complete.

退後 *T'wei⁴ hou⁴.* .... *To retire,* to retreat, to fall back, to withdraw.

主考 *Chu³ k'ao³.* .... The literary examiner who confers the degree of *chü-jên.*

臨近 *Lin² chin⁴.* .... *To draw near* (in time), to approach.

徇 *Hsün⁴.* ... To follow, to comply with; quick.

徇情 *Hsün⁴ ch'ing².* .... To comply with the wishes of another, to be partial to, to curry favor, *to favor.*

投帖 *T'ou² t'ie³.* .... *To send up a card or scroll,* to present compliments.

通報 *T'ung¹ pao⁴.* .... *To report,* to announce; general information.

NOTES.

2 **一概** here comes to mean "anything." If the order were changed to **他所說的不可一概憑信,** it would mean, *You must not believe all he said.*

4 In mathematical language a **萬萬** is an **億**, but in the language of common life **萬** is the highest numeral used, being duplicated one or more times to express higher denominations. **三萬萬** *Three times ten thousand times ten thousand;* i. e., *three hundred millions.*

6 **下了四十天雨** *There came down a forty days' rain.*

10 **刑名** is an assistant whose business it is to examine all criminal prosecutions and prepare the **批** or official reply, also to prepare drafts of all dispatches and reports. They are employed in all Hsien and Fu yamêns. In higher yamêns the office is called by a different name. It is a remarkable fact that the scholars of Shaohsing have a monopoly of this office in the whole empire. The reply to the **呈子**, or accusation, is, in civil suits, prepared by a different assistant, called **錢穀**.

12 **火砲** *Fire cannon.* **砲** is more frequently used alone. The Chinese speak of firing so many *cannon,* we of firing so many *shots.*

13 **比限** *To compare the term or limit.* Taxes in China are collected by constables or collectors called in different places **鄉約, 鄉保** and **地方.** The collection covers

第一百六課

我[1]和他是一輩。○一[2]樣的米麪、各人的手段。○丁[3]先生和丁太太的歲數一般大。○他[4]們都是一流的人。○家[5]裏的人口多了、那裏能一心呢。○我[6]知道你們現在都結成一黨了。○這[7]一羣羊盡是山羊、一隻綿羊也沒有。○棗[8]兒和核桃不可一例數。○天[9]主是三位一體的神。○這[10]一種雀子兒、我從來沒見過。○有[11]一

Translation.

1 I am of the same generation with him.
2 Though the rice and flour be alike, yet much depends on the skill [of the cook].
3 Mr. and Mrs. Ting are of the same age.
4 They all belong to the same set.
5 When there are many in the family, how can they all have one mind?
6 I know that you have now all formed yourselves into one clique.
7 This whole flock of sheep consists entirely of goats, there is not a single sheep in it.
8 Dates and walnuts must not be counted in the same way.
9 The Lord of heaven is three persons in one Godhead.
10 I have never before seen this species [of bird.

three months in the spring and three in the fall. Payments are usually made by the collectors every ten days, at which time all are assembled and their accounts examined. Those who have made prompt payment are complimented and sometimes rewarded, while delinquents are berated and not unfrequently beaten.

16 都 here gives the force of *at all* in English.

18 一塊 is more colloquial and more expressive than 一處, and equally *t'ung hsing.*

21 衣 is used without either of its usual defining words 裳 or 服, being made sufficiently definite by the preceding 穿. 人情 here means the presents which Chinese etiquette requires on occasion of weddings, births, funerals, feasts, etc.

22 There seems to be no *t'ung hsing* term for a highway robber. In Kiukiang all the terms in the text are rejected for 斷路.

24 The use of the term 靈魂 is largely Christian. The Chinese (heathen) usually use 魂 alone, or occasionally 魂靈, especially when speaking of the soul as disembodied. There is practically no distinction of meaning between 靈魂 and 魂靈.

26 姜太公, otherwise called 姜子牙, a legendary character of the twelfth century B. C. He is the most important personage in Chinese mythology. He was appointed by 元始天尊, *the most Ancient and Honorable One*, to assign to the gods their several ranks and duties. He is regarded as a sort of provost-marshal over the gods. This story of his bad luck in business is told of him when at home before he entered official life. 斷宰 is an official proclamation forbidding all slaughter of animals for food for a certain time. It is usually done in time of drought in order to propitiate the gods.

27 說, as here used, constitutes a very common idiom for expressing the idea that the thing spoken of is carried into immediate execution.

LESSON CVI.

One, expressing Sameness.

一 is joined with a variety of words for the purpose of classification or generalization, and is translated either *one*, or *the same*. The same forms are also used specifically, and when so used, 一 is rendered *the*, or *a*, or *whole*.

一輩 One generation,—the same generation.

一樣 One kind,—the same, alike.

一模 One pattern,—only used with 一樣

一模一樣 Precisely alike, just the same.

一般 One manner,—the same, like, equal.

一流 One current,—the same class or kind.

一心 One heart,—of the same mind, harmonious; the whole heart.

一意 One meaning,—of the same mind, harmonious, congenial.

一黨 One party,—the same party, the same clique or cabal.

一羣 One flock,—the same flock; the whole flock.

一例 One rule,—the same custom or way.

一體 One body,—the same body or substance; the whole body.

夥學生、天天從我門前過去。○你[12]不用揀、這都
是一路的貨。○這[13]一位是誰、答這是我一家的
叔叔。○牲[14]口市上來了一羣騾子、大約有二百
多匹個。○無[15]論騾馬牛羊、好些個在一塊兒、謂之
一羣。○在[16]這裏沒有你一家一黨的人嗎。○世[17]
上有一等人、自己不能擔扛事事、却好生事。○毒[18]蛇
一類的、誰告訴你們躲避將來的刑罰呢。○肥[19]
城出一種肥桃、是山東最有名的。○李[20]成文天
生各一路脾氣、沒有他如意的人。○你[21]看你的
頭髮、長的和囚犯一樣、快去薙薙罷。○若[22]是買

11 A company of school boys goes by my door every day.
12 There is no need of selecting, these goods are all of one quality.
13 Who is this gentleman? *Ans.* This is a distant relative of my father's.
14 A drove of some two hundred or more mules has arrived at the horse market.
15 A collection of either mules, horses, cows or sheep is called a herd.
16 Is there no one of your relatives or friends here?
17 There is a class of men in the world who, though unable to bear up under difficulties, are yet given to getting into difficulties.
18 Ye tribe of vipers, who hath told you to flee from the wrath to come.
19 Fei Ch'êng produces a kind of peach called the Fei peach, which is very widely known in Shantung.
20 Li Ch'êng Wên's natural disposition is *sui generis*, he is dissatisfied with everybody.
21 Look at your hair; it has grown as long as a prisoner's. Go and get it shaved at once.

一種 One seed,—the same kind or stock or sort or variety.

一夥 One company,—the same company or set.

一路 One road,—the same kind or quality.

一家 One family,—the same family or clan; the whole family.

一等 One order,—the same class, first class.

一宗 One clan,—the same clan or tribe; a class, a kind; a lot, a deal.

一族 One tribe,—the same ancestry, kindred.

一起 One rise,—the same company or set.

一類 One species,—the same class or category or character.

VOCABULARY.

段 *Twan*⁴. *To push with the hand;* a fragment, a piece, a section.

黨 *Tang*³. A gang, a band; a political party, *a faction, a clique;* a class, a sort.

例 *Li*⁴. *A rule,* a bye-law; custom, usage.

手段 *Shou*³ *twan*⁴. Skill, ability, might.

人口 *Jên*² *k'ou*³. Persons in a family, household:—Note 5.

山羊 *Shan*¹ *yang*². A goat.

綿羊 *Mien*² *yang*². A sheep.

核 *Hê*², *hu*². *Kernel,* seed; to scrutinize.

核桃 *Hê*² *t'ao*³. The walnut.

雀 *Ch'iao*³, *ch'iao*⁴. A bird, a small bird.

謂 *Wei*⁴. To say, to speak of; to designate, to denominate, *to call.*

擔事 *Tan*¹ *shï*⁴. To bear responsibility, to bear up under difficulties.

扛事 *K'ang*⁴ *shï*⁴. The same.

各一路 *Kê*⁴ *i*¹ *lu*⁴. Different from others, peculiar, *singular.*

囚 *Ch'iu*². *To imprison,* to incarcerate.

一個風箱匣、一年能省好些柴喇。○那[23]是常考一等的手、還能不中舉嗎。○竊[24]賊的和做賊的、都是一例問罪。○你[25]若不信看罷、那個女人、再不能和他一心一意的過日子。○在[26]鳳凰街上、有一對雙生抱、身量和面貌都一模一樣。○女[27]徒一起的人走乏倦了、又加心裏發慌、想找一個地方歇歇。○竊[28]賊和强盜、雖不一樣、然而却是一類。○他[29]雖然在遠支上、你們仍舊是一宗一族、不可彼此打罵。○[30]一樣的豆餅、怎麼兩樣的價錢呢、答必是法碼有輕有重。秤有大有小。○趕[31]到晚上回家的

22 If you buy a bellows, you can save a deal of fuel in the course of a year.

23 That is a man who always stands in the first class, can he fail to get his [second] degree?

24 One who secretes a thief is regarded as equally guilty with the thief himself.

25 If you don't believe it, wait and see. That woman can never live harmoniously with him.

26 On Phœnix Street there is a pair of twins who in size and looks are precisely alike.

27 Christiana and her company were weary with traveling and also agitated in mind, and sought a place to rest.

28 Although thieves and robbers are not the same, yet they belong to the same class.

29 Although he belongs to a distant branch, still you are of one family stock and should not quarrel.

30 How is it that the same quality of bean cake has two prices? *Ans.* It must be that the weights (scales) are different.

囚犯 *Ch'iu*^{2} *fan*^{4}. . . . . . . *A prisoner*, a convict.

風匣 *Fêng*^{1} *hsia*^{2}. . . . . . . A bellows, a blower.

風箱 *Fêng*^{1} *hsiang*^{1}. . . . . . . The same.

雙 *Shwang*^{4}. To double, to put two together; . . . . twins. See *shwang*^{1}.

雙生 *Shwang*^{4} *shêng*^{1}. . . . . Twins.

雙抱 *Shwang*^{4} *pao*^{4}. . . . . . Same:—Note 26.

竊 *Ch'ie*^{4}. *To steal*, to pilfer; clandestine, private; my opinion.

竊賊 *Ch'ie*^{4} *tsei*^{2}. . . . . A thief, a pilferer.

豆 *Tou*^{4}. . . . . Pulse, beans, peas.

法碼 *Fa*^{3} *ma*^{3}. Weights for weighing; *standard of weight.*

報信 *Pao*^{4} *hsin*^{4}. To announce, *to give notice*, to carry news.

旗下 *Ch'i*^{2} *hsia*^{4}. . . . . Bannermen, Tartars.

百姓 *Pai*^{3} *hsing*^{4}. The people, the common people.

看待 *K'an*^{4} *tai*^{4}. To behave towards, *to treat*, to regard.

朗 *Lang*^{3}. . . . . Clear, bright, distinct.

明朗 *Ming*^{2} *lang*^{4}. Bright, lustrous; clearly, *evidently*, manifestly.

明朗眼見 *Ming*^{2} *lang*^{3} *yien*^{3} *chien*^{4}. *Evidently*, palpably.

逃荒 *T'ao*^{2} *hwang*^{1}. . . . . . To flee from famine.

NOTES.

2 Lit., *With the same rice and flour, every man has his own skill*,—a ready-made saying often used as a comparison. The dictionaries carefully distinguish 段 from 叚 (read chia), but in common usage the latter is often written for the former.

5 There is nothing in this sentence as it stands to show whether it is to be taken hypothetically or not. In 人口 the noun and its classifier have changed places, making a term meaning *member of a family*, but only used, as here, when referring to the number of persons in a family.

7 The translation of this sentence sounds absurd. It is all right, however, in Chinese, because sheep and goats are regarded as essentially one species, all being called 羊.

8 Dates are usually sold by the quantity, walnuts by the piece, thus showing the superiority of the latter. The meaning of the saying is that men must not all be estimated alike.

9 三位一體 is the conventional form adopted in Chinese to express the Christian idea of the Trinity.

時候、以撒還沒到家、狗先跑來、彷彿報信的一般。○天32下如同一家、萬民都是一體、或是旗下、或是百姓、總是一樣看待。○前33天來了一起逃荒的、明朗(明明)眼見是你們一夥的、你怎麼硬說不是呢。○今34天你三叔家有甚麼事呢、問你怎麼看他有事呢、答我看見一夥子穿衣戴帽的人、往他家裡去。

31 In the evening when Isaac returned home, before he had reached the house, the dog ran out to meet him as if to give the news.

32 The whole empire is like one family, and all the people belong to one body. Whether bannermen or common people, all are to be treated alike.

33 Day before yesterday a band of refugees came, and it is very evident that you belong to the same company. Why do you persist in saying that you do not?

34 What is going on at your third uncle's to-day? *Ques.* What makes you think there is anything going on? *Ans.* I saw a lot of people in full dress going into his house.

13 一家的叔叔 *A family uncle.* The term *uncle* is here used vaguely for any relative of the same generation, and of the same family name, with the father.

14 牲口市 is a market for the sale of beasts used in farming, including horses, mules, donkeys and cattle. No word in the English language will exactly translate 牲口.

19 肥城 is a *Hsien* city south-west of Chinanfu. The district produces a peach of great size and delicious flavor.

20 各一路 *A way of his own*, that is, a way that is different from others, and hence *singular*.

21 Prisoners in China are not allowed to shave their heads.

23 手 primarily refers to skill of hand, but is often applied to skill of any kind.

25 The use of 再 as in this sentence is anomalous. It means *positively, certainly, in any case.* This usage is *t'ung hsing.*

26 雙抱 is so written, but is universally spoken *shwang*^{1} *pang.*^{4}

30 法碼 are used in weighing with scales (天平), and are here referred to as the standard used in gauging the steelyards. Weights and measures are very uncertain in China. It might almost be said that every man has his own. The variations are well nigh endless.

31 的 in the last clause is euphonic and redundant; with 的, the construction is, *like a news bringer*, without 的 it is, *as though bringing news*, but this difference of "construction" is something the average Chinese writer or speaker does not appreciate.

LESSON CVII.

EMPHATIC REDUPLICATION.

Compound adjectives and participial nouns are repeated for the purpose of strengthening the idea, the two words being repeated separately. This is the most common method of emphasizing. Almost any compound adjective may be thus reduplicated. The more common ones are illustrated in the lesson.

For additional list see Supplement.

VOCABULARY.

安生 *An*^{1} *shêng*^{1}. . . . . Quiet, orderly. (s.)

睦 *Mu*^{4}. . . . . *Harmony*, concord.

和睦 *Hê*^{2} *mu*^{4}. Peaceable, *harmonious;* to . . . . .cultivate harmony.

順當 *Shun*^{4} *tang*^{4}. Easy, *smooth*, facile, unembarrassed.

返 *Fan*^{3}. *To return;* to revert to; on the . . . . .contrary, but.

從容 *Ts'ung*^{2} *yung*^{2}. *At ease*, at leisure; in easy . . . . circumstances.

叨 *Tao*^{1}. To talk rapidly and incoherently, to . . . . . . gabble. Also *t'ao*^{1}.

嘮 *Lao*^{2}. . . . To talk without meaning, to prate.

嘮叨. To clamor, *to talk incessantly and to no point*; to murmur at.

絮叨 *Hsü*^{4} *tao*^{1}. To talk disconnectedly, *to . . . . .repeat again and again.*

誠實 *Ch'êng*^{2} *shï*^{2}. Sincere, honest, *upright*, ... ingenuous, *straightforward.*

虛套 *Hsü*^{1} *t'ao*^{4}. *Empty compliments*, the lan- . . . . guage and forms of etiquette.

第一百零七課

這[1]是實實在在的事情。○快[2]老老實實(安安生生)的念書罷。○在[3]賬目上、總要清清楚楚的。○弟[4]兄們和和睦睦的、那等不樂。○水[5]運歡歡喜喜走到自家屋裏去。○明[6]明朗朗(白白)我吃二百錢的虧。○這[7]書上講的詳詳細細的、你還不明白嗎。○他[8]的衣裳雖然不算好、却是乾乾淨淨的。○若[9]事情順順當當的、不過十天就返回來了。○不[10]用着急、從從容容的走罷、今天不論怎麼就到了。○你[11]這麼啐啐(絮絮)叨叨的、眞討人厭。○偺[12]們要誠誠實實的、不必動虛套子。○別[13]驚動他、叫他安安穩穩的睡罷。○王[14]老爺已經看得的的確確的、你還

TRANSLATION.

1 This is a positive fact.
2 Settle down quickly to your books.
3 In accounts clearness is all important.
4 When brothers are harmonious, everything runs smoothly.
5 Shwei Yün went to her own room delighted.
6 It is as clear as noonday that I lose two hundred cash.
7 It is minutely explained in the book, and yet you do not understand it?
8 Although his clothing would not be considered good, still it is perfectly clean.
9 If my business goes off smoothly, I will be back within ten days.
10 There is no need of hurrying; go at an easy pace; we will get there to-day in any case.
11 This repetitious way you have of talking is most disagreeable.
12 Let us be straightforward and put aside empty compliments.
13 Do not disturb him, let him sleep quietly.
14 Wang Lao Yie already knows it perfectly well, what room is there for further disputing?

的 *Ti*⁴. . . . . . . Real, certain; a target. See *ti*¹.
確 *Ch'iao*⁴. . . Firm, substantial; really, *certainly*.
的確 Certain, true, unmistakeable; in fact.
安頓 *An*¹ *tun*⁴. *Quiet*, at rest; comfortable; . . . . *gentle*, staid.
鄙 *Pi*³˒⁴. . . . . Low, mean; rustic.
鄙俗 *Pi*³ *su*². Common, mean, vulgar; shame- . . . . faced, *bashful*.
縮 *Soa*¹˒⁴. To draw back; *to shrink*, to contract; . . . . . to condense.
寒縮 *Han*² *soa*⁴ . . . . Retiring, *bashful*.
官樣 *Kwan*¹ *yang*⁴. Genteel, *well-bred*, gen- . . . . tlemanly; pompous.
大方 *Ta*⁴ *fang*¹. Genteel, *well-bred;* liberal- . . . . minded, generous.
痊 *Ch'üen*². . . . . Recovered from sickness, well.
愈 *Yü*²˒⁴. . . . . *Cured;* to exceed the more.

痊愈 Recovered, cured, *healed*.
盅 *Chung*¹. . . . . . . A small cup for tea or wine.
看守 *K'an*¹ *shou*³. To watch over, to guard, ... *to keep safely*.
墓 *Mu*⁴. . . . . . . *A grave*, a tomb, a sepulcher.
墳墓 *Fên*² *mu*⁴. . . . . *A grave*, a sepulcher.
懼 *Chü*⁴. . . . . *To fear*, to be apprehensive.
懼怕 *Chü*⁴ *p'a*⁴. To fear, *to be affrighted*, to . . . . dread, to stand in awe.
兢 *Ching*¹. . . . . Fearful, solicitous.
戰兢 *Chan*⁴ *ching*¹. To be alarmed, *to tremble*, ... to quake.
含 *Han*². To hold in the mouth; to contain; to . . . . cherish; to restrain.
含糊 *Han*² *hu*². Indistinct, *vague;* uncertain; . . . . indefinite; reserved.

強辯嗎。○15我父親今年八十歲、身體還是健結健結壯實壯實的。○16這些零零碎碎的東西、可以裝在箱子裏。○17女兒家應當穩安穩安重頓重頓的纔是。○18你不好寒鄙寒鄙縮俗縮俗的、叫人看着不大官方樣。○19平平安安的回去罷、你的病已經痊愈了。○20咱們爽痛爽痛快快的喝幾盅、時候不早喇。○21看守墳墓的人懼怕、戰戰兢兢、幾乎嚇死。○22我必得把家中的事、安排得妥妥當當的、纔能起身。○23你到底是願意是不願意、快說決痛斷快話、老是這麼含含糊糊的、像什麼呢。○24李昌齡好天分、可惜沒有個好言口談齒、說話嘟噥嘟噥攏攏攏攏的、叫人聽不出來。○25我不能去求告他、叫他看着小小器器的。○26那個孩子一點耳性沒有、必得煞諄煞諄實切實切的

15 My father is eighty years old this year, and his health is still quite robust.

16 These odds and ends you may put into the box.

17 Girls [or, young women] should by rights, be quiet and gentle.

18 You should not be bashful or people will think you are ill-bred.

19 Return in peace; your disease is already healed.

20 Let us quickly drink a few cups, the hour is not early.

21 And those who kept the grave trembled with fear, being frightened almost to death.

22 I must put my home affairs in good order before I can start.

23 Say definitely at once whether you are willing or not, and don't keep vacillating in this unseemly way.

24 Li Ch'ang Ling is quite gifted. It is a pity he has not a better utterance. He mumbles his words so that one can not understand him.

25 I am not going to make a poor mouth to him, and give him a chance to look down on me.

26 That child is very heedless; you will find it necessary to charge him very straitly.

齒 *Ch'ï3*. Front teeth; *words;* age; toothed.

口齒 *K'ou3 ch'ï3*. *Utterance*, enunciation.

言談 *Yien2 t'an2*. Speech, *utterance*.

嘟 *T'u1*. Thick, tongue-tied, lisping.

噥 *Nu3*. Indistinct, inarticulate, nasal.

嘟噥 To mutter, to *mumble;* to ravel out.

禿攏 *T'u1 lung3*. The same.

求告 *Ch'iu2 kao4*. To beg, to entreat, *to make a poor mouth.*

耳性 *Êr3 hsing4*. Capacity to hear, power of attention.

煞實 *Sha1 shï2*. Firm, close, compact; decided; forcible, pointed; *straitly.*

諄 *Chun1*. To enjoin, to reiterate; *emphatically*, earnestly.

諄切 *Chun1 ch'ie4*. Carefully, emphatically, *straitly.*

吹打 *Ch'wei1 ta3*. To play (as a band).

完全 *Wan2 ch'üen2*. Complete, entire; finished; *all.*

正直 *Chêng4 chï2*. Straitforward, *upright*, truthful.

彎 *Wan1*. Bent, bowed, crooked, curved.

彎曲 *Wan1 ch'ü1*. Crooked, *tortuous.*

謊詐 *Hwang3 cha4*. False, *deceitful*, dishonest, double-tongued.

端正 *Twan1 chêng4*. Correct, exemplary; *upright;* sedate, respectful.

歪扭 *Wai1 niu3*. Awry, askew, crooked; distorted; *lounging.*

囑咐他纔行。○你27的王到你那裏去、和和平平的、騎着驢後面跟隨一個驢駒子。○過28公子齊齊整整的備了千金聘禮、又擇了一個吉日、吹吹打打送到水家來。○我29在外頭十二年的工夫、現在回家、看見老少都還完完全全的、實在感恩不盡。○這30個心經、都是說心要正直、不要彎彎曲曲的、要誠實、不要詭詭詐詐的、要爽快、不要齷齷齪齪的。○人31坐着應當端端正正的、不可歪歪扭扭的、一點兒不穩重體統。

27 Thy King cometh unto thee peacefully, riding upon an ass with its foal following.

28 Kwoă Kung-tsï prepared a full set of very costly betrothal presents, and, selecting a lucky day, sent them accompanied by a band of music to the Shwei family.

29 I have been absent twelve years, and I cannot be sufficiently thankful that now on my return home, I find the family circle still unbroken.

30 This *Classic of the Heart* everywhere requires that the heart be upright and not tortuous, truthful and not deceitful, cheerful and not fretful.

31 When one is sitting, he should sit upright and not lounge in an undignified manner.

NOTES.

10 After 怎麼 either 着 or 的 or 樣 is understood.

13 The last clause might also with equal propriety be rendered *Let him go quietly to sleep.*

17 家 is added to 女兒 to generalize it.

19 As the sentence stands in the New Testament, 經 is omitted. Its use adds both to the euphony and perspicuity of the sentence. In Mandarin the 經 is rarely omitted, save in certain fixed expressions. It is never omitted when followed by a double word as here.

23 In Pekingese 老 as here used denotes time. It is not so used in Central or Southern Mandarin:—Les. 127. Sub.

28 吉日 is somewhat bookish. In common conversation 好日子 is nearly always used. For colloquial the 備 of the previous clause should also be expanded to 豫備.

30 心經 is the title of a book exhorting men to the cultivation of propriety and virtue.

LESSON CVIII.

REPEATED ACTION.

屢次 Frequently, constantly, continually, repeatedly. Often reduplicated for emphasis.

時刻 Every moment, constantly, incessantly. Often reduplicated for emphasis.

時時 Every time, always, constantly.

時常 Constantly, always, habitually.

常常 Continually, constantly, habitually.

往往 Frequently, every little while.

不閒着 or **不閒之** Without ceasing, continuously, incessantly, always.

不歇氣 The same. (s.)

不住的 Incessantly, continuously, all the time. A limiting word generally follows 住 (6) (10).

不斷 Continuously, without interruption.

動不動 Again and again, frequently, on every occasion, all the time.

値不値 The same. Widely used but not *t'ung hsing.*

得不得 Again and again, all the time, always, time after time. (N.)

常不常 The same. (s)

好不好 Over and over, again and again, frequently. (C. & S.)

弄不弄 Time after time, time and again, all the time. (C). Read *no⁴ pu⁴ no⁴* or *nung⁴ pu⁴ nung⁴*.

成天家, **整天的** Constantly, always, all the time, perpetually:—Les. 72. Note 1.

數次 A number of times, several times.

第一百八課

你[1]要時刻留神。○我[2]們兩個是常常的見面。○他[3]動不動(好不好)拿着死嚇人。○五[4]個人做了三天、還看不出做的生活(活)在那裏、只看見他們不閒着(之)吃烟。○我[5]整天家(的)就是愛(好)替古人擔憂、○他[6]們不住口的說了半天話。○我[7]脊梁上那個癤子、時刻往外流(淌)膿。○你[8]這樣不閒(歇)着做活、不怕累壞了嗎。○已[9]經告訴他數次、他總不理會。○孫[10]師傅心口疼、在家裏不住聲的叫喚(喊叫)、○你[11]值不值(得不得、常不常)的張着個瓢口(火盆)嘴哭、早晚把我哭死就好喇。○我[12]們雖然多年沒見、却不斷的有信。○這[13]裏緊靠大街、熱鬧(鬧熱)得很、時時刻刻有事、沒有安靜的時候。○王[14]成山是個好人、就是值不值(弄不弄、常不常)喝醉了酒、愛(光)罵人。○怎[15]麼小小的年紀、動

Translation.

1 You should give unremitting attention.
2 We two are constantly meeting each other.
3 In order to frighten people, she frequently threatens to kill herself.
4 These five men have been working three days, but it does not appear what they have done. It seems as if they were all the time smoking.
5 I am much given to sympathizing with the ancients.
6 They talked without ceasing for half a day.
7 That boil on my back is constantly discharging pus.
8 Are you not afraid you will injure yourself by working so constantly?
9 I have told him a number of times, but he pays no attention.
10 Mr. Sun is at home crying out incessantly with a pain in his stomach.
11 You are always bawling with your mouth open as big as a dipper (fire-pan); sooner or later your crying will be the death of me, and then you'll be satisfied, will you?
12 Although we have not seen each other for many years, yet we have corresponded without interruption.
13 This place adjoins the great street and is very much crowded; there is always something on hand—never a moment's quiet.
14 Wang Ch'êng Shan is a good enough man, the trouble is that he frequently gets drunk, and then he is given to abusing people.

Vocabulary.

屢 *Lü*³. Often, frequent; successively; constantly, repeatedly.

留神 *Liu*² *shên*². *To give attention*, to be on the alert, to be watchful.

生活 *Shêng*¹ *hwoă*². *Work*, employment, business. (c. & s.)

住口 *Chu*⁴ *k'ou*³. To stop speaking.

脊 *Chi*²˒³. The spine, *the backbone;* the ridge or comb of a roof.

梁 *Liang*². A bridge; a *ridge-pole;* a beam, a sleeper: a seam.

脊梁. *The back*, the spinal column.

膿 *Nung*², *nêng*². Pus, purulent matter.

歇氣 *Hsie*¹ *ch'i*⁴. To stop, to rest. (s.)

理會 *Li*³ *hwei*⁴. To regard, *to pay attention to*, to notice.

叫喚 *Chiao*⁴ *hwan*⁴. *To cry out*, to yell; to cry or call as animals:—Note 10.

瓢 *P'iao*². A calabash, a gourd; a gourd dipper, *a wooden dipper*.

哭死 *K'u*¹ *sï*³. To cry oneself or another to death:—Les. 183.

安靜 *An*¹ *ching*⁴. *Quiet*, calm, peaceful.

不動就腰疼腿疼呢。○他[16]一秋不斷的吃藥、也沒見出怎麼樣來。○人[17]家串門子、都有時有刻、你是時時刻刻的闖串。○他[18]害癲癇的(抽羊角瘋)病、屢次跌在火裏、屢次跌在水裏。○只[19]從離別以後、心中時常想念。○他[20]屢屢次次的欺負我、實在叫我過不去。○先[21]生到過南京沒有、○答 我已經去過數次。○我[22]們大嫂子、真是個殷勤人、從早到晚不住手的做活。○香[23]齡子好大飯量、若是由着他的性兒、能成天家不住嘴的喫。○無[24]論他們怎樣不好、那總是你的公公婆婆、不可得不得(弄不弄)惹他生氣。○試[25]驗格物的時候、往往弄壞了(踢蹬了)傢什伙。○你[26]動不動想着打人、那一回遭打出禍來、你就後悔不及喇。○從[27]來說家賊難防、他這樣摸摸撡撡(緝緝撡撡)的、誰能時時(時常)防備他呢。○俗[28]語說、

15 How is it that one so young is every little while having pains in his back and legs?

16 He has been taking medicine all the autumn without any apparent effect.

17 Other people have certain times for visiting, but you are continually at it.

18 He is afflicted with epilepsy, and frequently falls into the fire, and frequently into the water.

19 Ever since we parted I have been constantly thinking of you.

20 He is constantly insulting me. I really cannot put up with it.

21 Have you ever been at Nanking, sir? *Ans.* I have been there several times.

22 Our oldest brother's wife is a very industrious body, she works incessantly from morning till night.

23 Hsiang Ling-tsï has an enormous appetite, if you should let him have his will, his mouth would never be empty.

24 No matter how bad they are, still they are your father and mother-in-law. You ought not to be all the time vexing them.

25 In making experiments in natural science, it frequently happens that instruments are broken.

26 You are all the time full of the idea of fighting. One of these times you'll get yourself into trouble, and then it will be too late to repent.

27 It has always been said that thieves in the household are hard to guard against. Who can be always on his guard against such a light-fingered fellow as this?

串 Ch'wan⁴. To string on a string; *to go or pass through;* to connect, to league together; a string of anything:—Les. 125.

串門子 Ch'wan⁴ mên² tsï³. To call, *to visit*, to gad about.

闖門子 Ch'wang³ mên² tsï³. Same.

癲 Tien¹. Crazed, insane; convulsions, fits.

癇 Hsien². Convulsions, epileptic fits.

癲癇 Epileptic fits; convulsions.

羊角瘋 Yang² chiao³ fêng¹. Epileptic fits.

離別 Li² pie². *To part*, to take leave.

想念 Hsiang³ nien⁴. To think about, *to keep in mind*, to long for.

南京 Nan² ching¹. Nanking, the name was given in the Ming dynasty when the capital was moved to Peking.

住嘴 Chu⁴ tswei³. To stop eating.

公公 Kung¹ kung¹. A woman's father-in-law.

婆婆 P'oa² p'oa². A woman's mother-in-law.

驗 Yien⁴. To examine officially, to inspect, *to verify;* to hold an inquest.

試驗 Shï⁴ yien⁴. To try, to test, *to experiment.*

家賊 Chia¹ tsei². A thief in one's own family.

撡 Soa⁴. To feel after; to select, *to take.*

緝 Ch'i⁴. To pursue; *to search for.* See ch'i¹.

久病牀前無孝子、到病的日子久了、雖有孝子伺候、也難時時都對心思。○你[29]們也曉得犯法不好、却不住的犯法、這是甚麽緣故呢。○帮[30]助人不過在那一時、常常如此、誰能帮助得起呢。○東[31]鄰舍那個老頭子、實在不成脾氣、自己在外邊不住手（閒着）的賭錢、回家還要時刻找事、值不值好不好、摔盆摔碗、打老婆罵孩子。○遲[32]雲生屢屢次次來說閒話、拉閒聒兒、閒搗白、逢拉開話匣子、就是半天、誰有這麽些工夫陪伴他呢。○明[33]明是個水長蟲（蛇）、你們都稱他爲大王、給他燒香燒紙、請他聽戲、若他眞眞是神、你們這樣敬奉他、還能屢次被黃水淹了嗎。

28 The saying is, "A dutiful son is never found at the bedside of one who is long ill." When anyone is long ill, it is hard even for a dutiful son always to serve him to his mind.

29 You know it is not right to break the law, yet you are continually breaking it. What is the reason of this?

30 Helping others is only a temporary thing. Who can afford to keep on helping indefinitely?

31 The old fellow who lives to the east of us is certainly a hard case. When away from home he spends his time gambling, and when he comes home he is continually making trouble, ever and anon smashing the crockery, beating his wife and abusing his children.

32 Ch'i Yün Shêng is constantly coming over to gossip. Let him once get started he will run on for half a day. Who can afford the time required to entertain him?

33 Manifestly it is merely a water snake which you address as "The Great King," burning incense and paper to him and inviting him to enjoy theatricals. If he were really a god, would you, who thus worship him, still be flooded again and again by the water of the Yellow River?

摸摖 *Moă*¹ *soă*⁴. To feel after; to feel with the hand, *to finger*:—Note 27.

摸緝 *Moă*¹ *ch'i*⁴. The same. (s.)

孝子 *Hsiao*⁴ *tsï*³. A dutiful son.

找事 *Chao*³ *shï*⁴. To find fault, to pick a quarrel, *to make a disturbance*, to raise a row; to look for employment.

搗白 *Tao*³ *poă*². To gossip, to chat, to talk together. (s.)

聒 *Kwa*¹,⁴. *Incessant talking;* loquacity, jabber. Also *kwoă*¹.

閒聒 *Hsien*² *kwa*⁴. Idle talk, *chit chat.*

話匣子 *Hwa*⁴ *hsia*² *tsï*³. "Talk box", a facetious term for the mouth or the faculty of speaking.

伴 *Pan*⁴. A comrade, an associate; *to attend.*

陪伴 *P'ei*² *pan*⁴. *To entertain*, to bear one company.

大王 *Tai*⁴ *wang*². A rebel chief, a freebooter:—Note 33.

敬奉 *Ching*⁴ *fêng*⁴. *To worship*, to serve as men do the gods.

NOTES.

1 Or *You should always keep your wits about you.*

3 Lit., *Takes death* (meaning suicide) *and frightens people.* This is a common threat of Chinese women, and is really their only resort in order to bring their husbands or mothers-in-law to terms, or to get justice at their hands, and it is not unfrequently carried into effect.

5 That is, easily moved by the sorrows and sufferings of historical or fictitious characters.

10 **叫喚** is not properly applied to articulate sounds, though sometimes so used derisively. It is used of the call of almost all animals, thus covering many English words, as bark, bellow, bawl, bray, squeal, etc.

11 **瓢口** *A dipper mouth;* i. e. a mouth as big as a dipper. **火盆嘴** *A fire pan mouth;* i. e., a mouth as big as a fire pan.

第一百九課

若[1]要叫人看明白、必得加上一個小註兒。○這[2]塊手巾、不論怎麼洗也洗不乾淨。○這[3]是一點不含糊的事情、我記得十分清楚。○你[4]看你寫的黑墨烏嘴糊眼的、誰能看清楚了呢。○先[5]把事情辦停當了、再去聽戲罷。○我[6]當是你和他說妥當了、淨叫我去碰釘子。○我[7]若是不帶眼鏡、這樣的字、一點也看不真切親確。○李[8]姑娘過於靦腆、一句話說了半天、到底沒說清楚。○于[9]先生講這個題目、講了半天到底沒講透徹。○也[10]

Translation.

1 If you want people to understand it, it will be necessary to add an explanatory note.

2 No matter how you wash this handkerchief you cannot make it clean.

3 There is not the least doubt about it. I remember it with perfect distinctness.

4 Just look at your writing how it is blurred and blotted; who will be able to make anything out of it?

5 First dispose of your business properly, then go to the theatre.

6 I thought you had arranged it with him satisfactorily. You put me in a very embarrassing position.

7 Unless I wear spectacles, I cannot see this kind of print with the least distinctness.

8 Miss Li is entirely too diffident. She has been trying for half a day to get out one sentence, and after all did not speak it clearly.

9 Mr. Yü has been discoursing on this text for ever so long, and after all has not made it clear.

14 喝醉酒 *To drink drunk with wine.* 酒 is added for emphasis. 光 gives the idea of *given to*, but is rejected by the Peking teacher.

19 The style is that of a letter.

24 那 here fills the place of a personal pronoun and is so translated.

26 打出禍來 may mean, *to inflict a serious wound* and so become liable to prosecution, or the payment of damages; or it may mean, as we say, "*to hit the wrong man.*" Note that 那一遭 does not here mean *that time*, but *whichever time*, or *one of these times*.

27 摸摸揉揉的 *Laying hands on whatever is within reach, pilfering, light-fingered.* Only used in this sense when reduplicated. In the South 摸摸緝緝的 is used in the same way.

31 不成脾氣 *Not constituting a disposition*; i. e., wanting in the essentials of a right disposition. There are other phrases on the same model, thus we have 不成材料 *unsuitable for the purpose, worthless*, 不成敬意 *not sufficient to express respect.* 摔 here means *to set* or *throw down with a bang*, and hence, *to smash.*

33 Snakes that leave the water and come on land during a flood, are regarded as sacred and divine, being possessed by the god who controls the flood. They are often fed up and worshipped with expensive ceremonies by both officers and people. 黃水 is a contracted term for the flood water from the Yellow River. 大王 is a term found in novels and applied to noted robbers and freebooters. It was first conferred as a title on supposed supernatural snakes by Kanghi, the second Emperor of the present dynasty.

LESSON CIX.

Double Auxiliaries.

In addition to the several single auxiliaries already illustrated, there are a number of double words added to verbs to qualify their meaning. Those most frequently used are the following:—

明白 Clear,—added to verbs to express the clearness of the action, or its satisfactory completion.

清楚 Well defined,—added to verbs to express the perfect clearness and distinctness of the action.

完全 Finished,—added to verbs to express the entire completion of the action.

妥當 Satisfactory,—adds its force to the verb it follows. 妥 is also used alone.

停當 is the same as 妥當, but a little more colloquial.

乾淨 Clean,—adds its force to the verb it follows.

不知是我沒說明白、可也不知是他沒聽明白。○你[11]看他走將起來(走起來)、搖搖擺擺的、自己覺着是個景兒(很有滋味)喇。○就[12]是常辦公事的人、也必有個參差不齊、那能樣樣都辦得妥當呢。○無[13]論學綱鑑、學史記、不過記得大關節目、說到那些細微處、誰也記不完全。○先[14]把被套行李、預備妥當、苫(轎)子一來、我們就起身。○我[15]和寶興的賬、上月就算清楚喇。○多[16]虧當時我和他立下合同、上面寫的清楚、不然又叫他賴了去了。○學[17]問一道、是大海無邊、怎能

10 I do not know whether it was that I did not say it plainly, or that he did not hear it correctly.

11 See the air with which he struts along. He imagines that he is perfectly stunning.

12 Even one who is constantly transacting business will sometimes fall short. How is it possible to always give entire satisfaction?

13 In learning either annals or history one can remember only the general outline; as to the particulars, no one can remember them all.

14 Get the bedding and luggage ready beforehand, and as soon as the litter comes we will start.

15 My account with Pao Hsing was settled in full last month.

16 It is very fortunate that at the time I had an agreement drawn up with him in which everything was distinctly written out; otherwise he would have imposed on me again.

17 Learning is a great and shoreless sea.

眞切 Vivid,—adds its force to the verb it follows.

親確 Distinct,—adds its force to the verb it follows.

透徹 Perspicuous,—adds its force to the verb it follows.

齊全 Complete,—adds its force to the verb it follows.

將起來 An auxiliary form found in Chinese novels. It is used with verbs of motion and expresses an inceptive, or a progressive idea.

With this lesson we take leave of the subject of verbal auxiliaries; not that there are not more, both single and double, but because in most cases they are each limited to one or two special applications, each of which is best learned as an independent phrase.

VOCABULARY.

註 *Chu*⁴. To define, to explain; *a note*, an explanation, an emendation.

小註 *Hsiao*³ *chu*⁴. A note, *an explanation*, a comment:—Note 1.

黑墨糊眼 *Hei*¹ *mei*⁴ *hu*² *yien*³. Blotted, blurred, defaced.

黑墨烏嘴 *Hei*¹ *mei*⁴ *wu*¹ *tswei*³. The same.

停當 *T'ing*² *tang*¹. *In proper order*, satisfactory, all right:—see Sub.

親確 *Ch'in*¹ *ch'iŏ*⁴. *Clear*, distinct, well defined, sharp:—see Sub.

愐 *Mien*³. To reflect; *modest*, ashamed.

靦 *T'ien*³,⁴. Ashamed, *bashful;* to blush.

愐靦 Modest, *bashful*, shamefaced.

于 *Yü*². To proceed; *a surname:* also used as synonymous with 於.

徹 *Ch'ê*⁴. To penetrate; *clear*, perspicuous.

透徹 *T'ou*⁴ *ch'ê*⁴. To comprehend; *clear*, perspicuous; thorough:—see Sub.

參 *Ts'ên*¹. Uneven, not uniform. See *ts'an*¹, also *shên*¹.

差 *Ts'ï*¹. Having uneven points, rugged. See *ch'a*¹ and *ch'ai*¹.

參差不齊 *Ts'ên*¹ *ts'ï*¹ *pu*⁴ *ch'i*². Uneven, irregular.

綱 *Kang*¹. A bond of union, a principle, a rule.

把所有的書藉、都學完全了呢。○現18在兩社（鄉）因為這條河壩、又打起官司來喇、也不知這位大老爺、能給他們斷清楚了不能。○我19這樣盤腿坐着、光壓痲了脚、所以坐一會子、必得站將起來（站起來）、活動活動。○你20明天可以跟着去上工罷、我和掌櫃（尺、作）的已經說明白了。○那21間房子還沒收拾嗎、（答）收拾了一氣、還沒收拾妥當。○分22家總要分得清楚、免得分家不明、遺留後患。○他23所講究的、不過附會之說、仍舊沒講明白。○追24賊追出一大半子、這就

How can one ever learn all the books there are?

18 At present the two townships have gone to law again about this river embankment. It remains to be seen whether this magistrate will be able to settle the matter satisfactorily.

19 This sitting cross-legged always makes my feet numb, so that after sitting awhile I have to get up and move around a little.

20 You may go to work to-morrow with the others. I have arranged it with the manager (foreman).

21 Have you not yet put that room in order? *Ans.* I worked at it a little while but it is not yet finished.

22 In dividing the family inheritance, it is important to secure a clear understanding so as to avoid subsequent difficulties growing out of an unsatisfactory division.

23 His exposition simply runs in the old rut, after all he has not made it clear.

24 If one recovers the greater part of any stolen property, that is con-

---

鑑 *Chien*⁴. A mirror; an example; a precedent; a precept.

綱鑑 Historical annals, an outline history.

史 *Shï*³. A historian; *a history*, records.

史記 *Shï*³ *chi*⁴. A history, a chronological record.

節目 *Chie*² *mu*⁴. Divisions, heads, classification, *outline*.

大關節目 *Ta*⁴ *kwan*¹ *chie*² *mu*⁴. The general outline, the principal heads or divisions.

微 *Wei*¹. *Minute*, insignificant; subtle, hidden; slightly; rather:—Les. 177.

細微 *Hsi*⁴ *wei*¹. *Minute*, fine, very small.

被套 *Pei*⁴ *t'ao*⁴. A large bag or wallet for holding bedding and clothing.

行李 *Hsing*² *li*³. Luggage, baggage.

籍 *Chi*⁴. A book, a record. Also *chi*².

書籍 *Shu*¹ *chi*⁴. *Books*, records.

社 *Shê*⁴. The tutelary god of a particular place; a village; *a township*.

壩 *Pa*⁴. An embankment, a dike.

盤 *P'an*². To sit with the legs crossed under one.

盤腿 *P'an*² *t'wei*³. To sit tailor fashion as Chinese women constantly do.

活動 *Hwoă*² *tung*⁴. Loose, moveable; variable, *to move*, to exercise.

掌尺 *Chang*³ *ch'ï*³. *A foreman*, a head workman, a boss.

掌作 *Chang*³ *tsoă*⁴. The same.

遺留 *I*² *liu*². To bequeath, *to leave behind*, to transmit.

附 *Fu*⁴. To lean upon, to cling, to attach oneself to; to add to; a supplement.

附會 *Fu*⁴ *hwei*⁴ *To echo the words of another*; to gloss over; to speak at random.

成就 *Ch'êng*² *chiu*⁴. To complete, to finish, *to fulfil*.

遵 *Tsun*¹. To obey, to conform to, *to act as required*, to follow out. [to keep.

遵守 *Tsun*¹ *shou*³. To observe a law,

遵行 *Tsun*¹ *hsing*². *To perform what is commanded*, to obey.

算好、還能追齊全了嗎。○25貨都預備齊全了、只等車來就裝。○26我們的救主、已經成就了律法的義、凡律法當遵守的、他都替我們守完全了、當遵行的、他都替我們行完全了、所以我們雖然有罪、若肯悔改信主、就必得救。

sidered very good indeed. Did you suppose it was possible to get it all back?

25 The goods are all in readiness, and as soon as the carts come, we will commence loading.

26 Our Saviour has already fulfilled the righteousness of the law. Everything the law requires us to observe, He has completely observed for us; what it requires us to perform, He has completely performed for us; so that although we are sinners, yet if we will repent and believe in the Saviour, we shall certainly be saved.

NOTES.

1 小註 *A small comment*, is so called because usually inserted in small type and in double columns.

6 碰釘子 *To run against a nail*, which produces a sudden and painful revulsion of feeling, hence, *to be embarrassed, to be nonplussed.*

10 可 as here used, is little more than a mere expletive.

11 搖搖擺擺 *To swing and sway, to swagger, to strut.* The single form of this reduplication is rarely used. 覺着很有滋味 *Delighted with his own self-satisfaction;* 覺着是個景兒 *Thinks he is somebody worth looking at.*

14 轎子 might also refer to a sedan chair, but the mention of luggage implies that a mule litter was intended.

17 學問一道 *This business of learning.* 一道 is added for the purpose of specializing and emphasizing.

18 The use of 這 seems to imply that the officer in question was a new one, different from the former one.

20 There seems to be a great variety of terms for *head workman.* 掌櫃的, which is used in this sense in Peking, *generally* means the responsible man in a business firm, rather than a foreman or head workman.

22 遺留後患 *To leave behind an after trouble*, a phrase borrowed from books.

23 Chinese teachers are much given to repeating over and over again the original word or words with slight variations, and calling that an explanation. In expounding the classics (which is here referred to), they for the most part simply rehearse with slight variations and verbal expansions the words of the standard commentator.

26 凡律法當遵守的 *Whatever* [in] *the law* [we] *ought to observe.*

LESSON CX.

CONNECTIVES.

The more commonly used words of this class were given in Les. 12. This lesson adds others less frequently used, but equally important.

與 To give,—with, to, when joined with 同 it means, *as*, (2)

同 To unite,—together with, in common, and, the same.

連 To connect,—also, even, and. The normal place for 連 is at the beginning of a clause, and it is generally followed, after the subject, by either 都 or 也.

帶 A girdle,—together with, and, including.

連......帶. Both ...... and, between ..... and.

並 Two joined together,—together with, and, and also, moreover.

以及 Together with, in addition to, and also.

VOCABULARY.

並 *Ping^{4}.* Two joined together, unitedly; together with:—see Sub.; enforces a negative:—Les. 121.

玩笑 *Wan^{2} hsiao^{4}.* To jest, *to joke*, to talk in fun.

惱 *Nao^{3}.* *To get angry*, to feel irritated, to be indignant.

夫婦 *Fu^{1} fu^{4}.* ...... Husband and wife.

舛 *Ch'wan^{3}.* ...... *Opposed to*, perverse.

舛錯 *Ch'wan^{3} ts'o^{4}.* ...... An error, *a mistake.*

第一百十課

誰[1]好意思與你爲仇呢。○我[2]與你父親同年歲。○連[3]他帶我、都受了傷。○我[4]不過是與你玩笑、你就惱了嗎。○他[5]們議論他、連我咱們也帶上了。○我[6]明天必過去同他商量。○再[7]去見他、應該同着別人。○我[8]與他素不相識。○不[9]許他與匪類相交。○夫[10]婦是有福同享、有罪同受。○與[11]人方便、自己方便。○謝[12]兆年手上生長瘡、連胳膊都腫起來了。○若[13]不同他講明白了、以後怕有舛差錯錯。○與[14]我咱們無干的事、我咱們就不必管。○兒[15]子與爹娘、論不得是非。○我[16]合家的人、以及羊羣、都平安無事。○姜[17]大興如今賭起錢來喇、把房子連帶地、都輸淨了。○看[18]不得他是

Translation.

1 Who would have the face to act as your enemy?
2 I am of the same age as your father.
3 He and I were both wounded.
4 You ought not to get angry when I was merely joking with you.
5 In criticizing him they also implicated us.
6 I shall certainly go over to-morrow and consult with him.
7 When you go again to see him, you should take some one else with you.
8 I was not acquainted with him previously.
9 Do not allow him to associate with the profligate.
10 Husband and wife enjoy their blessings and bear their sorrows in common.
11 To accommodate others is to accommodate oneself.
12 Shie Chao Nien has a boil on his hand which has caused the swelling of his whole lower arm.
13 If you do not have a distinct understanding with him, I fear there will afterwards be some mistake.
14 It is better not to meddle with that which does not concern us.
15 A son should not contest a question of right and wrong with his parents.
16 My whole family, together with my flocks, are all getting along very well.
17 Chiang Ta Hsing has taken to gambling, and has lost both his house and his land.

差錯 *Ch'a^1 ts'o^4.* An error, *a mistake*, a misunderstanding, a blunder.

無干 *Wu^2 kan^1.* No part in, *no concern of.*

丈母 *Chang^4 mu^3.* A man's mother-in-law.

虛度 *Hsü^1 tu^4.* To live in vain, to waste or *squander* (time).

日月 *Ji^4 yüe^4.* Time.

傢具 *Chia^1 chü^4.* Fixtures, furniture, *effects.*

罄 *Ch'ing^4.* Exhausted, emptied; entirely, *wholly*:—Les. 149.

罄淨 *Ch'ing^4 ching^4.* Entirely finished, quite used up, *all gone*:—Les. 149, Sub.

白丁 *Pai^2 ting^1.* *A man without a degree*, a common man.

清吉 *Ch'ing^1 chi^2.* Perfect felicity, entire good fortune. (w.)

福安 *Fu^2 an^1.* Peace and happiness. (w.)

性命 *Hsing^4 ming^4.* *Life*, the vital principle, existence.

伯 *Pai^3.* A father's elder brother. Also read *po^2* in this sense, and in Shantung *pei^4*. See *po^2*.

大伯子 *Ta^4 pai^3 tsï^3.* A husband's elder brother:—Note 28.

小叔子 *Hsiao^3 shu^2 tsï^3.* A husband's younger brother.

擄 *Lu^3.* To plunder, *to take or carry captive.*

使費 *Shï^3 fei^4.* Outlay, *expenses.*

費用 *Fei^4 yung^4.* The same.

酬 *Ch'ou^2.* To pledge a guest; to recompense, *to requite.*

應酬 *Ying^4 ch'ou^2.* *To reciprocate friendship or kindness;* to entertain; intercourse, reciprocity; to give a fee to a superior.

個秀才、秀才却與秀才不同。○ 19 你這個沒大沒小的、連丈母都要笑了。○ 20 今若不隨哥哥去同生同死、却投那裏去。○ 21 不但是你們虛度日月、連我也白費了工夫咯。○ 22 李三元家失了火、把糧食衣裳、並了大小傢具、都燒得罄淨。○ 23 今天黃福財請了三桌客、連一個白丁也沒有。○ 24 父就是天、母就是地、那有爲人敢與天地爭是非呢。○ 25 有個騎牲口的女人過河、連人帶牲口、都跌在水裏。○ 26 敬請李先生大人、並合家淸福吉安。○ 27 一犯了案、連身家性命

18 Do not depend upon his being a graduate; there are graduates and graduates.

19 You presumptuous fellow; cracking coarse jokes even with your mother-in-law!

20 If I do not go with you now for life or for death, where shall I go?

21 Not only have you squandered your time, but I also have spent mine in vain.

22 A fire broke out in Li San Yüen's home, and his grain and clothes, together with all his effects, were entirely burned up.

23 Hwang Fu Ts'ai invited three tables of guests to-day, and there was not a single one without a degree.

24 The father is Heaven and the mother is Earth; where is the man who would dare to contest a point of right and wrong with Heaven and Earth.

25 A woman was fording the river on an animal, when the animal stumbled, and both woman and beast fell into the water.

26 My best wishes to his honor, Mr. Li, and his family.

27 If once you commit a crime, your own life and the lives of your family are all endangered.

簿 *Pu*⁴. A register; an account book; *a blank book*, a memorandum.

緣簿 *Yüen*² *pu*⁴. A subscription book for religious or charitable purposes.

賭博 *Tu*³ *pŏ*². . . . . . To gamble.

娼 *Ch'ang*¹. . . . . A singing woman, a courtesan.

妓 *Chi*⁴. . . . . . . A courtesan, a prostitute.

娼妓 A prostitute, a strumpet.

賊盜 *Tsei*² *tao*⁴. *A robber*, a thief, a highwayman.

盜賊 *Tao*⁴ *tsei*². . . . . . The same.

急忙 *Chi*² *mang*². Quickly, hurriedly; promptly, *suddenly*, for the time being.

樹林 *Shu*⁴ *lin*². . . . *A wood*, a grove; a forest.

䠀 *Ts'wan*⁴. *To leap*, to jump; to prance; to spurt out.

廊 *Lang*². . . . . *A verandah*, a porch, a gallery.

厦 *Sha*⁴. . . . . . . A projecting roof, a shed.

簷 *Yien*². . . . . . . The eaves of a house.

厦簷 Projecting eaves; *a projecting roof supported on pillars*.

花消 *Hwa*¹ *hsiao*¹. . . . . *Expense*, outlay.

酬謝 *Ch'ou*² *hsie*⁴. To reciprocate in kind, *to return a favor by a present*.

賀喜 *Hê*⁴ *hsi*³. . . . . . To offer congratulations.

酒飯 *Chiu*³ *fan*⁴. Food fit to be eaten with wine, a feast.

厮 *Sï*¹. . . . . *A servant*, a menial attendant.

小厮 *Hsiao*³ *sï*¹. *A serving boy*, a waiter; a little boy, a son.

鬟 *Hwan*². The hair dressed in a knot on the top of the head, *a tuft*.

丫鬟 *Ya*¹ *hwan*². A slave girl, *a waiting maid*. Note 35.

僕 *P'u*³,². . . . . . *A servant*, "your servant."

僕婦 *P'u*² *fu*⁴. . . . *A slave woman*, a nurse. (w.)

册 *Ts'ê*⁴. . . . . A list, *a register;* records.

花名册 *Hwa*¹ *ming*² *ts'ê*⁴. A general roll or *register*, a list of adherents.

卯 *Mao*³. The fourth of the twelve branches; 5 to 7 o'clock A.M., *morning*.

卯簿 *Mao*³ *pu*⁴. A muster roll,—so named because called in the morning.

都保不住。○28我們(俺)當家的(孩子爹)叫賊殺了、大伯子同小叔子、也都叫賊擄了去喇。○29我家中的使費(費用)太重、吃米燒柴、人情應酬、連經戲緣簿、每年總要(得)五百多吊錢。○30這些賭博場、並娼妓園子、正是賊盜出沒的所在。○31那獅子見他要跑、急忙躥出樹林、撲在他身上、連撕帶咬、把他傷了個不堪。○32今天我要拾掇客堂、可以將裏頭的椅子、和桌子、連小床、帶書架子、以及所有的零碎東西、都搬到廊子(廈簷)底下去。○33我的孫子今年進學、花消太多喇、連學

28 My husband was killed by the robbers, and his elder and younger brothers all carried away captives by them.

29 The expenses of my family are quite too heavy. What with rice and fuel, friendly contributions and social reciprocities, together with assessments for prayers and theatricals, I require over five hundred strings of cash each year.

30 These gambling dens and brothels are the rendezvous of robbers and thieves.

31 The lion seeing he was about to run, leaped suddenly out of the wood and pounced upon him, and what with tearing and biting, wounded him dreadfully.

32 I want to clean up the parlor to-day; you may carry out to the verandah the chairs, tables and sofas, also the bookcase, together with all the smaller articles.

33 My grandson getting his degree this year

NOTES.

3 連他帶我 The double conjunction emphasizes the fact that *both* were wounded, as if one ought to have escaped.

8 素不相識 *Previously not acquainted*, a ready made phrase.

11 A common saying answering to, "A kind act is never thrown away."

18 秀才與秀才不同 Lit. *graduates are not the same as graduates*, or, as we say in English, "*there are graduates and graduates.*"

19 沒大沒小 A very expressive phrase, meaning that the person disregards, or is insensible to, his relation to those above and below him.

24 父就是天母就是地, presents a stock sentiment of Chinese philosophy. The understanding of the common people takes the impersonal pantheistic terms of the learned, in what is practically a personal sense. To the common Chinese mind 天地 means God.

25 Note how 跌 is predicated of both the woman and the animal.

26 This is the stereotyped polite phraseology with which a letter opens.

27 犯了案 *To sin a suit*; i.e., to transgress the law so as to incur a prosecution. 身家性命 In letters, legal documents and books, 身 is used pronominally for the person speaking and sometimes, as here, for the person spoken to or about; *chia* is not an enclitic but is used in its primary sense. The combination is decidedly *Wên*.

28 孩子爹 Women address their husbands, and also speak of them to others, as *the children's father* or as *so and so's father*, using the name of the eldest son, or if there be no son, of the eldest daughter. Other persons also often take up and use the term used by the wife. Men also speak of their wives as the children's mother, etc. 當家的 "*the man of the house*," is more frequently used in the North than in the South. It is a curious fact that while 伯 or 伯伯 or 伯父 means a father's elder brother, a paternal uncle, 伯子 or 大伯子 means a husband's elder brother, a brother-in-law; and that while 叔 or 叔叔 or 叔父 means a father's younger brother, a paternal uncle, 叔子 or 小叔子 means a husband's younger brother, a brother-in-law. 姑 and 舅, and in some localities 姨, follow the same rule; thus 姑 or 姑姑 or 姑母 means a father's sister, a paternal aunt, while 姑子 (大姑子 and 小姑子) means a husband's sister, a sister-in-law.

29 經戲緣簿 A subscription book for raising money to pay for reciting prayers and holding theatricals. These subscriptions are practically *assessments* by the priests.

30 出沒的所在 *Place of appearing and disappearing*; i. e., *hiding place*,—a book expression.

33 送學 Shortly after the examinations are over and the degrees awarded, the magistrate of each district issues a notice, calling the new graduates to meet him on a certain day and be presented to the 老師. They go dressed up in conventional uniform to the magistrate's office, where he

規帶酬謝先生、以及送學時所用的藍衫靴帽吹手、並賀喜的客吃的酒飯等項、一共花了三百多吊。

○我[34]借給王雲山那三十吊錢、這三年一個利錢也沒得、如今他這一死、把我的錢、連本帶利全丟了。

○家[35]中上下所有的管家小厮、以及丫鬟僕婦的名字、一總記在花名册子上、營中兵丁的名字、一總記在卯簿上。

cost a great deal. His graduation fees and present to the teacher, together with the blue coat, boots, hat, musicians, and the feast for those who came to offer congratulations, etc., which were required on the occasion of his matriculation, involved, in all, an expense of over three hundred thousand cash.

34 During these three years I have not received a single cash of interest on that thirty thousand cash that I lent Wang Yün Shan, and now that he has died, my money, both principal and interest, is all lost.

35 The whole family, including stewards and servant boys, together with slave girls and serving women, are all to be entered on the general register; and the names of all the soldiers in the barracks are to be recorded on the muster roll.

treats them to wine, and then goes with them to the 老師, whose official residence is either in, or attached to, the temple of Confucius. They first go into the temple and worship the Sage, and are then formally presented to the 老師 as his pupils (in theory). When dismissed, each one mounts his horse, and, accompanied by musicians and banners, goes round the city or country to call on his friends; after which he is expected to entertain his friends at a feast. These formalities are not, however, compulsory, and those who are too poor to bear the expense, do not go at the invitation of the magistrate, and of course lose the glorification they might otherwise have had.

35 丫鬟 is probably derived from a special manner of wearing the hair indicative of servitude. Both 丫鬟 and 僕婦 are book terms. The colloquial terms are 丫頭 and 老媽.

LESSON CXI.

SIGN OF THE PERFECT PARTICIPLE.

既 is the sign of the perfect participle. It precedes the verb and is usually rendered *having* or *seeing*, sometimes *since* or *inasmuch as*. It is closely allied in meaning to 已經, but differs in that it is only used in a subordinate or participial clause, and implies a principal verb to follow.

既然 } 既是 } The same meaning as 既 alone, 然 and 是 are added for the sake of rhythm, serving also to strengthen slightly the force of 既

既自 Substantially the same as 既然 alone, but more colloquial, and also sometimes local.

既已 A contraction of 既然已經.

VOCABULARY.

既 *Chi*⁴. . . . To finish; since, seeing:—see Sub.

不算 *Pu*⁴ *swan*⁴. *To count oneself out*, to refuse, ... to disclaim; to go for nothing.

岳 *Yoa*⁴, *yüe*⁴, *yao*⁴. A wife's parents. A contraction of 嶽.

岳父 *Yüe*⁴ *fu*⁴. . . . . A wife's father.

養傷 *Yang*³ *shang*¹. To nurse a wound; *to defray the expense of recovery from a wound.*

管理 *Kwan*³ *li*³. *To rule over*, to govern, to . . . . control, to manage.

第一百一十課

他[1]既走了、由他他罷。○我[2]既說出來、就不能不算。○既[3]然打了他、還能不給他養傷嗎。○他[4]既早知道了、怎麼不早來告訴我呢。○他[5]自己既然沒提、誰好意思的問他呢。○事[6]情既已壞到這個樣子兒、大約難以再好。○你[7]既不嫁、就不該寫庚帖與我。○既[8]然不能替人家做、就當趕快去辭。○你[9]既然是新女婿、怎麼不給你岳父丈人去拜年呢。○我[10]既主意定了、你們都不得多言多語。○你[11]在小事上既有忠心、我要交給你大事管理。○既[12]然知道爹娘的恩了、為甚麼不孝順呢。○哥[13]哥既是不肯饒我、拿把刀來、割我這個顆頭去也就是了。○他[14]既是你的親戚、問他借幾百錢、那不是現成嗎。○你[15]既自是結吧、還這

Translation.

1 Since he has gone, let him do as he likes.
2 Having committed myself, I cannot but stand by it.
3 As you have beaten him, can you avoid bearing the expense of his recovery?
4 Seeing you knew it some time ago, why did you not come sooner and tell me?
5 As he did not mention it himself, who would have the face to ask him?
6 Seeing the business is damaged to this extent, it will probably be hard to right it again.
7 Seeing you do not intend to marry, you should not have given me a betrothal card.
8 Seeing you cannot do it for him, you should go at once and excuse yourself.
9 Being a new son-in-law, why do you not go and pay your father-in-law a new year's call.
10 As I have already made my decision, none of you need say anything more about it.
11 Inasmuch as thou hast been faithful in small things, I will make thee ruler over great things.
12 Since you know the kindness of your father and mother, why do you not honor them?
13 Well, brother, since you are not willing to forgive me, you might as well just take a knife and cut off my head.
14 As he is a relative, what difficulty is there in asking him for the loan of a few hundred cash?

多事 *Toă¹ shï⁴*. To meddle, to interfere, *to be impertinent*.

慮 *Lü⁴*. To think anxiously about, to cogitate, *to care for*, to plan.

大丈夫 *Ta⁴ chang⁴ fu¹*. A spirited magnanimous man.

梭 *Soă¹*. A shuttle.

箭 *Chien⁴*. *An arrow;* an archer; a bowshot; swift as an arrow.

忽 *Hu¹*. *To neglect*, to slight; careless; suddenly, unexpectedly :—Les. 115.

疎忽 *Su¹ hu¹*. Careless, *negligent*, lax.

赶攏 *Kan³ lung³*. To curry favor, to pay court to, to coax.

俯就 *Fu³ chiu⁴*. To accommodate oneself to, to curry favor with.

材 *Ts'ai²*. *Materials;* qualities; abilities.

材料 *Ts'ai² liao⁴*. *Materials;* ingredients; substance; capabilities.

辦置 *Pan⁴ chï⁴*. *To get ready;* to provide; to procure.

爽神 *Shwang³ shên²*. *Quick*, prompt, expeditious.

欠帖 *Ch'ien⁴ t'ie³*. A promissory note, a bond, an I. O. U.

警 *Ching³*. *To warn*, to caution; to urge one to reform.

麼多說話做什麼。○旣16然是我在這兒、看着我的面上、饒過他這一次罷。○那17一日沒有費用、旣有費用、就一日也少不得這個錢了。○你18旣沒親眼看見、怎麼知道的這麼詳細呢。○他19這正是多事、人家本主旣然願意、他還用不肯嗎。○旣20無遠慮、必有近憂。○若21是沒有學問、也還可說、旣然有這樣的學問、爲甚麼不去考呢。○22咱我們不要走、他旣擺上上了酒、還能不預備飯嗎。○他23旣自是心裏難受、你又去找他、他還能對你說好的嗎。○旣24然是個男子漢、大丈夫、辦事說話、不好婆婆娘娘老老婆婆婆婆媽媽的。○俗25語說、日月如梭、光陰似箭、光陰旣過去的這麼快、還可一刻疎忽嗎。○他26旣是欺軟怕硬的東西、就不用理他、你若去俯趕就攏他、他就

15 Seeing you stammer, why do you talk so much?

16 Seeing I am here present, forgive him this once for my sake.

17 What day is there when you have no outlay? This being the case, you cannot do even a single day without money.

18 Not having been an eye-witness, how do you come to know it all so minutely?

19 This is a pure impertinence of his. Seeing the original party is willing, what business has he to dissent?

20 Since you have no care for the future, trouble will be sure to overtake you soon.

21 If he had no literary attainments, there would be some excuse; but seeing he has the scholarship, why not go and compete?

22 Don't let us go; having set out the wine can he fail to have food ready?

23 Is it likely you will get a favorable response, seeing you are applying to him when he is already worried?

24 As you boast of being a man, you should not speak and act in an effeminate way.

25 The saying is, "Days and months fly like a shuttle; time speeds by like an arrow." Since time passes so quickly, we should not waste a single moment.

26 Since he is a fellow who insults the weak and cringes to the strong, it

警戒 *Ching*³ *chie*⁴. *To warn,* to caution; to threaten; to exhort.

省 *Hsing*³. To examine, to inquire into; to watch; *to awaken.* See *shêng*³.

悟 *Wu*⁴. *To arouse,* to awake; to perceive, to understand, to reflect.

省悟 *To awake to a sense of,* to become aware of, to become sensible of.

頑 *Wan*². Stupid, heedless, *immovable.*

愚頑 *Yü*² *wan*². Thick-headed, *obtuse,* stupid; heedless; mulish.

NOTES.

3 When one man wounds another in a fight, it is customary to require him to defray the expense of medical treatment, and in some cases pay for loss of time also, while the wound is healing.

7 與 is used for 給, see Les. 25.

9 Custom requires a son-in-law to pay his respects and carry a present to his father-in-law at the new year for three successive years, after which it is optional.

10 主意 may here be regarded as a compound verb and 定 as its auxiliary; or if taken as a noun, it is to be regarded as transposed for rhetorical effect from its usual position. The common order would be 我主意旣定了.

13 The phrase 把刀來 is probably elliptical for 把刀拿來, for 把 does not ordinarily take 來 alone as an auxiliary. 也 serves to connect the refusal to forgive and the beheading,—*since you will not forgive me, you might as well also cut my head off.*

17 這個 here refers back to the subject of discourse.

更長了價錢兒喇。○材27料既然都辦置就了、做起來也爽神。○他28這箇欠帖、到底是箇假的、從前要錢的時候、叫他蹧蹋的家裏老少不安、如今既已知道是假的、咱能叫他安穩嗎、總得照實告他一狀、叫他受點刑罰、纔能出我這口氣喇。○王29蘭堂眞是糊塗人、我警戒過他好幾次、他總不省悟、他既然這麼愚頑、吃虧是免不了的。

is best to pay no attention to him. Once begin to coax him, and he will presume all the more.

27 Having the materials all ready, it can be made very quickly.

28 This note of his after all is forged. When he was pressing for payment, he worried us so that neither old nor young got any rest. Now that we know it is false, shall we allow him to take his ease? Only by entering suit according to the facts, and giving him a taste of punishment, can I satisfy my resentment.

29 Wang Lan T'ang is a very foolish man. I have warned him several times, but he cannot be aroused [to a sense of his danger]. Seeing he is so obtuse, he will just have to suffer the consequences.

19 人家 and 本主 are in apposition, referring to the same person.

20 This sentiment is from the Confucian Analects, inculcating the wisdom of planning well for the future.

21 A full translation of 也還可說 would require, *there would then still be some excuse.*

22 In the entertainment of guests, wine is first set forth by itself and subsequently the food is brought on.

24 男子漢 expresses physical qualities, and 大丈夫 mental qualities. The two phrases together express very strongly the qualities of a vigorous manliness. 婆婆娘娘 is the reduplication of a noun after the manner of the adjectives in Les. 107, making a very expressive descriptive adjective.

26 欺軟怕硬的 is used as a compound adjective descriptive of the "fellow" here referred to. 長了價 *Raise his price,*—a figure taken from buying and selling.

LESSON CXII.

ANTITHETICAL PARTICLES.

A number of different words are used to connect clauses used in apposition or antithesis, of which the principal are the following:—

倒 To invert,—on the contrary, yet. 倒 is often used when it cannot be translated. It serves to intimate that the thing asserted is contrary to expectation; thus in the seventh sentence its use intimates or at least suggests, that a commonplace style was to have been expected.

反 To return,—on the other hand, on the contrary, contrariwise, and yet.

倒反 or **反倒**, On the contrary, etc. Joined together, the two words serve to strengthen each other. In some places the one order is more used, and in other places the other order.

偏 Inclined,—bent on, determined—generally indicates a trace of perversity or contrariness. The English language affords no real equivalent for this word.

轉 To turn,—on the other hand, it came to pass, it turned out.

乃 An antithetical book particle, often used in Mandarin. It expresses a mild opposition to something preceding either expressed or implied. It may sometimes be rendered,—but, yet, moreover, etc., but more frequently goes untranslated, having no proper equivalent in English.

VOCABULARY.

乃 *Nai*^{3}. But; doubtless; moreover, in fact; to wit, then:—see Sub. See *ai*^{3}.

長子 *Chang*^{3} *tsï*^{3}. The eldest son.

志向 *Chi*^{4} *hsiang*^{4}. *Will,* purpose, determination; inclination.

雅 *Ya*^{3}. Elegant, *genteel;* refined, polished.

第一百十二課

你[1]打算害人、倒害了自己。○我[2]想不到的倒得了。○明[3]明是你、你反拉扯別人。○他[4]不愛長子、反愛少子。○你[5]人兒雖小、志向倒不小。○你[6]不讓我來、我偏要來。○聽[7]他說的話很雅致、倒不俗氣。○我[8]不和你計較、你倒反反倒和我計較嗎。○他[9]的才學倒不怎麼樣、就是他的血心、乃是人所不及的。○當[10]說的他不說、反說了許多的廢話。○二[11]嫂子說得是、我倒忘了這一着。○你[12]做這把鉗子、倒有些手藝。○這[13]就是於人有益的、反轉於人有損了。○你[14]自己不正經、倒說人家不乾淨哩。○都[15]說無子女也

TRANSLATION.

1 You thought to injure another, but on the contrary you have injured yourself.

2 I obtained what I had not anticipated.

3 Clearly it was you, and yet you put it off on others.

4 He did not love the eldest, on the contrary he loved the youngest.

5 Although you are small of stature, your will is not small.

6 I am determined to come in spite of your prohibition.

7 His conversation appears to be quite elegant, and not at all commonplace.

8 When I do not dispute with you, you turn about and dispute with me, eh?

9 There is nothing special in his talents and learning, but his warm-heartedness is unequaled.

10 He did not say what he should have said, but on the contrary said a great many irrelevant things.

11 What you say is so, sister-in-law. I had quite forgotten this move.

12 You have shown considerable skill in making these pincers.

13 This is a case in which what was to have been beneficial, has turned out to be injurious.

14 You yourself are not free from reproach, yet you turn about and accuse others of dishonor.

15 Everybody says if you have no sons, daughters are as good; but it is not

---

致 *Chï*⁴. To induce; *to regulate;* a *Wên-li* causative; in order to; extreme, in the highest degree; to the extent of:—Les. 191.

雅致 *Genteel,* stylish, refined, elegant.

才學 *Ts'ai*² *hsüe*². *Talent and learning;* learning, acquirements.

血心 *Hsie*³ *hsin*¹. Heart, affection; *warm-heartedness,* sympathy.

廢話 *Fei*⁴ *hwa*⁴. Empty words, useless verbiage, *irrelevant talk.*

矯 *Chiao*³. To feign; to usurp; martial; obstinate, deceitful.

矯强 *Chiao*³ *ch'iang*². *To make false pretences;* unreasonable.

咬扯 *Yao*³ *ch'ê*³. To evade, *to trump up a case;* to incriminate others.

正派 *Chêng*⁴ *p'ai*⁴. Respectable, *exemplary,* well-behaved, modest.

半吊子 *Pan*⁴ *tiao*⁴ *tsï*³. *A half-witted fellow,* a simpleton, a lackwit, a numskull.

撒村 *Sa*¹ *ts'un*¹. To blackguard, to vilify, *to retail scandal.*

按 *An*⁴. To press with the hand, *to hold down;* to repress, to grasp; to examine:—see *an*¹.

揉 *Jou*². To bend, to twist; to supple up, to bring into subjection.

揉搓 *Jou*² *ts'o*¹. *To knead,* to twist and gouge; to crumple in the hand.

宦 *Hwan*⁴. One who serves, a courtier; *a dignitary.*

官宦 *Kwan*¹ *hwan*⁴. *Officials,* gentry.

好、那知道養了兩個女兒、乃是一對冤家、叫人難受不難受呢。○你16明明沒有理、偏要混矯强咬扯、○咱17們明明待他是厚、他反說是待他薄。○王18愼終乃是正派人家、不是那等半吊子、好撒村的人、所以說他怎麼來怎麼去的、我就是不大敢信。○怕19讀書做文章、倒愛說閒話、管閒事。○我20所願的我偏不做、我所恨的我倒去做。○你21年紀雖輕、聽你的話、倒很有大人的見識。○打22倒沒打喇、就是叫他按在地下、好一頓揉搓。○八23戒道、若是背着師傅浮水、轉連我墜下水裏去了。○他24是官宦人家、你要用錢謝他、倒不官様大氣喇。○起25先我看那布很好、打算兩疋都要他的、後來細看看、乃是用洋線織的、所以一疋我也沒要。○若26照你的話去做、不但不能救就

so, for I brought up two daughters and they have turned out to be my enemies. What a grief of heart it is!

16 You are plainly without a case, yet you persist in trumping up false issues.

17 Clearly we treated him generously, yet he says we treated him meanly.

18 Wang Shên Chung is an exemplary man, and not one of those half-witted fellows who are given to retailing scandal; therefore when all sorts of stories are told of him I am not inclined to believe them.

19 Disliking to study and write essays, he on the contrary relishes idle talk and meddling in affairs that do not concern him.

20 What I would, that I do not; what I would not, that I do.

21 Although you are young in years, your conversation indicates that you have quite a mature judgment.

22 He did not strike me, it is true; but he held me down and gave me a good shaking.

23 Pa Chiai replied, "If I try to swim with you on my back, master, the result will be that we shall both sink to the bottom."

24 He belongs to an official family, so it will not be in good taste for you to return the favor in money.

25 At first I took that cloth to be very good and proposed to buy both pieces of him; but afterwards upon closer examination, I found that it was woven of foreign thread, hence I did not take even one piece.

26 If we do as you say, not only will we

大氣 *Ta⁴ ch'i⁴*. . . . . Genteel, aristocratic. (s.)

織 *Chï¹*. . . . . To weave.

救急 *Chiu⁴ chi²*. To save from the emergency, ... *to remove embarrassment*, to tide over the difficulty.

就急 *Chiu⁴ chi²*. To suit the emergency, to . . . . meet the case.

脫空 *T'oă¹ k'ung⁴*. To have time or opportunity; . . . . to lose time; to lose a chance or opportunity.

半憨子 *Pan⁴ han¹ tsï³*. *A simpleton*, a half- . . . . witted fellow.

豐收 *Fêng¹ shou¹*. . . . . . . A bountiful harvest.

蝗 *Hwang²*. . . . . The locust.

蝗蟲 *Hwang² ch'ung²*. . . . . The locust.

攔 *Lan²*. *To hinder*, to stop; to obstruct; to . . . . . . screen off.

阻 *Tsu³*. . . . . To hinder, to impede, *to oppose*.

攔阻 To hinder, to interfere with, *to oppose*.

貧 *P'in²*. . . . . . . Poor, destitute.

貧寒 *P'in² han²*. . . . . . . *Poor*, destitute.

折乾 *Chê² kan¹*. *To substitute*, to commute, to . . . . exchange for.

乾折 *Kan¹ chê²*. . . . . . The same.

淡薄 *Tan⁴ poă⁴*. Weak,—as a solution or an . . . . emotion.

急、倒反加憂愁了。○我[27]不脫空兒的、整月家替他當差、反倒有了不是嗎。○那[28]個不識人的老剝皮、使用了許多心機、反害了自己。○張[29]家那個孩子、從小我看他很聰明、後來念書念的、倒成了半憨子獃子喇。○都[30]指望今年必要豐收、誰知以後來了蝗蟲、倒把莊稼都吃盡了。○你[31]不攔阻他們、反倒順着他們的口氣說、這是甚麼意思呢。○王[32]老四欠周老大的情、要謝他些東西、周老大如今貧寒的很、我看倒不如折乾乾折、謝他幾兩銀子好。○別[33]的學生都聽戲去了、你為什麼不去呢、答先生派我看屋房子、我倒想着去呢。就是摸撈不着去。○王[34]先生上回來的信、說在這個月初三要到、今天倒十四咯、還沒有來、大約光景是有甚麼講究啊。○古[35]人交友很淡薄、今人交友很親熱、但是用着朋友的時候、古人乃是一片眞心、今人乃是一片假意。

fail to remove the embarrassment, but on the contrary will rather make the matter worse.

27 I never lost any time, but served him month in and month out, and am I still to be found fault with?

28 That old skinflint tried a great many tricks, yet injured himself after all.

29 From a child I regarded that boy of the Chang family as very bright, but afterwards he became imbecile from overwork at his books.

30 All hoped this would certainly be a bountiful year, when, all unexpectedly, the locusts came and ate up all the crops.

31 You do not oppose, on the contrary you chime in with them; what is the meaning of this?

32 Wang the Fourth is under obligations to the elder Chou and is proposing to express his thanks by some presents; but as Chou the elder is very poor at present, I think it would be better to substitute a few taels of silver instead.

33 All the other scholars have gone to hear the play, why do you not go? *Ans.* The teacher has appointed me to watch the room. I would like to go, but have no opportunity.

34 In this last letter Mr. Wang said that he would be here by the third of this month. This is the fourteenth and he has not yet come. The probability is that something has occurred [to prevent].

35 In ancient times friendships were quite cool, in these days they are very warm; but in the time of need the ancient friend was true, while the friend of these days is false.

NOTES.

4 少子 is not a common combination. It is used here as the correlate of 長子 alone. A more colloquial form of the whole sentence would be, 他不愛大兒子倒愛小兒子.

8 In order to bring out the proper force of the sentence, the first 你 and the last 我 should be emphasized.

11 這一着 *This move or trick*,—a figure taken from chess playing. Read chao[1] in Peking, but tsoă[3] in Shantung.

14 乾淨 is here used figuratively of character or conduct.

18 半吊子 *A half string* [of cash] that is, *a half-wit*,—chiefly used as a term of reproach. 說他怎麼來怎麼去的 *Saying this and that about him, telling stories about him.*

20 偏 is here very forcible, but no English word will translate it. 倒 might be rendered *on the contrary*, but its force is more elegantly left to be implied in the relation of the clauses.

22 打倒沒打 *As for beating, he did not indeed beat me*,—a common idiom for expressing this special form of idea.

第一百十三課

先[1]生和你怎麼說來着呢。○南[2]北二京我都到過來咯。○初[3]三那天、你沒給你姥姥老娘婆婆去拜年嗎、答去來着去來。○只[4]是我圖甚麼來着來。○預[5]先沒告訴他、也不知他預備來了沒有。○你[6]若是不服、咱我們兩個就來。○還[7]用打算和人家怎麼樣嗎、來不來先先不先倒自己窩裏反了。○這[8]樣的大雨、你往那裏去來着的咧、快進來。○這[9]不過是他約摸的話、他還親眼看見來着喇。○我[10]這箇時辰表、原沒別的說、實係是孫友梅兄送我的、答却又來、既是孫兄送你的、你昨天怎麼說在上海拍賣買的呢。○我[11]是向他求幫、誰說

Translation.

1 What did the teacher say to you?
2 I have been at both the northern and southern capitals.
3 Did you not go on the third to pay your respects to your maternal grandmother? *Ans.* Yes, I went.
4 But what did I covet?
5 He was not told beforehand, and I do not know whether he is prepared or not.
6 If you are not satisfied, just come ahead [if you dare].
7 Why lay plans for dealing with others, when here already there is a rebellion in our own house.
8 Where have you been in this great rain? Come in quickly.
9 This is nothing more than a supposition of his: he did not see it himself.
10 There is no other explanation concerning this watch of mine; it was really given to me by brother Sun Yiu Mei. *Ans.* But see here: if it was given to you by Brother Sun, then why did you say yesterday that you bought it in Shanghai at auction?
11 I was applying to him for help: who

The use of 倒 implies a previous impression that he *had* been beaten. "Shaking up" scarcely translates 揉搓, as here used, nor does any other term in the English fighting vocabulary.

23 八戒 The servant and disciple of 唐僧, Les. 86, Note 25.

26 不識人 *Does not regard persons;* that is, has no regard for friendship, age or rank, *unprincipled, recreant, heartless.* 老剝皮 *An old extortioner* who, not satisfied with taking goods and clothes, is ready to tear off men's skins to satisfy his demands, *an old skinflint.* 老 is usually a term of honor, but here it is an intensive of reproach.

29 念書念的 *Studying he* [finally] *studied himself* [into a simpleton], an idiomatic form which English will not literally express.

LESSON CXIII.

Peculiar Uses of 來.

In addition to its regular and constant use as an auxiliary, 來 is also frequently used at the end of a clause or sentence in the place of 了. In Pekingese it is generally followed by 着, but not in Central or Southern Mandarin.

來 is also used out of its ordinary sense in the following special phrases.

來來 or 來來來, expresses a challenge,—come ahead, come on if you dare, we'll try it on.

來不來 expresses an absurd state of things, an unprecedented or unexpected turn of affairs,—here behold, here already, well! well!

先不先 is used in Southern Mandarin in the same way, and with substantially the same meaning as 來不來 in the North.

却又來 An exclamation arresting the speaker and preparatory to charging home on him an inconsistency,—there now, but then, well then, but see here.

他該我的呢、答却又來、他既然不該你的、怎麼說必得給你三十兩銀子呢。○你12怎麼這麼外道、我們從幾時分過彼此來着。來呢的呢○別13人都沒有動靜兒、你先來不不先來的先這麼怕、這樣兒那樣兒防備着、還是個漢子味氣兒嗎。○他14能多做就多做、不能多做就少做、從來誰和他計較過來呢。○這15些米沒用篩子篩一篩嗎、答篩了來着喇着、沒篩還能這麼乾淨嗎。○李16老二、趕自是李文山的兄弟、答却又來、你那天爲甚麼說、他們是爺兒父子兩個呢。○在17關東山的時候、那些麞麅、野鹿、狼、蟲、虎、豹、我都見過來。喇○聽18說人長瘌痢禿瘡、若把頭摸上一些個黏粥、叫狗舔一舔就好了、答我用過這個法子、叫狗舔過來着咯着、舔了也是不好。○我19早說他沒有那股子常恒勁兒、你却不信、你看他

said he owed me anything? *Ans.* Well then, if indeed he does not owe you, how is it that you say he must give you thirty taels?

12 What makes you so offish? Since when have we had separate interests?

13 Nobody else is making any move, and here you are already in a fright, taking this and that precaution: is this the mettle of a man?

14 If he can do more, let him do more; if he cannot, let him do less. Who ever found fault with him about it?

15 Have you not sifted this rice? *Ans.* Certainly I have. Would it be as clean as this if I had not sifted it?

16 Of course Li the Second is Li Wên Shan's brother. *Ans.* There now! why then did you say the other day that they were father and son?

17 When I was in the mountains in Manchuria I saw the musk ox, the spotted deer, the wild deer, the wolf, serpent, tiger and leopard.

18 I have heard it said that if one who has scald head will rub his head with rice gruel and have a dog lick it, it will get well. *Ans.* I once tried this plan of having a dog lick my head, but it did no good.

19 I said from the first that he did not have that amount of perseverance, but you would not believe it: and

VOCABULARY.

姥 *Lao*³. Maternal grandmother. Always doubled ...... in use. (N.)

老娘 *Lao*³ *niang*²...... Maternal grandmother.

預先 *Yü*⁴ *hsien*¹...... *Beforehand*, previously.

係 *Hsi*¹,⁴. Belonging to; concerning; the substantive verb in *Wên-li*.

實係 *Shï*² *hsi*⁴...... Indeed, *really*, in fact.

拍 *P'ai*⁴, *p'ai*¹. *To strike with the open hand;* to pat, to caress; to slap.

拍賣 *P'ai*¹ *mai*⁴......... To sell at auction.

外道 *Wai*⁴ *tao*⁴. Unfriendly, *offish*, cool, unsocial.

外氣 *Wai*⁴ *ch'i*⁴.......... The same. (S.)

篩 *Shai*¹.......... A sieve; *to sift*.

趕自 *Kan*³ *tsï*⁴. *Of course*, to be sure, assuredly, by all means.

麞 *Chang*¹.......... The musk deer.

麅 *P'ao*². A small spotted deer found in North China.

豹 *Pao*⁴........ The panther, the leopard.

瘌 *La*⁴.......... Severe, grievous; bald.

瘌痢 *La*⁴ *li*⁴.......... *Scald head.*

禿 *T'u*¹.......... The scald head.

禿瘡 *T'u*¹ *ch'wang*¹. The scald head, sores on the head.

黏 *Nien*².......... *Glutinous*, viscid; rice,

來不來先不先的就想着改行喇、現在你信不信呢。○張[20]价人和他女人打架、把鍋也砸了、屋裏的東西也摔了、還要點火燒房子、大家夥兒勸他、他一賭口氣就走喇、如今還不知往那裏去喇、答嗐、這不是糊來鬧嗎。○你[21]年前借我的錢、本利一個沒打、今年又推脫不還、我就不能答應你、答你不答應待要怎麼樣呢、來來來、你做甚麼、我就和你做甚麼。○這[22]爭過繼的、有弟兄幾個呢、答只弟兄兩個、問他父親弟兄幾個呢、答弟兄三個、問都有兒子嗎、答大分兒和二分兒大房和二房、都是兩個老絕戶孤寡、對却又來呀、他們弟兄兩個、已經頂着三分子家業、那還有他們爭的分兒呢。

sure enough, here he is already wanting to try something else. Do you believe it now?

20 Chang Chiai Jên had a fight with his wife; he broke the kettle to pieces and smashed the furniture, and was about to set fire to the house; and when all present joined to exhort him, he went off in a fit of passion and no one knows where he has gone. *Ans.* Humph! Isn't that a silly piece of acting?

21 You borrowed some money of me last year and did not pay a cash either of principal or of interest, and this year you still make excuses and won't pay up. I am not going to submit to it. *Ans.* Submit or not, what are you going to do about it? Just come and we'll have it out on any line you choose.

22 How many are there of these brothers who are contending about the privilege of being adopted? *Ans.* There are only two of them. *Ques.* How many brothers were there in their father's family. *Ans.* Three. *Ques.* Had they all sons? *Ans.* No, the two elder are both without sons. *Ques.* Well, well! when they two are heirs to the three portions what is there left to contend about?

黏粥 *Nien² chou¹*. Rice gruel, milled gruel, congee.

舔 *T'ien²*. *To lick*, to taste.

恒勁 *Hêng² chin⁴*. *Persistence*, perseverance, the gift of continuance.

常勁 *Ch'ang² chin⁴*. The same. (s.)

改行 *Kai³ hang²*. To change one's trade or occupation.

糊來 *Hu² lai²*. *To act the fool;* to make much ado about nothing.

价 *Chie⁴*. A waiter; good. (w.)

年前 *Nien² ch'ien²*. Before the last new year.

繼 *Chi⁴*. To connect; *to succeed;* to add to.

過繼 *Kwoa⁴ chi⁴*. To adopt as heir the son of a brother or cousin. Note 22.

絶戶 *Chüe² hu⁴*. A man or woman who has no children neither hope of any.

孤 *Ku¹*. An orphan; fatherless; alone, *solitary.*

孤寡 *Ku¹ kwa³*. Widowed and childless. Alone, solitary, *childless.* (s.)

NOTES.

3 Custom fixes the day on which a man and his children should make a new year's call on his wife's parents, but the day differs in different localities. In some places it is the second, in some the third, and in some the fourth day of the new year. The 去 before 拜 might with equal propriety be placed immediately after 沒. In Nanking 婆婆 is used both for mother-in-law and for maternal grandmother; which is intended can only be known from the connection.

7 窩 here refers to a company or set engaged in a common business or enterprise.

10 實係 is stronger than 實在, and is chiefly used in asseverating. 兄 is often used by friends in a complimentary way when addressing or referring to each other. The idea of selling at auction has been introduced into China by foreigners.

第一百十四課

大[1]熱的天、坐下風涼風涼涼快涼快再走罷。○你[2]若不信、可以試驗試驗。○家[3]裏有火、快進去暖和暖和罷。○材[4]料不彀數、就搭就搭接就接就罷。○若[5]是有用人的、煩老兄舉薦吹嘘。○你[6]自己尋思尋思思想思想、比方有人這樣待你、你願意不願意呢。○現[7]在還有我父親、我必得回家去商議商議、纔能定規。○埽[8]道路上那些樹葉子、太不好看、可以去打撢打撢。○在[9]家裏閒着發悶、不如出去溜打溜打遊逛遊逛。○出[10]門那能像在家裏一樣呢、好歹將就將就就是了。○勞[11]你的駕、進去通報通報、就說我家老爺要見。○孩[12]子要睡睏覺、你抱抱他、拍打拍打他就睡睏。

TRANSLATION.

1 The day is very hot: sit down and cool off a little, and then proceed.

2 If you do not believe, just try it.

3 There is a fire in the house, go in quickly and warm yourself.

4 The material is not sufficient, but try and make it answer.

5 If a vacancy occurs, may I trouble you to speak a good word for me?

6 Stop and think a moment: if, for example, any one should treat you in this way, would you like it?

7 My father is still living, I must go home and consult with him before I can decide.

8 The leaves on the front walk are too unsightly, go and sweep them up.

9 Better go out for a walk than sit idly at home giving way to your low spirits.

10 When on a journey one cannot have things as they are at home. You must put up with things the best way you can.

11 May I trouble you to go in and make an announcement for me, saying that my master wishes an interview?

12 The baby wants to sleep. Hold it in your arms and pat it a little and it will go off to sleep.

---

11 必 should be emphasized.

12 The ideal friendship is when the parties 不分彼此, *make no distinction of meum and tuum;* that is, each holds all he has at the disposal of the other.

16 爺兒兩個 *Father and son or daughter*, also applied to grandfather and grandson, or even to ancestor and descendant and includes collateral as well as direct relationship.

17 狼蟲虎豹 is a ready made list, in which 蟲 is put for serpents in general.

20 糊來 *A foolish proceeding.* This is an exceptional use of 來, not provided for in the subject of the lesson.

22 The Chinese have a great horror of dying childless, hence couples who are without male children generally adopt a brother's son, or the son of a cousin of the same family name, in order to have some one to inherit their property, care for them when old, and keep up worship at their graves. 大分兒, 二分兒, etc., is a common way of distinguishing brothers and sisters. 分兒 is equivalent to 分位兒, referring to order of age, and consequently of dignity. The Southern equivalent is 大房. The 老絕戶 is rejected by the Nanking teacher, not because it is not used, but because as here used it is too disrespectful.

LESSON CXIV.

REDUPLICATION OF COMPOUND VERBS.

Not only are single verbs reduplicated as illustrated in Les. 33, but also compound or double verbs. The force of the reduplication is substantially the same as in the case of single verbs. An 一 is never inserted as in the case of single verbs.

喇。○ 13 舖子裏的事情、都鬧(弄)壞了、非整理整理不行喇。○ 14 大小上司、都要孝敬(應酬)孝敬(應酬)、那裏孝敬(應酬)不到、那裏就不順當。○ 15 今天過十月一(朝)、可以稱幾斤肉、打幾壺酒、大夥兒犒勞犒勞。○ 16 我忘了(記)囑咐囑咐他、別叫他走漏消息。○ 17 你頭一次去、該在那裏多住幾天、好和教友們彼此認識認識。○ 18 叫他回娘家去、把肚子裏的悶氣、發洩發洩就好喇。○ 19 這兩天要來客、你可以把院子收拾收拾、省得叫人家笑話。○ 20 先生來有甚麼事呢、答沒有什麼事、就是來拜望拜望、請你們老爺的安。○ 21 你看那個釣魚竿子、扽掣扽掣的、必是魚上了鈎喇。○ 22 廚房有人好吃

13 Affairs in the shop have all been thrown into disorder, a straightening up is indispensable.

14 Superiors of all grades must be feed; wherever you fail to give a fee, there will be trouble.

15 To-day is the first of the tenth month; you may get a few pounds of meat and a few pots of wine and give all hands a feast.

16 I forgot to charge him that he must not let the secret leak out.

17 The first time you go, you should prolong your visit a little so as to get acquainted with the brethren.

18 Let her go and visit her mother and work off her low spirits, and she will be all right.

19 Some guests are coming in a few days; you must clean up the yard, lest they laugh at it.

20 What business have you come on, sir? *Ans.* I have no particular business; I merely came to call on your master and pay my respects.

21 See that fishing-rod how it bobs up and down, it must be that a fish has taken the hook.

22 "With a friend in the kitchen, you can get something to eat; with a

VOCABULARY.

風凉 *Fêng*¹ *liang*². . . . . . . Airy, *cooling*.

搭 *Ta*¹. *To put or hang on;* to build; to add; to get on with; to adapt to; to engage a passage.

就搭 *Chiu*⁴ *ta*¹. *To make a thing answer*, to adapt to circumstances.

嘘 *Hsü*¹. . . . . . .To breathe; *to blow;* to suck up.

吹嘘 *Ch'wei*¹ *hsü*¹. To blow; *to say a good word for*, to recommend.

尋思 *Hsin*² *sï*¹. . . . . . . *To consider*, to reflect.

埇 *Yung*³, *ying*³. A raised path or walk in front of a house.

埇路 *Yung*³ *lu*⁴. A raised or paved walk in front of a house.

埇道 *Yung*³ *tao*⁴. . . . . The same.

打掃 *Ta*³ *sao*³. . . . . . . *To sweep*, to brush up.

溜打 *Liu*¹ *ta*³. . . . . . . To walk for recreation.

拍打 *P'ai*¹ *ta*³. . . . . . *To pat;* to tap, to knock.

上司 *Shang*⁴ *sï*¹. . . . . A superior officer.

孝敬 *Hsiao*⁴ *ching*⁴. To honor and respect (as parents); *to give a present or fee to a superior officer:*—Note 14.

犒 *K'ao*⁴. . . . . To reward workmen with a feast.

犒勞 *K'ao*⁴ *lao*². A feast given to soldiers or workmen:—Note 15.

走漏 *Tsou*³ *lou*⁴. To leak out; *to let out a secret*, to tell, to divulge.

消息 *Hsiao*¹ *hsi*². . . . . . . News, word; *a secret*.

悶氣 *Mên*⁴ *ch'i*⁴. *Low spirits*, dejection, dumps, blues, melancholy.

洩 *Hsie*⁴. To leak, to ooze out, to drip; to divulge, to tell a secret.

發洩 *Fa*¹ *hsie*⁴. To let out, to give vent to, *to work off.*

飯、朝裏有人好作官、大人現在這樣重用你、你還不能提拔提拔我們嗎。〇小23兒鹵莽無知、若他遇見什麽爲難的事、望乞先生指教指教指點指點、〇逢24年過節的、你怎麽不上墳去祭奠祭奠、買幾張紙錢燒化燒化呢、答上墳添土、除去墳墓上的荆棘、這個無有不可、若是燒香燒紙的祭祀、那都是無知妄作。〇現25成的館子、咱們進去喫喝杯茶、坐坐歇息歇息、我的東就是了、答那裏的話呢、今天該是我的東喇。〇老26兄長了一個好鼻子、嘴巴子也很方正、又滿臉放光、這是主着要發大財、答托福托福、若兄弟當眞發了大財、却是借你老人家的錦言咯。

friend at court, you can obtain an office." Seeing His Excellency now depends so much on you, can't you give us a lift?

23 My son is heedless and ignorant; if he gets into any difficulty, I hope you will help him with your advice.

24 When the annual festivals come, why do you not go to the graves to offer sacrifices, and also buy a few sheets of paper money to burn? *Ans.* Going to the graves to add some earth or to clear away the brambles is all right; but as to burning incense and paper money as a sacrifice, that is all useless nonsense.

25 Here is a tea-house just at hand, let us go in and drink a cup of tea and sit and rest awhile. You are my guest. *Ans.* What are you talking about? It is my treat to-day.

26 You have a good nose and your lower jaws are square and your whole face is bright, all of which indicates that you are to become rich. *Ans.* I am certainly much obliged. If I do indeed succeed in making a fortune, it will be owing to your complimentary words.

釣 *Tiao*⁴. . . . . *To fish*, to fish for, to catch.

竿 *Kan*¹. . . . . A rod, *a pole*, a staff.

扽 *Tun*⁴. . . . . . . To shake, to move.

掣 *Ch'ê*⁴. To obstruct; to draw (as lots); *to pull;* . . . . . to grasp.

扽掣 To shake, *to bob up and down*, to dance.

重用 *Chung*⁴ *yung*⁴. *To depend upon*, to rely . . . . on; to have confidence in.

鹵 *Lu*³. . . . . . Rock salt, alkali; *rude;* insolent.

莽 *Mang*³. . . . . Thick grass; confused; *heedless.*

鹵莽 Rustic, rude; *heedless*, abrupt.

望乞 *Wang*⁴ *ch'i*³. . . . . I beg, I hope. (w.)

指教 *Chi*³ *chiao*⁴. To teach, to direct; *to advise,* to . . . . counsel.

指點 *Chi*³ *tien*³. To point out, to direct, to . . . . guide; *to advise.*

奠 *Tien*⁴. . . . . To enshrine; *to offer a libation.*

祭奠 *Chi*⁴ *tien*⁴. . . . . To sacrifice to.

紙錢 *Chi*³ *ch'ien*². Paper money, tinsel paper:— . . . . Note 24.

燒化 *Shao*¹ *hwa*⁴. . . . . . . To burn, to consume.

祀 *Si*⁴. . . . . *To sacrifice to*, to worship.

荆 *Ching*¹. . . . . *A bramble;* thorny, prickly.

棘 *Chi*⁴. . . . . . . *A thorn*, a bramble; troublesome.

荆棘 Thorns, brambles.

方正 *Fang*¹ *chêng*⁴. . . . . . Full, *plump;* broad.

托福 *T'oa*¹ *fu*². I'm much obliged, you're very . . . . kind.

錦 *Chin*³. Embroidered; elegant, flowery, *complimentary.*

錦言 *Chin*³ *yien*². Flowery language; *complimentary words.*

第一百五十課

你[1]怎麼忽然改了主意呢。○冷[2]不防的冒不通的猛過地裏把我嚇了一跳。○他[3]忽然變了脾氣、好起賭博來喇。○我[4]已經走出二三里路、忽拉巴（猛然）想起把傘忘記了。○他[5]岳父的名字、我遽然間想不起來。○新[6]衣裳是偶然有事情穿的罷咧。○我[7]猛然間看見他、一點也不認得。○勸[8]戒人的話、不可陡然就說。○請[9]問老長兄、今日爲甚麼突（忽）然要起行。○咱[10]們偶

Translation.

1 How is it that you have suddenly changed your mind?
2 Unexpectedly he gave me a fright.
3 He suddenly changed his bent and developed a passion for gambling.
4 I had already gone two or three *li* when it suddenly occurred to me that I had forgotten my umbrella.
5 His father-in-law's name I cannot recall on the spur of the moment.
6 New clothes are only to be worn on special occasions.
7 Seeing him unexpectedly, I did not recognize him at all.
8 In exhorting any one, it is not best to begin too abruptly.
9 Please tell me, my good brother, why you suddenly want to start to-day.
10 Should we suddenly meet with some

Notes.

1 Said to a passer by, by one who is resting in the shade at the roadside.

5 吹噓吹噓 *Blow a little for me*; i.e., *recommend me.*

8 埇路 properly *yung*[3] *lu*[4], but in actual use frequently spoken *ying*[3] *lu*[4]. It is also written 甬 by some, and by others 映.

11 我家老爺 *The honored head of our family*,—addressed by the gentleman's servant to the servant of the man upon whom his master has come to call.

14 All inferior officers are expected to send in a retaining fee to their superiors at the new year, as well as on certain other special occasions. If the fee is not sent in, the inferior will presently find his affairs embarrassed with difficulties. The giving of this fee is facetiously called 孝敬, *showing respect*, or 應酬, *making a return.*

15 The first day of the tenth month is a feast-day in honor of 城隍, the god of the city moat. On this and similar feast-days, custom requires that employers should give their workmen a half-holiday and a feast. This is technically called 犒勞, *feasting the weary.*

17 多住幾天 *Remain a few days longer*; i. e., *prolong your visit a little*, for the purpose referred to.

18 The "belly" is commonly regarded by the Chinese as the seat both of the intellect and the affections.

23 The language and style of a letter.

24 逢年過節的 requires 時候 understood to complete the construction. Paper money is burnt for the use of the dead. In the case of ancestors it is supposed to express affectionate remembrance, as well as to conciliate them and secure their good offices on behalf of their descendants; in the case of other gods it is a bribe to appease their anger and secure their protection. It consists of tinsel paper, that is, paper, having pasted on it a very thin leaf of tin to represent silver, or of brass to represent gold. It is folded and pasted in the shape of ingots of silver and gold. The poor also use yellow paper with holes punched in it to represent copper cash. 無知妄作 is book style.

25 我的東 *I am host, it's my treat.* 東 is put for 東家. A more colloquial form, at least in the North, is 我的請兒.

LESSON CXV.

Phrases indicating Suddenness.

The superabundance of words for expressing this idea shows that the Chinese language is in some respects richer than the English. A number of the following phrases are more or less local, and sundry of them are practically synonymous, differing only in the connexion in which they are used.

忽然 Suddenly, unexpectedly, all at once. This is the most common and universally used word for expressing the idea of suddenness.

猛然 or **猛然間** Suddenly, unexpectedly, all at once; abruptly. The 間 is added or not as the rhythm suggests. It may also be added to any of the following terms which end with 然.

遽然 Suddenly, abruptly, on the spur of the moment.

陡然 Suddenly, abruptly, all at once.

突然 Suddenly, unexpectedly, abruptly.

(爾/然)有了不測的事、他能替咱們出力。○ 11應當(卽/及)早預備、怕他猝然來到、就預備不及了。○ 12人至親的骨肉、(猛孤丁/冷孤丁/冷然間)的死了、免不得常常(想着/思慮)難(受/過)。○ 13昨日那場雨、下的實在急、(霎時間/一霎時/登時間)滿地是水。○ 14我們若是突然間他、他必心驚、不肯告訴。○ 15韓先生做文章、眞是好手、(登時/爽然/霎時)就是一篇。○ 16馬纔(要/待要)跑、叫我(抽冷子/偷冷的)一把揪住了。○ 17他看見人家賺錢享福、一時間眼就熱起來。○ 18火輪車跑的實在快、一(轉/眨)眼的工夫、就過去了。○ 19我今天去看大人的、正當熱鬧中間、在我身旁(冷孤丁/冷打驚/打冷驚)放了三聲大砲、把我嚇了一跳。○ 20把心已經放肆慣了、遽然要收回來、

misfortune, he will be able to help us.

11 We ought to prepare in good season lest he should come suddenly and we not be able to get ready in time.

12 When a very near relative suddenly dies, one cannot help constantly thinking of him and feeling sad.

13 That was a heavy rain yesterday; in a twinkling the earth was everywhere covered with water.

14 If we ask him abruptly, his suspicions will certainly be excited and he will tell us nothing.

15 Mr. Han is certainly skilled in writing essays, he does one up in no time.

16 The horse was just about to run, when I suddenly seized him and held him fast.

17 When he saw men making money and enjoying it, his cupidity was at once excited.

18 The cars run at a tremendous speed; they pass by in the twinkling of an eye.

19 I went to-day to see the reception of His Excellency, and just in the midst of the excitement I was suddenly startled by the firing off of three great guns at my side.

20 Having habitually allowed the mind to wander unrestrained, it is a very difficult thing to bring it suddenly under discipline.

猝然 Suddenly, abruptly, quickly.

爽然 Promptly, in a trice, in no time. (c.)

驟然 Suddenly, in a flash, with a start.

倏然 Instantly, instantaneously, all at once.

偶然 Suddenly, accidentally, without notice.

偶爾 The same as 偶然, but more bookish, at least in most places. Les. 161.

冷孤丁 All at once, suddenly, unexpectedly.

冷打驚 The same. (c.)

打冷驚 The same. (c. & s.)

冷不防 Unexpectedly, unawares.

冷地裡 The same. (s.)

冒不通 The same.

冷然間 Suddenly, all at once.

抽冷子 Suddenly, unexpectedly, unawares. A Peking term.

偷冷的 The same. A Southern term.

忽拉巴 All of a sudden, without warning. A Shantung term.

打不瞧 Before one is aware, unawares. A Shantung term.

一時間 In a moment, at once, at present.

一展眼 In the opening of an eye, }
一轉眼 In the turn of an eye, } in the twinkling of an eye.
一眨眼 In the wink of an eye, }

猛過地裡 Unexpectedly, unawares, suddenly. A Southern term.

一霎時 In a twinkling, in a moment.

霎時間 The same.

登時 or **登時間** In a moment, in a twinkling, in no time. Les. 162.

一旦 Some morning; suddenly, in a moment, as soon as. A book term used by scholars.

頃刻 or **頃刻間** In a moment, in a twinkling. A book term.

那可難哪。○那[21]少年人猛然抬頭、看鐵公子是個貴人行動、却不認得。○丈[22]夫在世、和他如膠似漆、忽然丈夫去了世、心裏就像沒着落似的。○剛[23]行到半路、驟然間起了狂風、把船撞在礁石石礁上、一頃霎刻時間就沉下去了。○今[24]日有個大漢子、和我打架、叫我抽打偷冷不冷子瞧一拳、打了一個仰搬臥脚蹬。○天[25]時是無定的、旱澇是常有的、當那有穿有吃的時節、多費多用、一旦遇了那荒年、你們都怎樣過呢。○前[26]日

21 The young man suddenly lifting his head, saw that Mr. T'ie had an aristocratic bearing, but did not recognize him.

22 While her husband was living, she was strongly attached to him; and when he suddenly died, she felt as if she had no dependence.

23 Just when they had accomplished half the voyage, there suddenly arose a violent storm which drove the ship on the rocks, and in a moment they went down.

24 A big fellow was fighting with me to-day, when, taking him unawares, I gave him one blow with my fist which sent him sprawling on his back.

25 The seasons are uncertain, floods and droughts are frequent. If when you have abundance you live extravagantly, by and by when a year of famine suddenly overtakes you, how will you all get a living?

VOCABULARY.

遽 *Chü*⁴. . . . . . . Hurried, agitated; suddenly.

偶 *Ou*³. An image, an idol; a mate; an even . . . . . number; a pair; abruptly; accidentally.

陡 *Tou*³. . . . . Steep, precipitous; suddenly.

爾 *Êr*³. The *Wên-li* second personal pronoun, ... you; an affirmative particle.

猝 *Ts'u*⁴. . . . . Abrupt, precipitate.

霎 *Sha*⁴. . . . . . A shower; an instant, a moment.

眨 *Cha*³, *chan*³. . . . . To wink; to twinkle.

驟 *Tsou*⁴. . . . . . Quick; suddenly, with all speed.

頃 *Ch'ing*¹'²'³. An instant, a moment, just now, ... at once.

旦 *Tan*⁴. . . . The morning light, clear; daylight.

倏 *Shu*⁴. . . . . Hastily, quickly, suddenly.

起行 *Ch'i*³ *hsing*². . . . . . To start on a journey.

測 *Ts'ê*⁴. To fathom, to sound; to measure, to . . . . . . guage, *to estimate*.

不測 *Pu*⁴ *ts'ê*⁴. Inscrutable; unexpected; a . . . . calamity, *a misfortune*.

即 *Chi*²'⁴. To approach; now, soon, *forthwith;* as . . . . to; that is:—Les. 160 and 162.

即早 *Chi*⁴ *tsao*³. Early, *in good season*, before- . . . . hand.

及早 *Chi*² *tsao*³. . . . . The same:—Note 11.

骨肉 *Ku*³ *jou*⁴. . . . . *A relative;* kinship.

思慮 *Sï*¹ *lü*⁴. To think anxiously, to ponder, ... *to brood over.*

難過 *Nan*² *kwoå*⁴. . . . In straits; troubled, *sad.*

肆 *Sï*⁴. To set forth; reckless, dissolute; *uncurb-* . . . . . . *ed;* used for 四 in accounts.

放肆 *Fang*⁴ *sï*⁴. *Unrestrained;* reckless; prof- . . . . ligate; wanton.

少年人 *Shao*⁴ *nien*² *jên*². A young man, a . . . . youth.

行動 *Hsing*² *tung*⁴. To move about; *bearing,* be- . . . . haviour; to ease one's self.

着落 *Choå*² *loå*⁴. Resting place, home; *depend-* . . . . *ence,* support.

狂風 *K'wang*² *fêng*¹. . . . A storm, a hurricane.

礁 *Chiao*¹. . . . . Half-tide rocks, shoal rocks.

礁石 *Chiao*¹ *shï*². . . . . . . Shoals, hidden rocks.

石礁 *Shï*² *chiao*¹. . . . . The same.

仰 *Yang*³. *To look up towards heaven;* to look . . . . up to, to respect.

臥 *Woå*⁴. . . . . *To lie down;* to rest.

仰搬脚 *Yang*³ *pan*¹ *chiao*³. *Sprawling on the* . . . . *back,* lying on the back with hands and feet in the air.

仰臥蹬 *Yang*³ *woå*⁴ *têng*⁴. The same:—Note [24.

上半天、我母親還好好的、到下半天出去的時候、偶然間倒在地下、得了個中瘋不語。○打[27]羣架、一點好處沒有、在打的時候、各人逞各人的剛强、一旦出了人命、就都直了眼挓挲手挓手喇。○起[28]頭都拿他當官宦人家、以後正說話的時候、他冷孤丁冒不通冷地裏提到他父親種的多少地、人都把嘴一癟撇、你說他漏洩底不漏洩底呢。○人[29]病到利害的時候、若是陡然覺輕些、就當快預備、因為這就是燈將滅而復明的理

26 Day before yesterday forenoon my mother was quite well, but in the afternoon when she was going out, she suddenly fell to the ground speechless with a stroke of paralysis.

27 There is nothing to be gained from joining in a free fight. While the fight goes on, each man relies on his own powers; but the moment some one is killed, all throw up their hands in consternation.

28 At first all considered him as belonging to the official class, but afterwards, while he was talking, he accidentally spoke of the number of acres his father farmed, upon which all the company made a grimace. Wasn't that a come down?

29 When any one is dangerously ill, if he all at once feels better, final preparation should at once be made, for this is like the lamp flaring up just before it goes out.

澇 *Lao*⁴. . . . *Flooded*, injured by excessive rain.

下半天 *Hsia*⁴ *pan*⁴ *t'ien*¹. . . . . Afternoon.

中瘋 *Chung*⁴ *fêng*¹. . . . . A stroke of paralysis.

直眼 *Chï*² *yien*³. To stare, *to look blank*, to be . . . . at one's wits' end, dismayed.

挓 *Cha*¹. . . . . . . To open out, to spread out.

挲 *Sa*¹. . . . . . To open out. See *soă*¹.

挓挲 *To spread out the hands and fingers in . . . . . token of being in a strait;* spread out loosely; disheveled.

挓手 *Cha*¹ *shou*³. To spread out the hands as . . . . in a strait.

癟 *Pie*³. . . . . Shriveled, limp; puckered.

漏底 *Lou*⁴ *ti*³. To be mortified, *to betray one's . . . . . antecedents*, to lose caste.

洩底 *Hsie*⁴ *ti*³. . . . . The same.

嚷 *Jang*³. . . . To vociferate, to shout. See *jang*¹.

興 *Hsing*⁴. . . . Joyful, elated, excited. See *hsing*¹.

戳 *Ch'oă*¹. To stab, *to strike or punch with a . . . . . stick;* to taunt, to nag; a stamp, a seal.

法國 *Fa*³ *kwoă*². . . . . France.

天空 *T'ien*¹ *k'ung*¹. . . . *The sky*, the air; space.

輕氣 *Ch'ing*¹ *ch'i*⁴. . . . . Hydrogen.

飄蕩 *P'iao*¹ *tang*⁴. To float, to soar; *to sail;* . . . . to roll (as a boat).

可巧 *K'ê*³ *ch'iao*³. Happily, *fortunately*, opportunely.

輪船 *Lun*² *ch'wan*². . . . . A steamship.

射 *Shê*⁴. *To shoot;* to spurt out; to issue forth; . . . . . . to radiate.

NOTES.

5 名字 A distinction is made between 名 and 字. The 名 is the original and ordinary name, the 字 is a second name or title, derived from the 名 by some classical or fanciful association. In common use, however, 名字 simply means name, and by rights should be written 名子, as is evident from the fact that it is frequently heard 名兒. Custom, however, has put 字 for 子 in this particular case. 姓 differs radically from both 名 and 字, being the family name or surname.

6 罷咧 is here equivalent to 不過, or to the book term 而已.

9 老長兄 *Old elder brother*, a term of respect approximately equal to *my good brother*, or *my good sir.*

11 The double form 卽早 and 及早, results from the use of hard and soft sounds. Where soft sounds prevail 卽 and 及 are read precisely alike, and either is correct; but where hard sounds prevail only 及 will answer, as 卽 is *everywhere* soft. This fact should determine the writing in favor of 及 which is everywhere correct; moreover the fact that hard sounds are the older and have been supplanted by soft sounds, shows that 及 is doubtless the original writing of the phrase.

呀。○他30們正在學房、山嚷怪叫的興鬨、叫先生抽冷子冷不防冷冷地裏進去、喝了一聲、就像喜鵲窩裏戳了一棍似的、倏忽然一點動靜也沒有了。○從31前法國有兩個人、坐輕氣球在天空飄蕩、不覺飄到大海之上、可巧看見海中有一隻輪船、他們就赶緊的將氣球落下、既落到海面、二人一齊跳在海裏、那氣球就突驟然騰空、彷彿一條箭射到天上去了。

30 They were in the schoolroom just in the full tide of their hilarity, whooping and yelling like demons, when the teacher, coming in unexpectedly, gave one shout: it was like striking a nest of young magpies with a stick; instantly there was not a sound to be heard.

31 Once in France two men ascended in a balloon, and while sailing in the air, were insensibly carried out to sea. Fortunately they caught sight of a steamship and, with all haste, caused the balloon to descend. When they touched the surface of the water, the two men jumped simultaneously into the sea, whereupon the balloon suddenly darted up, like an arrow shot skyward.

15 The peculiar force of 就是 cannot be matched in English.

17 眼熱起來 *To look with longing eyes, to wish for.*

19 Strictly speaking 的, as here used, should limit the seeing to the persons who went out to meet his excellency. This, however, is not the real meaning. A word like 光景 must be supplied after 的 in order to complete the construction. The proper sense is given without 的.

21 鐵公子 The hero of the Fortunate Union.

22 This sentence might also be rendered, *While her husband was alive, he was strongly attached to her*, etc. The sentence was probably made by a foreigner. If a Chinese had made it he would have said, either 二人 or 兩口, instead of 和他.

24 仰臥 *To fall* or *lie on the back*, and 蹬 *to spread* or *sprawl the feet.* The Peking phrase 仰搬腳 is not so readily analysed. Nanking rejects both phrases, and says 仰巴四义.

27 打羣架 *To fight in a flock;* that is, to engage in a free fight or general row. 出了人命 *There comes out a* [*loss of*] *life;* i.e., some one is killed and his life is to be accounted for to the law.

28 一撇 is used in the North and means to twist the lips to one side, 一癟 is used in the South and means to draw up or pucker the lips, both being expressive of contempt.

29 The preparation to be made, is to lift the dying man off the *k'ang* and dress him in his burial clothes. The 理 at the end drops out of the translation.

30 山嚷怪叫 *Hills resounding and hobgoblins howling,* used as a figure to describe the uproarious hilarity of school boys. 興 changes its usual tone, and also requires emphasis to bring out its force.

31 輕氣球 *A hydrogen globe,* that is, a balloon. 可巧 *Fitting the emergency.* In Peking 法 in 法國 is read *fa*⁴.

LESSON CXVI.

Phrases indicating Certainty.

定 Certainly, positively. 定 forms a number of combinations, as below, and is the most important word used for the expression of certainty.

一定 Certainly, inevitably; determined, invariable, for certain.

定然 Certainly, positively, surely.

必 Necessarily, certainly.

必定 Certainly, positively, inevitably; very certain; it must be.

必然 The same.

準 Certainly, surely.

一準 Certainly, positively, unquestionably.

定準 Positively, inevitably, assuredly.

着準 Assuredly, unquestionably, unmistakeably. (c.)

準成 Certainly, surely, inevitably. (c. & n.)

準行 The same. (s.)

定準不移 Undoubtedly, unquestionably, absolutely certain.

第一百十六課

先[1]生明天一定走嗎。○天[2]下事、有大利必有大害。○你[3]若是急賣、準要賠錢賒本。○凡[4]哄騙人的、必定不是好人。○留[5]他自己在那裏、必然要住不住下。○若[6]是我知道是爲這件事情請我、我斷不肯去。○他[7]一定要走、我留不住他。○行[8]好得好、是定而不可移的。○你[9]不賠我一個新的、我定不讓你。○我[10]看準了、必定是他偷的。○像[11]這樣的轄制人、人家定着準不能受。○等[12]我有錢的時候、定然要去買個時辰表。○別[13]人不能、這一準是王錦芳使的手眼。弄的手段。○看[14]你這個樣兒、必然是

TRANSLATION.

1 Will you certainly go to-morrow, sir?
2 In everything, that which affords large profits necessarily involves [the risk of] great loss.
3 If you urge a sale, you will certainly [lose money.
4 Whoever deceives another is certainly not a good man.
5 If you leave him there by himself, he will certainly not stay.
6 If I had known that it was on account of this business that he invited me, I should assuredly not have gone.
7 He is determined to go, I cannot detain him.
8 That he who does right fares well, is an invariable law.
9 I will positively not let you off unless you get me a new one.
10 I am quite satisfied that he must have stolen it. [sort of coercion.
11 He will assuredly not submit to this
12 When I get the money, I will certainly go and buy me a watch.
13 This is unquestionably one of Wang Chin Fang's tricks; no one else could do it.
14 Judging from your condition, it must be you have caught cold.

定而不可移 Fixed and unalterable, morally certain, invariable.

一定不移 The same.

堅定不移 Positively, incontestibly, assuredly, unmistakeably.

堅定着一 The same. (c.)

斷 Assuredly, positively.

斷斷 The same. Repeated for emphasis.

斷乎 Certainly, positively, undoubtedly, assuredly, absolutely.

斷然 The same.

確乎 Assuredly, undoubtedly.

確乎不移 Indisputably, assuredly, without the least doubt.

鑿鑿可據 Demonstrably, undoubtedly, indisputably. Bookish.

着準可據 The same. Colloquial. (c.)

絶 Absolutely, utterly.

絶然 The same.

決 Positively, unequivocally.

決然 The same.

萬 or **萬萬** Utterly, absolutely, positively,—always used with a negative.

VOCABULARY.

移 *I*². To transplant; *to move*, to shift, to migrate; to graft.

鑿 *Tsoă*². A chisel; to chisel out, to dig; to brand; *to verify;* secure.

賒本 *Shê*² *pên*³. To lose on an investment. (c.)

轄 *Hsia*². To govern, *to rule;* to regulate.

轄制 *Hsia*² *chï*⁴. To rule over, *to coerce*, to constrain, to keep under.

手眼 *Shou*³ *yien*³. Device, manœuvre, *trick*, bribe, corruption.

凍着的了。○論15到他的口才、確乎不在衆人以下。○雖16有千萬好話、他絕絶然不聽。○我17若不看他老了、斷乎不能白饒了他。○若18是中國肯修鐵路、定然準一年富似一年。○這19是的的確確的事情、斷然沒有差錯。○但20凡是個男子漢、都當有一定的志向。○事21情這麼一來、定着準難以了結。○現22在我左右兩難、沒有一準的主意。○他23若一點私弊沒有、斷不肯私自逃走。○這24是定而不可移的章程、斷乎不能更改。○人25死了以後堅定不移堅定着一斷然沒有脫生輪迴。○他26們兩個私通、這是確乎不移鑿鑿可據的事情。○不27莫要亂說、那林內是個清雅的去處、決然沒有妖精。○我28已經仔細訪問了、定準不移着準可據一定不移

15 As to fluency, he is certainly not inferior to others.

16 Although all the arts of persuasion [have been exhausted], he utterly refuses to listen.

17 If I had not regarded his age, I should certainly not have let him off scot-free.

18 If China were willing to build railroads, it is very certain that she would grow richer year by year.

19 This is an undoubted fact ; there is absolutely no mistake about it.

20 Every true man ought to have some decision of character.

21 Under these circumstances, the business will unquestionably be difficult to settle.

22 Just now I am in a great dilemma and cannot come to any settled conclusion.

23 If he had been guilty of no corruption at all, you may be sure he would not have secretly fled.

24 This is the invariable rule which absolutely cannot be changed.

25 There is positively no transmigration after death.

26 That they two have had some secret intercourse is an indisputable fact.

27 Do not talk at random. That grove is a quiet place where there are positively no ghosts.

28 I have already made careful inquiry ;

鐵路 *T'ie*³ *lu*⁴. . . . . A railroad.

但凡 *Tan*⁴ *fan*². *Whoever*, whatever ; whenever ; . . . . if at all, if in any case, if indeed:—Les. 157.

私弊 *Sï*¹ *pi*⁴. Bribery, *corruption;* fraud, ... embezzlement.

私自 *Sï*¹ *tsï*⁴. Privately, *secretly*, clandestinely, ... surreptitiously.

逃走 *T'ao*² *tsou*³. *To flee*, to run away, to . . . . abscond.

脫生 *T'o*¹ *shêng*¹. To transmigrate ; to be born . . . . into the world.

迴 *Hwei*². To come round to the starting point, ... to revolve.

輪迴 *Lun*² *hwei*². Transmigration, the doctrine . . . . of metempsychosis.

私通 *Sï*¹ *t'ung*¹. Clandestine communication, ... *secret or illicit intercourse.*

清雅 *Ch'ing*¹ *ya*³. *Quiet*, tranquil, still, retired.

妖精 *Yao*¹ *ching*¹. *A spectre*, a goblin, an elf, ... a satyr.

訪問 *Fang*³ *wên*⁴. . . . . *To inquire*, to look for.

罪惡 *Tswei*⁴ *ê*⁴. . . . Wickedness, *sin*, evil deeds.

橫 *Hêng*⁴ Perverse, mulish ; unreasonable, outrageous ; contrary, sinister. See *hêng*².

流淚 *Liu*² *lei*⁴. . . . . . To shed tears, to weep.

失和 *Shï*¹ *hê*². To disagree, to fall out ; *to declare war.*

漱 *Shu*⁴. . . . . *To rinse*, to wash.

粗蠢 *Ts'u*¹ *ch'un*³. . . . . Rustic, *boorish;* stupid.

粗笨 *Ts'u*¹ *pên*⁴. . . . . The same.

他是個有德行的人。○這[29]罪惡的報應、一定要受、斷乎免不了。○我[30]看他一臉橫肉、定然不是好人。○神[31]是神、人是人、若說人能成神、斷斷然沒有這個理。○等[32]他要飯的時候、給他頓飯吃倒可以、叫我保他做什麽、萬也不能。○看[33]他那樣流淚、和他所賭的咒、鑿鑿可據是屈他。○現[34]在這兩國打仗、是確乎不移的事、但不知是爲甚麽失和。○我[35]的父親每頓飯後、必要漱漱口、刷刷牙、這是一定之規。○你[36]若是當堂說這樣的話、準行成是要挨嘴巴子。○楊[37]本義那個人、生的過於粗笨蠢、想叫他有點文雅雅道儒雅意思、萬萬不能。○我[38]與你說明了罷、寺內決不進去了、茶是決不吃了、知縣

he is unquestionably a good man.

29 This retribution for sin is something that will inevitably come, and there is positively no escape.

30 I noticed that his face had a sinister expression; he is certainly not a good man.

31 Gods are gods and men are men. To say that a man may become a god is assuredly contrary to reason.

32 When he comes to want I will give him a meal, but recommend him for a place, I positively will not.

33 Judging from his weeping and his protestations, he is undoubtedly wronged.

34 That these two kingdoms are now at war is an indisputable fact, but how the peace was broken I do not know.

35 It is my father's invariable custom to rinse his mouth and brush his teeth after each meal.

36 If you use such language as this in the presence of the magistrate, you will certainly get a beating on the face.

37 That man Yang Pên I is by nature excessively boorish; it is vain to expect to give him any polish.

38 I now tell you plainly, the temple I positively will not enter, the tea I positively will not drink, the magistrate I positively will not see.

文雅 *Wên² ya³*. Cultivated, *polished*, refined, ... literary.

雅道 *Ya³ tao⁴*. Gentlemanly, *polished*, refined. (c.)

儒雅 *Ju² ya³*. Literary, refined, *polished*, ... cultured.

寺 *Si⁴*. A council chamber; *a Buddhist temple* ...... or monastery; a mosque.

知縣 *Chi¹ hsien⁴*. ... ... A *hsien* magistrate.

仵 *Wu³*. ... ... An opponent; *a mate*.

仵作 *Wu³ tsoâ⁴*. A surgical expert, a coroner:— ... ... Note 39.

天靈盖 *T'ien¹ ling² kai⁴*. ...... The forehead.

肘 *Chou³*. ... ... The elbow, the elbow-joint.

拐肘 *Kwai³ chou³*. ... ... The elbow.

踝 *Hwai³*. ... ... The ankle bone or joint.

雨星 *Yü³ hsing¹*. ... ... A rain drop.

NOTES.

2 害 does not here mean certain evil or loss, but rather the risk of it. Compare the common saying, "Nothing ventured, nothing won."

7 This sentence might also mean, *If he is determined to go, I cannot detain him.*

11 The 人家 is not adequately translated by *he*. It designates the person referred to in a way that English will not express.

20 Lit. *Whoever is a male Chinaman ought to have a fixed purpose.* A woman is not supposed to have a mind of her own.

22 左右兩難 *Left and right both (two) difficult*, that is, *a difficulty on either hand, in a strait betwixt two, in a dilemma.*

30 一臉橫肉 *seems* to use 橫 in its ordinary literal sense, after the style of our term "cross grained:" but on the

是決不見了。

39 ○件作訛、在天靈盖上、有鐵傷一處、右拐肘上有木傷一處、左踝子骨上、有木傷兩處、他怎麽知道一定是木傷是鐵傷呢。

40 ○六月二十四、是關老爺磨刀的日子、多少必下點雨、答那却不準成啊、前年天旱、一個六月沒下一個雨星兒、你忘記了嗎。

39 The coroner reports that there is a wound on the forehead made by an iron instrument, on the right elbow a wound made by a wooden instrument, and two wounds on the left ankle made by a wooden instrument. How does he know for certain that a wound has been made by a wooden or by an iron instrument?

40 The twenty-fourth of the sixth month is the day the God of War whets his sword; it is certain to rain at least a little. *Ans.* That is not certain. Year before last during the drought, it did not rain a single drop during the whole sixth month. Don't you remember?

contrary it changes its tone and takes its derived sense.

31 This is a Christian sentiment. All Chinese gods are supposed to be deified men.

32 頓飯吃 An 一 is elided before 頓.

35 一定之規 *A fixed or invariable rule,*—a book phrase in common use.

36 當堂 *In the presence of the court,* that is, of the magistrate.

39 仵作 is an attaché of the yamên, though not counted a 衙役. His special business is to go with the magistrate when investigating a case of murder or assault, and act as an expert in determining the character and extent of the wounds.

40 雨星 *A rain star,* that is, a *rain drop,* so called from the sparkling of drops of rain.

LESSON CXVII.

Specific Time.

The more common terms for the designation of time have already been given in Lesson 16. In this and the three following lessons, the various terms for expressing time are more fully set forth. The Chinese affords a large variety of such terms.

昨兒個 Yesterday,
今兒個 To-day,
明兒個 To-morrow,
後兒個 Day after to-morrow,
} These terms are local, being largely confined to the city of Peking.

夜來 Yesterday. Local in Shantung. In some places in the South, 夜來 means, last night.

大前日 or **大前天** The day preceding the day before yesterday.

老前日 or **老前天** The same. Used in some parts of the South.

大後日 or **大後天** The day following the day after to-morrow.

老後日 or **老後天** The same. (s.)

本月 This month, the present month.

本年 This year, the present year, that same year. 本 is rarely, if ever, applied to 日 or 天.

上月 Last month.

下月 Next month.

上年 Last year.

下年 Next year.

上禮拜 Last week.

下禮拜 Next week.

上 and 下 are not applied to 日 or 天, though we have 上半天 and 下半天.

大上禮拜 Week before last.

上上禮拜 The same.

大下禮拜 Week after next.

下下禮拜 The same.

今朝 This morning; to-day.

今早 This morning—Other terms for morning, as well as for noon, evening, and night, have already occurred in previous lessons.

今年 This year. 今 is not applied to 月, nor to 禮拜; instead of it, 這個 is used.

第一百十七課

請[1]先生把我上月的工錢給我。○大[2]後天是安息日、你別忘記喇。○他[3]不是前日來的嗎、答不是、是老大前日來的。○你[4]今年僱了幾個夥計、答僱了四個。○上[5]禮拜四是上月二十八。○下[6]禮拜三、我俺二哥娶成親家。○你[7]去年進京、在那裏住着、答在客店裏。○我[8]明兒個走、到下月二十五六就回來了。○他[9]昨昨兒天個還好好兒的、今兒天個就病了嗎。○我[10]哥哥僱給人家拉縴去喇、總得到下禮拜纔能回來。○上[11]年所念的書、今年忘記了一大多半。○我[12]後天先來拜壽、老大後天再來叨赴擾席。○你[13]若常常般勤作活、到下年我要加你的工錢。○今[14]年下雨太多、將來莊稼必然不收成。○後[15]兒天個他們老翁下葬、我得幫幫

TRANSLATION.

1 Will you please, sir, give me my last month's wages?

2 Two days after to-morrow is the sabbath. Do not forget.

3 Did he not come day before yesterday? *Ans.* No. He came the day before that.

4 How many hands did you hire this year? *Ans.* I hired four.

5 Thursday of last week was the twenty-eighth of last month.

6 Wednesday of next week, my second brother is to be married.

7 When you went to the capital last year, where did you lodge? *Ans.* At an inn.

8 I am going to-morrow, and will return by the twenty-fifth or twenty-sixth of next month.

9 Is he sick to-day? Why, yesterday he was quite well.

10 My elder brother has gone to track for a man who hired him, and cannot return before next week.

11 I have this year forgotten the greater part of the books I studied last year.

12 Day after to-morrow I am coming to make a birthday call, and the next day I am coming to the feast.

13 If you continue diligent in your work, next year I will increase your wages.

14 There has been too much rain this year, the crops will certainly be poor.

15 Day after to-morrow the patriarch of the family is to be buried. I must go and help them.

去年 or 舊年 Last year.
前年 Year before last.
明年 Next year. 明 is never applied to 月.
過年 Next year, after the new year.
來年 Next year, the coming year.
轉年 Next year, the following year.

後年 Year after next.
大前年 The year preceding year before last.
現前年 The same. (s.)
大後年 The year following year after next.
老後年 The same. (s.)

VOCABULARY.

工錢 *Kung*[1] *ch'ien*[2]. . . . . Wages.
縴 *Ch'ien*[4]. . . . . . . A tow-rope, a tracking line.
拉縴 *La*[1] *ch'ien*[4]. *To track;* to lobby for; to act the drummer.
拜壽 *Pai*[4] *shou*[4]. To make a birthday call:— Note 12.

叨 *T'ao*[1]. . . . . . . To desire; to receive; *to enjoy.* See *tao*[1].
叨擾 *T'ao*[1] *jao*[3]. . . . . . To enjoy an entertainment.
翁 *Wêng*[1]. . . . . . Venerable; *an old man.*

他們去。○[16]今朝有酒今朝醉、明日愁來明日當。○[17]前年上省
赶考、我們兩個走了一路。○[18]舊年是閏七月、大前年是閏三
月。○[19]你昨兒/夜來不是這麼說的嗎、答是這麼說的。○[20]現在沒有
錢贖、到轉/來年春分的時候再贖罷。○[21]依我的意思、叫他過/明年
再上一年學、到後年下來做買賣。○[22]我們已經定規、於本月
二十四日起身。○[23]他是大上/上上禮拜六來的、到這個禮拜二、一
共是十一天。○[24]下月初五、又到了會期喇、又得拿四吊錢的
股/本子。○[25]登州是靠/仗着吃關東糧、關東既然歉收、明年的糧
食是必貴的。○[26]他去年佔我的地、今年又佔我的地、若是過
年再這個様兒、我定然要不依他。○[27]知府已經卸事、新官還

16 While we have wine, let us drink our fill; the troubles of to-morrow let to-morrow bear.

17 Year before last when we went to the provincial capital to the examinations, we traveled in company.

18 Last year there was an intercalary seventh month, and three years ago, an intercalary third month.

19 Is not this what you said yesterday? *Ans.* It is.

20 I have no money to redeem it at present. I will redeem it in the spring of next year.

21 According to my idea, let him still go to school next year, and the year after leave school and go into business.

22 We have already decided to start on the twenty-fourth of this month.

23 He came week before last on Saturday. By Tuesday of this week it will be eleven days in all.

24 The fifth of next month the meeting of the company comes round again, and I must make another payment of four thousand cash.

25 Têngchow depends on Kwantung for grain. Since the crops in Kwantung are short, grain will certainly be dear next year.

26 Last year he encroached on my land, and again this year he encroached on it. If he does the same thing next year, I am determined to resist him.

27 The prefect has vacated his office, but the new incumbent has not yet arrived.

老翁 *Lao3 wêng1*. An old gentleman, *a patriarch*, a graybeard.

葬 *Tsang4*. To inter, to bury.

下葬 *Hsia4 tsang4*. To inter, to consign to the grave.

春分 *Ch'un1 fên1*. The vernal equinox.

登州 *Têng1 chou1*. A Fu city in Shantung fifty-five miles west of Chefoo.

歉 *Ch'ien4, chien4*. Scanty, deficient, scarce :—Note 25.

歉收 *Ch'ien4 shou1*. A scant harvest, *short crops*, scarcity.

卸事 *Hsie4 shi4*. *To vacate an office*, to relinquish a trust.

文書 *Wên2 shu1*. *A dispatch;* an official document; a deed.

二府 *Êr4 fu3*. A sub-prefect.

朦朦亮 *Mêng2 mêng2 liang4*. Break of day, morning twilight.

走水 *Tsou3 shwei3*. To take fire, to have a conflagration :—Note 29.

宴 *Yien4*. A banquet; rest, repose.

點心 *Tien3 hsin1*. Cakes, candies and nuts, *delicacies*, dessert.

丙 *Ping3*. The third of the ten stems or **天干字**, bright.

寅 *Yin2*. The third of the twelve branches or **地支字**, 3 to 5 A.M.

乙 *I4*. The second of the ten stems; curved; a pedantic form of 一.

丑 *Ch'ou3*. The second of the twelve branches; 1 to 3 A.M.

沒有來到、昨兒個(昨天)來了文書、叫二府代任。○[28]幸虧去年冬天裏、下了三四場大雪、所以麥子雖然都種晚了、今年還能收成。○[29]聽說上禮拜二、朦朦亮的時候、費縣當鋪走了水、把房子一總都燒了。○[30]王宴平現在熬到分兒(苦出來)喇、今早上我上他家裏去、正碰見他的兩個孫子、一個端着茶、一個端着點心、送給他吃。○[31]我今年二十九歲、是甲子年丙寅月乙丑日己卯時生的。○[32]大前日到大後日(老前日到老後日)、是七天的工夫、大前年到大後年(現前年到老後年)、是七年的工夫、但是上上禮拜到下下禮拜(大上禮拜到大下禮拜)、却只有五個禮拜的工夫。

Yesterday a dispatch came authorizing the sub-prefect to act as his substitute.

28 Fortunately last winter there fell three or four heavy snows, so that, although the wheat was all sown late, there may still be a full crop this year.

29 I hear it said that on Tuesday of last week, just at the break of day, the Fei Hsien pawn-shop took fire and the whole establishment was burned up.

30 Wang Yien P'ing has reached the goal of life. When I went to his house this morning, I met his two grandsons, one carrying a cup of tea, and the other some delicacies for him.

31 This year I am twenty-nine years old, having been born in the year *chia tsï*, in the month *ping yin*, on the day *i ch'ou*, and the hour *chi mao*.

32 From the day previous to day before yesterday, to the day subsequent to day after to-morrow, includes a space of seven days; from the year previous to year before last, until the year subsequent to year after next, is a space of seven years; but from week before last until week after next is only five weeks.

NOTES.

10 僱給人家 *Hired himself to some one.*

12 拜壽 *Worship age,*—to pay respects on the occasion of a birthday. It is only practiced in the case of persons of some age and distinction. Sometimes it is carried to the length of a prostration, but more generally it is simply a bow.

16 Notice how 朝 is used instead of 日 to avoid repetition, and then how 朝 and 日 are both repeated to add force and beauty to the saying.

24 會期 *The appointed time for the meeting of the company.* The Chinese are much given to forming small joint stock companies of a peculiar kind. Some man who wants to raise a sum of money, secures the consent of a number of friends to enter the company, and fixes the amount of the shares. He then makes a feast for the shareholders and each man pays over to him one share, which is always such an aliquot part of the whole stock as there are members in the company. At the end of a month or of two months, as the case may be, another meeting is held (but no feast given) and again each member pays in a share to the man who offers to accept the largest discount in order to get the money. The party who gets the money is said to 把 the 會. The same thing is done at each subsequent meeting until the number of meetings equals the number of members, when the company expires. The discounts apply only to those who have not yet used the money, those who have already done so always paying a full *share.*

25 歉 has the same meaning whether aspirated or not, but the two are used in different connections,—thus 歉收 is aspirated, but 歉年 is unaspirated.

26 There being no hedges or fences in China it is no uncommon thing for one man in ploughing to encroach on the land of another, and such encroachments often give rise to quarrels and lawsuits.

29 走了水 *The water left;* i.e., *a fire broke out.* This phrase sounds like slang, but is not so regarded by the Chinese. It is explained by saying that the reason the fire exceeded its bounds was because water was absent.

30 熬到分兒 *To endure to the full,* that is, to bear the toils and responsibilities of life until the coveted end of life is attained, which, in the average Chinaman's eye, consists in having an easy competence with children and grandchildren to wait on him. The Southern form 苦出來 has practically the same meaning. 苦 is used as a verb.

31 The Chinese reckon years in cycles of sixty, the years of the cycle being indicated by the combination of the ten stems, or 天干字, viz., 甲乙丙丁戊己庚辛壬癸, with the twelve branches, or 地支字, viz., 子, 丑, 寅, 卯, 辰, 巳, 午, 未, 申, 酉, 戌, 亥. The branches are applied to the stems six times in order, (not twelve times as would have seemed natural). See Williams' Dictionary, page 355. Months, days and hours are designated by the same sixty combinations taken in the same order.

The months begin with 丙寅 for the first month of the first year (甲子) of each cycle, and count in order to the end of five years, which exhausts the sixty combinations. The next five years begins with 己巳 for the first month, and repeats the cycle in the same order, and so on. Thus in

第一百十八課

你[1]怎麼到這早晚兒（嚐子）纔來。○現[2]今人情太薄了。○那[3]個老母雞、現時菢窩（菢蛋）。○還[4]有別的、我當下（時下）想不起來。○這[5]個樣子、現今不時興喇。○聽[6]說初成萬、現時發了大財。○那[7]是多年的事情、現今不必題。○我[8]這會兒（子）有事、沒有工夫。○這[9]時候（嚐）天實在短、一轉眼就黑了。○目[10]下糧食的行市、已經落了。○我[11]的肚子、這一陣疼的利害。○目[12]下說話、

TRANSLATION.

1 How is it that you have not come until this time?
2 At the present day, the generous impulses of humanity are greatly degenerated.
3 That old hen is just now sitting.
4 There is something else which I cannot at this moment recall.
5 This style is not in fashion at present.
6 I hear that Ch'u Ch'êng Wan has now become very wealthy.
7 That is a matter of many years ago; there is no occasion for mentioning it now.
8 I am engaged at present, and have no leisure.
9 The days are very short at present, it is dark in a twinkling.
10 Just now the price of grain has fallen.
11 My belly aches severely just now.

the case of all years designated by 甲 or 巳, the first month is 丙寅, the second 丁卯, etc.; in the case of all years designated 乙 or 庚, the first month is 戊寅, the second 己卯, etc. Intercalary months are not counted, but half of the month is attached to the previous and half to the succeeding month. The days are not derived from the months, but are taken from official lists in a printed almanac or book. They profess to have begun with 甲子, when the cycle was introduced in the 61st year of Hwang Ti, and to have repeated the cycle regularly until the present time.

The hours are derived from the days in the same way as the months are derived from the years, beginning, however, with 甲子, for the midnight hour of the first day of the cycle, and repeating every five days. The person in question was born in 1864 on the twenty-third of the first month between 5 and 7 o'clock A.M.

LESSON CXVIII.

PRESENT TIME—GENERAL.

今 Now, in present circumstances,—when used alone it is generally followed by 有 and serves to introduce a subject or sentence.

現今 Now, at present, at the present time, now-a-days,—not appreciably different from 現在.

現時 At present, at the present time, just now.

現下 The same. (Shantung.)

時下 At present, just now.

目下 At this moment, at present, just now, now, just at this present time.

刻下 At this moment, at the present time, just now.

當下 At this moment, just now, now.

脚下 At present, now; in the presence of.

眼時下 At present, just now, at this present time.

眼時間 The same.

此刻 At this moment, at present.

目今 At this present time, at present, just now. A book term.

眼前 At present, just now.

馬上 Just now, at this present moment. (Pekingese.) See Les. 162.

這嚐 At present, at this time, just now.

這嚐子 The same. (S.)

這嚐個 The same. (C.)

這早晚 The same. (N.)

這會兒 At present, at this time, now.

這一陣 At this moment, just now.

這個時候 At this time, at the present time, now.

這個當兒 At this time, at this juncture, now. (N. & C.)

這個當口 The same. (S.)

他有四十口人。○這[13]個當口兒、他們已經睡喇。○現[14]今的人、認眞辦事的少。○我[15]打算去、馬上沒有工夫。○直[16]收拾到這會兒、還沒收拾(俐㨰/俐束/熨貼)。○我[17](眼時下/眼時間/眼前)上天無路、入地無門。○此[18]刻沒有別的病、就是胸膈中憋氣。○他[19]前幾年不肯用工念書、現時知道錯了。○先[20]生刻下在家裏作甚麽、答在家裏閒着、沒有事情。○你[21]的父母現(在/下)還康健哪、答他們從前受過累、所以現(在/下)不什麽康健了。○慕[22]太太爲自己不能生育、目下情願叫慕老爺買(小婆子/個妾)。○他[23]早走喇、這個時候、大約能走二十里路。○你[24]們妞兒若不丟、現今也有十幾歲了。○馬[25]上我家裏的事太多、要一時之閒空也沒有。○刻[26]下的醫生、好的雖有、但是一百裏也不過挑出一個來。○[27](目今/脚下)閃

12 At this present time he has a family of forty.
13 By this time they are already asleep.
14 There are few men now-a-days who are truly faithful.
15 I was planning to go, but have not time just at present.
16 Have you been arranging things all this time and are they not yet in order? [dilemma.
17 I am just now in an inextricable
18 I have no other ailment at present save a feeling of oppression in my breast.
19 During the previous years he was unwilling to study. He now sees his mistake.
20 What are you just now doing at home? *Ans.* I am at home idle; having no employment.
21 Are your parents still hale and hearty? *Ans.* In former years their strength was overtaxed, so that at present they are not very vigorous.
22 Mrs. Mu, because she herself has no hope of bearing children, is now quite willing that Mr. Mu should procure an inferior wife (a concubine).
23 They started some time ago; by this time they have probably gone twenty li.
24 If your daughter had not died, she would now be in her teens.
25 My home affairs at present are too numerous; I can't get a moment's leisure.
26 Although there are some good doctors at the present time, yet you could not

VOCABULARY.

菢 *Pao⁴*. . . . . To incubate, to brood.

菢窩 *Pao⁴ wo̤¹*. . . . . To incubate, to sit.

菢蛋 *Pao⁴ tan⁴*. . . . . The same.

時興 *Shï² hsing¹*. . . . . . . Fashionable, in vogue.

㨰 *Lo̤⁴*. To pile up, to lay in a pile, *to arrange in order;* a pile, a parcel.

俐㨰 *Li⁴ lo̤⁴*. In order, ship-shape, *satisfactory;* finished. (N).

俐束 *Li⁴ shu⁴*. . . . . The same. (C.)

胸 *Hsiung¹*. *The breast,* the bosom; the feelings, the heart.

膈 *Kê²*. *The diaphragm;* a thin membrane; the mind.

胸膈 *The breast;* the diaphragm; the feelings.

憋 *Pie¹*. Irritable; restrained, *oppressed;* sad, melancholy.

憋氣 *Pie¹ ch'i⁴*. Unable to breathe, *oppressed,* smothered.

康健 *K'ang¹ chien⁴*. . . . . *Hearty,* vigorous.

慕 *Mu⁴*. To love ardently, to be fond of, to long for; *a surname.*

育 *Yü⁴*. . . . . *To bear;* to nurture, to rear.

生育 *Shêng¹ yü⁴*. . . . . To bear children.

得我前不巴歸村、後不巴着店、往那裏去投宿呢。○往[28]大衙門投手本、必遞門包、這是現今通行的規矩。○你[29]想他從正月就病、一直病到這早晚嗜子、什麼人能架得住呢。○王[30]老三的買賣已經歇關喇、眼目時下間艱難的很、連吃的都沒有。○近[31]來郭文彬的兒子、吃喝嫖賭無所不為、所以他目如今的愁腸、比那些年倒更多了。○現[32]今的世代、若沒有點刁鑽古怪的本事、還想着站立得住、那可不用打算。○已[33]經十五六歲的姑娘、成天家淨玩耍兒、也不學點針線、你這個當兒口不學、等到幾時纔學呢。○我[34]見告白上說、今有東關孫榮泉、於初三日晚間、在關帝廟聽戲、因不小心、失去牛角圖書一包、大小五塊、若有送到者、必謝錢五百文、決不食言。

pick out more than one in a hundred.

27 I am now left all alone, with no village in front and no inn behind; where shall I go to find lodgings?

28 In sending your card to any large yamên, it is necessary to fee the gatekeeper; this is now the universal custom.

29 Just think of it; he took sick in the first month and has been sick ever since; who could stand it?

30 Wang the Third has already closed up his business; at the present moment he is in great straits, not even having enough to eat.

31 Recently Kwoă Wên Pin's son has become dissolute and reckless, so that at present his troubles are still greater than in those former years.

32 If you think to hold your own in these days without some craft and exceptional skill, you will soon find out your mistake.

33 A girl fifteen or sixteen playing all the time and not even learning to sew! If you don't learn now, when will you learn?

34 I saw a placard which said, Sun Jung Ch'üen of the east suburb, while at the temple of Kwanti on the evening of the third listening to a play, lost, through carelessness, a parcel of horn seals, consisting of five in all. Any one returning them will receive a reward of five hundred cash. Positively no backing out.

妾 *Ch'ie*[4]. . . . . A concubine, a secondary wife.

妞 *Niu*[1]. A lass, a girl, *a daughter*. An unauthorized Pekingese character.

投宿 *T'ou*[2] *su*[4]. To find lodgings, to rest for the night.

手本 *Shou*[3] *pên*[3]. A folded ceremonial card :—Note 28.

門包 *Mên*[2] *pao*[1]. A doorkeeper's fees or perquisites.

近來 *Chin*[4] *lai*[2]. . . . . Recently, of late.

郭 *Kwoă*[1]. . . . . An inner wall; *a surname*.

彬 *Pin*[1]. . . . . . . Chaste, elegant.

腸 *Ch'ang*[2]. The intestines; *the feelings*, the affections.

愁腸 *Ch'ou*[2] *ch'ang*[2]. *Trouble*, worry, anxiety, sorrow.

世代 *Shï*[4] *tai*[4]. . . . . The world, *the times*.

刁鑽 *Tiao*[1] *tswan*[1]. To manœuvre, to intrigue, to scheme; *crafty*, cunning.

告白 *Kao*[4] *pai*[2]. An unofficial notice, *a placard*, an advertisement.

圖書 *T'u*[2] *shu*[1]. *An unofficial seal*, a stamp, a signet.

食言 *Shï*[2] *yien*[2]. To eat one's words, *to back out*, to retract.

第一百十九課

他[1]頭裏早頭來過好幾遍。○我[2]從來沒聽見這句話。○他[3]先前是個財主。○事[4]情沒來以先、該早預備。○他[5]向來不喜歡我。○若[6]是早已料到、還有法子。○他[7]把以向先來的老樣子都改了。○他[8]早已有病、至今沒好。○頭[9]裏是怎麼樣、現在還是怎麼樣。○[10]早朝飯以前、各人都要打辮梳頭子、洗臉。○我[11]們先前上過這樣的當、受了好

TRANSLATION.

1 He has come several times before.
2 I have never before heard this expression.
3 He was formerly a wealthy man.
4 You should have made preparations before the emergency arose.
5 He has never liked me.
6 If I had anticipated it beforehand, I could have provided for it.
7 He has changed all his former ways.
8 He was taken sick some time ago, and he has not yet recovered.
9 Let it be as it was before.
10 Before breakfast, every one is to comb his hair and wash his face.
11 We once before fell into this kind of a trap and endured a deal of suffering.

NOTES.

12 The force of 說話 does not appear in the translation. It is as if we should say, *At the present speaking he has a family of forty.*

14 認眞辦事 *To be faithful and earnest in regard to engagements or responsibilities relating to others.*

17 上天無路入地無門 *No road to ascend to heaven nor any door to enter the earth;* i.e., *no possible way of escape, utterly helpless.*

22 The occasion of a man in common life taking a second or inferior wife, is generally the barrenness of the first wife. In these circumstances she oftentimes not only consents to it, but even urges it. This inferior wife or concubine is generally called 小婆子 in the North, though 妾 is the proper term, and is sometimes used. A man who takes an inferior wife always has to take her from a lower rank of society than his own, and also has to pay for her, more or less according to circumstances. Though socially inferior to the first wife, the inferior wife has nevertheless bettered her circumstances both socially and financially.

27 閃 does not here indicate whether the person has been left alone by mistake or by some trick. The phrase 前不歸村後不着店, is frequently used figuratively of any one in embarrassing circumstances.

28 手本 is a folded red paper (ten folds) with black back, containing merely the name and style of the individual. It is used as a card of ceremony, but is always returned to the bearer.

31 無所不爲 *Nothing that he will not do, given to every vice, reckless.* The use of 那些 implies a knowledge on the part of the party addressed, of trials endured in previous years.

34 This is the usual form of notices put up offering a reward for lost articles. As usual in such cases, though professing to be colloquial, it still contains some *Wên-li* words and idioms. 送到者 is book style for 送到的. The 牛角 referred to is the horn of the water buffalo, of which the best stamps are made.

LESSON CXIX.

PAST TIME—GENERAL.

早 Early,—some time ago, long ago; in season.

早已 Formerly, some time ago, beforehand.

早裡 Formerly, of old, old, heretofore. (C. & N.)

早頭 The same. (S.)

早前 Once, once upon a time, previously, some time ago.

早先 The same.

早年 In former years, in ancient days, long ago.

頭裡 Formerly, some time ago, heretofore, before; with a negative,—never. (C. & N.)

頭前 or **前頭**. The same as **頭裡**.

先前 Once, once upon a time, formerly, before, a while ago; with a negative,—never.

先頭 or **先頭裡** The same.

些苦難。○[12]早先前爲這個雨字、我叫先生打了一板尺子。○[13]像如今的時症、頭前前頭都沒經過。○[14]在洪水以頭前的那些人、都活八九百歲。○[15]他從來沒受過逼迫。○[16]你以前所念的書、還該常常温習。○[17]二姑娘在那裏、答先頭我見他在客堂裏。○[18]這是他早頭頭裏的老毛病、現在又發作了。○[19]氣派還是往年的氣派、家道却不是往年的家道了。○[20]他頭裏借我四吊錢去、到如今一個也沒還我。○[21]早先前咱們在第一樓茶館裏會過、你忘了我嗎。○[22]早先年的人、比如

12 I once received a stroke of the ferule from my teacher on account of this character yü.

13 We have never before experienced an epidemic like the present one.

14 The antediluvians all lived to be eight or nine hundred years old.

15 He has never suffered persecution.

16 The books you have already studied you should frequently review.

17 Where is the younger miss? *Ans.* I saw her a little while ago in the parlor.

18 This is an old failing of his, which has now broken out anew.

19 The style is still that of former years, but the rate of expenditure is not what it once was.

20 He borrowed four thousand cash from me some time ago, and to this date has not repaid a single cash.

21 We met each other once in the Ti-i-lou Tea-house; have you forgotten?

22 The men of former times were all

先年 In previous years, former times.

從來 Heretofore, formerly; with a negative,—never.

從早 For a long time, for some time, for a great while.

從先 Once, formerly, a while ago.

以前 Before, heretofore, already, formerly.

以頭 The same, but much less current.

以先 Before, former, previous.

向來 Same as **從來**, but less current.

一向 All this time, from some previous time to the present.

古 Ancient times, generally joined with other words save where correlated with **今**.

古時 Anciently, ancient times, in olden time.

古年 The same.

太古 Primeval times.

上古 Primitive times, olden times.

中古 Mediæval times.

往日 In former days or times, in the past, heretofore.

往年 In former years or times, in bygone years.

老老年間 In old times, very ancient times, long long ago.

老輩子年間 In the times of our forefathers, in olden times.

VOCABULARY.

時症 *Shï² chêng⁴*. A prevailing disease, an ... ... epidemic.

迫 *P'oa⁴*. To urge, *to harass*, to force, to drive to ... . extremity.

逼迫 *Pi⁴ p'oa⁴*. ... ... *To persecute*, to harass.

氣派 *Ch'i⁴ p'ai⁴*. *Style*, air, pomp, pretension, ... show.

家道 *Chia¹ tao⁴*. Style of living, pecuniary circumstances, *rate of expenditure*.

茶館 *Ch'a² kwan³*. A tea shop, a temperance ... ... saloon.

憨厚 *Han¹ hou⁴*. ... ... *Generous*, liberal.

渾厚 *Hun² hou⁴*. ... ... The same.

璺 *Wên⁴*. ... ... A crack, a flaw.

今的人都更渾憨厚。○看[23]樣兒是早碰打的裂璺我早前先却一點沒留聒意睬。○你[24]怎麼認識這個人呢、答我們以前作過鄰街舍坊。○按[25]中國說、是今不如古、按西國說、是古不如今。○我[26]一向得老兄做件兒、實在於我大有益處。○那[27]個界石、是早年老輩子立的、你如今拔了、咱們就是一塲官司。○你[28]這個症候、是剛纔得的呢、是早先得的呢。○我[29]的房錢早已交足了、你還問我要嗎。○這[30]些事情、早向裏來都是我父親管的、所以我摸不着根底底細。○古[31]年時有名的聖

more generous than those of the present.

23 Judging from its appearance it is an old crack, but I had not previously noticed it.

24 How do you come to know this man? *Ans.* We once were neighbors.

25 According to Chinese ideas, the present is inferior to ancient times; according to Western ideas, ancient times were inferior to the present.

26 It has indeed been of great benefit to me that I have had you for my companion all this time.

27 That boundary stone was put up long ago by our forefathers. Your having now removed it, simply means a lawsuit for us.

28 Is this disease of yours a recent thing? or did you contract it some time ago?

29 I paid up my house rent in full some time ago. Why are you dunning me again?

30 These affairs were formerly all looked after by my father, hence I am unable to go into particulars.

留意 *Liu*[2] *i*[4]. . . . . . . To pay attention, *to notice.*

界 *Chie*[1,4]. *A boundary*, a limit, a terminus; a sphere, a condition.

界石 *Chie*[4] *shï*[2]. . . . . A boundary stone.

根底 *Kên*[1] *ti*[3]. Origin, ground, occasion; facts, *particulars.*

聖人 *Shêng*[4] *jên*[2]. A man pre-eminent in wisdom and virtue, a sage.

禹 *Yü*[3]. The founder of the Hia dynasty:—Note 31.

鞦 *Ch'iu*[1], *yiu*[1]. A breast strap, a crupper, a trace; *a swing.*

韆 *Ch'ien*[1]. . . . . . . A swing; to swing to and fro.

鞦韆 *Yiu*[1] *ch'ien*[1]. . . . . . . A whirlwheel, *a swing.*

燈草 *Têng*[1] *ts'ao*[3]. The wick of a lamp,—so called because it is the pith of a species of grass or reed.

温和 *Wên*[1] *hê*[2]. Genial, *affable;* peaceable, quiet.

起先 *Ch'i*[3] *hsien*[1]. At first, originally, at the outset:—Les. 126. Sub.

機關 *Chi*[1] *kwan*[1]. Trigger, handle; trick, *artifice*; turning point, clue.

馬脚 *Ma*[3] *chiao*[3]. An underhand trick or scheme; "the cloven foot":—Note 34.

狐 *Hu*[2]. . . . . *A fox;* suspicious.

狸 *Li*[2]. . . . . . *A fox;* a raccoon, a wild-cat.

狐狸 The fox.

尾 *Wei*[3], *i*[3]. *The tail;* the end, the last of; the hinder part, the stern of a ship.

尾巴 *I*[3] *pa*[1]. *The tail,* the hinder part, the stern of a ship:—Note 34.

誌 *Chï*[4]. . . . . . . To remember; to record; a mark.

誌石 *Chï*[4] *shï*[2]. A stone used as a test of strength:—Note 35.

制石 *Chï*[4] *shï*[2]. . . . . The same.

弓 *Kung*[1]. . . . . *A bow;* curved; five feet.

近日 *Chin*[4] *jï*[4]. . . . . . . Recent times, now. (w.)

盤古 *P'an*[2] *ku*[3]. . . . The first man:—Note 38.

闢 *P'i*[4]. To burst forth, to open up, *to set in order;* to develop.

開天闢地 *K'ai*[1] *t'ien*[1] *p'i*[4] *ti*[4]. Opening heaven and setting in order the earth,—a stereotype phrase for the creation or formation of the world.

羲 *Hsi*[1]. . . . . Breath, vapor:—Note 38.

農 *Nung*[2]. To cultivate, to farm; agriculture:—Note 38.

孟 *Mêng*[4]. . . . . Eminent; senior:—Note 31

人、就是堯舜禹湯文武周公孔子。○你[32]姐姐從鞦韆上掉下來、跌破了頭、現在好了沒有、答從早就好喇。○從[33]早先招呼着叫我點燈、一點燈草沒有、我怎麼點呢。○我[34]看見那人和你說話、頭裏(起先)很有溫和老實的樣兒、後來你說破了他的機關、他的利害就露出狐狸尾巴(馬脚)來了。○拿[35]大刀、抱誌(制)石、拉硬弓、這都是我往年的老本事、現在這些武

31 The noted sages of ancient times were Yao, Shun, Yü, T'ang, Wên, Wu, Chou-kung, K'ung-tsï.

32 Your sister fell out of the swing and cut her head; is she well yet? *Ans.* She has been well for some time.

33 He has been calling out to me for some time to light the lamp. But how can I light it when there is not a particle of wick?

34 I noticed that in talking with you he had at first a very affable and inoffensive manner; but by and by when you exposed his tricks, his evil purpose disclosed itself.

35 To handle the great sword, lift the standard stone and draw the stiff bow; these were the feats of bygone years, but now I can not essay such exercises.

Notes.

8 至今 is slightly bookish, though often used. 到如今 is the more common spoken form.

9 Or, *it is just as it was before.*

10 In the South 梳頭 is only used of women and children, not of men, who have queues.

12 The pupil probably mistook 雨 for 兩 or 丙, and got a stroke of the ruler to assist his memory. Striking on the hand with a ruler is almost the only mode of punishment used by Chinese teachers. 戒尺 is the more proper and general term for the ferule, though it is sometimes called 板子, especially in Peking. The bastinado used by magistrates is called 板子.

17 二姑娘 *The younger of two sisters.*

21 第一樓 The name of a two storied tea house in Shanghai. The 第一 means first in excellence, *first-class.*

29 The direct interrogative is here best rendered into English by an indirect interrogative.

31 We have here the stereotype enumeration of Chinese sages. They are arranged in the order of time.

堯 The first Emperor of reputed Chinese history. He is the great model of wisdom and virtue in a sovereign. His reign began B.C. 2357.

舜 The second Emperor of reputed history. He was chosen by 堯 and associated with him for thirty years in the government. He mourned for his predecessor three years and then formally assumed the government B.C. 2255.

禹 also called 大禹, *The Great Yü*, or 神禹, *The Divine Yü.* He is reputed to have been a descendant of Hwang Ti. He was chosen as his successor by 舜, and succeeded to the throne B.C. 2205, and became the founder of the Hia dynasty. The great achievement which procured for him the throne, was the draining of the land from a great flood, at which he labored incessantly for nine years.

湯 A wise and virtuous prince who overthrew the tyrant 桀 Chie, the last of the Hia dynasty, and became the founder of the Shang dynasty.

文 The Duke of 周. His original name was 昌, and his title 西伯, *Chief of the West.* He lived from 1231 to 1135 B.C., and after his death was canonized as 文王. He was renowned for virtue and wisdom. He revised the Book of Changes and wrote comments on it.

武 The son of 文王, to whose dukedom he succeeded B.C. 1169. His real name was 發, and he was canonized as 武王. His great achievement was the overthrow of the tyrant 紂辛, the last of the Shang dynasty, whose throne he took and became founder of the (周) Chou dynasty.

周公 The fourth son of 文王, and brother of 武王. He materially assisted his brother in obtaining the throne, and throughout his reign was his most valued counsellor. He drew up a code of laws for the empire, and is reputed as the inventor of the mariners' compass.

孔子 Confucius, the last and greatest of Chinese sages. His real name was 孔丘, and his title 仲尼. He lived from B. C. 557 to 479. He was neither emperor nor prince. His greatness was in his virtue, his wisdom and his learning. 孟子 Mencius, is not ranked as a sage (聖人) by the Chinese, but as a 大賢, *a great worthy.*

34 In this sentence, which is taken from the Pilgrims' Progress, 頭裡 is used in sense of *at first*, which is not its proper meaning, though said to be sometimes so used in Peking. 起先 is the better word for the connection. 露出馬脚來 *To reveal unawares some concealed charcater or design.* The figure probably comes from the discovery of some ambush or stratagem in war by the footprints of the horses. 尾巴 is spoken both *wei*³ *pa*¹ and *i*³ *pa*¹, but the reading *i*³ does not generally extend to the derived sense of 尾.

35 拿大刀 *To flourish aloft the heavy cutlass or halberd.* 抱誌石 This 誌石 or 制石 is a heavy oblong stone with niches cut in it for handles. The feat consists in lifting it up by main force on the knee, and then taking it in the arms and standing erect with it. 拉硬弓 *To draw a stiff bow*

藝、都試不得咯。○我[36]與你往日無寃、近日無仇、○傳[37]說在老輩(老老)子年間、人活到六十歲不死、就要活埋。○盤[38]古開天闢地的時候、爲太古、伏羲神農黃帝的時候、爲上古、從堯到武王的時候、爲中古、在孔孟前後數百年的時候、都渾而言之爲古時。

36 I never was, and am not now, at enmity with you.

37 There is a tradition that in old times if a man did not die before he was sixty years old, they buried him alive.

38 The time when P'an Ku opened the heavens and divided the earth was primeval time. The times of Fu Hi, Shin Nung and Hwang Ti were primitive times; the times from Yao to Wu Wang were mediæval times, and the times preceding and following Confucius and Mencius are spoken of, in a general way, as ancient times.

to the point of the arrow. These are the three chief athletic exercises of the Chinese.

38 盤古 The Chinese first man. He is a mythical character alleged to have been the first development out of chaos, and to him is attributed the setting in order of heaven and earth. Various wonderful stories are told concerning him.

伏羲 Also called 庖羲氏, the first Emperor of Chinese legendary history. The period commonly assigned to the beginning of his reign is B.C. 2852. He instructed the people in the arts of hunting, fishing and pasturage. He invented the eight diagrams, established the laws of marriage, and constructed musical instruments.

神農 *The Divine Husbandman.* He was the second legendary emperor and successor of 伏羲. He is reputed to have reigned from B.C. 2737 to B.C. 2697. He made ploughs, and taught the people agriculture. He also taught the people the use of plants for medicine, and instituted the holding of markets. He is now worshipped as the God of Agriculture.

黃帝 *The Yellow Emperor.* He was the third and last legendary emperor. He regulated the customs of the people and taught them how to make utensils of wood, pottery and metal, also how to build boats and construct wagons.

LESSON CXX.

FUTURE TIME—GENERAL.

後 Afterwards, subsequently; when directly following a noun,—after.

往後 Hereafter, henceforth, in future, since.

過後 Afterwards, subsequently, by and by.

以後 Afterwards, hereafter, after, in future, subsequently.

日後 In the future, at a future time, by and by, sometime. A book form, sometimes used in colloquial.

之後 A book form of 以後, but not unfrequently used in colloquial.

向後 In future, hereafter, henceforth. (L.)

然後 Afterwards, and then, then, subsequently.

隨後 At once, forthwith, thereupon, afterwards, following.

久後 Ultimately, eventually, by and by, ever.

末後 At last, finally, ultimately.

後來 Afterwards, hereafter, henceforth.

後頭 Afterwards, in future,—heard occasionally in this sense, but more commonly and properly used of *place* than of time.

後日 Properly *day after to-morrow*, but sometimes used indefinitely, especially in books,—in future, by and by, hereafter.

往前 or 這往前 Henceforth, from this time forth, after this. The Chinese seem quite at sea with reference to the use of 前 and 後 joined with 往.

往下 or 這往下 Henceforth, from this time forth.

往下去 The same. (N.)

改日 Some other day, again,—only used at parting where we would say good-bye.

底下 In the future, at some other time, by and by.

從今以後 or 從今後 or 從今之後 Henceforth, in future, from this time forth.

從此以後 The same.

第一百二十課

讓[1]人不算癡、過後得便宜。○往[2]後怎麼樣、現在還不知道。○再[3]往下(這往下)去天就漸漸的長了。○往[4]後你的閒事、我再不管。○先[5]試一試、不行然後再說。○我[6]要走喇、咱們改日再見(會)罷。○萬[7]不可起先(先頭)殷勤、後來(後頭)懶惰。○現[8]在貧賤、要求後日的富貴。○今[9]日是我家女兒、後日是別人家媳婦。○你[10]別看他當時生氣、過後還是一樣。○我[11]先換上衣裳、隨後就去。○你[12]以後(向後)上街、要先告訴我。○[13]再往前(這往前)去天暖和了、爐裏不用生火。○那[14]些不要緊的小事情、過後誰還記在心裏。○午[15]飯之後、二人又敘談了半天。○我[16]雖然不如人、還指望孩子們往後如人。○從[17]今以後(今後)你要小心、不可任口胡說(信口胡言)。○[18]以後(向後)他若再來

TRANSLATION.

1 To yield to others must not be considered foolish; the advantage of it will appear by-and-by. [know.
2 How it will be hereafter we do not yet
3 From this time forth the days will gradually become longer.
4 Hereafter I will not trouble myself about your affairs.
5 Try it first, and if it will not do, we will then talk about it again.
6 I must be going. We'll meet again some other day.
7 It will never do to be diligent at first and afterwards grow lazy.
8 Those who are now in humble circumstances should aspire to be wealthy by and by.
9 To-day she is our daughter, to-morrow she will be somebody else's daughter-in-law.
10 Don't mind his getting angry at the time; he will be all the same afterwards. [then go at once.
11 I will first change my clothes, and
12 Hereafter when you go on the street, I want you first to tell me.
13 From this time on the weather will be mild; you need not make a fire in the stove. [trivial matters?
14 Who can afterwards remember those
15 After dinner they talked together again a long while.
16 Although I am not equal to others, I want my children hereafter to be equal to others.
17 From this time forward you must be

VOCABULARY.

貧賤 *P'in² chien⁴*. *In humble circumstances*, poor, indigent.

敘 *Hsü⁴*. *To talk*, to converse, to discuss.

敘談 *Hsü⁴ t'an²*. *To talk together*, to converse, to chat.

任口胡說 *Jên⁴ k'ou³ hu² shwoă¹*. To speak recklessly or extravagantly, to talk at random.

信口胡言 *Hsin⁴ k'ou³ hu² yien²*. The same :— Note 17.

攪鬧 *Chiao³ nao⁴*. To act in a disorderly manner, *to raise a row*, to bluster.

蹧鬧 *Tsao¹ nao⁴*. The same. (s.)

過失 *Kwoă⁴ shï¹*. *A mistake*, an error; an offence.

鑑戒 *Chien⁴ chie⁴*. *A warning*, an admonition.

隨手 *Swei² shou³*. *At once*, without delay, while one's hand is in.

層次 *Ts'êng² ts'ï⁴*. *Order*, arrangement, gradation.

措 *Ts'oă⁴*. To place, *to arrange;* to employ.

懊 *Ao⁴*. Vexed; *to regret*.

懊悔 *Ao⁴ hwei³*. To repent, to regret, to reproach oneself, *to rue*.

貼心 *T'ie¹ hsin¹*. *Amiable*, gracious; intimate, affectionate.

蹧攪鬧、可以攆轟出他去。○你19這樣好吃懶做、久後怎麼成家立業呢。○今20日的過失、就是後日的鑑戒。○花21錢該隨手記賬、恐怕過後忘了。○做22論必得先鋪排出層次來、然後纔好措詞。○你23實在願意和他結親、就結罷、過後你可別懊悔。○這24個藥是飯前吃呢、是飯後吃呢、答就飯前飯後都可以。○這25以後你看見楊三來沒有、答從前年我見他一面、日往後再沒見他。○聽26說先生娶了一個好媳婦、真是先生的洪福。答看如今可是貼心貼意的、但不知往下怎麼樣。○莊27稼都是先發苗、後長稭、再後秀穗、末後穗上纔結子粒。○張28先生今天沒有工夫、等底下再同他商議罷。○你29這個瘡若不拿擠一拿擠、久後結作個疤瘌、纔難看喇。○

careful not to talk so recklessly.

18 If in future he comes again to make a row, just put him out.

19 If you are so gluttonous and lazy as this, how will you ever get on in the world?

20 The mistakes of to-day are warnings for to-morrow.

21 When you spend money, you should at once make an entry of it, lest you subsequently forget.

22 In writing an essay, it is necessary first to lay out the order of thought before proceeding to elaborate the language.

23 If you are so anxious to form a marriage engagement with her, then do so; but be sure you do not afterwards repent of it.

24 Is this medicine to be taken before or after meals? *Ans.* It may be taken either before or after.

25 Did you afterwards see Yang San? *Ans.* I met him once, the year before last, but since that time I have not seen him.

26 I have heard, sir, that you have gotten an excellent daughter-in-law, which is certainly a great blessing. *Ans.* At present she seems to be everything that could be desired, but I don't know how it may be by and by.

27 Grain first puts forth sprouts, then it rises into stalks, afterwards it sends forth ears, and finally it yields the grains.

28 Mr. Chang has no time to-day; wait till some other time to consult him.

29 If you do not press the pus out of this

貼心貼意 *T'ie¹ hsin¹ t'ie¹ i⁴.* Amiable and obliging, everything that could be desired.

苗 *Miao².* The young and tender sprouts of grain; descendants.

稭 *Chie¹.* Stalks of corn or grain.

末 *Moă⁴.* The end, the last; *final;* remnants; powder, dust:—Les. 127.

子粒 *Tsï³ li⁴.* A grain, a seed.

擠 *Chi³.* To crowd, to push; *to press,* to squeeze; to milk.

疤 *Pa¹.* *A scar,* a mark.

疤瘌 *Pa¹ la⁴.* *A scar,* a cicatrix.

花用 *Hwa¹ yung⁴.* To spend money, to expend; expenditure.

上任 *Shang⁴ jên⁴.* To enter upon the duties of an office.

貪 *T'an¹.* *To covet,* to desire inordinately.

貪贓 *T'an¹ tsang¹.* *To covet or take bribes,* venal, corrupt.

世界 *Shï⁴ chie¹.* The world, *the age.*

練武 *Lien⁴ wu³.* To practice with sword and spear, *to fence.*

打拳脚 *Ta³ ch'üen² chiao³.* To practice boxing, *to box:*—Note 32.

灰心 *Hwei¹ hsin¹.* To be disheartened, to give up, to lose hope, *to lose interest.*

疫 *I⁴.* A prevalent disease, an epidemic.

瘟疫 *Wên¹ i⁴.* An epidemic, *pestilence.*

別[30]看他這個時候、典房子賣地的花用、他受罪的日子還在後頭。○鄭[31]太爺纔上任的時候、還有個作清官的樣子、自從送他萬民衣萬民傘之後、反倒顯出貪贓來咯。○從[32]前馬道清很愛練武打拳脚、後來遇見一個會拳脚的、就在衆人面前和他比試、剛一交手、教人家扔出好遠的去、鬧了一個沒趣、從此以後他也就灰了心咯、再也不學咯。○從[33]來說、福不雙降、禍不單來、所以大亂之後、常有荒年、荒年之後、常有瘟疫。

boil of yours, it will ultimately leave a scar that will be very unsightly.

30 Don't be misled by his present reckless extravagance; his time of suffering is yet to come.

31 When His Worship Chêng first came into office, he seemed like an upright officer, but from the time he was presented with the complimentary cloak and umbrella, he began to show an inclination to take bribes.

32 Formerly Ma Tao Ch'ing was very fond of fencing and boxing, but before long he fell in with a skilled boxer and presently engaged with him in a public trial of skill. They had hardly closed before the other man sent him reeling back ever so far, thus turning the laugh upon him. From that time on he lost his interest in boxing, and ceased practising.

33 It has been said that "blessings do not come in pairs, nor do misfortunes come singly"; hence it is that after a rebellion there is generally a year of famine, and after famine, pestilence.

Notes.

1 A proverbial saying.

7 後頭 in the second clause is used to match 先頭 in the first. The sentence is from The Sacred Edict.

9 今日 and 後日 are here used indefinitely, as are the corresponding terms in English. The same is true of (20).

17 信口胡言, 信 here means *to accord with, to follow*, which is a very unusual sense.

19 成家 as here used means something more than simply to get married; it also includes the idea of maintaining a family. 好吃懶做 is a ready made expression.

24 都可以 *All will do;* i.e., *either will do.*

30 典房子賣地的 The addition of 的 turns the phrase into a participial adjective qualifying 花用.

31 萬民衣 is a rich silk robe or cloak presented to a magistrate by the people as a testimony of regard. The names of all the contributors are put on the cloak in gilt letters. 萬民傘 is a large silk umbrella or canopy presented for the same purpose. Sometimes both are presented, sometimes only the latter.

32 打拳脚 In boxing, the Chinese use the feet as well as the hands, learning to kick as well as to strike. 鬧個沒趣 *To provoke a ridiculous* or *shameful discomfiture, to be put to shame* or *confusion.*

LESSON CXXI.

Strong Negation.

無 Destitute of, without, none. When followed by an abstract noun it often answers to the termination *less*, as 無用 *useless*, 無能 powerless, etc.

非 No, not,—a book negative often used in colloquial and stronger than 不.

並 Altogether, at all,—always combines with a negative. 並 is also a copulative :—Les. 138.

無非 Simply, nothing more, for no other purpose. This double negative forms a strong affirmative, which appears in English in the form of the sentence, without any special word to represent it.

無不 Without not,—that is, always, in everything.

並非 Not, not at all, not in the least, by no means.

並不 The same,—but not quite so strong.

並沒 The same,—differing from 並不 as 沒 does from 不.

並無 The same.

第一百二十一課

他[1]自己並用不着、却不肯給人用。○今[2]天並沒有外人
來、誰能偷去呢。○無[3]是無非他就敢打你嗎。○你[4]這個
人只知道吃飯、並不知道米的艱難。○那[5]裏算客呢、我
們無非是自己叔爺兒姪兒們。○這[6]並不是我攆了他、是他自
己不愛幹了。○我[7]是無心說的、他却是有心聽了。○張[8]
成勳無非也是個人、他能學我就能學。○你[9]並摸不着
事情的根底、就亂插嘴嗎。○他[10]是營務出身、並非科甲
底子。○人[11]作事若能無過不及、這就是合乎中道。○在[12]
山上並無樹木、太陽的熱氣、如同火窰一般。○我[13]並不
是向你說、你來搭的甚麼帮腔(帮甚麼腔)呢。○朝[14]廷立下這個法

TRANSLATION.

1 He has no use for it himself, and yet he will not allow any one else to use it.
2 No outsider has been here to-day; who could steal it?
3 Would he venture to strike you without any provocation?
4 *You* only know what it is to eat, you do not know how hard it is to get what you eat.
5 Why speak of being guests? We are all in the family.
6 It was not that I drove him away, but that he himself was unwilling to remain.
7 I spoke without reference to him, but he took it as intended for him.
8 Chang Ch'êng Hsün is nothing more than a man; if he can learn it, I also can learn it.
9 Why do you keep thrusting in your talk when you understand nothing about the matter.
10 He served in the army originally and has no literary degree.
11 If in his actions a man is able to avoid both excess and deficiency, this is in harmony with the golden mean.
12 There were no trees upon the mountain, and the heat of the sun was like a furnace.
13 I was not talking to you; what are you putting in your gab for?

These four phrases have substantially the same meaning, but are used in different connections. The force of 並 is not usually translateable by any special word. It gives a strength to the negation which the English language will not adequately express. The insertion of *at least* or *at all* approximates it, but is neither so elegant nor so forcible as 並 is in Chinese.

VOCABULARY.

無心 *Wu^2 hsin^1.* *Unintentionally*, unwittingly, accidentally. [Les 159.

有心 *Yiu^3 hsin^1.* Intentionally, on purpose.

勳 *Hsün^1.* Meritorious service, patriotic.

營務 *Ying^2 wu^4.* *Military affairs or service*, the army:—Note 10.

底子 *Ti^3 tsï^3.* Foundation; original draft; a copy; *previous attainments*, antecedents; discount on full strings of cash—from 4 to 16 according to locality.

出身 *Ch'u^1 shên^1.* To spring from, to come from; *originally*, primarily.

合乎 *Hê^2 hu^1.* *To accord with*, to harmonize with. (w.)

中道 *Chung^1 tao^4.* The medium between extremes, the golden mean.

樹木 *Shu^4 mu^4.* *Trees*, woods; vegetation.

熱氣 *Jê^4 ch'i^4.* Heat, caloric.

窰 *Yao^2.* A kiln, *a furnace*; a brothel.

火窰 *Hwoa^3 yao^2.* A furnace.

度、無非禁止百姓們爲非、引導百姓們爲善。○他[15]這一遭來、並非向你借錢、是要給你兒子說個媳婦兒(丈人家)。○你[16]的膽子可也不小、並沒同我商議、你就應許了嗎。○袁[17]錫功那個人、凡託他的事情、無不盡心竭力。○他[18]們的喜樂、並非從心所發、不過是外面虛浮的喜樂。○阿[19]、他已經當了掌櫃的嗎、無怪說話這麼硬掙(硬氣)。○那[20]不過是古人的遺傳、並沒有實在的憑據。○你(您)[21]妯娌兩個、無非爲兩句話、還值得動手嗎。○孔[22]雀並不會嗓、他的貴重處、就在一個尾巴。○你[23]自己脚跟底下、並沒打掃乾淨、還出來說嘴喇。○他[24]並不是

14 The Emperor established these laws for the express purpose of prohibiting the people from doing wrong and leading them to do right.

15 He has come this time, not to borrow money of you, but to propose a father-in-law for your son.

16 Well, you are a bold fellow to promise him without having consulted me.

17 That man Yüen Hsi Kung does his very best in everything that is entrusted to him.

18 Their rejoicing does not come from the heart; it is nothing more than a transient, external rejoicing.

19 Oh! he has been made head-man, has he? That explains why he speaks so positively.

20 That is nothing more than an ancient tradition, having no trustworthy evidence.

21 There is nothing between you two sisters-in-law but a few words—nothing worth coming to blows about.

22 The peacock cannot sing; his excellence is in his tail.

23 You have not swept clean under your own feet, and yet you assume to disparage others.

24 He is not a *lin-shêng* at all, yet you persist in saying he is.

幇腔 *Pang*¹ *ch'iang*¹. A chorus, an accompaniment; *intrusive talk.*

廷 *T'ing*¹˒². . . . . . An audience-hall, a court-yard.

朝廷 *Ch'ao*² *t'ing*². The imperial audience-hall; *the Emperor.*

法度 *Fa*³ *tu*⁴. . . . . . . *Laws*, regulations, rules.

禁止 *Chin*⁴ *chï*³. . . . . .To forbid, *to prohibit.*

爲非 *Wei*² *fei*¹. *To do wrong*, to violate the law, to do evil.

導 *Tao*³˒⁴. . . . . *To lead*, to induce.

引導 *Yin*³ *tao*³˒⁴. *To lead*, to guide, to show the way, to induce.

爲善 *Wei*² *shan*⁴. *To do right*, to act virtuously, to be free from faults.

袁 *Yüen*². . . . . . . A robe; *a surname.*

虛浮 *Hsü*¹ *fou*². Superficial, unsubstantial; *transient*, fleeting.

硬氣 *Ying*⁴ *ch'i*⁴. *Positive*, peremptory, emphatic.

硬掙 *Ying*⁴ *chêng*⁴. Firm, inflexible; *positive*, peremptory; relentless.

錫 *Hsi*¹˒². . . . . . . Tin; pewter; *to confer*, to give.

遺傳 *I*² *ch'wan*². *A tradition*, a legend, a fable.

妯娌 *Chou*² *li*³. . . . . .The wives of brothers.

嗓 *Sao*⁴. . . . . To chirp, *to sing*, to whistle.

脚跟 *Chiao*³ *kên*¹. . . . The heel; *sole of the foot.*

說嘴 *Shwoă*¹ *tswei*³. To boast, to brag; to exalt oneself and *disparage others*, to run down.

廩 *Lin*³. A government granary; a stipend to an advanced 秀才.

廩生 *Lin*³ *shêng*¹. An advanced 秀才:—Note 24.

服事 *Fu*² *shï*⁴. . . . . . *To serve*, to minister to.

勾當 *Kou*¹ *tang*⁴. . . . .*Business*, job, affair.

素日 *Su*⁴ *jï*⁴. Commonly, ordinarily; formerly, *in the past.*

瞞哄 *Man*² *hung*³. *To deceive*, to impose upon, to hoodwink.

干罪 *Kan*¹ *tswei*⁴. To plead guilty, to own up; *to take the consequences.*

個廩生、你偏說他是個廩生。○
[25]哥哥在此、無非是服事人、這並
不是大丈夫男子漢的勾當。○
[26]既然天無二日、民無二王、天地
間還能有第二位上帝嗎。○[27]我
們深準知道他們二人、素日並無
寃仇、實在是相親相愛、如親弟
親兄一樣。○[28]小的實係是不知
道、並不敢瞞哄大人、若查出有
一點兒瞞哄、小的情願甘領罪。

25 Here you are simply serving others,—which is not the kind of business for a man of any spirit.

26 Since heaven has no second sun, and the people have no second king, do you think that in the universe there can be a second God?

27 We know for certain that in the past these two men have not been enemies; they have, in fact, loved each other like own brothers.

28 Your unworthy servant really does not know. I should not dare to deceive your honor. If you discover that I have practiced the least deception, I will cheerfully bear the penalty.

NOTES.

3 無是無非 *Without right and without wrong*; i. e., *without any cause, or grievance.*

4 你這個人 The use of 這個人 singles out the party addressed as worthy of contempt, as is sometimes done in English by saying the "you" with special emphasis and intonation, and then pausing and beginning the sentence anew.

5 叔姪 *Uncles and nephews*; i. e., *belonging to one family.* A Southern term.

10 營務 does not necessarily mean that the party was a soldier, but that he had employment in connection with military affairs.

11 無過不及 is the standard definition of the "golden mean," which forms the Chinese rule of virtue. 無 applies to 不及 as well as to 過, as if written 無過無不及.

13 Lit., *what accompaniment have you come to play*, implying that what was said was an intrusion in the interest of another.

24 廩生 is the first intermediate grade above the first degree of 秀才. It formerly entitled the possessor to an allowance of grain from the public granary, but now only gives the privilege of standing security for undergraduates, for which a small fee is received. It is of no special service in securing the second degree.

LESSON CXXII.

SPECIAL USES OF 見.

1. 見 is prefixed to many adjectives and nouns in the general sense of to manifest or show,—thus 見强 is to manifest improvement, to be better; 見效 to manifest efficacy, to be efficacious; 見怪 to manifest displeasure, to take offence or be offended. Thus used, 見 has no exact equivalent in English. "Seem" will not translate it, for seem implies doubt, which 見 does not. It is approximately equivalent to the substantive verb. It appears to be put for 現, as it often is in *Wên-li*, where, however, it also takes the sound of 現. This use of 見 is entirely *t'ung-hsing.*

2. 見 is prefixed to verbs in the sense of to bear or to stand,—見穿 to stand wearing, that is, to last; 見做 to stand doing, that is, to be tedious; 見燒 to stand burning, that is, to have the quality (in fuel) of lasting, etc. Some would write 健 rather than 見. This use of 見 or 健 prevails in Shantung, but is not *t'ung-hsing.* In Peking and the North 禁 *chin*^{1} (not *chin*^{4}) is used in the same way, and with the same meaning. The same usage also prevails in Nanking and the South, but there teachers incline to use 經. Inasmuch, however, as Southern Mandarin confuses the final *n* and *ng*, it is likely that there also the proper writing is 禁.

3. 見 is joined with 天 in the sense of *every*,—見天 day by day, *every day.* In Peking it is frequently expanded into 見天見.

For list of words following 見 and 禁 see Supplement.

第一百二十二課

這[1]種花洋布就是好看、一點也不經見禁穿。○人[2]過了五十歲、就不經見禁混了。○各[3]樣的藥都吃了、一點也不見效。○這[4]件生活活計看着不多、却眞經見禁做。○張[5]時鐸的兒子、在家裏見要死見要活的、我要去看看他。○聽[6]說這一百里路、不甚麼大、怎麼這麼經見禁走呢。○人[7]若是有飯吃、有事情做、一點也不經見禁過。○今[8]天我看他的文章、眞是大見長進、比從前强的多喇。○他[9]這二年實在見老、頭髮白了一半、臉上也有了皺紋喇。○現[10]在他的熱見輕一點、他的病却見重了。○保[11]興子在家裏出生花兒、七天還沒灌上漿來、昨天吃了一劑副藥、今天見好一點。○凡[12]血汗掙來的錢、纔經見禁花的喇、若是來的太容易了、饒讓他有百萬之富、也是不能經見禁花的。○13我們這偏僻地方、貨價是見神見鬼的、說賤就賤、說貴

Translation.

1 This quality of foreign print is only for looks, it is not at all serviceable.
2 When a man has passed fifty, he does not last long.
3 He has taken every kind of medicine without producing the least improvement.
4 This piece of work seems to be quite inconsiderable, but really it is a very tedious job.
5 Chang Shï Toă's son is at home in a very critical state. I must go and see him.
6 I have heard that this road is not a long hundred li: how is it that it seems so long?
7 When one has a good living and something to do, time slips away very quickly
8 I saw his essay to-day, and certainly he has made great improvement. He writes very much better than formerly.
9 He has grown old very rapidly these two years: half his hair is gray and his face is wrinkled.
10 His fever is now a little lower, but his disease is worse.
11 Pao Hsing-tsï is at home sick with the small pox. This is seven days, and the pustules have not yet filled with lymph. Yesterday he took a dose of medicine, and to-day he seems a little better.
12 When money is earned by the sweat of the brow, it is spent sparingly. If it comes too easily, even if a man has it by the million, it will soon be squandered.
13 In this out of the way place of ours, the prices of things are very uncertain. Without notice they suddenly rise, and then as suddenly fall.

Vocabulary.

禁 *Chin*¹. . . . . To bear, to stand. See *chin*⁴.

鐸 *Toă*². . . . . A kind of bell; to incite. (w.)

長進 *Chang*³ *chin*⁴. *To improve,* to grow in knowledge or skill.

皺 *Chou*⁴. . . . . . *Wrinkled,* shriveled, furrowed.

紋 *Wên*². Figures woven on cloth, a line, a mark, *a trace.*

皺紋 *Wrinkles,* furrows.

灌 *Kwan*⁴. To pour into and fill, *to fill up;* to pour down (as medicine), to drench.

僻 *P'i*⁴. Secluded, rustic; *departing from the right,* depraved; partial; cramped; Also *pei*⁴.

偏僻 *P'ien*¹ *p'i*⁴. *Out of the way,* secluded, bye; depraved; askew, lopsided.

𪖙 *Tsao*¹. . . *Decayed,* spoiled, useless. Also *ts'ao*².

𪖙爛 *Tsao*¹ *lan*⁴. . . . . . Decayed, *rotten,* spoiled.

就貴。○我[14]不說、你再三逼着我說、說出來你可別見怪啊。○荆[15]四寶的日子、這幾年怎麼樣、答不見好強、還是很巴結。○你[16]看用這些火輪機器作活、多麼見功。○這[17]些柴伙都[illegible]（朽）爛了、一點也不（經見禁）燒。○大[18]人不見小人怪過。○你[19]見天見天（見天）的淨下棋、也不嫌（絮）膩煩嗎。○[20]先生到我們家裏來、可別見笑啊、答好說、我們居家過日子、那家不是這個樣兒呢。○工[21]夫若不間斷、自然一個月比一個月的見強。○都[22]是一樣的糧食、怎麼歉了年、就不（經見禁）吃呢、答好年頭的糧食、一斗能稱六十斤、壞年頭的糧食、一斗只稱四十五斤、差着十五斤的分量、還能（經見禁）吃嗎。○那[23]年李大人上京引見、不能見景生情、（給教）皇上見了怪、以後他的官運就不見旺了、可見作大官的、也（要得）上人見喜哪。

14 When I declined to tell, you repeatedly urged me to do so; and now when I tell it out, you must not be offended.

15 How is Ching Sï Pao getting on these few years? *Ans.* About the same as ever. He is still very much embarrassed.

16 Look at these steam machines, how they turn out the work.

17 This firewood is half rotten. It burns up very rapidly.

18 A high-minded man does not take offence at men of low degree.

19 Do you not get tired of playing chess day in and day out?

20 You are welcome to our house, sir, but you must not laugh at us. *Ans.* There is no apology needed. What house where there is a family is not in the same condition?

21 If you work on without ceasing, each month will naturally show an improvement on the last.

22 The grain is all the same: how is it that in a scarce year it does not last? *Ans.* In a good year a bushel of grain will weigh sixty catties, but in a bad year it will only weigh forty-five catties: being less by fifteen catties in weight, how can it last?

23 The year that Li Ta Jên went to the capital to have an audience with the Emperor, he was unable to adapt himself to the circumstances, and the Emperor was not pleased. Since then his official fortune has not been prosperous; from which it is evident that even high officials must have the good-will of their superiors.

朽 *Hsiu*³. . . . *Rotten*, decayed; putrid; forgotten.

膩 *Ni*⁴. . . . . . . Greasy, oily; *smooth*.

膩煩 *Ni*⁴ *fan*². *Tired of*, disgusted with, sick of. (N.)

絮煩 *Hsü*⁴ *fan*². . . . . The same. (C. & S.)

見笑 *Chien*⁴ *hsiao*⁴. *To laugh at*, to ridicule; laughable :—Note 20.

間 *Chien*⁴. To divide, to separate; to put a space between; *to intermit;* to alienate; occasionally. See *chien*¹.

間斷 *Chien*⁴ *twan*⁴. To intermit, *to interrupt;* a break, an interval.

歉 *Chien*⁴. . . . See *ch'ien*⁴. Les. 117 :—Note 25.

年頭 *Nien*² *t'ou*². The season, *the year*, the harvest.

分量 *Fên*⁴ *liang*⁴. . . . . Weight, heft.

引見 *Yin*³ *chien*⁴. To have an audience with the Emperor.

官運 *Kwan*¹ *yün*⁴. *Official fortune*, chances of preferment.

旺 *Wang*⁴. Increasing, *prosperous*, flourishing, booming; fervid, violent.

可見 *K'ê*³ *chien*⁴. It appears, it is evident, it is seen :—Les. 180.

上人 *Shang*⁴ *jên*². A superior (official or otherwise).

第一百二十三課

你¹越放刁、我越打你。○這²本書越看越有滋味。○小³孩子是越慣越壞。○越⁴窮越見鬼。○越⁵怕人的事情、越傳得快。○仇⁶恨越深、忿怒越大。○我⁷已經輸了二十多吊現錢、索性再劉（出）上幾十吊、撈撈本。○前⁸日那場雪、越往東越大。○凡⁹人做壞事、都是越做越貪。○兵¹⁰是越雄壯越好。○人¹¹遇見意外的好事、就必越發歡喜。○說¹²他胖、他大𧑐兒發了喘喇（就越發喘）。○你¹³越讓他、他就越往前赶。○越¹⁴急越做

Translation.

1 The more obstreperous you are, the more I will whip you.
2 The more I read of this book, the more interesting it becomes.
3 The more children are indulged, the worse they are spoiled.
4 The poorer one is, the worse his luck.
5 The more anything fears exposure, the faster it spreads.
6 The deeper the enmity, the greater the anger.
7 I have already lost over twenty thousand cash. I might as well stake a few more tens and recover my money.
8 The snow that fell the day before yesterday—the farther east you go, the deeper it is.
9 The more any one gives rein to his lusts, the more he longs for their gratification.
10 The stronger and braver a soldier is, the better.
11 When any one meets with some very unexpected good fortune, his rejoicing is all the greater.
12 Speak of his being fat, and he pants all the more.

Notes.

2 不見混 *Cannot stand the wear and tear that flesh is heir to.*

12 血汗 *Bloody sweat*, expressive of severe toil. The same idea is more fully expanded in the saying, 這是一滴血一滴汗掙來的錢 *By drops of blood and drops of sweat has this money been earned.*

13 見神見鬼的 A figure drawn from the sudden and unexpected manner in which gods and demons are supposed to appear and disappear. 說賤就賤說貴就貴 is a very common idiomatic form, somewhat analogous to the English phrase, "no sooner said than done."

18 大人不見小人過 *The great man does not notice the offence of one beneath him.* As thus used, 見 does not illustrate the idiom of the lesson as does the reading with 見怪.

20 別見笑 A common form of apology, which seems rather embarrassing to a foreigner. 見笑 *To manifest laughter*, that is, *to laugh at.* *In Wenli* 見笑 means *to be laughed at*, but not so in Mandarin. 好說 *You speak too well*; that is, *you exaggerate, your apology is quite unnecessary.*

21 的 in this sentence is to be regarded as possessive to some noun understood, such as 學問 or 樣子.

23 見景生情 *To perceive the state of affairs and adopt a [corresponding] course of action*; that is, *to adapt one's actions or conduct to the varying circumstances of the case.*

LESSON CXXIII.

The Progressive Degree.

越 To pass over,—serves as a sort of progressive copula. It is generally used in pairs in correlative clauses, and gives the force of the English form,—the more . . . . . . the. . . . .

越發 All the more, yet more, still more. Sometimes used singly, and sometimes in pairs in correlative clauses. 越 without 發 is not used singly.

益發 A book form equivalent to 越發 and sometimes used in speaking, especially in the South.

大𧑐 Great store or lot,—still more, all the more. (c)

索性 To restrain or curb the nature or inclination, to stretch a point and do what would not otherwise be done; may generally be translated by the phrase, *might as well*; sometimes, *go ahead*, or *let us just*, will approximate the idea. It nearly always includes the idea of a venture.

不好、實在叫人發躁。○ 15 人家是越學越明白、你倒越學越糊塗。○ 16 從那個時候、我就越發小心。○ 17 越發有人在眼前、他就越發逞能強。○ 18 他小時也不怎麽樣、以後越長越有出息。○ 19 人家既然敢靠咱、咱就該越發拿出眞心來。○ 20 一不做、二不休、已經得罪了他、索性和他分個高低、就是了。○ 21 今天過熱、一點風絲兒也沒有、越喝涼水越渴。○ 22 我一看見這些筷子碟子、就越發覺得肚子餓了。○ 23 寃仇越結越大、情誼越交越深。○ 24 他的兩姨姊妹、生的實在標緻俊俏、叫人越看越愛看。○ 25 齊云方從小就不怎

13 The more you yield to him, the more presumptuous he becomes.
14 The more excited I grew, the worse I did. Dear me, but it was vexatious!
15 The more others learn, the wiser they become; but the more you learn, the more stupid you are.
16 From that time I was still more careful.
17 The more that spectators are present, the more strenuously he exerts himself.
18 There was nothing special about him when young, but afterwards the older he grew, the more promise he gave.
19 Since he trusts us, we ought all the more to deal sincerely with him.
20 "Either don't begin at all, or else don't quit till you have finished." Having offended him, I might as well settle once for all which is the better man.
21 It is excessively hot to-day; there is not even a breath of air; and the more cold water one drinks, the thirstier he becomes.
22 When I saw these chop-sticks and plates, I felt all the more hungry.
23 The more enmity is cherished, the greater it becomes: the more friendship is cultivated, the stronger it becomes.
24 His cousin is a very handsome girl; the more one looks at her, the more he appreciates her beauty.
25 From his youth Ch'i Yün Fang was not very bright, and during these

VOCABULARY.

越 *Yüe*^{4}. To pass over, to exceed, to transgress; to pass by, to skip:—see Sub.

躉 *Tun*^{3}. An overplus; a depôt, a storehouse; wholesale, by the lot:—see Sub.

索 *Soă*^{2}. To bind; to restrain, to curb:—see Sub. See *soă*^{3}. Also *soă*^{4}.

放刁 *Fang*^{4} *tiao*^{1}. To grow perverse or refractory or *obstreperous.*

仇恨 *Ch'ou*^{2} *hên*^{4}. *Enmity,* hatred; revenge.

忿怒 *Fên*^{4} *nu*^{4}. *Anger,* violent anger, indignation, resentment.

撈本 *Lao*^{1} *pên*^{3}. To come out without loss, *to get one's money back.*

雄壯 *Hsiung*^{2} *chwang*^{4}. *Brave and strong,* sturdy, stalwart.

意外 *I*^{4} *wai*^{4}. *Unexpected,* unthought of, surprising.

逞能 *Ch'êng*^{3} *nêng*^{2}. To try with all the might, to do one's level best, *to exert to the utmost.* (s.)

風絲 *Fêng*^{1} *sï*^{1}. *A breath of air,* a very gentle breeze.

碟 *Tie*^{2,4}. *A plate,* a saucer.

云 *Yün*^{2}. To speak, to say. (w.)

靈俏 *Ling*^{2} *ch'iao*^{4}. Quick-witted, clever, *smart,* sharp, gifted.

背晦 *Pei*^{4} *hwei*^{4}. Childish, imbecile, *doting.*

羸 *Lei*^{2}. Lean, emaciated; feeble, *infirm.*

麼靈俏(伶俐)、這二年越發(大蹇兒)老背晦(嬴堆)了。○你[26]悄悄兒(啞密密)的罷、你越發表明(白)、人家倒越發疑惑喇。○人[27]是越吃越饞、越閒越懶。○生[28]疥(瘡)長癬、到癢起來、越撓(擓)越刺撓。○明[29]明是陽症、他當作陰症治了、所以從吃那付藥、越發(大蹇兒)病得利害喇。○你[30]去告訴赶脚的、明天我要一早走、叫他來的越早越好。○若[31]想把省悟罪的心壓制、益發覺得罪重、壓制不住了。○俗[32]語說、差之毫釐、謬之千里、就是越差越遠的意思。○今[33]年山紬很貴、扯(截)個袍料兒、總得摸摸着(估估着/冒冒的)三吊錢、索性多花兩吊、扯(截)個綿綢的多麼局面。

two years, he has all the more become an old dotard.

26 Keep quiet. The more you explain, the more they suspect you.

27 The more [dainties] you eat, the more you long to eat; the more you lounge, the lazier you become.

28 When one has scabies or ringworm and it becomes itchy, the more one scratches, the worse it itches.

29 It is clearly a *yang* disease, yet he treated it as a *yin* disease; hence from the time that he took that medicine, he has grown steadily worse.

30 Go and tell the muleteer that I want to start early to-morrow morning and that the earlier he comes the better.

31 If you try to repress your convictions of sin, you will all the more realize the weight of your sins. These convictions cannot be repressed.

32 The saying is, "A miss of a hair's breadth becomes a mistake of a thousand li;" which means that a mistake once made grows greater and greater.

33 Pongee is very dear this year; enough for a gown will cost very nearly three thousand cash. How much better to spend another thousand or two for fine silk and have a genteel garment.

嬴堆 *Lei*^{2} *twei*^{1}. Wearisome, laborious, tedious. Infirm, feeble; *doting*. (s.)

啞密密的 *Ya*^{3} *mi*^{4} *mi*^{4} *ti*^{1}. *Quietly*, silently; on the sly:—Les. 154.

饞 *Ch'an*^{2}. To love good eating, *to hanker after dainties;* greedy, gluttonous.

癬 *Hsien*^{3}. Tetter; *ringworm;* scaldhead.

癢 *Yang*^{3}. To itch.

擓 *K'wai*^{3} To rub; *to scratch.*

撓 *Nao*^{2}. To disturb, to worry, to vex; *to scratch,* to irritate.

刺 *Ts'ï*^{4}. A prickle, a thorn; *to prick;* to stab; to pole a boat; to criticise, to lampoon.

刺撓 *Ts'ï*^{4} *nao*^{2}. *To itch,* to tingle.

壓制 *Ya*^{4} *chï*^{4}. *To repress,* to keep in subjection. Read *ya*^{1} *chï*^{4} in Peking.

毫 *Hao*^{2}. An atom, a mote, a particle; the ten thousandth part of an ounce.

釐 *Li*^{2}. A grain, a small particle, the thousandth part of an ounce.

謬 *Niu*^{4}, *miu*^{4}. *A mistake,* an error; false, fallacious.

山紬 *Shan*^{1} *ch'ou*^{2}. Undyed silk, pongee.

估 *Hu*^{4}. To rely on, to presume on.

摸摸着 *Moă*^{1} *moă*^{1} *choă*^{2}. *Very nearly,* about, approximately.

估估着 *Hu*^{4} *hu*^{4} *choă*^{2}. The same.

冒冒的 *Mao*^{4} *mao*^{4} *ti*^{1}. The same.

綿綢 *Mien*^{2} *ch'ou*^{2}. Fine silk, colored silk.

局面 *Chü*^{2} *mien*^{4} Correct in the style, *genteel,* presentable.

第一百二十四課

今[1]天在那裏打尖來。○快[2]打火
點起燈來。○這[3]個新媳婦打扮
的實在俏俊。○叫[4]打水的快打水
來。○你[5]去給我打一點糨子(糨糊)。○
刁[6]大年酷好打人的高興(興頭)。○他[7]
們都打場去了。○動[8]不動你就
摔打、你摔打給誰看呢。○你[9]看
王天喜、今天穿着兩件好衣裳、
走起來摔打摔打的、搧氣得很。
○天[10]東南上打閃、有八成是要

TRANSLATION.

1 Where did you stop at noon to-day?
2 Strike a fire [with flint and steel] at once and light the lamp.
3 This bride is dressed very beautifully.
4 Tell the water carrier to bring some water quickly.
5 Go and make a little paste for me.
6 Tiao Ta Nien delights in spoiling other people's fun.
7 They are all out thrashing.
8 You are all the time dashing things down [and breaking them]; for whose benefit are you doing it?
9 Look at Wang T'ien Hsi. He has got on a suit of fine clothes to-day, and goes strutting along fairly bursting with conceit.

NOTES.

2 Or, *The oftener I read this book, etc.*
4 To see a demon is not a good omen, and hence is put for bad luck.
9 Or, *The more a man indulges in evil practices, the stronger his evil propensities will become.*
14 實在 is here very emphatic, and very difficult of translation.
20 一不做二不休 *Do not act in the first place, or in the second place do not give over. It is better not to begin, than to begin and not finish.*
22 越發覺得肚子餓了 *I all the more felt my belly to be hungry.*
24 兩姨姊妹 *Cousins by maternal aunts;* i.e., the children of sisters, each of whom calls the other's mother 姨.
27 The idea of dainties is implied in the word 饞.
29 陽 and 陰, having no equivalents in the English language or thought, cannot be translated. Chinese medical practice is largely founded on a division of diseases and medicines into two classes, distinguished as 陽 and 陰.

LESSON CXXIV.

VARIOUS USES OF 打.

The word 打 has a wide range of use. It resembles in this the words *turn* and *take* in English. It is joined with both nouns and verbs to express a great variety of actions. Several examples of its use have already occurred.

打尖 To stop for refreshment when traveling, as opposed to stopping over night.

打火 To strike a match, to strike a light.

打扮 To dress, to array; dress, costume, toilet.

打水 To draw or bring or carry water.

打糨 or **打糨子** To cook or make starch or paste.

打高興 To take down, to spoil the fun, to take the wind out of one's sails.

打興頭 The same. (s.)

打場 To thrash out and winnow grain.

打閃 To lighten, to flash as lightning.

打僸 To dread, to shrink from. (c.)

打影子 The same. (s.)

打鞦韆 To swing.

打喳喳 To whisper.

打耳喳 The same. (s.)

打草稿 To draw out a rough draft, to write the first copy.

打賭 To wager, to bet.

打勝 or **打勝仗** To gain the victory.

打敗 or **打敗仗** To suffer defeat.

下雨。○喫[11]不窮、穿不窮、算計(打算)不到一世(纔受)
窮。○別[12]的我都不打發(打影子、偺怵)、就是打怵(打影子、偺着)
學算法。○打[13]更有打梆子的、也有打鑼
的。○世[14]上有三宗險、坐船騎馬打鞦韆。
○您[15]二位有甚麼怕人的話、這樣打着
喳(耳)喳(嗒)說。○我[16]剛纔打起草稿來、還沒有
謄清。○你[17]若不信、我(咱)們兩個(們倆)可以賭(打)個
東(賭)。○勝[18]敗是兵家的常事、那能單打勝
仗、不打敗仗呢。○你[19]會打算盤不會、答
我只會個小九九。○打[20]人休打臉、罵人

10 It is lightening in the south-east; most likely it will rain.
11 It is not food nor clothing that makes a man poor; but failure in managing will do it (keep him poor all his life).
12 I do not dread anything else save mathematics.
13 Some watchmen strike a *pang-tsï*, and some, a gong.
14 There are three dangerous things in the world; traveling by ship, riding on horseback and swinging.
15 What secrets have you two that you must speak in a whisper?
16 I have just now finished writing the rough draft, and have not yet made a clean copy.
17 If you don't believe it, we will make a bet (bet a treat).
18 Victories and defeats are the common experience of soldiers. How can you expect to be always victorious and never suffer defeat?
19 Can you reckon on the abacus? *Ans.* I only know how to add.
20 When you strike a man, do not

打算盤 To reckon on the abacus.
打點 To arrange; to equip, to fit out; to provide for; to smooth the way with money, to bribe.
不打緊 No matter, of no consequence. 打緊 is not used without the negative.
打把勢 To box, to fence.
打八式 The same.
打拳 To box, to fence, to fisticuff.
打獵 To hunt game.
打量 To suppose, to estimate, to consider.
打盹 To nod; to doze. to be sleepy.
打哈息 To yawn.
打呵欠 The same. (s.)
打包 To bud, to pullulate.
打躬 To make a profound bow with the hands joined and subsequently raise them to the head.
摔[1]打 To throw down forcibly, to dash down.
摔[3]打 To fling the arms, to strut; to fling abroad, to scatter.
呼打 To flap back and forth, to flutter; to palpitate, to throb.
喪打 To frown at, to scowl at; to snub.
檏打 The same.
掄打 To fling, to swing, to flourish.
For list of examples of the use of 打 see Supplement.

VOCABULARY.

扮 *Pan*[4]. . . . To dress up, to rig out; to beautify.
酷好 *K'u*[4] *hao*[4]. *To have a passion for*, to desire ardently; addicted to.
高興 *Kao*[1] *hsing*[4]. Elated, exulting, jubilant, *merry.*
興頭 *Hsing*[4] *t'ou*[2]. Elation, exultation; merriment, *fun.*
摔 *Shwai*[1]. To wrestle; to throw down forcibly, to dash or fling down. See *shwai*[3].
揚氣 *Yang*[2] *ch'i*[4]. . . . *Conceited*, puffed up.
八成 *Pa*[1] *ch'êng*[2]. Eight parts in ten, most likely:—Note 10.
怵 *Ch'u*[4]. . . . Timorous, fearful, *shrinking.*

休揭短。○若21是不用幾百銀子打點打點、就是挨到你的缺、也沒有你的官作。○我22們今天來打攪喇、答這不打緊、請再坐坐罷。○莫23妙於白天念書、晚上學着打把勢(八式、拳)○這24幾天不大疼喇、就是覺着裏頭咕嘟(呼打)咕嘟(呼打)的直跳、大約(光景)是作(鼓)膿喇。○他25光堵喪(喪打、檏打)人、人都不願意和他說話。○或26打飛禽或打走獸、總名叫打獵。○媽27啊、我們的水罐子叫誰打打喇、你看水直往下滴打滴打的。○劈28臉打了一個耳巴(瓜)子、回頭就跑。○我29

strike his face; and when you berate a man, do not cast his short-comings in his teeth.

21 Even though you do wait till your turn comes round, without spending a few hundred taels to pave the way there will be no office for you.

22 Our coming to-day has incommoded you. *Ans.* That is no matter: please sit a little longer.

23 The best way is to study in day-time, and practice boxing at night.

24 It does not pain me much these few days, but I feel it throbbing constantly; pus is probably forming.

25 He is given to snubbing people; so that no one likes to talk with him.

26 Whether hunting birds or beasts, the common name is hunting game.

27 Mamma, somebody has broken our water-pot: see how the water keeps dropping down.

28 Aiming at his face, he gave him a blow on the cheek, and then turned and ran.

29 I should not mind making you a

發怵 *Fa*¹ *ch'u*⁴. *To dread*, to shrink from, frightened.

傗 *Ch'u*⁴. Rough; timorous, *shrinking*.

梆 *Pang*¹. A hollow wooden block on which watchmen strike the hours.

坐船 *Tsoă*⁴ *ch'wan*². *To travel by boat or ship*, to travel by water.

喳 *Ch'a*¹. To whisper, to chatter. See *cha*¹.

耳喳 *Er*³ *ch'a*¹. A whisper in the ear.

稿 *Kao*³. Straw; *a first draft*, a rough copy, a sketch; a proof.

草稿 *Ts'ao*³ *kao*³. *The first* or *rough draft of a paper;* original copy.

謄清 *T'êng*² *ch'ing*¹. To make a clean copy, to copy out.

把勢 *Pa*³ *shï*⁴. The art of boxing or fencing with sword or spear.

八式 *Pa*¹ *shï*⁴. The same:—Note 23.

咕嘟 *Ku*³ *tu*¹. A bubbling, gurgling or murmuring sound; to rumble; to throb.

堵喪 *Tu*³ *sang*⁴. *To snub*, to bluff off.

飛禽 *Fei*¹ *ch'in*². Birds.

走獸 *Tsou*³ *shou*⁴. Beasts, quadrupeds.

獵 *Lie*⁴. To hunt wild animals, the chase.

劈臉 *P'i*¹ *lien*³. To stand square in front and strike.

耳瓜子 *Er*³ *kwa*¹ *tsï*³. The cheek bones, the side face.

耳巴子 *Er*³ *pa*¹ *tsï*³. The same.

掄 *Lün*¹. To whirl or swing around, to flourish. Also *lun*².

舞 *Wu*³. To gesture, to fence, to pantomime; *to flourish*, to brandish.

舞弄 *Wu*³ *nung*⁴. To befool, to play tricks on; *to flourish*, to brandish.

聖徒 *Sheng*⁴ *t'u*². A saint, a Christian.

哈 *Ha*¹ To open the mouth wide, to gape. See *ha*³, also *k'a*¹,⁴.

哈息 *Ha*¹ *hsi*². A gape, a yawn.

呵欠 *Ha*¹ *ch'ien*⁴. The same. (s.)

約束 *Yüe*¹ *shu*⁴. *To control*, to restrain, to keep in order.

希奇 *Hsi*¹ *ch'i*². Wonderful, surprising, *remarkable*, strange.

賞你三五兩銀子、也不打緊、可惜今日忘記帶來。○你[30]拿你的棍子出去玩罷、別在家裏舞掄弄打。○他[31]打量人去學聖徒的過失、還能彀有聖徒的德行、正是自己哄自己。○你[32]們毆打眊了嗎、答沒毆打眊、問沒毆打眊、怎麼打呵哈欠息呢。○昨[33]天我看見這花纔打包、今天就開喇。你說希奇不希奇。○人[34]有子弟、從小就要約束他、叫他學禮貌、打躬作揖、倒茶裝菸、站的地方、坐的位次、都叫他曉得方向。

present of three or five taels of silver, but unfortunately I forgot to bring any along to-day.

30 Take your stick out of doors to play, and don't flourish it about in the house.

31 He deceives himself in thinking that if a man imitates the faults of Christians, he will of course have their virtues.

32 Have you been taking a nap? *Ans.* No, we have not. *Ques.* If you have not been taking a nap, why then are you yawning?

33 Yesterday I noticed that this flower had just put forth a bud, and to-day it is in full bloom. Isn't that remarkable?

34 When a man has children and nephews, he should control them from their childhood, requiring them to learn to be polite, to bow and courtesy, to pour tea and light a pipe, and also teach them to keep their proper places both when standing and when sitting.

禮貌 *Li*^{3} *mao*^{4}. . . . . *Politeness*, etiquette.

躬 *Kung*^{1}. . . . . The body, the person.

揖 *I*^{1}. A bow with the hands to the breast; a . . . . . salutation.

作揖 *Tsoa*^{4} *i*^{1} To make a bow with the hands . . . . to the breast.

倒茶 *Tao*^{4} *ch'a*^{2}. . . . . To pour out tea.

裝菸 *Chwang*^{1} *yien*^{1}. . . . . To fill a pipe.

位次 *Wei*^{4} *ts'ï*^{4}. Position, rank, order of prece- . . . . dence.

方向 *Fang*^{1} *hsiang*^{4}. Direction, bearing; posi- . . . . tion, place.

Notes.

3 Properly speaking, 俊 refers to natural looks, and 俏 to dress.

10 八成 is a contraction for 八分之成. 十成 is a common expression to denote completeness; hence, 八成 is *eight parts in ten*, that is, *for the most part*, *most likely*. Other numbers are also used; as 五成, 六成, etc.

11 一世 *One world*; i.e., *a generation*, *a life time*. The term is derived from the idea of transmigration. So also are 出世, *to be born*, and 去世, *to die*.

17 賭個東 *To bet a treat*, 東 being put for 東家, the moneyed partner or party.

19 小九九 is the Chinese multiplication table. Each line stops when it reaches the square, so that no multiplier is ever greater than the multiplicand, and every process of multiplication is carried on in conformity with this idea. In the present case the numbers of the 小九九 are spoken of as an exercise in addition.

23 把勢 The postures of offense and defence taken in boxing. Others would write, 八式, the eight standard positions of arms and feet assumed in boxing.

LESSON CXXV.

Classifiers.

朶 A bunch or cluster,—classifier of flowers, clouds, etc.

文 A vein or band,—classifier of cash and coins.

軸 An axle,—classifier of maps and scrolls.

角 A corner,—classifier of dispatches.

封 To seal,—classifier of letters, dispatches, packets of silver, etc.

尾 The tail,—classifier of fishes.

北京大学中国语言学研究中心

早期北京话珍稀文献集成

主编 刘云

—— 西人北京话教科书汇编

分卷主编 翟赟 郭利霞 陈颖

下

官话类编

[美]狄考文 编著

国家出版基金项目
NATIONAL PUBLICATION FOUNDATION

第一百二十五課

看[1]這朶雲彩、好像是有雨的樣子。○不[2]受十分苦、難得一文錢。○這[3]張軸畫是張敔畫的牡丹、他要十兩銀子。○昨[4]天來了一封角文書、說七月二十二、學臺從省裏起馬。○你[5]那對頭、也有一段話說。○哥[6]哥既然想鯉魚吃、你可以去買幾條尾來。○我[7]今天見了一件奇事、看見五個人扛着一面大枷。○那[8]一天我到他家裏去、見他炕上、連一條領席都沒有。○這[9]是誰家的一所房宅子、好大氣派。○他[10]早上晨吃了一片頁兒饅頭、喝了四兩牛奶。○王[11]之東這步時運實在不濟、半年死了三個孩子。○如[12]今的世界、只要多有幾串銅錢、這就有了勢力喇。○我[13]給他帶

Translation.

1 This cloud looks as if it had rain in it.

2 It is hard to get even a little money without great labor.

3 This picture is a shrub peony painted by Chang Yü. He wants ten taels for it.

4 Yesterday there came a dispatch saying that the Literary Chancellor would start from the provincial capital on the twenty-second of the seventh month.

5 Your opponent has also something to say.

6 Since our brother longs for some carp to eat, you may go and buy him a few.

7 I saw a remarkable sight to-day. I saw five men wearing one large cangue.

8 The other day when I went to see him, I noticed that he did not have even a sheet of matting on his k'ang.

9 Whose residence is this? It is a very pretentious building.

10 This morning he ate a slice of bread and drank four ounces of milk.

11 Wang Chï Tung has had a run of exceedingly bad luck; within a half year three children have died.

12 In these times it is only necessary to have a little hard cash and you will have influence.

段 A section,—classifier of stories, sections of a book, plots of ground, etc.

面 The face,—classifier of drums, mirrors, gongs, saddles, etc.

領 A collar,—classifier of sheets of matting, window shades, and upper garments.

所 A place,—classifier of dwellings, houses, etc.

片 A flake,—classifier of sheets or patches, also of short spaces of time.

頁 A leaf or sheet,—classifier of things in sheets as leaves of a book, boards, panes of glass, slices of bread, sheets of foil or tinsel paper.

串 To string together,—classifier of cash, strings of beads or pearls, etc.

處 A place,—classifier of houses, places, etc.

步 A step,—classifier of circumstances.

貫 A string of one thousand cash,—classifier of sums of cash.

樁 A stake,—classifier of affairs. (L.)

扇 A fan,—classifier of gates, doors, windows, shutters, etc.

架 A frame,—classifier of clocks, scales, philosophical instruments, etc.

丸 A pellet,—classifier of medicines in pills.

味 A taste,—classifier of medicines.

頂 The apex,—classifier of hats, sedan chairs, state umbrellas, etc.

幅 A roll,—classifier of maps, pictures, scrolls, leggings, etc.

簍 A basket,—classifier of things in baskets or crates; as tea, oranges, etc.

來一封信、還有一封銀子、可以請他親自來取。○別[14]說他還有地、就是這三處房子的房租、五口人也吃不了。○到[15]兩軍對敵的時候、並看不見別的、就是看見一片烟。○雖[16]有萬貫的家財、死後連一文也帶不了去。○我[17]看這件事情、心裏就是不平、那有欺負人、欺負到這步田地的呢。○男[18]人能掙、還得女人能過、若是外頭掙一塊板、家裏丟一扇門、雖然能掙、也是白饒（贅、忙）上了。○郭[19]子彬的鐘表店舖、昨天晚上、叫賊偷了一架鐘、兩個掛表去。○可[20]以把這五味藥、研爲細末、做成三十顆丸藥（個丸子）、每天晚上吞一顆（吃一丸）。○這[21]幾天上街、可以找着買一面鑼、預備吃飯的時候好打。○就[22]是蓋

13 I have brought for him a letter and a bundle of silver. Ask him to come in person and get them.

14 Not to speak of the land he has, the rent of these three houses alone is more than sufficient for the support of a family of five.

15 When the two armies joined battle, nothing could be seen but a cloud of smoke.

16 Although you have a fortune of ten thousand strings [of cash], yet when you die you cannot take with you a single cash.

17 When I saw this affair I felt very indignant. How could any one wrong another to such a degree as this?

18 Not only must the husband be able to earn, but the wife must know how to save. If, while the husband earns a board in the fields, the wife runs through with a door at home, his being able to earn money will be of no avail.

19 Last night one clock and two watches were stolen by a thief from Kwoă Tsï Pin's watchmaker's shop.

20 Take these five ingredients, grind them into a fine powder and make them up into thirty pills,—of which take one every evening.

21 Within the next few days, when you go on the street, you may look for and buy a gong to be struck at meal times.

VOCABULARY.

軸 *Chou*^{2}. An axle, a pivot, axis of motion; a roller:—see Sub.

貫 *Kwan*^{4}. A string of cash; to string; to go through, to penetrate:—see Sub.

頁 *Yie*^{4}. The head; a leaf of a book or folio; a slat, a slice, a leaf:—see Sub.

幅 *Fu*^{2}. A strip of cloth; a hem; a border; a roll:—see Sub.

敔 *Yü*^{3}. An ancient musical instrument. (w.)

鯉 *Li*^{3}. The carp.

枷 *Chia*^{1}. A cangue or wooden collar:—Note 7.

宅 *Chai*^{2}, *chê*^{2}. A dwelling, a residence, *a private house;* a location, a site.

對敵 *Twei*^{4} *ti*^{2}. *To join battle*, to confront.

鐘表 *Chung*^{1} *piao*^{3}. *Clocks and watches*, a clock, a striking clock.

研 *Yien*^{2}. To grind, *to rub fine*, to powder; to search into.

柁 *T'oă*^{2}. A tie-beam or girder between pillars; the triangular frame over each partition, consisting of a girder, two rafters and an upright.

樑 *Liang*^{2}. A beam, *a girder;* a mast.

檁 *Lin*^{3}. The poles or beams which extend from one rafter to the other:—Note 22.

擱木 *Kê*^{1} *mu*^{4}. The wooden plate above a door or window. (c. & n.)

托板 *T'oă*^{2} *pan*^{3}. The same. (s.)

三間房子、也得買兩架樑柁、二十一根檁、再加上門窗托擱板木、還不得一宗成文的錢嗎。○有[23]一天下小雨、我見放牛的、頭戴一頂斗葦篷笠、身披一領件蓑衣、手拿一根棍子、遠遠的望着、眞像一幅好畫圖。○那[24]是天生的一段材、無論怎樣管他、總斷不了那宗風流氣。○前[25]兩天、一位朋友送給我一封筆、十錠塊墨、一簍茶葉、今天必得預備一點禮物送給他。○東[26]面那四幅畫屏、像是鄭板橋畫的、却沒落欵。○古[27]來拿賊的方法、是一個村堡蓋一座樓、樓上安一面鼓、若一家有了事、把鼓擂起來、人家都聽得、就將緊要的出路堵住、那賊往那裏跑呢。

22 Even if you build but three rooms, it will be necessary to buy two sets of beams, twenty-one rafters, and in addition, the doors and windows with the supporting plates over them. Will it not cost a lot of money?

23 One day when it was drizzling, I saw a cowherd wearing a straw hat on his head and a rush coat on his back and holding in his hand a long staff. Looking at him from a distance, he looked just like a well drawn picture.

24 That disposition is born in him. No matter how you control him there is no getting rid of that propensity to dissipation.

25 A few days ago a friend made me a present of a bunch of pens, ten sticks of ink and a basket of tea. To-day I must provide some present for him.

26 Those four sets of scrolls to the east look like the painting of Ching Pan Ch'iao, though his signature is not subscribed.

27 The ancient method of catching thieves was to build in each village a tower with a drum in it, then if any family missed anything the drum was beaten, and all hearing it at once closed up all the chief ways of exit, so that the thief had no means of escape.

成文 *Ch'êng² wên²*. A great many, a lot of [cash]. (Pekingese.)

放牛 *Fang⁴ niu²*. To herd cattle; to pasture cattle.

葦 *Wei³*. A rush, a reed; tall coarse grass.

笠 *Li⁴*. *A rain-hat made of coarse grass or bamboo splints;* a hamper; a crate.

葦笠 A coarse conical rain-hat.

篷 *P'êng²*. *Coarse matting;* an awning, a booth; a ceiling.

斗篷 *Tou³ p'êng²*. A coarse conical rain-hat made of straw. (s.)

蓑 *Soă¹*. A cloak of thatched leaves or grass.

蓑衣 *Soă¹ i¹*. The same.

畫圖 *Hwa⁴ t'u²*. A painting.

風流 *Fêng¹ liu²*. *Dissipated,* dissolute, rakish; gay, fast; stylish, refined.

茶葉 *Ch'a² yie⁴*. Tea leaves, tea.

屏 *P'ing²*. A screen; *a set of scrolls;* an ornamental tablet.

欵 *K'wan³*. To respect; *a signature,* an inscription; a kind; a section, an article.

落欵 *Loă⁴ k'wan³*. *To affix a signature,* to attach an inscription or stamp.

古來 *Ku³ lai²*. Of old, for a long time, *ancient,* from ancient times.

方法 *Fang¹ fa³*. Plan, *method,* expedient, arrangement; prescription.

村堡 *Ts'un¹ p'u⁴*. *A village,* a town.

擂 *Lei²*. To rub fine; *to beat,* to drum.

緊要 *Chin³ yao⁴*. Important—same as 要緊, but savors of book style.

有事 *Yiu³ shï⁴*. To have business, engaged; *to meet with something unusual,*—an accident or misfortune.

第一百二十六課

[1]養兒原爲防備老。○[2]我起根兒以來就厭惡他。○[3]起先你是這麼說的嗎。○[4]這本不是他所該管的事。○[5]起頭難些、久後就容易了。○[6]王文池的女人、原是財主家的姑娘。○[7]沒有法子、誰叫我底起根根兒裏、沒有出息呢。○[8]當初他來託付你、你就不該應承。○[9]我本來是浙江人、在這裏落戶入籍。○[10]我曉得他借的時候、原本本來就沒

Translation.

1 The primary idea in bringing up sons is to provide against old age.
2 I abominated him from the first.
3 Is this what you said at first?
4 This affair does not properly come under his jurisdiction.
5 At first it was rather difficult, but by and by it became easy.
6 Wang Wên Ch'i's wife originally belonged to a rich family.
7 There is no help for it: whose fault is it [but my own] that I have amounted to nothing?
8 When he first came to ask your good offices, you should not have promised.
9 Originally a Chekiang man, I have taken up my residence here.
10 I know that when he originally bor-

Notes.

3 張敔 was a noted Chinese painter,—specially noted for painting peonies.

4 Both 封 and 角 are *t'ung-hsing* as classifiers of dispatches.

6 As a classifier of fish, 條 is much more common than 尾, which is *Wên*.

7 A cangue is a heavy board or block of wood, about three and a half feet square, with a hole in the centre large enough to admit a man's neck. It is made in two halves, and is bolted together and locked around the neck. Culprits are usually sentenced to wear it a number of days, sitting at the gate of the yamên—sometimes at the gate of the person they have sinned against. Generally each culprit has his own cangue, but in some cases the board is made long, with two or more holes, and those who have been guilty of a like offense are locked in together.

8 那一天 at the opening of a sentence, is used much as the colloquial English, "*the other day.*"

12 幾串銅錢 *A few strings of copper cash*—a facetious amplification.

13 Broken silver is usually tied up in packets of fifty taels each, so that a packet *ordinarily* means this sum. A less amount is however also called 一封.

17 那有 is here very emphatic. It expresses both the surprise and the indignation of the speaker. The translation falls short of the Chinese.

22 A Chinese house has, properly speaking, only one pair of rafters over each partition. The 檩 extend between these rafters, the number of them usually being seven, one over the top of each wall, one at the comb, and two between. There is considerable confusion in the application of 桁 樑 and 檩 in different sections. Arches are not built over windows and doors, but the superincumbent wall is supported by a heavy wooden plate, for which each locality has its own name.

26 鄭板橋 was another noted painter.

LESSON CXXVI.

Beginning.

原 Originally, primarily.

原來 Originally, from the first; the fact is, properly, in the nature of the case.

原起 Originally, primarily; always.

原先 At first, primarily.

原本 Originally, primarily, at the outset, in the nature of the case:—Note (16).

原根兒 Originally, at first, in the first place. (C. & N.)

原起根兒 The same.

原底子 The same. (S.)

起先 At the first, at the outset; heretofore.

起頭 Originally, at first, in the beginning.

起首 The same.

起前 At first, from the first. (S.)

起初 Originally, primarily, at first, in the first place, in the beginning.

起初頭 The same. (N. & C.)

打算還。○他[11]們倆、起初相好、近來絶了交略。
○原[12]來世上、姓張姓王姓李的最多。○也[13]不
知是咱們給他弄壞了、也不知原底根子兒就是
這麽的。○鄭[14]福德起原先起不會滑逃學、如今却學
會了。○那[15]個孩子太精靈細喇、我起起根前根起就看着
他不好養。○這[16]原本是人家掙到的錢、那好
這麽勸不揹呢。○他[17]本情是對不住你、你却不
好直絶絶不理他。○太[18]初有道、道與神同在、道
就是神。○原[19]來那婦人是七月七生的、因此
小名叫巧雲。○這[20]塊地本來是姓張的、如今

rowed it, he did not intend to return it.

11 They two were originally good friends, but recently they have cut each other's acquaintance.

12 In point of fact, Chang, Wang and Li are the most common surnames in the world.

13 It is hard to say whether we spoiled it for him, or whether it was so originally.

14 Chêng Fu Tê was not originally given to playing truant, but he has now learned to do it.

15 That child was too precocious. I thought from the first he would not live to grow up.

16 This is money which he has worked for. It is wrong to hold it back in this way.

17 He has treated you badly it is true, yet it is not right for you to utterly disregard him.

18 In the beginning was the Word, and the Word was with God, and the Word was God.

19 That woman was born on the seventh of the seventh month, hence her little name is Skilful Cloud.

起根 From the first, in the first place, primarily, always.

根起 The same,—but less general.

根兒裏頭 Primarily, in the first place. (N.)

底起根裡 Originally, at first, in the first place. (N.)

底根兒裡 The same. (N. & S.)

本 Originally, properly.

本來 Originally; properly, the truth is, in fact.

本情 Original state of the case, in the nature of things, really, it is true, of course.

開頭 At first, beginning from, in the first instance.

開先 The same. (S.)

太初 In the beginning, at the birth of time.

當初 At the beginning, at the first, in the first place.

以來 From the first; heretofore.

自來 Heretofore, ever, all along, always,—with a negative, never. Also naturally.

從根 From the first, from the beginning,—with a negative, never. (N. & C.)

從頭 The same.

一起頭 In the first place, at the outset.

一開手 At first, at the start, at the outset.

一上手 The same.

VOCABULARY.

託付 *T'oă^{1} fu^{4}*. *To ask the help or services of*, ... to entrust to, to depend upon.

浙 *Chê^{4}*. A stream in Chekiang from which the . . . . . . province is named.

落戶 *Lao^{4} hu^{4}*. To reside, *to make one's residence*, to settle.

籍 *Chi^{2}*. . . . A list, a register, a docket:—see *chi^{4}*.

入籍 *Ju^{4} chi^{2}*. To be enrolled as a resident, to . . . . acquire citizenship.

滑學 *Hwa^{2} hsüe^{2}*. . . . . To play truant. (C.)

精靈 *Ching^{1} ling^{2}*. *Bright*, smart, precocious, ... quick-witted; ethereal.

同在 *T'ung^{2} tsai^{4}*. At the same place, together, ... *with*, in company with.

典在姓王的手裏。○21從明天開頭起、午飯後要兩點鐘上學。○22我起根兒臉自來心軟、架不住人央求。○23他原來起就臉皮薄、臉嫩這是我知道的。○24他打頭起首只有五千銀子的本、現今賺了有五十萬。○25你根兒裏頭起初頭是多少錢買的、答那時候有錢、買的貴。○26我的書、原起根兒起根兒就沒念好、如今荒疎的、更不像樣兒了。○27這些律法原本本來是為不孝不弟的人設的。○28起頭開先教訓人種莊稼的、是神農。○29你不信打聽打聽、從根頭來我在酒飯館子裏、沒有賬。○30你別說是價錢大、東西本情也就是好啊。○31起初連我也不信、以後仔細訪問、纔知道是有憑有據的事情。○32原打算要買

20 This piece of land belonged originally to one Chang, but is now mortgaged into the hands of a man named Wang.

21 Beginning from to-morrow, school will open in the afternoon at two o'clock.

22 I have always been tender-hearted and unable to resist entreaty.

23 I know he has always been bashful.

24 He had originally only five thousand taels of capital, but he has now cleared about five hundred thousand.

25 For how much did you buy it in the first place? *Ans.* I was rich then, and I paid well for it.

26 My scholarship was imperfect in the first place, and now by neglect it has become still more indifferent.

27 These laws were made primarily for the unfilial and unfraternal.

28 It was Shên Nung who first taught men to cultivate the earth.

29 If you do not believe [just go and] inquire. I have never had any account at a saloon or restaurant.

30 Do not suppose the price is high, for the goods are really first class.

31 Neither did I believe it at first, but afterwards, upon making careful inquiry, I found out that it was a veritable fact.

32 I originally intended to buy a pound of oil of peppermint and half a pound of olive oil, but subsequently, because

---

掯 *K‘ên3*. To oppress, to wrong, *to grind down;* . . . . . . to vex, to obstruct.

勒掯 *Lê1 k‘ên3*. To oppress, to squeeze, *to keep* . . . . . . *back what is due.*

臉軟 *Lien3 juen3*. Unable to resist entreaty, ... *tender-hearted*, lenient.

心軟 *Hsin1 juen3*. . . . . The same.

臉皮 *Lien3 p‘i2*. The face as expressive of . . . . emotions or character.

臉皮薄 *Lien3 p‘i2 poă2*. Shamefaced, *bashful*, ... diffident.

嫩 *Nên4, nun4*. . . . . . Delicate; weak, soft; *tender.*

臉嫩 *Lien3 nên4*. . . . . *Bashful*, diffident.

荒疎 *Hwang1 su1*. . . . . . . *To neglect*, to disuse.

像樣 *Hsiang4 yang4*. As it should be, passable, ... very fair.

不像樣 *Pu4 hsiang4 yang4*. Inferior, *indifferent;* out of bounds.

飯館 *Fan4 kwan3*. An eating-house, *a restaurant.*

磅 *P‘ang1*. . . . . . . A pound,—used for the sound.

薄 *Poă4*. . . . . Peppermint. See *poă2*.

荷 *Hê2*. . . . . . The small-leaved water lily.

薄荷 Peppermint.

橄欖 *Kan3 lan3*. . . . . The olive.

輪流 *Lun2 liu2*. *To take turns;* one by one in . . . . order.

元勳 *Yüen2 hsün1*. A distinguished patriot, ... especially one who aids in founding a kingdom or dynasty.

江山 *Chiang1 shan1*. Land, *territory*, realm, ... domain.

紳 *Shên1*. A sash; those who are privileged to . . . . . . wear sashes, *literati.*

一磅薄荷油、半磅橄欖油、後來因爲錢不彀、就每一樣買了半磅。○當33初分家的時候、他定規要跟着小兒子過、現在却是三家輪流着。○姚34期、原是東漢開國的元勳、一起頭打江山的就是他。○原35先紳士們、打算舉保保舉他、給他立一座節孝牌坊、以後聽說他不大穩當、就擱下了。○增36福小時節、還有點精氣神兒、後來越長越獃、答 他從根從頭原來就不帶精神、常常像發睖、佯向如同沒有魂兒似的。○無37論是交友、是交財、若是一開手上手能交到好處、以後自然越交越厚、就是有點不好、也叫以前的好處蓋掩了。

my money was insufficient, I bought a half pound of each kind.

33 Originally, when the family was divided, he decided to live with the youngest son, but now he lives by turns with the three.

34 Yao Ch'i immortalized himself in the founding of the Eastern Han dynasty. It was he who, in the first place, subjugated the land.

35 In the first place the literati intended to recommend the erection of a monumental arch commemorating her virtue, but afterwards, hearing that her reputation was not the best, the project was dropped.

36 When Tsêng Fu was still young, he showed some little vigor of mind ; but as he grew, he became more and more stupid. *Ans.* From the first he was not bright, and he had all the time a vacant stare as if he had lost his wits.

37 Whether in the intercourse of friendship or of business, if a good foundation is laid at the outset, afterwards, as a matter of course, the longer the intercourse continues the more cordial it will become; so that even if some little difference should arise, it is covered over by the former goodwill.

紳士 *Shên¹ shï⁴*. . . . Gentry, *literati* ; head-men.
舉保 *Chü³ pao³* . . . . Same as 保舉.
節孝 *Chie² hsiao⁴*. Chaste and faithful widowhood.
牌坊 *P'ai² fang¹*. A commemorative arch :— Note 35.
佯 *Yang²*. . . . .To feign ; *unreal*, feigned ; dreary.
佯向 *Yang² hsiang⁴*. To look blank, *a vacant look;* to dream, to muse. (L.)
睖 *Lêng⁴*. To stare, to look intently, to gaze ; *a vacant look, a stare.*
發睖 *Fa¹ lêng⁴*. To stare, to look daft ; *vacant*, dazed, stupified.
開手 *K'ai¹ shou³*. To begin ; at first, *at the outset.*
上手 *Shang⁴ shou³*. . . . . The same.
蓋掩 *Kai⁴ yien³*. *To cover up*, to conceal, to hide from view.

NOTES.

1 This sentence no doubt expresses the chief idea in the desire of the Chinese for sons, though the wish to have some one to offer sacrifices to them after death is also very potent.

9 落戶 means simply to reside or locate, while 入籍 means to be registered as a citizen. There seems to be no established rule in regard to this registry.

12 原來, as here used, is not to be understood as referring to the state of things in ancient or former times, but rather as giving emphasis to a fact both past and present. These are by far the most common family names in China.

15 好養 *Good to rear;* that is, *possible to rear*,—predestined to live and grow up to adult years.

16 原本 is used to add assurance to the fact stated, somewhat as we use the phrase, *in point of fact.* 掙到 means that the labor has been performed and the money is due.

19 巧雲 The star Atair in Cygnus. The mythological story is that 巧雲 is the seventh daughter of 玉皇上帝, and the wife of 牽牛郎 (Denab), and is wonderfully skilful in needlework and all feminine accomplishments. 牽牛郎 borrowed money from 玉皇上帝 for the expenses of his wedding. He failed to repay it, and 玉皇, to punish him, took 巧雲 home, and ever since allows

第一百二十七課

你[1]的上孟子(上孟)、還沒念到底嗎。○我[2]再三問他、到底沒問明白。○善[3]惡到頭終有報。○末[4]末了、我依了他。○罷[5]了罷了、終久是你有眼力。○這[6]個法子、歸齊(期、根)要使不上。○你[7]說不是罵我、到底是罵誰呢。○你[8]這樣懶、終久(期畢)是要要飯吃。○究[9]竟好是好的自己、壞是壞的自己。○你[10]這樣瞞哄人、終久還能瞞得住嗎。○誰[11]知他不將恩報、竟將仇報。○終[12]久親戚是親戚、朋友誰肯出這樣的力呢。○這[13]條路雖然遠點、到底可更方

Translation.

1 Have you not yet finished reading the first half of your Mencius?
2 I asked him again and again and after all did not get a satisfactory answer.
3 When good and evil have reached their measure, there will finally be a recompense.
4 Finally I assented to him.
5 Well, well, after all your insight was the best.
6 After all this plan will be impracticable.
7 You say you are not reviling me, whom then are you reviling?
8 If you are so lazy as this, sooner or later you will come to beggary.
9 After all the man who does right benefits himself, and the one who does wrong injures himself.
10 Deceiving people in this way [do you suppose] you can keep up the deception to the end?
11 Who would have supposed that instead of requiting with kindness, he would requite with injury?
12 After all "blood is thicker than water:"

her to visit her husband and two children only one day in each year; viz., on the seventh of the seventh month. Her mother-in-law takes revenge by compelling her, in that one day, to wash all the dishes the family has used during the year, and to tidy up the whole house. On that day she is worshipped as 巧女姐姐, or 織女姐姐 by Chinese girls and young women who hang up her picture, spread before it offerings of fruit and flowers, and make prostrations, praying her to impart to them some of her wonderful skill. This story has many variations in different localities.

20 姓張的 ought by rights to be 姓張的的, but one 的 is elided.

29 酒飯館 is a contraction for 酒館和飯館.

35 節孝牌坊 is an ornamental arch or gateway erected across a street, or at the side of a high-way, to commemorate the constancy of a young widow who has remained faithful to her mother-in-law until death; which is considered the acme of female virtue and filial duty. They are usually allowed on the recommendation of the literati of the woman's native place, made to the literary chancellor of the province. 不大穩當 *Not very stable* or *reliable*. In this connection it means, *virtue not reliable, character not above suspicion.*

36 精氣神兒 is a colloquial dissection and amplification of the term 精神.

LESSON CXXVII.

Ending.

到底 To the end, at last, after all, in the end, then.

到了兒 or **到末了兒** At the last, in the end, finally.

到臨了 At the end, near the close, finally.

竟 After all, finally.

究竟 At last, after all, ultimately, finally.

畢竟 The same—but slightly bookish.

期畢 In the end, finally, sooner or later.

歸期 After all, finally, ultimately, at last. (C. & N.)

歸齊 The same. This is the writing generally adopted in Peking. It does not, however, accord so well with the meaning as 期, moreover wherever hard sounds are used it is incorrect, as it is fundamentally a soft sound. 期 on the other hand is both hard and soft, and is correct everywhere. The tone is changed by the combination, from the first to the fourth, as is common in such cases.

便。○用14現錢買東西、始終到了必便宜賤一點。○多15少人
講情、他都不准、畢竟是你老先生的臉面大。○我16
終久不大明白、請先生再講一遍。○這17個孩子太
頑疲疲頑了、歸根兒結期不能成人。○他18們整天家的、彼此吹
毛求疵、究竟歸眞必鬧出一場大亂漏子。○我19怕你這樣
重用他、到了期畢到臨了要出故事葛籐。○他20名爲聖徒、究竟心
不誠實。○事21情雖然不全在你身上、終久歸實却有你
的分兒。○一22雙鞋上了兩天、也沒上起來、末了還
是我給他上起來的。○他23母親老總沒回家、也沒人
曉得他往那裏去了。○以24撒雖盡力要與他和好、

what friend would have exerted himself in this way?

13 Although this road is a little longer, yet in the end it is more convenient.

14 Buying for ready money, certainly is a little cheaper in the end.

15 Ever so many have tried to conciliate him but in vain; after all, honored sir, your influence with him was the greatest.

16 After all I do not quite understand: please, sir, explain it once more.

17 This boy is too ungovernable; he will never make a man.

18 They are constantly carping at each other; ultimately they are sure to get up a big quarrel.

19 I fear, if you continue to depend so much upon him, there will finally be trouble with him.

20 He is called a Christian, but after all he is not sincere.

21 Although the matter does not entirely rest with you, yet after all you have a share in it.

22 She worked two days at putting the soles on this one pair of shoes, and then did not get done. Finally I had to finish them for her.

歸究 In the end, finally, ultimately, after all.
歸實 The same. (s.)
歸眞 The same. (s.)
歸根兒 In the end, finally, after all, the upshot of it.
歸結 The same. (s.)
終 The end, at last, finally.
終久 In the end, to the end, sooner or later, after all.
始終 First or last, in any case, in the end, sooner or later.
至終 At the last, after all, in the end. (w.)
末了 At last, finally, in the last place, in conclusion.
末末了 The same. Doubled for emphasis.
老 After all, at all, with a negative, never. (N.)
總 After all, at all, in any case.
末尾 At the tail end, at the bottom, lastly.

VOCABULARY.

畢 *Pi*^{4}. . . . . Finished, ended; the last, final.
竟 *Ching*^{4}. To finish; the end, the utmost; at . . . . last, finally, after all.
眼力 *Yien*^{3} *li*^{4}. Power of vision; *discernment*, ... shrewdness, judgment.
講情 *Chiang*^{3} *ch'ing*^{2}. To speak on behalf of, to . . . . intercede, *to conciliate*.
疲 *P'i*^{2}. . . . . . Lassitude; *remiss*, careless, callous.
頑疲 *Wan*^{2} *p'i*^{2}. Mischievous, *ungovernable*, ... perverse; obstinate.
疲頑 *P'i*^{2} *wan*^{2}. . . . . The same. (s.)
疵 *Ts'i*^{1,2}. . . . . . . A scab; a failing, *an imperfection*.
吹毛求疵 *Ch'wei*^{1} *mao*^{2} *ch'iu*^{2} *ts'i*^{2}. To magnify . . . . trifling faults, *to carp*, to cavil.
以撒 *I*^{3} *sa*^{1}. . . . . Isaac.
批評 *P'i*^{1} *p'ing*^{2}. To criticise; to berate, *to* . . . . *overhaul*.
屍 *Shi*^{1}. . . . . A corpse.

却是至終不能。○李[25]德隆至今還沒得缺、究(歸)竟要作一輩子候補老爺。○起[26]頭我沒作聲、末了叫我好一個批評。○媒[27]人誇獎我們(借)親家、怎樣財主、究竟一無所有。○你[28]依你的法子、我依我的法子、我想到了兒、大家都能得好處。○劉[29]三起頭並不是個(無賴子、馬流人、流屍)、只因有些無二鬼、常勾引他、竟成了一塊大滾刀筋(肉)。○這[30]宗族、譬如一股水、流出去、分作幾條、分作幾十條、究竟都是這一股泉裏的水。○人[31]得功名、眞是一時的儌倖、你看林有能、府縣考都取在末尾、這回院考、碰着了題、竟進了個第五

23 Her mother never returned home, and no one knows where she went.

24 Although Isaac tried his best to keep at peace with him, yet after all he was not able to do so.

25 Up to this time Li Tê Lung has not obtained an office. He will finally be an expectant official all his life.

26 At first I said nothing, but finally I gave him a good overhauling.

27 The middleman vaunted about how wealthy our relative was, and here it turns out that he has nothing at all.

28 You follow your way and I'll follow my way, and I fancy that in the end we shall all come out right.

29 Liu San was not originally a dissolute fellow, but being constantly led astray by a set of renegades, he at last became a regular desperado.

30 This ancestry is like a stream of water which, flowing forth, divides into several branches or several tens of branches, nevertheless they all come from one source.

31 A man's getting a degree is in truth a mere accident of fortune. Look at Lin Yu Nêng; at the *Fu* and *Hsien* examinations he stood at the tail end, yet at the recent collegiate examination he

無賴子 *Wu² lai⁴ tsï³*. A vagabond, a tramp; a knave, *a dissolute fellow*.

馬流 *Ma³ liu²*....... *Dissolute*, profligate. (C.)

流屍 *Liu² shï¹*. A vagabond, a tramp; *a dissolute fellow*. (S.)

只因 *Chï³ yin¹*. Only because, inasmuch as, but since, *but*:—Les. 181.

無二鬼 *Wu² êr⁴ kwei³*. A rascal, a knave, a sharper, *a renegade*.

勾引 *Kou¹ yin³*. *To lead astray*, to entice, to decoy, to inveigle; to draw on.

滾刀筋 *Kun³ tao¹ chin¹*. A reckless and obstinate villain, *a desperado*, a wretch.

滾刀肉 *Kun³ tao¹ jou⁴*. The same:—Note 29.

分作 *Fên¹ tsoă⁴*. *To divide*, to separate; to parcel out.

儌 *Chiao³*...... To do, to act; *fortunate*, lucky.

倖 *Hsing⁴*..... Unusually fortunate, very lucky.

儌倖 *Good fortune*, luck, a happy chance.

院考 *Yüen⁴ k'ao³*. The literary examinations held in each prefecture by the 學院, or Literary Chancellor:—Note 31.

宋 *Sung⁴*........ To dwell; *a surname*.

撒 *Sa³*. To scatter, to sow, *to put forth*, to spill, to leak:—See *sa¹*.

撒潑 *Sa³ p'oă¹*. To do with one's might, *to make a strenuous effort*, a spurt.

放潑 *Fang⁴ p'oă¹*........ The same. (L.)

攢 *Tsan³*.......... To urge forward, to hasten.

攢勁 *Tsan³ chin⁴*. To do with one's might, *to make a strenuous effort*. (L.)

餻 *Kao¹*. A raised sweet cake, either baked or steamed.

雞蛋餻 *Chi¹ tan⁴ kao¹*....... A sponge cake.

攪和 *Chao³ hê²*......... To mix, to stir.

蛋黃 *Tan⁴ hwang²*........ The yolk of an egg.

蛋清 *Tan⁴ ch'ing¹*...... The white of an egg.

蛋白 *Tan⁴ poă²*.......... The white of an egg.

烤 *K'ao³*... To toast, *to bake*; to dry at the fire.

名秀才。○我[32]好意勸他、他老(總)不聽、咱們不如回去罷。○這[33]件衣裳、我已經用熱水、加胰子搓了、又上河裏過(擺)了、到底(歸齊)還不乾淨。○都[34]說宋成仁、挑不了二百斤柴伙、他撒了潑(放了潑、攢了勁)、竟是從三里橋挑來了。○福[35]田啊、點心已經沒有了、今天可以做個雞蛋糕、你不會我教給你、問怎麼做呢、答用雞蛋九兩、白糖九兩、白麪五兩、先把蛋黃和糖、使勁攪和起來、後加上麪、攪和勻了、末尾再把蛋白(清)打起沫(潑)來、都合在一塊兒、輕輕攪和起來、立時就烤。

happened on the right theme, and after all graduated in the fifth place of honor.

32 I exhorted him with the best intentions, but he quite refuses to hear. The best thing is for us to go back.

33 I have rubbed this garment with hot water and soap, and have taken it to the river and rinsed it, and after all it is still not clean.

34 Everybody said that Sung Ch'êng Jên could not carry two hundred catties of firewood, but by making a strenuous effort, he after all carried it from the three li bridge.

35 Fu T'ien, the dessert is all used up; you may make a sponge cake to-day. If you do not know how, I will teach you. *Ques.* How do you make it? *Ans.* Take of eggs nine ounces, white sugar nine ounces, and flour five ounces: first, thoroughly mix the yolks of the eggs and the sugar, then add the flour and stir till quite smooth: lastly, beat the whites of the eggs into a froth, and mix all together, stirring lightly, and bake at once.

Notes.

1 The works of Mencius are for convenience divided into two parts, called 上 and 下, which are usually bound in separate volumes. 到底 is here used in its primary sense, and, properly speaking, does not illustrate the subject of the lesson.

3 This is a very useful and important saying. It is not drawn from classical sources, but is found used by Buddhist and Taoist writers, and is very ancient. 到頭 qualifies 善惡, meaning that when good and evil conduct have reached the limit set to them by fate, or by the gods, there will then be a recompense. 終 is the usual writing, though 總 is sometimes found, and would seem more forcible. If it be used the sense is *certainly*, rather than *finally*.

9 A more literal rendering would be, *after all when one does good, the one who gets the good is himself, and when one does evil, the one who suffers the evil is himself.*

11 The use of 報 implies that the person referred to had been the recipient of favor. The translation gives the approximate force of 竟 without any special word.

15 臉面 is the "face" that the other party felt constrained to give to the party interceding, hence it is practically equivalent to *influence*.

22 To 上 a shoe, is to sew the sole fast to the upper.

25 得缺 *To get a vacancy;* that is, to get a position which has been made vacant by death or otherwise. 候補老爺, a humorous appellation which defies literal translation into English.

27 As soon as a betrothal is concluded the families begin to call each other 親家. It is not an uncommon trick for the go-between to deceive one party (or both) in regard to the circumstances of the other.

29 滾刀筋 or 肉 *Turn-knife-tendon* or *muscle*, that is, a piece of tendon or muscle so hard and tough that the knife glances off it, (some say so soft and flabby that it rolls under the knife),—a fellow so depraved that no appeal to virtue or reason, or even to force, makes any impression on him. 一塊 is applied contemptuously.

31 The candidates for literary degrees in each district are first examined by the district magistrate (縣考), and the best noted and reported. All the candidates in each prefecture are then assembled and examined by the prefect (府考), and the best noted. All this is preparatory to the examination by the 學院, who makes the circuit of his province twice in three years, and holds examinations in each Fu city, and confers the degrees. 碰着題 *To hit the theme.* It is a common thing for candidates to write out, in miniature hand, copies of superior essays on standard themes and conceal them on their persons, or to commit a number of such essays to memory, in hope that the theme given may prove to be one of these. When by such means a candidate finds himself in possession of a first class essay, on the required theme he is said to 碰題.

第一百二十八課

他[1]一見了家信、就歡喜的了不得。○這[2]兩句書、是一反一正。○先[3]生一來、學生就安靜了。○你[4]這麼一行一行的栽上、不是更好看嗎。○咱[5]們一來一往的、不覺有十幾年喇。○我[6]的記性不好濟、一轉眼就忘記了。○近[7]來天氣一冷一熱的、所以人多生病。○他[8]帶的這兩個女人、是他的一大妻一小妾。○若[9]不是鼓作膿、還能一掣掘握一掣掘握的疼嗎。○我[10]一見、就知道他不是個正經東西。○你[11]們若是一對一對的走、還齊整一些。○人[12]

Translation.

1 As soon as he saw the letter from home, he was wild with joy.
2 These two texts are diametrically opposite.
3 As soon as the teacher comes, the scholars are quiet.
4 When you plant them in rows this way, do they not look much better?
5 Without realizing it we have had intercourse for upwards of ten years.
6 My memory is poor: in a twinkling I have forgotten.
7 The weather has been changeable recently, hence there is much sickness.
8 One of the two women he has with him is his wife, and the other a concubine.
9 If pus were not forming, would it be a throbbing pain?
10 I knew at a glance that she was a bad character.
11 It will be more orderly for you to go in pairs.
12 When men begin to grow old, the marrow in their bones gradually dries up.

LESSON CXXVIII.

一 in Composition.

Although 一 has already served as the basis of three lessons, it requires still another.

When 一 is joined with a verb it marks the exact point of time of the action, and may be rendered, just as, the moment, etc. It is usually followed by a 就 in the next clause, and the two are together equal to, as soon as, whenever, etc.

When 一 is repeated with words of opposite meaning, it denotes alternation, transition, or enumeration: as,

一反一正 One the wrong, the other the right side, the reverse of each other, opposite sides; negative and positive.

一來一往 Coming and going, back and forth, intercourse.

一冷一熱 Cold and hot by turns, alternations of temperature, changeable.

一妻一妾 A wife and a concubine, the one a wife and the other a concubine.

一大一小 The same; also applied to other distinctions of rank, and of size.

一男一女 A man and a woman; male and female.

一漲一退 Advancing and receding by turns; ebbing and flowing; fluctuating.

一興一衰 Flourishing and declining by turns, progressing and receding, changing.

一紅一白 Red and white by turns, alternations of color.

一起一落 Rising and falling by turns; bobbing up and down; heaving. These are but specimens of many others like them.

When 一 is repeated with the same word, it denotes order of arrangement or succession: as,

一行一行 Row by row; in rows, in ranks.

一握一握 One grasp or compression after another, by throbs, pulsating.

一掘一掘 One dig or thrust after another, by throbs, lancinating. (c.)

一掣一掣 One pull after another, by jerks, by throbs; twitching, palpitating. (s.)

一上了年紀、骨髓就漸漸的枯了。○就[13]怕下大了、這麼
一陣一陣的下、還擋不住走。○天[14]主起初造人、是造一
男一女。○世[15]道一與一衰、好像海潮一漲一退似的。○
一[16]年一年的攢下去、自有富厚的日子來到。○他[17]不讓
我說話、我一說話、他就別字眼(挑眼)。○今[18]天眞晦(喪)氣、纔往外
一走、碰在門框上、把頭碰了一個大疙瘩。○我[19]的眼就
是見不得風、一見風就淌眼淚(流淚)。○身[20]體是靠靈魂得活、
所以魂一離身、人就死了。○他[21]肚子裏、必是有積塊(聚)、因
爲逢疼起來、就摸着一個一個(一塊一塊)的。○人[22]做事情、不怕多、
就是怕急、一急心裏就慌了。○我[23]見他臉上、一紅一白

13 Raining this way in showers need not prevent our going. What I fear is that it will rain hard.

14 When God at first created man, he created one man and one woman.

15 The progress of events in the world is a series of advances and retrogressions, like the rising and falling of the tides.

16 Laying by year by year, affluence will naturally ensue.

17 He will not allow me to speak. Whenever I speak, he finds fault with what I say.

18 I have been very unlucky to-day. Just as I was going out, I struck my head on the door frame and raised a great lump.

19 Somehow my eyes cannot endure the wind. As soon as the wind strikes them, the tears flow.

20 The body is dependent on the soul for life, hence the moment the soul leaves the body, death ensues.

21 There must be some obstruction in his bowels, for whenever the pain comes on, one can feel lumps.

22 In working, a large amount is not so much to be feared as is hurry, for whenever one is hurried, the mind becomes confused.

23 I saw the color come and go in his

一對一對 One pair after another, pair by pair; in pairs.

一陣一陣 One spell after another, by spells; intermitting.

一年一年 One year after another, by the year, yearly.

一個一個 Unit by unit, in detached pieces; one by one, seriatim.

一塊一塊 Piece by piece, in pieces, in bits, in lumps.

一層一層 Story by story, step by step, consecutively; in layers.

Phrases of this class are very numerous. All classifiers may be so used, also many words denoting time, quantity, or action.

VOCABULARY.

握 *Wo*⁴, *wu*¹·⁴. *To grasp*, to clench, *to compress;* a handful.

掘 *Chüe*². To dig, to excavate, to scoop; *to throb*, to lancinate.

髓 *Swei*³. The marrow.

骨髓 *Ku*³ *swei*³. The marrow in a bone.

世道 *Shï*⁴ *tao*⁴. The world, *the course of events*, the times.

海潮 *Hai*³ *ch'ao*². The tides.

漲 *Chang*⁴. To rise (as water); to expand, to dilate; to rise in price; *to advance.*

富厚 *Fu*⁴ *hou*⁴. Wealthy, *affluent.*

框 *K'wang*⁴. An outer frame, a border.

積聚 *Chi*² *chü*⁴. *An obstruction or compaction in the bowels;* an embolus.

積塊 *Chi*² *k'wai*⁴. The same.

扎實 *Cha*¹ *shï*². Strong, firm, secure; *forcible*, conclusive.

欺生 *Ch'i*¹ *shêng*¹. To insult or *impose upon strangers.*

口音 *K'ou*³ *yin*¹. Pronunciation; enunciation; *dialect*, brogue.

的、很喫不住。○你24聽他一層一層的、說的那個理、眞是扎實。○此25地的人、很欺生、一聽見口音不對、價錢就要的大大的。○這26必是鬼火、不能是燈籠、因爲人拿燈籠、不能這樣一起一落的。○鴛27鴦都是一對一對的、永沒有拆散的時候、所以姑娘們做新娘子(媳婦)、媽(娘)家都陪一對鴛鴦枕頭。○不28打官司則已、一打起官司來、我必帶着你的干証。○別29看他把耳朵耷拉着、很老實、可就是不讓女人騎、女人一上去、他就踢蹶子(打蹄子)。○我30在外頭、心裏是清清楚楚的、一進了這個大門、就轉不過向來(轉了向)喇、你說奇不奇呢。

face showing that he felt very much annoyed.

24 Listen to his arguments as he advances step by step; certainly they are quite conclusive.

25 The people of this place are much given to imposing on strangers. Whenever they notice that a man's dialect is strange, they at once ask a high price.

26 This must be a Will o' the wisp; it cannot be a lantern, for no one carrying a lantern would move it up and down in this fashion.

27 Mandarin ducks always go in pairs and never forsake each other; hence when young ladies get married, their mother's family always present them with a pair of mandarin-duck pillows.

28 If there is no lawsuit, that is the end of it; but if a lawsuit results, I will of course require your testimony.

29 Don't suppose from his drooping ears that he is entirely gentle, for he will not suffer a woman to ride him. Whenever a woman mounts him, he begins to kick.

30 As long as I am outside, I am all right [in regard to the points of the compass]; but as soon as I enter this great door, I lose my bearings. Isn't it singular?

鬼火 *Kwei*³ *hwoa*³. . . . . Ignis-fatuus.

鴛 *Yüen*¹. . . . . The drake of the mandarin duck.

鴦 *Yang*¹. . . . . . The hen of the mandarin duck.

鴛鴦 The mandarin duck,—noted for conjugal fidelity.

拆散 *Ch'ai*¹ *san*⁴. To separate, to sunder, to . . . . scatter, *to forsake*.

媽家 *Ma*¹ *chia*¹. . . . . A wife's mother's family.

干証 *Kan*¹ *chêng*⁴. . . . . *Testimony*, witness.

則已 *Tsê*² *i*³. *That is the end of it*, so be it:— . . . . Note 28.

耷 *Ta*¹. . . . . . Lop-ears; dragging, drooping.

耷拉 *Ta*¹ *la*¹. *To droop*, to drag, to hang down; . . . . to move in a slouching way.

蹶 *Chüe*³. . . . . To kick, a kick. Also *chüe*².

踢蹶子 *T'i*¹ *chüe*³ *tsï*³. *To kick*, to kick up . . . . the heels.

打蹄子 *Ta*³ *t'i*² *tsï*³. . . . . The same,

轉向 *Chwan*⁴ *hsiang*⁴. *To lose one's bearings*. . . . . to become confused.

NOTES.

8 妻 and 妾 are the proper words for *wife* and *concubine*, but they are not generally used in conversation, 大 and 小 being used instead, either alone as here, or joined with 老婆 or 婆子.

10 正經東西 *An orthodox thing*,—only used with a negative, and to express contempt.

19 見 as here used means *to endure* or *withstand*, which in fact is one of its regular mandarin meanings, and is the meaning which forms the basis of the second usage illustrated in Les. 122.

23 一紅一白 *One red one white; that is, red and white or flushed and pale by turns.*

25 This sentence was written in Nanking, (as might be inferred from the use of 此地,) but the fault of which it speaks is just as true of the Chinese elsewhere.

28 則已 is a book term used colloquially in the South but not in the North, save occasionally by educated men. Its colloquial equivalent is 就罷, or 便罷.

30 The Chinese always indicate direction and position by the points of the compass, and generally keep these points in their minds with remarkable accuracy.

第一百二十九課

去[1]年新安的電線、是從上海起、到北京止。○既[2]不爲名、又不爲利、你想他到底是爲甚麼呢。○人[3]的主意、不可忽然而天、忽然而地的、應當起初這樣、以後這樣、末了還是這樣。○若[4]單買一斤、要四十個錢、成包的、只管合三十六個錢、到底成躉總的買、强勝似零買。○地[5]球上的南北線、名爲經線、就是從南極起、到北極爲止。○那[6]些好花錢的人、起初也是捨不得、以後越花越肯花、末了就是願意花、也沒有甚麼花了。○你[7]既不能念書、又不願學手藝、到底打算怎麼度日呢。○

TRANSLATION.

1 The new telegraph line put up last year, extends from Shanghai to Peking.

2 If he is seeking neither reputation nor money, what then do you suppose he is seeking?

3 A man's purpose should not be subject to great and sudden changes, but what it is at first, it should continue to be, and remain the same to the end.

4 If you buy only one catty it costs forty cash; in whole packages the price is only thirty-six cash; in the end it is better to buy at wholesale than at retail.

5 The lines running north and south on the globe are called meridians. They extend from the south pole to the north pole.

6 Those who are so free with their money were also loath to part with it at first, but afterwards the more they spent the more lavish they became, until at last they found their desires ahead of their means.

7 Seeing you cannot get an education, and are not willing to learn a trade, what do you propose to do for a living?

LESSON CXXIX.

CORRELATIVE PARTICLES.

Ability to use a language effectively, and especially ability to use it for the expression of complicated thought, depends largely on the ready and effective use of correlative particles. They are the framework upon which the clauses expressing connected thought are hung. Such particles have of course been introduced to some extent in previous lessons, but for the purpose of aiding the learner in finding and acquiring their ready and accurate use, I have arranged a number of lessons on this basis, of which this is the first and simplest. The others, twelve in all, will follow at intervals :—

從 . . . 起 . . . 到 . . . 止, From . . . to.

到底 . . 强似 After all . . . better than.

到底 . . 勝似 After all . . . better than.

既不 . . . 又不 . . . 到底 If not . . . nor . . . really; or, since not . . . nor yet . . . after all; or, seeing not . . . and not . . . then.

起初 . . . 以後 . . . 末了 At first . . . afterwards . . . at last; or, at first . . . then . . . finally.

These translations are only approximate; they will vary somewhat with the subject and the connexion.

VOCABULARY.

成包 *Ch'êng² pao¹*. By the bundle or package, *wholesale*.

成躉 *Ch'êng² tun³*. By the lot, by the quantity, *wholesale*. (c. & s.)

成總 *Ch'êng² tsung³*. The same.

勝似 *Shêng⁴ sï⁴*. Superior to, *better than*, more advantageous.

零買 *Ling² mai³*. To buy at retail, or in small quantities.

地球 *Ti⁴ ch'iu²*. The earth; *a globe*.

官[8]府設立粥廠、是從今年十一月初一起、到轉來年二月初一止。○用[9]汽機、雖然多費本錢、然而折算起他所做的活來、到底用汽機勝似用人力。○每[10]禮拜派一個管事的、就是從這個禮拜一起、到下禮拜一為止。○太[11]太聽說老爺遇見了強盜、嚇的臉上起初紅喇、以後青喇、末了又黃喇。○李[12]玉春的舅子、在家裏發脾寒瘧子瘧疾、天天從半夜起、到天亮為止。○有[13]一個賣肉包子的、三天賣一籠屜、能掙能尋一百錢、又有一個人、一籠屜只掙尋三十個錢、一天却能賣十籠屜、這麼比較起來、到底少貪利強似多貪利。○他[14]看着我是倭儂廢老實、特為來找我的晦氣殃、起初說些好話、跟我借一吊錢、我不

8 The soup kitchen provided by the officials, opens on the first of the eleventh month of this year, and continues to the first of the second month of next year.

9 Although steam power costs more at first, yet if you take into account the work it does, it is better in the end to use steam than to use hand labor.

10 A monitor is appointed each week, beginning with Monday of this week and ending with Monday of next week.

11 When the lady heard that her husband had met with robbers she was so frightened that her face at first became red, and then turned livid, and finally pale.

12 Li Yü Ch'un's brother-in-law is at home suffering from ague. [He has an attack] every day, lasting from midnight until daylight.

13 A certain seller of meat dumplings sold one platter in three days, on which he cleared one hundred cash; another cleared only thirty cash on each platter, but in one day he could sell ten platters; from which it appears that after all it is best to be satisfied with small profits.

14 He thought I was a saphead (green), and came on purpose to victimize me. At first he spoke plausibly and wanted to borrow a thousand cash of me, but I refused to lend it to him. Afterwards he only wanted five hundred.

經 *Ching*[4]. The warp; what runs lengthwise; .... *meridians*. See *ching*[1].

經線 *Ching*[4] *hsien*[4]. .... Meridian lines.

度日 *Tu*[4] *jï*[4]. .... To live; *to make a living.*

官府 *Kwan*[1] *fu*[3]. .... An officer, officers.

設立 *Shê*[4] *li*[4]. To set up, to establish, to institute; ....to open; *to provide.*

廠 *Ch'ang*[3]. A shed; *a depôt*, a storehouse; a .... manufactory.

粥廠 *Chou*[1] *ch'ang*[3]. A soup kitchen where gruel .... is dispensed to the poor.

汽 *Ch'i*[4]. .... Steam, vapor.

汽機 *Ch'i*[4] *chi*[1]. .... A steam engine.

舅子 *Chiu*[4] *tsï*[3]. ....A wife's brother.

肉包子 *Jou*[4] *pao*[1] *tsï*[3]. A steamed mince .... dumpling.

脾寒 *P'i*[2] *han*[2]. .... Ague.

倭 *Woă*[1]. A name for Japan; zinc; crumpled; ....soiled; *weak.*

儂 *Nang*[4]. .... Slow, *dull*, irresolute.

倭儂 Dirty, slovenly, squalid; weak, *soft.*

倭儂廢 *Woă*[1] *nang*[4] *fei*[4]. A silly goose, *a sap-* ....*head*, a mooncalf.

特為 *T'ê*[4] *wei*[4]. Specially, *on purpose*, expressly. .... See Les. 159.

搌擁 *Ts'oă*[4] *yung*[3]. To coax and drag away, *to* .... *hustle off.*

真實 *Chên*[1] *shï*[2]. .... True, real, *genuine.*

交情 *Chiao*[1] *ch'ing*[2]. The mutual affection of .... friends, *friendship.*

盛 *Shêng*[4]. Abundant, exuberant; *prosperous;* ....flourishing; excellent. See *ch'êng*[2].

借給他、以後只借五百、我還是不借、末了就
放起刁來了、說我該他一百吊錢、叫我打了
一頓、旁邊的人、好歹把他拉扯(撮擁)着走喇。○往[15]
年間交朋友、到底有點眞實滋味、强似如今
的人交友、淨是嘴裏的交情、心裏並不實在。
○這[16]場雨下的到底不大、却仍舊强似一點
不下。○國[17]家强盛的根本、旣不在乎設立砲
局、又不在乎多買鐵甲船、到底是在什麼呢、
就是在乎振興學校、因爲學校若能振興、人
才自然衆多、國家自然就强盛了。

but I still refused. At last he grew outrageous and declared that I owed him a hundred thousand cash, upon which I gave him a sound drubbing, the bystanders hustling him off as best they could.

15 The friendships of former times were better than those of the present; they had something genuine in them, whereas now-a-days friendship is merely in words without any reality in the heart.

16 After all the rain was but slight, still it is better than that it should not have rained at all.

17 Since the source of a nation's prosperity is not in the establishing of arsenals, nor yet in the purchasing of many ironclads, in what then is it? It is in the advancement of education; for if education is advanced, of course men of ability will abound, which will necessarily make the nation prosperous.

强盛 *Ch'iang² shêng⁴*. Flourishing, *prosperous*; vigorous, puissant.

在乎 *Tsai⁴ hu¹*. Same as 在:—Note 16.

砲局 *P'ao⁴ chü²*. An arsenal.

鐵甲船 *T'ie³ chia³ ch'wan²*. An iron armored ship,—an ironclad.

振 *Chen⁴*. To shake; to stir up, *to excite;* to restore; to alarm.

振興 *Chên⁴ hsing¹*. To cause to flourish, *to advance*, to promote.

校 *Hsiao⁴*. A school house. Also *chiao⁴*.

學校 *Hsüe² hsiao⁴*. A school, a seminary; *education*, learning, science, (w.)

人才 *Jên² ts'ai²* *A man of ability*, a gifted man; talent. (w.)

衆多 *Chung⁴ toă¹*. Very many, numerous, *abundant*.

NOTES.

2 According to the translation, 爲 here *seems* to mean *to seek*. It really means *for the sake of*, and a verb must be supplied to complete the sense.

3 忽然而天忽然而地的 The 而 has here approximately the force of 就:—See Les. 138. 天 and 地 are used figuratively to express strong contrariety.

5 The south pole takes the precedence in China.

8 In scarce years, and in many places every year, the officers open kitchens in the winter, where rice or millet gruel is given out daily to the poor.

11 老爺 is rendered husband, because the connection shows that the person spoken of was the woman's husband.

12 脾寒 is a *t'ung-hsing* term for ague, but in Central Mandarin 瘧子 is more frequently used, and in the South 瘧疾.

13 The article referred to as a 屜 or 籠, is in Peking called a 籠屜, and in Chinanfu and elsewhere a 簹子. Different forms have probably given rise to different names. It is primarily a slotted bamboo frame fitting closely in the kettle and resting on its sides; bread and cakes are spread on it to be cooked or warmed by the steam from the water or food which is boiling beneath. This is a 簹子. A hoop is sometimes added which gives the article the form of a sieve, and it is then called a 屜. This hoop is sometimes attached to a matting top (or bottom if you please), instead of to the slotted 簹子, for which it serves as a cover, and the whole is called a 籠 or 籠屜. As many cakes or dumplings as this platter will hold for cooking is called 一籠, or 一屜.

14 老實 here means *green, pliant, spiritless*, but falls far short of the force of the expression with which it is mated.

16 在乎 is a book form, frequently used in colloquial. The 乎 is a mere euphonic particle, having no effect on the meaning of 在.

第一百三十課

[1] 人的好歹、我許品得出來。○[2] 那句話、也許（行許）他是無心說的。○[3] 說起那個人來、管許（占許）你必認得。○[4] 孩子這麼直咳嗽、許（敢）是喫的鹹菜多喇。○[5] 先頭他在棧房、如今也許還在那裏。○[6] 這條手巾、多半（少不）是前頭那個人掉的。○[7] 許（料）得是我記錯了、我却總覺着不能。○[8] 用一個擺渡、也許就載過去了。○[9] 今天英子沒來上學、想許（橫暨）是他母親病的更重喇。○[10] 家裏有白糖沒有、答 還許（許還、想還）有一點、却不能多。○[11] 莫不是尹先生來了、別人敲門、不能這樣急。○[12] 這第二番託他、莫非他又忘記喇。○[13] 你們倆、能暨起這個梯子來嗎、答 可以試試、管許（可許）不大離（不離經）。○[14] 我於世事上、再經

Translation.

1 I can generally form a fair estimate of a man's character.

2 It may be that he used the expression without thinking.

3 Speaking of that man—you most probably know him.

4 This continual coughing is probably because the child has eaten too much salt pickle.

5 A little ago he was in the ware-room, and probably he is still there.

6 This handkerchief was most likely dropped by that man in front.

7 Possibly my memory is at fault, but I hardly think it can be.

8 By using one ferry-boat we may perhaps get them taken over.

9 Ying-tsï did not come to school to-day. I presume his sick mother is worse.

10 Is there any white sugar in the house? *Ans.* There may still be a little, but there cannot be much.

11 It must be that Mr. Yin has come. No one else would knock so furiously.

12 It must be he has forgotten again this, the second, time that we have depended upon him.

13 Can you two set up this ladder? *Ans.* We'll try. Most probably we can.

14 When I have had a few more years of experience, I may perhaps be considered a man of good judgment.

LESSON CXXX.

Probability.

許 Probably, perhaps, possibly, likely, may be. 許 is the most generally useful and extensively used word for expressing probability.

行許 Perhaps, possibly, it may be. (c.)

管許 Probably, quite likely, most likely, in all probability.

占許 Probably, most likely. (c.)

可許 The same. (s.)

許得 Perhaps, possibly, it may be. (L.)

料得 The same. (s.)

想許 I presume, probably, it may be. (N.)

多半是 Most likely, most probably.

少不是 or **少不得** The same. (L.)

想 I dare say, I presume. (s.)

想必 Most likely, in all probability. (s.) See Les. 96.

要是 Most likely, probably, I presume.

敢 I dare say, perchance, possibly, probably, I venture.

巧了 May possibly, perchance, peradventure.

好像 It seems as if:—Les. 99.

或者 Possibly, it may be:—Les. 56.

莫不是 It must be that.

莫非是 The same.

橫豎 Probably, most likely, I venture.

庶幾 May perhaps, perchance,—a book term often used by educated men, but sounding a little pedantic.

歷幾年、庶幾(或者)可以算個明白人咯。○ 15 連好幾天、沒做一個好饅頭、莫不是麵肥(引子)(酵子)壞喇。○ 16 李潤田錯怪了我、我託人透說透說、許他就不生氣喇。○ 17 現在已經過了半夜、他還沒來、莫非是路上遭了什麼事情罷。○ 18 利豐家怎麼關了板(上了門)呢、答 管許(想必)是倒了罷。○ 19 他光說辦土貨、沒說辦洋貨呀、答 他巧了(好像)提過、我却不記得(記不得)。○ 20 上天若再加我幾年的壽數、完全我學易經的工夫、庶幾乎可以無大過了。○ 21 誰歡喜(喜)喫那點冷乾糧呢、還不許是耗子(老鼠)拉去了嗎。○ 22 兄弟你心中有些不樂、莫不是家裏有甚麼

15 I have not made a loaf of good bread for several days. It must be that the yeast is spoiled.
16 Li Jun T'ien has erroneously taken offence at me. If I get some one to explain to him, perhaps he will not be angry.
17 It is now past midnight and he has not come. It must be that he has met with some mishap on the road.
18 How is it that the Li Fêng firm have closed their doors? *Ans.* It is most likely they have failed.
19 He only spoke of buying native goods, not mentioning foreign goods at all? *Ans.* He may possibly have mentioned them, but I do not remember it.
20 If Heaven adds a few more years to my life, so that I may complete the study of the Book of Changes, I may, perhaps, be free from any serious faults.
21 Who would care to eat that bit of cold bread? May it not be that the rats carried it off?
22 You are unhappy in mind my brother. Something has been said by the family which has wounded your feelings, has there not?

VOCABULARY.

庶 *Shu*^{4}. A multitude, all; the mass; nearly, ...it may be, probably :—see Sub.

品 *P'in*^{2}. To classify, to distinguish, to discern, ... *to recognize.* See *p'in*^{3}.

鹹菜 *Hsien*^{2} *ts'ai*^{4}. Vegetables pickled in salt, ... seasoning :—Note 4.

棧 *Chan*^{4}. . . . . *A storehouse;* an enclosed pen.

棧房 *Chan*^{4} *fang*^{2}. A store-house, *a ware-room,* . . . . a godown, a depository.

渡 *Tu*^{4}. . . . To cross a stream or sea, *to ferry.*

擺渡 *Pai*^{3} *tu*^{4}. . . . . . *A ferry-boat;* to ferry over.

載 *Tsai*^{4}. To contain ; to lade a ship or cart ; *to* . . . . . . *convey;* to record ; a cargo. Also *tsai*^{3}.

尹 *Yin*^{3}. . . . . .To govern ; an overseer ; *a surname.*

世事 *Shï*^{4} *shï*^{4}. The affairs of the world, *the* . . . . *affairs of life.*

經歷 *Ching*^{1} *li*^{4}. To pass through, to meet with, ... *to experience,* to undergo.

麪肥 *Mien*^{4} *fei*^{2}. . . . . Yeast. (N.)

引子 *Yin*^{3} *tsï*^{3}. Ferment, barm ; *dry yeast:—* . . . . Note 15.

透說 *T'ou*^{4} *shwoă*^{1}. *To explain* or intercede on . . . . behalf of ; to sound.

半夜 *Pan*^{4} *yie*^{4}. . . . . .Half the night ; *midnight.*

土貨 *T'u*^{3} *hwoă*^{4}. . . . . Native goods.

洋貨 *Yang*^{2} *hwoă*^{4}. . . . . Foreign goods.

易經 *I*^{4} *ching*^{1}. The Book of Changes :—Note . . . . 20.

乾糧 *Kan*^{1} *liang*^{2}. . . . . Bread or cakes.

鼠 *Shu*^{3}. . . . . . . A rat, rodents.

老鼠 *Lao*^{3} *shu*^{3}. . . . . .A rat or mouse.

傷觸 *Shang*^{1} *ch'u*^{4}. To *offend,* to irritate, to . . . . chafe.

觸犯 *Ch'u*^{4} *fan*^{4}. To offend, to affront, *to wound* . . . . *the feelings;* to sin against.

砍快 *K'an*^{3} *k'wai*^{4}. Prompt, quick, ready, ...peremptory.

脆 *Ts'wei*^{4}. . . . .*Brittle,* short, crisp (as pastry).

言語、傷觸(觸犯)了你嗎。○後[23]天上東莊赴席、您家裏去幾個人、答現在還說不定、大約是去兩個、也許只去一個。○這[24]兩條金魚、我看給他三百錢、就是便宜價兒、他答應的却很砍快(響脆、脆快)、敢是我輸了眼力(色)、出的價錢大喇。○剛[25]纔過去一個女人、穿的繡(彩)花褲子、走起來倒倒險險(伶式伶仃)的、看他那個走像、想要是裏頭踹的蹺、答那個倒許啊。○此[26]處的人、詭計多端、你我雖是十分(投契、切洽、相投)也難保不中人的反間計、所以你若聽說我待你有過錯犯、你就親自來問我、我若聽說你待我有過錯犯、我也親自去問你、這樣、庶幾可以保全交情、不被人賣

23 How many of your family are going to the east village day after to-morrow to the feast? *Ans.* I cannot tell at present. Probably two will go, or possibly only one.

24 I thought that to give him three hundred cash for these two gold fish would not be too much. He replied very promptly however. Possibly I was mistaken and offered him too high a price.

25 A woman just now passed by wearing embroidered trousers and having a very unsteady gait. Judging from her style of walking, I suspect she was wearing false feet. *Ans.* That is not at all unlikely.

26 The people in this neighborhood are very perfidious. Although you and I are very intimate friends, yet it is not impossible that we may fall into some of their traps for estranging us. Therefore if you hear that I have treated you improperly in any way, come at once in person and ask me; and if I hear that you have treated me improperly, I will go in person and ask you. In this way perhaps we may protect our friendship from the deceitful tricks of others.

脆快 *Ts'wei⁴ k'wai⁴.* Brittle; crisp; prompt, quick, ready.

響脆 *Hsiang³ ts'wei⁴.* Prompt, decided. (s.)

仃 *Ting¹.* Alone, unsupported.

伶式伶仃 *Ling² shi⁴ ling² ting¹.* Tottering, staggering, *unsteady;* gingerly, carefully. (s.)

倒倒險險 *Tao³ hsien³.* *Unsteady;* reeling, staggering.

走像 *Tsou³ hsiang⁴.* Mode of motion, gait, *style of walking.*

踹 *Ts'ai³.* *To tread on,* to stamp, to trample.

蹺 *Ch'iao¹.* To elevate the feet; on tiptoe; a high-heeled shoe, *a false wooden support for the foot:*—Note 25.

詭計 *Kwei³ chi⁴.* Stratagem, artifice, trick, deception.

投契 *T'ou² ch'i⁴.* Friendly, *intimate.*

洽 *Hsia⁴.* To blend, to imbue; *intimate.*

切洽 *Ch'ie⁴ hsia⁴.* *Intimate,* cordial, ardent.

反間計 *Fan³ chien⁴ chi⁴.* A device by which to alienate friends.

過犯 *Kwoá⁴ fan⁴.* A transgression, *a fault,* a sin.

保全 *Pao³ ch'üen².* To preserve, to render safe, *to protect.*

賣弄 *Mai⁴ lung⁴.* *To betray,* to circumvent, to practice upon.

荷包 *Hê² pao¹.* A purse, *a pouch.*

砲臺 *P'ao⁴ t'ai².* A fort.

洩氣 *Hsie⁴ ch'i⁴.* *To be satisfied,* to be appeased, to put away one's anger.

伏氣 *Fu² ch'i⁴.* *To be satisfied,* to be appeased. (accent on *ch'i⁴.*) Note 28.

選 *Hsüen³.* *To select,* to elect, to vote.

挑選 *T'iao¹ hsüen³.* *To select,* to choose out, to pick out.

措手 *Ts'oá⁴ shou³.* To be available, to be practicable; *ready,* at hand.

弄了。○我[27]的烟袋荷包、在家裏到底沒找着、我細想想、昨天和你喝酒來、横豎擱在你家裏、書案桌子上、答許啊、等我回家給你找找。○奪[28]不回我們的砲臺來、我就是不伏洩氣、可以挑選五百精兵、今晚上給他個措手不及、去偷他的營、若是我們的官星顯的時候、巧了或者就奪回來了。

27 After all, I could not find my tobacco pouch anywhere at home, and, upon considering, I think it must be that yesterday when I was drinking wine with you, I left it on your book table. *Ans.* Possibly you did. I will look it up for you when I go home.

28 I cannot be satisfied unless we recapture our fort. You may select five hundred tried soldiers and, coming on them suddenly to-night, take them by surprise. If my lucky star should be in the ascendant, perchance we may recapture it.

NOTES.

1 許 is here used to express that peculiar shade of assumed humility which suggests a touch of self-conceit. The idea of probability is *implied*. The distinction in the tone of 品 is not made in Peking, where all meanings are *p'in³*.

4 鹹菜 Turnips or other vegetables pickled in brine and cut up into little bits. The Chinese put no salt in their rice or millet, but eat this *hsien ts'ai* with it instead. It is popularly supposed that eating too much of it will cause coughs and asthma.

10 Different teachers will give different opinions as to whether 還許 or 許還 is the better. So also in English we can say, *There is perhaps still a little*, or *There is still a little perhaps.*

15 There is much variety in the use of words for yeast. 引子, and 酵子, and 引酵, and 麪酵, and 發麪, and 麪肥, are all used in various places. 酵 expresses the idea of fermentation, and 引 that of propagation. In Shantung and Peking and perhaps elsewhere, 引子 means the yeast proper, either wet or dry, and 酵 the sponge.

18 The front of most Chinese shops consists of upright boards sliding in grooves. They are taken down in the morning and put up at night. Hence 關板 is to "*shut up shop.*" To close up for the night is 上板.

19 好像 is stronger than 巧了, and would require us to translate, *It seems as if he had, but I do not remember.*

20 易經 The oldest and most obscure of the Chinese classics. The diagrams on which it is founded are attributed to 伏羲, but the text was written by 文王, and afterwards expanded by Confucius. It is essentially a book of divination.

22 傷觸 is somewhat bookish; 觸犯 is the more colloquial form. 觸 alone is also used.

25 Chinese women, whose feet are larger than is esteemed pretty, often make a false foot of wood which they wear underneath the heel of their own foot, the toes and front part of which are bent nearly straight down as if standing on tiptoe.

26 詭計多端 *Abound in deceitful stratagems,*—a book phrase.

28 偷營 *To come suddenly upon the encampment of an enemy and capture it by surprise.* 伏氣 is to be distinguished from 服氣. 官星 *Official star.* Each officer, in theory at least, regards himself as under the guiding influence of some particular star.

LESSON CXXXI.

APPREHENSIVENESS.

恐 I fear, lest.

怕 I fear, I am afraid, I presume.

恐怕 I fear, I am afraid, lest, peradventure, I apprehend; probably. Though *properly* expressing apprehension of something undesirable, 恐怕 is often used, especially in the South, for simple probability.

恐其 The same as 恐怕, but a little more colloquial.

只怕 I only fear, it is to be feared; I suspect; but, peradventure.

只恐 It is to be feared, the danger is.

就怕 I am afraid, the fear is, lest.

就恐 The same.

惟恐 I fear, it is to be feared, lest perchance, peradventure.

第一百三十一課

臨[1]時恐怕預備不及。○我[2]大媽娘的病、恐其難好。○
老[3]爺怕沒喫過我們的菜罷。○到[4]落沒太陽的時候、
恐怕遶趕不回來。○別[5]的我都不怕、就是怕他不讓
說話。○他[6]說是要守寡、我恐怕他守不住。○若[7]是
仍舊忍耐、恐其把他越發慣壞了。○以[8]後要儉省
一點、恐怕錢不彀用的。○在[9]這樣繁華地方、我怕
你難作好人。○晚[10]上應該早早關門、恐其有賊進
來。○他[11]有一半點好處、惟恐就是怕人知不不知道道。○恐[12]怕
你把這件事、看得太容易了。○趕[13]急着做還怕做不
出來、那裏敢曠功呢。○應[14]當遠離匪類人、恐怕叫

Translation.

1 I fear that we will not have time to get ready at the last moment.

2 My aunt will not, I fear, recover from her disease.

3 I presume you, sir, have not before eaten of our dishes.

4 I suspect we shall not be able to get back by sunset.

5 I do not fear anything else; I only fear he will not allow me to speak.

6 She says she will remain a widow, but I apprehend she will not be able.

7 If we continue to indulge him, I fear we shall spoil him all the more.

8 Henceforth we must be a little more saving lest our money be insufficient.

9 In such a gay place as this, I fear you will find it hard to lead a virtuous life.

10 At night you should shut the door early, lest thieves get in.

11 When he does any little praiseworthy thing, he is so afraid people will not know it.

12 I fear you underrate the difficulty of this affair.

13 I fear I cannot finish even by hurrying; how then should I venture to idle away time.

14 You should keep aloof from dissipated

Vocabulary.

恐 *K'ung³*. Apprehensive, alarmed; suspicious; lest, supposing, perhaps:—see Sub.

惟 *Wei²*. To consider; just so, precisely; but, only; and so, only that:—Les. 150.

臨時 *Lin² shï⁴*. On the eve of, *at the last moment;* when the test comes.

繁華 *Fan² hwa²*. Gay, *fashionable*, festive; dissipation.

曠 *K'wang⁴*. Vacant, waste; spacious; to relax, to neglect.

曠功 *K'wang⁴ kung¹*. To neglect work or duty, *to idle away time.*

遠離 *Yüen³ li²*. *To keep aloof from,* to avoid, to give a wide berth.

飲 *Yin⁴*. To give an animal drink. See *yin³*.

走岔 *Tsou³ ch'a⁴*. *To take different roads;* to work at cross purposes.

替換 *T'i⁴ hwan⁴*. To substitute, to exchange, *to take turns.*

側 *Ts'ê⁴, chai¹*. Lateral, inclining, awry, uneven, tilted.

側稜 *Chai¹ lêng⁴*. Inclined, *uneven*, tilted, edgewise.

凸 *Tu³, ku³*. Projecting, convex, bulged. Also read *kung³* in Nanking.

橋凸 *Ch'iao² kung³*. Bulged, warped, *uneven*, tilted. (s.)

洩漏 *Hsie⁴ lou⁴*. *To leak out,* to come to light, to let out a secret.

矆 *Sa²*. To look about, to glance at.

矆目 *Sa² mu⁴*. To look about, to glance around, *to take a look.* (c.)

睆 *Hsüe²*. To look sharply, to look about.

睆目 *Hsüe² mu⁴*. To look askance, to look about, *to take a look* (N.)

瞥 *P'ie¹*. To glance at, to look askance at.

他拉下去。○就15怕他一得了錢、再不正經做工夫(活)。○驢16不吃草、恐怕是渴了、可以打點水來飲飲他。○若17差人迎他去罷、又恐走岔了道兒。○該18有兩個人替換着做、一個人怕扛不住。○安19在那個橋凸(側稜)着地方、恐怕倒了、打着孩子。○事20情就恐怕不做、若是做了、早晚還有不洩漏的嗎。○我21回去的遲晚了、恐怕一個老的兒(老兒的)不放心。○只22怕太太不喜歡來、若喜歡來、我們都很樂意。○恐23其他已經藏起來了、你可以到他家去瞥瞅眝目目瞅眝目目。(瞥25瞧)○這24匹馬好大龍性、若不牽着、恐怕撒歡跑了。○只怕這個法子、行來已久、未免虛應故事。○楊26

men lest they drag you down with them.
15 What I fear is, that if he gets the money, he will not afterwards do his work properly.
16 The donkey is not eating his food. I fear he is thirsty; bring some water and give him a drink.
17 If I should send any one to meet him, the danger is they might take different roads.
18 There should be two to work by turns. I am afraid one man could not stand it.
19 If you set it in that uneven place, I fear it may fall over and strike the children.
20 The only doubt is as to whether he did it. If he did it, there is no doubt but that it will leak out sooner or later.
21 If I am late returning, I fear the old folks will be uneasy.
22 I only fear your ladyship will not care to come; if you would like to come, we shall all be perfectly delighted.
23 I presume he has already hidden it. You might go to his house and take a sly look.
24 This is a very spirited horse. If he is not led, I fear he may get frisky and run away.
25 This method having been practiced for so long, it will necessarily, I fear, be a mere formality.

瞥瞥瞧 *P'ie*[1] *p'ie*[1] *ch'iao*[2]. To look about, to *take a look*, to glance around. (s.)

龍性 *Lung*[2] *hsing*[4]. *Spirited*, mettlesome (of horses).

撒歡 *Sa*[1] *hwan*[1]. *To frisk*, to prance, to gambol, to curvet.

已久 *I*[3] *chiu*[3]. A good while, *a long time;* equal to 已經久了.

未免 *Wei*[4] *mien*[3]. Not to be avoided, unavoidable; *necessarily.*

棠 *T'ang*[2]. A species of crab-apple.

彪 *Piao*[1]. Streaks, veins; ornate; foolish, *eccentric, silly.*

半彪子 *Pan*[4] *piao*[1] *tsï*[3]. A fool, an ass, a madcap, *a crack-brain.*

螞 *Ma*[3]. A leech; *an ant.* Also *ma*[4].

蟻 *I*[3]. An ant.

螞蟻 An ant.

白螞蟻 A white ant; *a good-for-nothing*, a loafer, a drone, a deadhead. (s.)

促織 *Ts'u*[4] *chï*[1]. The cricket.

鷹 *Ying*[1]. *The falcon*, eagle, hawk, etc.

鴒 *Ling*[2]. The lark, the wagtail.

百鴒 *Pai*[3] *ling*[2]. The thick-billed lark; a thrush.

對詞 *Twei*[4] *ts'ï*[2]. To bear witness; *to respond to a charge*, to answer.

敵手 *Ti*[2] *shou*[3]. An opponent, an antagonist, *a match;* the adverse party.

借字 *Chie*[4] *tsï*[4]. A promissory note.

欠據 *Ch'ien*[4] *chü*[4]. The same. (s.)

鴻 *Hung*[2]. The swan; vast, immeasurable; profound.

賣法 *Mai*[4] *fa*[3]. To sell the law, *to pervert justice for a bribe.*

言明 *Yien*[2] *ming*[2]. To state explicitly, *to agree*, to arrange definitely.

太爺眞是好官、無論甚麼官司、都是仔細又仔細、惟恐有閒屈了的地方。○他[27]也不是個文官、又不是個武將、我巴結他幹甚麼呢、答你巴結他、還是個有錢的大爺、若他眞是個文官武將、只恐你還巴結不上呢。○江[28]南棠那是個半彪子(白螞蟻)、從小只會鬥鵪鶉、放大鷹、(促織、玩百鴿、)所以叫他上堂對詞、恐其不是楊三的敵手。○莫[29]嫌官員都是貪贓賣法、若心裏沒有眞道感動、只恐你我做了官、也是如此。○立[30]借字(欠帖、欠據)人王學易、今借到李鴻發錢、一百二十吊整、言明月利一分、四年本利還清、恐後無憑、立此字(帖、據)存照。

26 Yang T'ai Yie is certainly a good magistrate. No matter what the case may be, he is exceedingly careful, lest perchance he should do some injustice.

27 He is neither a civil officer nor a military captain; why should I court his favor? *Ans.* You court his favor because he is a wealthy aristocrat. If he were indeed a civil or military officer, it is to be feared that paying court to him would be beyond your reach.

28 Chiang Nan T'ang is a crack-brained fellow. From his youth he has done nothing but fight quails and fly falcons (fight crickets and play with thrushes), hence I fear it will not do to have him appear in court as respondent. He is no match for Yang the Third.

29 Do not find fault with the officials because they all take bribes. If our hearts were not controlled by the truth it is to be feared that you and I, if we were officers, would also do the same.

30 The drawer of this note, Wang Hsüe I, has this day received of Li Hung Fa the sum of one hundred and twenty thousand cash, which is to bear interest at one per cent. per month, and it is agreed that principal and interest shall be paid in full within four years. Lest hereafter proof should be wanting, this note is given in evidence.

NOTES.

4 沒 is not here a contraction for 沒有, but means of itself properly, *to disappear.*

5 Chinese officials, when they think they already understand a case, or when they are bribed or influenced in other ways to take a given view of it, are in the habit of refusing peremptorily to allow the party assumed to be in the wrong to speak for himself, or to offer evidence.

11 The conditional character of the first clause is implied in the structure of the sentence. In some localities 知不道 is regularly used for 不知道.

15 As here used 工夫 means *work*, that is, that which occupies *time.* This use is not unfrequent.

17 走岔道 *To go by a branch road*, and so fail to meet one who goes by the other road, *to miss by taking different roads.*

20 This is a somewhat perplexing sentence. It is translated as referring to the past, and to an absent party. It is equally applicable to the present as a direct address. *The only uncertainty is about your doing it; once done it is sure to leak out sooner or later.*

21 老兒的 or 老的兒 is much used in the North for parents when speaking to others. It is somewhat inelegant, but not in the least disrespectful. The second form seems to be a sort of unconscious transposition of the first. In the South 兒 is omitted and 老的 used.

25 虛應故事 *Vainly fulfil the old thing*, that is, to follow a mere routine. A book phrase.

27 巴結 is here used in its more unusual sense of *paying court to, or fawning upon.* 武將 is rarely used, save as here in correlation with 文官.

28 鬥鵪鶉 *To fight quails*, 放大鷹 *to let loose the great falcon.* Fighting quails, and catching rabbits and small birds with falcons, are favorite amusements with Chinese sportsmen, especially in the North. 白螞蟻 *A white ant*, that is, one that has always enjoyed itself eating and resting within doors, and has never been bronzed by toil and exposure, hence *a house-plant, a loafer.*

29 貪贓賣法 *Covet bribes and sell the law*, a book expression in common colloquial use.

30 This is the usual form of a promissory note. One per cent. per month is considered very low interest for small amounts. Two per cent. is very common, and is what all the pawn shops exact. Three and even five per cent. a month are often asked, and not unfrequently paid.

第一百三十二課

倘[1]若他不肯來、也要揪他來。○設[2]若年少時學好了、就如生成的一般。○倘[3]或你不信、可以問問他連襟。○倘[4]若世上沒有惡人、怎能顯出善人來呢。○如[5]若有人欺負你、不要和他爭競。○設[6]或是我做得來的、我還能推辭嗎。○假[7]如別人輕慢你的父母、你心裏必不歡喜。○要[8]緊要買好的、如或錢不彀、請你給我借墊上。○倘[9]或來提問的時候、小人難以回話。○他[10]若賣了更好、設若不賣、可以再加上五百錢。○設[11]如這事在你自己身上、再不能說得這麼輕省。○倘[12]若說他不好、他心裏就慚愧怨恨。○應[13]該看事作事、如若不然、怕你要吃大虧。○他[14]做惡不改、倘和他交往、必定壞了我們的名聲。○莊[15]稼是好莊稼、設若不下這

TRANSLATION.

1 If he is not willing to come, then bring him by force.

2 If anything be well learned in youth, it becomes like a second nature.

3 If you do not believe it, you may ask his brother-in-law.

4 If there were no bad men in the world, how would good men be recognized as such?

5 In case any one insults you, do not contend with him.

6 If it were something I was able to do, do you suppose I would decline?

7 If some one should sneer at *your* father and mother, you would assuredly not be pleased.

8 Be sure and buy good ones; in case the money is not sufficient, please advance it for me.

9 If at any time the case is transferred [to a higher court], your humble servant will find it hard to make answer.

10 If he accepts the offer, so much the better; if not, then you may add five hundred cash.

11 If this business concerned *you*, you would not, by any means, speak so lightly of it.

12 If you reprove him, he is ashamed and hates you.

13 You should be guided by circumstances, otherwise you may suffer serious loss.

14 He is a hopelessly bad man; if we associate with him, our reputation will certainly be ruined.

15 The crops were good, and if this

LESSON CXXXII.

CONDITIONAL PARTICLES.

The common and most frequently used conditional particle is 若 or 若是, given in Les. 14.

倘 If, supposing that,—generally joined with 若 or 或.

倘若 If, supposing, premising.

倘或 If, etc.;—not sensibly different from 倘若, but a little more bookish.

如 If;—generally joined with 若 or 或.

如若 If, in case.

如或 If, in case,—not sensibly different from 如若.

設若 If, supposing that, suppose, if it should happen.

設或 If, provided,—not sensibly different from 設若.

設如 If,—same as 設若.

設使 If, suppose. A book term.

假若 If, in case, suppose.

假如 Same as 假若.

假使 Same as 設使.

場冰雹雹子、能有十分年成。○若[16]不見他就罷、如或見了他、請他務必到這裏來。○你[17]看這些孩子累你嗎、假若死了一個、管保你又不樂意了。○假[18]如妻子死了、還可另娶一個、這兄弟若是歿了、那裏還討得一個。○先[19]探探他的口氣、倘若看出他不願意、就不必再說。○勸[20]老兄別認親定這個道兒、設或中不了老兄的打算、將來怎麼樣呢。○幸[21]虧你來得早、如若是畧遲些兒、就趕不上了。○倘[22]或人做出畜類事來、就叫作衣冠禽獸。○你[23]們說、念佛就可以消罪、假如你做下歹事、犯了罪、到衙門裏高聲叫幾千聲大老爺、他就饒

hailstorm had not come, there would have been a bountiful harvest.

16 If you do not see him, no matter; but if you do, tell him he must be sure to come here.

17 You think these children are a burden to you, do you? But if one of them should die, I'll guarantee you would be dissatisfied.

18 In case your wife dies, you can marry another; but if a brother dies, where can you get another?

19 First sound him; if you see that he is unwilling, you would better not say anything further.

20 I exhort you, my good brother, not to be too confident of this plan; if it should not turn out as you expect, what then?

21 It is fortunate you came early; if you had come a little later, you would have missed [the opportunity].

22 If a man's conduct is brutish, he is called a beast in clothes.

23 You say that repeating the name of Buddha will take away sin. Suppose when you do wrong and commit a crime, you should go to the yamên and call out, "Your Honor," in a loud voice several thousand times; would the magistrate therefore forgive you?

VOCABULARY.

倘 *T'ang*[3]. . . . . . . If, supposing:—see Sub.

生成 *Shêng*[1] *ch'êng*[2]. By birth, *natural*, original, ... congenital.

連襟 *Lien*[2] *chin*[1]. Brothers-in-law; i.e., men . . . . . . whose wives are sisters.

輕慢 *Ch'ing*[1] *man*[4]. To treat with disrespect, ... to disparage, *to sneer at.*

提問 *T'i*[2] *wên*[4]. To transfer to a higher court . . . . . . for trial.

回話 *Hwei*[2] *hwa*[4]. To make answer, *to respond;* a reply, a response.

輕省 *Ch'ing*[1] *shêng*[3]. Light, unburdened; light, ... unencumbered; *light,* flippant.

慚 *Ts'an*[2] . . . . . . *Ashamed,* mortified.

愧 *K'wei*[4]. . . . . . *Ashamed,* abashed; remorseful.

慚愧 *Ashamed,* mortified; conscience stricken.

雹 *Pao*[2]. . . . . . Hail.

冰雹 *Ping*[1] *pao*[2]. . . . . . Hail, hailstones.

歿 *Mo*[4]. . . . . . *To die;* dead, lost.

認定 *Jên*[4] *ting*[4]. To be sanguine, to be confident, certain.

認親 *Jên*[4] *ch'in*[1]. . . . . . The same.

畜 *Ch'u*[4]. To rear, to feed; cattle, domestic . . . . . . animals. Also *hsü*[4].

畜類 *Ch'u*[4] *lei*[4]. . . . . . Brutes, cattle.

冠 *Kwan*[4]. *To cap;* to excel; to declare of age; . . . . . . to be married. Also *kwan*[1].

念佛 *Nien*[4] *fo*[2]. To chant the name of Buddha:—Note 23.

消罪 *Hsiao*[1] *tswei*[4]. *To take away sin or guilt,* . . . . . . to wash away sin, to absolve.

犯罪 *Fan*[4] *tswei*[4]. *To commit sin,* to transgress, ... *to violate law.*

延 *Yien*[2]. To extend, to protract; to involve; . . . . . . slow, dilatory; to invite.

了你嗎。○[24]假設使你延捱着、竟不問你要也罷了、究竟正項錢糧、依舊是脫不了的、你們喜歡拖欠、是為什麽呢。○[25]不知是誰、將一個倒臥（路倒、路斃）的送在我地裏、老族長說、不如寂寂（悄悄）的把他掩埋了、不用稟官、我看總是不對、假若走漏風聲、被人挾告、這不是個活亂（漏）子嗎。○[26]聽說你們外國、所住的房子、走的道路、用的器具、做的工程、好像是別有天地、設若只隔三五千路、我定要去逛逛、見見世面。○[27]設如和少年發達的人談起功名來、就當說是捷足先登、若和那些久望發達的人談起功名來、就當說是大器晚成。

24 If, by delaying, it came to pass that you were not ultimately compelled to pay, it might do; but in the end your legal taxes you cannot escape: why then are you so anxious to defer payment?

25 I wonder who brought a [dead] outcast and laid him on my land. The head of the clan says it would be better to bury him quietly without reporting to the magistrate, but I do not think so. If [I do so, and] a report of it gets out, and I am accused by some one, it will be a serious affair for me.

26 I hear that in the foreign country, the houses you live in, the roads you travel on, the utensils you use and the work you carry on, all seem as if it were a different world. If it were only a few thousand *li*, I would certainly visit you and see the sights.

27 If you should be talking about degrees to one who got his degree young, you should say, "The nimble foot gets up first"; if talking of degrees to those who have long been hoping for a degree, you should say, "Great utensils are long in reaching completion."

捱 *Yai*². To lean upon; *to put off*, to procrastinate; to bear, to suffer.

延捱 To put off, to postpone, *to delay*.

錢糧 *Ch'ien*² *liang*². . . . . Taxes.

拖欠 *T'o*¹ *ch'ien*⁴. *To defer payment*, to evade paying a debt.

斃 *Pi*⁴. . . . . To fall down dead, to die.

倒臥 *Tao*³ *wo*⁴. To fall and die; one found dead on the street or at the roadside, the dead body of an outcast.

路倒 *Lu*⁴ *tao*³ . . . . The same.

路斃 *Lu*⁴ *pi*⁴. . . . . The same.

掩埋 *Yien*³ *mai*². To hide in the ground, *to bury*.

寂 *Chi*⁴. . . . . . . Silent, *quiet;* lonesome, solitary.

風聲 *Fêng*¹ *shêng*¹. . . . . .A rumor, *a report*.

挾 *Hsie*². To presume upon, to extort, to squeeze, *to take advantage of*. Also *chia*¹.

挾告 *Hsie*² *kao*⁴. *To accuse at law*, to bring suit against in order to injure.

工程 *Kung*¹ *ch'êng*². *Work*, public works; handiwork; performance.

發達 *Fa*¹ *ta*². To prosper, to get rich; *to get a degree*, to succeed in life.

捷 *Chie*²,⁴. To gain a victory, to succeed; *prompt, quick;* alert, clever.

NOTES.

2 This sentence is given as it stands in the Sacred Edict. As spoken, however, 年少時 is not smooth. Either 年 or 時 should be omitted, or, better still, expand the expression into 年少的時候.

9 This is the language of a jailor or an underling in a yamên to whose safe keeping a prisoner of some consequence has been committed. 小人 is here used as a demeaning term instead of 我. The use of 來 intimates the coming of a messenger or deputy with orders for the transfer of the case. 回話 *Make answer concerning the condition or whereabouts of the prisoner.*

第一百三十三課

若[1]不是你、就必是他。○若[2]是行好、自能得好。○倘[3]若天道不好、只得改日再去。○設[4]或心裏沒有、口裏自然說不出來。○他[5]請我、不能爲別的事情、不是借錢、就是作保。○倘[6]若船僱不妥、只好打旱路走就是了。○若[7]不得着你老、恰巧走到這裏、我們只好死在他手裏。○若[8]是重看妻子、就必不輕看岳父岳母。○倘[9]若柴糧米草太貴、只可少買、不可多存。○設[10]或京裏改變小

Translation.

1 If it is not you, then it must be he.
2 If a man does good, he will of course receive good.
3 If the weather is unfavorable, there is no way but to go at some other time.
4 If it is not in his mind, of course it cannot come out of his mouth.
5 He cannot want to see me for anything else than either to borrow money or to ask me to go his security.
6 If you fail to hire a boat, you will just have to go by land.
7 If you, good sir, had not happened along in the nick of time, we could not have escaped death at his hands.
8 If a man has a high regard for his wife, he will, of course, not despise his father-in-law and mother-in-law.
9 When grain and fuel are very dear, it is best to buy but little and not keep much on hand.
10 If a change is made to the small

11 在你自己身上 *On your own body;* i.e., *concerned you.* 再 here takes special emphasis; *by any means* is an approximate rendering.

18 The sentence is from the Sacred Edict and accords with orthodox Chinese teaching. The idea it expresses is at variance, however, with the general sentiment of mankind, and even the Chinese while they approve the sentiment theoretically, do not often feel so in fact. Fraternal affection is not remarkably prevalent amongst them. Notice in 這兄弟 the use of the definite for the indefinite.

22 衣冠禽獸 *A clothed and capped beast,*—a book phrase.

23 念佛 To repeat 阿彌陀佛, that is, Amitâbba Buddha. This is done as a meritorious prayer or penance, as the Romanists repeat *pater nosters.*

24 Originally taxes were paid in grain, and are still in some parts of China, hence the term 錢糧, which is now applied to taxes generally. 糧 is also used alone, even when the payment is in money. 正項 *The regular or legal amount;* 項 is used as a classifier.

25 Of the three terms used, 路倒 is the official one. It is no uncommon thing for wandering outcasts to die on the road, especially in the winter. Chinese are very much afraid of having such an outcast die on their land or premises, as it generally involves them in considerable expense at the yamên. When a man finds such a corpse on his land or premises, he will, if possible without discovery, move it on to the land of his neighbor, or his enemy. Bodies are sometimes moved several times in this way. 活亂子 *An urgent or insuperable difficulty or embarrassment.*

26 別有天地 is a book phrase equal to 另一個天地, *another heaven and earth,* that is, *a different world.*

27 捷足先登 and 大器晚成 are both complimentary sayings in the book style.

LESSON CXXXIII.

Correlatives with If.

若是…就必 If . . . of course, then must.
若是…自能 If . . . of course, necessarily.
若是…只好 If . . . no way but.
若是…自然 If . . . of course, naturally.
若是…怎能 If . . . how can.
若是…未必 If . . . not likely, not probable, uncertain whether.

若不…就必 If not . . . then must.
若不…只好 If not, unless . . . then only, just have.
若能…免得 If can . . . and so avoid or prevent.
若能…省得 If could . . . and so avoid or save.

銅錢、貨物自然必落價。○若[11]是他家裏殼過的、未必就肯上關東。○若[12]是已經出了票、自然要得和他去對審詞了。○你[13]別欺負他是軟弱、倘若他就發潑了、你和他未必就能勝過他。○他[14]們天天不是罵、就是吵、我實在聽殼了。○你[15]看他和你相好嗎、若是你不買奉他、我看他未必肯幫助你。○設[16]或大老爺、親自放他當經承、旁人自然沒有法兒治。○若[17]是他肯留歇宿更好、倘若不肯留歇、我們只可去投店下處、就是了。○他[18]惹的亂子不少、你若是不給他調調處說調調處說、只好看他栽跟頭。○那[19]個人渾身是油、不是個油匠、就是個廚子。○若[20]能

cash in the capital, the prices of goods will naturally fall.

11 If he had sufficient to live on at home, it is not likely he would go to Kwantung.

12 If the warrant is already issued, of course you will have to go and stand trial.

13 Don't you assume that you can impose upon him because he is weak; if he should summon all his strength, it is not at all certain that you could master him.

14 They are either scolding or fighting every day. I am tired of hearing it.

15 You think he is your friend, do you? But if you do not curry favor with him, I question very much whether he will help you.

16 In case your worship should yourself appoint him head clerk, of course no one could hinder it.

17 If he is willing to lodge us, so much the better; if he is unwilling to lodge us, we shall have to go to an inn: that's all.

18 He has stirred up a deal of trouble, and unless you mediate for him, we shall have to witness his disgrace.

19 That man is all covered with grease; if not a painter, he must be a cook.

倘若...只好 or 只可 If... it is best, just have to, the only way is.

倘若...未必 If... not certain, not likely.

設若...未必 If... not likely.

設或...自然 If, in case... of course, naturally.

設或...就必 If... certainly.

[若]不是...就是 If not... then—, or, either... or. In this combination 若 is understood before 不是.

倘若...只得 If... it will be necessary.

VOCABULARY.

天道 *T'ien¹ tao⁴*. Heavenly doctrine, divine truth; *the weather.*

作保 *Tsoă⁴ pao³*. To go security, to become surety for.

岳母 *Yoă⁴ mu³*. Wife's mother.

改變 *Kai³ pien⁴*. *To change*, to modify, to alter.

貨物 *Hwoă⁴ wu⁴*. *Goods*, merchandise, commodities.

審 *Shĕn³*. To investigate; to discriminate, to examine and judge.

對審 *Twei⁴ shĕn³*. To confront in court, *to stand trial.*

發潑 *Fa¹ p'oă¹*. To put forth all the strength, with all the might. (s.)

買奉 *Mai³ fĕng⁴*. *To curry favor with*, to put under obligation; to bribe.

經承 *Ching¹ ch'ĕng²*. The head clerk of an office.

留宿 *Liu² hsiu³*. To invite to stay over night, *to keep over night.*

留歇 *Liu² hsie¹*. The same. (s.)

把他告倒了、管保衆人沒有不願意的、免得他常常横行。○不21過眼前沒有好手比着、倘若見了博學名家、他未必能免出得俗。○幸22虧他老三不在家、設若他在家裏、未必能了的這樣快當。○這23部書卷數很多、設或不號出來、就必亂了頭緒。○若24能學的會畫拉搨副對子、會寫個人名字、也省得一動筆的事情、必得求人。○若25是我們待他好、他自然也待我們好、若是我們待他不好、他怎能待我們好呢。○雖26然老的沒留下什麼、也不要灰心、若是五更起、半夜眠、起五更、睡半夜、少吃減

20 If you can carry the suit against him and prevent his constantly acting so outrageously, I can assure you everybody will be pleased.

21 It was simply that there was no first class man present with whom to compare. If he were to meet men of acknowledged ability, it is not likely he would appear more than ordinary.

22 Fortunately his third brother was not at home: if he had been at home, it is not likely it would have been settled so quickly.

23 This book is in a great many volumes; if we do not number them, they will certainly become misarranged.

24 If he can simply learn enough to scratch off door inscriptions and write people's names, it will save the necessity of being under obligation to some one every time any writing is to be done.

25 If we treat him well, he will naturally treat us well; if we do not treat him well, how can he [be expected to] treat us well?

26 Although your father did not leave

投店 *T'ou² tien⁴*...... To go to or stop at an inn.

投下處 *T'ou² hsia⁴ ch'u⁴*. To find a stopping .... place, to secure lodgings.

跟頭 *Kên¹ t'ou²*. On one's head, a somersault.

栽跟頭 *Tsai¹ kên¹ t'ou²*. To fall heels over head; *to make a fool of oneself*, to make an utter failure.

渾身 *Hun² shên¹*.... The whole body, *all over*.

油匠 *Yu² chiang⁴*........... A painter.

横行 *Hêng⁴ hsing²*. To act unreasonably; *outrageous conduct*, perversity.

博學 *Poá² hsüe²*. *Extensive learning*, profound scholarship; learned.

名家 *Ming² chia¹*. *One distinguished in his profession*, a noted artist.

快當 *K'wai⁴ tang⁴*. *Quick*, prompt, expeditious.

頭緒 *T'ou² hsü⁴*. A beginning, a clue, *order*, method; an ally, a champion.

畫拉 *Hwa⁴ la¹*. *To scratch off*; to scribble, to scrawl.

搨 *T'a¹*. To take a rubbing of an inscription on stone; an impression, a facsimile. *To scrawl*, to scribble. (s.)

對子 *Twei⁴ tsï³*. A pair of correlated scrolls or inscriptions.

眠 *Mien²*....... To close the eyes, to sleep. (w.)

便家 *Pien⁴ chia¹*. A wealthy family; *the rich*, the well-to do, gentle folks.

膽氣 *Tan³ ch'i⁴*.......... Courage, bravery.

帥領 *Shwai⁴ ling³*. A leader, a general, a commander-in-chief.

鴉片 *Ya¹ p'ien⁴*........... Opium.

罌 *Ying¹*.... A small jar with ears; a vase. (w.)

粟 *Su⁴*....... Rice in the hull, paddy.

罌粟 The poppy plant.

罌粟花 *Ying¹ su⁴ hwa¹*.......... The poppy.

氏 *Shï⁴*...... Family, clan; female; a surname.

秋審 *Ch'iu¹ shên³*. The autumnal assizes:—Note 30.

翻供 *Fan¹ kung¹*. To retract testimony previously given, to recant

監斃 *Chien¹ pi⁴*.... To die in prison:—Note 30.

用、自然能巴結到好處。○現27今的便家、倘若過窮了、未必不坑人、未必不騙人、未必能赶上偺弟兄們、還有點子窮志氣。○古28語說、膽小不得將軍作、若是沒有膽氣、怎能爲帥領呢。○中29國窮、就是窮在鴉片烟上、若能把種罌粟花的、與吃鴉片烟的、一概禁除掉、自然一年富似一年。○王30劉氏打了兩回秋審、翻了兩回口供、倘若這一回再翻了供、回來只得把他監斃了。

you anything, you should not lose heart, for if you rise early and retire late and economize in everything, your circumstances will necessarily improve.

27 If those who are now wealthy were poor, it is not certain that they would not defraud and cheat others. I question whether they would be as good as we who, though poor, still have some purpose to do right.

28 The old saying is, "A man of little courage will never be a general." If courage is wanting, how can one become a great leader?

29 The poverty of China is simply due to opium. If we could get rid of all who plant the poppy and all who eat opium, we should naturally grow richer year by year.

30 Mrs. Wang of the Liu family has been twice to the autumnal assizes, and has twice retracted her testimony; if she retracts this time, the only way will be to procure her death in prison.

NOTES.

2 自能 is an abbreviation for 自然能.

6 In many places 把 or 跟 or 從 would be used instead of 打.

7 着 is here used in a sense fairly equivalent to *happened*. When so used it is in many places read tsoă (not choă). It is only so used after 若, or other equivalent word.

10 Since the time of Hsien Fĕng a species of large cash have been used in Peking. They were intended to pass for ten ordinary cash, and accordingly have 當十 stamped on them. They are not, however, equal in weight to ten ordinary cash, and as soon as official pressure was relaxed, they ceased to pass at their nominal value, and were estimated at their real value. It is not the real, but the nominal price, that would change with the abolition of these large cash.

21 見 takes the sense of *to meet, to come into the presence of.* 免得俗, *to avoid being ordinary,* 出得俗, *to escape being ordinary.*

26 賑 is a book word, not ordinarily used in Mandarin. The Sacred Edict from which this sentence is taken, is commonly accounted Mandarin, but it is a rare thing to find in it a full sentence without some smack of *Wên-li.*

30 王劉氏 The common way of designating a woman when there is occasion to write her name, is to add to her husband's family name that of her own, followed by the character 氏. On cards, or where it is desired to show respect, a 門 is added, as 王門劉氏. In all important criminal convictions, especially in those involving a death penalty, it is required that the prisoner, together with a copy of the testimony, be sent up to the Provincial Judge (按察司) for examination and confirmation of the sentence. If the prisoner retracts his testimony and confession, the case is remanded for a new trial. The Provincial Judge holds his court annually in the autumn, hence the term 秋審. In embarrassing cases, or where corrupting influences are at work against a prisoner, it is not an uncommon thing for an accused person to be "done" to death in prison, by torture, starvation, cold, etc. This is spoken of as 監斃. A report is first sent up that the prisoner is ill, and afterwards another report stating that he has died of disease, and thus the case drops.

LESSON CXXXIV.

OPTATIVE FORMS.

願 To wish,—may, would that, I hope.

但願 May, would that, oh that, I trust.

The Chinese language has no means of expressing a strong desire so admirably as the English "Oh that." 但願 approximates it more nearly than any other term.

巴不得 To wish, to long, anxious that, would that.

第一百三十四課

願[1]你們一路平安。○但[2]願老爺的官爵高升。○當[3]夜武松巴不得到天明。○若[4]由得自己的性兒、恨不能一步到家。○我[5]巴不得和你們吃杯酒、親近親近。○張[6]順聽了這話、恨不得一口吞了這婆娘。○人[7]都巴不得(望不能)(望不到)養個好孩子、然而却不能個個都好。○我[8]實在想你、恨不能現在就面對面纔好。○但[9]願你們都體恤我、多方為我原諒一點。○他[10]嘴裏雖然說是不喜歡、心裏却是巴不能殼(望不能)的。○你[11]擠鼓(夾鼓)(眨眨)眼(眼)(眼睛)、不讓他說、我却恨不得他說出來。○我[12]如今恨不能快死、却就是死不掉了。○他[13]巴不得討你們大家的喜歡、但一人怎能稱服百人心呢。○人[14]到求救無門的時候、恨不能

TRANSLATION.

1 I wish you a safe journey.
2 I hope, sir, that you may meet with great preferment in office.
3 That night Wu Shung longed for the coming of the morning.
4 If he could have had his own will, he would fain have been home at one bound.
5 Would that I could take a cup of wine with you and enjoy your good fellowship.
6 When Chang Shun heard these words, he would fain have swallowed the woman at one gulp.
7 Every man is anxious to rear a good son, but then, all cannot be good.
8 I long very much to see you. Would that even now we could see each other face to face!
9 I trust you will all sympathize with me, and in every way make due allowance for me.
10 Although he affirms in words that he does not wish it, yet in his heart he longs for it.
11 You wink at him that he must not tell, whereas I only wish he would speak it out.
12 I long for a speedy death, but die I cannot.
13 He is anxious to please you all, but how can one man meet the wishes of a hundred?
14 When a man finds that he is unable

巴不能 or **巴不能殼** To long for, to wish, would that.

恨不得 To hate that one cannot,—to long for, to wish, would that, would like to, anxious to.

恨不能 The same.

望 I hope, I trust.

望不能 To be anxious, to long for. (c.) In Nanking 望不能 is also used in the sense of 難道.

望不到 To be anxious, to long for. (s.)

VOCABULARY.

爵 *Chüe*², *chiao*². A wine cup; a degree of nobility; *rank*, station.

官爵 *Kwan*¹ *chüe*². Official rank, office.

升 *Shêng*¹. A measure of ten 合, varying in different places from a pint to a gallon; to rise, to ascend; *to advance in office.*

親近 *Ch'in*¹ *chin*⁴. To draw near to, *to have fellowhsip with*, to show affection for, to caress.

婆娘 *P'oa*² *niang*². A married woman, a woman.

體恤 *T'i*³ *hsü*⁴. To feel for, *to sympathize with*, to enter into the feelings of.

多方 *Toa*¹ *fang*¹. *In every way*, by all means; taking pains.

夾 *Chia*¹·⁴. To carry under the arm, to squeeze, *to press between*, to insert between.

有人替他想個法子。○你[15]但說那等願你飽暖的話、送這些空頭人情、有甚麼滋味呢。○我[16]巴不能彀說他們好、但是照實話講、說不出好來。○就[17]怕你不肯學、既然要學、巴不能教你成人呢。○爲[18]他們爭吵的事、我巴不得給他們說熨貼了再走。○但[19]願老天爺、今年開恩、使得風調雨順、沒有蟲災、我們就可以飽食暖衣、過太平日子了。○上[20]去的時候、望老兄給我說幾句好話。○我[21]巴不得和你搭件兒去、就是這兩天的公事很忙、不得空呢。○望[22]他老人家多活幾年、看我們過過日子、我們年輕的人、到底有個倚靠。○我[23]的兒子同喜啊、我恨不得你此時在家、跟你說幾句話、把你母親託付你。○

to save himself, he is more than willing for some one else to find a plan for him.

15 What point is there in merely saying, "I wish you were full and warm," making this empty pretence of charity?

16 I only wish I could speak well of them, but I cannot do so truthfully.

17 I was only afraid you were not willing to learn; seeing, however, that you desire to learn, I shall be but too glad to give you the opportunity to make a man of yourself.

18 With reference to their quarrel, I very much wish I could bring about a settlement before I go.

19 Would that this year the Heavenly Sire would show favor, give wind and rain in season and not send a scourge of insects; then we should have plenty to eat and wear and live in peace.

20 When you go in, I hope you will speak a good word for me.

21 I should like very much to go in company with you, but the fact is my business is very pressing these few days, so that I cannot spare the time.

22 I hope the old gentleman will live a good number of years to advise us in our plans, that we young folks may have some one to depend upon.

23 My son, T'ung Hsi, I would that you were now at home that I might

擠鼓 *Chi*³ *ku*³. . . . . To wink. (N.)

夾鼓 *Chia*¹ *ku*³. . . . . To wink.

求救 *Ch'iu*² *chiu*⁴. *To seek an escape;* to pray . . . . for salvation.

稱 *Ch'ên*⁴. Suitable, *to suit;* corresponding, becoming. See *ch'êng*⁴ *and ch'êng*¹.

飽暖 *Pao*³ *nwan*³. Full and warm, fed and . . . . clothed.

開恩 *K'ai*¹ *ên*¹. To be gracious or merciful, *to show favor;* to grant a prayer.

災 *Tsai*¹. A calamity sent from heaven, divine . . . . . judgments, *a scourge,* a misfortune.

搭伴 *Ta*¹ *pan*⁴. To become companions, *to go . . . . in company with.*

降臨 *Chiang*⁴ *lin*². To descend from heaven, to . . . . come from above.

旨意 *Chi*³ *i*⁴. *The will or purpose of one in . . . . authority;* an edict.

護己 *Hu*⁴ *chi*³. Partial to oneself; *to look out . . . . for number one;* ungenerous.

蝙蝠 *Piên*¹ *fu*². . . . . The bat.

嘁 *Ch'i*¹. . . . . . The sound of indistinct talking.

嘁嘁喳喳 *Ch'i*¹ *ch'a*¹. *Chattering,* garrulous; . . . . to prattle, to jabber.

聒 *Kwoă*¹,⁴. To stun, to make the ears ring; . . . . clamor. See *kwa*¹,⁴.

站口 *Chan*⁴ *k'ou*³. A stopping place, a lodging . . . . place, a station.

果兒 *Kwoă*³ *êr*². Eggs,—a Pekingese term, not . . . . often used without the addition of 白; viz., 白果兒.

24 我們在天上的父、願人都尊你的名爲聖、願你的國降臨、願你的旨意行在地上、如同行在天上。○25 世上的人、護己的多、有了好處、都說是自己的、有了不好處、恨不能推得乾乾淨淨的。○26 他們兩個、都是屬蝙蝠的、黑夜裏有精神、常常到三四更天、還嘁嘁喳喳的說話、吵的旁人也睡不着、所以我巴不能他們快搬出去。○27 我走的饑又饑、渴又渴、緊慢也到不了個站口、望老先生賜點方便、家去給我烙兩張餅、打臥幾個雞果兒、末了給你錢由你收、隨你要多少錢好不好、答好啊、那裏不是交朋友呢。

speak with you and commit your mother to your care.

24 Our Father which art in heaven; Hallowed be thy name. Thy kingdom come. Thy will be done on earth as it is in heaven.

25 Most people in the world look out for number one. When anything praiseworthy occurs, they take the credit of it; when anything blameworthy happens, they are anxious to disclaim it entirely.

26 They two are like bats, lively after dark. They generally keep chattering until the third or fourth watch of the night, disturbing other people so that they cannot sleep; for this reason I wish they would soon move out.

27 I have been traveling until I am exceedingly hungry and thirsty, and I am unable to reach a stopping place. Will you kindly accommodate me, sir, by baking a couple of cakes and poaching a few eggs for me, and I will pay you your price. *Ans.* All right. It is always worth while to make a friend.

Notes.

9 The use of both 多方 and 一點 is somewhat redundant.

12 就是死不了 Or, *somehow I cannot die.*

14 求救無門 *To seek for escape, but find no opening,*—a book expression in common use.

15 空頭人情 *Empty-headed sympathy,—a sham favor, empty talk instead of substantial aid.*

16 Note how 講 is substituted for 說, because immediately followed by another 說.

18 爲 is here used, as it frequently is, in the general sense of, *as to, with reference to.*

19 風調雨順 *Winds gentle and rains seasonable,*—a book phrase often quoted. 飽食暖衣 *Food plenty, clothing warm,*—another book phrase.

22 他 and 老人家 are in apposition.

26 吵 expresses the action of those who make the disturbance, and 聒 the effect on the ears of those who are disturbed.

27 饑又饑渴又渴 Repetition with 又 is an intensive form of the book language, sometimes introduced in speaking, especially by educated men. 緊慢 here means, *in the exigency, for the time being,* which is a departure from its primary and ordinary meaning: 給你錢由你收 is a phrase based on the custom of handing the string of cash to the person to take off as many as he chooses. 給你錢留 is a shorter phrase with the same meaning.

LESSON CXXXV.

Exceptive Phrases.

非 Unless, save, without.
非離 Unless, without, no way but.
除非 Unless, except, aside from.
除了 Except, unless, exclusive of, none but.
離了 Without, aside from, except, save.
錯過 Aside from, except, without, but for.

第一百三十五課

常[1]走路、非有錢褡褡褳子不行。○除[2]了吃飯的時候、他一天到
晚常不在家。○錯[3]過周金山。別人沒有這樣的手段。○非[4]
罰他四十吊錢、我斷不能肯依他。○除[5]非你不在我門裏、你
既然在我門裏、就要得聽我的指派使。○錯[6]過是乾爹你來、任
誰也討使不了這個臉去。○非[7]劉大兄、誰能有此高見。○除[8]
非他常在家裏藏來着、汞不叫我看見、一看見可就跑不掉了
他。○要[9]開鎖、必得找合式的鑰匙、我看這事、除非了離你去、是
辦不成的。○[10]割配疥藥、雖有許多方法、但是非有硫磺不效。
○這[11]是一本好書、就是太深奧、非離離了先生講、不能明白。○
錯[12]過救主耶穌、誰都沒有功勞、贖人的罪。○他[13]要強霸霸佔我

TRANSLATION.

1 When you are constantly traveling, you cannot get on without a wallet.
2 The whole day long he is never at home except at meal times.
3 No one except Chou Chin Shan has such cleverness as this.
4 Unless he is mulcted to the amount of forty thousand cash, I can by no means consent.
5 [You cannot disobey my orders] unless you leave my family. While you are in my family, you must obey.
6 I would not have yielded the point to any other than to you, my adopted father, no matter who might have come.
7 Who save you, Brother Liu, would have such discernment?
8 [He cannot escape] unless he always hides and never lets me see him. If once I get my eyes on him, he will not get away.
9 If you want to open a lock, you must find the right key. As I see this business, unless you go, it cannot be accomplished.
10 Although there are many prescriptions for compounding itch medicine, yet without sulphur none is effective.
11 This is a good book, only it is too profound. Without a teacher to explain it, it is unintelligible.
12 Aside from Jesus the Saviour, no one has the merit necessary to atone for the sins of men.

VOCABULARY.

褡 *Ta*¹. . . . . . . A bag, a wallet.

褳 *Lien*². . . . . . *A pouch*, a waist-bag.

褡褳 *A wallet*, a pouch, a purse; drilling.

錢褡子 *Ch'ien*² *ta*¹ *tsï*³. A purse, a wallet:—Note 1.

指使 *Chï*³ *shï*³. *To order*, to direct, to instruct; to point out.

指派 *Chï*³ *p'ai*⁴. *To order*, to direct; to prescribe.

乾爹 *Kan*¹ *tie*¹. An adopted father:—Les. 72. Note 3.

來 *P'a*¹. To hide oneself, to lie low, to keep out of sight,—a colloquial local character.

高見 *Kao*¹ *chien*⁴. Good judgment, penetration, *discernment*:—Note 7.

硫磺 *Liu*² *hwang*². . . . . . . Brimstone, sulphur.

奧 *Ao*⁴. The southwest corner; mysterious, *obscure*, deep.

深奧 *Shên*¹ *ao*⁴. . . . . Difficult, *profound*.

霸 *Pa*⁴. . . . . . To rule by force, to encroach on.

霸佔 *Pa*⁴ *chan*⁴. *To take by force*, to usurp; to infringe, to trench upon.

强霸 *Ch'iang*² *pa*⁴. *To take by force*, to usurp, to seize illegally.

結果 *Chie*¹ *kwoa*³. To bear fruit, to yield; to finish, *to put an end to*, to kill.

五服 *Wu*³ *fu*². The five grades of mourning dress; ancestry:—Note 15.

訟 *Sung*⁴. . . . . Litigation; *a prosecution*.

的女兒、除非把我結果頭殺了、但凡有我這口氣、他就不用打算。○這[14]個孩子在白日天裏、誰愛抱就抱、但是一黑了天、天一晚了離了他嫣不行。○他[15]婆家並沒有親房近支、在五服的、就是還有柳芳林、錯過他出名、事還不能成喇。○他[16]兩個的官司、並不是不好說和、是中間有壞人唆訟、如今要了事、除非把那個壞人弄出去。○你[17]昨天冒犯你爺爺、到如今他還怒氣不息、也不吃飯、我看非你去磕頭賠禮、他是不能消氣的。○這[18]裏的肉架案子、從去年都齊了行喇、無論到那一家、錯過二百錢一斤、是不行的。○膠[19]和鰾都粘不住、非螺絲釘不行。○離[20]了莊稼漢上糧、上銀子、你們把什麽做兵

13 If he expects to take my daughter by force, [he cannot do it] except by first making an end of me. While I have breath in my body, he need not think of it.

14 In the day time, whoever pleases may take up the child; but as soon as night comes, no one will do save his mother.

15 She has no near relative of her husband's family. Of those for whom she would wear mourning, there is only Liu Fang Lin, and without his name the business cannot be settled.

16 The lawsuit between the two would not be difficult to compromise but that there is an evil-minded man stirring them up. There is no way, at present, to settle the matter unless that obnoxious man is driven out.

17 You offended your grandfather yesterday, so that his anger has not yet abated and he refuses to eat. In my opinion his anger will not be appeased unless you go and apologize and do him reverence.

18 Since last year, all the meat dealers of this place have combined to adopt a uniform price. No matter to which one you go, there is no buying for less than two hundred cash per catty.

19 Neither common glue nor fish glue will hold it; nothing but screws will serve the purpose.

唆訟 *Soā*[1] *sung*[4]. . . . . . . To incite to litigation.
怒氣 *Nu*[4] *ch'i*[4]. . . . . *Anger*, wrath, passion.
磕頭 *K'ê*[1] *t'ou*[2]. To knock the head on the . . . . ground as an act of worship or of ceremony, to kotow.
消氣 *Hsiao*[1] *ch'i*[4]. To abate one's anger, *to* . . . . *become reconciled.*
肉架子 *Jou*[4] *chia*[4] *tsï*[3]. *A butcher's stand*, a . . . . meat shop.
肉案子 *Jou*[4] *an*[4] *tsï*[3]. . . . . The same.
鰾 *Piao*[4]. . . . . *Fish glue*, gelatine.
螺絲釘 *Loā*[2] *sï*[1] *ting*[1]. *A wood screw;* a . . . . machine screw.
蠶 *Ts'an*[2]. . . . . The silkworm.
護衛 *Hu*[4] *wei*[4]. . . . . *To protect*, to defend.
冬至 *Tung*[1] *chï*[4]. . . . . The winter solstice.
夏至 *Hsia*[4] *chï*[4]. . . . . The summer solstice.
天文家 *T'ien*[1] *wên*[2] *chia*[1]. . . . . . Astronomers.

NOTES.

1 A 錢褡子 is a closed bag with a slit in the middle of the side, and serves as purse and hand-bag combined. It is usually carried over the shoulder, or if riding, across the saddle.

5 The structure of this sentence is highly idiomatic. The clause in brackets has to be supplied in order to exhibit the full idea in English. A free translation would be, *While you are in my family, you must obey my orders.* See also 8th and 13th sentences.

6 乾爹 and 你 are in apposition, the latter being added for emphasis as well as to express endearment and respect. 使不了這個臉去 *Cannot make use of this face*, that is to say, in the matter in hand I would not have yielded to the intercession of any other. The face referred to is that of the adopted father, and implies that the concession was made in order to avoid putting him to the blush for having failed in his suit.

餉、離了養蠶織布的、你們把什麼穿在身上呢、你們想到此處、還不該出力護衛他們嗎。○ [21]平常人只知日頭往南、行到最低的那一點兒上、就爲冬至、往北行到最高的那一點兒上、就爲夏至、但要算計、甚麼時候最高、甚麼時候最低、除了天文家、旁人都不會算。

20 Aside from taxes in grain and money paid by the farmers, what is there to supply your wages? Aside from those who raise silk worms and weave cloth, who is there to furnish you the clothes you wear? When you think of this, should you not strive to protect them?

21 Ordinary people simply know that when the sun has moved southward until it has reached its lowest point, that is the winter solstice; and when it has moved northward to its highest point, that is the summer solstice; but as for computing when it is at the highest and when at the lowest point, none but astronomers are able to do this.

7 高見 The 見 is put for 見識, and 高 is descriptive, including also a compliment to the person addressed.

8 跑不了他 Note the transposition by which the proper subject of the verb is made to come after it, which is a colloquial rather than a book form.

10 In *Wên-li* 硫 is generally used for sulphur, though 磺 is occasionally used. In Mandarin the two words are always joined.

13 口 and 氣 do not here combine into a phrase as they generally do. 氣 is accented and 口 may be regarded as a classifier.

15 親房近支 *Own house and near branch;* that is, *a near relative.* The expression is taken from books. 五服 are five kinds of mourning apparel, worn for different lengths of time by persons of different degrees of consanguinity. Persons whose ancestors of the fifth generation unite in one belong to the 五服, and are supposed to wear a certain kind of mourning for a certain time. Beyond this degree of consanguinity, the relationship is ignored.

19 和 is properly conjunctive, but here, being followed by 都 with a negative, it becomes *disjunctive.*

20 In most parts of the country 把 would be replaced by 拿 or 將.

21 天文家 The family (i.e., class) who make astronomy a study or profession. This use of 家 is both *Wên-li* and Mandarin

LESSON CXXXVI.

PHRASES OF ASSURANCE.

果 Really, in very deed,—not often used alone.

果然 Really, in fact, actually, indeed; sure enough.

果不然 The same. The insertion of this negative forms a curious solecism, as it practically makes no difference in the meaning. It may perhaps be explained by considering the phrase as an interrogative affirmative.

果眞 Really, in reality, sure enough, absolutely, actually.

眞果 The same,—but less widely used.

眞個 The same as 眞果 and probably a corruption of it. (N.)

當眞 Really, in very deed, in fact, for a fact, in earnest.

如果 If indeed, if in truth, in case.

VOCABULARY.

祝 *Chu*⁴. To pray for blessings, to bless (by praying for); to invoke.

河南 *Hê*² *nan*². The province of Honan.

震壓 *Chên*⁴ *ya*⁴. To intimidate, to overawe, *to frighten.*

半信半疑 *Pan*⁴ *hsin*⁴ *pan*⁴ *i*². Uncertain, *doubtful;* hesitating, halting between two opinions.

打死 *Ta*³ *si*³. To kill by blows, to kill:— Les. 183.

第一百三十六課

人[1]若果然不知道孝順、反不如禽獸了。○祝[2]雲亭眞果是這麽說的嗎、答眞果眞的、我不撒謊。○你[3]說你是往河南去、如果往河南去、從上路就該岔道。○我[4]從早就怕他不符前言、果眞他照這條路來了。○起[5]初我還半信半疑的、後來在朋友跟前打聽、果然是眞的。○我[6]不過是連打帶嚇嚇呼、震壓震壓他、還能當眞打死他嗎。○他[7]若果然能旣往不咎、那又成了聖人喇。○你[8]們如果願意在這裏住幾天、所需用的東西、這裏可以供給。○行[9]不二三里、見那石匣之中、果有一猴、露着頭、伸着手。○你[10]眞個要入一個股分嗎、或者是說着玩(作戲)呢、答君子口裏無戲言、那有說着玩(作戲)的

TRANSLATION.

1 If a man really does not recognize his filial obligations, he is beneath the beasts.

2 Did Chu Yün T'ing really say this? *Ans.* He really did. I am telling no lie.

3 You say you are going to Honan. If indeed you are going to Honan, you should have turned off this road at the last fork.

4 I have feared for some time that he would violate his promise; and, sure enough, this is just what he has done.

5 At first I only half believed it; afterwards I inquired of some friends and found that it was really true.

6 I was only beating and threatening him in order to frighten him. Do you suppose I would really kill him?

7 If he is indeed able to forgive and forget the past, then he must be accounted a sage.

8 In case you are really willing to stay here a few days, we can provide whatever you require.

9 We had not gone over two or three *li*, when, sure enough, I saw a monkey putting out his head and hands from within that stone box.

10 Do you in reality wish to take a share, or are you only in sport? *Ans.* "The superior man is not given to joking;" there is no sport about it.

咎 *Chiu*[1,4]. . . . A fault, an error; *to criminate.* (w.)

需用 *Hsü*[1] *yung*[4]. Required for use, necessary, ... *requisite.*

供 *Kung*[4]. To place before, to offer; to support, ... *to supply;* offerings. See *kung*[1].

股分 *Ku*[3] *fên*[4]. A share in a business or . . . . company.

戲言 *Hsi*[4] *yien*[2]. *Words spoken in sport,* a jest, ... humor, pleasantry.

打破 *Ta*[3] *p'oa*[4]. To break in pieces, to smash; . . . . *to break up,* to destroy.

公平 *Kung*[1] *p'ing*[2]. . . . . . *Just,* right, equitable.

定貨賬 *Ting*[4] *hwoa*[4] *chang*[4]. An order for goods, ... an order book.

脣舌 *Ch'un*[2] *shê*[2]. . . . . Talk, words, speech.

嘴舌 *Tswei*[3] *shê*[2]. . . . . The same.

磨嘴舌 *Moa*[3] *tswei*[3] *shê*[2]. To talk, to bandy . . . . words, to expatiate; to dispute, *to haggle.*

費脣舌 *Fei*[4] *ch'un*[2] *shê*[2]. . . . . The same.

覆 *Fu*[2]. Back and forth, to and fro; to overthrow, ... to upset; *to reply.*

回覆 *Hwei*[2] *fu*[2]. . . . . To answer, *to reply.*

瞎說 *Hsia*[1] *shwoa*[1]. To talk at random, *to talk* . . . . *nonsense;* to exaggerate, to tell lies.

呢。○他[11]們兩下做親、門當戶對、若果眞是你給他打破了、
這個天理、可就傷的大喇。○自[12]己果然和氣待人、那不和
氣的、也就跟着你學和氣了、果然公平處事、那不公平的、
也就跟着你學公平了。○豆[13]餅正在要跌落價的時候、益順
先定規買我二百片塊、後來又說、就是三百片塊也可以、我就
下上了三百片塊的定貨賬、如今價錢果然跌落了、他就和我磨賫
嘴脣舌說、他只定規二百片塊、我回覆他說、你爲什麼說三百
片塊也可以呢、你還能一口兩舌嗎。○昨[14]天孩子跑來家說、
外頭來了一個鬼子、我說你別瞎說罷、他就急急的說、眞
果個的、後來我出去一看、果不然是個外國人、下來勸善、叫

11 It is in every way appropriate for these two to marry. If you have really broken up the match, you have grievously violated the will of heaven.

12 If you yourself are really pacific in your treatment of others, those who are not peaceably inclined will learn from you to be peaceable. If you yourself are really just in your dealings, those who are unjust will learn from you to be just.

13 Just when the price of beancake was on the point of falling, I Shun decided to buy of me two hundred cakes, but afterwards added the words, "or three hundred if you like;" upon which I put him down for three hundred cakes. Now that the price has actually fallen, he haggles with me, saying he only bargained for two hundred. I replied, "Why then did you say 'three hundred if you like'? Can you go back on your word?"

14 Yesterday one of the children came running home saying, "A [foreign] devil has come." I replied, "Stop your foolish talk," but he answered excitedly, "It's really so." When I went out, I saw at once that it really was so—that a foreigner had come exhorting men to be good and to reverence Heaven and Earth and father and mother. Truly he was a laughable object.

可笑 *K'ê*³ *hsiao*⁴. . . . . . . *Laughable*, ridiculous.
硇 *Hsin*⁴. . . . . Arsenic :—Note 15.
砒 *P'i*¹. . . . . . . An ore of arsenic ; arsenic.
砒霜 *P'i*¹. *shwang*¹. White arsenic, arsenious . . . . acid.
滷 *Lu*³. . . . Crude soda ; *pickle*, brine :—Note 15.
服毒 *Fu*² *tu*². . . . . To take poison.
褪 *T'un*⁴. . . . . . . To disrobe ; to prune, *to trim.*
招風 *Chao*¹ *fêng*¹. . . . . To catch the wind.
攲 *Ch'ie*¹. . . . . Leaning, toppling over.

NOTES.

3 道 is much used in Mandarin books at the beginning of a clause or sentence, meaning *he said, or so and so said.*

4 不符前言 *Not to accord with previous words, to break one's word.*

7 旣往不咎 *Not resenting what is already past, not cherishing enmity for past offences.* 那又成了聖人喇 *That would be to become a sage.* One of the highest qualities of the so-called sage is that firm and self-contained equipoise of mind that is not disturbed by the wrongs endured from others.

11 做親 *To become kindred ; that is, to make a marriage alliance.* 門當戶對 *Gate suitable and door agreeing ;* that is, the wealth and social standing of the families are similar. 天理 expresses the highest idea the Chinese have of right. 傷天理 is to violate the highest law, and expresses the idea of wrong doing more forcibly than any other term in the language. 這個 limits 天理 in this particular case to the principle that marriage between suitable persons is an ordinance of heaven, to defeat which is a great wrong.

12 處事 *To transact affairs, to act,*—a *Wên-li* expression.

人敬天敬地敬父母、實在叫人可笑。○他15成天家、說是要吃砒䃀霜、要喝滷水、都看他是嚇呼人、那想到他當眞就服毒死了呢。○人16做好夢不靈、做壞夢準成、去年五月間、我做了一夢、夢見一羣牲口、向我亂踢亂咬的、一直把我咬醒了、自己心裏猜算、怕要有事、以後果不然叫那些勇好一頓打、幾乎要了命。○老17人的話、到底該聽、我的爺爺、從多日就告訴我、把房子後頭那棵樹褪一褪、免得招風、我却沒拿着當事、誰想這場大風、眞果個把樹颳歪敧了、把房子也壓壞了。

15 She was constantly threatening that she would eat arsenic or drink brine, but all supposed she was merely trying to frighten us. Who would have thought that she would really take poison and kill herself.

16 When one has a good dream, nothing comes of it, but a bad dream never fails. Last year in the fifth month I had a dream; I dreamed that a drove of animals came wildly kicking and biting at me, insomuch that I woke up. I turned the matter over in my mind and was afraid something would happen. Afterwards, sure enough, those soldiers gave me such a beating as came very near finishing me.

17 After all, the advice of old people should be heeded. My grandfather has been telling me for ever so long to trim that tree behind the house and prevent its catching the wind, but I paid no attention to the matter, when, sure enough, this high wind blew the tree over on the house and damaged it.

13 一口两舌 *Two tongues in one mouth; that is, one mouth speaking two things, going back on one's word.*

14 鬼子 or, as often, 洋鬼子, is not only called out at foreigners for the purpose of dishonoring and stigmatizing them, but is the term by which the people in common conversation universally designate foreigners. Its use is comparatively recent, and probably sprang originally from the idea of grotesqueness suggested to the Chinese mind by the hair, beard, and dress of foreigners.

15 服毒 *To submit to* [the taking of] *poison.* 服 is used for 吃, because the taking of the poison requires a constraint of the natural taste and feelings. 䃀 is a term used in foreign medical books. The Chinese write 信 alone. The name more recently adopted in chemistry and medicine for arsenic is 砒. 滷水 is the pickle used in making bean-curd. It is made of crude salt and contains more or less caustic soda, and is very poisonous.

LESSON CXXXVII.

General Intensives.

The more common words of this class were given in Lesson 15.

極 Very, extremely, exceedingly, to the last degree.

極其 Extremely, exceedingly, entirely, etc. 其 is added for euphony.

到極處 To the last degree, to the utmost, in the extreme.

甚 Very, to a high degree, exceedingly, specially.

儘 The extreme, very exactly, perfectly.

儘之 Continuously, indefinitely, so long.

着實 Decidedly, truly, emphatically; reliable, matter of fact.

十分 Entirely, perfectly, in the highest degree.

深 Deeply, thoroughly, fully.

得利害 Very severe, extremely, immoderately, extravagantly.

的利害 The same,—的 being evidently a corruption of 得.

數着 The best, the worst, etc.

到所以然 (To the reason why), consummate, with a vengeance, to the uttermost.

到所以然處 The same.

到家 *To the stopping place,* to the last degree, to the uttermost.

第一百三十七課

我[1]們在那裏極方便。○李[2]長松病得不甚重。○他[3]這樣强佔人家田產、可惡極了。○我[4]看他的心、偏的利害。○這[5]樣脾氣、着實不好。○有[6]話快說、別儘之就誤工夫。○河[7]邊有各種鮮花、十分好看。○他[8]說了無數的壞歪話、甚不中聽。○父[9]子兩個、樂極生悲、不能說出話來。○那[10]地方的風俗、眞是淫亂極了。○他[11]的三個姑娘、數着那個小的人物好。○柳[12]瑞廷在那裏住呢、答在前街上、儘東頭住。○我[13]看這樣辦法、極其妥當。○那[14]兩個人、心中甚拘執泥、不隨夥兒。○山[15]上有極大極密的樹林、甚是茂盛。○你[16]們兵民、都要着實小心謹愼。○他[17]縣考在儘末了、府考又在儘末了嗎。○這[18]時候不大疼了、就是纔搽

TRANSLATION.

1 We are very conveniently situated there.
2 Li Ch'ang Sung is not very sick.
3 His taking the land by force in this way, is detestable to the last degree.
4 In my opinion his mind is extremely biased.
5 This kind of a disposition is decidedly [bad.
6 If you have anything to say, say it quickly, and don't waste time indefinitely.
7 On the banks of the river were all kinds of fresh flowers which were extremely beautiful.
8 He said a great many unreasonable (offensive) things, very unpleasant to hear.
9 The extreme joy of father and son produced such emotion that they were unable to speak.
10 The customs of the place were indeed licentious in the extreme.
11 Of his three daughters, the physique of that youngest one is the best.
12 Where does Liu Jwei T'ing live? *Ans.* He lives on the front street at the extreme eastern end.
13 I consider this plan of action entirely [satisfactory.
14 Those two men are exceedingly obstinate and contrary.
15 On the mountain was an exceedingly large and dense forest which was very luxuriant.
16 You soldiers and people should all be very cautious and circumspect.
17 In the Hsien examination he was the very last [on the list]; in the Fu ex-

VOCABULARY.

甚 *Shên*^{4}. . . . . Very:—see Sub. See *shên*^{2}.

强佔 *Ch'iang*^{2} *chan*^{4}. *To take possession by force;* to usurp.

田產 *T'ien*^{2} *ch'an*^{3}. . . . . *Lands,* possessions.

歪話 *Wai*^{1} *hwa*^{4}. *Unreasonable,* preposterous; irrelevant, misleading.

淫 *Yin*^{2}. . . . To soak; *licentious,* lewd; excessive.

淫亂 *Yin*^{2} *lwan*^{4}. *Licentiousness,* debauchery, adultery.

人物 *Jên*^{2} *wu*^{4}. Personal appearance, form, *physique,* presence.

拘泥 *Chü*^{1} *ni*^{2}. Obtuse, pigheaded, *obstinate,* bigoted.

隨夥 *Swei*^{2} *hwoa*^{3}. To follow the crowd, to fall in with, to conquer, *to acquiesce.*

茂 *Mao*^{4}. . . . . . . Exuberant, flourishing; elegant.

茂盛 *Mao*^{4} *shêng*^{4}. *Luxuriant,* flourishing, prosperous.

謹愼 *Chin*^{3} *shên*^{4}. Careful, cautious, discreet, *circumspect.*

正大 *Chêng*^{4} *ta*^{4}. . . . . Important, *weighty.*

身段 *Shên*^{1} *twan*^{4}. . . . . Stature, size; *body.*

響亮 *Hsiang*^{3} *liang*^{4}. Resonant, clear, *ringing,* sonorous.

華麗 *Hwa*^{2} *li*^{4}. . . . . Elegant, *stylish,* fine.

悲嘆 *Pei*^{1} *t'an*^{4}. Sad, grieved, *distressed,* mournful.

上藥、疼得利害。○19孔子說的話、雖極平常、却極正大。○20你看着他無能嗎、在他莊上還數着他呢。○21你若能打、儘管給我打、打出禍來是我的。○22現在就要得去嗎、答不甚要緊、等一會兒也可以。○23我僱的這個老媽子、是好極咯、粗細工夫(活)他都會做。○24人死後還要復活、這是我深信不疑的。○25那個人的身量不大、聲音倒極響亮。○26論這房子、雖不十分華麗、然而所佔的地方、却極其清雅。○27我這些年、是靠山山倒、靠海海乾、思想起來、眞是悲嘆之極。○28你還不去進館、儘自在這裏賣獃作甚麼。○29那是已經受封誥的太太、你看他頭戴鳳冠、身穿蟒袍、脖頸子上掛着朝珠、實在體面到極處。○30村中雖有許多人家、却東一家、西一

amination was he the last again?

18 It does not hurt very much at present, but when the medicine was first rubbed on, it pained me very severely.

19 Although the sayings of Confucius are very plain, yet they are exceedingly weighty.

20 You think he is a man of no capacity, do you? The fact is, he is the best man in his village.

21 If you can fight, then fight your best for me; and if you hurt somebody, I'll pay the damages.

22 Must I go just now? *Ans.* It is not specially important, by and by will do.

23 This old servant woman I have hired is first rate. She can do both fine and coarse work.

24 That men will rise again after death, is something I fully believe.

25 That man is not large in body, but he has a ringing voice.

26 Although this house is not specially stylish, yet the position it occupies is very quiet.

27 Everything is against me these few years. I am distressed beyond measure whenever I think of it.

28 Have you not yet gone to school? What are you here so long for?

29 That is a lady who has received a title of nobility. See, she wears on her head a phœnix hat, on her shoulders an embroidered gown, and on her neck there hangs a string of pearls. Her dress is elegant in the extreme.

30 Although the town has a large popu-

賣獃 *Mai*⁴ *tai*¹ To fool away time, to dawdle, *to loiter*, to dilly-dally.

誥 *Kao*⁴. To enjoin upon, to order; *to grant a patent.*

封誥 *Fêng*¹ *kao*⁴. To confer a title or patent of nobility, to decorate.

冠 *Kwan*¹. A cap, *a hat*, a crown, a crest. See *kwan*⁴.

鳳冠 *Fêng*⁴ *kwan*¹. A hat or coronet with pendants and having a phœnix embroidered or gilded on it. It is worn by ladies of rank, and in some places by brides of all ranks.

蟒 *Mang*³. A python with yellow scales.

蟒袍 *Mang*³ *p'ao*². A ceremonial robe embroidered with dragons.

脖 *Po*². *The neck;* the navel.

頸 *Kêng*³. *The neck*, the throat.

朝珠 *Ch'ao*² *chu*¹. A long string of beads worn by officials.

跨 *K'wa*⁴. To straddle, to bestride; to pass over; a stride; *wide apart.*

跨拉 *K'wa*⁴ *la*¹. *Scattered*, sparse. (L.)

殘 *Ts'an*². To destroy, to kill; to injure; to spoil; broken, fragmentary; ravening, *cruel*;

殘忍 *Ts'an*² *jên*³. *Cruel*, unmerciful, hard-hearted.

胡琴 *Hu*² *ch'in*². A Chinese violin, a fiddle:—Note 32.

聲調 *Shêng*¹ *tiao*⁴. *Voice*, tune.

絃 *Hsien*². The string of a lute, violin, etc.

家、不甚相連（跨拉得很）、○說[31]某人性同虎狠、就是說他的性情、殘忍得利害。○[32]街（大）門口有個唱（賣）唱的、拉着四根絃的胡琴、唱的那個聲兒（調）、儘合着絃、實在好聽。○凡[33]是碼頭地方、風俗就不好、旱路碼頭更甚。○這[34]幾年的米、總掉不下兩吊六七百錢一石、有時賣兩吊五、那就是賤到家（底）喇。○他[35]外面皮兒、雖像愚蠢、心裏却奸猾到極處、法子多、圈套大、不論甚麼事、預先拿話勾引你、把你的主意套了去、然後他遠遠望着你、你一漏空、他就鑽進去了。○人[36]家急急的收拾行李、預備明天早早起行、你却儘之在那裏攪鬧（擾）、等人攆着纔走、眞沒眼色到所以然（極）處。

lation, yet the houses stand here and there very much scattered.

31 To say that a man's disposition is like that of a tiger or wolf, is equivalent to saying that it is outrageously cruel.

22 There is a minstrel at the gate playing a violin, and his voice is in perfect harmony with the instrument. It is a treat to hear him.

33 In every emporium of trade, morals are bad, and this is specially true of such as are inland.

34 For these several years the price of rice has not ranged lower than two thousand and six or seven hundred cash per picul. A few times it sold for two thousand five hundred, which was the very cheapest.

35 Although in appearance he seems stupid, yet at heart he is crafty to the last degree; his devices are many and his toils far reaching. No matter what the business is, he first approaches you plausibly and pumps you, and then stands off and watches. As soon as he catches you off your guard, he takes advantage of you.

36 He is anxious to put his luggage in order so as to start early in the morning, yet you insist on remaining and keeping up your uproar until you are driven out. You seem to be utterly wanting in a sense of propriety.

石 *Tan*4. *A measure of ten* 斗; A picul, one hundred catties :—Note 34.

愚蠢 *Yü*2 *ch'un*3. . . . . Silly, *stupid*, obtuse.

猾 *Hwa*2. . . . . Cunning, *treacherous ;* clever.

奸猾 *Chien*1 *hwa*2. Treacherous ; *crafty*, knavish ; . . . . subtle.

漏空 *Lou*4 *k'ung*4. To expose a weak place, to . . . . be off one's guard.

NOTES.

6 儘之 is sometimes written 儘自. Being nothing more than a euphonic ending, 之 is the better writing ; moreover the sound of 之 is everywhere correct, while 自 is in many places incorrect.

8 樂極生悲 is a book phrase meaning that *extreme joy gives rise to sadness*, that is, manifests itself in emotions that seem akin to sadness. The same phrase is also used to mean, *excessive joy is the precursor of sorrow.*

12 前街 may mean the front street as we understand front ; or it may mean, the south street as opposed to the 後街, or street to the north. 前 and 後 are frequently so used. The South Gate of Peking is called 前門. Les. 38, Note 15.

14 不隨夥兒 *To refuse to follow others or submit to the majority, contrary, intractable.*

21 打出禍來 *To strike out a calamity*; that is, to strike or fight so as to produce serious consequences.

24 深信不疑 *Profoundly believing and free from doubt*,—a book phrase.

25 倒 expresses the unexpected contrast between the size of the man and the strength of his voice.

27 靠山山倒靠海海乾 *When I trust in the hill, the hill falls over ; and when I trust in the sea, the sea dries up ;* a bold figure for expressing unprecedentedly bad luck.

32 賣唱的 *A street minstrel, one who sings for a living.* 胡琴 *A Mongolian lute*, which is played with a bow like a violin, though the original Chinese 琴 is a lute, which is played by striking with the fingers.

第一百三十八課

那[1]淨是些似是而非的話。○他[2]的漢丈、大而且胖。
○有[3]人自己不好、並且不教兒女學好。○他[4]那個
叫給人不服處、就是因爲能說、而不能行。○5拉拉拖邋疲疲人
不只是不能成事、且又往往誤事。○他[6]們倆、底根
兒裏相好、而且又連了幾層親。○和[7]親近人交往、
不但是要按理、並且更要看情。○人[8]都是學而知
之、那有生而知之的呢。○杜[9]占鰲天分既高、而且
工夫又純、還能沒有進益嗎。○若[10]是這麼浪費慣
了、不但折福、並且還要破家。○你[11]且在這路旁邊
樹林中、將就歇歇、養養精神再走罷。○他[12]已經病

TRANSLATION.

1 That talk is all specious fallacy.
2 His figure is large and also portly.
3 Some men are not good themselves, and moreover they do not train their children to be good.
4 The reason he cannot influence others is that he does not practice what he preaches.
5 The dilatory man not only fails to accomplish anything, but he frequently hinders the accomplishment of things.
6 They two were originally friends, and they have also become connected by several intermarriages.
7 In our intercourse with near relatives we must not only regard the claims of reason, but still more those of affection.
8 Men all get knowledge by learning. Where is the man who is gifted with it by nature?
9 Tu Chan Ao's talents are of a high order, and his time is wholly given to study; can he do otherwise than excel?
10 If this extravagance becomes habitual, he will not only curtail his happiness, but he will also bankrupt his estate.
11 Come, be content to rest here in this grove at the road side and refresh yourself before going on further.

34 石 is simply 石 *shï* with a dot added for the sake of distinction. It is not recognized by Kanghi and is frequently written simply 石, though *tan* is not a recognized pronunciation of 石. It is properly a *measure* of ten 斗, but is in practice constantly confused with 擔 *tan*, a *weight* or load of 100 catties. As a measure, it is exceedingly variable in different places, because the 斗 is so variable. In Têngchow a 斗 is about one and a third bushels, and consequently a 石 is over thirteen bushels. In some other places the 斗 is less than a peck, and the 石 of course proportionately small.

LESSON CXXXVIII.

TRANSITIONAL CONJUNCTIONS.

Both 而 and 且 have already appeared in sundry combinations in previous lessons, but their own special force remains to be considered.

而 And, yet, but. 而 often expresses a close connection or transition which has no corresponding word in English. It is properly a book word, but is often used in colloquial.

且 But, and, moreover, furthermore. The difference between 而 and 且 is often very little. They will frequently replace each other.

且 For the time being, temporarily, first. Thus used, 且 does not stand as a connective of clauses, but is thrown in directly after the subject in order to make a place for what follows, to serve as a stepping stone to it. It is in this case approximately equal to 暫且 or 先 or 就, but is less explicit.

而且 And, and also, yet, moreover.

並且 And, also, but, moreover.

When connecting clauses, 而 and 且, as well as 而且 and 並且, are nearly always followed by 又 or 也 or 再.

了五六個月、而且飯食又不佳、所以纔瘦枯了。○你13既然不老不少、而且也沒有殘疾、怎麼還討飯吃呢。○我14且問你、他不恭敬你、你還恭敬他（來着 咧來）沒有。○這15件事不如託來順罷、因爲他有工夫、而且也有成事的才幹。○不16當做而做的、與當做而不做的、都不合理之當然。○你17該把這張禱告文念熟了、並且常常照樣禱告。○你18且出去、等我們商議商議、再告訴你。○人19的聰明、不只得之於父、且更得之於母、所以男人念書、既能加上兒女的聰明、若是女人也念書、更能加上兒女的聰明。○學20問的大好處、就是在乎能開人的心竅、使心越用越靈、而且能知古今的事、通達萬物的理、使人無往

12 His being so thin is because he has been ill for five or six months, moreover his food also has not been the best.

13 Why are you begging, seeing you are neither an old man nor a child nor yet a cripple?

14 He did not show you respect [you say]; just let me ask you, did you show him respect?

15 It would be better to entrust this affair to Lai Shun, because he has the time to spare, and he also has the ability to put it through.

16 Doing what ought not to be done, and not doing what ought to be done, are both contrary to the principles of right reason.

17 You ought to commit this form of prayer carefully to memory, and constantly to pray after this manner.

18 Do you go out a little while and wait till we have consulted, after which we will inform you.

19 A man's mental endowments are derived, not alone from his father, but still more from his mother; therefore seeing the education of the father adds to the capacity of the children, still more will the education of the mother add to their capacity.

20 The great advantage of learning consists in its developing the faculties of the mind, so that the more they are exercised the more efficient they become; moreover by this means a man

VOCABULARY.

拉疲 *La¹ p'i²*. *Dilatory*, behindhand; negligent, careless, heedless.

拖疲 *T'o¹ p'i²*. The same. (S.)

拉遢 *La¹ t'a¹*. The same. (N.)

杜 *Tu⁴*. The russet pear; to stop, to impede; to shut off; *a surname*.

鰲 *Ao²*. A huge sea fish.

純 *Ch'un²*. Pure, unmixed; entirely, *wholly*; simple, guileless, sincere.

進益 *Chin⁴ i²*. Improvement, *progress*.

浪 *Lang⁴*. A wave, a billow; *profligate*; wasteful; unrestrained, lawless.

浪費 *Lang⁴ fei⁴*. *To spend extravagantly*, to squander, to waste.

折福 *Chê² fu²*. To lessen blessings, to cut off enjoyments:—Note 10.

破家 *P'o⁴ chia¹*. To lose property, *to bankrupt one's estate*.

飯食 *Fan⁴ shi²*. *Food*, victuals.

佳 *Chia¹*. Beautiful, *good*, superior, excellent.

瘦枯 *Sou⁴ k'u¹*. Poor, *lean*, ill-favored, emaciated.

殘疾 *Ts'an² chi²*. Deficient in limb or organ, *crippled*, maimed.

當然 *Tang¹ jan²*. That which ought to be, *right*:—Note 16.

禱 *Tao³*. *To pray to the gods*, to supplicate.

而不樂。○水21是二分輕氣、一分養氣、化合而成的。○大22哥、你這幾年出門很好阿、大有所望阿、答見笑、我有甚麼能幹耐呢、能幹甚麼呢、不過餬口而已。○人23一做了賊、不但是對不住天地鬼神、並且對不住親戚朋友、也不但是對不住親戚朋友、而且對不住父母兄弟、又不但是對不住父母兄弟、且是對不住妻子兒女、又不但是對不住妻子兒女、且更對不住自己的良心。○從24前買這樣的貂鼠馬褂、至不濟最公道也得四百兩銀子、你看這一件、顏色兒多麼黑、毛道頭兒多麼厚、又平正、且是風毛出得齊截、面子的緞子又厚、花樣兒也新鮮、又合如今的時樣兒、問你要三百銀子、還算多了嗎。

comes to know ancient and modern affairs, and to understand the laws of nature, so that wherever he turns he finds enjoyment.

21 Water is composed of two parts of hydrogen and one part of oxygen chemically combined.

22 Well, sir, you have been quite successful in your business these few years [I hear], and your prospects are good. *Ans.* You are too facetious. What capacity have I? What business can I do? It is all I can do to make a living.

23 When a man becomes a robber, he not only sins against the gods, but he also sins against his relatives and friends; and he not only sins against his relatives and friends, but also against his parents and brothers; and not only against his parents and brothers, but also against his wife and children; and not only against his wife and children, but still more against his own conscience.

24 Formerly a sable coat of this kind would have cost at least four hundred taels. Just look at this one, what a pure black it is, how thick the fur is and how smooth, and also how even is the border; the satin cover also is heavy, and the figure is new and just in the present style. Can it be considered dear at three hundred taels?

禱告 *Tao^3 kao^4*. To pray, to supplicate; *prayer*, ... supplication.

禱告文 *Tao^3 kao^4 wên^2*. A written form of .... prayer.

通達 *T'ung^1 ta^2*. To see through clearly, to .... *understand*, to comprehend.

養氣 *Yang^3 ch'i^4*. .... Oxygen.

化合 *Hwa^4 hê^2*. To combine chemically; to .... unite in one.

餬 *Hu^{1,2}*. ...... Congee; *to get a sustenance*.

餬口 *Hu^1 k'ou^3*. To get or make a living, to .... earn one's bread.

而已 *Êr^2 i^3*. And nothing more, only, simply, ... *barely*. (W.)

貂 *Tiao^1*. .... The Siberian sable.

貂鼠 *Tiao^1 shu^3*. .... *The sable*, the marten.

至不濟 *Chï^4 pu^4 chi^4*. At the very least, ... at least.

毛道 *Mao^2 tao^4*. .... Class or quality of fur.

毛頭 *Mao^2 t'ou^2*. .... The same. (S.)

平正 *P'ing^2 chêng^4*. .... Level, even, *smooth*.

風毛 *Fêng^1 mao^2*. A fur border or facing:— .... Note 24.

齊截 *Ch'i^2 chie^2*. .... *Even*, regular, smooth.

新鮮 *Hsin^1 hsien^1*. .... *New*; fresh, bright.

時樣 *Shï^2 yang^4*. *The prevailing style*, the .... fashion.

第一百三十九課

我[1]原不能走路、又加上今天起身晚了、所以到如今纔來。○那[2]個人用不得、常常爭競工錢、還帶着(之)不愛做工活。○我[3]覺着渾身發燒、就像火烤的一樣、又搭上害耳朶底(耳底)子、疼得連顋頰(顋)都腫了。○他[4]本來身子就弱、再加上病了這一場、所以連走的力氣都沒有。○這[5]幾天淘溝的氣味兒、很不好、又搭着天氣乍冷乍熱(忽冷忽熱)的、所以人都不能保養身子。○芹[6]子的(他)爹、發(犯)了心疼的病、直叫喚(喊叫)了四天、還帶着一吃藥就吐、你說愁

TRANSLATION.

1 I never was a good walker, and besides I started late this morning; hence it is that I have but just arrived.

2 That man is not useable; he is continually disputing about his wages, and moreover he does not like to work.

3 My whole body feels burning hot as if roasted by the fire, and in addition, I have such a severe ear-ache that the whole side of my face is swollen.

4 He was originally delicate, and having had this spell of sickness in addition, he has not even strength to walk.

5 These few days the stench from cleaning the drains is noisome, and in addition, the weather is very changeable, so that no one is able to preserve his health.

6 Ch'in-tsï's papa has had an attack of dyspepsia which has kept him groaning incessantly for four days, and moreover, when he takes any medicine he immediately throws it up. Isn't it trying?

NOTES.

1 似是而非 *As if it were but is not*, that which resembles truth or fact, but is not such, plausible.

8 學而知之 A book phrase meaning to acquire knowledge by the labor of learning, as opposed to 生而知之, to be endowed with knowledge by birth or intuition.

10 折福 *To cut off or deduct* (by evil deeds) *from the sum total of blessings allotted to each individual by the gods.* 破家 *To lose or waste money so as to involve the sacrifice of one's property and estate.*

14 且 is here thrown in to interrupt the sentence and make a place for the question immediately following.

15 不如 implies a comparison, the first half of which is unexpressed.

16 理之當然 *Reason's oughtness, right reason.* The phrase is often turned about and said 當然之理.

19 之 as here used is quite equivalent to 着 in meaning, and being used in imitation of book style is entirely *t'ung hsing.*

20 This sentence was made by a Chinaman who had tasted of Western education and knew its value. 無往而不樂 *Go nowhere without finding joy;* that is, finding enjoyment in everything.

23 對不住 *Cannot endure confronting, unable to face*, that is, *self-condemned*, hence, *to offend, to sin against.* 天地鬼神 *Heaven and earth, demons and gods;* a comprehensive summary of divine powers and beings, all of which are required to fully express the Chinese idea of divinity. The best translation of the whole is simply, *gods.*

24 風毛 is a narrow border of extra long fur sewed on along the edges where the satin outside is joined to the fur lining. 公道 *Just,*—from the side of the purchaser; that is, *cheap.*

LESSON CXXXIX.

CONJUNCTIVE PHRASES.

還帶着 or 還帶之 And moreover, furthermore.

再加上 And in addition, and furthermore, and still more.

再搭上 The same.

再者 And again, and further, and in the next place.

再是 The same.

又加上 And in addition, and besides.

又搭上 or 又搭着 The same.

人不愁人呢。○王7太太原來就俊俏(俏爭)、又搭上穿着紅綢子褲、綠緞子襖、戴着滿頭的翠花、看着眞如天仙一般。○請8你捎(帶)個口信給我的外甥、叫他十六日來聽戲、再者、叫他來的時候、可以從東路走、我好赶着牲口去迎他。○我9在二月陪送了一個姑娘、八月娶了一個媳婦、又加上蓋了五間房子、你想我有多少錢、還能有存項呢。○人10在監裏、帶着手銬脚鐐、又被鐵鍊捆鎖、這些刑罰、已經就彀受的、再搭上臭蟲咬、蚊子叮、連擓擓也摸不着(抓也抓不着)、眞是苦惱極了。○他11雖然長了十五歲、比起你來、還是個孩子、你好動手打他嗎、再者說、打狗看主面、他

7 Lady Wang is naturally handsome, and when, in addition, she is dressed in red silk trowsers and a green satin sacque and has her head covered with turquoise feather work, she really looks like a fairy.

8 Will you please carry word to my nephew to come on the sixteenth to the theatre, and further tell him, when he comes to come by the east road that I may take an animal to meet him.

9 In the second month I gave my daughter her marriage outfit, in the eighth month I brought home a daughter-in-law, and, in addition, I have built a house of five rooms; how much money do you suppose I have, that I should still have cash on hand?

10 When a man is in prison, and has on handcuffs and shackles and is bound with an iron chain; these inflictions are already all he can bear; but when, in addition, the bed-bugs bite, and the mosquitoes sting, and he cannot even scratch; he is indeed wretched in the extreme.

11 Although he is a youth of fifteen, yet in comparison with you he is but a child; does it become you to strike him? Besides it is said, "When you would strike a dog, have regard to his master." Suppose the boy did

VOCABULARY.

發燒 *Fa¹ shao¹*. *To feel feverish*, to burn with fever.

顋 *Sai¹*. The jaws, *the cheeks*.

頰 *Chia¹*. The lower jaw, *the cheek*, the chops.

顋頰 The cheeks, the jaws, *the side face*.

溝 *Kou¹*. A ditch, *a drain*, a sewer; a gutter, a ravine.

氣味 *Ch'i⁴ wei⁴*. Smell; *stench*, fumes.

保養 *Pao³ yang³*. To protect, *to preserve;* to keep, to cherish.

芹 *Ch'in²*. Celery; cress.

俏爭 *Ch'iao⁴ chêng¹*. Pretty, *handsome*, neat, elegant. (s.)

翠花 *Ts'wei⁴ hwa¹*. Artificial flowers made of the feathers of the turquoise king-fisher.

天仙 *T'ien¹ hsien¹*. An immortal, a genius, *a fairy*:—Les. 74. Note 26.

口信 *K'ou³ hsin⁴*. News sent by word of mouth, a message.

陪送 *P'ei² sung⁴*. To escort, to accompany ceremonially; *to fit out.*

存項 *Ts'un² hsiang⁴*. Money on hand, *cash;* money kept on deposit; reserve.

銬 *K'ao⁴*. Fetters for the hands, manacles. This character is not recognized by Kanghi, but is in general use in official documents.

手銬 *Shou³ k'ao⁴*. Manacles, *handcuffs.*

鍊 *Lien⁴*. To smelt, to refine; to work out by experience; to discipline; *a chain.*

捆 *K'un³*. *To bind*, to fasten; to gird.

捆鎖 *K'un³ soă³*. *To bind*, to chain, to pinion; to secure, to fasten.

臭蟲 *Ch'ou⁴ ch'ung²*. A bed-bug.

就是得罪你、你也該告訴我、等我給你出氣、你該自己打他這麼個樣子嗎。○文[12]王生來就有聖德、天下固然不能不服、又搭着紂王殘害忠良、暴虐黎民、所以民心就越發歸文王了。○人[13]都說是守業難、你看李雲慶家、一連五六輩子財主、現在他的三個兒子、又都巴巴結結的過日子、一個瞎枉花錢的也沒有、還帶著三個媳婦、也很和睦、永沒有爭吵打架之說、若都能像這樣守業、還有個守不住的嗎。○若[14]是好馬、腿必定結實、耐得勞苦、樣兒也好、又伶便、騎上如同飛鷹一般、你這匹馬、算個什麼、口也老了、下巴骨都耷拉了、再是腿也軟、肯打

offend you, you should have told me, and allowed me to give you satisfaction ; you ought not yourself to have beaten him in this way.

12 From his birth Wên Wang had the virtues of a sage, so that the nation could not fail to give him its allegiance, and when, in addition, Chou Wang maltreated his faithful officers and oppressed the common people, the hearts of the people all the more turned to Wên Wang.

13 Everybody says that preserving an inheritance is difficult. Look at Li Yün Ch'ing's family ; they have been rich for five or six consecutive generations, and now his three sons are all thrifty, not one is spending money foolishly, and moreover his three daughters-in-law are all very harmonious, there is never the least sign of quarreling or fighting. If all followed this example, would any fail to preserve their patrimony ?

14 In the case of a good horse, his legs are sound and will stand fatigue ; he is well shaped and his movements quick ; when you mount him, away he flies like a hawk. But this horse of yours—of what account is he ? He is old and his jaw droops, also his legs are weak and he has a habit of

蚊 *Wên*². . . . . *A mosquito*, a gnat.

苦惱 *K'u*³ *nao*³. Wretched, *miserable ;* forlorn, . . . cast down ; chagrined.

出氣 *Ch'u*¹ *ch'i*⁴. To aspirate ; to vent one's . . . anger ; to avenge, *to vindicate.*

紂 *Chou*⁴. . . . A trace, a breech-strap :—Note 12.

殘害 *Ts'an*² *hai*⁴. To treat cruelly, to *maltreat,* . . . to abuse.

忠良 *Chung*¹ *liang*². Faithful and virtuous . . . [officers]. (w.)

虐 *Nüe*⁴, *yo*⁴. . . . . . *Cruel,* tyrannical ; harsh.

暴虐 *Pao*⁴ *nüe*⁴. *To oppress,* to tyrannize over, . . . to ill-use.

黎 *Li*². . . . . Black ; *many,* numerous.

黎民 *Li*² *min*². The black haired people, the . . . Chinese people. (w.)

守業 *Shou*³ *yie*⁴. To preserve an inheritance ; . . . frugal :—Note 13.

勞苦 *Lao*² *k'u*³. . . . . . Labor, toil, *fatigue.*

伶便 *Ling*² *pien*⁴. *Quick,* active, nimble, agile, . . . prompt.

下巴 *Hsia*⁴ *pa*¹. . . . . The lower jaw.

下巴骨 *Hsia*⁴ *pa*¹ *ku*³. The jaw bone, *the* . . . *lower jaw.*

打前失 *Ta*³ *ch'ien*² *shï*¹. . . . . . . To stumble.

打前絆 *Ta*³ *ch'ien*² *pan*⁴. . . . . . . The same.

打踢絆 *Ta*³ *t'i*¹ *pan*⁴. . . . . . . The same.

傪 *Ts'an*⁴. . . . . Perverse ; mean, *contemptible.*

傪頭 *Ts'an*⁴ *t'ou*². Mean, contemptible, shabby, . . . *scrubby ;* stupid.

一來 *I*¹ *lai*². . . . In the first place :—Note 15.

直直 *Chï*² . . . . *Directly,* entirely, absolutely.

毀滅 *Hwei*³ *mie*⁴. *To destroy utterly,* to annihilate, to abolish.

前失、前絆踢絆誰肯費草費料的、養這麼匹儳頭馬呢。○你[15]說外國人來中國傳教、是我們中國人的好處、我一點也不信、一來他們當初進中國、乃是硬強進來的、天下還有將好處強送給人的嗎、二來傳耶穌道理、直直是毀滅聖教、聖教該是人毀滅的嗎、還有比孔夫子更大的聖人嗎、三來他們教訓人不拜菩薩、這就是眼中無神、教訓人不拜祖宗、這就是忤逆不孝、你想教人不敬神、不孝父母的、這還算是好道理嗎、再是他們各處立義學、開醫院、他們還能白花這些錢、白出這些力嗎、無非是巧奪民心、預備吞大清的江山就是了。

stumbling: who would waste provender keeping such a screw as this?
15 You say that foreigners coming to China to propagate their religion is a blessing to us Chinese. I don't believe a bit of it. In the first place, their entrance into China was originally by force, but who in the world undertakes to force good things on people. In the second place, the preaching of Christianity aims directly at the destruction of Confucianism. Ought the doctrines of the sages to be destroyed? Is there any greater sage than Confucius? In the third place, they teach men not to worship the Poosas; that is, to have no fear of the gods before their eyes, and they teach men not to worship their ancestors; that is, to be undutiful to parents. Do you consider that a good doctrine which leads men not to worship the gods nor to honor their parents? Moreover they are everywhere establishing charity schools and opening hospitals. Would they spend all this money and take all this pains for nothing? By no means. It is simply an ingenious plan for stealing the hearts of the people, and so preparing the way for gobbling up our imperial master's broad domain.

聖教 *Shêng⁴ chiao⁴*. . . . . Confucianism.

夫子 *Fu¹ tsï³*. *A sage;* a rabbi; an honored teacher.

菩薩 *P'u² sa¹*. An inferior Buddha; an idol, a god; a dear, a darling.

祖宗 *Tsu³ tsung¹*. . . . . . . Ancestors, progenitors.

忤 *Wu³*. . . . . . *Disobedient*, intractable, forward.

逆 *Ni⁴*. *Rebellious;* contrary; to oppose, to resist; to anticipate.

忤逆 *Undutiful;* refractory, incorrigible.

義學 *I⁴ hsüe²*. . . . . A charity school.

醫院 *I¹ yüen⁴*. . . . . . . A hospital; a dispensary.

Notes.

3 害耳朶底子 *To have a pain,* or ulcer, *in the bottom of the ear, to suffer from earache.*

6 芹子他爹 *Ch'in-tsï, his father.* This redundant expression is a common colloquial idiom, especially in the North. It is a general practice to designate parents by the names of their children.

9 By using 呢 at the end, the question is made to turn on the 多少 above, rather than on the last clause.

10 In former times manacles were made of wood, and the character 梏 was used, now they are generally made of iron, and 銬 has come into use.

12 聖德 *The virtues of a sage,* the highest type of mental and moral qualities. 紂王, otherwise called 紂辛, the most infamous tyrant known in Chinese history. He imprisoned 文王, but subsequently released him. He was defeated and dethroned by 武王, and with him ended the Shang dynasty. 殘害忠良暴虐黎民 is a set form of words in the book style.

13 守業 *To preserve and build up by prudence, diligence and economy the inheritance transmitted from parents,*—a virtue, which owing to the tendency of affluence to produce

第一百四十課

這[1]一尊大礮、是從英國買來的。○現[2]在
城裏有三班子戲、你是愛聽那一班子
呢。○我[3]們這莊上、有四口眼井、只有一眼口
甜水。○人[4]受是爭一口氣、神受是爭一炷爐香。○
一[5]個上半天頭晌講這五排帮書、儘彀先生受
的。○那[6]座廟名子、叫萬佛寺、因爲裏
頭有一萬尊佛。○北[7]門外頭、一點遮擋
沒有、不如壘砌上一堵扇牆、好擋擋北風。○
買[8]賣好做、夥計難搭、若是三股繩一齊
緊、還有不發財的嗎。○今[9]託人捎寄來山地洋

Trasnlation.

1 This large cannon was purchased in England.
2 There are three troupes of actors in the city at present; which company do you wish to hear?
3 We have four wells in our village, only one of which has good water.
4 As breath is to men, so is incense to the gods.
5 To lecture to these five classes in one forenoon is quite as much as you can stand, sir.
6 The name of that temple is the Hall of Ten Thousand Buddhas, because there are in it ten thousand Buddhas.
7 There is not the least shelter outside the north door; it would be better to build a wall to keep off the north wind.
8 Business is easy to do, [faithful] partners are hard to find. When the three strands of the rope tighten together, who could not make money?
9 I send by the bearer one sack of

indolence and dissipation, is held to be as difficult as it is admirable.

14 肯 is here equal to, *given to*, or *has a habit of*.

15 孔夫子 *Master Kung*, gives to the great sage his Western name, Confucius. For the use of 一來, *in the first place*, 二來, *in the second place*. See Les. 170 Sub. 忤逆不孝 *Incorrigibly disobedient and undutiful*,—a book phrase expressing the highest degree of filial impiety. 大清 is the dynastic title of the reigning Tartar dynasty.

LESSON CXL.

Classifiers.

尊 Honorable, eminent,—classifier of idols, Buddhas, cannon, etc.

班 A class, a set,—classifier of offices in yamêns, troupes of actors, etc.

眼 An eye, a hole,—classifier of wells—for which 口 is also used.

爐 A furnace,—classifier of incense urns.

帮 A company,—classifier of parties of men, classes in school, guitars, flutes, etc.

排 A row, a set,—classifier of ranks of soldiers, classes in a school, beds in a garden, etc.

堵 To close up,—classifier of walls.

股 A slice, a share,—classifier of strands in a thread or rope, shares in a company, etc.

包 To wrap; a bundle,—classifier of goods in bundles or packages.

筆 A pen,—classifier of accounts.

端 The beginning,—classifier of subjects in a discourse, pieces of silk, etc.

刀 A knife,—classifier of reams of paper, slices of bean curd, etc.

炷 A wick,—classifier of sticks of incense.

盤 A plate,—classifier of millstones, pieces of business, etc.

營 An encampment,—classifier of divisions of an army.

哨 To whistle, to patrol,—classifier of companies or squads of soldiers.

統 The whole,—classifier of tablets, tombstones, etc.

合 To combine,—classifier of doors, windows, hinges, etc.

捲 To roll up,—classifier of maps and pictures.

對 To pair,—classifier of things in pairs.

藥豆蛋山芋一包、上海大米四包、見字查收。○你[10]打聽臧家莊做甚麽呢、答在那裏有一筆賬、我得去要。○他[11]那院裏、不知是誰娶親、我看見門上掛着一幅端疋紅彩、門外貼着喜字。○那[12]是三吊錢的票子、買了兩刀毛邊紙、去一吊八、還淨賸一吊二。○他[13]們那裏、是金丹教和一炷香大行的地方、所以人都有個求永生的底子。○這[14]一排畦子、都種的芹菜。○南[15]屋是五間半、裏頭安的一盤磨、一盤碾子、還有幾個糧食囤摺子。○一[16]營兵分爲五哨、就是前後

potatoes and four bags of Shanghai rice. Please take delivery on receipt of this memorandum.

10 Why are you inquiring for Tsang-chia Chwang? *Ans.* I have an account there which I am going to collect.

11 I wonder who in his yard is getting married. I see a red cloth hung around the door, and the character "rejoice" pasted outside.

12 That was a three thousand cash note. I bought two reams of maopien paper which took one thousand eight hundred cash, and there is left just one thousand two hundred.

13 In their neighborhood the Golden-pill sect and the One-stick-of incense sect flourish, on which account the people generally have an antecedent idea of seeking immortality.

14 This row of beds is all planted in celery.

15 The south room is five spans and a half. In it there is a flour mill, a hulling mill and also several grain bins.

16 One regiment is divided into five

VOCABULARY.

班子 *Pan*¹ *tsï*³. . . . . A troupe of actors.

炷 *Chu*⁴. . . . . A wick, *a stick of incense.*

哨 *Shao*⁴. To sing (as a bird), to whistle; to call (as a guard); to patrol; *a company of a hundred men.*

遮擋 *Chê*¹ *tang*³. To ward off, to defend, *to shelter*, to hinder.

壘 *Lei*³. To pile up one on the other, *to build;* a heap; a rampart.

葯 *Yoă*⁴, *yüe*⁴, *yao*⁴. *Medicinal herbs;* another form of 藥.

山葯 *Shan*¹ *yao*⁴. . . . . The Chinese yam.

山葯豆 *Shan*¹ *yao*⁴ *tou*⁴. The potato (yam beans). (N.)

地蛋 *Ti*⁴ *tan*⁴. . . . The potato (earth eggs). (C.)

洋山芋 *Yang*² *shan*¹ *yü*⁴. The potato (foreign wild taro). (S.)

查收 *Ch'a*² *shou*¹. To examine and receive,—used on letters and parcels.

臧 *Tsang*¹. . . Generous, virtuous; a surname. (W.)

畦 *Hsi*¹. . . . . A bed in a garden.

永生 *Yung*³ *shêng*¹. Everlasting life, *immortality; ever living.*

芹菜 *Ch'in*² *ts'ai*⁴. . . . . Celery.

碾 *Nien*³. A hulling mill for rice or millet. Note 15.

囤 *Tun*⁴. . . . . . . An osier bin for holding grain.

碑 *Pei*¹. . . . . . . A stone tablet, a grave-stone.

刻 *K'ê*¹. . . . . . . *To engrave*, to carve. See *k'ê*⁴.

刼 *Chie*². To plunder, *to rob on the highway;* a Hindoo kalpa, a cycle, an aeon.

文約 *Wên*² *yüe*¹. An indenture, *a deed*, a bond.

名人 *Ming*² *jên*². A noted man, a celebrated character.

梅花 *Mei*² *hwa*¹. A prune blossom; *the flowering almond.*

蘭花 *Lan*² *hwa*¹. An orchidaceous plant with a fragrant flower.

昂 *Ang*². . . . . . To elevate; stately, grand; high priced.

並用 *Ping*⁴ *yung*⁴. *To use together*, to use at once.

左右中、一哨又分十棚。○17前面有一統座碑、請去看看上面刻的甚麼字。○18去年臘月間、就在這個地方、刧斷了一幫關東客、還殺了十七歲的一個人。○19別管是典房子、是買房子、上帶着幾扇合門、幾扇合窗、幾鋪炕、幾個鍋竈臺、文約上都要一一載明、不然、交房子的時候、怕有差錯。○20這一捲子畫、都是甚麼名人畫的、答有趙子昂的馬、王鐸的梅花、張敔的牡丹、鄭板橋的蘭花。○21不但禽獸之一公

companies ; the front, rear, left, right and middle ; and each company is divided into ten platoons.

17 There is a monument just in front ; please go and see what inscription is on it.

18 Last year in the twelfth moon a company of travellers from Manchuria was robbed just in this place, and one young man of seventeen was killed.

19 No matter whether you are mortgaging or buying a house, the number of doors and windows and k'angs and kettle-ranges which are included should all be distinctly specified in the deed ; otherwise, when the time for the delivery of the house comes, there is danger of a misunderstanding.

20 By what noted artists were the paintings on this roll made ? *Ans.* The horse is by Chao Tsï Ang, the flowering almond is by Wang Toă, the peony by Chang Yü and the orchid by Chêng Pan Ch'iao.

21 Not only are a male and a female of

黃表 *Hwang*² *piao*³. A special kind of yellow paper used to burn in sacrificing to the gods. Holes are punched in it, and it is then supposed to represent copper cash.

石匠 *Shï*² *chiang*⁴. A stone-cutter.

包工 *Pao*¹ *kung*¹. Work done by the job.

日工 *Ji*⁴ *kung*¹. Work done by the day.

卯子工 *Mao*³ *tsï*³ *kung*¹. The same.

Notes.

2 子 is added to 班 when it means a company of actors, but not when it means a class of constables in a yamên.

3 甜水 is *sweet water* as distinguished from 苦水, *bitter water*, that is water containing alkaline salts.

4 (Or,) *As men require breath, so the gods require incense.* The meaning of this proverbial saying probably is, that as a man's life depends on the breath he breathes, so a god's life and prosperity depend on the incense he receives. 佛 is frequently substituted for 神.

8 The strands of a rope are put figuratively for the persons associated in business.

9 Potatoes being of foreign introduction, and having received no settled name, the people of each port have given them a name of their own. There are others besides those in the text, as 地包 in Shantung, and 蕃崽 at Kinkiang.

11 On the occasion of a wedding, a long red scarf is festooned above the frame of the street door, and the character 喜 written on red paper is pasted in all prominent places in view of the bride's chair as it approaches the house of the bridegroom. This latter is for good luck, while the red scarf is simply a sign of festivity. The sentence implies that several families lived in the same courtyard.

13 There are a great many small religious sects in China. They are not really distinct from the great religious systems of the land, but rather included in them, though in most cases involving more or less of a protest against their errors and corruptions. The government is disposed to regard all such sects as seditious. The 金丹教 is a sect springing from Taoism, and gives prominence to the supposed "pill of immortality." This pill is called *golden*, partly to express its preciousness, and partly because transmuted gold is supposed to be an important constituent of it. The 一炷香 is a sect which lays great stress on prayers and penances. Their theoretical time for kneeling in prayer is the time it takes for one stick of incense to burn out.

15 A 碾 consists of a heavy stone roller called a 碾砣, mounted on a large flat stone five or six feet in diameter, called a 碾盤. It has an axle and is surrounded by a frame in which it turns like a wheel. The inner side of this frame pivots on a centre-post, and as the roller is drawn or pushed round it rolls with a slipping motion on the base, upon which the grain is spread to be hulled. A 摺子 is different from a 囤子, though used for the same purpose. The latter is a very large round osier basket, often from three to five feet wide, and from four to eight feet high. The

一母為一對、凡是兩個並用的東西、也都說是一對、比方一對花瓶、一對枕頭、一對旗桿、一對石獅子。○ 22 俺家他老爺、明天燒過五七、你今天進城、看見春子、叫他務必買四刀黃表紙捎帶來。○ 23 你可以去叫那個姓張的石匠來、我要和他商量、做一座統碑、看看是包工合上算、是卯子日工合上算。

birds and beasts called a pair, but everything in which two are used together is called a pair; for instance, [we say] a pair of vases, a pair of pillows, a pair of flagstaffs or a pair of stone lions.

22 To-morrow is the day for burning the fifth seven for the children's maternal grandfather. When you go into the city to-day and see Ch'un-tsï, tell him to be sure and buy four reams of yellow paper and bring them home with him.

23 Go and call that stone-cutter named Chang. I want to consult him about making a tablet so as to see whether it will be cheaper to have it done by the job or by the day.

former is made of long strips of matting about fifteen inches wide, carried round and round like the threads of a screw, each round being telescoped by half its width or more into the one below it. It usually has a low basket for a bottom, and is constructed gradually as the grain is filled in. In Shantung the strip of matting, not the bin, is called 褶子.

18 Notice how the omission of a subject for the verb really turns it into a passive.

20 These are the names of the most famous painters of China.

22 俺家他老爺 is a highly idiomatic expression. 家 joined with 他, stands for the children of the family, whose maternal grandfather is the person referred to. On the death of a parent the sons burn paper money on the recurrence of each seventh day, until seven times, that is, the forty-ninth day. Daughters are usually excused if they burn five times.

23 The term 卯子工, used in Peking, probably comes from the custom of calling the roll or counting the workmen in the morning.

LESSON CXLI.

SPECIAL INTENSIVES.

Mandarin abounds in special intensives. Some of these intensives are applied to a considerable number of adjectives, but the greater number are limited to one or two special ones. Many of them are evidently founded on resemblance, similar to our "snow white," "ice cold," "red hot," etc., but in many cases no such origin is apparent. If the real origin of the usage in each case were known, doubtless it would be found that all are based on some kind of resemblance. The fact that the figure intended is oftentimes unknown or uncertain, makes the proper writing in such cases more or less uncertain. Elegant and forcible speech depends in no small degree on the ready command of these qualifiers. Their proper translation is difficult, and in many cases impossible. Having no special intensives in English, we are compelled to use general intensives instead.

Four lessons are given to the illustration of this class of words, beginning with those applied to the greater number of words. The usage differs very much in different localities, necessitating many double readings, and even these do not represent nearly all the variations. The student should inquire of his teacher, not only concerning the readings given, but for others not given.

希 Rare, sparse,—generally includes an idea of depreciation. It is widely used, but more frequent in the South than in the North.

希破 Shamefully ragged, all in tatters.

希鈍 Miserably dull, dull as a beetle. (s.)

希慢 Very slow, awfully slow. (s.)

希爛 Extra soft, well cooked; rotten, falling to pieces; in pieces, in tatters.

希軟 Very soft or weak; quite limber or pliable.

希瘦 Very thin, miserably lean. (s.)

希碎 In small pieces, in bits, all to flinders.

希鬆 Exceedingly loose; very negligent.

希矮 Very low, excessively low. (s.)

希窄 Very narrow, excessively narrow. (s.)

第一百四十一課

他¹早晨只喝了兩碗精稀的水飯。○你²看爐裏還有火沒有、答還挺透旺呢。○這³把薙頭刀子精希鈍、薙不下頭髮來。○去⁴年纔做的新綿襖、他一冬穿的希破。○這⁵個老驢精希慢、就是一步一鞭子、也赶他不動。○許⁶老大、那眞是百折不回的人、心裏剛硬到極處。○希⁷爛的牛肉、你吃點兒罷、答你先切一點給我嘗嘗。○路⁸上精希爛瀼、一點也不好走。○這⁹樣的春風、有兩天就吹的迸乾喇。○纔¹⁰下了這場雨、地都挺透泡暄、實在好鋤。○做¹¹饝餑饝餑的麪、你調和的希

TRANSLATION.

1 This morning he only drank two bowls of very thin gruel.
2 Look if there is still any fire in the stove. *Ans.* It is burning briskly.
3 This razor is as dull as a beetle, it will not shave at all.
4 The new wadded coat I made for him just last year, he wore all to tatters in one winter.
5 This old donkey is awfully slow; give him a cut every step and you can't, even then, get him to go.
6 That elder Hsü is exceedingly self-willed, and intractable to the last degree.
7 Well cooked beef [for sale]. Have some to eat? *Ans.* First slice off a little for me to taste.
8 The road is extremely muddy, so that the walking is very bad.
9 With a spring wind like this, it will be as dry as tinder in two days.
10 Owing to this rain which has just fallen, the ground is quite mellow and very easy to hoe.
11 In making bread it will never

希賤 Exceeding cheap, cheap as dirt.

希嫩 Exceedingly tender.

精 Pure, fine, unmixed,—conveys the idea of entireness. Some teachers prefer to write 淨, and Southern teachers contend for 盡, which with them is read *ching*, and the meaning is quite correct.

精稀 Extremely thin.

精鈍 Extremely dull, dull as a beetle. (C. & N.)

精慢 Extremely slow, awfully slow. (C. & N.)

精瀼 Extremely muddy, terribly muddy.

精瘦 Extremely lean, thin as a rail. (C. & N.)

精窮 Extremely poor, poor as poverty.

精濕 Soaking wet, dripping wet. (C. & N.)

精矮 Extremely low, very short. (C. & N.)

精窄 Extremely narrow. (C. & N.)

透 To penetrate,—conveys the idea of through and through, thoroughly. Some teachers prefer to write 頭, but its meaning is not so appropriate.

透旺 Thoroughly flourishing, very vigorous.

透暄 Thoroughly mellow or light. (C.)

透濕 Thoroughly wet, soaking wet. (S.)

透酥 Thoroughly short or crisp.

透鮮 Thoroughly fresh, altogether fresh.

透活 Thoroughly alive; very loose. (C. & N.)

透亮 Thoroughly light, entirely clear.

迸 To crack, to split open. Some teachers prefer to write 崩, to fall—as a mountain.

迸乾 Splitting dry, dry as tinder.

迸脆 Exceedingly brittle, brittle as glass.

迸俏 Exceeding pretty, very pretty. (S.)

迸俊俏 The same.

剛 Hard, firm,—conveys the idea of rigidity.

剛硬 Rigorously hard or stiff, hard as steel, very rigid. (C. & S.)

剛結實 The same.

泡 A bubble, froth,—conveys the idea of lightness—read both *p'ao*⁴ and *pao*⁴.

泡暄 Very light, or mellow, light as froth, [(C. & S.)

漫 Diffused, to overflow,—conveys the idea of all-pervading.

漫窮 Excessively poor, utterly poor. (S.)

軟還行嗎。○ 12你臉上怎麼希精瘦呢、答這幾天瀉肚瀉的。○ 13別看他的門戶高、房屋大、家裏却是漫精窮。○ 14囫囫圇圇的一個大花瓶、叫您孩子給我打的希粉碎。○ 15鋪蓋都淋得透精濕、晚上怎麼睡覺呢。○ 16京裏的酥果子、是透酥透酥的、別處總做不出那個樣兒來。○ 17實指望他來接手辦、必要辦出個眉眼來、誰知還是希鬆平常。○ 18我實在看不中那個房子、希精矮、還帶着希精窄、不如去另找個大些的。○ 19今年的魚希很賤、連那活透鮮的鮁魚、纔賣十七八個錢一斤。○ 20那些屠戶、眞下得手、一個漫透活的畜牲、說殺就殺了。○ 21這些桃子、有的還剛硬結實、也有的都霹爛喇、給你三十個錢、包元

do to mix the dough too soft.

12 How is it that your face looks so very thin? *Ans.* It comes from the diarrhœa I have had for a few days.

13 Don't be deceived by the fact that he has a high gate and a large house; the family are as poor as they can be.

14 My big vase, perfectly sound, your children have broken all to pieces for me.

15 Our bedding is all wet through and through, how can we sleep to-night?

16 The shortcakes made in the capital are exceedingly crisp, no other place can produce them of the same quality.

17 I sincerely hoped that when he succeeded to the business, he would put matters and things in order; but I am disappointed to find that he is just as careless as others.

18 I really do not like that house at all, it is very low, and besides exceedingly cramped. It would be better to look for one a little larger.

19 Fish are dirt cheap this year, even perfectly fresh bonito only sell for seventeen or eighteen cash per catty.

20 Those butchers are too reckless, they will butcher a live animal without the least hesitation.

21 Some of these peaches are still as hard as bullets, and some are

漫活 Fully alive, very loose or moveable. (s.)

粉 Powder, the bloom of fruit,—conveys the idea of pulverulence.

粉碎 All in pieces, fine as powder. (s.)

粉嫩 Blooming fair or ruddy; very tender.

充 To fill,—conveys the idea of completeness.

充俊 Perfectly beautiful, very pretty. (c.)

潔 Clear, pure,—conveys the idea of purity.

潔白 Pure white, perfectly white.

沙 Granular,—conveys the idea of granularity.

沙嫩 Exceedingly tender or crisp. (s.)

When in any case a given intensive is not used and the dialect affords no other intensive to take its place, Chinese teachers incline to insert 挺 as an equivalent, which however is not a special but a general intensive:—See Les. 15.

VOCABULARY.

水飯 *Shwei*³ *fan*⁴. Rice water with the rice in it:—Note 1.

充 *Ch'ung*¹. To fill full, to satiate; to act in the capacity of; to fulfil; extreme.

潔 *Chie*². Clear, pure, free from sin or defilement, untainted.

薙頭刀 *T'i*⁴ *t'ou*² *tao*¹. A razor.

灢 *Nang*⁴. *Muddy*, sloppy, slippery.

迸 *Pêng*⁴. To drive off; *to crack open*, to split; to leap, to jump, to prance.

暄 *Hsüen*¹. Genial, pleasant; *light*, spongy; *mellow*.

瀉 *Hsie*⁴. To leak, to ooze; *to purge*.

瀉肚 *Hsie*⁴ *tu*⁴. To purge, to have diarrhœa.

好不好。○于22得水、渾身被賊砍的希爛、我一看見、實在肉痲。○秋23天的王黃瓜、纔從科上摘下來的時候、吃着是迸脆、味道是迸鮮。○凡24貼身的衣裳、不可漿糨得太硬、必得希軟的、穿着纔舒坦。○聽25你這麼一講、我心裏就透亮、如同開了兩扇門一般。○我26的槽板牙、早已掉了、前邊雖然還有幾個門牙、上下也不對齒、所以除非發得挺透泡暄的饅頭、一點也不能吃。○王27連升得了一個絕充迸俊俊俊俏的媳婦、潔白的臉、希粉沙嫩的皮、兩個杏核楕眼子睛眼、就和兩汪灣子水一樣。○張28八昨天黑夜、不知多會兒死了、起初他家裏的人、都當是他睡覺、到天亮去摸了一把、渾身都挺剛硬喇。

entirely rotten; what do you say to thirty cash for the lot?

22 Yü Tê Shwei's whole body was hacked to pieces by the robbers. It made my flesh creep to look at him.

23 In the autumn, cucumbers freshly plucked from the vines are exceedingly crisp and highly succulent.

24 Clothing worn next the skin should never be starched too stiff, it must be quite soft in order to be comfortable.

25 Since hearing this explanation of yours my mind is entirely clear. It is like the opening of a double door.

26 My double teeth have long ago fallen out, and although I still have several incisors in front, those above and below do not match; therefore unless bread is raised very light I cannot eat it at all.

27 Wang Lien Shêng has gotten a very pretty wife with a snow-white face and an exceedingly fresh complexion, and her two almond eyes are just like two pools of water.

28 It is not known at what time last night Chang the Eighth died. At first the family all thought he was sleeping; but, when day-light came, a touch of the hand disclosed the fact that his whole body was quite rigid.

門戶 *Mên² hu⁴*. . . . . . . A door, *a gate;* family.

酥 *Su¹*. A cheesy butter; crisp, flaky; *short* (as pastry):—Les. 142. Sub.

接手 *Chie¹ shou³*. *To succeed*, to follow, to come next.

眉眼 *Mei² yien³*. . . . . Outline, *plan;* expression.

活鮮 *Hwoa² hsien¹*. Fresh as life, perfectly fresh:—Les. 148 Sub.

鮁 *Pa⁴*. . . . . The bonito.

屠 *T'u²*. . . . . To kill; to kill and dress, to butcher—especially hogs.

屠戶 *T'u² hu⁴*. . . . . A butcher.

畜牲 *Ch'u⁴ shêng¹*. . . . . . A brute, *an animal.*

霉爛 *Mei² lan⁴*. Decayed and moldy, *rotten;* spoiled.

包元 *Pao¹ yüen²*. To include all, *the lot;* to be responsible for the lot.

王瓜 *Wang² kwa¹*. King of melons,—the cucumber:—Note 23.

黃瓜 *Hwang² kwa¹*. . . . . The same.

味道 *Wei⁴ tao⁴*. . . . . Taste, *flavor.*

槽 *Ts'ao²*. A trough; a flume, a sluice; *a groove*, a channel; a vat, a tub.

槽牙 *Ts'ao² ya²*. . . . . Back teeth, grinders.

板牙 *Pan³ ya²*. . . . . The same. (s.)

門牙 *Mên² ya²*. . . . . Front teeth, incisors.

楕 *Ku²*. A kind of wood; *the kernel or pit of a seed.* (Used for 核.)

汪 *Wang¹*. A wide expanse of water; a pond, *a pool.*

灣 *Wan¹*. A cove, a bay; a pond, *a pool;* an anchorage.

絕俊 *Chüe² chün⁴*. Perfectly beautiful:—Les. 148 Sub.

第一百四十二課

通希[1]嫩的韭菜、你還嫌老。○這[2]一陣怪冷的、關上那個門罷。○我[3]們雖是同縣、却還相隔老遠。○外[4]頭漫通爭亮的月亮、不用燈籠。○別[5]給他舀的溜太滿、恐怕他灑撒出來。○你[6]替我去說說罷、我自己去、漫怪怕害醜臊的。○他[7]昨天到我那裏、日頭還好老高的呢。○這[8]些水精通混喇、可以倒出去、再換一些。○我[9]吃這藕沙酥嫩脆的、實在美可口。

Translation.

1 Perfectly tender chives, and yet you object that they are old.
2 It is rather cold just now. Won't you shut that door?
3 Although from the same county, we are still a long distance apart.
4 The moonlight is quite bright outside, there is no need of a lantern.
5 Don't fill it brim full for him, lest he spills it.
6 Do you go and speak for me, I am too much ashamed to go myself.
7 Yesterday when he arrived at our place, the sun was still ever so high.
8 This water is all muddy; you may throw it out and get some more.
9 I find this water-lily root exceedingly tender and of a most delicious flavor.

Notes.

1 水飯 is different from 稀飯 or 黏粥 in that it is not boiled into a gruel, but is simply boiled soft and eaten swimming in the water in which it is boiled.

2 The translation does not convey the force of 呢. *Of course there is, it is burning briskly,* would approximate the idea.

6 百折不回 *A hundred breaks not bend back;* that is, he is like a stiff stick, so unyielding that a hundred efforts will not cause it to break and double back on itself.

7 The call of one at the wayside selling cooked meat.

10 暄 is here used by accommodation. There is no proper character to express the idea of *spongy* or *mellow.*

11 麪 is *dough* as well as *flour.* In the process of making bread, the dough is called *mien* until it has been made into rolls or loaves, and then it is called by the name given to it after it is baked. Vermicelli, however, is *mien* to the end.

18 大些的 *Larger by some,* somewhat larger.

20 More literally, *Verily those butchers find no difficulty in taking hold; they take the life of a vigorous animal without the least hesitation.*

23 Cucumbers are everywhere called *hwang*² *kwa*¹, but the original and correct writing is 王瓜. Writing 黃瓜 is a concession to the pronunciation.

26 不對齒 *The points* or teeth *not opposite,* 齒 being used for *points,* or as an alternate to avoid the repetition of 牙.

27 媳婦 is here translated wife, because beauty, which is the quality here attributed to her, would be valued by her husband, but not by her father-in-law, who would rather prize diligence, docility, etc.

LESSON CXLII

Special Intensives.

通 To permeate, the whole,—conveys the idea of through and through, entirely, wholly.

通嫩 Perfectly fresh, or tender. (C. & S.)

通亮 Perfectly light, very bright. (S.)

通混 Thoroughly turbid, or muddy. (C. & N.)

通紅 All over red, entirely red, a bright red.

通肥 All over fat, rolling fat, fat. (C.)

老 Old,—applied to words expressive of size and distance. Old things are supposed to have grown *great.*

老遠 Ever so far, very distant.

老高 Ever so high, very high or lofty.

老大 Ever so big, very large or great.

老厚 Ever so thick, enormously thick.

老粗 Ever so large, very large, or coarse.

老長 Ever so long, very long.

溜 To flow, to glide,—conveys the idea of evenness or smoothness, and is applied chiefly to lines and surfaces.

○那[10]塊冰溜希滑、得要小心纔能過去。○今[11]天怪漫熱、身上很覺着發懶。○通[12]紅的花兒、碧綠的葉兒、畫的實在現活。○這[13]兩個馱子、都精爭飄輕、不值得駝的。○你[14]想他孩子已經老大喇。他爸参爸還沒有二十五嗎。○可[15]以去找人、修理修理那個打毬塲、把他輥的溜坦平的。○你[16]自己在家裏不害怕嗎、答害怕倒不害怕、就是覺着怪希孤冷單清的。○可[17]以給我做個小綿襖、絮的精溜薄椤的、預備秋後穿。○你[18]快拿到河裏去洗罷、河裏澄碧清的水。○宋[19]家眞是個財主的

10 That piece of ice is very slippery, it will be necessary to take care in crossing it.

11 It is excessively hot to-day and I feel very lazy.

12 The painting is very life-like indeed with those bright red blossoms and emerald green leaves.

13 These two [mule] loads are quite light, less than animals ought to carry.

14 Just think, the son is already ever so big, and is the father not yet twenty-five?

15 You may go and find a man to put the ball ground in order. Have it rolled perfectly smooth.

16 Are you not afraid to stay at home alone? *Ans.* No, I am not afraid; but I feel somewhat lonesome.

17 You may make me a small wadded coat with quite thin wadding, ready for wearing when autumn sets in.

18 Take it at once to the river and wash it. The water in the river is quite clear.

19 The Sung family certainly have the

溜滿 Level full, brimming full. (C. & S.)

溜滑 Very slippery, smooth as glass.

溜平 Perfectly smooth, level as a board.

溜椤 Very thin, thin as paper. (C. & S.)

溜光 Very smooth, smooth as glass. (C. & N.)

溜圓 Perfectly round, round as a ball.

怪 Strange, monstrous. As an intensive 怪 is rather general than specific, there being no special limit to its application, save that it always implies something *unpleasantly* excessive. It is moreover only a semi-intensive, answering very nearly to our words *quite, rather, somewhat,* etc. Its use may perhaps be explained by considering it an exaggeration, as "horribly" is often used in colloquial English.

爭 To strive for precedence,—conveys the idea of pre-eminence. Some would prefer to write 增 to add.

爭亮 Exceedingly bright, glistening.

爭輕 Exceedingly light, light as possible. (C.)

爭肥 Exceedingly fat, rolling fat. (N.)

飄 To sway or float on the wind,—conveys the idea of buoyancy.

飄輕 Very light, light as a feather, light as air. (S.)

酥 Crisp, flaky,—conveys the idea of crispness.

酥脆 Very crisp, short, flaky, or brittle.

酥焦 Very crisp, short, or flaky.

焦 Scorched,—conveys the idea of brittleness.

焦脆 Very crisp, short as a crackling. (N.)

坦 A plain,—used by way of comparison.

坦平 Level as a plain, very level. (S.)

碧 Green jade stone,—used by way of comparison.

碧清 Extremely clear or limpid, clear as crystal. (S.)

碧綠 Emerald green.

油 Oil,—used by way of comparison.

油光 Very smooth, sleek as oil.

澄 Clear, limpid—conveys the idea of transparency. (C. & N.)

澄清 Transparently clear, clear as crystal.

赤 Red, flesh color,—conveys the idea of ruddiness.

赤紅 Very red, blood-red, flaming red.

樣子、你看他家出來的騾子馬和狗、個個吃
的爭/通/精肥。○女[20]人還能勝過男人嗎、他若再向
你生氣、不如讓他、免得叫他打的怪疼的。○
這[21]是早晨纔炒的落花生/長生果/花生、焦脆焦脆/酥焦酥焦的、你只
管多稱幾兩去吃罷。○淑[22]貞的右手第二個
指頭上、長了一個疔、連手背都腫的老厚、胳
膊也腫的老粗、還有老長的一道紅線、看着
眞嚇人的。○山[23]後那個泉眼/泉的水、管多會兒/子
都是澄/碧清、一眼能望到底。○六[24]九子奶奶/媳婦、今
天上他娘/媽家去喇、梳的溜/油光的頭、穿的湛/簇新

appearance of wealth. Look at the mules, horses and dogs which come out of their door; every one is rolling fat.

20 Can a woman overcome a man? If he gets angry with you again, it will be better to give up to him and avoid the pain of his blows.

21 These peanuts were just roasted this morning and are exceedingly crisp, you're safe in buying a supply of them to eat.

22 Shu Chên has a felon on the second finger of her right hand, so that even the back of her hand and her forearm are swollen up ever so thick, and there is a long red line [extending up her arm]: really it is something frightful to look at.

23 The water in that spring north of the hill is always clear as crystal, one can see straight to the bottom of it.

24 Liu Chiu-tsï's wife went home to see her mother to-day. Her hair was combed smooth as oil and she had on a brand new silk coat and

湛 Deep and clear,—conveys the idea of entireness.
湛新 Entirely new, brand new.
明 Bright,—conveys the idea of shining.
明亮 Shining bright, glistening.

精混 Extremely muddy, very turbid.
精輕 Extremely light, very light. (C. & N.)
精薄 Extremely thin. (C. & N.)
精肥 Extremely fat. (S.)
希滑 Exceedingly slippery, excessively smooth. (S.)
希冷清 Very cool; lonesome. (S.)
希醜 Exceedingly ugly, horribly ugly. (S.)
漫亮 Very light, bright as day. (S.)
漫熱 Very hot or warm, oppressively hot. (S.)
簇新 Entirely new, brand new. (S.)
透歡 Very animated, sprightly.
迸歡 Very animated, sprightly.

VOCABULARY.

碧 *Pi*^{4}. . . . . Green jade-stone.
澄 *Têng*^{4}, *ch'êng*^{2}. Clear, limpid; to clarify by settling; to pour off, to decant.
酥 *Su*^{2}. Curd, cheese; crisp, flaky, short; numb.
簇 *Ts'u*^{4}. . . . . An arrow head; a crowd, a group.
赤 *Ch'ï*^{4}. Carnation red, flesh color; naked; destitute, barren.
韭 *Chiu*^{3}. . . . . Chives, scallions.
韭菜 *Chiu*^{3} *ts'ai*^{4}. . . . . Chives, scallions.
藕 *Ou*^{3}. . . . Water-lily plant; the water-lily root.
可口 *K'ê*^{3} *k'ou*^{3}. . . . . Savory, *delicious*.
美口 *Mei*^{3} *k'ou*^{3}. . . . . . *Delicious*, savory, tasty.
發懶 *Fa*^{1} *lan*^{3}. *To be lazy*, to feel languid or weary; to be disinclined.
現活 *Hsien*^{4} *hwoa*^{2}. . . . . . . *Life-like*, natural.
爸 *Pa*^{4}. . . . . Papa,—always doubled in use. (N.)
輥 *Kun*^{3}. . . . . *To roll;* a rolling motion.
孤單 *Ku*^{1} *tan*^{1}. Alone; lonely, solitary, *lonesome*.

的紬子襖、(通/赤)紅的洋機褲子、管那裏紥裏的都好、就是兩隻大脚(希/怪)醜的。○西25國兵所用的洋鎗、都擦磨的明亮、到出隊的時候、叫太陽一照、眞如同明鏡一般。○馬26先生的小孩兒、長的實在(待/叫/得)人(親/愛/疼)、溜圓的一個大頭、(透/迸)歡的、兩個眼睛誰願意抱就抱、一點也不認生。○我27纔記事的時候、那個地方、不過多少存一點水、現在叫水沖了一道老長的大溝、非從橋上、不能過去。

bright red muslin trowsers. She was dressed up nicely in every respect, only that her two big feet looked horribly ugly.

25 The guns used by western soldiers are all polished up bright, so that when they are on parade, the sun shining on the guns makes them gleam like mirrors.

26 Mr. Ma's child has grown to be a very loveable boy, with his large round head and two laughing eyes. Whoever wishes may take him in their arms, he is not in the least strange.

27 When I was first old enough to remember, there was only a little water standing there; but now the water has washed a great gully which one cannot cross save by going over the bridge.

冷清 *Lêng*³ *ch'ing*¹. Cold, chilly; *lonesome;* cool, distant.

炒 *Ch'ao*³. To fry with constant stirring; to scramble eggs; to roast or brown (as peanuts or coffee.)

落花生 *Loà*⁴ *hwa*¹ *shêng*¹. Peanuts.

長生果 *Ch'ang*² *shêng*¹ *kwoà*³. The same:—Note 21.

花生 *Hwa*¹ *shêng*¹. The same.

淑 *Shu*⁴˒². Limpid; virtuous, uncorrupted. (w.)

貞 *Chên*¹. To inquire by divination; lucky; chaste, virtuous, undefiled.

疔 *Ting*¹. A venereal ulcer; *a felon.*

手背 *Shou*³ *pei*⁴. The back of the hand.

泉眼 *Ch'üen*² *yien*³. A fountain, *a spring.*

紥 *Tsa*¹, *cha*¹. *To wind around and bind,* to bandage, to tie securely.

裹 *Kwoà*³. *To wrap around,* to bind.

紥裹 *To dress up,* to accoutre, to trick out; to patch up, to mend.

洋鎗 *Yang*² *ch'iang*¹. A foreign gun, *a gun,* a pistol.

擦磨 *Ts'a*¹ *moà*². To rub, to scour, *to polish.*

NOTES.

7 呢 indicates a tone of surprise which cannot be expressed in a translation.

14 Lit., *Just think, his son is already ever so big, and is his father not yet twenty-five?* which, however, conveys a wrong sense, since one 他 stands for the father and the other for the son. Practically 他 is equivalent to the definite article, as in the translation.

15 A piece of ground devoted specially to ball playing is a foreign idea, but rolling is familiar to the Chinese, as they roll all their threshing floors.

17 秋後 does not mean *after the autumn,* but rather 立秋後, *after the setting in of the autumn.*

20 The person spoken of is probably the woman's husband. It is quite an ordinary occurrence for a man, especially a young man, to whip his wife.

21 The three terms given for peanuts represent approximately the Northern, Central and Southern names, but the Northern term is most widely used.

22 The 的 at the end of this sentence is represented in the translation by the word *something.* A more literal rendering would be, *really it is appalling to look at.* The 的 might be omitted without special detriment.

23 一眼 *One eye;* that is, *at one look, at a glance, readily.*

24 The addition of 兩隻 gives emphasis.

第一百四十三課

這[1]有什麼笑頭呢。○他[2]打鎗、一點準頭沒有。○山[3]前的景緻、很有看頭。○看[4]這件事的來頭、必要難辦。○我[5]家裏一個親人也沒有、還有甚麼戀頭呢。○你[6]該讓他一點、不可做到盡頭。○這[7]碗蠣羹、好體面（美）口頭。○他[8]的口頭語、帶着許多髒話。○我[9]坐在這裏就好、這裏有個靠頭兒。○孫[10]先生講書、人都嫌沒有聽頭。○像[11]我這等孤苦（老）人、你當（認）是還有甚麼奔頭嗎。○不[12]能說是不彀秤、不過是沒有抬頭、高頭、出秤。○這[13]些沒有滋味的話、有甚麼說頭呢。○他[14]

Translation.

1 What is there to laugh at in this?
2 He cannot shoot with the least accuracy.
3 The view south of the mountain is well worth seeing.
4 It is evident from the way this thing presents itself that it will be very hard to manage.
5 At home I have not a single near relative. What is there to hold my affections?
6 You ought to make some concession to him and not go to extremes.
7 This bowl of oyster soup has a very fine flavor.
8 His favorite expressions are characterized by a great deal of vulgarity.
9 Sitting here just suits me, as I have something to lean against.
10 All complain that Mr. Sun's expository lectures are uninteresting.
11 Do you suppose that a forlorn old man like me has anything to live for?
12 It cannot be said that it is short weight, it is only that it is not good weight.
13 What is the use of this insipid talk?

LESSON CXLIII.

頭 Joined to Verbs and Adjectives.

In addition to its use with nouns as in Les. 17, 頭 is also joined to verbs and adjectives. When joined to a transitive verb, it gives a meaning equal to, something to, or worthy of, as 聽頭 something to hear; that is, something worth hearing. When joined to an adjective, it gives the force of a noun of corresponding meaning. Intransitive verbs are used participially, and follow the use of adjectives. These statements have some exceptions and modifications, as appears in the following list. For additional list see supplement.

笑頭 Something to laugh at, worth laughing at, laughable.

準頭 Accuracy of aim, a definite object.

看頭 Something worth looking at, pleasing to the eye, a sight.

來頭 The aspect of an approaching event or person, looks.

戀頭 Something worthy of being longed for or attached to, attachment.

盡頭 The extreme, the uttermost, the bitter end, the last drop.

口頭 Taste, flavor,—口 being put by metonomy for 嘗.

靠頭 Something to lean upon, backing, support.

聽頭 Something worth hearing, entertainment, instruction.

奔頭 Something worthy of pursuit, an object, an aim.

高頭 Extra height, elevation, projection above:—Note (12).

抬頭 The same,—抬 being taken participially. It is also used to mean, worth carrying, weighty.

說頭 Worth saying, point, interest.

去頭 Worth going, worth while to go.

活頭 Living time, space or time to live, prolongation of life.

甜頭 Sweetness; a perquisite, a cumshaw.

不歡喜見我、我還有什麼去頭呢。○看15你這個樣子、怕沒有大活頭。○除16了他應得的工錢、一點甜頭外出息也沒有。○人17在世上、沒有幾天的混頭。○做18這桿手鎗、真得個好手頭。○夢19是心頭想。○這20種僟頭風箏、怎麼放得起呢。○李21紹祖得空就往那裏去、也不知那裏有他的什麼想頭。○幸22虧你的嘴頭上得塲能說、不然、就被他問倒了。○若23是他跟前有個小廝、那還有個盼望頭。○他24不愛出力、敢保在孫師傅那裏、沒有大住頭。○你25聽了誰的攛掇撮弄、為着什麼事情起這個念頭、我實在不懂喇。○這26個驢一分養頭也沒有、現擺放着大路他不走、單願意往

14 When he does not wish to see me, what point is there in my going?
15 Judging from your present appearance, I fear you have not long to live.
16 In addition to his regular wages, there are no perquisites at all.
17 In a few days man shuffles through this mortal life.
18 To make this pistol has certainly taken a high order of skill.
19 Dreams are the uppermost thoughts of the mind.
20 How can one fly such a rickety old kite as this?
21 Whenever Li Shao Tsu has time he runs over there. I wonder what allurement there is for him at that place.
22 It is fortunate you have a ready tongue, otherwise his questions would have put you in a predicament.
23 If she has a young son, she still has an object to live for.
24 He does not like to work; I venture he will not stay long with Sun Shï-fu.
25 To whose instigation have you been listening? Why you have taken up this idea I really do not understand.
26 This donkey is not at all worth his keeping: he will not go in the broad road before him, but is all the time wanting to sheer off to the side.

混頭 Time or space for shifting along.
手頭 Skill of hand, dexterity,—手 being put by metonomy for 巧.
僟頭 Vile, scrubby, rickety, good-for-nothing.
想頭 Longing, desire, allurement.
嘴頭 Capacity or faculty for talking; the mouth as the organ of speech.
盼頭 Something to hope for, expectation, incentive, inspiration.
望頭 The same.
住頭 Staying time, length of time.
念頭 Thought, idea, notion, opinion.
養頭 Worth supporting, worth keeping.
賺頭 Something gained, profit.
講究頭 Worth talking about, worthy of consideration.
玩頭 Amusement, entertainment.
樸頭 Something to resort to, dependence.
年頭 The harvests of the year, the season, the crops, — 年 being put by metonomy for 收.
添頭 Something added, an increase, a supplement.

VOCABULARY.

打鎗 *Ta*3 *ch'iang*1........ To shoot; to hunt.
景緻 *Ching*3 *chï*4........ Scenery, *view*, sight.
蠣 *Li*4........ Oysters.
孤苦 *Ku*1 *k'u*3...... Lonely, *forlorn*, desolate.
孤老 *Ku*1 *lao*3. Old and childless; *forlorn*, ...desolate.
外出息 *Wai*4 *ch'u*1 *hsi*2.......... Extras. [*perquisites*.
手鎗 *Shou*3 *ch'iang*1.......... A pistol.

路邊旁裏蹓。○大[27]約他不能賺錢、就是賺、也沒有大賺頭。○那[28]個混帳行子東西有甚麼大講究頭、斷不可題他。○實[29]指望到會上去玩玩、開開心就好了、那知道一點玩頭也沒有。○小[30]孩子在平日間、一時也離不開他媽媽、因此媽媽一死、就覺着沒有靠樸頭了。○徐[31]悟眞忽然起了修煉的念頭、用了好些日子的工夫、到底沒摸着門兒。○今[32]年這個年頭、眞是取借無門、憑着田地、賤貴都找不出要主買主來。○俗[33]語說、要價不嫌多、還價不嫌少、所以買東西的時候、不好一口還到了數、總要留點添頭。

27 He will not likely make any money, and if he does it will not be much.

28 What is there worthy of so much consideration in that worthless villain? Don't mention his name.

29 I confidently hoped that by going to the fair, the amusements and diversion of mind would set me all right; but it turned out after all that there was nothing worth seeing.

30 In ordinary circumstances a child cannot do, for even a little while, without its mother: hence when its mother dies, it feels without any dependence at all.

31 Hsü Wu Chên, all at once, took up the idea of becoming an ascetic, but, after trying for some time, he wholly failed to get hold of the clue.

32 In such a year as this there is not the least chance to borrow, and with houses and lands to sell, one can find no purchaser at any price.

33 The proverb says, "One cannot ask too high a price nor offer too low a one." Therefore in buying a thing, it is not best to offer at once all you are willing to give, but always leave room for rising.

箏 *Chêng*¹. . . . . A harpsichord; *a kite*.

風箏 *Fêng*¹ *chêng*¹. . . . . A kite.

攛 *Ts'wan*¹. . . . . To fling; to stir up, *to foment*.

掇 *Ts'oă*³. . . . To exchange, to mix up. See *toă*⁴.

攛掇 To excite by misrepresentation, to carry tales and foment a quarrel; to *instigate*, to inveigle.

撮弄 *Ts'oă*¹ *lung*⁴. To stir up, *to foment*, to . . . . egg on, to urge, to hustle.

行子 *Hang*² *tsï*³. . . . . . A tribe, a set, *a fellow*.

開心 *K'ai*¹ *hsin*¹. To dissipate care or trouble, ... *to divert the mind*, to relax.

平日 *P'ing*² *jï*⁴. *In ordinary times*, commonly, ... ordinarily.

修煉 *Hsiu*¹ *lien*⁴. To practice the austerities of . . . . an ascetic.

取借 *Ch'ü*³ *chie*⁴. . . . . To borrow money.

要主 *Yao*⁴ *chu*³. . . . . A buyer, a purchaser.

買主 *Mai*³ *chu*³. . . . . The same.

Notes.

8 口頭, as here used, belongs rather to Lesson 47 than to this one; yet 頭 is not regularly joined with 口, as it is with 骨 and 舌. 髒話 is the Southern form, in the North 髒 is rarely used without 骯 before it.

10 講書 here refers to expounding the classics, as is regularly done in Chinese schools.

12 It is the general custom to give *good weight*, by weighing with the beam of the steelyards considerably above the horizontal. This is spoken of in Peking as 抬頭, in Shantung as 高頭, and in the South as 出秤, *going beyond the scale*. It should perhaps be added that steelyards are generally made to weigh a little *light*.

17 Note the difference between 活頭 (15) and 混頭. The former has reference to living, simply; the latter regards the manner of living.

19 This is a puzzling sentence, and 頭 as here used hardly comes under the subject of the lesson. A friend suggests the following translation; *A dream is the surface thought of the heart.*

22 上得場 *Fit to appear on the arena, equal to the emergency.*

第一百四十四課

告[1]訴他是我的本分、至於聽不聽在他。○孩[2]子總得從小管、及至長成了人、再就管不好喇。○要[3]用可以拿去罷、論到錢上、咱們兩個、斷不可提。○我[4]就是怕有病、至於做活多少、那不要緊。○赶[5]我去了、已經鎖了門。○天[6]已經到了這個時候、等赶預備好得了、總要得到黑。○快[7]打打辮子罷、及等赶吃了飯、就該上學喇。○我[8]們但能看人的外貌、至於心裏的意思、誰能看得透呢。○有[9]一等人、專好播弄是非、及至人家鬧起事來、他就躲在一邊了。○我[10]走的畧遲晚點、赶我到了、他已

TRANSLATION.

1 My duty is to tell him; as to his heeding it or not, that rests with him.
2 Children should, by all means, be governed from the first. When they have grown to adult age, they cannot then be successfully governed.
3 If you wish to use it, take it; as for pay, that is not to be mentioned between us two.
4 What I fear is sickness; as to the amount of work to be done, that is of no consequence.
5 When I arrived the door was already locked.
6 It is already so late that by the time we get ready it will be dark.
7 Be quick and comb your hair; by the time you have eaten, it will be time to go to school.
8 We can only see a man's exterior; as to the designs of his heart, who can penetrate them?
9 There is a class of men whose chief delight is in stirring up strife, but as soon as the parties get to fighting they slip out of the way.
10 I started a little late and by the time

23 小厮 means properly *a slave or servant*, but is in many places applied to little boys, as 丫頭 is to little girls.

25 The first two clauses of this sentence might be regarded as independent interrogations, and the third an exclamation by way of comment, thus: *Whose instigation have you been listening to? For what reason have you taken up this idea? I really do not understand it.* The insertion of a 呢 after 攛掇, and another after 念頭, would fix this construction, but their omission does not necessarily exclude it.

26 現放着 ought by rights to apply to the person speaking, whereas Chinese teachers make it descriptive of the road. In this case 的 must be supplied after 着, or else 着 be changed to 的. I have translated as if 的 were written instead of 着.

33 Or, *The buyer is not offended at a high asking price, nor the seller at a low offer.*

LESSON CXLIV.

PREPOSITIONAL PHRASES.

至於 As to, with reference to, with respect to:—See Les. 191. Sub.

論到 As to, as for, with reference to, with respect to.

說到 The same.

論及 The same.

及 By the time,—not often used alone.

及至 When, but when, by the time.

及至於 But when, by the time, at the time.

及攻 By the time, when. (C.)

赶 By the time, as soon as. (C. & N.)

等 The same. (S.)

及赶 By the time, when, as soon as. (C. & N.)

及等 The same. (S.)

及到 The same. (S.)

赶到 By the time, at the time, when.

經喊了寃喇。○人11初時間做了壞事、心裏也過不去、及至做得一椿兩椿、膽子就大了。○你12已經使用了定錢、你就必得賣給我、論及別的、咱們說不着。○借13給他的時候、他是十分歡喜、及至於要的時候、他就惱了。○賈14丕齡就是嘴頭子蛤固硬扎、論及韜畧、他卻不及他哥哥。○他15只求有個好女婿就得中了、至於家裏貧富、絕然不論。○先16生的外祖父、好了沒有、答那裏好了呢、趕到及攻我去的時候、早就咽了氣。○論17及兩家的錢財、不差什麼、就是張家的人口多一點。○他18們怎樣打架、我都親眼見過、至於以後怎樣和息了、我卻一字不知。○他19調治痔瘡疔瘡、這一切的外科、還

I arrived he had already appealed for protection.

11 When a man first does wrong, his mind is ill at ease; but when he has done so once or twice, his courage increases.

12 You have already received the earnest money, and you must sell to me. There is no room to talk about anything else.

13 When I loaned it to him, he was highly pleased; but when I asked him for it, he got angry.

14 Chia P'ei Ling's tongue is extremely sharp, but in strategy he is inferior to his elder brother.

15 He simply seeks for a good son-in-law, whether poor or rich he does not care in the least.

16 Has your maternal grandfather recovered? *Ans.* No, indeed. By the time I arrived he had already breathed his last.

17 The two families are about equal in wealth, but the Changs have a somewhat larger family.

18 I saw their fighting with my own eyes, but as to how they were afterwards reconciled I know nothing whatever.

19 He treats hemorrhoids and syphilitic ulcers and this whole class of external

Vocabulary.

攻 *Kung*¹. To attack, to assault; to apply to; to arouse, to stimulate.

打辮子 *Ta*³ *pien*⁴ *tsï*³. To comb and plait the hair.

播 *Poă*³ To sow, to scatter; to publish abroad; to reject; *to shake, to winnow.*

播弄 *Poă*³ *lung*⁴. To move; to manage, to cheat; *to stir up.*

喊寃 *Han*³ *yüen*¹. To call for justice, *to appeal for protection*:—Note 10.

初時間 *Ch'u*¹ *shï*² *chien*¹. *At first*, at the start, in the beginning.

定錢 *Ting*⁴ *ch'ien*². Earnest money, money to bind a bargain.

丕 *P'ei*³, *p'i*³. Unequaled, distinguished.

蛤 *Kĕ*², *ka*². A frog; a lizard; *any bivalve shell.* Also *ka*¹.

蛤固 *Ka*² *ku*⁴. Severe, stern, savage, *fierce*, relentless. (C. & N.)

硬扎 *Ying*⁴ *cha*¹. Severe, stern, *fierce*. (S.)

韜 *T'ao*¹. A quiver, a scabbard; to sheath.

韜畧 *T'ao*¹ *lüe*⁴. Devices, *stratagems*.

祖父 *Tsu*³ *fu*⁴. Paternal grandfather.

外祖父 *Wai*⁴ *tsu*³ *fu*⁴. Maternal grandfather.

錢財 *Ch'ien*² *ts'ai*². Money; *wealth*.

和息 *Hĕ*² *hsi*². To make up a quarrel, to make peace, *to become reconciled.*

痔 *Chï*⁴. Piles, hemorrhoids.

痔瘡 *Chï*⁴ *ch'wang*¹. Piles; rectal ulcers.

算可以。若論到內科、臟腑裏的病、他却是一門不通。○包[20]運隆就是吃飯賽得過人的(趕個好的)、說到做活、十個也抵不住一個。○我[21]聽見背後裏、欻的一聲、趕我一回頭(及我一掉臉)、已經咬着了。○你[22]昨天到聖廟裏去、看見孔子甚麼樣兒呢、答說到他的樣兒、實在出奇、面目醜陋、五露朝天、一點也不好看、但他既有那樣的聖德、人可沒有嫌他醜的。○論[23]到求着成仙的人、眞有些誠心的、我在泰山上、看見一個洞、洞裏有個道士、從多年就在那裏打坐修煉、飲食一天減似一天、漸漸的也不吃、也不喝、趕到(及到)我看見的時候、他坐在那裏已經死了、身上只有皮包骨頭、指甲有半尺多長。

ailments very well, but as to the diseases of the internal organs he is entirely ignorant.

20 In eating, Pao Yün Lung counts a full hand (excels); as for work, ten of him would not count one.

21 I heard a growl behind me, and before I could turn my head he had bitten me.

22 You went yesterday to visit the temple of the sage: what does Confucius look like? *Ans.* He is certainly very remarkable in appearance, his features are uncouth and his face slants backwards, so that he is very far from good looking; but since he had such sagely virtue no one objects to his looks.

23 Speaking of those who seek immortality, there certainly are some of them sincere. At the T'ai Mountain I saw a cave and in the cave a Taoist priest who for many years had been sitting there disciplining himself. He took less and less nourishment each day until, at last, he neither ate nor drank at all. At the time I saw him he had already died sitting there, and his body was nothing but skin and bone, his finger nails being over half a foot long.

疔瘡 *Ting¹ ch'wang¹*. . . . . . . Syphilitic ulcers.

外科 *Wai⁴ k'ê¹*. Medical practice relating to . . . . the external parts and organs.

內科 *Nei⁴ k'ê¹*. Medical practice relating to the . . . . internal parts and organs.

臟 *Tsang⁴*. The thoracic viscera; the contents . . . . of the trunk.

腑 *Fu³*. . . . . The abdominal viscera.

臟腑 The internal parts and organs of the body.

賽 *Sai⁴*. To present thanks; to strive for superiority, to emulate, *to rival*.

欻 *Hu¹, ch'wa¹*. Suddenly; to bang, to whiz; . . . . to sniff, *to growl*.

掉臉 *Tiao⁴ lien³*. *To turn the head*, to look . . . . around, to turn about.

出奇 *Ch'u¹ ch'i²*. *Remarkable*, wonderful, ... strange, startling.

面目 *Mien⁴ mu⁴*. The face, *the features*, the . . . . countenance.

成仙 *Ch'êng² hsien¹*. To become an immortal:— . . . . Note 23.

誠心 *Ch'êng² hsin¹*. *Sincere*, honest, ingenuous, ... guileless.

道士 *Tao⁴ shï⁴*. . . . . A Taoist priest.

打坐 *Ta³ tsoa⁴*. To sit continuously as a means . . . . of ascetic contemplation.

NOTES.

5 Or, *By the time I arrived he (or they) had locked the door.* There is nothing to show whether 鎖 is to be taken actively or passively.

10 An 一 might be inserted before 點. When any one is violently assaulted or maltreated, he flies to the yamên and calls loudly on the magistrate for protection and redress.

第一百四十五課

人[1]以無事爲福。○不[2]可以外貌取人。○他[3]整天的家、專以賭博爲事。○以[4]此辛苦讀書、可以成名。○要[5]以公道爲主、兩家不可相虧。○小[6]人常以自己的私心、測度君子。○有[7]道的人、總以道爲是。○若[8]單以口舌與他相爭、甚是費力。○你[9]們作兒女的、不可以父母拘管爲仇。○漸[10]漸習以爲常、連覺也不覺了。○中[11]國的婦女們、多以出頭露面爲羞恥。○記[12]得古來的事情、以好的爲法、以不好的爲戒。○你[13]聽他這些無理的話、淨是以大壓小、以強壓

TRANSLATION.

1 Men regard freedom from trouble as happiness.
2 Judge not according to the outward [appearance.
3 He makes gambling his constant and sole employment.
4 Studying with such assiduity as this, he should get his degree.
5 Make justice your rule and let neither party wrong the other.
6 The mean man always makes his own selfishness the standard by which he measures the superior man.
7 Wisdom is justified of her children.
8 If you limit your contention with him to words, the case will be exceedingly difficult.
9 You who are children must not regard the restraints of your parents as proceeding from enmity.
10 Habit gradually becomes so confirmed that one is not even conscious of it.
11 Most Chinese women consider it a shame to show their faces in public.
12 Former things are kept in remembrance that the good may be used as examples and the bad as warnings.
13 Just listen to his unreasonable talk;

This is called 喊冤. In very urgent cases he also beats the drum at the inner door, placed there for the purpose, which (theoretically) compels the immediate attention of the magistrate.

12 The payment of a small portion of the price in order to fix a bargain is a common custom, especially in buying houses or lands.

18 一字不知 is an affectation of book style. The ordinary colloquial would be 一點兒不知道.

19 一門不通 *Does not comprehend a single step or principle, incompetent in every respect.* 門 is equal to 法門, *art, method, principle; department, branch.*

22 聖廟 *Holy temple*, that is, the temple of Confucius, which has in it an image of Confucius, and also of each of his chief disciples. There is such a temple in every *Hsien* city. According to tradition, Confucius was far from prepossessing in appearance. 五露朝天 *The five orifices facing heavenwards*, viz., the eyes, nostrils, and mouth. 朝天 means that the chin protruded and the forehead retreated, so as to give his face the appearance of being directed upwards.

23 成仙 *To become an immortal*, by a process intended to eliminate the gross and the sensual, and at the same time to nourish and stimulate the spiritual and the ethereal. This process consists in sitting erect and motionless with the features fixed in an attitude of contemplation (打坐), in holding the breath and acquiring the art of breathing only at long intervals, in gradually reducing the amount of food to a minimum, and in sundry other exercises and austerities.

LESSON CXLV.

THE INSTRUMENTAL VERB 以.

以 To use, to take, to regard as,—the common instrumental verb of the book language, but often used in Mandarin, especially in ready-made forms and phrases.

以爲 To regard as, to take as, to use as. In the majority of the cases in which 以 is used as an instrumental verb in Mandarin, it is followed by 爲, either directly or separated by a few words. 以 being a book word gives character to the whole lesson, most of the sentences being more or less *Wên*.

弱。○14人的良心、大不相同、常有這人以爲是的、那人倒以爲非。○15你不可爲惡所勝、應當以善勝惡。○16你們可不大家省悟、着實以農桑爲重嗎。○17像這樣渺冥茫無憑的事、人竟信以爲眞、都是因習而不察的緣故。○18應當以螞蟻蟻蛘和蜜蜂爲榜樣、效法他的殷勤。○91我初次上京、進了永定門、以爲是進了城咯、他們還說是城外、再進了前門、那纔是進了城咯。○20叫人暗暗的傳了一二十個能事的衙役、遠遠跟隨、以備使

he is squarely advocating [the principle] that might makes right.

14 The consciences of men differ widely. It frequently happens that what one man regards as right, another considers wrong.

15 Be not overcome of evil, but overcome evil with good.

16 Should not all take warning, and emphatically regard farming and silk raising as the important things?

17 That men should believe and regard as true anything so vague and unattested as this, is simply because they accept it without examination.

18 You should take the ant and the bee as patterns, and imitate their diligence.

19 The first time I went to Peking, I entered the Yungting gate and supposed I had entered the city, but was told that I was still outside the city, and that only after entering the South gate would I be inside.

20 He sent and secretly summoned ten or twenty efficient constables to follow him at a distance ready for service.

21 Do you suppose that he of the double

VOCABULARY.

私心 *Si*¹ *hsin*¹. *Selfishness*, partiality; underhand, secret.

度 *Toā*⁴. To guess, to estimate, *to measure*. See *tu*⁴.

測度 *Ts'ê*⁴ *toā*⁴. *To measure*, to estimate, to calculate, to fathom.

拘管 *Chü*¹ *kwan*³. *To restrain*, to control, to hold in check.

婦女 *Fu*⁴ *nü*³. Wives and daughters, women. Note 11.

露面 *Lou*⁴ *mien*⁴. *To show one's face*, to appear in public:—Note 11.

渺 *Miao*³. Indistinct, *vague;* boundless.

冥 *Ming*². Dark, *obscure;* the unseen world.

茫 *Mang*². Vast and vague—as the ocean.

渺冥 Indistinct, *vague;* uncertain, unattested.

渺茫 *Vague*, misty, indistinct; vast.

蛘 *Yang*³. The mantis.

蟻蛘 *I*³ *yang*³. An ant, an emmet. Read *ki*³ *yang*³ in many places.

蜜蜂 *Mi*⁴ *fêng*¹. A honey-bee, a bee.

榜 *Pang*³. To beat, to bamboo; a placard; *a list of successful competitors.*

榜樣 *Pang*³ *yang*⁴. A model, an example, *a pattern.*

效法 *Hsiao*⁴ *fa*³. *To imitate*, to copy, to pattern after.

跟隨 *Kên*¹ *swei*². *To follow;* to attend.

翎 *Ling*². *A plume*, a tail feather, a feather.

花翎 *Hwa*¹ *ling*². A peacock's feather, a variegated plume.

惹氣 *Jê*³ *ch'i*⁴. To provoke to anger, to irritate; to vex; *to quarrel.*

霸道 *Pa*⁴ *tao*⁴. The way of a tyrant, *oppression;* usurpation; intimidation.

附從 *Fu*⁴ *ts'ung*². *To follow*, to submit to, to obey; to become an adherent.

打光棍 *Ta*³ *kwang*¹ *kun*⁴. *To lead the life of a villain;* to act without regard to consequences; to live by one's wits; to play the sharper.

喚。○21你以爲大花翎家怕你嗎、人家是不願意和你惹氣啊。○22能作大惡、又能行大善、而且能以大善蓋掩大惡、使人只知他的善爲善、不以他的惡爲惡、這纔算是大光棍、就如從前有個李飛虎、若見那些富貴有勢力的人、橫行霸道、不幹正事、他就硬强問他要銀子、不給不行、要出一千八百來、就和附從他的人、夥吃夥用、一點不分彼此、若有窮人求他、都是三千五吊的帮助、你看現在這些打光棍的、有這麼一個嗎。

plume is afraid of you? He is simply averse to having a dispute with you.

22 It is the characteristic of an accomplished rascal that he is able to perpetrate great crimes while practising great virtues, and moreover is able to use these great virtues to cover up his great crimes, so that while men recognize his virtues they are oblivious to his crimes. For instance, there was formerly one Li Fei Hu, who, when he saw rich and powerful men given to high handed oppression and neglecting the ordinary virtues of life, would peremptorily demand money of them and would take no denial, and when he had extorted from them eight hundred or a thousand [taels], would use it for the common wants of himself and his followers, making no distinction whatever of *meum* and *tuum*. If a poor man appealed to him, he was sure to get a lift of from three to five thousand [cash]. Look at the present race of rascals will you? Is there one such among them?

NOTES.

6 小人……君子 In Confucian ethics these two terms are constantly recurring opposites. They are the *saint* and *sinner* of classical religion. 小人 is the *selfish, mean-spirited man*, 君子 is the *high-minded and honorable man*.

7 Or, *He that has truth always regards truth as right;* that is, a man of principle is always loyal to his principles.

9 Be careful to read 可 and 以 separately, and not, as they so frequently are, one word. 父母拘管爲仇 would be distinctly improved by inserting a 的 after 父母. It may mean, either enmity on the part of the parents, or an occasion of enmity on the part of the child. It is probably intended to include both ideas.

11 Some teachers insist that in the term 婦女, the 女 refers specifically to young unmarried women, and that it is properly used only when young women are included. Others say, what is undoubtedly true, that it is frequently used in an indefinite way for women at large. 出頭露面 *To show one's face, to appear in public; to be forward, to take the lead.* 露面 is a rhetorical repetition of 出頭.

12 This sentence might also be taken as an address or exhortation in the second person.

13 以大壓小以强壓弱 *Use the great to oppress the small, the strong to oppress the weak.* The second expression is from book language, and the first is an imitation of it added for emphasis.

15 爲 with 所 here makes a passive. A more literal rendering would be, *You should not become such as evil overcomes.*

17 習而不察 *To adopt without investigation,* a convenient and expressive book phrase in common use colloquially.

19 Against the south face of the wall of Peking city proper, called by foreigners the Tartar city, there is built an outer city wall (外城) of three sides, including within it the whole southern wall of the Tartar city, which has in it three gates, of which the central one is the 前門. The 永定門 is the gate of this outer city, which is in a line with the 前門.

20 以備 *For the purpose of being ready,*—a common book phrase occasionally used in colloquial Mandarin.

21 大花翎 A large or double peacock plume worn as a badge of honor. It is here used as an epithet for designating a particular well known man or family. The full force of 人家 cannot be preserved in a translation. 和你惹氣 implies mutual provocation and quarrelling.

22 夥吃夥用 *To eat and use in company;* that is, *in common.*

第一百四十六課

鹿[1]鳴高最愛賣誇富、其實那裏有個大錢。○雖[2]是一族人、其中也分親疎遠近。○人[3]都叫他獃傻子、其實他更不獃傻。○只[4]能知其當然、不能知其所以然。○古[5]人以爲地是平的、其實却是圓的。○這[6]其中的妙趣、只可意默會、不可言傳。○其[7]餘的事、等我回來再安排罷。○學[8]生偷閒調鬼、覺得是哄先生、其實正是哄自己。○昨[9]天說的妥妥當當如官如府的、今天忽然又反復了、這其中必有緣故。○他[10]說診評號脈、其實不過用指頭混摸了一回。○其[11]裏不知其外的事、我叫他猝然一問、把我問瞜了。○孔[12]夫子說、發憤忘食、言其人在熱心用功的時候、雖是饑餓、也覺不出來。○先[13]盛滿了那個鐔子、

TRANSLATION.

1 Lu Ming Kao is much given to boasting (making capital) of his wealth, while the fact is he is not worth a cash.

2 Although they are of the same clan, yet within the clan some are more nearly related than others.

3 Everybody calls him a simpleton, but, in fact, he is very far from being a simpleton. [the reason why.

4 Only the obligation can be known, not

5 The ancients supposed the earth to be flat, but in reality it is round.

6 The exquisite sentiment herein contained can only be conceived, it cannot be expressed in words. [I return.

7 The other matters I will arrange when

8 Students idle away time and play tricks thinking they are cheating the teacher, whereas they are really cheating themselves.

9 Yesterday it was settled quite satisfactorily, and to-day the settlement is suddenly repudiated. There must be some cause for this.

10 He said he was feeling my pulse, whereas he simply felt around at random for a while with his fingers.

11 Men are not acquainted with what lies beyond their own sphere. He suddenly asked me a question which quite nonplussed me.

12 Confucius said, "When I worked with ardor I forgot my food": that is to say, when a man gets very much

LESSON CXLVI.

MANDARIN USES OF 其.

其 holds approximately the same place in book language that 他 does in Mandarin, save that 其 is used freely of *things* as well as of *persons*. In Mandarin 其 is, for the most part, only used in certain connections and as a component of certain phrases. The following are the most common special phrases in which it occurs. It has already been used several times.

其實 In fact, in point of fact, in reality, whereas.

其中 Herein, amongst, in the midst of.

其間 In the midst of, amongst.

其餘 The remainder, the residue, the rest.

其裏 The inside, that which is within.

其外 The outside, that which is without.

言其 That is, that is to say, as much as to say.

取其 To take for, to consider as :—Note (16).

准其 To allow, to permit.

隨其 To follow ; to let, to allow.

聽其 To let, to allow.

究其實 In point of fact, the fact is, after all.

其餘的、可以倒在這個瓷盆鉢裏。○[14]你聽他說的極好、而究其實、一點道理不明白。○[15]我說行好的事、不可出於有心、是言其不可有貪圖的意思、並非要人專務外貌、把心裏的善念丟掉了。○[16]你和他交往、是取其他什麼長處呢、答我取其他性子直快爽、○[17]常言道、近朱者赤、近墨者黑、言其人不可濫交、因爲若和好人交往、不知不覺就學好了、若和壞人交往、不知不覺就學壞了。○[18]我出好心勸你、你倒撲喪起打人起來了、其實我在這事上、還有甚麼私弊嗎。○[19]俗語說、家貧出

interested in his work, he does not even realize that he is hungry.

13 First fill that jar, and the remainder you may pour into this crock.

14 You think he spoke very well, and yet, in point of fact, he knows nothing at all about the doctrine.

15 When I said one must not do good for a purpose, I meant by it that one must not have a selfish end, not that I would have men intent only on the outward appearance, discarding all virtuous purpose in the heart.

16 What excellence do you find in him that you cultivate his acquaintance? *Ans.* I am taken with his straightforwardness.

17 The common saying is, "That which touches vermillion becomes red, and that which touches ink becomes black;" that is to say, you should not associate promiscuously with others, for if you associate with good men, you will unconsciously practice their virtues; and if you associate with bad men, you will unconsciously learn their vices.

18 I exhorted you from the best of motives and yet you rebuff me; but then [do you think] I have any underhand design in this business?

19 The saying is, "When a family is poor, it has dutiful sons; when

VOCABULARY.

鳴 *Ming*². The cry of a bird or animal; to sound out, to resound.

誇富 *K'wa*¹ *fu*⁴. *To boast of one's wealth;* to profess to be rich.

賣富 *Mai*⁴ *fu*⁴. To make capital of one's wealth by displaying it.

所以然 *Soă*³ *i*³ *jan*². The reason why, the cause, the wherefore.

默會 *Moă*⁴ *hwei*⁴. *To conceive mentally,* to imagine; to take a hint.

意會 *I*⁴ *hwei*⁴. *To conceive mentally,* to feel the force of an idea which cannot be expressed in words.

言傳 *Yien*² *ch'üen*². *To express in words,* to state *viva voce.*

偷閒 *T'ou*¹ *hsien*². To steal time, to evade doing, to shirk, *to idle time.*

調鬼 *Tiao*⁴ *kwei*³. *To play tricks,* to hoodwink; to prevaricate, to shuffle.

診 *Chên*¹˒³. To examine, to verify, to ascertain.

診脈 *Chên*¹ *moă*⁴. To examine or feel the pulse. (N.)

評脈 *P'ing*² *moă*⁴. The same. (C.)

號脈 *Hao*⁴ *moă*⁴. The same. (S.)

憤 *Fên*⁴. *Ardent,* eager, excited; urgent desire or purpose.

發憤 *Fa*¹ *fên*⁴. To grow excited, *to act with intense ardor.*

熱心 *Jê*⁴ *hsin*¹. Hearty, zealous; earnest, eager, *interested.*

罈 *T'an*². An earthenware jar.

鉢 *Poă*¹. An earthenware basin or crock; a priest's or beggar's alms-dish.

孝子、國亂顯忠臣、這言其貧亂、如同忠孝的試金石一般、因爲家貧的時候、非眞孝子、斷不能奉養無愧、國亂的時候、非眞忠臣、斷不能捨身爲國。○到[20]船主查客的時候、必得有船票、方纔准其下船、若沒有船票、就必把他帶回去。○你[21]儘之和他作結寃做甚麽呢、從來說、成人不用管、管死不成人、我看不如聽隨其自便也就是了。○按[22]字的正音、是該說尾巴、我們這裏叫訛白了、都叫翼巴、其實下筆寫的時候、仍舊是寫尾不寫翼。

the country is in anarchy, patriots appear:" that is to say, poverty and anarchy are, as it were, the touchstones of patriotism and filial piety; for when the family is poor, only the truly filial are able to serve [their parents] perfectly; and when the nation is in disorder, only the truly patriotic are ready to sacrifice themselves for their country.

20 When the captain checks off the passengers, each one must have a ticket or he will not be permitted to land. If any one is without a ticket, he will certainly be carried back again.

21 Why do you keep continually vexing him? The saying is, "If he has it in him, he'll make a man without being governed; and if not, governing to death will not make a man of him." In my opinion you would better just let him have his own way.

22 According to the proper pronunciation of the characters we should say wei-pa, but we here incorrectly pronounce it i-pa, yet in writing we still write wei not i.

貪圖 *T'an¹ t'u².* *To covet*, to lust after, to hanker after, to wish for.

丟掉 *Tiu¹ tiao⁴.* To reject, to cast away, *to discard*, to throw away.

直爽 *Chï² shwang³.* *Straight-forward*, open, candid; prompt, ready. (N.)

直快 *Chï² k'wai⁴.* The same. (C. & S.)

濫 *Lan⁴.* To overflow; lawless, irregular; *promiscuous;* excessive.

濫交 *Lan⁴ chiao¹.* To associate promiscuously with others.

臣 *Ch'ên².* A vassal; *a minister*, a statesman.

試金石 *Shï⁴ chin¹ shï².* A touch-stone.

奉養 *Fêng⁴ yang³.* *To support dutifully*, to minister to respectfully.

結寃 *Chie¹ yüen¹.* To make an enemy, to provoke enmity; *to aggravate.*

作寃 *Tsoă⁴ yüen⁴.* To act the part of an enemy, to vex; *to aggravate.*

自便 *Tsï⁴ pien⁴.* At one's own convenience, *as one pleases.*

翼 *I⁴.* The wings of a bird; to assist; to defend.

下筆 *Hsia⁴ pi³.* *To write;* to begin to write; to compose.

NOTES.

2 遠近 is added chiefly for rhetorical effect. The reversed order is an accident, growing out of the fact that 遠 and 近 are commonly joined in this order.

3 The use of 更 implies a comparison with others, and suggests the idea that so far from being a simpleton, he is sharper-witted than the average of men.

4 Or, *It is only possible to know the oughtness of it, not the wherefore.* This sentence expresses its idea more elegantly and forcibly than the English language is capable of doing.

6 這 properly belongs to some such word as *sentence* or *phrase* understood, which has been displaced by the abrupt introduction of 其中. See also 9.

9 如官如府 *Perfectly satisfactory, all ship-shape; readily, easily.* A very common and very expressive local phrase. Its proper writing and analysis are both quite uncertain.

11 其裏不知其外的事 *He that is within does not know that which is without;* that is, a man is not expected

第一百四十七課

天¹這樣短、吃兩頓飯就合式。○這²一稞帽辮子、有多少綑、答這是一百二十綑、○給³我扯打五道青洋緞條兒、緣子緣條要三道直的、兩道斜的。○這⁴一罈子酒、至少有一百二十壺。○你⁵上濰縣的時候、請你給我買一件身皮襖、一條腰裙子。○西⁶遊記、分為二十卷、共一百回。○碎⁷倒沒碎、就是打了一道大裂璺。○這⁸桶橘子、是一百五十個、我纔已經數過了。○你⁹看你一綑高粱（粟秫）稭、和一紮韭菜一樣、那能值十

TRANSLATION.

1 When the days are so short as this, two meals answer the purpose.
2 How many bundles are there in this pile of straw braid? *Ans.* This one has one hundred and twenty bundles.
3 Cut off for me five strips of black farmers' satin facing. I want three strips straight and two bias.
4 A jar of liquor like this, will measure at least one hundred and twenty bottles.
5 When you go to Weihsien please buy for me a fur coat and a skirt.
6 The *Record of a Journey to the West* is divided into twenty parts, including in all one hundred sections.
7 He did not indeed break it to pieces, but he made a large crack in it.
8 This tub of oranges contains one hundred and fifty. I have just counted them.
9 Look at this bundle of sorghum stalks of yours. It is no larger than a bunch of chives. How can it be worth fifteen cash?

to know what does not pertain to his calling or position, or what overpasses his opportunities.

12 發憤忘食. These words are found in the Analects, and were used by Confucius with regard to himself.

16 Note that the Mandarinizing of 取其 so completely obscures the primary meaning of 其 as a pronoun, that 他 may be inserted immediately after it. The same thing often happens in the case of 盲其, but could not happen in the case of 准其 or 隨其 or 聽其, where 其 retains its proper pronominal force.

18 我出好心勸你 *I put forth a good heart to exhort you;* that is, *I exhorted you from a good motive.*

21 結冤 or 作冤 here means to cross the purposes of, and attempt to govern, a son who is restive and resentful under the restraint. 成人不用管,管死不成人 *To make a man [of a child] requires no governing, and governing to the death will not make him a man;* that is, he who has the elements of a manly character will attain the end without parental restraint, and he who has not, will fail even though governed to the uttermost.

22 呌白 *To call colloquially;* that is, *to mispronounce in colloquial usage.*

LESSON CXLVII.

SIGNIFICANT CLASSIFIERS.

Classifiers have been divided by some writers into distinctive and significant. By significant classifiers are meant such as express the quantity, measure or form, of the noun, and generally admit of translation by a special word. The distinction is not important, nor is it always very evident. Previous lessons have contained some such, though the most of them are collected in this lesson, which concludes the subject of classifiers.

頓 To bow the head,—classifier of meals, of beatings, beratings, etc.

稞 A stack of grain,—classifier of things in piles or cords.

綑 A bundle,—classifier of things in rolls or bundles.

道 A road,—classifier of things in strips or bands, also of bridges, cracks, etc.

罈 An earthenware jar,—classifier of things in jars, as wine, oil, etc.

壺 A pitcher or jug,—classifier of things in jugs, as oil, wine, etc.

身 The body,—classifier of coats, cloaks, etc.

腰 The loins,—classifier of skirts, aprons, etc.

卷 A roll; a section,—classifier of sections or parts of a book.

五個錢呢。○從¹⁰來說、和氣生財、這個人眞是一團和氣、怎能不發財呢。○那¹¹三道鬧、數那第一道難過。○我¹²看你鬢角上、常貼着兩張帖膏藥、是爲甚麼貼的呢。○這¹³塊方端硯是頂好的、你看看上頭不是有眼嗎。○西¹⁴邊那道河溝子、我打算商議合村疃、修上一道小橋。○我¹⁵用十二吊錢、買了一棵楸樹、有九拃捺半粗、能截鋸兩節、你看吃虧不吃虧。○這¹⁶些禮物、用兩擡食盒就送去了、值不不值得用四擡。○

10 It has been said, "A peaceable temper brings wealth." This man is the embodiment of good temper, how can he help getting rich?

11 Of those three locks, the first is the most difficult to pass.

12 I notice that you constantly have plasters stuck on each of your temples. What do you wear them for?

13 This Twan inkstone is first-rate; look, and you will see it has an eye on it.

14 I propose to consult the town about building a small bridge over that gully to the west.

15 I have bought a catalpa tree for twelve thousand cash. It is nine spans and a half in diameter and will cut two lengths. Do you think I have been cheated?

16 These presents can be sent in two racks of boxes; it is not worth while to use four racks.

回 A turn,— classifier of chapters in novels.

桶 A tub,—classifier of things in tubs or casks, as oranges, pears, etc.

𥶇 A handful,—classifier of bunches or bundles of kao-liang stalks, onions, etc.

紮 To wind around and tie,—classifier of things in bunches, as tape, cord, etc.

帖 A placard,—classifier of things pasted up or posted.

團 A lump,—classifier of things in lumps or pellets.

方 A square,—classifier of panes of glass, inkstones, etc.

拃 A span,—classifier of measurements made with the hand.

捺 A span,—classifier of measurements made with the hand:—Note (15).

節 A joint,—classifier of things in fixed lengths, as logs, verses, etc.

章 A chapter,—classifier of parts of a book, of documents, etc.

擡 To carry on a pole,—classifier of loads carried by two.

篇 A section of leaf,—classifier of poems, essays, and of leaves of books.

滴 A drop,—classifier of things in drops.

馱 A mule or donkey load or pack,—classifier of loads or packs.

擔 A load, a picul,—classifier of loads or piculs.

箱 A box,—classifier of things in boxes.

盒 A small covered box or can,—classifier of things in small boxes.

匣 A small box with moveable lid,—classifier of things in such boxes.

號 A mark,—classifier of lessons.

首 A head,—classifier of hymns, poems, etc.

桌 A table,—classifier of feasts.

VOCABULARY.

綑 *K'un*³. To bind, to tie up; a bundle, a coil, ... a roll.

捺 *Na*⁴. To press down; to span with the thumb . . . . . . and finger, *a span.*

拃 *Cha*¹. . . . . To span; *a span.*

𥶇 *Chien*³. A bunch, a handful. This character . . . . .is not authorized by the dictionaries, but is given in the *Wu Fang Yüen Yin.*

帽辮子 *Mao*⁴ *pien*⁴ *tsï*³. . . . . Straw braid.

緣條 *Yüen*² *t'iao*². . . . . Facing, binding.

上[17]卷是八章、一共四十篇。〇天[18]下事物之理、是無窮無盡、我們所知道的、不過像海中的一滴水、海邊的一粒沙。〇已[19]經買了二十馱子松柴、再去買上十三擔煤、今年就彀燒的咯。〇方[20]纔有個大黧(黧)花貓、上厨房偷什麼吃、給叫我打急了眼、他就往玻璃窗上一撞、撞碎了一方塊玻璃、跑出去了。〇他[21]今天纔買了四十箱火煤油、五桶柑子八十盒子牛奶膏、五百匣官鉛粉、二百五十斤哈啡、所以手裏不能有存錢。〇現[22]在我一

17 The first part has eight chapters, in all thirty-two leaves; the second part has nine chapters, in all forty leaves.

18 The principles involved in universal nature are infinite. Those which we know are but as a drop in the ocean or a grain of sand on the sea shore.

19 I have already bought twenty loads of pine-tops and when in addition I have bought thirteen piculs of coal, I will have sufficient fuel for the present year.

20 Just now a large brindled cat came into the kitchen to steal something to eat. I chased it until it grew desperate, when it gave one bound against the window breaking a pane of glass and so escaped.

21 He has just to-day bought forty boxes of kerosine oil, five tubs of oranges, eighty tins of condensed milk, five hundred boxes of white lead and two hundred and fifty catties of coffee, and therefore cannot have any ready money on hand.

22 At present I only recite one lesson a day. *Ques.* How much do you commit for a lesson? *Ans.* I commit

濰 *Wei*². A small river in Eastern Shantung running into the Gulf of Pechili.

濰縣 *Wei*² *hsien*⁴. A city on the river *Wei*, 200 miles west of *Chefoo*.

裙 *Ch'ün*². *A skirt*, a petticoat.

橘 *Chü*². An orange, the mandarin or loose-peel orange.

秫稭 *Shu*¹ *chie*¹. The stalks of *kao-liang*.

閘 *Cha*². A flood-gate; a dam; *a lock;* a sluice; a customs barrier; a guarded gate.

鬢 *Pin*⁴. The hair on the temples, *locks;* tresses.

鬢角 *Pin*⁴ *chiao*³. The temples.

膏藥 *Kao*¹ *yao*⁴. A medicated plaster.

河溝 *Hê*² *kou*¹. The dry bed of a mountain torrent, a gully.

食盒 *Shï*² *hê*². A set of large trenchers in a frame:—Note 16.

無窮 *Wu*² *ch'iung*². Endless, perpetual; boundless, *infinite.*

無盡 *Wu*² *chin*⁴. The same.

松柴 *Sung*¹ *ch'ai*². Pine bushes or brush dried for fuel.

黧花 *Li*² *hwa*¹. Dark spotted, *brindled.*

柑 *Kan*¹. The close-skinned Canton or Swatow orange.

牛奶膏 *Niu*² *nai*³ *kao*¹. Condensed milk.

鉛粉 *Ch'ien*¹ *fên*³. Carbonate of lead.

官粉 *Kwan*¹ *fên*³. The same.

啡 *Fei*¹. A phonetic character.

哈啡 *K'a*¹ *fei*¹. Coffee.

傳 *Chwan*⁴. A record; *a narrative, a biography;* traditions. See *ch'wan*².

雞片 *Chi*¹ *p'ien*⁴. Sliced chicken, fricasseed chicken.

拌 *Pan*⁴. To divide; to mix; *to make into a salad.*

肚 *Tu*³. The stomach. See *tu*⁴.

炸 *Cha*². To fry in oil or lard:—See *cha*⁴.

脂盖 *Chi*¹ *kai*¹. Minced meat wrapped in slices of fat pork.

淞 *Sung*¹. A river near Sungkiang Fu; to dress meat or fish by cutting into strings, covering with the yolk of an egg, frying in lard and lastly steaming.

滙 *Hwei*⁴. To deposit money; a check, a draft; to cook by cutting into shreds dipping in starch batter and then frying in lard.

天只背一號書、問一號念多少呢、答念三首詩、兩篇文章、五篇左傳。○ 23 進寶、你去告訴萬順樓的掌櫃的（老板）、叫他明天中晌（上午）、給我預備一桌八大八小的酒席（八八的酒席、老三道飯）八個小碗、要他一碗溜雞片、一碗拌肚、一碗炸脂蓋、一碗淞魚、一碗滙三絲、一碗燒肉、一碗爨腰子、一碗蜜餞蓮子、八個大碗、要他一碗炒蟹黃、一碗滙蹄筋、一碗溜蝦仁、一碗炸裏脊、一碗魚翅、一碗紅燉肉、一碗大海參、一碗炒魚肚、若再添菜、可以現點。

three odes, two essays and five leaves of the Tsoŏ Chwan.

23 Chin Pao, you go and tell the manager of the Wan Shun restaurant to prepare for me, to-morrow at noon, a dinner of twice eight bowls (three courses, old style). Let the eight small bowls be,—one of fricasseed chicken, one of pork tripe salad, one of pork rolls fried in oil, one of shred fish fried in lard, one a ragout of three kinds of meat dressed with starch and fried in lard, one of grilled pork cutlets, one of sliced pork kidneys stewed in gravy and one of candied lotus nuts. Let the large bowls be,—one of scrambled crabs' roe, one of shred pigs' feet sinews fried in lard, one of shelled lobsters dressed with broth, one of pork tenderloin fried in lard, one of sharks' fins, one of stewed pork basted with sugar, one of large trepang and one of smothered fish stomachs. If more is wanted we will order it at the time.

三絲 *San^1 sï^1*. Shreds of three kinds of meat, ...(as chicken, fresh pork, and ham,) a ragout.

爨 *Ts'wan^4*. A cooking range; a mess; to cook .... over again in a different form; *to parboil, then slice and stew in gravy.*

腰子 *Yao^1 tsï^3*......... The kidneys.

蜜餞 *Mi^4 chien^1*. Fruits preserved in honey .... or sugar, candied fruits.

蓮子 *Lien^2 tsï^3*......... Lotus nuts.

蠏 *Hsie^4*......... A crab.

蠏黃 *Hsie^4 hwang^2*........The roe of crabs.

蹄筋 *T'i^2 chin^1*.......The sinews of pigs' feet.

鰕 *Hsia^1*. *A lobster;* a shrimp; a prawn; a .... crawfish.

鰕仁 *Hsia^1 jên^2*......... Shelled lobsters.

裏脊 *Li^3 chi^3*......... The tenderloin.

燉 *Tun^4*.... To simmer slowly, *to stew,* to seethe.

參 *Shên^1*. The ginseng plant. See *ts'an^1* .... and *ts'ên^1*.

海參 *Hai^3 shên^1*. Bêche-de-mer, sea-cucumber, ... trepang.

魚肚 *Yü^2 tu^3*....... Fish stomachs; gelatine.

NOTES.

1 In the winter many of the poorer classes eat only two meals per day. In the North the non-laboring classes eat only two meals per day at all seasons.

6 西遊記 A Chinese novel, giving a mythological account of the adventures of 陳玄奘, commonly known as 唐僧, a priest who made a journey to the West in the seventh century in search of sacred books.

7 碎倒沒碎 *Broken it is not.* This form of expression implies that the party addressed supposed it was broken.

10 一團和氣 *A lump of good humor.*

13 The best inkstones come from the banks of a small stream called 端溪, in the province of Kwangtung, hence they are called 端硯. The "eye" on the inkstone is a sort of spiral making or whorl in the stone, supposed to indicate an extra quality.

15 There are two kinds of 楸樹, classed as Catalpa Bungeai and Catalpa Kaemferi. The latter grows as a forest tree in Manchuria. The logs are exported and extensively used for making coffins and furniture. The appearance both of the tree and of the wood is very similar to walnut. The common name in Shantung for the Kwantung variety is 核桃楸, *walnut ch'iu,* and the fruit is said to resemble a very small walnut. 兩節 *Two lengths,* that is, two coffin lengths. When lumber is cut in the forests it is cut into coffin lengths, about seven and a half feet, this being the chief use of lumber in China. Some teachers prefer 楠 as a better writing for this classifier.

第一百四十八課

你[1]這篇文章、做的眞是絶妙。○
絶[2]細的麪、他還嫌粗。○這[3]些杏
子兒、看着蒼皎黃、吃着却活焦酸。○可[4]
以告訴他、叫他給我搓一根絶
細的麻繩子。○我[5]一輩子不愛
吃牛肉、聞着就嫌他活喬齁羶。○我[6]
們掌秤最公道、你看不是坦四平
的嗎。○方[7]纔洗魚沒洗手、弄得
我手上活喬齁腥的。○金[8]雞納霜、原
是一種頂好的藥、就是活烈惡苦、叫

Translation.

1 This essay of yours certainly is most admirably done.

2 Extra fine flour, and yet he objects to its coarseness.

3 These apricots look quite yellow, and yet to the taste they are sour as vinegar.

4 You may tell him to twist for me a very fine hempen cord.

5 I have never in my life relished beef, I dislike its rank odor.

6 Our weighing is entirely fair: see, is not the beam perfectly level?

7 I have just been cleaning some fish and have not washed my hands, so that they have a very rank fish smell.

8 Quinine is a very excellent kind of medicine, but it is exceedingly bitter,

16 The dishes of food and other presents are spread out in large trenchers, which are then piled one on top of the other in a frame, each being supported on the rim of the one underneath. They are sometimes round and sometimes square. The frame supporting the trenchers is carried on a pole by two persons, constituting a 擡 or *load.*

18 天下事物之理 *The principles of all the affairs and things in the world.*

20 打急了眼 *Beat its eyes excited, or glaring.*

22 The 文章 here referred to are essays of standard excellence, which are committed to memory as models of style. 左傳 An amplification and exposition of Confucius' 春秋. It is said to have been written by 左邱明 and from him to take its name, *Tsoŭ's narrative.* Some however explain the term as *the assisting narrative*, that is, traditional explanations of the 春秋, handed down from generation to generation, and finally committed to writing when the art of Chinese writing was sufficiently developed to serve the purpose. It constitutes one of the five classics.

23 八八 is an abbreviation for eight large and eight small bowls. The three courses (道) are marked by the setting on of three rounds of candies and fruits (點心). *Old style* means *large* dishes. 溜 *To cut in bits or slices, cook and dress with gravy, to fricassee;* in some places, *to warm over again by steaming.* 燒, as here used is *to broil or grill on a gridiron.*

LESSON CXLVIII.

Special Intensives.

絶 To overpass,—conveys the idea of surpassing.

絶妙 Surpassingly excellent, most admirable.

絶細 Extremely fine, or minute, or slender.

絶密 Extremely fine or close, delicate.

皎 Bright,—expresses lustre and is applied to bright colors.

皎黃 Bright yellow, brilliant yellow. (c.)

皎藍 Bright blue, brilliant blue. (c.)

蒼 Azure,—conveys the idea of lustre.

蒼黃 Bright yellow, brilliant yellow. (s.)

蒼白 Azure white, iron grey:—Note (22)

活 Alive,—conveys the idea of activity, vigor.

活酸 Intensely sour (s.)

活腥 Very rank, intensely fishy. (s.)

活羶 Very rank, intensely fetid. (s.)

活苦 Intensely bitter, pungently bitter. (s.)

喬 Lofty; curved,—expresses excess and is applied to smells.

喬羶 Exceedingly rank, intensely strong or fetid. (c.)

喬腥 Very rank, a strong fishy smell. (c.)

喬氣息 Very rank, musky, nauseating. (c.)

人不願意吃。○9這些菜生齁鹹、你這
麼大口的吃、不怕咳嗽嗎。○10我今
天看見一個學生、穿着翠皎藍的大
衫、走起來眞是飄灑摁。○11放割癤子、必
得等他熟透了、若是沒熟透、就放割
的生疼。○12不論誰訂書、不能訂得
一斬四掌齊、若要一斬四掌齊、必得用切裁刀
切裁。○13糯米本是膠黏的、這個糯米
糕所以不黏、必是對上了秈大米。○
你14看人家那個小姑娘、今年纔九

so that one does not like to take it.
9 These vegetables are exceedingly salt. Are you not afraid that eating such great mouthfuls of them will bring on a cough?
10 I saw a school-boy to-day wearing a bright blue gown which looked very graceful as he walked along.
11 Always wait till a boil is ripe before cutting it. If cut before it is fully ripe, it is very painful.
12 No matter who stitches a book, he cannot make the edges perfectly even; in order to be perfectly even they must be cut with a paring knife.
13 Glutinous rice is naturally viscid as glue: the reason these glutinous rice dumplings are not gummy must be because they are made partly of common rice.

喬膙 Exceedingly rank, very offensive or pungent, ammoniacal. (C. & S.)

齁 To breathe with difficulty,—expresses the idea of stifling, and is applied to smells. This intensive has a very wide application in Pekingese, being applied to many things besides tastes and smells. Its use in other dialects is very limited.

齁羶 Stiflingly rank or fetid. (N.)

齁腥 Stiflingly rank or fishy. (N.)

齁鹹 Chokingly salt, excessively salt. (C. & N.)

齁氣息 Stiflingly strong or musky. (N.)

齁膙 Stiflingly rank or fetid, reeking. (N.)

惡 Evil,—conveys the idea of painful excess.

惡苦 Pungently bitter, wofully bitter. (N.)

惡醜 Shockingly ugly, ugly as sin. (N.)

烈 Burning,—conveys the idea of intensity.

烈苦 Intensely bitter, furiously bitter. (C.)

烈醜 Excessively ugly, horribly ugly. (C. & S.)

四 Four,—applied to lines and surfaces; in the case of lines some teachers prefer 矢.

四平 Perfectly level, everywhere level.

四齊 Perfectly even, entirely regular or uniform. (C. & N.)

絲 Unwound silk,—conveys the idea of uniformity. (C. & N.)

絲勻 Perfectly regular or uniform. (C.)

斬 To cut off,—conveys the idea of evenness.

斬齊 Perfectly even or uniform. (S.)

生 Raw,—conveys the idea of acuteness.

生鹹 Intensely salt, very salt. (C. & S.)

生疼 Intensely painful, acutely painful.

膠 Glue,—conveys the idea of stickiness.

膠黏 Sticky as glue, extremely viscid.

天 The sky,—conveys the idea of brightness.

天藍 Sky blue, bright blue. (N.)

翠 The purple-green feathers of the kingfisher,—conveys the idea of brilliancy.

翠藍 Brilliant blue, bright blue.

膙 Rank, pungent,—conveys the idea of fetid.

膙氣息 Disgustingly rank.

焦酸 Intensely sour, burning sour.

VOCABULARY.

皎 *Chiao*3. Pure white, effulgent, splendid, bright :—see Sub.

喬 *Ch'iao*2. High, lofty, aspiring; crooked :—see Sub.

烈 *Lie*4. Burning; ardent, impetuous; determined, inflexible :—see Sub.

斬 *Chan*3. To cut in two; to decapitate; to sever; temporary :—see Sub.

歲、紡的線兒絲勻勻勻絲淨勻淨的。〇尊15子
他女婿、惡烈醜惡烈醜的、一臉大黑痲疤
子、還帶着是個羅羅駱鍋鍋駝子腰腰。〇用16品藍
染布、當時是天皎翠藍的、可惜就是掉
色、幾天還得再染。〇古17語說、世事
如山齊處少、若一定要個一掌四斬齊、
那裏能呢。〇這18樣的針線、那能交
得下去呢、再做的時候、要絕密的
針腳、刮刮淨淨的。〇我19願意天天
去看他、只因他常咳嗽吐痰、家裏

14 Look at that little girl—only nine this year, and yet the thread she spins is as even as can be!

15 Tsun-tsï's husband is horribly ugly, his face is all covered with big dark pock-pits, and besides he is a hunchback.

16 Cloth colored with aniline blue is bright blue at the first, but the trouble is it fades. After a few days [exposure] it has to be dyed again.

17 The old saying is, "Human affairs are like hills, the even places are rare." If you are determined to secure entire uniformity you will certainly fail.

18 How can I deliver such sewing as this? The next time you must take very fine stitches, making them firm and smooth.

19 I should like to go and see him every day, but that he is constantly

臊 *Sao*¹. Rank; fetid,—as the smell of perspiration ..... or of urine; reeking, stinking. See *sao*⁴.

羶 *Shan*¹. *Rank*, fetid,—as the smell of goats or ...... sheep; noisome.

腥 *Hsing*¹. *Rank*, strong,—as the smell of fish ...... or flesh.

掌秤 *Chang*³ *ch'êng*⁴. To superintend weighing, ... to weigh.

金雞納 *Chin*¹ *chi*¹ *na*⁴.... ··· ....Cinchona.

金雞納霜 *Chin*¹ *chi*¹ *na*⁴ *shwang*¹.... Quinine.

大衫 *Ta*⁴ *shan*¹..... An unlined coat or gown.

揌 *Sai*¹.... To shake, to wave, *to flutter*.

飄揌 *P'iao*¹ *sai*¹........*Graceful*, airy, jaunty.

飄灑 *P'iao*¹ *sa*³.... .... The same.

裁刀 *Ts'ai*² *tao*¹. A knife for paring the edge of .... books or for cutting paper.

切刀 *Ch'ie*¹ *tao*¹.... ...... .The same.

糕 *Kao*¹. *Rice dumplings*; fruit jelly or jam; ...... sponge or other similar cakes.

秈 *Hsien*¹.... ... ... Common rice. (s.)

秈米 *Hsien*¹ *mi*³.... ... .The same.

勻淨 *Yün*² *ching*⁴.... ...... .Uniform, *even*.

羅鍋子 *Loă*² *kwoă*¹ *tsï*³....... A humpback.

羅鍋腰 *Loă*² *kwoă*¹ *yao*¹.........The same.

駱駝腰 *Loă*² *t'oă*² *yao*¹.... ...... .The same.

品藍 *P'in*³ *lan*²............. .Aniline blue.

掉色 *Tiao*⁴ *shai*³..... ... To lose color, *to fade*.

針腳 *Chên*¹ *chiao*³.... ...... .Stitches.

刮淨 *Kwa*¹ *ching*⁴.... ...... .Even, *smooth*.

氣息 *Ch'i*⁴ *hsi*². The smell of urine; *rank*, ...strong, stinking, fusty.

尿 *Niao*⁴.... ...... .To urinate; urine.

尿罐子 *Niao*⁴ *kwan*⁴ *tsï*³. *A chamber utensil*, ...a urinal.

馬桶 *Ma*³ *t'ung*³. *A chamber utensil*, a com- .... .mode.

頂棚 *Ting*³ *p'êng*². .....A ceiling:—Note 21.

虛棚 *Hsü*¹ *p'êng*².... .... The same. (c.)

仰板 *Yang*³ *pan*³.... .... The same. (s.)

NOTES.

4 The using of both 告訴 and 叫 is somewhat redundant, though adding to the explicitness of the order given.

8 Chinanfu rejects all of the three forms in the text and says 喬苦.

9 It is popularly supposed by the Chinese that eating too much salt will cause coughs and asthma.

10 In many places in Central and Northern Mandarin 飄灑 is spoken *p'iao sai*, and on this account is oftentimes

駒喬臊氣息、所以我不敢進去、一進去、就熏的惡心要吐。○這[20]個尿罐子、馬桶多少日子沒刷洗、弄的駒臊喬臊的、快拿去刷刷洗洗罷。○昨[21]天晚上躺在牀上、似睡不睡的時候、有個大蝎子、從頂棚虛棚仰板上掉在我的臉上、把我螫的生疼、一夜也沒睡着。○王[22]大人、就是看中李家那匹蒼白馬、希罕他走得穩、跑得又快、一天能跑四百里路。

coughing and expectorating, which gives the room such a rank smell that I dare not go in. Whenever I go in, the smell nauseates me, so that I feel like vomiting.

20 This chamber utensil has not been washed for ever so many days so that it has a very offensive smell. Take it out at once and wash it.

21 Last night when I was lying on the bed dozing, a large scorpion fell down from the ceiling on my face and stung me, causing such a severe pain that the whole night I did not sleep.

22 His Excellency Mr. Wang is specially pleased with that iron-grey horse belonging to the Li family. He is taken with its easy gait and its great speed, which is equal to four hundred *li* in a day.

---

written 飄摁, Some teachers adhere to 灑, but give it a second reading when meaning *to sprinkle*, viz., *sai*³ or *shai*³, which in fact is its original reading.

13 所以不黏 *The therefore of its not being glutinous;* that is, the reason why it is not glutinous.

14 人家, as here used, could only be translated into English by using the name of the person for which it is a substitute.

15 女婿 is here used for husband, being taken from the standpoint of the wife's parents, just as a man's wife is so generally called his daughter-in-law.

16 Aniline colors are extensively used in China, but the Chinese have not yet learned the art of so using them as to make fast colors.

18 那能交得下去呢 The language of an employer to an employe and may mean either, *How can I deliver such sewing to my customers*, or, *How can you deliver such sewing to me.*

21 The Chinese do not generally ceil their houses, and when in the case of a more pretentious house they do make a ceiling, it is usually paper pasted on a light frame of bamboo, cane or sorghum stalks. In some cases boards are used, either nailed on the undersides of the rafters, or on the joists of the second floor. In the North such ceilings are usually called 天花板. The term 仰板 is used either of a board ceiling, or of a second floor as seen from below. 虛棚 applies to a light paper ceiling enclosing a triangular space between itself and the roof. Besides the three terms here given, there is also the term 仰棚, which is widely used. Chinese houses know nothing of plastered ceilings, and ceilings of any kind are comparatively rare. 似睡不睡 *As if asleep but not asleep*, that is, *half asleep, dozing.*

22 蒼白 *Azure white;* that is, in the case of a horse, *iron grey.* As thus used, 蒼 *modifies* the meaning rather than *intensifies* it.

LESSON CXLIX.

SPECIAL INTENSIVES.

As the intensives in this lesson are each confined to one or two applications they are not separately defined. The special force of each intensive is indicated, as far as may be, by the first definition in each combination, which is *approximately* literal.

雪白 Snow white, immaculate white.

漂白 Bleached white, pure white, clear white.

滾熱 Boiling hot, scalding hot,—said even of solid things,—as cakes.

鬆臭 A rotten smell or stench, stinking, putrescent. (C.)

罄淨 Entirely exhausted, all gone, used up.

漆黑 Black as varnish, black as ebony, jet black, shining black. (C. & N.)

烏黑 Black as a raven or crow. (C. & S.)

墨黑 Black as ink, jet black. (C. & S.)

啊熱 Oppressively hot, stifling. (C.)

悶熱 Oppressively hot, very close, stifling.

澈白 Transparently white, pure white. (S.)

淹濕 Soaking wet, dripping wet. (C.)

漬濕 Soaking wet, wringing wet. (S.)

漬酸 A yeasty sour, intensely sour. (S.)

第一百四十九課

好[1]幾年沒見面、你的鬍子都雪白了。○温[2]泉的水、就是在冬天、也是滾熱。○你[3]說那塊肉沒壞、怎麼聞着活鬆鮈臭呢。○摸[4]着他身上焦滾熱、一點汗也沒有。○路[5]上被雨阻嘔截了三天、把盤纏花的罄淨。○[6]烏墨漆黑的頭髮、漂雪白的臉、眞是好人物。○今[7]天悶啊惡熱、喘不上氣兒。○月[8]季花有赤紅的、有澈喬雪白的、還有水粉紅色的。○一[9]連下了十來天雨、把柴伙淋的漬淹精濕。○那[10]個學生、穿的

TRANSLATION.

1 I have not seen you for quite a number of years; your beard is white as snow.
2 The water of a hot spring is scalding hot, even in winter.
3 You say that piece of meat is not spoiled. How comes it to have such a putrid smell?
4 His body feels burning hot to the touch, and there is not a trace of perspiration.
5 I was detained three days on the road by rain, and spent the last cent of my travelling money.
6 With hair as black as a raven and a face as white as snow,—truly she is a real beauty.
7 The heat is very oppressive to-day; one can hardly breathe.
8 Some monthly roses are bright red, some snow (clear) white and some pink.
9 It has been raining continuously for

絳紫 Crimson red or purple, a bright purple. (N.) [(C. & S.)
血紫 Blood purple, bright purple, livid.
蜜黃 Yellow as honey, bright yellow. (S.)
响乾 Snapping dry, dry as tinder. (N.)
顯青 A showy blue, bright blue or black, brilliant blue. (C. & S.)
顯乾 Perfectly dry, thoroughly dry. (C.) Possibly a mispronunciation of 响乾.
筆直 Straight as a pen, perfectly straight, straight as an arrow. (C. & N.) [(C. & S.)
順直 Straight as a line, perfectly straight.
燥熱 Scorching hot, hot as an oven, oppressively hot.
噴香 Diffusively fragrant, very fragrant.
細甜 Pervasively sweet, very sweet, deliciously sweet. (C. & N.)
鮮甜 Freshly sweet, deliciously sweet. (S.) Fresh things are sweet, stale things sour.
死辣 Deathly sharp or hot, intensely pungent or hot. (C.)
乾辣 Parching hot, intensely pungent. (N.)
死鹹 Deathly salt, intensely salt. (S.)
風快 Quick as the wind, quick as a flash.
鋒快 Sharp as a spear point, very sharp, a keen edge.
巴澀 Acridly astringent, highly astringent or puckery. (C.)
苦鹹 Bitterly salt, intensely salt. (C. & N.)
緋紅 Scarlet red, purple red, red as a beet.
焦熱 Burning hot, scorching hot; a raging fever. (C. & S.)
焦乾 Parching dry, dry as tinder. (S.)
惡熱 Excessively hot, oppressively hot, stifling. (N.)
喬白 Very white, white as can be. (C.)
活辣 Intensely hot or pungent, extremely peppery. (S.)
活臭 Intensely stinking, disgustingly foul or putrid. (S.)
活澀 Intensely astringent or puckery. (S.)
四直 Perfectly straight, straight as a line. (C.)
齁臭 Very stinking or foul, an overpowering stench. (N.)
齁澀 Chokingly astringent or puckery. (N.)
天青 Sky blue, navy blue; deep blue, blue-black. (N.)

絳血紫的袍子、皎蜜黃的套褲、很合時派。○[11]昌邑的漂
布匠、漂的布是雪白的、眞好極喇。○[12]响焦迸乾的南山
片菸、一點不能掉賠秤。○[13]你打裱的紙殼子、已經顯迸乾
喇、怎麼還不揭下來呢。○[14]這條路一點彎轉沒有、
筆順直的大路。○[15]天氣這樣燥熱、怕是要下雨罷。○
[16]這蘋果聞着是噴香的、吃在嘴裏也是細鮮甜的。○
[17]好體面涼菜、就是擱的醋蒜多了、弄的焦漬酸乾死活辣。○
[18]別看我這個驢驢子小、走的却風快、一天能走二
百里路。○[19]我先把刀子磨得鋒快的、給你把頭薙
一薙、把鬍子刮一刮、好上丈人家吃酒啊。○[20]做箭

over ten days, so that all the fuel is soaking wet.

10 That school-boy has on a deep purple coat and bright yellow leggings, exactly in the fashion.

11 The cloth bleached by the fullers of Ch'ang-i is white as snow. Nothing could be finer.

12 Perfectly dry leaf tobacco from the Southern Hills. Loss of weight is quite impossible.

13 The pasteboard you made is already fully dry. Why have you not taken it down?

14 There is not the least turn in this road. It is a perfectly straight highway.

15 I fear it is going to rain, the weather is so scorching hot.

16 This apple has a very fragrant smell, and it is also very sweet to the taste.

17 This is a very fine salad, save that they have put in too much vinegar and garlic making it fearfully sour and sharp.

18 Don't be misled by the small size of this donkey of mine, he is as fleet as the wind, he can travel two hundred *li* in a day.

19 When I have stropped the razor to a keen edge, I will shave your head and

Vocabulary.

漂 *P'iao*³. . . . .To bleach, to whiten by bleaching. . . . . Also *p'iao*¹.

澈 *Ch'ê*⁴. . . . . . . Pellucid, clear.

絳 *Chiang*⁴. . . . . A deep red, crimson.

响 *Hsiang*³. . . . . . . An abbreviated writing of 響.

燥 *Tsao*⁴. . . . . . . Dry, scorched, parched.

噴 *P'ên*¹. . . . . . . To spurt; to spread as an odor.

緋 *Fei*¹. . . . . . . Purple silk; lilac color, scarlet.

漬 *Tsï*⁴. . . . . . . Soaked, soggy, moldy, stained.

粉紅 *Fên*³ *hung*². . . . Pale red, pink :—Note 8.

水紅 *Shwei*³ *hung*². . . . . The same.

紫 *Tsï*³. . . . . Purple, purplish yellow.

套褲 *T'ao*⁴ *k'u*⁴. . . . . . . *Leggings*, overalls.

時派 *Shï*² *p'ai*⁴. The prevailing fashion, the . . . . mode.

漂布匠 *P'iao*³ *pu*⁴ *chiang*⁴. A bleacher, a . . . . fuller.

邑 *I*⁴. . . . *A walled city;* a camp; a capital.

片菸 *P'ien*⁴ *yien*¹. Leaf tobacco pressed in flat . . . . bunches.

掉秤 *Tiao*⁴ *ch'êng*⁴. . . . . To lose weight.

賠秤 *Shê*² *ch'êng*⁴. . . . . To lose weight.

裱 *Piao*³. *To paste on*, to mount as maps or . . . . . . pictures.

殼 *Ch'iŏ*⁴, *ch'üe*⁴. Husk; *skin;* bark; shell; . . . . crust.

紙殼子 *Chï*³ *ch'iŏ*⁴ *tsï*³. . . . . . . .Pasteboard.

彎轉 *Wan*¹ *chwan*³. Crooked, tortuous, round . . . . about, a turn.

凉菜 *Liang*² *ts'ai*⁴. . . . . . . A vegetable salad.

鋒 *Fêng*¹ The point of a spear, the tip; bristling; *keen*.

蒜 *Swan*⁴. . . . . . Garlic.

辣 *La*⁴. . . . . Acrid, pungent, *sharp*, hot; severe.

拿準 *Na*² *chun*³. To take accurate aim, *to go* . . . . *straight to the mark.*

必得做的四筆直纔好、多少有點彎彎、就不拿準喇。○他21們
弟兄兩個、大不一樣、一個是漆黑、一個是雪白、眞是一一龍母
生生九百種般、○這22些柿子沒漤透、咬在嘴裏活巴齁澀的。○亞23非利
加人、雖然皮色烏墨漆黑、他自己仍然以爲好看。○無24論是做
素菜、是做葷菜、淡了固然不好、死生苦鹹也是不好。○昨25天來
家、走了十里路的夜道、天又陰的漆黑、對面不見人、伸手
不見掌、我把跌了好幾個跟頭。○雙26子那個閨女、實在愐
腆、一提起他女婿來、把他羞的滿臉緋紅。○我27看見王三
截扯了一個馬褂子面兒、纔七十二個錢一尺、那個褡褳是
挺厚的、色是顯天青的、老遠看看、眞和哈喇一樣。

scrape your face in order that you may go to drink your father-in-law's wine.

20 An arrow should be made straight as a line. If it is warped in the very least, it will not fly straight.

21 They two brothers are entirely different, one very swarthy and the other very fair. How true it is that "one mother gives birth to many kinds."

22 These persimmons are not fully cured. They have a very astringent taste.

23 Although the color of the African's skin is jet black, yet he himself still thinks it beautiful.

24 No matter whether you are cooking vegetables or meats, it is, of course, not good to make them too fresh, nor is it good to make them very salt.

25 In coming home last night I came ten *li* after dark. It was cloudy and dark as pitch; you couldn't see a man before you nor a hand before your face. The result was that I got several tumbles by the way.

26 That little maiden, Shwang-tsï, is exceedingly bashful. The simple mention of her [intended] husband makes her blush scarlet.

27 I saw the stuff which Wang the third has bought for a short coat at only seventy-two cash per foot: the drilling is very thick and of a glossy blue-black color; from a distance it looks just like broadcloth.

百般 *Pai³ pan¹*. *Many kinds*, every kind, multifarious, various.

柿 *Shi⁴*. The persimmon, or China fig.

漤 *Lan³*. To pickle fruits in brine; *to ripen by steeping in hot water*:—Note 22.

澀 *Shê⁴, sê⁴*. Rough, harsh; *astringent*.

亞非利加 *Ya⁴ fei¹ li⁴ chia¹*. Africa.

葷 *Hun¹*. *Cooked meats*; dishes held to be inconsistent with a religious fast.

素菜 *Su⁴ ts'ai⁴*. Cooked vegetables, vegetable food:—Note 24.

葷菜 *Hun¹ ts'ai⁴*. Vegetables cooked with meat:—Note 24.

Notes.

3 Chinanfu rejects all of the three forms in the text, and says 喬臭.

8 粉紅 means *white and red mixed*; that is, *pale red or pink*, so that in this case 粉 modifies rather than intensifies the meaning.

10 絳紫 *Scarlet purple* seems a confusion or contradiction of terms, but it must be remembered that both terms are somewhat vague. 血紫 The Chinese take venous not arterial blood as the standard, and so say blood purple.

11 昌邑 A district city in Shantung, in the prefecture of Laichou.

12 南山 is said to be a range of hills in the prefecture of 台州 in Manchuria, which produces on its sides an extra fine quality of tobacco.

13 Pasteboard is made straight and smooth by being pasted against a board or a wall, and left there to dry.

16 The Chinese have no generic name for apple, but a specific name for each variety of apple. Foreign apples are usually called 蘋果 because they outwardly resemble this variety more than they do any other.

21 一母生百般 is a common phrase to express the idea that the children of the same parents are often very

第一百五十課

天[1]下惟有理可以服人。○大[2]家的東西、你不能獨自得了。○崔[3]冕任誰不怕、惟獨怕他老婆。○別[4]人都肯了、獨獨獨你不肯、是爲甚麼呢。○人[5]總得講理、不可一味的使鬧脾氣。○西[6]國有一種牙醫生、專門給人收拾牙。○你[7]獨自一個個去、叫我不放心。○禍[8]福無門、惟人自招。○他[9]一輩子沒做別的、專門一撥弄官司。○看[10]書不獨消閒遣、而且又長學問。○我[11]是專管一條、他是兼管一切。○人[12]生在世、惟夫妻二人、離散不開。○你[13]我是孤身在外、只恐有錯。○

TRANSLATION.

1 Right is the only thing in the world that commands universal assent.
2 You cannot appropriate to yourself alone what belongs to the whole company.
3 Ts'wei Mien does not fear anybody at all, except his wife.
4 Everybody else is willing, how is it that you alone are unwilling?
5 A man should be reasonable, and not give loose rein to his own idiosyncrasies.
6 There is in the West a class of [men called] dentists who make a special business of repairing teeth for people.
7 I am afraid to have you go all alone.
8 Calamities and blessings are conditioned entirely on a man's own actions.
9 He has done nothing all his life but manage lawsuits.
10 Reading not only whiles away time, it also advances one's scholarship.
11 I give my attention all to one thing; he has the whole under his control.
12 According to the constitution of human society, it is only husband and wife who are inseparable.

different, both in character and appearance. 一龍生九種 is another phrase for expressing the same idea. Its derivation is uncertain.

22 Persimmons are often plucked before they are quite ripe, and are *cured* by steeping them in warm water. This brings out the yellow color and takes away the astringent taste. Chinanfu rejects all of the three forms in the text and says 喬澀.

24 素菜 *Vegetables cooked alone without meat, fish or animal oil.* 葷菜 *Meats, including eggs, fish and animal oils, together with strong smelling vegetables, as onions and garlic.* 菜 is often used alone to include *all* admixtures of both. This distinction of 素 and 葷 is made by the Buddhists, who make merit by abstaining from 葷.

LESSON CL.

RESTRICTIVE PARTICLES AND PHRASES.

This lesson may be regarded as a continuation and completion of Lesson 49.

惟 Only, but, sole, except,—a book word, but often used in colloquial, especially when joined with 獨.

獨 Alone, only, specially,—often doubled for emphasis.

惟獨 But, only, save, except, sole.

一味的 Simply, with one single purpose, always:—Note (5).

專 Special, wholly, with all the mind, intent.

專門 Specially, wholly, solely.

專一 Solely, wholly, undividedly, merely.

獨自 or **獨自個** or **獨自一個** By oneself, all alone.

孤 Alone, single, solitary.

就是 Is not unfrequently so used as to take the place of 惟 or 獨, as in (14), (16).

別[14]的他都不要、就是想枇杷吃。○不[15]論是手藝、是學問、要精於那一樣、必得專一學那一樣。○我[16]莊上有一家姓丁的、去年八月害癟亂病、十口人死了九口、就是剩了六歲的一個孩子。○這[17]是合會的事情、你怎麼獨獨來找我呢、答能者多勞、先生既然能事、所以獨獨來找先生。○你[18]可以先去領教領教那些年高的人、然後再下手辦、不可自己獨出心裁。○平[19]常人的眼睛、都是一個瞳人、惟有舜和項羽的眼睛、是兩個瞳人。○人[20]家的兄弟、都如手足一般、惟獨我的兄弟、乃是前世的寃家。○他[21]們年輕的都做什麼、怎麼獨獨叫你老人家、磕磕絆絆 戰戰磕磕 抖抖擻擻的來呢。○若[22]是一味

13 You and I are abroad alone, and the danger is that we may make some mistake.

14 He longs for some bibos to eat, but wants nothing else.

15 In whatever you would be proficient, whether handicraft or learning, you must give it undivided attention.

16 There was a family by the name of Ting in our village, who took cholera last year in the eighth month, and of a family of ten, nine died leaving only one, a child six years old.

17 This matter belongs to the whole society, why do you specially come to me about it? *Ans.* "The capable man has most to do." Since you, sir, have the ability therefore we come specially to you.

18 Go first and learn awhile of those who are older, and only after doing this undertake the management yourself; you must not attempt to strike out independently.

19 Ordinary people's eyes have only one pupil, but Shun's and Hsiang Yü's eyes had each two pupils.

20 Other people's brothers are like hands and feet to them, but my brother is a born enemy.

21 What are all the young people doing, that they send you, aged sir, tottering along.

22 If you always forbear with him, he

VOCABULARY.

獨 *Tu*^{2}. Solitary, alone; by oneself, single; widowed; only, yet:—see Sub.

崔 *Ts'wei*^{1}. A high mountain; a surname.

冕 *Mien*^{3}. A crown, a coronet.

講理 *Chiang*^{3} *li*^{3}. To discuss the merits of a matter; *to be reasonable.*

鬧脾氣 *Nao*^{4} *p'i*^{2} *ch'i*^{4}. To indulge one's peculiar disposition, *to give rein to one's special idiosyncrasies;* to act contrarily.

使脾氣 *Shï*^{3} *p'i*^{2} *ch'i*^{4}. The same.

撥弄 *Po*^{1} *lung*^{4}. *To manage,* to manipulate; to stir up; to foment.

遣 *Ch'ien*^{3}. To commission, to send; *to let go.*

消遣 *Hsiao*^{1} *ch'ien*^{3}. To seek amusement, *to while away time;* to saunter about, to dissipate care.

消閒 *Hsiao*^{1} *hsien*^{2}. The same.

兼 *Chien*^{1}. To include, *to embrace;* along with; together with; equally; connected.

離散 *Li*^{2} *san*^{4}. *To separate,* to go apart, to scatter; to become estranged.

孤身 *Ku*^{1} *shên*^{1}. *Alone,* solitary.

枇杷 *P'i*^{2} *pa*^{1}. The bibo or biwa, the loquat of Central China.

領教 *Ling*^{3} *chiao*^{4}. To receive instruction, *to learn from,* to take lessons from; I am much obliged (for the information).

的忍耐他、他倒以爲你是無能膿包、就越發欺負你喇。○這[23]邊買賣、他們都不錯、惟獨我沒落下一個大錢。○衆[24]人唱完了詩、都躺下安歇、惟獨亞伯思想父親、睡不安穩。○雖[25]然他在世俗上、也做些好事、還不許是專爲務名嗎。○咱[26]們先生太不公道、明是他兒子領頭惹了禍、他却打了這些人、獨獨不打他兒子、○他[27]是欺負我孤單門獨戶、我就仗着理直氣壯、不受他欺負、所以纔鬧大發攤喇。○中[28]國所事奉的神、大概是在廟裏敬拜、惟有竈王竈君是在家裏敬拜。○女[29]人有天生下賤的、聽說上海有個婊子、連一位巡撫他都不嫁、獨獨看中一個戲子、偏嫁了他、這希奇不希奇呢。

will regard you as of no account (a soft-head), and will all the more insult you.

23 They all came out fairly well in this speculation save myself, and I did not realize a cash.

24 When the company had finished singing, they all lay down to sleep; but Abel kept thinking of his father and did not sleep soundly.

25 Although in the eyes of the world he has done some praiseworthy things, yet may they not have been done merely for the sake of a good name?

26 Our teacher is too unjust. It was clearly his son who took the lead in stirring up the trouble, yet he whipped all the others but never touched him.

27 He presumed to insult me because we are but a single family; while I, standing on the justice of my cause, refused to submit to his insults; hence it is that the strife has become so serious.

28 The gods served in China are for the most part worshipped in temples, but the Kitchen God is worshipped at home.

29 Some women are base by nature. I have heard that there was a prostitute at Shanghai who would not marry even a governor, but fell in love with an actor and married him. Was not that very remarkable?

年高 *Nien² kao¹*. Old men, men of experience, elders.

瞳 *T'ung²*. *The pupil of the eye;* the image reflected in the pupil.

瞳人 *T'ung² jên²*. The same.

羽 *Yü³*. Wings, plumes, feathers.

前世 *Ch'ien² shï⁴*. A former life; a previous state of existence.

磕磕絆絆 *K'ê¹ pan⁴*. Trembling, tottering from age.

戰戰磕磕 *Chan⁴ k'ê¹*. The same.

擻 *Sou³*. *To shake;* to arouse.

抖擻 *Tou³ sou³*. To shake, *to tremble;* to shiver, to quake; to arouse.

無能 *Wu² nêng²*. Impotent; inefficient; weak, good-for-nothing, *of no account.*

膿包 *Nung² pao¹*. A silly fool (lit., a bag of pus), a lackbrain, *a soft-head.* (s.)

領頭 *Ling³ t'ou²*. To lead the way, *to take the lead*, to go ahead.

大發 *Ta⁴ fa¹*. Grave, *serious*, important.

大攤 *Ta⁴ t'an¹*. The same. (s.)

敬拜 *Ching⁴ pai⁴*. To reverence, to worship.

竈王 *Tsao⁴ wang²*. The Kitchen God:—Note 28.

竈君 *Tsao⁴ chün¹*. The same.

下賤 *Hsia⁴ chien⁴*. *Base*, mean, low, vicious, depraved.

婊 *Piao³*. A prostitute, a harlot.

戲子 *Hsi⁴ tsï³*. *An actor*, a comedian.

第一百五十一課

他[1]的便宜、豈肯叫人得呢。○自[2]己不正、焉能正人。○這[3]等喪良心的錢、豈能長久嗎。○既[4]在矮簷下、焉敢不低頭。○叔[5]叔既不去、哥哥與兄弟、難道也不去嗎。○你[6]這婦人、焉知不能救丈夫呢。○百[7]姓都安安靜靜的、豈不快活嗎。○你[8]也太多疑、難道一個聖旨、敢傳假的。○蛟[9]龍豈是池中物。○我[10]給先生代勞行不

Translation.

1 Will he allow any one to get the advantage of him?
2 How can a man correct others who is not himself correct?
3 Can this kind of dishonest gain be lasting?
4 Since I am under authority, how dare I do otherwise than submit?
5 Seeing you, uncle, will not go, is it possible that my brothers will also refuse to go?
6 How do you, who are a wife, know that you cannot save your husband?
7 Is it not delightful when the people are all quiet and peaceable?
8 You are too suspicious. Do you think any one would dare proclaim a false Imperial Edict?
9 Is a dragon to be found in a fish-tank?
10 How would it be for me to take your

Notes.

5 一味的 *One taste;* that is, holding on persistently and without consideration to one idea.

8 A piece of Taoist moralizing in the book style, but constantly in the mouths of Chinese religionists.

11 兼 is a book term, not often used in Mandarin.

12 人生在世 *As man exists in this world,*—a common phrase, but difficult to translate. 夫妻 In Mandarin neither of these words is ordinarily used alone for husband or wife, but when joined together they form a common and easily understood term.

17 能者多勞 A proverbial phrase in book style, meaning that the services of the man who has ability are always most in demand.

18 領教那些年高的人 is equivalent to 領那些年高的人的教. The 領教 is used as if it were a single transitive verb. It is rather to be regarded as a passive,—*to be instructed by.* 獨出心裁 *To proceed alone and devise a plan;* that is, *to ignore the advice and the precedents of others and strike out for oneself, to act independently.*

20 前世的寃家 *An enemy from a previous state of existence, a transmigrated or prenatal enemy.*

21 獨 is not specially represented in the translation. It implies that there was a purpose in sending the old man, and that it was unbecoming in the circumstances.

27 理直氣壯 *When the cause is right the courage is strong.* The phrase is here appropriated and used as a whole, with the meaning given in the translation. 孤門獨戶 *Lone gate and single door;* that is, a single family living in a neighborhood where it has no relatives. The Chinese depend very much for protection on their relatives. A single family living alone feels weak.

28 竈王 or 竈君 or 竈神 is one of the most ancient of Chinese gods. His picture is pasted over the cooking range, and he is worshipped by every family at stated times, especially on the twenty-third of the last month when he ascends to heaven to make his annual report to 玉皇上帝, and on the last day of the year when he returns to his former place. He is the special patron god of the family. There are no temples built to him. There are various accounts of his origin. One of the most rational, though not the most popular, is that he was at first a man named Chan (mispronounced Tan) Tsï Kwoǎ 禪子郭 who invented fire by rubbing sticks together, and was hence regarded as a god and deified as the Kitchen God.

LESSON CLI.

Special Interrogatives.

豈 A direct interrogative particle, always expressing more or less of surprise or impatience. It stands at the beginning of a clause and expects a negative answer, unless a negative is included in the question, when it of course expects an affirmative answer. The clause or sentence beginning with 豈 sometimes ends with 嗎, sometimes with 呢, and sometimes without either 嗎 or 呢. There is no rule as to which shall be used in a given case, and the choice seems to be left largely to the fancy of the writer or speaker. As 豈 asks a *direct* question the concluding word *ought* to be 嗎. 豈 is sometimes translated *how* or *why*, but incorrectly as it is properly the sign of a *direct* question

行、答好說、豈不敢勞駕。○亙[11]古以來、只有臣替君死、焉有君替臣死的道理呢。○你[12]我彼此恭恭敬敬的、豈不好嗎。○他[13]們既然凡事都外着我、我焉得不自己打算自己的呢。○你[14]是我的恩人、你今有難、我豈有不救你之理。○趙[15]子龍若非全身都是膽、焉敢屢次擋曹兵。○這[16]原是我一生的毛病、我豈不知道嗎。○那[17]女子只好十八九歲、這婆子倒有八十歲、難道六十多歲還生產嗎。○王[18]三的姑娘、本不願意給于五的兒子、作媒的硬强作主、眞豈有此理。○事[19]情既然定了局、你又反復了、這豈

place? *Ans.* You are very kind, but I could not think of troubling you.

11 From ancient times it has only been known that a minister has given his life for his prince; what reason would there be in a prince giving his life for his minister?

12 Is it not the proper thing for us to treat each other with mutual respect?

13 Since they ignore me in everything, why should I not look out for myself?

14 You are my benefactor, and now that you are in trouble can I do otherwise than help you?

15 If Chao Tsï Lung were not the very embodiment of courage, would he dare repeatedly to withstand the soldiers of Tsʻao?

16 I know quite well that this has been a life-long fault of mine.

17 That young woman cannot be over eighteen or nineteen while this woman is fully eighty; can a woman of over sixty bear children?

18 Wang the third was from the first unwilling to give his daughter to Yü the fifth's son, but the middleman took it into his own hands and settled it. Nothing could be more unreasonable.

19 After the terms are fully settled you

難道 It is hard to say, how can you say? you don't mean to say, is it so?—an interrogative form used both in colloquial and in books. It expresses a strong presumption on the part of the speaker.

焉 How, why,—an indirect interrogative particle, generally used to express a strong affirmation. It stands at the beginning of a clause, and is generally used in connection with the following words, viz., 能, 敢, 知, 有, 得, which are arranged in the order of the frequency of their use. 焉 is primarily a book word, but is often used in Mandarin.

VOCABULARY.

豈 *Chʻi*^{3}. A direct interrogative particle:—see .... Sub. Also *kʻai*^{3}.

焉 *Yien*^{1}. A final affirmative particle in Wên-li; ....an initial interrogative particle meaning, how, why:—see Sub.

長久 *Chʻang*^{2} *chiu*^{3}. Continual, permanent, ... *lasting*.

低頭 *Ti*^{1} *tʻou*^{2}. To lower the head, to stoop; to ....yield, *to submit*.

多疑 *Toă*^{1} *i*^{2}.......... To be suspicious.

聖旨 *Shêng*^{4} *chï*^{3}. *An imperial edict;* the holy .... will or purpose of God.

代勞 *Tai*^{4} *lao*^{2}. To fill the office or perform .... the work of another.

蛟 *Chiao*^{1}......A dragon with scales:—Note 9.

亙 *Kên*^{4}.... A limit, *the extreme point;* universal.

亙古 *Kên*^{4} *ku*^{3}. Of old, *from the earliest times;* .... antiquity.

恩人 *Ên*^{1} *jên*^{2}...... *A benefactor*, a saviour.

一生 *I*^{1} *Shêng*^{1}......A life time, the whole life.

生產 *Shêng*^{1} *chʻan*^{3}. To give birth to; to bring .... forth, *to bear*.

豈有此理 *Chʻi*^{3} *yiu*^{3} *tsʻï*^{3} *li*^{3}. *Is it reasonable?* is it possible? *outrageous*, out of the question.

算是大丈夫嗎。○你[20]想明明的乾坤、朗朗的世界、若是他和姓李的、沒有苟且之事、姓李的焉敢來搶他呢。○他[21]們是口是心非、我是心口如一、豈不强過他們嗎。○楊[22]老四太豈有此理了、人家託他帶的銀子和信、他竟是把信燒了、把銀子昧下了。○你[23]看那個瘸子、走路多麼累贅、我們的身子、既然沒有殘疾、豈不當知足嗎。○子[24]路問事鬼神的道理、孔夫子說、未能事人、焉能事鬼、又問死的道理、孔夫子說、未知生、焉知死。○咱[25]們說話、再不能不符前言、若是不符前言、豈不成了匹夫了嗎。○那[26]是一部公用的書、你怎麼不讓別人看呢、答就是公用的書、也有個先來後

turn round and rue the bargain. Do you consider this manly?

20 If she had had no illicit intrigue with the man Li, how would he dare to come in the face of divine and human law and carry her off?

21 Their words are good, but their intentions are evil. My words and intentions are alike. Am I not better than they?

22 Yang the Fourth is too outrageous for anything. Some one sent some money and a letter by him, when, behold, he burned the letter and used the money.

23 Look at that lame man, how laboriously he walks. Since our bodies are free from deformity, should we not be content with our lot?

24 When Tsï Lu asked about serving the gods, Confucius said, "While you are not able to serve men how can you serve the gods?" He also asked concerning death, to which Confucius replied, "While you do not understand life how can you understand death?"

25 We will not fail to abide by what we have said. He who does not keep his word debases himself.

26 That is a book for public use, why is it that you will not allow anyone else to see it? *Ans.* Even if it is for public use, still "first come first served." When I am just in the midst of reading it must I give way and let him see it first?

坤 *K'un*¹. Obedient; earth; the moon; a wife, female.

乾坤 *Ch'ien*² *k'un*¹. Heaven and earth, the cosmos; *the moral law written in the heart;* male and female.

苟 *Kou*³. If; if indeed, if only; *illicit;* careless, inconsiderate.

苟且 *Kou*³ *ch'ie*³. *Illicit intercourse,* intrigue; careless, reckless.

昧 *Mei*⁴. Dark, obscure; to suppress; to embezzle, *to appropriate.*

瘸 *Ch'üe*². *Lame;* to limp, to halt.

累贅 *Lei*⁴ *chwei*⁴. Troublesome, *laborious,* embarrassing; tedious, repetitions:—Note 23.

符前言 *Fu*² *ch'ien*² *yien*². To fulfil a promise, to keep one's word.

匹 *P'i*³. A mate; mean, vulgar. See *p'i*¹.

匹夫 *P'i*³ *fu*¹. A common man, a plebian; *a base fellow,* a mean-spirited man.

公用 *Kung*¹ *yung*⁴. Common property; *for public* or *general use.*

獻 *Hsien*⁴. *To offer in worship;* to present to a superior, to hand up to.

供獻 *Kung*⁴ *hsien*⁴. *Offerings;* sacrifices.

上供 *Shang*⁴ *kung*⁴. To present offerings, to worship with an offering.

長命 *Ch'ang*² *ming*⁴. Long-lived, to live to old age.

短命 *Twan*³ *ming*⁴. Short-lived, to die prematurely.

到、難道我正看着的時候、還必得讓他先看嗎。○你[27]想想、從來說聰明正直的爲神、既是一個神佛、豈有貪圖你的元寶供獻、就保護你、若是不與他燒錢上供、神佛就惱你、降禍於你、這神佛也是一個小人了。○更[28]有把自己好兒好女、怕他養活不大、捨在廟裏、做了和尚道士、以爲出了家、在佛爺脚下、就長命了、我且問你、難道這些現做和尚道士的、個個都是活七八十歲、就沒一個短命的嗎。

27 Consider how it has long been said, "That is divine which is both wise and upright." Seeing he is a divine Buddha will he covet your silver and your offerings and so protect you? If, because you do not burn paper and make offerings to him, he is angry with you and sends misfortune on you, this divine Buddha is nothing but a base fellow.

28 There are still others who, fearing that their sons and daughters may not live to adult age, take them to the temples and devote them to the Buddhist or Taoist priesthood, supposing that by abjuring family ties and sitting at the feet of Buddha they will secure long life. I would ask such, is it a fact that all who have become priests have lived to be seventy or eighty years old and not one has been short-lived?

NOTES.

2 Notice how 正 is first an adjective, then a verb.

3 喪良心 *To lose the conscience, to become callous to the claims of right and justice.* 喪良心的錢 is money obtained by shamefully dishonest means.

4 Or, *The circumstances being such as they are, how can I do otherwise than acquiesce?* Lit. *Since I am under the low eaves how can I refuse to bow my head?*

8 This sentence stands in the Fortunate Union without any final particle, but according to the genius of the spoken language it ought to have a 嗎. It is not uncommon for writers of books to omit colloquial particles for the sake of brevity or of dignity.

9 It is uncertain whether 蛟 and 龍 should here be regarded as distinct animals, or 蛟 be regarded as defining the species of 龍. The sentence is proverbial, and used as a figure.

13 外 is here used as a verb.

15 趙子龍 One of the heroes of the "Three Kingdoms," distinguished for size and beauty of person, and noted for the most daring bravery. Liu Pei is reported to have said of him, 子龍全身都是膽, *Tsï Lung's whole body is gall.* The gall is regarded as the seat of courage.

20 乾坤 is put for the moral restraints of the higher law, and 世界 for the legal penalties of the state; so that the whole expression, 明明的乾坤朗朗的世界, is an elegant periphrasis for *divine and human law.*

22 The phrase 豈有此理 is here taken as a whole, and so qualified by 太. Still greater liberties are sometimes taken with this phrase; thus we sometimes hear 豈有此理得很.

23 累贅 In this particular phrase 累 is in many places read *lei*².

24 子路 was one of Confucius' disciples. The record of these questions is found in the Analects. It is worthy of note that while 子路 said 鬼神, Confucius in his reply only used 鬼. He was led to this no doubt by the rhetorical necessity of only putting one word in correlation with 人. His choice of 鬼, however, implies that in this connection 鬼 includes 神. That is to say, all gods are first men and then gods, which accords with Chinese theogony, and with the prevailing sentiment of the Chinese people. The sage cleverly evaded both questions.

27 聰明正直的爲神 is adapted from the words of the 左傳, which are, 神聰明正直而壹者也. It expresses the idea that the distinguishing traits in the character of a 神 are wisdom and virtue.

28 怕他養活不大 The 他 here stands for the children, and is really the object of 養活, as if the sentence read 怕養活他不大. The construction is *Wên-li* rather than Mandarin. Parents do not always go the length of really giving their sons to be priests, but only make a pretence of doing so by having them shave their heads and wear the usual garb of priests until grown up, when they throw off the disguise. Sometimes they give them to the priesthood conditionally for a time, and redeem them when half grown. Children devoted to the priesthood are supposed to be under the special protection of the gods and hence more likely to escape the accidents of youth, and grow up to manhood. 現 is *Wên* for 現在.

第一百五十二課

你[1]看這個法子怎麼樣、答我看未必行得去了。○人[2]怯場、那是天生的性情、不一定是因爲工夫不到。○要[3]知道說好話的、不一定不準成就是好人。○雖[4]是父母的心腸、也未必沒有偏向。○咱[5]我們的糧食、能接上新的不能、答我看能接得上、偺媽媽我媽媽却說不見得其能。○不[6]必然一回還清、就是陸續的之着還、也無不可。○他[7]自己可說是能行、其實到底能行不能行、也未可知。○每[8]課的生字、必得一般多嗎、答不必然、多幾個少幾個、都不要緊。○你[9]就是背地裏有肋、若是某人在眼前、未必見得其你敢說這些硬郎漢氣話罷。○現[10]在過了九點半鐘、怕他已經睡了、答不見得其能睡、他常行十點鐘纔睡覺。○天[11]下的事情不可

TRANSLATION.

1 What do you think of this plan? *Ans.* I scarcely think it will succeed.
2 Embarrassment springs from natural temperament, not necessarily from want of proficiency.
3 You ought to know that he who talks fairly is not certainly a good man.
4 Even the heart of a parent is not certainly free from partiality.
5 Will our grain hold out until the new crop comes in? *Ans.* I think it will hold out, but mother says she is doubtful of it.
6 It is not absolutely necessary to pay all at once. There is no objection to its being paid in instalments.
7 He himself however says it will answer, but whether after all it really will answer or not is uncertain.
8 Must there be the same number of new characters in each lesson? *Ans.* Not necessarily; a few more or a few less is not important.
9 You are very brave behind peoples' backs. If the party in question were present, it is doubtful if you would venture to speak so defiantly.
10 It is now more than half-past nine o'clock; I fear he has gone to bed. *Ans.* I scarcely think he has gone to bed; he does not usually retire until ten o'clock.
11 How things will turn out cannot be known beforehand. It is not certain

LESSON CLII.

PHRASES OF UNCERTAINTY.

未必 Not certainly, not necessarily, scarcely think.

未必然 Not certain, not likely, not necessarily.

不一定 Not certain, doubtful, contingent.

不必 Not certainly, not likely; need not, better not.

不必然 Not certainly, not necessarily.

不準成 Not certain, not sure, not settled, problematical.

不見其 Not likely, scarcely think, doubtful, dubious.

不見得 The same. (s.)

那見其 Do you suppose? You need not think, far from certain.

那見得 The same. (s.)

未必見其 Not very likely, doubtful, dubious.

未必見得 The same. (s.)

未可知 Who knows? no knowing, quite uncertain. Used at the end of a sentence to express a doubt of what has preceded.

逆料、今日看着是福、未必不是後日的禍、今日看着是禍、未必不是後日的福、所以只得聽天由命就是了。○別[12]混加批評、聖人還能有錯嗎、答這個也未必然、孔夫子說、苟有過、人必知之、他既然明說自己有錯、我們怎能說他沒有錯呢。○彭[13]儒林那是一位道學先生、不見得其能做出這樣僭分的事來。○但[14]凡是個眞耿直人、性子性體都是急躁、而性子性體急躁的人、却未必都是耿直。○大[15]概不能是遭了事情、必是路上被風雨阻住了、或者家中偶然有事、沒能應時起身、也未可知。○雖[16]說事大事小、

that what seems happiness to-day may not prove misfortune to-morrow, nor that what seems misfortune to-day may not prove a blessing to-morrow. Therefore the only way is to abide the decision of fate.

12 Do not make rash criticisms. The sage cannot be mistaken. *Ans.* That is not at all certain. Confucius said, "If I have any errors people are sure to know them." Seeing he himself plainly said he had errors, how can we say that he had none?

13 P'êng Ju Lin is an exemplary man. I scarcely believe he is capable of doing such an unwarrantable thing.

14 Every straightforward man has a hasty temper, but it does not follow that everyone who has a hasty temper is straightforward.

15 I hardly think he has met with any accident; it is most lkely that he has been detained on the road by the weather, or something has unexpectedly occurred at home so that he could not start at the time appointed. Yet who knows?

16 Although it is said, "whether great or whether small, meeting face to face

VOCABULARY.

怯塲 *Ch'ie⁴ ch'ang³.* Excited by the presence of spectators, *embarrassed.*

心腸 *Hsin¹ ch'ang².* *The heart,* feelings, affections.

偏向 *P'ien¹ hsiang⁴.* *Partial,* unfair, [to one side.

還淸 *Hwan² ch'ing.¹* *To pay off,* to pay in full.

陸 *Lu⁴.* Dry land, terra firma; detached, *in portions.* Also *liu⁴.*

陸續 *Lu⁴ hsü⁴.* Successively, one by one in order, *in instalments.*

肋 *Chin⁴.* *Strength,* force, energy, muscle.

硬郞 *Ying⁴ lang².* Muscular, vigorous; bold, *defiant.*

漢氣 *Han⁴ ch'i⁴.* Bold, manly, resolute; *defiant,* boastful.

常行 *Ch'ang² hsing².* Ordinarily, commonly, *usually.*

逆料 *Ni⁴ liao⁴.* To anticipate, *to know beforehand.*

彭 *P'êng².* Near; numerous; *a surname.*

道學 *Tao⁴ hsüe².* The science of morals, the teaching of the sages; consistent, *exemplary,* orthodox:—Note 13.

僭 *Chien⁴.* To arrogate to oneself, to usurp, to assume.

僭分 *Chien⁴ fên⁴.* To usurp, to assume without authority; *unwarrantable.*

耿 *Kêng³.* Bright; constant; *ingenuous.*

耿直 *Kêng³ chï².* Sincere, *straightforward,* downright, frank; unyielding.

性體 *Hsing⁴ t'i³.* Disposition, *temper,* temperament, character.

應時 *Ying⁴ shï².* According to appointment, at the proper time.

關係 *Kwan¹ hsi¹.* To concern, to have relation to, *to involve;* consequences, result, effect.

爽當 *Shwang³ tang⁴.* Prompt, *quick,* expeditious.

一到就了、但這是關係人命的事、未必見得其能了的這麼爽當。○我[17]勸你別任性喇、俗語說、官斷十條路、你雖然覺得有理、那見得其一定能贏官司呢、就是果眞贏了、也是贏的你叔叔、於你臉上並無光輝彩。○人[18]總要看眼色行事、咱們若是到人家家裏說閒話、人家的廚房、已經擺上飯了、咱們還不走、豈不躭誤人家吃飯嗎、人家當面雖不必說什麼、背後必說一點眼色沒有。○看[19]他說得這樣的確、敢許是我當初聽恍惚了、也未可知。○聽[20]說十里舖、有一帮子和尚化緣、一定要化五十吊錢、少一吊也不肯、聽那個說法、必是一些戒和尚、答那也不一定、還不許是些野和尚、假粧戒和尚的樣子、欺騙人嗎。

settles all;" yet it is not likely that this affair, which involves the life of a man, can be settled so quickly as this.

17 I should advise you not to be over-confident. There is a saying, "The verdict of a magistrate may take [any one of] ten roads." Although you think you have right on your side, yet it is far from certain that you will gain your case; and even if you really do gain it, you are gaining it against your uncle, which will not be any credit to you.

18 One should always act with due discernment. If I go into the house of another to have a chat, and when the cook has already set out the food, still do not go, will I not interfere with their meal? Although they may not say anything to my face, yet behind my back they will surely say that I have no discernment.

19 Seeing he speaks so positively it may be that in the first instance my hearing was at fault, and yet there is no knowing.

20 I hear there is a company of Buddhist priests at the ten *li* village collecting money. They are determined to get fifty thousand cash and will take nothing less. Judging from the report they must be ordained priests. *Ans.* That is not certain. May they not be a lot of vagabond priests falsely pretending to be ordained in order to deceive people?

任性 *Jên⁴ hsing⁴*. Obstinate, headstrong; reckless, *overconfident*.

光彩 *Kwang¹ ts'ai³*. Glory, splendor, lustre; honor, *credit*.

輝 *Hwei¹*. Glorious, refulgent, splendid.

光輝 *Kwang¹ hwei¹*. Glory, splendor, brilliance; honor, *credit*.

恍 *Hwang³*. Wild, mad; fluttered, confused.

惚 *Hu¹*. Minute; in doubt, hesitating.

恍惚 Flurried, confused, uncertain, *indistinct*.

化緣 *Hwa⁴ yüen²*. To raise a subscription for religious or charitable uses, *to collect money*, to levy a contribution.

粧 *Chwang¹*. To dress up, to adorn; to feign, *to pretend*, to assume a character.

假粧 *Chia³ chwang¹*. *To pretend*, to feign, to simulate falsely.

欺騙 *Ch'i⁴ p'ien⁴*. To cheat, to defraud, *to deceive*, to circumvent.

NOTES.

6 無不可 The more expanded colloquial form would be, 沒有什麼不可以處.

7 可 is inserted to convey the idea that notwithstanding the supposed improbability, he still thinks the plan will succeed.

9 劤, *strength* is here put for *bravery*. Some would write 勁.

11 聽天由命 is equal to 聽天命. This sentiment, which is often heard, looks like a belief in an overruling Providence; yet in fact it amounts to little more than a belief

第一百五十三課

他[1]爲何管我的閒事。○你[2]們的意思如何。○這[3]點事情、何足爲難。○若[4]不是他、還有何人。○在[5]家孝父母、何必遠燒香。○這[6]是我的事情、與你何干。○我[7]的身家性命、何等貴重。○有[8]麝自然來香、何必迎風站、何用大風揚。○你[9]的身體、從何處來、怎麼就不想念你的生身父母。○有[10]空兒、何不到我這裏走走呢。○做[11]甚麼要想甚麼、爲何不經心做呢。○不[12]分親疎、就動手、那如何使得呢。○說[13]了幾句戲言笑話何至這樣翻臉。○那[14]首詩唱得

TRANSLATION.

1 Why does he meddle in my private affairs?
2 What is your opinion?
3 What is there in this trifling affair that need present any difficulty?
4 If it is not he who else could it be?
5 If at home you honor your parents, what necessity is there to go great distances to burn incense?
6 This is my business. What concern is it of yours? [and family?
7 How precious are the lives of myself
8 If you have musk on your person the fragrance is self-diffusing. Why take pains to stand in the wind (what need of a hurricane to spread it)?
9 Where did your body come from? How is it you do not keep in mind the parents who gave you birth?
10 Why do you not come to visit me when you have leisure?
11 When you are doing anything you should fix your mind upon that. Why do you not take more care?
12 It will never do to strike right and

---

in blind fate. The personality of 天 is too vague to make 命 mean anything more than fate.

13 道學先生 One who not only teaches the doctrines of the sages, but professes to practice them, and protests against the laxity of modern times.

18 人家家裡 The first 家 belongs to 人. 咱們, though translated *I*, is used in a general sense as equal to *one, any one*. 廚房 is put for *cook*. This figure of speech is quite common.

20 It is a common thing for priests to fix on a certain sum which they determine to collect, apportion it among their constituents, and then insist on each man subscribing his apportioned share. A 戒和尙 is a priest who has been regularly ordained by an abbot, and has taken the vows or orders of the priesthood. He has on his head the round scars (from 3 to 12) of the burning moxa, and carries the certificate of the abbot by whom he was ordained. He is entitled to temporary entertainment in any temple in the empire, and may collect money in any of the eighteen provinces. A 野和尙 is an unordained priest who is not domiciled in any particular temple but wanders from place to place.

LESSON CLIII.

THE INTERROGATIVE PRONOUN 何.

何 is the *Wên-li* equivalent of 甚麼, but is also much used in Mandarin, especially in ready-made phrases. Of these phrases the following are the most important:—

爲何 For what,—why. 何 is often used alone in the sense of 爲何

如何 As what,—how, what.

何如 What as,—how, what, how about, what of. Always stands at the end of a clause.

何必 Why must,—why, why should, what occasion.

何干 What concern,—what business, what connection with, what relation to.

何等 What sort,—how (much, great, etc.)

何用 What use,—why.

何足 What sufficiency,—what need, why.

何至 What extent,—how come to the point of, why.

何苦 What bitterness,—why take the trouble, what sense, what occasion.

何苦來 The same.

太絮熟煩了、何不換首新鮮的呢。○你[15]們自己問心、如何過得去呢。○他[16]既然不聽好話、何必儘之勸他呢。○看[17]不中那個、你看這個何如。○爲[18]何只顧報這點子仇、竟把身子捨了呢。○吾[19]兄既是親身來了、也就是了、何必又送這些東西。○咱[20]們都是時常見面的人、何用這麼周旋、多禮。○既[21]然有這等學問、何愁不進學呢。○看[22]他的樣子倒不錯、但不知他的手藝何如。○你[23]常遊手好閒、你的父母妻子、何所倚靠。○今[24]天狀元遊街、你看轟轟烈烈的、是何等的聲勢。○他[25]吃虧倒罷了、是爲他自己的事情、你這是何苦呢。○你[26]變着法子難爲我、於你又沒有甚麽益處、這是何苦來

left without regard to friend or foe.

13 What is there in these few playful words to warrant taking such offense?

14 That hymn has been sung until it is worn out. Why not change to something new?

15 Just ask yourselves, how would it ever do?

16 Why persist in exhorting him seeing he will not listen to good advice?

17 If you do not fancy that one, what do you think of this one?

18 Why are you bent on venting this bit of spite even if it costs you your life?

19 It is enough for you, my dear fellow, to come to see me. Why also make these presents?

20 Why should we who are always meeting each other use so many formalities?

21 With such scholarship as this, why be anxious lest you should not get your degree?

22 He certainly presents a good appearance, but what skill he has remains to be seen.

23 While you continually loaf around in idleness what have your parents and family to depend upon for a living?

24 To-day the chwang-yüen is parading the street. See how imposing the display.

25 For him to suffer is all very well, the affair being his own, but why should you involve yourself?

26 Your persistent effort to annoy me

VOCABULARY.

何 *Hê*², ... Which? what? how? why?

麝 *Shê*⁴. . . . . . . The musk-deer; *musk.*

經心 *Ching*¹ *hsin*¹. With the mind; *to take care*, to give heed.

翻臉 *Fan*¹ *lien*³. To resent, *to take offense*, to flare up, to fly into a passion.

問心 *Wên*⁴ *hsin*¹. To take counsel of conscience, *to ask oneself.*

熟煩 *Shu*² *fan*² Repetitious, monotonous; *worn out*, humdrum, uninteresting.

親身 *Ch'in*¹ *shên*¹. . . . . . In person, personally.

旋 *Hsüen*². To come round to the same point, *to do or act in turn*; then, next, quick. Also *hsüen*⁴.

周旋 *Chou*¹ *hsüen*². To circulate, to bring about; *to treat with great attention or formality.*

多禮 *Toă*¹ *li*³. Much ceremony, many formalities, formal.

狀元 *Chwang*⁴ *yüen*². The highest graduate of the Hanlin:—Note 24.

遊街 *Yiu*² *chie*¹. To parade the street with music and banners:—Note 24.

轟轟烈烈 *Hung*¹ *lie*⁴. The din and rush of a great display; resounding, *imposing*, grand.

聲勢 *Shêng*¹ *shï*⁴. Parade, *display*; distinction, eclat; majesty, awe.

呢。○有27時想、這孩子不是我的、何必掛念、然而到底免不掉了爲他着急。○怎28麼間了半天、你一味的吞吞吐吐、支支吾、吾、你把我作何等人看待。○你29們百姓、拿着父母的遺體、生在太平無事的時候、有衣有食、何苦信從那些邪教、干犯王法、豈不是個大癡子嗎。○都30志達的文章、比李貞的何如、答嗯、都志達的文章、那能赶上李貞的呢。○我31請教你、他若是不依我、我把他全盤子端出來、好不好呢、答我勸你不必呀、但凡磨得開、也就是了、何苦認眞呢。○做32針線又何難之有呢、不論是幣撩緝擖、鈎纄靪衲、以及描畫扎繡、無非是手熟爲能。

brings you no advantage. Why take all this trouble for nothing?

27 At times I think, the child is not mine, why should I worry myself? but after all I cannot help being anxious about him.

28 Why is it that after questioning you half a day, you do nothing but equivocate and evade? What sort of a man do you take me to be?

29 What occasion is there for you people, bearing the body received from your parents, born in peaceful times and having clothing and food, to believe in those heretical sects and break the law? Are you not exceedingly silly?

30 How does Tu Tsï Ta's essay compare with Li Chên's? *Ans.* Humph! what comparison is there between Tu Tsï Ta's and Li Chên's essays?

31 What is your advice? If he takes issue with me, would it not be well to make the whole affair public? *Ans.* I would advise you not to do so. It is better to put a decent face on it if you can. What use is there in stating all the facts?

32 What special difficulty is there in the art of sewing? Whether it be to hem, to fell, to stitch or to close up, to sew in lining, to quilt, to sew on [buttons or tapes] or to stitch [a sole], to trace, to draw, to do ornamental work or to embroider, nothing is required but a practiced hand.

吐 *T'u*³. To spit out; to tell, to own up; to stammer, *to hesitate.* See *t'u*⁴.

吞吐 *T'un*¹ *t'u*³. *To hesitate*, to stammer; to mumble.

信從 *Hsin*⁴ *ts'ung*². *To believe in*, to follow the lead of.

邪教 *Hsie*² *chiao*⁴. A heretical sect.

干犯 *Kan*¹ *fan*⁴. *To break a law;* to offend against, to trespass.

請教 *Ch'ing*³ *chiao*⁴. *To ask for information or advice;* please tell me.

全盤子 *Ch'üen*² *p'an*² *tsï*³. The whole affair or business.

緝 *Ch'i*¹,⁴. To stitch. See *chi*⁴.

纄 *Yin*⁴. To baste, to quilt.

描 *Miao*². To trace, to copy; to draw, to sketch.

NOTES.

5 This is a Confucian protest against Buddhist and Taoist worship of the gods which often leads the worshipper to go long distances to worship at the shrine of noted deities. With Confucianists, reverence for parents is the cardinal virtue.

8 迎風站 *Stand in the face of the wind*, that it may spread the perfume, the possession of which you wish to be known. The saying is of course used as a figure.

13 何至, *why to the extent of*, is somewhat bookish. 何, being derived from book language, has a tendency to ally with itself similar words and forms.

19 吾兄, *my brother*,—is a book term occasionally used in colloquial. It is only heard in familiar and direct address. 吾, as a pronoun, is the *Wên-li* equivalent of 我, and its use in Mandarin is almost confined to this term.

第一百五十四課

外[1]頭的風尖溜溜的、請到家裏
來說話罷。○明[2]晃晃的太日陽頭、竟
下起雨來了。○你[3]跑顛顛的、往
那裏去呢。○那[4]個人用不得、逢
用了他、他就惡巴狠巴狠的要錢。○
柏[5]大嫂不過是外面老實、心裏
却是毒狠螫巴螫巴的。○要[6]切的楞薄薄生
薄生的、不要太厚。○這[7]件衣裳潮
糊糊的、可以拿出去晾一晾。○
箱[8]子裏裝的甚麼、檯着這樣沉

TRANSLATION.

1 The wind outside is quite sharp, please come into the house to talk.
2 The sun is shining brightly, and yet it is raining.
3 Where are you going in such breathless haste?
4 It is better not to employ that man. Whenever you employ him he demands exorbitant wages.
5 Mrs. Pai is very good-natured outwardly, but her heart is relentless.
6 Let it be cut in quite thin slices, not too thick.
7 This garment is quite damp. Take it out and air it.
8 What does the box contain, that it is so very heavy to carry.

23 子 after 妻 is not here an enclitic, as it often is in the same connection, but means sons or children.

24 When the examination for the Han-lin degree is held, the scholar who attains the first place is called a 狀元, *first diploma;* the second, 榜眼, *the eye of the list,* and the third is called 探花, *taking the flower.* It is the privilege of these three to be escorted in state with music and banners through the streets from the examination hall to their residences. This is called 遊街.

25 你這是何苦呢 *You this is what bitterness;* that is, *what occasion is there for you to suffer on account of his trouble.*

29 The use of 個 in the last clause of this sentence is grammatically inconsistent with the plural 你們 in the first,—a thing which Chinese scholars fail to appreciate.

31 請教你 is equivalent to 請你的教. 全盤子端出來 *Pass around the whole platefull;* that is, *tell the whole story.*

32 The insertion of 又 implies that the speaker had attainments in other things, and looked lightly on the art of sewing, as presenting no special difficulty. 何難之有 A book phrase occasionally heard in conversation.

LESSON CLIV.

SPECIAL DUPLICATE ADJUNCTS.

Many adjectives and some nouns and verbs take after them a special duplicate adjunct or qualifier. These adjuncts serve the double purpose of modifying and emphasizing the words to which they are joined, in a way which has no parallel in the English language. In many cases *quite* or *decidedly* fairly approximates the meaning, in other cases *so* or *such* or *too* is better. In a few cases the adjunct is intensive and may be rendered *very* or *extremely;* in other cases it modifies the meaning of the original word very little indeed, being used chiefly for emphasis. Many cases still remain in which the English language wholly fails to convey the true force of these peculiar forms. These adjuncts are especially characteristic of colloquial, and their fitting use adds much to the sprightliness and force of a speaker's style.

It is a special feature of this duplication that, irrespective of the fundamental tone, the second character of the doublet always takes the *first* tone. Thus 亮堂堂的 is not *liang*⁴ *t'ang*² *t'ang*² *ti*¹ but *liang*⁴ *t'ang*² *t'ang*¹ *ti*¹, and so of all. The duplication nearly always ends with 的. Some of these duplicates are common to several words, but the greater number are special. They vary very much in different localities, though a goodly number are quite *t'ung-hsing.* The whole number of these expressions is very large, and it is often difficult to decide what characters should be used in writing them. Four lessons will be devoted to their illustration. Owing to the necessity of the case, the translations given are oftentimes only approximate.

顛重顛重的呢。○這[9]個孩子眞不害怕臊羞、身上光溜溜的、就往外跑。○掌[10]櫃的不在眼前、有了事、也要快當溜當溜的去做、這纔是不做面子活。○劉[11]同岡是個直巴巴的心眼兒、並沒有一點轉彎抹角的地方。○老[12]的在家裏、眼巴巴的望你、你怎麽不早回去呢。○這[13]纔下來的王黃瓜、脆生生的、鮮溜溜的、實在好吃。○孫[14]世純不輕易說話、說出句話來、却乾煞重巴巴的。○他[15]今年累巴巴的、這個錢未必能都還。○[16]抽乍冷猛子的進了屋家裏就覺

9 This child has not the least shame; he is ready to run out without a stitch on him.

10 To do with dispatch whatever is to be done, even when the overseer is not present, is the way to avoid being an eye-servant.

11 Liu T'ung Kang has a straightforward disposition. There is not the least crookedness about him.

12 The old folks are anxiously expecting you at home; why do you not return as soon as possible?

13 These first new cucumbers are very crisp and fresh, their flavor is indeed delicious.

14 Sun Shï Ch'un does not often speak, but when he does say anything he says it with emphasis.

15 He is sadly embarrassed this year. It is not likely he will be able to pay all this debt.

16 Coming suddenly into the house, it seems quite warm.

溜 To flow—as a doublet imparts the idea of *smooth, facile, flowing.*

尖溜溜的 Quite sharp, very penetrating, quite raw. (c. & s.)

快溜溜的 Quickly, speedily, on the run.

光溜溜的 Entirely naked; quite smooth or bare or sleek; entirely destitute.

鮮溜溜的 Quite fresh, delicious (used of fresh vegetables). (c. & n.)

稀溜溜的 Quite thin, entirely fluid, flowing.

窄溜溜的 Quite narrow, contracted.

苦溜溜的 Quite bitter, decidedly bitter, too bitter. (c. & s.)

巴 To wish,—as a doublet imparts the idea of *urgent* or *intense.*

惡巴巴的 Wholly unprincipled, unconcionable, atrocious. (c. & s.)

狠巴巴的 Very severe or radical, relentless, malicious.

直巴巴的 Straightforward, out and out, entirely frank.

眼巴巴的 Looking eagerly, anxiously waiting, longing.

乾巴巴的 Emphatic, to the point, very stern.

煞巴巴的 Decisive, peremptory, categorical; stern. (c.)

重巴巴的 Very weighty, emphatic, decisive. (s.)

累巴巴的 Very much embarrassed, in straits, hard pressed.

生 Alive,—as a doublet imparts the idea of *tender, delicate.*

薄生生的 Quite thin, very thin, delicately thin.

脆生生的 Quite tender, crisp (applied to things edible).

白生生的 Quite white or fair, a delicate white.

輕生生的 Quite light or tender or easy.

糊 To paste,—as a doublet imparts the idea of *soft, warm, sticky.*

潮糊糊的 Quite damp, decidedly damp.

爛糊糊的 Very soft and tender.

呼 To breathe,—as a doublet imparts the idea of *warmth.*

熱呼呼的 Quite warm, agreeably warm, comfortable.

堂 Large, airy,—as a doublet imparts the idea of *spaciousness.*

亮堂堂的 Bright, brilliant; clear, lucid.

茂堂堂的 Flourishing, luxuriant, abundant.

着熱呼呼的。○這[17]時候亮堂堂的月亮、我看黑夜裏走路、倒比白日裏強。○雖[18]然皮色發黑、因為常搽粉、也就白肯生肯生的咯。○已[19]經煮的爛糊糊的、也就是牙口不濟也能吃。○老[20]兄現在也不缺吃、也不少穿、兒孫長的齊整整茂堂堂的、還担的甚麼愁腸呢。○我[21]的外甥、從前一大把子頭髮、自從害了一場瘟症、竟掉的光禿溜禿溜的。○這[22]個黏粥粥稀溜溜的、喝着實在順口。○你[23]去裁一張紙來、不要太寬、窄

17 With such bright moonlight as there is at present, I regard traveling by night as preferable to traveling by day.

18 Although her complexion is naturally dark, yet from the constant use of cosmetics she appears quite fair.

19 It is already boiled very tender, even one with poor teeth could eat it.

20 My good sir, you have plenty to eat and plenty to wear, and your children and grandchildren are all flourishing, what have you to worry about?

21 My nephew formerly had a very heavy head of hair, but since his attack of typhoid fever, it has fallen off until he is now completely bald.

22 This gruel is quite thin and exactly suits my taste.

23 Go and cut me a piece of paper; not too wide, a narrow strip will answer.

顛 To jog, to vibrate,—as a doublet imparts the idea of *rising and falling*.

跑顛顛的 On the run, on the trot.

沉顛顛的 Very heavy—bending the carrying pole. (C. & N.)

明晃晃的 Very bright, dazzling bright,—imparts the idea of *radiance*.

惡狠狠的 Relentless, unconscionable,—imparts the idea of *intensity*.

毒螫螫的 Poisonous, relentless, virulent,—imparts the idea of *virulence*. (C. & S.)

枵薄薄的 Quite thin,—imparts the idea of *thinness*. (C. & S.)

沉重重的 Decidedly heavy, weighty,—imparts the idea of *weight*. (S.)

快當當的 Quick, speedy, on the run,—imparts the idea of *juncture of time*.

白肯肯的 Quite white or fair,—imparts the idea of *similarity*. (S.)

齊整整的 Very uniform, quite regular, the full number,—imparts the idea of *completeness*.

光禿禿的 Quite smooth, entirely bald,—imparts the idea of *baldness*.

苦殷殷的 Quite bitter, very bitter,—imparts the idea of *abundance*.

苦澀澀的 Quite bitter, disagreeably bitter,—imparts the idea of *astringency*. (S.)

赤條條的 Stark naked,—imparts the idea of *slenderness*.

VOCABULARY.

晃 *Hwang*[3] . . . . . *Bright*, dazzling, flashing.

柏 *Poă*[4]. The cypress; the cedar; *as a surname*—read *pai*[3].

怕羞 *P'a*[4] *hsiu*[1]. To fear shame, *to feel ashamed*. (S.)

螫 *Shï*[4]. . . Poisonous; malignant:—See *chê*[1].

岡 *Kang*[1,3]. . . . . . . A peak, a range; a summit.

抹 *Moa*[3,4] To rub out, to blot out; *to go round a corner*; to rub on, to smear. See *ma*[1].

轉彎 *Chwan*[3] *wan*[1]. To make a turn, to wind about, *to go round a corner*.

抹角 *Moă*[4] *chiao*[3]. *To go or turn round a corner*; to round off a corner

乍猛的 *Cha*[4] *mêng*[3] *ti*[1]. *Suddenly*, all at once, in a moment. (S.)

皮色 *P'i*[2] *shai*[3]. Color of the skin, color, *complexion*.

搽粉 *Ch'a*[2] *fên*[3]. . . . . . To powder, to paint.

溜溜的就行。○這[24]是大葉子茶、下的多了、就苦澀溜般澀溜般的。○我[25]們空身行人、還走累喇、你看前頭那個大澀溜般哥、挑着一百多斤的擔子、走起來還輕生生的。○他[26]在家裏爲姑娘的時候、被這王三爺打了一頓、從此他算恨他到了骨頭咯、多會提起來、他就惡狠狠的罵。○說[27]起李光大失火來、眞有故事、那天夜裏、我叫虼蚤咬的還沒睡着、忽然聽見他家裏吆喝救火、我急忙跑去一看、見他赤條條的、在院子裏張羅開咯、早晚等到火要滅的時候、有人告訴了他、他這纔穿上衣裳去了。

24 This is the large-leafed tea; if you put in too much it will be bitter.

25 Even we who are walking empty-handed are tired out, yet just look at that big fellow in front; though carrying a load of over a hundred catties he still steps along as lightly as you please.

26 When she was a girl at home she was beaten by this man Wang San Yie, and from that time she has hated him thoroughly. The mere mention of him calls forth the fiercest abuse.

27 Speaking of the fire at Li Kwang Ta's, there is a good story about it. That night I was pestered by the fleas and had not yet gone asleep, when suddenly I heard some one in his house call out, Fire! I hurriedly ran over to see, when I found him in the yard perfectly nude, making a great ado. By and by when the fire was nearly put out, some one told him and only then did he think to go and put on his clothes.

肖 *Hsiao*⁴...... *Like*, similar; small; inferior.
牙口 *Ya*² *k'ou*³.... .... The teeth.
担 *Tan*¹.... .... A short writing of 擔.
瘟症 *Wên*¹ *chêng*⁴. Epidemic sickness, especially epidemic *typhoid fever*.
空行 *K'ung*¹ *hsing*². Without lading, unencumbered, *empty-handed*.
空身 *K'ung*¹ *shên*¹. Unencumbered, empty-handed; not pregnant.
虼蚤 *Kê*⁴ *tsao*³.... .... A flea
吆 *Yao*¹....... *To cry out*, to call to.
喝 *Hê*⁴. *To call out*; to scout at, to scold. See .... *hê*¹.
吆喝 To scold; *to call out*, to shout; to cry wares.
早晚 *Tsao*³ *wan*³. Sooner or later, first or last; .... *by and by*, when.

NOTES.

5 大嫂 is much used as a general title for women. A woman may be addressed as 大嫂 by people of near the same age, but one ten or more years older than the speaker should be called 大娘. The proper reading of 螫 is *shï*⁴. but it is often used for 蜇, and hence is read colloquially *chê*¹.

10 做面子活 *To do face work; i.e., to be an eye-servant.*

11 抹角 is rarely used, save as joined with 轉彎. In some places to rub *out or off* is read *moä*³, and to rub *on*, *moä*⁴, in other places both meanings are read alike; viz., *moä*³.

14 Peking teachers put 乾巴巴的 for 煞巴巴的, and Southern teachers put 重巴巴的. All agree as to the use of 巴, but differ as to the proper word with which to join it in this connection. The three terms are probably not entirely equivalent.

16 乍猛的 is a Southern term belonging to, but not included in Les. 115.

25 大哥, as here used, is somewhat depreciatory. When joined with a surname, as 李大哥, etc., or when used to a friend, or of a real brother, it is respectful and proper; but as a general term it is avoided, especially in direct address. This arises from the fact that 大哥 is used as a slang term by rakes and vagabonds.

27 那天夜裡 *The night of that day; i.e., that night.* 救火 *Save fire!* that is, Fire! Fire!

第一百五十五課

有[1]甚麼急事、你這麼慌張張的。○這[2]些飯已經壞喇、酸(滋滋/漬漬)的怎麼吃呢。○天[3]氣這樣暖和和的、咱們出去逛逛罷。○馮[4]太太雖然不算大俊俏、臉上却是富態態的。○這[5]雙羽綾鞋、我穿着緊綁綁的、不大合式。○再[6]不必買他的東西、每逢(制/較)他的秤、他就賴(糊糊/唧唧/滋滋)的。○吳[7]建章肚子裏、並沒有個眞見識、說起話來(霧罩罩/雲張張/霧騰騰)的、一點準頭沒有。○不[8]起眼的一個小瘡、時刻還疼絲絲的。○敢[9]是潲進雨來喇、怎麼窗臺上的東西、都濕(拉拉/漬漬)的呢。○這[10]個老婆眞是潑婦、整天家嘴裏

Translation.

1 What urgent business is on hand that you are in such a flurry?

2 This food is already spoiled. How can one eat sour stuff like this?

3 Seeing the weather is so mild, let us go out and take a walk.

4 Although Fêng T'ai-t'ai is not particularly handsome, yet her face has a genteel appearance.

5 I find this pair of satinet shoes rather tight; they do not altogether suit me.

6 It is better not to buy anything more of him. Every time you test his scales he makes a fuss about it.

7 Wu Chien Chang is wanting in good common sense. He talks all at random and entirely without point.

8 A trifling boil not worth noticing, yet it pains me all the time.

9 I presume the rain must have blown in. How else would the things on the window sill be so wet?

10 This woman is a regular virago; her mouth is always full of railing.

LESSON CLV.

Special Duplicate Adjuncts.

張 To expand,—imparts the idea of *increase*, or *excitement*.

慌張張的 In a state of confusion or alarm, all in splutter.

雲張張的 Cloudy, piles of clouds; flighty, at random, wildly. (c.)

漬 Water-soaked,—imparts the idea of *sogginess.*

酸漬漬的 Quite sour, a sourish taste, disagreeably sour, disgusting. (c. & s.)

濕漬漬的 Quite wet, very damp, soggy. (s.)

黏漬漬的 Disagreeably sticky.

水漬漬的 Soggy, watery, washy, wishy-washy.

滋 Luxuriant,—imparts the idea of *profuseness.*

酸滋滋的 Decidedly sour, too sour. (N.)

賴滋滋的 Grumbling, whining, fault finding. (s.)

唧 The hum of voices,—imparts the idea of *iteration.*

賴唧唧的 Grumbling, whining, fault finding. (c. & N.)

罵唧唧的 Continual scolding, constantly railing. (c. & N.)

哭唧唧的 Sobbing and crying, whimpering.

綁 To tie,—imparts the idea of *firmness.*

緊綁綁的 Pinching tight, too tight, quite firm or tense.

硬綁綁的 Very firm or solid, solid as a rock.

牢綁綁的 Quite firm or secure; quite readily, certainly. (c. & s.)

和 To harmonize,—imparts the idea of that which is *smooth, agreeable.*

暖和和的 Quite warm, agreeably warm.

平和和的 Mild, peaceable; average.

軟和和的 Quite soft, pliable, yielding.

孜 Unceasing,—imparts the idea of *continuity.*

罵罵咧咧（罵唧唧）的。○銀[11]子錢是人的血脈、所以發了財、臉上就樂孜孜（樂嘻嘻）的。○你[12]怎麼不好呢、答不知怎麼樣、就是覺着昏沉沉的頭發暈（發頭暈）。○鋪[13]着厚敦敦的褥子、蓋着軟和和的被、還能睡不舒服（熨貼）嗎。○人[14]若生的俏皮皮（俏生生）的、不但好看、就是做生活活也更爽俐（麻俐）。○楊[15]老四一輩子沒有好日子過、你看他別管多會兒（管多會兒、隨便那時）說話、是哭唧唧（哭啼啼）的、臉上一派的苦像。○看[16]你臉上喜孜孜的、有甚麼得意的事呢、答我的孫子、今年十四歲進了學、我怎能不喜呢。○我[17]的汗衫子該洗喇、出點汗黏漬（黏糊）

11 Money is a man's life-blood, hence when he gets rich his face wears a cheerful smile.

12 What is ailing you? *Ans.* I do not know what, save that I feel stupid and dizzy.

13 With a thick mattress spread under him and covered with a soft quilt, can he fail to sleep comfortably?

14 If a man is naturally well-proportioned, he is not only comely but he is also quicker at his work.

15 Yang the Fourth will never be a prosperous man. Just look at him; he always speaks as if he were ready to cry, and his whole face has a woe-begone expression.

16 You are looking very happy; what is it that pleases you? *Ans.* My grandson, who is fourteen this year, has just got his degree. How can I be otherwise than happy?

17 My undervest needs washing. Whenever I perspire a little, it becomes sticky and clings to my body.

18 Look at that boy of Sun Hsi Yüen's. Ever since they settled his betrothal he is as happy as the day is long.

樂孜孜的 Constantly smiling, cheerful.

喜孜孜的 Covered with smiles, very happy, in good spirits. (C.)

嘻 To laugh,—imparts the idea of *mirth*.

樂嘻嘻的 Smiling, happy. (S.)

笑嘻嘻的 Laughing, smiling, giggling, in a good humor.

潤 Moist, shining,—imparts the idea of *moistness* or *gloss*.

光潤潤的 Sleek, shining, smooth.

油潤潤的 Moist, soft and rich. (S.)

汪 A pool,—imparts the idea of *plenitude*.

油汪汪的 Quite moist, soft and oily.

淚汪汪的 Tears brimming, eyes full of tears.

富態態的 A genteel appearance, a well-to-do look,—imparts the idea of *style* or *mien*.

霧罩罩的 Foggy; muddled, indistinct, at random,—imparts the idea of *covering*. (C. & N.)

霧騰騰的 The same. Les. 166.

疼絲絲的 Aching, a fretting pain,—imparts the idea of *continuity*.

濕拉拉的 Very wet, dripping wet, soaking wet:—see Les. 166.

昏沉沉的 Stupid, confused in mind, very dull,—imparts the idea of *heaviness*.

厚敦敦的 Quite thick; quite generous, free-handed,—imparts the idea of *bountifulness*.

哭啼啼的 Ready to cry, tearful, weeping,—imparts the idea of *crying*. (S.)

俏皮皮的 Quite brisk, active; slender, well-proportioned,—directs attention to the *external appearance*. (C. & N.)

牢樁樁的 Quite firm, reliable; readily, certainly,—imparts the idea of *firmness*. (C. & N.)

硬刺刺的 Hard, gritty; quite tough,—imparts the idea of *hardness*.

賴糊糊的 Persistent fault finding, whining, grumbling. (N.)

俏生生的 Brisk, active; graceful, well proportioned. (C. & S.)

黏糊糊的 Disagreeably sticky, adhesive.

穩當當的 Steady, firm; readily, certainly.

光堂堂的 Very smooth, sleek, shining.

漬糊的、都貼在身上。○你[18]看孫喜元家那個學生、自從給他說上媳婦講上奶奶整天的是笑嘻嘻的。○眞[19]好結實孩子、渾身都硬綁綁的。○在[20]貴處的年成怎麼樣呢、答平和和的、不算大好、也說不出大不濟壞來。○有[21]你這樣的手藝、若是上京、一年牢椿椿牢綁綁穩當當的、能掙二百吊大錢。○人[22]若常吃好東西、臉上就光堂堂潤潤的、分外的好看。○會[23]做弄乾飯的、做弄的油汪汪潤潤的、眞是好吃、那些不會做弄的、不是做弄的硬刺刺的、就是水漬漬的、並沒有正經飯味。○那[24]獃子、當眞眼淚汪汪的哭將起來、口裏不住的絮絮叨叨、數黃道黑白、眞個果像死了人的一般。

19 What a very robust child. His whole body is as firm and strong as possible.

20 How are the crops in your neighborhood? *Ans.* Only ordinary. They are not very good, nor can one say they are very poor.

21 With such mechanical skill as you have, if you should go to the capital, you could certainly earn two hundred thousand cash per year.

22 When a man habitually lives on good food, his face has a soft, sleek appearance that is especially pleasing.

23 One who knows how to cook dry rice makes it rich and moist, and it is exceedingly palatable; but one who does not understand the art makes it either hard and gritty, or soft and soggy, so that it is entirely without its proper flavor.

24 That simpleton, sure enough, with eyes full of tears burst out crying, and kept up a continuous stream of incoherent complaints, just for all the world as if some one were dead.

VOCABULARY.

馮 *Fêng*². . . . . A *surname.* Also *p'êng*².

羽綾 *Yü*³ *ling*². . . . . . Satinet, lasting.

建 *Chien*⁴. To establish; to organize; to erect; to confirm; to build.

起眼 *Ch'i*³ *yien*³. Worthy of notice, considerable.

霧 *Wu*⁴. . . . . Fog, mist, vapor.

潲 *Shao*⁴. *Water driven by the wind;* to splash, to spray, to sprinkle.

潑婦 *P'o*¹ *fu*⁴. A shrew, *a virago,* a termagant.

罵罵咧咧 *Ma*⁴ *lie*². Continually scolding, *constantly railing.*

孜 *Tsï*¹. . . . Unwearied effort; unceasing affection.

嘻 *Hsi*¹. To laugh, to titter; the sound of merriment; delighted.

頭暈 *T'ou*² *yün*⁴. . . . . . Light-headed, *dizzy.*

敦 *Tun*¹. Honest, *generous;* sincere, solid; affluent; to consolidate; to urge.

舒服 *Shu*¹ *fu*². *Comfortable,* at ease, satisfied; well.

啼 *T'i*². *To cry,* to bewail, to weep; to crow; to scream.

一派 *I*¹ *p'ai*⁴. . . . . A branch; all, *entire.*

苦像 *K'u*³ *hsiang*⁴. A sorrowful appearance, a woe-begone expression.

爽利 *Shwang*³ *li*⁴. . . . . *Quick,* prompt.

汗衫子 *Han*⁴ *shan*¹ *tsï*³. . . . . . An undervest.

分外 *Fên*⁴ *wai*⁴. More than usual, extraordinary; *special,* extra. Les. 172.

第一百五十六課

已[1]經過去的事情、不必再究問了。○既[2]然是個舉人、諒來學問不大離譜 很糅 很齣。○今[3]天已經到了這個時候、索性等到明天早早走罷。○東[4]家既然看我不好、索性我也不討好了。○他[5]既是心裏焦、你又去俏皮 打趣他、豈不是火上加油嗎。○我[6]們已經約定了、諒來他今天不能不來。○夥[7]計既然搭不好、買賣諒來也必做不好。○你[8]已經給他謄了一大半子、索性一個人情送到底罷。○這[9]裏已經預備了你的飯、不必上街去吃。○既[10]然免不掉了打官司、索性

TRANSLATION.

1 The affair is already past, it is better not to rake it up again.
2 Seeing he is a chü-jên, it is not likely his scholarship is very inferior.
3 As it is so late to-day, you may as well wait till to-morrow and take an early start.
4 As my employer has a poor opinion of me, I might as well not try to please him.
5 Seeing his mind is already irritated, is it not simply pouring oil on the fire for you to go and twit him.
6 We have already made a definite appointment, so he will scarcely fail to come to-day.
7 Seeing he cannot get on with his employés, it is not likely his business will succeed.
8 Having copied more than half of it for nothing, you might as well finish it for him on the same terms.
9 Your food is already prepared here, you need not go on the street to eat.
10 Since we cannot avoid going to law, let us make a big row with him.

NOTES.

4 富態態的 expresses that fresh, soft, well-preserved look which results from good living and freedom from toil and exposure.

6 制他的秤 or 較他的秤 *To test* or *try his scales.* Purchasers frequently, in fact generally, weigh with their own scales the articles they buy, as a check on the dishonesty of the seller. There is *practically* no legal standard of weights and measures in China.

11 銀子錢 *Silver and cash;* that is, *money.*

15 一派的苦像 *A complete spread of sorrowful looks, a woe-begone expression.* The idea of the sentence is that the man's appearance betokens bad luck.

19 好 serves as an intensive, qualifying 結實.

24 眼淚 does not here form a compound term, but 眼 stands alone, and is qualified by 淚汪汪的. 數黃道黑 (or 白) *To recount the yellow and tell the black* (*or white*); i.e., *to go over and over with variations.*

LESSON CLVI.

CORRELATIVE PARTICLES.

已經...諒來 Having, already... likely, so.
已經...索性 Seeing, having... might as well, may as well.
已經...不必 Already..... need not, better not.
已經...何必 Since, having......... why.
已經...還能 Seeing, having..... can still.
既然...諒來, or 諒愁 Seeing, having... likely, probably.
既然...索性 Seeing, having..... might as well, let us.
既然...怎麼 Seeing, having... why, how.
既然...還能 Seeing, having... can still.
既然...既當 Seeing, having..... should, should have.
既然...只管 Seeing, having..... simply, go ahead.
既自 or 既然...豈不 Seeing...... is it not, will it not.
既...又 Having...... then, also.

和他大鬧一鬧罷。○我[11]心裏既已自糊塗、你又給我這些糨糊子吃、豈不叫我越發糊塗嗎。○他[12]已經打砸了我的飯碗、我索性和他拼對命就結了。○交[13]朋友總得言而有信、既滿口應許人家、臨時又荒唐了、這是一種甚麼人呢。○他[14]在路上、已經吃了一個饅餑頭子、大諒不能很餓。○俗[15]語說、人有名、樹有影、衆人既然都稱讚他、諒想來必是好人。○你[16]既打了他、又要叫他賠東西、還有這宗情理嗎、答嚼嚼嚼、那來的話呢。○崔[17]先生是個不念舊惡的人、他已經當面說了你、諒來不是能

11 I am already stupid; if you give me this paste to eat, will it not make me all the more stupid?

12 Since he has taken away my livelihood, I might as well finish the business by pitting my life against his.

13 In intercourse with friends one should always keep his word. What sort of a man is he who, having made an explicit promise to another, gives him the slip when the time comes.

14 He ate a roll on the road; it is not likely he is very hungry.

15 The proverb says, "Reputation is to a man as the shadow to the tree." Seeing that everybody speaks well of him, he is very probably a good man.

16 Having beaten him, what show of reason is there in your demanding that he make good the loss? *Ans* Tut! tut! tut! I had no such idea.

17 Mr. Ts'wei is a man who does not cherish the memory of a wrong. Having reproved you to your face, it is not likely that he will hereafter hold any enmity against you.

18 Seeing his ideas are so high, will it

VOCABULARY.

究問 *Chiu*^{1} *wên*^{4}. To interrogate; to pry into, ... to inquire; *to rake up*.

舉人 *Chü*^{3} *jên*^{2}. A graduate of the second de- . . . . gree, for which examinations are conducted in the provincial capitals.

猱 *Nao*^{1} . . . . . . Worthless, *inferior*, trashy.

嘈 *Ts'ao*^{2}. . . . . *Inferior*, trashy. See *tsao*^{1}.

俏皮 *Ch'iao*^{4} *p'i*^{2}. Quick, active, agile; light, ... trim; to tease, *to twit*.

打趣 *Ta*^{3} *ch'ü*^{4}. To tease, to chafe, *to twit*, to . . . . joke.

對命 *Twei*^{4} *ming*^{4}. To stake the life against that . . . . of another, to engage in a mortal combat, to fight to the death.

拼命 *P'in*^{1} *ming*^{4}. . . . . The same.

滿口 *Man*^{3} *k'ou*^{3}. Mouth filled with; clearly, ... *explicitly*, positively, fully,

讚 *Tsan*^{4}. . . . . . To commend, *to praise*.

饌 *Chüen*^{3}. A steamed dumpling; a roly-poly; . . . . a steamed roll.

稱讚 *Ch'êng*^{1} *tsan*^{4}. To praise, *to speak well of*, ... to eulogize.

記恨 *Chi*^{4} *hên*^{4}. To cherish hatred, to hold . . . . spite.

心意 *Hsin*^{1} *i*^{4}. Thought, purpose, *aspiration*, ... idea.

改嫁 *Kai*^{3} *chia*^{4}. To marry again (said of a . . . . widow).

節烈 *Chie*^{2} *lie*^{4}. Inflexible virtue; unyielding de- . . . . votion to a deceased husband.

值日 *Chï*^{2} *ji*^{4}. Day of duty, on duty:—Note . . . . 22.

謔 *Nüe*^{4}. . . . To ridicule; to mock, to trifle with.

謔薄 *Nüe*^{4} *pao*^{2}. . . . . . To taunt, *to tease*.

戳薄 *Ch'oä*^{1} *pao*^{2}. To taunt, *to tease*, to nag, ... to chafe.

認保 *Jên*^{4} *pao*^{3}. The graduate who becomes . . . . security for a candidate entering for the first degree.

再記恨你。○他[18]的心意既己自高、還要叫他聽人指派使、豈不是個難事嗎。○已[19]經定規不要他、何必爲這二三百錢、算計的這麼清呢。○他[20]們弟兄兩個、既然都懊悔分家、你索性勸勸他們、再合起來不好嗎。○你[21]想一個改嫁的婦人、既是怕人笑話、若和他談節烈的事、豈不是不知趣嗎。○你[22]也是個値日的、他也是個値日的、大老爺已經出了他的票子、你何必只是戳譃薄他呢。○認[23]保既然敢保他、我這個派挨保、怎麼不敢保他呢。○李[24]永勝已經犯了聖諱、還能指望進學嗎。○他[25]哥哥既然是個兵部

not be a difficult thing to make him subject to the will of another?

19 Having decided to dismiss him, why, for the sake of these two or three hundred cash, reckon the account so closely?

20 Since the two brothers are sorry that they divided the estate, would it not be well for you to exhort them to unite again?

21 Consider the case of a remarried widow. Being already apprehensive of ridicule, would it not show a great want of good taste to talk to her about the devotion due to the memory of a deceased husband?

22 Since, according to the regular order, it is his turn as well as yours, why, when the magistrate puts *his* name on the warrant, do you persist in taunting him?

23 Seeing the leading security is ready to guarantee him, why should I, who am but second, not venture to do as much?

24 Having used a forbidden character, what hope has Li Yung Shêng of getting a degree?

25 Seeing that his brother is one of the

挨保 *Ai² pao³*. The second or sub-security for a candidate :—Note 23.

派保 *P'ai⁴ pao³* . . . . The same.

聖諱 *Shêng⁴ hwei⁴*. Sacred names, tabooed characters :—Note 24.

代書 *Tai⁴ shu¹*. A lawyer, *a scrivener* :—Note 26.

兵部 *Ping¹ pu⁴*. The Board or Bureau of War in Peking.

尙書 *Shang⁴ shu¹*. A president of one of the Six Boards. Each board has two presidents, one Tartar and one Chinese.

乾老子 *Kan¹ lao³ tsï³*. Adopted father :—Note 26.

下力 *Hsia⁴ li⁴*. To use effort ; *to work energetically*, to strive.

腆 *T'ien³*. . . To go to excess ; to enrich, *to thicken*.

腆臉 *T'ien³ lien³*. *To put on a bold face*, to be brazen-faced, thick-skinned.

捨臉 *Shê³ lien³* . . . . . . The same. (s.)

厚臉 *Hou⁴ lien³*. . . . . The same. (s.)

探前 *T'an⁴ ch'ien²*. Early, *beforehand*, in anticipation of. (c.)

探先 *T'an⁴ hsien¹* . . . . The same. (s.)

諼 *Hsüen¹*. . . . . . Deceitful ; *to impose on*.

諼弄 *Hsüen¹ lung⁴*. . . . . . . To befool, *to cajole*.

鬧事 *Nao⁴ shï⁴*. To raise a row, to make a disturbance, *to get into a scrape*.

看笑話 *K'an⁴ hsiao⁴ hwa⁴*. To laugh at, to make fun of. (N.)

看笑場 *K'an⁴ hsiao⁴ ch'ang³*. . . . The same. (C.)

聽笑聲 *T'ing¹ hsiao⁴ shêng¹*. . . . The same. (s.)

分派 *Fên¹ p'ai⁴*. *To direct*, to prescribe ; to supervise, to lay out.

豌 *Wan¹*. . . . The pea—introduced from the West.

豌豆 *Wan¹ tou⁴*. . . . . Peas.

看柿 *K'an⁴ shï⁴*. . . . The tomato :—Note 28.

西紅柿 *Hsi¹ hung² shï⁴*. . . . . The same.

洋柿子 *Yang² shï⁴ tsï³*. . . . . The same.

嬰 *Ying¹*. . . . An infant, a babe. (w.)

嬰孩 *Ying¹ hai²*. . . . . An infant, a babe.

尙書、他怎麼只作一個知縣呢、(答)若不是他哥哥作尙書、他連個知縣也摸不着作。○俗[26]語說、是親必顧、劉代書既然是他乾老子、還能不爲他使勁兒(下力)嗎。○你[27]還(腆/捨/厚)着臉說呢、你既然知道他們是帮虎吃食的人、就當(卽早/探前/探先)防備、爲甚麼受他們的謏弄、鬧出這麼一場丟人的事來、叫大衆(看笑話/看笑場/聽笑聲)呢。○他[28]既然分派叫你種兩畦子豌豆、六畦子(西紅柿、/看柿/洋柿子)、你只管照他的話去種、多少不關你事。○[29]教子嬰孩、教婦初來、既慣他、又打他、那是斷乎使不得的。

presidents of the Board of War, how is it that he is only a Chihsien? *Ans.* If he had not had a brother who was president of a Board, he would not have been even a Chihsien.

26 The saying is, "Kin are ever kind." Seeing Liu the scrivener is his adopted father, can he fail to exert himself on his behalf.

27 Well you ought to be ashamed to tell it. Since you knew that they were fellows who would help a tiger eat his prey, you should have been on your guard. Why allow them to cajole you into such a disgraceful scrape as this, and make yourself a public laughing stock.

28 Since he has directed you to plant two beds of peas and six of tomatos, simply go and plant them as he told you; the quantity is no business of yours.

29 Discipline a child from infancy, and a wife from her marriage. It will never do to begin punishing after you have indulged the formation of bad habits.

NOTES.

1 已經過去的事情 properly means, *that which is already past*, but the general is here put for the particular, hence it means, *the affair is already past.*

2 嘈 is much used in some parts of the North as the equivalent of 歹, or or 不濟.

8 The use of 人情 implies that the copying was from the first a matter of favor not of wages.

11 To eat paste muddles a man's wits, because being thick and viscid it closes up the orifices of his mind (心竅).

12 打了我的飯碗 *Broken my rice bowl;* i.e., caused me to lose the employment upon which I depended for a living. 砸 is preferred in Peking.

13 言而有信 *Faithful to one's word,*—a book phrase.

14 饝子 In some places a 饝子 is a steamed roly-poly made with mince meat instead of with sweetmeats; in other places it is simply raised dough twisted into "rolls," and steamed.

15 The comparison is implied by the juxtaposition and similar construction of the phrases.

16 那來的話呢 is abbreviated from 那裡來的話呢.

17 念舊惡 *To cherish the memory of an old injury, to hold spite,*—a classical phrase used by scholars.

21 The structure of this sentence is irregular. The first clause may be regarded as independent, the regular construction beginning with 旣是.

22 値日 *The day on which one's turn comes.* The underlings in a yamên are divided into companies or sections, which take turns in receiving and executing the commands of the officer. The use of the term 値日 is confined to this connection. 只是 commonly means *only*, but it here means *to persist in.* It is frequently so used.

23 The 挨保, or *sub-security* (called 派保 in some places) is of much less importance than the 認保, or *principal security*, who is supposed to be personally acquainted with the circumstances of the candidate, and with whom the responsibility chiefly rests. It is required that both these securities have the degree of 廩生 or *preferred hsiu-ts'ai.* On this account they are commonly called 廩保.

24 The characters forming the personal names of deceased emperors of the reigning dynasty are "forbidden." To use one of them in an essay is an offence fatal to all hope of getting a degree, no matter what the merits of the essay may otherwise be.

26 是親必顧 *He who is a relative will certainly regard.* The 是 is emphatic, being used for 凡是 or 但凡是. The 代書 is a licensed scrivener, whose special business it is to draw up indictments and counter indictments. He is not, however, allowed to present them for his client, nor to plead the case as a lawyer. 乾老子 means the same as 乾爹, but would not be used in speaking face to face as would 乾爹.

28 看柿 *Mock-persimmon*, that is, *tomato.* Being recently introduced into China each locality has its own name for tomatos.

第一百五十七課

但[1]凡有牲口、誰肯自己推磨呢。○如[2]果不干你事、何不對天發盟誓。○但[3]凡能忍得住疼、我也不出聲吆喝。○這[4]場官司、萬一打贏了、往後却就好創喇。○如[5]果沒有大過犯、何妨從寬饒恕他呢。○但[6]凡是個有人心的、那有見死不救之理呢。○無[7]事防備有事、萬一久後他們和睦起來、你我豈不成了壞蛋嗎。○如[8]果車價這樣貴、何妨僱匹(頭驢)驢子騎騎。○但[9]凡賣得着、還能不賣給你嗎。○你[10]這樣敞着門、光着脊梁、萬一有

TRANSLATION.

1 Who that has a beast is willing to turn the millstone himself?

2 If it really does not concern you, why not take an oath before heaven to that effect?

3 If I could possibly endure the pain, I would not cry out.

4 If perchance we gain this lawsuit, we shall thenceforth get on all right.

5 If indeed he has not been guilty of any great offence, why not be generous and forgive him?

6 It is not to be supposed that any one with human feelings would stand by and see a man die without an effort to save him.

7 "While there is no difficulty provide against difficulty." If perchance by and by they should become reconciled, would not you and I be regarded as reprobates?

8 If carts are so dear, why not hire a donkey to ride?

9 If I could at all afford to sell [at this price], would I not sell it to you?

10 Leaving the door open in this way

LESSON CLVII.

CORRELATIVE PARTICLES.

但凡...誰肯 In case ... who is willing.

但凡...也不 If possibly, as long as ... would not, better not.

但凡...那有 In case, if .... would.

但凡...還能 If at all .... would.

但自...誰肯 While, in case ...... who is willing.

如果...何不 If indeed, if really ...... why not.

如果...何妨 If indeed, if really ... why not, what objection.

如果...豈肯 If indeed, if really ...... could or would be willing?

如果...能 If indeed, if really .....could or would be willing.

如果...還能 If indeed, if really ...... could or would be willing.

萬一...就 or **却就** If, if perchance..... ... then.

萬一...豈不 If, if perchance .... would or will not?

果然...難道 If indeed ....is it so? you don't mean to say.

VOCABULARY.

盟 *Mêng*[2]. ... ... An oath attested with blood.

盟誓 *Mêng*[2] *shï*[4]. To attest before the gods; *to take an oath;* to swear.

出聲 *Ch'u*[1] *shêng*[1]. *To call or cry out,* to make a noise.

打贏 *Ta*[3] *ying*[2]. To conquer, to triumph, *to gain the victory.*

何妨 *Hê*[2] *fang*[1]. What is there to hinder, *why not;* what objection.

從寬 *Ts'ung*[2] *k'wan*[1]. To be charitable, *generous,* lax.

人闖進來、却就有了笑話喇。○如[11]果是個貞潔女人、自己的男人、豈肯賣了他嗎。○但[12]凡是個本分人、那有領班戲子的呢。○但[13]凡有利的事、誰肯不爭着去做呢。○如[14]果他有那分子手藝、穿戴的還能彷彿花子一般嗎。○你[15]們常販這些私貨、眞是擔險、萬一被巡役搜出來、豈不是自投法網嗎。○可[16]以先上衙門看看、如果告示還不出、何妨再去遞張催稟呢。○火[17]是要緊當小心的、萬一有個失手差脚、燒了房子、却就被他害喇。○你[18]看孫進士是誰、如果他沒有甚麼短處、叫一個監生這樣汚村辱、他豈肯干休嗎。○人[19]都是

and going about stripped to the waist, if perchance some one should suddenly step in what a joke that would be.

11 If she were really a virtuous woman, would her own husband be willing to sell her?

12 What man of good character would be manager of a theater?

13 Who does not strive to have a share in whatever is profitable?

14 If indeed he has such mechanical skill as that, would he be dressed like a beggar?

15 You who are constantly engaged in smuggling are certainly playing a desperate game. If by any chance the detectives find you out, will you not have put your own neck in the noose?

16 Go first to the yamên and see, and if the proclamation is not yet issued, what objection is there to presenting a petition urging its issue?

17 It is important to be careful of fire, lest perchance your carelessness results in the burning of your house, which would be a great loss.

18 Consider who Sun the Chin shï is. If his skirts were indeed clear, would he tamely allow a man who is but a chien-shêng to lampoon him like this?

19 A man must be reduced to extremi-

饒恕 *Jao² shu⁴.* *To forgive;* to excuse, to pass over.

貞潔 *Chên¹ chie².* Virgin purity; chaste, *virtuous.*

穿戴 *Ch'wan¹ tai⁴.* Clothing; *to wear.*

擔險 *Tan¹ hsien³.* Dangerous, perilous; to run great risk.

網 *Wang³.* *A net;* a web; a law.

法網 *Fa³ wang³.* The toils or clutches of the law.

示 *Shï⁴.* To reveal, *to proclaim;* an edict, a proclamation, a revelation, a sign.

告示 *Kao⁴ shï⁴.* *A proclamation.*

催稟 *Ts'wei¹ ping³.* A petition urging action in a case at law.

失手 *Shï¹ shou³.* To let a thing fall; *to mistake through carelessness* or *by accident;* to pilfer.

差脚 *Ch'a¹ chiao³.* To make a misstep.

失手差脚 To make a mistake; an accident; *carelessness.*

進士 *Chin⁴ shï⁴.* A graduate of the third degree, the examinations for which are held in the Capital and open to all 舉人.

監生 *Chien⁴ shêng¹.* A literary degree obtained by purchase:—Note 18.

村辱 *Ts'un¹ ju³.* To stigmatize, *to lampoon*, to berate; to blackguard.

汚辱 *Wu¹ ju³.* To put to shame, to bespatter, *to lampoon*, to berate.

不得已 *Pu⁴ tê² i³.* No help for it, *in straits,* unavoidable:—Les. 179. Sub.

討要 *T'ao³ yao⁴.* To ask for, *to beg for.*

點破 *Tien³ p'o⁴.* *To disclose,* to divulge, to let out, to reveal.

委屈 *Wei³ ch'ü¹.* Injustice, *wrong.*

僥 *Chiao³.* Fortunate, *lucky.* Used for 儌.

僥倖 *Chiao³ hsing⁴.* A happy chance, *luck,* good fortune.

不得已纔討飯吃、但凡有一線之路、誰肯向人討要呢。○媒[20]人的話是靠不住的、如果他有八十畝地、還能三十多歲沒有家口下嗎。○你[21]以為他們都糊塗嗎、萬一有人點破你的機關、你就要吃大虧喇。○但[22]凡受過大委屈的、一輩子還能忘嗎。○不[23]可一味的圖創僥倖、萬一露出破綻、豈不悔之晚矣。○我[24]聽他的話總是支離、如果不是他的主謀、人家還能憑空去告他嗎。○你[25]忘了古語說、上山擒虎易、開口告人難嗎、自己但凡有法騰挪、也不向人倒挪借。○就[26]是那玉皇天尊、果然有這位神、他在

ties before he will beg. Who will beg from others while he has the least hope of getting on himself?

20 A middleman's word is not to be trusted. If indeed he owns eighty *mow* of land, would he be without a wife at thirty-odd years of age?

21 Do you suppose they are all fools? If perchance some one detects your trick, you will find yourself in a bad predicament.

22 Can any one who has suffered a great wrong ever forget it?

23 You should not trust too much to luck. If perchance the matter leaks out, it will be too late to repent.

24 As I understand his statement, it is clearly evasive. If the scheme were not of his devising, could they have trumped up the charge against him?

25 Have you forgotten the old saying, "To seize a tiger on the hills is easy, but to open your mouth to ask a favor is hard?" So as long as one has any way to shift for himself, he will not borrow of others.

26 As to the Most Exalted Pearly Emperor, if there be such a god, do you suppose that while enjoying himself

綻 Chan^4.... *A rent*, a rip; cracked, split; a hint.

破綻 P'oa^4 chan^4. A rent disclosing what is within, a flaw, a defect; a hint.

矣 I^3. A final particle used in *Wênli* to emphasize what precedes.

支離 Chï^1 li^2. *Evasive*, irrelevant; false, sophistical. 不支離 not far out of the way, about right.

主謀 Chu^3 mou^2......... *A scheme*, a project.

擒 Ch'in^2....... To seize, to arrest, *to take*.

開口 K'ai^1 k'ou^3. To open the mouth; *to begin to speak*.

挪借 Noa^2 chie^4. *Borrowing of one to pay another*, to borrow temporarily.

倒借 Tao^3 chie^4.......... The same.

塑 Su^4....... To model in clay.

統領 T'ung^3 ling^3. A commanding general, a commandant.

尅 K'e^4. To subdue; to repress; to deny oneself; *to do or take by force*.

送老 Sung^4 lao^3. To bury a parent or grandparent, to dress for burial.

裝老 Chwang^1 lao^3. To dress a parent or grandparent for burial.

NOTES.

5 從寬 *To follow the broad* [*path*]; i.e., *to be generous, to be lenient.*

6 In the translation, 理 is represented by the phrase, *it is not to be supposed;* that is, there is no such principle of human action as that, etc. The structure of the sentence is somewhat illogical.

7 成了壞蛋 *To turn out to be rotten eggs;* that is, to become a stench in the nostrils, to be regarded as offenders.

10 笑話 is here a noun,—*something to laugh at, a joke.*

16 If a petition is not acted on promptly, custom allows the petitioner to present a second petition, called a 催稟, or *petition of urgency.* A third even may be presented without offence.

18 The degree of 監生 entitles to greater privileges than that of 秀才, but is less honorable. It may be obtained by one who has not, as readily as by one who has, his first degree.

19 不得已 is equivalent to 不得不如此; that is, *without resource.*

23 露出破綻 *To disclose a rent;* that is, to let out what it is important to conceal. 悔之晚矣 A book phrase here quoted entire.

天上逍遙自在、難道用着你們塑他的金身、給他蓋房子住嗎。○再27不許你往外扔發石頭、萬一寃家路兒窄、一下把人打死、豈不是個活亂漏子嗎。○街28上傳說黃大人、因爲私尅兵餉、已經被統領殺了、我看這必是仇人咒他、如果是眞、他家裏豈能沒有信嗎。○父29母已經這麼大的年紀、連件送裝老的衣裳都沒有、萬一早上晚下、得個暴促急病死了、豈不瞎巴結了一輩子嗎。

in heaven, he needs that you should make him a gilded image and build a house for him to live in?

27 Hereafter you must not throw out stones. If by chance some one doomed to die should be passing by, and should be struck and killed, would it not be a dreadful calamity?

28 It is currently reported on the street that Hwang Ta-jên has been put to death by the commanding general for embezzling the soldiers' pay. I think the report must be the work of an enemy defaming him. If it were true would not his family have heard of it?

29 Our father and mother at such an age, and yet we have not even garments in which to bury them. If some morning or evening they should suddenly sicken and die, would not the toils of their whole life have been in vain?

---

25 易 and 難 are used emphatically, in contrast with each other. The structure is *Wên*. In Mandarin 告 is not used by itself in the sense of, *to ask*. It is so used in combination in the phrase 求告.

26 天尊 *Honored in heaven*, a title of dignity applied by the Taoists to their chief gods.

27 寃家路兒窄 *The road of enemies is narrow;* that is, *enemies are sure to meet*, or, *vengeance is sure to overtake its victim*. The phrase is a puzzling one, of which various explanations are given. It involves a mixture of ideas of metempsychosis, fate, providence and the agency of disembodied spirits.

28 私尅兵餉 *To withhold illegally a portion of the soldiers' pay.* This is a very common abuse in China. When confined within reasonable bounds it generally passes unnoticed.

29 This sentence assumes what is a prevalent idea in China; viz., that one of the prime objects of life is to provide a good coffin and good clothes, in which to be buried. The bounden duty of sons is to provide these things beforehand for their parents. The reason these things are so important is, that the deceased is supposed to appear in the next world in the dress and style in which he leaves this world, and his standing and circumstances there are supposed to be as much affected by these things as they would be here.

LESSON CLVIII.

Indefinite Pronouns.

This lesson is supplementary to the thirty-fifth lesson.

全 All,—the whole, completely, wholly.

全然 All,—completely, entirely,—with negative,—not at all.

共 All,—everybody; altogether.

俱 All,—the whole lot,—usually follows a list of particulars.

俱都 All,—every one.

俱以 All,—a book term in which 以 is added for euphony.

皆 All,—the whole number, all included.

皆都 All,—the same as 皆 alone.

盡 All,—everything; completely, entirely.

盡皆 All,—every single one, every last one.

盡情 All,—the whole business; entirely, perfectly.

大凡 All,—everyone, whoever; generally.

列 All,—of a company or class; nearly always joined with 位 and used as a complimentary term.

諸 All,—each and every one:—mostly used in special phrases.

共總 Altogether, in all, total.

統共 The same.

統總 The same.

第一百五十八課

事[1]情成破敗全在於你。○若[2]是和他好說、他算全然沒聽見。○列[3]位都請坐下、咱們常來常往、何必這樣多禮。○這[4]是人所共知的事情。○諸[5]位弟兄、請聽我的話。○兒[6]在外蒙神保佑、所作所為、盡皆順利。○豐[7]泰棧專辦洋廣雜貨、一應俱全。○旁[8]別的毛病皆可將就、惟獨手不老穩實、這是沒法將就的。○五[9]大洲的人數、雖然多如海邊的沙、但往上追到極遠之處、俱都以神為本。○踏[10]破鐵鞋無覓處、得來全不費工夫。○那[11]個人心裏眞是海量、一點也不古板板滯、大凡和他共事的人、沒有一個不賓服佩服的。○有[12]一等書獃子、只知道念四書、論到世事人情、他就全然不懂了。○你[13]看宮化東家裏、輩輩不做好事、

TRANSLATION.

1 Whether the affair succeeds or fails depends wholly on you.

2 If you speak mildly with him, he pays no attention to you at all.

3 Please be seated, gentlemen. Why should we who are constantly seeing each other be so formal? [knows.

4 This is something that everybody

5 Will all the brethren please give ear to my words?

6 Since leaving home, I (your son) have been favored with the protection of God, and everything I have undertaken has prospered.

7 Fêng-t'ai store: special dealers in all kinds of miscellaneous goods, foreign and Cantonese.

8 Other faults may all be borne with, but purloining is something that cannot be tolerated.

9 Although the inhabitants of the five continents are as numerous as the sand on the sea shore, yet if we follow up [their history] to the remotest antiquity, we find the source of all in God.

10 You may wear out a pair of iron shoes searching for a thing and not find it; when it turns up, it does so without the least trouble.

11 That is truly an honorable man, and not in the least narrow-minded. Of all who do business with him there is not one who does not defer to him.

12 There is a class of learned idiots who know nothing but to study the four

VOCABULARY.

皆 *Chie*[1]. All, all persons or things of the same class:—see Sub.

俱 *Chü*[1]. All,—collectively:—see Sub.

列位 *Lie*[4] *wei*[4]. You gentlemen, sirs.

順利 *Shun*[4] *li*[4]. Successful, *prosperous; unobstructed, facile.*

雜貨 *Tsa*[2] *hwoa*[4]. Miscellaneous goods, general merchandise; *groceries.*

洲 *Chou*[1]. An island; *a continent,* a region.

海量 *Hai*[3] *liang*[4]. Broad-minded, *honorable;* magnanimous; self-control.

踏 *Tsa*[1]. To tread on, to step on; *to walk.*

覓 *Mi*[4]. *To search for,* to seek, to hunt up.

板滯 *Pan*[3] *chi*[4]. Obtuse, thick-headed; *narrow-minded,* opinionated.

古板 *Ku*[3] *pan*[3]. Old-fashioned, set in one's way; *narrow-minded,* bigoted; obtuse.

共事 *Kung*[4] *shï*[4]. To act together with; *to be a business associate.*

賓 *Pin*[1]. A visitor, a guest; *to acknowledge,* to acquiesce.

賓服 *Pin*[1] *fu*[2]. To approve, to be pleased with; to submit to, *to defer to.*

書獃子 *Shu*[1] *tai*[1] *tsï*[3]. A learned idiot; a book worm:—Note 12.

如今他的子孫、俱以發達、那裏有天理呢。○世[14]人皆都說曉神仙好、只有兒孫忘不了、癡心父母古來多、孝順子孫誰見了。○雖[15]然這是書上的話、却也不可盡信、因爲孟子明明的說、盡信書、不如無書。○張[16]大哥你借斗麥子給我過年、好不好、答我統共共總還沒有一斗麥子、那裏有借給你的呢。○你[17]想他共總教的十來個學生、每個學生還拉不上一吊錢、他說沒法餬口、還算希奇嗎。○在[18]何處有嫉妒分爭、就在何處有攪亂、和諸般的惡事。○倉[19]猝之間、作成此事、那能盡美盡善呢。○你[20]猜四書五經、統共總有多少字呢、答我知道、四書上有二千三百二十八個字、五經上有二千四百二十六個字、統共總是

books. As to the affairs of the world and of society, they know nothing at all.

13 Look at Kung Hwa Tung's family; for generations they have been a worthless lot, yet now his descendants have all gotten rich. There *is* no such thing as justice.

14 The life of the genii is what all men approve, but the desire for children they cannot give up. Many doting parents there ever have been, but dutiful children who has seen?

15 Although this is recorded in a book, yet it must not be implicitly believed, for Mencius distinctly says, "It would be better to have no books at all than to believe everything that is recorded in books."

16 Brother Chang, can you lend me a bushel of wheat to put me over the new year? *Ans.* Altogether I have not got a bushel of wheat, how should I have any to lend you?

17 Just consider; he has in all only ten or twelve pupils, and his pupils will not average a thousand cash each. Is it strange that he says he cannot make a living?

18 Wherever envying and strife are, there is confusion and every evil work.

19 Having done it up on the spur of the moment, how can it be entirely perfect?

20 Guess what is the total number of characters in the Four Books and Five Classics. *Ans.* I know the number. There are 2328 in the Four

宮 *Kung*¹. . . . A mansion; a palace; a temple.

發籍 *Fa*¹ *chi*². *To get rich,* to become wealthy; . . . . to lay up money.

佩 *P'ei*⁴. To wear on the girdle, to keep as a . . . . . . souvenir, to remember; *to respect.*

佩服 *P'ei*⁴ *fu*⁴. To regard with approval; to . . . . .respect; *to defer to.*

嫉 *Chi*⁴. . . . . . . Envy, jealousy.

妒 *Tu*⁴. . . . . . . Jealous, envious.

嫉妒 To be jealous of, *to envy;* envy, jealousy.

攪亂 *Chiao*³ *lwan*⁴. *To confuse,* to throw into . . . . disorder, to disturb.

五經 *Wu*³ *ching*¹. The five classics:—Note . . . . 20.

倉猝 *Ts'ang*¹ *ts'u*⁴. In a moment, *on the spur* . . . . *of the moment;* hurried, flurried:—Note 19.

拐角 *Kwai*³ *chiao*³. An angle, *a corner;* to go . . . . round a corner.

醬 *Chiang*⁴. . . . Sauce used as a condiment, soy.

薑 *Chiang*¹. . . . . . Ginger.

椒 *Chiao*¹. . . . . . Hot spicy plants; pepper.

花椒 *Hwa*¹ *chiao*¹. . . . . . . Prickly-ash berries.

胡椒 *Hu*² *chiao*¹. . . . . . Black pepper.

曲折 *Ch'ü*¹ *chê*². Crooks and turns, ins and . . . . outs, *complications.*

褒 *Pao*¹. . . . . . . To admire, to praise.

貶 *Pien*³. . . To censure, to disparage; to dismiss.

四千七百五十四個。○這[21]條街往西轉彎、走到拐角、就是鄭家雜貨店、憑你買油鹽醬醋、棗子白糖生薑花椒胡椒茶葉俱全。○你[22]去問問馮連登罷、這件事的細微曲折、他雖不能盡情知道、却總知道個八九分。○俗[23]語說、管閒事落不是、大凡出頭管事的、還有不落褒貶的嗎。○入[24]伏以後、天氣到底是熱了、你看來來往往的人、皆都穿了夏布大褂。○依[25]我看、爲人只有兩件大事、一是多多掙幾吊錢、可以飽食暖衣、不受飢寒、二是常常出一點力、可以舒筋活血、不生疾病、除這兩件以外、別的俱是枉然。○孔[26]夫子當日周流列國、常常被人厭惡、可見世人所厭惡的、未必不是好人。

Books, and 2426 in the Five Classics, making 4754 in all.

21 Going west on this street you make a turn and presently come to the corner where is Mr. Chêng's grocery, at which you can buy everything in the way of oil, salt, sauce, vinegar, dates, sugar, ginger, prickly-ash berries, black pepper and tea.

22 Go and ask Fêng Lien Têng; although he may not be acquainted with all the details of this affair, yet he certainly knows the greater part.

23 It is a common saying that "he who meddles in the affairs of others will get into trouble." Who ever takes the lead in anything and yet escapes criticism?

24 It is undoubtedly hot after the beginning of midsummer. Notice how the passers by are all wearing grass cloth gowns.

25 In my opinion there are only two important things in life; one is to make a good lot of money, so as to have plenty to eat and wear and not suffer from hunger or cold, the other is to take a little regular exercise so as to keep up the tone of the system and prevent sickness. Aside from these two things all else is vanity.

26 When Confucius was traversing various countries, he was constantly hated by the people, from which we see that he who is hated by others is not necessarily a bad man.

褒貶 *Criticism*, fault-finding, disparagement.
夏布 *Hsia⁴ pu⁴*. . . . . Grass cloth.
大褂 *Ta⁴ kwa⁴*. . . . . A long coat, a gown.
飢 *Chi¹*. . . . . . Same as 饑.
飢寒 *Chi¹ han²*. . . . . . . Hunger and cold.
舒筋 *Shu¹ chin¹*. *To relax the muscles;* to . . . . take exercise. (w.)
活血 *Hwoa² hsie³*. To stimulate or accelerate . . . . the circulation.
疾病 *Chi² ping⁴*. An ailment, a disease, *sickness*, illness.
枉然 *Wang³ jan²*. *Vain*, useless; in vain, to no . . . . purpose.
周流 *Chou¹ liu²*. . . . . . To circulate, to traverse.
列國 *Lie⁴ kwoa²*. . . Various countries, all nations.

NOTES.

1 成破 is equivalent to 或成或破. 在於 is a redundant expression smacking of books.

6 The language of a letter from a son who is abroad, to his parents at home.

7 一應俱全 *One answer all complete;* that is, every inquiry [for goods] meets with an affirmative response. The phrase is thoroughly *Wên*. It is represented in the translation by the words *all kinds*. The whole sentence is the inscription on a signboard.

10 無覓處 *No place to find*, that is, *cannot be found*,—a book phrase not ordinarily used in Mandarin.

12 書獃子 *A book simpleton*, that is, a man of limited abilities who, by his exclusive attention to books, has unfitted himself for the practical affairs of life. 世事人

第一百五十九課

我[1]看你是明知故問。○倘[2]若家中有事、必特爲送信給你。○他[3]不叫我去、我偏要去。○還[4]能特特爲你自己、改了大衆的規矩嗎。○這[5]樣安排、是特意爲你打算。○沒[6]有別的事情、就是特特爲來給先生餞行。○看[7]朱九這個樣子、是滿打心裏要和咱們結寃、作對。○他[8]一生了氣、就故意的摔打給人看。○什[9]麽人不可好交、怎麽特特(偏偏)兒的交往一個無賴賴賴

Translation.

1 I believe you are asking just for the sake of asking.

2 If anything occurs at home, we will send a special message to you.

3 Since he forbids me to go, I am all the more determined to go.

4 Can the customs of the whole community be changed solely on your account?

5 It is arranged in this way with special reference to you.

6 I have no other business, I came simply to bring a lunch for your journey.

7 Judging from Chu Chiu's manner, he deliberately intends to act as our enemy.

8 Whenever he gets angry, he takes to slinging things about for effect.

9 Was there no one with whom to

情 *the affairs of the world and the amenities of life*,—may be regarded as a rhetorical transposition of 世人的事情.

14 This sentence is a verse from a ballad in the "Dream of the Red Chamber." In 神仙, the *persons* are put for the *state* of those persons. A man can only attain the immortality of the 神仙, by a life of severe asceticism, utterly inconsistent with marriage and the rearing of children. The rhythm of the verse requires that in 見了, the 了 should be read with more emphasis than properly belongs to it.

15 The sentiment here attributed to Mencius is one of his many sensible sayings. The original reference was to the 書經.

19 倉猝之間 is a book phrase rarely heard in colloquial. The whole sentence smacks of book style.

20 五經 *The Five Classics;* that is, 易經 or Book of Changes, 書經 or Book of History, 詩經 or Book of Poetry, 春秋 or Confucian Annals (commonly called 左傳), and 禮記 or Book of Rites. 四書五經 *Four Books and Five Classics*, is the common phrase by which the writings of the sages are designated. These comprehend all the books commonly studied in Chinese schools.

21 This is the language of a poster or advertisement, directing attention to a certain shop.

25 舒筋活血 *Expand the muscles and enliven the blood.*—an expression taken from medical language. The sentiment of the sentence is thoroughly Chinese.

26 周流列國 A book expression, rarely used except as applied to Confucius, who, accompanied by a number of his followers, visited the several petty kingdoms composing the empire, offering his services to the rulers as a teacher and reformer of government and manners.

LESSON CLIX.

Phrases of Special Intent.

特 Specially, expressly, of set purpose, solely.

特特 Emphatic for 特.

特意 Specially, expressly, fully intending.

特爲 On purpose, specifically, expressly, for the special purpose of.

故 On purpose, for the sake of.

故意 Purposely, of set purpose.

偏 Purposely, bent on, must needs, all the more, persistently, perversely, contrarily. Compare Les. 112.

偏偏 Emphatic for 偏.

着意 or 有意 Intentionally, deliberately.

誠心 Purposely, intentionally. (C. & N.)

安心 The same. (C. & S.)

處心 Intentionally, of purpose.

有心 The same.

打心裡 Of set purpose, deliberately, intentionally, sincerely, really. (N. & C.)

滿心裡 With full intent, fully expecting, sincerely.

單 or 單爲 Specially, specifically, simply.

本心裡 Of set purpose, deliberately; of oneself. (S.)

子肉的呢。○我[10]特爲去找他、他故意的躲了。○[11]單破出單爲出上你的工夫看孩子、你還叫他趴在水裏。○他[12]那是無心的話、並不是有着意說你。○叫[13]你往東、你偏往西、叫你打狗、你偏打雞。○我[14]打滿心裏要巴結想他成人、誰知他就是沒有出息。○應[15]當將自己心比人心、不可誠安心惹人生氣。○他[16]是沒看見、把你碰拐倒了、並不是處有心的。○你[17]這是打本心裏的話呢、還是嘴上牙外的話呢。○老[18]兄既是特意爲我預備的、我只得領情謝就是喇。○我[19]特爲大聲叫你、你故意的不答應、這豈不是誠處有心要討打嗎。○我[20]囑咐你不要上樹、你偏要上、萬一從上頭掉下來、却就要了你的命喇。○明[21]曉得子弟不是、偏要護短、反說小孩子家、

associate, that you must needs make friends with a vagabond?

10 I went expressly to find him, but he purposely avoided me.

11 It was your only business to watch the child, and yet you allowed him to creep into the water.

12 That was only a thoughtless speech of his. He was not intending to reprove you.

13 When told to go east, you perversely go west; when told to strike the dog, you perversely strike the chickens.

14 I was sincerely hoping that I could make a man of him, but I find there is no outcome in him.

15 You should measure others' feelings by your own, and not purposely stir up people's indignation.

16 He did not see you and so knocked you over. It was quite unintentional.

17 Do you really mean this, or is it only mere talk?

18 Seeing you have prepared it specially for me, I cannot refuse to accept the favor.

19 I took pains to call you in a loud voice, and you purposely did not answer. You are trying to earn a flogging, are you?

20 I charged you not to climb the tree and yet you persist in doing so. If by chance you should fall down, that will be the end of you.

21 You know very well that the young people were to blame, yet you persist

VOCABULARY.

滿心 *Man*³ *hsin*¹. The whole heart, wholly; . . . . bent on, bound to:—see Sub.

作對 *Tsoä*⁴ *twei*⁴. . . . . . . To act as an enemy.

無賴肉 *Wu*² *lai*⁴ *ju*⁴. A tramp, a renegade, a . . . . worthless scamp:—Note 9.

趴 *P'a*². . . . . . . *To creep*, to crawl. Also *p'a*¹.

巴想 *Pa*¹ *hsiang*³. To desire greatly, to long for, ... *to hope for*. (s.)

領謝 *Ling*³ *hsie*⁴. To return thanks; *to accept a* . . . . . . *favor* [for which thanks are due].

護短 *Hu*⁴ *twan*³. To screen a fault, *to condone;* . . . . to excuse.

柱 *Chu*⁴. . . . A pillar, a post; a main dependence.

好事 *Hao*⁴ *shï*⁴. To be a busybody, to love scan- . . . . dal; *to be fond of amusement.*

誕 *Tan*⁴. To boast, to tell lies; *disorderly;* to . . . . bear children; to increase.

調誕 *Tiao*⁴ *tan*⁴. To tell lies, to talk at ran- . . . . dom; *mischievous*, incorrigible.

調脾 *Tiao*⁴ *p'i*². *Mischievous*, perverse, incorri- . . . . gible.

蛤 *Kê*¹, *ka*¹. . . . . A crepitating sound. See *kê*².

鉿 *Kê*⁴. . . . . . A creaking sound.

蛤吧蛤吧 *Kê*¹ *pa*¹. *To crack*, to snap, to . . . . crepitate, to click.

鉿扎鉿扎 *Kê*⁴ *cha*¹. . . . . The same.

不過玩耍玩耍罷了、何妨呢。○姜[22]廷柱的那個孩子小廝、真調誕脾、他爬在房子上、蹓的些瓦蛤吧蛤吧鉿扎鉿扎的、我說你快下來罷、他說我偏不下去。○那[23]個老頭子實在好事玩、隔着十來里路、還單爲騎着牲口去聽戲。○成[24]年家東跑西顛南跑北奔南奔北跑的、打本心裏要積攢一點過日活、沒料想心比天高、命如紙薄、掙一個口吃一個口、至今還是光溜溜精光光的。○我[25]特意的要挖酷挖酷他、纔說了兩三句、他就徉徜粧徉走了。○你[26]看他紥裏穿紥的、就和個四不像子四不像一樣、見了女人就大搖大擺、鑑着脖頸子喝喝咧咧伸着頸脖子唧吶吶的唱、故意的粧模做樣給人看。○我[27]就是見不得他身上那個氣味、他偏偏坐在我旁邊、你說漚人不漚人煩人不煩人嫌人不嫌人。

in condoning their、faults, having even the face to say, "What does it signify? the children were only playing."

22 That boy of Chiang T'ing Chu's is a mischievous young rascal. He climbed up on the house and was walking over and cracking the tiles. I said to him, "You come down at once," to which he replied, "I won't do it."

23 That old fellow is certainly fond of amusement. He will mount his donkey and ride a distance of ten odd *li* simply to attend a theater.

24 I have been working hard year after year hoping to accumulate a little property (lit. livelihood), but alas, though my aspirations were high, fortune was all against me; as fast as I could earn a mouthful it was eaten up, so that to this day I have not a cent to my name.

25 I was fully intending to give him a good berating, but before I got well started he turned up his nose and walked off.

26 Look at him, dressed up like a dude. When he meets a woman he swaggers and struts, and with head in the air, strikes up some rollicking ditty on purpose to show himself off.

27 The thing I cannot abide is the rank smell he has about him, yet he persists in sitting beside me. Isn't it provoking?

東跑西顛 *Tung*¹ *p'ao*³ *hsi*¹ *tien*¹. To hurry hither and thither; to strive; *to work hard.*

南跑北奔 *Nan*² *p'ao*³ *pei*³ *pên*⁴. The same.

南奔北跑 *Nan*² *pên*⁴ *pei*³ *p'ao*³. The same.

過日 *Kwoă*⁴ *jï*⁴. A living; savings; *property,* money.

過活 *Kwoă*⁴ *hwoă*². The same.

精光光 *Ching*¹ *kwang*¹. Quite destitute, *without anything.*

徉 *Yang*². To ramble, to rove; to saunter idly.

徜 *Ch'ang*¹. To and fro, unsteady.

徉徜 Playful, unconcerned; *disdainful*

鑑 *Ch'ên*¹. To stretch out.

穿紥 *Ch'wan*¹ *tsa*¹. *To dress up,* to accoutre, to trick out.

四不像 *Sï*⁴ *pu*⁴ *hsiang*⁴. Nondescript, outlandish:—Note 26.

脖頸子 *Poă*² *kêng*³ *tsï*³. The neck, the back of the neck.

頸脖子 *Kêng*³ *poă*² *tsï*³. The same. (s.)

喝喝咧咧 *Hê*⁴ *lie*¹. *Vociferous,* stentorian, uproarious.

吶 *Na*⁴. To call aloud, to shout. Also *noă*⁴.

唧吶吶 *Chi*¹ *na*⁴ *na*⁴. *Vociferous;* inarticulate shouting.

漚 *Ou*¹. To soak, to macerate; to rot. To disgust, to exasperate. (N.)

第一百六十課

你[1]就滿身是口、也賴不過去了。○就[2]打着他的時運高、也未必能撈出本錢來。○別[3]講我沒有錢、就是有錢、我還能還他的賭博賬嗎。○你[4]所問的、我實係是不知道、即使便知道、也不敢告訴。○你[5]們是同胞弟兄、就打之着有點不是、仍舊應該彼此包涵。○縱[6]然我不去、你就該不來嗎。○他[7]每月只掙兩三吊錢、就五六口人子花消、即使便能以儉省、也是養活不過來的。○你[8]單

TRANSLATION.

1 Even if your whole body were full of mouths, you could not lie out of it.
2 Even supposing he should have the best of luck, it is not likely that he can recover his capital.
3 Not to speak of the fact that I have no money, even if I had money, I would not pay his gambling debts.
4 I really know nothing of the matter you are inquiring about, and even if I did know, I would not dare to tell you.
5 You are own brothers, and even if some wrong has been done, you should still mutually forbear.
6 Even though I did not go, was that a sufficient reason for your not coming?
7 He only earns two or three thousand cash a month and has a family of five or six to provide for, so that even if he does know how to economize, he will not be able to support them.

NOTES.

1 明知故問 *Knowing perfectly well yet make a point of asking.*

9 什麽人不好交 *What man is not fit to associate with?* that is, are there not enough of good people with whom to associate, that you, etc.? 無賴肉 The writing of this phrase is hypothetical. 無賴 is *to live by one's wits without any legitimate means of support.* 肉 denotes the want of a self-respecting personality. Some write 無賴油 explaining the 油 from 油子 or 老油子, *an oily tongued slippery fellow.* Others write 無來由, *a tramp without antecedents;* i.e., without family, friends or property. The fact that in China a man's sense of obligation depends so much on his connection with family and friends, gives some color to this writing. 無賴的 is used in the South and 無賴子 in the North.

13 Said to one who is provokingly contrary.

17 牙外的話 *Words outside the teeth;* that is, jesting or deceitful words which mean nothing. 嘴上的話 *Mere talk, empty words.*

18 領謝 differs from 領情 in that the latter always implies the acceptance of the favor, whereas the former is sometimes used as a polite form of declining a favor.

22 我偏不下去 means more than, *I won't do it.* It means, *I won't do it just because you order me to do it,* or, *the more you tell me to come down the more I won't come down.*

26 四不像 was originally applied to a mythological animal that was neither bird, beast, fish nor reptile, but a composite of all. The term has been adapted, and is used of one who is neither 士, 農, 工 nor 商, neither *scholar, farmer, artizan* nor *merchant,* that is, *a clown, a dude; a man without any profession or means of living.* 粧模做樣 is a rhetorical transposition of 粧做模樣.

LESSON CLX.

HYPOTHETICAL WORDS AND PHRASES.

就 or **就是** Even if :—Les. 44. Sub. 4 (1).

就算是 Even supposing, even if, even on the supposition.

就打着 or **就打之** Even if, even on the supposition.

雖就是 Even should, even although.

即便 Even if, even in case.

即使 The same. (s.) A book term.

即或 Even if, even in case.

縱 If, even if, even although.

縱然 Even if, even though, even allowing.

縱就是 Even if, even supposing, even admitting.

人獨馬騎萬不可去、就是你有力氣、也當知道好漢打不出村
去。○有[9]理行遍天下、無理寸步難行、縱然他們人多、就不講
理了嗎。○這[10]個情我實在不願意去討求、即便我去、也恐怕討求
不下來。○學[11]生在專心致志的時候、縱然聽見街上有玩要活
龍的、他的心也不外散。○莫[12]說你打不過他、就算是能打過
他、豈不惹下後患了嗎。○看[13]他那個灑脫的樣兒、縱有些小
過錯、也不足為怪。○曹[14]正道、若是閉了關的時候、縱有一萬
兵、也上去不得、你二位焉能上去。○你[15]這個人實在扯拉拉疲疲忽、借
了人的傢什、永遠不送、就算是失落不棹了、也不怕躭誤人家
用嗎。○人[16]有能事的、有不能事的、能事的、雖就是半路上變

8 You must not think of going single-handed. Even if you are strong, you must remember that one fighting man cannot put to rout a whole town.

9 With reason on one's side, he can go anywhere; without it, it is hard to take a single step. Even if their number is great, will they not listen to reason?

10 I am very loth to go and ask this favor; and even if I do go, I fear I shall not be successful.

11 When the student's mind is intently engaged in study, his attention would not be distracted even though he heard that they were exhibiting a live dragon on the street.

12 The fact is you are not able to beat him; and even supposing you were able, would you not be laying up trouble for the future?

13 Judging from the free and easy way he has, it would not be at all strange if he had some trifling faults.

14 When once Ts'ao Chêng Tao has closed up the barriers, even if you had ten thousand soldiers you could not force them; how then can you two do it?

15 You are certainly a careless fellow, borrowing people's tools and never returning them. Even supposing you do not lose them, are you not afraid you will disoblige the owners?

16 Some men have tact, others have not. When a man has this faculty, even should the aspect of an affair change

VOCABULARY.

縱 *Tsung*⁴. Remiss, careless; to indulge, to give rein to; even if, allowing, supposing; perpendicular. Read *Tsung*¹·³·⁴ with different meanings, but with no uniformity in usage.

胞 *P'ao*¹, *pao*¹. The placenta; *uterine;* a vescicle, a blister; a fish bladder. Note 5.

同胞 *T'ung*² *pao*¹. Uterine brothers, *own brothers.*

灑脫 *Sa*³ *t'oǎ*¹. Careless, *free and easy;* reckless, headlong.

拉忽 *La*¹ *hu*¹. Negligent, heedless, *careless;* slovenly.

扯疲 *Ch'ê*³ *p'i*². . . . The same. (s.)

變卦 *Pien*⁴ *kwa*⁴. Change of circumstances, a new turn of affairs:—Note 16.

扶持 *Fu*² *ch'i*². To hold up, to support; to assist, to help.

揣 *Ch'wai*³. . . To feel after; to estimate, *to guess.*

揣摸 *Ch'wai*³ *moǎ*¹. To feel after; to think over; to surmise, *to fancy*

估摸 *Ku*¹ *moǎ*¹. To estimate, to conjecture; *to fancy,* to imagine.

領理 *Ling*³ *li*³. *To lead,* to conduct, to show the way.

領路 *Ling*³ *lu*⁴ . . . The same.

矬 *Ts'oǎ*² . . . A person of small stature, a dwarf.

瘰 *Loǎ*³, *lei*³ . . . Scrofulous ulcers, king's evil.

癧 *Li*⁴ Scrofulous swellings or ulcers on the neck.

了卦、他也能隨機應變、把事辦妥了。○已[17]經十五六歲的東西、還能跑沒有掉了嗎、答 即便沒有不了、跑不掉、你一時間找不着他、他家裏活不見人、死不見屍、能不問你要嗎。○古[18]語說、單絲不成線、孤樹不成林、他縱有頂天的本事、沒有人扶持還能行嗎。○我[19]揣摸着、他不敢去告、縱然就是去告、他也佔不了不得佔上風。○若[20]是要臉的人有了錯處、縱然人家不說他、他也很覺慚愧、若是不要臉的人有了錯處、縱然人家說他、他也不知羞恥。○這[21]樣的匪類人、還能養出個好兒子來嗎、縱就是有個好兒子、也必叫他領路領理壞了。○你[22]要說張家那個矬矮姑娘嗎、他母親生瘰癧疙瘩、害癧子頸、不但脖頸子上有瘡、連胸膛和胳肘

when it is half done, yet he can adapt himself to the circumstances and bring it to a satisfactory issue.

17 Can a youngster of fifteen or sixteen lose himself entirely? *Ans.* Even suppose he cannot be entirely lost, yet if, for the time being, you cannot produce him, will not his family, not finding him either alive or dead, demand him at your hand?

18 There is an old saying, "A single filament of silk does not make a thread, a single tree does not make a grove." Even if he had the most transcendent ability, he could not succeed without the help of others.

19 I fancy he will not venture to go to law; and even if he should, he will not make any thing by it.

20 When a man who has any self-respect is in the wrong, even though no one should reprove him, he still experiences a deep sense of humiliation; but when one who has lost all self-respect is in the wrong, he feels no shame even when reproved.

21 Can a dissipated man like this bring up a virtuous son? If he should have a good son, he is certain to lead him astray.

22 Are you about to propose for that dwarf girl of the Changs'? Her mother was afflicted with scrofulous sores, having ulcers not only on her

瘰癧 A scrofulous ulcer, an indolent sore.

癧子頸 *Li⁴ tsï³ kêng³*. A scrofulous ulcer on the neck.

膛 *T'ang²*. Fat, plump; a protuberance; *the breast.*

胸膛 *Hsiung¹ t'ang²*. The bosom, *the breast,* the thorax.

胳肘窩 *Kê² chou³ woă¹*. The armpit.

癆 *Lao²*. Any wasting disease.

癆病 *Lao² ping⁴*. Phthisis, *consumption;* any wasting disease.

輔 *Fu³*. *To help,* to second, to assist.

輔助 *Fu³ chu⁴*. *To help,* to assist, to succor, to lend one's aid.

繫 *Hsi⁴*. Let down by a rope, to suspend; *a suspension cord,* a handle. Also *chi⁴*.

削 *Hsiao¹*, *hsüe¹*. To pare off, to shave, *to scrape;* to extort; to deprive of.

NOTES.

4 是 is often omitted after 實係, but its use adds emphasis. As 係 (*Wên*) and 是 (*Mandarin*) are really equivalents, the fact that 是 is thus used after 係 shows the extent to which the meaning of 係 is obscured in the phrase 實係.

5 同胞弟兄 *Sons of the same mother.* If 胞, as now defined by medical men, means placenta (not womb) then this phrase is a misnomer.

8 單人獨馬 (or 騎) *A single man, or a single horse* (or *horseman*), a phrase derived from war, meaning that

窩裏、也都有瘡、而且又有癆病、還能不傳在他身上嗎、即便不傳、你娶這麽一個矮矬子、身體那樣軟弱、他還能以輔助你嗎。○現23在挑八根股繫繩、也不過是針尖削鐵的一點利兒、就算是他的賣頭好、一天掙個百兒八十的、頂了天喇。○從24來說、有病亂投醫、不定是什麽方兒、就治好了、即或到底治不好、那是他命該如此、於我們心裏也算安穩咯。

neck, but also on her breast and armpits, and moreover she also has consumption, which diseases cannot but be transmitted to her daughter. Even if not transmitted, should you marry such a dwarf, with so weakly a body, can she be any help to you?

23 At present the money made by peddling is like the moiety of iron scraped from the point of a needle. Even granting that he is a good salesman, at the very most he can only make eighty or a hundred cash per day.

24 It is said, "When you are sick, call all the doctors you can." There is no knowing what prescription may cure him; and if after all he fails to be cured, it will be because it was so ordained by fate; our minds also will be at rest.

---

a single soldier, whether on foot or horse, is useless against numbers. The derived meaning is obvious.

11 專心致志 *Mind single and purpose fixed;* that is, *the mind concentrated on one object, absorbed in thought.* A ready made book phrase. 活龍 *A live dragon.* The reference is to the feast of lanterns on the 15th of the first month, when dragons composed of lanterns strung together are carried through the street, forming a spectacle of attractiveness which few boys could resist. Much less could they resist the exhibition of a real live dragon on the street.

16 能事 *To have a capacity for managing things.* 事 is used as a verb. 變了卦, *change of diagram,*—a figure taken from the diagrams in the Book of Changes, which are used in divining and fortune-telling.

19 佔上風 *To obtain the place or seat nearest the wind,*—whoever is next the wind gets the first and freshest breeze, hence the meaning, *to get the advantage of.*

23 挑八股繩 *To carry eight strands of rope.* Peddlers carry their stock in two baskets or boxes, each suspended by four ropes. 針尖削鐵, *to scrape iron from the point of a needle;* that is, to make very small profits. 百 does not usually take 兒 after it. It is here added to separate the 百 from the number following. 賣頭好 may mean either *makes good sales,* or *is a good salesman.*

LESSON CLXI.

Phrases of Recurrent Time.

間或 Occasionally, sometimes, in case.

偶爾 Unexpectedly, occasionally, by times:—See Les. 115. Sub.

輕易 Lightly, thoughtlessly, not often. With a negative—seldom, rarely, scarcely ever.

半晌 For the most part, seldom, rarely,—always followed by a negative. (c.)

成久 For the most part, ordinarily. With a negative, rarely, hardly ever. (s.)

幾工 Always with a negative,—rarely, hardly ever. (c.)

Vocabulary.

發市 *Fa¹ shï⁴.* To make sales, to have customers.

發利市 *Fa¹ li⁴ shï⁴.* The same. (s.)

僻 *Pei⁴, pi⁴.* Quiet, private, *secluded,* out of the way. See *p'i⁴.*

僻靜 *Pei⁴ ching⁴.* Secluded, out of the way, bye, *retired.*

知心 *Chï¹ hsin¹.* *Congenial;* like-minded, sympathetic.

倍 *Pei⁴.* Fold, times; *to double.*

第一百六十一課

這[1]句話、在本地並不是簡直的不說、間偶或爾也有說的。○如[2]今的官、輕易沒有動大板子打人的、常行都是小板子。○那[3]些大洋行、輕易(半晌/半天)不見他發利市(市)、逢發利市(市)、却就不在少處。○我[4]們這裏太僻靜喇、幾工兒(輕易)見不着個人來。○若[5]是到了人地兩生的地方、輕易遇不見個知心的人、一旦遇見的時候、心裏必加倍的親熱。○這[6]都是好錢、間或(卽或)有一個半個(半個)小的、也都好使(用)。○近[7]來上陣打仗、大半晌(大概)沒有用弓箭的、差不多都是用鎗砲。○李[8]殿魁那個人、輕易不生氣、今日怎麼生了這麼大的氣呢。○你[9]是個希客、輕易(成久)不到我們家裏來、快請坐罷。○這[10]樣的字眼兒、就是閒書上、間偶

TRANSLATION.

1 This expression is not entirely unheard in this neighborhood; it is used occasionally.

2 At the present time, magistrates do not often punish with the large bamboo, they commonly use the small bamboo.

3 Those large foreign hongs seldom seem to have a customer, but when they have one their sales are always heavy.

4 Our place here is entirely too retired. We rarely see any one.

5 If one goes where both people and place are strange, he seldom meets with a congenial spirit; when however he does meet with such a one, he is sure to be doubly drawn towards him.

6 These are all good cash, if occasionally there are one or two small ones they will still pass.

7 In the wars of recent times bows and arrows have rarely been used. Nearly all use muskets and cannon.

8 That man Li Tien K'wei rarely gets angry; how comes it that he got into such a passion to-day?

9 You are quite a stranger. It is a rare thing that you come to our house. Please take a seat.

10 This phraseology is occasionally found in novels, but I have never come across it in the classics.

加倍 *Chia*[1] *pei*[4]. To add as much again, *to double.*

一半個 *I*[1] *pan*[4] *kê*[4]. *An occasional one,* one here and there, a few.

一個半個 *I*[1] *kê*[4] *pan*[4] *kê*[4]. The same. (s.)

上陣 *Shang*[4] *chên*[4]. To go into battle.

殿 *Tien*[4]. A grand hall, a palace, temple.

字眼 *Tsï*[4] *yien*[3]. Form of speech, *phraseology,* words.

閒書 *Hsien*[2] *shu*[1]. *Novels*; light literature—which is lightly esteemed by the Chinese.

經書 *Ching*[1] *shu*[1]. Classical books, the writings of the sages.

寡婦 *Kwa*[3] *fu*[4]. A widow.

路兵 *Lu*[4] *ping*[1]. Guards on the highway, patrolmen.

失事 *Shï*[1] *shï*[4]. To lose by thieves or robbers; *to have a mishap.*

鼎 *Ting*[3]. A three-legged caldron; firm, settled.

狡 *Chiao*[3]. Crafty, wily; specious.

狡猾 *Chiao*[3] *hwa*[2]. *Crafty,* cunning, subtle, treacherous.

獻勤 *Hsien*[4] *ch'in*[2]. *To make capital of one's zeal for another;* to act the sycophant, to toady. Note 13.

寵 *Ch'ung*[3]. To be partial to; *to favor,* to prefer; to indulge, to dote on.

爾或有用的、經書上從來沒見。○俗[11]語說、寡婦門前是非多、現在他男人既然死了、若沒有要緊的事情、不好輕易往他家裏去。○走[12]路還是走大路妥當、間或有險要的地方去處、都有路兵看守、幾工成久少有失事的。○朱[13]萬鼎爲人極其狡猾、常在魯大人跟前獻功勤、十分得寵、所以逢他說話、輕易沒有敢駁文的。○要[14]飽總得家常飯、要暖還得粗布衣、我家裏並非沒有山珍海味、只是輕易半晌成久吃不着、也並非沒有綾羅緞疋、只是輕易半晌成久穿不着。○這[15]以後我叫他拾漏子錯拾怕了、在他跟前、輕易不敢說話。○簍[16]子莊上我親家、好不通情理、我輕易不到他家裏去、那一天我去了、心裏指望吃他一頓好飯、他竟端上

11 The saying is, "Many scandals flit about a widow's door." Seeing her husband is now deceased, if you have no important business, it is best for you not to go there when you can avoid it.

12 When traveling it is best to go by the great road, since in case of any special danger there is a guard of soldiers at hand. It is a rare thing that there is any mishap.

13 Chu Wan Ting is an exceedingly crafty man. He is constantly bringing his services to the notice of Lu Ta-jên with whom he is in high favor, so that when he says a thing no one lightly ventures to oppose.

14 For satisfying the appetite ordinary diet is the best, and for warmth coarse clothing is the best. It is not that we have no delicacies in our house, but ordinarily we do not eat them; nor is it that we have no silk and satin, but ordinarily we do not wear them.

15 Since that time I have been tripped up by him so often that I have grown wary, and seldom venture to say anything in his presence.

16 That relative of mine in Lou-tsï-chwang has no idea of the fitness of things. I seldom go to his house, but one day I went hoping to get one good meal off him, when, behold, he simply set out a saucer of salt

獻功 *Hsien⁴ kung¹*. *To make capital of one's merit;* to curry favor, to act the flunkey.

得寵 *Tê² ch'ung³*. *To be in favor*; to be indulged.

駁文 *Poă² wên²*. To contradict, to take issue with, *to oppose*.

家常 *Chia¹ ch'ang²*. Common, *ordinary*, usual, every-day.

山珍 *Shan¹ chên¹*. Savory dishes from the hills, game.

蘿 *Loă²*. . . . . . . Parasitic plants.

蔔 *Poă¹, pei⁴*. . . . . . . A fragrant white flower.

蘿蔔 Radishes, turnips, carrots, etc.—variously used in different places, especially with respect to turnips.

花言巧語 *Hwa¹ yien² ch'iao³ yü³*. A pompous, affected, or specious style of speech.

巧言花語 *Ch'iao³ yien² hwa¹ yü³*. The same.

實實落落 *Shï² loă⁴*. Real, bona fide, veritable; *plain, substantial.*

苟儉 *Kou³ chien³*. Stingy, mean, shabby; a niggard, *a skinflint.*

嗇鬼 *Sê⁴ kwe³*. . . . . . A miser, a niggard. (s.)

猫兒頭 *Mao¹ êr² t'ou²* . . . . An owl.

解手 *Chie³ shou³*. To attend to a call of nature, to ease oneself.

跌死 *Tie¹ si³*. To fall and kill oneself, to be killed by a fall:—Les. 183.

一碟子鹹蘿蔔、拿上兩個窩窩頭、女親家／親家母還花言巧語／巧言花語的說、到我們這裏、不用鬧虛套子／虛之套之、全是實實落落的、我嘴裏不說心裏說、像這樣的實落、輕易却沒大有、偶爾／間或有一半個、也必是為窮所逼、斷沒有和這個老苟儉／嗇鬼一樣的。○

17 這些妖巧講究、我輕易不信、惟獨說貓兒頭叫喚、必定主着不祥、這個我可十分相信、在我莊的西廟上、有個姓于的道士、前年四月間犯了癆病、吐血很重、到第三天晚上、聽見一個貓兒頭、在院子樹上叫了三聲、又笑了三聲、他就很覺喪氣、後來到了半夜、他要出來解手、一出門跌了一個跟頭、一下跌死了、你看到底靈不靈呢。

turnips and a couple of kao-liang cakes, his wife meanwhile going on to say, in the most plausible style, "When you come to see us there is no occasion for putting on a great show of formality, so we just have everything plain and substantial." I said nothing, but I thought to myself: It is not often one gets treated quite so plainly as this; and if occasionally such a case should occur, it is from the necessities of poverty. I venture you will not find another like this old skinflint.

17 I don't generally believe in these superstitious notions; but that the hooting of an owl is a sure sign of bad luck, I do most thoroughly believe. At the temple to the west of our village there lived a Taoist priest by the name of Yü. In the fourth month of the year before last he was taken with consumption, and began to spit a great deal of blood. On the evening of the third day he heard an owl on a tree in the yard give three hoots and three laughs, which he felt was a very bad omen. Afterwards, getting up in the middle of the night to attend to a call of nature, he tripped as he went out of the door, and falling headlong killed himself. Could any omen be more undoubted than that?

NOTES.

2 The 大板子 is a strip of bamboo about three or four inches wide and five feet long, and is wielded by the executioner with two hands. The 小板子 is about two or two and a half inches wide and three feet long, and is usually wielded with one hand. The beating is done on the bare thighs, the culprit being held down on his face by two lictors, one sitting on his shoulders and the other on his feet.

4 The 來 at the close serves simply as a final particle, equivalent to 了 or 喇.

6 間或 Though used freely in many places is not much used in Peking, and 即或 is here supplied in its place by the Peking teacher. It is not, however, the equivalent of 間或 which is followed in the translation. If 即或 be followed, then "if occasionally" should be *even if*.

9 希客 *A rare guest*, one whose visits are "few and far between." 快 is used to express cordiality, but will hardly bear translating.

13 獻勤 means to make a business of bringing one's diligent services prominently to the notice of a master or superior, and so curry favor and gain confidence. 獻功 means substantially the same thing, but is a less offensive term.

14 山珍 is rarely separated from its companion phrase 海味, though the latter is frequently used alone. 珍 is not often used of things to eat, but is so used in this phrase in allusion to the cost and difficulty of procuration. 緞疋 *Webs of satin*. The addition of 疋 gives the idea of a considerable quantity. There is also the analogous phrase, 布疋.

15 拾漏子 or 錯 *To gather up a slip or mistake;* that is, *to trip up, to catch*. 找 is also used instead of 拾.

16 窩窩頭 Cakes in the shape of a bird's nest; usually made of kao-liang meal, sometimes of corn meal. They are largely eaten by the poorer classes in Northern China. The 窩 is not always repeated. 女親家 or 親家母 *A son's wife's mother*, or *a daughter's husband's mother*. Both terms are widely used though neither is entirely *t'ung-hsing*. 親家婆 is also used.

第一百六十二課

請[1]你少等一等、立時就好得喇。○他[2]們一聽說、隨即去看了一遍。○他[3]把東西一交給我、隨時就回去了。○我[4]出去買一點菜、立刻就回來。○有[5]話一直的說出來就是了、何必這麽半吐半咽半含半吐半吞半吐的。○我[6]們抄出他的批來、隨即寫了一個訴呈、攔轎路輿遞上去了。○他[7]們打完了晌尖中尖中伙即時就起了身。○人[8]已經病到那個分兒、就是治的得法、也不能立時痊愈。○你[9]不必回下處、就從這裏一直的去罷。○馬[10]曰德眞是聰明過人、無論甚麽書、看過一遍、立刻就明白了。○就[11]打着他見信立時起行、這時候也不來

Translation.

1 Please wait a little; it will take but a moment.

2 As soon as they heard of it, they went at once and took a look.

3 As soon as he had delivered the things to me, he at once returned.

4 I am going out to buy a few vegetables and will return immediately.

5 If you have anything to say, speak it out; why so much humming and hawing?

6 When we had secured a copy of his verdict, we at once wrote a defence and handed it in from the roadside.

7 When they had finished their lunch, they started forthwith.

8 When a man's disease has reached such a point as that, even though the medical treatment insures recovery, yet the patient cannot be well in a moment.

9 You need not return to your lodgings; why not go directly from here?

10 Ma Yüe Tê's ability is really extraordinary. No matter what book it is, let him but read it over once, and forthwith he knows all about it.

11 Even supposing he started the moment he received the letter, he

LESSON CLXII.

Instantaniety.

This lesson is closely connected with Les. 115.

立時 Instantly, immediately, in a moment.
立刻 The same.
立卽 At once, immediately, forthwith.
登時 Instantly, in a moment, immediately. (s.)
隨卽 At once, forthwith.
隨時 At once, forthwith, immediately.
隨就 Forthwith, without delay.
隨赶着 At once, forthwith, immediately. (N.)
隨跟之 The same. (c.)
隨跟身 The same. (s.)
卽時 Forthwith, instantly.
一直的 Forthwith, straightway, directly.
馬上 At once, promptly, quickly :—Les. 118.

Vocabulary.

半吐半咽 *Pan⁴ t'u³ pan⁴ yien⁴.* To hesitate, to stammer, *to hum and haw.* (N.)

半含半吐 *Pan⁴ han² pan⁴ t'u³.* The same. (c. & s.)

半吞半吐 *Pan⁴ t'un¹ pan⁴ t'u³.* The same. (c. & s.)

訴呈 *Su⁴ ch'êng².* A counter accusation; *a defense,* a vindication.

輿 *Yü².* A chariot, *a carriage;* to contain.

攔轎 *Lan² chiao⁴.* To stop an official chair to present a petition :—Note 6. (N.)

攔路 *Lan² lu⁴.* The same. (c.)

攔輿 *Lan² yü².* The same. (s.)

不得到。○地12已經旱透了、你看澆上兩瓢水、隨隨趕跟着之就吃滲掉喇。○一13提我的錢沒有了、他臉上立刻發紅、諒來是他偷的。○王14文祥並沒來辭行、竟一直的走了嗎。○賣15主既然鬆了口、應當隨即和他立約立字、恐其事緩有變。○該16你做的、你就一直的去做罷、你這麼當有作無的、還能混過去嗎。○你17看路上有多少人、管保隨隨隨趕跟跟着之身就叫人家撿拾去喇、你往那裏去找呢。○王18先生進來連坐也沒坐、只說了幾句話、立即轉身走了、也不知他有甚麼要緊的事。○若19用電線傳信、不論相隔多遠、從這頭一發、那頭立登時就知道了。○罷20喇、你馬上交來三百兩、也准你罷。○受21人之託、必當

could not have arrived by this time.

12 The ground is already dried through. Notice how when you pour on a few dipperfuls of water, it is absorbed at once.

13 When I spoke of my money being missing, his face instantly flushed; in all probability he is the man who stole it.

14 Wang Wên Hsiang did not come to say good bye, but just went straight off?

15 The seller having yielded assent, you ought forthwith to have drawn up an agreement, lest delay should lead to a change of mind [on the seller's part].

16 Whatever you ought to do, go ahead and do it. You cannot get out of it by ignoring the matter in this way.

17 Look at the number of people there are on the road. I'll warrant you some one picked it up immediately. What chance is there of your finding it?

18 Mr. Wang came in but did not even sit down; he simply said a few words and turned about and left at once. I do not know what important business was on hand.

19 In sending a message by telegraph, no matter what the distance, as soon as the message is started from this end it is instantly known at the other end.

20 All right; pay over three hundred taels promptly, and I'll let you off.

曰 *Yüe*1,4... To speak, to utter; designated, *called.*

過人 *Kwoă*4 *jên*2. Beyond others, beyond the ... ... average, *extraordinary.*

澆 *Chiao*1.... To irrigate, to water; *to pour on.*

滲 *Shên*4...... To leak; to soak into, *to absorb.*

辭行 *Ts'i*2 *hsing*2. *To take leave*, to bid adieu .... (used of the person departing).

賣主 *Mai*4 *chu*3.... ... The seller.

鬆口 *Sung*1 *k'ou*3 *To yield assent*, to concede, ... to agree to.

緩 *Hwan*3. Slow, lax; easily, gently; *to delay*, ... to neglect. (w.)

立約 *Li*4 *yüe*1. To make a covenant; to sign ... articles of agreement; *to write a deed.*

立字 *Li*4 *tsï*4....... To write and sign a deed.

親口 *Ch'in*1 *k'ou*3. With one's own mouth; *ex- ... ... plicitly.*

遲延 *Ch'i*2 *yien*2. *To delay*, to put off, to pro- .... crastinate, to loiter.

欽 *Ch'in*1.... To respect; *imperial*, governmental.

欽差 *Ch'in*1 *ch'ai*1. An imperial commissioner; .... *a minister*, an envoy.

升轎 *Shêng*1 *chiao*4. To get into or mount a se- ... ...dan chair:—Note 23.

姑媽 *Ku*1 *ma*1.... ... A father's sister.

軋 *Ya*4. The creaking sound of a wheel; *to grind ... ... or crush on a* 碾.

颷 *Hsüen*4....... A revolving wind.

颷風 *Hsüen*4 *fêng*1.... ... ... A whirlwind.

抛 *P'ao*1. To cast off, to reject; *to throw over- ..... board;* to deduct; to project, to fling.

錨 *Mao*2....... *An anchor*, a grappling iron.

艙 *Ts'ang*1. The compartments of a ship; *the ... ... hold.*

忠人之事、你既然親口應承了、就當立刻給人去辦、不要遲延叫人着急。○十[22]點鐘的時候、有一位米先生來找你、看見你不在家、隨隨隨跟跟赶身之着就走喇。○欽[23]差怎麼來的這樣快呢、答欽差到了公館、吃了飯立即升轎、連歇息也沒歇息。○等[24]我換上衣裳、隨就同之着你走。○他[25]說還有一點點事兒、辦妥當了、馬上就來。○我[26]的姑姑姑媽正在那裏套着牲口軋碾子碾、見我去了、隨時卸了牲口、就帶領我到家裏去咯。○我[27]們一知道來了颶風、隨即落了篷、抛下錨、又盖嚴艙口、免得灌進水去。

21 "When you receive a trust from any one, you should faithfully execute it." Having explicitly made the promise, you should redeem it at once and not cause anxiety by your delay.

22 About ten o'clock there was a Mr. Mi came looking for you. When he found you were not at home he immediately went away.

23 How did the minister arrive so quickly? *Ans.* When he reached the hotel he took dinner and forthwith got into his chair and started. He did not even take time to rest.

24 Wait till I have changed my dress, and I will go with you at once.

25 He says he has a very little business, and that as soon as it is finished he will come at once.

26 My aunt was just hitching up the donkey to hull millet, but seeing me coming, she at once unharnessed the donkey and lead (escorted) me into the house.

27 As soon as we knew that a whirlwind was approaching, we at once took in sail and cast anchor, and also battened down the hatchway to prevent the water from pouring in.

Notes.

5 半吐半咽 *Half spitting out, half swallowing*, or 半含半吐, *half holding in, half spitting out*, a fair equivalent of *hum and haw.*

6 The 批 is the comment or verdict of the magistrate on the indictment of the prosecutor. This verdict is usually posted in front of the yamên, or it may be obtained in advance from the under officer having it in charge by paying him a small fee. When a man is accused he always puts in a vindication or counter indictment. Custom allows any man or woman to present a petition or indictment to an officer as he is going along the street in his chair. The party usually kneels in the middle of the street in front of the chair holding up the paper in his or her hand, when the chair-bearers will stop (especially if tipped) and allow of its presentation.

7 晌尖 means the noonday halt for food and rest. 中尖 and 中伙 are both used in the same sense in the South.

15 事緩有變 *A thing delayed may change,*—a book expression. 緩 is used colloquially, only in a few such phrases.

16 當有作無 *To regard that which is as if it were not, to ignore.* The reverse phrase 當無作有 is also used.

21 The use of 之 usually indicates that the expression in which it occurs is derived from books.

23 升轎 is formal and official. The term in *common* use is 上轎.

LESSON CLXIII.

Adversatives of Surprise.

誰料 Who would have thought, to everybody's surprise.

誰知 But behold, what do you think, to my surprise.

不料 Behold, who would have supposed, unexpectedly.

那知 Dear me, but do you know, don't you know.

殊不知 Don't you know, but in fact, whereas in fact. (Bookish.)

豈知 The fact is, but you know,—with a negative—don't you know, you ought to know.

竟不知 Yet after all, but behold.

第一百六十三課

昨[1]日那樣的晴天、誰料今天下這樣的大雨。○我[2]指望勸勸他就好了、誰知越勸他、他越生氣。○我[3]在那裏向東蹲着、不料叫他一把推在坡崖子底下、把手腕子掛了。○爲[4]這麼一點小事、誰料鬧到這麼個分兒。○我[5]當是這二兩年他歸了正道、那知他還是無所不爲。○小[6]時看着他極好、誰料他長成這麼個物件東西。○別[7]人蹧蹋我倒還罷了、不料自己的弟兄、也蹧蹋起來喇。○丁[8]鳳鳴、縣府考都不怎麼樣、誰料院考竟進了個第一。○我[9]打算樸投了他去、他必然有些幫助、誰知他竟反臉無情抹面無情、○自[10]己喫喝嫖賭吹、却不叫後人跟他學、殊不知上梁不正底梁下梁歪、有其父必有其子。○你[11]怎麼拄着枴棍兒呢、答前日我給孫家修理房子、不料從脚手跐脚跳架上掉下來、

TRANSLATION.

1 As clear as it was yesterday, who would have thought that to-day there would be such a heavy rain?

2 I hoped that a little exhortation would make it all right, but, to my surprise, the more I exhorted him the angrier he became.

3 I was squatting there facing the east when, all unexpectelly, with one push he threw me down the bank and sprained my wrist.

4 Who would have thought that a quarrel like this would have arisen from so small a matter?

5 I supposed that during these two years he had reformed; but, dear me! there is still nothing too bad for him to do.

6 When he was a boy he was very promising; who would have thought he would grow up to be such a renegade as this?

7 It is quite enough for others to abuse me; who would have supposed that my own brother would join in the abuse?

8 At the district and prefectural examinations, Ting Fêng Ming was only mediocre, but, to everybody's surprise, at the general examinations, he got his degree and stood first on the roll.

9 I thought when I applied to him, that he would certainly give me some assistance but, to my astonishment, he treated me with cold indifference.

10 He himself indulges in every kind of dissipation, yet does not allow his offspring to imitate him; but don't you know that "when the upper beam is out of true, the lower one also

VOCABULARY.

晴 *Ch'ing*². . . . . . . *Clear*, cloudless; blue sky.

殊 *Shu*¹. To kill, to exterminate; unlike, differ- . . . . ing; really, very.

蹾 *Tun*². . . . . . . *To squat*, to sit on the heels.

掛 *Ch'oă*¹. To pierce, to harpoon; to jar by a . . . . fall, *to sprain*.

物件 *Wu*⁴ *chien*⁴. An article, an object, a thing, ... a concrete something; a blockhead, a good-for-nothing; a *renegade*.

拄 *Chu*³. . . . . . . To prop; *to lean upon*.

枴 *Kwai*³. . . . . A staff, *a crutch*.

枴棍 *Kwai*³ *kun*⁴. . . . . A staff, *a crutch*.

跐 *Ts'ï*³, *ts'ai*³. To tread, to trample; to stand . . . . upon, to set the foot on.

脚手 *Chiaoă*³ *shou*³. . . . A scaffold, scaffolding.

跐脚 *Ts'ï*³ *chioă*³. . . . . . The same:—Note 11.

跳架 *T'iao*⁴ *chia*⁴. . . . . The same.

把腿跌壞了。○看[12]他所穿戴的、眞好像個富家公子、那知道從頭到脚都是借的。○前[13]日指望騙他來、打一頓出出氣、不料轉被他打了個不堪。○他[14]只覺着先生不管他、這是待他好、豈知若是不管他、這正是看不上他、不願意爲他費事。○罷[15]了罷了、我從多年和你交往、竟不知你身上、有這麼大的工夫。○那[16]些沒有見識的人、都以爲富貴在乎風水、殊不知或富或貴、全是上天爲主、於風水毫無相干。○他[17]仗着官銜大、權柄大、就橫行霸道、欺壓黎民、覺着沒有人可制(擋兒)喇、殊不知天外有天、人外有人、叫劉大人一本把他叅倒了。○起[18]先我還存着一個照應他的心、怕他年輕不會辦事、竟不知他

will be askew?" "Like father like son."

11 How is it that you are using a crutch? *Ans.* Day before yesterday I was repairing a house for the Sun family, when what should I do but fall from the scaffolding and hurt my leg?

12 Judging from his dress he appears to be a wealthy young aristocrat, but do you know, the entire suit is borrowed.

13 I hoped when I inveigled him over here the day before yesterday, that I would have the satisfaction of giving him a beating, when, behold, he turned the tables on me and gave me a frightful pommeling.

14 He simply thinks that when the teacher does not punish him, he is treating him kindly, while the fact is, if he does not punish him, it is because he has given him up and is unwilling to take any more trouble with him.

15 Well, well, I have been acquainted with you all these years and yet I never knew you had such skill as this.

16 People of no independence of judgment imagine that riches and honor depend on *fêng-shwei*, whereas in fact, both riches and honor depend on the will of Heaven and have nothing whatever to do with *fêng-shwei*.

17 Presuming on the possession of a high rank and great power, he acted in a reckless and unscrupulous manner, oppressing the people and imagining that nothing could withstand him. But you know, "There is no height that has not a height above it, and no man who has not his superior." Liu Ta-jên by one bill of charges upset him.

公子 *Kung*¹ *tsï*³. Son of a prince; son of a rich family, *an aristocratic young man;* a fop, a swell.

風水 *Fêng*¹ *shwei*³. Geomancy:—Note 16.

相干 *Hsiang*¹ *kan*¹. Involved in, connected with; *to have to do with.*

銜 *Hsien*². To control; *rank,* official title.

官銜 *Kwan*¹ *hsien*². Official title or position, *rank,* office.

欺壓 *Ch'i*¹ *ya*⁴. *To oppress,* to despoil, to wrong; to insult.

叅 *Ts'an*¹. Same as 參.

道行 *Tao*⁴ *hang*². Skill or training in any art or craft or vice.

韻 *Yün*⁴. *A rhyme;* a chord; to rhyme.

詩文 *Shï*¹ *wên*². *Odes and essays,* prose and poetry; literary composition.

嚴緊 *Yien*² *chin*³. *Severe,* exacting, strict.

施教 *Shï*¹ *chiao*⁴. *To teach,* to instruct; to propagate doctrines.

甘苦 *Kan*¹ *k'u*³. Bitter experience, hard lot; sorrow; *straits,* trials.

的道行、比我們都大。○你[19]們都以爲能做八股文章、六韻詩、這就是個好學問兒喇、豈不知天下的學問無數、還有許多比詩文更要緊的、所以光會作詩文、怎敢自稱爲好學問兒呢。○俗[20]語說、嚴師出好徒、因此有的先生、就一味的嚴緊、無論學生大小、說打就打、殊不知凡事都有個中道、若是過於嚴緊、必常招惹學生的氣、這也不是善於施教的法子。○你[21]實在不知窮人的甘苦、我們有錢的人買糴米糧、固然逢買糴就是幾斗幾石、那知那些窮人、就是買幾升幾碗、也是不容易的。

18 At first I had an idea of helping him, fearing that being young he would not know how to manage his affairs, when, behold, his training is superior to that of any of us.

19 You all think that ability to write an essay in eight divisions and a poem in six rhymes, is what constitutes good scholarship, but do you not know that the learning of the world is boundless, and that there are many things more important than odes and essays? How then can he who is proficient only in writing odes and essays count himself a good scholar?

20 The proverb says, "A strict master makes good pupils," hence there are teachers who depend solely upon severity, no matter whether pupils are large or small they ferule them on every occasion, whereas the truth is that in all things there is a golden mean. If one is too severe he will keep his pupils always angry at him, which is not characteristic of good teaching,

21 You really know nothing of the straits of the poor. When we who have money buy grain, we buy several bushels or several tens of bushels, but with these poor people, mind you, to buy even a few gallons or a few pints (bowls) is difficult.

NOTES.

6 The use of 東西 to express contempt is *t'ung-hsing.* 物件 is also used in the same way in Northern and Central Mandarin, and expresses a still stronger contempt. It is applied either to imbecility or to viciousness.

8 Examinations are held in each Fu city twice in three years (the year of the triennial examination in the provincial city being omitted). The first of these examinations is called 歲考, and is both civil and military, including both those who have a degree and those who are seeking a degree. The second examination, called 科考, is only civil, and those who have a degree are not required to attend, save those who propose to compete at the ensuing triennial examination. Both the 歲考 and the 科考 are called 院考. The names of the successful candidates are posted up in order of merit. Hence the first is the most honorable, though the degree is the same.

9 抹面無情 *He stroked his face ignoring all friendship*, that is, he stroked his face with his hand and put on an expression of utter indifference. 反臉無情 *He turned his face away ignoring all friendship.*

10 吃喝嫖賭 These four have long been considered the cardinal vices of dissipation, but China is now compelled to add a fifth; viz., opium smoking, which is what is intended by 吹.

11 There is no *t'ung-hsing* term for scaffolding. In Peking it is called 脚手; in Eastern Shantung, 跐脚; in Chinanfu, 架子; along the Yangtse, 跳架 or 跳板; and doubtless there are still other terms in use.

13 轉 expresses the unexpected "turn" that affairs took.

15 工夫 is put for *skill*, because skill is the result of time spent in practice. Thus used, it nearly always refers to boxing, unless otherwise indicated.

16 風水 *Wind (or air) and water*,—a supposed subtle influence or ether pervading the crust of the earth, which by its movements produces and controls growth and decay, life and death, prosperity and adversity. Those who profess to understand and explain it, draw their stock of terms and phrases chiefly from the Book of Changes.

17 一本 *One volume or book.* 本 or 本章 is used technically of a memorial presented to the Emperor.

18 道行 is borrowed from the language of religious devotees.

第一百六十四課

只[1]要你拿定主意、無論誰也制不了你。○我[2]只當他上學去了、誰知他上南關去聽戲呢。○只[3]用老爺的片子到了、管保立時就開釋開放喇。○只[4]要走的正坐的正、那怕他們怎麼說呢。○孩[5]子們只知好飯可口、那知錢財的艱難。○我[6]只當是要來一個人、誰料來了這麼些呢。○只[7]用請他們喝幾壺、管保他們不能不應允。○你[8]只用不作聲、他還能再找你嗎。○我[9]素常

TRANSLATION.

1 Only make up your mind firmly, and nobody can successfuly oppose you.
2 I supposed that of course he had gone to school, when, behold, he had gone to the south suburb to attend a theater.
3 Simply let your Excellency's card be sent in, and I venture to say he will be liberated at once.
4 Only let your "walk and conversation" be upright, and you need not fear what they say.
5 Children simply know that good food suits their taste, what do they know of the difficulty of getting money?
6 I supposed only one man was coming, who would have thought that all these were coming?
7 Only invite them to drink a few bottles, and I'll warrant you they will not refuse [your request].
8 Just you keep quiet, and there is no

19 Eight is the orthodox number of divisions in a literary essay. These divisions are not announced or numbered, but are rather paragraphs or rhetorical parts. This method of division, which is essential to an essay that would take a degree, is said to have been introduced by 王安石 of the Sung dynasty. The regular form of an ode at the end of an essay, is six verses of four lines each, of which the second and fourth rhyme, the six rhymes also rhyming with each other.

21 甘苦 is formed after the model of quality by opposites (Les. 50), but the stress in this case all falls on the 苦, 甘 serving rather as an intensive.

LESSON CLXIV.

CORRELATIVE PARTICLES.

只要...無論 Only ... no matter, nobody.
只要...那怕 Only ... ... need not fear.
只要...那管 Only ... even if, no matter.
只要...就是 Only ... ... even if.
只用...管保 Only, simply ... ... I'll venture, I'll warrant.
只用...那管 Only ... ... need not care, what care, even if.
只用...自然 Only ... ... naturally, as a matter of course.
只用...還能 Only, just ... ... no danger, [cannot.
只用...無論 Only ... ... no matter.
只當...誰知 Supposed, thought ... ... most unexpectedly, would you believe it.
只當...誰料 Supposed ... ... behold, who would have thought it.
只覺...那知 Supposed ... ... whereas, when in fact.
只知...那知 Only, simply ... ... not, but yet, to my surprise.
只覺...誰料 Supposed ... ... who believe.
只以爲...誰知 Supposed of course ... ... behold, unexpectedly.
只以爲...不料 Supposed of course ... ... unexpectedly, suddenly.
只說...那知 Said, supposed ... ... yet, behold.
只說...歸期 or 歸實 Said, supposed, ... yet notwithstanding, yet after all.

只以為沒有仇人、誰知昨天有人給我貼(糊)了個匿名(沒頭)(白頭)帖。○人[10]只知生前快樂、那知死後受苦。○只[11]要不做虧心事、那怕半夜鬼叫門。○只[12]要問心過得去、那怕閻羅斷是非。○只[13]用自己的男人看中(好)了、那管公婆怎麼樣呢。○只[14]說王大成已經忌(禁)了賭喇、那知一個正月、又輸了四五十吊。○這[15]裏現成的鎖鍊子、只用把他鎖起來、還能跑了他嗎。○他[16]的眼睛、前年疼了一年、只說要疼瞎了、歸實(歸期)還好好的。○樊[17]昌發一點惻隱之心沒有、不知甚麼為憐憫人、只用叫他得了手、那管人家喫虧不喫虧呢。○從[18]這一仗看起來、

danger of his disturbing you again.

9 I have all along supposed I had no enemies, when, behold, yesterday some one assailed me in an anonymous placard.

10 Men only regard the enjoyments of the present life; who considers the suffering of the life to come?

11 Only do not violate conscience, and you need not fear the devil knocking at your door at midnight.

12 Only keep the approval of your own conscience, and you need not fear the judgment of Yien Loă.

13 Only keep the good opinion of your own husband, and you need not care what your father-in-law or mother-in-law may think.

14 It was said that Wang Ta Ch'êng had renounced gambling, and yet during the first month he has again lost forty or fifty thousand [cash].

15 Here is a lock and chain ready to hand; only fasten him with them and he will find it hard to escape.

16 His eyes pained him all the year before last, and it was supposed he would lose his sight, yet after all, they are now entirely well.

17 Fan Ch'ang Fa is destitute of all pity; he does not know what mercy is. Only let him get the advantage, and what does he care whether others suffer or not.

18 It is evident from this one battle that Gen. Hwang has no strategic

VOCABULARY.

釋 *Shï*⁴. To unloose, *to liberate;* to dissipate; to cease; Buddhist.

開釋 *K'ai*¹ *shï*⁴. To release, *to liberate,* to make free.

釋放 *Shï*⁴ *fang*⁴. To let loose, to set free; *to liberate,* to emancipate.

允 *Yün*³. To permit, *to assent,* to promise.

應允 *Ying*¹ *yün*³. *To assent,* to agree, to promise.

素常 *Su*⁴ *ch'ang*². Commonly, ordinarily; *all along,* hitherto.

匿 *Ni*⁴. *To hide,* to abscond; clandestine.

匿名 *Ni*⁴ *ming*². Anonymous.

生前 *Shêng*¹ *ch'ien*². The present life.

虧心 *K'wei*¹ *hsin*¹. To violate conscience, to do what is known to be wrong.

閻 *Yien*². A village gate, a hamlet, a lane.

閻羅 *Yien*² *loă*². The Buddhist Rhadamanthus:—Note 12.

鎖鍊 *Soă*³ *lien*⁴. Lock and chain, shackles.

樊 *Fan*². An enclosed space; *a surname.*

惻 *Ts'ê*⁴. *To pity,* to sympathize with.

隱 *Yin*³. Retired; covered; private; painful, *compassionate;* to keep back, to avoid.

足見黃大人沒有韜畧、只用多少有點韜畧、無論怎麽就打勝了。○他[19]光看書上的講究、只覺着照像是容易事、那知其中的巧處很多。○作[20]官只用有好斷才、又有愛民如子的心、自然必作清官。○都[21]說李光斗難伺候、我看一點不難、只用摸着他的脾氣、無論怎樣就行了。○學[22]問一道、只用肯專心致志、自然必能造就到好處。○你[23]放心罷、只要有我這口氣、到了時候、那管是借是當、也必還你的錢。○我[24]的小兒進了一個武秀才、只說有一百兩銀子就彀了、那知連學規帶請客、花了一百五十多兩。○人[25]那能一點錯處沒有呢、只要知過必改就是了。○我[26]只覺着他是知己的朋友、纔把家眷全

skill. With only a little knowledge in that direction, he could not have failed to win a victory.

19 Simply looking at the directions in the book, he thinks that taking photographs is a very simple affair, whereas it involves a large amount of practical skill.

20 Only let an officer have judicial ability, and a heart that loves the people as his own children, and he will as a matter of course be a good officer.

21 Everybody says that Li Kwang Tou is hard to serve, but I don't see any difficulty; only once understand his peculiarities, and no matter what you do it is all right.

22 Scholarship is a thing in which it is only necessary to have a single and resolute purpose, and you will naturally attain to excellence.

23 Never fear; only let the breath remain in my body, and I will repay you the money when the time comes, even if I have to borrow or pawn.

24 When my younger son got his military degree, he said that if he had one hundred taels it would be sufficient, whereas finally, including fees and feast, he spent more than one hundred and fifty.

25 Where is the man without any faults at all? If only he is willing to reform his errors when he knows them, it is well.

26 I supposed he was a true friend when

惻隱 Sympathy, compassion, *pity*, fellow-feeling.

得手 *Tê*² *shou*³. To get an opportunity, *to get the advantage*.

照像 *Chao*⁴ *hsiang*⁴. To take pictures with a camera, to photograph.

造就 *Tsao*⁴ *chiu*⁴. To build up, to progress, *to attain*, to accomplish.

舵 *To*⁴. . . . . A rudder.

偏離 *P'ien*¹ *li*². To diverge, to turn aside, to deviate, *to incline*.

遼 *Liao*². . . . . Distant, far away.

遼遠 *Liao*² *yüen*³. Far off, *at a distance*, remote.

死屍 *Si*³ *shï*¹. . . . . A dead body, a corpse.

抽身 *Ch'ou*¹ *shên*¹. To start backward; to withdraw suddenly.

NOTES.

2 The addition of 呢 at the end emphasizes the surprise expressed by 誰知

4 走的正, 坐的正 *Moving straight, and sitting straight*; that is, straight, or correct in everything. 走 and 坐 are used figuratively to comprehend the active and passive aspects of life.

9 匿名帖 *An anonymous placard*, also called a 沒頭帖 (usually read as if written 木頭帖), *a headless card*; that is, one without a superscription.

12 閻羅, or more frequently, 閻王 or 閻君 *the ruler and judge of the lower world*,—a Buddhist divinity introduced into China during the Sung dynasty. The

託付他、誰料他存心不艮、竟把我的老婆孩子都賣了呢。○人27心主宰萬事、就如舵管船一般、只用舵正當、船就自然一直向前、若是舵不正當、船就自然偏離左右。○你28先頭裏怎麼在潤喜跟前、說他爺爺的不是呢、答我只當是他走了、誰知道他在鍋臺旁邊 竈空裏 竈橫頭蹾着呢。○姜29似山上關東、十五六年沒有音信、他妻子只以爲他死了、去年秋裏纔嫁了人、不料他今年又回來喇。○30老 遼遠的望着、我只當是行路的、在路旁睡 躺着歇息、誰料走到跟前、還是一個死屍、嚇得我抽身就跑了。○這31個一棍子、那個一石頭、打了有一袋菸的工夫、我只說是要打壞喇、誰知他爬起來、揚揚不睬就走了。

I entrusted my family entirely to him, and yet, contrary to all anticipation, he proved a treacherous villain, and actually sold both my wife and children.

27 The heart controls everything just as the rudder controls the ship. Only let the rudder be amidships, and the vessel will naturally go straight forward; but if the rudder be not amidships, the vessel will naturally incline to one side or the other.

28 Why did you a little while ago in Jun Hsi's presence find fault with his grandfather? *Ans.* I quite supposed he had gone, when behold he was squatting in the chimney corner.

29 Chiang Sï Shan went to Manchuria and nothing was heard of him for fifteen or sixteen years. His wife supposed of course he was dead and only last fall married again, when this year he most unexpectedly returned.

30 Looking from a distance, I just supposed it was a traveller lain down at the roadside to rest, but when I came near, behold, it was a dead body. I was so frightened that I drew back with a start and ran away.

31 They beat and pelted him, some with sticks and some with stones, for as much as ten minutes. I quite expected he would be badly disabled, but, to my surprise, he got up and walked off as if nothing had happened.

---

people often speak of 十殿閻君, *the rulers of the ten temples;* that is, one for each of the ten court rooms of the Buddhist hell. The fifth (五殿閻君) is often spoken of as the fiercest of the ten.

14 只說 *Only say;* that is, the only talk heard on the subject was that he had reformed. The first month is the great time for gambling. Many who resist temptation all the rest of the year fall at this season.

15 跑了他 It would seem as if 他 were the object of the verb. It is not, however, but, notwithstanding its position, remains the subject. The whole clause is equivalent to 他還能跑了嗎.

20 愛民如子, *to love the people as one's own children,* is the acme of excellence in an officer. 淸官 means properly, *an upright officer who does not take bribes,* but is often used, as here, to include all the excellencies of an able and faithful officer.

24 When one gets a degree he has to pay the 老師 a graduation fee, more or less according to his ability, and custom requires him to make a feast for his friends, so that altogether, getting a degree is an expensive piece of good fortune.

25 知過必改, *knowing a fault will certainly reform,* is here quoted as a ready made book phrase.

26 存心不艮 *The purpose of the heart not good.* 不艮 is emphatic, and the phrase always refers to some deceitful or treacherous purpose.

27 主宰 is here used as a verb. The comparison assumes water free from currents and the wind "dead aft."

28 竈空. The space or corner at the side of the cooking range.

31 這個一棍子那個一石頭 *This one a stick and that one a stone;* that is, some with sticks and some with stones. 一袋菸的工夫 *The time of smoking one pipe.* This is often used as a measure of time, and means *about* ten minutes. 揚揚不睬 *Tossing the head in a careless way, putting on an air of indifference.*

第一百六十五課

你[1]纔吃了飯、又要什麼吃嗎。○要[2]知將來、但看已往。○我[3]們正要
去見你、不料你竟來喇。○待/若[4]要知道禮貌/性、總得/總要長到十來多歲。○
昨[5]天晚上正在半夜的時候、忽然有人喊叫有賊、把我驚的再沒
睡着。○要[6]知心腹事、但聽口中言。○孩[7]子纔不哭了、你又鬪弄/惹他、
眞眞討厭。○先[8]生正在位上寫字、不料從頂棚/仰棚/仰板窟窿裏、掉下一條
大長蟲/蛇來。○這[9]門親事待/若要成、必得叫他們兩個打對面/照面。○若[10]
要叫我與他和好、/改好/取和除非他親自來認錯。○你[11]妹妹把你外甥送喇、
現在必得你去保他、纔能出來。○這[12]場官司若要翻、非離投奔馬
老爺不行。○小[13]姑娘正在睡着/睡沉的時候、忽然狗咬/叫了一聲、把他吵/聒/鬧
醒了、他就直哭不歇着/歇息。○放[14]空船不能十分穩當、若要穩當、總得

Translation.

1 You have just eaten your dinner, and are you already wanting something to eat?
2 To know the future, it is only necessary to look at the past.
3 We were just on the point of going to see you, when, to our surprise, here you really come.
4 To understand etiquette requires an age of considerably over ten years.
5 Last night, just at midnight, some one suddenly called out, "Thieves!" and gave me such a fright that I could not get asleep again.
6 If you would know the thoughts of a man's heart, just listen to the words of his mouth.
7 The child had but just quit crying, and here you are teasing him again. Really you are too exasperating.
8 While the teacher was at his desk writing, a huge snake unexpectedly fell down from a hole in the ceiling.
9 If this match is to be brought about, it will be necessary for the two to see each other.
10 If I am to make peace with him, there is no way but for him to come in person and acknowledge his fault.
11 Your sister having accused your nephew of undutifulness, in order to procure his release, it will be necessary for you to go and become security for him.
12 To get a reversal of the verdict in this case, it will be necessary to secure the services of Ma Lao-yie.
13 While the little girl was sleeping soundly, the dog suddenly gave a

LESSON CLXV.

Correlative Particles.

纔 ... 又 Just......again, now, already.

若要 or 待要 ... 總得 If, in order to......must, necessary.

若要 or 待要 ... 必得 If, in order to......must, necessary.

若要 or 待要 ... 除非 or 非離 If, in order to......must, necessary, no way but.

要知 ... 但看 In order to know...... only necessary to look.

要知 ... 但聽 In order to know...... only necessary to listen.

正 ... 忽然 Just when, while...... suddenly, unexpectedly.

正 ... 不料 Just when, while...... suddenly, unawares, behold.

正 ... 可巧 Just when, while...... when luckily.

必得 ... 纔 It is necessary, must...in order [that.

上滿了載。○魯[15]鏡心那眞是一個名醫、就是架子太大、若要請他看病、至少也得二兩銀子的贄見禮（藥敬）、還必得用轎子去接他、他纔肯來。○車[16]王爺正在拉車赶脚的時候、不料皇上的旨意到了、叫他作鐵帽子王。○若[17]要人不知、除非己不爲。○大[18]家正在那裏免三去四的吆喝、不料衙役從後門裏進去、把賭錢的和看熱鬧兒（眼兒）（邊局）的、都拿了去喇。○這[19]個灰色雞、眞不填還（還債）人、纔下了十來個蛋、又要賴菢菢窩。○夜[20]間正要出汗的工夫、不料他把被都掀了、所以今天不但不見好强、倒越發見重喇。○必[21]得先種下、然後纔能收成、你若不先愛人、怎能指望人愛你呢。○前[22]日我對一位先生講道理、他也批駁我、我也批駁他、正說得高興的時候、不料從旁邊來了一個

bark and woke her up, and she has cried ever since.

14 An empty ship cannot be perfectly steady; to secure steadiness it must be filled with cargo.

15 Lu Ching Hsin is indeed a noted physician, but he holds himself quite too high. If you want to call him, you must give him a present of at least two taels, and also send a chair for him, or he will not come.

16 When the Carter King was following his calling as a carter, there suddenly came to hand an imperial edict creating him an Iron Crown Prince.

17 If you would not have others know of it, the only way is not to do it.

18 Just when the whole company were noisily engaged at the game, the police unexpectedly came in by a back door and arrested both gamblers and lookers on.

19 This gray chicken does not pay for her keeping. She has only laid ten or a dozen eggs and now she wants to sit.

20 During the night, just as the perspiration was about to break out on him, he unexpectedly threw off the quilts, so that to-day he is not only no better but on the contrary is worse.

21 You must sow before you can reap. If you do not first love others, how can you expect that others will love you?

22 Day before yesterday I was talking with a gentleman on the doctrine, and we were having quite a spirited discussion, but, just when the interest was at its height, a drunken fellow

VOCABULARY.

禮性 *Li³ hsing⁴*. . . . . . Politeness, etiquette. (s.)

鬪弄 *Tou⁴ lung⁴*. To aggravate, *to tease;* to irritate, to chafe. [Note 21.

仰棚 *Yang³ p'êng²*. . . . . . A ceiling. Les. 148

照面 *Chao⁴ mien⁴*. To see face to face:—Note 9.

投奔 *T'ou² pên⁴*. To appeal to, to depend upon, *to ask help of.*

放空 *Fang⁴ k'ung¹*. To go or travel empty or unloaded (as a ship, cart, etc.).

贄 *Chï⁴*. A present to a superior; a fee to a teacher.

贄見禮 *Chï⁴ chien⁴ li³*. A present or a fee to a teacher or to a professor of any art.

看眼 *K'an⁴ yien³*. . . . . . To be a spectator.

填還 *T'ien² hwan²*. *To repay,* to reimburse; to requite.

還債 *Hwan² chai⁴*. To pay a debt, *to discharge an obligation.*

賴菢 *Lai⁴ pao⁴*. . . . . . To sit on an empty nest.

批駁 *P'i¹ poă²*. To reverse the decision of a lower court; to rebut, *to refute.*

醉漢 *Tswei⁴ han⁴*. . . . . A drunken man.

醉鬼漢、嘴裏胡言亂語的、把那位先生衝走喇。○古23語說、量小非君子、無毒不丈夫、又說打蛇不死、轉背傷人、所以若要免去後患、必得給他一個剪斬草除根。○今24天我打張芙蓉門前走、見他穿的衣裳十分襤褸、頭上梳着一個小鬏髻、還戴着兩枝芍藥花、剛纔出了大門、看見我又回去喇。○李25憲章眞是苦命、一輩子生了一個兒子小廝男娃、正在有用的時候、忽然得病死了。○同26治四年八月間、我和李作福、在關東被紅鬍子擄去、坐在車上、我們正打算怎樣可以逃命、可巧遇見了李作福的一個親戚、是早年被紅鬍子擄的、那時已經當了頭腦、他向我們使丟了一個眼色、叫我們不要言語、後來到晚上、他就暗暗的把我們放了。

happened along and, by his incoherent talk, drove the gentleman away.

23 The old saying is, "He who has a narrow mind cannot be a superior man; he who cannot rise above his feelings cannot be manly;" also, "Strike a serpent without killing it, and it will turn back and wound you:" therefore if you would avoid trouble hereafter, you must finish him root and branch.

24 To-day as I went by Chang Fu Jung's door, I saw her in a very ragged dress, with her hair done up in a little knot and wearing in it a couple of peonies. Just as she came out of the street door, she saw me and turned and went in again.

25 Li Hsien Chang has truly had a hard lot. In all his life he has had only one son, and just when he came to be of some use, he sudddenly took sick and died.

26 In the fourth year of T'ung Chï in the eighth month, I and Li Tsoă Fu were taken captive in Manchuria by the red-bearded robbers. We were sitting on the cart, and just planning how we might escape with our lives, when, luckily, we met with a relative of Li Tsoă Fu's who had been taken captive by the red-beards years ago, and was at that time a leader among them. He gave us a wink not to say anything, and afterwards at night he secretly let us go.

轉背 *Chwan*⁴ *pei*⁴. To turn round; *to turn back.*
芙蓉 *Fu*² *jung*². . . . The rose mallow.
襤 *Lan*². . . . Torn in shreds, ragged.
褸 *Lü*³. . . . The lapel of a coat; *soiled*, dirty.
襤褸 *Ragged*, tattered; worn out, soiled.
鬏 *Chwa*¹. The hair done up in a knot on top of the head.
髻 *Chi*⁴. . . . The tuft or knot of a woman's hair.
鬏髻 The hair done up in a tuft or knot.
芍 *Shwoă*², *shao*². . . . The peony.
芍藥 *Shao*² *yao*⁴. The roots of the peony; *the peony.*
憲 *Hsien*⁴. . . . To govern; a law, a precept. (w.)
逃命 *T'ao*² *ming*⁴. To flee for life; *to escape with life.*
頭腦 *T'ou*² *nao*³. A chieftain, *a leader*, a ring-leader.

NOTES.

3 The use of 覺 implies that the person referred to had been expected, but for some reason his coming had been despaired of.

5 睡着 Here, as also in the thirteenth sentence, 着 is used emphatically.

9 打個照面 *Strike a face to face*: that is, to see each other face to face, though not necessarily to converse together. It is not often that this is demanded on the occasion of a first marriage, but it generally is in the case of

第一百六十六課

晴[1]了天再走罷、今日還是霧騰騰的。
○大[2]街上亂轟轟的、不如從小街上
走。○要[3]麻俐俐的做、不要帶作不作推前擦後
的。○這[4]個肉到底硬刺刺争争的、沒大煮
好。○裕[5]德號的錢疲拉拉的、一樣的
價不賣給他。○二[6]嫂子走起來劤快搗
搗的、腳底下實在麻俐。○眼[7]睜睜的
我看見是他拿去了、他還翻眼不承
認。○你[8]走的喘嘘嘘的喝凉呵呵的、吃冷水不怕
受病嗎。○熱[9]騰騰的飯、我們喫點兒

TRANSLATION.

1 Do not go until it clears up. It is still quite foggy to-day.

2 The main street is so much crowded that it would be better to go by a side street.

3 Do it up promptly and don't dilly-dally.

4 This meat after all is tough as leather; it is not sufficiently boiled.

5 Money is so hard to collect of Yü Tê, that, the price being the same, we will sell to others rather than to them.

6 Our second brother's wife has an energetic step and moves round with wonderful celerity.

7 It was he who took it. I saw him do it, as plainly as possible, and yet he turns round and denies it.

8 Are you not afraid that drinking cold water when all out of breath from running will make you sick?

9 Here is steaming hot rice. Had we

a second marriage. 照面 is rarely used, save in this special connection. In the North 對面 replaces it.

11 When a son becomes incorrigibly undutiful, his parents may accuse him to the magistrate and demand his punishment. This is to 送. It may be done by a father or widowed mother, or by a grandfather or widowed grandmother, or, in the case of an orphan, by a paternal uncle. It always results in severe punishment, and, in the case of a parent who disowns his son, may cause him to be put to death.

15 架子太大 *Framework too large*; that is, he puts on too much style, is too pretentious.

16 At the founding of the present dynasty, the title of prince was conferred on the eight leaders who assisted in founding the dynasty. In token that this title was to be hereditary and perpetual, an iron cap or crown was given to each, and they were in consequence called 鐵帽子王. In the course of time, one of these hereditary kings was guilty of crimes which cost him his life, and having no son, his title was given to his nearest collateral heir. This good fortune fell on a young man who, at the time the imperial edict arrived, was serving as a carter, and was in consequence dubbed, 車王爺.

18 免三去四 This phraseology has its explanation in the gambling game they were playing.

23 無毒不丈夫 *Without severity* (poison) *not manly*; that is, he who is not able to restrain his sympathies and disregard trifles, has not the strength of a true manhood. 打蛇不死 is the same as 打不死蛇, the object being inserted before the qualifier. 剪草除根 *Clip off the grass and remove the root, to destroy utterly*—"*root and branch.*"

26 紅鬍子, *redbeards*, is the term commonly applied to the bands of predatory robbers that abound in Manchuria. They wear false red beards as a mask, and to give them an appearance of fierceness.

LESSON CLXVI.

SPECIAL DUPLICATE ADJUNCTS.

騰 To ascend,—as a doublet, imparts the idea of *rising* and *expanding*.

霧騰騰的 Ascending vapor; foggy, misty.

熱騰騰的 Steaming hot.

慢騰騰的 Slow, deliberate, pompous.

轟 To rush,—as a doublet, imparts the idea of *rushing and noise*. Some would prefer to write 鬨.

亂轟轟的 The confused noise of many coming and going, bustling, crowded.

臭轟轟的 Very rank, stinking, noisome.

鬧轟轟的 Thronged, crowded, bustling.

拉 To drag,—as a doublet, imparts the idea of *dragging after* or *extending beyond proper limits.*

疲拉拉的 Dilatory, lax, paying money in driblets.

低拉拉的 Overcome with grief, the eyes brimming with tears.

酸拉拉的 Shuddering, aghast, flesh creeping.

再走不好嗎。○你10老實實的罷、不要動手動脚的。○你11看他睖睜睜的、越說他、他越不服。○他12身上雖是滾熱、頭上却是汗露津露津的。○那13個是李長庚的兒子、答就是那個小點點的。○外14邊冷颼颼的、快給孩子再套上件衣裳罷。○孫15先生不不矜慌不不躁忙、說起話來慢騰悠騰悠的、眞是一個文雅人。○我16不願意從那裏經過、那裏靠大糞場、臭轟轟的。○他17雖然老了、身上還壯實實的、就和一個小小夥漢子子一樣。○用18他的秤、稱一百斤、用咱們的秤、低拉拉的九十五斤。○連19羣子就是好唱、整天家嘴裏唱哼謳唧謳唧的。○你20嘗着什麼味兒、答沒有別的味兒、就是苦參

not better eat a little before we go?

10 Behave yourself, and stop fidgeting with your hands and feet.

11 See what a sullen look he has. The more he is reproved the more insubordinate he becomes.

12 Although his body is very feverish, his head is quite moist.

13 Which one is Li Ch'ang Kêng's son? *Ans.* That very little fellow is he.

14 It is quite chilly out of doors; put some more clothes on the child immediately.

15 Mr. Sun is very self-possessed, and in conversation he speaks with deliberation. He is truly a man of refinement.

16 I do not like to go by that road. It passes close by the compost yards, where there is a most noisome smell.

17 Although he is old, he is still quite vigorous—just like a young man.

18 With his scales, it weighs one hundred catties; with ours, the beam is decidedly low at ninety-five.

19 Lien Ch'ün-tsï is very fond of singing; he is all the time humming at something.

20 What flavor do you get from it? *Ans.* Nothing more than a slightly bitter taste.

低拉拉的 Decidedly low, drooping.

實 Solid, real,—as a doublet, imparts the idea of *reality, solidity.*

老實實的 Quiet, well-behaved, steady.

壯實實的 Quite strong, vigorous, robust.

結實實的 Quite firm, strong, robust.

麻俐俐的 Quickly, promptly, briskly,—imparts the idea of *celerity.*

硬爭爭的 Quite tough, gelatinous; obstinate,—imparts the idea of *resistance.* (C. & N.)

睖睜睜的 A sullen look, a glare, a sinister expression,—imparts the idea of *staring.*

眼睜睜的 In plain sight, before the eyes.

孤單單的 All alone, solitary, lonely,—imparts the idea of *singleness.*

喘嘘嘘的 Quite out of breath, panting,—imparts the idea of *breathing hard.* (C. & N.)

喘呵呵的 The same. (C. & S.)

毛伈伈的 Shuddering, flesh creeping, hair on end,—imparts the idea of *creeping.*

劤搗搗的 Quite vigorous, energetic, buxom,—imparts the idea of *stepping firmly.* (S.)

快搗搗的 Quite prompt, energetic, brisk.

小點點的 Quite small, very little, wee, tiny,—imparts the idea of *smallness.*

汗露露的 Perspiring freely, quite moist,—imparts the idea of *dew, moisture.* (C. & S.)

汗津津的 The same.

冷颼颼的 Whistling cold, quite chilly, raw,—imparts the idea of *blowing, rushing.*

慢悠悠的 Quite slowly, deliberate, self-possessed,—imparts the idea of *enduring.* (C. & S.)

唱謳謳的 Singing in a low voice, humming; musical,—imparts the idea of *monotonous sound.* (C.)

苦參參的 Bitter as ginseng, decidedly bitter, slightly bitter,—used by way of comparison.

參的。○你[21]褡子褡褳裏裝的什麼東西、鼓膨膨飽鼓鼓的。○我[22]吃這新玉米包米六穀餅子、甜甘甘絲絲的、艮硬硬硬爭爭的、給我饅頭也不換。○如[23]今時興這種大袖子、長山山拖拖的纔好喇。○叫[24]你淨乾立落乾立落的得二百吊錢、經紀用錢一概不管、這還不好嗎。○你[25]身體這樣軟弱、總要下力喫飯、喫的結實實的、我纔放心。○興[26]隆號的買賣實在興旺、不論多喒、門市上總是鬧轟轟的。○上[27]無父母、下無妻子、就是孤單單伶伶的我一個人。○不[28]知多少人來保他、只看見芽杈杈豎杈杈直豎豎的跪了一堂。○孫[29]大哥一輩子生了十個孩子、一個也沒養活、昨天在這裏說起來、眼裏酸拉拉的、眞可憐嗟嘆人。○這[30]個

21 What have you in your wallet that bulges it out so much?

22 According to my taste, these new-corn cakes are very sweet and gelatinous. I would not exchange them even for wheat bread.

23 These large sleeves are very fashionable at present. They should be real long by rights.

24 If you realize two hundred thousand cash clear of all incidental expenses, would you not be doing very well?

25 As you are so weak, you should try to eat more. I cannot be satisfied until a good appetite has made you strong and well.

26 The Hsing Lung is certainly doing a very prosperous business. The door is thronged at all hours.

27 I am all alone in the world, without either parents or family.

28 I do not know how many came to go his security. I simply saw a miscellaneous crowd kneeling in the court-room.

29 Brother Sun has had in all ten children born to him, and has not succeeded in bringing up one of them. Yesterday when he was here, it was truly pitiable to see his eyes fill with tears when he spoke of it.

30 This bèche-de-mer is stewed till it is

鼓膨膨的 Quite distended, plump, round,—imparts the idea of *fullness*.

飽鼓鼓的 Bulging, distended, big-bellied,—imparts the idea of *expansion*.

甜甘甘的 Quite sweet, very sweet,—imparts the idea of *sweetness*.

艮硬硬的 Gluey, gelatinous; tough, leathery,—imparts the idea of *resistance*.

長山山的 Quite long, lengthy,—used by way of comparison. (C. & N.)

長拖拖的 Quite long, trailing, dragging,—imparts the idea of *trailing after*. (C. & S.)

淨乾乾的 Clear of, exempt from, entire,—imparts the idea of *exemption from*. (C. & N.)

淨立立的 Clear of encumbrance, exempt, complete,—imparts the idea of *standing alone*. (C.)

淨落落的 Clear of encumbrance, complete,—imparts the idea of *unembarrassed*. (S.)

孤伶伶的 Quite alone, solitary,—imparts the idea of *lonely*.

芽杈杈的 Studded with points or branches, bristling, uneven, serried,—imparts the idea of *forked*. (N.)

豎杈杈的 Studded with branches or spines, uneven, rugged. (C. & S.)

直豎豎的 Studded with upright points or projections, serried,—imparts the idea of *upright*. (C. & S.)

年輕輕的 Quite young,—imparts the idea of *lightness*.

齊截截的 All at once, all alike, uniform,—imparts the idea of *evenness*. (N.)

齊雙雙的 One after the other, in close succession,—imparts the idea of *duplication*.

勝巴巴的 Quite overcome (with fear), shuddering. (S.)

哼唧唧的 Humming; grunting, groaning.

甜絲絲的 Quite sweet, deliciously sweet.

海參燉的艮硬硬硬爭爭的、美之極喇。○秦[31]悅德眞是好命、還年輕輕的、就有齊截截雙雙的三個兒子。○若[32]是屋裏有個死屍、人進去就覺着毛伈伈伈拉拉膨巴巴的、可見人死如虎、虎死如羊、○楊[33]三那塊地、到底是賣給朱六咯、昨天晚上、我到朱六家裏去、他們剛纔彊纔寫完了文書文契、中人正在那裏畫押、答叫我、我也是賣給朱六、眼睜睜的多賣二十吊錢、穀過兩個多月的日子、還能死死等着停着、叫自己本家勒掯了去嗎。

a perfectly firm jelly—a most delicious dish.

31 Ch'in Yüe Tê is a very fortunate man. While yet quite young he has three sons of nearly the same size.

32 If there is a corpse in a room, one feels a shudder when he enters; from which we see the truth of the saying, "A dead man is like a tiger, and a dead tiger is like a lamb."

33 That piece of land of Wang the Third's, was after all sold to Chu the Sixth. Yesterday evening I called on Chu the Sixth, and they had just finished writing the deed and the witnesses were about to sign it. *Ans.* If it were I, I also would sell to Chu the Sixth. Manifestly the price is higher by twenty thousand cash,—enough to support a family for over two months. Why should he wait indefinitely for one of his own family to take it off his hands for less than it's worth?

VOCABULARY.

颼 *Sou*¹... Chilly, the sound of the wind, rustling.
悠 *Yiu*¹. Sorrowful; far-reaching, remote; reiterated.
謳 *Ou*¹.... To sing, to hum; a song, a ditty.
膨 *P'êng*².... Fat, bloated, puffed out.
杈 *Ch'a*⁴. A pitchfork; the crotch of a tree; a prong; a stump.
翻眼 *Fan*¹ *yien*³. To change looks, *to play false*, to back out of.
承認 *Ch'êng*² *jên*⁴. *To admit*, to own up, to confess.
小夥子 *Hsiao*³ *hwoa*³ *tsï*³. *A youth*, a stripling, a young chap.
小漢子 *Hsiao*³ *han*⁴ *tsï*³. A boy, a youth, *a young man.*
玉米 *Yü*⁴ *mi*³....... Indian corn:—Note 22.
包米 *Pao*¹ *mi*³....... The same.
六穀 *Liu*⁴ *ku*³....... The same.
艮 *Kên*³.... Tough, gluey, *gelatinous.* Also *kên*⁴.
用錢 *Yung*⁴ *ch'ien*². A middleman's fee,—usually a percentage on the price.
興旺 *Hsing*¹ *wang*⁴. To prosper, *to flourish*, to thrive.
門市 *Mên*² *shi*⁴. The street frontage of a store or shop.
嗟 *Chie*¹....... To sigh, to lament.
嗟嘆 *Chie*¹ *t'an*⁴. To sigh, to lament, to regret, *to pity.*
悅 *Yüe*⁴....... Gratified, pleased, delighted.
伈 *Shên*³. Aghast, horrified; *shuddering*, the flesh creeping.
文契 *Wên*² *ch'i*⁴....... An indenture, a deed.
中人 *Chung*¹ *jên*².... A middleman, a witness.
押 *Ya*². To sign; to affix a seal; a signature, a mark:—see *ya*¹.
畫押 *Hwa*⁴ *ya*².... To sign a legal document.

NOTES.

3 推前擦後 *To shirk the front and shuffle to the rear*; that is, *to hesitate, to dilly-dally, to vacillate.*

7 翻眼. *To change the eyes*, that is, to change an expression of approval or assent to one of disapproval or dissent, hence *to go back on, to back out of, to play false.*

15 不慌不忙 *Not excited not hurried, self-possessed.* Sedateness and sobriety are essential to the reputation of a Chinese scholar or literary man.

16 臊 is very expressive as applied to a stench. We have something analogous to it in the term "noisome."

第一百六十七課

凉[1]亭上風颼颼的、不如上那裏去坐坐。○這[2]棵白梅花素淡淡的、不及那棵紅色的現活。○做[3]文章須要顯亮亮的、不要蒙頭蓋臉(面膪)。○不[4]要太大、小可可的就好。○這[5]家子的白麪、調(和)起來青(黑)須(碌)須(碌)的一點不白。○成[6]天家在家裏、死挺(獃)挺(獃)的不動彈、還能有飯吃嗎。○上[7]海眞是一個大碼頭、整年的沒有一時不熱鬧鬧的。○這[8]種菓子酸溜溜的、甜蜜(絲)蜜(絲)的、實在好喫。○纔[9]

TRANSLATION.

1 It is cool and airy in the summer house. We would better go and sit there.

2 This white almond flower is chaste and plain; not so showy as that red one.

3 In writing an essay you should be perspicuous, and not use an obscure, ambiguous style.

4 I don't want it too large; just a neat fit is the thing.

5 The flour from this firm becomes dark when mixed. It is not at all white.

6 Lying round home all the time and not making the least effort,—it is no wonder you have nothing to eat.

7 Shanghai is indeed a great metropolis of trade. There is no time in the whole year when it is not full of bustle.

8 This species of fruit is both tart and sweet, and is very delicious.

22 The Chinese do not prize a light and dry corn bread, but rather that of a moist and gummy consistency. In the North, Indian corn is also called 棒子 *pang*[4] *tsï*[3].

24 經紀 *An expert.* Nearly all kinds of buying and selling are done through the hands of a professional broker or expert, who of course gets a fee—generally from the seller, but in some cases from the buyer as well.

28 All persons are required to kneel in the presence of a magistrate. Such as have a degree are nearly always invited to rise and stand. Others also may be invited to rise and stand at the pleasure of the magistrate.

29 養活 usually forms a phrase meaning *to nourish*, and, as usual in such cases, the stress is thrown on the first character. Here, however, the words are used independently, and without special stress on either.

31 好命 *A happy fate, fortunate, lucky.* To have several sons while yet young, is the height of good fortune, chiefly because it secures a support in old age.

32 人死如虎虎死如羊 *A man dead is like a tiger*, because after death the soul has power to take vengeance; *a tiger dead is like a lamb*, because he has no soul. This saying seems to have come down from a time anterior to the advent of the doctrine of transmigration in China. It shows the instinctive belief in the future existence of the *human* soul.

33 Signing a Chinese legal document does not consist in writing the name, but in making or affixing a mark. This mark is usually a simple cross, but scholars frequently write as their mark a monogram of some motto, as 正大光明, which is the one most widely used. 叫我, as here used, is equivalent to, *if it were I, if I were in his place.* 死 is used as an adverb meaning *indefinitely*.

LESSON CLXVII.

SPECIAL DUPLICATE ADJUNCTS.

This lesson concludes the subject of duplicate adjuncts. For additional list see Supplement.

風颼颼的 Airy, breezy; chilly,—imparts the idea of *blowing*.

顯亮亮的 Quite plain or clear, manifest, perspicuous,—imparts the idea of *light*.

高亮亮的 Quite high, light and airy. (c.)

小可可的 A neat fit, close-fitting,—imparts the idea of *perfect conformity*.

青須須的 Somewhat dark, blackish, discolored,—imparts the idea of *somewhat*.

黑碌碌的 Quite dark, blackish,—imparts the idea of *discoloration*. (s.)

死挺挺的 Quite motionless, supine, inflexible,—imparts the idea of *rigidity*.

死獃獃的 Listless, lumpish, dronish,—imparts the idea of *listlessness*.

癡獃獃的 Vacant, silly, puzzle-headed.

來的這個人在學嗎、怎麼說話文縐縐的呢。○看[10]你臉上嫩俏和俏和的、實在不像五十多歲的人。○外[11]邊鬧嚷嚷的、有甚麼事呢。○李[12]三今天喝醉了罵街、叫人把頭打的血淋淋的、看見真是肉麻。○做[13]的時候多擱上點鹽、鹹津湛津湛的可以多吃幾頓。○剛[14]纔喝了一些稀飯、涼森陰森陰的實在舒坦。○不[15]要炒煳了、炒的黃嫩朧生嫩朧生的就得喇。○他[16]在關東當紅鬍子、把性子縱創野喇、如今來家還是橫虎丟霸虎丟霸的。○預[17]備得現成成的材

9 Is this man who has just come a graduate? How is it that his conversation has such a literary flavor.

10 Your soft, fresh face certainly does not look like that of a man over fifty years of age.

11 What is going on that there is such a clamor outside?

12 Li San got drunk to-day and began reviling on the street, when some one pommeled his head till it was dripping with blood. The sight of it was enough to make one's flesh creep.

13 In making it, put in a liberal allowance of salt; being thoroughly salt, it will last the longer.

14 I have just eaten some rice gruel—quite cold, and I feel very much refreshed.

15 Do not parch them till they are burned. If parched a light yellow, it will be sufficient.

16 He was a robber while in Manchuria, which developed in him a savage disposition, and even now since he has come home, he acts in a reckless way.

熱鬧鬧的 Bustling, busy, crowded,—imparts the idea of *bustle*.

甜蜜蜜的 Sweet as honey, quite sweet,—used by way of comparison. (C. & S.)

文縐縐的 Having a literary wrinkle, pedantic, professorial. The primary sense of 文 suggests the use of 縐, the expression being figurative and, as here used, slightly humorous.

嫩俏俏的 Soft, fresh, youthful, sprightly,—imparts the idea of *beauty*.

鬧嚷嚷的 Clamorous, the noise of wrangling,—imparts the idea of *vociferation*.

血淋淋的 Dripping with blood, bloody, blood trickling down,—imparts the idea of *dripping*.

鹹湛湛的 Quite salt,—imparts the idea of *moisture*. (C. & S.)

涼森森的 Quite cool, cold; cooling; chilly,—imparts the idea of *coolness*.

涼陰陰的 Quite cool; cooling; chilly,—imparts the idea of *cold*. (S.)

黃嫩嫩的 Pale yellow, tinged with yellow,—imparts the idea of *tenderness*. (N.)

黃朧朧的 Pale or light yellow,—imparts the idea of *dim light*. (C.)

橫虎虎的 Reckless, violent, overbearing,—imparts the idea of *fierceness*.

橫丟丟的 Reckless, turbulent, violent,—imparts the idea of *recklessness*. (C.)

橫霸霸的 Reckless, overbearing, domineering,—imparts the idea of *usurpation*. (S.)

現成成的 All prepared, ready to hand,—imparts the idea of *readiness*.

素淡淡的 Quite plain, modest, chaste,—imparts the idea of *plainness and insipidity*.

冷淡淡的 Quite cool, distant, unfriendly.

大發發的 Quite large, extra large,—imparts the idea of *increase*. (C. & N.)

大樣樣的 Very large, ample,—imparts the idea of *style*.

大道道的 Quite large, broad, wide,—imparts the idea of a *highway*. (S.)

肉頹頹的 Gross, expressionless, lubberly,—imparts the idea of *grossness*.

氣誖誖的 Flushed with anger, bursting with rage,—imparts the idea of *fierce anger*.

氣忿忿的 Very angry, flushed with anger, imparts the idea of *irritation*.

氣恨恨的 Very angry, scowling, fuming,—imparts the idea of *hatred*.

現活活的 Gay, showy, flashy,—imparts the idea of *life*, *activity*.

料、你當是要做還費事嗎。○自[18]從叫我說了那一回、他逢見了我、就冷淡淡的。○小[19]孩子一天長似一天、所以給他做衣裳、總要大(樣樣/發發/道道)的。○我[20]看他肉穠穠的一個臉、癡獃獃兩個眼、半點也不帶聰明。○你[21]沒見他氣(諍諍/忿忿/恨恨)的、在照壁前頭站着嗎。○已[22]經五十多歲的人、還紫裏的(現活活/華奢奢)的。○我[23]看見他笑睞睞的下來了、必是有點喜事。○他[24]看見人家中舉會試、心裏也(急齁齁/熱腸腸/眼巴巴)的、然而自已却不肯用功。○我[25]昨日碰見一個狼、幾乎叫他喫了、

17 Having the material all prepared, do you suppose it will be any great trouble to make it?

18 Ever since I reproved him that time, he always treats me coldly when he meets me.

19 Children grow larger every day, so that in making their clothes it is better to make them quite large.

20 His face appears quite gross, and his eyes have a vacant expression. He is without the slightest indication of intelligence.

21 Did you not see him standing just in front of the screen ready to burst with rage?

22 Over fifty years old, and yet tricked out in such a showy style!

23 I saw him coming out smiling pleasantly. He must have met with some good fortune.

24 When he sees some one attain the degree of *chü-jên* or *chin-shï*, his heart is filled with eager longing, nevertheless he is not willing to apply himself to study.

華奢奢的 Showy, gaudy, garish,—imparts the idea of *display*. (C.)

笑睞睞的 A pleasant smile, a broad grin,—imparts the idea of *half-closed eyes*.

急齁齁的 Eager, craving, yearning,—imparts the idea of *breathless emotion*. (C. & N.)

熱腸腸的 Quite eager, craving, yearning,—imparts the idea of *strong desire*. (C. & S.)

驚慌慌的 Frightened, nervous, all in a tremor,—imparts the idea of *distraction*.

辣觫觫的 Tingling sharp, quite pungent,—imparts the idea of *tremor*.

紅鋪鋪的 Blooming red, rosy, glowing,—imparts the idea of *diffusion*.

高梢梢的 Quite high, lofty, elevated,—used by way of comparison. (S. & N.)

寬綽綽的 Roomy, quite large, spacious,—imparts the idea of *amplitude*. (C. & N.)

寬敞敞的 Quite large, roomy, extensive, ample,—imparts the idea of *spaciousness*. (S.)

紫英英的 Bright purple, purplish,—imparts the idea of *elegance*.

紫微微的 Slightly purple, purplish,—imparts the idea of *minuteness*. (S.)

紫夠夠的 Deep purple, dark purple,—imparts the idea of *excess*. (C. & N.)

紫烏烏的 Deep purple, dark purple,—imparts the idea of *blackness*. (S.)

胖敦敦的 Quite fat, plump, lusty.

酸溜溜的 Quite sour, tart.

嫩和和的 Quite tender, youthful. (S.)

鹹津津的 Quite salt, decidedly salt. (S.)

黃生生的 Light yellow, a yellow tinge.

VOCABULARY.

颾 *Liu*². . . . . The sighing sound of the wind.

縐 *Chou*⁴. Crape; wrinkled, corrugated, variegated; crisp.

碌 *Lu*⁴. . . . Green jasper; rough; toilsome, laborious.

森 *Shên*¹. Overgrown with trees; somber, cool; severe, stern.

到如今提起來、我心裏還是驚慌慌的。○這26就是前年生疳積的那個孩子、你看他如今長的胖敦敦的、臉上紅鋪鋪的、一點病也沒有。○湯27裏叫我擱的胡椒多了、恐怕太辣、答不怕、辣觫觫的纔好喇。○租28郭家屯那處房子、就是太窵遠了、其實那個房子高梢亮梢亮的、寬敞綽敞綽的、人住着倒極暢快。○若29說紫微英微英的、就是說他少帶一點紫色、十分鮮明、若說紫烏夠烏夠的、就是嫌他太紫、成了黑紫色。

25 I met a wolf yesterday, and barely escaped being eaten up by him. Even yet when it is mentioned, I find myself all in a tremor.

26 This is the child that was suffering from innutrition the year before last. See how fat he has grown. His cheeks are rosy, and he is perfectly well.

27 I have put too much pepper in the soup; I fear it will be too hot. *Ans.* Never fear; it's all the better for being a little fiery.

28 That house in Kwoă-chia-t'un is too inconvenient of access to rent; although the house itself is quite high and roomy, and would make a very cheerful residence.

29 If you speak of a thing as being bright purple, you mean that it has a tinge of purple and is very brilliant. If, however, you speak of a thing as being a dead purple, you mean that the purple is too deep, amounting to a black purple.

朧 *Lung*². . . . . . The rising moon; obscure, dim.

穤 *Nai*⁴. . . . . . . Stupid; gross, defiled.

奢 *Shê*¹. . . . . . Wasteful, extravagant; gay, fast.

眯 *Mi*³. Sand in the eyes; blinking, eyes half . . . . . . shut.

觫 *Su*⁴. . . . . . To trouble; to shudder; to tingle.

梢 *Shao*¹. The end of a branch, the extremity, ... the small end.

夠 *Kou*⁴. Enough, sufficient; adequate. Often . . . . . . interchanged with 彀.

動彈 *Tung*⁴ *t'an*². . . . . To move, to stir.

整年 *Chêng*³ *nien*². The whole year, the year . . . . through.

在學 *Tsai*⁴ *hsüe*². Having the first degree:— . . . . Note 9.

煳 *Hu*². . . . To scorch; to burn in cooking.

半點 *Pan*⁴ *tien*³. . . . A very little, the least bit.

𧩰 *Hêng*⁴. To look at angrily; to *berate*, to . . . . scold.

照壁 *Chao*⁴ *pi*⁴. A wall before a door or en- . . . . trance serving as a screen.

會試 *Hwei*⁴ *shï*⁴. To compete for, or to take, the . . . . degree of 進士.

疳 *Kan*¹. A disease characterized by enlarge- . . . . . . ment of the belly and atrophy of the limbs, tabes mesenterica.

疳積 *Kan*¹ *chi*¹. . . . . . . The same. (s.) Rickets.

屯 *T'un*². . . . To collect; *a village*, a camp.

窵 *Tiao*⁴. . . . . . Deep, cavernous, remote.

窵遠 *Tiao*⁴ *yüen*³. Remote, out of the way, ... bye; inconvenient of access.

暢 *Ch'ang*⁴. Joyous, exhilarating; penetrating; . . . . spreading.

暢快 *Ch'ang*⁴ *kwai*⁴. Happy, in good spirits, ... cheerful.

NOTES.

3 蒙頭蓋臉 is a rhetorical duplication, used as a figure to denote an involved and obscure style. The three forms are Northern, Central and Southern.

9 在學 To get the first degree is, theoretically, to enter the government school supposed to be taught by the 老師, which, however, as a matter of fact, does not exist.

12 罵街 To walk along the street back and forth, railing and reviling at the top of the voice, not usually mentioning names, but by indirect allusions directing the abuse at this or that individual. It is not an infrequent occurrence in country villages.

20 帶 *To carry*, that is, in this case, *to manifest.*

24 會試 *To assemble and essay*; that is, to compete at the capital for the degree of 進士. The phrase is also sometimes used to signify the obtaining of the degree.

第一百六十八課

今[1]日洗了一天衣裳、實在使累的慌。○我[2]和他會過一面、記得他胖布刺拉(布刺)的。○王[3]大人原來是反叛出身、後來投降的、所以現在雖然作了官、仍舊還是兇布刺拉(布刺、布濆)的。○你[4]到如今纔來、叫人眞急得轂受(慌)。○這[5]件事眞是可惱、連我也氣的慌。○你[6]吃的飽布刺拉(布刺)的、還來打花花哨喇(拿人開心)。○挑[7]這五六十斤的擔子、還嫌壓的慌嗎。○放[8]這麼大的砲、他也不怕震的慌。○僱[9]個牲口搭搭脚兒罷、我看你走得太累的慌。○[10]乾(光)急沒法下手、實在叫人躁得轂受(慌)。○若[11]嫌熱的慌、可以把衣裳脫了罷。○別[12]看他臉上惡布刺拉(布刺)的、心裏却極

Translation.

1 I have been washing all day, and am terribly tired (done up).
2 I met him once, and I remember he was excessively fat.
3 Wang Ta-jên is a man who was originally a rebel, but afterwards submitted. Hence it is that, although he is now an officer, he still has altogether a savage disposition.
4 Your not coming until this time is enough to make one very anxious.
5 This business is certainly aggravating; even I am out of all patience.
6 You have eaten as much as you can hold, and now you come here to get off your jokes.
7 You don't feel overburdened with this load of only fifty or sixty catties, do you?
8 He does not mind the shock from the discharge of even so large a cannon as this.
9 Hire a donkey and rest your legs a little. I see you are quite tired out.
10 To be in [such] suspense and yet unable to do anything, is extremely trying.
11 If you feel oppressed with the heat, you can lay off some of your clothing.
12 Don't be misled by the forbidding

LESSON CLXVIII.

Intensives of Unpleasant Excess.

得慌 or **的慌**, is an intensive somewhat like 得很 in form, but of much less extensive application, and indicating a different kind of intensity. It is only applied to feelings of mind or body, and conveys the idea of exhaustion, or that peculiar feeling of distress which seeks in vain for relief from an unpleasant sensation. It is quite *t'ung-hsing*, but has a much wider use in some sections than in others, and is oftener heard in colloquial than found in books. The original form is doubtless that with 得, but 的 is now generally substituted for it. In cases in which 的慌 is not used, 轂受 is substituted for it, but the shade of meaning is not quite the same.

布刺的 is an intensive generally applied only to physical appearance, and expresses an unseemly or offensive excess. It is colloquial, but entirely *t'ung-hsing*, being changed in the South to 布刺拉的. The writing is somewhat uncertain. 布刺, *to spread out to criticism or reprehension*, gives perhaps the best approximation to the meaning. 巴刺 is a possible if not probable writing, the sound of 巴 being slightly modified in speaking.

布濆的 is an intensive used in Northern and occasionally in Central Mandarin, and having very much the same force as 布刺的. The proper characters are somewhat uncertain. Some would write 不及, but this gives no clue to the chief idea implied; moreover, 及 being hard, is only correct where all sounds are soft. The lesson embraces the most common words with which these intensives are used. Others will be found in the supplement.

良善。○13天過於冷、就是在家裏、還覺凍的殼受(慌)。○14只因多日沒見、心裏很想得慌。○15不要惹他、他睖布刺拉的(布刺)光淨打人。○16你的心口疼、覺得脹的慌不、答 就是覺得脹的疼。○17張有能眞是海量、遇着這樣的事、總沒見他愁的慌。○18人家都希罕男孩子、你怎麼倒希罕女孩子呢、答 我嫌這些男孩子鬧布潰的淨禍害人。野布刺的光作害人。野頭野腦的光闖禍。○19就是鐵石的人、聽了他的那個話、也沒有不慘得慌的。○20你這麼獃布刺拉的(布刺)、一點精神沒有、不怕人家偷甚麼去嗎。○21這一連好幾天不(沒)能出門、又加上事情不順、所以心裏很悶的殼受(慌)。○22那屋裏有蛇蚤、又有臭蟲、黑夜(夜裏)實在叮(咬)得慌。○23葛石巖的日子、這二年也敗落喇、雖然不算大窮、却是過的累布刺拉的(布刺)。○24你這個麪淨小麩子、而且也有沙、誰吃誰嫌牙

expression of his face, for he has a most kindly heart.

13 The weather is so excessively cold that even in the house I am freezing.

14 I have not seen you for so long that I long exceedingly for you.

15 Do not irritate him; he is irascible and given to striking people.

16 Do you feel any sense of distention with your dyspepsia? *Ans.* I do feel a painful sense of distention.

17 Chang Yin Nêng is certainly a man of great self-control. Though meeting with such things as these, he showed no sign of being worried.

18 Other people all desire sons; how is it that you on the contrary desire daughters? *Ans.* I dislike boys because they are so terribly boisterous, and are always getting into mischief.

19 Even a man of iron or stone could not listen to what he said without a strong feeling of sympathy.

20 Are you not afraid some one will steal your things? you are so absent-minded and pay no attention to anything.

21 I have not been able to go out for these several days, and besides matters have not been going smoothly, on account of which I feel very much depressed.

22 That room is infested both with fleas and bed-bugs. I was much worried through the night with their biting.

23 Kê Shï Yien has also been failing in circumstances these two years. Although he cannot be called very poor, yet he finds it hard to make the ends meet.

VOCABULARY.

叛 *P'an*⁴. . . . . . . To rebel, to revolt.

反叛 *Fan*³ *p'an*⁴. . . . . To rebel; a rebellion.

降 *Hsiang*². To submit, to return to allegiance; . . . . to cause to submit; to hold under the influence of:—see *chiang*⁴.

投降 *T'ou*² *hsiang*². To give up and submit to . . . . authority (of a rebel).

作官 *Tsoă*⁴ *kwan*¹. To be a magistrate, to fill . . . . office.

可惱 *K'ê*³ *nao*³. Provoking, vexatious, *ag-* . . . . *gravating*.

良善 *Liang*² *shan*⁴. Good, *kind-hearted;* humane, benevolent.

禍害 *Hwoă*⁴ *hai*⁴. Injury, calamity; to get into . . . . mischief; to involve in trouble.

作害 *Tsoă*⁴ *hai*⁴. To get into mischief; to . . . . involve in trouble or loss.

野頭野腦 *Yie*³ *t'ou*² *yie*³ *nao*³. Wild, turbulent, boisterous, unruly:—Les. 184.

巖 *Yien*². . . . . . A precipice, a cliff; hazardous.

磣的慌。○他[25]妯娌三個、見天（天天）打的鬼哭狼號、連四鄰都嫌鬧得慌（彀受）。○你[26]使的慌就歇一歇、累的慌就少做一點、餓的慌就去吃飯、乾的慌就去喝水、睏的慌（盹的慌）就去睡覺（睏覺）。○高[27]俅仗着有點浮聰明、凡事以强壓弱、就是不言不語在那裏坐着、也是那布刺（布刺拉）的、無論叫誰一看、就知道他不是個正經東西。○王[28]秉福那個人、眞酸極喇、不但臉上的樣子酸、走起路來酸、就是說出句話來、也是酸布漬（酸漬漬）的。○你[29]這位老大娘（老太）、整天家坐在這裏、替人家洗衣裳、從來有多少水、被你弄髒咯、你到百年之後、恐怕就是紮十隻牛給你、也替你喝不了這些混水啊、答 咳、一個窮老婆子、光活還顧不過來、那裏還顧得死怎麼樣呢、現在別的我都不愁、就是兩條腿很踡的慌、腰也疼的慌、兩隻胳膊都常累得酸布漬的。

24 This flour of yours is full of fine bran, moreover it also has sand in it. Whoever eats of it complains of its grittiness.

25 These three sisters-in-law are fighting continually, so that the whole neighborhood is disturbed by their crying and shrieking.

26 If you are tired, rest a little; if you are oppressed with work, do a little less; if you are hungry, go and take a meal; if you are thirsty, go and take a drink; and if you are drowsy, go and take a sleep.

27 Kao Ch'iu relies on his having a little superficial shrewdness and so tyrannizes over others in everything. Even when he is sitting quietly and saying nothing, he has a sinister expression. Whoever looks at him can see at a glance that he is a knave.

28 That man Wang Ping Fu is certainly a most disagreeable fellow. Not merely are the expression of his face and his style of walking disagreeable, but even his talk is quite disgusting.

29 Well, old grandmother, sitting here as you do every day washing clothes for people, how much water do you suppose you have defiled in all these years? When you are gone ten paper cows will not be sufficient to drink up all this dirty water for you. *Ans.* Humph, a poverty-stricken old woman like me, finds it hard enough to get a living, let alone busying myself with what is to come after death. My only worry at present is that my legs get so stiff sitting, and my back aches, and my arms are so used up that they hurt me all the time.

敗落 *Pai^{4} loà^{4}.* To decline, *to fail,* to wane; to go to ruin.

麩 *Fu^{1}.* Bran.

磣 *Ch'ên^{3}.* To grate on the nerves like biting on sand.

四鄰 *Ssŭ^{4} lin^{2}.* The neighbors on all sides, the neighborhood.

號 *Hao^{2}.* To scream, *to shriek,* to howl, to wail. See *hao^{4}*.

睏覺 *K'un^{4} chiao^{4}.* To sleep. (c.)

俅 *Ch'iu^{2}.* An ornamented cap.

不言不語 *Pu^{4} yien^{2} pu^{4} yü^{3}.* Saying nothing, silent.

老大娘 *Lao^{3} ta^{4} niang^{2}.* An elderly woman, old lady:—Note 29.

咳 *Hai^{1}.* An exclamation of surprise or of dissatisfaction. See *k'ê^{2}*.

踡 *Ch'üen^{2}.* To double up the legs as in sitting on them, to double up, to draw in.

第一百六十九課

連[1]我還不能、何況是你。○大[2]事不知辦了多少、何況是這點小事呢。○他[3]並不彀我自己打的、何況有你幫助呢。○這[4]個字連先生都不會講、何況是學生呢。○你[5]就是最小心、也難沒有錯處、何況這樣疎忽懈怠呢。○荒[6]唐的道兒、他一步也不肯走、況且公事上、又很小心、很勤謹。○犯[7]神的律法、已經就是大罪、況又辜負他的恩典。○就[8]是買銀子、還要得有點抬高頭喇、何況是買柴伙呢。○廟[9]裏的神、連自己也不能保佑、何況是保佑人呢。○窮[10]苦家、誰肯把女兒嫁他呢、何況耶勤學那個討人嫌的

Translation.

1 Even I am not able, how much less are you able!

2 I have managed any number of important affairs; how much more can I dispose of this trifling matter?

3 He is no match for me alone; how much more when I have you to help me!

4 Even the teacher cannot explain this character, much less can a pupil.

5 Even though you take the greatest pains, it will be difficult for you to avoid mistakes; how much more then if you are so careless and lazy?

6 He will have nothing at all to do with any questionable course of conduct; much more in the case of official business, in which he is most careful and assiduous.

7 To break God's law is of itself a great sin; how much greater [the sin] when, in addition, his grace is also abused.

8 Even if I were buying silver, you would have to give a little extra weight; how much more when I am buying fuel?

9 The gods in the temples cannot even protect themselves, much less can they protect men.

Notes.

1 使的慌 *Tired, "used up,"*—much used in Shantung, but not *t'ung-hsing.* 累的慌 is *t'ung-hsing*, but is not exactly equivalent, meaning rather, *overburdened, distressed by excess of labor.*

6 打花花哨 *Get off your euphonious twitter,*—applied in derision to one who is trying to say smart things. 拿人開心 *To enjoy oneself at the expense of another, to make game of.*

9 搭搭脚 *Take a passage for your feet*, that is, rest your legs by riding.

10 For this use of 乾, see Les. 94.

16 不 is emphatic, standing for the negative side of the question.

25 鬼哭狼號 *Demons crying and wolves yelping;* a forcible figure to describe the crying and screaming of the sisters-in-law in their quarrels.

27 以强壓弱 *Using main force to oppress the weak,*—a book phrase.

29 老大娘 is a widely used term of respect. It may be addressed to any elderly woman whose age and position does not entitle her to be addressed as 老太太. It is a widespread belief amongst Chinese women that to defile clean water is sin, and that they will be punished for it in another world by being compelled to drink all the water they have defiled in this world. Paper cows are burned that they may help them through with the disagreeable task. The phrase 百年之後 is a euphemism for "after death."

LESSON CLXIX.

The Comparative Conjunction.

況 Moreover, still more, besides. Not often used *alone* in Mandarin, though frequently so used in *Wên-li.*

何況 How much more, or how much less; still more, or still less,—much used in correlation with 尙且, see Les. 175.

況且 Still more, still further; moreover besides; especially.

樣兒。○你[11]的身子也是父母生成的、何況身外之物、豈不更屬父母嗎。○這[12]一頓現成的飯、何足掛齒、況且你的甚麼東西我沒吃過啊。○你[13]就是親眼看見他的過錯、也証不住他、何況是風聞聽來的呢。○爲[14]這暫時的榮耀、人還費事去求、何況爲天上永遠的榮耀、豈不更當求嗎。○就[15]算他是個會說的、也說不過這個理去、況且他的嘴很笨訥鈍呢。○連[16]自己的親姑媽姑、他還沒上沒下的罵、何況是我們呢。○必[17]定叫人家儘其所有的、都給了你、能彀嗎、況且給是人情、不給是本分。○你[18]看外人比我年紀大、我還要這樣敬重、何況是我的親哥哥呢。○我[19]若穿上好的、不但不

10 Who is willing to give his daughter in marriage to a poor family? how much less to such a disreputable fellow as Lang Ch'in Hsüe!

11 Your bodies, even, were generated by your father and mother; and do not things outside your bodies still more rightfully belong to them?

12 What is there worth speaking of in this one common meal? especially as there is nothing of yours of which I have not eaten.

13 You could not prove the crime against him even if you had seen it with your own eyes, how much less when it is a mere rumor.

14 When men take pains to seek even this transitory glory, should they not much more seek the everlasting glory of heaven?

15 Even supposing he were a plausible speaker, he could not maintain this position; how much less seeing he is exceedingly slow of speech.

16 In defiance of all propriety he reviles even his own aunt; how much more will [he revile] us.

17 Can you expect a man to give you everything he has? especially as to give is a favor, and not to give is no wrong.

18 Consider how I am expected to show respect even to a stranger who is my senior, how much more to my own elder brother.

VOCABULARY.

懈 *Hsie*^{4}. . . . . . .Remiss, negligent, listless, slow.

懈怠 *Hsie*^{4} *tai*^{4}. Dilatory, remiss; indisposed . . . . .to work, *lazy*.

勤謹 *Ch'in*^{2} *chin*^{3}. Diligent, assiduous; industrious.

辜 *Ku*^{1}. . . . A fault, a crime, a sin; to hold guilty.

辜負 *Ku*^{1} *fu*^{4}. To misuse; to abuse; to prostitute; to squander.

戥 *Têng*^{3}. A small steelyard specially constructed . . . . . . for weighing silver and gold.

窮苦 *Ch'iung*^{2} *k'u*^{3}. Poor, poverty-stricken, indigent.

訥 *Noă*^{4}. Slow of speech, awkward speech, stammering.

姑姑 *Ku*^{1} *ku*^{1}. . . . . A paternal aunt.

職 *Chï*^{2}. To oversee; official duty; province, ... function.

武職 *Wu*^{3} *chï*^{2}. . . . . Military office, military.

羞愧 *Hsiu*^{1} *k'wei*^{4}. . . . . Ashamed, mortified.

執法 *Chï*^{2} *fa*^{3}. Taking the law as guide, according to law.

按法 *An*^{4} *fa*^{3}. . . . . The same.

妝 *Chwang*^{1}. . . . . The same as 粧.

妝飾 *Chwang*^{1} *shï*^{1}. *Adornment*, dress, style; . . . . outward gloss.

煎 *Chien*^{4}. To scald; to steep; to temper. Also . . . . *chien*^{1}.

蘸 *Chan*^{4}. . . . . . .To dip, to immerse; to temper.

發條 *Fa*^{1} *tiao*^{2}. . . . . . A coiled spring; a spring.

得成樣兒、而且不舒服、況且我們這武職的差使、也用不着好衣裳。〇一[20]時官府把你問倒、自己也覺得羞愧、況你若告下謊狀、官府執按法還要問你個反坐。〇你[21]們這小信的人、野地裏的草、今日還在、明日就丟在爐裏、神還叫他有這樣的妝飾、何況你們呢。〇你[22]是不明白蘸煎發條的法子、你想那已經烤過兩回的都斷了、何況是一回沒烤過的、豈不更要斷了嗎。〇論[23]到學英文、這本是一件頂要緊的事情、凡有志求學問的、都當學習、因為今日的天下、一切有用的上等學問、和有名的書籍、差不多全屬英文、所以一通英文、就能通天下的學問、可以加增人的知識、開廣人的眼界、這豈不是念書的一大樂嗎、不但這樣、而

19 If I wear fine clothes, they are not only unbecoming but also uncomfortable; besides, we who belong to the military class do not need elegant clothes.

20 If at any time the magistrate should ask you a question that knocks you off your feet, you would yourself feel ashamed; and moreover if you have brought a false charge, the magistrate may, in accordance with the law, inflict on you the punishment which the accused would have had to suffer.

21 If God so clothe the grass of the field, which to-day is, and to-morrow is cast into the oven, shall He not much more clothe you, O ye of little faith?

22 You don't understand the method of tempering springs. Just think; if a spring, whose temper has been twice drawn, breaks, how much more will one break whose temper has not been drawn at all.

23 The learning of English, of which you speak, is indeed a very important matter. Every one who aspires to be a scholar should learn it. For nearly all the most useful and important sciences known in the world at the present time, together with all the most noted books, are in English. Hence when a man knows English, he has access to the learning of the world, and can enlarge his knowledge

學習 *Hsüe² hsi².* To learn by repetition or practice; to study; to acquire an art.

上等 *Shang⁴ têng³.* Superior, first-class; *important.*

加增 *Chia¹ tsêng¹.* To add to, to increase, *to enlarge.*

知識 *Chi¹ shi².* *Knowledge,* discernment, insight, capacity.

開廣 *K'ai¹ kwang³.* To enlarge, *to extend.*

眼界 *Yien³ chie⁴.* Boundary of sight, scope of vision, *mental horizon.*

教習 *Chiao¹ hsi².* A teacher, a professor.

譯 *I⁴.* To explain; to interpret.

繙譯 *Fan¹ i⁴.* To interpret; *to translate.*

精通 *Ching¹ t'ung¹.* Thorough, well-versed; *competent,* finished.

效用 *Hsiao⁴ yung⁴.* To labor for, to exert oneself on behalf of, *to serve.*

較比 *Chiao³ pi³.* To compare.

財利 *Ts'ai² li⁴.* *Money;* profit, gain.

佔先 *Chan⁴ hsien¹.* To outstrip, to excel; *to get the advantage.*

上達 *Shang⁴ ta².* To ascend, *to rise;* to advance in honors; to strive for excellence or superiority.

捷便 *Chie² pien⁴.* Convenient, brief; pointed; *labor-saving.*

且英文、也是國家所等用的、你看現在所有作西學教習的、全是用的西國人、作西學繙譯的、也是用的西國人、倘若本國有能精通英文的、爲國家効用、較比用西國人、豈不是一大光彩嗎、何况在功名道上、在財利道上、也都是通英文的人佔先、所以凡有志上達的、或是想着成大功、立大業的、都當知道、這英文就是一個捷便門、就是一條四通八達的路、要緊想法子學、而且也要學到好處。

and extend his mental horizon; and is not this one of the chief enjoyments of a scholar? Not only so, but English is needed by the government. You observe that all teachers of Western science and all translators of scientific books, who are employed, are foreigners. If there were natives of our own country who were competent scholars in English, and could serve the government in this capacity, would it not be much more creditable than to use foreigners? Moreover, both in getting degrees and in making money, those who have a knowledge of English have the advantage. So that all who desire to rise, or to attain distinction, or to acquire a fortune, should know that the English language is the labor-saving plan, the high way, in fact, to success. Be sure you find a way to learn it, and learn it well.

NOTES.

2 It will be noticed that some of the sentences containing 何况 end with 呢, and some do not. There is no evident reason why they should not all end with 呢.

12 掛齒 *To hang on the teeth*; i. e., *to speak of*,—only used as following 何足.

16 沒上沒下 *Ignoring upper and lower*; i. e., *in defiance of the obligation to respect superiors.*

17 More literally, *Is it practicable to require that a man shall certainly give you everything that he has?*

19 不得樣 or 不成樣 *Inappropriate, not befitting, not in style.*

20 問倒 *To ask searching questions which nonplus the person examined and convict him of falsehood.* 反坐 *To sit in the opposite seat*; i. e., *to take the place of the accused*; to impute to one the crime of which he falsely accuses another, and punish him accordingly. This is a recognized principle of Chinese law.

22 發條 is a comparatively recent term, devised in all probability to designate the spring of a watch,—發 describing the use of the spring, and 條 its form. The term has now, however, come to be applied to springs of all kinds and shapes. In Peking to temper steel is *chan*⁴ and in Shantung *chien*⁴, the proper characters being in both cases uncertain. The *Wên-li* term is 焠 *ts'wei*⁴ which is sometimes used colloquially at Nanking.

23 四通八達 *Four ways open and eight ways communicating*; that is, *giving access to all quarters, a high way*:—see Les. 186.

LESSON CLXX.

ENUMERATION OF PARTICULARS.

又...又 Both ... and.

又...却又 (　　) ... but yet, and yet.

又...而又 (　　) ... and yet, and besides.

The first 又 is untranslatable; it is implied in the order of the sentence.

一來...二來, etc. In the first place ... in the second place, etc.

一不...二不 Neither ... nor. With a negative, cardinal numbers are often thus used instead of the ordinals.

一則...一則 }
一則...二則 } First ... second, etc. The first form, which simply repeats the 一則 with each particular, is sometimes used, especially in books, but the proper numbers are most generally used.

第一百七十課

他[1]天生得又聾又啞。○我[2]的嘴又拙、心又笨。○這[3]些糧食、又潮濕又賠虧斗。○自[4]己又不按理行、而却又想着叫人說個好、這豈不是難事嗎。○他[5]家裏又不缺喫、又不缺穿。○那[6]個人的心術不好、又狠毒、又詭詐。○我[7]看買個鍍銀的好、一則體面、二則不長銹。○凡[8]事又好出頭、而却又不敢擔事、所以他常常自己找一些些個難爲。○又[9]有德又有才的人、天下找不出多少來。○我[10]和他一不沾係親、二不帶係故、怎麼能偏向他呢。○一[11]樣的事情、叫有心眼兒的人辦、又省力、又快當。○你[12]又要好的、而却又捨不得錢、那有又好又賤的貨呢。○行[13]又不是、止又不是、實在叫我進退兩難。○怪[14]不得姜家的媳婦不當意、又饞又懶、而且又不和他女婿一心。○約[15]瑟爲甚麼不給他弟兄們打算官職呢、答一

TRANSLATION.

1 He was both deaf and dumb from his birth.

2 My speech is awkward and my mind [is dull.

3 This grain is both wet and short in measure.

4 You act unreasonably and yet you desire men to praise you. Is not this an impossible thing?

5 At his home there is no lack either of food or of clothing.

6 That man's heart is depraved; he is both cruel and treacherous.

7 I think it would be better to buy a silver-plated one. In the first place, it is genteel; and in the second place, it will not rust.

8 He wants to lead in everything, and yet he is afraid to take responsibility; hence he is constantly getting himself into difficulty.

9 But few men are to be found in the world who are both virtuous and gifted.

10 I am neither a relative of his nor an old friend; why should I be partial towards him?

11 When a thing is done by a man of ability, it is so done as to both save labor and secure despatch.

12 You want a superior quality, and yet you are loth to pay the price. Where will you find goods that are both cheap and good?

13 It will not do to proceed, neither will it do to stop. Truly I am in an embarrassing position.

14 It is no wonder that the Chiang family are not pleased with their daughter-in-law. She is both greedy and lazy, and besides, she is not true to her husband's interest.

VOCABULARY.

虧斗 *K'wei*¹ *tou*³. *Short measure;* to lose measure.

賠斗 *Shê*² *tou*³. *To lose measure,* to fall short.

銹 *Hsiu*⁴. Rust, an oxide.

沾 *Chan*¹. To moisten, to imbue; to soil; to receive [favors], *to enjoy;* to participate in, to have to do with; to be infected by.

當意 *Tang*¹ *i*⁴. *Pleased with,* acceptable, agreeable.

官職 *Kwan*¹ *chï*². Office, official rank.

分散 *Fên*¹ *san*⁴. To scatter, to disperse.

聚集 *Chü*⁴ *chi*². To assemble, *to gather together,* to collect.

驚眼 *Ching*¹ *yien*³. To stir up a craving for, to excite desire.

來他們本是牧羊的人、未必有作官的才學、二來作官必分散、難以再聚集在一處、三來分散在伊及人當中、免不得隨他們的風俗、去拜假神。○你[16]留這麼些現錢做什麼、叫人家看見驚眼、倒不如買點銀子藏着、一則省得有人來借、二則免得有賊來偷、你就沒有這點打算嗎。○吳[17]天保眞是個有福分的人、你看他活的時候、家裏又發功名、又發財、他一死了、立時就敗落喇。○凡[18]來歷不明、蹤跡可疑的人、都立刻舉報出來、斷不可容在甲內、一則免得失事、二則免得帶累。○這[19]裏脚的風俗、一來不合天理、二來不合人情、怎麼說是不合天理呢、因爲天給人的四肢百體、各有其用、而脚的用處、是在乎能站能走、但是一裏起來、却就難站難走了、況且孩子在七八歲、正是

15 Why did not Joseph provide official positions for his brethren? *Ans.* First, they were shepherds, and probably had not the talents and education necessary for officials; second, if they became officials, they must needs separate, and it would be difficult for them to come together again; third, if scattered amongst the Egyptians, they could not avoid following their customs and worshipping false gods.

16 Why do you keep so much ready [copper] cash to excite the cupidity of beholders? It would be much better to exchange it for silver, which you can hide away. In the first place, you will be saved from borrowers; and in the second place, you will avoid its being stolen by thieves. Haven't you this small amount of forethought?

17 Wu T'ien Pao was evidently a favorite of fortune. See how while he lived, his family increased both in honors and riches, but as soon as he is dead, their good fortune at once departs.

18 All persons of uncertain antecedents or of suspicious conduct, you should report at once and by no means harbor them in the neighborhood; first, to avoid theft; and second, to avoid complications.

19 The custom of foot-binding is, in the first place, contrary to reason; and, in the second place, contrary to natural affection. Why is it contrary to reason? It is so because each of the several members of the body which Heaven has given to men, has its proper use, and the use of the feet is to stand and walk; but if they be

---

福分 *Fu*² *fên*⁴. Portion of happiness, lot, *fortune.*

蹤 *Tsung*¹. A vestige, a footstep.

跡 *Chi*⁴. *A trace;* vestiges; effects.

蹤跡 Footprints; traces, vestiges; *antecedents.*

舉報 *Chü*³ *pao*⁴. *To report,* to state, to give an account of.

裹脚 *Kwoâ*³ *chiao*³. To bind the feet as Chinese women do.

肢 *Chï*¹. The limbs, the members of the body.

虧損 *K'wei*¹ *sun*³. A deficiency, a defect; to injure, to impair; *to stunt.*

旗裝 *Ch'i*² *chwang*¹. Manchu dress,—especially that of the feet.

强壯 *Ch'iang*² *chwang*⁴. Strong, vigorous, *robust.*

疼痛 *T'êng*² *t'ung*⁴. Pain, suffering.

難堪 *Nan*² *k'an*¹. Difficult to bear; *intolerable,* insupportable.

得劤 *Tê*² *chin*⁴. The advantageous application of strength; to get the advantage.

又長骨頭又長肉的時候、若是裹腳、必要虧損他的身體、所以說是不合天理、怎麽說是不合人情呢、因爲女兒本來是軟弱的、即便和旗裝一樣、也大不如男人强壯、何况又裹了腳、不但頭四五年疼痛難堪、而且終身受累、永遠沒有得勁的時候、所以說是不合人情、既然不合人情、又不合天理、爲父母的、還可仍舊給女兒裹腳嗎。

bound, standing and walking are made very difficult. Besides, at seven or eight years is just the age when the bones and muscles are developing, and if the feet are bound, the child's body will certainly be stunted in its growth. Hence I say that the custom is contrary to reason. Why is it contrary to natural affection? It is so because girls are by nature delicate, so that, even with feet dressed as Manchus, they are far from being as robust as men; how much more when their feet are bound. Not only do they suffer intolerable pain during the first four or five years, but they are handicapped all through life, and are never able to use their strength to advantage. Hence I say it is contrary to natural affection. Seeing then that it is contrary both to natural affection and to reason, is it right for parents to continue binding their daughters' feet?

NOTES.

5 The translation given assumes that 他 refers to a child, or to some subordinate member of the household. It may, however, with equal propriety be referred to the head of the family, in which case the translation should be, *In his family, etc.*

10 故, as here used, stands for 故交, *an old acquaintance.* 係 is equivalent to 是. It is a *Wĕn-li* character, but as used in this phrase, is thoroughly colloquial.

11 The use of 一樣 *suggests* the idea that the same thing done by some one else would not be so well done.

13 進退兩難 *Advance and retreat alike difficult, in a dilemma, in a strait betwixt two,*—a very common and expressive phrase.

18 Cities and large towns are formed by the officers into wards or companies of ten families each, which are called 甲. The names are registered, and if any one of the ten is guilty of a misdemeanor the whole company are involved and are compelled to share the consequences.

19 裹脚 *To bandage the feet;* that is, to compress or "bind" them as Chinese women do. The more common colloquial term is 包脚. 四肢百體 *Four members and hundred* [parts of the] *body.* There is an ellipsis of some word equivalent to *parts or organs.* The phrase is a summary expression for the whole body.

LESSON CLXXI.

SPECIAL TERMS OF POLITE ADDRESS.

The Chinese are much given to the use of exaggerated terms of politeness, especially in case of limited acquaintance, or when meeting in a ceremonious way. A number of these terms have already occurred in previous lessons. The list here given, while not exhaustive, is sufficient for all practical purposes.

貴 Honorable—applied to names, ages, affairs, dwellings, cities, countries, etc.

貴姓 What is your honorable surname? Most of these complimentary terms, when used in direct address, carry with them the force of the question appropriate to the case.

貴處 What is your honorable residence? that is, from whence do you come?

貴府 Where is your honorable residence? that is, where do you live? where is your home?

貴寓 Where are your honorable lodgings or apartments?

貴縣 What is your honorable district or county?

貴國 Your honorable country, or which is your honorable country?

貴庚 What is your honorable age? Applied chiefly to young persons, but not to children.

貴甲子 What is your honorable age?

第一百七十一課

沒[1]領教、尊貴姓啊、答賤姓王。官印大名尊諱呢、答
賤名天榜。大號台甫呢。答草字登雲。貴
處縣答敝處縣是蓬萊。貴庚、答今年癡長
二十歲。貴科、答我兄弟是乙酉科僥
倖的。敢問登翁要到何處、有何貴幹、
答要到祥符縣去處館。貴席、答不敢
稱席、不過代辦來往的書札。阿哦、原來
是書啟老夫子、失敬失敬、答好說、不敢
當。○家[2]有賢妻、男兒人不遭橫事。○老[3]先
生今年高壽貴甲子、答已經虛度六十八喇。

TRANSLATION.

1 I have not the pleasure;—what is your honorable surname? *Ans.* My humble surname is Wang. Your distinguished name? *Ans.* My humble name is T'ien Pang. Your great title? *Ans.* My vulgar title is Têng Yün. From what honorable place (county) do you come? *Ans.* My obscure residence is P'ênglai. What is your honorable age? *Ans.* This year is the twentieth of my imbecile life. In what honorable class did you get your degree? *Ans.* Fortune favored your younger brother in the class of I-yiu (1885). May I presume to ask where you are going, and what is your honorable business? *Ans.* I am going to fill a position in the district of Hsiangfu. May I inquire what is your official position? *Ans.* I cannot claim to have any official position; I am going to act as corresponding clerk. Ah! then, you are a reverend secretary. I beg pardon. I beg pardon. *Ans.* You compliment me overmuch.

2 A man who has a good wife does not get into trouble.

3 Venerable sir, what is your great age?

These characters being the first of the 天干 and 地支 are taken as representative. This term is applied to persons of greater age than the former, though not to the very old.

貴幹 What is your honorable business? i. e., occasion of your coming?

貴科 Which was your honorable class? The use of this term implies that the person addressed has a degree.

貴席 What is your honorable office? Only used of the official assistants in a yamên. The theoretical reference is to such as eat at special tables, not with the common herd.

賤 Mean. Mostly used with names and surnames in response to 貴 in the preceding question.

賤內 My unworthy wife.

敝 Deteriorated, worthless. Applied to places, in response to 貴 in the question.

敝處 My contemptible residence, or neighborhood.

敝縣 My contemptible district or county.

敝國 My contemptible country.

敝寓 My contemptible lodgings.

官印 Official style or name. The first character assumes an official status, and the second is used in allusion to printed cards, or an engraved seal.

大 Great,—in addition to its use to signify elder, 大 is used as a complimentary term in a few cases.

大名 Great or honorable name.

大號 Great or honorable designation. The 號 is a name or style taken by educated men, and is supposed to have some fanciful connection with the 名. Some few persons have a 名, a 號 and a 字, but most persons only have two names, the second one being called either 號 or 字.

大人 Great man, honored sir,—used in letters as a term of respect after 父親, 母親, 夫子, 先生, etc. In classical use 大人 is the correlative of 小人, in official language 大人 is the honorary title given to certain grades of officials.

小 Small,—besides the term 小的 (which see) 小 is occasionally used as a demeaning term.

小弟 Insignificant younger brother, your humble servant.

小號 Insignificant designation or firm.

○剛[4]纔家去的是令正嗎、答就是賤內、見笑見笑。○諸[5]位到了寒舍、在下有幸了。○先[6]生貴國、答做國是美國。○我[7]當是令尊還在、竟是去世多年了嗎。○我[8]這幾年沒到府上去、現在令堂還康健啊、答承問承問、現在家母還不甚衰弱。○我[9]成日家要到貴府去看看、到底沒能彀去。○先[10]生這次來考、貴寓在那裏、答做寓在狀元街。○先[11]生家中都有甚麼人、答有家嚴父、家慈母、還有一個家兄、一個舍弟、一個小犬犬子、一個小

Ans. I have already wasted sixty-eight years.

4 Is that your worthy wife who has just gone into the house? *Ans.* That is my humble housekeeper,—a ridiculous object.

5 Your unworthy servant is fortunate in having you, gentlemen, come to his humble dwelling.

6 What is your honorable country, sir? *Ans.* My unworthy land is the United States of America.

7 I supposed your honored father was still living. Is it many years since his decease?

8 I have not been to see you for several years. Is your honored mother still in good health? *Ans.* You are very kind, thank you. My mother is not as yet greatly enfeebled.

9 I have long desired to go to visit your honorable residence, but have not yet been able to do so.

10 Where is your honorable stopping place during the present examinations, sir? *Ans.* My unworthy apartments are on the Chwangyüen street.

11 What family have you at home, sir? *Ans.* I have my father and mother,

小犬 Small dog,—a demeaning term for a son.

犬子 Canine son,—a demeaning term applied to a son, either large or small. 子 is not an enclitic but a noun qualified by 犬.

台甫 Exalted title,—a polite way of referring [to the 號.

草字 Grass characters or name,—grass expressing the idea of common or unworthy.

草舍 Thatched cabin, my humble dwelling.

寒舍 Cold cabin, my cheerless dwelling.

高壽 What is your venerable age?—only used in addressing old people.

翁 An old man. Age is honorable; hence this term is applied by way of compliment even to comparatively young men. It is always joined to the first of the two characters constituting the name, the other being omitted.

令 Good, worthy of regard,—chiefly applied to family relationships.

令尊 Your worthy sire.

令堂 Your worthy mother.

令郎 Your worthy son.

令愛 Your worthy daughter.

令正 Your worthy wife. 正 refers to the *wife* as distinguished from a concubine.

令昆仲 Your worthy brothers.

Besides the above, 令 is also applied to 兄, 弟, 姊, 妹, 叔, 姪, etc.

老 Old,—largely used as a term of respect.

老夫子 Aged master, respected sir,—applied to a teacher, or to a professor of any fine art.

老人家 Old gentleman. Frequently joined with the pronoun 你 or 他.

老先生 Venerable sir.

老 is also joined with many relationships as, 父親, 母親, 哥, 兄, 兄台, 弟, 弟台, etc.

家 Family,—is used by the speaker to designate members of his own family, but expresses no special disrespect or otherwise.

家嚴 Family discipline, my father. Used of parents after death, rarely while they are living.

家慈 Family forbearance, my mother.

家 is also used with 父, 母, 兄, 伯, 叔, etc.

賢兄 or **賢弟** Worthy younger brother.

女、再者還有拙荆。○閣[12]下是行幾、答小弟
是排行第八。○兄[13]台在那裏發財、答在天
津衛受罪。甚麽寶號、答小號是東興玉。
○天[14]色已晚、請老兄到草舍住宿、等明天
吃了早飯再走罷。○看[15]閣下必是個斯文
人、不然、怎麽一臉書氣呢。○有[16]一位李長
春先生、你不是認識他嗎、這位相公就是
他的令郎、那位姑娘是他的令愛。○自[17]古
道、送君千里、終有一別。○怎[18]麽老先生要
走嗎、答外頭有個朋友、找我去看看病、失

also one older and one younger brother, a young son and a little daughter, and also my stupid thorn.

12 Which son are you, sir? *Ans.* Your younger brother is the eighth in order.

13 Where are you getting rich (i. e., doing business)? *Ans.* I am toiling away in Tientsin. What is the precious title of your firm? *Ans.* Our insignificant title is Eastern Flourishing Jewel.

14 It is already quite late, sir; I shall be pleased to have you spend the night under my humble roof, and you can go on after breakfast to-morrow morning.

15 From your appearance, sir, I judge you are a literary man; otherwise whence this academic expression of countenance?

16 There is a Mr. Li Ch'ang Ch'un whom you know, do you not? This young gentleman is his son, and that young lady is his daughter.

17 The old saying is, "Though you accompany a guest a thousand *li* there must be a farewell at last."

18 How is this? must you go, respected sir? *Ans.* A friend without inquires for me to go and see a patient. Please excuse me.

賢妻 A virtuous or prudent wife,—not used in direct address.

舍弟 A younger brother who shares the same cabin, my younger brother.

舍妹 My younger sister, is also used.

在下 The one beneath, your humble servant,—a depreciatory term for oneself.

拙荆 Stupid thorn, my wife.

閣下 Dweller in a lofty house, respected sir, —a formal term expressing high respect, and much used in conversation in some places; in other places rarely used, save in letters or books.

台下 The exalted one at whose feet I stand, honored sir. Less used than 閣下.

尊駕 Exalted sitter in the carriage. Riding in a carriage is a mark of a gentleman. It is similar to, but less used than 閣下.

尊嫂 Respected sister-in-law.

尊姓 What is your exalted surname? 尊名 is also used.

尊諱 Exalted agnomen, honorable name.

愚 Stupid,—a depreciatory substitute for 我, used in letters.

愚弟 Stupid younger brother, is also used [in the same way.

失陪 I am wanting in courtesy, please excuse me,—said when taking an early leave.

失敬 I have failed to show the respect I should have shown,—used when a stranger is suddenly recognized as being more than he was supposed to be.

承問 Thank you for asking, you are very [kind.

少見 I have not seen you for a long time; you have been much missed,—generally doubled and used in response to the greeting of a friend whom one has not seen for some time.

彼此 [The fault is] mutual, I am equally to blame,—always doubled, and used in response to some phrase or expression implying an apology.

久仰 I have long respected you, your reputation has preceded you.

久違 I have absented myself too long. I have too long neglected you,—belongs properly in the mouth of the party who has been absent,

陪失陪。○19台下在此、已經年久、眼中熟人甚多、望祈留意、若有地方、代爲吹噓吹噓。○我20勸老弟一句好話、千萬不要起這座墳、因爲這座墳正在穴眼上、一起就走了地氣脈喇。○昨21天小弟將扇子撇丟在府上、明天來的時候、煩尊駕帶來。○敬22請賢兄並尊嫂大人、及令姪天福均安、愚弟在外、諸事如心、勿勞惦念。○貴23縣有位衣成章先生、可認識嗎、答就是小弟、對久仰久仰、先生的品學俱高、果然是名不虛傳。○貴24處

19 You, sir, have been in this place a long time, and have a large circle of acquaintances. Please then keep me in mind, and in case a situation offers, I beg you will recommend me for it.

20 I will give you a little good advice, my respected brother. Do not for the world move this grave, for it is just on the center of the vein. If you disturb it, the good luck will all be dissipated.

21 Yesterday I forgot my fan at your residence. May I trouble you, respected sir, to bring it with you when you come to-morrow?

22 To my excellent brother, my respected sister-in-law and my worthy nephew T'ien Fu; greeting. Everything is satisfactory with your unworthy brother; you need have no anxiety.

23 There is in your honorable district a Mr. I Ch'êng Chang; are you acquainted with him? *Ans.* Your humble servant is he. I have long desired to meet you. Your character and scholarship are alike exalted. Your reputation is well deserved.

24 The green hills and flowing streams of your honorable neighborhood are most charming. *Ans.* You flatter us, sir. Our

but in practice is used indiscriminately by friends who have not seen each other for some time.

寶號 Precious firm-name; what is the name of your respected firm?

寶眷 Your precious family.

台 Exalted, is used as a term of respect after the names of various relationships as 兄台, 弟台, 伯台, 叔台, 父台, etc., also 老台 aged or honored sir.

These terms being for the most part the language of mere conventional politeness, do not carry with them nearly the force that their literal signification would seem to imply. It is worthy of note that these stilted terms of politeness for the most part associate with them a high style of Mandarin.

Vocabulary.

台 *T'ai*². Eminent, exalted, your honor:—see Sub. ...... Also used as a short writing of 臺.

甫 *Fu*³...... To begin; a second name or style.

賢 *Hsien*². *Worthy*, virtuous; one whose gifts .... and virtues exceed those of others, but do not equal the sage or 聖人:—see Sub.

犬 *Ch'üen*³ .... A dog, a cur:—see Sub.

違 *Wei*². To oppose, to disobey; to leave, to ...... avoid, *to neglect*:—see Sub.

酉 *Yiu*³. Ripe, mellow; the tenth of the twelve ...... branches.

處館 *Ch'u*³ *kwan*³. To fill the position of a .... teacher or secretary or clerk.

代辦 *Tai*⁴ *pan*⁴. *To do or act instead of;* to exe- .... cute for another; a deputy.

書札 *Shu*¹ *cha*². Letters, despatches, petitions .... etc.; *correspondence.*

啟 *Ch'i*³. ...... To explain; to open; to report.

書啟 *Shu*¹ *ch'i*³. An official writer, a secretary; .... *a scrivener.*

橫事 *Hêng*⁴ *shi*⁴. A misfortune, a disaster, a .... calamity, trouble.

山清水秀、眞是幽雅極喇、答先生過於誇獎、我們敝處山瘦地薄、實在不像地方。○老[25]兄回來喇、回來喇、久違久違、少見彼此、少見彼此、府上老世伯、老伯母、和令昆仲、都納福啊、托尊駕的福、都很平安。○去[26]年令尊壽誕、令郎又完婚、我都沒去道喜、少禮得很哪、答好說、去年家父的生辰、他老人家不願叫人知道、小兒完婚、甚是倉猝、所以都不敢驚動了。○若[27]不十分切己的朋友、雖自己年長、也當自稱爲弟、或是親

obscure neighborhood is very uninviting with its bare hills and sterile soil.

25 You have returned have you, worthy elder brother? Yes, I am back again, I beg pardon for neglecting you so long. Don't mention it: we have missed you very much (the neglect is mutual). Are your venerable father, respected mother and brothers all well? Thanks to your kind wishes; they are all quite well.

26 Last year, when your worthy sire passed his birthday, as also when your son celebrated his nuptials, I quite failed to present my congratulations, which was a great want of civility. *Ans.* Don't mention it. Last year my honored father did not wish his birthday made public, and my son's wedding took place quite suddenly, hence no special ado was thought advisable in either case.

27 Unless [the person addressed] be a very intimate friend, although you are yourself the elder, you should still speak of yourself as younger brother. In the case of relatives or very dear friends, all who are of the same generation, and younger than yourself, should be

---

住宿 *Chu⁴ hsiu³*. To stop for the night, to lodge all night.

斯 *Sï¹*. To split; this, that; presently.

斯文 *Sï¹ wên²*. Scholarly, literary.

書氣 *Shu¹ ch'i⁴*. The air of a literary man, an academic look.

年久 *Nien² chiu³*. For many years.

祈 *Ch'i²*. To pray, to beg; to request.

望祈 *Wang⁴ ch'i²*. Same as 望乞.

代爲 *Tai⁴ wei⁴*. Instead of, on behalf of.

穴 *Hsüe²˒⁴*. A cave; a den; a pit; a sinus, *a cavity;* a grave.

如心 *Ju² hsin¹*. According to one's mind, pleasing, *satisfactory.*

勿 *Wu⁴*. Not, do not,—a book term; used in Kiangnan for 不.

惦念 *Tien⁴ nien⁴*. To think of, *to be anxious about.*

幽 *Yiu¹*. Shady; solitary; retired; obscure.

幽雅 *Yiu¹ ya³*. Retired and beautiful, serene and quiet shade.

世伯 *Shï⁴ poă²*. Old uncle,—used in writing, in conversation 老大爺 is used.

伯母 *Poă² mu³*. The wife of a father's elder brother,—used in writing, 大娘 being used in conversation.

昆 *K'un¹*. Alike; together; *elder brother.*

昆仲 *K'un¹ chung⁴*. Brothers. (w.)

壽誕 *Shou⁴ tan⁴*. The day which marks the age; birthday.

完婚 *Wan² hun¹*. To celebrate a marriage:—Note 26.

生辰 *Shêng¹ ch'ên²*. Time of birth,—more bookish than birthday.

切己 *Ch'ie⁴ chi³*. *Intimate,* cordial.

年長 *Nien² chang³*. Elder, older.

在行 *Tsai⁴ hang²*. To be included in any craft; skilled in any art or craft, expert; *according to the requirements or proprieties of the case;* reasonable.

敢問 *Kan³ wên⁴*. May I presume? I venture to inquire,—used apologetically.

身分 *Shên¹ fen⁴*. Rank, standing; estate,

戚、或是知己的朋友、凡是同輩年少的人、都當稱他爲賢弟、惟有親兄弟、稱是稱胞弟。○出門的人、和人說話、彼此稱呼、總要在行、或稱先生、老先生、老伯台、老叔台、你老人家、或稱大哥、二哥、大爺、二爺、老兄台、老弟台、總要稱得合身分。

addressed as worthy younger brother, except that an own younger brother should be addressed as own brother.

28 In the conversation of a stranger with others, the respective styles of address used should always be in harmony with the proprieties of the case. Whether the address be sir, or respected sir, or respected elder uncle, or respected younger uncle, or you, good sir; whether it be oldest brother, or elder brother, or oldest uncle, or second uncle, or respected elder brother, or respected younger brother; it should in all cases accord with the standing of the person addressed.

Notes.

1 沒領教 *Have not received information;* that is, *I have not the pleasure of knowing your name.* The phrase is often used alone, the following 貴姓 being understood. 尊姓 and 貴姓 are equally *t'ung-hsing*, but the latter is much more commonly used. This sentence shows how briefly the Chinese can sometimes ask and answer questions by simply speaking the leading words.

2 This sentence is a common saying,—a compliment to the sagacity and influence of woman.

4 見笑 is used apologetically on account of the assumed inferior looks of the wife.

8 啊 is here used as an interrogative particle, or rather, it is the euphonic ending of a clause which is made interrogative by the inflection of the words. The difference between this form and that with 嗎 is, that 嗎 leaves the answer quite equivocal, while this form assumes or anticipates an affirmative answer.

12 行幾 *Which in order,*—only used of brothers, and arises from the custom of designating brothers by numbers. 排行第八 is a stately way of saying 行八.

14 天色已晚 *The color of the sky is already late,*—alluding to the fading light of sunset, a book expression frequently used by street ballad-singers.

17 君 is used by compliment to a guest. The saying is used when parting from a guest, after escorting him a short distance.

20 穴眼, *the eye of the cavity,* is the principle or central portion of the supposed passage or vein on which the grave is situated, and through which the propitious influences circulate. 地氣, *earth breath,* is the subtle essence which is supposed to permeate and animate the earth, and which constitutes the basis of the *fêng-shwei.* 地脈, *earth pulse,* is another name for the same essence, which is supposed to circulate in the earth as the blood does in the body.

22 This is the stereotype phraseology of the first part of a letter written home.

23 品學俱高 *Character and scholarship both excellent,*—a book expression.

25 納福 *To receive, or be in possession of, happiness.*

26 The Chinese regard an engagement as a quasi marriage, so that the *actual* marriage is but the *completion* of what was before begun, hence the term 完婚.

LESSON CLXXII.

Overplus.

Nearly all the terms connected with this idea gather round the word 外, outside, as appears below.

以外 Besides, in addition to, aside from.

格外 Beyond the bound or rule, special, extra, more.

分外 Beyond what is required, extra, especial, unusual.

另外 In addition, extra.

餘外 Besides, aside from, more than.

額外 Beyond the requirements of the case, extra.

越外 Excessive, gratuitous. (s.)

之外 A book term equivalent to 以外.

偏外 Much more, all the more, extra. (c.)

旁不相干 Irrelevant, beside the mark. (c. & n.)

餘裏掛外 Projecting within and hanging over without, irrelevant, useless. (l.)

多餘 Superfluous, unnecessary, to no purpose.

白多 The same. (s.)

浮餘 Superfluous, unnecessary; surplus, remainder. (n.)

餘浮 Surplus, overplus, remainder. (c.)

第一百七十二課

除[1]這個以外、再沒瞧見別的嗎。○求[2]大老爺格外施恩、童生再不敢喇。○一[3]樣的故典事、叫他一說、就分偏外有滋味。○請[4]先生另外抄出個底子來、預備以後對証。○月[5]亮到了中秋、分外的明亮。○請[6]兄台格外費心、小弟過後必來感情。○我[7]的饑空荒是沒處挪倒借的喇、你跟我要、也是白淨多多講餘的。○除[8]了這個以外、我沒有別的快樂。○這[9]是前有車後有轍的事情、還能越餘外間你要嗎。○我[10]因身體軟弱、比別人格偏外的怕冷。○我[11]們是按着人數買的、一個沒多有餘的的沒多有。○他[12]並沒說出個正經理來、淨說了些餘旁裏不掛相外干的話。○平[13]常煮做飯可以拘數、但這幾天有客、必得格外多煮做一點。○他[14]不聽好話、勸他也是多餘的。○沒[15]有別的東

TRANSLATION.

1 Did you see nothing besides this?
2 I beseech your honor to show me special mercy. I will not dare to repeat the offence.
3 The same story acquires an entirely new interest when he tells it.
4 Kindly write off an extra copy, that it may be preserved as a voucher.
5 In mid-autumn the moon is especially brilliant.
6 I trust, my dear fellow, you will take extra pains. Your unworthy brother will not fail to requite the favor in due time.
7 It is impossible for me to raise the money to pay my debts, so that your dunning is all to no purpose.
8 Aside from this I have no other happiness.
9 This is something for which there is abundant precedent. Do you suppose I would demand of you more than the regular amount?
10 Being physically weak, I am much more sensitive to cold than others.
11 We bought according to the number of persons. There is not a single one too many.
12 He did not give any satisfactory explanation, but simply said a lot of irrelevant things.
13 Ordinarily in cooking one can estimate just the quantity required; but these few days, having guests, it is necessary to cook a little more than usual.
14 It is futile to exhort him. He will not listen to good advice.

VOCABULARY.

童生 *T'ung*² *shêng*¹. A student who has attended the examinations one or more times, an undergraduate.

額 *Ê*²˒⁴. The forehead; a fixed quantity; *what is settled by law or custom.*

故典 *Ku*⁴ *tien*³. A precedent, a quotation; *a story*, a tradition.

對証 *Twei*⁴ *chêng*⁴. To prove, *to verify*, to substantiate.

感情 *Kan*³ *ch'ing*². To be thankful; *to return a favor.*

轍 *Chê*². The track of a wheel, a rut; *a precedent.*

拘數 *Chü*¹ *shu*⁴. To fix a number, *to estimate*, to judge.

塢 *Wu*³. A bank, a low wall, an entrenched camp.

船塢 *Ch'wan*² *wu*³. A dry dock.

理當 *Li*³ *tang*¹. *Ought*, by rights, in duty bound.

西。只有那兩個箱子、餘外還有我的行李。○這[16]八百錢、是我額外送你的酒錢、答多謝先生的賞。○爲[17]修這個船塢、他一共領了二十萬銀子、這其中不能沒有浮餘(餘浮)。○你[18]既然有這樣的名師、理當分外恭敬纔是、怎麼倒藐視(輕慢)他呢。○除[19]你之外、再沒有人能成全我這件事、因此我又來煩瑣你咯。○我[20]的眼睛已經疼花喇、一喝點酒、就格外的瘖曶。○王[21]先生說話淨蓋人、(壓量人)(掐尖子)明明人家說的有理、他偏想個法子、顯出人家沒有理來。○[22]民間交(兌)糧納稅、雖說有一定的額數、但是一經官吏書差的手、總必額外多要一點(些)、○人[23]失(喪)了家眷、固然沒有不難受的、但是若有撇(丟)下的小孩子、人就偏(格)外的難受。○我[24]那裏還有多餘(餘浮)着幾吊錢、你若是不彀用的、只管拿

15 Aside from those two boxes, there is nothing save my personal luggage.

16 These eight hundred cash are an extra present for yourself. *Ans.* Many thanks for your kindness.

17 He received in all two hundred thousand taels for building this dry dock, of which he cannot but have something left over.

18 Having so distinguished a teacher, you ought to treat him with unusual respect. How is it that you treat him with contempt?

19 There is no one except you who can carry this business through for me, so I have come again to trouble you.

20 My sight has already become blurred through this pain in my eyes, and whenever I drink a little wine, it is still more indistinct.

21 Mr. Wang is given to browbeating people. When the other party is clearly in the right, he still finds some way of showing that he is in the wrong.

22 Although the taxes and duties paid by the people are supposed to be fixed by schedule, yet in passing through the hands of the officers and collectors, something extra will of course be demanded.

23 A man is of course grieved when he loses his wife, but in case she leaves little children, he feels the loss still more keenly.

24 I have there a surplus of a few thousand cash. If you are in need of it, just take it and use it.

煩瑣 *Fan² soă³*. *To trouble*, to worry, to bother, ... to harass.

瘖 *Ma²,³*. . . . . . . Bleared, indistinct.

曶 *Hu¹,⁴*. . . . . . . To see obscurely.

瘖曶 Eyes blurred, *indistinct vision*.

壓量 *Ya⁴ liang²*. To presume, to domineer, *to* . . . . *browbeat*, to snub. (c.)

掐 *Ch'ia¹*. . . . To claw ; to grab; to twist; to plait.

掐尖子 *Ch'ia¹ chien¹ tsï³*. To domineer, to . . . . usurp the first place, *to browbeat;* to share illicit gains. (s.)

兌糧 *Twei⁴ liang.²* To pay tax either in grain . . . . or money.

納稅 *Na⁴ shwei⁴*. . . . . To pay duty.

吏 *Li⁴*. *An official ;* a subordinate, a deputy; a . . . . . . secretary.

額數 *Ê² shu⁴*. The legal rate, *the regular* . . . . *schedule.*

恙 *Yang⁴*. Nervous, out of sorts ; indisposed ; . . . . a sickness, *an ailment.*

病病恙恙 *Ping⁴ yang⁴*. Unwell, *ailing*, out . . . . of sorts.

吸氣筒 *Hsi¹ ch'i⁴ t'ung³*. . . . . . . An air-pump.

通力輪 *T'ung¹ li⁴ lun²*. . . . . . A balance wheel.

手工 *Shou³ kung¹*. . . . . . Cost of workmanship.

去用。○你25們別想我是個浮餘兒(多餘兒)、若是沒有我、你們自己却了不了。○慕26本仁的東家、一下子交給他二十個元寶、叫他到上海去辦貨、又另外給他三十兩碎銀子做盤費。○他27已經那麼大的年紀、又常病病恙恙的、所以大鍋的飯、一點也吃不下去、必得另外弄(做)小鍋的喫。○你28們這些路過人太多了去喇、一天沒有一百、也有八十個來討錢的、我們也是居家過日子的人、那裏有這麼些多餘錢來給你們呢。○這29個吸氣筒、原用不着通力輪、加上一個也是淨多餘的。○叫30銀匠打首飾、有管四分手工的、有管五分手工的、那些格外費工的、還有兩對兩的。

25 You need not think that I am a supernumerary; you cannot settle the matter yourselves without me.

26 Mu Pên Jên's employer gave him twenty ingots of silver at once, and sent him to Shanghai to lay in goods; and in addition gave him thirty taels of small silver for traveling expenses.

27 Being so old and constantly ailing, it is impossible for him to eat the ordinary food of the family. It will be necessary to cook something specially for him.

28 You traveling mendicants are quite too numerous. There are not less than eighty or a hundred of you coming each day. How should we, who also have to earn our living, have money to spare to give to all of you?

29 This air pump has no need of a balance wheel; to add one is entirely superfluous.

30 When silver ornaments are ordered of a silversmith, the charge for making is in some cases forty, and in some cases fifty per cent of the weight of the silver, and in case the work is very elaborate, the charge is equal to the weight.

NOTES.

2 Any one who has attended one literary examination is entitled to the appellation 童生. In this case, the party calls himself 童生 in order to bring to the notice of the magistrate the fact that he is a literary man.

9 前有車後有轍 *The wagon in front leaves its track behind;* that is, there are precedents by which the matter is determined.

22 官吏書差 *Magistrates, officers, clerks and police.* 書 stands for 書辦. The 官 and 書 are collectors of taxes, and the 吏 and 差 are collectors of customs.

24 多餘 as here used—in the sense of *surplus* or *remainder*, is vouched for by Peking teachers, but it is not so used in Shantung, where it is used only in the sense of *superfluous* or *unnecessary*.

26 辦貨 *Manage goods;* that is, to lay in and transport home a supply of goods for sale.

27 大鍋的飯 *Food cooked in the large kettle;* that is, the ordinary family fare as opposed to 小鍋的飯; that is, delicacies cooked in small quantities and with special pains.

28 太多了去喇. This addition of 去喇, after adjectives preceded by 太, or a word of similar import, is a colloquialism much in vogue in some places.

LESSON CLXXIII.

EMPHATIC ASSENT.

赶自 or **赶自的** Certainly, of course, I should say. (C. & N.)

自然是 Naturally, of course, to be sure.

可不是 Of course, that's so, you're right, exactly so.

可不是罷咧 The same,—罷咧 being [added for emphasis.

第一百七十三課

爲[1]我們的事、還能叫人家受掛誤拖累嗎、答那是自然的。○先[2]生不用開錢、今兒晚上的酒飯、都算我的、答那兒來裏的話、我喫喝的、還能叫你開錢嗎。○周[3]文錦這幾年沒有進項利路、却不像受窮的樣子、答趕自是那還間、他女人有一千多銀子的體己私房、還不彀他的嚼過花消嗎。○俗[4]語說、不見兎子不撒鷹、偺們沒看見他的東西、還能給他錢嗎、答那是一定的。○我[5]一個寡居婦、拉着這麽些孩子、見天天天又要吃又要穿、眞不是玩兒的、答可不是嗎那麽不是、難是不錯的。○我[6]們從早盼望你得兒子、好來喫你的喜麪蛋、這一回却是必要喫的喇、答那是不用說講的、就怕衆位不賞臉。○馬[7]雲龍不過十二三歲、就記得好幾部書、文章做的也很

TRANSLATION.

1 Can we allow others to be embarrassed with our affairs? *Ans.* Of course not.

2 You need not pay, sir; let this evening's wine and refreshments stand to my account. *Ans.* What are you talking about? Do you suppose I will let you pay my score?

3 Chou Wên Chin has had no income (means of living) these several years, and yet he does not seem badly off. *Ans.* Well, I should say not. His wife had over a thousand taels laid up of her own, which is enough for his living, is it not?

4 The proverb says, "Don't loose the falcon till you see the hare." Do you think we will pay him the money before we get the goods? *Ans.* Of course not.

5 It is truly no trivial matter for a widow, as I am, to bring up all these children,—finding food and clothing for them every day. *Ans.* That's so. It is difficult, no mistake.

6 We have long been hoping you would have a son that we might get a feast out of you, and now we must certainly have it. *Ans.* That goes without saying. I am only afraid you will not do me the honor.

7 Ma Yün Lung, though only twelve or thirteen years old, has memorized several books and also writes quite a good essay. He will surely make

那麽不是 Of course, that's so. (s.)

那是自然的 That's a matter of course, that's understood.

那是一定的 That's certain, that's so, that's a fact.

那是已就的 That's understood, you may rest assured of that. (c. & n.)

那是已在的 That's understood, that's a foregone conclusion. (c. & n.)

那是實話 That's a fact, that's so, that's sure.

那是不用說的 That goes without saying, of course.

那是不用講的 The same. (s.)

那何用說 The same as the last, but put in the interrogative form for emphasis.

那還間 Why ask that? of course not. (s.)

那兒的話 What are you talking about? what do you mean?

那來的話 The same.

那裏的話 The same.

In the above phrases 那 is emphatic and hence emphasized. Its tones must be carefully distinguished.

着 That's so, just so, exactly. Much used in some localities to express full assent, and is oftentimes repeated after each sentence. It is not essentially different from 嗻 (Les. 70), which writing is preferred by some teachers.

可以、往後必有個出息、答自然是、這樣的聰明、還能不發達嗎。○盧[8]相臣太不認交情了、跟他借件單袍子穿、他橫豎支吾着不借、他若再跟我們借東西、也不用借給他、答那是自然之已在的。○我[9]對你們告訴罷、人說家下小口、總要知道根底、因為這不是個騾子馬、不合式還可以再倒挑換、答那是實話。○他[10]若帶着人來打架、你們這些小夥子、要緊助我一膀之力、答那何用講說、偺們都是自己、不幫助你幫助誰呢。○我[11]若和自己親愛的人多日沒見、覺着見了、不知有多少話要說、及至果真見了面、又覺着無話可說、你看這奇不奇、答可不是罷嗎咧。○從[12]來說、前人開路後人行、若我待我的父母不好、將來

his mark by and by. *Ans.* Of course he will. Such talents cannot fail of success.

8 Lu Hsiang Ch'ên is *too* unneighborly. I asked him to lend me an unlined coat to wear, but he shuffled about and made all sorts of excuses for not lending it. When he comes again to borrow anything of us, we will not lend it to him. *Ans.* That's understood.

9 I tell you what it is, when a man bargains for a wife, he wants to know the bottom facts; for it's not as in the case of a mule or a horse, which if unsuitable, one can exchange. *Ans.* That's a fact.

10 If he brings men with him to fight, you young fellows must not fail to come to my assistance. *Ans.* Of course we will. We are all of one family. If we do not help you, whom should we help?

11 When for a long time I have not seen one whom I love, I feel as if I had no end of things to talk about; but when I actually see him, I then feel as if I had little or nothing to say. Strange, isn't it? *Ans.* That it certainly is.

12 The old saying is, "Men walk in the steps of their predecessors." If I treat my parents badly, will my children treat me well? *Ans.*

VOCABULARY.

掛誤 *Kwa⁴ wu⁴*. Trouble, *embarrassment;* to involve in.

拖累 *T'oă¹ lei⁴*. The same. (s.)

開錢 *K'ai¹ ch'ien²*. To give out money; *to pay*, to pay off.

利路 *Li⁴ lu⁴*. *Means of living*, employment, occupation. (c.)

嚼過 *Chüe² kwoă⁴*. Outlay, expenses, livelihood, *living*.

寡居 *Kwa³ chü¹*. To live in widowhood; *a widow*.

賞臉 *Shang³ lien³*. To show respect, *to honor;* to compliment.

挑換 *T'iao¹ hwan⁴*. *To exchange*, to transpose, to interchange. (s.)

倒換 *Tao³ hwan⁴*. To exchange.

親愛 *Ch'in¹ ai⁴*. To love dearly.

蜡 *Cha¹,⁴*. An imperial sacrifice for the fruits of the year :—Note 13.

兵船 *Ping¹ ch'wan²*. A war-ship, a man-of-war, a gunboat.

營子 *Ying² tsï³*. The Chinese city at Newchwang.

走動 *Tsou³ tung⁴*. To have intercourse or dealings with, *to associate with;* to have a movement of the bowels.

數過 *Shu³ kwoă⁴*. *To lecture*, to berate.

託夢 *T'oă³ mêng⁴*. To appear to in a dream.

源 *Yüen²*. A fountain, a spring; *source*, origin.

來源 *Lai² yüen²*. *Source*, origin.

我的兒子、還能待我好嗎、答喳着、這纔是好話喇。○昨[13]兒在八蜡廟、遇見費老四帶着孫子聽戲、看他大有享福的樣兒、答赶自自然是的、他大兒子在兵船上、每月挣十二塊洋錢、第二個在水師營、每月挣六兩銀子、第三個在營子、喫三釐小分子、有這麼三個好兒子、還能不享福嗎。○張[14]喜從早就不願意和他走動、今天叫他這一數過、管保再就不上門兒喇、答那是一定已就的。○都[15]說人死了不明白、不明白、死的俺孩子爹、昨天夜裏託夢給我、跟我要個馬褂子、若果眞不明白、怎麼知道回來要東西呢、答可不是。○雨[16]的來源、大概是出於海、因爲海水被烈日一曬、就化爲氣、答喳着。化氣就自然上升、答喳着。升到空中、就是雲彩。答喳着。但是空中比地面上更冷、所以雲彩就縮爲水點兒、水點兒落在地上、這就是雨、答喳着、這遭我可明白下雨的道理喇、領教領教。

Exactly so. That is sound doctrine.

13 I met Fei the Fourth yesterday at the Pacha Temple listening to the play with his grandchildren. He looked as if he were in very prosperous circumstances. *Ans.* Of course he is. His oldest son is on a man-of-war getting twelve dollars per month, the second son is in the naval encampment getting six taels per month, and the third is in a business house in Newchwang sharing three per cent of the profits. Having three such good sons, why should he not enjoy life?

14 Chang Hsi has been unwilling for some time to associate with him, and after the lecture he read him do-day, I venture he will not darken his door again. *Ans.* You may rest assured of that.

15 People say we are not conscious after death. Last night my deceased husband appeared to me in a dream, and asked me for a short coat. If he were indeed unconscious, how would he know to come back and ask for things? *Ans.* That's a fact.

16 The sea is the chief source of the rain. It is because the hot sun shining on the sea turns the water into vapor. *Ans.* Just so. Now the vapor naturally rises. *Ans.* Exactly. And when it rises it becomes clouds. *Ans.* Just so. But it is colder in the upper air than on the surface of the earth, therefore the clouds soon condense into rain drops, and these drops of water falling on the earth make the rain. *Ans.* Just so. I now understand the philosophy of rain. Thanks. Thanks.

NOTES.

1 那是自然的 is an emphatic assent to the negative implied in the question, and hence in effect makes a negative and must be so translated.

5 拉 is used of rearing children, in allusion to the effort required to "drag along" the load of care and toil. 不是玩 *No joke, no fun in it,*—a very common phrase.

6 喜麪 *Vermicelli of rejoicing.* In North China, vermicelli (noodles) is the essential dish at all ordinary feasts of rejoicing. In the South, eggs take the place of vermicelli.

10 一膀之力 *One shoulder's strength;* that is, *assistance, a lift.* 自己 is constantly used, as here, to signify, *belonging to the same family, or to one's own family.*

13 八蜡廟 A temple dedicated to the gods of grasshoppers, or locusts. There are eight of these gods, supposed to have authority over as many kinds of insects. The sacrifice referred to by the term 蜡, (or as originally written 䄍), probably had reference to deliverance from the ravages of insects. Grasshoppers are commonly called 螞蚱, and 蜡 is not now applied to them.

第一百七十四課

徐[1]先生最老實不過。○
這[2]樣混帳東西、非打不可。○
他[3]是武秀才又能待怎麼樣呢、武秀才還能喫了人不
成。○劉[4]家那個小黑驢、最快捎不過、你去借他的騎騎
罷。○今[5]天並沒有人來、難道一個鞍子、還能長上腿
自己跑了不成。○我[6]看他未必肯來、答他不來却不
行中。○馮[7]太太那個人、最直率爽不過、是說是、非說非、再
不能露面藏私藏頭露面。○難[8]道你這些話、都是從肺腑裏掏
出來的眞話不成。○那[9]樣不識高低的人、非强壓着他
不行。○天[10]父待我們罪人的恩典、極大無比。○他[11]這
樣打死我的親兵、非償命不行。○你[12]們回去告訴馬

TRANSLATION.

1 Mr. Hsü is simple-minded to the last degree.
2 Nothing less than a flogging will answer for such a scoundrel as this fellow is.
3 Suppose he *is* a military graduate, what can he do? Can a military graduate eat up people?
4 That little black donkey of the Liu family's is very fleet. Go and borrow it of them and ride.
5 No one has been here to-day. Do you mean to say that a saddle could grow legs and run away of itself?
6 I think it is very doubtful whether he will be willing to come. *Ans.* But he *must* come.
7 Mrs. Fêng is an uncommonly straightforward person. With her, right is right and wrong is wrong. Deceit is wholly foreign to her character.
8 Do you mean to assert that what you have said is downright honest truth?
9 With such a short-witted fellow as this, there is no way but to use force.
10 The mercy of our Heavenly Father toward us is great beyond comparison.
11 Having killed one of my body-guard, I insist that he shall pay the penalty with his life.
12 Do you go back and tell Ma Shu

LESSON CLXXIV.

FINAL NEGATIVE INTENSIVES.

The following negative finals form a somewhat miscellaneous class, which, for want of a better term, I have characterized as *intensives*.

不過 Not to be exceeded, to the last degree, exceedingly, very,—used to strengthen the force of a previous intensive.

不可 Cannot but,—nearly always preceded by 非, giving the sense of nothing less, nothing short of, etc.

不行 Will not do, can't be allowed, must.

不中 Will not serve the purpose, must, positively must. (c. & s.)

無比 Beyond compare,—used to strengthen the force of a previous intensive.

不成 Expresses an emphatic protest, and is used at the end of an interrogative clause, which is generally introduced by **難道**. It has no answering word in the English language. It forms a very forcible idiom and is entirely *t'ung-hsing*.

VOCABULARY.

捎 *Shao*¹. The arrow leaving the bow; rapid, ... *fleet*.

鞍 *An*¹. . . . . . . A saddle.

率 *Shwai*⁴. To follow, to conform to; *to lead*, to . . . . cause to follow; a leader, a guide; a term in a proportion; a resumé; suddenly.

書紳罷、非他自己來見我不可。○[13]反過來你瞧不上(看不中)我、復過來你也瞧不上(看不中)我、難道我必得上你眼睛裏去住不成。○[14]我見過他的文章、雖然用的典故不多、却最清楚不過。○[15]你這樣的不孝、我非送你的忤逆不可。○[16]我怎麼不敢跟他去呢、難道他家裏還有王命不成。○[17]你們逢少甚麼、就來問我要、難道我就是個有的不成。○[18]若是喫湯菜、非用羹匙(調羹)不可。○[19]聰明人能中舉會試、愚笨人就拉倒了不成、若是好好用功、自然也能上進。○[20]你們想想、他罵我一兩句、我受了他的、難道他就高貴了些、我就虧損了些不成。○[21]你到那些兵船上去看看、無論是機器、是鎗砲、都擦得明亮、凡露船面的地方、

Shên that nothing will answer but for him to come to see me himself.

13 This way you are dissatisfied with me, and that way you are dissatisfied with me. Must I see everything just as you do?

14 I saw one of his essays, and although there were not many quotations in it, yet the style was exceedingly lucid.

15 If you are so undutiful as this, I shall be compelled to report you [to the magistrate] as incorrigible.

16 Why don't I dare to go with him? Do they have the power of life and death at his house?

17 Whenever you need anything you come to me. Do you think my resources are without limit?

18 When eating a vegetable stew, one cannot manage without a spoon.

19 Because it takes a talented man to get a second or third degree, must a stupid man therefore not try at all? If he is diligent, he also will not fail to make progress.

20 Consider the case: if he gives me a few words of abuse and I submit to it, does it therefore follow that he is somewhat the gainer and I somewhat the loser?

21 Go on board those men-of-war and you will see that both the machinery and the guns are polished up bright, and all the exposed parts of the deck are

直率 *Chï² shwai⁴.* *Straightforward,* downright, frank, open-hearted.

掏 *T'ao¹.* To pull out, to drag out; to draw; to tug at.

親兵 *Ch'in¹ ping¹.* Armed attendants, body-guard.

償命 *Ch'ang² ming⁴.* To pay the penalty with life.

湯菜 *T'ang¹ ts'ai⁴.* Vegetables served with broth or soup over them.

愚笨 *Yü² pên⁴.* Dull, *stupid,* doltish.

用功 *Yung⁴ kung¹.* To study, to apply the mind; to practice, *to be diligent.*

上進 *Shang⁴ chin⁴.* *To make progress,* to advance.

船面 *Ch'wan² mien⁴.* The deck of a ship.

刷洗 *Shwa¹ hsi³.* Th scrub, *to scour,* to mop.

修飾 *Hsiu¹ shï¹.* To adorn, to embellish, to trick out, *to make neat,* to tidy up.

摳 *K'ou¹.* To pull, drag or *dig out;* to bring to light, to solve.

滴溜溜 *Ti¹ liu¹ liu¹.* Round, bulging, full; *glaring.*

溜豎豎 *Liu¹ shu⁴ shu⁴.* Staring, *glaring.*

訣 *Chüe².* Parting words; an art, a rule; *a mystery,* a trick; occult.

訣竅 *Chüe² ch'iao⁴.* Mystery, secret; *clue,* rationale.

都天天刷洗、眞是極乾淨無比。○依22我的意思、非罰他請十桌客不可、但有衆位的面子、你們看怎麼好就怎麼好。○若23是將好話說、不賠也不要緊、你既然說出這樣喪良心的話來、錯過賠我不行。○饞24老婆懶修飾、專聽門外賣東西、除非東家跑西家闖、不做針線只會浪、這樣的老婆、非休退了他不可。○這25裏找找不着你、那裏找找不着你、今天可叫我碰見喇、非給我錢不行中、答我沒有錢却怎麼樣呢、你還能叫我上地裏摳去不成。○別26看他瞪着兩個眼睛滴溜溜暨溜暨的、心裏却最傻糊儸塗不過、無論遇見什麼事情、一點也料鋪不開、並看不出事情的訣竅來。

scoured up every day. Nothing could exceed their perfect cleanliness.

22 According to my idea, nothing short of fining him ten tables of guests should be accepted; but in deference to you, gentlemen, let it be just as you think right.

23 If you had spoken reasonably, I would not have insisted on your making good the loss; but since you have chosen to speak in this unconscionable way, I shall accept nothing short of reparation.

24 A greedy wife, too lazy to keep herself neat, always listening for the step of the huckster, and forever gadding about, who will do no sewing, but gives herself to wantoning;—there is nothing to be done with such a wife but to divorce her.

25 I have been looking everywhere for you in vain. Now that I have happened on you to-day, I will not let you off unless you pay me. *Ans.* But what if I have no money? Can you make me dig it out of the ground?

26 Don't be misled by those bright glowing eyes of his. In point of fact he is thick-headed to the last degree. He hasn't the least faculty for managing anything; he never gets the clue to things.

NOTES.

4 The use of 的 makes 他 refer to the owner; if it were omitted, 他 would naturally refer to the donkey.

7 露面藏私 *Show the face, but conceal an evil purpose,—to speak fair words when evil is intended.* 藏頭露面 *Conceal the head but reveal the face*, has practically the same meaning.

8 肺腑裏掏出來 *Brought forth from the lungs and viscera.* Sentiments and intentions proceed not only from the "heart," as with us, but from the "inward parts" generally.

9 不識高低 *Not to recognize the difference between high and low;* that is, *not able to see a point, obtuse, short-witted.*

16 王命 *Royal authority.* The power of life and death, aside from the processes of law, is conferred upon certain officers. Such officers are said to have 王命; that is, the authority to condemn and execute at will, such as is possessed by a 王 or prince.

24 The first part of this sentence is a four line verse with two rhymes. It epitomizes in terse but forcible language the characteristic faults of a worthless wife.

LESSON CLXXV.

CORRELATIVE PARTICLES.

就是...還能 If should ... could, would.	就是...也不 Even, even if ... not.
就是...也得 Even if ... must.	就是...也强似 Better even ... than.
就是...也要 Even if ... will, must.	不但...而且 Not only ... but also.

第一百七十五課

不[1]用哭喇、你就是哭三天三夜、他還能再活過來嗎。○喫[2]大烟不但是花冤錢、而且還蹧蹋身子。○他[3]們兩個、那些鈎搭連環的事、就是神仙也斷不清。○實[4]在沒有新的、舊的也可以、答就是舊的、也得有啊。○我[5]和劉五子的冤仇、不但這輩子解不開、就是再一輩子、也解不開。○他[6]連個題講尚且作不好、何況是作滿篇呢。○人[7]不但要善良像鴿子、也要靈巧像蛇。○種[8]莊稼那能看二分利呢、所以就是賣地還賬、也强似年年給人拿利。○講[9]着給他一半現錢、他尚且不願意賣、何況要全賒着呢。○孝[10]子不但養活父母、而且他又敬愛他。○晉[11]惠公說、一個平常人尚且不可侮慢、何況我為國君呢。○無[12]論是說話是作行文、不但

Translation.

1 Come, come, stop crying. If you should cry for three days and nights, it would not bring him to life again.

2 Opium smoking not only wastes money, but it also destroys the health.

3 The tangle of these two men's affairs is such that even the genii could not decide between them.

4 If you really have no new ones, old ones will do. *Ans.* But what if I haven't even old ones?

5 My enmity with Liu Wu-tsï, not only cannot be allayed in this lifetime, it cannot even be allayed in the next lifetime.

6 He cannot even write an explanation of the theme, how much less can he write a complete essay.

7 A man should not only be harmless as a dove, he should also be wise as a serpent.

8 It is impossible to realize twenty-four per cent profit at farming. Hence it is better to sell land and pay one's debts, than to pay interest year by year.

9 He is not willing to sell, even when offered one-half ready money, how much less if it is all on credit.

10 A dutiful son not only supports his father and mother, he also honors and loves them.

11 Prince Hwei of Chin said, "You ought not to insult even a common man, how much more me, your prince."

12 Both in speaking and in writing you should aim, not only at brevity, but

不但...更 Not only...... but still more.

不但...就是也 Not only...... but even, but also.

不但...倒 Not only...... but on the contrary.

不但...也 Not only............ also.

尚且...何況 Even......how much more.

尚且...何況更 Even............how much more.

尚且...更 Even if......... much more.

Vocabulary.

善良 *Shan⁴ liang²*. Good, upright, honorable; .... *harmless.*

鴿 *Kê¹*...... *A dove;* a pigeon.

敬愛 *Ching⁴ ai⁴*. To respect and love, to revere, *to honor.*

晉 *Chin⁴*. To flourish; *name of an ancient feudal kingdom.*

要求其簡捷、更要求其顯亮明白。○若13是能作一部好書、不但於當世有益處、就是於後世也有益處。○叫14他欺貧詥到幾時是個頭兒呢、這回遭就是劉上一死、也要和他拔拔這個鋼眼見個高低見見血。○連15僱人幫助、尙且累得丟盔撩甲的、若不僱人、更不知累到甚麼樣兒喇。○外16人尙且要愛、何况自己的兄弟、更要相親相愛。○我17就是願意學醫道、因爲懂得醫道、不但能利己、而且也能濟世。○他18不但爲人打算事情、打算的周到、就是在交接應酬上、也沒有比他再通世務路的了。○他19覺着是賈大人的鄉親、賈大人必賞他個臉、歸根期不但沒討出臉來、反倒討了個無趣。○你20想有官壓服、惡人尙且橫行、若沒有官壓服、豈不更要橫行嗎。○俗21語說、酒肉朋友、柴米

still more at clearness and perspicuity.

13 If you can write a good book, it will be a benefit, not only to the present, but to succeeding generations.

14 How long must I put up with his domineering? This time we'll see who is the better man, even if it costs me my life.

15 If even with hired help we are fatigued beyond endurance, to what extreme would our fatigue reach if we had no hired help at all?

16 You ought to love even strangers, how much more should you love your own brothers.

17 The thing I want to learn is medicine; for if one understands medicine, not only can he benefit himself but he can also be a blessing to society.

18 Not only is he thorough in planning matters for others, but also in the varied intercourse of life, there is none more conversant with the amenities than he.

19 He thought that as he had been Chia Ta-jên's neighbor, Chia Ta-jên would certainly treat him with politeness; whereas he not only did not receive any consideration, but on the contrary was subjected to humiliation.

20 You should consider; if bad men are violent even with officers to restrain them, how much more violent would they become if there were no officers to restrain them.

21 The proverb says, "Feasting makes good friends; fuel and rice keep the peace between husband and wife." Hence when a man becomes very poor,

侮 *Wu*³. . . . . . *To insult;* to ridicule; to neglect.

侮慢 *Wu*³ *man*⁴. *To insult,* to contemn; to set . . . . at naught.

行文 *Hsing*² *wên*². *To write,* to compose in . . . . writing; to send a dispatch.

作文 *Tsoŭ*⁴ *wên*². To write, to compose in . . . . writing.

簡捷 *Chien*³ *chie*². . . . . . *Brief,* terse, concise.

顯亮 *Hsien*³ *liang*⁴. *Clear,* perspicuous; evident, ... manifest.

鋼 *Kang*¹. . . . . *Steel;* hard, tough.

鋼眼 *Kang*¹ *yien*³. . . . Eye of a steel cone plate.

盔 *K'wei*¹. . . . A defence for the head, a helmet.

撩 *Liao*⁴. To brush off; *to throw away;* to . . . . leave, to forsake :—See *liao*².

周到 *Chou*¹ *tao*⁴. Everywhere, catholic; com- . . . . plete, *thorough.*

交接 *Chiao*¹ *chie*¹. *Intercourse,* fellowship; . . . . communication.

世路 *Shï*⁴ *lu*⁴. *The customs and fashions of the* . . . . . . *world;* obsequious, complaisant.

世務 *Shï*⁴ *wu*⁴. . . . . The same.

鄉親 *Hsiang*¹ *ch'in*¹. *Residents of the same* . . . . *neighborhood,* neighbors.

壓服 *Ya*¹ *fu*². *To restrain,* to keep down, to . . . . . . curb, to control.

夫妻、所以人到過於窮了、不但朋友看不起、就是自己的妻子、也看不起。○你22的腿疼還沒好嗎、答那裏好了呢、前日叫一個拉駱駝(搖串鈴)的針了兩針、不但不見輕、倒越發見重喇。○他23光懶也好、或者是光饞也好、這個不但是懶、而且又饞、你說怎麼過日子呢。○張24二先生眞會辦事、無論多大的事情、叫他一辦、不但不板、而且一個人也不得罪、眞是圓通的很。○從25那一遭我算惺了腦子喇(傷了心)、就是有人託俺(我)親爹來說、我也不給人做媒了。○到26大旱的時候、不但有莊稼人、掘龍潭、打旱魃、許願求雨、就是一切的客商官員、也是如此。○從27來說、好馬不備雙鞍韂(喫回頭草)、烈女不嫁二夫、(郎君)(男)所以這家子就是踢蹬的(倒敗得)家產盡絕、房角地角一點沒有、我也不抱怨、那家子就是蹅(跕)着金銀上炕、我也不貪圖。

not only do his friends slight him, but even his own wife becomes estranged.

22 Is not the pain in your leg well yet? *Ans.* No, I should say not. Day before yesterday I got one of those camel-leading (bell-ringing) quacks to stick a couple of needles into it which made it, not only no better, but decidedly worse.

23 If she were only lazy, it would not matter; or if she were only greedy; but this one is not only lazy but greedy as well. How do you suppose I can make a living?

24 Mr. Chang the Second is an accomplished business man. No matter how extensive the business he undertakes, it is accomplished without difficulty. Nor does he offend a single person. He is certainly a very clever man.

25 From that experience I learned a lesson. Even if anyone should get my own father to ask me, I would not be go-between for him.

26 When there is a great drought, not only do farmers seek rain by digging up the dragon pool, destroying the drought demon and making vows, but even merchant travelers and officials all do the same.

27 The saying is, "A good horse will not carry two saddes (not eat leavings); and a virtuous woman will not marry two husbands." Therefore even if this family squander their inheritance so that they have neither house nor land, I will not reproach myself; and if that family be decked out in silver and gold, I will not covet it.

串鈴 *Ch'wan⁴ ling².* A bell in the shape of a ring:—Note 22.

圓通 *Yüen² t'ung¹.* Clever, tactful; accommodating; versatile.

惺 *Hsing¹.* *To consider;* to comprehend, to take in; to recall.

潭 *T'an².* Deep; a pool or pond.

魃 *Pa².* The demon of drought.

旱魃 *Han⁴ pa².* The same:—Note 26.

許願 *Hsü³ yüen⁴.* To make a vow; to promise with an oath.

客商 *K'ê⁴ shang¹.* A commercial traveller, a merchant.

韂 *Ch'an⁴.* A saddle and flaps; a saddle.

鞍韂 *An¹ ch'an⁴.* A saddle.

倒敗 *Tao³ pai⁴.* To fail, to come to grief; to ruin; *to squander.* (s.)

抱怨 *Pao⁴ yüen⁴.* To regret, *to reproach oneself;* to be spiteful.

跕 *Tien³.* To limp; to stand or walk on tiptoe, to walk softly. Also *tie¹.*

第一百七十六課

不[1]是張三好滋事、乃是李四挾
嫌找尋他（仇尋事）。○爲[2]君固然是難、但
是爲臣也不容易。○雖[3]然他當
下貧窮、焉知後來不富。○此[4]乃
兩相情願、不許反悔。○穿[5]衣裳
固然是粗糙（不濟）的省錢、但仍舊是
穿好的上算。○夫[6]妻不算兩個
人、乃是一體的。○他[7]固然不可
和你抬槓（拌嘴）、但是你也不該打他。
○潘[8]秀雲不是莊戶人家、乃是

TRANSLATION.

1 It was not that Chang the Third wished to pick a quarrel, but that Li the Fourth had a grudge against him, and set upon him.
2 To be a king is of course difficult, yet to be a minister is far from easy.
3 Although he is poor at present, yet who knows but that hereafter he may be rich.
4 This agreement is made with the full consent of both parties, and must not be broken.
5 Inferior clothing is of course cheaper, and yet after all it is more economical to wear good clothing.
6 Husband and wife are not two, but are one flesh.
7 He should not dispute with you, it is true, nor ought you to strike him.

NOTES.

3 鈎搭連環 *Hooks locked and links connected;* i.e., *entanglements, complications.* The phrase violates the usual symmetry. It ought to be 鈎搭環連.

5 This sentence assumes the transmigration of the soul, and that the wrongs done in this existence will be carried forward to the next one for adjustment.

6 題講 *An exposition of the theme,* an introduction setting forth the main points of the text. It is also frequently called 起講, *to set forth an exposition.* 滿篇 *A full or complete essay;* that is, one having all the requisite parts. 篇 is used with reference to the folded sheet on which the essay is written.

11 惠公 A prince of the kingdom of 晉, whose personal name was 夷吾. He used these words when in exile.

14 拔鋼眼 *To draw through the steel eye;* that is, to settle by trial who is the better man. The figure is taken from the drawing of wire through the eye of a steel cone-plate. 見個高低 *To see who is the better man.* 見見血 *To see blood;* i.e., *to carry it through to the bitter end.*

15 丟盔撩(卸)甲 *To throw away the helmet and drop the armor;* that is, to do so in the haste and exhaustion of flight,—a strong figure to express great hurry and fatigue.

21 The idea of the saying is that in order to retain a man's friendship, one must be able to reciprocate his invitations (to feasts, etc.), and to retain the affection of a wife one must be able to support her.

22 拉駱駝的 *A camel-leader;* that is, an itinerant doctor who goes about with a camel, partly to carry his outfit, and partly to serve as an advertisement. In the South the doctor carries his own pack and advertises himself by a special kind of bell called a 串鈴.

23 It is very evident from the sentiment of this sentence that the speaker is a young man who is speaking of his wife. The use of 這個 is highly characteristic.

25 惺了腦子 *To get the brain waked up, to learn by dear experience, to cut one's eye-teeth.*

26 掘龍潭 *To dig up the dragon pool.* In time of great drought the people sometimes go to the temple of Lung-wang and dig up the dry pool in the temple yard, which is supposed to be the home of the dragon. This is done to make him uncomfortable and frighten him, so that he will send rain. 打旱魃 Destroy the Drought Demon. Drought is attributed to the agency of a malicious demon who is supposed to reside in the coffin of some dead person. The corpse in the coffin in which he resides does not decay, and the grave mound remains moist when the ground all around is dry. The explanation of this is that the demon compels the dead man to carry water every night and water the grave. The supposed remedy is to tear open the grave and the coffin, pull the corpse to pieces and scatter the pieces in various places. This very thing is frequently done, despite the protestations of the friends of the dead. These things are not only done by the ignorant, but by the educated as well.

27 雙鞍韉 does not mean a double saddle, but a change of saddles, which implies a change of owners.

LESSON CLXXVI.

CORRELATIVE PARTICLES.

不是 . . . . . . 乃是 Not . . . . . . but.

乃 . . . 不 Indicates the adversative correlation of the clauses, but has no answering words in English. The use of 乃 adds a slight emphasis, somewhat approximating the force of *indeed,* or *in fact.*

固然 . . . . . 但是 . . . . . . 也 Of course, indeed . . . . yet,

書香子弟。○柳[9]樹甲雖然聰明、其實沒有甚麼書底子兒。○固[10]然是當論理、但是絕不論情、仍舊不能和睦人。○此[11]乃朝廷大事、不可多嘴。○安[12]息日做生(活)活、固然是犯罪、就是去玩耍、也不是正理。○殺[13]人固然該償命、但是情有可原、作官的仍舊是向活的、不向死的。○格[14]物乃是一種深奧學問、不是十天半月就能學明白的。○官[15]封印以後、雖然說是不許告狀、其實若有不法的大事、仍舊擋不住告。○人[16]的壽數原不可定、雖然今日還沒(尙未)死、焉知明日還活着。○作[17]事務要合乎中道、因爲不及固然是不好、就是過了也是一樣的不好。○雖[18]然衆人

8 P'an Hsiu Yün is not a rustic but the scion of a literary family.

9 Liu Shu Chia, although bright, is not in reality a profound scholar.

10 The right is to be kept in view of course, nevertheless to have no regard at all to sentiment, is not the way to make peace.

11 This is important imperial business, and should not be lightly criticized.

12 It is of course a sin to work on the Sabbath, and even to spend the time in amusement is not the proper thing.

13 A murderer should of course pay the forfeit with his life, yet the circumstances may afford occasion for clemency, and magistrates naturally favor the living rather than the dead.

14 Natural science is a profound subject, which cannot be mastered in ten or fifteen days.

15 Although it is said that suit cannot be entered after the magistrate has closed his seals, yet if there should be any flagrant violation of the law, suit may still be instituted.

16 The years of a man's life are uncertain. Although one does not die to-day, yet how does he know that he will be alive to-morrow?

17 In your conduct you should always follow the golden mean, for while neglect of duty is of course wrong, to

固然......但是......仍舊 It's true, of course... ...yet.

固然... ...就是... ...也 Of course ... ... yet, ...and even.

雖然...焉知 Although ... yet, yet who knows.

雖然...其實 Although ... ... yet.

雖然...其實...仍舊 Although ...... yet ... still.

雖然...却...乃 Although... yet... but.

VOCABULARY.

滋事 *Tsï¹ shï⁴*. *To pick a quarrel;* to stir up, to create a disturbance.

挾嫌 *Hsie² hsien²*. To estrange, to be or to set at variance; *to have a spite or grudge at,* to be at outs.

挾仇 *Hsie² ch'ou²*. To be enemies, *to have a spite or grudge at.*

找尋 *Chao³ hsün²*. To accuse, *to set upon,* to charge, to take to task.

貧窮 *P'in² ch'iung²*. ... ... Poor, needy.

槓 *Kang⁴*. ... ... The same as 杠.

抬槓 *T'ai² kang⁴*. *To dispute in a loud voice,* to altercate, to wrangle.

拌嘴 *Pan⁴ tswei³*. *To dispute,* to controvert, to bandy, to chaffer.

潘 *P'an¹*. ... ... A river in Honan; *a surname.*

莊戶 *Chwang¹ hu⁴*. ... ... *Rustic,* farmer.

書香 *Shu¹ hsiang¹*. Redolent of books, literary, scholastic.

書底 *Shu¹ ti³*. Education, *scholarship,* acquirements.

都說他是好人、若不仔細查問、焉知他不是鄉愿一類的呢。○人19辦紅白大公喜事、固然不可過於儉省、但也不可過於奢華、總要量力而行。○先20生教導學生、就如父母教導兒女一般、雖然打他、而其實却是愛他。○為21元帥的、固然必得有威嚴、三軍纔肯遵令、但若沒有愛心、三軍仍舊不能悅服。○我22本是一個異鄉人、雖然常與人有不和的事、却不是我去招惹惹呼人、乃是人來招惹惹呼我。○窮23家的姑娘、他固然不要、就是富家的姑娘、若沒有好門第、好人物、他仍舊是不要。○正24經話固然要聽、就是街市上、那些閒雜人等的話、也要放長耳朶聽聽。○這25話雖是他們在背地裏說的、

exceed the bounds of propriety is equally wrong.

18 Although everybody says he is a good man, yet if you do not carefully inquire, how can you be sure that he does not belong to the class of specious impostors?

19 In conducting weddings and funerals one should not of course be too parsimonious, nor should he make too great a display, but should always keep within his means.

20 A teacher instructs his pupils just as parents teach their children. Although he punishes them, yet in fact, he loves them.

21 A general must be strict, it is true, that so the soldiers may obey his commands; yet if he shows no affection, they will not yield a cheerful obedience.

22 Originally I was not a resident of this place; and although I often have trouble with others, it is not that I pick quarrels with them, but that they pick quarrels with me.

23 Of course he does not want the daughter of a poor family, and he will not accept even the daughter of a rich family, if the standing of the family is not good, or if the young lady is not comely.

24 Legitimate conversation you should of course give attention to, and even the

封印 *Fêng*1 *yin*4. To lock up the seals; to close a public office.

查問 *Ch'a*2 *wên*4. *To inquire*, to search.

鄉愿 *Hsiang*1 *yüen*4. A smooth-tongued specious fellow, *an impostor*, a wolf in sheep's clothing:—Note 18.

奢華 *Shê*1 *hwa*2. Extravagance, *display*.

教導 *Chiao*1 *tao*4. *To instruct*, to teach.

威嚴 *Wei*1 *yien*2. August, severe, stern.

遵令 *Tsun*1 *ling*4. *To obey* orders, to observe a command.

悅服 *Yüe*4 *fu*2. *To obey cheerfully*, to assent cordially, to approve.

異鄉 *I*4 *hsiang*1. A new-comer, a settler; a stranger.

招惹 *Chao*1 *jê*3. To irritate, to vex, *to pick a quarrel*.

惹呼 *Jê*3 *hu*3. To irritate, to stir up, to provoke, *to pick a quarrel*.

門第 *Mên*2 *ti*4. *Standing* (of a family), reputation, character, social position.

閒雜 *Hsien*2 *tsa*2. Idle, *loafing; disreputable*; rowdy.

冶 *Yie*3. To fuse, to smelt.

縲 *Lei*3. *To bind as a criminal;* to secure.

紲 *Hsie*4. To tie, to secure, *to fetter*.

縲紲 *Bonds*, imprisonment.

貝 *Pei*4. Precious, valuable; money, treasure.

寶貝 *Pao*3 *pei*4. Precious; *a treasure*.

禍根 *Hwo*4 *kên*1. A root of evil, a source of misfortune.

也不一定就是實情、因爲住(做)衙門的人、甚麼法子都有、焉知不是隔壁告狀、特爲說給大老爺聽呢。○公[26]冶長雖在縲絏之中、其實却不是他的罪、所以出監之後、孔子還情願將自己的女兒給他作妻。○東[27]莊上淘金的、得了一塊大金、有九斤半重、誰不說是得了寶貝呢、那知道因爲分贓不平、出了人命、把金都花淨了、另外又賠上若干、從此知道這金乃是他們的禍根、並不是他們的寶貝。○我[28]們所顧念的、不是看得見的、乃是看不見的、因爲看得見的、是暫時的、看不見的、是永遠的。

gossip of loafers on the street should not go unheeded.

25 Although this was spoken in secret it is not certainly the truth, for there is no end to the tricks of yamên people. How do you know that they were not playing a part,—talking on purpose for your honor to hear?

26 Although Kung Yie Ch'ang was in bonds, yet he was not in fact guilty of any crime, hence after his release, Confucius of his own accord gave him his daughter to wife.

27 The gold diggers in the village to the east found a nugget of gold weighing nine and a half catties. Who would not say that they had found a treasure? And yet because of an unsatisfactory division a murder resulted, on account of which they spent all the gold and a deal of money besides, from which we see that this gold was really a source of misfortune rather than a treasure.

28 We regard not that which is seen but that which is unseen; for that which is seen is temporary, but that which is unseen is eternal.

Notes.

1 Note that 尋找 and 找尋 mean different things, or at least are used in different ways; the former means to *seek for, to search*, the latter means *to look for*, for the purpose of accusing or taking to task—"to go for."

4 This is one of the stereotyped forms of words used at the end of written agreements.

9 書底 refers to the time and strength spent in school committing and expounding the classics, which are supposed to be the foundation of all learning.

15 封印 is the technical term for locking the seals and shutting up a public office for a vacation or a holiday.

16 尙未 is a book expression equivalent to 還沒. It is not used in colloquial, save by scholars who wish to air their learning.

18 Confucius says of the 鄉愿 that he is 德之賊也, *a thief of virtue*,—one who puts on the semblance of virtue for the sake of popularity, but who is not really virtuous.

19 公事 is here used out of the ordinary sense to mean a wedding or a funeral. This use is not *t'ung-hsing*. In Peking 大事 is used in the same way. Red is the prevailing color at weddings, and white at funerals, hence 紅公事 or 紅大事 is a wedding, and 白公事 or 白大事 is a funeral. The phrase, 紅白喜事, seems altogether inappropriate, seeing that a funeral can hardly be classed as a 喜事. The term is nevertheless used in some sections. The funeral of a person who dies over eighty years of age is called a 喜喪.

21 三軍 *The three armies*; that is, the right, left and centre; but often used as here in the sense of, *soldiers, forces, army*.

24 閒雜人等 *Miscellaneous idlers and the like*. 放長耳朶聽 is, so to speak, to stretch the ears so as to hear the more and hear on all sides, not as a participant in the conversation, but incidentally as a bystander.

25 隔壁告狀 *To state the case from an adjoining room*; that is, to talk in one room on purpose to be heard in another. An officer will sometimes listen by stealth to the talk of his underlings or his prisoners, hoping thus to get at the truth; while they, knowing or supposing he is listening, play off on him by saying to each other, as if secretly, the very things they want him to hear and believe.

26 公冶長 was accused of murder, but was not convicted. Confucius subsequently gave him his daughter in marriage, thus testifying his belief in his innocence.

27 分贓不平 *Divide the booty unjustly*. The term 贓 is probably used, because those who found the gold attempted to divide it secretly, without sharing with the whole company. The phrase is a ready made one, more properly used of dividing spoil.

第一百七十七課

可[1]以把那張桌子、些微的往南磨一磨。○這[2]塊木頭彊將彊將兒的穀材料。○請[3]你把這事的根本來歷、畧畧說給我聽。○拿[4]來我再銼一銼、答你別銼大喇、絲來毫去銼一點就行喇。○先[5]生沒有工夫、不過畧畧兒的講了一遍。○我[6]去的時候、彊將彊將兒的赶上送他們走。○這[7]塲雨下的不大、不過僅僅可可有三指。○柳[8]老二的病、今天稍微好一點。○這[9]些飯是昨天賸的、微微的有一點酸味兒。○你[10]給的價兒還不穀本、些微的添一添、就賣給你。○這[11]個藥搽在瘡口上、稍微有點兒疼。○有[12]一等擔不起大財的人、畧有一點富裕身分就狂的了不得。○這[13]並不是我生事、他若是些須讓

TRANSLATION.

1 You may push that table just a very little to the south.
2 This piece of wood is barely sufficient.
3 Please give me a brief account of the origin and progress of this business.
4 Bring it here and I will file it some more. *Ans.* Be sure you do not file it too much. File it off just the least bit and it will do.
5 The teacher was pressed for time, and only explained it over once in a cursory way.
6 When I went I was barely in time to see them off.
7 This has not been a heavy rain, barely three fingers deep.
8 Liu the Second is slightly better to-day.
9 This rice was left over from yesterday and is slightly sour.
10 The price you offer is not sufficient to cover cost; make it a little more and I will let you have it.
11 When this medicine is rubbed on the mouth of the ulcer it causes a slight smarting.
12 There is a class of men who cannot stand much money. Just let them acquire a little wealth, and they are puffed up beyond endurance.
13 It is not that I am quarrelsome. If he gave me the least chance of escape, I would drop the matter.
14 It has been said, "A three years severe drought will not starve a

LESSON CLXXVII.

ADVERBIAL DIMINUTIVES.

些微 A little, just a little, a trifle.

稍微 A very little, trifling, slightly.

微微 A little, a very little, slightly, the least bit.

僅僅 Barely, merely, only.

可可 Barely, merely, neatly, scarcely. (S.)

彊彊 Barely, just, merely.

將將 The same. Those who use soft sounds incline to use this character; but it will not do where hard sounds prevail, as it is originally soft. The meaning of 彊 is equally suitable, and the sound is everywhere correct.

絲來毫去 A very little, a very trifle, the least bit.

些來小去 The same.

一星半點 A very little, the least mite or particle.

畧 A little, the least bit, any.

畧畧 A very little, just a little; slightly; briefly; cursorily.

畧微 Just a little, a very little.

些須 The least, a very little, trifling.

些小 Just a little, a very little, a wee bit. (N.)

畧小 The same. (S.)

多少 More or less, a very little, a fraction.

頗頗 Slightly, measurably, somewhat. (C.)

點路我走、我也就拉倒了。○從[14]來說、大旱三年餓不死廚子、一星半點的、些來小去的他還能一點不吃嗎。○論[15]慕家那處宅子、倒很整齊齊整、就是畧窨一點兒。○施[16]大哥這一塲取在那裏呢、答將將兒僅僅的掛上個名兒。○他[17]的少、你的多、把你的些須勻一點兒給他、就公道喇。○你[18]回家和你父親畧畧頗頗的提一提、看他願意不願意。○如[19]今的人、有三錢的不和有倆錢的結交、些小畧微富一點兒、眼裡就瞧不起人喇。○就[20]算是不好、究竟是個瑪瑙嘴子、雖然微微多少偏一點膛、若不細看也看不出來。○他[21]欠我們櫃上二百多吊、到如今一個沒還、若是些來小去的、我們還能這樣着急嗎。○搭[22]夥計總得彼此將就、若些須有

cook." Can you expect him to refrain entirely from eating a single particle of anything?

15 That residence of Mu's is indeed quite complete, but it is a little too contracted.

16 How did Brother Shï come out in this examination? *Ans.* He barely succeeded in getting his name posted up.

17 His are less and yours are more. Divide off a very little of yours to him, and you will then have a fair division.

18 You go back home and sound your father on the subject and see if he is willing.

19 In these days the man who has three cash will not associate with the man who has but two. When a man gets a very little money, he does not condescend to look at ordinary people.

20 Inferior—if you like; and yet it is a carnelian mouth-piece. Although the bore is a little to one side, it is not noticeable without careful examination.

21 He owes our firm over two hundred thousand cash, and up to this time has not paid a cash. If it were only a trifle, do you suppose we would be so anxious about it?

22 Those who go into business together should be mutually forbearing in their intercourse. It will not do to get angry and dissolve partnership for every trifling mistake.

Vocabulary.

稍 *Shao*¹. Gradually; slightly, partially; for the most part, rather.

頗 *P'oa*¹. Partial; an excess; very; a little; somewhat, rather.

銼 *Ts'oa*⁴. A file; *to file*, to trim.

富裕 *Fu*⁴ *yü*⁴. Rich, affluent, *wealthy*; in easy circumstances.

結交 *Chie*¹ *chiao*¹. Intercourse, fellowship; *to associate*, to have dealings.

瑪瑙 *Ma*³ *nao*³. Veined stones, as,—*carnelian*, agate, opal.

散夥 *San*⁴ *hwoa*³. *To dissolve partnership*, to quash an agreement; to disperse; to quit.

寃屈 *Yüen*¹ *ch'ü*¹. *A wrong*, a grievance.

辭賬 *Ts'ï*² *chang*⁴. To leave or quit a position, *to throw up a situation.*

翡 *Fei*³. The cock of the blue-green kingfisher.

翡翠 *Fei*³ *ts'wei*⁴. Jadite, chrysoprase.

搬指 *Pan*¹ *chï*³. A broad ring worn on the thumb by archers.

磴 *Têng*⁴. A ledge, a step; delay, *hesitancy.*

艮 *Kên*⁴. A limit; to stop, to hesitate; perverse: —See *kên*³.

學館 *Hsüe*² *kwan*³. A school.

話音 *Hwa*⁴ *yin*¹. Stress of voice, intonation; *a hint*, a suggestion.

偏沉 *P'ien*¹ *ch'ên*². Out of balance.

掖 *Yie*⁴. To seize or raise by the arm; *to insert or thrust into;* to tuck into.

點差錯、不可就吹燈散夥。○在[23]人家門裏作活、就是稍微有點寃屈、也當忍耐、不可一直的辭賬。○光[24]洗澡的水、就給他預備不好喇、畧熱一點、他就嫌燙的慌、畧冷一點、他又嫌冰扎的慌、再沒有這麼難伺候的喇。○這[25]個翡翠搬指、好是好、就是我帶着畧畧大一點兒。○誰[26]還怕誰嗎、若果然要見個高低、很合我的式、若畧打個艮磴兒、也不是好漢子。○這[27]場官司人都說很難、你看我如今打得頗頗的有點眉眼咯。○我[28]再不叫孩子念書喇、你看我從小用了多少功、花了多少錢、這纔進了學、以後求親告友謀了個學館、僅僅的掙二十來吊錢、彀做甚麼的呢。○明[29]人不用細說、只用畧畧漏點話音兒、管保他就聽出來了。○前[30]頭那個馱子綁得好、後頭這個綁的偏沉了。答絲來毫去偏一點、也不要緊、塞掖上個小石頭就墜過來喇。

23 When you are working for another, even if you suffer some trifling wrong, you should be patient and not hastily throw up your situation.

24 One cannot even prepare his bath-water to suit him. If it is the least bit too warm, he complains of being scalded, and if it is the least bit too cool, he complains of being chilled. Few men are as hard to serve as he.

25 This jade-stone ring is good, it is true, but it is the least mite too large for me.

26 You think I'm afraid of you do you? If you really want to see who is the better man, I am quite ready for you, and whoever shows any sign of backing out is no man.

27 Everybody said this suit would be difficult, but you see, I have carried it on in such a way that there is now a fair prospect of success.

28 I'll not send my children to school any more. Look how much labor I have expended from my youth, and how much money I have spent, in order to obtain a degree, and then only by dint of appealing to my relatives and friends did I secure a school, and it only brings me a little over twenty thousand cash [per year]. What does that amount to?

29 It is not necessary to state a thing in detail to a clever man. You only need to give him a slight hint, and you may be sure he'll understand.

30 That load in front is properly bound, but this one behind is out of balance. *Ans.* It is the least trifle uneven, but that is no matter; insert a small stone under the rope, and it will restore the balance.

NOTES.

7 三指 *Three fingers;* that is, the width of three fingers.

9 The language used may apply either to taste or to smell.

12 身分 here means *money, property,* in which sense it is not *t'ung-hsing*—not being so used in Peking.

13 讓點路我走 *Allow a little road* [*for*] *me to go.* The expression would be more elegant if 我走 were changed to 給我, as it often is; yet the form of expression in the text is quite common.

15 In some sections 宅子 is constantly used for house instead of 房子; in other sections it is only used occasionally, and generally denotes all the houses in a court including the court itself.

16 This sentence would be precisely the same if addressed to the person himself.

19 三 is put for 三個, and is read sa^1.

20 A carnelian mouth-piece to a pipe is much valued.

22 吹燈散夥 *Blow out the lamp and disperse the company.* The expression is probably taken from gambling; when one gets angry or disgusted, he blows out the light and so breaks up the game and scatters the company.

26 誰還怕誰嗎 *Who is afraid of whom?* that is, *do you think I am afraid of you?* 打個磴 *To make a halt, to hold back.* 打個艮 *To show* [*a sign of*] *hesitation.* The former expression is Northern, the latter Central and Southern.

第一百七十八課

今[1]年一春沒大下雨、看這個光景、麥子必不收成。○兩[2]國又添兵、又預備兵器、看那個景況、兩下必要打仗。○那[3]塊地已經出到一百吊一畝、他還不賣、看這個樣兒、恐怕買不下上來。○他[4]今日應了明日、明日應了後日、看那個樣子、他原沒打算還錢。○老[5]三下半年、常上大烟館裏去磨轉轉、看這個情形、怕他已經學成匪類馬流下流了。○這[6]處宅子、前面是走馬大門、後邊有車門、周圍都是羣房、看這個氣派、定管規保裏邊也不能錯。○新[7]進士來了報子、道喜

TRANSLATION.

1 This year it has scarcely rained during the entire spring. From the look of things the wheat will certainly be a failure.

2 The two nations are both increasing their armies and preparing arms. Judging from appearances there will certainly be war.

3 I have already offered to the amount of one hundred *tiao* per acre for that piece of land, and he still will not sell. From the appearance of things I fear it cannot be bought.

4 To-day he promises that he will pay to-morrow, and to-morrow he promises that he will pay the next day. I judge from the way he acts, he has no idea of paying the money.

5 The latter half of the year Lao San has been constantly hanging around the opium shop. From the look of things I am afraid he has already fallen into dissolute habits.

6 This compound has in front a large gate for the entrance of horses; behind it has a wagon gate, and all around are rows of houses. Judging from the general style, I'll warrant that the inside is also in keeping.

7 The announcement of the new Chin-

LESSON CLXXVIII.

PHRASES OF INFERENCE.

The following phrases are all very similar in meaning and use. The definitions give the approximate literal meaning rather than the actual words found in the translations, which are modified to suit the connection. In all the phrases, either 這 or 那 may be used.

看這個光景 Judging from the appearance of things.

看這個景況 Judging from the appearance of affairs.

看這個樣子 Judging from the manner or style of things.

看這個樣式 Judging from the fashion of things.

看這個式樣 Judging from the shape of things.

看這個情形 Judging from the appearance of circumstances.

看這個形勢 Judging from the posture or situation of things.

看這個局勢 Judging from the condition or state of the game.

看這個行動 Judging from the course or bearing of things.

看這個舉動 Judging from the course or tenor of things.

看這個架子 Judging from the form or appearance of things.

看這個架式 Judging from the configuration of things.

看這個氣派 Judging from the style of things.

的客、只是一頓光頭麪、看這個光景、新進士回家祭祖、必不能有大舉動。大張羅有大排場○李[8]大人帶着礦師、又上金狗山驗礦去喇、看這個行動、金狗山的礦是必要開的。○外[9]頭的日光、怎麼又黃又暗呢、看這個樣子、必是日蝕護日○上[10]一次大決課、前幾名都是五吊錢的獎賞、看今科這個樣式、每人兩吊錢就不少喇。○麒[11]麟街上那個長痲瘋的人、已經生了蛆喇、看那個樣子架式、再活不過今天去。○我[12]退一步、他就往前赶一步、我再退一步、他又往前赶一步、看這個形勢、他是打心裏要找我的饑荒。晦氣○太[13]太在堂屋裏捶衣裳、聽說來了報子、並沒動身、只管捶他的衣裳、看這個樣子、眞有個太太的氣象。○孫[14]大人在酒席筵前、喫也不大願喫、喝也不大願喝、看這個形勢、我們託他的事、未必能替我們出力。○他[15]們兩個作買賣的時候、就很投契、

shï has come, and those who went to congratulate him, were simply treated to a meal of plain vermicelli. Judging from this, when he comes home to sacrifice to his ancestors, there will be no great ado made.

8 Li Ta-jên has again taken a mining engineer and gone to Chin-kou Hill to prospect for a mine. From the look of things the mine at Chin-kou Hill will doubtless be opened.

9 What makes the sunlight without so yellow and dull? From the appearance of things there must be an eclipse coming on.

10 On the last occasion at the test examination, several of the highest names each received a reward of 5000 cash. Judging from the appearance of things this time, 2000 cash is the utmost that each man will get.

11 That man on Ch'ilin street who has leprosy, already has maggots on him. Judging from his condition, he cannot live over to-day.

12 When I yield a step, he advances a step; when I yield another step, he advances another step. It is evident that he intends to make trouble for me.

13 Madam was in the middle room pounding clothes, and when she heard that the announcement had come, she never moved, but kept right on with her work as before. From this it is evident that she has indeed the style of a lady.

14 While sitting at the feast Sun Ta-jên seemed reluctant either to eat or to drink. I judge from his manner that he will probably not exert himself in the affair we have entrusted to him.

15 When they were in business they were very intimate, now they each

VOCABULARY.

兵器 *Ping¹ ch'i⁴.* Arms, weapons, implements of war.

磨轉 *Moă⁴ chwan⁴.* To hang around, to loaf, to loiter.

情形 *Ch'ing² hsing².* The appearance or look of things, circumstances.

周圍 *Chou¹ wei².* Around, surrounding.

礦師 *Kung³ shï¹.* A mining engineer.

蝕 *Shï².* To eat away, to encroach on; to eclipse, to be eclipsed.

日蝕 *Ji⁴ shï².* An eclipse of the sun.

護日 *Hu⁴ i⁴.* The same:—Note 9.

决課 *Chüe² k'ê⁴.* A final or test examination:—Note 10.

現在兩家的孩子、也都長得很好、彼此常送東西、看這個舉動、必是要結兒女親家。○我[16]見他家裏、是用白綾子糊房、紅緞子包恭凳、看那個氣派、真彀個人伺候的。○那[17]人的言語穩重、舉止端方、看這個行動、必是大家出身。○素[18]常我和他們並沒有來往、今天他忽然請我喝酒、而且那些陪我的人、也都不像好人、看這個局勢、他們必是要算計(牢籠)我。○前[19]五天我去問他們多會開船、他們說還有七十個酒罈沒上、等上完了就開、昨天我又去問他們、他們說還有二百個酒罈沒上、看這個情形(架子)、不知多會兒纔走喇。○法[20]蓮和尚喫大烟、將廟中的東西變賣淨了、自從會首們警戒他以後、他就起了誓、永不再喫、如今已經三年了、看這個式樣、是不能再開的喇。○李[21]老二這個人、我看他這個架子、是有點兒要揩不住。

have a growing family of fine children, and are constantly making each other presents. Judging from the appearance of things their children will no doubt intermarry.

16 I noticed that in his house they used white lining satin to paper the rooms, and red satin to cover the commode. Judging from the style of things it will be as much as a man can do to wait on them.

17 That man's language is courteous and his manner dignified. Judging from his bearing he must belong to a good family.

18 Ordinarily I have had no intercourse with them, but to-day they have suddenly invited me to a feast; and moreover all the other guests are suspicious characters. From the look of things I suspect that they are setting a trap for me.

19 Five days ago I went and asked them when the vessel would sail. They said there were seventy jars of wine yet to be put on board, and that as soon as these were loaded, they would sail. Yesterday I went again and asked them. They said there were still two hundred jars of wine to load. Judging from the aspect of things it is hard to say when they will go.

20 Fa Lien the priest smoked opium and sold off everything in the temple; but when the trustees of the temple reproved him, he took an oath that he would never smoke again. That is now three years ago. Judging from the circumstances it is not likely he will begin to smoke again.

21 I judge from the appearance of this man Li the Second, that he will hardly stand it.

大課 *Ta³ k'ê⁴*. . . . . The same.

麒 *Ch'i²*. . . . . . . The male of the Chinese unicorn.

麟 *Lin²*. . . . The female of the Chinese unicorn.

麒麟 A fabulous beast of auspicious omen.

痲瘋 *Ma² fêng¹*. . . . . Leprosy.

蛆 *Ch'ü¹*. . . . . Maggots bred in putrid flesh.

架式 *Chia⁴ shï⁴*. *Condition*, circumstances; . . . . appearance, outlook.

堂屋 *T'ang² wu¹*. The middle room of a Chinese . . . . house, a hall.

恭凳 *Kung¹ têng⁴*. . . . . A commode.

舉止 *Chü³ chï³*. Deportment, behavior; manner, style. (w.)

局勢 *Chü² shï⁴*. Position [of the game], situation, *outlook*.

揩 *Chï¹*. To prop up; to withstand, to bear up, ... to endure, *to stand*.

第一百七十九課

老[1]雖愛少、無奈奈何少不愛老。○他[2]看着沒法推賴諉、無奈纔說了實話。○天[3]地間還有愛死的人嗎、都是無可計奈何纔尋死啊。○朋[4]友家賀喜、親戚家弔喪、本不願意應酬、然而都是不得已的事情。○這[5]是我們的家務事、別人都無可奈何。○我[6]已經打了你、你可治不得我。○人[7]若不是窮到了無奈的地步、誰肯要飯吃呢。○你[8]現在又有勢力又有錢、誰能治得你呢。○我[9]巴

TRANSLATION.

1 Although parents love their children, yet somehow the children do not love their parents.

2 Only when he saw that evasion was impossible did he come to the point of telling the real truth.

3 Is there a man in the whole world who chooses to die? It is only when men are in desperate straits that they seek death.

4 Friends in offering congratulations, and relatives in presenting condolences, are not really desirous of making presents, but the circumstances give them no choice.

5 This is our own family affair; no one else can do anything about it.

6 I have thrashed you, and it is impossible for you to get any satisfaction out of me.

7 Save as a last resource, who is willing to beg.

8 At present you have both prestige and money, who is able to get the better of you?

NOTES.

1 沒大下雨, *it has not rained much*, is very different from 沒下大雨, *there has been no great rain.*

3 那塊地 would seem to be the subject of the verb, but it is not—a subject must be supplied.

6 走馬大門 A front gate large enough and high enough to admit a man on horseback.

7 光頭麪 A meal consisting entirely of *mien*,—which is considered very good, though not stylish. When a man gets a degree, special couriers carry the news to his friends, taking their chances of the pay they may get. When he himself returns home, he sacrifices to his ancestors, and is expected to invite his friends to a feast.

9 The Chinese traditional explanation of an eclipse is that the sun (or moon) is being eaten up by a great dog. The phrase 護日, *protecting the sun*, is derived from the practice of beating on drums and pans to frighten away the dog, and so save the sun.

10 Throughout the provinces the prefects hold a monthly examination of such graduates as choose to present themselves, giving a small stipend to a number of the best. Shortly before the triennial examination at the provincial capital, a special examination called a 決課 or 大課 is held, and those who attain a certain degree of excellence receive an allowance for traveling expenses.

11 再 has here the force of *certainly, or in any case.* Its use implies that the man had unexpectedly lived from day to day, but that he certainly could not live another day. Leprosy is more generally called 大痲瘋.

13 That a wife should show no sign of excitement or pleasure on such an occasion as that of her husband getting a degree, is supposed to be the height of decorum and of lady-like bearing.

14 酒席筵前 *In the presence of the feast;* that is, at or during the feast.

15 結兒女親家 *Make themselves kindred by contracting marriage alliances between their children.*

LESSON CLXXIX.

IMPRACTICABILITY.

奈何 What is to be done? *i. e.*, there is no help, no resource; yet nevertheless: also sometimes used as a verb,—to do to another, to put through.

無奈 Unable, no resource; yet; only; alas!

無奈何 Without resource, no help, no other way; only; last resort.

沒奈何 The same.

無計奈 No means of doing anything, no help for it, in straits.

不得去淨這私慾心、無奈就是不能彀。○治10得了病、治不了命、若是命裏該死、那是沒有治的。○若11是有錢、我很願意借給他、無奈我也不彀用的。○誰12願意賣房子地呢、但是到了過不去的時候、無奈也只得賣。○楊13老八從來不會還錢、今天怎麼當了衣裳、還張六的錢呢、答那是不得已喇、他滿心不願意當、張六又不答應。○起14先我看一個人就扛來喇、試驗試驗治不不得行、必得倆人去擡。○現15在來投奔老爺、眞是出於無計可奈奈了、但凡有一線之路、也不好意思來。○起16先他不應許當街磕頭、人家再三不肯、不得已

9 Would that I could get entirely rid of this corrupt heart; but alas! I cannot.

10 You may cure the disease, but you cannot control fate. If it is ordained that he should die, there is no help for him.

11 If I had the money, I would willingly lend it to him; but it is out of the question when I haven't even enough for myself.

12 Who is willing to sacrifice house and land? Yet when one gets into a strait, he has no resource but to sell.

13 Heretofore Yang the Eighth has not been given to paying his debts; how does it come that to-day he has pawned his clothes and paid Chang the Sixth? *Ans.* It was because he could not help it. He was very loth to pawn them, but Chang the Sixth gave him no choice.

14 At first I thought one man could bring it on his shoulder, but on trying I found it impracticable. It will require two men to carry it.

15 My coming now to seek help of you, sir, is because I am in a very great strait. If I had any resource at all, I would not think of coming.

16 At first he would not agree to kotow on the street, but the other party was inexorable. Only when he found there was no help for it did he finally assent.

無計可奈 The same. (s.)

無計奈何 The same.

無可奈何 Impossible to do anything, in a tight place, in an extremity, at the end of one's tether.

無何可奈 The same.

無可如何 The same.

不得已 No help for it, no choice, no other way, unavoidable, in straits.

不得而已 The same.

治 or **治得** To manage, to bring to terms, to put through;—with a negative, 治不得, unable to control or manage, impracticable.

無法可治 Out of one's power, impracticable, no resource.

沒有治兒 Impracticable, helpless, hopeless, incorrigible.

VOCABULARY.

奈 *Nai*⁴. The crab-apple; a remedy, a resource; how? what way?

諉 *Wei*³. To implicate; to shirk, to evade.

推諉 *T'wei*¹ *wei*³. To make excuse, *to evade*; to retract, to back out.

推賴 *T'wei*¹ *lai*⁴. *To evade*, to back out; to throw the blame on another. (s.)

烟癮 *Yien*¹ *yin*³. The craving of the appetite for opium.

烟頭 *Yien*¹ *t'ou*². The amount of opium smoked in a given time.

纔應承了。○若[17]是嫂子這麼混帳、還可以說說道道、就是打他幾下、也無不可、但這是個兄弟媳婦（小嬸兒）（弟媳）、實在無法可治。○我[18]還有一計、偏要奈何他一場。○信[19]是信他不過、但此時捉不着他的短處、却奈何他不得（無可奈何他）。○王[20]元亨抽（喫）鴉片煙、是一點治頭兒沒有的、一來他沒主意、絕然不想着戒忌、二來烟頭（癮）太大、就是要戒忌也戒忌不掉了。○難[21]道朝廷喜歡打人殺人嗎、只因百姓們不學好、不聽教訓、沒奈何只得用刑罰去治他。○起[22]先他不跟着走、叫賊兵打了兩馬棒、又要拿刀殺他、不得而已（無計奈）纔跟着走了。○那[23]年的年成很不好、又加上

17 If it was an elder brother's wife that was so hateful, I could talk back to her, or I might even slap her a few times; but this is a younger brother's wife, and I can do nothing at all with her.

18 I have one more plan, and I am determined to have another tussle with him.

19 We do not believe him of course, but since we are unable just now to fix any fault on him, we can do nothing to him.

20 Wang Yüen Hêng's opium smoking is past all remedy. In the first place, he has no will-power and no desire whatever to break off; in the second place, the habit has too strong a hold (he takes too much); even if he did desire to break off, he could not.

21 Do you think the emperor takes pleasure in beating men or putting them to death? It is only because the people will not be virtuous and heed instruction that, as a last resort, he employs punishments to control them.

22 At first he refused to go with them, whereupon the robbers struck him a couple of blows with a cudgel, and were about to kill him with a sword, when he yielded to necessity and followed them.

23 That year the crops were very poor, and besides, the family, both children and adults, were constantly sick, so

賊兵 *Tsei² ping¹*. Organized robbers, banditti; rebels.

棒 *Pang⁴*. A club, a cudgel; a drumstick.

馬棒 *Ma³ pang⁴*. A large rattan cudgel or whip carried by mounted robbers.

祠 *Ts'ï²*. To sacrifice to ancestors; ancestral.

祠堂 *Ts'ï² t'ang²*. An ancestral hall or temple:—See Les. 86. Note 5.

家雀 *Chia¹ ch'iao³*. The sparrow.

麻雀 *Ma² ch'iao³*. The same.

杌 *Wu⁴*. A stump; a square stool.

杌凳 *Wu⁴ têng⁴*. A square seat or stool.

獨凳 *Tu² têng⁴*. A square bench or stool for one person.

蹺 *Ch'iao¹*. Same as 蹻.

蹺脚 *Ch'iao¹ chiao³*. To stand on the toes, to walk on tip-toe.

跕脚尖 *Tien³ chiao³ chien¹*. To stand on tip-toe.

虛假 *Hsü¹ chia³*. False, empty, *vain;* imaginary.

尊長 *Tsun¹ chang³*. The senior members of a family or clan.

罰棍 *Fa² kun⁴*. To condemn to be scourged; *to beat*, to scourge.

跪香 *Kwei⁴ hsiang¹*. To kneel while a stick of incense burns out.

點畫 *Tien³ hwa⁴*. *To make signs with the finger;* to gesture, to point out.

指戳 *Chï³ ch'oă¹* *To make signs;* to gesture, to point out.

大人孩子不斷的有病、所以到轉年春天、我們就沒法過了、出上工夫要着喫、也要不出來、無何奈可奈何纔把小姑娘賣給他了。○在24祠堂厦簷底下、有一窩麻家雀、無奈沒有梯子構不着、答我看樑摞四條杌凳子、獨凳、跐着腳尖蹺着腳就構着喇。○我25明知道拜祖宗是虛假的事、但是我不拜、尊長們不依、又要罰棍、又叫跪香、不拜不行、沒奈何我纔屈着良心去拜了。○從26前我見那些打滿遍街罵滿遍巷的老婆、若說男人管不住他、我就十分不服、誰知現在我也攤了這麽一個、眞是無可奈如何、無論怎樣打他、他就是要罵、那一天叫我直打得沒有氣兒、纔住了手、尋思想着他再可不敢罵了、那知道他甦醒過來、嘴裏雖然罵不出聲兒來、還是用指頭指點指戳點畫着罵。

that the following spring we were reduced to want. We took to begging, but despite our efforts we could not get enough to live on, until finally, driven by necessity, we sold our younger daughter to him.

24 There is a nest of sparrows under the eave of the ancestral hall; the trouble is I cannot reach them without a ladder. *Ans.* I think that by getting up on four stools placed on top of each other, and standing on tiptoe, you can reach them.

25 I know quite well that worshipping ancestors is a vain superstition, but when I did not worship, the senior members of the family took me to task, and were about to give me a beating and make me do penance, and so compel me to worship. Only when there was no help for it, did I do violence to my conscience by worshipping.

26 It used to be that if any one said that a man could not control those women who set whole streets at defiance with their violence and vituperation, I was up in arms at once. Very unexpectedly one such has now fallen to my lot, and I am at my wits' end. No matter how you beat her she persists in reviling. One day I beat her until she fainted before I stopped, thinking that after that she would certainly be afraid to revile me, but what do you think? When she came to again, although unable to speak audibly, she signed defiance with her fingers.

Notes.

10 There is throughout this sentence a play on the word 治, which means both *to cure*, and *to control* or *bring under subjection.* The Chinese are thorough-going fatalists.

15 一線之路 *A road the size of a thread, the least possible opening or chance.* The use of 之 shows that the phrase is a ready made one taken from books.

17 According to Chinese ideas of propriety, a man may be quite free in his intercourse with his *elder* brother's wife, but not with his *younger* brother's wife. In like manner he may be free with his wife's *elder* sister, but not with her *younger* sister.

20 烟頭 means the amount of opium smoked per day, which is here taken as a measure of the strength of the opium habit. It is not always a true guage, however, as some men can smoke much more than others can without falling greatly under the power of the habit. **烟癮** means the strength of the appetite itself, irrespective of the quantity smoked.

25 跪香 To kneel in front of a shrine or tablet with a stick of lighted incense held in the two hands, and so remain until the incense stick is burned out, which requires from an hour to an hour and a half. It is sometimes done voluntarily as a penance, and sometimes required as a punishment.

26 Notice the vividness of the phrase **罵不出聲兒來**. The inarticulate motion of her lips was assisted by the significant gestures of her fingers. When a woman gets in an uncontrollable passion, she will sometimes go out on the street and pour out a torrent of abuse until she wears herself out.

第一百八十課

他[1]既然能起來上街、可見病的不很重。○俗[2]語說、大事不如小、小事不如了、可知起事不如息事好。○他[3]天生叫人可愛、人家不能不愛他。○都[4]說王六有了錢喇、這樣的冷天、連個袍子沒穿、可見還是沒有錢。○思[5]想起來、眞是令人可嘆。○湯[6]先生雖然沒有甚麽大本事、但是他傳道的熱心、眞是可取。○這[7]是可行可止的事情、成也可、不成也可。○他[8]們爲百十個錢、就傷了和氣、從此可知朋友是假的、惟有錢是眞的。○孫[9]國祺一點好處也沒有、不是明明的欺壓人、就是暗暗的給人播弄是非、眞是萬人可恨。○我[10]們(姥姥/老娘/家婆)家、蓋了一座好齊整

TRANSLATION.

1 As he is able to get up and walk out, it is evident that he is not very sick.

2 The proverb says, "A trivial quarrel is better than a grievous one, and a settlement is better than a trivial quarrel;" from which it is evident that to settle a quarrel is better than to raise one.

3 He is by nature lovable, one cannot help loving him.

4 They say that Wang the Sixth has gotten rich, yet on such a cold day as this he is out without even a wadded coat, from which it is evident that after all he has no money.

5 It really makes one sad to think of it.

6 Although Mr. T'ang has no great talents, yet his earnestness as a preacher is worthy of all praise.

7 This is not an essential matter, it may be dispensed with. If it is accomplished all right; and if not, all right.

8 Their friendship was sacrificed for a matter of a hundred cash, from which it is plain that friendship is a sham, money is the only thing that is real.

9 There is nothing good about Sun Kwoă-Ch'i. If he is not openly imposing on people, he is secretly making trouble for them. He is detested by everybody.

10 At our maternal grandmother's they have built a very fine looking tiled

LESSON CLXXX.

可 AS A VERBAL PREFIX.

可, prefixed to a verb, turns it into a verbal adjective, having in general the force of English adjectives ending in able, as **可憐** *pitiable*, **可愛** *lovable*, etc. The number of verbs to which **可** is commonly applied is not great, though it may, if occasion require, be used with many others.

可見 Visible,—it is evident, it is seen, it appears, which shows.

可知 Knowable,—it may be known, from which it appears, which proves.

These two phrases differ from those following, in that they are not generally used as adjectives, but rather as inferential connectives.

可愛 Lovable,—winsome, prepossessing.

可嘆 Deplorable,—sad, heart-rending.

可取 Worthy of being chosen, agreeable, taking.

可行 Doable,—that which may be done, that which may proceed.

可止 Stopable,—that which may be dispensed with, that which may be quitted.

可恨 Abominable,—hateful, detestable.

可惜 Regrettable,—what a pity! alas!

可惱 Provoking to anger, exasperating.

可巧 By chance, accidentally, happily.

可託 Reliable,—trustworthy, to be depended on.

可敬 Respectable,—worthy of respect.

的瓦房、可惜山牆上開門、還帶着是個偏向斜的、實在不官樣成樣。○常[11]言道、一日夫妻百日恩、從此可見夫妻的情分、比誰都大。○雖[12]然他這椿事叫人可惱、然而仍有可取的地方。○纔[13]要問他、可巧又來了一位親戚、把話頭兒打斷了。○李[14]崇眞那是千金可託的人、把錢交給他、是千妥萬當。○劉[15]滙川既有那樣的聰明本事、還能這樣柔和謙遜、實在叫人可敬可愛。○事[16]情雖然壞在他手裏、其實也有可原、不過爲他年紀輕、見識短、並不是出於故意的。○雖[17]然有說他這個那個的、都是無根的流言、一點也不可憑、答雖不可憑、却是叫人可疑。○最[18]

house, but what a pity they made a door in the end, and that too to the one side. It is decidedly not in good taste.

11 The common saying is, "One day husband and wife implies a hundred days' kindness," from which we see that the sympathy of husband and wife is greater than that of any other.

12 Although this business of his makes one indignant, yet there are still some redeeming features about it.

13 Just as I was about to ask him, a friend happened in and broke up our conversation.

14 Li Ch'ung Chên is a perfectly reliable man. Nothing could be more satisfactory than to deposit the money with him.

15 Though so wise and gifted, Liu Hwei Ch'wan is yet able to exhibit such mildness and courtesy that one cannot but respect and love him.

16 Although the business came to grief in his hands, yet there is some excuse for him. It was simply the result of his youth and inexperience, and not that he wished it to be so.

17 Although there were various stories afloat about him, yet they were only vague rumors, entirely untrustworthy. *Ans.* Although untrustworthy,

可原 Excusable,—pardonable, allowance to be made for.

可憑 Reliable,—trustworthy, to be depended upon.

可疑 Questionable,—doubtful, dubious.

可怕 Terrible,—to be feared, to be dreaded.

可惡 Detestable,—hateful, abominable.

可殺 Killable,—deserving of death, ought to die.

可留 Sparable,—deserving to be spared.

可觀 Admirable,—worthy of being looked at, elegant, beautiful, showy.

VOCABULARY.

息事 *Hsi² shï⁴.* *To settle a quarrel*, to come to an agreement, to make peace.

祺 *Ch'i².* Fortunate; felicitous.

家婆 *Chia¹ p'oa².* A maternal grandmother. (s.)

山牆 *Shan¹ ch'iang².* The gable, the end of a house.

偏斜 *P'ien¹ hsie².* To the one side, off or aside from the centre.

成樣 *Ch'êng² yang⁴.* Becoming, *in good taste*, seemly.

常言 *Ch'ang² yien².* A common saying, a trite saying.

情分 *Ch'ing² fen⁴.* Affection, attachment; kindness, *sympathy.*

崇 *Ch'ung².* Lofty, eminent; honorable; to exalt; to adore, to reverence.

川 *Ch'wan¹.* A mountain stream.

可怕的、是父母溺愛不明、你看王光輝、從作嬰娃孩娃的時候、他父母就慣他、現在無所不幹至、到處去誆騙人、可知慣子如殺子、這話誠然不錯。○19俗語說、有緣千里來相會、無緣對面不相逢識、又說千里姻緣一線牽、可見交友結親、都是有緣分的。○20梁老老梁婆子、常說幾天幾天沒吃甚麼、身上却肥胖得很、可知他說的不是實情話。○21宋某人實在可惡極了、口稱要送人家的姑娘去上女學、却揀那好的、自己留着作妾、其餘的都給人家賣了、凡評論這事的人、都說那是可殺不

yet they were sufficient to raise doubts.

18 The thing most to be feared is that parents will be blinded by affection. Look at Wang Kwang Hwei. From the time he was a child his father and mother indulged him, and now he goes everywhere swindling people, and there is nothing too bad for him to do, which shows that the saying, "To indulge a son is no better than to kill him," is verily true.

19 The saying is, "When there is a pre-existing affinity, friends will come a thousand *li* to meet; and when there is none, they will not become acquainted though face to face;" again, "Those destined for each other in marriage, though a thousand *li* apart, are yet led by one thread;" from which it is evident, that friendships and marriages all have their predetermining laws.

20 That old woman Liang is continually saying that she has eaten nothing for so many days, and yet she is as fat as she can be, which shows clearly that what she says is not really true.

21 That man Sung is worthy of utter detestation. Giving out that he was taking people's daughters to the girls' school, he nevertheless selected the best one and kept her for a con-

---

柔和 *Jou*^{2} *hê*^{2}. . . . . *Mild*, meek, forbearing.

遜 *Hsün*^{4}. . . . . . . Conciliatory, humble, retiring.

謙遜 *Ch'ien*^{1} *hsün*^{4}. Humble, conciliatory, yielding, *courteous.*

流言 *Liu*^{2} *yien*^{2}. Idle talk; unfounded rumors; *stories.*

溺 *Ni*^{4}. To sink; to suffocate; to be fond of, *to dote on.*

溺愛 *Ni*^{4} *ai*^{4}. To love to excess, to dote on; *blind to the faults of.*

誆 *K'wang*^{1}. . . . . . To talk wildly, to lie, *to cheat.*

誆騙 *K'wang*^{1} *p'ien*^{4}. *To swindle,* to embezzle; to defraud, to fleece.

誠然 *Ch'êng*^{2} *jan*^{2}. In very deed, *verily,* assuredly.

緣分 *Yüen*^{2} *fên*^{4}. Predestined fitness or adaptation, an antecedent affinity.

珊 *Shan*^{1}. . . . . . . Coral.

瑚 *Hu*^{2}. . . . . . . A sacrificial vessel.

珊瑚 Precious coral,—the red or pink variety.

頂子 *Ting*^{3} *tsï*^{3}. The "button" worn on top of the hat as a sign of literary or official rank:—Note 22.

水文 *Shwei*^{3} *wên*^{2}. A water-mark or vein in a stone or crystal.

作意 *Tsoŭ*^{4} *i*^{4}. The train of thought or skeleton of an essay or discourse; *ideas.*

氣調 *Ch'i*^{4} *tiao*^{4}. The measured cadence of literary composition or of a chant, *rhythm,* tune.

觀 *Kwan*^{1}. To look at, to observe, to note. Also *kwan*^{4}.

幹員 *Kan*^{4} *yüen*^{2}. . . . . . . A gifted officer of state.

招搖 *Chao*^{1} *yao*^{2}. To raise a disturbance, to draw a crowd; *to make an ado.*

可留的東西。○這[22]個珊瑚頂子、顏色(色頭)真好、可惜有這一點毛病。答 那是一道水文、算不得毛病。○去[23]年我看他的文章、還在糊塗陣裏、今年我看了看、又有作意、又有氣調、實在大有可觀。○張[24]大人真是國家的幹員、可惜他有個舅子、名叫朱洪江、仗着自己是官親、到處去招搖撞騙。

cubine, and the others he sold. Every one who speaks of it says, such a rascal should be put to death without fail.

22 The color of that coral button is very fine; what a pity it has this small defect. *Ans.* That is a natural vein, and cannot be regarded as a defect.

23 When I examined his essays last year, they were all a mass of confusion. This year I have been looking at them, and I find they have both ideas and rhythm, and are very readable.

24 Chang Ta-jên is really one of the talented officers of the land, but unfortunately he has a brother-in-law called Chu Hung Chang, who makes capital of his relationship, and goes about making a great ado and swindling people.

NOTES.

7 Or, *This is a thing that may be carried on, or it may be dropped; if completed, all right; if not, no matter.*

10 The Chinese consider it a great incongruity to have a door in the end of a house.

13 話頭兒 *The thread of the discourse.*

14 千妥萬當 *Perfectly satisfactory.* See Les. 186.

18 溺愛不明 *Blinded by excessive affection,*—a book phrase.

19 緣 here means the supposed occult and inscrutable chain of causes or attractions which operate to bring together those who have an affinity for each other, or who are predestined to be joined together. No English word is adequate to translate it.

20 In the North, 肥 is only used of animals or of meat, never of persons. In the South it is sometimes used of persons also.

22 頂子 The Chinese "button," as it is called by foreigners, is of various kinds. All who have literary degrees, high or low, are thereby entitled to wear a gold (gilded brass) button. Officers wear buttons of various kinds, according to their rank. The lowest is glass, in two grades; the lower being milk color and the higher, clear (crystal). The next rank is blue, in two grades; the lower being jade-stone and the higher, sapphire. The highest is red, also in two grades; the lower being red coral and the higher, ruby. In each case the more brilliant or transparent color indicates the higher rank.

23 糊塗陣 *A confused array, a demoralized order of battle,*—a forcible phrase to express the confusion and disorder of that which should be methodical. 氣調 The Chinese lay great stress on the rhythmic flow of the style. Their reading and reciting is a sort of chanting. Whenever a Chinese scholar falls on a piece of good writing, he spontaneously takes to chanting it as he reads.

LESSON CLXXXI.

CORRELATIVE PARTICLES.

This lesson illustrates a few correlative particles in sets of three.

別說……卽便……也 } To say nothing of…… …even if…… …( ).
別講……卽便……也 } What signify…… …even if…… …( ).

As here used, 也 has no answering word in English.

諒來……若不……還能 Most likely, probably…… …if not…… …would.
本當……只因……所以 Ought by rights…… …but because,…… …therefore.
雖然……若是……還能. Although…… …yet if…… …might.
若………雖然……也. If, when…… …although…… …yet.
雖然……只因……所以 Although…… …yet because…… …therefore.
別講……就是……還值得 To say nothing of…… …even if…… …worth while.
雖然……只要……還能. Although, even though…… yet if, only…… will be, may.

第一百八十一課

別莫[1]說你父親還給你掙下點家業、卽便一點沒掙下、你也不能把他扔丟了。○雖[2]然我沒親眼看見、諒來必是你先罵他、你若不先罵他、他還能打你嗎。○前[3]日本當親自來給大人慶壽、只因偶然得了一點寒疾、不敢見風、所以不能親來。○他[4]不用仗着武秀才來嚇呼我、莫別說他是個武秀才、卽便是個文舉、我也不能去求招告賠他。○看[5]聞頭一堂、官司本該打贏了、只因錢沒花到、所以纔打輸喇。○我[6]想起在學堂辜負那些光陰、心裏眞是懊悔、因爲我的明悟才分天分雖然不好、若是肯用上工夫、還能多認識幾個字。○聽[7]這個口話音、諒來他還是有錢、若不然、還能想着開當鋪嗎。○像[8]

TRANSLATION.

1 To say nothing of the fact that your father laid by something of an inheritance for you, even if he had laid by nothing, you could not cast him off.

2 Although I did not see it with my own eyes, yet I venture to say that you first reviled him. If you had not first reviled him, would he have struck you?

3 I certainly ought to have come in person day before yesterday to offer my congratulations on your birthday, sir, but on account of having taken a slight cold I could not venture out in the wind, and so was unable to come in person.

4 He need not think to frighten me with his military degree. What does a military degree signify? Even if he had a civil degree of the second rank, I would not go and make suit (own up) to him.

5 Judging from the first hearing, this suit ought certainly to have won; but because there was not enough money used, it was lost.

6 When I think of the time I wasted in school, I feel very sorry; for although my talents are inferior, yet if I had realized the importance of improving my time, I might have known many more characters.

7 Judging from this language, he probably has some money after all. If not, would he be thinking of opening a pawn shop?

8 To say nothing of his having had some experience, even if he had had no ex-

VOCABULARY.

慶壽 *Ch'ing*[4] *shou*[4]. To present congratulations on the birthday,—sometimes accompanied by a present.

寒疾 *Han*[2] *chi*[2]. A cold, indisposition caused by a cold.

招賠 *Chao*[1] *p'ei*[2]. To confess and make amends, to confess and apologize.

打輸 *Ta*[3] *shu*[1]. . . . . . To be worsted, *to lose.*

明悟 *Ming*[2] *wu*[4]. Intellect, *talent,* genius; intelligent, brilliant.

才分 *Ts'ai*[2] *fên*[4]. . . . . . *Talent,* parts.

口話 *K'ou*[3] *hwa*[4]. Style of speech, *language,* expression.

分辨 *Fên*[1] *pien*[4]. *To distinguish;* to pick out and assort; to separate.

蔽 *Pi*[4]. . . . . To repress; *to obscure;* to screen.

蒙蔽 *Mêng*[2] *pi*[4]. To cover up, to screen, to smother; *to blind,* to hoodwink.

沾染 *Chan*[1] *jan*[3]. To contaminate, to soil; *to corrupt.*

蛾 *Ê*[2]. . . . . A moth, a miller.

蝴蝶 *Hu*[2] *tie*[2]. . . . . . A butterfly.

他那樣的聰明、莫別說他還經練過、即便沒經練過、保管管保也辦不錯。○老[9]兄爲小弟的親事、這樣費心、本當應允纔是、只因沒有父命、所以不敢遽然應承。○雖[10]說良心能以分辨是非、只因內被私慾蒙蔽、外被世俗沾染、所以眞是眞非、連良心也分辨不清楚了。○[11]莫別講是爲個蛾兒、就是爲個蝴蝶、你已經十來多歲的東西、還値得放開大喇叭喉嚨子哭嗎。○人[12]既然都這樣傳說、諒來是不屈他、若不然、一人和他有仇、還能人人都有仇嗎。○官[13]沒有不讓人和息的、雖然已經被傳到案、只要有人調處、遞上一張告和和息呈子、也能把事情按下。○人[14]若不被聖靈重生、雖然願意行善、也不知善爲何物。○爲[15]我們的事、勞起動這麼些人來說和、莫別講還不能吃大虧、即便吃個三千五吊錢

perience, with his abilities, I warrant he would manage it successfully.

9 Seeing you, good brother, have taken so much pains about my betrothal, I ought by rights to assent; but inasmuch as I have not yet had my father's consent, I cannot venture to promise at once.

10 Although we say that conscience can distinguish right and wrong, yet because of the blinding effect of lust within, and the corrupting effect of the world without, it comes to pass that true right and wrong, even the conscience, is not able clearly to distinguish.

11 It is only a moth: and even if it were a butterfly, is it worth while for you, a great thing over ten years old, to set up such a bawling about it?

12 Probably he is not unjustly accused, seeing everybody reports it in this way. If it were not true, although one man might be his enemy, yet surely all would not be his enemies.

13 No magistrate refuses the privilege of a settlement. Even although the parties are already summoned, only let there be some one to act as mediator, and a notice of settlement be presented, and the case may be arrested.

14 When a man has not been renewed by the Holy Spirit, although he wishes to do good, he does not understand what it is to do good.

15 Having put all these gentlemen to the trouble of coming to mediate in this business of ours, to say nothing of our not suffering any serious loss, even if we should lose three or five

喇 *La*³. . . . . A prolonged sound. See *la*¹.

叭 *Pa*¹. . . . . An open mouth.

喇叭 A trumpet, a clarionet.

重生 *Ch'ung*² *shêng*¹. To be born again; regeneration.

行善 *Hsing*² *shan*⁴. *To do good*, to do works of benevolence; to do righteously.

起動 *Ch'i*³ *tung*⁴. To disturb, *to put to trouble.*

維 *Wei*³. . . . . . Connected with; whereas. (w.)

記仇 *Chi*⁴ *ch'ou*². *To hold a grudge*, to cherish a purpose of revenge.

如初 *Ju*² *ch'u*¹. . . . . As at first, as before.

復初 *Fu*⁴ *ch'u*¹. *To restore as it was originally;* to begin again, to revert.

遇險 *Yü*⁴ *hsien*³. To meet with danger or accident.

變故 *Pien*⁴ *ku*⁴. *An unforeseen occurrence*, an emergency; an accident.

見影 *Chien*⁴ *ying*³. To see a trace or indication or sign of.

錢穀 *Ch'ien*² *ku*³. A collector of taxes; *a treasurer* or cashier.

書信 *Shu*¹ *hsin*⁴. . . . . . *Letters*; correspondence.

的虧、也當叫衆位圓上臉。（給衆位個臉）○李[16]維坤的大長處、就是不會記仇、人雖然得罪了他、只要給他賠個禮、他就能照舊如初（仍舊復初）的和人相好。○我[17]雖然想着快快回家、只因公事還沒有完、現在不能脫身、所以只得等到年底了。○看[18]上海來的電報、算計保大昨天就該來到烟台、但是到如今沒來、諒來必是遇險、（必有變故、必有失事）若是沒有遇險、（變故、失事）還能到如今不見影兒嗎。○州[19]縣衙門裏的師爺、不是一樣、管批呈子的叫刑名、管地丁錢糧的叫錢穀、管寫稟帖書信的叫書啟、凡作州縣官的、雖然大半是聰明人、只因公事太多、一個人擔當不了、所以必得用這三樣的師爺。

thousand cash, we ought to yield to their wishes in the case.

16 The good point about Li Wei K'un is that he never holds spite. Even though one offends him, yet if an apology be made, he will be just as friendly as ever.

17 Although I am anxious to return home as soon as possible, yet because my business is not finished I cannot get away at present, but will be compelled to remain till the end of the year.

18 Judging from the Shanghai telegram, the *Pou-ta* should have reached Chefoo yesterday, but up to the present time she has not come. Something unusual has most likely occurred. If there had been nothing unusual, could it be that up to this time there should be no sign of her?

19 The assistants in Chou and Hsien offices are not all of one grade. Those who have charge of opinions rendered on indictments, are called prosecuting attorneys; those who have charge of land and poll taxes, are called treasurers; those who have charge of writing petitions and letters, are called secretaries. Although Chou and Hsien magistrates are, for the most part, able men, yet because the public business is more than one man can attend to alone, they find it necessary to use these three kinds of official assistants.

NOTES.

2 諒來必是 Or, *It must be so.*

3 寒疾 *A cold ailment,*—any slight disease caused by exposure to cold.

4 文舉 A civil, as opposed to a military, Chüjên.

5 一堂 *One hall or court*; that is, *one hearing.* A suit is rarely finished at one hearing. The magistrate adjourns a case at any point he chooses, and calls up another. One case may, and often does, have many hearings.

7 還, as used in the first clause, implies that his having money had been doubted or denied; as used in the second clause, 還 adds emphasis to the question.

10 眞是眞非 *True right and true wrong;* that is, *an unerring discernment of what is right and wrong in each case.*

13 Lawsuits are a trouble to magistrates, and rarely a source of much profit, hence they are generally quite willing to have them settled by compromise. The 和息呈子 or 告和呈子 is presented, in the name of the parties, by the mediator or middleman, and embraces a statement of the terms of settlement.

14 In this sentence, which is from the Pilgrim's Progress, 行善 is used to signify *righteous living*, but it is more commonly used by the Chinese to signify *acts of benevolence performed with a view to acquiring merit.*

15 叫衆位圓上臉 *Cause these gentlemen to complete their face; that is, not put them to shame.*

16 不會記仇 *Not know how to hold spite;* that is, *not naturally given to holding spite.*

18 烟台 The Chinese name of Chefoo, being the name of the fishing village which originally occupied the site. The name "Chefoo" comes from a village on the other side of the harbor, at which it was originally supposed the foreign town would be built, and which in fact has a much better anchorage. **變故** *A changed cause;* i.e., *an unforeseen turn of affairs.*

19 地丁 *Land and poll,* which sums up taxes proper in China. Buildings and personal property are not taxed. Business men are *supposed* to pay tax in duties, which are levied afresh almost every time the goods are moved.

第一百八十二課

若[1]是請客之家、無酒更好、就是有酒、也不可多食。○若[2]看樓房街道、買賣興旺、上海本是一個頂好的地方、但看那些酒樓茶舘、男女混雜、却是一個頂壞的地方。○我[3]們各人都帶着乾糧點心、所以他若是留飯更好、就是不留飯、也餓不着。○若[4]看他這樣窮苦、本當賙濟賙濟他、但看他有錢就花、實在不堪配可憐。○若[5]是他叔叔到底沒有兒子、固然必要過繼他、萬一人家有了兒子、他豈不是白指望了嗎。○若[6]看他臉上的氣色、一天兩天還不礙事、但看他的脈、却不敢保。

Translation.

1 If the host does not provide wine, so much the better; and even if there is wine, one should not give rein to appetite.

2 If you regard the fine buildings, and streets, and the flourishing business of Shanghai, it must be accounted a very excellent place; but if you look at the wine galleries and tea houses and promiscuous commingling of the sexes, it must be considered a very corrupt place.

3 We have all brought a lunch along. If he invites us to stop for dinner, so much the better; and if he does not, we will not suffer from hunger.

4 If one considers his poverty, he should by rights have assistance; but when one considers that he spends his money as fast as he gets it, he does not really seem worthy of pity.

5 If his uncle eventually has no son, he will of course adopt him; but if perchance his uncle should have a son, this hope would all come to nothing.

6 Judging merely from the color of his face, there is no danger for one or two days; but when his pulse is considered

LESSON CLXXXII.

Correlative Particles—Double.

The lesson gives a specimen of the manner in which correlatives are joined together in couples for the expression of more involved ideas. There are many such combinations. The translations given are necessarily somewhat imperfect.

若是 ... 更好 ... 就是 ... 也不 If ... so much the better ... even if, still if ... not.

若看 ... 本是 ... 但看 ... 却是. If regard, if look at... naturally must ... but if... must.

本 and 却 will not bear literal translating.

若看 ... 本當 ... 但看 ... 實在 If consider... would naturally, should... but if... really.

若看 ... 本當 ... 但看 ... 還當 If consider ... ought by rights ... but if ... should.

若看 ... 還 ... 但看 ... 卻 If look, judging from ... ( ) ... but if, but when ... ( ).

As here used, 還 and 卻 have really no answering words in English.

若是 ... 固然 . 萬一 ... 豈不 If ... of course... but if perchance, in case... (not ?)

豈 Can only be rendered by the sign of a question, being in these cases the sign of the interrogative affirmative.

若是 ... 固然 ... 就是 ... 仍舊 If ... of course ... and if, and yet ... equally.

若按理 ... 雖就是 ... 但想到 ... 仍舊 Although ... yet according to justice ... yet when we consider, yet influenced by ... better after all, may after all.

It is here impossible to put the English in the same order as the Chinese.

○若[7]按理說、他夜間來偷我們的樹、雖是罰他也不爲過、但想到他是我們本家的姑爺（女婿）、旁人又沒看見、總是該寬恕他纔是。○到[8]那天、你實在不能脫身、就不必爲難（煩難）、因爲你若是能來幫助更好、就是不來幫助、也不至於誤事（丟差）。○劉[9]天祿已經這麼大了、要給他定親、總得商議商議他、若是啞密密的定了、以後若能合他的意、固然大家都好、萬一不合他的意、豈不得受他一輩子的埋怨嗎。○若[10]看秦英打死了皇親國丈、本當斬首、給國丈償命、但看他父秦山有功、今在西涼被困、還當暫且寬饒、差他救父回朝、將功折罪。○若[11]按公道、他這樣倚勢欺人、就該趁此機會告他一狀、但想到千金置產、萬金置鄰、仍舊該寬讓他、只求過得去也就罷了。○

it is hard to say [what may happen].

7 Although according to justice it would be no more than right to punish him for coming in the night and stealing our trees, yet when we consider that he is a son-in-law of ours, and that no one else saw him we would better after all be lenient with him.

8 If on that day you really cannot get away, you need not feel troubled; for although, if you can come and help, it will be much better, still your not coming will not involve any failure.

9 Liu T'ien Lu being already so old it will be necessary to consult him in making a marriage contract for him. If we settle it up on the sly, then afterwards, in case she suits his mind, of course all will be well; but in case she should not suit his mind, will we not have to bear his life-long reproaches?

10 If we regard simply the fact that Ch'in Ying killed the Emperor's father-in-law, we ought by rights to behead him in order to avenge the death of the imperial father-in law; but if we consider the worthiness of his father Ch'in Shan, who is at present besieged in Shiliang, we should reprieve him temporarily, and send him to rescue and bring back home his father, and so atone for his crime by meritorious service.

11 Seeing he thus uses his power to tyrannize over others, we ought in justice to embrace this opportunity to prosecute him; but considering that whilst "a thousand taels will buy a farm, it takes ten thousand to buy a

VOCABULARY.

樓房 *Lou² fang²*. *A two or more storied house*; . . . . an upper room.

酒樓 *Chiu³ lou²*. . . . . An up-stairs saloon.

氣色 *Ch'i⁴ sê⁴*. *Color of the face*, looks; expression; appearance.

爲難 *Wei² nan²*. To regard as a difficulty; in difficulty, in straits, *troubled*.

煩難 *Fan² nan²*. . . . . The same.

誤事 *Wu⁴ shï⁴*. . . . . . . *To fail*, to break down.

丟差 *Tiu¹ ch'ai¹*. To disappoint the expectations of another, *to fail*, to blunder, to make a mess of.

皇親 *Hwang² ch'in¹*. The Emperor's relatives by marriage.

國丈 *Kwoă² chang⁴*. The Emperor's father-in-law:—Note 10.

斬首 *Chan³ shou³*. . . . . . To behead.

寬饒 *K'wan¹ jao²*. To deal leniently with, to show mercy; to *reprieve*.

寬讓 *K'wan¹ jang⁴*. To make allowance for, *to tolerate*, to put up with.

聽[12]說王玉琨、和他哥哥又合起來喇、依我看來、若是能常常和睦、在一塊兒過固然是好、萬一過不上來、再分開、可就叫人恥笑大喇。○舜[13]的兄弟象、天天想着殺舜、到舜為天子的時候、若按俗理說、雖然就是把象殺了、也是公道、但舜想到手足的情分、仍然還好好的待他、可見舜眞無愧爲聖人了。○如[14]今小場的文章、最喜的是快馬輕刀、若是用功不到、固然不能進學、就是費力太大、仍舊不能進學。○我[15]有一個朋友、在河南桐栢縣作知縣、這幾天有意要去找他討個差使、却沒拿定主意、若到了那裏、他不忘舊交、固然必有照應、萬一高攀不上、豈不白跑這一遢嗎。

neighbor," it will be better after all to put up with him,—only so that we don't entirely lose face.

12 I hear that Wang Yü K'un and his elder brother are living together again. As I look at it, it is of course all right if they can indeed continue to live in peace, but if perchance they fail to live together harmoniously and separate again, people will make great fun of them.

13 Shun's younger brother Shang was every day wanting to kill him. When Shun became emperor, although according to the ordinary ideas of justice it would have been perfectly right to put Shang to death, yet Shun, influenced by fraternal affection, continued to treat him as kindly as ever; from which it is clear that Shun is not unworthy to be accounted a sage.

14 In the primary examinations at present, the popular thing is a sprightly superficial style; hence, while one who is not diligent cannot of course succeed, yet he who overdoes the matter will equally fail.

15 I have a friend who is magistrate in the T'ung-pai district of Honan. I have been thinking these few days to go and see him and ask him for something to do, but have not yet made up my mind. If, when I get there, he does not ignore the old acquaintance, I would of course be provided for; but if perchance I should fail to obtain recognition, I should have all my journey for nothing.

琨 *Kun*¹. . . . . A kind of precious stone.

恥笑 *Ch'ih*³ *hsiao*⁴. To laugh out of countenance; . . . . to ridicule, *to make fun of.*

天子 *T'ien*¹ *tsï*³. . . . The Emperor:—Note 13.

手足 *Shou*³ *tsu*². A figure for brothers, or for . . . . fraternal affection.

費力 *Fei*⁴ *li*⁴. To expend effort; to take pains; . . . . laborious.

舊交 *Chiu*⁴ *chiao*¹. Former friendship, *old acquaintance.*

攀 *P'an*¹. . . . . To grasp, to climb, *to reach up to.*

高攀 *Kao*¹ *p'an*¹. *To claim acquaintance or friendship;* to aspire to.

Notes.

3 留飯 seems to say *keep or leave food*, but it really means *to invite one to stay for a meal.*

5 人家 here refers to the uncle, and is practically equal to a simple personal pronoun, though more definite in its reference.

7 The structure of this sentence is somewhat involved. 他夜間來偷我們的樹 is used parenthetically.

10 秦英 was the emperor's nephew, and though a mere stripling, was of giant strength. While he was out fishing, one of the emperor's fathers-in-law came along with

第一百八十三課

哎[1]呀我的媽媽媽呀、疼死我喇。○他[2]因爲羞愧難當、就出去弔死了。○昨[3]兒晚上、我母親跌了一跤、幾乎跌死。○口[4]子外頭碰壞了一隻船、把人都淹死了。○任[5]憑怎樣催他、他也不着急、真能把人急死。○只[6]當是他存出好心、給我父親治病、誰料一副劑藥把我父親磂藥毒死了。○但[7]凡是個有臉有皮的人、也就羞死煞了。○孩[8]子死是病死了、難道你不在家、我還能害死他不成。○這[9]條狗不看門家、光偷嘴、不如灌死他就結了。○賊[10]兵進了城、見人就殺、遇着小

TRANSLATION.

1 Oh, my mother! This pain is killing me.
2 Because he was mortified beyond endurance, he went out and hanged himself.
3 Last night my mother stumbled and fell and almost killed herself.
4 A ship has been wrecked outside the harbor and all on board drowned.
5 No matter how you urge him, he never gets in a hurry. It is really enough to worry one to death.
6 I of course supposed he was sincerely trying to cure my father, when, behold, by one dose of medicine he poisoned my father to death.
7 Anybody who had the least sense of shame would have been mortified to death.
8 The child's death was caused by disease. Is it a supposable thing that I took his life in your absence?
9 This dog will not watch the house, and is always filching something to eat. We might as well strangle him (with water) and be done with him.

h's retinue making a great ado, and frightened away the fish. This angered 秦英 and, being spurred on by his companions, he set on the offender, and dashing him down, rent him asunder by his great strength. The story is recorded in the history of the Tang dynasty, and being frequently acted in theaters, is familiar to the people. 國丈 *State father-in-law.* The fathers of the Emperor's wives and concubines are so called,—perhaps because the "state" has the "privilege" of maintaining them and their families. 回朝 *Return to the palace, or the immediate society of the emperor.* 將功折罪 *To make amends for crime by meritorious deeds,*—a recognized principle of Chinese governmental policy.

11 倚勢欺人 *To rely on power or prestige and so insult or oppress others.* 萬金置鄰 In China much more stress is laid on having good neighbors than is usually the case in the West, not so much for the sake of gentility as for security and help in difficulty.

13 象 was the half-brother of 舜, being the offspring of the father's second marriage. Both the father and the younger son sought to compass the death of the elder son. 天子 *Son of heaven,*—the Emperor is so styled because he is supposed to reign by the direct appointment of Heaven, and to be the representative or vicegerent of Heaven. 俗理 *Common reason,* the commonly accepted principles of right or justice, the lower as contrasted with the higher law or principle.

14 快馬輕刀 *A swift horse and a light sword,* a figure used to set forth a sprightly and incisive style. 費力太大 *Put forth too much effort;* that is, by excessive pains and care make the essay too heavy and labored.

LESSON CLXXXIII.

THE AUXILIARY VERBS 死 AND 煞.

死 To die,—is used as an auxiliary after verbs denoting the means or manner of killing. Though properly an auxiliary, 死 is not unfrequently used as a mere intensive. In has already been used a number of times in previous lessons.

煞 To kill,—is used as an auxiliary after verbs denoting the means or manner of killing. It is frequently, perhaps generally, used as an intensive, though it has the form and construction of an ordinary auxiliary. It is rarely used in Southern Mandarin.

孩子、扯捽着腿就摔死了。○正[11]當這隆冬數九的時候、身上一點兒綿衣裳沒有、有多少凍不死的呢。○我[12]正在大樹底下避躲雨、忽然打了一個霹炸靂雷、差一點叫給他震死。○你[13]怎麼把他打死了呢、答他拿刀來砍我、叫我從下邊一脚踢死了。○雞[14]吃了有毒的蟲子、毒氣都攻在腦子裏、所以雞到年數多了、他的頭就能毒煞死人。○我[15]和湯人傑比套拳拳脚、沒隄防、軟肋裏被他打了一下、希乎把我疼煞死。○王[16]天喜的孩子傷了風、渾身發熱、王天喜就煎了一副麻黃湯給他吃了、又蓋上四五牀被、要摀漚逼出點汗來、誰知這一摀漚逼、竟把個孩子摀漚厥死了。○別[17]的病一

10 When the rebels entered the city, they killed every one they saw. If they came across a child, they took it by the legs and dashed it to death on the ground.

11 Just in the depth of winter, and without a stitch of wadded clothing! How many are there who would not freeze to death [in the same circumstances]?

12 While I was sheltering myself from the rain under a large tree, there suddenly came a clap of thunder the shock of which came very near killing me.

13 How did you happen to kill him? *Ans.* He drew a knife and was about to cut me, when I gave him a kick from beneath and killed him.

14 When chickens eat poisonous worms, the poison all collects in their brains; hence when chickens get very old, their heads are poisonous.

15 I was boxing with T'ang Jên Chie and, failing to guard myself, he gave me a blow on my floating ribs the pain of which nearly killed me.

16 Wang T'ien Hsi's child took a cold and his whole body was feverish, whereupon Wang T'ien Hsi prepared him a sweating draught, and, giving it to him, covered him with four or five quilts in order to force out the

VOCABULARY.

難當 *Nan*² *tang*¹. Hard to bear; *beyond endurance*, in a strait.

跤 *Chiao*¹. . . . . To trip, to *stumble*, to fall.

口子 *K'ou*³ *tsï*³. . . . . A harbor, a port.

看家 *K'an*¹ *chia*¹. To watch the house or home. (N.)

猱 *Nao*⁴. . . . . To poison.

隆冬 *Lung*² *tung*¹. Intense cold, the depth of winter.

數九 *Shu*³ *chiu*³. The nine times nine days following the winter solstice.

霹 *P'i*¹. . . A clap, a report; the crash of thunder.

靂 *Li*⁴. . . . . A clap, a peal.

霹靂 A clap or peal of thunder.

炸雷 *Cha*⁴ *lei*². . . . . A clap of thunder. (S.)

毒氣 *Tu*² *ch'i*⁴. A poisonous vapor or gas or essence; poison.

比拳脚 *Pi*³ *ch'üen*² *chiao*³. To make trial of skill at boxing, *to box*.

套拳 *T'ao*⁴ *ch'üen*². *To box*, to practice boxing.

隄 *Ti*¹. . . A dike; to oppose, *to guard;* to fill up.

隄防 *Ti*¹ *fang*². *To guard against;* to be ready for, to ward off.

肋 *Lei*⁴. . . . . The ribs.

軟肋 *Jwan*³ *lei*⁴ . . . . . The floating ribs.

煎 *Chien*¹. To fry in oil; to simmer; *to decoct medicines*. See *chien*⁴.

麻黃 *Ma*² *hwang*². . . . . The horsetail.

摀 *Wu*³. . . . . To cover with the hand, to muffle.

點沒有、就是喉嚨腫的嘆喘不出上氣來、硬瘪死了。○馬[18]五招死老崔婆子、一直跑上了嶗山、只覺着在那裏沒有事喇、誰料他在夢中吐了實情、竟被即墨縣官拏住、打遞解打回來了。○榮[19]大老爺問案、最決斷、不過心裏一掂算畫會打稿要怎麽問就怎麽問、若有不遵斷的、輕者掌打嘴嘴巴、重者打小板子、或一千或八百、就是屈死煞、也也要得出具結結○葛[20]畢氏、和姦夫楊乃武串同一氣、用毒藥害死本夫、被人告了、楊乃武是個大財主、就用錢上下打點、直打了十來年的官司、從本縣打到北京、也沒問成他謀害本夫的罪名、眞是錢能通神哪。

perspiration, when what should he do but smother the child to death.

17 He had no other disease, save that his throat was so swollen that he could not get his breath, and he simply smothered to death.

18 When Ma Wu had choked old Dame Ts'wei to death he fled at once to the Lao Mountains, thinking that there he would be safe; but, behold, all unawares he let the secret out in his sleep, and finally was arrested by the Chimoǎ magistrate and sent back to his own district for trial.

19 Yung Ta Lao Yie is a man of the greatest positiveness. He at once forms an opinon of how the case stands, and as he thinks, so it must be. If any one dissents from the verdict, the lighter punishment is slapping on the face, and the heavier, a beating with the light bamboo, one thousand blows, or perhaps eight hundred. Even if wronged to death, you have to make a settlement.

20 Mrs. Kê of the Pi family with her paramour, Yang Nai Wu, conspired together and procured the death of her husband by poison. Being accused, Yang Nai Wu, who was very wealthy, bribed both the lower and the higher officials, so that after a suit of over ten years, carrying the case from the district magistrate to the capital, no conviction was obtained for the murder. Verily money is all-powerful.

瘪 *Pie*¹. A suppurating ulcer; to hold in, restrain; tenesmus; *to smother.*

嶗 *Lao*².... Certain mountains:—Note 18.

解 *Chie*⁴.... To send under guard. See *chie*³, and *hsie*⁴.

遞解 *Ti*⁴ *chie*⁴. To send under guard from one jurisdiction to another.

掂算 *Tien*¹ *swan*⁴. To weigh, to estimate; to consider, *to form an opinion.*

畫會 *Hwa*⁴ *hwei*⁴. To picture in the mind, *to conceive*, to imagine.

打稿 *Ta*³ *kao*³. To make a first draft; to plan, to project, to estimate.

打嘴巴 *Ta*³ *tswei*³ *pa*¹. To beat on the face:—Note 19.

掌嘴 *Chang*³ *tswei*³. To slap on the face, to beat on the face.

具結 *Chü*⁴ *chie*². To draw up and sign a settlement of a lawsuit.

出結 *Ch'u*¹ *chie*². To arrange and draw up a settlement of a lawsuit.

姦 *Chien*¹. Illicit intercourse of any kind; to debauch.

姦夫 *Chien*¹ *fu*¹. A husband who is guilty of adultery, an adulterer.

串同 *Ch'wan*⁴ *t'ung*². To connect together; *to band*, to ally.

毒藥 *Tu*² *yao*⁴....... Poisonous drugs, *poison.*

謀害 *Mou*² *hai*⁴. To harm seriously or fatally by a secret plot; to plot against.

通神 *T'ung*¹ *shên*². Moving the gods; *all-powerful*:—Note 20.

第一百八十四課

大[1]丈夫作事、敢作敢為當。○這[2]個學生神鬼頭鬼腦的、精神外漏。○我[3]好心好意的告訴他、倒反討了個無趣。○你[4]這個孩子、怎麼無是無非無涉無千就打人呢。○他[5]們兩個眞是絕情絕意、一點夫妻的滋味情腸也沒有。○已[6]經僱給人家、還能自由自在的、像在家裏一樣嗎。○只[7]用合家無災無病、雖就是窮一點、過的也有心腸。心與○當[8]時他滿應滿許滿口應許要給我

Translation.

1 A resolute man dares to act and to bear the responsibility (to undertake).
2 There is something outlandish about this pupil. He looks a great deal brighter than he really is.
3 I told him with the best of intentions, and got snubbed for my pains.
4 You little rascal, you! what makes you strike people without any provocation?
5 They two have in fact lost affection for each other; the proper conjugal feelings are all gone.
6 Having hired yourself to another, can you still be as independent as if you were at home?
7 Only let a family be free from trouble or sickness, and although they live frugally, they will still keep in good spirits.

Notes.

1 哎呀, as here used, goes somewhat beyond the definition given in Les. 93. It is here an expression of mingled surprise and pain. 娘 is often used instead of 媽, though never doubled. When a man is in trouble he calls on his mother, and when one man wishes to revile another he reviles his mother, thus indicating that in China, affection for the mother is ordinarily stronger than that for the father.

7 有臉有皮 is equivalent to 有臉皮, which is thus amplified for emphasis; see next lesson.

9 灌死 to strangle by pouring water into the mouth, or by holding the head or mouth and nose under water.

11 隆冬數九 *In the nines of the ascendant winter, in mid-winter.* It is customary to count time by nines from the 冬至, or *winter solstice*, until nine times nine days are counted, which includes the coldest weather and brings the spring.

16 麻黃湯 A draught made by the decoction of a variety of herbs, of which the principle one is the horsetail, and used as a domestic sudorific for the cure of colds. 給他吃了 does not mean, *ate it for him*, but, *gave him to eat*,—給 being used as a principle verb. 把個孩子 This use of 個 is colloquial, but quite *t'ung-hsing*. It is a contraction for 那個.

18 嶗山 A range of hills or mountains in the district of 卽墨, on the southern side of the Shantung promontory, noted as the site of many Taoist temples. 吐了實情 *Spit out the facts*, or as we say, "let out the truth."

19 Beating on the face is considered a lighter and less shameful punishment than beating with a bamboo. The beating is done with a short heavy leather strap of two thicknesses sewed together, and resembling a Chinese leather shoe sole. 輕者...重者 A common and very neat form of expressing the limits of lightness and severity. The same form is used with other adjuncts, 大者..小者, etc.

20 本夫 *The husband of the woman in question.* The terms here used are those current in legal documents. 通神 means properly *to connect with the gods, to affect or move the gods*, and hence, *to be possessed of* or *endued with, divine effect or power, all-powerful.*

LESSON CLXXXIV.

Quadruplet Phrases.

Both written and spoken Chinese shows a strong liking for four character phrases. They abound in all kinds of writing, as well as in colloquial Mandarin. Though extensively used in colloquial, they generally have their origin in books. Those most commonly used have been arranged in four classes, and one lesson will be given to each.

The present lesson illustrates such quadruplet phrases as have the first and third characters the same, the second and fourth being analogues; or *vice versâ*, the second and fourth the same and the first and third analogues. In most cases the analogous words form a phrase, which, for rhetorical effect, is separated into parts by the

還這筆賬、怎麼一個大錢沒還你呢。○我[9]和你無寃無仇、你這樣無緣無故的來找我做什麼呢。○卜[10]先生最沉重排塌端方不過、狂言狂語一點沒有。○我[11]看見他揑手揑脚的、在後窗底下聽了多時。○雖[12]是些個一些八面風的話、却能把人說得心服口服俯伏在地的。○別[13]看他外面憨頭憨腦癡頭癡腦的、心裏却是詭詐得很。○[14]順絲順緒順情順理的事好辦、有頭有尾的話叫人愛聽。○一[15]舉一動總要謙卑、若是大模大樣的、就討人嫌了。○眼[16]見是實、耳聽是虛、那些風言風語的話、何足憑信呢。○這[17]蒼蒼之天、並沒有一定的界限、乃是無邊無岸的。○世[18]間的

8 He promised at the time, most positively, to pay this account for me. How is it that he has never given you a cash?

9 There is no enmity between you and me. Why then do you come without any apparent reason to throw the blame on me?

10 Mr. Pu is very sedate; he never speaks extravagantly.

11 I saw him stealing on tip-toe to the back window, and listening a long time.

12 Although what he says is nothing but rattling declamation, yet he has the knack of gaining people's complete confidence.

13 Don't be misled by his simple appearance, his heart is very deceitful.

14 Well-regulated business is easy to manage; methodical speech is pleasant to listen to.

15 Take care to be unpretending in all your deportment. If you are ostentatious, you will provoke the aversion of others.

16 What is seen is real; what is heard is uncertain. What is there that is worthy of credence in these floating rumors?

repeated word. Dialectic differences have caused the introduction of several phrases belonging to the subsequent classes.

敢作敢當 Ready to assume responsibility, self-reliant; decision of character.

敢作敢爲 Ready to undertake, resolute.

鬼頭鬼腦 Outlandish, ludicrous, comic; lackadaisical.

神頭鬼臉 The same.

好心好意 With the best intentions, in the kindness of one's heart, well meant.

無是無非 Without cause, unprovoked.

無涉無干 Without cause, unprovoked; extraneous, irrelevant.

絶情絶意 Affection lost, estranged.

自由自在 At liberty, free, unconstrained.

無災無病 Free from trouble and sickness, well and happy.

滿應滿許 To promise positively, an unreserved promise.

無寃無仇 Without enmity, on good terms.

無緣無故 Causeless, unprovoked, without a reason.

狂言狂語 Extravagant language, braggadocio; rudeness, incivility.

揑手揑脚 To walk lightly, to walk stealthily on tip-toe, to tread gingerly.

心服口服 Full or hearty assent, cordial approval.

憨頭憨腦 Lumpish, lubberly; gawky.

癡頭癡腦 Simple, silly, vacant, maudlin.

順絲順緒 In a regular and orderly way.

順情順理 Proper, reasonable, regular.

有頭有尾 Methodical, systematic.

一舉一動 In everything, in the whole deportment.

大模大樣 Ostentatious, pretentious, pompous.

風言風語 Floating rumors, hearsay.

無邊無岸 Boundless, illimitable.

糊裏糊塗 Foolish, inconsiderate, haphazard, topsy-turvy.

事、何必認眞、只是睜着一個眼、閉着一個眼、糊裏糊泥磨裏糊塗糊塗磨留的混兩天就是了。○他[19]成天家整天的、不是和這個吵、就是和那個鬧、而且勸不聽勸、打不怕打、眞是無法無天。○實[20]心實意的朋友有多少、大概都是假仁假義、臨事靠急臨時就急就不行了。○柳[21]同安有一口四五六的楸木棺材、他要五十吊錢、公理公道的、能值四十五吊。○這[22]等唆事的人、眞眞可惡、並沒有影兒的事情、他能謅得有根有稍有頭有尾的。○孫[23]國瑞今年攬了十八個學生、都是般大般小、十來多歲、其中有一多半是纔開蒙的。○這[24]個說話有條有

17 This azure sky has no definite boundary, but is illimitable.

18 Why should one be over-conscientious in the affairs of this life? It is better with half-shut eyes to flounder hap-hazard across its narrow span.

19 He is all the time getting into a rumpus with somebody; moreover he will not listen to advice, nor is he afraid of a whipping. He is simply incorrigible.

20 How few true and faithful friends there are. The great majority are hollow-hearted. When the time of trial comes, they are found wanting.

21 Liu T'ung An has a four five six catalpa coffin, for which he wants fifty thousand cash. A fair price would be forty-five thousand.

22 The class of busy-bodies is truly detestable. They will fabricate a story in all its details, when there is not a shadow of foundation for it.

23 Sun Kwoă Jwei has this year secured a school of eighteen pupils, all good sized boys in their teens, the most of them being beginners.

24 This one speaks in good logical order,

糊泥糊塗 The same. (s.)
磨裏磨留 Indistinct, confused, vague.
無法無天 Lawless, insubordinate, reckless, incorrigible.
實心實意 Sincere, true and faithful.
假仁假義 Hypocritical, false, hollow.
臨事靠急 When the trial or test comes, the hour of trial:—Les. 195.
臨時就急 The same:—Les. 195.
公理公道 Equitable, honest, fair, just.
有根有稍 With all its parts, in detail.
有頭有尾 The same.
般大般小 Half-grown, medium sized.
有條有理 In logical order, systematic.
有滋有味 Interesting, fascinating, spicy.
有情有趣 The same.
閒坐閒耍 Idle, unemployed, indolent, frivolous.
閒坐閒玩 The same.
無理無法 Foolish; unlawful, criminal.
銜天銜地 Exaggerated, extravagant, preposterous, bombastic.
不三不四 Insolent, saucy, abusive.
得過且過 To evade, to shirk, to slight.
怯頭怯腦 Faint-hearted, fidgety; green.
縮頭縮腦 The same.

VOCABULARY.

無趣 *Wu² ch'ü⁴.* Out of countenance, mortified; *snubbed;* no fun in it.

涉 *Shé⁴.* To ford a stream; to implicate, *to concern;* connected with.

情腸 *Ch'ing² ch'ang².* Affection, sympathy; *feeling,* emotion.

自由 *Tsï⁴ yu².* At liberty, one's own master.

卜 *Pu³.* To divine; to guess; *a surname.*

理、那個說話有滋有味[有情有趣]、兩個人眞是棋逢對手。○ 25個不安分守己、愛吃好的、愛穿好的、閒坐閒玩耍、就做出許多無理無法的事來。○王26老三就是說句實話、也是衒天衒地的樣子、叫人不敢實信他。○刁27鳴春不但不肯認錯、而且嘴裏還不三不四的。○有28一等混事的人、無論做什麼、是得過且過、一點不肯認眞、這樣的人、我實在不願意和他共事。○今29天我在齊化門外頭、叫小掠[起手/扒兒手]把口袋裏的錢吃[起/扒]了去喇、答 誰叫你不小心、別說你這怯頭怯腦[縮頭縮腦]的樣子、就是久在大城裏頭的人、出去還得留神呢。

and that one is very interesting. The two are really very well matched.

25 Whenever a man departs from the line of duty and learns to love fast living, spending his time in idleness and frivolity, he will presently be guilty of many foolish and unlawful things.

26 Even when Wang the Third does speak the truth, he does it in such a bombastic way that one does not venture to believe him.

27 Tiao Ming Ch'un not only will not admit his fault, but he even talks insolently.

28 There is a class of easy-going people who slight everything they do, having no idea of ever doing their best. I dislike exceedingly to work with such people.

29 To-day outside the Ch'ihwa gate, the money I had in my bag was stolen by a pick-pocket. *Ans.* That was your own carelessness. Even old residents in the city need to have their wits about them, much more such a clodhopper as you.

沉重 *Ch'ên² chung⁴*. Weight; weighty, important; serious, grave, *sedate*.

俯伏 *Fu³ fu²*. To fall on the face, to bow in submission.

謙卑 *Ch'ien¹ pei¹*. Meek, humble; modest, *unpretending*.

界限 *Chie⁴ hsien⁴*. .... Boundary, limit.

岸 *An⁴*....... *Shore*, bank, beach; goal.

棺 *Kwan¹*. ... ... A coffin.

棺材 *Kwan¹ ts'ai²*. ... ... A coffin.

唆事 *Soa¹ shï⁴*. To set at variance, *to intermeddle*, to incite a quarrel.

開蒙 *K'ai¹ mêng²*. *To enter school for the first time;* to give the first lesson.

世間 *Shï⁴ chien¹*. ... *The world;* human affairs.

對手 *Twei⁴ shou³*. To encounter an opponent; an opponent, *a match*, a rival.

衒 *Hsüen⁴*. To praise; to brag, *to boast;* vainglorious; exaggerated, extravagant.

實信 *Shï² hsin⁴*. To believe implicitly, to confide in; to really believe.

掠 *Lüe³,⁴*....... *To rob;* to plunder, to raid.

扒 *P'a²*. To lie down flat; to crawl; *to sneak*. ...... See *pa¹*.

小掠兒 *Hsiao³ lüe³ êr²*. A petty thief, a pick-pocket. (N.)

起手 *Ch'i³ shou³*. ... ... The same. (C.)

扒兒手 *P'a² êr² shou³*......... The same. (S.)

NOTES.

2 精神外漏 *Intelligence developed externally;* that is, a precociously intelligent look or expression but with no mind or talent corresponding.

7 有心 or 有心腸 *Have heart;* that is, *hopeful and contented, thrifty.* The more common meaning of 有心 is, *intentional.* 有興 *Have joy;* that is, *hopeful, cheerful, in good spirits.*

12 八面風的話 *Speech that turns about to the eight points from which the winds blow, specious declamation.*

13 憨頭憨腦 and 癡頭癡腦 are not quite

第一百八十五課

凡[1]官場中的事情、本當公事公辦、但如今沒有一樣不是有名無實的。○他[2]們沒說別的、淨說了一些家長里短的話。○各[3]國的政事雖不一樣、而究其實、却是大同小異。○這[4]部三國志、少頭缺尾的、叫人沒法子看。○莊[5]稼人總得起早連睡晚的做、光愛睡懶漢早覺那還行嗎。○看[6]不得他說的好、他却是嘴甜心苦。○老[7]兄這兩天長吁短嘆、心中有什麼難事呢。○諸[8]葛亮用兵、眞是神出鬼沒的、叫人一點也測度不到。○自[9]己專好損人利己、却想

Translation.

1 All legal matters ought to be transacted in accordance with justice, but, at the present time, there is nothing connected with them that is not a sham.
2 Their talk was nothing but a lot of scandal.
3 Although the governments of different countries are not the same, yet when carefully examined they are found to be alike in the main.
4 This copy of the History of the Three Kingdoms is so imperfect that one cannot read it.
5 Farmers must work early and late; it will never do to lie abed long in the mornings (like a sluggard).
6 Do not be misled by his plausible talk. He has a honeyed tongue but a cruel heart.
7 What is troubling you, my friend, that you go sighing around these last few days?
8 Chu Kwoă Liang's military strategy was truly marvelous. No one could possibly anticipate his movements.
9 Though caring for nothing but to benefit

equivalent. The former gives the idea of a full, fat, expressionless face, the latter that of a doltish, half-witted look.

17 蒼蒼之天 *The heaven which is the blue sky*, as distinguished from Heaven as used for the presiding deity. 之 is not, as commonly, a possessive, but serves rather as a relative or appositional particle.

20 臨事靠急 *Approaching the affair and drawing near to the [time of] anxiety*; that is, *when the time of need or trial comes*. The connection shows that 事 is used in the sense of *trouble*.

21 四五六 is used to designate a coffin with bottom four inches thick, sides five inches thick, and top six inches thick. Coffins are made heavy in order to resist decay.

24 棋逢對手 *The chess-player meeting his match*,—said of competitors or opponents who are well matched.

27 不三不四 It is not easy to see how this phrase comes to mean what it does.

29 齊化門 is the more southerly of the two gates in the east wall of Peking. The stone road leading to T'ungchow proceeds from it.

LESSON CLXXXV.

Quadruplet Phrases.

The phrases illustrated in this lesson are such as have the first and third characters either analogues or opposites, the second and fourth being *usually* related in the same way.

有名無實 Illusory, deceptive, unreal, sham.

家長里短 Neighborhood gossip, scandal.

大同小異 Nearly alike, essentially alike, only slightly different.

少頭缺尾 Imperfect, incomplete, defective.

起早睡晚 Early and late.

起早連晚 The same.

嘴甜心苦 Honeyed words but a cruel heart, hypocritical, double-faced, false.

長吁短嘆 To sigh, to groan, to lament.

神出鬼沒 Marvelous, astonishing, unaccountable.

損人利己 To benefit self at the expense of others, to overreach, to defraud.

求福免禍 To attain happiness and escape misfortune.

着求福免禍。○你10父親東跑西顛、東奔西跑豈是容易掙這幾個錢、你可以這樣浪費嗎。○劉11玄德使龐鳳雛作一個縣官、豈不是大材小用嗎。○那12個人不能成全大事、無論做甚麼有始無終、一點常性恒心沒有。○既13然是個忠臣、那有貪生怕死、不敢諫諍之理呢。○他14地裏打的粮食、並不彀半年吃的、全仗着東扯西拉的過日子。○我15左思右想、就是沒有投路奔、但凡有一點投路奔、我早就跳了槽喇。○夫16妻們應當你敬我愛、不可整天家吵吵鬧鬧的、不成體統。○我17們都是一樣的

yourself at the expense of others, you yet hope to be happy and escape misfortune.

10 Has it been an easy thing for your father to earn by incessant toil these few cash, that you should squander them in this way?

11 When Liu Hsüen Tê sent P'ang Fêng Ch'u to be a district magistrate, was it not a case of putting great abilities to an unworthy use?

12 That man will never accomplish anything great. Everything he does is left unfinished. He hasn't a particle of perseverance.

13 If you are a faithful minister, how can you decline to reprove [the Emperor] simply because you are afraid of losing your life?

14 The grain he gets from his land is not enough for half a year's consumption; his chief dependence for a living is in borrowing this to pay that.

15 In spite of all my planning I find no opening. If there had been the least chance, I would have thrown up my position long ago.

16 Husband and wife should love and

東跑西顛 To run hither and thither, to bustle, to toil, to be at great pains.

東奔西跑 The same.

大材小用 Waste or misuse of materials or talent.

有始無終 Unfinished, abortive.

貪生怕死 Clinging to life, preferring life to duty.

東扯西拉 Borrowing this to pay that, by hook and crook.

左思右想 To cast about in every direction, in a quandary, at one's wits' end.

你敬我愛 Mutual respect and affection.

厚此薄彼 To treat one better than another, to be partial.

翻來覆去 This way and that, over and over, again and again.

打爹罵娘 To maltreat father and mother.

隱惡揚善 To conceal the evil and proclaim the good.

口是心非 Deceitful, double-faced, false, hypocritical.

推前擦後 To evade, to shirk, to wriggle out of.

辭前挨後 The same.

有益無損 Beneficial and involving no danger, safe.

言差語錯 Misunderstanding; sharp or unpleasant words.

嫌貧愛富 To slight the poor and pay court to the rich.

大公無私 Just and equal, equitable, even-handed.

賞善罰惡 To reward the good and punish the evil, to judge and administer justice.

改惡從善 To reform, to turn over a new leaf.

轉禍爲福 To turn misfortune into happiness.

改頭換影 To change, to transform; to metamorphose.

改頭換面 The same.

似是而非 Specious pretence, fallacious.

公事公辦 In accordance with justice:—Note 1.

現世現報 Present or manifest retribution.

有憑有據 Certain, veritable, incontestable, well established.

人、在你跟前也都沒有錯處、你怎麼該厚此薄彼呢。○你[18]們翻來覆去、是要把這個不是推在我身上、我還就是覺着一點不是沒有。○都[19]說沒有神靈神靈、你看李滋源常常打參罵娘、叫給雷一下打死了、這不是現世現報嗎。○天[20]下揚善而又揚惡的人很多、眞眞能以隱惡揚善的、却很希少。○這[21]等口是心非的人、實在討人厭惡。○說[22]不出他有別的毛病、就是凡事推前擦後辭前挨後的、一點上緊的緊趲着緊的意思沒有。○鐵[23]銹的功用、能以補血、乃是一種有益無損的好藥。○一[24]年三百六十天常在一塊兒、那能一

respect each other, and not violate propriety by continually scolding and quarrelling.

17 We are all on the same footing, and no one of us has been guilty of any offence against you. Why then should you treat some better than others?

18 You are twisting this way and that way in order to throw the blame on me, and yet I cannot feel that I have done anything wrong.

19 Everybody says there are no [puissant] gods; but just look how Li Tsï Yüen, who was constantly abusing his father and mother, was struck dead by lightning. Was not this a manifest retribution?

20 There are plenty of people in the world who will spread abroad both good and evil reports, but very few who will really conceal the evil and tell the good.

21 This class of deceitful people is very detestable.

22 I cannot say that he has any other fault, save that he is always disposed to shirk, and hasn't a particle of energy.

23 The effect of iron rust is to invigorate the blood. It is an excellent tonic, and free from all danger.

24 How can those who are constantly

VOCABULARY.

官場 *Kwan¹ ch'ang².* Governmental offices and business; *legal*, official.

政事 *Chêng⁴ shï⁴.* *Government*, administration of law; civil affairs.

懶漢 *Lan³ han⁴.* A lazy fellow, a sluggard.

吁 *Hsü¹.* Ugh! humph; *to sigh*, to groan.

難事 *Nan² shï⁴.* Difficulty, *trouble*, embarrassment.

玄 *Hsüen².* Dark, abstruse, profound.

龐 *P'ang².* A lofty house; *a surname.*

雛 *Ch'u².* A chick, a young bird, a fledgeling.

常性 *Ch'ang² hsing⁴.* "The gift of continuance," *perseverance*, grit.

諫 *Chien⁴.* To reprove, to urge to reform.

諍 *Chêng¹.* To remonstrate with a superior.

諫諍 To reprove and advise a ruler or superior, to remonstrate.

投路 *T'ou² lu⁴.* Opening, resort, resource; *chance*, opportunity.

跳槽 *T'iao⁴ ts'ao².* To seek a better situation, *to throw up position*, to strike:—Note 15.

神靈 *Shên² ling².* Divine intelligences, *the gods;* divinity.

希少 *Hsi¹ shao³.* Very few, rare.

緊趲 *Chin³ ch'ên⁴.* Diligent, industrious; *energetic.*

着緊 *Choa² chin³.* The same.

功用 *Kung¹ yung⁴.* *Effect*, result, operation.

退親 *T'wei⁴ ch'in¹.* To break a marriage contract.

賴婚 *Lai⁴ hun¹.* To seek to evade the fulfilment of a marriage contract.

訟師 *Sung⁴ shï¹.* A pettifogger:—Note 27.

轉動 *Chwan³ tung⁴.* To revolve, to turn, to turn over.

二二忽忽 *Êr⁴ hu¹.* Hesitating, wavering, indistinct, *confused*,

點言差語錯沒有呢。○從[25]前他見楊家興旺、就託兩三起人、把女兒許給人家、如今楊家敗落喇、他又想着和人家賴退親、這不是明明嫌貧愛富嗎。○天[26]道既是大公無私、自然必要賞善罰惡、所以若能改惡從善、這就是轉禍爲福了。○怪[27]不得沙景雲當訟師哪、這個人眞有轉動乾坤的手段、明明是有憑有據的事情、他竟改頭換面影、說出一些似是而非的理來、把人弄的疑二疑二惑忽惑忽的了。

associated together, avoid having some little misunderstandings?

25 Some time ago, when he saw that the Yang family were prospering, he made several proposals and eventually betrothed his daughter to them; and now that the Yang family are in adversity, he wants to break the engagement. Is not this a clear case of despising the poor and paying court to the rich?

26 Since the ways of Heaven are perfectly just, the good will certainly be rewarded and the evil punished. If, therefore, you will reform and practice virtue, then blessings instead of calamities will be the result.

27 No wonder that Sha Ching Yün follows the profession of law. He is a man of really transcendent ability. The most clearly established facts are so entirely transformed by his specious arguments that one's mind is all in confusion.

NOTES.

1 公事公辦 *Public business should be characterized by justice.* It is worthy of note that 公, which properly means *public*, comes also to mean *just*, implying perhaps that that only which is public, is supposed to be just. 公事公辦 is also used with the meaning,—*That which pertains to all should be managed in common*, or *with the concurrence of all.*

2 家長里短 *Family long, alley short*; that is, the criticisms of each other's shortcomings made by those living in the same family or in the same alley.

4 三國志 A historical novel written during the Yüen dynasty by 羅貫中. The narrative includes the chief characters and events of the period during which the rival houses of 魏, 蜀 and 吳 were struggling for the mastery,—the heroic epoch of Chinese history. It is regarded by the Chinese as their best novel. It is written in easy *Wênli*, with an occasional flavor of Mandarin.

8 神出鬼沒 *As gods and demons appear and disappear*; that is, in the surprising and unaccountable manner in which gods and demons appear and act and then as suddenly vanish.

9 求福免禍 *Seek blessings and avoid misfortunes*; that is, attain the blessings conferred by the gods on the virtuous and escape the misfortunes sent on the vicious. Both 禍 and 福 refer primarily to the awards of the gods, as is indicated in the common radical with which they are written,—the radical under which are classed all the characters denoting divine beings, acts, offices and worship.

11 劉玄德, better known as 劉備, began life as a seller of straw shoes, but rose to be a fellow soldier with the famous Chang Fei and Kwan Yü, in the period of the "Three Kingdoms." He was known as 漢中王 until he proclaimed himself Emperor in A. D. 220. He is known in history by his imperial title 昭烈帝, of the 蜀漢 dynasty. 龐鳳雛 was an officer of remarkable ability under him, whom he at first appointed as a local magistrate, before he had learned his commanding talents.

13 忠臣 The Chinese theory of the duty of a faithful minister is, that in case of dangerous imperial errors or vices, he ought to reprove his sovereign even at the risk of his life.

15 跳了槽 *Jumped the trough*, a figure taken from animals' feeding, when they leave an empty trough and strive for a full one.

18 我還就是覺着 The translation scarcely conveys the full force of this expression. *But you see, I think*, if spoken with proper emphasis, will approximate it.

19 神靈 *Divine intelligences*,—a term commonly used to designate the whole class of (supposed) divine beings. 靈神 *A live or efficient god*; that is, one who has the knowledge, power and will to execute judgment on those who offend him, and to hear the prayers of those who pray to him.

23 補血 *To supply the deficiencies of the blood, to invigorate the blood.*

25 退親 differs from 賴婚, in that the former *may* be justifiable, but the latter never is.

26 天道 sometimes means *the weather*, but here it means *the way of Heaven*; that is, *the providential government of Heaven*. The four phrases here used are stock phrases in Chinese moral teaching, and well illustrate the terseness and vivacity which such ready made phrases impart to the style.

27 訟師 is one who hangs about yamêns and fattens on the fees he gets for giving advice to anxious litigants, as well as for assisting them in various illicit ways by collusion with the underlings. Such business is illegal, and such men are held in detestation by magistrates. Lawyers or counsellors in the Western sense are not known in Chinese courts.

第一百八十六課

[1]陳日興太執拗（拘板）了、一點三還九轉（三彎九轉）也沒有。○[2]他這樣隔三跳兩（隔二騙三、丟三歇五）的用功、那能見長進呢。○[3]你有甚麼不對（合）心思、嘴裏這麼念三道四（言三語四）的。○[4]這塊木頭七歪八扭的、一點不成材料。○[5]他三番兩次的來纏磨我、眞討人嫌。○[6]總要規規矩矩、不可七抓八拏的。○[7]人若不知三綱五常、與禽獸有甚麼兩樣處呢。○[8]當家三日狗也嫌、七言八語的還能免嗎。○[9]不消着急、這不是三天五日可了結的事。○[10]以後我在背地裏問他、他還是橫三豎四的支吾。○[11]你這些櫻桃、怎麼七大八小的、還帶着裏頭淨蒂把（把）把。

Translation.

1 Ch'ên Yüe Hsing is entirely too pig-headed. He hasn't the slightest idea of how to adapt himself to circumstances.

2 How can he make progress when he studies in such an irregular way?

3 What are you dissatisfied about that you keep up such a grumbling?

4 This piece of wood is bent and twisted out of all shape and not fit for anything.

5 He came again and again, importuning me in the most annoying way.

6 You should behave properly, and not keep meddling with things.

7 If a man ignores the human relations, in what does he differ from the brutes?

8 "Act as head of the family for three days, and the very dogs will be dissatisfied with you." Can you expect to escape all criticism?

9 It is not worth while to get in a hurry. This is not a matter that can be finished up in three or four days.

10 I afterwards asked him privately, but he still tried in every possible way to evade.

11 How is it that these cherries of yours are so unequal in size? and what is more they are chiefly stems.

LESSON CLXXXVI.

Numerical Quadruplets.

Many four character phrases are formed of two numbers combined with two analogous words. These numbers sometimes have a reason for their use, but frequently seem to be chosen quite at random. The lesson embraces the most commonly used phrases of this class.

三還九轉 Adaptation to circumstances, resources, expedients.

三彎九轉 The same.

隔三跳兩 By fits and starts, by spells, irregularly.

隔二騙三 The same.

丟三歇五 The same. (s.)

念三道四 To find fault, to grumble, to croak.

言三語四 The same. (s.)

七歪八扭 Bent or twisted out of shape, crooked, gnarled.

三番兩次 Several times, time and again.

七抓八拏 To snatch and grab; to meddle with, to take without leave.

三綱五常 The three relations,—prince, father and husband; and five virtues,—benevolence (仁), rectitude (義), courtesy (禮), knowledge (智), and faithfulness (信). The whole phrase is a comprehensive summary of human duty.

七言八語 Diverse opinions, criticisms, conflicting views.

三天五日 Three or four days, a few days.

橫三豎四 This way and that way, up and down, back and forth, every way.

七大八小 Irregular in size, different sizes.

三差兩錯 Mistakes, misunderstandings.

一差二錯 The same.

○ 倘[12]若有個三差兩錯、一差二錯、我可是來找你呀。○ 他[13]的年紀太大、說話顛三倒四的。○ 任[14]你千思萬想、那知老天爺有一定的安排。○ 他[15]叫我三拳兩腳、打了個不亦樂乎。○ 一[16]條線的事情好辦、若是七股八杈、七杈八股、七頭八杈的、就叫人難插手了。○ 他[17]一家人、都一點外務沒有、眞是十子九成、盛水不漏。○ 別[18]大意過、太大意了、依我看十有八九不行。○ 每[19]月掙不上三千兩吊錢、君三民七、君七民八的、還打不過點兒來。○ 我[20]本不愛管他的閒事、但他再三再四的央求、也只得給他調說調說、調處調處。○

12 If it turns out that there are any mistakes, I will hold you responsible.
13 He is too old; his speech is rambling.
14 Prepare and plan as you will, you will find that the purposes of God will still come to pass.
15 I administered a few kicks and blows, which gave me a sense of supreme satisfaction.
16 A systematic piece of business is easy to manage, but in a complicated affair it is hard to know where to take hold.
17 There is not an immoral member in the whole family. It is a clear case of nine parts in ten (no leakage).
18 Don't be overconfident. In my opinion there are eight or nine chances in ten that it will not work.
19 Hardly earning as much as two or three thousand cash per month, when divided up I find it insufficient to make the ends meet.
20 I am loth to have anything to do with his affairs, but he has importuned me over and over again, so that I cannot but speak a word for him.
21 This collector was most unrelenting, and he came, too, just when I had no

顛三倒四 Inverted, disordered, confused, rambling, incoherent.

千思萬想 To devise various plans, to think anxiously, to scheme.

三拳兩脚 A few blows and kicks, a belaboring, a drubbing.

七股八杈 At loose ends, heterogeneous, complicated, tangled.

七杈八股 The same.

七頭八杈 The same.

十子九成 Nine out of ten grow and mature.

十有八九 Eight or nine chances in ten, "ten to one."

三千兩吊 Two or three thousand cash.

君三民七 To divide up, to distribute:—Note 19.

君七民八 The same.

再三再四 Again and again, over and over again, time and again.

七拚八湊 To "make a raise" by sacrificing this for that, to scrape or get together, to gather up.

吆三喝二 To cry out again and again; clamor, hue and cry.

吆二喝三 The same.

千辛萬苦 Toils, privations, hardships, inconveniences.

連三疉四 One thing upon another, piled up, in close succession.

連三帶四 The same.

三言兩語 A few words or sentences, in short, summary.

七折八扣 Seven or eight parts in ten:—Note 26.

七顛八倒 In confusion, topsy-turvy.

七嘴八舌 Conflicting opinions, miscellaneous criticisms.

三日打魚兩日曬網 Unprofitable, unproductive.

○這[21]個要討賬的、實在蛤固利害、又趕上家裏沒有錢、東家討、西家借、七拼八湊的對付了五百錢、好歹撮弄他走了。○快[22]給他點冷飯、打發他走罷、叫他儘自吆三喝二吆二喝三吆吆喝喝的做甚麼呢。○買[23]賣人東跑西奔南跑北奔、千辛萬苦的巴結、無非爲利起見。○[24]這幾年的生意不濟好、又加上男婚女嫁、連三疊帶四的辦事、實在穀我架弄的。○可[25]惜夜來昨天我不在家、若是我在家裏、三言兩語盤倒那先生、管保有場好笑。○放[26]賬的買賣、到還錢的時候、

money in the house; by borrowing of one and another and putting odds and ends together I made up five hundred cash, and managed to send him off the best way I could.

22 Quickly give him a little cold victuals and send him away. Why keep him here crying after us without ceasing?

23 The merchant travels hither and thither, subjecting himself to all sorts of inconvenience, solely for the sake of gain.

24 Business has been poor these few years, and besides all this my sons and daughters have been getting married, piling up matters on me until it is about all I can stand.

25 I am sorry I was not at home last night. If I had been there, I could have wound up the gentleman in a few words, and there would have been a good laugh, I'll warrant you.

26 In doing a credit business, when pay-day comes, what with small cash

VOCABULARY.

陳 *Ch'ên*². To spread out in order, to marshal; to state in order; stale, used up; a *surname*.

執拗 *Chï*² *niu*⁴. Obstinate, self-opinionated, *pig-headed*.

拘板 *Chü*¹ *pan*³. Stiff, set, *pig-headed*.

櫻 *Ying*¹. The cherry.

櫻桃 *Ying*¹ *t'ao*². The cherry, cherries.

蒂 *Ti*³. The peduncle or stem of a flower or fruit.

蒂把 A stem of flower or fruit.

亦 *I*⁴. And, also, moreover, likewise. (w.)

插手 *Ch'a*¹ *shou*³. *To take or catch hold;* to meddle, to interfere.

外務 *Wai*⁴ *wu*⁴. That which is outside one's calling or duty, misdoing, *immorality*.

大意 *Ta*⁴ *i*⁴. Chief idea; sanguine, elated, *confident*.

要賬 *Yao*⁴ *chang*⁴. To collect debts or accounts.

起見 *Ch'i*³ *chien*⁴. With the object in view, for the sake of; motive;—always stands at the end of a clause.

架弄 *Chia*⁴ *lung*⁴. To endure, *to stand;* to pretend, to brag.

放賬 *Fang*⁴ *chang*⁴. To sell on credit.

扣 *K'ou*⁴. To deduct, *to discount;* to hook; to buckle; to button.

主事 *Chu*³ *shï*⁴. To control, to superintend, *to be the head*.

NOTES.

4 不成材料 *Not fit for material, not fit for use.*

6 七抓八拏 sometimes means, *to snatch or meddle with things in an uncivil or disorderly way;* sometimes it means, *to take in a surreptitious or underhand way.*

8 The dog is dissatisfied, because the master of the house is so economical that nothing is left for him to eat.

15 不亦樂乎 *Is it not pleasure?* an expression quoted from the Analects, and there used of the pleasure experienced in meeting a friend from a distance, but here applied in a humorous way to the satisfaction felt when an enemy or an opponent is put to the worse.

16 一條線的事情 *An affair on one thread;* that is, *following one chalk line,*—that which is connected in a regular order, "one line of things."

17 十子九成 *Of the seeds sown, nine out of ten grow and yield grain.* 盛水不漏 *The vessel does not leak;* that is, *all profit and no loss.*

又有毛小錢、又有短數、又抹零、又扣底、七折八扣的並不賺錢。○好[27]好的事情、叫糊塗人一辦、就弄的七顛八倒、一點眉眼沒有。○家[28]有千口、主事一人、若是七嘴八舌的、那還能行嗎。○人[29]無論做甚麼、總要有恒常心性、能以長忍久耐、倘若三日打魚、兩日曬網、將來進益必有其限。

and short count, cutting off fractions and deducting discounts, you realize only seven or eight parts in ten, so that finally there is no profit left.

27 A straightforward matter in the hands of an incompetent man, soon gets so involved that there is no head or tail to it.

28 Though the family be numerous yet it has but one head. If each one wants to have things his own way, it will be impossible to get along.

29 In whatever he undertakes, a man should be persevering and exercise patience. If he spends three days fishing and two days drying his nets, he will make but little progress.

19 君三民七 *The king three parts and the subject seven,*—referring originally to the proportion paid in taxes, but commonly used of apportioning anything according to the requirements of the case. In the Southern form, the numbers seven and eight seem to be used at random. 點, besides its many other meanings, means also *to count out in order, to check over.* This is its meaning in the expression 打不過點來; that is, *insufficient to meet all of the various uses for which it is required.*

23 Different dialects give us nearly all the changes that can be rung on 東西南北, with 跑 and 奔,—all meaning the same thing.

24 男婚女嫁 *The male taking a wife and the female marrying a husband;* that is, the marriage of sons and daughters.

26 小錢 Thin, imperfect cash are in the South called 毛錢. In paying cash in quantity, especially when paying accounts at the end of the year, it is a common thing to pass off strings of cash that are 短數, *short in count.* 抹零 The debtor pays the round numbers, neglecting the odd numbers and expects, indeed in a sort compels, the creditor to accept that much less. 扣底 The sales having been in each case for small amounts, really represent 滿錢, *full count,* but the payment being in the round sum and consequently subject to 底子, the 底子 becomes in fact a discount. 七折八扣, *cut down to seven or eight parts in ten,* is here used to summarize the losses, and may include, besides those here mentioned, unsaleable goods taken in exchange, partial payments, insolvent debtors, etc., by all of which the gross amount is discounted.

29 長忍久耐 is a transposition of 長久忍耐, after the model of the phrases in Les. 185.

LESSON CLXXXVII.

INFERENTIAL PHRASES.

總而言之 In a word, in conclusion, to sum up.

總之 In general, to sum up.

如此看來 Thus we see, from which it is evident.

從此看來 From which we see, from which it appears or is evident.

由此觀之 From which it appears, thus it is evident.

由是觀之 The same,—是 being used for 此, which is its original book sense.

這樣看起來 or 這麼看起來 From which it is evident, thus it appears, from which it would seem.

這麼說起來 From which statement we see, in such a case.

這等說起來 The same.

VOCABULARY.

誡命 *Chie⁴ ming⁴*. . . . . Commandments.

嗆 *Ch'iang⁴*. To irritate the throat; to choke; . . . . to suffocate; *to smoke out.*

蚊帳 *Wên² chang⁴*. . . . . A mosquito net.

波斯 *Po¹ ssŭ¹*. . . . . Persia.

攻打 *Kung¹ ta³*. . . . . *To attack,* to fight.

尼 *Ni²*. . . . . . . To follow, to accord with; a nun.

希利尼 *Hsi¹ li⁴ ni²*. . . . . Greece.

第一百八十七課

上帝的誡命雖有十條、總而言之、却都包在一個愛字裏面。○2熏嗆煍蚊子雖便賤意、却是年年費草、用蚊帳雖貴、却只一年花錢、從此看來、還是掛蚊帳上算。○當3初波斯王、用一百萬兵攻打希利尼國、倒被希利尼的二萬兵打敗了、如此看來、兵是貴乎精、不貴乎多。○常4見弟兄們爭鬧、彼此連話都不說、一到和外人打起架來、也不論誰惹的事、就都一齊動手、由此看來、弟兄總比外人更親。○王5元吉那個人太靠不住喇、前幾天我託他一件頂要緊的事情、他也滿口應承了、歸根期他却一點沒辦、把我的事情就誤了、答這様麼看起來、他原不是你的心腹人、你怎麼敢重託他呢。○那6些好酒的人、時刻手不離盅、盅不離嘴、一到喝醉了、輕者就誤事情、重

TRANSLATION.

1 Although the commandments of God are ten, yet they are all summarily comprehended in the one word love.

2 Although smoking out mosquitoes is cheaper, yet grass has to be bought every year; although using a net involves a greater outlay, the expense is once for all; from which it appears that using a net is, after all, the more economical.

3 Once upon a time the King of Persia attacked Greece with a million of soldiers, and yet they were defeated by twenty thousand Greeks; from which it is evident that the great desideratum with soldiers is skill and valor, not numbers.

4 You often see brothers quarreling until they will not even speak to each other, but as soon as a quarrel arises with an outsider, no matter who is in the fault, they all pitch in together; from which it appears that, after all, brothers are nearer than strangers.

5 That man Wang Yüen Chi is *too* unreliable. A few days since I entrusted some very important business to him, he also promised most positively, and yet after all he did not attend to it, and my business went by default. *Ans.* From this it would seem that he was not your sincere friend. What possessed you to put such confidence in him?

6 These wine-bibbers who never know when to leave off their cups, when once they get drunk, at the very least, neglect their business, and in more serious cases, involve themselves

貴乎 *Kwei4 hu1.* To value, to estimate highly; *to regard as valuable.*

甘美 *Kan1 mei3.* Delicious, *luscious.*

亂性 *Lan4 hsing4.* To confuse the mind, *to disorder the faculties.*

傷身 *Shang1 shên1.* To wound the body; *to injure the health;* to undermine the constitution.

耍虛子 *Shwa3 hsü1 tsï3.* To fall into dissipated habits, to sow one's wild oats. (N.)

耍匪類 *Shwa3 fei3 lei4.* The same. (C.)

不成常 *Pu4 ch'êng2 ch'ang2.* To leave the path of virtue, to become dissipated. (S.)

折騰 *Chê2 t'êng2.* To spoil, to ruin; to use up; *to squander.* (N.)

踢弄 *T'i1 lung4.* To spoil, to ruin; *to squander; to sell at a sacrifice.* (C.)

步行 *Pu4 hsing2.* To walk, to go on foot.

蹾 *Tun1.* To strike; to thump, *to jolt.*

者還要惹下大禍、從此看來、酒味雖然甘美、却是亂性傷身子的毒藥。○于⁷小喜(要虛子、/要匪類/不成常)把房產田地都(折騰/踢弄/舞弄)淨了、他媽說他、他說還有老婆孩子沒(折騰/踢弄/舞弄掉)喇、這麼樣看來、連他的老婆孩子、將來也是要(折騰/踢弄/舞弄掉)的。○要⁸僱轎他嫌太貴、坐小車他嫌擎的慌、東洋車又去不了、他自己也不能步行、你說怎麼樣呢、答這等說起來、他只可以不去就是了。○要⁹想叫兒子孝順、就不該打罵妻子、因爲兒子見母親挨打受罵、就必埋怨父親、既然埋怨父親、還能孝敬父親嗎、而且人這樣輕看妻子、久而久之、兒子也必輕看母親、既然輕看母親、還能孝敬母親嗎、由(此/是)觀之、凡苦待妻子的人、就是教導兒子不孝順了。○若¹⁰中國只安幾個砲局子、開幾個船廠、却不重西國學問、使民間設

in very great misfortunes; from which we see that although the taste of wine is luscious, yet it is a poison that disorders the faculties of the mind and undermines the health.

7 Yü Hsiao Hsi, becoming dissipated, squandered all his houses and lands. When his mother scolded him, he replied, "I have not yet disposed of my wife and children." From this it looks as if he probably would finally sell even his wife and children and squander the money.

8 He is not willing to spend the money to hire a chair; the jolting of a wheelbarrow he will not put up with; a jinricksha cannot go, and he is himself unable to walk. What do you think can be done? *Ans.* In these circumstances there is no way but for him to give up going.

9 If you wish your son to be dutiful, you must not maltreat your wife; for if a son sees his mother ill-treated, he will reproach his father; and reproaching his father, how can he honor him? Moreover if a man thus dishonors his wife, by and by the son will disregard his mother; and when he disregards her, how can he honor her? Thus it is evident that whoever maltreats his wife, teaches his son to be undutiful.

10 If China merely establishes a few arsenals and builds a few navy yards, but does not lay stress on Western science, and have the people establish scientific schools, she can never make her army efficient; for without Western learning, although the people

船廠 *Ch'wan² ch'ang³.* A ship yard; *a navy yard.*

强兵 *Ch'iang² ping¹.* *To secure an efficient soldiery,* to strengthen the army.

製 *Chï⁴.* To cut out; to fabricate, *to make.*

製造 *Chï⁴ tsao⁴.* To manufacture.

軍器 *Chün¹ ch'i⁴.* Implements of war, *arms.*

精妙 *Ching¹ miao⁴.* *The highest excellence,* exquisite; ingenious.

運用 *Yün⁴ yung⁴.* *To make use of,* to apply; to adopt.

能人 *Nêng² jên².* A man of ability.

武備 *Wu³ pei⁴.* *Military force or strength;* to recruit and organise troops.

臥房 *Wo⁴ fang².* A bedroom.

新郎 *Hsin¹ lang².* A bridegroom.

新郎官 *Hsin¹ lang² kwan¹.* The same. (s.)

新婦 *Hsin¹ fu⁴.* A bride.

洞房 *Tung⁴ fang².* A bridal chamber.

嚴密 *Yien² mi⁴.* *Private,* retired; secret, close; non-committal.

立格物學房、斷乎不能强兵、因爲若沒有西國學問、雖能製造軍器、也不能精妙、雖有汽機、也不能運用、雖有大砲、也不能拿準頭、雖是兵多將廣、也沒有多少能人、總而言之、學問乃是武備的根本、倘若學問興起、國家自然就强盛了。○人[11]睡覺的房子、名謂臥房、新郎官(新郎)和新娘子(新婦)的臥房、名謂洞房、這麼說起來、洞房比臥房、格外有個嚴密肅靜的意思、又格外有個仙境的情趣(滋味)。○到[12]了親友家、就是見了底下人、也有個稱呼、比方看門的稱門公(佬)、買東西的稱買辦、管賬的稱先生、料理家務的稱管家、廚子稱廚師(司務)、伺候書房的稱書僮、其餘做零碎事的、稱打雜的、或稱帮忙的、就是叫一聲老張老李、也無不可、總之、見人應當和氣謙恭、不可一味的高傲自大、反倒叫人瞧不起了。

may manufacture arms, they cannot make really good ones; although they have engines, they will not be able to use them; although they have great guns, they will not know how to fire them accurately; although they have a multitude of soldiers and numerous generals, yet there will be few men of ability. In a word, learning is the foundation of military strength. If learning flourishes, the nation, as a natural consequence, will become powerful.

11 The room where one sleeps is called a bed-chamber, the bedroom of the bridegroom and bride is called the bridal chamber; from which we see that a nuptial chamber, as compared with a bed-chamber, suggests the idea of privacy and quiet, and has also a specially romantic flavor.

12 When you visit the family of a relative or friend, even those of inferior station whom you meet, should be addressed in a becoming manner. For example, the man who watches the door should be addressed as porter; the man who makes purchases, as butler; the man who keeps the accounts, as clerk; the man who oversees the affairs of the household, as steward; the cook, as professor of the culinary art; the school-room waiter, as footman; and others who are men-of-all-work, as waiters or attendants. Even to address as old Chang, or old Li, is quite admissible. In general, you should treat all you meet with courtesy and deference, and not exhibit a haughty and self-important spirit, thereby incurring people's contempt.

肅 *Su*⁴. . . . . . Reverence; awe, dread; courteous.
肅靜 *Su*⁴ *ching*⁴. . . . . *Quiet*, undisturbed.
境 *Ching*⁴. Boundary; abode; neighborhood, ... district, *place*; state, condition.
仙境 *Hsien*¹ *ching*⁴. Fairy-land; *romantic*, unreal.
親友 *Ch'in*¹ *yu*². . . . . . Relatives and friends.
門公 *Mên*² *kung*¹. . . . . A doorkeeper, a porter.
佬 *Lao*³. . . . . . . A burly old man.
門佬 *Mên*² *lao*³. . . . . A doorkeeper. (s.)
買辦 *Mai*³ *pan*⁴. . . . . A butler, a purveyor.
僮 *T'ung*². . . . . . *A slave boy;* a slave girl.
書僮 *Shu*¹ *t'ung*². A school-room servitor or attendant.
打雜 *Ta*³ *tsa*². To serve as man-of-all work, to act as coolie or waiter.
謙恭 *Ch'ien*¹ *kung*¹. Respectful, deferential; *unassuming.*
高傲 *Kao*⁴ *ao*⁴. . . . Proud, *haughty*, imperious.
自大 *Tsŭ*⁴ *ta*⁴. . . . . . Self-important, conceited

第一百八十八課

倘[1]若妯娌們不生外心、家是難以分的。○夫[2]妻們若不相得、嫉妒比誰都大。○丁[3]學祿爺兒(父子)們、連一個修德的也沒有。○他[4]做爺兒們、(男子漢)碰見這個尚且扎掙不住、何況你是娘兒們(婦人家)呢。○作[5]惡的人們、任憑怎麼樣的喫齋念經、修橋補路、焉能消解了他的罪惡呢。○紳[6]衿富戶們、常有仗着勢力

TRANSLATION.

1 If sisters-in-law do not become estranged, the family is not easily divided.

2 If husband and wife have not confidence in each other, no jealousy can compare with theirs.

3 Ting Hsüe Lu, father and sons—there is not one well-behaved man amongst them.

4 If he, a man, when placed in these circumstances could not endure it, how much less could you who are a woman!

5 How impossible it is for evil doers to escape the consequences of their sins, how much soever they may abstain from meats and repeat prayers, build bridges and repair roads!

6 The literati and the wealthy frequent-

NOTES.

1 總而言之 is a book phrase, but is in constant use in Mandarin. It usually stands after, and sums up several particulars, but is so used in this sentence that it may be fairly rendered, *summarily*.

2 Mosquitoes are smoked out by burning a coarse rope made of fragrant weeds, which will smoulder a long time, giving out a plentiful smoke, that drives out the mosquitoes, but does not seriously inconvenience the sleepers.

3 精 is here used to express that which is held to constitute the highest excellence in a soldier, viz., perfection in discipline and skill in the art of war. 貴乎 is slightly bookish.

5 心腹人 *Heart-belly man;* that is, one whose friendship enters into his innermost feelings, and hence is real and sincere.

6 手不離盅盅不離嘴 A ready made couplet, vividly describing one who is excessively given to drink.

7 It is not an uncommon thing for gamblers and opium smokers to sell their wives and children in order to get the means of gratifying their evil propensities.

9 This sentence was written by a Christian. It is doubtful whether any heathen Chinese ever constructed such an argument.

10 兵多將廣 *Soldiers many and generals abundant,*—a ready-made phrase expressing the idea of an extensive military organization.

11 新郎 and 新婦 are both decidedly bookish, being rarely if ever used in colloquial. 新郎官 is, however, used colloquially in the South.

12 底下人 is a general term signifying inferiors, and including subordinates of all classes. 先生 is used in this case, because the service involves writing. 書僮 is a book term and characterizes an office only known in the houses of the very wealthy. 帮忙的 applies to a servant or helper hired for a special occasion. Such a mode of address as 老張, would only be allowable in case the parties were acquainted with each other.

LESSON CLXXXVIII.

SPECIAL USES OF CERTAIN WORDS.

們 Though usually found only with the personal pronouns, 們 is sometimes used, as noted in Les. 3, with other words denoting persons. In this lesson are illustrated some of its more unusual, but perfectly legitimate uses.

甚 In Mandarin books, 甚 is not unfrequently found used alone in the sense of 甚麼. It is simply an attempt to write the colloquial *sha*², which, as noted in Les. 17, is a widely used colloquial contraction of 甚麼. Thus used 甚 should be read *sha*², as it is spoken.

嘛 This character is occasionally found in books, as a colloquial contraction for 什麼. More commonly this contracted form is written simply 麼, which in this case is read *ma* in the North and *mê* in the South.

欺壓民人的、若碰着那種不徇情的官員們、也是一樣的治罪。○烹[7]訇的响了一聲、濺濽起好些的油點子、把那小童們臉上、燙了幾個燎漿大泡。○每[8]年燈節這幾天、買賣人們、無不家家懸燈結彩、惹得城廂內外這些人們、沒有一個不要看看的、眞是熱鬧無比。○弟[9]兄們、姊妹們、姪兒們、孫子們、都分親的和叔伯的、往上推論、就是爺爺們、老爺外公

ly take advantage of their position to oppress the common people. If, however, they happen on an official who is no respecter of persons, he punishes them just the same as he would any one else.

7 With a sudden report there spurted up several drops of boiling oil and scalded the faces of the young acolytes, raising a number of large serous blisters.

8 Every year during the several days of the feast of lanterns, the business houses all hang up lanterns and transparencies, exciting everybody in the whole city and suburbs with a desire to see, and making a season of unequaled interest.

9 Brothers and sisters, and nephews and grandchildren, are all divided into those of the first degree of consanguinity and those more distant. Ascending to elders, the same principle

怎 Normally, 怎 always takes either 麼 or 樣 after it (and 怎樣 is really a contraction for 怎麼樣), but in books it is sometimes used alone,—rarely in colloquial, and is then generally followed either by 能, 好, 敢 or 的.

咋 A colloquial contraction of 作什麼, chiefly, though not exclusively, used as a reply when another calls, as "What is it?" is often used in English. It is extensively used in Northern and Central Mandarin, but not in Southern. It must be distinguished from 嗏 *cha*, which is Pekingese, and is simply an affirmative reply.

等 When 等 stands at the end of a clause, either alone or joined with 類 or other similar word, it means, *and such, and the like, and so on*, including all of the class of persons or things referred to. When 等 is doubled at the end of an enumeration of particulars, it is equivalent to *etc.* When joined to a pronoun, as in 伊等, it is practically equivalent to a plural.

VOCABULARY.

嘛 *Ma*². A colloquial character used as a contraction for 什麼:—see Sub.

咋 *Cha*⁴. A hoarse noise; a contraction for 作什麼:—see Sub.

外心 *Wai*⁴ *hsin*¹. Disaffection, alienation, *estrangement*.

修德 *Hsiu*¹ *tê*². To maintain a good character, to be virtuous, *to be well-behaved*.

齋 *Chai*¹. *To abstain from;* fasting, penance; dignified.

喫齋 *Ch'ï*¹ *chai*¹. To abstain from meat.

念經 *Nien*⁴ *ching*¹. To repeat prayers.

衿 *Chin*¹. The same as 襟.

紳衿 *Shên*¹ *chin*¹. *The literary class*, the gentry.

富戶 *Fu*⁴ *hu*⁴. The wealthy.

民人 *Min*² *jên*². Common men, the people.

治罪 *Chï*⁴ *tsuei*⁴. To condemn, *to punish*.

烹 *P'êng*¹. To boil; to decoct; to scald.

訇 *P'ing*¹. A report, an explosion.

濺 *Chien*⁴. To dash up, to sputter, *to spurt;* to tinge; to soil.

濽 *Tsan*⁴. To splash, *to spurt*, to sputter.

燎 *Liao*². To scorch, *to burn;* to illuminate; a signal light.

燎漿泡 *Liao*² *chiang*¹ *p'ao*⁴. A blister raised by fire.

燈節 *Têng*¹ *chie*². The feast of lanterns on the 15th of the first month:—Note 8.

們、叔叔們、舅舅們、以及姑姑們、姨姨們、
也是如此。○請[10]你去看看他來作甚麼。
○賢[11]姪如何來得這等早、有甚麼話說。
○你[12]可以打聽打聽、他姓甚名誰、○我[13]
自然必賞他銀兩、却干你甚麼事。○我[14]
當是他眞果是個明公百曉、仔細盤問起來、
甚麼事都不懂得。○他[15]不跪我也罷了、
怎倒叫我去跪他呢。○你[16]給我這樣丟
人、我怎能白饒了你呢。○玉[17]英道、說那
裏話、我兩個從小兒的結髮夫妻、與他

applies to paternal and maternal grandfathers, paternal and maternal uncles, as also to paternal and maternal aunts.

10 Please go and see what he has come for.

11 Well my esteemed nephew, what have you to talk about that you have come so early?

12 I wish you would inquire and ascertain his surname and name.

13 I will of course present him with some silver, but what business is it of yours?

14 I supposed that he was really a master in his profession, but upon careful questioning I found he was a complete ignoramus.

15 That he does not kneel to me is enough, how can you possibly ask me to go and kneel to him?

16 How can I excuse you for causing me such mortification?

17 Yü Ying replied, "What are you talking about? We two were affianced in our youth, and I have borne

懸 *Hsüen*². *To suspend;* to be anxious; in suspense, undecided.

結彩 *Chie*¹ *ts'ai*⁴. To ornament by festooning with cloth or paper hangings.

城廂 *Ch'êng*² *hsiang*¹. City and suburbs.

叔伯 *Shu*² *poa*². Family relationships which come through 叔 and 伯:—Note 9.

外公 *Wai*⁴ *kung*¹. A maternal grandfather. (s.)

推論 *T'wei*¹ *lun*⁴. To carry out an argument or train of reasoning, to infer, *to proceed in the application of a principle.*

銀兩 *Yin*² *liang*³. A few taels. (w.)

明公 *Ming*² *kung*¹. A master of any art or science.

百曉 *Pai*³ *hsiao*³. *Master of any art or science,* one who knows it all. (s.)

盤問 *P'an*² *wên*⁴. *To question,* to interrogate, to pump.

屬員 *Shu*³ *yüen*². Subordinate officers.

忙活活的 *Mang*² *hwoa*² *hwoa*² *ti*¹. Quite busy, *pressed with work.*

水菸 *Shwei*³ *yien*¹. Tobacco prepared for smoking in a water pipe:—Note 22.

說事人 *Shwoa*¹ *shï*⁴ *jên*². A mediator; *a middleman.*

查明 *Ch'a*² *ming*². To make careful examination, to search into.

稟覆 *Ping*³ *fu*². To report to a superior.

叔弟 *Shu*² *ti*⁴. A cousin, a contraction of 叔伯兄弟.

貿 *Mao*⁴. To barter, *to trade,* to deal.

貿易 *Mao*⁴ *i*⁴. To do business, *to trade,* to exchange commodities, to barter.

竹 *Chu*². The bamboo.

籃 *Lan*². A basket with a bale or handle.

六畜 *Liu*⁴ *ch'u*⁴. Domestic animals,—the horse, cow, sheep, chicken, dog and hog.

百獸 *Pai*³ *shou*⁴. Wild animals, beasts.

昆蟲 *K'un*¹ *ch'ung*². Insects, including also reptiles.

串珠 *Ch'wan*³ *chu*¹. A reference book, a marginal reference:—Note 26.

卽如 *Chi*⁴ *ju*². *Such as,* for instance. (w.)

地理 *Ti*⁴ *li*². *Geomancy;* geography.

聖賢 *Shêng*⁴ *hsien*². Sages and worthies.

草木 *Ts'ao*³ *mu*⁴. Vegetation.

生男育女、怎麼的不認得。○你18既是大遠的來了、又是頭一回向我開口、怎好叫你空手回去。○他19如今已經吃了俸祿、却不能管理屬員、這樣無用的官、還要他幹甚麼(嘛)。○現20在莊稼地裏忙活活的、你要進城去做甚麼(嘛)(做麼事)、答有點閒事兒。○他21也沒傷你、也沒惹你、你要打他做甚麼(咋)(做麼事)。○洪22喜在這裏沒有、問做甚麼(咋)(做麼事)、答你給我買四兩水菸去。○官23批的是叫族長與說事人等、查明稟覆。○今24有我叔弟來此貿易、請將所寄下之皮箱、與竹籃等物、託他

him sons and daughters. How should I not know him?"

18 Having come a long distance, and this being the first favor you have asked of me, how could I send you back empty-handed?

19 He has already drawn his salary, but is unable to control his subordinates. What advantage is there in retaining such an incompetent officer?

20 Why must you go into the city just now, when farm work is so pressing? *Ans.* I have a little special business.

21 He neither wounded you nor irritated you; what are you striking him for?

22 Hung Hsi, are you there? *Ans.* Yes. Well, go and buy four ounces of water-pipe tobacco for me.

23 The officer gave judgment that the head of the clan, with the middlemen, etc., should make examination and report.

24 My cousin is going to your place to trade. Will you please have the leather trunk, bamboo basket, etc., left with you, put in his care to bring back.

貸 *Tai4*. . . . . To lend, to loan.

借貸 *Chie4 tai4*. . . . . To loan money.

遂 *Swei2*. . . . *To accord*, to follow; then; finally.

結連 *Chie1 lien2*. *To gather together*, to band together, to confederate.

理論 *Li3 lun4*. *To reason*, to argue, to remonstrate.

棍徒 *Kun4 t'u2*. . . . . A base fellow, a ruffian.

毆傷 *Ou1 shang1*. . . . . To wound in a fight.

殞 *Yün3*. . . . . To die, to perish. (w.)

殞命 *Yün3 ming4*. *To lose life*, to perish, to die.

痕 *Hên2*. . . . . *A scar*, a mark; a trace; a flaw.

傷痕 *Shang1 hên2*. . . . . A scar, *a wound*.

NOTES.

3 爺兒們 *Father and son or sons.* It is uncertain from this term whether one or more sons is meant, though the subsequent part of the sentence implies several.

4 爺兒們, as here used, is a Pekingese term, and means a man as distinguished from a woman. The term is not heard in Eastern Shantung nor anywhere in Southern Mandarin. The term 娘兒們 is formed in the same way, and means a woman as distinguished from a man. 兒 is to be regarded as an enclitic. This use of 們 is anomalous.

5 喫齋 *To eat abstinence;* that is, to abstain from meat and eat only vegetables. 修橋補路 *To build bridges and repair roads*,—done in order to acquire merit with the gods.

7 This sentence is from the *History of Robbers.* The character 烹 is incorrectly used, as it means *to boil*, but not to *burst* or *resound.* The proper character is 訇. 點子 is rather a particle than a drop. A 滴 is a drop as it drips or falls from its attachment; a 點 is a drop in its detached or isolated state.

8 燈節 *The feast of lanterns*, which is held on the 14th, 15th and 16th of the first month, when the business streets of towns and cities are illuminated, and frequently covered with matting. 懸燈結彩 *To hang out lanterns and transparencies, and to festoon doors and gateways with cloth or paper hangings.*

9 叔伯 The children of one's 叔 and 伯, that is, cousins of the same family name, are called *shu-poă* brothers and sisters; and starting from this point the term *shu-poă* is extended through father and mother, until it eventually comes to be applied to all terms expressive of family relationship, except that of father and mother, son and daughter. The extension is made by assuming the heirship of all who are *shu-poă* to father or mother, as well as all to whom they have become heir through their fathers and mothers, and so on, the special term expressing the relationship being in each case changed to suit the difference of generation. Thus your

father's *shu-poă* 哥哥 are your *shu-poă* 大爺, your
father's *shu-poă* 姐妹 are your *shu-poă* 姑姑, your
mother's *shu-poă* 弟兄 are your *shu-poă* 舅舅, your

帶回。○空[25]中的鳥、和海裏的魚、是天主第五天造的、至於六畜百獸、以及昆蟲等類、都是第六天造的。○串[26]珠上所記的典故、乃是一類一類的、即如天文類、地理類、聖賢類、草木類、等等。○你[27]看世上這些人、雖然貴賤貧富等等不一、而要發財之心、都是一樣的。○孫[28]文洲因借貸不遂、即結連棍徒王連城、與崔鎮山等、齊至門前大罵、身之長子出與理論、竟被伊等毆傷、幾乎殞命、現有傷痕、與李德茂李德盛李德潤等、俱可爲証。

25 The birds of the air and the fish of the sea were created by God on the fifth day, while the various kinds of beasts, with the insects, etc., were all created on the sixth day.

26 The parallel passages given in the reference book are all arranged by subjects, such as astronomy, geography, biography, botany, etc.

27 Look at the people in the world, will you; although they all differ greatly in rank, wealth, etc., yet they are all alike in possessing a desire for riches.

28 Sun Wên Chou, because I would not lend him the money he wanted, gathered a set of ruffians, consisting of Wang Lien Ch'ing, Ts'wei Chên Shan and others, and came in a company to my door and reviled me outrageously. My eldest son going out to reason with them, was set on by them and beaten almost to death; in proof of which there are his wounds and the testimony of Li Tê Mao, Li Tê Shing, Li Tê Yün and others.

father's *shu-poă* 孫子 are your *shu-poă* 姪兒, your son's *shu-poă* 姪兒 are your *shu-poă* 孫子, &c., &c. These relationships are carried out to the fifth generation, and the intricacies involved in them are not inferior to those involved in the handling of an irreducible equation of the third degree, notwithstanding which, every old woman in China can trace them out and rattle them off as glibly as a smart boy can say the multiplication table. A working knowledge of these relationships is well worth acquiring, for the sake of the great advantage it affords in social intercourse, especially with the women.

17 結髮夫妻 *Betrothed from the time when the hair was tied up in little knots or fillets.* 怎的 is an obsolete form found only in books.

18 向我開口 *Open your mouth to me;* that is, ask of me a favor, especially a loan of money.

22 The tobacco smoked in water-pipes is prepared from inferior or refuse tobacco by softening with oil, coloring yellow with sulphide of arsenic, or green with sulphate of iron and copper, then compacting in a press and shaving into shreds.

26 串珠 *Strung beads,* a term applied to books of classified extracts from celebrated authors. Sometimes the 串珠 is confined to the classics or to certain classical books. The term has been adopted by foreigners to signify *marginal references.*

27 等等不一 *Kind kind not alike;* that is, *various kinds, many classes.*

28 This sentence gives the principal part of a short indictment (呈子), and the style is of course somewhat *Wên.* 借貸不遂 *In lending not accordant;* that is, not accommodating him when he wanted to borrow. 身 is commonly used in writing for the pronoun I, and is generally written a little to the one side. 與 takes 他 understood after it. 理論 is a little more bookish than 論理, and is used in a somewhat different way.

LESSON CLXXXIX.

MALE AND FEMALE.

Special terms for designating the male and female of various animals prevail in Chinese, very much as in English. A few have already occurred. Others are brought together in this lesson. Foreigners often make themselves ridiculous from not knowing these terms and their proper use. [(7).

男女 are confined almost entirely to persons.

公母 are the most general terms for designating and distinguishing the male and female of birds and animals.

雌雄 are used in *Wênli* to designate the male and female of birds of all kinds. In colloquial 公 and 母 are used.

第一百八十九課

無[1]論是男是女、若過於輕飄佻、就難免衆人輕視。○纔[2]菢出來的小鴨子、怎能分出公母來呢。○小[3]公豬叫豵、小母豬叫豚、大公豬叫脚秧豬、蕃滋生小豬的叫老母豬。○論[4]到看門家、騲母狗和公牙狗一樣、但是人都嫌他下狗、所以都不願意要騲母狗。○這[5]個兒騾太烈棱鬧、不如我騎他罷、兄台可以騎那個騍騾、還穩當一點。○我[6]們莊稼人、夜裏若沒有公雞啼打鳴、怎能知道時候早晚呢。○我[7]養公牙郎貓養彀了、成天家光老不在着家、那赶上養個母女貓好呢。○人[8]多亂、龍多旱、媳婦多了婆婆弄做飯、公雞多了不啼打鳴、母雞多了不下蛋。○俗[9]語說、騍馬上不得陣、是比方女人不

TRANSLATION.

1 If the conduct of either men or women be unduly frivolous, they cannot avoid being lightly esteemed by others.

2 How can you distinguish the male and female of little ducks just out of the egg?

3 A male pig is called a *tsung;* a female is called a *t'un*. A male hog is called a boar, and a hog that breeds pigs is called a sow.

4 As far as watching the house is concerned, a bitch is quite the same as a dog; but every one objects to having a bitch, because they dislike her pups.

5 This he mule is too unruly; it will be better for me to ride him. You may ride this she mule; she is a little safer.

6 If we farmers had no cocks to announce the morning, how could we know the time?

7 I have had enough of keeping tom-cats; they will never stay at home. How much better to keep a tabby.

8 "Where people are many, there is confusion; where dragons are many, there is drought; where daughters-in-law are many, the mother-in-law does the cooking; where roosters are many, the morning goes unannounced; where hens are many, no eggs are laid."

9 The common saying is, "A mare is not fit to go into battle;" which is a

牝牡 are used is *Wênli* to designate the male and female of domestic animals, especially of such as are used in sacrifice. In colloquial **公** and **母** are used, except where special names exist.

The special names used in the lesson are defined in the vocabulary.

VOCABULARY.

雌 *Ts'ï*^{2}....... *The female of birds;* weak.
牝 *P'in*^{3}....... The female of beasts.
輕飄 *Ch'ing*^{1} *piao*^{1}. *Frivolous*, gay, rollicking; light, slender.
輕視 *Ch'ing*^{1} *shï*^{4}. *To esteem lightly*, to look down on, to despise.
佻 *T'iao*^{1}....... Unsteady, careless, unreliable.
輕佻 *Ch'ing*^{1} *t'iao*^{1}. *Frivolous*, trifling, light-minded, gay.
豵 *Tsung*^{1}....... A shote, *a male pig;* a litter.
豚 *T'un*^{2}....... A sucking pig; *a female pig.*
秧 *Yang*^{1}....... Young grain, sprouts, shoots.
秧豬 *Yang*^{1} *chu*^{1}....... A boar. (N.)
脚豬 *Chiao*^{3} *chu*^{1}....... A boar. (C. & S.)
滋生 *Tsï*^{1} *shêng*^{1}. *To bear*, to produce; to multiply, to teem.
蕃 *Fan*^{2}... Luxuriant; *to increase;* numerous.
蕃生 *Fan*^{2} *shêng*^{1}....... To generate, *to bear.*
老母豬 *Lao*^{3} *mu*^{3} *chu*^{1}....... An old sow.
牙狗 *Ya*^{2} *kou*^{3}....... A male dog. (C. & N.)
騲狗 *Ts'ao*^{2} *kou*^{3}....... A bitch, a slut. (S.)
兒騾 *Êr*^{2} *loă*^{2}....... A male or jack mule.

能替男人辦理事情、正彷彿騍馬不能替兒馬上陣打仗一樣。○叫[10]驢和兒騾、雖然筋力更大、但是論到拉車、或是莊稼地裏用、還是養草驢和騍騾好、因爲他更聽使喚(調度)、沒有反性的時候。○你[11]別嫌女娃孩(娃兒)多、俗語說、少一般不成世界、倘若人都養男娃孩(娃兒)、沒有養女娃孩(娃兒)的、天下豈不都絕了後代了嗎。○凡[12]天地間的活物、無論飛禽走獸、昆蟲鱗介、一概都分公的母的、並且都按公母之理相傳。○這[13]四個山羊、都是公的、那八個綿羊、有三個公的、五個母的。○有[14]一家財主、夜裏做了一夢、夢見一個欠錢的人來說、我來還你老人家的賬、說完這話、就進牛圈(欄)去了、這財主醒來、聽見外面有人說、我

figure to indicate that a woman cannot do the business of a man, just as a mare cannot take the place of a stallion in war.

10 Although jackasses and jack mules are stronger, yet for draught or for farm work it is better to keep she asses and mules, for the reason that she asses and she mules are more docile and do not become unruly.

11 Do not be dissatisfied that you have so many daughters. The saying runs, "Minus one half, the world could not subsist." If all reared sons and none daughters, would not mankind find themselves without descendants?

12 All living things on the face of the earth,—birds, beasts, insects and fishes,—are divided into male and female, and all are propagated by the union of the sexes.

13 These four goats are all billy-goats; but of those eight sheep, three are rams and five are ewes.

14 A certain rich man had a dream one night. He dreamed that one of his debtors came and said to him, "I have come, good sir, to pay you your account;" and when he had said this, he disappeared into the cow-stable. When the rich man awoke he heard some one outside saying, "Our cow has given birth to a calf." He afterwards made inquiry and found that this same debtor had in fact died that

稜 *Lêng*². . . . A rafter; an edge; *unruly*, vicious.
騍 *K'ê*⁴. . . . . . A mare.
騍騾 *K'ê*⁴ *loă*². . . . . A she mule.
打鳴 *Ta*³ *ming*². To announce the morning as . . . . cocks do by crowing.
啼鳴 *T'i*² *ming*². . . . . The same. (s.)
郎貓 *Lang*² *mao*¹. . . . . . A he cat, a tom cat. (N.)
牙貓 *Ya*² *mao*¹. . . . . The same. (c.)
女貓 *Nü*³ *mao*¹. . . . . A she cat.
騍馬 *K'ê*⁴ *ma*³. . . . . A mare.
兒馬 *Êr*² *ma*³. . . . . A stallion.
叫驢 *Chiao*⁴ *lü*². . . . . A jackass.
筋力 *Chin*¹ *li*⁴. . . . . *Strength*, muscle.
騲驢 *Ts'ao*³ *lü*². . . . . A she ass, a jenny.

調度 *Tiao*⁴ *toă*⁴. To transpose and arrange, *to* . . . . *manage*, to manipulate.
反性 *Fan*³ *hsing*⁴. *To become unruly* or violent; to grow cantankerous.
鱗 *Lin*². . . Scales of fish; overlapping like scales.
介 *Chie*⁴. . . . . To aid; to involve; mail, *armor*.
鱗介 The scaly tribe,—fishes, turtles, etc.
牸 *Tsï*⁴. A cow,—sometimes used in books for . . . . . the female of other domestic animals.
牸牛 *Tsï*⁴ *niu*². . . . . A cow.
犍 *Chien*¹. . . . . . A bull, an ox.
投生 *T'ou*² *shêng*¹. To come into the world, *to* . . . . *be born from another state of existence into this.*
綏 *Swei*¹. . . . . Quiet, modest; *coy*, amorous. (W.)

們的母牸牛、下了一個小犢子、後來訪聞那個欠錢的人、果眞就在這夜裏死了、纔知道這個小犢子、原是那欠錢的人所脫投生的、特爲來塡還他。○飛[15]禽的公母論雌雄、走獸的公母論牝牡、這是書中常見的分別、其實也不必盡然、若獨有飛禽論雌雄、怎麼詩經說有狐綏綏、有註狐是雄狐的呢、若獨有走獸論牝牡、怎麼書經說牝雞司晨呢。○所[16]有的活物、有的不分大小、都一樣的叫法、就像小狗、還是叫小牙狗、小母狗、小貓、還是叫小牙貓、小女貓、但是也有大小不一樣叫法的、就像小牛、叫咩子、小羊叫羔子、小驢小馬小騾子、都叫駒子、小鼈和小兎子、有叫羔子的、也有叫崽子的。

night. Thus he knew that his debtor had transmigrated into this calf for the express purpose of repaying the account.

15 The male and female of birds are called *ts'i* and *hsiung*, and the male and female of beasts are called *p'in* and *mu*. This is the distinction constantly observed in books, and yet not always so. For if birds alone are classed as *ts'i* and *hsiung*, why then does the Book of Poetry say, "The lonely fox moves coyly"? while the commentator says that a *hsiung* fox is referred to; and if beasts are always classed as *p'in* and *mu*, why then does the Book of Records say, "The *p'in* fowl rules the morning watch"?

16 Of all living things, some make no difference in the names by which the full grown and the young are called, all being called by the same names, thus young dogs are called little male dogs, and little female dogs, also young cats are called little male cats and little female cats. There are some, however, in which the old and the young are not designated in the same way, thus a young cow is called a calf, a young sheep is called a lamb, a young ass, horse or mule is called a colt and a young turtle or rabbit is sometimes called a *kao* and sometimes a *tsai*.

司晨 *Sï*[1] *ch'ên*[2]. . . . . . .To herald the morning.
書經 *Shu*[1] *ching*[1]. The Book of History:— . . . . Note 15.
咩 *Mie*[1]. . . . . .The bleating of a sheep; a calf:— [Note 16.
羔 *Kao*[1]. . . . . A lamb, a kid.
鼈 *Pie*[1]. A turtle,—much used as a symbol of . . . . lasciviousness.
崽 *Tsai*[3]. The young of turtles, rabbits, monkeys, ... etc., a cub,—a favorite word in Chinese billingsgate.

NOTES.

3 The terms here applied to swine are in common colloquial use.

4 The antecedent of 他 is properly the term 母狗, at the end of the sentence. 下 is used of the bringing forth of all animals, as well as of the laying of eggs.

6 打鳴 and 啼鳴 mean to announce the morning by crowing, but do not mean to crow at other times, or in general, which is expressed by 叫.

7 着 here means *to remain, to stay.* The terms for male and female cats differ much in different places. The use of 女, as in Pekingese, is somewhat anomalous.

8 In the first couplet, 了 is not used because the words are used singly; in the second couplet, it is used because the words are used in pairs. Its use or otherwise is very often, at it is here, a mere matter of taste or of balancing of clauses.

14 你 adds force to the address, and being accompanied by a proper title, is entirely respectful. Such stories as this are common among the people, and form the main ground of belief in the theory of transmigration.

15 書經, *the Book of History*, also called the *Book of Government*, was originally compiled by Confucius, from the historical remains of previous times, covering the dynasties from B. C. 2400 to B. C. 721. It originally embraced 100 books, but is incomplete at the present time.

16 咩 The composition of this character would indicate its application to the young of sheep, and it is so defined in the dictionaries. In actual practice, however, it is only applied to the young of cattle.

第一百九十課

食[1]言那便不是大丈夫。○你[2]不賠錯便罷、怎麼倒怪着我們、向我們橫鼻子豎眼的呢。○從[3]祖宗分枝下來、叫九族。○求[4]你細訪一訪、便知是眞是假了。○人[5]往往爲一點小事、便失了和氣。○秀[6]才不出門、便(能)知天下事。○衆[7]人打量(估猜)了他一會、便問、你是那裏來的。○你[8]不留我們住(宿歇)便罷了、怎麼倒攆着我們走呢。○男[9]子有德便是才、女子無才便是德。○他[10]仗着自己知道幾句書、便以爲飽學。○凡[11]得無義之財的、便是行了偷竊。○我[12]若讓過這一遭、鄉里便都來欺負我。○你[13]若是薄待了兄弟、

TRANSLATION.

1 He is not an honorable man who goes back on his word.

2 It is enough that you get off without begging our pardon; why do you turn about and show your ill will by turning up your nose and leering at us?

3 The several lines of descent from an ancestor are called the nine clans.

4 I ask you to make careful inquiry, and you will find out whether it is true or not.

5 It frequently happens that persons are estranged from each other by a mere trifle.

6 A hsiu-ts'ai, without crossing his threshold, knows the affairs of all the world.

7 They all regarded him doubtfully for a little and then asked, "Where do you hail from?"

8 Is it not enough that you do not invite us to lodge, without turning about and driving us away?

9 A man's virtue is regarded as an endowment; a woman's want of endowment is regarded as a virtue.

10 Because he knows a few passages of the classics, he imagines himself a profound scholar.

11 Whoever takes unjust gain, is guilty of theft.

12 If I yield this one time, the whole neighborhood will be ready to impose upon me.

LESSON CXC.

便

便 (pien), is the higher Mandarin equivalent of certain uses of the more colloquial 就. It marks the logical dependence of two clauses. It may sometimes be rendered, *thus* or *in that case*, but is generally not translateable by any special word. It is much used in book Mandarin and occasionally in conversation.

VOCABULARY.

賠錯 *P'ei[2] ts'o[4].* To apologize, to make amends.

橫鼻 *Hêng[2] pi[2].* To turn up the nose as an expression of contempt.

豎眼 *Shu[4] yien[3].* To stare in anger or contempt; to leer, to glare.

分枝 *Fên[1] chï[1].* To divide into branches:—Note 3.

九族 *Chiu[3] tsu[2].* Nine generations of a family connexion:—Note 3.

估猜 *Ku[1] ts'ai[1].* To conjecture, to wonder; *to regard doubtfully* or inquiringly.

便是薄待了爹娘。○强[14]盜不得財的問流罪、得財的問斬罪。○今[15]日得將軍搭救、便是重生父母、再養爹娘。○他[16]不問便罷、若是問起來、我却沒有好話答應／答對他。○若不從有了教化、便把普天下各樣的人、都整齊得一樣了。○你[18]可以說實話、你是誰家的小厮、這些話是誰教你的、我便饒你。○再[19]請少坐、聽學生說完、便知其實。○我[20]若跟你要銀子、便是勒掯你、焉有兄弟情常／分。○你[21]們若是認得理眞、便知道心裏光光明明的、就是天堂、心裏黑黑暗暗的、便是地獄。○我[22]有個草頭方兒、能治大

13 If you treat your brother meanly, it is just the same as if you treated your parents meanly.

14 A robber who gets no money, is condemned to banishment; while a robber who gets money, is condemned to be beheaded.

15 Your rescuing me to-day, sirs, is as if you had given me a second term of life.

16 If he does not ask, let it pass; but if he asks about it, my reply will not be mild.

17 Since civilization has prevailed, all kinds of people in the world have been reduced to order.

18 Speak the truth and tell me whose servant boy you are and who told you to say these things, and I will let you off.

19 Please sit a little longer and listen till I finish, and you will know the facts.

20 If I should take your silver, it would be taking advantage of your necessities, and how would this comport with the affection of a brother?

21 If you had a clear understanding of things, you would know that to have a mind cheered by the consciousness of well-doing, is heaven; while to have a mind beclouded by the consciousness of evil-doing, is hell.

22 I have a domestic recipe that is effective in the worst cases. I'll guarantee that it will cure him.

飽學 *Pao^3 hsüe^2*. A well-versed scholar, a man of large attainments.

偷竊 *T'ou^1 ch'ie^4*. To steal, to pilfer.

鄉里 *Hsiang^1 li^3*. Neighborhood.

流罪 *Liu^2 tswei^4*. A crime punishable by banishment.

斬罪 *Chan^3 tswei^4*. A crime punishable by decapitation.

搭救 *Ta^1 chiu^4*. To save, to rescue.

答對 *Ta^1 twei^4*. To reply, to answer; to retort, to respond.

情常 *Ch'ing^2 ch'ang^2*. Affection, attachment:—Note 20.

和美 *Hé^2 mei^3*. Peaceable, harmonious; unruffled family affection. (w.)

濶 *K'woá^4*. Same as 闊.

寬濶 *K'wan^1 k'woá^4*. Wide, extensive, roomy; magnanimous, *great-souled*.

唆挑 *Soá^1 t'iao^3*. To stir up, to incite,—same as 挑唆.

載 *Tsai^3*. A year, a revolution of the seasons. See *tsai^4*.

NOTES.

3 分枝下來 *To descend in constantly subdividing lines*,—a peculiar expression only used as here. The 九族 are usually defined as including four generations of ancestors and four of descendants, which, with the generation of the individual in question, makes up the nine. This seems a little inconsistent with the evident meaning of the sentence which contemplates nine generations of descent in regular order from a common ancestor. It is a peculiar fancy which makes the count proceed from the middle. It must be

病、管許醫得他好（管保給他治得好）便了。○你[23]們看陳褒家、因爲人和美（和睦）、便把狗都感化的好了、難道人倒不如狗嗎。○他[24]們裏頭、有幾個性如烈火的漢子、倘或一言半語衝撞了他、便壞了大事。○我[25]們聽說瑞蓮遭了口舌、有尋死的心腸、便赶緊打發人去安慰他、勸他心裏要開濶（寛濶）一點、不要過於難受。○平[26]安便是福、若今日吵、明日鬧、就是手中有幾個錢、心裏也不舒服。○會[27]說話的兩頭瞞、不會說話的兩頭傳、若把人家的事情唆挑起來、便是壞蛋了。○那[28]個月有三十天、就爲月大、若只二十九天、便爲月小。○請[29]父親放心、兒再住上一年半載、將外邊的賬目收齊、便就回家。

23 Look at the family of Ch'ên Pao; by their harmony they have moved the very dogs to be at peace. Do you mean to say that men are inferior to dogs?

24 There are amongst the number several men of the most fiery temper. If by speaking a few words we should offend them, it might ruin important interests.

25 When we heard that Jwei Lien's reputation had been assailed, and that she was meditating suicide, we at once sent some one to comfort her, and to exhort her to exercise a little more fortitude and not be too much depressed.

26 Peace of mind is what constitutes happiness. If you are scolding and quarreling every day, even with your hands full of money, your mind will be ill at ease.

27 "A discreet man will not tell everything to either party, but an inconsiderate man carries tales for both parties." He who incites others to quarrel, is a mean villain.

28 When a month has thirty days, it is said to be great; and if it has only twenty-nine days, it is said to be small.

29 Please do not worry, father. After remaining a year, more or less, in order to collect outstanding accounts, I will return home.

---

remembered that each generation includes the collateral descendants from previous generations.

6 A very common saying, intended as a compliment to the general information possessed by the educated man, yet in point of fact the average graduate knows absurdly little about anything beyond his own neighborhood.

8 宿 is more freely used in Shantung than it is either North or South.

9 This sentence is a play on the words 才 and 德. The meaning is that a virtuous character is a man's best endowment, while a woman's want of special endowments is the best assurance of her virtuous character. In China clever women do not have the best reputation.

11 無義之財 *Gain gotten by unrighteousness, unjust gain.* 行了偷竊 *Has done theft*; that is, *is guilty of theft.* 行 is commonly used where we say "*guilty of.*"

14 The principle here enunciated is well recognized in Chinese law, viz., that the money aspect of a crime is of prime importance. A murder for money is held to be a greater crime than a murder from malice.

20 情常 *Affection principle*; that is, that affection which accords with the 五常, or *five relations.*

21 This sentence, which is taken from the Sacred Edict, is intended to combat the idea that there is any veritable heaven or hell. 心裡光光明明的 A mind which has nothing to conceal, either from human law or from the ears of society, and so does not fear the light. Moral feelings as in the sight of God, are not intended.

22 草頭方兒 *A recipe of herbs*; that is, a domestic recipe made up of common herbs, which can be procured without buying. 便了 is here the more stately equivalent of 就是了.

24 一言半語 *One word and half a clause, a few words, a word here and there.*

25 遭口舌, in the case of a woman, generally means reports impugning her virtue.

28 In China all months consist of either twenty-nine or thirty days, and are called 小 or 大 accordingly. The respective months are not the same, however, from year to year, but are varied in accordance with the time of new moon. If the change to new moon occurs before midnight, that day belongs to the old month, and if after midnight, it belongs to the new month.

29 一年半載 *One year and a half revolution of the seasons*; that is, *a year or thereabouts, a year more or less.*

第一百九十一課

我[1]雖然很窮、却不至於偷人家的。○只[2]三十里路、我一個空行（空身）人、還要二百錢嗎、甚至不然（甚不然）、我還能以步行。○他[3]本來醜是不錯的、却不至於像你所說的。○耶[4]穌降世一千八百七十年、法國被德國打敗了、甚至京城被破、皇上也被擄去。○念[5]書固然是當勤苦、然而也不可勤苦過度、以致累壞了身體。○我[6]父親纔死的那幾天、我實在想的慌（想的很慌）、甚至一閉眼、就是他在我跟前。○那[7]逃城的路上、逢有岔路、就有指路牌、使人不至（致）錯走了道路。○那[8]些好賭錢的、逢賭起錢來、就沒有厭彀、甚至於三天三夜不騰挪窩的也有。○林[9]師母生了一個奶癰、折磨的不像人樣兒了、甚至於吃飯還必須人餧他。○你[10]目下吃一點虧、還不至悞了你女兒終身。○炕[11]上若

Translation.

1 Although I am extremely poor, I have not come to the point of stealing.

2 Only thirty *li*, and I a man without luggage, yet you want two hundred cash! If there is no other way, I can walk.

3 She is naturally homely, it is true, but not to the degree you speak of.

4 In the year of our Lord 1870, France was so effectually defeated by Germany that even the capital was taken and the Emperor made a prisoner.

5 Study should of course be prosecuted with untiring diligence, and yet this diligence should not be carried to such an extreme as to destroy the health.

6 The first few days after my father's death, my thoughts were constantly reverting to him, insomuch that whenever I shut my eyes, I seemed to see him before me.

7 At every fork in the road on the way to the Cities of Refuge, there were sign-boards, so that men might not mistake the road.

8 Those who are addicted to gambling, when they begin to play, never know when to stop, insomuch that there have been cases in which they did not stir from their places for three days and three nights.

9 Mrs. Lin has had an abscess in her breast, which has completely prostrated her, so that she cannot even eat without some one feeding her.

10 By suffering a little present loss you will avoid blighting your daughter's whole life.

11 If we can all crowd upon the k'ang we will all sleep there; and if not,

LESSON CXCI.

Sequential Phrases.

The following phrases are all derived from books, but the most of them are in common use, and are very convenient and expressive.

甚至 So that, so that even, inasmuch as, even if, insomuch that.

甚至於 The same,—**於** being added for the sake of rhythm.

甚至不然 or **甚不然** If no other way, if not . . . then, otherwise.

至於 To the point or degree of, so that. Note that, as here used, **至於** differs from its use in Les. 144.

不至 or **不至於** So as not, so that not, not to the degree or extent of.

不致 or **不致於** Same as **不至** but more bookish.

以致 or **以致於** So as to, so that, insomuch that.

能擠得下、我們都在炕上睡、甚至不然、(甚不然、)我就打個地鋪。○[12]神憐愛世人、甚至將獨生子賜給他們、叫凡信他的、不至滅亡、必得永生。○[13]慕成愛他的主人、至於替他一死。○[14]當初他們是爲孩子打架起釁、因此漸漸疎淡(疎遠)、以致兩家成了讐咯。○[15]長毛反的時候、我的房子和東西、都叫賊放火燒了、甚至連宗譜牌位、都失落了。○[16]藥是不可多吃的、我的家兄、小時吃藥太多、以致於(以至於)傷了元氣、因此一輩子常筋骨疼。○[17]這良心責備人眞是利害、要安慰也安慰不了、要壓制也壓制不下、甚至教他難爲的、如同傻(癡)了一樣。○[18]患難生忍耐、忍耐生老練、老練生盼望、盼望不致於(至於)羞恥。○[19]這一回裝載、本來太多、但是早晨(早上)開船的時候、是

then I will make a bed on the floor.

12 God so loved the world that He gave His only begotten Son, that whosoever believeth on Him, should not perish but have everlasting life.

13 Mu Ch'êng loved his master so much that he gave his life for him.

14 The first occasion of misunderstanding was a quarrel of the children's, and from this they gradually became estranged, until at last the two families became enemies.

15 At the time of the long-hair rebellion, my house and effects were all burned by the rebels, so that even my family register and ancestral tablets were lost.

16 Medicine should not be taken to excess. When my elder brother was young, he took so much medicine that he injured his constitution, and in consequence of it he has all his life suffered from rheumatism.

17 These upbraidings of conscience are truly terrible. You try to quiet them, but they will not be quieted; you try to suppress them, but they will not be suppressed; insomuch that you are worried by them to the verge of madness.

18 Tribulation worketh patience; and patience, experience; and experience, hope; and hope maketh not ashamed.

19 We were in fact too heavily loaded on this voyage. In the morning, however, when we set sail, we had a fair wind and sped along quite briskly, but in the afternoon, quite unexpectedly the wind turned suddenly about to the north and began to blow

VOCABULARY.

降世 *Chiang*⁴ *shï*⁴. To be born from a previous state, to descend to the world.

勤苦 *Ch'in*³ *k'u*³. Unwearied effort; *untiring diligence.*

過度 *Kwoă*⁴ *tu*⁴. Extreme, excessive.

岔路 *Ch'a*⁴ *lu*⁴. A fork in the road; a diverging road.

挪窩 *Noă*² *woă*¹. *To change the place* or residence; to move, to stir.

騰窩 *T'êng*² *woă*¹. The same. (s.)

癰 *Yung*¹. *An abscess,* a carbuncle.

奶癰 *Nai*³ *yung*¹. A mammary abscess.

折磨 *Chê*² *moă*². To wear out, to use up; to harass, to jade.

餧 *Wei*⁴. To feed,—animals or children or the sick.

憐愛 *Lien*² *ai*⁴. To compassionate, *to love tenderly;* kind-hearted.

滅亡 *Mie*⁴ *wang*². To suffer destruction, *to perish,* to be lost utterly.

起釁 *Ch'i*³ *hsin*⁴. Origin of a quarrel, *occasion of trouble or misunderstanding.*

疎遠 *Su*¹ *yüen*³. Distant, cool, *estranged,* disaffected.

讐 *Ch'ou*². Enmity,—same as **仇**.

個順風、跑的倒還不慢、誰知到下半天、忽然轉了北風、越颳越大、大浪如山倒、船彷彿要沉的樣子、甚至船面上都上了水咯、老大看看不好、便嚷叫招呼扒載、一直扒去一半、還是不行、後來砍眠了大桅、好歹纔保住了。○夫20妻不和的根源根由多半是從男人糊塗起的、或是嫌妻子出身貧賤、或是嫌妻子容貌醜陋、或是嫌妻子性情蠢笨、因此與他不和、甚至動不動就吆喝打罵、如同奴婢一般、何不想你這些不如意處、豈是你妻子願意如此的嗎、而且定親一事、原是憑着父母之的命、媒妁之的言、若有不如意處、就不該定他、既然定了他、又娶了他、就不該嫌他、你想想是不是呢。

stronger and stronger; the waves ran mountain high and the vessel seemed ready to founder, insomuch that the whole deck was flooded with water. The captain, seeing that the danger was imminent, called out to lighten the ship, which was done until half the cargo was thrown overboard. This proving still insufficient, the main mast was next cut away, after which we managed to outride the storm.

20 The occasion of disaffection between husband and wife generally springs from the folly of the husband. He is dissatisfied with his wife because she came of a poor family, or because she is homely in appearance, or because she is naturallp dull, and hence does not try to live peaceably with her, insomuch that on every occasion he is ready to scold or to strike or to revile her, as if she were a slave. Why do you not consider? Do you suppose it pleases your wife that she gives you all this dissatisfaction? Moreover, the betrothal was originally made in accordance with your parents wishes and upon the representations of the go-betweens; and if you had cause of dissatisfaction, you should not have made the betrothal. Having betrothed her and married her, you should not now be dissatisfied with her. Consider now, if this is not the proper view of the case.

放火 *Fang*⁴ *hwoă*³. . . . . To set on fire.

譜 *P'u*³. . . . . . . A list, *a register*, a record.

宗譜 *Tsung*¹ *p'u*³. A family or genealogical register.

牌位 *P'ai*² *wei*⁴. . . . . . . The ancestral tablet.

元氣 *Yüen*² *ch'i*⁴. That strength and vigor of vital principle which belongs to the individual by birth; *the constitution.*

責備 *Tsê*² *pei*⁴. To reprove, to admonish; to scold, *to upbraid.*

患難 *Hwan*⁴ *nan*⁴. Trouble, misfortune, *tribulation.*

老練 *Lao*³ *lien*⁴. . . . . *Experience,* wisdom.

開船 *K'ai*¹ *ch'wan*². . . . . To set sail.

順風 *Shun*⁴ *fêng*¹. . . . . A fair wind.

老大 *Lao*³ *ta*⁴. . . . . The captain of a boat.

嚷叫 *Jang*³ *chiao*⁴. . . . . . . To call out, to shout.

扒載 *Pa*¹ *tsai*⁴. To lighten a ship by casting cargo overboard.

桅 *Wei*². . . . . . The mast of a ship.

根源 *Kên*¹ *yüen*². Root, origin; source; rise; *occasion.*

根由 *Kên*¹ *yiu*². Origin, source, ground, cause, *occasion.*

容貌 *Jung*² *mao*⁴. . . . . Appearance, looks.

奴 *Nu*². . . . . . A slave.

婢 *Pei*⁴. . . . . . *A slave girl;* a maid-servant.

奴婢 Male and female slaves; *a female slave.*

妁 *Shwoă*²,⁴. A go-between in arranging marriages. (w.)

媒妁 *Mei*² *shwoă*⁴. . . . . The same. (w.)

第一百九十二課

1 那裏何曾有好人。
2 未曾舉意神先知（老天知）。
3 我頭前曾吃過這樣的虧。
4 他不曾妄殺一人。
5 你勸我吃藥、何嘗不是好話。
6 那是他不願意、我何嘗不願意呢。
7 周襲鴻曾發過大財、却沒置下產業。
8 你在我莊上住了幾天、曾見過我父親沒有。
9 未曾防備、被他一尾巴打了一個跟頭。
10 那個人曾受過大苦、也曾享過大福。
11 我還未曾說你、你倒躺（睡）在地下放刁（放賴）。
12 他雖然聽見了、却假粧未曾聽見。
13 這麼一點事情

Translation.

1 When was there ever a good man there?
2 Before the thought has arisen the gods know (God knows) it.
3 I once suffered a similar loss.
4 He never wrongfully put a single man to death.
5 It was really very kind of you to exhort me to take the medicine.
6 It was he that was unwilling; when was I ever unwilling?
7 Chou Hsi Hung has, from time to time, made a great deal of money, but he has accumulated no property.
8 You remained several days in my village; did you see my father?
9 Not being on my guard, I was knocked heels over head by one flop of his tail.
10 That man has endured great suffering, and has also enjoyed great prosperity.
11 Even before I have begun to scold you, you throw yourself down and begin to play off.
12 He pretends that he did not hear, though he heard well enough.

Notes.

7 In Peking, the two forms 致 and 至 do not differ in sound, but in Shantung, the two characters belong to different syllables, and the use of 致, as here, would not be intelligible as spoken, and as written, is regarded as *Wên*. Sign-boards at cross-roads or forks in the road, are unknown in China; hence the term 指路牌 is a made-up term.

10 Said by a magistrate to a man who was engaged in a lawsuit concerning the marriage engagement of his daughter.

13 幕成 was a bondservant of 幕懷古, a noted minister of the Ming dynasty. The servant was so much attached to his master that when, through the machinations of 唐欽 *T'ang Ch'in*, an unscrupulous imperial favorite, the master was ordered to be put to death, the servant freely gave himself to suffer death in his master's stead.

15 The 牌位, or *ancestral tablet*, is a small painted board about five inches wide and from twelve to fifteen inches long. It is usually surrounded by a flaring carved frame and is fastened upright on a small oblong wooden base. On this board is written the surname and title of the deceased.

17 The 這 is to be regarded as applying to the whole expression 頁心責備, rather than to 頁心 alone.

19 浪如山倒 *Waves like mountains falling over*, in allusion to the falling over of the crest of the waves.

20 媒妁之言 *The words of the middle-men*; that is, the bargaining and arranging which took place through them. 妁 is only used in Mandarin in this particular book phrase.

LESSON CXCII.

Special Forms for Past Time.

曾 Sign of indefinite past time, used in book Mandarin and occasionally in colloquial. It always precedes the verb.

不曾 Never, never did, not in any case.

未曾 Not yet, before, never before.

何曾 When? when ever? why? on what occasion?

嘗 Formerly, usually,—used as a sign of the past in Wênli and occasionally in Mandarin. Its use in Mandarin is confined to the following phrases:—

未嘗 Not in any case, never.

何嘗 Why? when? for what reason?

曾經過多少人說和、也沒說開。○你[14]看劉德佩、所以不能成名、弄的半途而廢的、何嘗不是吃了他躐等的虧呢。○你[15]曾聽過這個故事沒有、答 我小時候聽見過。○不[16]知為什麼、門戶都開了、却不曾失了東西。○他[17]曾在衙門當過差、所以官場中的事、他全明白。○往[18]常來的家信、却不曾有這個圖書、只是隨手寫的。○未[19]曾聽人的口供、就先定人的罪、還有這個理嗎。○不[20]必恰照原文繙、就是畧改一點、也未嘗不可。○我[21]的哥哥、從來不曾有這病、如何心疼就便死了。○聖[22]書說、沒有義人、連一個也沒有、細看起來、何嘗不

13 Ever so many men have tried to settle this trifling affair, but without success.

14 Look at Liu Tê P'ei; the reason he has made a failure and cannot get his degree, is simply because he is suffering the consequences of his irregular preparation.

15 Have you ever heard this story? *Ans.* I heard it when I was a child.

16 I do not know how it is; the doors were all open, but nothing was missing.

17 He once filled a position in the yamên, hence he is thoroughly posted in official matters.

18 Heretofore home letters have not usually had this stamp on them, but were simply addressed in the ordinary way.

19 Is it consistent with reason to condemn a man before his testimony has been heard?

20 You need not translate with slavish literality. There is no reason why slight deviations may not be made.

21 My brother has never been subject to this disease. How is it that he has taken cramp in the stomach and died?

22 The Bible says there is not one righteous man, no, not one; and care-

VOCABULARY.

曾 *Ts'êng*². Past, already, finished, once:—see Sub. Also *tsêng*¹.

妄殺 *Wang*⁴ *sha*¹. To put to death unjustly.

產業 *Ch'an*³ *yie*⁴. Inheritance; *property*; estate.

放賴 *Fang*⁴ *lai*⁴. To become obstreperous; to demand satisfaction for a trumped-up offence; *to play off.*

途 *T'u*². A road, a path; *a pursuit.*

躐 *Lie*⁴. To leap over, to overstep; *to omit.*

躐等 *Lie*⁴ *teng*³. To leap over and omit, to skip, to pass by; *irregular.*

原文 *Yüen*² *wên*². The original text.

炮 *P'ao*², *pao*¹. To roast, to bake.

炮烙 *Pao*¹ *loa*⁴. The burn with a red-hot iron.

嚴刑 *Yien*² *hsing*². Cruel punishments, tortures.

無故 *Wu*² *ku*⁴. *Without cause;* unjust, unprovoked; fortuitous.

殺害 *Sha*¹ *hai*⁴. To kill, *to put to death;* to slaughter.

邦 *Pang*¹. A region, a country.

邦國 *Pang*¹ *kwoa*². States and kingdoms, nations.

至理 *Chï*⁴ *li*³. Self-evident truths, axioms, ultimate truth or reason,—especially moral truth.

傀 *K'wei*³. Gigantic; a monster.

儡 *Lei*³. To contend fiercely.

傀儡頭 *K'wei*³ *lei*³ *t'ou*². A puppet show, Punch and Judy.

木人戲 *Mu*⁴ *jên*² *hsi*⁴. The same. (s.)

提戲 *T'i*² *hsi*⁴. The same.

點主 *Tien*³ *chu*³. To consecrate an ancestral tablet;—Note 27.

是呢。○賊[23]到受刑的時候、也未嘗不後悔、無奈已經落在法網、後悔也悔不及了。○商[24]紂乃是一個無道的昏君、最暴虐不過、他曾用過炮烙嚴刑、無故殺害忠良。○好[25]班子我們寫不起、不濟(好)的眼前又沒有、甚至不然(甚不然)我們寫一臺傀儡頭(木人)(提)戲唱一唱、也未嘗不可。○嘗[26]思大道不限於邦國、至理可通於中外、既是大道至理、何用論及出於那一國呢。○點[27]主是不能不點的、就是沒打算出來、請誰作個點主官好、我們本家、也有廩生、也有拔貢、現在

ful observation shows that this is actually the case.

23 Robbers never fail to repent when the time of punishment comes, but having once fallen into the toils of the law, repentance is of no avail.

24 Chou of the Shang dynasty, was an unprincipled and reckless prince, and cruel to the last degree. He used the inhuman torture of the red hot pillar, and without any cause put faithful and virtuous men to death.

25 A good company [of actors] is beyond our means, and no inferior company is at present available. If there is no other way, we might engage a puppet show to come and perform.

26 I have always considered that fundamental principles are not confined by national boundaries, and that ultimate truth is common to all. Since truth is fundamental and ultimate, why speak of the country from which it comes?

27 The tablet must of course be consecrated, but I have not thought of any

點主官 *Tien³ chu³ kwan¹*. The officiating minister in the ceremony of consecrating an ancestral tablet.

貢 *Kung⁴*. Presents offered as homage or tribute; superior, *the best of its kind.*

拔貢 *Pa² kung⁴*. A selected or first honor graduate:—Note 27.

黌 *Hung²*. Name of a famous college built in the Han dynasty by the Emperor Shun-ti.

黌門 *Hung² mên²*. Literary, *academic;* in virtue of scholarship.

敬惜 *Ching⁴ hsi¹*. To gather up carefully or reverentially,—as paper.

褙 *Pei⁴*. Paper or cloth pasted together into pasteboard.

紙褙子 *Chï³ pei⁴ tsï³*. Pasteboard.

NOTES.

2 This sentence is a common and very useful saying, not however derived from classical sources, but frequently found in Taoist and Buddhist tracts. It is often said 未從舉意神先知. The term 神 will of course be taken as singular or plural according as the speaker is a monotheist or a polytheist. 老天 is sometimes used instead of 神, especially in the South, and, in this connection, is as near an approach to the idea of the true God as is often made by the Chinese.

5 *Why was it not kind of you to exhort me to take the medicine?* that is, *It was really very kind, etc.*

8 Or, *How many days were you in my village? Did you see my father?* As written, the Chinese expresses either meaning equally well; as spoken, the stress thrown on 幾 is very different in the two cases.

9 一尾巴 *One tail;* that is, one stroke or flop of the tail.

11 The use of 睡, as here, seems somewhat ridiculous, but it is vouched for by an experienced teacher as good Southern Mandarin.

14 所以 *The therefore;* that is, *the reason.* 半途而廢 *To fail half way, to make a failure, to come to nothing,*—a book phrase in common use.

18 When a stamp is used it is struck twice across the seam on the back which seals the letter; otherwise the date is written along the seam, so as to be partly on one side and partly on the other.

20 未嘗不可 *Not in any case may not;* that is, *it is allowable, no objection to, may,*—a common and very expressive phrase.

24 商紂 The common title by which 紂王, the last prince of the Shang dynasty, is commonly known. 炮烙嚴刑 An inhuman mode of torture, consisting in compelling the victim to embrace or climb a red hot hollow copper pillar.

都不在家、下王家王培基是個舉人、他和我們老人家又不對勁兒、再打算只可以請秀才了。答既然沒有廪貢舉人可請、我看請個黌門秀才、也未嘗不可。○[28]現在中國、最講究敬惜字紙、以爲碎紙上若是有字、就當恭恭敬敬的收拾起來、收拾的多了、可以用火燒了、若是用脚踹了、或是堆在灰塵裏、或是用他打紙褙子、都是汚穢聖人的字、是有大罪過的、其實經書上、却未曾有這教訓、我看現在的人、講的也太過了。

suitable person whom we can invite to officiate. We have in our family both advanced and first honor graduates, but at the present time none of them are at home. Wang P'ei Chi, of lower Wang-chia, is a chü-jên, but he was not on good terms with the old gentleman. I cannot think of any one else we can ask, except simply a hsiu-ts'ai. *Ans.* Seeing there is no available graduate of a higher degree, whom we can invite, I see no reason why we should not invite an academic graduate.

28 In these times in China, there is much stress laid on the careful gathering up of paper with characters on it. It is considered that all odds and ends of such paper should be reverentially gathered up, and, when a quantity is accumulated, burned with fire. To tread it under foot, or scrape it up with the sweepings, or use it to make pasteboard, is to dishonor the characters used by the sages, and is a very great sin. Yet no such teaching is found in the classical books, and in my opinion people at the present day lay quite too much stress on it.

It was devised by 紂王 and only used by him. 忠頁 sometimes means, *faithful and good men in general*, and sometimes it is used as a contraction for 忠臣頁民, *faithful ministers and virtuous people*.

25 寫 here means *to hire or engage*. It is only so used in connection with engaging theatrical companies.

26 嘗思大道不限於邦國至理可通於中外 This is the first sentence of the introduction to Dr. Martin's Evidences of Christianity,—not Mandarin, but elegant *Wênli*.

27 點主 designates the ceremony of consecration by which the ancestral tablet is invested with its special and sacred character. The last letters of the inscription on the tablet are either 神主, *divine lord*, or 神主之位, *seat or throne of the divine lord*. The full inscription is first written on the tablet with black ink, save that 神主 is written 神王. A literary graduate (the higher the better) is then invited to come to the house of the deceased and 點主. This personage is called 點主官, and performs the ceremony in full official dress. Several friends serve as attendants, one of whom acts as master of ceremonies. When all things are ready, the 點主官 is invited to a raised seat behind a table, in imitation of official form. The master of ceremonies then calls out to the son or sons, 跪, *kneel*, which they do in front of the table. Next, addressing himself to the coffin, he calls out 請主詣公案前, *will your lordship please advance to the front to the official desk*. An attendant then uncovers the tablet and places it before the 點主官, who takes up a vermilion pen and affixes the dot to the 王 making it a 主; at the same time the master of ceremonies calls out, 請主歸靈位, *will your lordship please proceed to your spirit seat*. The tablet is then removed to its proper place, and the sons light incense, present offerings and make prostrations before it. No tablet is worshiped until after this ceremony of investiture, which is in fact a sort of canonization or deification of the deceased. 拔頁 At each 科考 or triennial examination of the *hsiu-ts'ai* graduates, this special degree of 拔頁 is conferred on the one who stands first. Besides the honor, it entitles its possessor to the privilege of competing at the Capital for the degree of chin-shï, without first obtaining the degree of chü-jên.

28 In nothing does Confucian Phariseeism come out more conspicuously than in the care taken to avoid desecrating printed or written paper. Chinese school-rooms are always provided with a box or basket in which all scraps of writings are carefully put. At city gates, and in other public places, baskets inscribed with 敬惜字紙 are often hung up for the reception of stray bits of printed paper. If a scrap of such paper meets a Chinaman's eye on the ground he will generally pick it up and tuck it away in some safe place. To gather up such paper and so prevent its desecration is considered a work of merit. Les. 29, Note 19.

第一百九十三課

寧[1]可少念一點、也不要貪多念不熟。○我[2]寧可出去討飯吃、也不能受你的打罵。○能[3]上大廟去作鬼、不上小廟去爲神。○我[4]們寧肯落個拒絕人的名兒、再也不肯和他交往。○寧[5]可一日沒錢使、不可一日壞行止。○但[6]凡是個眞忠臣、（寧可／寧自）死了、也不事奉二主。○寧[7]可捨財救人、不可圖財害人。○寧[8]肯和他打場官司、把錢花在衙門裏、還（勝似／强似）叫他白白賴了去。○我[9]（能可／能肯）叫官（折磨／折蹬）死、也不肯拔刀自刎。○你[10]當拿定主意、（寧可／寧自）得罪他、也不可（扯謊／撒謊）。○寧[11]可將就用自己的、免得捨臉求人。○他[12]寧肯甘心受屈、不肯叫你被

TRANSLATION.

1 It is better to learn a little less than to aim at getting much and so fail to learn it thoroughly.

2 I would rather go out and beg for my bread than put up with your scolding and beating.

3 I would rather be a devil in a great temple than a god in a small one.

4 We would rather get the name of being churlish than have anything more to do with them.

5 I would rather be without money for a day than be a vicious man for a day.

6 He who is a really faithful minister will die rather than serve a second master.

7 Better give money to save others than covet money to the injury of others.

8 I would rather go to law with him and spend my money in yamên fees than have him wrest it from me for nothing.

9 I would rather be tortured to death by the magistrate than take a knife and kill myself.

10 You should make up your mind that it is better to offend him than to tell a lie.

11 It is better to put up with one's own, and so avoid continually asking favors of others.

12 He prefers to suffer wrong rather

LESSON CXCIII.

CORRELATIVE PARTICLES.

The correlatives illustrated in this lesson gather for the most part around the words 寧 and 能, 可 and 肯, and exhibit the various ways the Chinese have of saying, *rather... than or better... than.* The variety at their command (with varying shades of meaning) shows the superior richness of their language in this particular case. 能 is a colloquial substitute for the more bookish 寧. Some would always *write* 寧, but read *nêng*, thus giving *nêng* as a second reading to 寧; the more common way, however, is to write 能.

寧可 or **寧自** .... **也不** or **不可** Better, rather ... than.

寧可 is more widely and generally used than **寧自**.

寧可 ... **免得** Better, rather ..... than, and avoid.

{寧肯, 寧可} ... {也不, 不肯, 强似, 勝似} Better, rather... than.

{能肯, 能可} ... {也不, 不肯, 不可, 强似} Better, rather... than.

It is difficult, if not impossible, to preserve in English, the varying shades of meaning expressed by these several forms.

能 ... **不** Better, rather ... than.

寧 ... **不** Better, rather ... than.

寧 ... **莫** Better, rather ... than, and not.

害、待你眞是恩重如山。○各[13]樣事情上、寗可吃點虧、不可同人爭鬧。○寗[14]肯送他幾個盤纏、叫他快走、還勝似叫他老在這裏白住。○像[15]這樣儱賴不賢的女人、能肯能可能可打光棍子、打光棍漢打單身子也不受他的躋蹧。○寗[16]可樸實、莫學奢華。○寗[17]選高郞、不選高房。○他[18]是個捨命不捨財的人、寗肯出劉上身子受罪、也不肯花一文錢。○姜[19]太公、寗自寗可隱遁在渭水釣魚、也不肯輔保紂王。○依[20]我看、能肯能可自己受忙、還強似僱一個不聽說的人。○寗[21]可失去百體中的一體、免得全身丟在地獄裏。○寗[22]爲太平犬、狗莫作亂世人。○能[23]叫家寬、不叫屋寬、所以房子窄狹窄巴一點、那是小

than to have you injured. His treatment of you is exceedingly generous indeed.

13 In all circumstances it is better to suffer a little wrong than to get into a fight.

14 I would rather give him a little something for traveling expenses and send him off at once than have him remain here indefinitely.

15 Such a termagant of a woman as this! I would rather go without any wife than submit to her hectoring.

16 Better be unassuming and not affect vain display.

17 Better chose a good husband than a fine house.

18 He is a man who would part with his life rather than with his money. He would subject his body to hardship rather than spend a cash.

19 Chiang T'ai Kung preferred to go into retirement and fish in the Wei rather than support King Chou.

20 In my opinion one would better worry through the work himself than hire one who will not obey.

21 It is better to lose one of the members than that the whole body should be cast into hell.

22 "Better be a dog in time of peace than a man in time of anarchy."

23 "To have a rich patrimony is better than to have a big house." A somewhat

VOCABULARY.

寗 *Ning*^{2,4}. Rest, quiet, to soothe; to prefer, rather:—see Sub.

寗可 *Ning*^{4} *k'ê*^{3}. Would rather, would be better:—see Sub.

寗肯 *Ning*^{4} *k'ên*^{3}. Would rather, would prefer:—see Sub.

寗自 *Ning*^{4} *tsï*^{4}. The same.

能肯 *Nêng*^{2} *k'ên*^{3}. Same as 寗肯.

能可 *Nêng*^{2} *k'ê*^{3}. Same as 寗可.

拒 *Chü*^{4}. To reject, *to repel*, to cast off.

拒絕 *Chü*^{4} *chüe*^{2}. To reject, to cast off, to disown.

行止 *Hsing*^{2} *chï*^{3}. Actions, conduct.

忠臣 *Chung*^{1} *ch'ên*^{2}. A faithful or devoted minister or public officer.

捨財 *Shê*^{3} *ts'ai*^{2}. *To contribute in charity;* liberal, large-hearted, generous.

圖財 *T'u*^{2} *ts'ai*^{2}. *To be covetous;* mercenary, venal.

刎 *Wên*^{3}. To cut cross-wise, to divide.

自刎 *Tsï*^{4} *wên*^{3}. To cut one's throat, *to kill oneself.*

儱 *P'ai*^{4}. Exhausted, debilitated, feeble; rude, *uncivil:*—Note 15.

儱賴 *P'ai*^{4} *lai*^{4}. Slatternly, filthy; ill-tempered; *vixenish.*

單身 *Tan*^{1} *shên*^{1}. Alone, *unmarried.* (s.)

躋 *Chi*^{1}. To ascend, to rise; to fall, to ruin.

躋蹧 *Chi*^{1} *tsao*^{1}. To worry, to annoy; to badger, to harass, *to hector.*

捨命 *Shê*^{3} *ming*^{4}. To give one's life, to part with or lose the life.

事。○張24聚去年一年、只攤了一張票、今年開徵後、寧可再差他、不可改差別旁人。○說25事人、是寧叫事中、不叫事公、若一定要個公平、永遠也了不成。○寧26隔千層山、不隔一層板、就是說人的骨肉至親、雖是活隔千山萬水、還强似死隔一口棺材。○請27看那些作賊的、一犯了案、不但自己的皮肉家產、不得自主、就是自己的妻子兒女、也不得自主、如此看來、寧可甘心受窮、也不可起意偷盜。○人28心大不相同、就像在荒年的時候、有人說、寧肯父子離散、各自逃命、還强似都在一塊餓死、又有人說、寧肯在一塊餓死、也不肯彼此離散。

contracted house is a small matter.

24 During the whole of last year only one warrant fell to Chang Chü. This year, after business is resumed, it will be better to send him again than to pass him by and send others.

25 A mediator seeks to bring about an agreement, rather than to secure justice. If he made justice a *sine qua non*, he could never effect a settlement.

26 "It is better to be separated by a thousand ranges of hills than by the thickness of one board;" that is to say, a living relative separated by half the globe, is better than a dead one separated by [the boards of] a coffin.

27 Just look at the case of robbers. When they are arrested, not only are their own persons and property beyond their control, but also their wives and children; from which you see that it is better cheerfully to bear poverty than to harbor the thought of robbery.

28 People's ideas are very different. For instance, during the famine year some said, "It is better for the family to separate and each one flee for his life than for all to remain together and starve;" while others said, "It is better to starve together than to separate."

遁 Tun^4. . . . . . To hide; to vanish; *to retire.*

隱遁 Yin^3 tun^4. To disguise oneself; *to go into retirement;* to hide.

渭 Wei^4. . . . . . A river in Shensi.

輔保 Fu^3 pao^3. . . . . *To support,* to uphold. (w.)

百體 Poă^2 t'i^3. *All the members of the body,* the whole body.

亂世 Lan^4 shï^4. . . . . . Anarchy.

窄巴 Chai^3 pa^1. Narrow, *contracted;* straightened in circumstances.

窄狹 Chai^3 hsia^2. . . . . . Narrow, *contracted.*

徵 Chêng^1. To levy; *to collect; to summon;* evidence, proof:—Also tsï^3.

開徵 K'ai^1 chêng^1. To open official business—especially the collection of taxes.

至親 Chï^4 ch'in^1. Nearly related; a very near relative.

自主 Tsï^4 chu^3. *One's own master,* at liberty, free.

起意 Ch'i^3 i^4. To take up an idea, to get a notion; *to harbor a thought.*

偷盜 T'ou^1 tao^4. . . . . To steal, *to rob.*

NOTES.

3 A 鬼 *is a servant or waiter;* that is, in a temple he occupies a subordinate position, attending on the commands of the god. A 神 *is a master or lord;* that is, in a temple he sits in the seat of authority and commands his subordinates. This is one of the characteristic distinctions between a 鬼 and a 神. The sentence gives the Chinese view of the comparative desirability of "*reigning* in hell" or "*serving* in heaven." Milton probably expressed the characteristic spirit of his race when he attributed to Satan the opposite sentiment.

6 The Chinese hold to an exceedingly high standard of devotion in a public servant of the Emperor.

12 恩重如山 *Favor as weighty as the hills, very great favor,*—a book phrase.

第一百九十四課

寗[1]可多用幾兩銀子、也要買頂好的。○與[2]其打死人、不如被人打死。○事[3]到頭、不自由、這一遭我寗肯傾了家、也要和他碰一碰。○與[4]其借給他、終久不還、我就寗肯白送給他、還落一個整人情。○我[5]這回上濟南府、寗肯多走幾里、也要到曲阜去看看孔廟。○與[6]其事情壞了後悔、那赶上在事前多加斟酌呢。○如[7]今有客來、都是這鳳姑娘周旋接待、今日寗可不見太太、倒要見他一面、纔不枉走這一遭兒。○我[8]已經試驗過了、寗肯少貪點利、

TRANSLATION.

1 I would rather buy the best even if it does cost a few more taels.
2 It would be better to be murdered than to commit murder.
3 "When things become desperate, responsibility ceases." I'll have it out with him this time, even if it costs me everything I have.
4 Rather than lend it to him never to be returned, I would prefer to give it to him outright and have the credit of the gift.
5 During this trip to Chinanfu I intend to visit Ch'üfu and see the temple of Confucius, even if I have to go a few *li* out of my way.
6 How much better to consider the matter well beforehand than to let it go wrong and have to repent of it.
7 At present when guests come, this Miss Fêng always does the honors in receiving them. I must see her today, even if I miss seeing the lady of the house; otherwise my trip will be all for nothing.
8 I have already made the experiment.

15 憊 is read *pai*⁴ by the dictionaries, but in colloquial practice everywhere, North and South, it is *p'ai*⁴. 光棍漢 is a Southern expression. In the South 光棍 does not mean *single* or *unmarried*, save as joined with 漢. Kiukiang, however, rejects both expressions and substitutes 打單身.

17 The first 高 is figurative, the second literal. 郎 here means *a husband*. The couplet is a common saying in book style.

22 犬 is *Wên*, 狗 colloquial.

23 家 is here put for *patrimony, circumstances, living.*

24 改差 *To change the service or sending;* that is, to pass by one in favor of others.

25 The fear of going to law makes the Chinese willing to submit to a wonderful amount of wrong. Arbitrators and mediators presume on this fact and often propose the most unjust terms of settlement, thus giving the strongest and the most quarrelsome all the advantage.

LESSON CXCIV.

CORRELATIVE PARTICLES.

寗肯 / 寗可 ... 是 / 也要 / 也要 / 還要 / 倒要 ... Better, rather ... than. Or reversing the Chinese order,—Rather, will ... even if. The varying shades of meaning expressed by these several forms, it is difficult, if not impossible, to preserve in English.

與其 ... 不如 / 與其 ... 不及 As compared with ... would be better. Or reversing the Chinese order,—Rather than ... it is better, it would be better.

與其 ... 寗肯 As compared with .. rather. Or—Rather than ... would be better, would prefer.

與其 ... 何如 / 與其 ... 那赶上 Rather than ... how much better? or How much better ... than?

與其 ... 寗 Better ... than. (w.)

These forms with 與其 are favorite book Mandarin forms, but are not often used in conversation, unless by literary men.

還是賣現錢上算。○與⁹其吃各樣的藥不見效、不如自己靜
靜兒的養着倒好。○嗐¹⁰這不識字的人、眞是個睜眼瞎子、往
後寗可僱人做生活活、也要替出孩子來、念幾年書。○與¹¹其做
一個抗糧的滑頭戶、何如做一個守法度的良民好呢。○馬¹²貴
生的脾氣、眞是古怪古董、你看他雖然窮的有上頓無下頓、但每
逢過節的日子、寗肯把鞋押了、還要吃一頓好飯。○應¹³當量
力而行、不可輕戰、與其到底勝他不過、不如早早求和、還强
似荼毒生靈。○與¹⁴其等父母死了、去殺豬宰羊的祭祀、那趕
上趁着父母活的時候、不斷他的口腹、依隨他的心願呢。○
念¹⁵書雖然是好事、也要得看人的天分如何、與其念個學而不

It is better to be content with a little less profit and sell for ready money.

9 It is better to wait on nature, with good nursing, than to keep taking all sorts of medicine to no purpose.

10 Och! but a man who can't read is no better than a blind man. Hereafter I will hire help to do the work rather than not give the children the opportunity to go to school for a few years.

11 How much better to be a good citizen who keeps the laws, than to be a slippery fellow who tries to evade paying his taxes.

12 Ma Kwei Shêng is certainly a queer fellow. Although, as you see, he is so poor that when he eats his breakfast he does not know where his supper is to come from, yet whenever a feast day comes round, he will pawn the shoes on his feet rather than fail to have a good meal.

13 You should measure your action by your strength, and not lightly go to war. Rather than waste life in vain by failing to conquer, it would be much better to sue at once for peace.

14 How much better while your parents are still alive to supply their need and follow their wishes, than to wait till they are dead and then sacrifice hogs and sheep to them.

15 Although education is a good thing, yet it depends on what the person's abilities are. Rather than make a failure, and be unfitted for anything,

VOCABULARY.

與其 *Yü³ ch'i².* . . . . . . As compared with, rather.

傾 *Ch'ing¹.* To overturn, to subvert; *to squander;* to pour out.

傾家 *Ch'ing¹ chia¹.* *To lose everything,* to become bankrupt.

斟 *Chên¹.* To pour out; *to deliberate,* to consider.

酌 *Choă²,⁴ chao¹,⁴.* To pour out; *to deliberate;* to choose.

斟酌 *To deliberate,* to consider, to reflect.

抗 *K'ang⁴.* . . . . . *To resist,* to oppose, to rebel.

抗糧 *K'ang⁴ liang².* To resist or evade the payment of taxes.

頑戶 *Wan² hu⁴.* An obstinate or *slippery fellow,* a hard case.

滑戶 *Hwa² hu⁴.* *A slippery fellow,* a hard case, a knave.

古董 *Ku³ tung³.* Antiquities, curios; curious, odd, singular, *queer.*

荼 *T'u².* . . . . . A bitter herb; *to harm.*

荼毒 *T'u² tu².* Poisonous weeds; *to destroy wantonly,* to slaughter.

生靈 *Shêng¹ ling².* Animate beings, all living things, *life.*

祭祀 *Chi⁴ sï⁴.* . . . *To offer sacrifices;* a sacrifice.

口腹 *K'ou³ fu⁴.* . . . . Food; *necessities.*

依隨 *I¹ swei².* *To follow;* to agree with, to acquiesce.

心願 *Hsin¹ yüen⁴.* . . . . *Wish,* desire.

成、任什麼不會做、還不及早早的下學(出學)做莊稼。○16若照我們的賬算、他還欠我們三百餘吊、照他的賬算、我們倒欠他五百餘吊、他那裏要呈要告的、我們還是求人說和爲妙、與其和他打官司、把錢花在衙門裏、寧肯找個一百八十吊的給他、免得去跪官跪廳(跪官跪府)的。○17王孫賈以爲孔子有求作官的心、又覺着自己是衛國的權臣、凡要求用於衛君的、莫妙如求他作個引進、因此借俗語問孔子說、與其媚於奧、寧媚於竈、何謂也、孔子參透他的心思、就回答說、不然、獲罪於天、無所禱也、這就是說、媚奧媚竈都不可以、惟獨當以天爲主、倘若得罪了天、就沒有別處可禱告了。

it would be better to quit school in good season and go to farming.

16 According to our account he still owes us over three hundred thousand cash, but according to his account we owe him five hundred thousand, and he declares he will bring suit. It will be better for us, however, to arrange a compromise. Rather than go to law and spend the money in the yamên, it would be better for us to give him one hundred thousand or eighty thousand and so avoid the humiliation of the court room.

17 Wang Sun Chia, supposing that Confucius had thoughts of seeking office, and considering himself an influential officer of the kingdom of Wei, and that those who sought office of the king of Wei could not do better than seek his good offices, came therefore to Confucius, and availing himself of a common saying asked, "What is meant by, 'It is better to pay court to the furnace than to pay court to the south-west corner?'" Confucius, seeing through his purpose, answered him saying, "Not so, he who offends against Heaven, has no one to whom he can pray;" that is to say, you should pay court neither to the god of the furnace nor to that of the south-west corner, but should appeal to Heaven alone; for if one has sinned against Heaven, there is no one else to whom he can pray.

下學 *Hsia*⁴ *hsüe*²...... To quit going to school.
出學 *Ch'u*¹ *hsüe*². *To leave school;* to finish .... an education.
跪官 *Kwei*⁴ *kwan*¹........ To kneel before an [officer.
跪廳 *Kwei*⁴ *t'ing*¹.......... To kneel in court.
跪府 *Kwei*⁴ *fu*³.......... The same.
權臣 *Ch'üen*² *ch'ên*². *An influential minister;* .... an imperial favorite.
引進 *Yin*³ *chin*⁴. To introduce and recom- .... mend.
獲 *Hwoă*⁴....... To catch; to get, to obtain.
獲罪 *Hwoă*⁴ *tswei*⁴...... *To sin against;* to sin.

Notes.

3 事到頭不自由 very closely approximates, "*Necessity knows no law.*"

5 曲阜, a *hsien* city in south-western Shantung, near which Confucius is buried. The grave is about a mile from the city wall in the midst of a large and beautiful walled cemetery in which are also buried the seventy-six generations of Confucius' lineal descendents, in all many hundreds of graves. There is also within the city a magnificent temple in his honor, commonly known as 孔廟. Both the temple and the cemetery are kept up at government expense.

10 No "authorized" word of the English language will fully express the force of 瞎, as here used. The rather questionable expression *By George!* comes very near the meaning. 睜眼瞎子 *An open-eyed blind man;* that is, one who has eyes and seems to see but does not see.

16 跪官跪廳 is 跪官廳 expanded, and 跪官跪府 is 跪官府 expanded:—Les. 184. All the parties in a lawsuit are required to kneel in the presence of the magistrate.

第一百九十五課

蘿[1]蔔是一樣好菜、吃了能以消食化痰。○你[2]別/莫癡心妄想、他的姑娘還能到了你手裏嗎。○依[3]我看、你不如推聾粧啞、權當是沒聽見就是了。○孩[4]子們眞好打發、一個雞蛋、就哄的歡天喜地的。○今[5]天忽然眼跳心驚、許/想是家中遇着甚麼事喇。○女[6]人家若沒有個針線笸籮/簸兒/箸兒、那些針頭線腦的、怎麼收拾呢。○嘴[7]快心直的人、雖然容易得罪人、到底却更好交。○今[8]年又豐收、又太平、眞是風調雨順、國泰民安。○要[9]學拳棒/把勢、必得眼尖手快/眼精手快纔能學

TRANSLATION.

1 The radish is an excellent vegetable; when eaten it aids digestion and clears the throat.

2 You need not keep striving for a thing so impossible. Do you suppose his daughter could come into your possession?

3 In my opinion you would better pay no attention, but just act as if you had not heard it.

4 Children are very easy to satisfy. A single egg has made him wild with delight.

5 To-day my eyes suddenly began to twitch and my heart to palpitate; it may be (I suspect) that something has happened at home.

6 If a woman has no work-basket, where can she put the odds and ends of her sewing?

7 Although a plain-spoken and straightforward person is apt to offend others, yet he is after all the easiest to get on with.

8 This year there is a bountiful harvest, and peace prevails. We have been blessed with propitious winds and seasonable rains, public tranquillity and domestic quiet.

9 In learning the art of boxing (fen-

17 求用於 *To ask office or employment from,*—a *Wênli* form of expression. **奧** *The south-west corner*, which being most distant from the door, represented darkness and mystery. There is no god known in China as **奧神**. There was probably a vague reference to Heaven, as the mysterious One to whom the **竈**, or, *God of the Furnace*, was subordinate. Wang Sun Chia's intimation was, that it was best to approach the superior through the subordinate. Confucius resented his use of the term **媚**, and in response gave utterance to the remarkable saying here quoted. No heathen sage ever gave utterance to a more pregnant or important sentiment.

LESSON CXCV.

QUADRUPLET PHRASES.

The phrases illustrated in this lesson are such as have the first and third characters analogous verbs or adjectives, and the second and fourth nouns; or, *vice versâ*.

消食化痰 Dissolve the food and clear away the mucus, promote digestion and clear the passages.

癡心妄想 To seek an unattainable object, to pine after, to hanker for.

推聾粧啞 To pretend not to hear or understand, to pay no attention, to take no heed.

眼跳心驚 Eyes twitching and heart palpitating, nervously apprehensive.

歡天喜地 Leaping with joy, wild with delight.

針頭線腦 Odds and ends of sewing.

嘴快心直 Plain-spoken and straightforward, blunt and candid.

風調雨順 Winds propitious and rains seasonable, wind and rain in due order and proportion.

國泰民安 The nation tranquil and the people at rest, general peace.

到好處。○你[10]昨天指雞罵狗、直罵了一天。難道我還聽不出來嗎。○那[11]等心驕氣傲的人、眞是難以和他共事。○他[12]叫反賊蹧蹋怕了、所以一聽見反的信息、就嚇得的魂飛魄散的。○諸[13]位都受屈喇、答好說好說、今天眞是酒醉飯飽、不說蹧擾喇。○他[14]無論做甚麼、總是拖泥帶水的、沒有個擺俐俐俐束擺時候。○我[15]不能爲這幾吊錢、虛心下氣的去看他的臉。○城[16]裏的女人、光會搽胭抹粉的、粗重工活一點也不能做。○和[17]外鄉人打

cing), one must have a sharp eye and a quick hand in order to attain proficiency.

10 Yesterday you kept on the whole day reviling the dog over the heads of the chickens. Do you suppose I did not know what you meant?

11 It is very hard indeed to work with that class of haughty, self-conceited people.

12 The ruthless violence of the rebels has made her so nervous that as soon as she heard the rumor of rebellion she was frightened out of her senses.

13 I am sorry you have all fared so poorly. *Ans.* Far from it I assure you. We have to-day eaten and drunk our fill. Excuse us for the trouble we have given you.

14 No matter what he does, he does it in a slovenly manner. He never gets anything properly done.

15 I'll not, for the sake of these few thousand cash, go meekly and subject myself to his disdainful looks.

眼精手快 A keen eye and a quick hand.

眼尖手快 A sharp eye and a quick hand.

指雞罵狗 To revile one over the shoulders of another.

心驕氣傲 Self-conceited, haughty.

魂飛魄散 Frightened out of one's senses, scared to death, bereft of one's wits :—Note 12.

酒醉飯飽 To eat and drink to the full, to partake heartily.

拖泥帶水 Slovenly, negligent, hodge-podge.

虛心下氣 Meek and submissive, with bated breath.

搽胭抹粉 To powder and paint, to trick out gaudily.

坐家欺客 To take advantage of being amongst friends and so insult strangers.

盖廟築塔 To build temples and erect pagodas.

修橋補路 To repair bridges and mend roads.

捨飯放生 To dispense food and release those condemned to die.

望風撲影 To look at the wind and pounce on a shadow, to speak or act at random.

溝滿濠平 Gullies and gutters all full, abundant rain.

循規蹈矩 To conform to the rules, to follow the routine, punctilious [Note 21.

生枝雕葉 To draw out in detail :—

按部就班 To follow the prescribed order, orderly, well-behaved.

遠走高飛 To go far and fly high, an extravagant idea, a wild adventure.

設身處地 To imagine oneself in the place of another :—Note 24.

順水推舟 To row with the stream, to drift with the current, to go with the crowd.

擔驚受怕 To endure fright and suffer fear, in a state of fear and alarm.

提心弔膽 A state of trepidation, breathless anxiety :—Note 26.

家破人亡 Property lost and life gone, ruined in person and estate.

忘恩負義 Forgetting favor and abusing grace, ungrateful.

平淡無奇 Nothing uncommon, ordinary.

平平無奇 The same.

超羣出衆 Extraordinary, exceptional, above the average.

掐尖出色 Excelling others, capping the climax, first class, exceptional.

架、即便不是坐家欺客、人家也必說是坐家欺客。○蓋[18]廟築塔、修橋補路、捨飯放生、這都是積陰功的法子。○摸[19]不着底細、你好望風撲影的說嗎。○我[20]們那個地方也是大雨、下的溝滿濠平的。○你[21]看他生枝雕葉的、眞是說的活眼兒(活現)見、那想到他能撒(扯)謊呢。○趙[22]長春眞是一個好學生、凡事都是循規蹈矩、按部就班的、一點錯亂沒有。○請[23]問你近來有什麼妙見識、情願捨了相好的街坊、

16 City women only know how to paint and powder; heavy (coarse) work they cannot do at all.

17 If you have a fight with a stranger, even though it is not the native insulting the stranger, yet people will surely say it is.

18 Building temples and pagodas, repairing roads and bridges, dispensing food and saving life;—these all are ways of making merit.

19 Is it right for you to speak at random, when you are not acquainted with the facts?

20 We also had a great rain at our place which filled all the gutters and gullies.

21 Just think how vividly he pictured it all out in order. Who would have thought he was telling a pack of lies?

22 Chao Ch'ang Ch'un is an exceedingly good pupil. He observes the rules in everything, being most regular in his habits and without the least misconduct.

23 Please tell me what wonderful idea you have got of late, that you are willing to leave good neighbors and go on this wild adventure.

VOCABULARY.

笸 *P'oă*³. . . . A flat open basket without handle.

籮 *Loă*². . . . . . . A wide open basket; a sieve.

笸籮 A flat open basket without handle.

笺 *K'ao*³. . . An open basket without handle (s.)

拳棒 *Ch'üen*² *pang*⁴. . . . . Boxing and fencing.

信息 *Hsin*⁴ *hsi*². . . . . . News; report.

魄 *P'oă*⁴. The animal soul; the senses,—as distinguished from the reason.

蹧擾 *Tsao*¹ *jao*³. To make an ado, to create a disturbance; to annoy, *to trouble.*

摞俐 *Loă*³ *li*⁴. . . . . . In order,—same as 俐摞.

胭 *Yien*¹. . . . . . The throat; rouge.

築 *Chu*². To beat or ram down hard,—as in making a mud wall; to erect, *to build.*

陰功 *Yin*¹ *kung*¹. Merit in the eyes of the gods and available in the next life as an offset to sins.

濠 *Hao*². . . . . . A moat, a ditch, a gutter.

雕 *Tiao*¹. . . . . To engrave, *to carve;* to adorn.

活眼兒見 *Hwoă*² *yien*³ *er*² *chien*⁴. Life-like, *vivid,* realistic.

活現 *Hwoă*² *hsien*⁴. . . . . The same.

循 *Hsün*². To follow; *to comply with,* to accord; docile.

蹈 *Tao*⁴. To tread on, to disregard; *to tread in the footsteps of,* to conform to.

錯亂 *Ts'oă*⁴ *lan*⁴. Confused, disordered, irregular.

狀師 *Chwang*⁴ *shi*¹. A lawyer, an attorney, *an advocate*:—Note 24.

辯理 *Pien*⁴ *li*³. To contest or argue the right or wrong of a thing.

干己 *Kan*¹ *chi*³. . . . . To concern oneself.

舟 *Chou*¹. . . . . . A ship, a vessel of any kind.

槍 *Ch'iang*¹. . . . . A spear, a lance.

赫 *Hê*⁴. . . . Bright, gleaming; elegant; *majestic.*

赫赫有名 *Hê*⁴ *hê*⁴ *yiu*³ *ming*². Illustrious; *brilliant reputation;* prestige.

超 *Ch'ao*¹. To leap over, *to excel,* to surpass; to save, to release.

獨自遠走高飛呢。○狀[24]師替人辯理、必得設身處地、纔能辯到好處。○這[25]不干己、誰肯得罪仇人呢、也不過順水推舟、好歹了結就是了。○你[26]常這樣動刀動槍的、不但妻子兒女、老婆孩子擔驚受怕、就是父母、爹媽也常爲你提心吊膽的。○你[27]看唐欽、受了慕懷古的提拔、反將慕懷古害了個家破人亡、誰不說他是忘恩負義的東西呢。○起[28]初聽說的時候、眞是赫赫有名、誰料見了面、竟是一把平平無奇平淡無奇的手、竝沒有甚麼超羣出衆招尖出色的地方。

24 When an advocate pleads a man's cause, he must conceive himself in the place of his client in order to manage the case well.

25 Who is going to make an enemy on account of business that does not concern himself? Simply drift with the current and, in some way or other, bring the matter to an end.

26 By constantly flourishing your weapons in this way, not only are your wife and children kept in a state of apprehension, but your parents also are in a constant state of trepidation.

27 Just look how T'ang Ch'in, after being helped by Mu Hwai Ku, turned about and procured the destruction of Mu Hwai Ku and his estate. Who does not pronounce him an ungrateful wretch?

28 When I first heard of him, he had a great reputation; but when I saw him, he turned out to be a man of but very ordinary attainments,—in no respect excelling the generality of men.

NOTES.

4 打發 here means, to send away satisfied one who is demanding something, hence *to satisfy, to please.*

6 的 at the end of **針頭線腦**, gives practically the force of, *sort, and the like.*

9 拳 refers to boxing proper, and **棒** to fencing with a club or shillalah.

12 魂飛魄散 *Soul flown and senses scattered.* **魂** is the *rational soul,* **魄** *the animal soul or breath.* According to Chinese psychological ideas a man has **三魂** and **七魄**.

13 不說蹧擾 *We will omit the usual polite apologies for the trouble we have given you.*

15 看他的臉 *See his face,*—to beg for a favor of one who is not willing to grant it, and so be compelled to submit to whatever ungracious words or looks may accompany either the refusal, or the unwilling granting of the request.

18 The three phrases here used are stock phrases for expressing the various ways of making merit. **放生**, is to save life by releasing birds or animals held in captivity, or prepared for slaughter. This is a distinctively Buddhist idea.

21 生枝雕葉 *To produce branches and strike out leaves,* as a picture grows under the hand of the artist or engraver; that is, *to draw out and describe in detail, to portray, to picture.*

24 狀師 is a term coined to fit the idea of the word "lawyer" or "attorney." No such profession is known or allowed in Chinese courts. **設身處地** *Suppose* [*one's own*] *body to occupy the place* [*of another*]; that is, to regard oneself as standing in another's shoes and so be able to give vivid and faithful expression to the feelings of the party represented.

25 得罪仇人 *To offend an enemy;* that is, to offend one so as to make him an enemy.

26 提心吊膽 *The heart rising* [*into the throat*] *and the gall suspended;* that is, *in a state of breathless anxiety and alarm.*

LESSON CXCVI.

QUADRUPLET PHRASES.

The phrases illustrated in this lesson consist of analogous nouns, which serve as the summary of a subject. A few common phrases of five nouns each are also added.

東西南北 The four cardinal points, all quarters.

起承轉合 The four steps in writing an essay:—Note 2.

仁義禮智 The four cardinal virtues.

春夏秋冬 The four seasons.

第一百九十六課

船[1]在大洋之中、若沒有個羅經、就分不出東西南北來。○要[2]作文章、必得先明白起承轉合四個字。○誰[3]沒個仁義禮智的天性、誰不該鄭重學校呢。○請[4]看春夏秋冬、四季循環不已、誰能使他如此呢。○肉[5]和麪都齊全喇、就是油鹽醬醋、還沒辦預置備好。○要[6]作官、總得能斷出個是非曲直來纔行、你看王魁五、他明白甚麼呢、那個纔是個酒囊飯袋喇。○聊[7]齋那一部書、差不多淨說的是妖魔鬼怪。○不[8]用木匠的傢伙、我家裏錛鑿斧鋸都有。○他[9]不但是文章見長、就是詩詞歌賦、也不在衆人以下。

TRANSLATION.

1 When a ship is in the midst of the ocean without a compass, it is impossible to distinguish the four cardinal points.

2 In order to write an essay, one must first understand the four words: state, expand, illustrate, combine.

3 Who has not the natural instincts of benevolence, justice, propriety and reason? Who is there who should not value education?

4 Look, if you please, at the ceaseless revolution of the four seasons; spring, summer, autumn and winter. Who is able to produce these changes?

5 The meat and flour are all ready, but the oil, salt, sauce and vinegar are not yet prepared.

6 He who would be a magistrate, must be able to judge between right and wrong, falsehood and truth. Look at that man Wang K'wei Wu. What does he know? He is really nothing more than a receptacle for wine and bread.

7 That book called Liao Tsai is made up almost entirely of stories of elves, fiends, demons and ghouls.

8 There is no need of carpenters' tools. I have in the house adze, chisel, hatchet and saw.

9 Not only are his essays improved, but in writing odes, chants, songs and poems, he is not inferior to others.

10 The great turtle, gavial, serpent and

油鹽醬醋 Condiments, trimmings.
是非曲直 Right and wrong, truth and falsehood; justice and truth.
妖魔鬼怪 Evil spirits, hobgoblins.
錛鑿斧鋸 Carpenters' tools.
詩詞歌賦 Poetry of all kinds.
黿鼉蛟龍 Mythological monsters.
魚鼈鰕蟹 Marine animals.
娼優隸卒 The disqualified classes.
飛潛動植 The four kingdoms of living things.
生死禍福 The four springs of human action.
喜怒哀樂 The four common passions or [feelings.
禮義廉恥 The four principles of morals.
鷄狗鵝鴨 The lesser domestic animals.
牛驢騾馬 The greater domestic animals.
槍刀劍戟 Weapons of war.
之乎者也 Euphonic particles:—Note 18.
酒色財氣 Vicious appetites or passions.
耳目口鼻心 The five senses:—Note 20
心肝脾肺腎 The five viscera.
金木水火土 The five elements.
青黃赤白黑 The five colors.
仁義禮智信 The five virtues.
酸甜苦辣鹹 The five tastes.
宮商角徵羽 The five musical notes.
東西南北中 The five quarters.

○黿[10]鼉蛟龍、魚鼈鰕蟹、這都是屬乎鱗介的東西。○按[11]中國的例條、凡是娼優隸卒的子弟、一概不准進考場。○天[12]地間有生氣的東西、固然多得不可勝數、但要分類言之、也不過是飛潛動植而已。○禮[13]義廉恥他全然不知、還冒充的什麽斯文呢。○人[14]的生死禍福、都是天命所定、絲毫由不得人、所以孔夫子說、死生有命、富貴在天。○葛[15]長松就和個土牛木馬（木頭人）一樣、喜怒哀樂好像一點沒有。○由[16]百川頭十年還當糧食販子、如今家裏雞狗鵝鴨、牛驢騾馬、都成了羣

dragon; the fish, tortoise, lobster and crab; all belong to that class of animals which have scales.

11 According to Chinese law, the children of prostitutes, actors, lictors and jailers, are all excluded from the competitive examinations.

12 Although the living things in the world are indeed numerous beyond computation, yet when they are classified, they are all comprehended under birds, fishes, beasts and vegetables.

13 What literary culture is he pretending to, when he is wholly ignorant of propriety, uprightness, purity and modesty?

14 A man's life, death, misery and happiness, are all determined by the decree of Heaven; not a jot or a tittle lies within human control. Hence Confucius says, "Life and death are determined by fate; wealth and honor rest with Heaven."

15 Kê Ch'ang Sung is like a wooden man; he seems quite insensible to pleasure, anger, sorrow or joy.

16 Ten years ago Yiu Pai Ch'wan was only a grain dealer; now he has at his home droves of chickens, dogs, geese, ducks; cows, asses, mules and horses; from which we see that after all, making a fortune is no great matter.

VOCABULARY.

羅經 *Loă² ching⁴* . . . . . . A mariner's compass.

羅盤 *Loă² p'an²* . . . . The same.

天性 *T'ien¹ hsing⁴*. The nature conferred by . . . . . . Heaven, natural disposition, qualities or *instincts*.

鄭重 *Chêng⁴ chung⁴*. To value, to regard as important; earnest; weighty.

循環 *Hsün² hwan²*. To come round in order; . . . . . . to revolve, to rotate.

不已 *Pu⁴ i³*. Without ceasing, endless, interminable.

囊 *Nang²*. . . . A bag, *a sack*, a purse; perquisites.

酒囊 *Chiu³ nang²*. *A wine-sack*, a wine-bibber, ... a sot.

飯袋 *Fan⁴ tai⁴*. . . . . . . *A rice-bag*, a glutton, a [gormand.

聊 *Liao²*. . . . . . To depend on; then; perhaps.

錛 *Pên¹*. An adze,—usually a wooden head . . . . . armed with a steel-edged cap.

歌 *Kê¹*. . . . . . To chant; an ode, a poem, *a song*.

以下 *I³ hsia⁴*. . . . . Beneath, *inferior to*.

黿 *Yüen²*. . . . . . The great sea-turtle.

鼉 *T'oă²*. . . . . . A large water-lizard, the gavial.

例條 *Li⁴ t'iao²*. . . . *Laws*, administrative rules.

優 *Yiu¹*. Excellent; abundant; excessive; tranquil; to play with; *an actor*.

隸 *Li⁴*. . . . . . . To control; underlings, *lictors*.

卒 *Tsu²,⁴*. Underlings; *a jailer;* a soldier, a private; a pawn in chess; to die.

考場 *K'ao³ ch'ang³*. The examination hall, *the literary examinations*.

勝數 *Shêng⁴ shu³*. Capable of being counted, ... a limited number,—generally with a negative.

潛 *Ch'ien²*. Hid in the water; retired, private; . . . . . . *fish*—as a species.

喇、可見日子要發旺起來、也不值什麼。○每17到皇上出來的時候、那些御前侍衛、都拿着槍刀劍戟、眞是耀眼爭光的。○對18着莊稼人、必得說個莊戶話、你這樣之乎者也的、他那能明白呢。○呂19洞賓去赴蟠桃會、王母娘娘阻擋他說、你這種神仙、酒色財氣無一不好、蟠桃會上不用你來、洞賓說、酒色財氣別說我好、就是王母娘娘也未嘗不好、王母娘娘說、我怎麼好酒色財氣呢、洞賓說、王母娘娘若不好酒、蟠桃會上的酒、是從那裏來的、王母娘娘說、我縱然好酒、却

17 Whenever the Emperor goes out, his attendants and body-guard all carry spears, knives, swords and halberds. It is truly a glittering pageant.

18 In talking to farmers you should use common language. How can they understand this grandiose talk of yours?

19 When Lü Tung Pin went to attend the P'an-t'ao Festival, the Royal Mother [seeing him about to enter], objected, saying, "Such a genius as you, who are given alike to wine, lust, avarice and anger, cannot be allowed at the P'an-t'ao Festival." Lü Tung Pin replied, "It is not I alone who am given to wine, lust, avarice and anger, but the Royal Mother is also given to them." The Royal Mother answered, "How do you make it out that I am given to wine, lust, money and anger"? Lü Tung Pin replied, "If the Royal Mother were not given to wine, whence the wine used at the P'an-t'ao Feast"? The Royal Mother answered, "If I *am* given to wine, I am *not* given to lust." Lü Tung Pin replied, "If the Royal Mother is not given to lust, then who gave birth to the Nine Celestial Fairies?" The Royal Mother replied, "If I *am* given to wine and lust, I am *not* given to avarice." Tung Pin replied, "If the Royal

植 *Chi*[2,4]. To plant; to set up; erect; *vegetation*, plants.

廉 *Lien*[2]. Economical, frugal, *pure*, incorrupt.

冒充 *Mao*[4] *ch'ung*[1]. *To pretend*, to sham; to play off, to personate.

絲毫 *Sï*[1] *hao*[2]. *A jot or tittle*, an iota.

販子 *Fan*[4] *tsï*[3]. A dealer in any commodity.

發旺 *Fa*[1] *wang*[4]. To prosper, to flourish, to get on in the world, *to make a fortune*.

御 *Yü*[4]. To drive a chariot; to wait upon; to superintend; *imperial*, royal.

御前 *Yü*[4] *ch'ien*[2]. The imperial presence; chamberlains, *imperial attendants*.

侍 *Shï*[4]. Near to; *an attendant*, a waiter.

侍衛 *Shï*[4] *wei*[4]. Imperial body-guard.

劍 *Chien*[4]. A two-edged sword; a rapier.

戟 *Chi*[3]. A two-pointed lance, a halberd.

爭光 *Chêng*[1] *kwang*[1]. Very bright, brilliant, splendid.

耀眼 *Yao*[4] *yien*[3]. Dazzling, *glittering*.

呂 *Lü*[3]. A musical pipe; tones; *a surname*.

蟠 *P'an*[2]. To curl up, *to coil;* squirming.

蟠桃 *P'an*[2] *t'ao*[2]. The flat whorled peach; the fabled tree of life.

阻擋 *Tsu*[3] *tang*[3]. To hinder, to prevent; *to object to*.

好酒 *Hao*[4] *chiu*[3]. To love wine, given to drink.

好色 *Hao*[4] *sê*[4]. Given to lust, lascivious.

好財 *Hao*[4] *ts'ai*[2]. To love money, covetous.

好氣 *Hao*[4] *ch'i*[4]. *Given to getting angry*, acting from the impulse of anger; spirited, touchy.

香火 *Hsiang*[1] *hwoä*[3]. Incense and paper money.

膚 *Fu*[1]. *The skin;* superficial.

肝 *Kan*[1]. *The liver;* irritable.

腎 *Shên*[4]. *The kidneys;* to harden.

徵 *Chï*[3]. One of the five musical notes. See *chêng*[1].

不好色、洞賓說、王母娘娘若不好色、九天仙女是誰生的、王母娘娘說、就算我是好酒色、我却不好財、洞賓說、王母娘娘若不好財、蟠桃會上的香火、都是叫誰收了、王母娘娘說、依你說來、我算好酒色財、却斷不好氣、洞賓說、王母娘娘既不好氣、就該叫我來。○耳[20]目口鼻心膚爲五官、心肝脾肺腎爲五臟、金木風水火土爲五行、青黃赤白黑爲五色、仁義禮智信爲五常、酸甜苦辣鹹爲五味、宮商角徵羽爲五音、東南西北中爲五方、君臣父子夫婦昆弟朋友爲五倫、年高富足康寧有德壽終爲五福、詩經書經易經禮記春秋爲五經。

Mother is not given to avarice, who gets the incense and paper money at the P'an-t'ao Festival?" The Royal Mother replied again, "Well, suppose that I am, as you put it, given to wine, lust and avarice, I am not, however, given to anger." Tung Pin replied, "If the Royal Mother is not given to anger, you ought to allow me to enter."
20 The ears, eyes, mouth, nose and heart (skin), are the five senses; the heart, liver, spleen, lungs and kidneys, are the five viscera; metal, wood (air), water, fire and earth, are the five elements; blue, yellow, red, white and black, are the five colors; benevolence, uprightness, propriety, wisdom and fidelity, are the five virtues; sour, bitter, sweet, pungent and salt, are the five tastes; kung, shang, chioă, tsï and yü, are the five notes; east, west, south, north and middle, are the five quarters; prince and minister, father and son, husband and wife, elder and younger brother, friend and friend, are the five relations; old age, riches, peace, virtue, and death from the weight of years, are the five blessings; the Book of Poetry, the Book of History, the Book of Changes, the Book of Rites and the Book of Annals, are the five Classics.

Notes.

2 The Chinese have an elaborate system of rules for the writing of a standard literary essay, which are explained and illustrated with great painstaking by school teachers. The translations of the four terms here given are only approximate, as no single words of ours will adequately render them.

6 The force of "that man" is given by the 那 in the clause below.

7 聊齋 A book of legends and fabulous exploits, the full title of which is 聊齋誌異. It was written by 蒲松齡, a Shantung scholar, and published in A.D. 1710. The book is valued for its vigorous and elegant style.

9 In China every literary man is supposed to write poetry.

12 生氣 *Living breath*; that is, *the breath of life*,—which is very different from the ordinary meaning, *to become angry*. The difference arises from the double sense of 生, which means both to *produce* and *living*. 分類言之 *To speak of by classes, to classify*.

18 之乎者也 Four of the most common *Wênli* euphonic particles,—used to describe a pedantic style interlarded with *Wênli* words and phrases.

19 呂洞賓 A noted Taoist of the T'ang dynasty versed in all the arts of magic, and who it is said finally attained immortality. In the 12th century temples were erected to him under the title of 純陽子. 王母娘娘, also called 西王母 *The goddess of the "Western Heaven,"* a prominent character in the exploits of 孫悟空, as related in the 西遊記. Her birthday comes on the third of the third month, and is largely observed in some parts of China. The 蟠桃會 is a festival in honor of 王母娘娘, supposed to be held in the Western Paradise, and to be attended by large numbers of gods and genii. It is so called because of the 蟠桃, or *flat spiral peach*, which is to be had at this festival, and the eating of which confers immortality. The story of 呂洞賓 going to this feast and his presence being challenged by the goddess, is not in the 西遊記, but is a popular tradition.

20 The original classification of the senses has the heart as the fifth, it being put for *reflection*. In his Evidences of Christianity, Dr. Martin pointed out this error and the omission of *touch*, and substituted 膚 for 心, which change is generally approved. 官 is used for sense, because each organ *controls* its particular sensation. The mistaken use of 木 as one of the elements, was also pointed out by Dr. Martin, and 風 suggested as a substitute. The Chinese musical

第一百九十七課

李[1]光大就是喜歡戴高帽子兒。○這[2]一回、我和他不是魚死、就是網破。○事[3]情既然做了、還有不透風的牆嗎。○說[4]話不可單踢打瘡疤、叫人落不下臺來。○他[5]正是雨後送傘、我不領他那個空頭情。○單[6]巴掌拍不響、若只一個人的不是、那能打起架來呢。○死[7]了李存孝、顯出王彥章來喇。○總[8]要因才施教、光這樣恨鐵不成鋼的催逼、倒越發把他催糊塗了。○畢[9]先生就是能以吹毛求疵、挑人家的錯、自己脖子後的灰、一點也看不見。○你[10]這樣關之着門起國號、就是不行、必得和我到大街上去講說講說。○已[11]經有現成的樣子、依照着着葫葫蘆蘆畫畫影瓢、還有畫不出來的嗎。○單[12]仗着能說不行、鸚鵡嘴巧、却說不過潼關去。○水[13]淺養不過魚

TRANSLATION.

1 What Li Kwang Ta delights in is to wear a tall hat.

2 I'll have it out with him this time. Either the net will break or the fish will have to die.

3 When a thing is once done, is there any wall that will not let the wind through?

4 In your conversation you should not be always hitting the tender spot and putting people to shame.

5 He is simply bringing me an umbrella after the rain is over. I will not accept his pseudo friendship.

6 A single palm will not clap. If but one is in the wrong, how can you raise a fight?

7 When Li Ts'un Hsiao died, it brought Wang Yien Chang to the front.

8 Instruction should always be proportioned to the ability of the student. To urge him forward beyond his powers of acquirement, is sure to result in all the greater confusion of mind.

9 Mr. Pi is an adept at pointing out other people's pecadillos, but he is quite unaware of the dirt on the back of his own neck.

10 I won't submit to this style of underhand assumption. You must come out on the street and discuss it with me.

11 You had a ready-made pattern. Who could not sketch a dipper (a shadow) with the gourd before him?

12 Trusting merely in your ability to

---

scale consisted originally of the five notes here given, which correspond respectively to C, D, E, G, A, of the Western diatonic scale. In the Han dynasty two additional notes were added, viz., 變徵 or 徵 flat; that is, F, and 變宮 or 宮 flat; that is, B, thus completing the scale, with 徵 or G as key-note. The seven syllables 凡工尺上一四合, given in lesson 103, are used in singing, and correspond to *do*, *re*, *mi*, *fa*, etc. of Western musical notation.

LESSON CXCVII.

PITHY METAPHORS.

The Chinese have in current use a large number of common, but expressive, figures and allusions by means of which they add both force and spice to their ideas. A few such have been introduced in previous lessons. A number of the most common and pithy ones are collected in this lesson, as specimens of many others. The meaning in many cases is evident. In the case of a number, hints are given in the notes. When not understood, a Chinese teacher will take pleasure in explaining them.

來、他光留我、不添錢還行嗎。○張[14]日新並不是個嚼咬牙的人、總是死人底下有活鬼、把他撮弄的。○你[15]的爆熗、爲甚麼叫人家點火呢、你當是看殯的、還怕殯大嗎。○人[16]都是這山望着那山高、其實另找個地方、也不一定就能多弄錢。○老[17]虎不吃回頭食、我既然和他算了賬、就不能再回去了。○不[18]如早早告訴他、這樣雪裏埋死屍、還能埋得住嗎。○他[19]若山上叫的好、我們就山下應的好、他若沒有好吹、我們還能有好打嗎。○這[20]是會上的捐錢、我若是於中取利、到了水落石出的時候、叫衆人一口唾沫就淹死了。○他[21]是欺負我老虎沒有呀啊、那知道騎驢的不濟不中、還有掌鞭的趕脚的呢。○這[22]是他的正

talk will not answer. A parrot's lips are clever, but they will not serve beyond T'ung-kwan.

13 Water that is too shallow will not support fish. For him simply to invite me to stay, without raising my wages, will not answer.

14 Chang I Hsin is not a factious man. It must be that there is a live demon under the dead man stirring him up.

15 Why do you allow other people to set off your fire-crackers? Do you suppose the spectators are afraid that the funeral will be too grand?

16 When one is on this hill, he always thinks the other hill the higher. The fact is, when you find another situation, it is not at all certain that you will better yourself.

17 "A tiger does not eat stale meat." Having settled the account with him, I'll not go back to him again.

18 You would better tell him at once. Can you conceal a dead body by burying it in the snow?

19 If he calls well on the hill, we will respond well from the valley. If he does not blow well, how can we beat a good accompaniment?

20 This money is the contribution of the Church. If I should make a profit out of it, when the water falls and the rock crops out, a few mouthfuls of spittle would drown me.

21 He insults me as being a tiger without teeth, does he? but let him

VOCABULARY.

彥 *Yien*⁴. . . . . . . Elegant; excellent. (w.)

催逼 *Ts'wei*¹ *pi*¹. . . . *To urge*, to press, to drive.

國號 *Kwoá*² *hao*⁴. National name or style; dynastic title.

鸚 *Ying*¹. . . . . . . *A parrot;* a cockatoo.

鵡 *Kê*¹. . . . . . . A wild goose; *a parrot.*

鸚鵡 A parrot.

潼 *T'ung*². . . . . A tributary of the Yellow River.

潼關 *T'ung*² *kwan*¹. A noted pass on the Yellow River in Shansi, where it is joined by the T'ung river.

嚼 *Chiao*¹. . . . . . . To eat, to chew, to bite.

嚼牙 *Chiao*¹ *ya*². Disputatious, *captious*, touchy, querulous.

咬牙 *Yao*³ *ya*². To gnash the teeth; petulant, snappish, *captious.*

捐錢 *Chüên*¹ *ch'ien*². To contribute money; *the money contributed.*

取利 *Ch'ü*³ *li*⁴. To take interest; *to make a profit.*

唾 *T'oá*⁴, *t'u*⁴. . . . . To spit; *saliva.*

唾沫 *T'u*⁴ *moá*⁴. . . . . *Saliva*, spittle.

早遲 *Tsao*³ *ch'i*². . . . . Sooner or later. (s.)

魁星 *K'wei*² *hsing*¹. The chief star of the great dipper :—Note 26.

點狀元 *Tien*³ *chwang*⁴ *yüen*². To attain the degree of 狀元 or first graduate of the Hanlin.

管、必得先商議他、水大還能漫過橋去嗎。○醜[23]媳婦免不了見公婆、你光覺着沒有臉去、早晚(早遲)還脫得了嗎。○孫[24]文慶不過是騎着人的馬、架着人的鷹、所以說話怪氣昂昂的、其實那也不是個咬狠的狗。○我[25]還能叫你墊錢嗎、總是汗打(從)病人身上出、還能把送殯的埋在墳裏嗎。○鹿[26]桂枝、最好以己之長、顯人之短、凡是魁星點狀元、都是他的、武大郎顯魂、都是人家的。○你[27]看如今這些候補官、鑽頭覓縫的、甚麼門路投不到呢。○這[28]可不是誇嘴、咱們的孩子、從來不做這樣半吊子事情、答你筐裏那有爛杏兒、你的麥

remember that although the rider of the donkey is not of much account, there is still the man with the whip.

22 This belongs to his jurisdiction ; you must first consult him. Even high water is not higher than the bridge.

23 "The homely daughter-in-law cannot avoid being seen by her husband's parents." You feel ashamed to go, but sooner or later you cannot help going.

24 The reason Sun Wên Ch'ing talks so loftily, is simply because he is riding another man's horse, and carrying another man's falcon. The fact is, however, that he is not the kind of a dog that will take hold of a wolf.

25 I cannot ask *you* to pay the money. "It is the sick man who must sweat." Who thinks of burying in the grave the friends who go to the funeral ?

26 Lu Kwei Chï is very much given to using his own strong points to expose the weak points of others. Every first degree the reigning star foretells, is his ; and every ghost of misfortune that appears, belongs to some one else.

27 Look at these expectant officials ; there is not a crack they don't worm into, nor a door they don't try.

28 I can say without boasting that our son has never been guilty of such a

縫 *Fêng*4. A seam ; *a crack;* a chance, an ...... opportunity. See *fêng*2.

筐 *K'wang*1.... An open basket without handle.

太歲 *T'ai*4 *swei*4. A great year,—that is, every .... 12th year from the beginning of a cycle ; *a year god:*—Note 30.

叢 *Ts'ung*1,2. A copse ; crowded together, abounding. (w.)

芝 *Chï*1...... The plant of immortality.

蔴 *Ma*2...... The hemp plant ; *sesame.*

芝蔴 Sesame—from which 香油 is made.

船行 *Ch'wan*2 *hang*2....... A shipping office.

彌 *Mi*2... To close up ; to complete : more. (w.)

陀 *T'oă*2...... A steep and rugged path. (w.)

阿彌陀 *Oă*1 *mi*2 *t'oă*2........... Amitâbha.

龍王 *Lung*2 *wang*2. The Dragon-king, the Rain-god ; Neptune.

NOTES.

4 落不下臺來 *Not able to let down (or come down from) the stage ;* that is, *out of countenance, put to shame.*

7 李存孝 and 王彥章 Two famous athletes of the after Han dynasty, of whom the former excelled the latter in strength and eclipsed his fame. When the former died, the latter had the field. The exploits of the two men are constantly introduced in theatrical plays, hence the currency of the saying.

8 恨鐵不成鋼 ; that is, 恨不能鐵要成鋼. Iron becomes steel by fierce heat and much labor, which is here compared to the pressure used to urge a student forward in his studies.

10 關着門起國號 *To close the doors and lay claim to the empire ;* that is, *to make extravagant pretensions which will not bear the light of publicity.*

12 潼關 A famous pass on the Yellow River in Shansi. There is a popular tradition that parrots South of this pass can talk, while those North of it cannot, and that those from the South, brought North through the pass, always lose the power of speaking.

15 Why do you let another man manage your affairs ? Do you suppose he cares how much trouble he gets you into.

18 It is vain to bury the body of a murdered man in the snow, in hope of concealing the murder.

子那裏有黑麪呢。○如[29]今的世界、是牆倒衆人推、所以人到倒運的時候、是鬼也朝（望）着颳颴風。○俗[30]語說、好漢不吃眼前虧、你怎麼單上太歲頭上去動土呢、答 我劃上拿着雞蛋碰石柱子、也要碰他一下。○叢[31]天柱那個人、成天家陳穀子爛芝蔴的、也不知那裏來的那麼些話、還帶着說的驢脣不對馬嘴、叫人聽着眞不入耳。○若[32]看他說話的樣子、眞是滿臉的天官賜福、但看他所作的事情、却是一肚子男盜女娼。○我[33]已經上船行去打聽明白了、前日壞的那號船、名叫大孝子、咱們的孩子坐的船、名叫水兎子、所以只管放心罷、答 阿彌陀佛、別管怎麼樣、咱們的孩子沒跟了龍王爺去就好。

silly piece of business as this. *Ans.* Oh no! *Your* basket has no rotten apricots in it; *your* wheat never makes dark flour.

29 In these times everybody pushes at a crumbling wall; hence when fortune fails a man, every demon blows a whirlwind at him.

30 The saying is, "A valiant man does not invite defeat with his eyes open." How is it that you persist in flying in the face of T'ai-swei? *Ans.* I'll risk it. I will have a round with him, even if it *is* smashing an egg against a stone pillar.

31 Ts'ung T'ien Chu is constantly spinning out old wives' stories; the wonder is where all his talk comes from; and moreover, he rattles on in a hap-hazzard way that is most unpleasant to hear.

32 If you regard his manner of speaking, his face beams with a celestial benediction; but if you look at his conduct, his heart is filled with violence and uncleanness.

33 I have already been to the shipping office and made inquiry. The ship that was wrecked day before yesterday, was called the Most Filial Son, the ship that our boy sailed in was called the Water Rabbit; so that you may set your heart at rest. *Ans.* Amitâbha Buddha! Only so that our boy hasn't fallen into the hands of Neptune it is all right.

20 於中取利 A *Wênli* expression, but frequently used in colloquial.

22 The bridge is above the water, otherwise it would not be a bridge. You cannot avoid consulting the man to whom it legitimately belongs to control the business in question.

23 公婆 A contracted combination of 公公 and 婆婆.

26 魁星 This star is regarded as the palace of the God of Literature, and is put by metonymy for the god himself. He is the patron divinity who presides over literary examinations and directs the conferring of degrees on worthy candidates. 武大郎, having been murdered is supposed to appear as a vengeful ghost, and his apparition is a sure sign of ill-luck, (See Les. 83, Note 19).

27 鑽頭覓縫 *The drill seeks the crack;* that is, the drill is bound to get in, and is sure to find a crack if there is one.

29 倒 refers to the wall being weak, and down in places. 是鬼 is equal to 逢是鬼, *every demon—even the least one.* 望 is here equivalent to 向. Whirlwinds are attributed to demons, and, especially in certain circumstances, are regarded as ominous of evil.

30 好漢 He is not considered a *valiant man* who exposes himself to certain defeat. He should be *shrewd* enough to submit temporarily, if necessary, and await a better opportunity to exhibit his prowess. 太歲 is a star god who presides over the year. He moves or turns about each year to a different quarter North, South, East or West. In breaking ground for a grave or a house it is important to avoid offending him by digging in the wrong place. The interpretation of his movements and his preferences forms a part of the art of Feng-shwei. He is very irascible, and when angered visits with calamities.

31 不入耳 *Not entering the ear;* that is, *such as the ear dislikes to hear.*

32 天官賜福 The president of the 吏部, now called a 尙書, was in former times called 天官, and as he was the head of the bureau of civil office, all the emoluments of office came through him, and to enjoy his favoring smile was to be in luck. Others say that 天官, as here used, refers to a guardian spirit or patron divinity of each family, through whose agency and by whose favor blessings are obtained.

33 阿彌陀佛 *Amitâbha Buddha,* here used as a devout expression of thankfulness, similar to, Thank God!

第一百九十八課

人[1]家都會彎彎曲曲、咱們是衚衕(巷子)裏赶驢、直打直。○你[2]當是我還和他望長久遠嗎、不過是沙鍋(砸填搗)蒜、一槌子的買賣。○他[3]不好、有他老的教訓、你這不是狗拿耗子、(狗捉老鼠)多管閒事嗎。○哎[4]呀李茍儉大哥、今天穿上新衣裳去咯、這可是大姑娘做新娘子(媳婦)頭一回(遭)啊。○他[5]把李成美蹧蹋的太苦咯、眞是王胖子跳井、下不去的事情。○這[6]個人情、非陶先生講不下來、答你把我誇獎的、眞是一張紙畫了個鼻子、好大臉哪。○那[7]樣的兒子、還能養他老嗎、依我說、那是雞菢鴨子、枉費了心。○我[8]們交人是單論心術、不論貧富、他却不然、他是單上老虎頭上抓抓

TRANSLATION.

1 Others can make shifts and turns; with us it is driving a donkey through an alley—straight ahead.

2 Did you suppose I intended to continue permanently in his company? It was nothing more than pounding garlic in an earthen stew-pan—a matter of one stroke.

3 If he is bad, let his parents correct him: are not you just a dog catching rats—meddling in other people's business?

4 Hurrah! brother Li Kou Chien has his new clothes on to-day. This is the young lady become a bride—for the first time.

5 He abused Li Ch'êng Mei too outrageously. It's a veritable case of fat Wang jumping into the well—won't go down.

6 This favor none but you, Mr. Tao, could have procured. *Ans.* You praise me as though you took a whole sheet of paper to sketch a nose—give me an enormous face.

7 Will a son like that support him in his old age? In my opinion it is a hen hatching ducks—a waste of care.

8 In making friends we regard character, not position. Not so with him; he seeks to catch his lice on (to scratch) a tiger's head—wants to curry favor with the great.

LESSON CXCVIII.

WITTICISMS.

The Chinese term here translated witticism is 坎, which means literally a pit, a trap, a turning point, and figuratively, a witticism, including innuendos, double-entendre, witty allusions, etc. These witticisms are generally spoken of as 調坎; read by some *t'iao*² *k'an*³, an adjusted device or turn, a play upon words; by others *tiao*⁴ *k'an*³, a moveable trick or turn, an ingenious transposition of words or figures. Colloquial Chinese abounds in such witticisms, but the majority of them are local in their use, and very many of them involve vulgar allusions. I have taken pains to collect a number of such as have the widest currency, and are presentable in print.

VOCABULARY.

搷 *Tien*¹. *To pound as in a mortar*, to bruise, to thump.

槌 *Ch'wei*². A mallet, a maul, a bat, a beetle.

陶 *T'ao*². A kiln; to please; correct.

虱 *Shï*¹. A louse.

抓癢 *Chwa*¹ *yang*³. To scratch oneself, to scratch an itchy place. (s.)

搒 *Pên*¹. To fumble; *to reach after*, to pull down; to push apart, to bend aside.

堂口 *T'ang*² *k'ou*³. Ability to plead or state a case in court.

虱子、(癢) 最好搽攀大頭子。○這[9]家子是怕那家子的堂口好、那家子就怕這家子有門路、所以他們是麻稭(檾稭)棍兒打狼、兩頭兒害怕。○人[10]家待他不好、那是他脚上的泡、自己走的、還埋怨誰呢。○他[11]任甚麼不會做倒罷了、還又好吃、又好穿、你說將來怎麼過日子呢、答可不是、那纔是鷹嘴鴨子爪、能吃不能拿的東西。○人[12]那能都是伶俐、沒有蠢笨的呢、但蠢笨也得不大離格(離經)、這個是擀麪杖吹火、一竅不通。○他[13]指望花幾吊錢、打官司能轉轉臉、究竟花了錢、還輸了官司、真是大姑娘下館子、人錢兩丟。○纔[14]有了幾個錢、他就鬧這些架子、看起來總是小廟的菩薩(神)、問怎麼講、答

9 This party fears that party's ability to plead; and that party fears this party has a friend at court; hence they are [like a man] attacking a wolf with a hemp stalk—both parties afraid.

10 If others treat him badly—that is a blister on his foot, raised by his own walking. He has none to blame but himself.

11 I could put up with her utter inefficiency, but, in addition, she wants the best of food and clothes. How do you think I can make a living? *Ans.* Sure enough. It is a case of hawk's beak and duck's claws—able to eat but not to catch.

12 Of course all cannot be bright and none stupid, and yet stupidity must be within reasonable bounds. With this fellow it is like using the rolling-pin to blow the fire—entirely impenetrable.

13 He hoped that by spending a few thousand cash in a lawsuit, he could put a fair face on the business, but in the end he spent his money and lost his suit. In fact it was the young lady visiting the saloon—girl and money both lost.

14 As soon as he gets a little money, he begins to make all this spread. Evidently he is, after all, only the god of a small temple. *Ques.* What does

---

檾 *Ch'ing*³. A species of hemp growing five or six feet high.

蠢笨 *Ch'un*³ *pên*⁴. Obtuse, *stupid*, dull, thick-headed.

擀麪杖 *Kan*³ *mien*⁴ *chang*⁴. . . . . A rolling-pin.

轉臉 *Chwan*³ *lien*³. To come off with a good face, to get well out of a difficulty.

培 *P'ei*². To heap up earth; to cultivate; to assist.

癩 *Lai*⁴. Any pustular eruption of the skin; mange, *leprosy*, scabies. (s.) See *lai*¹.

蝦 *Ha*², *hê*². . . . . A frog, a toad. Also *hsia*¹.

蟆 *Moă*¹, *ma*¹. . . . . A frog, a toad.

蝦蟆 A frog, a toad.

天鵝 *T'ien*¹ *oă*². . . . . A crane.

坐堂 *Tsoă*⁴ *t'ang*². *To sit on the judgment seat*, to hold court, to try a case.

跪鎖 *Kwei*⁴ *soă*³. To kneel on chains:—Note 16.

跪鍊子 *Kwei*⁴ *lien*⁴ *tsï*³. . . . . The same.

壓杠子 *Ya*¹ *kang*⁴ *tsï*³. A mode of torture:—Note 16.

跴杠子 *Ts'ai*³ *kang*⁴ *tsï*³. . . . . The same.

扛枷 *K'ang*² *chia*¹. . . . . To wear a cangue.

和而流 *Hê*² *êr*⁴ *liu*². *Following the current*; compliant, pliable.

冒失鬼 *Mao*⁴ *shï*¹ *kwei*³. A dare devil, *a reckless genius*.

刀筆 *Tao*¹*pi*³. A pen like a knife, a pungent writer, *a specialist* in writing indictments.

覿 *Ti*² . . . To see face to face, to have audience.

從來沒見過大香火。○李[15]培基那個樣子、還想着說陳宅的姑娘、那不是癩蝦蟆想吃天鵝肉、枉費了心思嗎。○昨[16]天我上衙門、遇見官坐堂、逼問連子的口供、又跪跪鍊子鎖、又跴壓杠子、跴壓的兩回沒有氣兒、看着眞可憐人、答他那是木匠扛枷、自作自受、誰叫他偷人家的呢。○到[17]對詞的時候、我也不能格外厚着你、也不能格外厚着他、我是竈王爺上天、有一句說一句。○雖[18]然不可和而流、但是當今的時勢、也不可太板滯了、總得八仙桌子盖井口、隨的方就的圓纔行。○增[19]福眞是冒失鬼一個、不管做甚麼、是老虎入山洞、顧前不顧後的。○這[20]張呈

that mean? *Ans.* He has never enjoyed any large sticks of incense.

15 A man like Li P'ei Chi thinking to marry a daughter of the Ch'ên family! Isn't that a leprous toad wanting a crane for a roast—a vain wish?

16 I went to the court-room yesterday, and happened in when the officer was on the bench extorting a confession from Lien-tsï. They made him kneel on a chain and then pressed him with a pole until he fainted twice. It was indeed a pitiful sight. *Ans.* That was the carpenter wearing the cangue—suffering the result of his own doings. Who required him to steal?

17 When the trial comes on I will neither be partial to you, nor will I be partial to him. Like Tsao Wang when he goes up to heaven, I will speak according to the facts.

18 Although one should not simply float with the current, yet in these times it will not do to be too unyielding. When it is a case of covering the well with a square table, you must accommodate the square to the round.

19 Tsêng Fu is one reckless genius. He goes at everything like a tiger entering into a cave—cares for the front, not for the rear.

覿面 *Ti² mien⁴*. . . . . Face to face. (w.)
奉承 *Fêng⁴ ch'êng²*. To compliment, *to flatter; . . . .* to pay court to.
後媽 *Hou⁴ ma¹*. . . . . . A step-mother.
後老婆 *Hou⁴ lao³ p'oă²*. . . . . . A second wife.
生生 *Shêng¹ shêng¹*. Simply; just, sheerly; *literally.*
活活 *Hwoă² hwoă²*. . . . . The same.
忠厚 *Chung¹ hou⁴*. Large-hearted, generous, *kindly.*

NOTES.

1 直打直 *Straight strike straight, or, straight and still more straight;* that is, *straightforward without turning to the right hand or to the left.*

2 望長久遠 *Looking towards a long drawn out continuance;* that is, *expecting or desiring a permanent continuance,*—a redundant colloquial quadruplet phrase. 買賣 is frequently used colloquially in the sense of *affair.*

5 It is not known why the ideal fat man is called Wang.

6 How big must that face be which requires a whole sheet of paper to draw a nose!—even such a face would it require to receive without blushing your extravagant praise.

8 貧富 *Poverty or wealth;* that is, *position in society.* 大頭子 *A prominent or influential man whose favor is worth courting.* In China the tiger is the king of beasts.

12 A bamboo tube is often used to blow the fire when kindling it. There is a pun on the word 竅, it being used literally for a hole or opening through which to blow, and figuratively for the seven supposed avenues of knowledge to the mind.

13 A respectable girl would compromise her reputation by going into a wine-shop.

14 小廟的神 A god in a small temple is not supposed to be accustomed to the enjoyment of large sticks of incense. 菩薩 is much more used in the South than in the North, largely taking the place of 神 in popular usage.

15 Notice how 癩 and 天 are balanced against each other in the structure of the sentence.

16 跪鎖 *To kneel with bare knees on a pile of coiled*

子、雖是刀筆先生寫的、却是王胖子的褲帶、希鬆平常。○我21這不是當面奉承你、我看老兄現在如同囊中之錐、不久就要出頭喇。○王22化南要打發他大兒子上關東、我看這可是羊肉包子打狗、有去無回、問怎麽說呢、答怎麽說、你知道他這個兒子、在他後媽手裏受了多少氣呢、要吃沒有吃的的吃、要穿沒有穿的的穿、動不動還要打打罵罵、王化南也作不下了後老婆子的主兒、所以他這一走、活生活生是叫他後媽逼出去了、而且那個小子、長的多麽伶俐、爲人多麽忠厚、那裏不能成家立業、他還回來作什麽呢。

20 Although this indictment was written by a specialist, yet it is like the girdle of fat Wang—loose and ordinary.

21 In speaking thus I am not simply flattering you. As I see it, my brother, you are like an awl in a sack. You'll show your head before long.

22 Wang Hwa Nan is sending his eldest son to Manchuria. In my opinion this is throwing a mutton dumpling at a dog—all outlay and no income. *Ques.* How is that? *Ans.* How is it! Don't you know that this son has suffered a deal of abuse at the hands of his step-mother? He could neither get anything to eat nor anything to wear, and was frequently beaten and reviled. Wang Hwa Nan also is quite unable to control this second wife, so that his son has been literally driven away by his step-mother. Moreover, the boy is naturally very bright, and he has a very kindly way with him; he can succeed in the world anywhere; why should he return?

chains. 鎖 appears to be used for 鎖鍊. The Southern form is the more correct. 壓杠子 A mode of torture in which the prisoner is made to kneel, while a carrying-pole is laid across the legs behind the knees and another placed under the arms, which are tied together and forced backward for the purpose. One lictor then stands on each end of the lower pole and lifts on the upper one. These modes of torture are frequently combined. They are extra-legal, but are very frequently resorted to by magistrates.

17 In making his report to 玉皇上帝, *Tsao Wang* is generally credited with telling the strict truth.

19 冒失鬼一個 *One reckless devil;* 一個, as here used *after* the descriptive term, is quite like the English use of *one* before it.

20 刀筆先生 A writer who, figuratively speaking, uses a knife for a pen. Commonly applied to the 訟師 who hang about yamêns and manage lawsuits.

22 When you throw a dumpling at a dog, instead of hurting the dog, he eats the dumpling and you lose it and get no return for it. 沒有的吃 is an inversion of 沒有吃的. Similar inversions are frequently heard in the North.

LESSON CXCIX.

PUNS.

The Chinese word for a pun is 雙關, *a double relation.* The fact that nearly all the syllables in the Chinese language are repeated in a large number of words, greatly facilitates punning. Notwithstanding this fact, however, punning is not more frequent in Chinese than in English. Perhaps the very facility offered detracts from the spice of the pun. A Chinese pun is *spoken* but cannot ordinarily be *written*, save by doubling the line as I have done, which, however, is like explaining a joke. Occasionally the pun turns on the double use of a single character, in which case the pun becomes like a pun in English. (4), (10), (16), (18). The translation of these puns, as such, is of course impossible; even to indicate their existence in a suitable manner, has been found a matter of no small difficulty.

第一百九十九課

那[1]個人是牆頭上種白菜、難交澆。○我[2]比常年不能多花、也不
能少花、還是外甥打燈籠、照舊舅。○咱[3]們說話辦事、都是杵頭
掉在碓臼裏、實石打打實石。○這[4]個學生一點出息沒有、究竟是兩
眼抹石灰、白瞎。○我[5]在他手下、直直成了小爐匠的櫃子、動
手就是錯銼。○你[6]是二十四孝、大閒賢人。○你[7]說這話、眞是兩手
捧壽桃、有理禮。○看[8]不得他初去的時候香甜、歸歸實期是薙頭的
扁担、長長遠軟不了。○你[9]去可要小心一點、別叫他們毀喇、答我
告訴你罷、老虎拉車、沒有敢趕的。○他[10]的尊長們說他倒罷了、
若是我們說他、豈不叫他說、我們是一根筷子吃藕、挑眼嗎。
○那[11]個孩子實在不成孩子、答送送子子生孫娘娘破了褡子、纔不成盛。

TRANSLATION.

1 That man is like cabbage planted on the top of a wall,—very hard to {water. / keep on good terms with.}

2 I cannot give more than common, nor will I offer less. It is still the nephew carrying the lantern,—{lighting his uncle. / as before.}

3 All *we* say and do is like the pestle falling into the mortar,—{stone upon stone. / truth upon truth.}

4 There is no outcome to this pupil; finally it will be a case of rubbing lime in both eyes,—{clear blind. / a total loss.}

5 In his employ, I find myself like the tool-chest of a traveling tinker,—every movement is {a stroke of the file. / a mistake.}

6 You are an embodiment of filial piety, —a great {saint. / idler.}

7 What you say is like presenting longevity cakes with both hands,—{very polite. / very reasonable.}

8 Don't be misled by his affability at first. After all he will be like a barber's carrying stick,—wanting in {length and flexibility. / continuance.}

9 If you go, you must be a little careful and not let them use you up. *Ans.* Let me tell you; when a tiger pulls the wagon, nobody {drives. / dares.}

10 For the older members of the family to reprove him is all right; but if we do it, he will be sure to say we are eating water-lily root with one chop-stick,—{lifting by a hole. / hard to please.}

11 Really that child is not going to come to anything. *Ans.* It is only when the Goddess of Maternity tears her satchel that the child {drops out. / comes to nothing.}

VOCABULARY.

常年 *Ch'ang*² *nien*². In ordinary years, commonly.

石灰 *Shï*² *hwei*¹. .... Lime.

香甜 *Hsiang*¹ *t'ien*². *Affable*, agreeable, delicious, sweet.

捧 *P'êng*³. To hold in both hands; *to present respectfully in both hands*, to offer.

長遠 *Ch'ang*² *yüen*³. *Continuous*, lasting, permanent.

送生娘娘 *Sung*⁴ *shêng*¹ *niang*². The goddess who bestows children:—Note 11.

子孫娘娘 *Tsï*³ *sun*¹ *niang*². .... The same.

送子娘娘 *Sung*⁴ *tsï*³ *niang*². ..... The same.

呱 *Wa*¹. To cry, *to bawl*; to groan, to sob:—Note 13.

成功 *Ch'êng*² *kung*¹. Accomplished, *finished*, consummated.

孩子咯。○有[12]三個匠人、一塊兒給人說事、木匠說、我們給他一句鋸兩開、鐵匠說、給他一合火成功、石匠說、不然、還是一起一起的來。○做[13]什麼這麼喞喞呀喇呱呱呀喇的、眞是蝦子蓋量棗、什麼聲升兒。○這[14]一連多少日子、不是下就是陰、總沒有露太陽的時候、今日却是新媳婦哭男人、號好天。○從[15]來說、大人不見小人過、若和他鬭、不丟人嗎、對我也不是個大人、答你不是大人難道是個小人不成。○有[16]個窮人、過年沒有錢買香、就將一個枯樹不子燒起來、供養財神、財神格外歡喜、就叫他發了大財、所以到第二個年節、那人特爲買了頂高的線香、供養財神、財神見今年的香、大不如上年的那麼粗、就嘆了一口氣、底下的人說、老爺不要動怒、如今的人、都是越有越細。○孫[17]保安在年輕

12 Three artizans once joined together as mediators in a certain case. The carpenter said, "Let us cut the knot in two with {one saw-cut." / one word.} The blacksmith said, "Let us settle the business up {at one heat." / by a compromise.} The stone-cutter said, "Not so; let us rather proceed {a stone at a time." / step by step.}

13 What are you making such a hubbub about? It is a veritable measuring of dates with a lobster shell—what a {peck! / noise!}

14 For these ever so many days it has been either raining or cloudy, with no sunshine at all, but to-day it is the bride wailing for her husband,—{calling on Heaven. / a clear day.}

15 It has been said that the man of high degree does not take offence at the man of low degree. Will we not be disgracing ourselves to quarrel with him? *Rep.* But I am not a man of high degree. *Ans.* Well, supposing you are not, you hardly count yourself a mean man do you?

16 A poor man had no money to buy incense at the new year, so he took a half rotten stump and burned it as an offering to the God of Wealth. The God of Wealth was especially pleased and made him rich. Therefore at the next new year, the man took pains to buy the best quality of fine incense and offer to him. He, seeing that the sticks of incense were ever so much less than that offered the year before, drew a long sigh. His servants said to him, "Don't be angry, your worship. In these times the more a man has the {smaller / closer} he becomes."

號天 *Hao² t'ien¹*. To call to Heaven for help in distress, to wail.

好天 *Hao³ t'ien¹*. A clear day, a fair day, *fair weather*. [Note 16.

不 *Tun¹*. ... *A stump*, a stub; a block of wood:—

樹不 *Shu⁴ tun¹*. ... A stump.

供養 *Kung⁴ yang³*. To present offerings to the dead; to worship with offerings of food and incense.

財神 *Ts'ai² shên²*. The God of Wealth:—Note 16.

年節 *Nien² chie²*. ... New year's festival.

動怒 *Tung⁴ nu⁴*. *To grow angry*, to lose the temper. [vaunt.

自誇 *Tsï⁴ k'wa¹*. ... *To boast*, to brag, to

答道 *Ta¹ tao⁴*. To speak in reply, *to reply*, to respond. [farrier.

獸醫 *Shou⁴ i¹*. ... A veterinary surgeon, a

問道 *Wên⁴ tao⁴*. ... *To ask*, to question.

連忙 *Lien² mang²*. Hurriedly; *excitedly*, quickly, hastily.

的時候、花錢就和花泥錢的一樣、現在忽然回了頭、不但捨不得花錢、又殷殷勤勤的過日子、那眞是船板做棺材、飄流了半輩子、到老來纔成人。○依[18]我說、他不自誇還少丢點人兒、誰不知他母親是個巫婆、和一個衙役搭夥計、纔有了他呢、答這名謂抱着孩子進當舖、自己當人、人家却不當人。○有[19]一隻病虎、被孫眞人治好了、從此這虎就在孫眞人門下聽用、這一天、孫眞人打發虎去下帖請客、客一位也沒來、孫眞人就問虎說、某先生怎麽沒來呢、虎回答說、叫我吃了、又問某先生呢、虎說也叫我吃了、孫眞人大怒、罵那虎說、你這畜牲、既不會請客、怎麽又去吃人。○王[20]二稜的父親和爺爺、都是當獸醫出身、有一天他問一個行路的人說、客作什麽生意發財、那客答

17 When Sun Pao An was a young man, he spent cash as if they were made of common clay; but he has now suddenly reformed, and not only is sparing in the use of money but is diligently making a living. That's a veritable case of making a ship's side into a coffin,—{floating / dissipating} half a lifetime and in old age {containing / becoming} a man.

18 In my opinion he would disgrace himself less if he boasted less. Who does not know that his mother was a sorceress, who took up with a yamên runner and gave birth to him? *Ans.* His case is what is called carrying a child to the pawn shop,—he {wished to pawn a man / considers himself a man} but {pawnbrokers / others} do not {take man on pawn. / consider him a man.}

19 A sick tiger was once cured by Sun Chên Jên, and ever afterwards the tiger served in his family. One day Sun Chên Jên sent the tiger to carry round his card inviting some guests to a feast. But not a single one of the guests came. Sun Chên Jên asked the tiger, saying, "Why has not so and so come?" The tiger replied, "I ate him." He then asked for so and so. The tiger said, "I ate him also." Upon this Sun Chên Jên got angry and reviled the tiger, saying, "You beast you! Since you do not know how to invite {guests / others} why do you go and eat {them?" / theirs?}

20 Wang Êr Lêng's father and grandfather were farriers by profession. Meeting a traveler one day, he asked him what line of business he was in. The stranger replied, "I am

NOTES.

3 實打實 is a colloquial intensive, equivalent to 實實在在.

4 There is here a double pun—one in the use of 白 and one in the use of 瞎. To gratify spite on an enemy lime is sometimes thrown or rubbed in the eyes, producing blindness.

5 When a tinker files an article, he supports it on the top of his tool-chest, and also steadies his file by having a handle on its outer end, which works back and forth through a ring on the top of the same tool-chest.

6 The 二十四孝 is a small book or tract containing twenty-four stories of notable instances of filial piety. It is sometimes distributed by zealous religionists as a work of merit.

7 壽桃 are cakes made in the shape of peaches, with the character 壽 imprinted on them in red. A plate of them is sent as a complimentary present on the occasion of a birth-day.

8 The regulation *pien-tan* used by barbers to carry their kit is both *short* and *stiff*.

11 子孫娘娘 The goddess by whose favor parents beget children, and to whom women pray for the coveted blessing of bearing children. She is sometimes confounded with 觀音, though not by any means the same as the well known Goddess of Mercy. The term most commonly used in Shantung is 送生娘娘, the goddess who presents or brings the children to the mother. She is popularly represented as carrying the children in a bag or satchel thrown across her shoulder. In the South 送子娘娘 is also used.

12 一鋸兩開 *Divide into two at one cut of the saw.* A single millstone, either upper or lower, is called 一起 *one lift*,—the 起 being used as a classifier.

道、沒有生意、我是個耍手藝的、王二稜只當他說是耍獸醫的、就跳上前去、把那客打了一個跟頭、那客連忙爬起來問道、你爲什麼打我呢、我說耍手藝、還說耍你來嗎、王二稜說、你若耍我倒還罷了、你耍我爹爹和我爺爺、我還能讓你白耍了嗎。○有[21]一個花子粧啞吧、在街上要錢、常用手指碗、又指口、呀呀的叫、有一天他拿着兩個錢、去買酒吃、吃完了說、再添些給我、賣酒的說、你向來不會說話、今天怎麼說起話來咯、花子說、向來我沒有錢、怎麼能說話呢、今天有了兩個錢、自然就會說話了。○姓[22]孫的僱了一個夥計、因爲多日未曾吃麪、臉上很不歡喜、東家問他說、你這幾天怎麼不歡喜呢、他回答說、我們離家在外的人、多日沒有見麪面、那裏那些歡喜呢。

not in business; I am a mechanic." Wang Êr Lêng supposing he said, "I make game of farriers," rushed at the stranger and knocked him headlong. The stranger, picking himself up, asked excitedly, "What did you strike me for? Was my saying I was a mechanic any insult to you?" Wang Êr Lêng replied, "If you made game of *me*, I could put up with it, but do you suppose I will let you go free when you make game of my father and grandfather?"

21 A certain beggar was accustomed to go along the street pretending that he was dumb, pointing to his rice-bowl and then to his mouth and uttering inarticulate sounds. One day he took two cash and went and bought a drink of wine. When he had drunk it all up, he said, "Give me a little more." The wine-seller said, "Heretofore you were unable to speak; how is it that you can speak to-day?" He said, "Heretofore I had no cash, how could I speak? To-day I have {two / a few} cash and as a matter of course I can speak."

22 A man named Sun hired a workman, and because for a long while he got no vermicelli to eat, the workman's face had an unhappy expression. His employer asked, "How is it that you look so sad these days?" to which he replied, "How should we, who are away from our friends, keep all the while smiling, when we do not see {their faces / vermicelli} for so long?"

13 唧喇呱喇, or 唧呀呱呀 *Fussing and crying; the confused noise of children talking and shouting and crying, hubbub, uproar.* The 喇 and 呀 are added in each case in order to separate and emphasize the other words.

15 "Mean" here makes the same pun in English that 小 does in Chinese.

16 不 is a colloquial character made by cutting off the top of 木 which makes a *wooden stump*. 財神 is the most popular and universally worshiped god in China. He is regarded as being the deified spirit of 比干, *Pi Kan*, a relative of the famous tyrant 紂辛. Pi Kan reproved the tyrant for his vices, upon which the tyrant ordered him to be put to death and his heart taken out, to see if there were really seven orifices (竅) in it, as was popularly reported. He was subsequently canonized as the God of Wealth.

17 There is here a double pun—one in 飄流 and one in 盛(成)人.

18 搭夥計 *To become companions*—as applied to a man and a woman—to live together temporarily as husband and wife, without any recognized marriage.

19 孫眞人 A famous physician of the Tang dynasty, whose real name was 孫思邈. There is a pun in both 請客 and 吃人.

20 耍手藝 *To play at a trade*; that is, *to work at or follow a trade.* This derived use of 耍 came probably from the effort of the artizan to polish and ornament his work so as to please and gratify the taste of the purchaser.

21 The pun here turns on the double use of 兩個 and involves a fling at the egotism of those who have *a little* money.

第二百課

你[1]別鬧、我打破個謎兒給你猜、一棵小樹刺鋪拉、開花結實又開花、你猜是什麼、答是棵棉花。○看[2]不見擋上一層、是甚麼呢、答眼鏡。○爲[3]你纔做、做了你又不喫、打一物籠嘴。籠嘴笊鐵○越[4]洗越骯髒、不洗倒乾淨、打一物水。○左[5]看三十一、右看一十三、左右一齊看、三百二十三、打一字非。○高[6]家的頭、李家的腳、陳家的耳朶反安着、打一姓郭。○小[7]小諸葛亮、坐在中軍帳、擺下八卦陣、捉拿飛虎將、打一活物蜘蛛。○手[8]掌大小一隻船、紅娘子在裏邊、一

TRANSLATION.

1 Don't be naughty and I'll make a riddle for you to guess. A little tree with spreading branches. It blooms, and when the fruit is ripe, it blooms again. Guess what it is. *Ans.* A stalk of cotton.

2 When you can't see, you put a screen between. What is it? *Ans.* Spectacles.

3 It was made (because you / for you to) eat, and now that it is made you do not eat. *Fits an article.* A muzzle.

4 Washing makes it more and more dirty; it is cleaner without washing. *Fits a thing.* Water.

5 Looking at the left it counts 31, at the right 13, and at both sides together 323. *Fits a character.* 非.

6 Mr. Kao's head, Mr. Li's foot, and Mr. Ch'ên's ear set on the wrong side. *Fits a surname.* 郭.

7 A wee wee Chu Kê Liang, sitting in an adjutant's tent, spreads out his radial array, to take prisoner the swift tiger braves. *Fits a living thing.* A spider.

8 A boat as large as your palm, containing a lady dressed in red. Down comes a shower of misty rain, but the boat comes along and all is dry. *Fits a utensil.* A charcoal iron.

LESSON CC.

RIDDLES AND EPIGRAMMATIC DISTICHES.

The Chinese term for a riddle, puzzle, or enigma is 謎語, or oftener in colloquial, simply 謎兒, which is pronounced mêr—as if written 悶兒. A considerable number of riddles and puzzles may be turned up, if one gets hold of a man who has a taste for such things and knows where to go to find them. I have not, however, heard of any published book specially devoted to riddles and enigmas. Some Chinese riddles evince considerable ingenuity, while others are but indifferent efforts. Many of their riddles contain puns, and some are based on puns. Nearly all have at least one rhyme. Many of them are based on the dissection of characters. Puzzles are often made by a ridiculous transformation of some passage from the classics, as (17), (19).

A much more popular and widely cultivated playing upon words is the 對兒 or 對子, an epigrammatic distich, which consists of two lines of equal length and corresponding structure, but of different though correlated sentiment. Nouns are mated with nouns, verbs with verbs, particles with particles; also numbers with numbers, places with places, virtues with virtues, etc. The last words do not usually rhyme, and the tones should be opposite. The 對子 is a favorite style of embodying and exhibiting weighty or complimentary sentiments, as in the common 對聯, or wall scroll, and in 門對子, or door mottoes. Some of these 對子 are the product of much thought and skill, and exhibit the capabilities of Chinese writing to its best advantage. A number of collections of them are published. 對子 become a means of amusement and a test of literary skill, when one person proposes the first line and challenges another to match it. The proposer is of course supposed to be able to furnish the required line if the other party fails.

陣霧露雨、船到水就乾、打一用物 熅斗。○小[9]小明光棍、常在繡房裏混、穿過一些綾羅綢緞、陪伴一些美色佳人、打一物 針。○一[10]家分兩院、兩院子孫多、多的倒比少的少、少的倒比多的多、打一物 算盤。○弟[11]兄兩個一樣高、腰裏綑着黑絲縚、大哥大哥等等我、我上陰間走一遭、打一物 水筲。○荒[12]郊野外一塊材、能工巧匠作出來、讀書的公子拉一把、他把公子抱在懷、打一物 圈椅子。○自[13]幼兒紅顏美俊、被他人纏繞得黑瘦三分、不料他心不良棄舊換新、倒忘了原當初結髮之親、打一物 舊紅頭繩。○二[14]人重疊高過天、十女共耕半畝田、我不騎羊羊騎我、千里姻緣一線牽、打四字 夫妻義重。○目[15]字加兩點、莫作貝字猜、貝字欠兩點、莫作目字猜、打

9 A bright little slip of a fellow, constantly lounging in the ladies' boudoir; used to {wearing / running through} silk and satin, and to being the companion of blooming beauties. *Fits an implement.* A needle.

10 A certain family lived in two courts with many children in each, and, strange to say, the greater were less than the lesser and the less were more than the greater. *Fits an article.* An abacus.

11 Two brothers just the same height; around each waist a sash of black; wait, brother, wait for me, while I take a trip to hades and back. *Fits an article.* A pair of water-buckets.

12 A stick of timber in the wild woodland, wrought by the artificer's skillful hand. A gentleman student {gives it a pull / takes hold of one} and it folds him to its breast. *Fits an article.* A bow-backed chair.

13 From youth I was ruddy and beautiful, but a fellow wound me around him and made me one-third black and thin, and then—would you think it—ungratefully cast me aside for a new one, forgetting the original affiance of youth. *Fits an article.* An old red hair-string.

14 Two men piled up higher than heaven. Ten women together farming a half acre of land. I don't ride on a sheep, but a sheep rides on me. Mates distant a thousand miles still drawn by one line. *Fits four characters.* With husband and wife kindness is all-important.

15 An eye adding two dots, but don't guess a treasure; a treasure wanting two dots, but don't guess an eye. *Fits two characters.* 貿資.

VOCABULARY.

鋪拉 *P'u¹ la¹*. To spread out with the hands; .... scattered about, *wide-spread*.

開花 *K'ai¹ hwa¹*....... To bloom, to blossom.

箍 *Ku¹*....... *A hoop;* a fillet; to hoop.

箍嘴 *Ku¹ tswei³*....... A muzzle. (N.)

籠嘴 *Lung² tswei³*.......... A muzzle. (C.)

笊 *Chao⁴*....... A bamboo skimmer; a ladle.

篱 *Li²*....... A skimmer.

笊篱 A perforated skimmer made of wire or bamboo. *A muzzle*, a blind. (S.)

中軍 *Chung¹ chün¹*. The adjutant commanding .... the forces under a governor or governor-general.

八卦 *Pa¹ kwa⁴*. The eight divining diagrams .... invented by Fu-hi and which form the ground work of the Book of Changes.

捉拿 *Choa¹ na²*.......... *To catch*, to seize.

飛虎 *Fei¹ hu³*. *A flying tiger;* a fabulous .... animal.

蜘 *Chï¹*....... An insect; *a spider*.

蛛 *Chu¹*..... The spider.

二字賀資。○16一個年輕的婦人、在碾子上碾米、忽然來了一個人問路、婦人因爲不便答話、就向旁邊路上、把手一擺、那人就隨着去了、誰知無巧不成故事、這婦人的婆婆、恰巧從家裏出來、他見媳婦向人擺手、那人也走得很慌、就疑惑他們有了私約、回家告訴他的兒子、他兒子就把婦人打了一頓、這婦人說、你打我知曉、必然有人挑、心裏明似鏡、只爲路一條、打一物燈籠。○17南面而坐、北面而朝、象憂亦憂、象喜亦喜、打一物鏡子。○18鑿壁偷光夜讀書、打一三國人名孔明。○19大爺的牛不喫草、打四書一句伯牛有疾。○20瞎子打雨傘、打四書兩句蓋有之矣、我未之見

16 A young woman was at the mill hulling rice, when suddenly there came by a stranger asking the way. Because it was not appropriate for the woman to speak, she pointed out the road by a motion of her hand, and the stranger passed on. But, "every freak of fortune gives rise to a story," and so sure enough the woman's mother-in-law came out just in time to see the motion of her daughter-in-law's hand and the man hastening on his way. She at once suspected they had some secret intrigue and went back into the house and told her son, and he in turn gave his wife a beating. The woman remarked: Your {carrying / beating} me, I know quite well is the work of somebody's {lifting / instigating}; but my heart is clear as a mirror, it was simply on account of the road. *Fits an article.* A lantern.

17 It sits on the south side but faces towards the north. When {Shang / the form} is sad, {Shun / the image} also is sad. When {Shang / the form} is pleased, {Shun / the image} also is pleased. *Fits an article.* A mirror.

18 He bored a hole in the wall to get light to study by at night. *Fits a character in the Three Kingdoms* {K'ung Ming. / a light-hole.}

19 My uncle's cow won't eat grass. *Fits a sentence in the Four Books.* {Pê-niu / uncle's cow} is sick.

20 A blind man carrying an umbrella. *Fits two clauses in the Four Books.* {Perhaps there are, but I have not seen any. / I have a cover, but I have never seen it.}

蜘蛛 The spider :—Note 7.
霧露 *Wu⁴ lu⁴*. . . . . Fog, *mist*, spray.
綉 *Hsiu⁴*. . . . . . . Same as 繡.
綉房 *Hsiu⁴ fang²*. A young ladies' chamber, *a lady's boudoir.*
佳人 *Chia¹ jên²*. . . . . A beautiful woman.
縚 *T'ao¹*. . . . *A sash*, a band, a fringe; an edging.
陰間 *Yin¹ chien¹*. . . . The unseen world, hades.
郊 *Chiao¹*. *Waste land*, common; a sacrifice to heaven and earth.
野外 *Yie³ wai⁴*. . . . . A wilderness, *barren fields.*
荒郊 *Hwang¹ chiao¹*. A waste common or wilderness.
圈椅子 *Ch'üen¹ i³ tsï³*. . . . . . . A bow-backed chair.
繞 *Jao³,⁴*. . . . . To wind around, to compass.
纏繞 *Ch'an² jao⁴*. *To wind around*, to wrap; to coil.
重疊 *Ch'ung² tie²*. In layers, in folds; *piled up*, doubled.
擺手 *Pai³ shou³*. *To wave the hand*, to beckon.
私約 *Sï¹ yoä¹*. A secret agreement; *an illicit intrigue.*

也。○有[21]一個好酒的對對子兒說、一壺在手、東不管、西不管、就死也不管、三杯入肚、天不怕、地不怕、即老婆亦不怕。○春[22]讀書、秋讀書、春秋讀書讀春秋、東當舖、西當舖、東西當舖當東西。○琴[23]瑟琵琶、八大王一樣頭腦、魑魅魍魎、四小鬼各別心腸。○冰[24]凉酒、一點兩點三點、丁香花、百頭千頭萬頭。○野[25]外黃花、好似金釘釘地、都中白塔、猶如玉鑽鑽天。○乾[26]隆皇上出了一個對子兒說、一大天上日月明、良月為朗、何申對的說、長巾帳中子女好、少女為妙。○王[27]先生病重的時候、知道父子快要分離、彼此都甚悲傷、就出了一個對子、給他兒子說、憐蓮子心中苦、他兒子說、離梨兒腹內酸。

21 A distich for a wine-bibber ran thus:—with a bottle in his hand he don't care for the east, he don't care for the west, he don't care even for death itself; with three cups in his belly he's not afraid of heaven, he's not afraid of earth, he's not even afraid of his wife.

22 Study in the spring, study in the autumn, spring and autumn keep up study, studying {Spring and Autumn / The Annals.}: a pawn shop on the east, a pawn shop on the west, east and west a pawnshop, pawning {east and west / things.

23 Lute, harpsichord and guitar; eight great kings, heads all alike; a brownie, an ogre, a nyx and a naiad; four little imps, each with different viscera.

24 Ice, cold, wine; one dot, two dots, three dots: a clove's fragrant blossom; the head of a hundred, the head of a thousand, the head of ten thousand.

25 The daisy growing on the common like a golden nail stuck in the earth: a white pagoda in the city like a pearly drill piercing heaven.

26 The Emperor K'ien Lung once proposed [one line of] a distich—One great heaven above, sun and moon [make] bright, the fair moon gives radiance. Hê Shên matched it saying, In the long curtained tent sons and daughters are good, but the little maiden is the fairest.

27 When Mr. Wang was very ill, knowing that father and son must soon separate, and both being filled with

知曉 *Chï*[1] *hsiao*[3]. To know, to be aware:—Note 16.

琵琶 *P'i*[2] *p'a*[2]. A guitar or viol.

魑 *Ch'i*[1]. A mountain elf, a brownie.

魅 *Mei*[4]. An ogre, a demon.

魍 *Wang*[3]. A water-demon, a nyx.

魎 *Liang*[3]. A naiad.

丁香 *Ting*[1] *hsiang*[1]. A clove.

丁香花 *Ting*[1] *hsiang*[1] *hwa*[1]. A clove blossom; the lilac.

黃花 *Hwang*[2] *hwa*[1]. The daisy, the dandelion.

申 *Shên*[1]. To extend, to expand; the 9th Chinese hour—3 to 5 p.m.

分離 *Fên*[1] *li*[2]. To diverge, to scatter, *to separate.*

灯 *Têng*[1]. A contracted form of 燈.

夕 *Hsi*[1,2]. *Evening*, dusk; late.

湖 *Hu*[2]. A lake.

江湖 *Chiang*[1] *hu*[2]. Rivers and lakes; wandering, *far-traveled*, peripatetic.

本身 *Pên*[3] *shên*[1]. Oneself, *own*, self.

事業 *Shï*[4] *yie*[4]. Calling, pursuit, occupation, *profession.*

○此28木是柴山山出、丁火爲灯夕夕多。○海29水潮、朝朝潮、朝潮朝落、山松長、常常長、常長常青。○有30連襟兩個、大的是書香人、朝第二個是江湖客、講明各就本業、作對一聯、大的說、三字同邊綢緞紗、三字同頭官宦家、穿遍了綢緞紗、纔是個官宦家、第二個說、三字同邊江海湖、三字同頭大丈夫、走遍了江海湖、纔是個大丈夫。○有31三個人、定規各人取兩個字、貼着本身的事業作對兒、頭一個是木匠說、尸至爲屋、一森三木、木木木、不知蓋了多少屋、第二個是賣酒的說、水酉爲酒、一品三口、口口口、不知喫了多少酒、第三個是種莊稼的說、豆頁爲頭、一犇三牛、牛牛牛、不知點了多少頭。○蘇32小妹把

grief, he gave a distich to his son, saying,
{I am sorry my son that your heart is grieved.
{The water-lily seed is bitter within.
The son replied {Leaving your son fills your {The pear is sour at the core. breast with sadness.

28 This wood makes firewood, and every hill yields it: a stick on fire makes a lamp, and night by night there are many.

29 The tide in the sea-water flows, morning by morning a tide; one morning it rises, another it falls. The pine on the mountain grows, day by day it grows, and it grows ever green.

30 Two brothers-in-law, the elder a literary man and the other a merchant traveler, agreed together to make each a line of a distich, each adhering to his own profession. The elder said, Three characters with the same side, silk, satin and gauze; and three others with the same top, officer, statesman and family; when they're all clothed with the silk, satin and gauze, then they become the family of a statesman. The younger matched it thus, Three characters with the same side, river, sea and lake; three characters with the same top, great, rod and man; when you've traveled over all the rivers, seas and lakes, then you become a valiant man.

31 Three men agreed to make distich lines, each adhering to his own profession and basing his line on two characters. The first, who was a carpenter, said, Corpse arrive makes a house; one forest of three trees, trees upon trees, it's hard to tell how many houses they'll build. The second, who was a liquor merchant,

---

尸 *Shï*[1]. . . . . . . *A corpse;* an effigy; useless.

犇 *Pên*[1]. . . . . . . An unusual writing of 奔.

游 *Yiu*[2]. . . . . . . To float; to drift; to rove.

言道 *Yien*[2] *tao*[4]. . . . To speak, to declare, to say.

恍然 *Hwang*[3] *jan*[2]. Fluttered, startled; with a . . . . start, *in a flash*, suddenly.

酒令 *Chiu*[3] *ling*[4]. The key of the drink:— . . . . Note (33).

當場 *Tang*[4] *ch'ang*[3]. During trial or examination; . . . . at the time, *then and there.*

爻 *Yao*[2]. . . . . . . To lay crosswise; to mix.

乂 *Ch'a*[1]. . . . To cross the arms; a crotch; *a fork.*

杈 *Ch'a*[1]. . . . . . . To prod; *to stick;* to nip.

檜 *Hwei*[4]. . . . . . . The cypress tree.

唉 *Ai*[1]. An exclamation or sigh of sorrow; an . . . . . . expression of deprecation. See *ai*[2].

喪心 *Sang*[4] *hsin*[1]. *To do wrong knowingly;* to . . . . violate conscience.

啐 *Ts'wei*[4]. To smack the lips; to spit; pish! . . . . . . *pugh!* bosh!

洞房的門關好、出了一個對兒、給他丈夫秦少游、言道多會對上、多會纔能開門、他丈夫拆開一看、寫的是閉門推出床前月、把他丈夫悶了半夜、也沒能對上、後來蘇東坡、願意觸動他的靈機、就找了一塊甎頭、向花缸裏一丟、水中的月影紛紛亂動、他丈夫恍然大悟、立時提筆對上說、投石沖開水底天。○33有三個人一同吃酒、定規以對對兒爲酒令、當塲對不上的、罰酒三杯、頭一個說、一個朋字兩個月、二物一色霜和雪、一月下霜、一月下雪、第二個說、一個出字兩座山.二物一色錫和鉛、一山出錫、一山出鉛、來到第三個、他却故意的不說、那

said, Water and grain make liquor; one series with three months, month after month, it's hard to tell how much liquor they'll drink. The third, who was a farmer, said, A bean and a leaf make a head; one scurry of three cows, cows upon cows, it's hard to say how many bobs of their heads there were.

32 Miss Su shut the door of the bride-chamber and put forth one line of a distich to her husband Ch'in Shao Yu, saying, When you've matched it, I'll open the door, and not till then. Opening the paper her husband found written, "I close the door and shut out the moonlight in front of the bed," which put him at his wits' end for half the night to no purpose. At last Su Tung P'oă, in order to suggest an idea to his mind, took a piece of a tile and, holding it over a flower pot filled with water, dropped it in, causing the image of the moon in the water to shimmer and shake. Upon this a bright thought flashed upon the bride-groom, and he at once took up his pen and wrote, I throw a stone and split open the sky beneath the water.

33 Three men were drinking wine together, and agreed to match distichs as a forfeit. Whoever failed to respond then and there, was to drink three cups. The first one said, A shed composed of two months; two things of one color,—frost and snow;

Notes.

1 破, means properly *to split* or *tear open*, and seems to apply more naturally to solving a riddle than, as here used, to making or propounding one. It is in fact used in both senses, and Chinese scholars differ as to which is the original and more appropriate sense. 剌鋪拉 *Thrusting out a spread*,—a peculiar phrase, coined apparently for this special case. In reading the accent is thrown on 拉.

3 打一物 *Strikes, (or refers to) an article*; that is, *fits an article*. Such a phrase is generally added to riddles as a guide to the solution.

6 This riddle is based on the short hand method of writing numbers. The numbers one, two and three, which consist of parallel strokes, are distinguished by being written alternately, horizontal and perpendicular.

7 諸葛亮, being one of the most renowned of Chinese generals, is made to represent the spider. With the Chinese, strategy is the fundamental idea of generalship and of the art of war. 蜘蛛 is the book term for a spider. The colloquial name, both in Northern and in Central Mandarin, is 蛛蛛. The eight, or rather the eight times eight, diagrams are generally arranged by geomancers in radial lines in concentric circles, making a figure not unlike a spider's web.

10 The understanding of this riddle depends on distinguishing between *value* and *number*, both of which are expressed by 多 and 少.

13 There is throughout this riddle an underlying reference to a marriage alliance, as if between the hair-string and the wearer.

16 知曉 is a facetious combination of 知道 and 曉得, only found in light literature, or in witty sayings. Why under the circumstances the woman made the riddle she did, is far from evident.

17 象憂亦憂 is from the Analects, and was said of *Shun's* noble treatment of his unworthy brother *Shang*. It is necessary to take 象 for the person standing *before* the mirror, not for the image *in* it, as the meaning of the word would more naturally suggest.

兩個就再三的催他、他回答說、我要對上、只怕你們二位見怪、那兩個人說、只要你對上、我們就不見怪、如是他就開口說、一個爻字兩把叉、二物一色你和他、一叉扠你、一叉扠他。○岳[34]飛被秦檜害了、所以後來的人、就在岳飛的墳墓前、做出秦檜夫妻的像來、一個跪在左邊、一個跪在右邊、又替他們作出一副對子來、乃是彼此相怨的話、在秦檜這一邊說、唉、僕本喪心、有賢妻何至如是、他妻子那一邊說、啐、婦雖長舌、非奸相不到今朝。

one month the frost falls and the other, the snow. The second said, Out—composed of two hills; two things of one color,—tin and lead; one hill yields tin, and the other yields lead. When it came to the third he declined to give his, and when they urged him repeatedly, he replied, If I tell you mine, I fear you two may be offended. The two, however, said, Only so you match the line we will take no offence. Upon this he went on and said, A mixture, composed of two forks; two things of one color,—you and he; one fork sticks you, and the other sticks him.

34 Because Yoă Fei suffered death by the instigation of Ch'in Kwei, men in after-times put effigies of Ch'in Kwei and his wife at the grave of Yoă Fei, one kneeling at the left, and the other at the right, and wrote a distich expressing their mutual recriminations. That at the side where Ch'in Kwei was, ran, Alas! I did indeed do wrong, but if I had had a prudent wife, I should never have come to this. That on the side where the wife was, ran, Pugh! I had a long tongue 'tis true, but if I had not married a traitorons minister, I should never have seen this day.

---

18 The words here quoted refer to a noted scholar of the Han dynasty, named 匡衡, who, because he could not afford a light to study by, made a hole in the partition and allowed his neighbors' light to shine through on his book.

19 The sentence referred to is from the Analects. 伯牛 was a disciple of Confucius. 大爺, or 大爺爺, is a colloquial rendering of 伯.

26 The Emperor K'ien-lung was noted for his literary taste and accomplishments. This distich is ingenious in that a mere dissection of characters makes a continuous sense. 何申 was a Tartar prince, able but unscrupulous and avaricious. He was subsequently put to death by K'ien-lung, and his enormous wealth confiscated.

29 The alliteration (in sound) is here well carried out.

32 蘇小妹 A sister of Su Tung P'oa, who had a share of her brother's genius. Her husband was also a literary man of some celebrity.

33 When friends are drinking wine together, they resort to a variety of games of chance or skill to heighten the enjoyment of the occasion, the forfeit paid by the loser being, not to pay the score, but to drink so many cups of wine. The object of each party is to make the other drunk.

34 岳飛, a noted military chieftain who flourished in the Sung dynasty during the reign of the Emperor Kao-tsung. He was the implacable enemy of the Tartars, who were then invading the country from the North, and for his patriotism has been much extolled by Chinese historians. 秦檜, a noted statesman who served under the Emperors Kin-tsung and Kao-tsung. He was taken prisoner by the Tartars and treated with great consideration by them. After his return he counseled making peace with the Tartars by partitioning the empire, and his advice prevailed with the Emperor Kao-tsung. Because 岳飛 opposed him and his policy of peace, he caused 岳飛 to be accused and, on a shallow pretext, put to death. For this treacherous act, and for his unpatriotic counsel to make peace by dividing the empire, he has been execrated by all succeeding generations.

END OF LESSONS.

SUPPLEMENTAL VOCABULARY

OF

SECOND READINGS.

A number of the second readings noted in the vocabularies, it was not found convenient to introduce in subsequent lessons. Such readings of course remain undefined. They are here brought together and defined for the information of the student, and are included in the general index.

葛 *Kê*[3]. . . . . A surname. See *kê*[2].

說 *Shui*[4]. To persuade, to urge; to solicit . . . . patronage, to drum. See *shwoă*[1].

藏 *Tsang*[4] A storehouse; a retreat; a safe. . . . . See *ts'ang*[2].

王 *Wang*[4]. To rule as a king. (w.) See . . . . *wang*[2].

塗 *T'u*[2]. Mud; to daub; to fill up a crack; to . . . . . . dirty; to blot out. See *tu*[1].

肉 *Ju*[4]. . . . . Cinnamon. See *jou*[4].

溜 *Liu*[4]. . . . . . . A current, a stream. See *liu*[1].

咽 *Yien*[1]. . . . . . . The throat, the gullet. See *yien*[4].

塞 *Sê*[4]. To stop up, to obstruct, to hinder; . . . . . . dull, stupid. See *sê*[1].

訂 *Ting*[4]. To settle; to criticize; to collate; . . . . . . to adjust. See *ting*[1].

舍 *Shê*[3]. To put away, to neglect, to set aside. . . . . . . See *shê*[4].

拽 *Yie*[4]. To trail, to drag after, to pull. See . . . . . . *chwai*[4].

嘔 *Ou*[3]. . . . . . . To quiet, to pacify. See *ou*[1].

讀 *Tou*[4]. . . . . . . A clause; a stop. See *tu*[2].

奇 *Chi*[1]. . . . Odd, single; a remainder. See *ch'i*[2].

操 *Ts'ao*[4]. . . . A principle, a purpose. See *ts'ao*[1].

累 *Lei*[3]. To tie together; to accumulate, to heap . . . . . . up; often. See *lei*[4]. *The distribution of meanings is unsettled.*

補 *P'u*[3]. The square embroidered patches which . . . . . . are the insignia of office. See *pu*[3], and *p'u*[1].

摩 *Moă*[2]. . . . . . To polish, to smooth. See *moă*[1].

估 *Ku*[4]. . . . Second-hand, no fixed price. See *ku*[1].

妻 *Ch'i*[4]. . . . . . To give to wife. (w.) See *ch'i*[1].

淋 *Lin*[4]. To filter, to dribble, to slaver. See . . . . . . *lin*[2].

鮮 *Hsien*[3]. . . . . . Rare, scarce. (w.) See *hsien*[1].

汨 *Ku*[3]. . . . . . . To mix, to rise. (w.) See *mi*[4].

蒙 *Mêng*[3]. . . . . . . 蒙古 Mongolia. See *mêng*[2].

披 *P'i*. To open, to uncover; to rive apart. . . . . . . See *p'ei*[1].

賈 *Ku*[3]. . . . . . To sell, to traffic. See *chia*[3].

渾 *Hun*[4]. . . . . . . Confused, chaotic. See *hun*[2].

彈 *Tan*[4]. . . . A bullet, a ball; a pill. See *t'an*[2].

卷 *Chüen*[3]. . . . . . To roll up, to curl. See *chüen*[4].

唵 *An*[1]. . . . To gobble up with the mouth. See *ê*[2].

摟 *Lou*[1]. . . . To rake together, to drag. See *lou*[3].

卡 *Ch'ia*[2]. . . . . . To pinch, to clamp. See *ch'ia*[3].

蔓 *Wan*[4]. . . . . . A vine, a tendril. (w.) See *man*[2].

熨 *Yün*[4]. To iron clothes; a charcoal smoothing iron. See *yü*[4].

契 *Hsie*[4]. The name of a statesman in the reign . . . . . . of Shun. See *ch'i*[4].

榰 *Ch'a*[2]. . . . . . A crack, a flaw, a joint. See *ch'a*[1].

蹶 *Chüe*[2]. To stumble, to slip; to leap. See . . . . *chüe*[3].

校 *Chiao*⁴. To collate, to revise; to judge of; . . . . stocks for the feet. See *hsiao*⁴.

螞 *Ma*⁴. . . . . A locust. See *ma*³.

畜 *Hsü*⁴. To feed, to rear; to lay up, to hoard. . . . . . . (w.) See *ch'u*⁴.

挾 *Chia*¹. To clasp under the arm, to pinch; . . . . to hide away, to appropriate. See *hsie*².

掄 *Lun*². To select; by turns, rotation. See . . . . . . *lun*¹.

衰 *Ts'wei*¹. A proportional part in Chinese . . . . alligation. See *shwai*¹.

豈 *K'ai*³. . . . . . Delighted, joyous. (w.) See *ch'i*³.

陸 *Liu*⁴. Used in official documents for 六. . . . . . . See *lu*⁴.

漂 *P'iao*¹. . . . . To float, to drift. See *piao*³.

稱 *Ch'êng*⁴. A scale or steelyard. The same as 秤. . . . . See *ch'êng*¹.

旋 *Hsüen*⁴. To revolve, to whirl round; dizzy. . . . . See *hsüen*².

趴 *P'a*¹. . . . To fall or lie full length. See *p'a*².

跕 *Tie*¹. . . . . . . To fall, to dart down. See *tien*³.

繫 *Chi*⁴. . . . To tie, to fasten on, to bind. See *hsi*⁴.

觀 *Kwan*⁴. . . . A temple, a hermitage. See *kwan*¹.

曾 *Tsêng*¹. Great—said of generations as great- . . . . grandson, etc. See *ts'êng*².

蝦 *Hsia*¹. . . . . . A shrimp, a prawn. See *ha*².

馮 *P'êng*². To ford a river; to rely on. See . . . . *fêng*².

SUPPLEMENT.

I.

LISTS OF SUPPLEMENTARY WORDS AND PHRASES.

It was originally intended to print the following lists in connection with the several lessons to which they belong. Inasmuch, however, as they are intended chiefly for reference, or as exercises for advanced students, it has been deemed more suitable to put them in a supplement. They represent a variety of dialects. The student can ascertain from his teacher which words or phrases are current in his own dialect. Even a cursory examination of these lists will give the student a useful, general idea of the range of the several idioms involved. It will also give useful employment to a teacher in off hours to have him construct short sentences illustrating these examples, which can then be read as exercises. The lists are not exhaustive, but are sufficient for all practical purposes.

LESSON XXVII.

把 劍 撓子 鞭子 笊籬 鑰匙 條帚 掃帚 刷子 鑷子 鉗子 鎚子 蠅甩子 鞋拔子 火鉗子 火剪 篦子 梳 傘 銼 鑿 鏇 鐧

件 汗衫 褲子 袍子 袷襖 綿襖 大襖 小襖 大褂 小褂 褂子 衣裳 公事 外套 單褂 馬褂 背褡

塊 緞子 綢子 豆腐 饅頭 水牌 磨石 玉石 玻璃 洋鐵 木頭 石頭 煤 錫 鉛 銅 板 紙 梨 餑餑 王瓜 甜瓜 果子 補襯 布 土墼 墨 皮子 劈柴 硯台 粉子 銀子 繩子 油炸鬼 餅 糖 甎 炭

位 師娘 少爺 相公 公子 太子 娘娘 公主 大人 宰相 皇上 神 親戚 客 董事 紳士 師傅 老太爺 總爺 副爺 將軍 小姐 姑娘 奶奶 師母 醫生 會友 執事 長老 牧師 教師 朋友 學生 老翁 令愛 令郎 師兄 表兄

LESSON XXXVIII.

條：道 河 衚衕 領子 綫 龍 蛐蟮 虫子 口袋 手巾 凳子

狐狸 和約 例 律法 規矩 溝 裙子 辮子 褲子 鐵鍊子 扁担

隻：象 脊 鴿子 班鳩 袖子 套褲 靴子 鳫 犬 豹 虎

兎子

匹：駱駝 牲口

頭：親事 駱駝 蒜

LESSON XL.

出來：潤出來 淋出來 濾出來 過出來 找出來 翻出來 學出來 念出來 温出來 剜出來 爬出來

搓出來 [illegible]出來 淌出來 流出來 飛出來 鑽出來 驢出來 吐出來 掏出來 漫出來 漲出來 撒出來 撇出來

說出來 撥出來 織出來 紡出來 煎出來 燒出來 銼出來 磨出來 分出來 除出來 乘出來 邊出來 捶出來

合出來 擺出來 洗出來 吸出來 鼓出來 碾出來 簸出來 伸出來 繙出來 畫出來 抹出來 帶出來 講出來

開出來 起出來 漏出來 撈出來 舀出來 明出來 寫出來 貼出來 變出來

出去：帶出去 領出去 抱出去 拿出去 送出去 搬出去 抬出去 赶出去 轟出去 攆出去 逃出去

吐出去 滾出去 颳出去 拽出去 拉出去 拖出去 扛出去 逐出去 哄出去 推出去 掀出去 取出去 掃出去

發出去 跳出去 貼出去 衝出去 分出去 淌出去 流出去 飛出去

進來：拉進來 闖進來 推進來 抓進來 擒進來 爬進來 赶進來 扛進來 抬進來 拿進來 搬進來

發進來 調進來 遞進來 接進來 背進來

進去：戳進去 拉進去 拖進去 抱進去 砸進去 頂進去 拉進去 背進去 釘進去 爬進去 放進去

幘進去 鑽進去 塞進去 捅進去 接進去 遞進去 背進去 請進去 楦進去

LESSON XLI.

過來
捎過來 抬過來 掀過來 拉過來 牽過來 奪過來 搶過來 正過來 挪過來 提過來 丟過來
扔過來 栧過來 送過來 撥過來 張過來 跟過來 跳過來 兌過來 換過來 躥過來 漫過來 跑過來 拖過來
挽回過來 趴過來 鑽過來 推過來 跨過來 帶過來 領過來

趴過去 鑽過去 遞過去

回來
搶回來 原回來 跑回來 牽回來 頂回來 贖回來 贏回來 退回來 轉回來 捎回來 交回來
打回來 追回來 趕回來 敗回來 圈回來 抱回來 叫回來 買回來

過去
跑過去 拖過去 捎過去 請過去 掀過去 抬過去 牽過去 拉過去 撥過去 穿過去 丟過去
拿過去 扔過去 栧過去 飛過去 跟過去 糊弄過去 搬過去 推過去 兌過去 躥過去 漫過去 跨過去 跳過去

回去
追回去 趕回去 搶回去 跑回去 贖回去 牽回去 拉回去 帶回去 贏回去 捎回去 退回去
賸回去 打回去

LESSON XLII.

本
聖諭 舊約 新約 聖書 曲子 皇曆 新報 卷子 冊子 文章 詩
字帖 史記 綱鑑 串珠

部
字彙 周禮 春秋 禮記 左傳 易經 書經 詩經 四書 代數 數學

行
生意 手藝 鴈 文章 淚 花 莊稼 樹

張
把 鋤 鐮 鋸 杴 鐝 發票 票子 謄黃 告示 弓
膏藥 嘴 案子 滙票 功牌 路票 文書 杈 呈子 契 約 梳

管
簫 笛子

錠
硃墨 金子 銀子

句：言語 古語 土話 官話 閒話 文話 俗話 淡話 笑話 文章 詩

古文 詞 賦

套：箱櫃 衣裳 首飾 把戲 戲法 故事 曲子 拳 話 書 傢伙

花盆 盆 木梳 謊話 口供 盃 碟子 盤子

LESSON XLVII.

頭：紉頭 墊頭 駕頭 伙頭 斧頭 行頭 錢頭 年頭 彩頭 兆頭

青頭 襯頭 節頭 寫頭 肩頭 源頭 當頭 項頭 替頭 椿頭 眉頭

LESSON LI.

法則 寒冷 飢餓 喜樂 憂愁 喜悅 羨慕 謙虛 驕傲 整奘 零碎 下賤 尊貴

勞苦 懊悔 放肆 門戶 分別 引誘 迷惑 斷絕 房屋 君王 婦女 釋放 綑綁

倔彊 過失 差錯 拖累 簡捷 淺薄 深厚 疑惑 決斷 羞辱 榮耀 俊俏 醜陋

誠實 汚穢 潔淨 公義 仁愛 慈悲 懇切 引導 挽回 豪傑 英雄 粗魯 担當

界限 憑據 曉諭 禀報 觀看 聞聽 誇奬 原本 回轉 改變 彎曲 直率 活潑

良善 兇惡 邪僻 端正 通達 羞恥 盼望 警戒 勸勉 黑暗 光明 管轄 約束

較比 法度 律例 性情 樹木 靈魂 身體 教化 意思 因由 緣故 生活 修理

惱怒 怨恨 嫉妒 激發 恩惠 疾病 健壯 偷竊 賞賜 刑罰 經歷 連絡 順從

悲哀 吉慶 原諒 算計 斟酌 度量 窄狹 寬綽 敗壞 成全 均勻 柔軟 剛硬

驅逐 辭別 推諉 攬承 表明 顯露 隱藏 治理 伺候 暴虐 保佑 冷淡 親近

官宦 諂諛 稱讚 稱呼 虧欠 缺少 滿足 拆散 錢財 瞞哄 欺騙 逃走 行走

蠢笨 靈巧 儆醒 殷勤 懶惰 懈怠 疎忽 謹慎 茂盛 衰敗 興旺 忍耐 逼迫

要飯 討賬 犯罪 喝水 完全 效驗 辯駁 和睦 爭競 預備 遲鈍 急促 爵祿

礦工 燒火

LESSON LII.

人

託人 着人 差人 屈人 惱人 笑人 喜人 惡人 賺人 害人 愛人

臊人 招人 戀人 服人 混人 辱人 坑人 賴人 嘆人 勒人 讓人 求人 煩人

派人 欺人 擄人 饞人 疼人 嚇人 驚人 貼人 告人 添人 用人 尋人 僱人

嫉妒人 諂諛人 奉承人 引誘人 教導人 嚇唬人 勸化人 啟發人 幫助人 憐恤人 鬥弄人 慪人 難人

勒掯人 勒索人 刻薄人 刻苦人 抬舉人 小看人 褒貶人 誇獎人 蹧蹋人 欺壓人 原諒人 提拔人 讒謗人

議論人 親熱人 急煞人 嘟囔人 責備人 督責人 教訓人 附就人 差遣人 耍弄人 壓勢人 壓量人 訛詐人

轄制人 賣弄人 連合人 挖苦人 衝撞人 度量人 感動人 安慰人 逆料人 疑惑人 坑害人 譏誚人 麻繁人

骯髒人 唐突人 堵喪人 招呼人 喝呼人 獻醜人 試探人 指使人 朦弄人 瞞哄人 催促人 刻村人 挾制人

窺探人 稱呼人 謀害人 隨希人 分派人 倭儸人 咒詛人 輕慢人 寬恕人 刁賴人 誣告人 囉唆人 勞動人

使喚人 拒絕人 圈弄人 折磨人 交往人 訓誨人 扶持人 周旋人 接待人 激發人 應酬人 安排人 率領人

伺候人 稱讚人 將就人 調戲人 誘惑人 迷惑人 引導人 鼓舞人 藐視人 調弄人 成全人 唆挑人 託賴人

開導人 警戒人 勉勵人 勸勉人 齷齪人 凌辱人

LESSON LXVIII.

棵科

松樹 梧桐樹 核桃樹 柿子樹 花紅樹 李子樹 桃樹 杏樹 秫稭 竹子 草

迎春花 荷花 梅花 菊花 芍藥 芭蕉 柑子樹 橘子樹 桑樹 楸樹 榆樹 柳樹 楊樹

稻子 麥子 豆子 秫秫 芋頭 山葯 蔓菁 生菜 芹菜 韭菜 蒜 水仙花 百合花

葫蘆 茄子 王瓜 甜瓜 西瓜

乘 車子 水車 牛車 磨子 碾 碓 機 櫃子 廚櫃 架子 篩子	**口** 缸 甕 刀 劍 鐘 鍘 井 棺材 好話 屋 鍼
砟	釘 箱子 螺絲釘 味兒
根 繩子 柱子 汗毛 鬍子 洋線 絲線 絛子 帶子 皮條 筷子 旗杆	**疋** 布 緞子 哈喇 綾子 洋縐 山紬 綿紬 篾 槳 櫓
槔 香 竹子 杆子 棍子 鞭子 菸袋	**輛** 馬車 東洋車
堆 甎頭 瓦碴 石灰 木頭 木花 鉋花 粮食 草 柴 煤 雪	**間** 屋子 客屋 飯屋 廚屋 廳屋 客廳 樓房 舖子 空屋 厠屋
糞 土 人 齷齪	**副** 鈴鐺 帶子 蹄子 肝腸 眼鏡 襖袖 紙牌 骨牌 骰子 手飾 牌釦
雙 靴子 套褲 眼睛 手 脚 父母 鞋傍子 鞋底	棺材板 心腸 腸子 對子 對聯 辮頭線 屏子 套褲

LESSON LXXII.

家 釋家 媽家 文家 武家 店家 鄉家 咱家 奴家 孤家 佛家 通家	喜主家 喪主家 翁婿家 皇上家 便家 船家 舖家 上家 下家 仙家 說家 喝家 好家
會家 名家 酒家 創家 姨家 女人家 老婆家 娘們家 娼婦家 婊子家 鄰舍家 東鄰家 西鄰家	男家 女家 苦主家 寒家 名家
老爺家 老娘家 舅舅家 姑姑家 姐姐家 妹妹家 女婿家 叔叔家 大爺家 妯娌家 姑嫂家 婆娘家 買賣家	

LESSON LXXIII.

發

發頭疼 發筋骨 發渴 發病 發顛狂 發迷 發驚瘋 發燒 發狠言 發沉 發福 發邁態 發大懸 發藍 發烏 發黑 發青 發綠 發白 發喘 發木 發抖 發狠 發懶

發咆哮 發夢 發氣 發火 發兵 發活 發旺 發苗 發芽 發科 發達 發怵 發暗 發光 發明

LESSON LXXIV.

開

撥攧開 行開 傳開 安不開 弄開 伸開 量開 夾開 裂開 沖開 剝開 劃開 割開 解開 排開 勻開 均開 派開 攤開 挪開 推開 搬開 破開 擘開

攻開 看開 崩開 捐開 砍開 鑿開 刨開 泡開 披開 撒開 扒開 撥開 撬開 裂開 掙開 橕開 化開

LESSON LXXV.

住

擋住 板住 吃住 抓住 耐住 護住 躺住 留住 掩住 牽住 瞞住 攔住 穩住 搗住 握住 揩住 跴住 按住 黏住 粘住 釘住 欺住 拴住 保住

搡住 懲住 圍住 圈住 証住 吸住 降住 捆住 墊住 扯住 混住 頂住 把住 停住 擒住 捉住 塞住 站住 坐住 攔住 騎住 綁住

LESSON LXXVI.

到

跟到 貴到 賤到 醜到 惡到 寃到 禮到 話到 印到 寫到 講到 間到 等到 拉到 解到 擠到 推到 點到 念到 唱到 請到 聽到 看到 論到

長到 窮到 帶到 領到 逛到 直到 睡到 逃到 活到 輪到 流到 教到 充到

時到 嚷到

LESSON LXXXV.

多

多綠 多紅 多小 多窨

多麼

多麼樂 多麼歡 多麼俏 多麼緊 多麼輕 多麼乖 多麼白 多麼黑 多麼狂 多麼愚 多麼點

多麼有名 多麼光面 多麼響 多麼笨 多麼巧 多麼香 多麼瘦 多麼肥 多麼胖 多麼亮 多麼辣 多麼酸 多麼喜

多麼光滑 多麼好吃 多麼好聽 多麼好看 多麼結實 多麼舒坦 多麼整齊 多麼體面 多麼光彩 多麼凉快 多麼容易 多麼便宜 多麼順利

多麼會過 多麼會講 多麼了亮 多麼清楚 多麼華麗 多麼好使 多麼聲勢 多麼儉省 多麼方便 多麼開脫 多麼親熱 多麼寬快 多麼富足

多麼穩重 多麼規矩 多麼方正 多麼鬆開 多麼緊醒 多麼清靜 多麼雅致 多麼痛快 多麼省力 多麼大方 多麼伎倆 多麼伶俐 多麼暢快

多麼爽當 多麼扎實 多麼柔妥 多麼聰明 多麼靈精 多麼精怪 多麼精細 多麼和氣 多麼温客 多麼挺妥 多麼揚氣 多麼顯亮 多麼氣派

多麼繁華 多麼進功 多麼俊俏 多麼喜笑 多麼滑鍚 多麼囉唆 多麼費事 多麼累贅 多麼活便 多麼靈通 多麼煞實 多麼砍快 多麼爽神

多麼嫩俏 多麼老當 多麼死手 多麼老實 多麼熱鬧 多麼實誠 多麼俏皮 多麼清秀 多麼出眼 多麼起發 多麼妥當 多麼穩當 多麼平和

多麼快樂 多麼乾淨 多麼平正 多麼勻和 多麼儒雅 多麼顯眼 多麼清亮 多麼靈分 多麼筋致 多麼俐束 多麼殷勤 多麼暖和 多麼詳細

多麼有勁兒 多麼有眼色 多麼準成 多麼出手 多麼孝順 多麼連俐 多麼醒眼 多麼安頓 多麼快活

LESSON XCI.

動

扯動　盪動　鏟動　夾動　擁動　撥攋動　抈動　搯動　撥動　走動　行動

轉動　扛動　掘動　推動　活動　引動　激動　蹎動　拼動　鼓動　打動　勞動　感動

砍動　割動　切動　扎動　弄不動　撐不動　拿動　背動　搖動　請動　抱動　掀動　搬動

喚不動　撐不動　拖不動　牽不動　輥不動　叫不動　提不動　指使動　求動

倒

拉倒　昏倒　打倒　擁倒　跪倒　掀倒　滑倒　撲倒　撞倒　碰倒　摔倒

慌倒　閃倒　壓倒　掀倒　拼倒　搬倒　蹎倒　傾倒　震倒　沖倒　盤倒　間倒　說倒

做倒　磕倒　醉倒　酸倒　拿倒　噴倒　擠倒　顛倒　淋倒　泡倒　張倒　按倒　帶倒

犯

坐不犯　走不犯　做不犯　說不犯　制不犯　打犯　架犯　扛犯　挑犯　駝犯　背犯

耐不犯　弄不犯

LESSON XCII.

及

忍耐不及　跑不及　想不及　等不及　做不及　寫不及　打算不及

迭

拾掇不迭　收拾不迭　打不迭　擋不迭　逃不迭

掉

打掉　丟掉　勾掉　弄掉　起掉　去掉　抹掉　搓掉　刷掉　棄掉　喪掉

走掉　扭掉　磕掉　賣掉

LESSON XCVIII.

處

不便處　衰敗處　興旺處　好看處　美處　賤處　貴處　笑處　喜處　強處　妙處

各處　遠處　近處　錯處　怕處　服人處　不及處　不濟處　不服處　糊塗處　熱鬧處　軟弱處　驕傲處

LESSON C.

牀　鋪盖　凉席　蚊帳　帳子　地毯　馬褥子　炕席

枝　筆　箭　令　令箭　鉛筆　桅桿　烟鎗　耳挖　簪子　旂　鞭子

矛　竹子　藕

座　門樓　油房　大廳　官廳　當舖　牌坊　鹽店　客店　酒店　鐘樓　鼓樓

大殿　亭子　營盤　墳　碑　墻　神龕　香亭　講書堂　壇　舖子

陣　雪　雹子　霧　笑　哭　鬧　雷　怒　冷　烟　魚

雁　人　心疼　鬼哭　陰風　仙風　颼風　打罵　瘋癲　忙　亂

塲　戰　飢荒　雹子　露　霜　病　空夢　辛苦　哭　笑　打

罵　是非　人命　熱鬧　笑話

鋪　榻　青韮

桿　長槍　鳥鎗　火鎗　大纛　大旂　左督旂　旂子　矛子　棍　竹棍

盞　茶　油　飯

穗　黍子　稷子　稌子　胡秫　玉胡秫　辮穗　帽穗　粟

層　意思　浮雲　玻璃　親戚　大殿　房子　紙　臺階　槅板

顆　黍子　秈米　大米　稌子　粳米　包米　棒子米　黃豆　綠豆　豇豆　黑豆

小豆　豌豆　穭豆　沙　人頭　丸藥　珍珠

粒　黍子　稌子　秈米　大米　粳米　包米　棒子米　黃豆　綠豆　豇豆　黑豆

小豆　豌豆　穭豆　沙

掛　鐘　表　錢　門簾　窗簾子　竹簾子　數珠　朝珠　鍊子　鬏子　鬍鬚

LESSON CI.

盡 受盡 寒盡 水盡 月盡 自盡 窮盡 殺盡 耗盡 得盡	**定** 保不定 平定 擬定 判定 派定 安定 約定 立定 拘定 持定 料定
完 挑完 搬完 賣完 分完 印完 批完 寫完 學完 講完 使完 用完	注定 算定
看完 拾掇完 收拾完 刷完 做完 切完 耡完 耩完 耕完 種完 算完 推完 拾完	**成** 繙成 軋成 收成 研成 湊成 慣成 煉成 說成 做成 學成 變成
澆完 抹完 裁完 割完 擇完 洗完 打完 編完 織完 紡完 禱告完 唱完 聽完	綑成 織成 紡成 編成 燒成
蒸完 燙完 梳完 薙完 點完 發完 包完 拔完	

LESSON CII.

見 撞見 尋見	想破 鼓破 氣破 猜破 畫破 洗破 搓破 割破 挖破 掛破 跌破 碰破 戳破
透 熱透 冷透 涼透 凍透 潤透 浸透 泡透 磨透 看透 熟透 刺透	揭破 粘破 剺破 搓揉破 嚇破 擊破 敲破
估透 鼓透 壞透 猜透	**壞** 凍壞 寫壞 做壞 治壞 病壞 氣壞 管壞 教壞 窮壞 慣壞 學壞
破 踹破 搗破 弄破 磨破 砸破 擠破 扎破 刺破 拆破 攻破 打破	蹧蹋壞 擺弄壞 碰壞 累壞 穿壞 醃壞 澇壞 旱壞 乾壞 說壞

LESSON CIII.

航海法　量地法　整理法　殘忍法　刻薄法　糊塗法　槍法　殺法　改法　變法　分法　狠法　毒法

走法　冷法　熱法　急法　弄法　告法　量法　治法　鍼法　官法　用法　**法**

炮製法　藏掩法　憋氣法

書法　革法　聚法　化法　留法　歸法　理法　行法　句法　勸法　創法　喝法　吃法

LESSON CVII.

磨磨蹭蹭　試試呼呼　楸楸扯扯　婆婆媽媽　唧唧咕咕　咕咕囔囔　怕怕恥恥　拘拘束束　嚴嚴實實　子子孫孫　世世代代　破破爛爛　掄掄打打

均均勻勻　停停當當　圓圓全全　精精細細　體體面面　悲悲慘慘　四四方方　正正當當　旺旺盛盛　俐俐東東　小小器器　巴巴結結　商商量量

唧唧噥噥　慌慌張張　昏昏沉沉　擁擁擠擠　多多少少　疤疤拉拉　靜靜板板　轟轟烈烈　猴猴氣氣　鬼鬼氣氣　熨熨貼貼　公公道道　整整齊齊

規規矩矩　滋滋潤潤　永永遠遠　滑滑錫錫　嘻嘻哈哈　砍砍快快　脆脆快快　輕輕省省　瞭瞭亮亮　顯顯亮亮　親親熱熱　冷冷淡淡　勻勻和和

疑疑惑惑　奇奇怪怪　精精爽爽　羅羅唆唆　思思拉拉　鼓鼓漲漲　仔仔細細　叮叮鐺鐺　口口舌舌　爭爭兢兢　趴趴叉叉　瑣瑣氣氣　哼哼唧唧

懇懇切切　窈窈窕窕　糊糊弄弄　謹謹慎慎　飄飄流流　準準成成　穩穩當當　寬寬綽綽　富富裕裕　斯斯文文　大大樣樣　淒淒凉凉　殷殷勤勤

軟軟和和　言言語語　說說道道　摔摔打打　伺伺候候　遮遮掩掩　瞞瞞藏藏　踺踺打打　跳跳打打　魁魁偉偉　威威武武　坦坦然然　說說笑笑

囫囫圇圇　周周正正　風風流流　潑潑實實　樸樸實實　分分明明　緊緊巴巴　冒冒失失　徠徠猷猷　迷迷伴伴　親親確確　孤孤單單　悠悠忽忽

結結吧吧　喀喀吧吧　亂亂道道　煇煇煌煌　勞勞碌碌　密密雜雜　跟跟蹌蹌　影影綽綽　曆曆留留　晃晃蕩蕩　客客氣氣　柔柔和和　烈烈決決

兩兩三三　渺渺冥冥　恍恍惚惚　反反復復　清清靜靜　清清閒閒　堅堅固固　實實落落　恭恭敬敬　雅雅道道　本本分分　蹀蹀躞躞　諂諂誳誳

吞吞吐吐　爽爽當當

搢搢擁擁　現現成成　委委屈屈　哭哭啼啼　挺挺妥妥　搖搖晃晃　熱熱鬧鬧　花花搭搭　平平和和　舒舒坦坦　搖搖擺擺　浪浪蕩蕩　三三兩兩

LESSON CXIV.

安安學說和查量比活表伸消紫 | 解打請通搖見擦撕擠拿糊遮招
置排習和睦考比量動明明停裏 | 說聽示報晃識磨巴巴巴弄擋呼
安安學說和查量比活表伸消紫 | 解打請通搖見擦撕擠拿糊遮招
置排習和睦考比量動明明停裏 | 說聽示報晃識磨巴巴巴弄擋呼

提訴瞞原摩均調演粉刷漿辭帮 | 檢約道叙鬆清門開算盤療撣撥
說說藏諒挲勻和習飾洗洗別助 | 點模謝談散閒弄導計算治撈攋
提訴瞞原摩均調演粉刷漿辭帮 | 檢約道叙鬆清門開算盤療撣撥
說說藏諒挲勻和習飾洗洗別助 | 點模謝談散閒弄導計算治撈攋

照照畫斟思打比校對質蹧拷盤 | 順理發添勸打熱樂評整鎮透穿
顧應拉酌量量較對証証蹋問問 | 理正明補戒樸鬧活論治壓說通
照照畫斟思打比校對質蹧拷盤 | 順理發添勸打熱樂評整鎮透穿
顧應拉酌量量較對証証蹋問問 | 理正明補戒樸鬧活論治壓說通

訪磕儘查翻嚇逼套安安安順說 | 會養保料遷遼圍助分停回彎改
問問問拉騰唬問問慰穩停說說 | 悟活養理就望護威派息轉轉調
訪磕儘查翻嚇逼套安安安順說 | 會養保料遷遼圍助分停回彎改
問問問拉騰唬問問慰穩停說說 | 悟活養理就望護威派息轉轉調

美擠誇可央哀騰吹打修教温派 | 審殺自滋
言鼓獎憐告告挪打算理訓習解 | 量浮在潤
美擠誇可央哀騰吹打修教温派 | 審殺自滋
言鼓獎憐告告挪打算理訓習解 | 量浮在潤

LESSON CXXII.

見 見見見見見見見見 | 經 經經經經
大小長短多少歹欺 | 用老胖瘦

LESSON CXXIV.

打 打打打打打打打打打打打 | 打打打打打打打打打打
傘食雷霹光鼾呼九旋交交 | 結地嘴鎗戲旅執挺場墻
　　　靂棍睡嚕天兒易待 | 交鋪巴　　　事　子　

打飽呃　打鋪拉　打嚏噴　打呃料　打跟頭　打千兒　打結子　打戰戰　打戰　打柴　打腔　打擂台　打擂

打磨　打差　打岔　打官司　打坑　打話把　打油　打春　打老婆　打狗　打洞　打眼兒　打哈哈

打扇　打點　打鐘　打鼓　打疙瘩　打動　打斷　打印　打圍　打頭的　打頭兒　打探　打牌

打碑　打鐵　打開兒　打雜兒　打釘子　打底子　打地基　打麻繩　打褙子　打伙食　打燈籠　打提溜　打磉子

打信兒　打鋪兒　打唋兒　打藕兒　打懼　打䂫　打骰子　打毽兒　打手摹　打曆習眼　打呑吐　打舒身　打掌

打滾兒　打棍　打戒尺　打板子　打合同　打回覆　打仰臥浮　打稟帖　打旱魃　打壙　打礦　打花花哨　打條石

打啞吧語　打電報

打急抓　打齊臺　打團團圍　打蹄子　打前絆　打前失　打辮子　打坐　打抽豐　打殃　打瓦　打飢荒　打照面

LESSON CXXV.

朶　花　香草

軸　影　佛像　直條子

角　烟　土　洋錢

封　香

段　書　文章　意思　理　故事　地　路橋　街　鋪子　柱子

面　旂　鞍子　鏡子　牌　鏊子

領　箔

所　莊院　公館　牢獄　班房　樓房　瓦房　草房　官宅　祠堂　古廟　講堂

洋樓　洋行

片　雲彩　樹林　肉　心　好心　熱心　血心　忠心　冰心　苦心　好意

頁　書　玻璃　字　信　饝饝　餑餑

步　運氣

頂　篼子　轎子　帳子　風帽　暖帽　秋帽　緯帽　涼帽　草帽　帽子

串　山楂　珠子　魚

幅　紅彩　珠子　行樂　簾子　册頁　帖　被單子　被

處　地　洋樓　講堂　古廟　祠堂　官宅　宅院　宅子　草房　瓦房　樓房
寺院　園地　場園　草場　傷　買賣　差地　官地　廟地　墓田　塋地

簍　糕餅　菸葉　紙　書　鰕醬　糖　油

貫　錢

架　鷹　眼鏡　食盒　蚊帳　帳子　天平　葡萄

扇　牆　磨子　屏風　槅子　牌　窗

味　藥引子

樁　生意　奇事　新聞　故事　物　營生　東西

丸　月亮

LESSON CXL.

幫　轎夫　吹手　夥　羊　饑民　船　先生　學生

尊　菩薩　神

排　兵　人

班　行人　女旦子　三小子　匠人　夥計　流教　賊　强盜　媽子　衙役

股　怒氣　利錢　本錢　賬份子　辮子　勁兒　霧氣　氣　烟　賊　水
惡味　味兒　人馬　鯨吞　毒氣

眼　鎗　針

爐　燒鴨　燒雞　燒餅　灰　炭　火

包 膿 鹽 湯 水 肉 菓子 茶食 烟土 菸 糖 衣裳

蛆 痰 金銀 首飾 血

筆 生意 飢荒 好字 字

刀 毛太紙 毛六紙 建連紙 川連紙 下箋紙 中箋紙 上箋紙 花箋紙 草紙 火紙 紙

榜紙 阡紙 高麗紙 緞摺紙 冥衣紙 刷印紙 古連紙 毛八紙 燈花紙 沙碌紙 海箋紙 連史紙 杠連紙

假面紙 毛頭紙 西紙 五色紙 西青紙 青紅紙 木紅紙 南紅紙 桑皮紙 甲紙 軟連紙 長行紙 蠟箋紙

表心紙 巨紅紙 石丹紙 白露紙 曹黃紙 油紅紙 灰平紙 包裹紙 赤金紙 烏金紙

盤 生意 買賣 架子 鞍子 爐 機 棋

營 兵馬 官軍 官兵 勇

哨 人馬 勇

統 天下 江山

合 墨鏡 硯池 米 草

捲 鋪蓋 衣裳 綢子 紙 布

對 茶杯 高照 紗燈 燈籠 燈台 蠟台 環子 鐲子 匣子 布 粉盒

頭棍 御棍 甘蔗棍 獸刀 鬼頭刀 三尖刀 象鼻刀 拳蛇 拳鑽 朝天凳 鉞斧 金瓜 蓋碗

書僮 鴛鴦 夫妻 棍 鎖鍊子 板子 鞭子 串鑼 耳箭 令箭 牌 旂 過路

野雞 班鳩 喜鵲 牛 羊 猪 鴿子 鴨子 雞 丫鬟 童男女

LESSON CXLI.

希 醜 冷清 滑 鬆 髒

精 拙 肥 輕 混 細 薄 光 淡

透 肥 歡	迸 硬 緊 歡
粉 白 細 | 潔 淨 綠	漫 行 好 可以 過得去 殼用的 熱 怕 亮醜

LESSON CXLII.

老 時節 一會子 歇 深 寬	怪 氣 好 急 難 暈 咬 癢 懶 臊 臭 寃
通 黃 透	悶 笨 巧 快 慢 膩 餓 乏 緊 疑惑 暖和 難受 淒涼
爭 清 新 楞 綠 明	惡心 不濟 煩躁
溜 長 窖 尖 彎	焦 熱 乾 躁 急 黃 酥 黏 綠 悶 黑 酸

LESSON CXLIII.

頭 與頭 開頭 閃頭 衝頭 過頭 喫頭 喝頭 守頭 幹頭 題頭 要頭	間頭 喚頭 打頭 挨頭 折頭 扣頭 長頭 賠頭 穿頭 巴結頭 咬頭 贅頭

LESSON CXLVII.

頓 打 罵 責備 耍笑 要戲	稞 草 柴 木頭 劈柴 棒子 蘆柴 松柴 麥稭 麥穰 秫稭 穀草

	豆稭 條子 甎 洋貨 洋布細 火油箱 碗 書
細	葱 韭菜 草 芥菜 芹菜 麥子 秫稭 穀草 條子 莊稼 海帶
	松柴 柴伙 洋布 繩子
道	河 光 虹 山澗 堤 文書 本章 摺奏 縫
罈	醋 油 蝦醬 鹹菜 腐乳
壺	茶 水 漿
身	衣裳 袍子 馬褂
綹	繩子 頭繩
團	爛泥 艾子 邪氣 絨 雪 火 丸子 彈子
帖	藥方 告示
方	甎 牆 板 豆腐
拃 搽	長 寬 厚 深
節	竹子 書 長 高 話 情理 烟衝
擡	轎
滴	油 酒 淚 墨
馱	柴伙 劈柴 貨
擔	草 柴伙 行李 馱子 水 筲 水菓子 菜
箱	書 藥 洋火 火藥 洋鎗
盒	肥皂 官粉 奶油 糖漿 蜜餞菓子
桶	柚子 靛 油 漆 水 糖 麪 糞 針
卷	書 經書 子書 史記 綱鑑 閒書 小說 經
回	書 閒書 小說

章 書算 法	**號** 船簿呈卷牌房買貨 子子子子子賣
篇 書賦話論古歌 文	**桌** 酒飯客祭

LESSON CXLVIII.

絕 瘦	**生** 酸	**膠** 糍	
喬 黃白臭苦酸澀醜		**惡** 熱戰搶罵霸	
皎 白	**四** 直	**齁** 臭苦辣酸澀	
活 醜現討辣臭澀 厭		**天** 青	

LESSON CXLIX.

雪 亮	**漂** 亮	**血** 紅	**蜜** 甜
滾 開燙	**罄** 乾光空 淨	**顯** 綠	**鮮** 紅亮
啊 煖	**澈** 清亮	**死** 緊懶蠻慢兒橫沉冷利混 害帳	

LESSON CLIV.

密糊糊的　黑糊糊的　黏糊糊的　濃糊糊的　綠生生的　黃生生的　藍生生的　俏生生的　毒巴巴的　勝巴巴的　澀巴巴的　窄巴巴的　穩巴巴的

禿溜溜的　喜溜溜的　淺溜溜的　賤溜溜的　扁溜溜的　順溜溜的　輕溜溜的　長溜溜的　急溜溜的　滑溜溜的　酸溜溜的　勻溜溜的　細溜溜的

LESSON CLV.

艮騰騰的　慢騰騰的　氣騰騰的　熱騰騰的　腥剌剌的　磣剌剌的　饞拉拉的　笨拉拉的　低拉拉的　疲拉拉的

酸拉拉的　伈拉拉的　疼孜孜的　美孜孜的　嫩和和的　順和和的　柔和和的　露漬漬的　膿漬漬的　滑漬漬的　鼓張張的　暈張張的　昏張張的

LESSON CLXVI.

俏爭爭的

亮爭爭的　風颼颼的　清颼颼的　涼颼颼的　亂搗搗的　忙搗搗的　跑搗搗的　嚴實實的　煞實實的　扎實實的　硬實實的　獷轟轟的　臊轟轟的

LESSON CLXVII.

黃乾乾的　獨伶伶的　實落落的　亂杈杈的　豎椿椿的　水汪汪的　潤滋滋的　淺薄薄的　狠盤盤的　喘呼呼的　樂顛顛的　溜舒舒的　腫胖胖的

高量量的　轂輪輪的　粗輪輪的　俊俏俏的　黑烏烏的　綠微微的　麻辣辣的　忙活活的　怒恨恨的　亂嚷嚷的　吵嚷嚷的　直挺挺的　響亮亮的

懶塌塌的　輕妙妙的　死板板的　軟箐箐的　直苗苗的　花斑斑的　惡猴猴的　稀郎郎的　窮栖栖的　活現現的　光滑滑的　毛毫毫的　矮趴趴的

LESSON CLXVIII.

得慌：熏得慌　暈得慌　樽得慌　癱得慌　邊得慌　磨得慌　擠得慌　烤得慌　臊得慌

的慌：勒的慌　鬧的慌　曬的慌　饞的慌

布刺的

滑布刺的 仇布刺的 笨布刺的 蠢布刺的 窩布刺的 衚布刺的 黑布刺的 刁布刺的 拗布刺的 傻布刺的 彪布刺的

佯布刺的 烏布刺的 混布刺的

LESSON CLXXXIII.

死

釘死 刺死 壓死 燒死 澇死 旱死 乾死 餓死 碰死 嚇死 氣死

夾死 擠死 踹死 笑死 哭死 砸死 砍死 吹死 熏死 病死 殺死 絞死 勒死

無用死 糊塗死 腫死 咬死 累死 窮死 樂死 喜死 撚死 揘死

煞

笑煞 吹煞 恨煞 勒煞 燙煞 乾煞 餓煞 熏煞 悶煞 嚇煞 氣煞

無用煞 糊塗煞 腫煞 咬煞 累煞 窮煞 樂煞 喜煞 堵煞 糊煞 擠煞 踹煞 哭煞

LESSON CLXXXIV.

開言開語 不卑不亢 不冷不熱 不硬不軟 不高不矮 不大不小 不言不語 半公半私 半人半鬼 半陰半陽 半眞半假 半信半疑 半含半吐

百巧百能 百發百中 百戰百勝 明爭明講 倫買倫賣 年前年後 脚前脚後 公事公辦 直打直飛 細吹細打 聾聲聾氣 脚踹脚蹤 貼心貼意

能文能武 能說能道 一生一世 滿收滿出 滿打滿算 盡心盡力 離心離德 人山人海 講打講鬧 講長講短 衚頭衚腦 瞜頭瞜腦 嫌好嫌歹

現世現報 像模像樣 二心二意 同心同德 猴頭猴腦 不仁不義 不忠不孝 作福作威 揚武揚威 沒上沒下 沒大沒小 沒反沒正 口大口小

知人知己 頭緊脚緊 身大力大 橫算豎算 算來算去 走來走去 能硬能軟 大出大賣 大包大攬 大鑲大緣 大哭大叫 大吃大喝 大手大脚

直絲直縚 直哭直罵 多才多藝 知進知退 年吃年用 獨門獨院 苦巴苦掖 聽說聽道 看上看下 聲答聲應 有好有歹 有哭有笑 隨得隨失

順心順意 如心如意 眼巴眼望 硬搶硬奪 自作自受 自賣自身 自消自滅 自怨自恨 自思自嘆 自說自道 自言自語 志大言大 話到禮到

現躉現賣 救苦救難 大慈大悲 全聖全善 全權全能 無生無死 無形無像 無盡無休 無窮無盡 無始無終

LESSON CLXXXV.

積少成多
寒來暑往
指東說西
喜新厭舊
男盜女娼
生前死後
頭上腳下
陽奉陰違
明擒暗縱
明升暗降
超前越後
承上起下
前思後慮

夫倡婦隨
男左女右
男婚女嫁
同父異母
好生惡殺
苦盡甜來
朝出夜歸
去舊換新
改邪歸正
棄邪歸正
棄假崇眞
好善惡惡
有頭無尾

生離死別
裏奸外曹
窮家富路
裏鉤外連
內憂外患
上和下睦
男扮女裝
父慈子孝
長話短說
左歪右扭
有眼無珠
有爵無祿
文東武西

老有少心
眉來眼去
南爭北戰
東擋西殺
大事小情
大街小巷
裏應外合
城裏關外
福善禍淫
天父地母
去惡向善
厭故喜新
折長補短

出死入生
天昏地暗
天高地厚
舍近圖遠
南跑北奔
東跑西奔
夜聚晝散
凶多吉少
捨己爲人
有嘴無心
上行下效

天狠地狗
緜來毫去
大驚小怪
大哭小叫
倚官嚇民
倚大壓小
倚强壓弱
屈打成招
虛告實審
假公濟私
輕說重報
閃輕躲重
胎前產後

LESSON CLXXXVI.

三頭六臂
一官半職
一呼百諾
一倡百和
一順百順
一了百斷
萬無一失
說千道萬
千說萬道
千言萬語
千山萬水
千人萬馬
十米九糠

緊七慢八
歪七裂八
歪七扭八
七个八个
七零八落
七青八黃
七死八活
七疼八癢
七高八矮
七高八低
七長八短
七上八下
七損八傷

一子兩業
一句兩開
一刀兩斷
一車兩馬
三魂七魄
三兄四弟
三節兩壽
千錯萬錯
一舉兩得
三敦四錯

三分五落
五零七亂
五零七散
五花六花
三花五花
三恍兩恍
三起兩落
三教九流
三從四德
三賢四德
馬二騙三
結二連三
重三道四

十有九成
九江八河
五湖四海
四通八達
四平八穩
左五右六
前三後四
三朋四友
三親六故
三年五載
三言五語
四蓬五亂
四分五落

LESSON CXCV.

探頭舒腦
老街舊鄰
一口同音
一口同聲
合口同聲
同心合意
斬鋼截鐵
咬鋼嚼鐵
咬牙切齒
替手換腳
福輕命薄
天昏地暗
起誓發願

起咒發誓
跺腳捶胸
爭名奪利
甜言蜜語
巧言花語
嬌生慣養
身小力薄
家成業就
心滿意足
指手畫腳
耳聾眼花
風吹草動
順風打旂

油頭粉面 鳴鑼擊鼓 觸目警心 奇思妙想 鬼哭神號 神差鬼使 神清夢穩 神清氣爽 嘴拙心笨 沽名邀譽 忠臣義士 頂盔貫甲 眉清目秀

讀書念卷 開門見山 深溝陡澗 海濶天空 青山綠水 修身養性 克己復禮 清心寡欲 邪情惡欲 捨死拼命 礶頭撒野 風花雪月 花街柳巷

灰心失志 傾家敗產 呼天號地 藥石成仇 忠言逆耳 良藥苦口 水長船高 仗義疎財 興利除害 貪贓賣法 致君澤民 作官爲宦 光宗耀祖

牙清口白 人困馬乏 助紂爲虐 手到病除 飽食暖衣 冬溫夏凉 悔罪改過 宿娼嫖妓 揚眉吐氣 賊眼流星 轉彎抹角 回心轉意 喪胆失志

年頭月盡 銅傍鐵底 倚官仗勢 油嘴滑舌 冰消瓦解 水閣凉亭 烟熏火燎 掐訣念咒 畫符念咒 頭昏腦悶 關門閉戶 謹言慎行 堵漸防微

臙滿肉肥 探囊取物 如膠似漆 酒池肉林 搖頭擺尾 瞞心昧己 出類拔萃 行遠自邇 登高自卑 皇親國舅 稱孤道寡 傾心吐胆 日久年遠

龍睛虎眼 髈大腰粗 虎背熊腰 指桑罵槐 敲山震虎 打草驚蛇 指山賣磨 胡言亂語 胡思亂想 少吃儉用 急手忙腳 飄江過海 改頭換腦

弄神搗鬼 看風駛船 見景生情 絕子斷孫 旁門左道 分門別戶 雲山霧罩 奇頭怪腦 昏頭脹腦 驚魂失色 聚精會神 耀眼爭光 龍睛虎目

幸災樂禍 脚大臉醜 張牙舞爪 死皮賴臉 撒謊調脾 驚天動地 正顏厲色 和顏悅色 死心塌地 上樹跳井 無風起浪 拙嘴笨舌 伶牙俐齒

沾親帶故 觸類旁通 借事爲由 平心靜氣 安居樂業 綢袍緞褂 細皮白肉 紅口白牙 人多勢衆 戶大人多 門當戶對 高樓大厦 順情達理

胡打亂敲 欺孤滅寡 打公罵婆 無功食祿 登山爬陵 堵門塞戶 積怨作仇 舌乾脣焦 摳心挖膽 心驚肉跳 披頭散髮 惜皮愛肉 坐井觀天

貨眞價實 銅打鐵鑄 泥塑木雕 誣良爲盜 皮開肉綻 頭破血出 鼻青臉腫 妻離子散 筋出力盡 狠心狗肺 人強馬壯 兵荒馬亂 赤手空拳

LESSON CXCVI.

天地君親師 公侯伯子男 覺悟記思像 喉舌脣齒牙

元亨利貞

金銀銅鐵 男女老幼 方圓平直 吹彈歌舞 鰥寡孤獨 加減乘除 雨雪風霜 綾羅綢緞 天地人物 福祿壽禧 孝廉方正 農工商賈 前後左右

花草樹木 貧富貴賤 衣衾棺槨 日月星宿 父母妻子 盃盤碗盞 旂鑼傘扇 切磋琢磨 筆墨紙硯 抑揚頓錯 烟茶酒飯 行動坐臥 樓臺殿閣

II.

DIALOGUES AND ORATIONS.

It was primarily intended to accompany the following dialogues and orations with a vocabulary and notes, but the great pressure of other engagements has prevented the accomplishment of this purpose. They will prove interesting and profitable reading for the student. They will be found to contain a large variety of useful terms.

The orations are selected from a number prepared in the Tungchow College, as specimens of Chinese oratory.

Dialogues.

1 盤問西事 Inquiry into Western Affairs.
2 備造樓房 Preparations for building a Foreign House.
3 家務常言 Domestic Conversation.
4 媒人說媒 A Go-between arranging a Marriage Engagement.
5 追討賬目 Collecting Accounts.
6 構訟小品 A Specimen of Litigation.
7 風水 Wind and Water.
8 買賣講價 Making Bargains in Business.
9 生童考試 Candidates attending Examinations.
10 親眷相稱 Essay—Mutual Relationships.

Orations.

1 太甲悔過 T'ai Chia's Repentance.
2 武王誓師 King Wu Charging his Generals.
3 孟子 Eulogy on Mencius.

盤問西事

在光緒十年八月間、有美國的范牧師、和福山的丁先生、一同上青州府去傳道、走到朱橋、天色已晚、就上利興店住宿、剛喫過晚飯、來了一位趙先生、問起西國的許多事來、先是問丁先生、後又親自問范先生、今將他們所談的話、記在下面、○趙說○你這位客、是那裏呀、○丁說○好說、我是從烟台來的、○趙說○是什麼生意發財、○丁說○沒有生意、我是一个傳道的人、和一位外國先生、要往青州府去、○趙說○哦、你是跟着鬼子下來的嗎、○丁說○我看你老先生、本是一个知禮的人、怎麼張口叫人鬼子呢、○趙說○不叫他鬼子、叫什麼呢、○丁說○該稱他是外國先生、○趙說○失言失言、請問你給他當通事、一個月掙多少銀子呢、○丁說○我和他出來、原不是爲多掙錢、乃是情願帮助傳道、所以一个月、也不過是五六吊錢、○趙說○他們也是越來越精細喇、初過來的時候、給他當通事的、一個月總掉不下／少不了十拉多兩銀子、如今連一半也掙不出來了、○丁說○天下的人、都是如此、但凡能省、還有不省的嗎、○趙說○這也是理、但一個月掙五六吊錢、却也不犯着去隨他們了、○丁說○據閣下這樣說來、難道人就是錢要緊嗎、世上的好事、就是賠錢、還有做的喇、○趙說○喫誰向誰、你旣隨了他們、也只得順着他們說就是了、○丁說○我原來是咱們天朝／大朝的人、現在還是天朝／大朝的人、怎麽說是隨了他們呢、○趙說○你隨了他們的教、豈不是隨了他們嗎、○丁說○隨教、那不算是隨了他們、因爲耶穌教的道理、就是老天爺／天老爺的道理、這老天爺／天老爺乃是天下萬國的老天爺／天老爺、他們當敬拜、我們也當敬拜、所以我們隨教、並不是隨了他們、若說是要隨他們、只怕他們還不要呢、○趙說○他們若不圖人隨他、也必別有所圖、不

然、他們爲什麽來到我們國裡呢、○丁說○你說他們別有所圖、在你看他是圖什麽呢、○趙說○那个我可不知道喇、誰知道他是圖什麽呢、○丁說○先生你不知道、還不能尋思尋思／思想思想嗎、大槪人以外國人所圖的、無非是圖名圖利、或是圖謀天下、這麽着／的先生仔細想一想、若說他圖名罷、到處人都叫他鬼子、這還算个好名嗎、若說是圖利罷、他們下來傳道、花許多盤費、送人無數的書、又開學房、又設醫院、都是花錢的道兒、這豈是圖利嗎、若說是圖天下罷、誰不曉得外國人的鎗砲利害、他們就必發大兵來、硬强爭奪、那能差這麽幾個傳道的先生、規規矩矩的勸化人呢、別的不講、只看咸豐年間、英國和法國打破了北京、他們若要奪中國的江山、豈不是容而且易嗎、從這些地方看起來、鑿鑿可據、他們不是圖名利、也不是圖天下的、○趙說○這樣、他們到底是爲什麽來的呢、○丁說○就是因爲他們先得了耶穌道理、知道人都有罪、非悔改信耶穌、死後難免罪報、不能得天堂的永生、所以纔來到中國、告訴我

們免罪報、得永生的法子、至於別的心思、是一點兒沒有的。○趙說○我聽說跟着他們念書的、都被他們載(裝)到外國去了、○丁說○那都是瞎話、我就是跟着他們念書的、出學堂門已經有八九年了、怎麼他們沒載(裝)了我去呢、就是我的同窗、共有七八十號人、也沒載(裝)去一個、所以你別聽那些瞎話、你想他要我們幹(作)什麼呢、○趙說○那些上女學的、可有叫他們載(裝)了去的、○丁說○這個先生親眼見過嗎、○趙說○見倒沒有見過、人家却都這樣說呢、○丁說○我知道你必是聽人說的、這都是混造謠言、沒有影兒(子)的事情、因為我的家裡、就是一個女學生、和他一同上學的姑娘們、現在已經都出了閣(門)、那裏有被他們載(裝)了去的呢、○趙說○你跟的這位外國先生、有家眷沒有、○丁說○有家眷、連孩子都一大羣(陣)喇、○趙說○人家都說他們的女人、比男的大、這個是真是假呢、○丁說○那兒來的話、他們拿着女人、不像我們這樣輕賤就是了、若說女人大似男人、天下並沒有這樣的地方、○趙說○怎麼聽我們莊上

創烟台的說、他們的女人、說甚麼(怎樣)就是甚麼(怎樣)呢、○丁說○那也不怪、因為外國女人、都念過書、論他們的聰明本事、差不多和男人一樣、所以男人作事、必商議他、就是男人不在家的時候、或是事多忙不過來、女人也能代辦、其實女人仍舊是順從男人、○趙說○這樣、他們開女學堂、是男先生教呢、還是女先生教呢、○丁說○大概女學堂的事、都是外國師娘(師母)經管的、教書却是我們本地的男先生、或是女先生、都有教的、○趙說○在他們學堂裏、都念什麼書呢、○丁說○也就是念四書五經、另外還學天下通行的學問書、就是天文地理格物算法等類、○趙說○如今去念書的、還是隨便(任)什麼都管嗎、○丁說○不能隨便(任)什麼都管、如今不管衣裳、不管鋪蓋、却還管飯、管筆墨書紙、和先生的束脩、○趙說○這也是他們行的一件好事、一年得(要)花一宗好錢喇(呢)、○丁說○趕自花一宗好錢、○趙說○他們花這些錢、是自己掏腰呢、還是他們的王子發給呢、○丁說○又不是他們自己掏腰、又不是他們的王子發給、是他

們本國信道的人、所捐出來的、○趙說○他們一年有多少出息、○丁說○一個人有一千多塊洋錢的進項、因爲外國人的身工／身價比我們貴、就是當苦力的、一天至少還挣一塊洋錢喇、○趙說○他們的銀錢、總是比天朝的更厚、／大朝的寬餘可惜我現在老了、若在年輕的時候、我也願意入這一教、○丁說○我怕先生看錯了、這耶穌教、並不是爲那些求財的人預備的、乃是爲那些求永生的人預備的、若爲在今世發財入教、入也入不進去、若爲死後得永生入教、越老纔越要緊喇、○趙說○若不嫌老、我有心見見這位外國先生、他叫見不叫見呢、○丁說○怎麼不叫見、只怕我們不肯見啊、我們若肯見他、就沒有個不叫見的理、○趙說○他懂得我們的話嗎、○丁說○懂得、學的很好的官話喇、○趙說○我們見他們、當行什麼禮呢、○丁說○沒有什麼格外的禮、也就是作揖請安、和我們本地人一樣、○趙說○他現在沒睡覺啊、○丁說○睡覺還早喇、我領你進去見見他罷、○趙說○怎麼好勞動你呢、○丁說○那不要緊、○

趙說○還要請教先生、這位外國先生姓什麼呢、○丁說○姓范、就是奚范彭鄖的范字、○兩個人到了上房門口、丁先生先進去見范先生說、有一位趙先生、願意進來談談、○范說○很好、請他進來罷、○丁先生遂即請趙先生進去、一見了面、趙先生就作揖問安、范先生也回禮讓坐、○趙說○先生喫了晚飯嗎、○范說○已經吃過多時了、趙先生也喫了嗎、○趙說○也喫過了、先生今年高壽啊、○范說○不敢當、我今年四十八歲、○趙說○先生的口音、倒很清楚喇、○范說○我已經學了多年、說的也不算很好、○趙說○貴國是那一國呀、○范說○敝國是美國、○趙說○美國的大小、比中國怎麼樣呢、○范說○有中國十八省、帶上滿洲、蒙古、伊犂、西藏、青海、攏總合起來那麼大、○趙說○哎呀、這不是很大嗎、大約地土也比這裡肥、○范說○實在比這裡肥、因爲那裡都是新開的地、所以土肥得很、○趙說○那邊都是種甚麼莊稼、○范說○常種的莊稼、就是麥子、稻子、包米、山藥豆白薯、地蛋地瓜、洋山芋山芋這四五樣、○趙說○哦、那裡還有包米和(白薯 地瓜 山芋)嗎、○范說○怎麼說是還有呢、連中國的包米和(白薯 地瓜 山芋)原起都是從美國來的、○趙說○是嗎、這個我今天纔聽見說、從前的時候、只知道鴉片烟是從那邊來的、○范說○論到那種東西、却不是從美國來的、多半是從印度國來的、其實這幾年就是從印度來的也很有限、因爲你們本國已經種開了、現在有好幾省、差不多淨種罌粟、○趙說○可不是啊、我們中國眞是被大烟害的苦喇、在美國也有喫的沒有、○范說○聽說這幾年、也有一半個喫的、但是民間急急的要斷、所以大烟在美國害人、不能像中國這樣的利害、○趙說○這裡看美國、是看東呢、是看西呢、○范說○也可說是看東、也可說是看西、○趙說○怎麼又看東又看西呢、○范說○因爲地是圓的、好像大球一般、中國在這一面、美國在那一面、所以從中國往美國去、向東向西、都能到得了、○趙說○美國若在地那一面、那裏的人、豈不是頭朝下了嗎、○范說○我恐怕越說、先生越不明白、這是關乎天文的講究、按天文的理、

是(日頭 太陽)吸着地球、地球就圍繞(日頭 太陽)運行在太虛之間、地球以外、任那裏都是無邊的虛空、因此地球這面的人、就以這面的虛空爲天、地球那面的人、就以那面的虛空爲天、總而言之、人無論在地球那一方、都是脚踏地、頭頂天、所以如今我在中國固然覺着頭朝上、從前我在美國、也是覺着頭朝上、○趙說○請問先生、剛纔講到地球在空中運轉、是怎樣轉法呢、○范說○地球原有兩個轉法、一是自己滾着轉、每轉一次、就是一天、一是繞着(日頭 太陽)轉、每轉一個大圈、就是一年、○趙說○明明天往西轉、怎麼說是地轉呢、○范說○你看天上的日月星辰、都是東出西落、好像是天往西轉、那知道所以看着天往西轉、正是因爲地往東轉、好比船在海上、明明是船往前走、但人在船上看着、竟是水往後走、又比方對月亮看雲彩、明明是雲彩往南跑、看着却是月亮往北跑、論到地向東轉、看着天像西轉、也是如此、○趙說○若果眞是地轉、我們轉到底下的時候、豈不掉下去了嗎、○范說○不能掉下去、因爲地球有極大

的吸力、凡在上面的山海人物、都吸住了、所以人在地球上、無論轉到那面、只覺得頭上有天、腳下有地、永遠沒有掉下去的時候、○趙說○聽先生講這個地、也像該是圓的、然而我心裏、總是含含糊糊的、○范說○圓的一定是圓的、若不然的時候、往東往西、還能都上美國去嗎、○趙說○上美國的這兩條道、路是那一條更近呢、○范說○東道更近、○趙說○走東道路有多遠呢、○范說○若一直筆直的走、有二萬多里、但火輪船、不能一直筆直的走、所以大約有三萬里路、○趙說○先生來的時候、在船上走了幾天呢、○范說○走了二十八天、○趙說○哎喲、這個火輪船、怎麼跑的這樣快呢、這不是一天能跑一千多里路嗎、○范說○是、一天總能跑一千多路、○趙說○先生在我們中國、有多少年哪、○范說○今年來了二十年整、○趙說○府上在那裡呢、○范說○敝處在烟台東山上、○趙說○先生在那裡是開學房學堂呢、是在講書堂裡呢、○范說○我的正事、是開學房學堂、但是每年在春秋兩季、總必騰出幾個月來、下來傳道、

○趙說○先生共有多少學生、○范說○現在有六十多個、○趙說○哎呀、這也儘殼先生忙的咯、那裡還有出來的工夫呢、○范說○論到有工夫、可實在是沒有工夫、但是我心裡有兩樣頂要緊的事、不得不出來告訴人、○趙說○什麼要緊的事、○范說○頭一樣、就是說人死了、不能拉倒、因為人在老天爺天老爺跟前、通統有罪、死後必受罪報、就是下地獄、永永遠遠的受苦、所以人當早早醒悟、快快求一個免罪的法子、○趙說○有什麼免罪的法子、○范說○那就是第二樣、我要告訴人的、人要想着免罪、自己的法子全不行、惟獨老天爺天老爺所設的法子纔行呢、因為老天爺天老爺曾打發他的兒子降世為人、名叫耶穌、特為來作救主、死在十字架上、因此我們雖然有罪、只用悔罪改過、信靠耶穌、耶穌就肯擔當我們的罪、老天爺天老爺看耶穌的情面、也肯饒赦我們的罪、這是老天爺天老爺特為給人預備免罪的法子、所以先生若要脫離地獄的永刑、得着天堂的永福、非信靠這位救主不可、○趙說○總是敬天敬地、行好、好啊、○范說○

敬天敬地、這是先生自己的話、耶穌道理、却不是叫人敬天敬地、是教人敬天地的主宰、因爲天地原是有形的死物、敬他不但沒有好處、而且還是得罪我們所當敬拜的老天爺天老爺○趙說○先生從來回家幾邊呢、○范說○只回去了一遭、○趙說○家裡都有什麽人哪、○范說○我的父母雙全、還有一個兄弟、一個妹妹、○趙說○先生跟前有幾位令郎、○范說○我沒有兒子、只有四個女兒、○趙說○你們貴國的人、若老了無子、也行說討小嗎、○范說○沒有爲生子說討小的、必得喪了妻、纔可以另續一個呢、○趙說○行過繼不行呢、○范說○也沒有過繼的、○趙說○那邊沒有上墳拜墓的禮嗎、○范說○這上墳拜墓、原是一個糊塗風俗、凡耶穌教行開的地方、總沒有上墳拜墓的、因爲按眞理說、應當獨獨拜老天爺天老爺、至於在我們老的上人身上、雖然應當生養死葬、死後常追念他、却斷不可拜他的墳墓、也不可以他爲神、去拜他的牌位、若是拜了、就是大大的得罪老天爺天老爺、所以先生不要看上墳拜墓是一件好事啊、○

趙說○先生曉得如今栽這些線杆子、到底是什麽意思呢、○范說○沒有別的意思、就是用他傳信、○趙說○傳信怎麽看不見呢、○范說○因爲是用電氣傳、電氣順着鐵絲走、人是看不見的、○趙說○有時聽見一欻欻的響、那就是傳信嗎、○范說○那是風颳的、不是傳信、傳信的時候、又不能看見、又不能聽見、○趙說○旣然又不能看見、又不能聽見、傳到頭怎麽就曉得了呢、○范說○在頭上當頭有一個機器、能寫出來、○趙說○罷了、能了、人家當初怎麽做得出來呢、○范說○那也不是一日之工想的、○趙說○從發信到見信、得要用多少工夫呢、○范說○並不用多少工夫、無論是幾千里、或幾萬里、這頭一發、那頭立時就曉得了、正好像我當面對你說話一樣、○趙說○這電氣到底是個什麽東西、能這樣快呢、○范說○電氣就是空中所打的雷啊、○趙說○哎呀、那個東西還好傳信嗎、○范說○中國只知道雷能擊人、但按格物的理、不但能用他傳信、還能用他點燈、用他鍍金、又能用他治病、○趙說○人有癆病、好不好用電氣治呢、○范說○治癆病不好用電氣、是先生有癆病嗎、○趙說○可不是啊、我原來就是一個癆病底子、但這幾年、犯(發)的更重、每逢到冬天的時候、常常咳嗽吐痰、痰裡也常帶血、○范說○像這樣的病、很不容易治、先生不如到烟台施醫院去、在那裡有一位出名的外國醫生、請他給你看一看、○趙說○烟台那位醫生、是眞果的捨藥呢、還是要謝儀呢、○范說○不要謝儀、都是白白捨給人家、還不但是白捨藥喇、而且又預備現成的房子、現成的牀鋪、就是病的利害的、也有人上心伺候、○趙說○那倒好極喇、可惜今年天冷了、我不能去、赶來年暖和的時候、我可必去求求醫、○范說○我也看先生該去纔是、但先生要緊要禱告老天爺(天老爺)、求他叫你的病能彀好了、更求他饒赦你的罪、叫你死後上天堂、在天堂那裡、就永遠沒有這樣的病了、○趙說○今天晚上、多多領(討)教喇、先生可以歇(歪着)歇息歇息罷、○范說○怎麼先生不坐了嗎、○趙說○外頭已經打三更咯、等以後到烟台再見(會)罷、○范說○等到烟台再見(會)、請罷、

備造樓房

有英國一位雅素先生、要修一座樓、就對王有容先生說、我打算盖一座兩層樓、不知得(要)多少材料、用多少工、我預備了二千兩銀子、也不知彀不彀、○王先生說、那但看雅先生要怎樣蓋法、是蓋多高多大、總得先畫出一個樣子來、叫木瓦匠看看、樣樣盤算盤算、然後纔能知其大畧、○雅說、○我已經畫了箇圖樣、將地基和各牆的尺寸、連門窗的大小、以及屋內的長短寬窄、都開的明明白白、但不知瓦匠是那箇好、木匠是那箇靠得住、○王說○論瓦匠的手藝、是劉瓦匠好、但他所用的人、三饞十懶的、不正經給人家做、至於孫瓦匠、手藝雖然不見好、他所用的人、却有些好手、做營生(生活)也勤苦、○雅說○這麼着(的)、我們就用孫瓦匠就是喇、木匠是那箇好呢、○王說○我看素常用的李木匠就好、先生也知道他的手藝、○雅說○好、這幾天你可以把他們叫來、商議商議、○王先生說完了話、就出來了、到第二天、雅

先生又請他進去、問他說、這地方買磚瓦是怎麼講究的呢○王說○論磚有好幾路講究、有青磚、二色子、黑磚、共分三路、價錢也不一樣○雅說○怎麼叫作青磚○王說○這樣磚燒出來的時候、是箇灰色、磚的聲音也响亮○雅說○怎麼叫作二色子和黑磚呢○王說○這二色子磚燒出來的時候、是兩樣色、有灰色、有黑色、所以叫他二色子、至於黑磚、燒的時候、並沒燒熟、顏色又是黑的、所以叫黑磚○雅說○磚的成色既不一樣、行市怎麼樣呢○王說○是按着成色扣錢的○雅說○這麼着的、我們就買點黑磚和二色子、預備房子裏面用○王說○很可用得、因爲裏面的牆壁子、雨淋不着、水也濕不着、就是砌上土坯土墼、也沒有壞○雅說○先生去叫木瓦匠來沒有○王說○叫過他們來、他們說、下半天必來○雅說○好、等他們來再說罷○到了下半天、木匠先來了、見了王先生說、聽說雅先生要蓋座樓房、打算預備點木料○王說○得多少木料○木匠說○不知道是怎麼箇蓋法○王說○雅先生畫了箇圖樣在這裏、上頭都開的明白、你看看就知道喇○木匠看了一遍、又仔細算計了一回、就說、總得五百料木頭○王說○做甚麼用那麼些木頭○木匠說○蓋造樓房、全是一棵木頭、少了就不彀用的○王說○我們先見見雅先生再說罷○二人既見了雅先生、木匠就說、方纔聽見王先生說、先生打算蓋座樓、要先預備點材料○雅說○得多少材料呢○木匠說○我剛纔和王先生說來、總得五百料木頭○雅說○做甚麼用這麼些木頭○木匠說○照着先生開的圖樣、說給先生聽聽、客廳客堂和書房的地板、廚房和飯廳吃飯堂的地板、過道的地板、二層樓上的地板、和地板底下的托樑、樓下的護貼牆板、二層樓上的護貼牆板、再是這些門框、門墳心、門旁的貼板、門上的擱木、下頭的門磡、這些窗的窗框、窗旁的貼板、窗上的擱木連窗台、還有支厦子的六根柱子、八架大柁樑、三根頂樑柱、四副叉手、四根擎天柱、二十二枝檁、一枝脊杦、再還有托簷板、天花板、椽子、以及樓梯、扶手、欄杆、這一切的東西、還不得五百料木頭嗎、若要用望板、板笆就是五百料也不彀、○雅說○這麼着、的你就先去買木頭罷、却不知道現在的木頭甚麼價錢、○木匠說、○今年的青楊白楊、都是貴的、楸木桐木、更不用說、就是口北松的價碼不大、算上車價也不過一吊四五百錢一料、○雅先生問王先生說、咱們前頭買的甚麼行市呢、○王說○前頭買的口北松、是一吊三百五一料、今年較比起來也不算貴、○雅說○若本地木頭、有好成色的、隨現在的行市看着買就是喇、至於大料、我要着人到海口上去買、○木匠說完了話、出來和王先生說、今年的木頭、也就是難買、○王說○雅先生叫你去買、你先去買買看、可有一件、千萬要留神、不要買輸了眼力、○木匠說○那是自然的、還能不算計着買嗎、○到第二天、孫瓦匠也來見王先生、王先生說、昨天打發人叫你、你怎麼不來呢、○瓦匠說○昨天回家晚了、所以今天早早的來咯、聽說雅先生要蓋座樓房、是眞的嗎、○王說○是、在這裏有箇圖樣、你仔細看看、就知道喇、○瓦匠看了一回就說、勞王先生的駕、進去通報通報、我們見了雅先生、再作商議罷、王先生隨卽見了雅先生說、瓦匠來了、要見見先生、○雅說○叫他進來罷、○瓦匠進去、雅先生說、我要蓋座樓房、不知瓦作的材料、得用多少、○瓦匠說○請先生先說說、要蓋甚麼樣的、○雅說○要蓋一座坐北向南的二層樓、磚砌山牆、石打地基、瓦作房蓋、四角歸圓的、至於房間的寬窄大小、我畫了個圖樣、在王先生手裏、你看看就知道喇、○王說○先生畫的圖樣、孫師傅、司務已經見過了、現在請他打算打算、都用甚麼材料、各樣材料預備多少、○瓦匠說○瓦作用的材料、就是磚瓦、石頭、石灰、這是幾樣頂要緊的、可先定規他二萬青磚、其餘二色子和黑磚、可照五千定規、不彀的時候再添、定規磚的時候、總要和窰上講明白、磚出了窰、准我們去驗看驗看、看中了纔許他送、瓦窰上的瓦、也叫他送二萬來、不彀用的再添、而且也要和他講明白、准我們驗看、若沒有瘖瘂破碎、纔許他送來、至於石灰石頭等項、那些都好說、○雅說○你可以和王先生商議、看着定規就是喇、○瓦匠遂同王先生出來、到外書房說、窰上的磚、買的時候、得長（眼力/眼色）、○王說○怎麼說○瓦匠說○先生不知道嗎、現在我們這個地方、開了兩座窰、南窰上的磚、燒的成色很好、價錢也不大、就是做磚的泥鬆、不（耐/扛）年數、北窰上的磚、燒的和南窰上一樣、價錢大、難講、但是他做磚的泥、又細又有筋、能多（耐/扛）年數、○王說○等他們窰上來的時候、再和他定規罷、○瓦匠說完了話、就走了、

○雅先生一日叫了王先生進去說、我聽見說、這裏蓋房子的木瓦匠、有（卯子工/僱工）的、有包工的、到底包工好、是（卯子工/僱工）好呢、○王說○若論修蓋的結實、是（卯子工/僱工）好、論省事、却是包工好、但只一件、如今的人、奸滑的多、若是和他們包工、待他有不合式的地方、他就給你（使壞/淨混）、若是（卯子工/僱工）、就不能有這些弊病、但做一天是一天的工錢、他就（挨延/挨遲）些日子、到房子蓋起來、總比包工多（耐/扛）年數、○雅說○這麼（着/的）、咱們就商議着（卯子工/僱工）就是了、

○王先生出來、恰巧碰見南窰主、來攬買賣、王先生讓在書房內坐下、南窰主說、雅先生修蓋樓房、用多少磚呢、○王說○用多用少、你得說箇價錢、○窰主就將青磚、並二色子、和黑磚、各樣價錢、說了一遍、○王說○這是（實落/實在）價錢嗎、○窰主說、○這都是賣開的行市、○王說○好、等我商議商議雅先生、明天再來見話罷、○到第二天、北窰主也來了、王先生問了問各樣磚的價錢、兩家較比起來、差不多少、王先生說、你們都要說少了不賣的價錢、我好給你們商議、若行市太大了、恐怕生意做不成、淨白跑腿、○兩家窰主一齊答應說、這就是最少的價錢、你只管去商議罷、管保能成、○王說○好、你們有事先去做罷、等下半天再來定規、○他們去後、王先生見了雅先生、說南北兩家窰主都來過了、他們說的磚價相仿、○雅說○甚麼行市呢、○王說○他們說、每萬青磚、一百吊錢、其餘的二色子、和黑磚、按着扣錢、○雅說○比前年買的磚、價錢一樣不一樣呢、○王說○比前年多着十幾吊錢、○雅說○今年怎麼這樣貴、○王說○他們說、今年柴草貴、較比前年的行市、總得一百吊錢、纔賣得着、○雅說○柴草雖貴、也差不了

那麼些錢、你總得要用點經紀、和他們講、不可由着他們的斗量。○王說○這麼着的可以給他多少錢呢。○雅說○你看着和他們講、他們實在說是今年柴草貴、只可給他加上五吊錢、行就行、不行也就不要了、○王先生出來的時候、兩家窰主早已來了、王先生問北窰主說、你的磚、到底甚麼價錢賣、○北窰主說、我並沒多說錢、再少了就不够本喇、兩個爭論了一回、到底沒能說定、○南窰主說、你老人家不是不知道、今年各樣的燒草、都比去年貴、就是一百吊錢賣磚、也沒有甚麼賺頭、若再少了更不用說喇、○王說○我纔和雅先生商議來、雅先生說、去年買的磚、是八十五吊錢、今年怎麼就得一百吊錢呢、若實在是少了不賣、不一定必得今年修蓋、明年也可以修蓋、後來好歹圓全圓成到九十吊錢、再多一文也不要、若是這個價錢賣、就立合同、若是這個價錢不賣、也就可以不要了、○南窰主說、先生既說到這裏、我們實在不好意思再爭了、只是求求先生的面子、多支幾吊錢做個本、好去買草○王說○好、我上去給你們說說、○這時候南窰主、將北窰主叫到背地裏說、夥計呀、怎麼樣呢、我看價錢爭到盡處喇、再要爭、買賣恐怕散了、他若多開幾吊錢給我們、就答應了罷、○北窰主說、我看也是、我們隨着辦罷、○兩個窰主、又進來說、二色子和黑磚、怎麼講呢、○王說○還是按常規扣下錢錢就是喇、○兩個窰主說、好、就是罷、我們拜託你老人家、要緊費心給說說、多支幾吊錢纔好咯、○王說○忘不了你們的錢哪、遂卽進去見了雅先生說、窰上的磚、照九十吊錢定規了、他們要想多支幾吊錢壓合同、可以給他多少呢、○雅說○他們可以靠得住、你打算去罷、○王說○他們也是多年的老買賣、準可以靠得住、我打算每人先給他四十吊錢、好不好呢、○雅先生說、好、王先生就出來、對窰主說、我們寫合同罷、無論用多用少、都是你兩家均着分做、○窰主說○就是那麼着的罷、我們的合同、也請先生代筆寫寫就完了、○王先生應允、先替南窰寫了一張、上面寫的是立合同南窰許全忠、攬到英國雅先生、青磚二萬、二色磚五千、黑磚五千、言明價錢、青磚九十吊、二色磚八十吊、黑磚七十吊、車脚在內、定於三月初八日送到、不許有悞、恐後無憑、立合同存證、當收錢四十吊、保人孔中樓、光緒十二年正月十八日立、替北窰寫的合同、也是一樣、後來又替雅先生寫了一張、給南窰、上言立合同英國雅素買到南窰許全忠青磚二萬、二色磚五千、黑磚五千、言明價錢、青磚九十吊、二色磚八十吊、黑磚七十吊、定於三月初八日送到、不許有悞、恐後無憑、立合同存證、當支錢四十吊、保人孔中樓、光緒十二年正月十八日立、寫給北窰的合同、也是如此、兩家既將合同收好、王先生就對窰匠說、你們的磚、算定規妥當了、往後送磚的時候、總得總要我們先驗看、驗看好了、纔許送來、〇窰主說、那是自然的、說完了話、他們就走了、〇接着瓦窰主、又來賣瓦、對王先生說、聽說雅先生蓋樓、要蓋瓦的、這幾年我們的瓦、都是加工細作的、可以照顧照顧、〇王說〇你來賣瓦、先把價錢說說、〇瓦戶說〇聽說你們用的磚、已經定妥了、價錢比去年高、我們的瓦、不是好說的嗎、先生看着罷、〇王說〇我怎麼看法、總得你自己說說、〇瓦戶說〇前頭有車、後頭有轍、磚既長了錢、瓦也難落價、都是因爲今年的柴草貴、所有的窰貨、沒有一樣不貴的、〇王說〇不用說廢話、快說價錢就是喇、〇瓦戶說〇去年的青瓦、每萬三十二吊、今年柴草這一貴、就可以照四十二吊開了、〇王說〇你們的瓦、比不得他們的磚、磚的價錢貴、因爲送磚的道路遠、是貴在脚錢上、不是貴在磚上、至於你們的窰、離城最近、送瓦很覺方便、價錢若太大了、那還行得嗎、我經手多少年、也沒想着四十多吊錢買瓦、〇瓦戶說、我算沒說、你老人家看着怎麼講、就怎麼講、〇王說〇去年的瓦、原是三十二吊錢、今年柴草貴、我給你商議商議、照三十五吊錢開、也就滿可以了、你賣就賣、你若不賣、這個價錢、到別個窰上、也能買得出來、〇瓦戶聽見到別個窰上去買、就急忙對王先生說、多年都是買我的瓦、這回要買別人的、叫人家看着也不像件事、你說三十五吊、就是三十五吊、賠着本我也要賣、不圖這次還圖下次喇、〇王說○這麼着的、我去見見雅先生、對他說明白了、我們就寫合同○王先生見了雅先生說、瓦窰上纔來賣瓦、他說了四十二吊錢一萬、我嫌他的價錢太貴、他說今年柴草貴、所有窰中燒出來的東西、通都長錢、他又說、磚旣長了錢、瓦就難落價、我和他講到三十五吊、他心裏還是猶豫不定的○雅說○上年買的瓦多少錢呢、○王說○上年買的是三十二吊、今年多加三吊錢○雅說○他少了不賣嗎○王說○他說這是最少的價錢、若再少了、就不够本咯○雅說○若實在是少了不賣、和他定規就是了、○王先生出來、照雅先生的話、說了一回、就定規先要四萬、彼此寫的合同、也和買磚的合同相彷、言明瘖瘂破碎、瓦戶照章賠補、當交壓合同錢十吊、各人收執一張、就散開了○此後賣石灰的、賣石頭的、都也講明了價錢、立了合同、再有推細沙子沙的、以及打土坯士墼的、也都定規日期來做活、○有一天、青石坑的主人來見王先生、說石板買了沒有、若沒買、咱們是老主顧、○王說○自然是買你的、現在要用坐窗四塊、連枕石二塊、盤臺子的石板六丈、通用出山淨、得多少錢一尺呢、○坑主說○坐窗連枕、淨出來得八百錢一尺、盤臺石只淨一面、也得六百錢一尺、○王說○還得說說不○坑主說○說說就說說、怎麼說罷、○王說、咱們兩個一口價、也不用囉囉唆唆、坐窗連枕、照七百五給你、開盤臺子石板、照五百五開、行不行呢○坑主說○我說的價、都是賣開的價、你老先生要落矮錢、我恐怕對不起別處呀、○王說○價錢是在各人講、還有生熟不一樣、若是來個生客、十年九不遇的買一回、你們沒有下次的盼望、價錢也許大一些、頭一件、這裏的修造差不多每年一次、第二件、我們這裏用石板、都是用你的、不圖這次、還圖下次、常言說、淡薄一分利錢吃飽飯、十分利錢餓死人、若是要的價錢狠了、不一定就買你的呀、○坑主說○到底你們念書的人、就是能說、死人也叫你說活了、有你老人家這張嘴、還有成不上來的買賣嗎、就照你老人家還的價錢、去商議罷○王先生遂卽去見雅先生說、我們應該用的石板、現在同坑主講妥了、○雅說○甚麼價錢呢、○王說○坐窗連枕七百五一尺盤臺子石板五百五一尺、○雅說○這個價錢開的怎麼樣呢、也沒打聽打聽人家是怎麼開的、○王說○連年就是這個價錢、○雅說○既是常行的價錢、就和他定規罷、○王先生遂跟之/遂隨身出來、立了合同、彼此交收了、○雅先生又把王先生、請進書房問他說、房子的材料齊了不齊、○王說○材料都齊了、就是下脚子/傢伙還不齊、○雅說○都是少甚麼東西、○王說○就是紮脚手/跐脚的杆子、繩子、抬石頭的紮法繩、/麻辮子/麻索子和托子、盛石灰的槽子/斗子和灰兠子、還有抬筐、擔筐、鍬钁/鍬鐝抬扁担、這些東西、○雅說○咱們當不了用、早早預備、好動工、○王說○還有件事、商議先生、這房子上的箔/笆、不知用甚麼的、○雅說○本地都是用甚麼的、○王說○本地有用荊條編的、有用秫秸勒的、也有用葦箔的、也有用望板/板笆的、○雅說○我看不如用望板/板笆好、○王說○要用望板/板笆、還得再添木頭、○雅說○這麼着/的、你告訴木匠去買罷、再是瓦匠來了、可以告訴他、牆根脚/牆基要打得結結實實的、不許糊弄、若有糊弄的地方、叫我看出來、我却不能讓他、○王說○大約他們可不敢混我們、再還有一件事、就是這些木瓦匠、到底是卯子工/僱工呢、是包工呢、○雅說○花錢蓋房子、總要蓋的結實、我看着包工、總不如卯子工/僱工做的好、我聽說人家包工蓋的房子、不是今日脊漏、就是明日瓦壞、那不是白花了錢嗎、○王說○卯子工/僱工就是囉唆一點、不但得/要時刻經心、到第五天上、還得酒飯犒勞他們、○雅說○你告訴他們說罷、總要用幾把好手藝的、殷殷勤勤的做營生/工夫、那一個不正經做、立時就不要他、到蓋起房子的時候、必要格外多給他酒錢、至於犒勞、我這裏不能預備、他們只可每天照工錢外、每名給他加上五十個錢、總比他吃犒勞上算得多、○王說○這麼的、他們那一個敢不正經做呢、○王先生從書房出來、着人叫了木瓦匠來、將雅先生安排的章程、說了一遍、○木瓦匠都說、雅先生既是卯子工/僱工、又給他們加錢、再不正經給先生做、那眞是沒有良心了、我們再求先生、問問雅先生、幾時開工、我們好安排人、○

王先生隨時進去商議明白了、出來對他們說、雅先生已經定規到三月初六開工、今天是二月二十八、還有八天、○木瓦匠答應說、好、到那天我們都一早來、

家務常言

婆婆　孫李氏

長子　國寶　長媳　趙氏　長子之子天來子

次子　國棟　次媳　張氏　次子長女桂齡　次女喜齡

三子　國華　三媳　劉氏

婆婆○我今天要到東街、你二嬸娘家去瞧瞧(看看)你三個人在家裡、趕緊的把活兒(營生)(生活)做做、若有不知道的、或是不會的、就問問你大嫂子、叫他告訴怎麽做、○大媳○我也有不會的、恐(看)告訴錯了呢、○婆婆○不要緊、你比他們來的年數多、又做慣了、大概不能錯、我要去喇、○衆媳○媽媽早些回來呀、省得黑天沒日(黑燈下火)的、叫人不放心、○婆婆答應一聲就走了、不多時走到東街、問道二嬸子在家裏嗎、○二嫂○在家裏呀、進來罷、哎喲、我的老妯娌、你好啊、○孫李氏○我好啊、二嫂子你好啊、○二嫂○我倒好喇、他們小妯娌都好啊、○孫李氏○都好啊、他們都叫我問二嫂子好、○二嫂○叫他們惦記着(罣着)快坐下歇歇兒罷、○孫李氏○你的年忙完喇、○二嫂○我們(俺)沒有甚麽忙、不過多少做點子就是喇、你家的人多、過年的東西、諒來都忙完喇罷、○孫李氏○算了(罷罷)罷、人倒不少、整天家(成天的)不知忙些甚麽、俗語說、人多亂、龍多旱、母雞多了不下蛋、一點兒不錯、○二嫂○到底還是人多好、自古道、人齊山也倒、有人有世界、看看你現在熬(守)得兒子媳婦、都雙雙對對的、就是受點累也願意、○孫李氏○二嫂子你不知道(曉得)、今天我特意要到你家裏來清閒清閒、在家忒鬧的過不得喇、○二嫂○我看你的三個媳婦、順情順理的都好、小孩子們又聽說、這都是因爲你平日教導的好啊、○孫李氏○題起他們順情順理來、我告訴給二嫂你聽聽、大媳婦來了多年、家裏的事情、都摸着門兒了、也學的會做、就是不願做、只顧做他男人和四個孩子的東西、這二媳婦、三個孩子的鞋脚衣裳、也顧不了、連自已整天家頭不像頭、脚

不像脚、不但沒本事做、又懶又滑、還常說扭話(橫話)氣人、第三個的、三個孩子穿的都整整齊齊的、也能做、就是嘴不成嘴、動不動就罵人、愛說閒話、愛挑眼、大家受不了他的氣、你想家口大了、孩子們多了、那能都管着穿呢、○二嫂○可不是嗎(那待是啊)○孫李氏○所以從去年、我立個規矩、一年每個房頭給他一吊五百錢、或買花紡、或買布穿、小子(小厮/小孖)會上學、就穿合衆(公衆)的、各人管各人自己的男人孩子、這老大家、小子(小厮/孖兒)們都大了、只有一個女兒穿的還不巴結、老二家、小子(小厮/小孖)纔兩歲、還有兩個無用的丫頭子、自己又不願紡花、怎麼會不襤褸呢、老三家、孩子們也還都小、不能穿合衆(公衆)的、所以老二和老三、常嘟囔我不公道、指使他們做點甚麼、這個就懶得動彈(動身)、那個就掉嘴滑舌的、俗語說、耳不聽、心不煩、聽了心裏不自然、成天家(成天的)生不了的閒氣、所以我到你家來告訴告訴、解解我的愁、二嫂子你可別(莫)見笑啊、○二嫂○嗐、我的老妯娌、你怎麼說來、我那得你這麼個人來說說話、還敢見笑嗎、家務事誰家能沒有、只要你做老的、能拿得起、

放得下、該說的說、該指使的指使、公公道道的、他們就不敢說別的、不知我說的對不對、○孫李氏○二嫂子說的眞不錯、我就是這個主意、○二嫂○今天也不知道老妯娌你來、也沒預備點好飯、我做點便飯你吃、你可別嫌哪、○孫李氏○千萬的別費事、○二嫂○沒有事費啊、○話分兩頭、再說三媳婦因爲婆婆出門、交付大媳婦、心中不服、就對大媳說、他奶奶(婆婆)今天不在家、這說不了、羊羣裏跑出駱駝來、顯着你是個大牲口喇、晌午(中上)做甚麼吃呢、○大媳○昨天晌午(中上)吃甚麼、今天還做甚麼吃、○三媳○去年的皇曆、今年可不好使(用)喇○大媳○依着你要怎樣做呢、○三媳○他奶奶(婆婆)臨走囑咐叫問你、就沒有錯、○大媳○這麼着(的)、你願做甚麼吃、再問問他二嬸子願做甚麼、就做甚麼好不好、○三媳○怎麼單問那鷹嘴鴨子爪的人、能吃不能拿的東西、○大媳○您二嬸子、今日他奶奶(婆婆)不在家、我們商議着做甚麼飯吃、○二媳○我不管家裏甚麼東西不都在您手裏、問我不及問您的波稜蓋正沒味、○三媳○這不

是、我先說不用問他、你偏問他、天不早喇、咱們擀麪吃好不好、○大媳○他奶奶婆婆回來不依、怎麼樣吃、○三媳○他不依有我、○大媳○好啊、這麼着的你快去擀、我就添火坐鍋、添鍋燒火○只有二媳、仍舊坐在炕上紡花、不但不動彈、嘴裏還嘟嘟囔囔唧唧咕咕的說、人家的孩子穿大家的、俺的孩子淨穿自己的、使殺怎麼樣紡、也賺不了穿、這兩個小劈材子、死一個也好、我也輕省輕省、○三媳○二嫂子別鼓氣喇、你每年不是也領吊半錢嗎、誰還比你多嗎、是你比別人還邋遢無能呢、○正說話之間、二媳的大女兒桂齡、哭着來見他媽、他媽問他說、你這該死的哭甚麼、○桂齡○大娘大媽打我、○二媳○打你、你不會不哭、何必要哭沒廉恥、不害羞、我看你頭頂火炭不覺熱、○大媳○您二嬸子、你怎麼說話不清不混的、桂齡在那裏把鍋臺、看鍋頭我摑擊他一指頭、叫他閃開、還犯着你說這樣的話嗎、○二媽○饒除倒是打了俺我的孩子、俺我罵孩子、倒罵出不是來了嗎、我知道又出來個二號二行婆婆、○大媳○你放屁、現在還有老的、誰管你、常言道、好狗看住自己的家、你這不識好

歹的東西、我沒那麼大工夫和你打膛、○此時三媳、已經將飯擺好、長子國寶、和他兩個兒子、連作活的老王、都來家吃飯、老王說、今天吃麪、是誰過生日、○三媳○今天是特爲犒勞夥計、就算給你過生日罷、○及至男的吃飽走了、大媳說、他們已經吃飽喇、我們也都吃罷、二媳的兩個女兒、剛纔拿起碗麪來、二媳就指着他女兒罵起來了、說、你們這些不要臉的東西劗子、就是得了饞癆喇、怎麼這樣嘴急急食呢、○三媳○你這個不害羞的浪榿架子、是有娘養、沒娘教、大嫂子說一聲都吃飯、就該快來饢搡饡胃、還要說長道短的罵人、我問你、這些不要臉的東西劗子、都是誰、你指給我看看、我要撕扯掙你、你纔得了饞癆饞痞、又有懶癆懶痞呢喇、○兩個爭吵了半天、還是他大嫂子說、快拉倒罷、不要鬭那些沒味的嘴、他奶奶婆婆不久就回來了、叫他聽見、不知道我們又怎麼鬧來、再是叫街坊鄰舍家聽見笑話、二人這纔不言語了、○既刷完了鍋、大媳和三媳、各人忙各人的鍼線、只有二媳、氣的上炕睡覺去了、○到了半過晌、孩子跑來家說、我奶俺婆

奶／婆回來喇、〇大媳婦爲吃麪的緣故、沒有話說、不敢來見、〇三媳婦一聽見婆婆回來了、就急忙出來迎接說、媽媽回來了嗎、〇婆婆〇回來喇、〇三媳〇媽媽今天不在家、俺還照你的規矩、晌午／中上吃的麪啊、〇婆婆〇今天沒有過生日的啊、〇三媳〇做活的老王、是今天生日、〇婆婆〇哦、老王的生活做的不錯、他過生日、也該吃頓麪條子、好拴着他的腿、〇大媳〇媽媽怎麼回來這麼早呢、〇婆婆〇我有心同你二大娘、再說會話、一陣一陣的耳朶熱、我惦記着家裏、恐怕有甚麼事情、就早早回來了、正說話的時候、老王挑了一擔水來、倒在缸／甕裏、〇婆婆〇老王啊、你的記性很好、還想着你的生日、〇老王〇老太太啊、我小時候、常忘記自己的生日、自從我的娘告訴了我、我這纔記住喇、他說吃麪那天、就是你的生日、今天我又過生日喇、說着大家笑了一頓、都也沒有言語的、因爲各人心裏都明白、却沒受老人家的氣、〇次日婆婆向三個媳婦說、今天是臘月二十喇、你們各人給男人孩子、把穿的戴的、都做齊全了沒有呢、〇大媳〇他爺們有去年過年的衣裳、只有兩雙襪子沒成就、躭誤不了他們過年、〇婆婆問二媳婦說、你呢、〇二媳〇別說沒有東西、就是有也做不起來了、〇婆婆又問三媳婦說、你呢、〇三媳〇我從來不怕做活計／營生／生活、就是巧媳婦作不出沒米的粥來、〇婆婆〇你織的那些布、都那裏去了、〇三媳〇我自從娶過／將進門來、頭一年給我吊半錢的棉花、還管着男人穿戴、若是攤／遇着個做莊稼的男人、衣裳還好將就些、就是攤／遇着個做買賣的男人也好、因爲錢頭是便宜的、腰裏／腰捴子／胯裏／胯夾的、不過是左眼的眵、抹在右眼裏、這個偏偏攤／遇着個書獃子、連箱子帶櫃裏、不是書就是字紙、並沒有那樣的家當、偏要上城裏去念、跟着城裏學的那路窮排塲、捺底子鞋不穿、布帽子不戴、學了個大尾巴狠的樣子、就打着人家請他十回、他請人一回、也得若干錢花、都不是從我手頭撙／搾出來的嗎、那還有存下的、倒是每年合裏／公衆給一吊五百錢、又有這三個孩子穿、我又不會偷、還有個甚麼法掙得呢、〇婆婆〇怎麼逢說起話來、你就不三不四的、嘴裏罵不絕聲的、一點規矩沒有、往後你就不使喚媳婦嗎、你沒有別的東西、連兩墨(疋)粗布也沒有嗎、○三媳○若是不嫌、粗布還有啊、○婆婆○咱們這個日月、能和有錢的人家一樣穿戴嗎、叫他大爺買上幾十個錢的品色、把粗布染染、舊的湊補上裏子、只要整整齊齊、新新鮮鮮的也可以見得高人貴客、○二媳○人家有粗布的就嫌、我這個不嫌的又沒有、○三媳○那却不行、真的假不得、假的真不得、你織了多少布、做了多少衣裳、還算計不出來嗎、○婆婆○快把你的布拿出來、好叫他三嬸子替你做做、○三媳○這一分派、可就拉了倒喇、○國寶○您三嬸子、你不要生氣、我纔聽得明白、咱(我們)媽媽不是硬派你、是催他二嬸子的布、他二嬸子若做不起來、能不請你幫幫他嗎、就是不請、居家過日子、都是魚帮水、水帮魚、我已經遇着了、您是話不透機、您三嬸子看我的臉面、聽我的話、給他做做罷、○三媳○我並不是格外咬牙(打牙)、咱們家裏、誰的東西我沒做過呢、怎麼連妯娌的東西也派起來了、不論甚

麼事、就是天牌打地牌嗎、大哥哥既然說到這裏、臉面置千金、我就是抱十二分委屈、還好不做嗎、叫他拿了來罷、○國寶○好啊、原是能者多勞、○婆婆○桂齡啊、你三嬸子帮着你媽做鍼綫、你可以給他哄着孩子、○桂齡○我不能、○二媳○你怎麼不能、你看你脚上連雙新鞋沒有、你不抱孩子、也不能給你做新鞋過年哪、我告訴你說、你別把兩隻脚好好包之、看人家瑞香、和你一天包的脚、現在人家包的溜轂輪的、你這個還挓挱在五下裏、大人給你包一包、你就哭阿叫阿的疼、自己又捨不得包、整天家拖着裹脚頭子、走起來又倒坐、又歪歪像個甚麼東西、你現在不包、單等到你婆婆家纔包嗎、恨起來、我就給你兩笤箒疙瘩(柄)、天地間沒有你這樣的賤才東西、快去抱孩子去、○三媳○不用他抱、我給他嬭一嬭、他就睡喇、○二媳○你嬸子不用你抱孩子、你就去梳梳頭罷、○桂齡○我自己不會梳○二媳○八九歲的東西、自己連頭也不會梳、過來我給你梳梳罷、了不得了、這些虱子都滾成蛋(毬)喇、別(莫)動、我給你

搯搯罷、你看看這些蟣子、直到頭髮稍都是、就像那大米乾飯樣、○婆婆○多少日子也不知給孩子刮刮(篦篾)頭、還唧咕孩子長虱子喇、○二媳○天生這種沒出息的東西、長了這麽幾根黃毛、早早叫虱子咬掉了纔好喇、○婆婆○快給他梳梳紮起來、要做甚麽、好叫他三嬸子帮着你做、你們妯娌兩個忙鍼綫、我和你大嫂子就忙吃的、○大媳○今年打算蒸多少乾粮媽啊、○婆婆○蒸他五篦(屜)子年糕、五篦(屜)子粿餾(絲糕)四篦(屜)子肉包子、三篦(屜)子栥餑餑、兩篦(屜)子粿餅、三十個大供、再蒸上篦(屜)子秫秫栥角子、好打發要飯的就得喇、○從此合家大小、都忙過年的東西、有一天國寶的兒子、對他爹爹說、過年這幾天、人家都有新帽子、我這個帽子、又舊又不時興、等赶集的時候、給我買個帽子、再給我買雙時樣的好鞋、○他爹爹說、今年將就將就罷、過年再買、○他孩子見父親不願意、就求他二嬸子、和他三嬸子的情面、他爹却(挪)不過去、好歹纔買了個帽子給他孩子、又給那些女孩子們買些花粉、連家裏女人們應用的東西、這一

天、年已經忙完了、二媳來和三媳說、若不是你帮着做、我們娘兒們、只得披着囫圇布過年、○三媳○誰叫你不會做、你比別人還少長那一樣嗎、○二媳一扭就走喇、去撿(拾)自己雞下的蛋、却找不着、抓着雞摸一摸、精瘪的肚子、就生氣說、蛋也不知叫那個賊根子撿去了、○三媳對大媳說、二劈材子不知在外念嘟什麽、還罵雞罵狗的、○二媳○我說你來嗎、我的雞下的蛋、不知叫誰撿(拾)去了、還能擋住人家說嗎、○三媳○算了罷、這算你有理、我不敢惹你、○國寶○這是那個孩子屙(㞎)的這些屎、難道鼻子聾(瞎)了、聞不見、眼睛也瞎了、看不見嗎、若是來了客、這是個甚麽樣子呢、○三媳○那定是桂齡姊妹們屙(㞎)的、自己沒空、也該指使個孩子收拾了、○二媳○雞蛋叫人撿去、也找不出個主兒來、院子的屎尿、就是我(俺)的孩子屙(㞎)的、吃東西也找不着我們娘兒們、有了不是、就都是我們的、○大媳○你說話要清楚一點兒、這是他三嬸子(三嬸)說是您孩子、我還說來嗎、○二媳○我還說你說的來嗎、你出來逞的什麽頭、我說吃東

西找不着我們娘兒們、還不是嗎、那一天赶集的、買的梨和落花生、您各人都拿了自己房裏去吃、就給我(俺)孩子兩個落花生、若挪在別人身上、還能肯嗎、○三媳○有出息的營生(事情)、偏偏不做、但學着爭嘴、眞不要臉、○大媳○各人都省兩句罷、您三嬸子、你怎麽管多會兒不會說句柔和(柔安)話、○三媳○兎子跳在墳頭上、要粧大的喇、○大媳○你可了不得了、人家不論說甚麽話、你張口就罵人、○三媳○說句笑話、是罵人嗎、我看你不懂(覺曉)甚麽、○大媳○這都不是罵人嗎、○三媳○可眞(鑿可)不是、○婆婆○聽見他們爭吵不止、就從屋裏出來說、你們(您)這些死東西、只坐了一塊兒、沒有好話說、不是他罵你、就是你罵他、就是我這個老東西、當你們(您)的害、幾時我死了、你們就沒有管轄咯、說着氣的掉了兩滴眼淚、纔要抽身往屋裏走、天來子跑進來說、奶奶(婆婆)啊、俺(我)三叔回來咯、○婆婆○是嗎、從這幾天我就盼(望)他、○國華○媽媽好啊、○婆婆○好啊、不是從十五放了學嗎、怎麽到今天纔回來呢、○國華○因爲算書房(學堂)一年的大賬、又算了舖家的賬、又有同窗們請客、又加上先生收了若干的對子、帮助他寫了些、好容易今天纔辭別了先生、和衆位同窗、媽啊、你怎麽不舒坦嗎、○婆婆○沒不舒坦、我纔睡了點覺、快叫他們收拾點飯你吃、去歇息罷、○到了臘月二十九日傍晚、二子國棟、也回了家、先問母親和哥嫂們好、孩子們也上前來問好、吃了晚飯、大家敘談了一回、婆婆說天不早喇、有話等明天再說罷、又對國棟說、你走的很乏了、去躺(倒)下歇歇兒罷、○國棟就往自己房裏來了、見了他妻張氏說、我來家看看、老少都歡歡喜喜的、像過年的樣兒咯、○二媳○有歡喜的、却臨不到我這裏、幸虧你今天來了家、不然、我二人不見其(得)就能見面了、○國棟○怎麽咯、○二媳○婆婆嫂子的氣、都好受、就是這個三老婆(婆娘)、我題起他來、就氣的渾身亂戰戰、他張口就罵人、凡事壓人三分點、若是不受他的、他還要動打、你看他長的、就是那母老虎、誰能和他打、又加上他的孩子、學的和他那個混帳媽媽一樣、把咱的孩子欺負的、比小一輩子還不如(也不同)、叫我實在沒法和他們一塊兒過、不如死了好、○國棟○聽你的話頭、我知道你的心思了、你是願意自己過是不是、你不想想、你自己能過嗎、我成年家在外邊、衣裳不用你做、又不用洗漿光三個孩子、你也(拾掇/紮裹)不起來、你看看你自己、頭不像頭、腳不像腳、咱們共總一百多畝地、除去養老長孫、不過分二十來畝地、莊稼我從小就沒做、是必得僱人去了、炭錢、還有火錢嗎、再說、你是能上場、你是能送飯、你是能裁、是能縫呢、(打淨撈乾、/好乾淨的)我每年不過掙那五十六十吊的錢、這生意東家還不定做不做、你看(他三叔/三叔叔)雖然在外念書、舉手不動、分開他能過好了、我們却過不住、你若不信、就看看他今年的事、他三嬸子、也是領了(合的/公衆)一吊五百錢、他全買了棉花、不到三月的工夫、紡做綫織成兩個大布、就賣四吊大錢、遂跟着又買上三吊大錢的花、不到半年、織了四個大布、只賣了兩疋、又是四吊來錢、還留了兩疋、盡殼他和孩子穿的、你算算他這一年、甚麼事情也沒躭誤做、淨得了五吊大錢、還剩下兩疋大布、你也是領了一吊五百錢、又加上我私下給你稱了兩三回花、你紡的也不過僅殼您娘兒們穿的、你(想想/尋思)若是分開、咱們這個日子、還有個過嗎、你說你要尋死、你不(惦記着/罣着)大人、難道你就不(惦記着/罣着)這三個孩子了嗎、我勸你(拉着/帶着)孩子好好過罷、不必有別的心思喇、○二媳○我盼望你來家、好作個主、給我出出氣、該有個活路纔是、不料想不但不給我出氣、反倒隨附人家、現在可沒有別的法子了、死了就是喇、○國棟見妻子這樣糊塗、想了多時、想出個妙法來說、你不聽我勸、是一定要尋死嗎、○二媳○我沒法子和他們過了、一定要死喇、○國棟○這麼(着/的)你就死罷、俗語說、老婆是穿的衣、去了舊的換新的、不過這三個孩子(得/要)安排、這個也難爲不着、我把桂齡給他大娘、把喜齡交給他三嬸子、管保學些好(針綫/針黹)、久後到他婆家、再不會受氣、天興子過年十歲、也好上學喇、就穿(合/公衆)的、交給他(奶奶/婆婆)照看着、或者我另尋個好的、也不叫他管別人的衣裳、只叫他(收拾頭腳/收頭收腳)修理自己體體面面的就好、不到三年五載、女兒都出了閣、兒子娶了媳婦、我們兩口子淸淸閒閒、歡歡樂樂的過到老、這就應了俗語說、有福的逼死無福的。○二媳聽說把女兒交在他三嬸子手裏、嚇了個了不得、又聽他男人、待後來的妻子這麼好、他是有福的、逼死我這無福的、心中大被感動、把淚一擦、就說我還不死喇、我活着、不是個釘、還是個刺喇。○國棟○你不如死就是了、這不是刀也有、繩子也有。○二媳○叫我死、我偏又不死喇、可不能把我的孩子們、落在別人手裏、你說有福的逼死無福的、我要等着看看、這有福的到底是誰。○國棟○你若聽勸悔改、這些福眼望着就是你的了、你若不聽我的勸、你白白的死了、淨把些孩子撇給人家喇。○早晨起來、大媳和三媳說、夜裏他二叔叔和他二嬸子、不知說些甚麼、嘓嘓噥噥的直說了半夜。○三媳○那個浪東西、見了他男人、說黃道黑的、不知編些甚麼瞎話喇。○二媳聽見了、就說、我們在房裏說話、愛說什麼就說什麼、你擋不住我們說、你爲什麼背後罵人、你纔是浪東西喇。○三媳摑了大媳一把、說了不得了、叫他聽見了、嚷嚷起來、怎麼對住俺二哥伯伯呢。○大媳就滿臉陪笑、對二媳說、您二嬸子、你別莫生氣、我和他三嬸子、是因爲他弟兄們都回了家、歡喜的特爲和你鬪趣啊、想你別的日子能生氣、今天還能生氣嗎、你看過一年家、老的少的、大人孩子、都熱熱鬧鬧的、氣從那裏生呢、就是氣也是歡氣的、說着大家笑了一頓、就過去了、

媒人說媒

男親家王想　其子連升

女親家欒可　媒人高見

從前有個木匠、姓高名見、住在高家莊、卻常在王家莊做活、有一天高見來到王家莊王想家做活、在門口碰見一位相公、就問他說、你這位相公好面熟、我一時怎麼想不起來呢。○相公○我姓王名叫連升、一向在固莊念書、輕易不來家、我們初次見面、怎麼能認得呢、這裏當家的就是我的父親。○高見○原來是小東家嗎、今年貴庚。○連升○癡長十七歲了。○高見○你丈人家是那裏呢。○連升○還沒有丈人家。○高見○怎麼

的着、從來沒有人提過嗎、○連升○提過、但是所提過的、高的不成、低的不就、都不合我父親的意、○高見○我和你父親相好、我給你做個媒罷、○連升○好啊、多謝、○高見對王想的長工老張說、你在王家做活、有幾年了、○老張○三年有零、○高見○這麼說來、他的家產田地、你該曉得罷、○老張○好地有五十畝、陳粮陳草的、倒是好日子啊、○高見○爲什麼沒給他兒子說講親呢、○老張○他家內外有個難多嘴的緣故、雖常有人提過、總是不能成就、又要門戶對、又要家道足、姑娘還要人品好、若要放心、還得先見見面、因有這些難處、所以就不容易說講了、○高見○要給人做媒、必得先曉得兩家的底細、一來門戶相當、二來男女相配、這纔是做媒的道理、我卻曉得有一個好姑娘、諒來必中他的意、○於是高木匠就做活去了、後來老張乘着機會對王想說、高木匠打聽我家大相公定親的事、上半天對我說、他知道一個好姑娘、人品不錯、家底門戶也相稱、有意要說給大相公、○王想○這個姑娘是那裏呢、○老張○是那裏他倒沒對我說、不如你親自去問問他罷、○王想對他家裏說、有喇、等到晚上、你炒上點菜、燎上壺酒、叫老張去把高木匠請來、說說這個親事、○王婆○好啊、只管請他罷、你和他喝着酒、仔細打聽打聽他罷、○老張○這麼着、我去請他晚上到這裏來罷、○王想○好啊、等等你去請他罷、○老張做了一會活、就到高木匠那裏說、上半天你提到給連升作媒的事、我已經和東家說喇、他叫我來請你晚上到他家裏說會話、○高見○好啊、就是這麼着的罷、○到了晚上、高木匠來到王想家、王想見了就說、○高師傅來喇、進來吃菸罷、○高見○菸是整天家成天的吃、○王想○今天晚上請你、諒來你也知道、俗語說、成不成、酒兩瓶、我們先喝幾盅再講、○高見○何必這樣費事呢、這纔是癡人作保、饞人說媒喇、○王想叫一聲說、快拿酒來喃、○老張○有喇、○王想○這個酒力薄、高師傅多吃上幾杯罷、○高見○酒薄意不薄、自古道君子之交淡如水、就是不吃不喝、也必成人之美、○王想○你要提的親、是那家的姑娘、○高見○欒家村欒可有個姑娘、我今天看見令郞、纔想起來了、○王想○他的門戶家業、怎麽樣呢、○高見○門戶很好、家業雖不算大、卻也有碗飯吃、○王想○你怎麽知道那姑娘的好歹呢、○高見○我在他家做活、親眼見過他的模樣也標緻、性情也溫柔、而且粗細都來得及、○王想○多大歲數了、○高見○聽說是十八、○王想○我兒子十七歲、不知年庚對不對、○高見○男十七女十八、一個屬鼠、一個屬豬、大三婚裏、倒恰合式、○王想○這麽一來、這門親事、我就拜託老兄罷、○高見○你闔家若願意、管許一說就能成、○王想○闔家沒有不願意的、或行或不行、你就給我一個回信罷、○高見○今天叫你花錢費事、實在不安、○王想○不成敬意、○高見○我這兩天是在這邊做活、爲這門親事、明天還得家去喇、告辭了、○王想○上緊的辦罷、我不遠送喇、○王想送到門口、回來就對家裏說、○你們都聽見了、高木匠來所提的親、你們都看好嗎、○王婆○若是說妥了、倒是門好親事、○王想對他兒子連升說、你的意思如何、○連升○婚姻的事、本是天作之合、又有父母之命、爲兒的應當順從、○王想○好、等高木匠的回信罷、○高木匠回家、對他家裏說、我爲王想的兒子提親、要上欒家去一邊做媒咯、○高婆○旣是這樣、早去早回來、○高木匠來到欒家門口、遇見欒可說、欒兄好啊、○欒可看是高木匠、就說、託高師傅的福、我倒好啊、你家裏的人都好嗎、○高見○多謝掛念、雖不怎樣大好、平安就是福了、○欒可○請到家裏吃菸罷、○高見○我正要到你家裏來、○欒可○你是個忙人、爲什麽事、到我這裏來呢、○高見○無事我不來、特爲給令愛提親做媒來的、○欒可○好啊、我說你無事怎麽能來呢、○高見○是好、若是不好、我斷不能來提、眞眞是好、○欒可○高師傅旣是來作媒的、就請把這個好、說給我聽聽、○高見○論到門戶家業、固然是好、就是人物年庚、也很合式、○欒可○是那一家呢、○高見○是王家莊一個莊稼財主、叫王想、他兒子叫連升、一家人忠厚老實、也是很好的日子、○欒可○什麽樣的日子、○高見○好地五十畝、住宅一大片、家裏養的有牛有馬、僱工也有好幾個、陳粮陳草、還有好些存項錢、姑娘過去、吃不了、穿不了、○欒可○他兒子多大了、學什麼事業、○高見○年庚十七、現今在學堂念書、人品文雅、相貌出衆、○欒可○這樣說來、可算得忠厚人家、詩書門第了、○高見○那也算得是了、目下欒兄意思如何、若是看中這門親事、就可以應許了、好歹你我是要窮手藝的人、工夫値錢、○欒可○憑你說的、卻也甚合意、我這邊就算應了罷、你可以到王家去回覆一聲、我也要同他媽商議商議、○高見○我就告辭了、改日再說、不用送、○欒可○那有不送之理呢、○高見○請罷、○欒可把高木匠送走了、就對他家裏和女兒說、纔來的那個高木匠、是特爲女兒提了一門親事來的、我看十分合式、當下也就算應了、○欒婆○是什麼地方的人、姓什麼、叫什麼、○欒可○論名倒是有名的、就是王家莊的莊稼財主王想家的兒、○欒婆○他有多少田地、○欒可○好地約有五十畝、住宅房子、也很

整齊、○欒婆○他有幾個兒子、○欒可○他只有一個兒子、名叫連升、是很好的孩子、○欒婆○他的兒子做什麼、○欒可○現今在學堂念書、倒是生就的聰明、○欒婆○多大歲數了、○欒可○今年十七、年庚也對、○欒婆○我們女兒十八、屬豬的、你算一算、大婚裏對不對、○欒可○男十七女十八、大三婚裏也不錯、○欒婆○你要了多少定親禮、衣服有幾件呢、○欒可○定禮東西、我一點倒沒要、○欒婆一聽沒要兩個字、就變了臉、說定禮東西、一點不要、你就給我作主、把女兒應了親嗎、○欒可○女大不可留、留來留去結寃仇、何必爲這點兒子定禮衣服講究呢、只要他過去、不愁吃、不愁穿、就是了、況且女兒是人家的人、長到一百歲、也是要給人家的、○欒婆○我女兒纔十八、怎麼就說是他大了、你說不可留、我說正該留、到了日期、自有人求、○欒可○自古道女兒養十七八、不是塡房、就是作妾、怎麼沒有人求呢、○欒婆○你好不成人性、女兒是你親生的、怎麼忍得咒駡他塡房做妾呢、而且塡房不塡房、做妾

不做妾、你不能以定規。○欒可○你這個儱賴不賢的老不賢德的老婆堂客、今天你要把我氣死了。○這時候、女兒見他媽爲定親禮、同他爹漚氣、又見他爹說了女兒養到十七八、不是墳房就是作妾的閒話、也就埋怨他爹哭着說、什麼話不好說、單要說做妾呢、○欒婆見他女兒哭了、心裏更加難受、說、你這個老討厭討賤的、今天我要和你對了這個命罷、我女兒並沒有得罪你、你倒把他氣的這個哭、○欒可一見他家裏這樣說法、就搚起拳頭、要來打他、女兒見他爹來打他媽、就急忙上前拉住他爹、跪下哭着說、爹啊、你別生氣、今天我媽惹着你老人家、你也不用打、也不用罵、只求你就我身上、消消氣罷、○當時有個鄰居、名叫硬正、聽見這番吵鬧、就跑進來說、老鄰居啊、你家裏從來風吹草動、半點沒有、今天是爲的什麼呢、○欒姑娘○是因爲我惹的他兩個老人家生氣、○硬正對欒可說、你這是爲的什麼呢、還值得搚着拳頭、瞪着眼睛、好像打架的樣子嗎、○欒可○你問問這個老不賢德的東西、我該不該打他呢、○欒婆○你當是什麼、他作事不講情理、還要打罵我娘兒們、○欒姑娘○不是的、是爲我惹的他、○硬正○你從小聽說、這會子大了、更不能惹你爹生氣、○欒婆○眞是爲女兒的事、○硬正○你說給我聽聽、○欒婆○今天高木匠爲我女兒來做媒、給王想的兒子提親、○硬正○提親做媒是好事、何用生氣呢、○欒婆○這個老討厭討賤的、也不要定禮、也不要衣服、也不商議我們、就把這門親事答應了、○欒可○家有千口、主事一人、我應了親、這就是個不是嗎、○欒婆○應親不要定禮、還算有理嗎、○硬正○爲什麼不要呢、這幾年我們這裏時興的都是要禮物、○欒可○究其實並不是不要、○硬正○你若是要了、又沒有這場爭吵了、○欒可○你只知其一、不知其二、我因爲王家的家道既好、不要也少不了掉的、所以不提定親禮、這是兩家的體面光彩、○欒婆○不要衣裳、女兒過去穿甚麼、不要首飾、女兒過去戴甚麼、這還那裏找體面光彩呢、○欒可○若是現要定禮多少、衣服多少、豈不是拿着女兒賣銀錢嗎、拿着女兒賣銀錢、女兒過去、雖然穿的好、戴的好、還能不被人小看輕看嗎、到臨了、還是個不體面光彩、○欒婆○照你這樣說、給女兒定親、不該要禮了、○欒可○我只爲女兒終身打算、至於定禮的事、媒人總要爲我提到講及、你看體面不體面講究不講究○欒婆○天下要定禮衣服的還少嗎、○欒可○大概各處各風俗、○硬正○你們老兩口、說來說去、都是爲疼愛女兒、一樣的心、○欒可○不是一樣、若是一樣、今天倒不打架了、○硬正就轉身對欒姑娘說、你媽今天恨你爹、只爲沒要定禮、恐怕穿的衣裳、戴的首飾、不如別人好看、他心裏就難過、這不是疼愛你嗎、○欒姑娘因爲有點害羞、就低聲說、是疼愛我、○硬正○再說你爹今天恨你媽、是恐怕他把終身大事看輕、把定禮看重、所以沒要定親禮、這也是疼愛你罷、○欒姑娘仍舊低聲說、也是疼愛我、○硬正○時下有的是門戶也不對、男女也不相配、只一味的講定禮、彷彿是個買賣、那個給的多、就賣給那個、這樣做法、算疼愛不算疼愛呢、○欒姑娘仍照前低聲說、不算疼愛、也不算體面光彩○硬正○你爹爲

你終身要緊、你媽爲你穿戴的要緊、自古道有不孝順的兒女、沒有不慈愛的爹媽、這樣看來、眞是不錯、○欒婆○今天多虧鄰居你來了、沒叫我娘兒們挨他的打、○硬正○常言道遠親不如近鄰、○欒可○今天叫鄰居見笑、只怪老婆糊塗、女兒啼哭、我也有些粗魯、○硬正○家務事那家沒有、還敢見笑嗎、況且喜事口舌多、你看那個喜字、上是十一口、下是廿口、總是七言八語的、○欒可○等親事妥當過禮的時候、請你來作個陪客罷、○硬正○我就是帮着做個媒人也何妨呢、○欒可○旣然如此、託你問問我家裏這個作主的、我應了親事、他肯不肯、○當這時候、欒婆因爲硬正同他女兒說的一番話、纔聽出他男人的意思來、就說、一來有鄰居的媒人、二來你的意思、我纔明白了、答應親事、還是你做主、我沒有不依的、○硬正○你們闔家都願意這門好親事、我也願意作個饞媒人、等我見高見再說罷、我走咯、○欒可○勞駕勞駕、○硬正○好說好說、○且說那高見從欒家回來、就對他家裏說、妥當了、欒可把

親答應了、我爲這件事眞得意了、我要上王家去商量商量、幾時可以吃個定親酒、○高婆○欒家都要的什麼定親禮呢、○高見○一點沒要、○高婆○這纔是體面人家、快些去罷、別耽誤人家的婚姻、○高木匠就來到王家、見了王想說、欒家都願意、因爲您是忠厚人家、詩書門第、可定個日子、就吃定親酒罷、○王想○勞動了高師傅、耽誤工夫、又跑了腿、○高見○這算不得什麼、該當是你們兩家的婚姻、男女的緣分、常言道千里姻緣一線牽、我這不過從旁撮合撮合作合作合就是了、○王想就吩咐說、快預備酒飯罷、○老張○飯早已預備下喇、○王想○拿上來罷、○高見○這又饕餮了、○王想○這不過是便飯、請問欒家要的都是什麼定禮呢、○高見○欒家只爲親事要緊、並沒提到要什麼、○王想○眞是體面人家了、可惜不要倒不如要好、○高見○怎麼說不要倒不如他要好呢、○王想○要的定禮有拘數、不要當更作個臉面、比他要的還該又多又好纔對呢、○高見○荒唐了、我竟把這層忘記了、○王想○今

天三月二十三、定個日子四月初八罷、○王婆○四月初八太急促了、恐怕辦備定禮和別的東西、來不及喇、○高見○這件喜事、總要快當纔好、耽誤日子多了、恐怕有變、○王想就決意說、是咯、一言爲定、四月初八、雙月雙日、取個吉利罷、○高見○好啊、我也好給欒家一個信、叫他到了那個日子、有個預備、今天吃了個酒醉飯飽、我要走喇、○王想○不送喇、請、○高見一直來到欒可家、欒可接着高見、請到家裏說、你從那裏來呢、○高見○我從王家莊來的、○欒可○吃袋菸歇歇罷、○高見○還不什麼累啊、○欒可對家裏說、快去把硬正請過來吃茶罷、○欒婆○我也正打算去請他來、○欒可○請他快過來罷、○欒婆隨就跑去對硬正說、高師傅來了、請你過去吃茶、就走纔好喇、○硬正○我不用請、一叫就到、○欒婆○同我一塊兒走罷、○硬正過來、見了高見說、高師傅在這裏嗎、我曉得你來必是爲王欒兩家的親事、現在怎麼樣了、○高見○王家也答應了、○硬正對高見說、早前我聽見欒兄談及閣下爲他

家姑娘、成全大事、我就心裏說、這件喜事、辦的兩家合式、若不是高某人、斷乎不能成功、後來欒兄又把我拖出來、說是好事成雙、所以我今天纔過來嘴饞。○高見○旣然有兄台出來、這事就更好辦了、你作女家媒人、我作男家媒人罷、○欒可對他家裏說、預備酒飯罷、○欒婆○現成的、○高見○又來添忙招忙了、○欒可對兩個媒人說、王家已經答應親事、定規多喒過禮呢、○高見○定規四月初八、○硬正○喜事總是逢雙日子好、但不知王家預備的什麼定禮、你該曉得罷、○高見○那是要臉的體面人家、總不能錯、○硬正○你怎麼知道不能錯呢、○高見○我在他家是三月二十三、他就擇定四月初八過禮、王家嫂子、嫌其日子太急促了、恐怕買首飾衣服、辦備不及、○硬正○聽他這樣的安排、大約是不能錯的了、○欒婆○衣服定禮、不先要下、我心裏總是有些疑惑、○高見○我又聽見王想的話、他說、那邊不要、我倒反要多花了、○欒可○這眞是要臉的體面人家、○硬正○自古道爭之不足、讓之有餘、○高見○天不早了、我要走喇、○欒可○又勞動高師傅了、○高見○您都坐着、不要送了、○欒可○請罷、○硬正○我也要家去咯、○欒可○你也要家去嗎、請了、○再說高見從王家走了以後、王婆對王想說、媒人都是成雙成對的、纔像件事、有四個的、有六個的、有八個的、至少也是兩個、現在只有高師傅一人、怎麼樣呢、○王想○是啊、還當找上一個纔是、○王婆○你看再找上誰呢、○王想○我看找南莊鄭多事罷、○王婆○自己莊上還有人、爲什麼單要請他呢、○王想○因爲他這幾年、常爲我家連升提親、雖是沒成、可也跑了腿、費了心咯、○王婆○你說請他、就去請罷、晚了、恐怕就誤了、○王想立時起身、不多時來到南莊、恰巧找着多事、就說、我今天是特來請你的、○多事○請我做什麼呢、○王想○我和欒家欒可結了親、是木匠高見的媒人、已經擇定了四月初八吃個定親酒、你去、就是兩個媒人了、○多事○很好啊、我去算個媒人也可、○王想○就是這麼着罷、我要回去喇、○多事○不吃菸喇、請罷、○王想去後、多事忽然想起一門親事、就問他家裏說、我的連襟愛財的女兒多大歲數了、○鄭婆○已經二十多歲喇、○多事○二十多歲、不給他找個婆婆家嗎、○鄭婆○因爲他爹要的定禮東西太多、所以養到如今、○多事○這様、必得財主家纔能說喇、○鄭婆○他爹並不論貧富、也不論歲數大小、只要多給定禮東西、他就應咯、○多事○王想倒是個莊稼小財主、定禮東西、諒必能給、○鄭婆○王想今天找你做什麼、○多事○爲聘欒家村欒可的女兒叫我算個媒人、○鄭婆○你應了他嗎、○多事○我當時雖然應了、後來卻又想起偺的外甥女兒來、願意另把他說給王想家、○鄭婆○那好說(講)嗎、○多事○想個法子、先給他打個破頭楔兒、然後再給他提這門親事、○鄭婆○這個法子可也許行、可以試試看罷、○多事等了幾天、上王家去見了王想、就說、我這幾天、爲你和欒家這門親事、費的心眞不小、纔打聽明白了、○王想○叫你費心、怎麼様、到底好不好、○多事○他的日子門戸都好、○王想○那層不好、

○多事○他的家裏不好、○王想○怎麼不好、○多事○他莊裏有兩句口話說、心眼糊塗手又拙、撒謊(扯謊)罵人頭一個、你想有這様的媽、還能理練(理料)出好女兒來嗎、○王想○常言道買豬不買圈、只求他的女兒好、就中了、○多事○別的不好、都不要緊、但他的女兒、往後可是你家裏的人、○王想○是啊、你見過嗎、○多事○費了這幾天的工夫、纔看見他○王想○什麼様子、○多事○別提了、他生就的奇相、身量又矮、腳又大、而且臉小鼻子歪、還帶着又疤又麻、眼睛又斜斜的、眞可算得個十不全喇、○王婆聽到這裏、就埋怨王想說、我說叫你打聽打聽、你不肯聽、我看如今怎麼辦呢、○王想○不合意就拉倒、還有什麼難處呢、○王婆○自古道只有女家不給、那有男家不要呢、○多事○雖然這様說、但結親必有憑據、現今定禮沒過去、庚帖也沒寫、這事情到底是空的、你要罷婚、誰還能擋住你嗎、○王婆○這句話、倒把我提醒了、這門親事、我們散了罷、不用爲難、○多事見他們兩個、都有後悔之意、就又加上兩句說、

欒家這媒人、我是不作的了、免得後來招些埋怨、若是講到別處、我可作個正媒、○王想○這正虧了你喇、若不是你細心去訪一訪、不但將來啞吧吃黃連、說不出的苦、而且還對不住我的兒子了、○多事○這算什麼、我要走喇、○王想○不送喇、請、○過兩天、高見聽人傳說、王家要廢黃這門親事、慌忙跑來見王想說、你同欒家作親、是彼此願意、已經應允、爲什麼又要拉倒呢、○王想○有兩個緣故、叫我不放心、○高見○那兩個緣故呢、○王想○第一定禮東西我沒有、第二沒親眼看見過他姑娘、○高見○定禮東西、原來欒家沒要、如今要看看他姑娘、也可以的、這門親不能叫你們廢黃喇、○王想○姑娘若叫我先看看、定禮東西也不能少的、○高見○要看還要背着欒家、因爲那邊的風俗、不肯叫姑娘出頭露面、先丟些醜、○王想○只要能看得見、你怎樣說、就怎樣好、○高見○定規四月初三、你先到我家裏、自有個妙法、叫你看見他、○王想○定就日期、我必到的、○高見○一言爲定、那頭也曾出來一個媒人、名叫硬正、我去和他商議商議、就必能行、○王想○好、那頭既然也出來個媒人、你去商議商議、我不攔擋你、○高見○我要去喇、○王想送出來就說、請罷、○高見一直來找硬正說、王欒兩家親事、不曉得什麼人打了破頭楔了、○硬正○不怕人家打破頭楔、王家有你、欒家有我、○高見○王家要看見姑娘纔放心這件事情、卻就叫我爲了難喇、○硬正○他暗地看看、不算爲難、因爲我是鄰居、找點別的小閒事、叫他姑娘到我家裏來、你們也要來到我家裏來的時候、我就叫他從裏往外走、你們就從外往裏走、兩下照個面、就能看個眞切了、○高見○已經定規四月初三、晌中飯前的期、到期就照你所說的行罷、○到了日期、王想來見高見說、怎麼定規了、○高見○我們上硬正家裏去、你看見硬嫂子往外送的那個姑娘、可就是你媳婦了、○王想○我們去罷、○高見○好啊、這就走罷、○旣到了硬正的門口、高見就敲門說、硬大哥在家嗎、○硬正○在家裏、請進來罷、○這時候、欒可的女兒果然在他家裏、聽見有人來就說、你家來了客了、我要走喇、○硬婆說、我去送你罷、○欒姑娘說、可以。○硬婆送他出了大門、見了高見和王想、丟個眼色、王想把欒姑娘上下一看、心裏就歡喜極了、○硬正把王想和高見讓到家中、就問王想說、可當意嗎、○王想○很好、今天這門親事、我可放了心了、○高見○你放心、我也放了心喇、這是誰在你家裏使的壞哪、○王想○是鄭多事、他說的壞話、○高見○你怎麼聽他的話呢、○王想○那天我家裏對我說、只高師傅一個媒人、不像件事、至少也該有兩個、因此我就想起鄭多事、去找他做個副媒人、○高見○什麼人都可做個副媒人、爲什麼單去找他呢、○王想○因爲他從前爲我兒子的親事、也是多過嘴的、○高見○這找的好、幾乎把這門親事打破了、○王想○若早曉得有硬兄作媒人、我何必找鄭多事呢、○硬正○多事這樣使壞、他到底圖些什麼呢、○王想○我聽別人說、是爲他連襟愛財的女兒打算、○硬正○這就是了、○高見○若不是我先看出來、有人說了壞話、這門親事、只好散了、○王想○多謝高師傅、實不枉叫個高見、○硬正○有我的媒人、管有幾個多事、想叫我們另打主意、是萬萬不能的、○王想○有兄台、那怕這事不正過來呢、○高見○俗語說、是婚姻、雷打不散脫、你不用謝我們二人、只求你把定親禮物、好好的預備罷、○硬正○自古道有錢不爲兒女花、待要留着做什麼、我們可不必爲他操心了、○王想○我們各人回家罷、等到四月初八、預備好了定禮、請你二位交給欒家就是了、○二人說好、大家就散了、不幾天到了四月初八、高見同硬正來對王想說、定親禮物預備妥當了嗎、○王想○都預備妥當了、○高見○都是什麼、○王想○這裏有禮單、你看看就知道了、也念給硬兄聽聽、○高見○這個禮單、寫的很清楚、○王想○是請先生寫的、○高見念着說、

謹具

豚肉貳方

喜果肆盤

首飾壹頭

綢緞肆件
打鐲銀廿兩
工費錢拾串

奉申
聘敬

右上

大姻望　翁欒老親家先生大人笑納是荷

眷姻弟王想率男子壻連升頓首拜

高見
冰人
硬正

王想○還有媒柬、你看寫的對不對、○高見○我不敢褒貶、因爲是各處的規矩、比方你纔說的這個媒柬、我那裏就叫金單、也有的地方叫婚書、也有的地方叫庚帖、大約寫的不錯、○王想○你可以看看、○高見一面看、一面念着說、

敬求
金諾
恭候
玉音

右上

大姻望　翁欒老親家先生大人閣下

眷姻弟王想率男子壻連升頓首拜

王想○寫的對不對、○高見○雖然各處不同、大概都是這樣意思、大約寫的不錯、○王想○既是不錯、煩硬兄就領着這些挑的抬的去罷、○高見○今天所預備的、叫我們很增光了、○王想○恐怕還不能中欒家的意罷、○硬正○欒家看見這些東西、必然喜歡、我們吃杯喜酒、兩家親事就成了、○王想○天不早了、○高見○我們快走罷、○到了欒家、欒可接着說、老兄們來了、這實在叫你們費心喇、○高見○理當理當、○欒可○快進家裏去歇歇罷、○高見○請看看那邊送來的東西、當意不當意罷、○硬正○不用看啊、管保十分當意、○欒婆○哎呀、還是要臉的人家、預備的東西、實在不錯、○硬正○自然不錯、那些不要臉的人家、鬼頭蝦蟇眼的、咱就不希和他辦事啊、○欒可○王家預備這些

東西、二位老兄費心不少了。○高見○沒費甚麼心、要臉的人家、又是孩子們終身的大事、豈能在這事上偷省嗎、○欒婆○快給挑抬的人酒錢、叫他們先回去罷、○欒可○我這裏光貪說話、還把這事忘了喇、每人該給他多少錢呢、○高見○多少不要緊、給他幾個酒錢就是了、○欒可○每人給他二百大錢、衆位看着怎麼樣、○高見○不少不少、○欒婆○天不早了、快坐席罷、○欒可○請二位老兄上坐、○高見○不敢不敢、○欒可○理當理當、○高見○今天又叫老兄費事了、○欒可○沒有事費、薄酒淡飯、老兄們包容就是了、○酒飯已畢、欒家寫了領謝和允婚的回帖、高見硬正拿着回帖、到王家去回覆了、遂各自回家、說媒的事、就完結了、

追討賬目

三義號　掌櫃的　全會

莫法治　莫學滑　莫不結　莫學文

三義號掌櫃的、對他夥計全會說、全夥計、你明天下鄉去(要/討)邊賬罷、○全會○(要/討)誰的賬、○掌櫃的○上莫家莊去找莫法治、他欠的錢、到底沒給、叫他們(要/討)(滑/疲)喇、非你去不可、(別/莫)讓他再(搪/抗)喇、○全會○別人家的賬、都好(要/討)、惟有莫法治的賬、提起來叫我也頭疼、○掌櫃的○還就是你去(要/討)纔好、自古道、養軍千日、用軍一時、○全會○無論他有什麼法子、他總是該我們的、不去(要/討)他總不想着還、我明天一早就去罷、○掌櫃的○吃了飯也可以、○全會○要找他、必得趁早、吃了飯去、怕找不着他、○掌櫃的○任憑你罷、○到第二天、全會早早(起/動)(身/身)、傍走到莫家莊的時候、恰巧碰見了莫法治、就問他說、那不是莫大哥嗎、○莫法治○是啊、全掌櫃的要往那裏去、○全會○特爲來找你、你要往那裏去呢、○莫法治○我也是去(要/討)筆賬、好還你們的錢啊、○全會○我不能等你(要/討)了錢來再還我、你今天可先還我的再說、○莫法治○你這個全掌櫃的、怎麼不講理呢、○全會○我怎麼不講理、○莫法治○我(要/討)不(了/到)錢來、(使/用)甚麼還你呢、○全會○這就是個理嗎、若是別人亦不給你、你也一輩子不還賬嗎、○莫法治○自古道錢是通

寶、他給我、我還你、這纔是國寶流通喇。○全會○你今天無論怎麼巧說、想着不給我錢、是萬不能行的。○莫法治○你說這話錯喇、我們正在這路上、你看看天上不下錢、地上也不長錢、我到別處要了給你、你又不叫我去。○全會○你說天不下錢、地不長錢、我說天也下錢、地也長錢、你看今年雨水不缺、莊稼十分收成、這不是天上下的錢、地裏長的錢嗎、莊稼主是指望好年景、糶糧賣草纔有錢、買賣家是指望放出去、收回來、纔有錢、現在這樣的好年頭、打的大囤滿、小囤流、你還說天不下錢、地不長錢嗎、這樣的年頭、你再不還錢、你的賬就不用還喇、○莫法治○我不能不還賬、你得給我點期限、限期或賣糧、或賣草、或是摘借摘借、倒借倒借積借積借預備彀了、給你送去、何等不好呢、○全會○不說送去、倒還罷了、若提起送去、叫人又氣又惱、你從前說年節送到、又應許五月節送到、現在八月節又過了、你送的錢在那裏呢、○莫法治○我欠您多少錢、還值得生這麼大的氣嗎、○全會○去年冬裏、已經當面算清、淨欠錢七吊五百、難道你就忘記了嗎、○莫法治○賬不對、只欠您五吊五百錢、○全會○你又用這個賬不對的法子搪我、已經預備着你喇、我把賬本拿來了、你看看是七吊五不是、○莫法治○這可是七吊五、我想着沒有這麼些錢、恐怕你們是記錯了罷、○全會○這都是一筆一筆的對出來的、○莫法治○我託你到櫃上先給我細查查、如果不錯、我就是還您、心裏也不委屈、○全會○自古道、地憑文書官憑印、買賣家憑賬本、你要不抱屈、除非我不要、○莫法治○你就是不要、我也必還、○全會○你說必還、拿錢來呀、○莫法治○家有萬貫、還有一時不便、怎麼等了我一年多、再等幾天、你好意思不准嗎、○全會、○這就等的有日子了、再不能等咯、○莫法治○罷呀、全老兄你這樣逼勒我、就是要討了錢去、你也摸得不着使用、爲甚麼兩個不交交一個呢、○全會○你這樣說法、更不能行、我摸得不着使用、我就不要了嗎、吃着人的濕的、拿着人的乾的、用我出來送人情嗎、○莫法治○走罷、跟我到家裏、好好請請你、替我到櫃上說幾句好話、我們就是好朋友喇、走罷、我也不去要討賬喇、○全會○就是到你家裏吃了喝了也不能算你還了賬、我就跟你去罷咧、○到了門口莫法治就叫門說、開開門、來了客喇、既進去又說、我們到南屋裏坐罷、又對他兒子莫學滑說、快去點個火來、○他兒子莫學滑、快跑家去、點了火來就站在旁邊伺候、○全會○這位學生是誰、○莫法治○我的大小子小廝小兒啊、○全會○今年十幾歲喇、○莫學滑○我今年十六、○全會○長的這個身量、該娶親喇、○莫法治○擇的明年九月二十的日子、便向他兒子說、進去把酒飯端上來罷、○全會○正來攪擾喇、○酒飯已到、二人各拿起筷子、一面吃、一面閒談、全會先吃完了、放下筷子、○莫法治○酒不喝、飯也不吃了嗎、○全會○酒足飯飽、○莫法治○拿了去罷、○莫學滑對他爹說、家裏裏頭叫你、○莫法治同他兒子走到外頭說、叫我做什麼、○莫學滑○這個客來做甚麼、○莫法治○他來要錢、○莫學滑○該他什麼錢、○莫法治○從去年欠下他的雜貨錢、○莫學滑○該他多少錢、

○莫法治○七吊五、○莫學滑○我們錢櫃裏有錢、拿給他罷、○莫法治○再該他幾天還行、○莫學滑○該錢有管轄、還錢兩無交、自古道、戀債不富、○莫法治○不用你管、有我搪他、○莫學滑○早晚當了還喇、○莫法治遂又進去對全會說、我這筆賬、不用你再跑腿喇、今年必給你交上、只求你替我再擔這幾天、○全會○我們從先說的明白、雖然吃了你的、喝了你的、今天不給我錢、還是不行、○莫法治○你說不行、要怎麼樣呢、人肉也不好吃、人血也不好喝、你還能拉我投井不成、○全會○你聞名訪訪、我是誰、你說這幾樣、難不住我、你要慣罷、人肉幾個錢一斤、人血多少錢一碗、你若賣、我就買、你還得先把錢給我、我好照顧你點、誰那個草雞了、不是眞朋友、你又說、不能拉你投井、走罷、我一定把你拖了井裏洗洗、好割點乾淨肉吃、○莫學滑見他二人動了手、急忙出去、要找個人來拉架、恰巧碰見莫不結在街上、就請他快快進去拉架、這莫不結本是莫家莊的一位體面人、善會勸人和睦、他就進去、滿臉陪笑、

走到近前說、你二人是爲甚麼這樣吵鬧、看着我的老臉、彼此撒手罷、○全會○我來要討賬、他說了一些嗓子牙齒外的話、看定了我不能做、我今天要做個樣給你們衆位瞧瞧、○莫不結○要錢討賬、何用動手呢、請問貴姓、在誰家發財、○全會○我姓全啊、在城裏三義號跑外櫃、○莫不結○今天這個不是、是莫法治的、因爲全掌櫃的、到我們這裏來是客、你有錢說有錢的話、沒有錢就說沒錢的話、怎麼好這樣的混嚷嚷呢、○莫法治○老大爺你說的不錯、我沒有錢、是說的沒錢的話、我這麼說不行、那麼說還是不行、把我逼急了、我就說人肉也不好吃、人血也不好喝、你還能拉我投井不成、他就動手說、我要拖你井裏洗洗、好割點乾淨肉吃、○莫不結○這是話赶話擠的、全掌櫃的不要生氣、三義號和我們莫家莊、交往買賣多年、彼此都有交情、不可傷了和氣、○全會○我很不願傷了和氣、無奈他抗賬的法子過多、我一槪是照着理給他破的、您若不信、我把今天的事、說給你老人家聽聽、他頭一個法、用的是要討賬還錢的法、第二個、是指天地作難爲人的法、第三、是討限期拖日子的法、第四、是用賬不對的法、第五、是用送人情的法、第六、你們都看見了、是鐵門閂的法、你問問他、那個法子、我不是照着討賬的理回覆的呢、○莫不結○聽你說的這些話、你算全會照理討莫法治的賬了、○莫法治○我從來沒遇見這個樣討賬的、我們倆是針尖對着麥芒、我和你是勢不兩立、做到底、○全會○你還有甚麼法子、只管拿出來、我還是按理問你要、並不含糊、○莫不結爲他們講和說、你二人要聽我勸、自古道、打架望人拉、告狀望人留、不料我今天碰着喇、只爲這七吊五百錢、不值得惹氣、莫法治、你到底是該人家的、你就是能打了他、他還是要錢、他若打了你、你還得還賬、講到打官司罷、這七八吊錢、並不彀盤纏、全掌櫃的、我給你們了結、你願意不願意呢、○全會○多謝你老人家費心罷、○莫不結○莫法治、你願意了結不願意呢、○莫法治○我願意了結、可就是沒有錢呢、○莫不結就出來問莫學滑說、你們家裏有錢沒有、若是沒有、我給你們先借上(出來)、○莫學滑○我們錢櫃裏有六吊錢、○莫不結說、好啊、遂即進來對全會說、你們的賬上、是欠七吊五百大錢、二年沒交、還是七吊五、我勸你多不如少、少不如了、今天就交五吊大錢、把賬了結、可以不可、○全會○你老人家爲的是好、我該遵命、但是有兩樣難處、一則七吊五百錢、少給兩吊五、連本錢也不彀、二則我是外櫃、不能作主、○莫不結○把這個難處、我和你兩個擔了罷、你賠上一吊五、到櫃(店)交上、我賠上一吊、在這裏交上、現在我就交你六吊錢、拿到櫃上、你就說是我不結說的、請給他勾賬、○全會○六吊錢清他的賬、憑我實在交不下去、若說出你老人家來、掌櫃的必樂意了結、就是罷、自古道、臉面值千金、拿錢來罷、我好再找別人去、○莫不結○莫學滑、你去拿六吊錢來、○莫學滑回答說是、○莫不結又對莫法治說、你這筆賬、六吊錢給你還清了、省了一吊五百錢、因爲有我的面子、○莫法治○多虧老大爺、你給我了結的很妥當、○莫學滑○這是六吊錢、交給全掌櫃的罷、

○全會○這是好錢嗎、○莫學滑○好錢啊、一個小錢也沒有、又不短數、○全會見錢已經到了手、就對莫法治說、今天得罪你了、○莫法治○是我對不起你啊、○全會又對莫不結說、叫你老人家費心了、我要走喇、○莫不結○你還往那裏去找誰、○全會○要去找東邊住的莫學文、○莫不結○他是個富裕日子、怎麼還該下你們的賬呢、○全會○欠的還不少呢、○莫不結○甚麼錢哪、○全會○他那年捐功名、借了櫃上六十吊錢、從前的利錢不欠、只是這兩年的利錢、一個沒給還有欠的雜貨錢若干、○莫不結○你不如在這裏坐坐、我叫莫學滑去叫他到這裏來見你、好不好、○全會○好、只是我有些不好意思勞動你們、○莫不結○你到這裏來、叫他們跑點腿算甚麼呢、○全會○我要勞駕了、○莫不結吩咐莫學滑說、你去叫莫學文來就說三義號全掌櫃的在這裏等他、叫他快來、○不多時莫學文來了、就說全掌櫃的早來了嗎、到我家坐坐罷、○全會○你已經來了、我就不去喇、就在這裏說說話罷、你

知道我是個跑外櫃的、沒有別的話說、爲的是討要賬、○莫學文○別人的賬、我不管、我的賬、不用你討要、到了時候、就給您送去、○全會○甚麼時候、纔算到了、○莫學文○年底爲期、就晚了嗎、○全會○你若是今年新拉的、可以捱到年底、並且你用我們的錢、是八月裏、七月底利錢就到期、何況還有陳欠的利錢、○莫學文○沒拖拉下你們的利錢、我那年不交、○全會○你若交轂了、現在我不能來討要、從你那年用這六十吊錢、算到今年七月底、是五年整、你一共交利錢是三十六吊、淨欠二年的利錢、就是二十四吊、還有貨物錢十幾吊、你若早還了、我們再借出去、每年不是又得利錢六七吊嗎、不是我們相好、去年底我們就不肯了、你倒說今年年底交上就晚了嗎、這是甚麼話呢、○莫學文○現在我不但不能還、我還要借幾十吊呢、○全會○自古道、好借好還、再借不難、你這個主、怕借給你嗎、若是前賬不清、免開尊口、○莫學文○今天若是把利錢貨錢還上、你還能再借給我嗎、○全會○能啊、○莫學文○我恐怕你收回去、不放給我、我也沒法、○全會○斷無此理、比方你是個莊稼主、今年把各樣糧食、收在倉裏好用、若是不再種上、倉糧用完、再吃甚麼呢、買賣也是如此、淨收不放、何處得利、淨放不收、使用甚麼、○莫學文○全掌櫃的說的不錯、可惜我今天不能還上陳欠、你還肯再借給我嗎、○全會○那自然不能再借、不但不借給你、你今天還得還陳欠、纔是正理、○莫學文○倒叫我爲了難了、有喇、老大爺你是個年高有德的人、我和全掌櫃的這個賬、你都聽見了、現在叫我爲了難喇、○莫不結○你們兩個人的事、並不爲難、因爲全掌櫃的待你不錯、很瞧得起你、你應該把陳欠算算、清楚了你再借也好、○莫學文○你既說不爲難、我就託你老人家、給我買點心罷、○莫不結○你借錢必得找出指頭來、○莫學文○指頭我有、過年打下麥子來、糶錢還他、○莫不結○你得找出押頭來、○莫學文○押頭也有、家後那二畝地罷、○莫不結○很好、你現在要用多少錢、○莫學文○有二十吊錢、就過去了、○莫不結○全掌櫃的、我在你面前、要討點臉兒、不知行不行、○全會○北京的大柳樹、南京的沈萬山、人的名、樹的影、你老人家若說了話、不行的也必行喇、○莫不結○你算算莫學文連本帶利、加上貨物錢、一共是多少、○全會○本錢是六十吊、利錢二年、欠的二十四吊、貨物錢十吊零二百、共合錢九十四吊二百、○莫不結○對不對、○莫學文○大概不錯、○莫不結對全會說、今天叫你又收又放、收他九十四吊二百錢的賬、前後本利貨錢全清、你現有錢六吊、給他五吊八、湊成一百吊、放給莫學文、當立帖據為憑、家後地二畝作押頭、有我莫不結為保人、你肯不肯、○全會、○既有你老人家給兩家為美、不好意思不肯、○莫學文○這纔有現錢五吊八百、不彀用的、再叫他多借上十吊、我將就着用罷、○莫不結對莫學滑說、莫學文不會寫字、你替他立張借帖、好交給全掌櫃的帶回、再多寫上十吊錢、○全會○不好再多、這裏沒錢、○莫不結、○過日到櫃上去取、今天不要、○全會○你老人家說了、我不好不答應、○莫不結○罷呀、一個人情送到底罷、○借帖已經寫完、莫不結對莫學滑說、你念給大衆聽聽、○莫學滑念道、

立借帖人莫學文、因為手中匱乏、同中人借到三義號大錢壹伯壹拾吊整、情願將自己房後地二畝、東至于姓、西至莫姓、南至道心、北至頂頭、四至分明、作為抵押、該錢筆下交足、言明年利二分行息、如若年利不到、准保人耕種墊利、本利不到、准保人將地交與三義號為主、任憑耕種典賣、不與莫姓相干、倘有莫姓親族爭差、有莫學文一面承管、恐後無憑、立字為証、

中保人莫不結十

代筆人莫學滑十

光緒十七年十月初二日　莫學文立

搆訟小品

有張三控李四霸產行兇一案、○呈詞○具呈人張三、年四十五歲、係某鄉某社某村居民、為霸產行兇懇恩驗究事、竊身於某年某月、因年饑不能餬口、將身村南祖業地五畝、央人說合、價賣於李四耕種、當立文契、同

中言明、雖係價賣、地價僅得半值、三年內任 身 原價回
贖、現有中說人管老二可傳問證、詎料伊覰地價廉、陡
生奸計、霸不放贖、身 向伊理講、反觸伊怒、將 身 頭顱毆
傷、命危旦夕、似此霸產行兇、情實難甘、不得不叩懇仁
天恩准相驗究追、以懲强橫而安懦弱、頂祝上呈、○末
後寫抱告子張小○呈報以後、縣官帶領刑房、招房、仵
作、三班差役、下鄉驗傷、鄉約地方伺候公館、縣官入了
公館、用過茶和點心、便吩咐地方把受傷的抬出相驗、
仵作仔細驗看、報明傷痕、刑房落淸傷單、傷單上寫的
是驗明張三、左額角有傷一處、深約二分、右臂邊有傷
一處、深約分許、寬長五分、非是木傷鐵傷、皆係磕傷、仵作
這樣稟報、刑房這樣落筆、因爲
李四在暗中將他們攢了一把、官看完了、又親自相驗
了一番、心中明白、當場將抱告的張小、訊了幾句口供、
吩咐將張三抬回家中養傷、又吩咐帶着被告李四、一
同回衙門去了、李四到了衙門、刑房向李四說、你何不
補張呈子、訴說張三誣賴刁控呢、於是李四到承發房、
買了格印紙、狀式拿到代書房、寫了訴狀、留下四百大錢、拿

着呈子回衙、正碰着官有堂事、沒到承發房掛號、一直
到大堂前、頭頂狀子、雙膝跪下、口稱靑天大老爺在上、
小的李四有寃狀上呈、懇求大老爺作主、衙役接過狀
子、雙手獻到公案、○呈詞○具呈人李四、年五十一歲、
係某鄉某社某村居民、爲誣賴刁控、據實訴明事、竊 身
於某年某月、買到張三地五畝、憑中說妥價錢七十千
整、當立文契錢契兩交、並無回贖字樣、現有中說人管
老二可傳問證、文契審呈、詎料伊因年得豐收、悔地價
廉、勁行回贖、身 伏思地價雖廉、而饑饉之時、銀錢亦不
同豐年、地隨時價、人所共知、身 向伊理說、伊因理缺、自
行磕傷刁賴、反以霸橫等情控 身 在案、似此橫刁、王章
安在、不得不據實訴明、懇恩電斷、焚祝上呈、○縣官閱
畢、當堂問他說、你爲甚麼霸張三的地畝呢、○李四○
小的不敢行霸、○官○你既不敢行霸、年限滿了、就該
讓他回贖、你爲甚麼不許他贖、反倒行兇呢、○李四○
大老爺的明見、他是逞刁誣告小的、小的不敢打人、他
的地本是賣給小的了、有一天他扛着錢、硬找小的贖

地、小的和他說、你的地已經賣了、為甚麼又來贖呢、且你賣地用中人、贖地怎麼不用中人呢、你把中人管老二叫來、他說是典的、我情願叫你贖、他若說是賣的、我(咱)們(們)兩箇、算沒有事、後來張三就把管老二叫來、管老二也說是賣的、小的又把文約拿出來、當着四鄰都看了、實係死契不錯、衆人就批評他幾句、他自覺抱愧、無言對答、就上酒館裏喝了個大醉、到小的的門口、撞頭撒賴、把頭撞破了、倒說是小的打的、小的實在萬分寃屈、○刑房在官旁邊低聲說、在鄉下聽着、也都說是碰的、刑房這樣回官、必是李四的錢、使翻劤了、俗語說、錢會說話、就是如此、　○官○先把李四押下去、等着張三傷痕平復了、我再給你審問虛實、○李四○謝大老爺的恩典、○原差將李四押在班內、這(班)分壯班、快班、皁班、名叫三班、三班輪流管押、　李四既發三班輪流管押、恐不便當、央請王麻子同各班的頭兒、說明班規、每班許他二百錢、衙門口的錢、(一百是一吊、)該管的這班、另外許下一吊、連刑招房上下都安排妥當、所以李四雖是被押、卻不曾受着憋曲、等了幾天、官要出票、就着管案的刑房、寫立票稿、送給內宅門、轉交刑名師爺、將稿核定、發給刑房謄清、再將清稿、送給宅門、轉交縣官、縣官用硃筆標了三日限期、添上值日的紅名、簽押用印、發回刑房、即從刑房落班、票上的紅名是李保、於是李保拿着票子、帶領散役、下鄉傳案、此時張三傷已平復、隨票到案、仗着自己是原告、又有重傷、楊楊得意、原差問他要鞋錢、分文沒有、班規房規、不曾安排、那知事從下辦、吏不舉、官不行、不開點名單(點單、到單)難以拘着過堂、挨了幾天、張三看看無法、這纔許下一吊錢、安排了衙門、原差這纔到刑房、給他開了點單、送到宅門、宅門遂將他的案卷、着刑房查出來、同點單一並送給官看、官將坐堂的時候、茶房在大堂前、高聲傳叫刑房、招房、三班頭、老爺坐堂喇、但見各科房的經承、三班頭役、各人戴着紅纓帽子、齊站公堂伺候大老爺、一聲點響、官已經升坐公堂、這箇時候、大板子、小板子、嘴巴子、各樣刑具、皁班俱已帶到、喊堂已畢、刑房就將兩造的案卷、擺在公案、官先將原告張三的案卷、揭開看了、後又看了李四的案卷、吩咐原差帶張三、原差齊聲傳呼說、帶張三、常言說、好見的閻王、難見的小鬼、張三雖是個無賴刁徒、究竟是鄉里愚民、沒曾打過官司、被差役這一聲吆喝、早已嚇的渾身抖戰、面如土色了、小衙役將張三帶到公堂前、衙役齊聲說、跪下、官說、抬起頭來、張三的頭上、還包着一塊藍布、官問張三說、你的傷好了沒有、張三說、還沒好、官遂吩咐說、將他的包頭揭開看看、仵作揭開一看、那傷已經好有八九分了、仵作報道、傷見平復、○官○張三、哪你的傷漸漸好了、官司還想要打嗎、○張三○李四欺負小的無能、他典小的的地、不準小的回贖、倒是小事、還要行兇打人、太沒天理王法了、大老爺不給小的伸出寃來、小的眞屈死了、○官○那李四如果昧了良心、霸種你的地畝、還要恃强行兇、憑空打人、你大老爺定要按律辦他、只怕你是自己撞破了、希圖借傷刁賴、據你這一面之詞、我是不能遽然就信的呀、○張三○大老爺案下有神、小的不敢撒謊、○官○你敢和李四對質嗎、○張三○小的情愿、○官○帶李四、○李四走到公堂、跪在案前、官問李四說、○抬起頭來、你霸種張三的地、又要恃强打人、你可知王法利害嗎、○李四○回大老爺的明見、小的不敢違背王法、若是小的眞果打他、情愿干罪、他明是自己撞破了、誣賴小的、○張三○你的頭爲甚麼不自己撞破、誰不是父母的遺體、誰肯自己撞破、自己受疼呢、○李四就向張三說、○當着大老爺說話、要憑天理、我有幾個腦袋、敢憑空霸你的地、又敢行兇呢、你說是我打的、有甚麼見證、○張三○你說是我碰的、有甚麼憑據呢、○李四○碰頭的時候、有中人管老二勸你沒有、○張三○你打我的時候、有趙胡氏來拉你沒有、○他兩個在大堂上、互相爭吵、縣官惱怒、把驚堂一拍、說道、你們兩個不要胡吵、○衙役高聲說、大老爺叫你們別莫胡吵、聽大老爺的吩咐、兩個這纔不言語了、○官問張三說、○張三、這鬬毆的事情、來往的人甚多、你怎麼單扯拉上個婦人作見證呢、明係無賴刁徒、希圖取巧、拿嘴巴子來、○張三遂叩頭說、求大老爺的恩典、小的一時的糊塗、求大老爺格外恩典、○

衙役○給大老爺磕頭罷、○官○你們打架的時候、就沒有別人勸說嗎、○張三○還有孫海、也勸說來、○官問李四說、是有孫海勸說來嗎、○李四○有、○官○好、我就添傳你們的見證、○遂取過硃筆來、在票子上、標了管老二和孫海的名子、勒了限期、官遂吩咐原差、將原被告都押下去、又另問了兩件案子、只聽三聲點響、縣官退堂而去、○再說、為張三一案、原差接過添傳的票子、不敢怠慢、即時下鄉、將管老二孫海傳到稟案、又開點單過堂、官吩咐先叫管老二、管老二跪在堂前、官問說、你是給張三作中人的嗎、○管老二○是小的、○官○李四霸張三的地畝、還行兇打人、你都親眼見過來嗎、○管○小的實不瞞大老爺、作中人的是一手托兩家、不能厚此薄彼、李四是忠厚人、自小不會打架、張三的地、本是先典後賣、有一日張三找着小的、要硬作典契、向李四贖地、小的不敢將無作有、所以沒肯替他去贖、因此不合他的意思、他就惱了、回家喝了個大醉、扛着錢自己去贖、李四不贖給他、他就和他打架、小的

聽說、恐怕鬧出事來、連忙去看、正遇着張三在李四的門口撞頭撒賴、碰的頭上血淋淋的、小的上前勸他、他不但辱罵小的、還說小的和李四扭成繩兒、一口同音的賴他的田地、○官○到底李四打他來沒有、○管○小的實在沒見打他、○官○是了、再傳孫海、○衙役齊聲說、傳孫海、原差帶着孫海到堂前、衙役齊聲說跪下、○官○你就是孫海嗎、○孫○小的是孫海、○官○你在家裏作甚麼生活、○孫○小的在家種莊稼、○官○張三和李四打架、你給他拉過架來嗎、○孫○小的給他拉過架來、○官○你既給他拉過架來、你可知張三頭上的傷、是打的呢、是碰的呢、○孫○那日小的出來檢糞、見他二人打架、小的見李四把張三打的滿臉是血、小的就赶緊上前拉勸、李四勢甚兇惡、不但不受人拉勸、反把小的摔倒在地、小的也就不敢拉了、○官○他使的是甚麼兇器、○孫○他使的是斧子、○官○胡說、他自己並沒稟報是斧子、你偏說是斧子、這明明是張三刁賴李四、買出你來作見證、你既敢扛帮硬證、又

敢這樣的胡說、豈不是找着挨打嗎、○孫○小的不敢撒謊、說的都是實話、○官○混帳東西、還要強嘴、給我杖嘴四十、我看他強嘴不強嘴、○孫○大老爺恩典哪、大老爺恩典哪、小的不敢撒謊啊、○那掌刑的不容分說、惡狠狠的、如狠似虎、走上前來、把孫海的頭、向旁邊一扭、刮打刮打的、一氣打了四十個嘴巴子、這四十下、比別人的四十下不同、因爲張三未曾替孫海花刑杖錢、所以這些皂隸、心中有些氣忿、如同瞎子打孩子一樣、一下是一下的、只這四十下、把孫海的嘴、打的鮮血淋漓、腫的好像猪嘴一般、○官又問孫海說、○張三的頭、到底是碰的、是打的、照實的說、○衙役在旁邊說、○大老爺叫你照實的說、快說罷、○孫○小的說實話、大老爺不信、再叫小的說甚麼呢、○官○你眞說實話、你大老爺還能不信嗎、你再說這樣的實話、還要加重的打、○孫○大老爺打死小的、小的也沒有二樣話、○官一聽見、立時摔簽說、拿小板子來、○衙役喊了一聲、就拉下去了、往下拉的時候、孫海就伸了兩個指頭給衙役、衙役知道他的意思、所以直打了一百、皮連紅也不紅、官吩咐掌刑的、給我狠打、那知衙役得錢、也沒有白使的、打人也都是有手法的、所以第二個掌刑的、雖然報數的聲音、格外的狠、打的響聲、也格外的大、又打了一百、還是未曾破皮、官看出破綻、就向掌刑的發怒說、○我把你這兩個狗才、從先他沒許你們錢、四十下就打破了嘴、現在他許了你們錢、二百板子、還打不破皮、我的官、你們就替我作了嗎、你們使了他的錢、也得陪他挨板子、快換新板子來、定要五下子見血、錯了一樣受刑、○說着、從旁邊過來一個衙役、手裏拿着一個又厚又重的新竹板子、把兩個掌刑的、每人打了二百、都不過五下、腿就開了、孫海在旁邊看見、正然害怕、官又問他說、○你到底說實話不說、○孫海暗暗想道、我那兩吊錢的勁兒、已經用盡了、若再不說實話、斷乎不能輕饒了、因此含糊說道、也許他是碰的、○官○混帳、碰的就是碰的、怎麼叫作也許、再給我着實的打、○孫○大老爺息怒、小的說實話就是了、張三帶着小的作干證、教小的說不是碰的、小的已經上了他的當、只求大老爺恩典罷、○官冷笑說、○我早知道他是碰的、你既說了實話、就下去具結、於你無事、○衙役○給大老爺磕頭罷、○孫海磕了一個頭、原差領着到招房具結去了、官在此時又另傳一案、方纔問畢、孫海借了二百大錢給代書、將結拿着當堂遞上、○結狀○具結狀孫海、今爲與甘結事、依奉結得張三呈控李四逞兇霸產一案、蒙恩訊明、實係自行碰傷、並非李四用斧砍傷、小的情愿遵斷、不敢妄作見證、甘結是實、○縣官看了、遂着孫海當堂畫了個十字押、又向孫海吩咐說、○你既是個莊稼漢子、應當老老實實的、遇有打架鬬毆的事情、只可從中說和、豈可替人妄作見證、攬管閒事、向後在家務要安分度日、再要如此、定行從重究辦、○孫○謝大老爺的恩典、○原差○下去罷、○官○傳張三、○張三上來、跪伏案前、○官○你的干證孫海、已經結明你是碰傷、還嘴強不嘴強呢、○張三○小的不是自己碰的、實係是他打的、○官冷笑說、使甚麼打的、○張三○

他也使斧子砍、也是棍子敲、○官又冷笑說、○好多兇器、一個人打一個人、手中能使幾樣家伙呢、莫別說孫海不肯替你作見證、就是憑我驗的說、棍打、沒有木傷、說斧砍、沒有刃傷、足證你是放刁圖賴、○張三○小的不是誣賴、○官發怒說、○混帳忘八蛋、你不是誣賴、難道是你大老爺驗假了不成、給我拉下去打、○皂頭啊的一聲、將張三拉到堂下、褪下褲子、頭西脚東、按在地下、一氣打了六百小板、打的皮開血流、肉都飛了、張三不住聲的喊求說、求大老爺恩典哪、可打死小的喇、小的再不敢了啊、○官○放起來、○張三起來、提上褲子、仍舊跪在案前、○官問他說、還說是打的不說呢、○張三哭淋淋的說、○雖然不是打的、也和他打的一樣、若是他好好的贖地給我、我也不肯打架、○官○爲地當說地的話、你偏事外放刁、自找打挨、我且問你、你的地、當日是先典給他、以後又賣給他沒有、○張三○也算賣、也算典、○官把驚堂木一拍說、○混帳、賣就是賣、典就是典、怎麼賣也算典呢、○張三○大老爺是青天、小的這塊地、好年成能值二百吊大錢、於光緒元年、小的取他五十吊大錢、原說是二分行息、指地作保、寫立典契、誰知連着歉年、小的付不上錢、到第二年李四就將地種去了、到第三年春天、小的沒有糧食餬口、因此又煩地經紀管老二串說明白、除他典價以外、僅僅加錢二十吊、要立賣契、小的很不願意、但家中等着買米度命、那時取借無門、眼看一家老少都要餓死、他又勒掯小的多了不給、無奈立了文契、當日寫文約的時候、原是死契活口、所以小的說賣也算典○官○怎麽叫做死契活口呢○張三○當場雖然是賣、他許着年成好了、還讓小的回贖、現在年成好了、小的湊足了錢、找着中人前去贖地、他竟不依贖、又把中人買通了、一口同音的說是沒有活話、小的和他理論、他不但不服說、反說出一些強梁話來、小的氣得無法、纔大喝了一頓、和他鬧了、小的家裏、現有八十多歲的老母、若贖不出地來、指着甚麽奉養呢、求大老爺施恩公斷罷○官○下去聽着、○又吩咐傳李四、李四上堂跪下、官問他說、○張三的地、是你先典後買的嗎、○李四○是、○官○有活話沒有、○李四○沒有活話、○官○張三怎樣說是有呢、○李四○大老爺明見、原本說話爲空落筆爲蹤、若是許他回贖、就仍然是典、不是賣了、既是賣、怎麽還要回贖、大老爺不信、小的把文約呈上看看、有活話的字跡沒有、○官把文約看了、就說、○文契上雖沒寫着、究竟有這個話沒有呢、○李四○小的不曾想着有這樣的話、○官○傳中人、○管老二上堂跪下、官問道、○張三的地、是先典後賣的嗎、○管○是、○官○當日寫約的時候、有許他回贖的話沒有、○管○有是有的、小的和他說的明白、賣是斬釘截鐵、亦斷葛籐、若想要贖、除非是理下求情、但地有時價、馬有走價、以後要贖、非照時價不可、小的是這樣和他說的活話、他也是照這話答應的、但現在時價能值一百五十吊大錢、他不按時價、硬照原價去贖、所以李四纔不贖給他、○官把兩造和干證的話、都聽明白了、要想斷案、吩咐傳張三、問道、○你的地已經賣了、文契上並無活話字樣、中人應許的、是照時價回贖、原來地有時價、各處都是如此、你想照原價回贖、於理不合、且歉年的時候、賣地的很多、先典後賣的也不少、地價通是便宜的、現在年成好了、地是貴的、你想照原價回贖、誰能肯呢、○張三見風不順、恐怕輸了官司、就苦苦的央求說、○小的幸虧命長、活這五六年、纔積蓄了四五十吊錢、若照時價、再做五六年工、也不夠數、只是小的的母親已經八十多歲了、每日吃糠咽土、小的不忍老娘受苦、指望贖過地來、打幾斗糧食、老娘吃幾頓飽飯再死、小的這纔甘心、求大老爺格外施恩公斷罷、○說到這裏、放聲大哭、把官的心哭軟了、遂把李四叫到堂上、說、○你願意贖給他不願意呢、○李四○他不照時價、小的不願意贖給他、○官○這地雖是賣契、他當初卻是指地作保、並非甘心出賣、你可念張三是個窮漢、家中又有老母、你有錢還可別處另買、讓他回贖祖業的地、幇他畧盡一點孝心、這也是你大大的陰功、我也不叫他只照原價、虧負於你、也不照時價、難爲於他、聽你大老爺的公斷、叫他湊上一百吊大錢給你、可願意不願意呢、○李四聽了這一番話、自覺官司雖沒十分贏、卻也有裏有面、官又未曾屈逼於我、若不答應、一來心裏下不去、二來又怕得罪了官、因此就聽官的吩咐說、○憑大老爺的公斷罷、○官○好、○又問張三說、你遵斷不遵斷呢、○張三○小的先回家去湊錢、若是湊足了、必遵大老爺的吩咐辦理就是了、○官○這麽着、都下去具結罷、○於是張三李四等、一齊下堂、到了招房、寫了結狀、遂又一齊到了堂上、○官看張三的結狀、○具遵依甘結人張三、具到前控李四兇霸典產一案、蒙恩訊明、着出大錢一百吊、向李四贖地、小的情愿遵斷、甘結是實、○又看李四的結狀、○具允服甘結人李四、具到張三控小的兇霸一案、蒙恩訊明、斷令張三給大錢一百吊、將該地贖回、小的情愿遵斷、甘結是實、○官吩咐叫各人親手畫了一個十字押、就退堂而去、張三李四、各回下處、就來了要錢的了、房裏要錢、班裏要錢、差頭要錢、小衙役要錢、代書要錢、掌刑的要錢、這纔是贏也得錢、輸也得錢、把張三和李四、一陣鬧糊塗了、錢數既都計較明白、那錢少的、現開付了、該不下的、又借了借、其餘的、討了限期、招了店保、應許以後來送、此後又告訴店家、預備酒飯、請了差役人等、吃喝已畢、又同店家算清了酒飯總賬、纔各人回家去了、

風水

信風水人張宗堯　不信風水人張老二
看風水人王先生　辯風水人李先生

張宗堯對他兄弟說、老二啊、你吃了飯、上東莊請王先生來看看咱的房子、有不合式處沒有、○老二說、又爲甚麼要看房子、○張宗堯○這二年、咱家裏不是這個長病、就是那個有災、生意買賣也不賺錢、我疑惑咱的房子、必有不合式處、請王先生給咱看看、另修理修理纔好、○老二○我看着不必、這二年咱家裏長病的多、也是不錯、但病災關乎人的命運、也關乎養身謹與不謹、房子那能管着人長病呢、至於買賣不賺錢、其中也有個別的緣故、並不關房子的事、○張宗堯○甚麼緣故、○老二○去年我對你說過數次、你總不聽、○張宗堯○你說甚麼我不聽呢、○老二○我說孫掌櫃的、不可再用他了、你說爲甚麼不可用、我說孫掌櫃的、口甜心苦、面善心惡、所以人都叫他孫麗貓、自去年咱莊裏有兩句話說、瘦了張宗堯、肥了孫麗貓、你想想這兩句話、是甚麼意思、不是因爲他抵盜咱的錢財嗎、我說了數次、你總不信、今日反疑惑咱的房子有不合式處、豈不是糊塗了嗎、○張宗堯○老二啊、你原來有個自是的病、不聽我說、不信風水、叫我心裏實在生氣、○老二○我不是不聽你說、只是這風水的講究、實在不足信、○張宗堯○不是不足信、是你不肯信、你看咱莊裏趙學仁家、前二十年、只五六十畝地、自從他信了我的話、請王先生給他改了大門、水道、另遷了墳塋、以後、人財兩旺、你不知道嗎、再看陳尙友家不信風水、我再三勸他、他總不肯信、自作聰明、蓋了一座大門樓子、犯了七殺、沒有二年的工夫、死了一個牛、一個孩子、買了一匹馬、又叫人家告着了、花了五十多吊錢、誰不知道呢、再

說咱祖父到了四十二歲、沒有兒女、請了一位鄭先生來、給咱看房子、看完了、對咱祖父說、這樣的房子、不但人不旺、就是錢財也不能存、因爲你的房子、前寬後窄、和簸箕相似、將錢財都簸出去了、所以主着不能存財、北房東頭屬艮、艮爲少男、艮位上少着一間、那能有兒呢、北房西頭屬乾、乾爲老父、乾位上又少着一間、所以又不利於老人、若要改正、當從北房東頭西頭、各接上一間、房子自然就方起來了、二年以後、管許你有兒、也保你人財兩旺、咱祖父信了鄭先生的話、將房子改正好了、到了第二年、就有了咱父親、家道也漸漸的好了、咱父親又有了咱兄弟二人、我也有兒有女、咱的日子、比從前又强了許多、這也算得是人財兩旺了、從此看來、有憑有據、你爲甚麼不信呢、○老二○你說可信的憑據、正是我不信的憑據、○張○那麼是你不信的憑據呢、○老二○趙學仁家發了財、眞是因爲得着好風水嗎、原是他父親和他叔叔分家、詭弊出一宗銀子來、有意買地、又怕他兄弟疑惑他、因而請王先生給他改大門、遷墳塋、假妝得了好風水、發了家、誰還不知道呢、至於陳尚友家、死了牛、死了孩子、更不關蓋大門犯了七殺的事、○張宗堯○是因爲甚麼、○老二○是因爲那一年是生瘟的年頭、又是傷牛的年頭、咱莊裏死的孩子很多、死的牛也不少、那能關蓋大門樓子犯了七殺的事呢、○張宗堯○他買了一匹馬、人家爲甚麼忽然的告着他呢、○老二○他買的那匹馬、是黑道上的、他這樣偷買盜賣、人家那能不告着他呢、○張宗堯○你說這兩家的事、也似乎有理、自從鄭先生給咱改正了房子、說是人財兩旺、可算應驗了罷、你爲甚麼還不信呢、○老二○這箇我也不信、○張宗堯○又爲甚麼不信呢、○老二○我先請問你、咱祖父祖母、甚麼年紀去的世、○張宗堯○咱祖父七十二歲、咱祖母四十六歲、○老二○咱父親母親甚麼年紀去的世、○張宗堯○咱父親去世的時候五十整、咱母親去世的時候七十九歲、○老二○哥哥說到這裏風水的講究、眞是不足信了、○張宗堯○怎麼說呢、○老二○鄭先生說咱的北房西頭、接上一間、管許老人活大年紀、爲甚麼咱祖父活了七十二歲、咱祖母只四十六歲就去了世呢、○張宗堯○咱的房子、是個坤門、坤爲老母、或者因爲大門矮的緣故、○老二○坤門矮就不利於老母嗎、○張宗堯○是、○老二○這麼着咱父親爲甚麼活了五十歲、咱母親爲甚麼反活了七十九歲呢、○張宗堯○我也不能明白、其中必有緣故、○老二○鄭先生說北房東頭、接上一間、管保多有孩子、爲甚麼只你有兒女、我已經四十多歲、還沒有兒女呢、就是咱的日子、比從前見好、也是人事天命兩下湊付、不是風水先生、叫咱好的、總而言之、死生有命、富貴在天、何必信那些糊塗講究呢、○張宗堯○你旣不信、我也不能强逼着你信、我自己去請王先生就是了、○張宗堯走到東莊、找着王先生說、王先生好啊、○王○我好啊、張大哥好嗎、○張○我也好啊、○王○快到家裏歇息歇息罷、○張○不必在這裏躭誤工夫、請先生趁着涼快(風涼)時候、到我家裏去坐坐罷、○王○有甚麼事情、○張○請先生還有

別的事嗎、○王○忙甚麼、在我家裏喫了飯、過晌再去不好嗎、○張○不必不必、我來的時候、已經吩咐孩子們、去買鮮魚了、我自己做的金盤露酒、也淋下來了、正要請先生去嚐嚐、咱就走罷、○王○張大哥說好便好、○走不多時、到了張的客廳(屋)裏、張吩咐孩子們說、○點過火來、給你王大爺喫菸、再去開壺茶來、○王○張大哥叫了我來、到底是爲甚麼呢、○張○這幾年我家裏長病的很多、買賣也不賺錢、我疑惑是房子的毛病、請先生來看看、再改正改正、○王○你的房子、前二年我已經看過、直到如今、我還記得、沒有甚麼大毛病、○張○請先生再看看纔好啊、○王○再看也不難、○於是二人一同出去、把房子周圍看了一遍、回到客廳(屋)裏坐下、○王○沒有大不合式處、就是大門略矮一點、再高起一尺多來、就合式喇、○張○旣沒有大不合式處、這幾年爲甚麼人財不旺呢、莫非是我們的墳塋不好嗎、○王○你說的不錯、我也想起來了、就是你們墳塋不好的緣故、○張○墳塋還是那個墳塋、爲甚麼前四五

十年好、這幾年又不好了呢、○王○前幾年我曾對你說過、只是你不理會、如今應驗喇、你服我的眼色不服、○張○我原來信服你、○王○你的墳塋、是下元運、所以前四五十年、主着發福、自從交了上元甲子、你的墳塋、就落了運了、所以你的日子人口就漸漸的衰敗了、從今以後、不但人財不能兩旺、還怕大不好喇、○張○有甚麼不好處○王○我說你也不信、○張○我斷不能不信、○王○還怕家破人亡喇、○張○請先生再給我改正改正、好不好、○王○改也無益、比方人若交了運、無論做甚麼、沒有不好的、若落了運、就是有天大的本事、也不行了、○張就憂憂愁愁的說、用甚麼法子、就好了呢、○王○必須另遷墳塋、○張○另遷墳塋、我也願意、只怕沒有好地呀、○王○有一塊頂好的地、離這莊也不很遠、那個氣力、那個結局、眞是不多得的啊、○張○甚麼局勢呢、○王○經上說、乾山乾向水朝乾、乾峯出狀元、就是這個局勢、○張○既是乾山、怎麼還有乾向呢、○王○不是我兄弟誇大口、不但你不明白、就是當今的地理先生、他也不能明白一個字啊、○張○因爲甚麼呢○王○因爲他看的書、不是地理大全、就是地理原眞、地理五訣、入地眼尋書、至於靑囊經的講究、他一字也不懂、那能懂得這個呢、○張○請先生把這塊地的好處、講給我聽聽、行不行、○王○講也不難、但怕洩漏天機、必遭天譴、○張○我是個門外漢、你說我也不能明白、就是明白一點、我也不和人家說、也不算洩漏天機啊、○王○這塊地、收入坤龍、三伏三見、頂大的力量、有訟卦乾卦兩水、彎彎曲曲、會於泰卦、消於同人、泰卦上更有秀峰突起、而立泰卦之向、泰在乾宮、否卦外三爻屬乾、謂之天地交泰、眞三元不敗之大地也、○張○我一點也不明白、請先生再從淺顯處、說給我聽聽、○王○乾山乾向水朝乾、就是乾宮卦內的山、作乾宮卦內的向、收乾宮卦內的水、則龍、向、水、三者俱歸生旺、就是了、○張○我到底不明白、請先生莫嫌煩瑣、再按着山水的形勢、講給我聽聽、好不好、○王○按着山水的形勢說、這塊地的結局、也甚合式、後龍上主峯漸垂頭、甚合元武垂頭的局式、前山高起、秀麗有情、又合朱雀翔舞的局式、左山活軟寬淨、又合青龍蜿蜒的局式、右山彎折低俯、又合白虎馴頫的局式、山既這樣、水也自然合局、這樣的地、眞是不多得的啊、○張○旣有這樣的好地、爲甚麼人家不用呢、○王○嗐、那些小小的地理先生、那能認得這樣的地呢、○張○咱二人相好、不是一年了、何不早將這塊地送給兄弟呢、○王○不是我的地、我甚麼法送給你呢、○張○先生但和我說這塊地在那裏、我用法子買了來、就是你送給我了啊、○王○這倒可以、但天生大地、以待善人、不可輕易與人啊、○張○咱雖不敢說是個善人、也沒作過大惡啊、先生若肯送給我、我必大大的報答先生的情、○王○張大哥你用甚麼報答我、○張○我必送二十兩銀子給先生買茶喫、○王○不要撒謊、○張○決不食言、○王○我不是貪財、送你這樣的地、實在也值這些謝儀、○張○我若是買到手、待遷墳塋的時候、還得先生來點穴啊、○王○這穴地、除了我以外、沒有一個能點的、因爲看地不難、點穴難、況這塊大地、點穴更不容易、若點着正穴、下葬的時候、必有青龍引路、白虎守穴、鸞鳳弔臨的祥瑞、若點不着正穴、不但不能發大富貴、還主着更凶喇、○張○因爲甚麼、○王○比方人住在鄉村裏、雖無大吉、也無大凶、若住在朝廷以上、一有不好、必有殺身滅門的禍、陰陽是一理啊、○張○我明白了、若後來點穴、再應驗你的話、我還要大大的報謝你、○王○再錯不了、○正說着話、忽然有人叫門、○張○我看看是誰叫門、○張開門一看、說、我當是誰、還是李先生嗎、○李○我聽着人說王大謌先生來了、○張○來了多時喇、請先生裏邊坐坐、○李○我正要找王先生談談、那能不進去呢、○李見王說、王先生好嗎、○王急忙起來說、好啊、李先生好嗎、○李○我也好啊、○張王一齊說、李先生快坐下喝茶罷、○李○都請坐、我在外邊聽見人說、張大哥請王先生來了、我特來看看先生、嗐、還是很康健啊、○王○老了、一年不如一年了、○李○王先生這幾年不住的看陰陽宅、料必見了些好地、到底有效驗沒有、○王○好地原不很多、就是有幾塊好地、點不着眞穴、雖好也不好了、○李○怎麽點不着眞穴、○王○因爲他看的書不好、○李○甚麽書、是好地理書、○王○第一部地理書、名靑囊經、原本作黃石公著、又有一部地理書、名葬經、是晉朝郭璞所著、又有靑囊奧語、天玉經、寶照經、是唐朝楊益所著、又有靑囊序、是楊益的弟子曾求己所著、這幾部書、都是發明靑囊經的義理、所以爲眞地理書、其餘的書、皆不足憑、○李○地理書上、所論的吉凶禍福、可信不可信呢、○王○說是不可信、自古帝王聖賢、沒有一個不信地理的、何況我們這些草莽之人呢、○李○帝王聖賢、那個信地理呢、○王○夏商以前、無所考究、但看他建都的地方、都是山水環抱、形局完密、若不信地理、他的京都、爲甚麽都佔着好地方呢、到了公劉遷豳的時候、相陰陽、觀流泉、高原下隰、無不看到、已略言其法、以後周公營洛邑、孔子使子貢給他看墳塋、都分分明明的言吉凶、使人趨避、到了秦末漢初、黃石公出世、深知天下的龍氣、皆以崑崙爲太祖、那山周圍八萬三千里、共分八龍、五龍入外國、三龍入中國、這八龍叫幹龍、從幹龍分出來的叫枝龍、又以幹龍爲太祖、由大至小、遞分不窮、其龍皆上應天星、分九宮、八卦、五行、陰陽、以定吉凶、於是著有靑囊經三卷、以發明其理、晉唐諸公、又各有註解、後世明理之士、以其說歷證古人的遺跡、無不恰合、亦皆著書立說、互相印證、如此看來、自古至今、那有不信的呢、○李○你說古帝王信地理、以他的京都爲憑據、實在不算憑據、因爲後人偏信地理、看見古帝王建都的地方、就特意尋找他的好處、其實帝王所倚仗的、原不在此、至於公劉遷豳、雖是看山水看地勢、也不可專說他是找好風水、因爲要立京城、沒有不找披山帶河、土厚水深的地方的、也沒有不隨山川的形勢、論他的陰陽向背的、再說周公營洛邑的事、也不是專爲找好風水、○王○既不是找好風水、爲甚麽單單的上洛邑立京呢、又爲甚麽果然應了他的占卜、坐了八百多年皇帝呢、○李○這也不難解說、周家舊日的京都、一在於豐、一在於鎬、皆偏於西邊、武王得了天下、四方的諸侯朝會、有很遠的、有很近的、甚不公平、洛邑居九州之中、所以成王登了極、命周公營洛邑、爲朝會諸侯之地、至於周家坐了八百年皇帝、是因爲他祖祖輩輩的功德、也不關洛邑的地脈好歹、若不論功德、但論地脈、到了八百年的時候、洛邑還是好好的、爲甚麼又失再天下呢、總而言之、有德者昌、無德者亡、這是正大情理、何必信那些糊塗講究呢、我再請問先生、孔子叫子貢給他看墳塋的事、出於何經何典呢、○王○我也不知道、我可常聽見別人說、○李○既不見經傳、以我看來、直是齊東野人之語、不必信啊、○王○孔聖人的事、你也不信嗎、○李○我不是不信孔聖人、我是不信這個說、你仔細想想、聖人活着的時候、尚且不貪富貴、不圖功名、他豈能叫子貢給他看塊好地、貪圖死後的功名富貴嗎、這等講說、眞是可笑啊、我再請問先生、人既死了、埋在地裏、甚麼緣故、就管着他的後世子孫富貴貧賤呢、○王○地理書上、都講的很明白、人人都該知道、○李○甚麼講究、○王○後世的子孫、都是和他祖宗一脈相傳、骨肉雖分、神氣相通、所以葬在好地、他的兒孫、必受蔭發福、葬在不好的地、他的兒孫、必被累受禍、比方樹根栽在好地方、枝葉就必茂盛、且能開花結果、樹根栽在不好的地方、枝葉就必衰敗、不能開花結果了、○李○這個講究、也不足信、我想古時的帝王、他的墳塋、必是頂好的、他的兒孫、爲甚麼忽然失了天下呢、看到這裏、後世的富貴貧賤、全在祖宗的功德、不在地脈的好歹、不用說了、○王○地理中有轉移造化的妙術、可爲知者道、難爲外人言、先生是門外人、我也難與先生强辯、咱們另說別的罷、○李○我聽見聖經上有話說、隱微的事、是屬乎神的、從此看來、地理卽有好歹、也是屬神經管、地之好者留以待善人、地之歹者留以待惡人、其中隱微、原非人所能知、豈是地理先生所能作主的嗎、自古帝王聖賢、建都相宅、也不過是上律天時、下襲水土、法其自然之運、因其一定之理而已、又豈同如今的地理先生、妄言吉凶禍福、以欺哄世上的人呢、先生自誤誤人、我很願叫醒先生、望先生萬勿見怪、○王○你還有甚麽說的沒有、○李○有方纔所說的這些話、不過說看地理的沒有益處就是了、至於他的害處還沒曾說到、先生若不見怪、我也願把他的害處、說給先生聽聽、○王○你說有甚麽害處呢、○李○那些小小的害處、我也不必細講、但說中國因爲風水的緣故、滿地金銀財寶、全不敢動、恐怕傷了地脈、以致國家貧窮、不能强盛、這豈不是喫了你們大大的害嗎、○王○你說這話、直是不通、地理先生的講究、不過說不可掘壞地脈就是了、何曾說地中的金銀財寶不可動呢、因爲世人多半固滯不通、所以連地中的金銀財寶也不敢動了、怎麽埋怨我們這看地理呢、○李○西國人不論地理、凡有金銀財寶的地方、一概掘出、難道他就掘不破地脈嗎、爲甚麽人民富貴、國家强盛、絕不像我中國這個樣子呢、○王○西國人也不盡是富貴之家、那些貧賤的、焉知不是因爲掘破地脈使然、昔日朱夫子嘗說、此地不發、是無地理、此地若發、是無天理、你不信我、你也不信他嗎、再看世上的人、居山者其性多剛、靠水者其性多柔、通都大邑之人多半聰明俊秀、僻鄉陋壤之人多半愚魯醜陋、你雖不信、非地理不足信、哪其中另有個緣故啊、○李○甚麽緣故、○王就變了臉說、夏蟲不可語冰、秋蟬不可語雪、就是這個緣故、○李也變了臉說、看天看地看陰陽、窮的沒處葬他娘、講風講水講地理、窮的家裏沒的喫、這是甚麽緣故、○張看着二人都變了臉、就快快的起來說道、不同不相爲謀、請了罷、請了罷、○李出去了、○張○王先生不必生氣、咱們喝酒喫飯罷、○王○好啊、○喫喝完了、王先生辭別回家、張老二出來送王先生走、正走着的時候、張老二對王先生說、○先前李先生所講的那些話、爲弟的在門外也曾聽見來、雖未免有些唐突、卻也有一些至理名言、萬望王先生和我哥哥採他合理之處、仔細尋思、庶幾不再被風水迷惑、○王先生和張宗堯無言答對、俱各掃興而散、

買賣講價

某城老年生意人王立○街坊少年手藝人李通糶糧米的○開布店的○賣柴草的○賣水菜的

王立對他家裏說、今天九月初二喇、我去糴幾斗糧食罷、○家裏○糧食還彀一月二十天吃的、現在糴不糴、不甚麼要緊、○王立○不要緊是不要緊、這却正是個好糴糧的時候、現在莊稼都收拾完喇、場也打下來喇、夥計也都好散工喇、凡是莊稼人、大概都折湊糧食、好還虧空（饑荒）、開付夥計的工錢、所以現在糴糧、比別的時候都便宜、○家裏○好啊、早晚也當不了糴、現在若是有錢、你就去糴罷、○於是王立背着斗就走了、剛一出門、遇見了李通、也背着斗、從那邊來了、○李通○王大爺要上市去糴甚麼呢、○王立○我打算糴幾斗穀、幾斗胡秫（秫秫）、再是糴把（點）黃豆、還糴二斗小米子、你去糴甚麼呢、○李通○我也是去糴斗小米、糴幾斗穀、若是麥子合式、還糴二斗麥子、王大爺是常趕集的老手、借你的經紀、使一使罷、○王立○好說、我也是糊泥糊塗的、○二人一面說着閒話、一面打聽那些糶糧下市的人、把各種糧價都打聽明白了、到了市上、二人東瞧西瞅、眼往兩邊使劤兒、忽然看見一分好成色的穀子、王立就走到近前、攄起一小把來、攤在手心一看、又撚出米來看了、問道、這穀要多少錢呢、○孫興○剛纔賣了二斗、是八百二十個錢、這個還算八百二就是了、○王立○不管人家買的多少錢、這個給你七百八、行不行、○孫興○七百八不好、賣七百八的也有、他却沒有這樣的穀、你看看這個穀、多麼成、多麼乾淨、○王立遂用手使劤往下一抄、抄出一把、又看了看、就說這穀實在不算十分乾淨、裏邊的小沙、還不少喇、○孫興○這樣的穀、你還嫌有沙、場園上打的東西、還能一點沙沒有嗎、○王立隨手又試了試斗、說斗也不見好、○孫興○這是足足的六碗斗、只多不少、○王立○你到底賣不賣呢、○孫興○七百八賣不着、你要就算八百一十個錢、○王立○總得八百下裏講、我們爽爽當當的給你七百九十個錢、○孫興○就是八百也賣不着、○王立○你有幾斗呢、○孫興○共拿了八斗、賣了二斗、還有六斗、○王立○你若是七百九賣、我們就裏/穡莊、○孫興○就是裏/穡莊、那個價兒也買不了、要買還得添錢、○王立○再不添喇、你不賣就罷、我們往裏去看看、○孫興○你們只管比着這個樣子去看罷、若是糴不中、再回來、○王李二人、往裏挨樣又看了幾分子、都沒講究上來、心裏就有定數了、一轉身看見一個熟人、名叫李忠、老遠招呼說、王大爺來糴甚麼、我有三斗胡秫/秫秫、一斗黃豆、你不要啊、○王立○你這胡秫/秫秫怎麼賣呢、○李忠○咱們都是熟人、我好意思間你多要錢嗎、你先看看東西何如、看好了東西、價錢好說、○王立先抄出一把來看了、又使/用牙咬了、就說看色氣還不大離/差、就是咬頭不好、○李忠○這是晒了兩遍的胡秫/秫秫、咬着崩牙、你還說咬頭不好嗎、○王立○還帶着太嫩、推不出麪子來、○李忠○這個胡秫/秫秫、你還嫌嫩嗎、這天生是那種黃胡秫/秫秫、不是那種黑胡秫/秫秫啊、○王立○咱們先別爭好歹、你要多少錢一斗罷、○李忠○你從市上過來、行市你必知道、剛纔

人家給我八百錢、我不賣、現在你來買、只可少賣幾個、還算八百錢就是了、○王立用斗量過、就說還有少頭沒有、○李忠○沒多要錢啊、○王立用手打了個九字碼兒、說、我也不少給你、就算這個零、你給我送去罷、○李忠○九個零、太虧我了、就是八百錢賣給你、也能少賣二三十、你也不是不知道行市、再少給錢就不對了、○王立○爲這十個、你不必再爭競了、合式我還要梢着你這斗黃豆、○李忠○好啊、這麼一塊兒講講罷、若是黃豆你再少給、咱們有言在先、我可是一定不賣、○王立○兩家情願、纔是買賣、你不賣、我還能强買嗎、說着、就將黃豆撥攋着看了一回、說這個怎麼算罷、○李忠○這個咱們也不用說空話/謊、就是一口的價兒、你若要、就開上一吊零五十個錢、不要、還是我的東西、○王立○你要的胡秫/秫秫價兒、還不大離格/經兒、這黃豆、你却要到行市外裏去了、你看市上、那有五十個零的黃豆呢、○李忠○怎麼沒有、剛纔俺/我的親戚、賣了六十個零、豆子還不如我的喇、○王立○這也算不得拔頂/頂好的豆子、

不過是中等貨、你看裏頭有多少青豆子、也不大很乾、○李忠○有一半個青豆子、關甚麼事呢、你說不乾、我咬個、叫衆人聽聽、是不是崩乾的呢、這個豆子、眞是市上數得着的、○王立○數得着也罷、數不着也罷、我再看看斗怎麼樣、○李忠○斗和(胡秫/秫秫)斗是一樣、錯了管罰、○王立○這麼(着/的)罷、咱們都是熟人、也用不着三說兩講的、這豆子、我給你三十個零就是了、你願意賣、就都給我送去、○李忠○不行、那三斗(胡秫/秫秫)、一斗你少給十個錢、我指望豆子、你肯給個公道價兒、不料你又少給二十、虧的我太大了、○王立○我早知道、你要從豆子裏、找(胡秫/秫秫)錢喇、所以並不是我還的價兒少、分明是你要的價兒大了、就是罷、我知道你不吃虧呀、○李忠○罷了罷了、你這個老頭子、眞有經紀、○王立○畧等一會兒、你自己給我送去罷、你也認識我的門兒、○李忠○好啊、○王立對李通說、合市沒有(壓住/好似)孫與那分子穀的、擡到手裏、眞和沙子一樣、就是八百錢、買了也合算、咱們倆回去(對付/買了)他的罷、○李通○好啊、回去(接就/買了)他的罷、○王立見了孫與、就說怎麼還沒賣嗎、○孫與○我單等着賣給你呢、○王立○(天生/定規)不值八百錢啊、若是值八百錢、到這時候、早賣出去喇、○孫與○給八百錢的、已經過去好幾個主兒喇、我還想着多賣呢、○王立○你想着多賣、還得人家多給呀、我看給你七百九、就不少了、○孫與○若是七百九賣、頭一回我就賣給你喇、○王立○這盤子買賣、只差十個錢、若是來兩回不成、實在太磨不開了、咱們倆、把這十個錢分了、好不好、○李通從旁邊勸着說、這麼很可以喇、叫他多出五個、你再讓他五個、早早賣了就是喇、○孫與○六斗你都要啊、○王立○都要、畧(等一等/打個辰)兒、我就回來、你再去送、又回頭問李通說、你要多少、○李通○我留二斗罷、○王立○好啊、這麼(着/的)我留四斗、○李通○先頭我看見、那邊有一斗米、成色很好、○王立上前看了看、說、不要那樣的米、你看金黃的色兒、那却是陳穀米、加鹹水做作出來的、咱們總是糴莊戶米、不要那些糧販子的米、○往前走了不多幾步、遇見一個莊戶大哥、出着一斗小米、身後還坐着一斗未出、人遞到一吊四百錢、他還不賣、王立接着看了一看、一點夾帶沒有、粒實又均勻、軋的又細、碎米也沒有幾個、沙也不多、斗又很蒙、就對賣米的說、這樣的米、一吊四百錢、你還不賣嗎、○賣米的○你看這樣的米、還不好嗎、一吊四百錢、我自然不賣、○王立○既是好、人家怎麼不買呢、○賣米的○他是不認貨呀、有了認貨的就買了、○王立○你到底要多少錢、說個實落價兒罷、○賣米的○少了一吊四百四不賣、○王立○給你一吊四百一何如、○賣米的、○別說你給四百一、就是四百三也買不了、○王立○當眞少了不行嗎、○賣米的○你當是還有說謊的嗎、○王立假裝要走、那賣米的同伴、急急招呼說、回來回來、我給你們兩家作個合局(轉彎)的、你也別(莫)一定要四百四、叫掌櫃的再添二十、你賣給他罷、○王立○添二十我不要、說着抽身就走、○合局(轉彎)的又招呼說、罷呀、回來、你再添十個、叫他賣給你罷、○賣米的○好、賣了賣了罷、我有二斗、你都要啊、○王立○斗怎麼樣呢、○賣

米的○都是一個斗掀的、錯了一個錢不要、○王立對李通說、這麼着(的)、咱們一個人一斗罷、○賣米的○現在就往下送罷、○王立○少停一停、我們回來再送、○二人又往前走、看見一個糶麥子的、剛纔講定了價兒、一吊四百六十個錢一斗、還剩下三斗、王立看過以後、就暗暗的對李通說、這分麥子很成(好)、皮兒又薄、而且又乾又淨、價錢又很公道、雖然氣色畧黑一點、那是因爲打場的時候、不甚大乾、其實出麪、還是一樣、不如就價兒糴他的罷、○李通○王大爺看着好就好、○王立就對糶麥子的說、糴你這三斗、價錢還有少頭沒有、○糶麥子的○一吊四百六、這就是賣價、剛纔你沒看見嗎、○李通○好、都給我送去罷、○二人所要糴的旣糴完了、就招呼糶粮的人、送下來了、走到王立門口、李通對糶糓米的說、你們給王大爺倒下、然後送到後街、從十字口往東走、我就在街南第三個門裏住、○王立到了家裏、先一樣一樣過了斗、看看都不差、就倒下了、然後拿出算盤來打着、對孫與說、你一共四斗七百九十五合

錢、共該三吊一百八、你算算對不對、○孫興○對啊、你打的還能錯了嗎、○王立又對賣米的說、你的一斗、是一吊四百六、我快拿錢給你們、你們好往後街去送、於是從家裏兩手拿出錢來、右手遞給孫興說、這是三吊錢的票子、一百八十個滿錢、左手遞給賣米的說、這是一吊四百六十、○孫興○有現錢、給我幾吊現錢不好嗎、○王立○票子還不是錢嗎、你放心罷、若是換不出錢來、囘來再交給我、○賣米的○這個錢不好、怎麼這麼些小錢呢、○王立○錢還能一般大嗎、就是官錢、和當鋪錢、也不能都一般大、只用沒有新小錢、這就是好錢、○賣米的○你看、這不是個新小錢是甚麼呢、你給我換換這一掛罷、○王立○一吊四百錢裏、只有這一個新小錢、怎麼夾着使不了（用不掉）呢、快將就着罷、○賣米的○你都過手來沒有、○王立○這都是親自過手的錢、○賣米的、招着數了二百、果然不錯、就裝在錢褡子裏走了、剛走出門、李忠就送秫秫（胡秫）和黃豆來了、倒下以後、王立問李忠說、你算着該是多少錢、○李忠○秫秫（胡秫）七百九十個錢一斗、三斗該是兩吊三百七、再加黃豆一斗、一吊零三十、共該三吊四百整錢、對不對呢、○王立○一點不錯、拿錢去罷、○李忠光點了點大數、後問錢怎麼樣呢、○王立○這都是挑的好錢、一個不好使的沒有、○李忠○有一半個小錢、倒不甚要緊、無論怎麼、就使出去了、就是怕短數、○王立○這都是我一手數過的錢、管保不短數、就是了、你若實在不放心、你就挨掛掐掐、或是下掛數數、○李忠○數他幹甚麼、咱們也不只交易了一囘、若是你這囘哄我、再就不見面了嗎、於是將錢收好、趕着牲口就走了、

到了九月三十晚上、王立的家裏對王立說、你應許給他奶奶做件大綿襖、這幾天他重念了好幾囘、不如去買點布、趁着大閨女（女兒）還沒囘去、快給他做起來罷、○王立○買罷咧、要甚麼布呢、○家裏○要一疋細莊布做表兒（面子）、還要一疋粗糙（糲）的好做裏兒、○王立○我看買洋布穿合算、○家裏○他奶奶不要洋布、嫌他破了、連點鋪襯都沒有、○王立○隨他罷、○家裏○你去的時候、

帶着給我截五尺綠洋機布、做條褲子、○王立○好啊、○第二天早飯以後、王立的大閨女女兒聽說他爹要去買布、就商議他爹說、爹啊、今天去買布、不好給俺我賒半疋粗洋布啊○王立○怎麼不好呢、○大閨女女兒○你給賒了、我家去就叫他快預備錢、至晚一個月就送來了、○王立○行啊、自己吃了袋菸、拿着錢、就往大街去了、先到了源興家問道、有細莊布沒有、○掌櫃的○有啊、買多少呢、○王立○合式買個兩三疋、○掌櫃的○看看這疋怎麼樣、○王立○這個不好、漿糨太大、○掌櫃的○再看看這疋、○王立○這個還是不好、綫條又鬆、又不均勻、○掌櫃的○莊布這就算好的喇、○王立○不要這個、沒有再好的嗎、○掌櫃的○再有頂高的、錢可多喇、○王立○貨高價取、齊買好貨、還怕錢多嗎、○掌櫃的○你看這疋、多麼細密、多麼平正、○王立○這疋還是不大對我的心思、綫太細、太薄楞了、○掌櫃的○這是淸水貨呀、一點漿糨也沒有、若是加水一洗、就和牛皮一樣、看不得綫細、○王立○這樣的賣甚麼數兒、○掌櫃的○零賣三十五個錢一尺、成疋的都賣一吊六百四、你若是買個兩三疋、我們圖需多賣點、就算一吊六百二一疋、○王立○那裏有這樣的行市、我方纔在天成家、他只要了一吊五百二、○掌櫃的○一分貨、一分價、要一吊五百二的、他也沒有咱們這樣的貨呀、○王立○你這貨也不見得很好、你看綫又細、面子又窨、並裁不出數來、○掌櫃的○綫不怕細、只要勻和、你看看這布多麼勻邊有多麼齊織的多麼緊正、就是面子也不能再寬了、○王立○一疋有多少尺呢、○掌櫃的○足足四十八尺、○王立○你量給我看看、○掌櫃的○這不是一尺、二尺、三尺、四尺、一共十二頁整整的足四十八尺、還有半尺的零頭、○王立○我也不少給你、一疋一吊五百四十個錢、你賣、我還要買別的、○掌櫃的○不行、差的太遠了、說着就將布收去、擱在鋪架裏邊、○王立○一吊五百五怎麼樣、○掌櫃的○一吊五百五也不穀本、○王立抽身就走了、○掌櫃的○回來回來、你給八十個零罷、○王立○多了不要、○掌櫃的○

六十個零、你要不要、我打心裏要拉你這個主顧、○王立轉過身來說、六十個零就算六十個零罷、○不料那掌櫃的竟拿出一疋次一等的放在櫃臺上、說這個布、連本也拉不出來、你要幾疋呢、○王立○還要一疋粗布、不怕綫大、只要結實就好、○掌櫃的○這疋結實、○王立○這是洋綫經織的、○掌櫃的○洋綫經碍甚麼事呢、那些好洋布、還趕不上粗布穿嗎、○王立○說是這樣說、人家却都不愛要、還有別樣的沒有、○掌櫃的○有倒有喇、却沒有不是洋綫經的、○王立○這個布面、和那個一樣嗎、○掌櫃的○長是一樣長、寬還略寬一點、我比量給你看看、○王立○這個實實落落的、你要多少錢、○掌櫃的○不好意思多要、你開一吊一百五十個錢就是了、○王立○我也不留添頭、給你一吊一百錢、你不賣就罷、○掌櫃的○再多你要不要、○王立○再多一個、我也不要、我到底沒大看中、○掌櫃的○就是罷、還要甚麼呢、○王立○不要別的、算算賬罷、○掌櫃的算了、就說共該兩吊六百六十個錢、○王立

○這裏有兩吊錢的票子、再開六百六十個現錢、○掌櫃的接過票子、吩咐一個夥計、到錢舖去照了一照、不多時回來、說不錯、○王立○不錯、我要走喇、纔走出門去、掌櫃的對夥計們說、終久買的不如賣的精、○再說王立從源與家出來、就往一個熟洋布店裏去了、那洋布店的掌櫃的、名叫宋欽、一見面、就笑喜喜的問道、王大哥來買甚麼、快坐下吃袋水菸罷、○王立一手接過水菸袋、一手按着水菸、說來買半疋粗洋布、再截幾尺綠洋機、○宋欽吩咐夥計說、把那個虎獅牌的拿出來、○王立看了看說、這就是我上回截的那一路啊、○宋欽○就是那路、這不是頭號虎獅牌的嗎、○王立○這個怎麼算呢、○宋欽○和你還是別人嗎、我這是二兩七錢三分銀子買的、關四吊二百錢一疋、你買半疋、就算兩吊一百、賺你四十個錢、就和發價一樣了、○王立○好啊、掌櫃的看着罷、○宋欽又叫夥計拿出綠洋機來、問道這個要多少呢、○王立○不要這種色太飽了、光落色、沒有那種帶黃色的嗎、○宋欽○有啊、這是

眞色的、截幾尺罷、○王立○截條褲料、有五尺就彀了、○王立○算算該是多少錢罷、○宋欽用算盤打着說、洋布是兩吊一百四、綠洋機你沒問價、再便宜一點算着、算你五十二個錢一尺罷、五尺是二百六、共該兩吊四百錢、○王立○今天錢不大便易、我先把綠洋機錢開上、那個洋布暫且掛幾天、好不好、○宋欽笑着說、哎喲、還是掛賬嗎、○王立也笑着說、掌櫃的不用害怕、等不幾天、我就給你送來、○宋欽○害怕倒不害怕、你這樣的主兒、還怕甚麽呢、我是因爲價錢算的很輕、若再掛賬、更沒有錢掙了、○王立○咱們這個賒賬、和現錢也差不許多呀、說着、就將布夾在胳肢窩裏回家去了、又過一月、到了冬月初頭、王立對他家裏說、這幾天太暖和温煖了、有個不久要反天下雪的樣子、趁早該買下幾馱子柴火、○家裏○快去買罷、一下起雪來、柴火就貴了、○於是王立到了草市、先問經紀說、今天柴草賣甚麽數兒、○經紀○穀楂松柴有賣三個八的、豆楂不過三個五六分錢、說話之間、有一個賣松柴的叫張三、上前來說、掌櫃的買松柴、我這裏有幾馱子、來看看罷、○王立○要多少錢一斤、○張三○你給四個錢罷、○王立○你這松柴不十分乾、我不要、○張三○你說我這松柴不乾、可是褒貶喇、你貴姓啊、○王立○我姓王、○張三○王大爺、你再看看、到底乾不乾、○王立○松柴也不十分乾、還要頂大的價、我那邊看看、回來再說、○張三○要價無多、還價無少、你到底還個價兒嗎、○王立○回來再還價罷、○又有一個賣松柴的、叫李四、向王立說、你來看看、我這兩馱子、這眞正是穀楂喇、○王立○看樣像是豆楂的、○李四○豆楂有這個樣兒嗎、我這是穀前裏砍的、你撅撅是不是骿手呢、○王立○小枝骿手、大枝却不是甚乾、○李四○就是大枝也乾透了、不信、我撅給你看看、○王立○你要幾個錢、○李四○你得給我四個二分錢、○王立○四個裏邊行不行、○李四○四個裏邊、沒有買賣、這是大山的松柴呀、你看枝子、就和骨頭一樣、毛稍明亮、稞在家裏、一點也沒過雨壓的多麽結實、○王立○不用再看了、你裏邊不賣就罷、○旁邊又有一個賣草的、叫楊五、向王立說、掌櫃的別走、你給他多少錢、○王立○我給他三個半錢、○李四○少了不賣、○楊五○中間無人事不成、我給你們(您)說句罷、就是三個七分錢、你不好不賣、他也不好不買、○李四○價忒少喇、○王立○多了我還不要喇、○李四○好啊、過秤罷、○經紀拿過秤來、一馱稱了二百一十斤、一馱稱了一百八十五斤、○稱過以後、楊五對王立說、我那裏還有一馱松柴、兩馱棒子、掌櫃的也稱稱罷、○王立○沒有錢買這麽些、○楊五○這纔用幾個錢、等下雪以後就貴喇、趁好天多買點子罷、○王立○你得少要幾個錢、我纔買喇、○楊五○咱們是隨行就市、我多要了、你也不給呀、○王立走到跟前、看了看說、這麽你要多少錢罷、○楊五○你纔買的松柴、是三個七、我這馱子、你還開三個七、棒子也不用多說、你開四個半就是了、○王立○這馱松柴、你要三個七、就算三個七、就是棒子、要的價兒大了、○楊五○這個價兒、實在不大、你問問掌秤的、我要的價兒、大不大呢、○王立○也不用問這個問那個、我看給你四個二分錢、就不少了、○楊五○四個半這就是賣價、我若是要謊、就問你要四個七、四個八喇、○王立○論你要的離格、也不大離格、但是買賣爭毫釐、一分貨、一分價、你沒有頂高的貨、就賣不出頂高的價錢來、必得少賣三分二分的、○楊五就用鞭桿把棒子敲了幾下、說你聽聽這個棒子、一登稜的響、眞是又成又乾、又直立、又沒有大塊、不論是皮毛、是身子、那裏有比這個好的呢、若是比較起來、就是賣四個六七也不算多、○王立○再給你加上一分罷、○楊五○不在那一分錢上、若只差着一分、那個小狗不賣給你、○李四對王立說、請掌櫃的給他再添上一分罷、四個三、到底還是虧他一點兒、○王立○添一分、就添一分罷、○於是經紀過了秤、一馱松柴是一百七十七斤、兩馱棒子、一馱稱了二百四十八、一馱稱了二百三十六、楊五對經紀說、這一馱怎麽掉了八斤呢、請你再掛一掛、○經紀又稱一回、仍舊是二百三十六斤、李四和楊五、各自開付秤錢、松柴每馱十二個、棒子每馱二十個、旣都開付明白、就發馱子、王立領着、一直送到門口、將松柴棒子卸下、搬到屋裏去、然後王立拿出手秤來、把架子一盤一盤的稱了、就對李四說、你的兩馱松柴、帶毛是三百九十五斤、去兩盤架子二十三斤、淨松柴三百七十二斤、三個七合錢、一吊三百七十六、又對楊五說、你的一馱松柴、帶毛是一百七十八斤、去十斤架子、淨松柴一百六十八斤、三個七合錢、六百二十一、兩馱棒子、帶毛是四百八十四斤、去兩盤架子二十四斤、淨棒子四百六十斤、四個四合錢、兩吊零二十四、加松柴錢、共該兩吊六百四十五、你們算算對不對呢、○楊五○我的松柴錢、掌櫃的算的不對罷、○王立○怎麽樣不對呢、○楊五○我算着該是六百二十二、○王立○買你兩吊六百錢的柴火、咬你六分錢、這還值得爭競嗎、○楊五○從來說咬五不咬六、這是糴粮買草的規矩、○王立○規矩也不是官規矩、咬我四分和咬你六分、也差不許多、你讓還得讓這一個喇、○楊五○那不要緊、只要掌櫃的知道就是了、可得給幾個好錢啊、○王立○咱們的錢沒有不好的、儘管拿去使用罷、○楊五因爲有事、將錢看了看、點了點、就拿着走了、只有李四、因爲要贖祟當、就對王立說、掌櫃的這錢不好啊、○王立○怎麽不好、都是一樣的錢、楊大哥沒嫌不好、怎麽獨獨你嫌不好呢、○李四○不瞞掌櫃的說、我是要贖祟當、這裏頭的小錢太多、請掌櫃的給我幾個好錢罷、○王立○你要贖當、我可沒有當舖錢給你、○李四○不一定要當舖錢、只請掌櫃的給換些比這樣好的就行喇、○王立○再換還是這樣的錢、○李四○這麽着的我要下掛挑喇、○王立○好、你下掛挑罷、若有不好使的、我就給你換上、好使的你還是得將就、○李四將錢數過、把小錢交給王立說、這是三十六個小錢、還短着三個錢的數、你再找出三十九個錢來就對了、○王立○短數我給你補上、這十二個黃鵝子、我也給你換上、那二十四個、都是二疋皮子、無論買甚麽、都能買得出來、我不能給你換、○李四偏要叫換、二人就吵起來了、正吵鬧之間、從旁邊來了一人、爲他們說和、從二十四個之中、又挑出八個來、對王立說、你再給他換上這八個罷、○王立○看着你這位的臉面、我給他換上就是了、於是連短數、又找出二十三個錢來、李四纔拿着走了、

又過了幾個禮拜、到冬月二十一日、王立對他家裏說、今天過冬、我要到街上去買點菜○家裏○我看不如買擔白菜、黃芽今天包頓餃子、賸下的留着過年、○王立○好啊、就找了一個簍子、提籃拿着香油罐子、一直到他常買東西的、一個水菜舖裏、掌櫃的問道、王大哥都買甚麼、○王立○打二兩香油、稱一斤鰕米、二斤葱、半斤芫荽、○掌櫃的、一樣一樣的都稱好了、王立說、給贅上幾科菠菜罷、家去好作個青頭、○掌櫃的○好啊、你看這些有好幾兩、○王立○算一算開賬罷、○掌櫃的○二兩香油是十八個、一斤鰕米、打上五十六、二斤葱、打上二十六、半斤芫荽、算四個、一共該是一百零四個錢、○王立○給你一百整錢就是了、○掌櫃的○不好抹零兒、你共總買了百十個錢的東西、還架住抹去四個零兒嗎、你看我算的價錢、那一樣不比人家便宜呢、○王立○我常在這裏買東西、再多照顧點就有喇、○掌櫃的○不論照顧多少、也得賣出本錢來纔行、○王立○好、我再給你添上兩個罷、這可不用說別的喇、○掌櫃的○罷罷罷、就是這麼着的罷、○王立把東西裝在簍子裏、說、我把簍子擱在這裏、先到菜市上去買擔白菜、回來再拿、○掌櫃的○好啊、○王立到了菜市、一連問了兩三個主兒、打了打價錢、比着平日、每斤能貴三四分錢、因此自己心裏說、今天過節、買的太多、未免太貴、不如少買幾斤吃着、等過日再買、於是來到一個菜攤子問道、你這白菜賣多少錢一斤、○掌櫃的○四個八啊、稱多少呢、○王立○給你四個三罷、○掌櫃的○四個三不賣、就去應酬別人去了、○王立○怎麼樣、你到底賣不賣呢、○小掌櫃的○你若是給四個八、怎麼不賣、光這樣打撈、還能買了東西嗎、○王立○你這小掌櫃的、實在會說話、來買你們的東西、怎麼說打撈呢、○老掌櫃的見王立翻了臉、就把他兒子嚇呼了一頓、急忙給

王立賠禮說、請你老兄消氣、那個畜類東西、不會說話、你看着我的面上、不要怪他。○王立○他若眞是個小孩、誰能怪他、從來說和氣生財、又道是買賣不成仁義在、說話那好這麼衝呢。○掌櫃的○可不是呢、那個東西、眞不知道甚麽。○王立就又到了一個菜攤子上、問白菜賣多少錢。○掌櫃的○那不是買的還沒走、你問他是多少錢罷。○買菜的○四個半哪、白菜不錯、很可以買得。○王立就揀了兩科、對掌櫃的說、給我稱稱這兩科罷。○掌櫃的○這兩科高高的十六斤、共該七十二個錢。○王立開上錢、拿着白菜、回到水菜舖裏、拐着簍子、就回家去了、

生童考試

某縣某村、有一個考童的、姓趙名鍾英、家業很富足、他父親名趙志學、也是個念書的人、只是考了一輩子童生、沒能進學、生了兩個兒子、大的名趙鍾傑、也念了七八年書、因爲天分魯笨、他父親就叫他棄儒就農、第二個就是所說的趙鍾英、他的天分很高、從八歲上學、跟他父親受業、到十三歲的時候、已經把四書五經、念了個通熟、講了個完全古文唐詩、以及一切時行文章詩賦、也念了許多、又日日學習字帖、於王柳顏歐趙諸名家字帖、和時行館閣體、都能摹仿上來、十四歲的時候、他父親就叫他作詩作文、不彀一年的工夫、就能作八韻詩、全篇文章、全篇賦、這固然是因着他有天分、也幸虧虧了他父親是個有學問的人、親自教導他的兒子、所以能有這樣的功效、不然的時候、縱然有天分、也未必造就的這樣快、但是趙鍾英的父親很知道自己的身分、因爲自己考了一輩子、沒能進學、知道必是有不合時派的地方、恐怕自己教自己的兒子、兒子也犯了父親的毛病、一輩子不能得功名、所以先把他兒子的書底子、預備好了、就決意給他另請先生、當趙鍾英十五歲的時候、他父親把自己所教的學生、挑出幾個念的書、和趙鍾英相彷彿的、與趙鍾英配成一帮、共計學生八人、可出束金二十五吊、打算另請先生、如是先和衆學生的父兄商議明白、怎樣派錢、怎樣派飯、諸事已妥、就

請了一位先生、這先生也是有品行、有才學的、一位老秀才、只是於摹仿時派上、不甚通達、所以也不必題到他的姓名、這先生上學以後、見趙鍾英才學出衆、又是正東的學生、就另眼看待、格外費心、數課以後、聽見縣考的信息、便勸他應試、趙鍾英縣考覆試到底、接着考府考、又得覆試到底、他父親和先生、都盼望趙鍾英可以進學、誰知到了院考的時候、竟是一場空夢、挨到下科、仍是如此、轉眼就是三四科、趙志學心中焦急、恐怕他的兒子、一輩子也和他自己一樣、光陰似箭、趙鍾英已經娶親、一日趙志學爲他兒子功名的緣故、正在憂悶之間、趙鍾英的丈人忽然來探望閨女(女兒)此人係趙志學幼年的同窗、姓高名識、原是個拔貢底子、由朝考二等、補授本省教諭、現在任滿回家、風聞他的女壻才學過人、數科不能進學、所以借着看閨女(女兒)的緣故、特來詳查此事、入門以後、一切周旋、俱不必題、到晚上、親家二人在一處叙談、趙鍾英在旁邊伺候、○高識○風聞我女壻、很有才學、怎麽考了數科、沒能進學呢、○趙志學○大概是才學不好、若是好的時候、何至如此、但是我因爲自己一輩子沒能進學、所以爲你的女壻、特特的請一位秀才先生教着、那先生教的也很用心、無奈於功名路上、仍是不利、只怕我父子們、都是命裏不該有功名罷、○高識○功名有命、是不錯的、但是看人的才分如何、也就可以約摸人的功名如何、有的只能進學、有的只能中舉、有的只能中進士、有的能拉翰林、點狀元、也有可上可下的才分、總而言之、必須人事盡了、纔可聽天由命、而且現今功名路上、樣樣都有個訣竅、不明白其中的訣竅、縱有才學、也難取勝、若是有實在的工夫、又得了其中的訣竅、大半沒有不得功名的、至於當得而不得、和不當得而得、又有一等命主乎其間、不是人所能逆料的、○趙志學○我現今請的先生、也是個秀才、於進學的訣竅、料想也該明白、○高識○親家、你別(莫)這樣說、大約每科進學的、二十個人以裏、若以才學訣竅而論、不過有五個是必能進的、還有五個是必不可進的、其餘十個、都是可進可不進的、要問其所以然、實係令人難解、現今親家所請的這位先生、固然是才學兼優、但於進學的訣竅上、未必十分明白、他所以能進學處、也未必不在可進可不進的數內、若果如此、他教的學生、那能保百發百中呢、○趙志學○是了、我從來沒聽見這些講究、今日纔得領教、眞是如夢初醒、現在叫你的女壻、把他先生批的文章、拿來你看看、好不好呢、○高識○可以的、我也很願意明白其中的緣故、○趙志學就吩咐他兒子、把近二年從先生批的文章、拿來遞給他丈人、○高識看了幾篇、就說、學生的才分工夫很好、先生批的也很費苦心、但是於功名的訣竅上、卻不甚合式、若要找近道兒、必須換換先生纔好、○趙志學○據親家看來、從那位先生好呢、○高識○城裏有一位老歲貢韓百川先生、當了多半輩子鎗手、於功名的訣竅上、甚是熟練、兄台諒來也知道此人、現今在城裏觀音廟裏設館、學生有二十多人、近科進學的、多半是他的門生、要求明師、莫如此人、○趙志學○要從此人受業、必須進城入廚、但近來在城裏念大書的、於吃喝嫖賭吹等事、大半無所不爲、一入其中、只怕所得不及所失、要把韓先生請到家中、勢又有所不能、我的意見、想要求一個次一等的、請到家中教讀纔好、○高識○有了、去年韓先生手下、進了一個大徒弟、名叫于大春、此人本有大才、兼有實學、只因不明白功名路上的訣竅、所以考了數次前名、沒能進學、無計奈何、投到韓先生門下受業、不上二年、盡得了韓先生的秘訣、上年新進、將來必要勝過他的先生、但時下聲價還不甚高、且家底寒微、必須以教學爲業、只用三四十吊錢、就可以請來、○趙志學○好極喇、親家認識此人嗎、○高識○認識倒認識、○趙志學○親家能替我去請此人不能啊、○高識○怎麼不能呢、但不知學生共有幾人、束脩可出多少、○趙志學○今年學堂中共是八人、攤學價四八三十二吊、下年另請先生、可攤五八四十吊、設或別的學東、有不願意的、我一個學生、也給先生四十吊錢、好不好呢、○高識○很好、等明天去請他便了、○說罷、各自安寢、第二天酒飯已畢、高識親自去見于先生、通說此事、于先生已經應允、高識便回到趙宅、住了一宿、次日就回家去了。○且說趙志學、已經爲他的兒子、另請了一個好先生、心滿意足、過了新正十五以後、就預備車馬、打發人去接(搬)于先生、接(搬)到以後、衆東家輪流管飯、趙志學家管待的格外豐厚、自不用說、開課後、于先生見趙鍾英的文章、隔着進學不遠、遂將一切訣竅、傳授與他、及至縣考來到、趙鍾英考得第三名、接着府考、又考得第五名、考完回家、工課更加嚴密、有一天趙鍾英對他先生說、今天我哥哥去赶集、看見院考的條子(條示)、是九月初三日調齊、又聽見門斗說、大人初四日下馬、先生打算幾時起身呢。○于先生○大人初四日下馬、初五日謁廟放告、初六日開棚考古、我們初一日走也就誤不了啊。○初一日、東家預備兩個牲口、送了一天、到了初二、師徒兩個、打發送的回去、各人打起圓包(包袱)來、一早就背着走、走到下半天、六點鐘的時候、趙鍾英對他先生說、我的脚磨起泡來喇、疼的實在不能走喇、咱們早住店歇着、好不好。○于先生○好啊、

我的脚倒不疼、就是腿酸了(疼一點)、這裏有個興隆棧、那是我的熟店、飲食很公道、又沒有臭蟲。○到了店門口、掌櫃的看見、說于先生來喇、裏邊坐坐、在上房有先生的一位鄉親、你們打個伴兒、明天一塊兒走罷。○于先生○好啊。○進去一看、原是他的同鄉李長煦、彼此敘了久別、讓了座。○于先生○今天住得太早啊。○李先生○不用說喇、常在書房裏不動彈、一點力氣也沒有、剛走了多半天、脚也腫了、腿也癱了、一步也走不動了。○于先生○咱們(我們)是同病相連、我師徒倆、也是如此。○李○西廂上說的好、荒村雨露眠宜早、野店風霜起要遲、咱們(我們)早早住下、歇息歇息罷、先生啊、這位令徒、是親(及門)受業呢、是批外課(附課)呢。○于○親(及門)受業的。○李○甚麼榜印。○于○他叫趙鍾英啊。○李又向趙鍾英說、哦、縣考第三、府考第五、就是閣下嗎、這纔是聞名沒見面咧、正在妙年、又考在前名、今科必進無疑了。○趙○先生過獎了、縣府考、不過是徼倖而已、院考進不進、尚在未定之間、那敢指望必進呢。○于○先生用了飯沒有。○

李○沒有、我們一塊兒喫罷、○于○好啊、掌櫃的、有甚麼飯呢、○店家○有單餅、綠豆水飯、豆腐菜、還有雞子、炒肉、又有活鮮的鯉魚、○于○可以先打半斤燒酒、炒五個雞子、煎兩條鯉魚、○不多時、店家把酒和菜、都送上來了、○于○連飯也送來罷、○店家○天還早喇、已經住下了、慢慢的多喝幾兩、解解乏罷、忙甚麼呢、○于○還是早喫了早歇着好、○三人喫喝完了、于就大聲叫道、掌櫃的啊、算賬來、再帶一壺水來啊、○店家連聲答應、手提水壺來說、都算我的罷、○于○好說、共該多少錢呢、○店家拿算盤打着說、半斤燒酒、七八五十六、五個雞子、算四十、兩個魚、少算一點、打上五十、再打上三張餅、三三見九十六碗水飯、六六三十六、共該二百七十二個錢、○三人湊上錢、店家把錢拿去、○李○今天的飯錢、算的不少啊、○于○比較起來、還算不甚麼多喇、別（莫）說這幾年歉收、就是豐收的年頭、每逢考的時候、那個店家、不狠狠的算錢呢、○李○總而言之、考的人沒有錢、也得裝個有錢的、就是了、○于○李先生、這

幾年還在外邊設館嗎、○李○今年在東莊教着幾個小學生、並沒有進場的、一年三十來吊錢、除去（批外課　附課）的束脩、再除去三（個）屆考的糜費、也就賸不多了、○于○你的考運、想是不好、怎麼考了這些年、還不進呢、○李○一不埋怨學台、二不歸咎考運、總是自己才學不高、我有帶的幾篇文章、求先生指教指教、看有甚麼毛病、○于先生看了一遍、說看你這文章、力量是有的、府縣考可以覆試到底、院考可就不行喇、因為小考的利器、總在清醒靈快四個字、第一眉目要清、不可蒙頭蓋面、遇着截上截下題、必須分清題界、不要挨搽不清、第二出落題字、總要緊醒、方能豁人心目、第三字句要靈便、不要笨拙、第四句法要爽快、不要拖累、若不照着清醒靈快去作文、任你使九牛二虎的力氣、也是枉然了、現在你文章的毛病、是用意太深、不分大小題、都要竭力去作、比方舉千斤之重、使得紅了臉、舉一毛之輕、也使得紅了臉、豈不是枉費氣力嗎、你若把這個毛病改了、我敢保你這科準進、等到進學以後、再學大場墨卷、可

就近邊了、○李○如此說來、成宏天崇諸大家、不必揣摹、只取那巧搭分品小題芝蘭一類的小文章、加工誦讀、學習個快馬輕刀、在小場就可以取勝了、○于○就是如此、割雞焉用牛刀呢、○正說話之間、又進來一個保等的秀才、名叫王希孟、彼此問了姓名、就說、○剛纔在外邊聽見于先生講小考的文法、實係不錯、但如今最尙的是字、若是卷子寫的俊秀光圓、就佔三分便宜、文章雖多少差池一點、也可以望進、○李○先生說的不錯、但咱們鄉下的學兒、多是半耕半讀、指頭很硬、有多少寫好字的呢、○王○鄉下的學兒不會寫字、不光爲他的手硬、一來是沒有講究、二來是沒有工夫、三來是見的字體少、四來是捨不得買好筆好墨、你看濰縣城裏的先生、多半會寫、從來拔貢優貢翰林狀元、全出在城裏、鄉下輕易沒有、這是因爲甚麼呢、就是因爲城裏大小學堂講究的是字、常常摹倣殿試策的式樣、筆墨上也捨得花錢、十一二歲的學生、就用徽墨湖筆、到臨場的時候、有用二百錢買一枝筆的、有用三百錢買一枝筆的、進拔貢場、還有用一兩銀子一枝的、咱們用幾十個錢買一枝筆、大毛不過幾根、做的欠工夫、修剔的又不乾淨、所以大不如湖筆飽滿、所用的墨也大不及徽墨、寫在卷子上、那能叫人愛看呢、○于○工欲善其事、必先利其器、想咱們二三十個錢買一枝筆、二三十個錢買一塊墨、別(莫)說是咱們、就是晉唐宋諸大家復生、也是難以寫好字的、○王○現今詩賦也大行、你看取古的正場的文章、只用敷衍過去、也就進了、○于○賦學一門和作文差不許多、頭一段渾寫大意、就是八股的起講、底下也分層次出落題字時令情景題字句總要鮮豔、好似春花嫩柳、史事題必須慷慨悲歌、從血性中流出、○李○如今經解還行不行呢、○于○考經的、多是帶本子、若是沒有本子、別(莫)說漢宋諸儒的講、就是原文大字、也怕記不完全喇、但是取了經學、也和取古的一樣佔便宜、○李○聽先生的話、眞是傾心吐膽、請將作詩的訣竅指教指教、○于○我於時派詩上、原不甚見長、後來聽了明人的講論、這纔覺得容易了、因爲作詩的規模、也與作賦作文、大同小異、這是平常先生、都知道的、至於對法、其首末二韻、不甚要緊、當中的四韻、一韻對草木、一韻對顏色、一韻對數目、一韻對疊字、若是記的典故多、要作三首四首詩、只用改頭換尾(影)、一湊合就得了、這雖然不可拘定死套、然而差不多的題、都能用上、○李○不錯不錯、這可算得是個秘傳了、再請問先生、我看院考牌示上、有算學二字、這是近年的新例、我到底不明白是個甚麼事情、○于○算學就是六藝中的數學、黃帝臣隷首作九九數、並算法九章、若遇深奥難算的、又有天元術勾股術以助之、西國算法、有四率、借根方、勾股八線、等類、如今讀書人、專會舞文弄墨、題起算學、全然不懂、及到作官的時候、任憑師爺和書吏擺弄、好像一個傀儡頭、雖然有耳朶、有眼睛、有鼻子、有嘴、卻全仗有人提弄他替他說話、朝廷知道數學、是要緊的、且於日用、學業、富國強兵、等事、大有關切、所以在經古場添上算學、無奈考試官一點不懂、只得找些算學的典故、考試生童、所以題不會出、卷子也不會看、茍且了事就是了、○王○先生講數學、實在是好、再請先生、把禮樂射御書、講給我們聽聽、○于○論及這些、我實係不敢說是明白、不過略曉一二、因爲聖門中的冉有、尚且說如其禮樂、以俟君子、何況經秦火以後、禮樂失傳、就是禮記、儀禮、周禮、所載吉凶軍賓嘉五大禮、多半是出於漢儒的附會、所以我不敢輕談、至於十二律呂隔八相生、本朝有黃鐘通韻一書、與漢宋諸儒的講究、大不相同、各持己見、不知誰是誰非、只可束書高閣拱手作別而已、說到射學、如今文武分爲兩家、所以讀書人、就與射隔膜了、古時出軍行圍、以車爲尙、因此御車也是最要緊的、但如今不用車戰、車之制度也都改變、赶車的人、也變爲卑賤了、惟有書法一道、許氏說文本六書、發倉頡造字的本意、而萬事萬物的義理、都可從六書中發明出來、若論寫的好歹、須本王右軍永字八法、鐵畫銀鈎、寫中鋒不寫偏鋒、方能成個家數、○王○領教領教、現在天不早喇、咱們睡罷、等明天路上再談、○于李趙同聲答道、明天再談罷、○店家

○先生們、都要安歇嗎、○于○已經二更多喇、我們明天要早點兒走、掌櫃的早給我們僱一程驢啊、○李○依我說、暫且不必僱驢、今天咱們把腿脚都跑壞了、明天早起、可以慢慢的走着、遛遛腿、等到打過早尖、再僱一程驢不晚、○于○好啊、這麽着咱們睡罷、○第二天、纔放朦朦亮的時候、各人收拾行李、叫開店門、背着圓包包袱走了、走不多遠、王先生說、○中國上古的時候、拔取人才、都是鄉舉里選、何等的不好呢、現在以文章取士、光爲這院考府考、叫我們花多少錢、跑多少腿、受多少罪、又屈了多少人才呢、○于○誰說不是、所說的鄉舉里選、乃是舉人之德、選人之才、既被鄉里舉選、自無不眞之理、現在獨獨以文章取士、是單有意取人的文才了、且即以文才而論、究竟錢買的、送情的、總能居一大半、眞才不過是一小半就是了、○王○嗐、若提起場中私弊、眞是一言難盡、總而言之、孔方兄就是好東西、有了孔方兄就有的是功名、○李○先生說有孔方兄就有功名、那郤還得會用的、像我、就是有錢、也不曉得怎樣用法、

○王○這些事、我可明白喇、縣府考有買案首的、有買前十名的、到了院考、有辦內稿鎗的、有辦薦卷的、有竄冒的、有磕連號的、有下箱子的、有用冒子的、還有狗咬狗的、○李○這些樣數、從前也曾聽見說過、就是不知道底細、○王○府縣考買個案首、大約用五六百銀子、若於官有情面、也許還能省二百、買個前十名、不過幾十兩銀子、因爲案首是沒有不進的、前十名郤不能定準、至於院考辦內稿鎗、是外邊有人和裏邊的人通線、講明了價錢、立下帖子、裏邊的人、和看卷子的師爺勾通、到了場期、看卷子的師爺、把文章做了、從後堂傳遞前堂、從前堂傳給巡風的、巡風的早和本童訂對明白、等到內稿下來的時候、巡風的站在本童的號頭上、以聲示意、本童聽見、望見、就裝作犯規的樣子、或吃菸、或亂號、或與鄰號交頭接耳、巡風的看見、就進入大號、手拉本童的手、要把他拉出去見大人受刑罰、本童再三求饒、方纔撒手、這時候、已經把內稿交在本童手中、這是眞內稿鎗、斷無不進之理、大約用銀五六百、或六七百不等、

還有一種假內稿鎗、俗名窩冒、就是鎗手勾通院役、於進場的頭一天晚上、偷進院內、藏在一邊、等出下題來、鎗手作文、院役傳遞、若是進了、也得花五六百兩。○辦薦卷、是勾通裏邊的人、和師爺打下勾手、把本童的文章、加上幾句好批語、學台一眼看高、一眼看低、隨着大流、也就進了、但是辦薦卷、最容易撞騙、有許多不通師爺的、若是師爺不打薦條、也就罷了、師爺打了薦條、那撞騙人的、把薦條暗暗的抄出來、交給本童、若是進了、就撞他三百兩、或五百兩、若是不進、也得給三十兩或二十兩的小頭。○磕連號、是本童和鎗手、俱是考童的、先和院書勾通、院書把二人的坐號、磕在一處、進了場的時候、二人連號並坐、諸事就方便了、這個辦法、約用三四百兩。○用冒子、是和廩保勾通、就是鎗手冒充本童的名子、頂替着進場、到點名的時候、正在燈下、十分倉猝、只用廩保不說、學台怎能知道、後來得了功名、就算本童的了、這個辦法、也掉不下三四百兩。○還有下箱子的、是隨棚舞弊的人、平素預備許多時派文章、有寫在紙本上的、有寫在綾子上的、每付大約有文章二三千篇、名叫箱子、有願用的、在外邊講明價錢、箱子客和前堂的搜檢翻子家馬勾通、於進場的頭一天、先把文章箱子、交給搜檢翻子家馬彼此定下暗號、等到點進名去、那搜檢翻子家馬假裝搜翻的樣子、就把箱子遞給本童、帶進場去了、此等名爲內下的箱子、又有一等外下的、是在外邊、把箱子帶在身上、點進名去的時候、搜檢翻子家馬不認眞摟翻他、但是這兩個辦法、是碰時運、也許碰不着、若是碰着文章進了、大約用百十兩銀子。○至於狗咬狗、也有叫民治民的、就是一同進場的人、在場裏講定買賣價錢多少、都是本童當面自講、所說的這些詭弊、不過是舉其大概、這麼看起來、窮童生要進個學、不是極難的嗎。○于○王先生所說的、這都是銀錢秀才、是通場瞞哄學台一人、還有一種情誼秀才、是學台一人瞞哄通場、因爲凡作學台的、光年兄年弟、也有三百六十個、各省各府的都有、再結交幾個朋友、高攀幾個堂官、也是各省各府的都有、一旦放了學差、誰好意思不給誰個面子呢、所以那些紳

衿鄉宦的子弟、有許多不知文章怎樣作法、竟是進了
學、你說氣人不氣人呢、○李○依我看、氣也罷、不氣也
罷、細論起來、還是自己的工夫不到、學問不佳、若是工
夫到、學問高、還能到底不進嗎、一旦進了、我想一個正正
大光明名公得的秀才、比起那些銀錢秀才、情誼秀才、終久體
面得多喇、○王○那是自然的、但是論到進學、還有許
多的小事、也當知道、也當小心、有些鄉學兒並不曉得
場中的規矩、又沒受過明人的指教、一進了場、心裏就
慌張得很、因此有越幅的、有空白的、有倒字的、有鑽頂
的、有當抬頭不抬的、有犯聖諱的、還有污卷的、這些事
情、雖然看着不甚要緊、然而小事卻能害大事、○于○
這些毛病、大概都是忙中發慌的緣故、若是心裏不慌、
凡事謹慎小心、怎麼會越幅鑽頂、怎麼會污卷呢、凡有
疑惑的字、簡直的不用、怎麼會倒字犯諱呢、○說着說
着、到了棧頭、打了早尖、王先生辭別先走了、○趙鍾英
○先生啊、咱們僱一程驢罷、我的脚又走不動喇、○于
○好啊、可以叫掌櫃的、給咱們僱兩個頭驢罷、○李○僱

驢沒有墊頭、是最難騎的、幸虧你們還帶着被褥套、預備
僱驢、我沒有被褥套、可以把我的行李、和你們的湊成一
塊兒、裝起來作墊頭、我也不騎驢、也不叫你們白揹、我
給你們攤上個分兒、好不好、○于○怎麼還用攤分兒、
搭着件一塊走、這算甚麼呢、咱們就僱兩個牲口、路上
倒換着騎罷、○到了晚上、用過晚飯以後、于先生說、○
這條路、我走一回、殼一回、這幾年我就窮在這條路上、
○李○窮秀才、富舉人、這番先生考個壹等、到下年鄉
試中個解元、往下就好了、○于○那趕自好、就怕沒有
那個命運、○李○先生上科進學、共花了多少錢呢、○
于○不花不花、還花了七八十吊、拉下有五十吊錢的
虧空、○李○咱們這等考窮考的、怎麼還花這麼些錢
呢、○于○先生光聽說辦功名的、必得有錢、那知道正正
大光明名公得的也是非錢不可、當初我是撥的府學、廩保領
我到府學去拜老師、老師很忙、並沒有工夫講我的學
規、我就站在一旁、聽見老師對那個新進的說、你別莫妝
糊塗、你這個秀才、只值一百銀子嗎、那新進的說、門生

實係不能、老師說、你不能、還有能的喇、新進的說、門生不明白、老師說、你是妝糊塗呢、你是當眞不明白呢、你的丈人家、不是丁宅上嗎、你女人的妝奩會少了嗎、箱裏櫃裏會沒有體已嗎、就是你女人沒有體己、你丈人肯叫你把秀才扔了嗎、你丈人肯了、你丈母娘也不能肯、你丈母娘肯了、你女人也必不能肯哪、又向一位新進的說、進了學立刻都窮喇、海岱門那個碓房、不是你們家的嗎、纔不多幾天、滙了二千銀子的滙票來、不是滙到你家嗎、不是你哥哥親自到煙台去取來的嗎、我們三年熬一個歲考、文武生的學規、不過七八百銀子、除去院規、再除去書斗的二成、我們夥計兩個、並不能足六百銀子、你當是還有甚麼出息嗎、從來人的名樹的影、誰還瞞得住誰嗎、你們有錢的門生、當幫助幫助窮老師、何苦在窮老師身上、打那些窮算盤、使那些窮經紀呢、又對那一位新進的說、你不是張家的外甥嗎、你進了學、難道不是他的光彩嗎、八十兩銀子、不難湊辦啊、不必再計較喇、這纔回頭向我說、我曉得你不是個有錢的、但是牟家是你的親姑姑、四十兩三十兩總能相幫、即不相幫、也可以挪借出來、老師說到這裏、又向他們說話、幸虧我的廩保、不給老師赶網、好歹講了二十兩銀子、及到覆出試來、就了不得喇、報子的要錢、房東要錢、學書要錢、門斗要錢、禮房要錢、吹手也要錢、礮手也要錢、把大門的也要錢、聽差的也要錢、轎夫也要錢、鬧的我手忙脚亂、一點主意沒有、幸虧管飯的在一旁說道、先生不用着忙、只用和他們講明了多少錢、我給先生開付、等先生回家的時候、我和先生一塊兒走、我的飯錢、和開付他們的錢、都如數帶回來了、管飯的這句話、好似趙子龍打開金鎖陣一般、後來我一個一個的和他們講明、一總算起來、在府裏花了六十多吊、回家又請了幾桌客、共花了足足的八十吊錢、雖然不算太多、但是咱們的家道不稱、又沒有好親戚、以後賣了二畝地、纔把這陣饑荒擋過去了。○李○在這條功名路上、有這麼些窮神惡鬼、如同搶刼的一般、無怪現在作官的、差不多都惡狠狠的要錢、大概都是這條路上學壞了○于○不但是學壞了、而且預先拉下虧空、若是一點贓不貪連本錢也賺不回來、又怎能指望發財呢○李○看如今的時勢用功念書還不如用功弄錢、倒是個求功名的捎道兒○于○嗐這些事情、越說越叫人可歎、我們不如早早的睡覺歇着罷、明天好早早到府○第二天將到府城門、李說○我和你們二人說話說熱喇、咱們賃房子在一塊兒寓着、好不好、○于○正合我的意思○恰巧來了一個熟識管飯的、名叫吳之用、急忙上前問道○先生們都來喇、府上都好啊○于先生說、好啊、你向來發財呀○吳○託福託福、還給先生賃處房子罷○于○可以的、我們原沒打算照顧別人去○吳○請先生們到飯館去坐坐、喫點飯、歇息歇息、我就打發人去找房子○三人就到飯館去了、不大的工夫吳之用來說在這東邊、許家有三間房子、自己佔着一間、裏邊鍋竈桌子椅子樣樣都有、又很清靜、和他講到兩吊錢、再少一個他也不賃○于○那個房子、我從前看過、也很便當、就定規賃他的罷○

三人跟吳之用、到了下處、于先生對趙鍾英說○今天初四、大人下馬、後天開棚考古、聽說這位大人不以古場爲重、考西府的時候、取古的往往不進、再者、我們今天纔進來、明天就預備進場、也太倉猝了、依我看、我們可以不進古場罷、至於正場、定準是先考生、後考童、你和李先生進場還早喇、可以安安靜靜的看點文章、或是寫幾個字、場前萬不可任意閒玩○初五日早飯後、于先生同着趙李二人、到了老師公館、拜望了廩保、看了看大人排的單子、知道某縣和某縣合棚、某縣是某日進場、到了考生的日子、于先生進場保等、考了個一等第一名、管飯的慌慌張張、前來報喜、大門旁貼上一個連中三元的報條、那時喝喜酒的要喜錢的出的出、進的進、鬧鬧鬨鬨、就是一天零半夜、把個李先生樂極喇、對趙鍾英說、您先生考了一等、這就是咱們倆的喜信、昨夜我做了一個夢、夢見于先生坐在山頂、甚是榮耀、你我也隨後跟着往上爬、今日于先生考了第一、是應驗了山頂上的夢、焉知你我不都跟着進學呢、○趙

○夢不足憑、憑各人的命罷、其實這個夢、也有些吉兆、○于先生既把自己的事、安排妥了、晚上對他的學生和李先生說、○後天就進場喇、明天上半天、你們該去塡年貌、投卷子、要緊別莫躭誤進場啊、○第二天、趙李二人、先到禮房、每人買了兩本卷子、一本謄文章的、一本默聖諭的、又買了一張互結、然後到公館裏、塡寫年貌、記上自己的年歲、身量、面貌、三代、並業師某人、認保某人、挨保某人、又在卷面上、寫上自己的名子、在互結上、也寫上業師認保挨保的名子、還有同考挨排的五個名子、就去求認保和挨保畫押、請老師用印、諸事已畢、遂就把卷子帶互結、投到禮房去了、○到了下半天、趙鍾英到街上買辦場具、就是粉子、蠟燭、單帖、夾紙、水壺、帶子、還有粽子、火燒食、和雞蛋糕、都是兩個人的、李先生在下處研墨、添墨盒子、又把硯台、筆墨、仿圈、聖諭、都預備停當、各人把各人的收拾起來、伺候黑夜進場、○于○別的都有了、就是李先生還少一頂秋帽子、一身外套子、○李○我已經託付管飯的、他應許給借、正說話的時候、管飯的來說、帽子和外套子、都借來喇、就是不大很好、○李○甚麽好歹、有這件東西就得了、好的誰肯往外借呢、這個就滿行啊、○管飯的○學院掛的牌、是四更三點放頭礮、就可以起來洗臉、五更一點放二礮、就可以喫飯、早去伺候着、五更三點放三礮、就開門點名、先生要預備甚麽飯呢、○李○黑夜起來、都是不愛喫、一個人要兩碗匾食罷、○管飯的○好、這麽着、先生們只管睡罷、聽更聽礮的事、都在我身上、萬萬不至誤事、○到放頭礮的時候、管飯的來叫趙李二位先生、起來洗了臉、及至放二礮的時候、二位先生用過了飯、就到考院前等候聽點、到了三礮、開了院門、就點起名來了、先在外邊經過縣點、又到大門前經過府點、然後往前魚貫而入、學台在二門底下東邊、西面坐、廩保在西邊、東面站、禮房唱名、童生應名、唱保、廩保接唱、學台用硃筆點名、童生接着卷子、到了龍門底下、被摟檢摟翻子翻過一回、這纔進去、各歸各號、天將要明的時候、就出下題來了、首題是方千里者九的九字、次題是登泰山、詩題是九日登高得高字、趙李二位先生、照着于先生所講的一切訣竅、聚精會神的把兩篇文、一首詩、斟酌的十分妥當、繳的頭卷出的頭場、都暗暗的得意、到了下處、于先生把他們兩個的文章一看、不覺喜孜孜的說、李先生今科再不進、就算是大人瞎眼了、鍾英的文章、也有指望、但不如李兄的準成、我等着喝喜酒罷、○李○常常的不進、也就不敢指望了、○于○今科不進、我就輸上一隻眼睛、○等到張出榜來、他們兩個、果然進了、跑報的星夜奔走、報到家中、插上紅旗、貼上報條帖、合家老少都是歡喜、又把報條帖送到各家、貼得滿街通紅、把那些不進的學生、一陣饞的都加工念書了、○再說于先生在府裏領着二位新進、拜了保師、又到老師的公館、拜了老師、遂就邀同保師、講明了學規大禮、李先生窮、用錢二十吊、趙先生富、用錢八十吊、又到禮房下處、說明覆試的卷子錢、李三吊、趙五吊、到了第二天、二人覆出試來、那一些同窗朋友、沾親帶故的、一齊都來了、喝酒的喝酒、借錢的借錢、這個要買雙鞋、那個要買封筆、十千二十吊、不大的工夫、就花淨了、這些朋友還沒走完、院裏的人役、又來了一大羣、擁擁擠擠、亂吵亂鬧、要錢的無數、噯、進學雖然是件好事、沒有錢打發、也很作難、人都知道他心裏歡喜、誰卻知道他心裏焦急呢、及至考試已畢、進院謝恩的時候、戴着新帽新頂、穿着新衣新靴、合府新進的生員、一同進去、參拜了大人、聽了發落、領了花紅、回到下處、各人收拾行李回家、一路之上、揚揚得意、到底比那些不進學的、自覺另一樣滋味、且是到了店裏、都稱他們新進老爺、誰不另眼看待呢、前幾次沒進學的時候、自覺討愧、無顏見鄉里父老、所以進莊難、進家也難、見弟兄難、見妻子更難、往往離家不遠、這就挨挨遲遲、到黑天纔敢進莊、這一回趙李二位、既都進了、就惟恐到家不早、一進莊內、但見老老少少、慌慌張張、稱的稱讚的讚、瞅的瞅、看的看、一時把合疃的人、都驚動了、趙先生到了家中、有他的父母在堂、先給他父母磕頭、後見哥嫂行禮、合家歡喜的了不得、雖然只一人得了功名、大家也都覺着成了貴人了、他的婦人站在一旁、口裏雖然沒說甚麼、心中的歡喜、卻比別人更深一層、趙先生和大家說完了話、纔來到自己房中、打趣他婦人說、你今天饒秀才、明天饒秀才、這回可叫你想了來了、他婦人回覆說、小小的一個秀才、不能滿我的心意、早晚盼望你中了舉人、會上進士、點了翰林、然後走馬上任、我做了官太太、幫助你爲國盡忠、留美名傳到萬世、這纔能解我的饞喇、再說李先生、父母早已去世、來到家中、雖然有他婦人、歡天喜地的迎接、究竟不如有爹娘更好、想到這裏、李先生不覺的落下淚來、這就是人逢喜事倍思親的話了、二人歇了一夜、印了報條帖、使人送給親友、趕着定了日期、請客賀喜、但見那些賀喜的人、有送對聯的、有送靴帽的、有送喜果的、有送喜貲的、酒擔食盒、來往不斷、金頂紅纓、出入不息、熱熱鬧鬧、一連數天、誰不欽敬、誰不羨慕、○請了客以後、忽然門斗送了信來、說某日某時送學、趙先生就去約會李先生進城、○李○我這麼大年紀纔進、在人跟前、也沒有甚麼光彩、且是送過學、至少也得十千八吊、我過的這日子、還去得起嗎、這一樣實在不能奉陪、你自己去罷、○趙先生年少高興、就和他先生進了城、借了丁宅上的一匹雪獅子馬、前後披掛、鞍韂鞴轡、都是額外出色、十五六歲的馬童、一個生的又俊俏、又伶俐、打扮的又整齊、又精彩、趙先生插上花、戴上帽、換上靴子、穿上藍衫、前後身十字披紅、居然就像一個小狀元、到了大堂前頭、和同學的人、拜謁了知縣、就各人上馬、那些武生們上馬、又爽快、又麻俐、叫人愛看、至於這些文生上馬、再三的上也上不去、如同蝦蟆趴陡崖一般、眞是令人可笑、上馬以後、新進生員、都騎馬在前、知縣坐轎在後、順着大街、遊遊蕩蕩、往老師衙門來了、街兩旁舖戶人家、男男女女、爭着觀看、賽着誇獎、恰巧有個花子、迎面來了、左手打着刮打板、右手打着撒拉機、隨口唱了四句話、說新進秀才來送學、光棍漢子尋老婆、這個比方甚麼意、滋味輕易撈不着、兩旁的人聽見、沒有一個不笑的、○到了儒學以前、騎馬的下馬、坐轎的下轎、知縣領着文武新生、進了文廟、行三跪九叩禮、拜了聖像、接着到了明倫堂、給兩位老師、行了相見的禮、禮既行完、知縣挑轎回衙、衆生員們、拜客的拜客、回家的回家、進學的事、就完結了、

親眷相稱

親眷是從男女嫁娶起首、男迎女叫娶、女歸男叫嫁、嫁娶之先、有媒人說親、若男兒幼小、父母託媒人給兒子聘妻、叫給兒子說媳婦、說丈人家、若男子歲數大了、父母又不在了、自己託媒人聘妻、叫說家口、也說成家、女子幼小、父母託媒人給女兒擇婿、叫給閨女(女兒)說婆婆家、說成了、就叫定了親、男以禮娶女、叫娶親、叫將(擡)媳婦、也叫合婚、完婚、用文話稱讚說、花燭之禧、合巹之禧、若婦人去世、男人又娶妻、叫續娶、繼娶、續絃、女以禮嫁男、叫出嫁、出閣、出門子、也叫做媳婦、用文話稱讚說、于歸大吉、若丈夫死了、婦人就爲寡婦、孝婦、若再嫁一男人、就叫改嫁、俗話叫走、文話叫再醮、嫁娶未久、男家叫女爲新媳婦(婦、娘子)女家叫男爲新女壻(郎、姑爺)長久叫夫婦、夫妻、也叫兩口子、女稱男爲丈夫、對外人提起丈夫來、俗話說、俺當家的、我們當家的、俺外頭的、我們家的(爺們、大爺)有孩子就說孩子他爹、若上了年紀、就說俺老頭子、我們老頭子、寫信給丈夫、稱賢夫某人、夫君某人、男稱女爲妻子、爲夫人、也叫他、夫妻兩口家、其名就叫他、他叫他、他他叫他他、有孩子的、叫孩子他(娘、媽)書內記的是卿、對外人提起妻子、常說俺家裏、我們家裏、也說(俺、我的)老婆、我們內人、文人相談、就說卑內、賤內、拙荆、外人問及妻子、就稱寶眷、貴內、令正、令內助、令夫人、大坤範、婦人自稱叫醜婦、賤妾、婢子、寫信給妻子、就稱賢妻某氏、夫妻生孩子、在懷抱的時候、叫(嬰孩、娃娃)男的叫兒子、外人問起來常說、你跟前的(學生、相公)也稱令郎、令器、令嗣、令公郎、間有功名人的兒子、叫少爺、若有好幾個兒子、就稱大少爺、二少爺、問先生的兒子、稱世兄、問先生的(閨女、女兒)稱世妹、對着外人提自己的兒子就說、我跟前的小厮、文人說犬子、或說小犬、也說小兒、女的叫閨女、女兒、妞兒、妮子、也叫嫚子、丫頭子、對着外人就說醜女、弱女、(小女、弱息)外人問起來就說、你跟前的姑娘、也說千金、文話稱令愛、若有好

幾個女兒就分大姑娘、二姑娘、兒女稱父親叫爹爹、爸爸、外人間起來文話稱令尊、對着外人提說稱家父、家嚴、嚴君、兒女叫母親是娘媽、媽媽、外人間起來、稱令堂、令慈、對着外人稱家慈、家母、慈母、兒女稱父親的妾叫姨、姨娘、文話稱庶母、生母、稱外人的庶母說如母、兒女寫信給父母自稱不孝男、不孝女、同父的男子是親弟兄、比自己大的叫哥哥、又分大哥二哥、寫信給親哥哥稱胞兄、對着外人說家兄、外人尊稱說令兄、稱哥哥的妻是嫂嫂、嫂子、對着外人稱家嫂、外人尊稱說令嫂、比自己小的叫兄弟、又分二兄弟、三兄弟、寫信給兄弟、稱賢弟、對着外人稱舍弟、胞弟、外人尊稱說令弟、稱兄弟的妻子是弟妹、兄弟媳婦、弟婦、對着外人稱舍弟婦、外人尊稱說令弟婦、哥哥兄弟的兒子、是姪兒、女兒是姪女、對着外人稱舍姪、小姪女、外人尊稱、令姪、令姪女、同父的女子是親姊妹、比自己大的叫姐姐、也分大姐姐、二姐姐、對着外人稱家姐、也叫家姊、外人尊稱說令姊、姐姐的丈夫、俗話叫姐夫、文話稱姐丈、對着外人稱家姊丈、家姐丈、外人尊稱說令姊丈、比自己小的叫妹妹、也分二妹妹、三妹妹、對着外人稱舍妹、也說小妹、外人尊稱、令妹、妹妹的丈夫、稱妹丈、也叫妹夫、對着外人稱舍妹丈、外人尊稱說令妹丈、稱父親的父親是爺爺、對着外人說家祖、也說家祖父、若已去世、說先祖、父親的母親、叫奶奶、婆婆、媽媽、對着外人說家祖母、也說祖母、外人尊稱、不過加一令字、稱父親的爺爺、叫老爺爺、也叫太爺、對着外人稱曾祖、父親的祖母、稱老太太、也叫老奶奶、對着外人稱曾祖母、父親的太爺、老爺爺、太太、老奶奶、叫老太爺、老老爺爺、老太太、老老奶奶、對着外人就說高祖、高祖母、凡去世的都可以加先字、稱父親的哥哥、是大爺、大伯、大爹、伯伯、也分大爺、二大爺、對着外人稱家伯、伯父、外人尊稱說令伯、賢伯、大爺的妻子、叫大娘、大媽、寫信稱伯母、稱父親的兄弟、是叔叔、也分二叔、三叔、對着外人稱家叔、叔父、外人尊稱說、令叔、叔叔的妻子叫嬸子、嬸娘、寫信稱嬸母、伯伯叔叔的兒女、還叫哥哥兄弟、姐姐妹妹、對着外人通稱叔伯弟兄、叔伯姊妹、父親的姊妹叫姑姑、姑媽、對着外人稱姑母、稱姑姑的兒女、也叫哥哥兄弟、姐姐妹妹、對外人提說、姑表弟兄、姑表姐妹、叫姑姑的丈夫是姑夫、也稱姑丈、稱母親的父母、是老爺、老娘、對着外人稱外祖父、外祖母、叫母親的弟兄是舅舅、對外人提說、舅父、娘舅、親娘舅、舅家母舅、叫舅舅的妻是舅母、妗母、妗子、稱舅舅的兒女、也叫哥哥兄弟、姐姐妹妹、對着外人稱表弟兄、表姊妹、叫母親的姊妹是姨、對着外人說、姨母、稱姨的丈夫是姨丈、也叫姨夫、稱姨的兒女、也是哥哥兄弟、姐姐妹妹、對着外人說兩姨弟兄、兩姨姊妹、稱父親的老爺老娘是老老爺、老老娘、父親的舅舅舅母、叫舅爺爺、舅奶奶、舅婆婆、母親的舅舅舅母、叫舅老爺、舅老娘、外舅爺爺外舅奶奶、兒子的妻子是媳婦、或兒媳、兒媳婦、女兒的丈夫叫女婿、對着外人稱小婿、外人尊稱說令婿、賢婿、令坦、令東牀、無論已嫁娶、未嫁娶、女稱丈夫的父母是父母、對人提說、公公、婆婆、書中記翁姑、總而言之、丈夫的一家人、丈夫叫什麼、妻子也叫什麼、祇是對着外人說起來、却有分別、丈夫的哥哥稱大伯子、兄弟稱小叔子、姐姐是大姑子、妹妹是小姑子、丈夫到了妻子的娘家、稱呼他家中的人、也和妻子一樣、對外人提說、卻有分別、就是妻子的父親、稱丈人、岳父、泰山、母親叫丈母、岳母、叫妻子的兄弟、是舅子、比妻子大的叫大舅子、比妻子小的叫小舅子、妻子的姐姐、是大姨子、妹妹是小姨子、妻子的姪兒叫妻姪、內姪、兒子生女、叫孫女、孫女的丈夫叫孫女女婿、生子、叫孫子、孫子的妻子叫孫子媳婦、孫子生子、叫重孫、也叫曾孫、曾孫生子叫玄孫、再往下算、出了五服、就算不得眷屬了、女兒生女叫外孫女、外孫女的丈夫叫外孫女婿、舅舅叫他是外甥女、外甥女婿、女兒生子、叫外孫、外孫的妻子叫外孫媳婦、舅舅叫他是外甥、外甥媳婦、外孫生子、叫重外孫、也叫外重孫、往下就不是至親了、眷屬以外、凡同族的人、俱照以上說過的稱呼、祇是對着外人說話、得加上一家的同族的三個字、如同族的哥哥兄弟之類、至親以外、一切瓜葛的親戚、也是一樣的稱呼、祇是對着外人說話、得加一表字、如表大爺表叔叔

之類、

太甲悔過

我眞是苦啊、自從出了亳都住在桐宮以裏、好像作了個落運的夢一般當這時候富貴榮華不能享受、公卿大夫不能指揮、九州牧伯也不能調動四海的百姓更不能治理、單單住在這先王的陵寢一旁整天家憂憂愁愁、永沒有個快樂的時候、這是因爲什麽緣故呢、莫非阿衡伊尹、他仗着是俺商家的大臣有一些創業的功勞因此起了一个支巧的念頭把我放在這裏呀、雖然如此、他到底是爲臣的、我仍舊是爲君的、爲臣的這樣待君、既不是義所當然、又不是理所當然、更不是分所當然、他爲什麽如此待我呢、最可怪的就是伊尹作了這樣越理僭分的事、各路諸侯、還不快快興兵來討他的罪、到如今還是半點動靜沒有、是他們不肯興討嗎、未必然、是道路阻隔住了嗎、未必然、是他們和伊尹通同作弊嗎、也未必然、哎、伊尹哪、伊尹哪、你爲什麽立這樣歹毒的心、作這樣奸詐的事、把我充發在這裏呢、我眞是苦啊、我眞是苦啊、沒有法兒、只得平心靜氣、再思再想、哎呀、明白了、明白了、這個緣故全在我自己身上、並不與別人相干哪、因此我就起了一個終身不解的怨恨、怨恨誰呢、怨恨百姓罷、百姓都安分守己、不反不亂、不能怨恨他們、怨恨牧伯罷、牧伯們都是下治理百姓、上服事王朝、各自盡他當盡的職分、又不能怨恨他們、怨恨在朝的公卿大夫罷、公卿大夫都是甘心樂意、事奉商朝、並沒有支離乖巧的心、更不能怨恨他們、究竟是怨恨誰呢、我就是怨恨我自己、我還要極力的治理、治理誰呢、治理百姓罷、百姓有有司治理、用不着我治理國政罷、國政有大臣治理、也用不着我治理朝綱罷、朝綱有冢宰治理、更用不着我、別人全不用我治理、還是得治理我自己、到了這分田地、我眞是苦啊、憑心自問、哎、太甲啊、太甲啊、你本是先聖成湯的孫子、應當給他續職、繼續之廣行王道、大開商家的江山纔是、爲什麽先王一崩、你就顛倒他的律法、擾亂他的典章呢、爲什麽竟把師保所說的一切話、看作無用、一點兒不肯遵守、一點兒不肯思想呢、爲什麼自作罪孽、無路逃脫、反失了那諒陰的大禮呢、抬頭一看、這新修的陵寢、豈不是我先祖成湯的故墓嗎、低頭一看、我身上穿的這齊衰、豈不是爲先祖成湯所帶的孝嗎、我的先祖啊、我的先祖啊、我眞是苦啊、按家道說、我是一個不孝的孫子、按國政說、我是一個無道的昏君、按天理說、我是一個腥聞在上的罪魁、哎呀、我眞是苦啊、我眞是苦啊、怎麼對住了我的先祖成湯呢、怎麼對住了我的師保阿衡呢、怎麼對住了在朝的百官呢、怎麼對住了九州的諸侯呢、怎麼對住了四方的黎民呢、我眞是苦啊、思想起來、眞眞是把我羞煞、把我臊煞、把我淡煞、無處遮飾了、但是回頭一想、聖賢不能無過、過而能改、善莫大焉、像我太甲正當這幼冲之年、從此悔罪改過、處仁遷義、也不妨爲有道的明君、是是是、有了、且看我修道去也、

武王誓師

衆將士們哪、各人拿着刀、執着槍、站立得穩、靜聽我言、古人有句話說、育養我的、就是我的君后、暴虐我的、就是我的寃仇、當今的獨夫受、暴虐極了、殘害極了、拿着群臣的性命、如禽獸一般、看着百姓的生死、連雞狗不如、成日家荒淫無道、殺戮忠良、苦害生靈、動不動就說、天下是我的天下、誰能把我怎麼樣呢、所以就遠君子、近小人、敗倫喪德、古今所未有之惡、他都做出、雖以夏桀的惡、來和他比量比量、也比不上去、差的還多、就如恩愛夫妻、誰忍的加害、但受將他的皇后、先挖去兩個眼、後炮烙了兩隻手、只見鮮血直流、油如水滴、皇后疼的滿地亂滾、疼哭不止、一直的疼死了、咳、恩愛夫妻、受尚如此忍心、在別人身上、更不用說了、所以去諫諍他的、不是被殺戮、就是受炮烙、杜元銑因諫諍、叫受殺死、梅栢去諫諍、被受炮烙、商容膠隔黃貴妃因諫諍、叫受摔死、把丞相比干、活扒了心、把上大夫楊任、活剜了眼、又用油烹了東伯侯、使囚車囚了箕子、還有許多、不能盡提、想這些忠心爲國的良臣、受這樣的慘毒苦害、殺戮、眞令人言之痛心、更有無緣無故受刑的、就如我父

親、有什麼不是來、竟被囚禁了七年、南伯侯有什麼罪來、竟身受大辟、又有我長兄伯夷考有什麼罪來、竟被受活活的用刀一塊一塊的割死、剁成肉丸、包作包子、强逼着我父親吃我長兄的肉、咳、傷心哉呀、傷心哉、更向百姓重重的要稅、誰若拿不上、沒有別話說、不是掛竿打板、就是跪鎖壓杠子、所以百姓雖筋出力盡、東借西取、求親告友、仍舊還有許多拿不上的、因此流離失所的、無處不有、甚至餓死父母、凍死妻子的、也是不少、眞暴虐極了、且又捉了百姓去修鹿台、巨橋、酒池、肉林、叫崇侯虎督工、若有錢的、行上賄賂、家中有二人、就去一個、無錢的、就是家中只一人、也是得去、崇侯虎不分白黑、口罵鞭打、往前直催、所以累死的人、橫仰豎欹、這裏一個、那裏一個、千千萬萬、不可勝數、遂死遂埋在鹿台之中、家裏連屍骸也不能見、成日家工場中、是號哭連天、直如殺人場一般、且鹿台之下、又挖一條深溝、放上大小無數的毒蛇、蝎子、名爲蠆盆、將女人剝去衣服、摔將下去、被毒蛇纏在身上、也有鑽在口裏的、蝎子螫的青一塊腫一塊、但見已經死的、那麼直挺挺的躺着、叫毒蛇去吃、尙未死的、是反來復去、直蹦亂跳、疼的鬼哭狼號、誰見了誰不落淚、而受反以此取樂、其心何忍、但受之惡、還不只如此、又造一些銅柱、抹上脂油、下邊點着烈火、逼着人從上頭走、掉下去落在火中、燒的是咬牙切齒、油如汗滴、這裏去一塊皮、那裏去一塊肉、你哭我叫、要死不得死、要活不得活、眞殘忍極了、受反以此和妲己取笑、眞忍哉其心也、又看見冬天過河的人、遂吩咐與我捉來、用鎚子將脚脛敲碎、拿出骨髓來觀看、此人疼個賊死、就是醒過來、也成了廢人、父母不能再事奉、妻子不能再養活、你想害的這家苦不苦呢、受之暴虐、還有更甚的、就是將孕婦割開觀看、但見去拿婦人的時候、把那一家人嚇的戰戰兢兢、齊哭亂號、夫不忍舍妻、妻不忍離夫、更有五尺之童、扯着他母親的衣裳、嗚嗚直哭、不肯鬆手、他母遂哭着說、我兒、你母親不能再抱養你了、咱們娘們今日相別、再永不得相見了、說完淚如雨下、殘臣將小孩一脚踢倒、拉着婦人去了、不多時拿了好幾個孕婦、都在受跟前用刀子割開、割開一個、就死兩個、哎、受的暴虐、十天十夜也說不完、想這些無知的百姓、無故受這些荼毒、暴虐、殘害、殺戮、如在烈火滾油之中、眞是傷心悲哉、百姓們就都過責我、不快快興兵、我如今若再不興兵伐受、一不合天意、二不合民心、更不知受能暴虐到什麼分、就是與受同惡、所以奉天討受之舉、無容推辭、我不能不伐、不得不伐、更不敢不伐、今日定要與受決個雌雄、定個勝負、爲萬民除害、爲忠臣報仇、廢棄商受、使百姓同得平安、就是後世百姓、也得享安樂、並且流芳百世、青史垂勳、你們都抬起頭來、向正北望望、來了來了、人馬望不到邊、你看那前邊的紅旗、不是助受爲虐的惡來嗎、那左邊的青旗、不是助受害人的飛蓮嗎、那右邊的白旗、不是督工殘民的崇侯虎嗎、那中央的黃旗、豈不是荒淫無道、苦害生靈、滅絕紀綱、殺害忠良、炮烙蠆盆、敲骨剖胎、神人共怒的獨夫受嗎、衆將士們、生死禍福、勝敗存亡、就在眼前、千夫長、百夫長、及各路諸侯、都大起膽子、盡上力量、勇往直前、不捉住獨夫受、不要回頭、走走走、

孟子

世人皆稱孟子爲大賢、其實稱他爲聖人、也是理當論孟子生的時候、沒聽說有二龍繞室、五老降庭、孟子死的日子、也沒記有弟子爲他帶孝、國君來行喪禮、然而在他以前的聖人、如堯舜禹湯文武周公孔子所傳的道、若以後沒有孟子、必早已墜於地、在他以後的學者、如韓愈周子二程朱熹諸人所守的道、若其先沒有孟子、必早已失其傳、試思當戰國的時候、以異端迷惑人的有告子、以邪說引誘人的有許子、無父無君的有楊子墨子、善陳善戰的有孫子吳子、人人都流於異端、誰還知道忠孝、國國皆貴尚爭戰、誰肯遵守王法、幸虧有孟子出來、闢邪說、放淫詞、黜五霸、貶桓文、唇槍舌劍、將一切旁門左道、殺了個望影而逃、使爲子的知道孝、爲臣的知道忠、爲國君的知道仁義、得聽王道、誰還能帮助他呢、誰不當佩服他呢、想當日、孔子將堯舜的道理發明出來、宰予稱他的事功賢於堯舜遠矣、這樣、孟子

又將孔子的道、重新証明出來、豈不更賢於孔子許多嗎、那可不論到他的事功呢、若說孟子的事、從少就可稱道、但就他長大周流列國的時候、更見出他是頭一個會引導人君的、如齊宣王以好勇推諉、孟子遂引出文王好勇來、宣王以好貨推諉、孟子便引出公劉好貨來、宣王以好色推諉、孟子又引出太王好色來、再如以羊易牛那塊事、連齊王自己也沒法解說了、孟子還爲他說、無傷也、是乃仁術也、王是光看見牛觳觫、沒看見羊觳觫、像齊王那樣的昏昧、都教孟子感動的說、夫子之言、於我心有戚戚焉、可見孟子、是盡力要救正一切的國君、到他年老的時候、因材施教、更能發揮聖賢的奧妙、就如養氣一事、乃是要緊的一步工夫、孔子還沒有提到、孟子可和他的門徒詳細講明、再如知言一事、也是要緊的學問、別人都未提明、獨有孟子、向他的門人陳明、詳觀孟子七篇、實足推倒一世的辯士、開拓萬古的心胸、所以當時滕文公、特爲越着國去聽他的教訓、曹君的兄弟、九尺四寸以長、還想着到他門下受業、

可見孟子在名教中更可算爲巨擘、孟子生平吐辭爲經、稱爲文章的祖始、現在且不必讚美他的文章、孟子固然深懂得天時地利人和、現在也不必誇獎他的武畧、現就着他言必稱堯舜、可知他的言語、是何等的整重、以尙志爲事情、可知他的心思、是何等的高超、不受齊王的兼金、辭却萬鍾的俸祿、可想到他的行爲、何等的廉潔、不肯往見諸侯、又說說大人則藐之、可想到他的氣象、是何等的剛方、而且勸齊王賑饑、無愧於仁、格梁王之貪心、無愧於義、不肯踰了位和右師說話、無愧於禮、預先裡知道盆成括必見殺、無愧於智、無怪乎人說孟子之功、不在大禹以下、無怪乎說孟子之德、絕類離倫、無怪乎刑部尙書錢唐、情願爲孟子被射、且曰臣得爲孟子死、死有餘榮、正見得孟子是教人服氣的、是憂心世道的、是挽回人心的、鄒國雖然不大、有孟子也不算很小、戰國雖是不好、有孟子也不至大壞、這樣看來、可以與山河竝壽的是孟子、可以與日月爭光的也是孟子、可以媲美千古的是孟子、可以流芳百世的也

是孟子、我中國直至今日、得稱爲文物之邦、中華天朝、有三綱五常、有君臣上下、有禮義廉恥、全賴孟夫子這一臂之力、總而言之、孟子從小到大、到老、言語當稱讚、心思當稱讚、行爲當稱讚、氣象當稱讚、並他的文武仁義禮智都當稱讚、所以稱他爲大賢、在孟子抱屈眞抱屈、稱他爲聖人、在我看理當又理當、

Syllabic Index of Characters and Phrases.

PEKING.

In the following index the single characters under each syllable are arranged in order according to the number of the strokes in each. The phrases pertaining to each character follow it in the order of the number of strokes in the second character. A tone mark to a character indicates that it has another reading. The phrases pertaining to such characters are distributed under their proper readings. The arrangement of the syllables is *strictly* alphabetic. Letters with diacritic marks always *follow* the primary letter. The numbers refer to the pages.

A

阿[1] 250
阿[3] 250
阿彌陀 607
阿彌陀佛 384
啊[1] 152
啊 251
啊[3] 518
啊熱 437

Ai

乃[3] 235
哀 49
哀告 49
哎 235
哎呀 249
哎喲 249
哎喲嚇喝 236
挨[1] 196
挨保 463
挨[2] 193
捱 204
唉[1] 621
唉[2] 251
崖 139
涯 157
噯 251
矮 47
愛 53
: 145
愛惜 123
愛惜皮肉 278
愛意 145
礙 52
礙口 283
礙事 52

An

安 34
安心 472
安分 54
安生 295
安息日 34
安排 110
安然 220
安頓 296
安置 162
安歇 181
安慰 154
安靜 299
安穩 180
岸 561
按[1] 52
按法 507
按部就班 598
按[4] 313
案 100
俺 223
唵[1] 624
暗 48
暗地 287
暗處 266
鞍 525
鞍韂 530
鵪 197
鵪鶉 197

Ang

昂 408
骯 60
骯髒 60

Ao

拗 See Niu
欸 235
欸喲乃呀 236
奧 391
傲 69
嗷 235
嗷喲哎呀 236
熬 119
懊 342
懊悔 342
襖 26
鰲 401

Cha

扎[1] 245
扎[2] 163
扎掙 163
扎實 369
乍 93
乍猛的 456
乍富 223
拃 431
咋 574
炸[4] 140
炸裂 140
炸雷 556
炸[2] 432
眨 324
挓 325
挓手 325
挓挲 325
紮 See Tsa
詐 38
喳[1] 178
喳喳 176
閘 432
蜡 523
蹅 469
劄 67
劄刀 67
雜 77
雜貨 469
雜亂 78
: : 102
雜亂無章 124

Ch'a

叉 621
扠 621
杈 498
岔 168
岔路 585
查 281
查收 408
查明 575
查問 533
差[1] 45
差一點 138
差不多 138
差不來往 138
差不許多 138
差不着一點 138
差不幾多 138
差不離 138
差不離形 138
差池 115
差沒一點 138
差脚 466
差錯 306
茶 60
茶葉 359
茶舘 338
喳[1] 355
插 276
插手 568
插嘴 276
搽 81
搽粉 456
搽胭抹粉 598
察 95
鍤[1] 277
鍤[2] 624
鍤 67

Chai

宅 358
窄 See Tsê
側 378
側稜 378
債 110
摘 193
擇 231
擇日子 233
齋 574

Ch'ai

拆 190
拆散 370
差[1] 134
差人 134
差役 281
差使 223
柴 27
柴伙 27

Chan

占 206
占卦 206
占許 374
佔 178
佔上風 478
佔先 508
沾 510
沾染 549
苫 See Shan
眨 See Cha
站 71
站口 389
站立 194
粘 131
斬 435
斬首 553
斬罪 582
斬齊 435
湛 280
: 416
湛新 416
棧 375
棧房 375
盞 273
綻 467
暫 52
暫且 52
暫時 264
戰 159
戰兢 296
戰戰磕磕 443
氈 274
囅 507

Ch'an

產 206
產業 588
諂 261
諂媚 261
禪子郭 444
鏟 67
: 132
纏 115
纏手 144
纏磨 125
纏繞 619
鑱 112
鑱頭 112
饞 352
韉 530

Chang

丈 51
丈人 184
丈夫 51
丈母 306
仗 30
杖 134
長[3] 45
長上 45
長子 312
長進 348
長孫 181
張 18
: 99
: 458
張狂 61

Yiu

Yüă

Yung

Yü

Yüe

Yüen

Yün

Radical Index of Single Characters.

Double readings are all given. When tonal the tones are marked; when syllabic the second reading is inserted. The numbers refer to the pages.

“早期北京话珍本典籍校释与研究”丛书总目录

早期北京话珍稀文献集成

（一）日本北京话教科书汇编

《燕京妇语》等八种

华语跬步

亚细亚言语集

北京风土编·北京事情·北京风俗问答

伊苏普喻言·今古奇观·搜奇新编

四声联珠

官话指南·改订官话指南

京华事略·北京纪闻

（二）朝鲜日据时期汉语会话书汇编

改正增补汉语独学

高等官话华语精选

速修汉语自通

速修汉语大成

中语大全

修正独习汉语指南

官话华语教范

无先生速修中国语自通

官话标准：短期速修中国语自通

“内鲜满”最速成中国语自通

（三）西人北京话教科书汇编

寻津录

语言自迩集

官话类编

华语入门

汉语口语初级读本·北京儿歌

北京官话：汉语初阶

北京话语音读本

语言自迩集（第二版）

言语声片

华英文义津逮

汉英北京官话词汇

（四）清代满汉合璧文献萃编

清文启蒙
清话问答四十条
一百条·清语易言
清文指要
续编兼汉清文指要
庸言知旨
满汉成语对待
清文接字·字法举一歌
重刻清文虚字指南编

（五）清代官话正音文献

正音撮要
正音咀华

（六）十全福

（七）清末民初京味儿小说书系

新鲜滋味
过新年
小额
北京
春阿氏
花鞋成老
评讲聊斋
讲演聊斋

（八）清末民初京味儿时评书系

益世余谭——民国初年北京生活百态
益世余墨——民国初年北京生活百态

早期北京话研究书系

早期北京话语法研究
早期北京话语法演变专题研究
早期北京话语气词研究
晚清民国时期南北官话语法差异研究
基于清后期至民国初期北京话文献语料的个案研究
高本汉《北京话语音读本》整理与研究
北京话语音演变研究
文化语言学视域下的北京地名研究
语言自迩集——19世纪中期的北京话（第二版）
清末民初北京话语词汇释